Reading *and* Writing *from* Literature

SECOND EDITION

JOHN E. SCHWIEBERT

Weber State University

Houghton Mifflin Company   Boston   New York

"Books are the best of things, well used; abused, among the worst. . . . They are for nothing but to inspire."

—RALPH WALDO EMERSON

Senior Sponsoring Editor: Dean Johnson
Editorial Associate: Bruce Cantley
Project Editor: Rebecca Bennett
Associate Production/Design Coordinator: Lisa Jelly
Senior Manufacturing Coordinator: Marie Barnes
Senior Marketing Manager: Nancy Lyman

Cover Design: Sarah Melhado Bishins
Cover Image: Tolstoy, Fjodor (1783–1873). Branch of flowers, butterflies, and flies. Russian State Museum, St. Petersburg, Russia.

Text credits appear on pages 1103–1110, which constitute an extension of the copyright page.

As part of Houghton Mifflin's ongoing commitment to the environment, this text has been printed on recycled paper.

Printed in the U.S.A.

Library of Congress Catalog Card Number: 00-103026

ISBN: 0-618-03962-7

123456789-DOC-04 03 02 01 00

Contents

iii

Appendices

Preface

Designed for use in literature courses that are also writing courses, *Reading and Writing from Literature* offers a fresh new approach to reading and writing in those classes. The book invokes a "conversation" model of reading and writing that empowers students to interact proactively and constructively with all texts, both literary and their own.

Reading and Writing from Literature presents reading as the primary resource for writing. Rather than only writing *about* literature, student users of this book write *from* literature; they use texts to produce texts. Being personally and culturally diverse, students are encouraged to identify and use those aspects of a text that interest them most as starting points for composing. Throughout the book, the guiding assumption is that, by creating, students also become stronger readers of the literature of past and present.

Inviting Students to Read and Write Intertextually

The theoretical basis of this book can be distilled into a single word—intertextuality, the primary engine that drives composing. In this book, "text" is defined broadly to include all kinds of printed works, such as stories, poems, essays, and plays, as well as non-print phenomena such as movies, pictures, songs, conversations, and experiences. Intertextuality posits that every "text" is related to and evokes other texts, that one text is enmeshed in others. To compose a story, poem, or essay is not to invent something out of nothing but to produce a new text out of a complex and interwoven fabric of other texts already "written into" the writer's life.

For a writer, reading is useful because it facilitates getting the texts of one's life on paper. The process begins when the writer reads a springboard text, such as a short story. Some aspect of the story—a character, an image, a phrase, a described incident—resonates with other texts in his or her life, thereby bringing these texts to consciousness. The writer composes a piece of his or her own, and the focus of the resulting composition is not the springboard text but the writer's *intertextual web*—the intricate and unique fabric of texts that constitutes who that writer is.

Intertextuality provides a rationale for reading and for writing in response to reading: through the process of writing, ideas can be articulated that might not have surfaced if the writer hadn't read and written from that particular text.

In addition, intertextuality explains how a person can respond in writing to another text and still produce work that is individual, exciting, and "independent": because each person's intertextual web is unlike anyone else's.

Finally, intertextuality provides a rationale for the student to pursue an ongoing, lifelong program of reading and writing. By demonstrating that no text, great or humble, is final, autonomous, or definitive, intertextuality validates every act of composing. In addition to being seen as ends-in-themselves, student texts and literary texts alike can be read temporally as parts of a continuing interplay of words and ideas, as "pre-texts" for additional thought, creation, and recreation.

Rhetoric Chapters

This textbook is organized into rhetoric chapters and anthology chapters. The rhetoric chapters introduce students to techniques of reading, writing, and sharing that they can use throughout the term. Chapters are short and accessible enough that students can master most of the material on their own with minimal expenditure of in-class time.

Part I, "A Conversation Model of Writing and Reading" (Chapters 1–4), presents writing and reading as conversational acts in which students "talk back" to the texts they read and use the conversation as a springboard for creating texts of their own. In addition, Part I introduces the "reading notebook," the special kind of journal students can use for collecting their own writings—notes, thoughts, responses to literary works, and creative writings of many kinds that may be prompted by the texts they read. The reading notebook breaks down the wall between composing for school and composing for life and a lifetime; while developing techniques of reading and writing that will be useful to them in this course, students also learn strategies for producing meaningful writings of their own independently of this class or this textbook.

Part II, "Writing Essays About Literature" (Chapters 5–8), emphasizes the intertextual or recursive process of such composing. Students' essays do not materialize out of nothing; they are generated from previous work and from literary texts, the texts in their own notebooks, and the texts of lecture and discussion. With strategies described in Part II, students learn how to use these texts to make a new text, i.e., an essay about literature.

Part III, "Creating a Writing Portfolio" (Chapters 9–10), shows students how to assemble a portfolio of their best writing for the quarter or semester. A portfolio is the result of a sustained process of recursive reading and writing in which students set aside their failed or mediocre work and concentrate on perfecting their best.

Part IV, "An Introduction to the Major Genres" (Chapters 11–15), introduces students to the genres of literature (short stories, poetry, nonfiction/essays, plays, and notebooks and journals) represented in the anthology. The chapters acquaint students with key literary terms and concepts that will help them to talk and write about short stories, poems, essays, and plays. In addition, Part IV is intended to increase students' technical knowledge of the genres so that they can write in multiple forms themselves.

The Anthology of Readings

Part V, "A Thematic Anthology of Readings" (Chapters 16–21), offers an anthology of 171 readings in the four major genres, arranged under six thematic headings: Gender and Relationships, Families, Experience and Identity, Individual and Society, People and Cultures in Conflict and Change, and Work and the Quality of Life. I have chosen a thematic arrangement over a genre-based arrangement for two reasons: first, to avoid breaking whole texts into fragmentary "elements" (those of the short story, of poetry, of drama), which is the almost inevitable result of a genre-based organization; and second, to place primary emphasis on issues and experiences that relate intertextually to students' lives.

In making selections I have worked consistently for variety: a mix of familiar authors and less-familiar, of frequently anthologized works, and infrequently collected ones. Texts in each thematic grouping represent a diversity of perspectives and experiences, as the Gender and Relationships chapter (Chapter 16) illustrates. Doris Lessing's story about male objectification of the female body ("A Woman on a Roof") is balanced by Scott Russell Sanders's male perspective on the same subject, "Looking at Women." Readings about wounded female and male identity are complemented by passionate and gentle love poems, such as Walt Whitman's "I Heard You Solemn-Sweet Pipes of the Organ" and Liz Rosenberg's "In the End, We Are All Light." Texts that focus on relationships as romance are balanced by Francine du Plessix Gray's discussion of alternative relationships in her essay, "On Friendship."

Finally, in order to encourage strong responses from students of diverse backgrounds and both genders, I have weighted selections toward the modern and contemporary and have included a significant number of multicultural and international selections.

Interchapters on Notebooks and Journals

Interspersed among the thematic chapters in Part V are six interchapters on writers' notebooks and journals. New to the second edition, the interchapters include selections from the notebooks and journals of five writers and provide students with practical ideas for creating and sustaining notebooks and journals of their own. The interchapters can be assigned and discussed in class, assigned but not discussed, or ignored at instructor discretion.

Apparatus to Accompany Readings

I believe that students accustomed to making their own texts will also become better readers of others' texts. A student who *writes* stories has a special motivation to understand the story elements of point of view, character, and plot because those elements have a context within his or her work as a creator. Similarly, students who write poems have an incentive to understand meter, metaphor, and diction in order to apply them in their own composing.

Accordingly, the book's apparatus is aimed primarily at prompting students to write as well as read. Such apparatus includes:

- Parts I–IV of *Reading and Writing from Literature,* described above.
- Activities for Writing and Discussion following approximately 60 percent of the selections. These activities are designed to motivate many kinds of writing in addition to literary analysis. Activities involve students in both creative and analytic work as well as in sharing their own work and ideas.
- Additional Activities for Writing and Discussion at the end of each thematic section. The Additional Activities encourage students to make connections among the various readings within the section. In addition, they help students develop habits of recursiveness as they review and reconsider those readings and the notebook writings they have composed in response to them.
- Numerous examples of student-written texts, both within individual chapters and in the appendices, that will stimulate students in their own composing.

Features New to the Second Edition

- More readings. The second edition includes 169 short stories, poems, essays/nonfiction works, and plays—20 percent more than the first edition. Over 40 percent of the readings are new.
- More Activities for Writing and Discussion. The activities, with their emphasis on provoking creative as well as analytic responses from students, were a popular element of the first edition. In the second edition nearly 65 percent of the readings are followed by activities, up from 50 percent in the first edition.
- A new thematic section, Work and the Quality of Life, that includes five short stories, eighteen poems, five essays, and a play.
- Seven new units on notebooks and journals—an introductory chapter, which demonstrates the purposes and uses of notebooks and journals with examples from an international range of writers; and six interchapters that profile individual writers, present sample entries from their notebooks, and provide exercises for students.

Summary: Distinctive Features of Reading and Writing from Literature, *Second Edition*

- Treats reading and writing as thoroughly interrelated: rhetoric chapters and other apparatus assure that students are always writing as they read and reading as they write.
- Empowers students both to *study* literature and to *use* literature as a springboard for making texts of their own.
- Provides guidelines for a reading notebook that students use recursively: they accumulate writings—notes, thoughts, responses to readings, drafts, revisions—reread them regularly, and continuously revise their selected best work.
- Offers activities and apparatus that get students to look repeatedly at literary texts and their own texts, thereby promoting habits of recursive reading, thinking, and writing.
- Includes an anthology of 162 readings (short stories, poems, essays, and plays) that are weighted toward the contemporary and multicultural to encourage strong responses from students of diverse backgrounds.
- Features a simple and uncluttered apparatus that students can use in class and on their own, without detailed guidance from the instructor.
- Contains numerous examples of student writings in many forms, both creative and analytic.
- Gives students incentives and strategies for continuing to read and write conversationally once this particular course is over.

Acknowledgments

The earliest support for this project came from my students and from my colleagues Candadai Seshachari and the late Lee McKenzie. To them I am deeply grateful, as I am also for the ongoing encouragement of Judy Elsley, Priti Kumar, Sally Bishop Shigley, Bob Smith, and Mali Subbiah. Many thanks to the excellent and supportive editorial staff at Houghton Mifflin: Dean Johnson, who oversaw the project during composition and review; Rebecca Bennett, who guided the book through production; and Bruce Cantley, who assisted with permissions and with patient and cheerful replies to my many queries.

A number of persons helped immeasurably in preparing for this edition, and I wish to acknowledge them here:

Troy Boucher, Southwestern College (KS)
Dominic Delli Carpini, York College of Pennsylvania
W. Curtis Currie II, University of Tennessee-Knoxville
William A. Davis, Jr., College of Notre Dame of Maryland
Irene Fairley, Northeastern University (MA)
Lynn Jeffress, Oregon Coast Community College

Vivian Colias Jones, Montgomery College (TX)
Bruce R. Magee, Louisiana Tech University
Andrew Manno, Ranitan Valley Community College (NJ)
Marilyn McDowell, University of Tennessee-Knoxville
S. Paul Rice, Coastal Carolina University (SC)

Finally, personal thanks to Bob Hogge, Mali Subbiah, Michael Wutz, and Jim Young for their friendship and inspiring conversation; to my parents, Olive and Lloyd Schwiebert; to my wife, Ann Jefferds; and to my children, Jack and Elizabeth, who have taught me more about "the life of the mind" than books ever can.

J. E. S.

A Conversation Model of Writing and Reading

P art I of *Reading and Writing from Literature* presents writing and reading as conversational acts in which you "talk back" to the texts you read and use the conversation as a springboard for creating works of your own. In addition, Part I introduces you to the "reading notebook," the special kind of journal you will use in the course for collecting your own writings—notes, thoughts, responses to literary works, and creative writings of many kinds that may be prompted by the texts you read. The reading notebook breaks down the wall between composing for school and composing for life and a lifetime. While developing techniques of reading and writing that will be useful to you in this course, you will also learn strategies for producing meaningful writings of your own independently of this class or this textbook. Thus, the ultimate aim of Part I is to make you a strong and independent reader of literature—and an active writer—for life.

1

Why Don't You Let It Out Then?

Walt, you contain enough, why don't you let it out then?

—WALT WHITMAN

For only that book can we read which relates to me something that is already in my mind.

—RALPH WALDO EMERSON

Three Writers

Robin wants to write a story about something that has been on his mind a lot lately: husbands and wives. Sitting at his word processor he begins, "Every marriage is improved—or destroyed—by the fires of time." He likes the sound of that and is poised to continue, when inspiration suddenly dies. He searches for something new and profound to say about love; he ransacks his brain for some original characters and situations . . . in vain. Discouraged, he types another sentence or two and gives up.

Robin is anxious about being "original." His anxiety destroys his creativity.

Suppose he approaches the writing task differently. He thumbs through a book of short fiction to find other stories about husbands and wives and discovers "The Story of an Hour" by the nineteenth-century American Kate Chopin. After reading several paragraphs he has become fascinated by the character of its heroine, Louise Mallard. Mrs. Mallard has just learned that her husband has been killed in a railroad accident. Seated by her bedroom window she slips into a reverie about her past and future. Complex emotions beset her. She sobs; then, as she stares blankly at a distant patch of blue sky, an unfamiliar feeling steals over her. Chopin writes:

When she abandoned herself a little whispered word escaped her slightly parted lips. She said it over and over under her breath: "Free, free, free!" The vacant stare and the look of terror that had followed it went from her eyes. They stayed keen and bright. Her pulses beat fast, and the coursing blood warmed and relaxed every inch of her body.

Robin circles this passage and scribbles in the margin, "She *relaxes* at the thought of her husband's death?" Louise's emotions set Robin thinking about fractured relationships, in which one partner prefers freedom to attachment. Thought follows thought, and soon he is remembering his Uncle Jules, who seemed to experience a kind of rebirth following the death of his wife, Aunt Maria. Robin begins writing the story of Uncle Jules and Aunt Maria. "The Story of an Hour" prompts him to write. While his own story is about a husband and wife, it in no way duplicates Chopin's. In short, his work is "original."

Sally keeps a personal diary. Unfortunately, while she thinks of plenty to write when her life is exciting or awful, on most days (which are humdrum) she draws a mental blank. Each day's entry sounds like every other's. Her own writing puts her to sleep.

A friend, Max, suggests her writing may be suffering from egocentrism and that she should seek prompts for writing from her environment. "Writers do it all the time," says Max. "They eavesdrop, look at people, watch movies, hang around shopping malls. . . ." Heeding Max's advice, Sally indulges in one of her favorite activities, watching TV, hoping it will stimulate her imagination. One evening she sees a TV version of Daniel Keyes's "Flowers for Algernon" and learns that this is a short story told entirely in the form of a diary (Algernon's). Inspired, Sally puts her own favorite literary form to work: she writes a story, in diary form, about a would-be writer who "can't" write.

Erica has always loved the sea. Her family vacationed on Lake Superior when she was growing up. As a child she built sandcastles and combed the beach for shells. Now, every time she gets near water, she dances or merely stands still, transfixed and staring at the horizon, watching cloud shadows roll over the waves, beholding the most fabulous sunsets imaginable. Erica wants to write about the sea. Every time she tries, however, she gets mired in false and overblown phrases that frustrate and embarrass her.

One day, while reading a biographical note on American playwright Eugene O'Neill, she notices the title of one of O'Neill's plays, *Beyond the Horizon*. The mere title does something to her—and for her. She circles it . . . repeats it to herself a few times out loud. She doodles in the margin: a conch shell, a snail, a long horizontal line. As she thinks, repeats, and doodles, memories and images long dormant rise to consciousness: memories of family trips, of childhood, of her own daughter playing in the sand, of sea-conversations and sea-books. She feels herself transported to those days at Lake Superior and writes the poem she has "always wanted to," about the particular feelings a child-turned-adult has when gazing at the horizon. It turns out to be a poem about love and aging and the integration of child and adult. The poem pleases her.

All three of these writers—Robin, Sally, and Erica—wanted to write but had no "way in" to their writing. All three were stuck—either not moving at all (Robin), or writing in circles (Sally), or producing "false" work that didn't reflect the writer's true feelings (Erica). Each transcended the problem by "reading" another text—a short story, a TV show, the title of a play—and using it to catalyze his or her imagination.

How did Robin, Sally, and Erica use the texts they read?

First, consider what they *didn't* do. They did not:

1. Read the text and slavishly imitate it. Robin does not try writing "like" Chopin because that does not interest him. What does interest him are some similarities between Chopin's characters and people he has known in his own life. Likewise Sally and Erica. "Flowers for Algernon" and *Beyond the Horizon* give them the initial impetus to create but recede in importance as Sally and Erica actually write.

2. Read passively. Robin, Sally, and Erica are not mere consumers of texts; they are also *producers*. They follow their reading by creating texts of their own.

3. Read to "master" the total text. The three writers pick up on particular aspects of the text that interest them at the moment. Robin concentrates on the commitment theme. Sally is indifferent to the themes, characters, and plot of "Flowers for Algernon"; what attracts her are the point of view and form—first-person point of view in diary form. As for Erica, she doesn't even bother to read O'Neill's play, let alone "comprehend" it. The mere title suffices to prompt her memories and imagination and give her momentum for writing.

Robin, Sally, and Erica do not write to comprehend the texts they read; they simply seize upon elements of those texts that they can *use* in order to write themselves. Instead of attempting to understand the texts in total, they converse with those aspects of the text that interest them. Like a participant in a two-way conversation, each of these writers composes something (in this case, a written text rather than a spoken statement) that sustains an ongoing conversation. Because these conversations never end, and because the writer is contributing just one bit more to the discussion, the pressures on the writer to compose "brilliantly" and "profoundly" are greatly reduced.

Robin, Sally, and Erica imagine a particular model—a conversation model—of the relationship between themselves as writers and the texts they use to help them write. The existence of this model is all-important to their success as writers.

A Conversation Model of Writing and Reading

The conversation model says that you interact or *converse* with a text when you read it. Even as you are learning from the text, you yourself are bringing something *to* it, namely, your own background, experiences, thoughts, prior knowledge, biases, and opinions. The conversation model honors your right to *talk back* to the text.

According to the conversation model our minds are not empty receptacles waiting to be filled. As living, sentient beings, each of us brings to a text a history of thoughts, experiences, ideas, and readings. Who you are shapes what meaning you "get" from a text. That is, what essay X "means" is not something intrinsic to the text alone; what it means is largely shaped by the personal and cultural makeup of the reader who reads it.

For example, when I read a short story the "meaning" of the text is partly determined by who I, the reader, am; by what I already know about the subject of the story; by what my feelings, biases, or attitudes are about that subject; and by a whole range of other factors such as my race, gender, previous reading, and personal and cultural experience. In other words, I not only "receive" information, ideas, images, and so on from the story; I also bring my *self* to it. Recall how Robin, for instance, brought his experience of Uncle Jules to his reading of "The Story of an Hour"; his unique individual experience prompted him to read and use Chopin's story in a way that would not have occurred to a different reader. Reading thus becomes a process of negotiation—a sort of conversation—between the distinctive reader "me" and the author and text of the work I am reading.

As an example, imagine you pick up an essay about "the meaning of education." A shudder of insecurity passes through you: "Looks tough. And this writer has a Ph.D. What am *I* going to get out of this?" You are thinking passively. You overlook that you have been in school for many years yourself. Even if you haven't spent your free time reading books and articles on education, you possess another resource that equips you to "converse" with this reading: your dozen or so years as a learner, as a participant in the educational system. You know what it is like to do assignments, and you have encountered all variety of teachers, students, and teaching methods. Even though you are not yet ready to read and respond to the text before you as an educational scholar or expert, you do have expertise of a kind. This expertise—your own life and experiences as a student—gives you a way in to any piece of writing about education.

In short: *you know more than you realize.*

This is what American poet Walt Whitman had in mind when he wrote,

> *Walt, you contain enough, why don't you let it out then?*

It's one of the most democratic lines in all literature. Instead of bowing to the Voice of Authority, which says, "You don't know enough yet to write; read some more *first*," Whitman discovers that he already knows (and you and I know) "enough" to join the conversation *now*.

Of course, you can always know more and write *better*—and reading and writing can be seen as lifelong endeavors to improve your knowledge and verbal dexterity. Whitman, for instance, read voraciously—everything from history and literature to astronomy, mysticism, criticism, human physiology, philosophy, and geology. His notebooks fill six thick volumes. However, he didn't postpone writing as something to be done only *after* reading; he read and wrote simultaneously. He fused reading and writing into one and treated the whole as a continuous two-way conversation, between himself and the world, himself and the written word, himself and experience.

ACTIVITIES FOR WRITING

1. In your own words, summarize the conversation model. What new understanding, if any, does the conversation model give you of your own habits as a reader and writer? Do you read "conversationally"? How or how don't you? When or when don't you?

2. Practice conversational reading and writing with the following exercise from *Personal Fiction Writing* (New York: Teachers & Writers Collaborative, 1984) by Meredith Sue Willis. Read the dialogue excerpt, below, from Tillie Olsen's novel, *Yonnondio: From the Thirties.* Then write what you imagine might have happened just before or after this dialogue. That is, write a prequel or sequel to the dialogue.

> No one greeted him at the gate—the dark walls of the kitchen enclosed on him like a smothering grave. Anna did not raise her head.
> In the other room the baby kept squalling and squalling and Ben was piping an out-of-tune song to quiet her. There was a sour smell of wet diapers and burned pots in the air.
> "Dinner ready?" he asked heavily.
> "No, not yet."
> Silence. Not a word from either.
> "Say, can't you stop that damn brat's squallin? A guy wants a little rest once in a while."
> No answer.
> "Aw, this kitchen stinks. I'm going out on the porch. And shut that brat up, she's driving me nuts, you hear?" You hear, he reiterated to himself, stumbling down the steps, you hear, you hear. Driving me nuts.

3. In the following essay, Cynthia Ozick describes one of her earliest memories, what she calls her "[f]irst inkling." Read the essay. Then respond conversationally by describing, with as much sensual detail of sight, sound, taste, smell, and touch as possible, your own earliest memory. To make this past moment feel as immediate as possible, you might use Ozick's second paragraph as a model and write in the *present* verb tense.

EXISTING THINGS

CYNTHIA OZICK

First inkling. If I were to go back and back—really back, to earliest consciousness—I think it would be mica. Not the prophet Micah, who tells us that our human task is to do justly, and to love mercy, and to walk humbly with our God; but that other still more humble mica—those tiny glints of isinglass that catch the sun and prickle upward from the pavement like shards of star-stuff. Sidewalks nowadays seem inert, as if cement has rid itself forever of bright sprinklings and stippled spangles. But the pavement I am thinking of belongs to long ago, and runs narrowly between the tall weeds of empty lots, lots that shelter shiny green snakes.

The lots are empty because no one builds on them. It is the middle of the summer in the middle of the Depression, childhood's longest hour. I am alone under a slow molasses sun, staring at the little chips of light flashing at my feet. Up and down the whole length of the street there is no one, not a single grownup, and certainly, in that sparse time, no other child. There is only myself and these hypnotic semaphores signaling eeriness out of the ground. But no, up the block a little way, a baby carriage is entrusted to the idle afternoon, with a baby left to sleep, all by itself, under white netting.

If you are five years old, loitering in a syrup of sunheat, gazing at the silver-white mica-eyes in the pavement, you will all at once be besieged by a strangeness: the strangeness of understanding, for the very first time, that you are really alive, and that the world is really true; and the strangeness will divide into a river of wonderings.

Here is what I wondered then, among the mica-eyes:

I wondered what it would be like to become, for just one moment, every kind of animal there is in the world. Even, I thought, a snake.

I wondered what it would be like to know all the languages in the world.

I wondered what it would be like to be that baby under the white netting.

I wondered why, when I looked straight into the sun, I saw a pure circle.

I wondered why my shadow had a shape that was me, but nothing else; why my shadow, which was almost like a mirror, was not a mirror.

I wondered why I was thinking these things; I wondered what wondering was, and why it was spooky, and also secretly sweet, and amazingly *interesting*. Wondering felt akin to love—an uncanny sort of love, not like loving your mother or father or grandmother, but something curiously and thrillingly other. Something that shone up out of the mica-eyes.

Decades later, I discovered in Wordsworth's *Prelude* what it was:

. . . those hallowed and pure motions of the sense
Which seem, in their simplicity, to own

An intellectual charm;
... those first-born affinities that fit
Our new existence to existing things.

And those existing things are *all* things, everything the mammal senses know, everything the human mind constructs (temples or equations), the unheard poetry on the hidden side of the round earth, the great thirsts everywhere, the wonderings past wonderings.

First inkling, bridging our new existence to existing things. Can one begin with mica in the pavement and learn the prophet Micah's meaning?

Making New Texts from Old: Intertextuality

Pen, paper, and book make an ideal community.

—Anonymous

I n college John took a literature class in which he was assigned to read *Moby-Dick*. *Moby-Dick* is a long novel, and the class spent four days analyzing it. John worked hard, produced a term paper on *Moby-Dick*—and shortly thereafter forgot the book and nearly everything he had learned about it. Then, two years later, something interesting happened. John was writing a short story with a first-person ("I") narrator; his progress was stalled, when suddenly, out of the murk of his subconscious, there returned to him the opening sentence of *Moby-Dick*: "Call me Ishmael." This sentence, in which the novel's narrator introduces himself, echoed in John's consciousness as he resumed and finished his story. A single sentence—a mere three words—suggested a sense of directness that helped him quickly and easily transpose his thoughts to paper.

When he mentioned this experience to a friend who had studied *Moby-Dick* in depth, the friend told him that he had misinterpreted the line "Call me Ishmael"—that it was not about "directness" but about "indirectness and evasion." John thought about this and replied, "You may be right. I only know that that line—whatever it means—helped me produce the best writing I've ever done."

A line from Shakespeare's *King Lear* says, "Nothing will come of nothing." Change the terms in that sentence a bit and you have a truism about the process of writing: *Something will come from something.* Writers have long complained about the dreaded "blank page"; the blank page only exists if you allow it to. Do you want or need to write? Then put something in front of you—a story, a poem, a paragraph—and react to it. Words will come, and sentences will accumulate; and if you react to something that strikes you in a special way the sentences will probably be interesting—or have the potential to be. At its most basic, *writing is reading—reacting*.

What it is about a particular reading that prompts you to write doesn't have to be something major; often—as the examples of John and of Robin, Sally, and Erica in the previous chapter illustrate—it will be something small: a theme, a character, an image, a phrase. The size of the catalyst is not important. What does matter is how powerfully it resonates with your own life and imagination.

A Four-Step Process for Writing from Reading

How can you do as John did and identify the powerful connections you have with a text? How can you then use those connections to produce satisfying writing of your own? Here is a four-step process that builds on the conversation model discussed in Chapter 1. You can apply the process to all your reading   to the short stories, poems, essays, plays, and notebooks and journals in this book and to a range of other texts that you encounter in daily life. Note that you do not have to rigidly follow the steps. Some people prefer to combine steps one and two or to skip step three. Begin by trying all the steps; then adapt them to your own style and needs.

1. *Do a first reading of the text.* Concentrate on immersing yourself in its rhythms, ideas, conflicts, plot, themes, characters.

2. *On a second reading, annotate passages that strike you.* Perhaps you like an idea, a phrase, a character, or an image, or perhaps you are struck by a section of dialogue, or maybe you are puzzled or mystified by a passage. Underline or bracket any such item. (This assumes, of course, that your copy of the text is your own and not a library's.) Also, in the margins, jot down:

- *Questions* that a passage raises for you
- *Analytical comments*, i.e., what you think about a passage
- *Summaries* of what a passage is saying (for more about summarizing see p. 100)
- *Connections* that a passage suggests with anything else you have read, thought about, or experienced

The marks you make in a text are called *annotations*. Annotation is as basic to readers and writers as hammers are to carpenters or spoons to cooks. It is your main means of identifying the resonant points of connection you have with a text; these points, in turn, can motivate you to write, as "Call me Ishmael" catalyzed John.

Many great writers are annotators; they talk back to what they read, using the writings of others to start their own thought processes. A famous example is William Blake, eighteenth-century poet and artist. As he read a book by Sir Joshua Reynolds, a leading artist with whom he disagreed passionately, Blake was furiously taking notes, developing, in a mass of annotations, his own theory of art.

Here are some excerpts from Reynolds's text (*Discourses on Art*) followed by Blake's annotations (the unusual capitalization is Blake's):

Blake: (general comment on the *Discourses*): This Man was Hired to Depress Art.

Reynolds: How incapable of producing anything of their own, those are, who have spent most of their time in making finished copies, is an observation well known to all who are conversant with our art.

Blake: Finished! What does he Mean? Niggling Without the Correct & Definite Outline? If he means That Copying Correctly is a hindrance he is a Liar, for that is the only School to the Language of Art.

Reynolds: But this disposition to abstraction, to generalizing and classification, is the great glory of the human mind.

Blake: To Generalize is to be an Idiot. To Particularize is the Alone Distinction of Merit. General Knowledges are those Knowledges that Idiots possess.

Reynolds: When we read the lives of the most eminent Painters, every page informs us, that no part of their time was spent in dissipation.

Blake: The Lives of Painters say that Rafael died of Dissipation. Idleness is one Thing & Dissipation Another. He who has Nothing to Dissipate Cannot Dissipate. The Weak Man may be Virtuous Enough, but will Never be an Artist. Painters are noted for being Dissipated & Wild.

Some of the notes Blake jotted down in this fashion resurfaced, verbatim or transformed, as lines in his published work. Blake used his annotations to develop his own thoughts, which in turn overflowed into his formal writing.

Ralph Waldo Emerson (1803–1882) was another annotator, though he preferred to write his annotations in separate notebooks rather than in the margins. Emerson thought of himself as a "creative" reader. Some of his notes were strikingly *dissociative* in character; that is, they didn't seem obviously relevant to the texts he was reading but were nevertheless triggered by them. For instance, as a young man a book on reason and revelation inspired him to write a paragraph about the uninhabited parts of the world being perhaps "the abodes of other orders of sentient beings invisible or unexperienced."[1] Emerson's habit of using reading to stimulate writing stuck with him all his life. To a young ac-

---

1. Quoted in Robert D. Richardson, Jr., *Emerson: The Mind on Fire* (Berkeley: University of California Press, 1995, p. 11.)

quaintance he once summed up his philosophy of reading as follows: "[O]nly read to start your own team."

The key to successful annotating is that you trust the *first thoughts* that occur to you as you read, and write them down. If you are used to doubting the value of your every thought, this requires conscious effort and practice. You may be more accustomed to trusting in second thoughts, those socially acceptable or "correct" thoughts that censor the first ones as "dumb," "ridiculous," or "irrelevant." Reject these second thoughts and cleave to the first. There will be time later for revising and refining your first thoughts.

In a sense good annotating requires *un*learning; often it is less a matter of thinking harder than of thinking *less* hard. Rather than straining to write the "correct" or intellectually "comprehensive" response, you relax, as William Blake did, to write whatever occurs to you. For example, here is how Tyler annotated the opening paragraph of Kate Chopin's "The Story of an Hour" (p. 181):

> Knowing that Mrs. Mallard was afflicted with a <u>heart trouble</u>, great care was taken to break to her as gently as possible the news of her husband's death.

My good elderly friend had heart trouble too. Jack had a valve replacement.

At first Tyler's annotation may seem odd and irrelevant; after all, it refers to his "good elderly friend," who isn't even a character in Chopin's story. However, Tyler trusts his first thought enough to write it down and leave questions of relevance till later.

This trust pays off, as the initial memory of his "good elderly friend" stirs other memories. One thought reminds him of another, which reminds him of yet another, and another, and so forth: "Jack Hislop lived next door for the majority of my youth. He was like a grandfather to me. . . . I remembered how Jack would joke about his heart, 'I've got a pig valve in my heart, oink-oink.' That would always make me laugh." Shared times with Jack, Jack's appearance and mannerisms, fragments of conversation—all these surface, one after another, in Tyler's consciousness. Ultimately, out of these memories he composes a three-page portrait entitled "Grandpa Jack." Here is a portion of what he wrote (a copy of the complete portrait can be found in Appendix A):

> As a little boy I would go over to visit [Jack] almost every day after school. One day I ran over to his house and found him lounging on the patio in his back yard. "Take a seat, partner," said Jack as he pulled up a chair for me. He fed me some cold watermelon and a large glass of "sodi water," as he called it. While I was enjoying the fruit Jack told me a story about when he was a young sheepherder. "I was no older than you, partner, maybe eleven years old. . . . Me and Pa and a few of my brothers were high on Durphies' Peak taking the sheep down to a nearby watering hole." His eyes were flashing as he was trying to point out where they were, since the mountain was in a broadside view. "A few sheep took off

up a narrow canyon, and I got roped into chasin' after 'em. I rode up the canyon a little way and seen 'em up ahead so I galloped my horse to catch 'em. When I caught those little rascals I started herding 'em back down to the watering hole. On the way down the canyon my horse started to get jittery because some bushes started to shake up ahead, and out charged a huge brown bear." Jack was standing now giving the motions of the incident. Jack blurted, "Holy Shit!" then apologized to me because his wife didn't like him to cuss. "The damn horse started to buck and my two dogs went into a barking frenzy. The bear was huge, it was at least ten feet tall when it reared up on his hind legs. The dogs distracted the bear long enough allowin' me to ride up and around to safety."

If you read "The Story of an Hour," the text that inspired "Grandpa Jack," you will find that it focuses on a woman and her feelings about marriage and her husband. Tyler's annotation (and the text it engendered) is about a colorful old friend and has virtually nothing to do with women, husbands, or marriage. What then? Is it merely eccentric and irrelevant? "Yes" and "no." If you take Chopin's text as the central point of reference, then his annotation is indeed irrelevant; however, if you take as the main point of reference the overlap between Chopin's text and the texts of his own life, Tyler's annotation is right on target. After all, it prompts him to articulate an aspect of his life he might never have written about otherwise without the stimulus of Chopin.

A footnote: At home and in class Tyler found enthusiastic readers for his essay. How interesting that so individual a response could have broad appeal to others. At the heart of annotation is a paradox. The more individual it is—the more spontaneous and intuitive—the more it seems to tap into something *universal* in human experience. "Speak your latent conviction," said Emerson, "and it shall be the universal sense"; or, more simply, if you like it, other people will tend to like it, too.

Here is a second example of annotation. Margaret is a middle-aged wife and mother who has recently entered college. She reads and annotates the following poem by Linda Pastan (p. 336):

MARKS

My husband gives me an A
for last night's supper,
an incomplete for my ironing,
a B plus in bed.
My son says I am average,
an average mother, but if
I put my mind to it
I could improve.
My daughter believes
in Pass/Fail and tells me

Annotations:

he likes the supper, but anything else? Hm. Sounds like she does all the work—or lots—and then has to get grades for it (pouring salt in the wounds)

More work . . . Is this son shiftless like mine? He should talk!

Hard! Anything less than an "A" really hurts

The "typical" family: father, mother, son, daughter. Everyone rates her

I pass. Wait 'til they learn——Wow! She gonna kill herself?
I'm dropping out.   get a divorce? take a break?
                          This'll shake 'em up

Note the individuality of Margaret's annotations. Like Tyler, Margaret writes spontaneously and directly about the points at which the literary text speaks to her. By annotating she focuses her attention less on the poem itself than on the overlap between the poem and various aspects of her own life—her own experiences, knowledge, thoughts, and feelings.

3. *Read over your annotations; then take several minutes to list the most powerful thoughts and impressions the text inspires in you.* Here again, trusting your first thoughts is crucial. Instead of writing down the sorts of ideas you think you *ought* to have, put in your list what you *want* to put there. For instance, after Margaret has read and annotated "Marks," she makes the following list:

- I like the phrase 'Wait 'til they learn/I'm dropping out.' It sounds like an ultimatum.
- Idea: being a wife/mother like being in school. Grades, grades, grades! Always someone grading you.
- I relate to this woman.
- How will she drop out?
- I get a picture of this woman working hard all day and her husband comes home and expects everything to be done for him hand and foot. The son and daughter show up for meals but are always running off to have fun somewhere.
- This house sounds like lots I know. Starting with *mine*.
- Who gets grades? Kids. The mother never gets to grow up!

4. *Review your list; identify your most intense point of response, and compose a text of your own.* To see some of the kinds of texts you can write at this stage, look ahead to the section entitled "Ten Ideas for Writing in a Reading Notebook" in Chapter 3. Margaret reviews her list of thoughts and impressions and finds her prevailing response is a sense of identification with the speaker in the poem. She explores this identification in a text of her own.

School of Hard Knocks

Grading doesn't begin and end with school. It goes on all our lives. That's what this poem showed me. Wives and mothers especially; we're always being graded!

I got married right out of high school and I thought I was done with getting grades. Little did I know I was just going from one school to another. And I don't mean college. I mean marriage.

There are several classes in this "school."

Marriage 101 is living with a husband. In my case a husband I hardly knew. A nice man and a good provider and all, it turned out, but also a lout who expected me to wait on him hand and foot. Cook the meals, wash the dishes, clean the house, do the errands, entertain the company.

A typical scene: I'm cleaning the bathroom in 95 degree heat, sweat   5
pouring down my face, and he's in the livingroom watching baseball and drinking a beer. His buddies are with him and when the snack tray's empty they yell at me to "please" get more. If I'm a little slow I get a dirty look (that's a "C"). If I yell "Help yourself" and don't come at all I get a growl and some angry comments about "women" (that's an "F"). If I load up the tray and deliver it with a smile it's a "B." To get an "A" I have to do some extra credit—give them their potato chips plus a new round of beers ("A" if the beers are cold, "A−" if they're not).

Marriage 201 is kids. I love my kids, don't get me wrong. They were cute babies and except for the terrible two's the sweetest children I'll ever see. But since they hit their teens it's been a downhill road.

They treat me like their live-in cook and maid. I spend an hour in a hot kitchen making supper—something a little special, chicken cooked a new way—and they shovel it down without a word, it might as well be an old sock fried in batter. No "thank you's" or "This is great"—they're in too big a hurry to get somewhere—a dance, a game, and other places I probably don't want to know about.

I guess they'd give me a "B" for cooking—not good enough for praise, not bad enough to make them throw up (an "F"). If they don't like what I give them you can bet I hear about it. "Mom, what is this?" "Mom, are we supposed to eat this meatloaf or use it for a paperweight?" That's a "C−"—if they even bother to force it down, that is. A grade of "D" means "give it to the Dog."

Kids grade like most of the teachers I had in school. If they like it they don't tell you, and if they hate it they don't let you forget.

Next we come to Marriage 301: middle age. In my generation this   10
means a daughter going on to college and asking you why you became a homemaker and mother instead of getting "a real job." So I could have you and have conversations like this, I say. She looks at me confused like I must be lying. A real job. Boy! I'll tell you about a real job. . . . *This* is a real job. But it's not the job she's interested in.

I'm 45 years old and was on the verge of burnout when I decided to go back to school this fall. I'm a college freshman now at the same school my daughter graduated from a year ago. My son's a sophomore. And I'm getting grades. Am I living my life backwards, or what? I wonder some-times. I seem to be going back to my childhood: teachers giving me grades. And the teachers get younger and younger. My Math professor's a girl hardly older than my daughter. When she gave me my first test back with a "B" it reminded me of fried chicken! Déjà vu!

Only a mother would understand.

Note that this process of writing from reading leads Margaret to write, as Tyler did, about a number of things that aren't exactly *in* the springboard literary text but are suggested by it. For instance:

- Beliefs traditional in Margaret's culture about appropriate sex roles for men and women—and counterbeliefs that challenge the traditional roles
- The habits and behaviors of her own husband and kids and of other husbands and kids
- Mealtime conversations (those in her own home and perhaps analogous ones she has heard—or heard of—in other homes)
- Memories of various dinners such as chicken and meatloaf
- The particular feelings one has cleaning bathrooms on hot days
- The addiction of some men to TV sports
- The politics of classrooms like grading and teacher-student relations
- Ageism and sexism (both her direct observations of them in life and what she has observed, indirectly, through magazines, books, cosmetics ads, TV shows, movies, and so forth)

You might represent Margaret's reading graphically as follows:

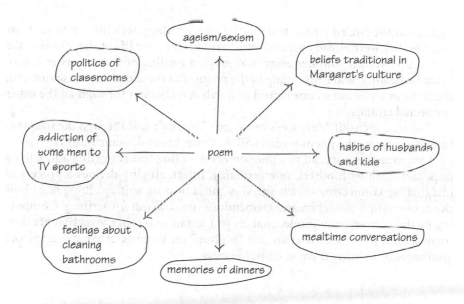

The point in the center is her starting point for writing, i.e., Pastan's poem. The arrows outward lead to the ideas, themes, beliefs, observations, experiences, and memories that she stumbled onto through the process of composing "School of Hard Knocks" and that generated her original focus.

Add a few more lines and you have an image of a web:

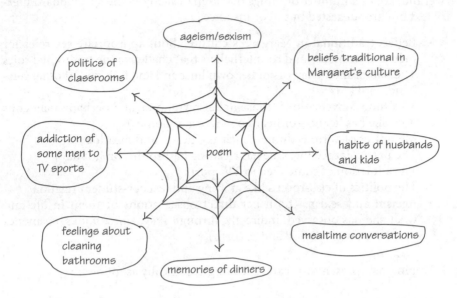

Again, call the circled items "texts"—the texts of Margaret's life. They are texts because they were already present and "written" into her life at the moment she picked up "Marks," and her essay is as much a reading of these texts as it is of Pastan's. Reading and responding to the poem stirs these texts to consciousness, the same as a motion in one strand of a web reverberates through all the other connected strands.

The true focus of Margaret's essay isn't "Marks"; it is the weblike intertextual connections the poem evokes with her own life and imagination.

Language theorists call this phenomenon, of one text activating and talking back and forth with others, *intertextuality*. Intertextuality defines a process of imaginative connecting that is the very pulse beat of writing. It explains how the conversation model creates tremendous momentum for writing. Composing by the conversation model enables you to tap into other texts that are dormant within you—texts that are just "waiting" for some external influence, i.e., another text, to bring them to consciousness.

Applying the Four-Step Process

Now try the Four-Step Process for yourself on the following short poem. Like Tyler and Margaret, strive to focus not on the "meaning" of the work itself but on the overlap of the text with the texts of your own life and imagination. If you wish, do the first three steps collaboratively, with a group or as a class. For Step Four ("compose a text of your own"), strive to write at least three hundred words.

WAITING FOR THE IDIOT TO GO AWAY

PETER SHARPE

The sweet tomato face annealed to itself
in all directions and pressed sloppily
to the car window.
    I sat five years old asking
'why does he do that' and 'why is he like that'.   5
His name was Benji, he was really
35 or 38 years old and he drooled
and was short. I never got
an answer from my father, who
stared straight ahead, his foot tapping   10
nervously on the accelerator pedal,
lips tight and knuckles whitening
on the wheel, 'pretend he isn't there'
he told me.
    I had my first remembered lesson   15
in the social graces: the world
was imperfect, and this was embarrassing.

When you have finished, reflect on the Four-Step Process in your notebook.
How did this mode of responding compare with the ways you have written in
response to literature in the past? What do you like or dislike about the writing
you produced for Step Four? If your piece pleased you, excellent; if not, bear in
mind that *no* writer produces great work every time he or she sits down to
write. Some of what a writer writes is good, and much—perhaps even most—is
"bad" or disappointing. What matters is that out of the patient and continual
practice of conversational reading and writing, *good writing will eventually
come.* To put your "bad" writing in perspective, glance ahead to the section on
"Revising" (p. 55) in Chapter 4

Some Implications of Intertextuality

The experiences of Tyler and Margaret show that you don't need a brilliant
imagination in order to write well; already woven into your life is a rich web of
texts that merely require the catalyst of an outside text, such as "The Story of an
Hour" or "Marks," in order to be realized on paper (or computer screen). The
texts Margaret and Tyler wrote did not materialize out of nothing; they
emerged out of other texts—"The Story of an Hour," "Marks," and the texts of
Tyler's and Margaret's own lives. The French painter Pierre Auguste Renoir
could have had people like Tyler and Margaret in mind when he wrote, "The
artist who uses the least of what is called imagination will be the greatest."

This notion—that every text comes out of other texts—may upset some deeply embedded beliefs you have about the "originality" of stories, poems, plays, and other works. You may suppose, for example, that a creation like *Hamlet* was woven entirely out of Shakespeare's imagination and owed little or nothing to the example, structure, style, and themes of other works. But—alas—such a notion is contradicted by evidence. Scholars have shown that Shakespeare probably drew liberally upon other texts when he wrote *Hamlet*. The acting company to which he belonged was performing a *Hamlet* by an earlier author in the 1590s, several years before Shakespeare wrote his own play. He would have known the earlier play and most likely have performed in it. This early play was, in turn, indebted to still older versions of the Hamlet story dating as far back as the twelfth century.

Aside from these obvious intertextual borrowings, we can generalize about other texts that must have echoed, consciously or subconsciously, in the Bard's mind as he composed *Hamlet*: his boyhood experiences of plays and entertainments in his native town of Stratford; the plethora of plays by his fellow playwrights, whose works he either performed or saw produced in London and at court; the many structural and stylistic conventions, e.g., soliloquies and asides, of Elizabethan tragedy; the texts of classical poetry and rhetoric; his intensive training and experience as an actor; his firsthand knowledge of stage mechanics and directing; and any number of personal and cultural "texts" that are more difficult to name exactly but that doubtless played a part.

We can infer from the example of Shakespeare—and of countless other creators—that there is no such thing as an "original" work in the pure sense.

Our traditional sense of printed texts is tacitly hierarchical. A creation like *Hamlet* or *Moby-Dick* ranks at the top of the hierarchy, while newspaper editorials, song lyrics, pop novels, and your own writings rank lower. A work by William Faulkner or Alice Walker—both internationally famous authors—rates high on the scale, while the story you compose is "just (blush) something I wrote." Of course, this hierarchy makes sense in some respects; by most people's standards, your short story isn't as "good" as Faulkner's. But such ratings rest on culturally and individually based notions of literary value and cause us to forget that there are other ways of looking at texts—for instance, the intertextual way.

Intertextuality focuses attention less on questions of literary value than on textuality itself. From that admittedly limited but too often ignored perspective, no text is "better" than another. Intertextuality democratizes. All pieces of writing are equal in terms of their shared identity and utility *as texts*.

A consciousness of intertextuality empowers you as a reader and writer. Every text—everything you read and everything you write—flows out of and into other texts. No text is closed off or completely self-sufficient. No text represents the Last Word.

Your awareness of intertextuality renders any text you read more accessible and more human. Take *Hamlet*, for instance. If you view it as "perhaps the greatest play ever written by perhaps the greatest writer who ever lived," it overwhelms you; it makes you afraid to write yourself. After all, who are you to meddle with a masterpiece like that? Your fear and insecurity are one with that of thousands of English students down through the decades who have balked helplessly at an assignment to "write an essay about *Hamlet.*"

On the other hand, if you view *Hamlet* as the outcome of a complex interaction of many texts—and as a prompt for countless others, e.g., the volumes and volumes of Shakespeare criticism that have been written; the plays, poems, stories, screenplays, musicals, and other imaginative works that have been partially prompted by *Hamlet*—then the play becomes less a holy relic and more a part of the complicated, ever-expanding web of human discourse. *Hamlet* is a strand in the web, a remark in an endless conversation that originated long before Shakespeare's time, reverberates in the present, and will echo and reecho long beyond today.

Viewed from some outlying perspective that takes in all of human time, *Hamlet* appears as just another turn—a brilliant and memorable turn, to be sure—in an ongoing conversation. It is of the nature of conversation to invite additional turn-taking. Reading *Hamlet,* you are welcome to respond to it; you are welcome to add your bit to the conversation.

It may help to think of this visually. Divorced from a notion of intertextuality, a text looks something like this:

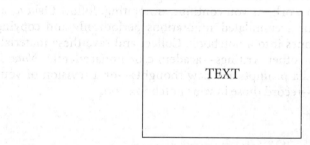

Its edges are hard and defined, closed off to creative reading and responding. Viewed through the lens of intertextuality, on the other hand, the text looks like this:

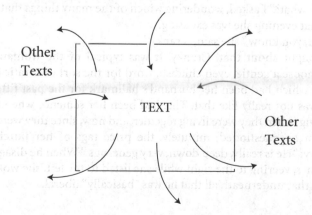

The edges are broken, open, allowing a fluid intercourse of this text with others—past, present, and future; printed and unprinted.

ACTIVITIES FOR WRITING

1. Use the "Four-Step Process for Writing from Reading" to respond to either of the texts printed at the end of this chapter, by Ellen Goodman and Barbara Crooker.
   a. Read through the text a first time without marking it (unless you feel moved to do so).
   b. On a second reading, annotate.
   c. Alone or with a group, create a list of the most powerful thoughts and impressions the piece inspires in you. Don't worry if items on your list seem to go off on a tangent from the text itself.
   d. Identify your favorite item or items in the list of thoughts and impressions and use it/them to create a text of your own that is at least three hundred words long.

2. As mentioned earlier, William Blake incorporated some of his annotations into his published work. As you continue annotating, follow Blake's example by rereading your accumulated annotations periodically and copying any especially striking ones into a notebook. Collect and save these materials for possible use in your other writings—academic or nonacademic. *Note:* If rereading your marginalia prompts any new thoughts—or a revision of your original marginal note—record those in your notebook, too.

LIVE-IN MYTHS

ELLEN GOODMAN

"He is not really like that," she said apologetically as her husband left the room.

"Like what?" I asked, wondering which of the many things that had happened that evening she was excusing.

"Well, you know," she said, "cranky."

I thought about that. Cranky. It was typical of the woman that she would choose a gentle, even childish, word for the sort of erratic outbursts of anger which had been her husband's hallmark for the past fifteen years.

He was not really like that. This had been her sentence when they were first dating, when they were living together, and now, since they were married.

When he questioned, minutely, the price tags of her purchases, she would say: "He is really, deep down, very generous." When he disagreed with her politics, veering to the right while she listed to the left, she would cheerily insist that underneath all that he was "basically" liberal.

When he blamed her for the condition of the house, as if he were a lodger, and blamed her for the children's illnesses, as if her negligence had caused their viruses, she would explain, "He is really very understanding."

Even when he was actually his most vital self, amusing and expansive, full of martinis or enthusiasm or himself—and she disapproved—she would forgive him because he wasn't really like that.

This time, dining with them out of town one brief night, I saw that this was the pattern of their lives together—a struggle between realities. His real and her "really."

I had known the wife since college and the husband from their first date. When they met she was a social worker and he was, it seems, her raw material. Was he the case and she the miracle worker? At times she looked at him that way.

Her husband was erratic and difficult, but he had a streak of humor and zaniness as attractive as Alan Arkin's. Over the years, he had grown "crankier" and she more determined in her myth-making.

This trip, for the first time, I wondered what it must be like to be a text living with an interpreter. To be not really like that. And what it must be like for her, living with her myth as well as her man.

I know many other people who live with their ideas of each other. Not with a real person but with a "really." They doggedly refuse to let the evidence interfere with their opinions. They develop an idea about the other person and spend a lifetime trying to make him or her live up to that idea. A lifetime, too, of disappointments.

As James Taylor sings it: "First you make believe / I believe the things that you make believe / And I'm bound to let you down. / Then it's I who have been deceiving / Purposely misleading / And all along you believed in me."

But when we describe what the other person is really like, I suppose we often picture what we want. We look through the prism of our need.

I know a man who believes that his love is really a very warm woman. The belief keeps him questing for that warmth. I know a woman who is sure that her mate has hidden strength, because she needs him to have it.

Against all evidence, one man believes that his woman is nurturing because he so wants her to be. After twenty years, another woman is still tapping hidden wells of sensuality in her mate, which he has, she believes, "repressed."

And maybe they are right and maybe they are wrong, and maybe they are each other's social workers. But maybe they are also afraid that if they let go of their illusions, they will not like each other.

We often refuse to see what we might not be able to live with. We choose distortion.

Leaving this couple, I thought about how much human effort can go into maintaining the "really." How much daily energy that might have gone into understanding the reality—accepting it or rejecting it.

How many of us spend our lives trying to sustain our myths, and how we are "bound to be let down." Because most people are, after all, the way they seem to be.

Really.

You might find yourself particularly drawn to Goodman's reflections in the last several paragraphs, or, just as easily, you might focus your annotations and response on the people and situations portrayed in the first half of the piece. What are this wife and husband like? Do they remind you of any people from your own experience? Do you know—or can you imagine—"people who live with their *ideas* of each other" [italics added] rather than with their authentic selves? These questions suggest just a few of the many points of connection you might find with this text.

Patty's Charcoal Drive-In

Barbara Crooker

First job. In tight black shorts
and a white bowling shirt, red lipstick
and bouncing pony tail, I present
each overflowing tray as if it were a banquet.
I'm sixteen and college-bound,   5
this job's temporary as the summer sun,
but right now, it's the boundaries of my life.
After the first few nights of mixed orders
and missing cars, the work goes easily.
I take out the silver trays and hook them to the windows,   10
inhale the mingled smells of seared meat patties,
salty ketchup, rich sweet malteds.
The lure of grease drifts through the thick night air.
And it's always summer at Patty's Charcoal Drive-In—
carloads of blonde-and-tan girls   15
pull up next to red convertibles,
boys in black tee shirts and slick hair.
Everyone knows what they want.
And I wait on them, hoping for tips,
loose pieces of silver   20
flung carelessly as the stars.
Doo-wop music streams from the jukebox
and each night repeats itself,
faithful as a steady date.
Towards 10 P.M., traffic dwindles.   25
We police the lot, pick up wrappers,
The dark pours down, sticky as Coke,
but the light from the kitchen
gleams like a beacon.
A breeze comes up, chasing papers   30

in the far corners of the darkened lot,
as if suddenly a cold wind had started to blow—
straight at me from the future—
I read that in a Doris Lessing book—
but right now, purse fat with tips,
the moon sitting like a cheeseburger on a flat black grill,
this is enough.
Your order please.

35

Building a Reading Notebook: Ten Ideas for Writing from Reading

Everything has been said before. There's nothing new to write about—always the same old things, the same old lies and the same old loves and the same old tragedy and joy. But you can write about them in a new way, your own way.

—EUGENE O'NEILL

Famous Writers at Work

How do writers produce their finished works? Do their stories, poems, essays, and plays materialize magically out of nothing? As suggested in the previous chapter, writers produce texts out of already existing texts. The examples of this are virtually limitless.

Anton Chekhov (1860–1904) was one of the world's greatest short story writers. Through much of his career he kept notebooks in which he recorded ideas for stories, brief character sketches, snippets of dialogue, memorable images and quotations, and thoughts. Many of these items furnished materials for his published stories. Toward the end of his life he said that he had enough ideas stored up in his notebook "for five years of work."

Playwright Eugene O'Neill (1888–1953) had an enormous impact on the development of modern drama and was awarded the Nobel Prize for Literature in 1936. Behind O'Neill the great dramatist is O'Neill the notebook writer. In his notebooks O'Neill recorded his "readings" of his own life and of the world around him. The plays that made him famous evolved out of notes, sketches, and outlines that he collected in these notebooks. Often this involved a remarkably slow process of accretion and reworking. For instance, one of his best plays, *The Iceman Cometh,* evolved from notes he made as many as twenty years before the play was published.

Emily Dickinson (1830–1886), who was all but unpublished during her lifetime, left behind nearly eighteen hundred poems which did not appear in their first complete and scholarly edition until almost seventy years after her death. Rather than pushing to place her work in periodicals or publish them in books, she wove many of her poems into hand-made booklets and shared poems with family and friends in her personal letters. The fact that some poems appear in more than one letter, or in multiple versions, and sometimes in letters that are dated many years apart, suggests that Dickinson amassed large stores of poems and poetic fragments that she regularly mined and reworked for her own satisfaction and for inclusion in her favorite form of publication—the personal letter. Interestingly, Dickinson never made money or gained much public reputation from writing during her lifetime; she loved the process of creation itself.

These are glimpses of writers at work. While the details of habit and behavior differ from one writer to the next, certain commonalities emerge: they collect material; at various times they reread and rework it. Composing is the process of "conversing" with the accumulated notes—reviewing, expanding, revising, and reordering them. The strategy that drives Chekhov's and O'Neill's notebooks and Dickinson's booklets and letters is simple: to accumulate writings that can be reread later and selectively discarded—or reworked and revised into more finished writing. Such is the principle behind the reading notebook.

Using Reading as a Springboard for Writing

Simply defined, a reading notebook is a place where you do as Chekhov, O'Neill, and Dickinson did and "springboard" off of texts that you read. These texts may be printed works, such as the stories, poems, essays, plays, and notebooks and journals in Part V of this book; or they may be unprinted "texts," such as movies, TV programs, pictures, songs, memories, personal relationships, experiences, or conversations. You use these texts, which suffuse your everyday life, as prompts for your own writing.

Ten Ideas for Writing in a Reading Notebook

Use your notebook for producing all kinds of writings that get you involved, personally and imaginatively, in what you read. Here are some suggestions. You can find additional examples of each of these "Ten Ideas" in Appendix A.

1. *Converse with specific points in the text that strike you.* In conversations with other people you do a number of things: agree, disagree, question, comment, joke, continue a point, and so on; you can converse in similar ways with the texts you read. For example, Stephanie read Ray Bradbury's "[A Story About Love]" (p. 207) and commented on several quotations that were key to her:

> "It's the privilege of old people to seem to know everything. But it's an act and a mask, like every other act and mask. Between ourselves, we old ones wink at each other and smile, saying, How do you like *my* mask, *my* act, *my* certainty? Isn't life a play? Don't I play it well?"

This statement is so very true. Everyone has a mask and plays a part. The only exceptions are children, until they reach a certain age and then they become like the rest of the actors. People play a part and wear a mask because they're afraid of rejection and persecution. No one likes to have their feelings hurt or their egos smashed in.

> "When you're twenty-seven if you still know everything you're still seventeen."

This statement is profound. I think what she means is that if you are 27 and think you know everything, you haven't lived enough, matured enough, or experienced enough to be more than 17. You may have the body of a 27 year-old, but your mind is that of a seventeen year-old.

> "[T]he average man runs helter-skelter the moment he finds anything like a brain in a lady."

This statement strikes me as one spoken by someone who knows. From personal experience, this statement is a fact. I think the key word here is "average." It takes a man who is secure enough in himself and who can see beyond the mask to know when he's got something in a woman with a brain. This is not an average man. That man is an extraordinary man.

> "Kindness and intelligence are the preoccupations of age."

I agree that people become wiser with age, but I don't think that kindness is necessarily a preoccupation of age. Most people try very hard to be kind and spare others' feelings. If she is talking about genuine kindness, then perhaps that is a preoccupation of age. Genuine kindness is a part of the real person; kindness is just another one of the masks we wear.

2. *Write about any personal connections you have with the reading.* Margaret's writing from "Marks," quoted in Chapter 2, is a good example.

3. *Write a letter to the author and/or a return letter from the author to yourself.* This is a good way to gain more confidence in yourself as a reader. Instead

of effacing yourself before the author, you address the writer familiarly and person-to-person. You can write to the author about most anything—from your evaluation of the work to your thoughts about a theme, a character or characters, life issues, or literary technique. Stan read Emily Dickinson's "The Soul Selects Her Own Society" (p. 613) and a few other Dickinson poems, as well as some biographical material. Confused by the poetry but fascinated by the unusual life of its author (see Appendix D), he wrote the following letter:

Dear Ms. Dickinson:

I hope you won't think I'm disrespectful, but I have a few questions for you. You seem a little unapproachable to me. Your poems are some of the most difficult I've ever seen—they hardly seem to be written in English.

I wonder if there is some connection between the meaning of your poems and your lifestyle.

Why did you shut yourself off from the world? Why, after a certain point in life, did you wear only white? Why did you write so many hundreds of poems without publishing them?

I could go on, but this is probably enough questions for now.
Sincerely,
Stan

P.S.—Please write back in language I can understand.

P.P.S.—I have my own theory of why you shut yourself off. I think you did it as a way to have maximum control over your own life. Live like a recluse and no one will bother you. You get a father who brings home cash, keeps bread on the table, and stays downstairs. You get a sister who can manage the little chores you don't feel like doing and who also stays downstairs—unless you ask her up. You have a servant or two to clean, cook, do the laundry, and you've got it made. You can bake, garden, and do just enough domestic chores to put "experience" into your poems, and you are running the house while everyone else just thinks you are "poor brilliant Emily" who's a little crazy in the head. You shut yourself off, in short, as part of a conscious strategy to control your family and amuse the neighbors so they would leave you alone to do what you wanted to—write.

Dear friend:
Such bolts of clarity
Inspire your charity—
E. Dickinson

4. *Write an imaginary interview with the author or with a character in a story, novel, or play.* This idea has the same basic advantages as letter writing. The interview format lets you see, hear, and address the author as a flesh-and-blood

person. Use your interview to ask the author questions about his or her text, style, characters, ideas, and life, for example.

5. *Compose a prequel or a sequel to a story.* Have you ever felt disappointed to see a story end? Perhaps you enjoyed the plot or identified with the characters and themes and could gladly have inhabited the world of that story—or novel or play—a while longer. Composing a prequel or sequel is an excellent way to do just that. You can sustain the lives of the characters beyond the author's pre-scribed ending, or you can imagine what the characters did, thought, and expe-rienced before the story proper begins. This is also a relaxed and pleasurable way of imitating the author's tone, style, and methods of characterization; that is, it is a good way of broadening your own storytelling repertoire.

Helen and Bill, the main characters in Bradbury's "[A Story About Love]," become acquainted one summer day in a drugstore. They fall in love despite a vast difference in age—she is ninety-five and he is thirty-one—and have only a brief relationship before she dies. In the story "reincarnation" is mentioned. This gave Trent the idea to invent a sequel, "written in a Southeast Asian style," that incorporates Buddhist mythology and the idea of reincarnation. "Bud-dhism," Trent explains, "teaches that human beings can be reincarnated in one of two ways: first, they can improve because of good actions in this life; second, they can regress if they involve themselves in unclean activities."

As William left the house of Helen, she truly desired to be with him. She hoped there was a way because her feelings for him were strong. At this time Buddha looked down and was filled with mercy.

He said to those enlightened about him, "This mortal truly possesses the love necessary to obtain the wish of her heart." He paused, then con-tinued: "But does the other possess the same quality?"

Ong Dia, one of the enlightened, spoke: "We must test the mortal to see if he has this quality."

Buddha replied, "Yes, we must do even as you say, Ong Dia."

Buddha then turned to Tao Quan and said, "Tao Quan, you must go down to the earth and test this mortal. Create a situation in which the mortal voluntarily chooses to do an act of love and mercy; if he chooses not to do this act, then he will not obtain the wish of his heart, and he will have to suffer regression in the great pattern of reincarnation."

The night that Helen died was hard for Bill, and he was having diffi-culty dealing with it. Just at this moment, a man ran up behind him. The man drew out a knife and demanded Bill's wallet, then ran away. Bill felt as though he had nothing to lose so he chased the man into the woods. They ran for a few minutes, then the thief tripped and fell. The thief was sliding down the edge of a hill which turned out to be a cliff. The bottom appeared to be some twenty feet down. The thief was hanging on to some foliage but was slipping fast.

The thief exclaimed, "Help me, please help me." Bill was scared, he did not know if he should help him. What if the man decided to use the knife and kill him anyway? Bill did not think long, he extended his hand to help the thief up.

Bill pulled the man up, and no sooner had he done so than he witnessed one of the most awesome spectacles he had ever seen. The thief changed form and seemed to float in the air. He then took on his true form, Tao Quan, one of the gods. Light and brilliance shone from his countenance.

Tao Quan spoke to him saying, "Great is the love and mercy possessed by you, mortal. You saved the life of one who had persecuted you and did it with the chance of losing your life; Buddha is smiling upon your action this night. Because of this thing you have done, you will receive the desire of your heart."

That night Bill was full of joy, but he did not know how his wish to be with Helen would be granted. He went to bed. The next morning he awoke and noticed nothing different. However, he felt a need to go to the drugstore.

He went in and everything seem to be the same; so he approached the snow-marble fountain. The man asked, "What'll it be?" Bill responded, "Old fashioned lime-vanilla ice." A shout of joy echoed throughout the store.

A beautiful young woman came running towards Bill. She looked familiar to him, and they embraced. He looked into her eyes and saw that it was Helen, except now she was young again. They held each other for a long time, then Bill whispered to Helen, "I love you." She answered, "I've waited for this day for 95 years. I love you too."

6. *Rewrite a text from a point of view different from that presented in the original text.* "Point of view" refers to the perspective from which a story is told. Any two witnesses to—or participants in—an event are apt to report different versions of what happened. Thus, events or impressions that seem to be definite and "factual" can change more or less drastically depending on who narrates and interprets them. (For more on the role of point of view in storytelling, see p. 131.)

Nathan found Chopin's "The Story of an Hour" was "too morose" for his taste, so in his response, he says, he " 'livened' it up by taking an outsider's perspective. Along the way I intertwined a little humor as well." Nathan rewrote "The Story of an Hour" from the point of view of the family physician in Brently and Louise Mallard's hometown. Since the physician appears only briefly in Chopin's short story, Nathan had to invent narrative details out of his own imagination:

"I want my mommy!"

The voices from the exam room could be heard out in the waiting room, making people very nervous. Inside the exam room a doctor struggled with his little patient as the father tried in vain to soothe the child.

Eventually a nurse brought in a lollipop which appeased the child somewhat, and the commotion subsided as the doctor quickly finished the child's checkup.

"There is a slight irritation in his ear due to an earlier rash which has flared up again. It should pass in a day or two," the doctor explained to the now frazzled yet relieved father.

As the father and son in tandem left, the doctor heard the nurse down the hall exclaim, "Next!" Wearily he waited for the next in a never-ending stream of patients, complaints, and anxious mothers of small children. It was always the same, day after day, month after month. Not that he minded, of course. The pay was good, the benefits many, and most of all, he knew it was a vital service he rendered to the people of his community. No, he didn't mind the work; it was just that he had seemingly fallen into a rut. Nothing ever changed. He wished that once in a while something so out of the ordinary would happen that he could get a fresh new perspective on everything.

The next person complained of stomach cramps. He prescribed the correct medication, and told the lady to see him again in a week if the pain still persisted.

Now he thought back to that very morning. He had expressed his feelings to his wife and wondered aloud to her what he could do about it. She had offered some words of encouragement, but said that it was something that he needed to work out for himself. Her last words as he exited the house were, "Maybe this'll be the day things change." He hoped she was right.

Suddenly his thoughts were interrupted by a nurse bringing hurried news of a train crash nearby. He acted quickly, telling the nurse to take over, and dashed out to his car.

When he got to the scene of the accident he was astounded by what he found. He had envisioned hundreds of people screaming, trapped inside a burning train. Instead, what he found was almost comical. The train had hit a herd of cattle while they crossed the tracks. The accident was an hour old when he arrived but appeared as if it had just happened moments ago. The engine had derailed, a fire had started, and the result was a fire that burned several head of cattle. One of the derailed cars contained superglue, and the whole conglomerate mess appeared as the largest, stickiest pile of hamburger the doctor had ever seen.

There were only minor injuries to the people involved, however, so when he got a call about a man involved in the wreck who had wandered home with a head injury he quickly drove to the person's house. When he got to the proper house he discovered the man was perfectly healthy, but his wife had just died. The situation was explained in this manner: the husband "died," the woman rejoiced, the "dead" husband returned, the wife then died, and now the husband rejoiced. The doctor thought it'd make a good Shakespearean play. He then determined the cause of death to be joy from hearing deathly news followed by extreme shock and grief on seeing the dead return. The doctor left satisfied at having his wish fulfilled at seeing the extraordinary.

7. *Rewrite a work into a different genre.* For instance, rewrite all or part of a short story as a poem, or a poem as a play, or a play as a letter, and so forth. Craig, a new father, was moved by Donald Hall's poem "My Son My Executioner" (page 335), in which the speaker/father ruminates on the theme of passing time. Hall's speaker glimpses his own mortality in the young life of his infant son. Craig rewrote the poem as a prose meditation by the father:

> I have such strange feelings as I cradle this child. On the one hand, a feeling of joy and happiness to be holding this new life that is bound to me so intimately. On the other hand, this infant child is like a mirror that shows me myself in a new and sudden light: for an instant it seems I am *myself* being cradled, and the large face looking down at me is my own father's. So *this* is what it's all about, I think: My own father is now an old man . . . his father's father is dead . . . life and death. At some level the fact that I am myself dying doesn't bother me because, for this moment, when everything is just an inseparable part of the living and dying, the individual *ME* doesn't matter, doesn't exist. It's a tender feeling I have as I contemplate my son's joyous life, which is all to come, and my own relentless decay. I almost envy myself this tenderness because such moments are so rare . . . moments of perfect wisdom, to be counted on the fingers of one hand.

8. *Borrow an incident or theme from a work to write a piece of your own based on a similar incident or theme.* The train wreck mentioned in Chopin's "The Story of an Hour" reminded JoEllen of a tragedy that occurred in her hometown when she was growing up, when two boys were killed by a train. "Even though I never really knew the family well," she wrote, "the story of these two boys being killed by a train had an impact on me." JoEllen borrowed the incident of the train death to create her own narrative and imagined herself into the story as the narrator/sister of the two boys.

> Life was casual in the small town of Kaysville. All the necessities were there: a good school, a small grocery store, a bank and the theatre. For such a small place a movie house was a luxury. Many people from neighboring towns came to see the big screen almost weekly. In our family, going to the movies was a monthly ritual. We lived on a farm on the west side of the tracks. Every day was filled to the brim with chores, school, and then chores again. My job was to feed the chickens and slop the

pigs. My two brothers helped pa milk the cows and feed the horses. Life was busy, but good.

The summer of '62 is when things changed. . . .

The rains never came that year. The crops were a complete loss and money was very tight. My brothers, now fifteen and sixteen, were looking for jobs off the farm to help ma and pa make ends meet. School was our only outlet from the frustrations we felt at home. One morning as we rode the bus to school we watched the passing train. As it thundered by we talked of its great power and strength. My oldest brother fantasized about what life would be like engineering a train and traveling all over the country. He felt his future was wide open in front of him. If he only knew. But none of us can predict what will happen in the future.

The day began with the rooster crowing to wake us for our morning chores. Our steps were a little lighter because it was Friday and we knew that we were going to the movies that night. The school day dragged on like most Fridays do, but finally the bell rang and we were out the door into the fresh fall air. We hurried through our chores and met ma in the kitchen fixing our supper. We urged her to hurry for we didn't want to miss a moment of the movie we had been waiting for. Ma and pa opted to stay home that night because of the lack of money or lack of interest—I'm not sure which. My oldest brother could drive, so he got the keys to pa's pickup and the three of us left ready for a break from reality on the farm. As we approached the train tracks my brother flipped on the radio and blasted it in our ears at a level that showed his enthusiasm for life. The night was pitch black with no moon in sight. What happened next was so quick that I can only guess. The powerful train that my brothers had admired only a few days before thundered upon us with no chance of escape. The impact on the driver's side sent me out of the window and to the side of the tracks. My brothers weren't as lucky. As I heard and felt the meshing of metal against metal and the screeching of wheels, I knew my life would never be the same.

9. *Borrow the genre or form of a work to create a piece of your own cast in the same genre or form.* A good example here is Daniel Keyes's story "Flowers for Algernon," which is a narrative related entirely through diary entries. Recall how Sally, mentioned in Chapter 1, borrowed Keyes's form to create a story about a "blocked" writer. While the theme of her story differed totally from Keyes's, the diary form provided a release for emotions and experiences Sally had not been able to articulate in other ways.

Unusual forms like that of "Flowers for Algernon" sometimes generate the most interesting and surprising responses. Eugene O'Neill wrote a one-act play, *Before Breakfast*, which has two characters, only one of whom actually speaks and appears onstage. (The play is a one-way conversation in which a wife, in the kitchen, talks to her husband, who is offstage in the bedroom.) Jean borrowed

O'Neill's formal technique to write a short one-way "dialogue" of her own in which a daughter talks on the phone with her mother and the mother herself is never actually heard. Incidentally, O'Neill himself got the idea for *Before Breakfast* from August Strindberg's one-act "monologue" play, *The Stronger.*

(10.) *Draft a fictional biography or autobiography of a character in a story, poem, or play.* One reason we enjoy literary texts is because they leave much to our own imaginations. Authors reveal selected facts about their characters and leave it to us to "fill in" gaps and missing details. You can use your notebook to reconstruct the life of a character who particularly intrigues you.

This list of "Ten Ideas" is by no means exhaustive. As you compose in your own notebook, you will doubtless discover other ideas for writing. The only rule is to write what you *want* to write, not what you feel you *should* write.

Review List of the Ten Ideas for Writing

1. Converse with specific points in the text that strike you.
2. Write about any personal connections you have with the reading.
3. Write a letter to the author and/or a return letter from the author to yourself.
4. Write an imaginary interview with the author or with a character in a story, novel, or play.
5. Compose a prequel or a sequel to a story.
6. Rewrite a text from a point of view different from that presented in the original text.
7. Rewrite a work into a different genre.
8. Borrow an incident or theme from a work to write a piece of your own based on a similar incident or theme.
9. Borrow the genre or form of a work to create a piece of your own cast in the same genre or form.
10. Draft a fictional biography or autobiography of a character in a story, poem, or play.

ACTIVITIES FOR WRITING

On the following pages are a short story (Elizabeth Bowen's "The Demon Lover"), a poem (Edward Field's "A Journey"), and a personal essay (N. Scott Momaday's "The Indian Dog"). Respond to any one of these readings using the Four-Step Process for Writing from Reading described in Chapter 2. For Step Four use one of the "Ten Ideas" in Chapter 3 and compose a response of at least three hundred words.

THE DEMON LOVER

ELIZABETH BOWEN

Towards the end of her day in London Mrs. Drover went round to her shut-up house to look for several things she wanted to take away. Some belonged to herself, some to her family, who were by now used to their country life. It was late August: it had been a steamy, showery day: at the moment the trees down the pavement glittered in an escape of humid yellow afternoon sun. Against the next batch of clouds, already piling up ink-dark, broken chimneys and parapets stood out. In her once familiar street, as in any unused channel, an unfamiliar queerness had silted up; a cat wove itself in and out of railings, but no human eye watched Mrs. Drover's return. Shifting some parcels under her arm, she slowly forced round her latchkey in an unwilling lock, then gave the door, which had warped, a push with her knee. Dead air came out to meet her as she went in.

The staircase window having been boarded up, no light came down into the hall. But one door, she could just see, stood ajar, so she went quickly through into the room and unshuttered the big window in there. Now the prosaic woman, looking about her, was more perplexed than she knew by everything that she saw, by traces of her long former habit of life—the yellow smoke-stain up the white marble mantelpiece, the ring left by a vase on the top of the escritoire; the bruise in the wallpaper where, on the door being thrown open wildly, the china handle had always hit the wall. The piano, having gone away to be stored, had left what looked like claw-marks on its part of the parquet. Though not much dust had seeped in, each object wore a film of another kind; and, the only ventilation being the chimney, the whole drawing-room smelled of the cold hearth. Mrs. Drover put down her parcels on the escritoire and left the room to proceed upstairs: the things she wanted were in a bedroom chest.

She had been anxious to see how the house was—the part-time caretaker she shared with some neighbors was away this week on his holiday, known to be not yet back. At the best of times he did not look in often, and she was never sure that she trusted him. There were some cracks in the structure, left by the last bombing, on which she was anxious to keep an eye. Not that one could do anything—

A shaft of refracted daylight now lay across the hall. She stopped dead and stared at the hall table—on this lay a letter addressed to her.

She thought first—then the caretaker *must* be back. All the same, who, seeing the house shuttered, would have dropped a letter in at the box? It was not a circular, it was not a bill. And the post office redirected, to the address in the country, everything for her that came through the post. The caretaker (even if he *were* back) did not know she was due in London today—her call here had been planned to be a surprise—so his negligence in the manner of this letter, leaving it to wait in the dusk and the dust, annoyed her. Annoyed, she picked up the letter, which bore no stamp. But it cannot be important, or they would know . . . . She took the letter rapidly upstairs with her, without a stop to look at the writing till she reached what had been her bedroom, where she let in light. The room looked over the garden and other gardens: the sun had gone in: as the clouds sharpened and lowered, the trees and rank lawns seemed already to smoke with dark. Her reluctance to look again at the letter came from the fact that she felt intruded upon—and by someone contemptuous of her ways. However, in the tenseness preceding the fall of rain she read it: it was a few lines.

> Dear Kathleen: You will not have forgotten that today is our anniversary, and the day we said. The years have gone by at once slowly and fast. In view of the fact that nothing has changed, I shall rely upon you to keep your promise. I was sorry to see you leave London, but was satisfied that you would be back in time. You may expect me, therefore, at the hour arranged. Until then . . .
>
> K.

Mrs. Drover looked for the date: it was today's. She dropped the letter on to the bed-springs, then picked it up to see the writing again—her lips, beneath the remains of lipstick, beginning to go white. She felt so much the change in her own face that she went to the mirror, polished a clear patch in it and looked at once urgently and stealthily in. She was confronted by a woman of forty-four, with eyes staring out under a hat-brim that had been rather carelessly pulled down. She had not put on any more powder since she left the shop where she ate her solitary tea. The pearls her husband had given her on their marriage hung loose around her now rather thinner throat, slipping in the V of the pink wool jumper her sister knitted last autumn as they sat around the fire. Mrs. Drover's most normal expression was one of controlled worry, but of assent. Since the birth of the third of her little boys, attended by a quite serious illness, she had had an intermittent muscular flicker to the left of her mouth, but in spite of this she could always sustain a manner that was at once energetic and calm.

Turning from her own face as precipitately as she had gone to meet it, she went to the chest where the things were, unlocked it, threw up the lid and knelt to search. But as rain began to come crashing down she could not keep from looking over her shoulder at the stripped bed on which the letter lay. Behind the blanket of rain the clock of the church that still stood struck six—with rapidly heightening apprehension she counted each of the slow strokes. "The hour arranged . . . . My God," she said, "*what* hour? How should I . . . . ? After twenty-five years . . . ."

The young girl talking to the soldier in the garden had not ever completely seen his face. It was dark; they were saying goodbye under a tree. Now and then—for it felt, from not seeing him at this intense moment, as though she had never seen him at all—she verified his presence for these few moments longer by putting out a hand, which he each time pressed, without very much kindness, and painfully, on to one of the breast buttons of his uniform. That cut of the button on the palm of her hand was, principally, what she was to carry away. This was so near the end of a leave from France that she could only wish him already gone. It was August 1916. Being not kissed, being drawn away from and looked at intimidated Kathleen till she imagined spectral glitters in the place of his eyes. Turning away and looking back up the lawn she saw, through branches of trees, the drawing-room window alight: she caught a breath for the moment when she could go running back there into the safe arms of her mother and sister, and cry: "What shall I do, what shall I do? He has gone."

Hearing her catch her breath, her fiancé said, without feeling: "Cold?"

"You're going away such a long way."

"Not so far as you think."

"I don't understand."

"You don't have to," he said, "You will. You know what we said."

"But that was—suppose you—I mean, suppose."

"I shall be with you," he said, "sooner or later. You won't forget that. You need do nothing but wait."

Only a little more than a minute later she was free to run up the silent lawn. Looking in through the window at her mother and sister, who did not for the moment perceive her, she already felt that unnatural promise drive down between her and the rest of all human kind. No other way of having given herself could have made her feel so apart, lost and foresworn. She could not have plighted a more sinister troth.

Kathleen behaved well when, some months later, her fiancé was reported missing, presumed killed. Her family not only supported her but were able to praise her courage without stint because they could not regret, as a husband for her, the man they knew almost nothing about. They hoped she would, in a year or two, console herself—and had it been only a question of consolation things might have gone much straighter ahead. But her trouble, behind just a little grief, was a complete dislocation from everything. She did not reject other lovers, for these failed to appear: for years she failed to attract men—and with the approach of her thirties she became natural enough to share her family's anxiousness on this score. She began to put herself out, to wonder; and at thirty-two she was very greatly relieved to find herself being courted by William Drover. She married him, and the two of them settled down in this quiet, arboreal part of Kensington: in this house the years piled up, her children were born and they all lived till they were driven out by the bombs of the next war. Her movements as Mrs. Drover were circumscribed, and she dismissed any idea that they were still watched.

As things were—dead or living the letter-writer sent her only a threat. Unable, for some minutes, to go on kneeling with her back exposed to the empty room, Mrs. Drover rose from the chest to sit on an upright chair whose back was firmly against the wall. The desuetude of her former bedroom, her married London home's whole air of being a cracked cup from which memory, with its reassuring power, had either evaporated or leaked away, made a crisis—and at just this crisis the letter-writer had, knowledgeably, struck. The hollowness of the house this evening cancelled years on years of voices, habits and steps. Through the shut windows she only heard rain fall on the roofs around. To rally herself, she said she was in a mood—and for two or three seconds shutting her eyes, told herself that she had imagined the letter. But she opened them—there it lay on the bed.

On the supernatural side of the letter's entrance she was not permitting her mind to dwell. Who, in London, knew she meant to call at the house to-day? Evidently, however, this had been known. The caretaker, *had* he come back, had had no cause to expect her: he would have taken the letter in his pocket, to forward it, at his own time, through the post. There was no other sign that the caretaker had been in—but, if not? Letters dropped in at doors of deserted houses do not fly or walk to tables in halls. They do not sit on the dust of empty tables with the air of certainty that they will be found. There is needed some human hand—but nobody but the caretaker had a key. Under circumstances she did not care to consider, a house can be entered without a key. It was possible that she was not alone now. She might be being waited for, downstairs. Waited for—until when? Until "the hour arranged." At least that was not six o'clock: six had struck.

She rose from the chair and went over and locked the door.

The thing was, to get out. To fly? No, not that: she had to catch her train. As a woman whose utter dependability was the keystone of her family life she was not willing to return to the country, to her husband, her little boys and her sister, without the objects she had come up to fetch. Resuming work at the chest she set about making up a number of parcels in a rapid, fumbling-decisive way. These, with her shopping parcels, would be too much to carry; these meant a taxi—at the thought of the taxi her heart went up and her normal breathing resumed. I will ring up the taxi now; the taxi cannot come too soon: I shall hear the taxi out there running its engine, till I walk calmly down to it through the hall. I'll ring up—But no: the telephone is cut off. . . . She tugged at a knot she had tied wrong.

The idea of flight . . . . He was never kind to me, not really. I don't remember him kind at all. Mother said he never considered me. He was set on me, that was what it was—not love. Not love, not meaning a person well. What did he do, to make me promise like that? I can't remember—But she found that she could.

She remembered with such dreadful acuteness that the twenty-five years since then dissolved like smoke and she instinctively looked for the weal left by the button on the palm of her hand. She remembered not only all that he said and did but the complete suspension of *her* existence during that

August week. I was not myself—they all told me so at the time. She remembered—but with one white burning blank as where acid has dropped on a photograph: *under no conditions* could she remember his face.

So, wherever he may be waiting, I shall not know him. You have no time to run from a face you do not expect.

The thing was to get to the taxi before any clock struck what could be the hour. She would slip down the street and round the side of the square to where the square gave on the main road. She would return in the taxi, safe, to her own door, and bring the solid driver into the house with her to pick up the parcels from room to room. The idea of the taxi driver made her decisive, bold: she unlocked her door, went to the top of the staircase and listened down.

She heard nothing—but while she was hearing nothing the *passé* air of the staircase was disturbed by a draught that travelled up to her face. It emanated from the basement: down there a door or window was being opened by someone who chose this moment to leave the house.

The rain had stopped; the pavements steamily shone as Mrs. Drover let herself out by inches from her own front door into the empty street. The unoccupied houses opposite continued to meet her look with their damaged stare. Making towards the thoroughfare and the taxi, she tried not to keep looking behind. Indeed, the silence was so intense—one of those creeks of London silence exaggerated this summer by the damage of war—that no tread could have gained on hers unheard. Where her street debouched on the square where people went on living, she grew conscious of, and checked, her unnatural pace. Across the open end of the square two buses impassively passed each other: women, a perambulator, cyclists, a man wheeling a barrow signalized, once again, the ordinary flow of life. At the square's most populous corner should be—and was—the short taxi rank. This evening, only one taxi—but this, although it presented its blank rump, appeared already to be alertly waiting for her. Indeed, without looking round the driver started his engine as she panted up from behind and put her hand on the door. As she did so, the clock struck seven. The taxi faced the main road: to make the trip back to her house it would have to turn—she had settled back on the seat and the taxi *had* turned before she, surprised by its knowing movement, recollected that she had not "said where." She leaned forward to scratch at the glass panel that divided the driver's head from her own.

The driver braked to what was almost a stop, turned round and slid the glass panel back: the jolt of this flung Mrs. Drover forward till her face was almost into the glass. Through the aperture driver and passenger, not six inches between them, remained for an eternity eye to eye. Mrs. Drover's mouth hung open for some seconds before she could issue her first scream. After that she continued to scream freely and to beat with her gloved hands on the glass all round as the taxi, accelerating without mercy, made off with her into the hinterland of deserted streets.

A JOURNEY

EDWARD FIELD

When he got up that morning everything was different:
He enjoyed the bright spring day
But he did not realize it exactly, he just enjoyed it.

And walking down the street to the railroad station
Past magnolia trees with dying flowers like old socks   5
It was a long time since he had breathed so simply.

Tears filled his eyes and it felt good
But he held them back
Because men didn't walk around crying in that town.

Waiting on the platform at the station   10
The fear came over him of something terrible about to happen:
The train was late and he recited the alphabet to keep hold.

And in its time it came screeching in
And as it went on making its usual stops,
People coming and going, telephone poles passing,   15

He hid his head behind a newspaper
No longer able to hold back the sobs, and willed his eyes
To follow the rational weavings of the seat fabric.

He didn't do anything violent as he had imagined.
He cried for a long time, but when he finally quieted down   20
A place in him that had been closed like a fist was open,

And at the end of the ride he stood up and got off that train:
And through the streets and in all the places he lived in later on
He walked, himself at last, a man among men,
With such radiance that everyone looked up and wondered.   25

THE INDIAN DOG

N. SCOTT MOMADAY

When I was growing up I lived in a pueblo in New Mexico. There one day I bought a dog. I was twelve years old, the bright autumn air was cold and delicious, and the dog was an unconscionable bargain at five dollars.

It was an Indian dog; that is, it belonged to a Navajo man who had come to celebrate the Feast of San Diego. It was one of two or three rangy animals following in the tracks of the man's covered wagon as he took leave of our village on his way home. Indian dogs are marvelously independent and resourceful, and they have an idea of themselves, I believe, as knights and philosophers.

The dog was not large, but neither was it small. It was one of those unremarkable creatures that one sees in every corner of the world, the common denominator of all its kind. But on that day—and to me—it was noble and brave and handsome.

It was full of resistance, and yet it was ready to return my deep, abiding love; I could see that. It needed only to make a certain adjustment in its lifestyle, to shift the focus of its vitality from one frame of reference to another. But I had to drag my dog from its previous owner by means of a rope. It was nearly strangled in the process, its bushy tail wagging happily all the while.

That night I secured my dog in the garage, where there was a warm clean pallet, wholesome food, and fresh water, and I bolted the door. And the next morning the dog was gone, as in my heart I knew it would be; I had read such a future in its eyes. It had squeezed through a vent, an opening much too small for it, or so I had thought. But as they say, where there is a will there is a way—and the Indian dog was possessed of one indomitable will.

I was crushed at the time, but strangely reconciled, too, as if I had perceived intuitively some absolute truth beyond all the billboards of illusion.

The Indian dog had done what it had to do, had behaved exactly as it must, had been true to itself and to the sun and moon. It knew its place in the scheme of things, and its place was precisely there, with its right destiny, in the tracks of the wagon. In my mind's eye I could see it at that very moment, miles away, plodding in the familiar shadows, panting easily with relief, after a bad night, contemplating the wonderful ways of man.

Caveat emptor. But from that experience I learned something about the heart's longing. It was a lesson worth many times five dollars.

Writing and Reading for Life and a Lifetime

> The poet must be continually watching the moods of his mind, as the astronomer watches the aspects of the heavens. What might we not expect from a long life faithfully spent in this wise? The humblest observer would see some stars shoot. . . . A meteorological journal of the mind.
>
> —HENRY DAVID THOREAU

Chapters 1 to 3 introduced you to the concept of the reading notebook. This chapter looks at ways of sustaining the process of keeping a notebook during this class and for a lifetime.

Why sustain it? First and foremost because keeping a notebook of your thoughts and creations is a rewarding activity in and of itself. In our fast-paced age a notebook is a vehicle for taking control of your own time and mind. As the poet Denise Levertov observes, "A writer's notebook is a way of keeping in touch with your inner life in the midst of the rush of daily preoccupations." A second reason for sustaining the notebook is to generate ideas and materials that can be developed into finished pieces of writing that please you and that can be shared either orally or through written publication.

The process of building a notebook can be reduced to a single simple idea: *write in quantity and revise selectively.* Writing in quantity provides you with a trove of collected writings to which you can frequently return as editor. As noted in Chapter 2 *it's easier to make something out of something already there than out of nothing.* Walt Whitman (1819–1892), American poet, illustrates this process.

Walt Whitman and the Notebook Pyramid

Whitman was a person with writing habits. He carried paper everywhere. If he was out walking, in his room, alone or in public, and he got an idea, or if he encountered something striking in a book or newspaper, he jotted it down on a slip of paper. In the course of a day he might collect a few notes or several dozen: quotations, observations, stray lines, and thoughts.

At home he sometimes sorted related notes into envelopes.[1] A different envelope for each embryonic poem:

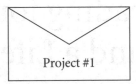
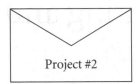

When he felt he had accumulated enough inside an envelope or file to make a poem, he emptied the contents onto his desk. Then, patiently, he moved the paper slips around, arranging them into order, pattern, and sequence and adding more material as necessary. Sometimes the pattern emerged quickly; he ordered the slips and transcribed them to make a rough draft. Other times the pattern emerged partially. Fine: he didn't force it, just left it for another day. Still other times the slips resisted any pattern or produced one that struck him as flat and uninteresting. That pile of scraps he gathered up and tossed.

Whitman sustained this process of collecting, sorting, dumping, and arranging over weeks, months, and years. Collectively, the notes evolved into a book, *Leaves of Grass*. In its final edition, published in the poet's old age, *Leaves* contained some four hundred poems. A life's work. And it all grew out of simple notes.

Whitman claimed that he "never forced anything,"—which is not to say he didn't revise compulsively (after all, how many of us spend thirty-five years, as he did, writing, rewriting, and expanding a single book?); but it was all done in a leisurely way.

Although Whitman lived in the nineteenth century, the process driving his work is as valid today as it was then. It involves:

- **Collecting** large numbers of notes and writings
- **Organizing** them for easy retrieval
- **Rereading** the notes and writings thus collected and organized
- **Revising** the useable material into finished work

You can visualize these activities as a pyramid:

---

1. Described here is *one* of Whitman's methods for composing. Like most writers, Whitman used different processes in different contexts.

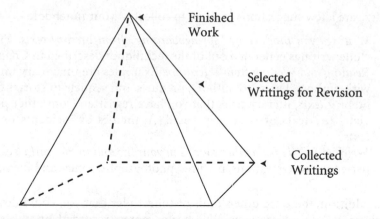

At the bottom and broadest part of the pyramid are collected writings, the huge and uncensored totality of all your work. As you proceed upward and the pyramid narrows, you come to that relatively smaller portion of your total output that you select for revising. At the apex of the pyramid is finished work, the volume of which is a very small percentage of the total. More will be said about this finished work, and how to realize it, in Part III of this book.

Like Whitman, all productive writers find ways of organizing the paper flow and development of their ideas from first notes to finished texts. While the precise mechanics of the process differ from writer to writer and task to task, these four activities, in some form, are basic to all successful composing.

Collecting

In every work of genius we recognize our own rejected thoughts.

— RALPH WALDO EMERSON

Kim, a would-be writer, can easily relate to this quotation. Again and again she has recognized in "work[s] of genius" her "own rejected thoughts." "I've thought of that!" "I could have written that!" "I could have done it better!" All are thoughts that occur to her frequently as she reads her favorite authors. Each statement has an element of truth; Kim's problem is that she failed to honor her thoughts by writing them down when they occurred to her. Instead, she let her internal censor wave them aside as "stupid" or "unimportant," and what might have matured into good writing died stillborn.

The first and last rule of collecting is "Do not censor." When you are collecting, *no* idea is too "stupid," "trite," or "insignificant" to write down. If it occurs to you, it's important—not necessarily "final" or "finished" but important.

Here are a few suggestions of items to collect in your notebook:

- *Writings you produce by "springboarding" from literary texts.* These include writings generated out of the techniques described in Chapter 3 of *Reading and Writing from Literature*. Examples are imaginary interviews with authors, letters to authors, prequels and sequels to stories or other literary texts, literary texts that you have rewritten from other points of view, and texts of your own based on themes or incidents in literary texts.
- *Writings you do from other sources in your life and in the world,* such as experiences, conversations, pictures, photographs, songs, and films.

In addition, there are other kinds of collectibles that you could describe as "quick-notes." These are generally shorter notes, recorded on the spot, on scraps of paper or in a small notepad. Note taking is essential not just to writers but to creative people in all fields of endeavor. A random list of some famous people who were (or are) notetakers includes Robert Frost, Abraham Lincoln, Ludwig van Beethoven, F. Scott Fitzgerald, John Lennon, Peter Ilich Tchaikovsky, Charles Darwin, Albert Einstein, James Joyce, Joseph Heller, Annie Dillard, Katherine Mansfield, Igor Stravinsky, Leo Tolstoy, Andre Gide, Joyce Carol Oates, Martha Graham, Toni Morrison, Jim Morrison, Theodore Roosevelt, Aaron Copland, Eugene O'Neill, Joan Didion, Allen Ginsberg, Anton Chekhov, and Virginia Woolf.

When Abraham Lincoln had a thought he wanted to save for later reflection or use he scribbled it down on a scrap of paper and stuck it inside the lining of his tall hat. Lincoln's law partner Billy Herndon wrote that his hat was "an extraordinary receptacle. It was his desk and memorandum book." Johann Wolfgang von Goethe (1749–1832) was a prolific writer in all literary forms and author of the epic *Faust,* one of the preeminent classics of world literature. Like Lincoln, he was also a habitual notetaker, dashing off ideas on envelopes, theatre programs, visiting cards, bills, or whatever paper came to hand, even getting up in the middle of the night to write if a thought came to him. He advised other people to do the same:

> [T]he daily thoughts and feelings which press upon the poet will and should be expressed. . . . [I]f the poet daily seizes the present, and always treats with freshness of feeling what is offered him, he always makes sure of something good, and if he sometimes does not succeed, has, at least, lost nothing.

> If you treat, at present, only small subjects, freshly dashing off what every day offers you, you will generally produce something good, and each day will bring you pleasure.

Goethe's term, "poet," should be understood to mean something broader than "a writer of verses." Though you may never write or publish a line of verse, if you make a habit of faithfully recording your thoughts, impressions, and observations you will be, de facto, a "poet"; that is, someone who approaches the moment mindfully. Poets think and feel like everyone else but differ in that they make a practice of writing their thoughts and feelings down.

Recording quick-notes enables you, in the words of Henry David Thoreau, to "write often" and "upon a thousand themes, rather than long at a time." The following types of notes—thoughts and observations; striking images, phrases, and facts; anecdotes and ideas for writing; and quotations read or heard—are some suggestions but there are many other alternatives.

Thoughts and Observations; Striking Images, Phrases, and Facts

One famous recorder of thoughts and observations is G.C. Lichtenberg (1742–1799), a German mathematician and scientist. During his student days Lichtenberg began keeping notebooks for collecting scientific jottings as well as miscellaneous notes on all aspects of life and society. By the end of his life he had accumulated thousands of these miscellaneous reflections, many of which originated as marginal annotations of readings. Here are some samples:

> Often when an acquaintance goes past I step back from my window—not so much to spare him the trouble of making a bow as rather to spare myself the embarrassment of seeing that he has not made me one.

> We cannot truly know whether we are not at this moment sitting in a madhouse.

> He stood there looking as sad as a dead bird's bird-bath.

> At the comedy, whenever something seemed ridiculous to him, he looked around for someone to laugh with him. When I noticed this, I never came to his aid but looked steadily away.

> A golden rule: one must not judge people by their opinions, but by what those opinions make of them.

Lichtenberg is interesting, in part, because he did not devote his life to note taking; nor was he a professional writer in the usual sense: he had a "regular" job, wrote scientific articles, and had a family and children and other responsibilities. He could as easily have been a grocery clerk, a custodian, a shoemaker, a student, an engineer, a homemaker, an accountant, unemployed, or retired. Like most of us, he found that thoughts were constantly darting through his mind, often when he was trying to concentrate on something else, such as a mathematical or scientific problem. Lichtenberg is proof that anyone, however busy, can find moments to record their thoughts and observations and so live life more attentively.

Jules Renard (see p. 844), French novelist and playwright, began keeping a journal of his thoughts and observations at age twenty-three as a means of training himself "to reproduce in compressed and resistant [prose] life completely pure and completely simple." Interestingly, Renard referred to his notes as "my daily prayer," and in fact his notes do suggest almost sacred efforts to savor and preserve the sensuous details of life.

When the little peasant girls see us from a distance they turn around to smile.

Our egoism is so excessive that, in a storm, we believe the thunder to be directed only at us.

The ostrich: a giant chick.

Papa. The swollen veins of his temples. Moles are digging around and ravaging him under the skin.

In the path, the caterpillar plays a soundless little tune on its accordian.

When a sparrow has said "Peep!" it thinks it has said everything there is to say.

D. H. Lawrence (see p. 406) collected his thoughts and published them in 1929 as a book entitled *Pansies,* a pun on the French word for "thoughts," *pensées,* which was also the title of an earlier collection of thoughts composed by the seventeenth-century French mathematician/philosopher Blaise Pascal. Lawrence wrote his thoughts in poem form because, as he claimed in the preface to his book, "it has always seemed to me that a real thought, a single thought, not an argument, can only exist easily in verse, or in some poetic form." Most of the poems, like the following examples, are quite short and may represent intuitive flashes: Lawrence wrote that his *Pansies* were "to be taken as . . . casual thoughts . . . as fleeting as pansies, which wilt so soon, and are so fascinating with their varied faces while they last."

Elephants in the circus
have aeons of weariness round their eyes.
Yet they sit up
and show vast bellies to the children.

I know I am noble with the nobility of the sun.
A certain peace, a certain grace.
I would say the same if I were a chaffinch or tree.

Poet Rita Dove (see p. 341) remarks that she "couldn't live without [her] notebooks. . . . Into my notebook goes anything that is interesting enough to stop me in my tracks—the slump of a pair of shoulders in a crowd, a newspaper story, a recipe, 'chewy' words like *ragamuffin* or *Maurice*." Dove's notes show her trying out images and rhythms for her poems:

Strike a stone
to see if it's thinking of water.

Purse as womb.

A porcelain cup overturned on a plate: an iridescent igloo.

You can take notes anywhere—on a bus, in a grocery or cafe, on a busy downtown street, or in the rugged outdoors. Mary Oliver (see p. 470) reports that "For at least thirty years, and at almost all times, I have carried a notebook with me, in my back pocket. It has always been the same kind of notebook— small, three inches by five inches, and hand-sewn. . . . [O]ver the years the notebooks have been laced with phrases that eventually appear in poems." She adds: "In the spring and fall notebooks, especially, there are pages where the writing is blurred and hard to read. Spring and fall are the rainy seasons, and almost all of the entries are made somewhere out of doors." Some examples:

It's better for the heart to break
than not to break.

Something totally unexpected,
like a barking cat.

All culture developed as some wild, raw creature strived to live better and longer.

Hasn't the end of the world been coming absolutely forever?

You can find out more about the notebooks and journals of Mary Oliver and of other writers by reading Chapter 15 and the "interchapters" included in Part V of this book.

Anecdotes and Ideas for Writing

Many writers are compulsive collectors of anecdotes and stories, and it's easy to see why: besides being enjoyable in themselves, collected stories provide a treasury of materials that can be expanded and/or incorporated into essays or longer narratives. Here are some student-written examples:

> Dream story: I am not able to find my house. I take the same streets, but all the houses are different.

> A bookstore at night when all of the customers have left and the lights are turned out—the characters come alive and their separate personalities are introduced to each other. Huck Finn meets Jane Eyre. Robert Frost learns how to save your soul when you're pregnant in the 90s.

> Psychologist for a movie company has to evaluate the mental state of a high school crush. The crush must have full mental capacity to appear in next film. Crush has drug problems.

Other good examples appear in the notebook of Anton Chekhov (see p. 883), Russian short story writer and playwright:

> The grandfather is given fish to eat, and if it does not poison him and he remains alive, then all the family eat it.

> A young man made a million marks, lay down on them, and shot himself.

> A man and woman marry because both of them don't know what to do with themselves.

Toward the end of his life Chekhov remarked, "I've got five hundred sheets of unused material in [my notebooks], enough for five years of work."

Quotations Read or Heard

For centuries writers have kept so-called "commonplace books" for collecting memorable or striking quotations from reading, conversation, or other sources. John Milton kept a commonplace book; so did Thomas Jefferson. Shakespeare alludes to commonplace books in *Hamlet* and may have used one himself. Quotations stimulate reflection and invention and can also be incorporated as examples or illustrations in your stories, essays, or other writings. Here are a few sample quotations collected by students:

> If every person could have exactly what he wanted, he would be no better than he is now. (Herakleitos)

> Any time that is not spent on love is wasted. (Torquato Tasso)

> Everything that seems empty is full of the angels of God. (St. Hilary)

(Overheard): Do good work and you will no longer act like a bum.

(Overheard): I walked past a classroom and heard the professor ask, "Does anybody in this room have a mother?"

He who isn't busy being born is busy dying. (Bob Dylan)

While to collect quotations is to copy down other people's words, it is also a way of recognizing and recording what sings inside yourself. Meditating on a favorite quotation—"absorbing" it as Walt Whitman liked to say—attunes you to the kind of verbal music you like and might *create*. John Milton's poetic voice (not to mention his astonishing memory) was enhanced by his practice of copying out, rereading, and memorizing passages of poetry and poetic prose that he liked. Thus seen a favorite quotation is as much your *own* as anything you write yourself. What you copy down from another, with passion, is the poetry inside you.

To collect items of the "quick-note" variety, you need to be able to get ideas on paper when they occur to you. So what do you do when you have a great idea but no place to put it? If you say, "I'll write it down when I get home," you probably never will, or you will have forgotten what your idea *was* by the time you reach pen and paper or your computer.

To eliminate this problem, do what many of the writers included in Part V of this book have done and carry a pocket-sized spiral notepad with you at all times. That way you can be sure that no interesting thought you have will go unrecorded. Whenever you get an idea for writing—from a literary text, a film or TV show, a conversation, a song—jot it down in your notepad.

Good writers are habitual quick-note takers. They write ideas on cards, napkins, scraps of paper, letters, backs of envelopes, restaurant menus, the palms of their hands—even on walls. William Faulkner is said to have outlined one of his novels on the walls of a hotel room, not a process I recommend but an extreme example of the lengths to which writers may go when they need to write *now*.

On May 14, 1925, the English novelist Virginia Woolf scribbled the following in her diary:

This is going to be fairly short; to have father's character done complete in it; and mother's; and St. Ives; and childhood; and all the usual things I try to put in—life, death, etc. But the center is father's character, sitting in a boat, reciting "We perished each alone."

These hastily written words—a mere two sentences—anticipate the structure of Woolf's great semiautobiographical novel *To the Lighthouse*, which she published two years later, in 1927. This quick sketch defined the original vision that helped Woolf plan and carry the work to completion.

British poet Stephen Spender had a similar habit of collecting ideas for writing:

> My method . . . is to write down as many ideas as possible, in however rough a form in notebooks. I have at least twenty of these, on a shelf beside my desk, going back over fifteen years. I then make use of these sketches and discard others.

Notice particularly how Spender uses these notes. He accumulates vast numbers—everything that occurs to him, without worrying about "quality"—and then sifts through them to determine which he will use, i.e., develop, revise, and possibly publish, and which he will discard. What he uses is only a fraction of the total accumulation, but without making lots of notes—from brilliant to ordinary to downright dull—he might never have written down the "good" ideas that eventually became poems.

Organizing What You Collect

As you accumulate diverse writings in your notebook, it's useful to develop a plan for organizing them so that you can easily retrieve and reread them. *How* to organize is largely a matter of individual taste, but here are two basic suggestions:

1. Begin each entry in your notebook by recording the date, time, and place where you are writing, e.g., "8/16/00, 8:20 A.M., kitchen." This notation is useful in two ways. First, date, time, and place provide a record that enables you to trace your intellectual and imaginative growth over weeks, months, and years; it's fun, in 2001, to look back at what you were reading, thinking, and producing in 2000. Second, the date/time/place notation shows you where and when you work best. If you notice that you produce 90 percent of your best writing at the "kitchen table" or in the "library," that tells you something about yourself as a writer. It tells you *where* you are most productive, just as recording the time tells you *when* you are most productive. After keeping a notebook for a while, you may realize that you write best between 7 and 9 A.M. in your bedroom or between 10 and 11 P.M. in your living room, for example.

2. Over time you may discover that you address certain themes or topics repeatedly. Consider organizing your notebook around these topics or themes. During his long life Emerson filled over 250 notebooks and journals and indexed them according to topic (e.g., "Fate," "Country Life," "Beauty and Art") so that he could access all the materials on a given topic easily. You may want to adapt Emerson's strategy for your own use. For instance, insert dividers, with appropriately labeled tabs, e.g., "stories," "ideas for writing," "family issues," "love," "thoughts," "quotations," within your notebook:

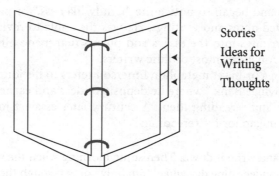

Or create individual paper file folders for each topic:

Or, if you prefer to organize electronically, create word-processing files for each category. Of course, the topics or categories you create *now* are not fixed; you can change them or create new categories at any time, as your own life and interests change.

Organizing like this eliminates the pressure to act immediately on a writing or note once you have collected it. The item goes into the appropriate section of your notebook, or into the appropriate electronic or paper file, and it *stays there*. Even if you don't do anything with the item for months or years, it's in a place where you can retrieve it instantly when you want it.

Rereading

> I can no more manage these thoughts that come into my head than thunderbolts. But once get them written down, I come & look at them every day, & get wonted to their faces, & by & by, am so far used to them, that I see their family likeness, & can pair them & range them better, & if I once see where they belong, & join them in that order they will stay so.
>
> —RALPH WALDO EMERSON

Though the language of this quote is somewhat archaic, the message is simple: *it is valuable to write things down and then, later on, to "look at them" again.* By rereading the materials in his notebooks "every day," Emerson got "used to" those materials and began to notice the "family likeness," or patterns, among his many assorted notes and writings. He was then able to revise and develop his notebook writings into the essays and poems that made him one of nineteenth-century America's most prolific writers.

Elsewhere, in a brilliant metaphor, Emerson refers to his journals and notebooks as his "Savings Bank," where he deposited ideas and earned "interest" on them by saving and rereading them. A century later essayist Joan Didion invokes the same metaphor for rereading:

> See enough and write it down. Then some morning when the world seems drained of wonder, some day when I am only going through the motions of what I am supposed to do—on that bankrupt morning, I will simply open my notebook and there it will all be, a forgotten account with accumulated interest, paid passage back to the world out there.

No writer can wake up with fresh inspiration for writing every day of his or her life. Rereading gives you something to do when your mind is too dull for producing new writing. It epitomizes a major theme of this book: *One of the best stimuli for new writing is old writing, both other people's and your own.*

Here are some practical steps for rereading:

1. Reread your notebook regularly, with pen or pencil in hand.
2. Underline or bracket words, phrases, sentences, paragraphs, or longer entries that interest you—for whatever reason.
3. In the margins annotate or "talk back" to those items that strike you. Write about:
   a. Additional thoughts the item suggests to you
   b. Why the item interests you
   c. How you might like, at some point, to expand the item

For example, Liz, a student, writes the following entry in her notebook:

I don't need a future, I just need to believe in a future.

When she rereads this note a month later, Liz is stimulated to a further thought, which she jots in the margin (her shorthand is slightly edited here for clarity):

I don't need a future, I just need to believe ⟵————— Use in a story of "mad musician": likes being disconnected from reality, needs her own reality
in a future.

On another occasion Liz rereads an entry and reacts to it as follows:

Definition of a success: someone whose work   ⟵———Write a letter about
is their fun.   this to Meg?

The beauty of this process of "talking back" to your own writing is that it can be endlessly extended. What you write in the margin beside one of your entries can, in turn, be a prompt to still further expansion. Thus, over time, a short entry with a marginal comment can evolve into something much larger, such as a full-fledged essay, story, or poem.

Revising

Revision means, literally, to "look at again." In a sense this whole book, with its emphasis on intertextuality, on rereading and rewriting texts, is about revising. In fact, reading and writing are always revisionary acts because they are acts of thinking, which is itself always recursive.

Here, however, we consider "revision" in its more limited and conventional sense, as the process of taking a piece of your writing and reworking it to make it better. Two key questions are: *When* should you revise? *What* should you revise, and what should you leave as is?

Brenda Ueland, a writer and teacher of writing, once observed:

[T]here are wonderfully gifted people who write a little piece and then write it over and over again to make it perfect,—absolutely, flawlessly perfect, a gem. But these people only emit about a pearl a year, or in five years. And that is because of the grind, the polishing, i.e., the fear that the little literary pearl will not be perfect and unassailable. But this is all a loss of time and a pity. For in them there is a fountain of exuberant life and poetry and literature and imagination, but it cannot get out because they are so anxiously busy polishing the gem.

Ueland suggests that many of us choke off our confidence and productivity at the roots by working too hard on one piece of writing and failing to write in quantity. *We work on one piece of writing only, and revise that to death, rather than writing in large quantities and revising selectively.*

Consider four kinds of writing:

1. Writing you revise carefully
2. Writing you revise quickly
3. Writing you leave unrevised
4. Writing you throw away

All four of these kinds of writing are important, and it is important to do each. Any successful and prolific writer will tell you that. While it is true that good writers revise some work painstakingly (Ernest Hemingway said he rewrote the opening of his novel *A Farewell to Arms* twenty times!), they also do a good deal of writing that they revise quickly, or leave unrevised, or simply throw away.

Popular myth portrays the writer as someone who gets "inspired" and then, in one swift motion, creates a masterpiece. In fact, the writer's work—or workshop—is far messier and imperfect than that. Writers have layers of material within their workshops:

- Short notes—hundreds, thousands, everything from quick notes recording images or phrases, to quotations from books or conversations, to visual sketches (of characters, themes, natural objects, for instance), to paraphrases of major ideas for future works (stories, poems, memoirs, essays, plays). Some of these notes are "strays" or "orphans," that is, the writer has no idea what she may do with them—they just interest her in some way. Others take a ready slot in the writer's work in progress. Some are expanded or joined to other larger works. Some of these never get used; many or most get reread some time.
- Outlines
- Paragraphs or other chunks of text that are written and awaiting a slot within some larger piece of work
- Rough drafts
- Revised and edited works that the writer—or publisher—deems unpublishable
- Texts in diverse stages of revision
- Works that are virtually "done" but missing some small detail that will make them complete.

Eugene O'Neill kept a notebook in which he recorded ideas for plays, plot scenarios, character ideas, arrangements for sets and scenes, and other thoughts that came to mind. Reading his notebooks affords a useful glimpse into the creative process and the principles of mass generation of ideas and selective revision that guide it. For every one play he conceives, drafts, revises, polishes, and brings to production, there seem to be dozens of others that die at conception, or at the outline stage, or in some medial phase of revision. From 1925 to 1934 he worked on a play about an emperor of ancient China that he ultimately abandoned. That was okay because he had lots of other plays in the works that he loved enough and felt good enough about to finish.

Were the abandoned plays, sketches, and ideas a waste of O'Neill's time? No. They were simply by-products of the process, efforts that probably had to be made in order for O'Neill to create the plays for which he is famous.

An especially striking example of a writer producing in quantity and revising selectively is Russian novelist Leo Tolstoy, who drafted several hundred pages of a novel about Czar Peter the Great and then threw them away because he was "no longer interested" in Peter the Great!

When you do only extensively revised writing, a problem develops. Call it "thinness." You get better, perhaps, at editing, at performing microsurgery on texts, and at repairing faulty punctuation and grammar, but your ability to generate large quantities of text atrophies from lack of practice. Your writing output is paper-thin—almost nonexistent. You are like a stream that has dried to a trickle. By contrast, bold and prolific writers are like great gushing rivers that overflow their banks so powerfully that nothing can slow or stop them.

A moment ago I mentioned Tolstoy, who tossed his novel in progress into the wastebasket after drafting hundreds of pages. During his long life, Tolstoy also wrote *War and Peace,* one of the longest, best novels of all time, and enough volumes of short and long fiction, correspondence, moral and religious philosophy, and educational essays to fill several yards of library shelf space. Tolstoy wrote in abundance. Is all his work of equal excellence? No. It ranges from the brilliant to the average to the downright bad.

Consider Walt Whitman, whose literary output was nearly as vast as Tolstoy's. His secret? He wrote constantly and abundantly—sometimes magnificently, sometimes ordinarily, sometimes sloppily and poorly. Out of this immense pool of writings—poems, notes, plans, sketches, outlines, drafts, fragments—he selected a relatively small portion (those works he cared about most) for careful revision into finished work. The great majority of his writings he left unfinished, unrevised, or partially revised.

Tolstoy and Whitman wrote in quantity and revised selectively.

Cultivate a sense of *selectivity* in your writing. Practice doing all four kinds of writing I mentioned above—carefully revised, quickly revised, unrevised, and throw away—and select only the works you care about most for careful revision. Your reading notebook is a place for you to produce writing in abundance. By writing regularly in your notebook, you accumulate ample raw material that you can either revise and publish or simply use as a way of pursuing the ongoing task of making meaning.

ACTIVITIES FOR WRITING

1. Buy a small notepad that is easily transportable in a bag, pocket, or purse.
    a. For the rest of the quarter or semester, use this notepad for collecting thoughts and observations, striking images, phrases, and facts, anecdotes and ideas for writing, quotations read or heard, or other kinds of notes. Concentrate on recording your ideas on-the-spot and in exactly the words they occur to you, however awkward or strange. Reread your notes periodically and make any revisions or additions that occur to you. If rereading one note makes you think of something else, jot down the new idea *immediately.*
    b. At the end of the term, compile a small selection of your best or favorite notes and quotations. If your instructor requests it, attach a

preface in which you discuss your experiences with note taking. What kinds of notes did you take? When and where did ideas most frequently occur to you? What methods did you use for recording them, and how well did those methods work? How could you integrate this habit of note taking into your life after or outside of college?

2. For the next class (or for some class meeting later in the term) bring a half dozen or so favorite quotations that you have collected in your notebook. With a partner or small group, comment on the qualities you like in the quotations, such as metaphors, phrasing or word choice, sound effects, or ideas. In addition, point out anything you find mysterious or ineffable about the quotations that makes them inexhaustibly rich for you.

3. Try copying your quotations onto note cards so that you can carry a selection in your pocket or bag and flip through them when away from your desk. In his autobiography Walt Whitman describes how he did this with his favorite quotations, so that they could be "absorb'd over and over again" and "sink into [him]."

4. Rereading activity (repeat often):
   a. Reread all or a portion of your notebook, with pen or pencil in hand.
   b. Underline or bracket words, phrases, sentences, or longer passages that strike you, for whatever reason.
   c. Reread the marked passages and choose one that seems most interesting to you now, share and discuss the passage with a partner, small group, or friend.
   or
   In the margins annotate or "talk back" to those notes that strike you. Write about:
   • Additional thoughts the item suggests to you
   • Why an item interests you
   • How you might like, at some point, to expand the item
   d. If you wish, revise a favorite passage using one of the revision strategies in Chapter 9 or some other strategy of your own choosing.

Part

II

Writing Essays About Literature

Part I of *Reading and Writing from Literature* showed you ways of producing writings that are sometimes described as "creative" or "imaginative." In Part II we turn to what is probably the most commonly assigned type of composition in literature-based writing courses: the essay about literature. There are some important differences between the kinds of writing addressed in Parts I and II. For example, writings produced in Part I are typically ungraded and may assume a great variety of forms, such as stories, poems, personal memoirs, dialogues, letters, and many others. The kind of writing emphasized in Part II, on the other hand, is normally done for a grade and in some more narrowly prescribed form, generally that of the expository or argumentative essay. (Expository and argumentative essays are short works of nonfiction prose that pose a main point or thesis and support it with evidence and examples.)

How, then, do Parts I and II interconnect? In some ways, the writings you produce as a result of techniques outlined in Part I have a life of their own and can be collected, revised, and enjoyed independently of Part II. Long after you have finished this particular class, you can continue using the "Four-Step Process," the "Ten Ideas," and other techniques to build up a body of writings for your intellectual or esthetic pleasure, for sharing, and perhaps even for formal publication. At the same time, Part I prepares you for Part II. Part I strategies enable you to engage literary texts in meaningful ways that will help you when you compose essays about literature. In addition, Part I has introduced you to habits of conversational reading and writing—habits as basic to writing good essays about literature as they are to producing creative and imaginative work.

5

Ways of Planning: Thinking and Writing Recursively

Look, and look again.

—ANN E. BERTHOFF

Putting Essays About Literature into Context

For some students the assignment to "write an essay about literature" is a source of anxiety. Perhaps "essay about literature" triggers memories of failure, of interpreting a story or poem "incorrectly" and receiving a bad grade, or it may conjure feelings of apathy and distance ("What does this assignment have to do with my life?"). The aim of this part of *Reading and Writing from Literature* is to defuse these feelings and demonstrate strategies for working your way naturally through such essays.

The essay about literature is a diverse genre. It includes essay exams, critical analyses or "explications" of literary texts, argumentative papers, personal narratives that are grounded in a reading of a literary text (or texts), and essays that involve outside research. Sometimes the topics for such essays are assigned by an instructor; other times you, the student, are asked to devise a topic yourself.

Essays about literature have multiple purposes. One function is broadly personal; they can reward you—the writer—by prompting you to discover interconnections among literary texts and the texts of your own life. A second function is pragmatic: essays about literature provide instructors and others with a means of evaluating your ability to write. Essay assignments often require you to do an "objective" text-focused analysis that may suppress overt

61

mention of the personal. While such essays may be less emotionally engaging for you than personal or creative types of writing, being able to write them is usually critical for succeeding in class and in school.

Cultivating Recursive Habits of Thinking

Perhaps the major value of writing essays about literature is this: they help you develop recursive habits of thinking. "Recursive" means "running back again," or, as Ann Berthoff puts it in the epigraph to this chapter, looking and looking again. Recursiveness is the very stuff of thinking, which (in turn) is the stuff of essay writing.

If the preceding paragraph made you pause, and you reread it to understand or assess it, you were thinking recursively. When you write down a few sentences and look them over with the aim of expanding them, you are again thinking recursively. When you share your interpretation of a story or poem in class and reconsider it in the light of alternative opinions offered by your instructor or classmates, you are again being recursive.

Recursiveness provides a powerful term for understanding what you do when you write an essay about literature. Returning to Part I's theme, you use texts (literary texts, the texts in your notebook, the texts of lecture and discussion, for example) to make a text. Your new thoughts and writings don't come out of nothing but out of "running back" over previous work or "texts." Thus, when you're "stuck" in your writing or your thinking, there is an alternative to panic or to doing nothing; you can go over materials you have already generated and use them to move yourself forward. Writing an essay about literature is not a monolithic task that is to be achieved—or irredeemably failed—in a single step. Instead, it is a steady and incremental process that relies on looking and looking again—on rereading, writing, rewriting, and discussing.

In short, you don't need to be brilliant to think or write well; you do need recursive habits of thinking.

Working Toward Your Essay Before It Has Been Assigned

It follows from the preceding discussion that essay writing begins long before you receive the actual assignment to write one. From day one of class you begin accumulating materials that can provide you with topics and ideas for essays. These materials include the textual annotations you have made on the assigned stories, poems, essays, and plays anthologized in Part V of this book, notes of class lectures and discussions, writings in response to literature that you have been collecting in your reading notebook, and notes on small group discussions. All of these materials—these "texts"—provide scraps of overlapping textual fabric from which to stitch and sew together new creations.

Two of these types of materials—textual annotations and notebook writings—have already been discussed in Part I. Others, such as notes on lectures and class discussions, are fairly self-explanatory. One important kind of daily activity that hasn't been talked about yet is small group work.

Sharing and Learning in a Small Group

A small group (typically composed of three to five members) can be among your most stimulating resources in a literature or composition class. Groups embody the spirit of recursiveness, which is rough and multidimensional. Recursive thinking does not proceed forward in a straight line from brilliance to brilliance; the shape of its movement is more analogous to a web that darts in multiple—even contradictory—directions. Like webs, groups relate and contradict and interconnect. That is what makes them useful and fun. Margaret Fuller, a nineteenth-century essayist, described the group process beautifully. Of her own "conversation" groups she wrote:

> I am so sure that the success of the whole depends on conversation being general that I do not wish any one to join who does not intend, *if possible*, to take an active part. No one will be forced, but those who do not talk will not derive the same advantages with those who openly state their impressions and consent to learn by blundering, as is the destiny of [human beings] here below.

A good group "blunders" its way to understanding, doesn't treat any opinion as "dumb" (so long as the opiner is willing to consider differing opinions and grow from them), and is as lively and various as human thought itself. A small group is an excellent forum for sharing your readings of literary texts and issues. In addition, your group can give you feedback at various stages of planning, drafting, revising, and editing your essays.

Your instructor may encourage group sharing as a regular class activity. Here is one rather generic format for sharing that you can relax or modify as you and your group mates become more familiar with each other. For purposes of illustration the focus of group discussion is assumed here to be a literary text. However, a small group can also meet to share opinions about members' writings in-progress or any other subject of interest to group members and/or the instructor.

1. Form into your group.
2. Share your responses to the assigned literary text for that day. For instance:
   a. Identify a passage in the text that was "most significant" to *you* and explain why,
   or

    b. Read aloud the notebook entry you wrote in response to the text (remembering that you may skip over passages that are too personal or that you are uncomfortable sharing),

    or

    c. Summarize the notebook entry you wrote and share any ways that it enriched your reading of the text.

3. After you have presented, group members can respond by

    a. Pointing out something in your sharing that they found "interesting"

    or

    b. Expressing how they responded to the text differently than you did.

4. Repeat this process, with each member of the group taking a turn as presenter.

Techniques for Note Taking in Small Groups

Make a habit of taking notes on your group discussions, even if some of the ideas presented are ones you disagree with or consider "silly" or "dumb." Note taking improves your listening skills, makes you more conscious of alternative points of view, and provides you with a record of discussion that you can refer to later when writing your essays.

    Here are two good ways to develop habits of note taking:

    1. *Write while you listen.* Try taking a steady stream of notes as your group mates read their writing or ideas aloud. For instance, here are the notes one student took as he listened to Tyler read the potrait "Grandpa Jack" from Chapter 2 (see pp. 13–14):

> Jack—neighbor
> visits Jack
> Jack "lounges"
> Jack down-to-earth
> like Jack's talk
> tells story
> sheepherding incident
> "eyes flashing"
> colorful
> good story/details/suspense

Sometimes writing while you listen can help you to concentrate and to overcome the inertia of not writing (or listening) at all. In addition, of course, you can use items off your list to provide feedback to the writer.

    2. *Write after you listen.* Sometimes it's hard to listen and write at the same time—hence this alternative strategy. After a member of your group has read,

you and the others can take one minute to jot down reactions to what you just heard. What struck you? What *issues* does the writing raise for you? Where could you use more information or development? Following the minute of silent writing, group members can hand their written reactions to the author or share their reactions orally.

Finding a Topic: Rereading (and Writing from) the Writing You Have Already Done

As mentioned, when you are assigned to write an essay you do not have to start from scratch. You begin with an already ample storehouse of writings that can provide ideas and prompts for essays. Begin work on your essay by rereading all of your textual annotations, notebook entries, notes on lectures, and notes on class and small-group discussions. Read with pen or pencil in hand. Whenever you find any item that strikes you, for whatever reason, bracket or underline it. When you are finished, reread all the items you have bracketed or underlined. In the margin beside each, write yourself a note explaining what it is about this passage that grabs you.

Turning Your Favorite Interest into a Workable Topic

Based on your review of your annotations, notebook, and lecture and discussion notes, you can define a workable topic for your essay. There are many ways to do this. Your instructor may introduce you to "brainstorming," "quick-writing" (or "freewriting"), or other activities for coming up with topics. Another good place to begin is with the apparatus included in this book. You can find topics by combing the "Activities for Writing and Discussion" that follow many of the short stories, poems, essays, and plays in Part V or by looking through the "Additional Activities for Writing and Discussion" that conclude each thematic section in Part V.

For example, Joe knows that he wants to write something about Doris Lessing's short story "A Woman on a Roof" (p. 200). Lessing's story concerns a woman sunbather whose nakedness stirs complex reactions, e.g., attraction, excitement, anger, in two male roofers named Stanley (in his thirties) and Tom (seventeen). One of Joe's annotations, made in the middle of the story, suggests to him a topic for an essay: "They [Stanley and Tom] have different perspectives—in a sense contradictory." Joe reads the "Activities for Writing and Discussion" that follow the story and decides to write on Activity #5:

> Stanley and Tom react to the woman differently. Stanley feels rage toward her, while we are told that Tom feels a "bond between the woman and

himself" (p. 204). Discuss the differences in their reactions. Is Tom (a) "better" or "kinder" than Stanley, (b) simply different from Stanley, or (c) really no different from Stanley?

Developing a "Working Thesis"

A thesis states the main point you are going to make in your essay; it normally appears in the opening paragraph or near the beginning of the essay. A "working thesis" is one you adopt tentatively in order to begin your essay while remaining open to the possibility of revising it in the course of composing.

A clear thesis benefits both writer and readers. First, it gives you—the writer—a manageable focus for your work. A carefully limited thesis can save you from straying off your subject. Second, a thesis helps your readers. A thesis is to an essay as a map is to an unfamiliar city. If you are entering Chicago for the first time, you want a map to show you where you are going. Similarly, a thesis lets your readers know what lies ahead so that they have a context for understanding each of your paragraphs and sentences as the essay unfolds.

You can devise a working thesis in any of several ways. Some writers like to discover a thesis by "quick-writing" (see the following section). Others develop a thesis by using Step Three (list the most powerful thoughts and impressions the text inspires in you) in the "Four-Step Process for Writing from Reading" described in Chapter 2. Start by finding a text or passage that interested you and that you annotated heavily. For example, Sam rereads the following passage in Henry David Thoreau's "Where I Lived, and What I Lived For" (see p. 930) and the annotations he made in his notebook:

I went to the woods because I wished to live deliberately, to front only the essential facts of life, and see if I could not learn what it had to teach, and not, when I came to die, discover that I had not lived. I did not wish to live what was not life, living is so dear; nor did I wish to practise resignation, unless it was quite necessary. I wanted to live deep and suck out all the marrow of life, to live so sturdily and Spartan-like as to put to rout all that was not life, to cut a broad swath and shave close, to drive life into a corner, and reduce it to its lowest terms, and, if it proved to be mean, why then to get the whole and genuine meanness of it, and publish its meanness to the world; or if it were sublime, to know it by experience, and be able to give a true account of it in my next excursion. For most men, it appears to me, are in a strange uncertainty about it, whether it is of the devil or of God, and have *somewhat hastily* concluded that it is the chief end of man here to "glorify God and enjoy him forever.". . .

[ANNOTATIONS]

Thoreau went to Walden to experience what life really is, whether that might be good or bad.

doesn't want to *waste* life but be "deliberate" (= "intentional," "careful in deciding," "slow")

"Spartan-like": scaling life to essentials. What is essential?

beautiful paragraph! something to put on the refrig.

you can only *know* by experience

taking others' opinions without thinking

create story of someone *today* who lives like T.

T. wants to think, to evaluate all he's doing in his life

Noting that his strong response to this passage makes it a promising focus for an essay, Sam then redoes Step Three of the Four-Step Process and comes up with several ideas for a working thesis. Since a thesis is a complete sentence, he tries to phrase each item in his list of thoughts and impressions as a complete sentence.

- I want to save this paragraph, put it somewhere, maybe even memorize it.
- The idea of living deliberately is a good one; we need to slow down, especially in this hectic modern life. Think and examine everything, especially what we do *routinely*. **Thesis** possibility: Thoreau calls us to examine the way we live, especially what we do routinely without thinking. (Find other passages that support this.)
- Thoreau's point is not about *where* you live but *how*, and *how* is to live deliberately. Thesis possibility: Thoreau's point is not that we must go to the woods as he did but that we must keep the woods—something wild—inside us(?)
- I'm not ready to move to the woods, but I have memories of being in nature and the peace it brings. I could write about this in a personal essay. My own Walden pond is a boulder up Ogden canyon; I go there to "live deliberately."
- Do you go to the woods or do the woods come to you? Do you have to go to the woods to live deliberately or do you just have to get the

woods inside your mind? Is Walden a matter of what you do or what you think, or both? Walden in L.A.? New York?
- In *Dead Poet's Society* this paragraph was quoted. Seize the day, live life to the full. Thoreau brings back memories of that movie.

You can also develop a thesis by posing a question around some problem:

- "Is Mr. Green's behavior in the story 'A Loaf of Bread' ethical?"
- "Why do Mrs. Hale and Mrs. Peters in Susan Glaspell's *Trifles* conceal the evidence that implicates Minnie Wright in the murder of her husband?"
- "Why does Louise Mallard in 'The Story of an Hour' seem to want to be 'free' of her husband, even though he has always treated her affectionately?"

Then formulate an answer to the question to create a working thesis:

- "Mr. Green is unethical; he consciously exploits customers in the poor (mainly black) neighborhood and then blames society for his own wrongdoing."
- "Mrs. Hale and Mrs. Peters feel an empathy for Minnie Wright that ultimately overrides their sense of obligation to the law."
- "Though her husband is loving toward her, Louise Mallard wants to be 'free' to experience the independence she has never been allowed to have."

These three examples illustrate some important qualities of a "good" or "strong" thesis:

1. A good thesis is nonobvious. The third example would be greatly weakened if it were changed to read, "Mrs. Mallard yearns for freedom." That would merely be stating the obvious since at the story's climax Mrs. Mallard rhapsodizes about being "Free, free, free!"

2. A good thesis makes a worthwhile, interesting contribution to the "conversation" on the topic. Again, the third example illustrates, as it promises to touch on some interesting aspects of "The Story of an Hour," for instance, the rather surprising fact that Mrs. Mallard seems to want to be rid of her husband even though he has been kind to her, and the idea that freedom and self-fulfillment can be quashed by factors, such as marriage, which are normally viewed as self- and life-enhancing. Similarly, the second sample thesis, about *Trifles*, implies a discussion of interesting conflicts between personal conscience and the law.

In Joe's case a question has already been posed for him in the "Activities for Writing and Discussion" after "A Woman on a Roof":

Is Tom (a) "better" or "kinder" than Stanley, (b) simply different from Stanley, or (c) really no different from Stanley?

From the question Joe derives the following working thesis: "Despite his gallant intentions, Tom is essentially no different from Stanley in Doris Lessing's 'A Woman on a Roof.'"

Planning Your Essay: Quick-Writing

The key to planning is flexibility: writers may use different methods to plan different essays. Joe uses a technique called quick-writing. The purpose of a quick-write is simple: to get something—however crude—on paper or screen that can move you forward in your writing and serve as a reference point (perhaps) for instructor or peer feedback. Quick-writing is easy:

- Write for a limited time period (perhaps ten to fifteen minutes) and *stop*.
- Write quickly and continuously.
- Censor nothing; permit yourself to write down everything—brilliant, mediocre, or "dumb"—that occurs to you.
- Do not worry about making grammar, spelling, punctuation, or other sentence-level errors; simply push forward.

Here is Joe's quick-write:

"Young Tom" in "Woman on a Roof" is really in the same boat as Stanley. "The bond between the woman and himself" is something covert and not outwardly observable. His feelings manifest themselves in the form of elaborate fantasies that he has every evening when he gets home and he somehow imagines that the "woman" has knowledge of these or is somehow informed of his supposed "bond" with her. At the end, young Tom even manages to feel slighted by the woman's apathy towards him as if she has wronged him by reacting in this way. Stanley certainly manifests his feelings in a more direct and observable way.

The woman has made herself unavailable to Stanley who may observe the candor of the relationship Stanley has with Mrs. Pritchett, a woman who has made herself accessible to him and he manages to have a reasonable relationship though it is made possible via the flirtatious nature of their interaction.

Stanley may be capable of dealing with women in only a sexual way and the woman on the roof's uncaring, unmoved manner has been in effect an invalidation of Stanley's sexual persona or merely a rejection—something that Stanley is not accustomed to or perhaps just a rejection in this manner.

Note that quick-writing is a step, not an end in itself; Joe's writing is rather disjointed, but he now has some basic ideas to mull over and develop into a draft. We will come back to these "basic ideas" in a moment.

Also, notice that quick-writing is not only an activity for the "planning" stage of writing; you can quick-write at any time in the course of composing an essay or any other piece of writing. You can quick-write to develop a thesis, to recast an awkward or confusing paragraph, to "rough out" an introduction or conclusion, to regain focus when your mind wanders, or simply to break the inertia of not writing. Quick-writing is a quintessentially recursive activity.

Planning Your Essay: Listing and Sequencing

Another way to plan is by listing the points you want to raise to support your thesis. First, do a brainstorm list; that is, write down any points that occur to you without worrying about their order. Then reread the list and rearrange the items, as necessary, into a logical sequence.

For an example of listing and sequencing, consider Lori's work for an essay on Charlotte Perkins Gilman's story "The Yellow Wallpaper." "The Yellow Wallpaper" is about a married woman in a profound mental and emotional crisis. Her husband, John (a physician), has prescribed complete rest and has moved her to a house in the country, where she is confined to a single garishly wallpapered room. The wife becomes obsessed with the wallpaper, perceiving images in it of a trapped woman trying to escape, and eventually tears the paper from the walls. Critical opinions differ over the end of the story: Has the woman achieved a liberation of some kind, or has she gone insane? In her working thesis and list of supporting points, Lori argues the latter:

> Working thesis: The narrator went insane at the end of the story, but justifiably so.
>   Why justifiably?
>   John's treatment was that of a Dr. whose last concern is his wife
>   John laughs at her—practical—he doesn't believe she's sick
>   she admits that he may be the reason she doesn't get better
>   he assures friends and relatives she's fine; she's stuck
>   doesn't let her work
>   she can't be herself around him
>   he "takes all care from me" instead of taking care of her
>   It's a human characteristic that, when left in one place, alone, people start to think weird things
>   She is insane (examples at end)
>   insanity was her escape (?)

Lori then rereads and refines her list and classifies related items into groups. Finally (as indicated here by the arrow she has drawn), she arranges the groups into a meaningful sequence:

1. Insane
    examples at end (quotes)
    it was her way of *escape*
2. John's treatment was more like punishment
    left her alone; no variety
    told her she wasn't sick
    didn't let her work
3. It's a human characteristic that, when left in one place, alone, people start to think weird things
    like analyzing wallpaper and giving it a smell
    she has no one to be intimate with/so she becomes intimate with the wallpaper
    she was forced to be in a horrible place and she couldn't deal with it.

Like Joe, Lori now has some ideas with which to work. She follows her list with a quick-write:

At the first of the story we have a depressed woman. She is slightly depressed and dealing with a mild nervous condition but overall a pretty healthy person. Her husband, John, decides to take his wife away for a while (to hide/rest) and they move into an old abandoned mansion. This could have been a good arrangement. She might have even grown better, but John gave her a cruel schedule to follow. She was told not to work, be around people, or even write. Her eating and sleeping habits were closely monitored, and she got worse. She was kept in a big room with only a heavy bed, bars on the windows and hideous wallpaper. At first she would write her feelings, but after a while she became too weak for that and layed(?) in bed and stared at the wallpaper. She could not grow close to John (in fact, there was a growing gap between them), so she became intimate with this wallpaper. She analyzed its color, texture, patterns, and even gave it a "smell." This woman was forced to live in a horrible place deprived of work, beauty, freedom, and exercise, and she couldn't deal with it.

She is trapped. She is entirely too weak to get out of a world that's destroying her. All she has left is the wallpaper, so she finds a woman in that wallpaper and she displaces/uses her as an avenue to her feelings. The woman is symbolically trying to get out and the narrator is determined to help. She begins stripping the wallpaper off the walls around the room, and in doing so, liberates herself from this mentally torturous reality.

Creeping about, she is finally free. Call it insane, but this is the only "out" she had. Reality didn't hold anything for her. So, she stepped out.

Getting Feedback from a Peer or a Small Group

As they formulate theses and plan their essays, Joe and Lori can benefit from peer feedback. Like quick-writing and listing, feedback is useful at all stages of writing an essay (or any other text). Two common misconceptions about feedback are that its aim is to "tear apart" the other person's paper and that its message is primarily negative. In fact, some of the most helpful and motivating feedback is positive. Its focal aim is not to hurt but to help. In a partnership or small group, the objective is always to assist each other toward better writing.

Different stages of writing call for different kinds of feedback. Here are two general suggestions for feedback during early stages of writing:

1. Offer at least some positive and encouraging comments. What writers most need at this stage is momentum to get all their ideas on paper. Positive comments can help create that momentum. Make your comments as specific as possible. A reaction such as "Joe, I like how you contrast Stanley's treatment of Mrs. Pritchett with his treatment of the woman on the roof, though I'm not sure I understand it" is quite helpful. It tells Joe that his point is worth developing but needs clarification. On the other hand, a response of "Great piece! Don't change a thing!" is of dubious value. Your feedback, of course, should also be sincere. You don't have to applaud writing that fails to meet the assignment just because you want to be supportive.

2. Since essays often change radically during the drafting, revision, and editing stages, focus on larger issues (appropriateness to the assignment, focus, potential for development) rather than on such sentence-level matters as wording, grammar, and spelling.

Here are a few questions that you and your group might address during the planning stages of writing an essay:

When you have developed a working thesis and are starting to plan your essay:

- Is the thesis appropriate to the assignment? Example: If your assignment says to write on one of the "Activities for Writing and Discussion" at the end of "A Woman on a Roof" and your thesis is on "The Story of an Hour," you need a new thesis.
- Is the thesis nonobvious? Does it promise to make an interesting contribution to the "conversation" about the chosen topic?
- Is the thesis supportable within the prescribed word length for the assignment (e.g., three hundred words, five hundred words, one thousand

words)? Example: If your instructor wants an essay of "around one thousand words," you will have trouble covering the following thesis: "Charlotte Perkins Gilman's 'The Yellow Wallpaper' is a critique of nineteenth-century treatments of nervous disorders." Such a thesis would require considerable development and outside research. You would do better to narrow the thesis to something like "John's medical treatment of the narrator helps precipitate her final crisis."

After you have composed one or more quick-writes on your topic:

- Which points relate to and support the thesis? Which, if any, do *not* (and should therefore be cut)?
- Which points seem strongest or most interesting?
- Which points need more explanation or development?

Joe applies these questions to his quick-write on "A Woman on a Roof" and also gets feedback on the questions from his group mates. Then, as shown below, he marks up his quick-write to indicate points for development. With these notes, he begins the transition from quick-write to draft.

"Young Tom" in "Woman on a Roof" is really in the same boat as Stanley. "The bond between the woman and himself" is something covert and not outwardly observable. His feelings manifest themselves in the form of elaborate fantasies that he has every evening when he gets home and he somehow imagines that the "woman" has knowledge of these or is somehow informed of his supposed "bond" with her. At the end, young Tom even manages to feel slighted by the woman's apathy towards him as if she has wronged him by reacting this way. Stanley certainly manifests his feelings in a more direct and observable way.

Outwardly, Tom and Stanley react differently. Inwardly, their reactions are similar

The woman has made herself unavailable to Stanley who may observe the candor of the relationship Stanley has with Mrs. Pritchett, a woman who has made herself accessible to him and he manages to have a reasonable relationship though it is made possible via the flirtatious nature of their interaction.

Similarity with Tom's inward fantasies

Stanley may be capable of dealing with women in only a sexual way and the woman on the roof's uncaring, unmoved manner has been in effect an invalidation of Stanley's sexual persona or merely a rejection—something that Stanley is not accustomed to or perhaps just a rejection in this manner.

Compare/contrast their reactions—outward reactions/ inward reactions Conclusion: the nature of unspoken relationships?

Checklist of Activities for Planning an Essay about Literature

Develop habits of recursive reading and writing:
- Reread your notebook regularly, and mine it for ideas for writing.
- Share with your peers to develop your ideas and gain new perspectives.
- Practice habits of note taking and of reviewing and annotating your own notes.

Find a topic:
- Review your notes and notebook.
- Brainstorm or quick-write for possible topics.
- Peruse the "Activities for Writing and Discussion" and the "Additional Activities for Writing and Discussion" that follow many of the reading selections in Part V.

Develop a working thesis:
- Brainstorm or quick-write your way to a thesis, or
- Use Step Three of the "Four-Step Process for Writing from Reading" (p. 15), to make a list of possible theses, or
- Pose a question around some problem your thesis can answer.

Evaluate your thesis:
- Is it appropriate to the assignment?
- Is it nonobvious, and does it promise to make an interesting contribution to the conversation about the topic?
- Is it supportable within the prescribed word length for the assignment?

Do a quick-write of your essay, or
Make a list of points to support your thesis (and then arrange the points into a logical sequence or outline).

Get feedback at various stages from a partner, small group, and/or your instructor.

6

Ways of Drafting:
Building a Barn
in a Tornado

> I don't give a hoot what the writing's like. I write any sort of rubbish that
> will cover the main outlines of the story, then I can begin to see it.
>
> —FRANK O'CONNOR

Beginning with Limited Expectations

I t's one thing to develop a thesis for an essay, make a list of ideas, and do a
quick write or two; quite another to produce a draft. Somehow a "draft" suggests something *substantial*.

The best way to approach drafting is with limited expectations. Rid yourself
of the notion that a draft is a nearly "finished" piece of writing, and think of it,
instead, as a *rough approximation* of an essay. When you draft you are trying to
get all your ideas on paper (or screen) in whatever rough form you can. Concerns about quality and finish are far away.

You may want to keep the following images in mind as you draft:

1. *A safety net.* Spread beneath you as you draft is an immense safety net
called "revision," which makes injury impossible, no matter how hard or far
you fall. Revision is your invitation to return to your draft and redo it, as much
as you'd like, later on.

2. *Building a barn in a tornado.* This was novelist William Faulkner's
metaphor for drafting. Imagine yourself in the ultimate race against time. You
have to hang on to your hammer and drive the nails *fast* before they blow away.

75

Two Ways of Drafting

Two basic procedures for drafting are "starting from scratch" and "cutting and pasting." Which approach you use depends on the quality of the writing you have done on your topic so far. If your predraft writings such as notes, lists of ideas to develop, and quick-writes are confused or unsatisfying, you may prefer the "start-from-scratch" method. On the other hand, if your predraft writings read well and already begin to suggest usable "pieces" of a draft, then cutting and pasting is good.

Starting from Scratch: Writing a "Throwaway" or "Rehearsal" Draft

Start from scratch when you have a topic but the preliminary writings you have done for it are too poorly written to include in your essay. First, review your writings, getting the important ideas firmly fixed in your mind. Then write a quick draft. To highlight its tentative nature, call it a "throwaway" draft or, if you prefer, a "rehearsal" draft.

Starting with a fresh sheet of paper (or a clear screen), and without looking back at your preliminary writings, write the draft. Begin by accepting that what you produce will probably be food for the trash bin—compost, waste material, junk. Your main goal in this draft is to *approximate* the shape you want your final text to have.

Here are a few guidelines for throwaway drafting:

- Focus yourself by jotting down your working thesis.
- Write quickly for a limited time period (twenty to thirty minutes works well).
- Make sure the draft has a beginning and an end, however sketchy.
- Do not concern yourself with getting the "correct" phrasing or with providing supporting examples, as fumbling over these matters will break your momentum and disturb your train of thought.
- Whenever you get stuck and can't think of a word, phrase, or sentence, leave a blank and push on. If you are undecided between two different words or phrases, include both and separate them with a slash, e.g., "She loved/enjoyed the book." Aim to achieve an overall shape for the piece, and worry about details later.

Here is the throwaway draft Joe wrote for his essay about "A Woman on a Roof":

Lessing on Men and Women

In Doris Lessing's "A Woman on a Roof," two men/roofers become fascinated with a woman who sunbathes nearby them as they work. While Stanley hoots and _____ angry at the woman, Tom—the younger—sees himself as the woman's protector. Yet, despite his gallant intentions, Tom is essentially no different from Stanley in his treatment of the sunbathing woman.

Outwardly, the two men react quite differently. With the initial sighting of the "woman on a roof" Stanley raises questions about the woman's near-nudity, and, later, he begins acting out at the woman, whistling and hooting at her. Though he is seemingly annoyed at her and her state of near-nudity, he seems inextricably drawn to her and his annoyance deepens with her indifference.

Tom's actions are, at first, little different from Stanley's: he snickers at Stanley's derisive comments about the woman, he goes with Stanley to spy on the woman, and he even stands by Stanley as Stanley hurls epithets at the woman after Tom has come to see himself as the woman's champion. The woman's indifference angers Tom as much as it does Stanley and, ultimately, he comes to feel a resentment in himself toward the woman, even hatred.

Stanley's relationship with the *other* two women of the story, his wife and Mrs. Pritchett, gives us a glimpse of some of his inner motivations. Some of his earlier anger with the "woman on the roof" seems to stem from his feelings about his wife. "If my wife lay about like that, _____" (fill in quote) Stanley says. It seems his annoyance with the sunbathing woman could be related to his inability to control her the way he, probably, controls his wife. Stanley is able to regain that sense of control through his relationship with Mrs. Pritchett and we see him responding positively to her as she seems to be receptive to his physical charms.

Control is also the primary issue in Tom's relationship with the woman on the roof. When he first sees her, he wants to possess her apart from his cohorts, as his own. Tom stands near Stanley as Stanley rages against the woman, hoping that she doesn't associate him with Stanley (reword?); he comes to see himself as having to save the woman from Stanley and even has involved fantasies about becoming the woman's lover. But when the woman does not sunbathe one day, Tom feels betrayed. Her appearance the following day reassures Tom, and the fact she can't be seen by the others makes her seem more like his own. By the end of the story, however, when Tom comes face to face with the woman's indifference, he feels slighted in much the same way that Stanley does.

It is the woman herself who sees Tom, for all his romantic intentions, as no different from Stanley. When Tom finally speaks to her, the woman tells him to go away and that, if he gets a thrill out of "seeing women in bikinis," he should "go to the Lido." Tom feels stung by what he perceives as her mis-perception of his actions and goes away hating the woman, suggesting that the woman saw him with the utmost clarity of all.

What happens to the throwaway draft after you have written it? From its name you might assume it ends up in the wastebasket, and this does occasionally happen. Even then, however, you will not be disappointed because your expectations were modest. You may need to change your topic, do some more preliminary quick-writes, or get feedback from your instructor or classmates about what to do next. On the other hand, like Joe, you may be pleasantly surprised by the quality of your throwaway. Sometimes, when you have low expectations for a draft (telling yourself you're going to "throw it away" when it's done), you end up producing something better, richer, and more exciting than you do when you grit your teeth and say, "This *will* be a masterpiece." Thus, you might end up not "throwing away" the draft at all. You may find that doing a rough draft is basically a matter of filling out and elaborating on the throwaway. Finally, no matter what you do with the draft, you will be going back over it; you will be using it recursively to move your work forward.

Joe reviews his draft in the light of four questions that you might apply to your own throwaways:

1. What are the strengths of the draft, and where is it working well? Identify specific passages.
2. What do you need to do in order to advance to a rough draft? Identify specific passages that need work and why.
3. Which points relate to and support the thesis? Which do not (and therefore should be cut)?
4. Which points could use more explanation or examples?

To observe Joe's next step, see "From Throwaway Draft to Rough Draft," below.

Cutting and Pasting

Cutting and pasting involves taking various pieces of preliminary writing you have already done on your topic and combining and arranging them to create a draft. You can cut and paste by either of two general methods: on screen with a word processor or on paper.

As you accumulate a number of entries on a topic that you want to develop into a finished piece of work, e.g., "nonconformity or madness in Ray Bradbury's 'The Murderer'" or "escape themes in 'The Yellow Wallpaper' and 'The Story of an Hour,'" a word processor is enormously helpful. With word processing you can type related notebook items into a word-processing document. That way you can see them all, together and in one place, on screen. You are "getting all the cards on the table." At this point the "cards" may be extremely disorganized. Nevertheless, you are 51 percent of the way to a finished text because you have all your ideas before you. Now you can begin arranging, rearranging, adding, and deleting materials toward accomplishment of a draft.

To illustrate: suppose the pages below are in your notebook, and the circled parts—"A" and "B"—are passages that please you in their current form:

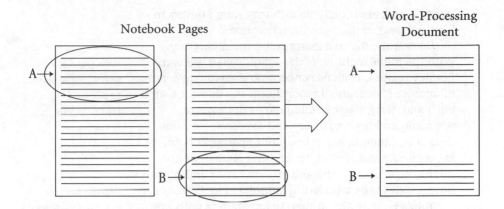

As illustrated, you can "cut" these passages out of your notebook and "paste" them into a *new* word-processing document as parts of a rough draft.

If you lack access to word processing, you can rearrange the pages in your notebook so that entries on your topic are physically juxtaposed. This is where a looseleaf notebook is advantageous. For instance, if entries from October 8 and October 14 talk about "differences between Stanley and Tom in 'A Woman on a Roof,'" put them physically together (within your notebook or in a file folder) so that you can begin to see connections between what you wrote on those two days. This is an excellent way of organizing your ideas, of moving from the notebook writing stage to the draft stage. (I have presented "starting from scratch" and "cutting and pasting" as if they were mutually exclusive activities. They aren't. Often you will end up creating a part of your draft by cutting and pasting and other parts by writing from scratch.)

From Throwaway Draft to Rough Draft

Here is the rough draft that Joe wrote after doing his throwaway. The marginal notes indicate some of the more significant changes he has made from his throwaway draft.

The Clarity of Control:
Lessing on Men and Women

Expands title to be more descriptive

In Doris Lessing's "A Woman on a Roof," two men become fascinated with a woman who sunbathes nearby them as they work. While Stanley hoots and hollers and actually expresses a sense of rage at the woman, Tom, a younger man, comes to see himself as the woman's protector. Yet, despite his gallant intentions, Tom is essentially no different from Stanley in his treatment of the sunbathing woman.

Outwardly, the two men react quite differently. With the initial sighting of the scantily clad woman, Stanley raises questions concerning the woman's state of undress ("Someone'll report her if she doesn't watch out") and, later, begins acting out at the woman, whistling and hooting at her and expressing a great deal of agitation at her subsequent apathy. Though he is seemingly annoyed at her and her state of near-nudity, he seems inextricably drawn to her and his annoyance deepens with her "gesture[s] of indifference."

Tom's actions are, at first, in conspiracy with Stanley's actions: he snickers at the derisive comments Stanley makes about the woman, he "makes the trip" with Stanley to spy on the woman and, even once he comes to see himself as the woman's champion, he stands by Stanley as Stanley hurls epithets at her. The woman's indifference angers Tom much in the same way it angers Stanley and, ultimately, he comes to feel a resentment in himself toward the woman, even hatred. He feels her "unfairness pale him," and, when it rains at the end of the story, he feels a sense of triumph over her.

It is in Stanley's relationship with the other two women of the story, his wife and Mrs. Pritchett, that we glimpse some of his inner motivations. Some of his earlier anger with the "woman on the roof" seems to stem from his feelings about his wife. "If my wife lay about like that," Stanley says, "I'd soon stop her," and it is here that we are able to discern that his annoyance with the sunbathing woman could be related to his inability to control her much in the same way he, no doubt, controls or seeks to control his wife. Stanley is able to regain that sense of control through his relationship with Mrs. Pritchett and we see him responding positively to her as she seems to be receptive to his physical charms.

Control is the primary issue in Tom's relationship with the woman on the roof, as well. When he first sees her, he wants to possess her apart from his cohorts, to keep her for his own. On one of his trips to spy on the woman, Tom makes the report that "she hadn't moved, but it was a lie. He wanted to keep

Here (and elsewhere) adds quotations to illustrate points

Details supplement ideas that were hinted at in throwaway

Expands discussion of Mrs. Pritchett and how Stanley's relationship with her illuminates his relationship with "woman"

what he had seen to himself: he had caught her in the act of rolling down the little red pants over her hips. . . ." Tom stands near Stanley as he rages against the woman, hoping that she doesn't associate his proximity with complicity; he comes to see himself as having to save the woman from Stanley and even has involved fantasies about becoming the woman's lover. But when the woman does not sunbathe one day, Tom feels betrayed. Her appearance the following day re-assures Tom as does her moving to a part of the roof where the men could not see her, because he feels that she's "more his when the other men couldn't see her." And, by the end of the story, when Tom comes face to face with the woman's indifference, he feels slighted in much the same way that Stanley does.

Extensive expansion of last 2 paragraphs with quotations, examples, and rewording of undeveloped ideas

It is the woman on the roof's perception of Stanley and Tom that is most telling, for she sees Tom, with all his romantic intentions and farflung illusions, as being virtually indivisible from the howling, ranting and hateful Stanley. When Tom finally speaks to her, after he has (in his mind) come to her rescue at the end of the story, the woman tells him to go away and that, if he gets a thrill out of "seeing women in bikinis," he should go somewhere where he'd "see dozens of them, without all this mountaineering." Tom feels stung by what he perceives as her mis-perception of his actions and goes away hating the woman, sug-gesting that the woman had not mis-perceived the situation at all, but that, perhaps, she had seen Tom with the utmost clarity of all.

Checklist of Activities for Drafting

- **"Start from scratch"** if none of your predraft writings is successful. Write a "throwaway" or "rehearsal" draft.
- Follow your throwaway with a **rough draft.**
- **"Cut and paste"** if portions of your predraft writings are successful. "Cut" the successful portions and "paste" them together. Then add other paragraphs, as needed, to complete your essay.
- **Get feedback** at various stages of drafting from a partner, small group, and/or your instructor.

7

Ways of Revising: Caring and Not Caring

Teach us to care and not to care . . .

—T. S. Eliot

Putting Revision into Context

Chapter 6 suggested that you approach drafting with low expectations. Not so revising. The very nature of revision is to "go over" and make better. The further along you get in revising a text, the higher your standards of quality become. At the quick-writing stage you have no standards at all. By the time you reach final proofreading, at the other end of the composing spectrum, you ought to be an archperfectionist. Keep in mind, however, that not every text you begin writing is worth revising. For more about that review Chapter 4, pp. 55–57.

To title this chapter "Revising," as if announcing a new topic in *Reading and Writing from Literature,* is somewhat misleading. Realize it or not, you have been revising constantly throughout this course. To revise means "to look . . . again" (*Oxford English Dictionary*), and "looking again"— a.k.a. "conversing" or being "recursive"—has been the perennial theme of this book. In developing habits of recursiveness, you have automatically developed habits of revision as well. A litany of revision techniques you have already learned and practiced would read like a repetition of the table of contents for Chapters 1 through 6. Any of the following is, potentially, an act of revision:

- Conversational reading and writing
- Annotating
- Notebook writing and sharing
- Listing and sequencing
- Quick-writing
- Revising from group or instructor feedback
- Reading aloud
- Throwaway/rehearsal drafting
- Cutting and pasting

All of these techniques and habits can help you revise an essay about literature. If it weren't for the problem of redundancy, all could be addressed again in this chapter. The best way to use this book is not to read about these techniques once and never come back to them but—you guessed it—to use the book recursively. "Run back" to these strategies again and again—any place, any time. If one cannot help you in a particular situation, perhaps another can.

Thus, this chapter does not "introduce" revision or presume to confine it to a single chapter unto itself; it merely revisits it in the somewhat distinctive context of revising an essay about literature.

Talk to Your Draft from the Point of View of a Hypothetical Critic

Someone once said that writers have two absolutely indispensable needs, a passion for what they are writing and an attitude of ruthless objectivity toward their own creations. This is a paradox at the very heart of revising. As a writer you need to care and not care; you need to care deeply about what you are creating and yet be ready—in an instant—to destroy your writing if it's not working.

Most of us feel vulnerable—naked—when we revise; we long for a suit of armor to steel us for the task and to defend ourselves from the expected "blows" of readers. Together, passion and objectivity constitute this armor. If you are passionate enough about what you are making, if you care enough about the task, the destruction of your text won't matter; you will simply collect yourself and begin again. If you are objective enough, you will never encounter a harsher critic than yourself, so no attack or defeat will astonish you.

To be a good reviser, do everything possible to cultivate both passion for your task *and* objectivity about it. Part I dealt with passion, but here, now, is a word about objectivity. In the context of revision, the opposite of objectivity is attachment—attachment to your text. Writers who are attached to their texts regard any criticism, however useful or appropriate, as a personal affront. They reject criticism, whether self-generated or from others, and thus eliminate any chance of making their texts better.

One excellent way of developing objectivity is to talk—in writing—to the text of your evolving essay and to do so from a particular point of view. Author Jules Renard posed a good model when he said, "I read what I write as though I were my mortal enemy." As you look over your draft, put yourself in the shoes of your severest critic or at least of an interested but critical reader. For instance, if you are writing an essay critical of cell phones, imagine you are someone who values and depends on a cell phone and assess your draft from that person's perspective. Imagine what she would question, challenge, or dislike and what you might say to modify her views. Then question and critique your draft (write in the margins of it) as that person might.

For example, here I am talking to an earlier draft of the introduction to this chapter. My drafts tend to be long on feeling and short on clarity, and so the reader I imagined for myself was an interested but critical English instructor who hates sloppy language and ideas.

> By this point in *Reading and Writing from Literature*, you are no stranger to revision. To revise means, literally, "to see again"; and "seeing again"—a.k.a "conversing" or "recursiveness"—has been the constant theme of this book. In developing habits of conversing and recursiveness, you have (necessarily) developed habits of revision as well. Speaking practically, you have already developed a repertoire of strategies for revising. Refresh your memory of these as often as necessary/Refer back to these as often as necessary. If one cannot help you in a particular situation, perhaps another can.

Margin notes:
EXPAND. Good ideas but flat

Good link with earlier chapters

Use a different word?

Sounds preachy & patronizing(?)
Why should I *care*?

Since the "I" who writes in the margins is my hypothetical critic and not myself, no emotions attach to my paragraph. I don't care about *it*, only about having my ideas come across clearly and effectively.

Practice writing questions and comments in the margins of your own draft as a hypothetical reader might. Jot down:

- **Reactions:** "I understand." "Gets dull here." "This needs reworking."
- **Questions:** "What's your point?" "Why are you telling me this?" "What do you mean?" "So what?"
- **Needs:** "Example, please!" "Clarify/explain." "I need to see some evidence to support this."

The more you write, the more weblike you will find the nature of writing to be; every process and activity is interconnected with every other. *How* do you get better at recording "reactions," "questions," and "needs" in the margins of your drafts? By experiencing, whenever possible, feedback from other people. Such feedback teaches you how and what readers think. Every time you discuss your work with instructors, peers, or anyone else, you strengthen your capacity to identify with readers of your own work.

Global and Local Revisions

Being large in scope and complex, revision tends to raise questions like "Where do I start?" It is useful to separate revision concerns into "global" and "local." Among global concerns are matters of topic selection, thesis, focus, purpose, organization, and clarity. Local concerns include sentence-level issues of grammar, spelling, punctuation, and usage. Though writers often mix their writing on the two levels, generally you should deal with global concerns first and local ones later. After all, it doesn't pay to revise sentence "X" to perfection if you are going to throw it out a few minutes later because it doesn't fit your thesis. Why do surgery on a toe if you're going to amputate the foot? The strategies in this chapter follow a general progression from global to local.

A Short Checklist of Questions for Global Revision

Here are a few questions for addressing global revision concerns. You can use the questions by yourself or in collaboration with a small group.

- Does the draft meet the requirements of the assignment? Is it the appropriate length? Does it address an appropriate topic? A brilliant paper that fails to meet the assignment is probably going to get a poor grade.
- Does the draft have a clear thesis or purpose? If so, what is it?
- Does each paragraph relate to and support the thesis? Which paragraphs, if any, do not?
- Are ideas logically or coherently arranged so that one paragraph follows clearly and understandably from another?
- Does the essay include adequate evidence or examples to support and illustrate the various points? Where, specifically, could you add more?
- Does the essay have a clear conclusion?

Postdraft Outlining

An outline is a familiar device for planning an essay, but you may not realize that it can be equally useful to do an outline *after* drafting. Postdraft outlining helps you look at your draft closely, and it can also help you respond to the "Checklist of Questions." Here are the steps:

1. Read through your whole draft. Then, at the bottom of the last page, write a statement that summarizes what you think the whole paper "does" (that is, what its thesis or purpose is).

2. Reread your draft again, paragraph by paragraph. When you finish reading a paragraph, write in the margin beside it a statement summarizing what you think that paragraph "does," i.e., how it functions in your paper.
3. Beside each paragraph, you can also record your emotional reactions to that paragraph, for instance, "My interest really picks up here," "I find this suspenseful," "I'm feeling bored here," or "I'm losing interest here."
4. When you are finished, review the marginal comments you have written and ask yourself the following questions:
   a. Do your ideas seem to be in a logical order? Does one paragraph and idea follow clearly and logically from another? Draw arrows in the margins to indicate places where you want to rearrange paragraphs or information.
   b. Does each paragraph and idea have a reason for being in the essay? That is, does each paragraph relate to and support the thesis? If not, so indicate.
   c. Are there any places where you need to add more information? or perhaps eliminate some information? or clarify a point? Mark any such places and, if possible, add or delete the information.

Here is Joe's postdraft outline for his paper about "A Woman on a Roof." Skim through the essay, paying particular attention to the "outline" comments in the margins and at the end of the essay.

The Clarity of Control:
Lessing on Men and Women

In Doris Lessing's "A Woman on a Roof," two men become fascinated with a woman who sunbathes nearby them as they work. While Stanley hoots and hollers and actually expresses a sense of rage at the woman, Tom, a younger man, comes to see himself as the woman's protector. Yet, despite his gallant intentions, Tom is essentially no different from Stanley in his treatment of the sunbathing woman.
>*thesis/intro*
>
>*Tom is no different from Stanley*

Outwardly, the two men react quite differently. With the initial sighting of the scantily clad woman, Stanley raises questions concerning the woman's state of undress ("Someone'll report her if she doesn't watch out") and, later, begins acting out at the woman, whistling and hooting at her and expressing a great deal of agitation at her subsequent apathy. Though he is seemingly annoyed at her and her state of near-nudity, he seems inextricably drawn to her and his annoyance deepens with her "gesture[s] of indifference."
>*Comparison of outward reactions—Stanley moves from puritanical concern to rage*
>
>*inexorably(?)*
>
>*Add page #'s for quotations*

Tom's actions are, at first, in conspiracy with Stanley's actions: he snickers at the derisive comments

Stanley makes about the woman, he "makes the trip" with Stanley to spy on the woman and, even once he comes to see himself as the woman's champion, he stands by Stanley as Stanley hurls epithets at her. The woman's indifference angers Tom much in the same way it angers Stanley and, ultimately, he comes to feel a resentment in himself toward the woman, even hatred. He feels her "unfairness pale him," and, when it rains at the end of the story, he feels a sense of triumph over her.

It is in Stanley's relationship with the other two women of the story, his wife and Mrs. Pritchett, that we glimpse some of his inner motivations. Some of his earlier anger with the "woman on the roof" seems to stem from his feelings about his wife. "If my wife lay about like that," Stanley says, "I'd soon stop her," and it is here that we are able to discern that his annoyance with the sunbathing woman could be related to his inability to control her much in the same way he, no doubt, controls or seeks to control his wife. Stanley is able to regain that sense of control through his relationship with Mrs. Pritchett and we see him responding positively to her as she seems to be receptive to his physical charms.

Control is the primary issue in Tom's relationship with the woman on the roof, as well. When he first sees her, he wants to possess her apart from his cohorts, to keep her for his own. On one of his trips to spy on the woman, Tom makes the report that "she hadn't moved, but it was a lie. He wanted to keep what he had seen to himself: he had caught her in the act of rolling down the little red pants over her hips. . . ." Tom stands near Stanley as he rages against the woman, hoping that she doesn't associate his proximity with complicity; he comes to see himself as having to save the woman from Stanley and even has involved fantasies about becoming the woman's lover. But when the woman does not sunbathe one day, Tom feels betrayed. Her appearance the following day reassures Tom as does her moving to a part of the roof where the men could not see her, because he feels that she's "more his when the other men couldn't see her." And, by the end of the story, when Tom comes face to face with the woman's indifference, he feels slighted in much the same way that Stanley does.

Tom's outward reaction initially a self-mirroring of Stanley; moves to the end of story. Tom's feelings of hatred

Need to mention that resentment occurs as result of her rejecting him?

Gauging Stanley's internal state via his external relationships with women: it all equals the attempt to gain and maintain control

Clear

Expand?

Control is the catalyst in Tom's motivations re: the woman on the roof as well— speaks in terms of possession— motivation the same as Stanley's

Redundant with end of 3rd paragraph?

It is the woman on the roof's perception of Stanley and Tom that is most telling, for she sees Tom, with all his romantic intentions and farflung illusions, as being virtually indivisible from the howling, ranting and hateful Stanley. When Tom finally speaks to her, after he has (in his mind) come to her rescue at the end of the story, the woman tells him to go away and that, if he gets a thrill out of "seeing women in bikinis," he should go somewhere where he'd "see dozens of them, without all this mountaineering." Tom feels stung by what he perceives as her mis-perception of his actions and goes away hating the woman, suggesting that the woman had not mis-perceived the situation at all, but that, perhaps, she had seen Tom with the utmost clarity of all.

> *We see that it is the perception of the woman that is illuminating—she views both Tom and Stanley as being the same leering fiend*

> *Despite Tom's intentions, he is driven by the same thing that drives Stanley: <u>control,</u> and the woman perceives this more aptly than either Tom or Stanley.*

Joe's draft is already quite strong. The postdraft outline indicates a clear thesis with effective organization and supporting points. Joe does, however, identify a few places for revision. For instance, he raises a question about clarity in the third paragraph, makes a note to "expand" at one point (the end of paragraph #4), and locates a possible redundancy between the third and fifth paragraphs.

Having Other People Outline Your Draft

Postdraft outlining enables you to see your draft more objectively. You can also benefit from having other people, particularly a peer or a small group, do outlines of your draft so that you have one or more alternative perspectives to compare with your own. Here's how to do it:

- Bring an extra, *clean* copy of your draft with you to class.
- Sit with a partner.
- After you and your partner have finished doing postdraft outlines of your own papers, exchange papers so you are now looking at your classmate's draft and he or she is looking at yours.
- Now repeat steps 1 through 4 above on your *partner's* draft.
- Finally, with your partner compare how you analyzed each other's papers. This can tell you a lot about how well your paper is working. For instance, if your partner's summary of thesis or purpose for your draft (step #1) differs from what you intended, you probably need to make your thesis clearer. Similarly, if your partner's analysis of one of your

paragraphs suggests that he or she is interpreting it differently from what you meant, then you need to think about revising for greater clarity. If your partner writes, in the margin beside your third paragraph, "I am losing interest here," perhaps you need to revise that paragraph to make it more vivid or exciting, or perhaps you need to consider getting rid of it.

Getting Writer-Initiated Feedback

The postdraft outline is an example of reader-initiated feedback; that is, it involves readers describing their reactions to your work while you—the writer—mainly listen. While such feedback is useful, there may be times when you want input on specific problems or issues that concern you about your draft. Hence the value of *writer*-initiated feedback. This is where you, as writer, indicate to your partner(s) specific kinds of feedback that you want that may not be addressed through postdraft outlining.

Before meeting with your partner or group, take a few moments to answer the following questions:

- What do you feel are *strengths* of your draft in its current form? Write down the strengths.
- What specific passages in the draft need more work and why? Identify particular passages in the margins.
- Where in the draft would you like suggestions from your partner or small group?

Share your responses to these questions with your partner(s) or group and read your draft aloud to them. Then ask your partner or group members to respond to the specific areas of need you indicated and take notes on their suggestions.

As you request feedback, keep in mind how thick or thin your skin is. If you thrive on tough criticism, you can ask for it. On the other hand, if tough criticism tends simply to destroy your confidence, devise your request for input so that it will elicit gentler comments of the sort that you want and need in order to improve your draft. After all, the ultimate goal of this or any other revision activity is to get the input that will help you move boldly forward toward a better piece of writing.

Developing Your Essay with Illustrative Quotations and Examples

Poet William Stafford once said that he could reduce revision to a single word: "more." Stafford meant that his most frequent response to others' writing was "tell me more." Clearly, one of the major defects in many rough drafts is a lack of supporting quotations or examples. The key here is *development:* you can make your ideas clearer and more vivid for readers by illustrating those ideas.

Compare the following two versions of a paragraph in Joe's "The Clarity of Control: Lessing on Men and Women." The first version omits quotations and examples, while the second includes them.

> Control is the primary issue in Tom's relationship with the woman on the roof, as well. When he first sees her, he wants to possess her apart from his cohorts, to keep her for his own. Tom stands near Stanley as he rages against the woman, hoping that she doesn't associate his proximity with complicity; he comes to see himself as having to save the woman from Stanley and even has involved fantasies about becoming the woman's lover. But when the woman does not sunbathe one day, Tom feels betrayed. Her appearance the following day reassures Tom, as does her moving to a part of the roof where the men could not see her.

> Control is the primary issue in Tom's relationship with the woman on the roof, as well. When he first sees her, he wants to possess her apart from his cohorts, to keep her for his own. On one of his trips to spy on the woman, Tom makes the report that "she hadn't moved, but it was a lie. He wanted to keep what he had seen to himself: he had caught her in the act of rolling down the little red pants over her hips. . . ." Tom stands near Stanley as he rages against the woman, hoping that she doesn't associate his proximity with complicity; he comes to see himself as having to save the woman from Stanley and even has involved fantasies about becoming the woman's lover. But when the woman does not sunbathe one day, Tom feels betrayed. Her appearance the following day reassures Tom as does her moving to a part of the roof where the men could not see her, because he feels that she's "more his when the other men couldn't see her." And, by the end of the story, when Tom comes face to face with the woman's indifference, he feels slighted in much the same way that Stanley does.

Notice how the quotations and examples serve to ground discussion more carefully in the text's details. Notice, also, how Joe introduces his quotations; rather than simply insert them without context or explanation, he integrates them seamlessly into his own prose.

To prompt yourself to use more examples in your writing try this: Read over your draft; wherever you introduce a point follow it up with a new sentence beginning, "For example, _____" or "For instance, _____" and fill in the blank. "The woman on the roof is not trying to attract the men's attention. For instance, after the second day she moves to a different part of the roof where the men will not see her." In some cases you may decide that no example is necessary, but the simple phrase, "For example," creates a momentum for inserting your illustrations. Later you can delete some of the "For example" phrases and rework your transitions to eliminate choppiness and redundancy.

Local Revision: Copyediting Your Text

When you draft or do global revisions, imagination is an asset. By contrast, when proofreading, you want to be like a machine that focuses in on individual sentences and words and coldly examines them for errors. The problem is, after rereading your text a dozen times during the drafting and revision stages, you may reach a point where you can no longer "see" it; the words and sentences run together in a confused blur. How can you see your text afresh? Here are two suggestions:

Do a "micro" postdraft outline. While the regular or "macro" postdraft outline described earlier in this chapter focuses on revision at the *paragraph* level, a "micro" outline focuses on *sentences*. Simply follow the directions on page 85 for postdraft outlining, with one difference: wherever you see the word "paragraph" replace it with "sentence." You can either apply the "micro" process to your whole text or to troublesome parts of it.

Proofread your text backward. This is an excellent way of seeing your text objectively.

1. Get a clean hard copy of your text and sit alongside a partner.
2. Turn to the last page of your text and place a sheet of paper over it so that everything is covered except the final sentence.
3. Read the final sentence aloud slowly, with pen or pencil in hand. With your partner, examine the sentence for any of the following:

   - Typographical mistakes, e.g., you typed "tch" for "the"
   - Missing words, e.g., "He bought book"
   - Spelling errors, e.g., you typed "seperate" for "separate"
   - Punctuation errors, e.g., you omitted the apostrophe from the contraction in "She cant"
   - Other errors to which you may be prone, e.g., sentence run-ons, comma splices, mistakes in capitalization

4. If you or your partner find any errors, correct them. If you are uncertain whether an error exists or how to correct it, consult a good English handbook.
5. Raise your cover sheet so that the second-to-last sentence is exposed and repeat steps 3 and 4 on that sentence.
6. Continue in like manner through the rest of the text so that the last sentence you proofread is the first sentence of your paper.

If this process seems a bit tedious, keep in mind that its larger purpose is to train you to read carefully and with an editor's eye. The reward is a better and more professional-looking text. Over time and as your eye improves, you can modify the steps as appropriate.

"Lightning" Revision: Reading Your Writing Aloud to a Peer or a Small Group

Reading aloud was just recommended as a method of copyediting. In fact, reading aloud is useful at any and all stages of composing an essay about literature (or any other text). You can read your lists of ideas, your notes, your working theses, your quick-writes, your drafts, your revised drafts (or parts of drafts)—anything.

Reading aloud is helpful in at least two ways. First, it can show you whether a particular writing project is worth pursuing. If you are too embarrassed to read a piece aloud, it *may* mean your work is severely flawed and that perhaps you should start over with a different idea. (A poet friend treated this as a litmus: if he hesitated to read his precious poem aloud he knew the poem wasn't precious, and he destroyed it.) Second, reading aloud is an excellent device for "lightning" revision. Often you can make improvements in your work when reading it aloud that you wouldn't when reviewing it silently. You can read aloud to yourself, but it is even better if you read to a partner or small group because the presence of an audience can intensify your concentration. Observe these three simple steps:

1. Begin without apology ("This is really stupid . . .") or introduction ("Well, you know I'd better explain this before I read it . . ."). Simply plunge in and read. It's a fast way to thicken your writer's skin.
2. Read slowly, with pen or pencil in hand. Whenever you come to a place where you want to make a change (correct a typo or spelling error, alter a word or phrase, add or eliminate a phrase or sentence), simply pause and make the revision. Continue thus throughout your text. Remember: this is a method of *rapid* revising, so don't belabor it; only make changes that occur to you spontaneously.
3. When you have finished, congratulate yourself; you have made your work public, and that takes courage. Reading aloud is a mode of instant publication.

Checklist of Activities for Revising

- "Talk" to your draft from the point of view of a hypothetical critic or reader.
- Focus on global revisions first and local revisions later.

- Do a postdraft outline.
- Have other people do postdraft outlines of your draft.
- Get writer-initiated feedback.
- Develop your essay with illustrative quotations and examples.
- Copyedit your text.
- Do "lightning" revision while reading your writing aloud to a peer or a small group.

8

Documenting Research Essays

[T]he man who thinks for himself becomes acquainted with the authorities for his opinions only after he has acquired them and merely as a confirmation of them, while the book-philosopher starts with his authorities, in that he constructs his opinions by collecting together the opinions of others: his mind then compares with that of the former as an automaton compares with a living man.

—ARTHUR SCHOPENHAUER

Chapter 7 dealt with an essay about literature that focuses on one literary text (or possibly two or three, if the essay is a comparison). Most likely, the text you wrote about was one of those included in Part V of this book. Thus, readers could find your text without the aid of a bibliography and research documentation was unnecessary. In this chapter we turn to essays that draw on outside sources. Such sources may include primary texts, e.g., literary texts such as short stories, poems, essays, and plays, as well as secondary sources, e.g., works of literary criticism, biographies, and other texts *about* literature rather than the literature itself. For these essays documentation is a necessity; that is, you must acknowledge, in an appropriate format, the sources of your information and ideas.

Writing research essays is a familiar, though more complex, example of the conversational and intertextual models of reading and writing you have worked with so extensively throughout this book. It involves the finding and stitching together of patches of overlapping text. Rather than addressing the intricacies of finding and evaluating sources (tasks with which a good librarian can help you), this chapter focuses on how to *use* sources:

- When and how should you acknowledge your sources?
- How can you read sources and understand them?
- How can you incorporate ideas or information from sources into your essay?

• What rules should you use for citing your sources and preparing a bibliography or "Works Cited" page?

A Sample Research Essay

Throughout this chapter, the following essay by Kristin will serve as an illustration. Refer to it, as necessary, as you read the chapter or prepare your own research essays. Boxed notes in the margins refer to terms or ideas that are explained in this chapter. For another example of a documented research essay, see "Your Passing Thoughts: Ralph Waldo Emerson" on page 95.

"The Yellow Wallpaper": A Critical Survey

Charlotte Perkins Gilman's "The Yellow Wallpaper," written over one hundred years ago, is the narration or journal of a woman who is severely oppressed by her husband. While she is suffering from a "nervous disorder," a result of post-partum depression, he takes her to an old abandoned house and demands that she rest from all her work. He does not allow her to think or act for herself. She is afraid to speak out against him, so she records her feelings and impressions in her journal which becomes the text for the story.

> Title of essay centered on page

> Titles of short stories, poems, essays, and other kinds of short works are enclosed in quotation marks

"The Yellow Wallpaper" has undergone a variety of interpretational changes in its hundred year history. Its original audiences thought of it simply as a tale of horror or a depiction of mental breakdown. Consequently, it was ignored by most literary critics immediately following its publication. It was not until the latter part of the twentieth-century that the onset of the feminist movement demanded a closer look at the symbolism behind "The Yellow Wallpaper." Jean E. Kennard suggested "that the recent appearance of feminist novels has . . . led us to find in the story an exploration of women's role instead of the tale of horror . . . its original audience found" (qtd. in Shumaker 588). At a 1989 Modern Language Association convention in Washington, D.C., Elaine R. Hedges called "The Yellow Wallpaper" "the most well-known rediscovered work by a nineteenth-century American woman." At present "The Yellow Wallpaper" is firmly established in the literary canon appearing in all major literary anthologies (222).

> Kristin introduces quotations and integrates them into her own prose

> Example of a parenthetical reference omitting author's last name

Subsequent to its republication, "The Yellow Wall-paper" has been subject to many critical studies. Feminist critics from North America to Europe have used its text as an explicit illustration of the degrading and detrimental effects of women's life in a male dominated society.

Michelle A. Masse, from the department of English at Louisiana State University in Baton Rouge, wrote a critical essay on "The Yellow Wallpaper" entitling it "Gothic Repetition." She employed a variety of techniques in her interpretation. She utilized feminist criticism throughout the work, but also used psychoanalytic and formalist. Much of the essay concentrated on Gilman's use of repetition in her phrases and symbols creating a classic Gothic tale. Though this was the primary purpose of the essay, it was not as important as her explanations for the narrator's motivations and actions.

Masse begins by describing the narrator's loss of identity as a direct cause of her anxiety. Because of John's infantilizing treatment she is forced to deny her identity as an adult, mother, and intelligent human being (702). Using names such as "darling," "little goose," and "little girl" in addressing her and compelling her to stay in a room previously used as nursery or asylum forces her, according to Masse, to see herself as a child and ambiguously joins children with infantilized women (702).

Masse states that the narrator is subject to Freud's theories of displacement and repression. "At a certain pitch of intensity, she ostensibly moves away from talking about herself to discussion of safe inanimate objects . . . " (705). This is shown on page 88 of Gilman's text when the narrator states, "John says the very worst thing I can do is to think about my condition, and I confess it always makes me feel bad. So I will . . . talk about the house." Not being able to consciously deal with her submission and gradual loss of identity, she displaces and represses her feelings onto the house. She also displaces the restrictions placed upon her by her husband/doctor onto the woman she sees imprisoned behind the wallpaper (Masse 701).

Example of a paraphrase or summary

Example of a parenthetical reference using author's last name

The key symbol in this work is the yellow wallpaper. Its bulbous eyed, crawling, fungus-like pattern becomes the object of the narrator's unconscious attempts to resolve her problems. She is determined to find the pattern behind the paper because, as Masse states: "[she] believes that there must be a logical principle . . . determining the pattern of the paper, because there are supposed to be rules for such things, just as there must be comprehensible reasons for gender expectations" (707). Her attempts to find order and control within the paper are in vain. After staring at the paper for a number of hours, she writes: "just as you get well underway in following, it turns a back-somersault and there you are. It slaps you in the face, knocks you down, and tramples upon you. It is like a bad dream" (Gilman 95). Just as she cannot conquer and control the paper, she cannot conquer and control her husband. Masse says "The paper, unlikely concretization of authority's horror though it is, is inescapable and aggressive when challenged" (Masse 708). The narrator becomes angry with the "everlastingness" of the paper (Gilman 91), symbolizing the continuity of oppressiveness. Masse points out that the narrator believes others have been subjected to the paper and angered by it and worries that it will continue to be detrimental to women (708). The narrator spends many long hours studying the paper and eventually "sees what the cultural codes found in this story reveal: a trapped woman" (Masse 708).

Masse states that the narrator finally finds freedom, autonomy and power through her identification with the woman in the wallpaper. "[The narrator] has finally recognized her dilemma, measured the scope allowed to her, and disabused herself of belief in the benevolent intention behind those limits" (Masse 709). She no longer struggles to deal with her prohibited identity. Although her escape is destructive and only partial, it is nonetheless an escape to the only freedom available to her. She has finally spoken and been heard by John (Masse 709).

This essay is very detailed and specific. Masse did many close readings of "The Yellow Wallpaper," and most of her symbolisms can be traced back to certain words in the text. I am in strong agreement with her interpretation of the story's conclusion and of the wallpaper's symbolism as a representation of her sense of repression and submission. I too feel that the

Examples of paraphrasing

narrator displaced many of her feelings onto the wallpaper, refusing to talk or write about them. This essay, however, seemed very complex and only a few
parts opened up the text and gave me a better understanding of it. Masse concentrated on too many symbols, and thus her essay was not clear and concise.
Her lack of focus made it difficult to discern what was
actually being discussed.

   Conrad Shumaker, of the University of Central
Arkansas, describes "The Yellow Wallpaper" as:

> a question that was . . . and still is—
> central . . . to the place of women in
> American culture: What happens to the
> imagination when it's defined as femi-
> nine (and thus weak) and has to face a
> society that values the useful and the
> practical and rejects anything else as
> nonsense? (590)

Block-indented quotation (use when a quotation runs to 5 or more typed lines)

In a block-indented quotation, the terminal punctuation precedes the parenthetical reference

Through the use of feminist criticism, Shumaker
shows how the narrator's husband tries to force her to
shut out all imaginative powers and be logical. He,
like most males of that day, is unable to see anything
that is not practical and materialistic. Anything illogi-
cal, like his wife's problem not really being physical
or her "work" helping her to improve, is unfathomable
to him. He wants only to deal with physical causes
and effects (Shumaker 591). By labeling his wife's
imagination as a negative force, John can control her
and maintain his materialistic view of the world (Shumaker 593). John represents reason to his wife, so
when her feelings contradict him it is automatically
her sensitivity that is at fault because she cannot
question his authority (594). The narrator believes
that John loves her just as John believes that she is
obedient to all of his demands. Although neither is
true, this shows that they both are doomed to act out
these roles until the disastrous end (595). Shumaker
points out the irony in the fact that the reason John
fails to cure his wife is because of his deeply rooted
belief and faith in materialism, "a faith that will not
allow him even to consider the possibility that his
wife's imagination could be a positive force" (592).
The chilling conclusion of the story, as seen by Shumaker, is a very limited amount of freedom for the
narrator. The most important thing accomplished is
the fact that "she has discovered . . . and finally re-

vealed to John, the wife he is attempting to create—
the woman without illusions or imagination who
spends all her time creeping" (598).

Kristin's essay continues for several more pages, but this portion of it is adequate for our purposes here. Her essay ends with the following "Works Cited" page, which lists all of the sources to which she referred in her essay:

Works Cited

Gilman, Charlotte Perkins. "The Yellow Wallpaper." *Literature: An Introduction to Critical Reading.* Ed. William Vesterman. New York: Harcourt, 1993: 87–100.

Golden, Catherine. " 'Overwriting' the Rest Cure: Charlotte Perkins Gilman's Literary Escape from S. Weir Mitchell's Fictionalization of Women." *Critical Essays on Charlotte Perkins Gilman.* Ed. Joanne B. Karpinski. New York: G. K. Hall & Co., 1992: 144–58.

Hedges, Elaine R. " 'Out at Last?' 'The Yellow Wallpaper' after Two Decades of Feminist Criticism." *Critical Essays on Charlotte Perkins Gilman.* Ed. Joanne B. Karpinski. New York: G. K. Hall & Co., 1992: 222–33.

Lane, Ann J. *The Charlotte Perkins Gilman Reader.* New York: Pantheon Books, 1980.

Masse, Michelle A. "Gothic Repetition: Husbands, Horrors and Things That Go Bump in the Night." *Signs* 15 (1990): 679–709.

Shumaker, Conrad. "Too Terribly Good to Be Printed: Charlotte Gilman's 'The Yellow Wallpaper.' " *American Literature* 57 (1985): 588–99.

When You Need to Cite or Acknowledge a Source

Like Kristin, you need to acknowledge any source that you quote, summarize, or paraphrase. To quote is to use the exact words that are in the source text. To paraphrase or summarize is to put the cited material into your own words (a paraphrase usually involves a shorter passage of text and a summary a longer one). Paraphrasing or summarizing is the process of cutting textual fragments to the size and shape you want and skillfully stitching them together so that the whole appears almost seamless.

Acknowledging sources is important for two main reasons. The first is *intellectual honesty*. The ideas are someone else's, not your own. Therefore, you need to give the other person credit for the idea or words. Using another's words or ideas without acknowledgment, as if they were your own, constitutes plagiarism, a serious offense. The second is *as a courtesy to your readers*. A citation of an outside source shows readers where they need to look if they desire further information on your topic.

In a research essay, try to use quotations sparingly. If you overuse quotations, your essay may read like a patchwork of other people's ideas and your own presence as author of the essay will suffer. In addition, copying ideas word for word from a source is a purely mechanical process; you don't necessarily think about what you read. On the other hand, when you summarize or paraphrase, you must process what the passage means. The reward of your effort is that you understand the material to a degree that you wouldn't if you merely copied it verbatim.

How to Paraphrase or Summarize

Here are some suggested steps for paraphrasing or summarizing a passage:

Step #1: Read through the passage a first time to get a sense of the content.

Step #2: Reread the passage, underlining and jotting down key ideas; that is, annotate.

Step #3: Determine the hierarchy of ideas (which idea is most important, next most important, and so on).

Step #4: Write out the most important points and find a way to link them together into one or two sentences.

Step #5: Edit the sentence(s) for clarity and conciseness.

For example, suppose you want to summarize the second paragraph of Kristin's essay. Steps #1 (read), #2 (annotate), and #3 (determine the hierarchy of ideas) are indicated by the following underlinings and marginal notes:

"The Yellow Wallpaper" has undergone a variety of interpretational changes in its hundred year history. Its original audiences thought of it simply as a tale of horror or a depiction of mental breakdown. Consequently, it was ignored by most literary critics immediately following its publication. It was not until the latter part of the twentieth-century that the onset of the feminist movement demanded a closer look at the symbolism behind "The Yellow Wallpaper." Jean E. Kennard suggested "that the recent appearance of feminist novels has . . . led us to find in the story an exploration of women's role instead of the tale of horror . . . its original audience found" (qtd. in Shumaker 588). At a 1989 Modern Language Association convention in Washington, D.C., Elaine R. Hedges called "The Yellow Wallpaper" "the most well-known rediscovered work by a nineteenth-century American woman." At present "The Yellow Wallpaper" is firmly established in the literary canon appearing in all major literary anthologies (222).

Marginal notes:

Interpretations of the story have changed over time

Early—seen as sensational story: critics didn't pay attention to it

Feminist movement has focused new attention on the story—see it as symbolic

Step #4: Write out the most important points and find a way to link them together into one or two sentences:

Interpretations of "The Yellow Wallpaper" have ⎯⎯⎯⎯ ~~with the growth of feminism~~
changed significantly since the story's original publi-
cation. While early readers saw it mainly as a sensa- ⟨critics⟩
tional story, feminists ~~who have focused new~~ ⟨the story⟩
~~attention on the story~~ / feminist have treated ~~it~~ seriously / ~~critics pay more attention~~ / ~~story~~ is seen as ⟨and have it⟩
symbolic of the status of women in the 19th century.

Step #5: Edit the sentences for clarity and conciseness:

Interpretations of "The Yellow Wallpaper" have changed significantly
since the story's original publication. While early readers saw it mainly
as a sensational story, with the onset of feminist criticism the story has
been treated seriously by critics and been seen as symbolic of the status
of women in the 19th century.

You can see how hard it is to portray the process of summarizing on paper.
You can't retrace the exact mental shifts and turns this reader went through to
produce his final summary. That is okay. The important thing is to have a sense
of the steps involved and to recognize the recursiveness of the process. For instance, notice the crossed-out words, inserts, and arrows that show the reader
rethinking and revising.

There are several additional points to make about this example.

First, if this process seems overly time-consuming, realize that the five steps
are a slow-motion description of what you do when you summarize. As you
gain more practice at the process you will inevitably collapse the steps into an
abridged form.

Second, summarizing is an intellectually empowering process in and of itself, independent of the summary you produce. Simply by going through the
intellectual process of the five steps, you strengthen yourself as a reader (and
tone your recursive "muscles").

Third, there is not one "correct" wording for a summary. If you tried summarizing the sample paragraph yourself and came up with something slightly
different, that is fine, though your summary ought to express similar content.

Fourth, summarizing is affected by context. The final content of your summary or paraphrase will change somewhat depending on the particular purpose you have for summarizing. For instance, suppose you are reading Kristin's
essay as part of your research for writing an essay about "sensational literature
in nineteenth-century America." In that case, what Kristin's second paragraph

has to say about twentieth-century feminist critics will be irrelevant to your purposes. Your essay might include a summary more like the following:

> Many stories regarded today as "classics" were viewed as merely sensational stories when they were first published. Charlotte Perkins Gilman's "The Yellow Wallpaper" is a good example (Richards 1).

Parenthetical References; MLA Documentation Style

The "(Richards 1)" that concludes the above sample is called a "parenthetical reference." It indicates that the information is not something you came up with yourself but that you found on page one of a text by Richards. In Modern Language Association (MLA) documentation style, parenthetical references replace traditional footnotes.

The term "documentation style" refers, in part, to the particular set of rules you follow for citing sources in a research essay. Documentation styles vary from discipline to discipline. If you are writing a paper in an English class, you will probably use the MLA style, which is based on the *MLA Handbook for Writers of Research Papers;* in a psychology class you will use the APA (American Psychological Association) style; and for a paper in biology, the CBE (Council of Biology Editors) style. The important thing is not to memorize the rules for all of these styles but to learn how to understand and follow *a* style consistently. It's like using a cookbook. You don't need to memorize all the steps in a recipe; you just need to know where to look them up and how to read and follow them. If you can read and follow the rules for MLA style, you will be able to learn the rules of style for other subjects and follow them accurately, too.

The following are several common variations of MLA-style parenthetical references:

- **Parenthetical reference including author's last name.** A parenthetical reference usually includes the author's last name and the page number(s) where the information appears:

> Not being able to consciously deal with her submission and gradual loss of identity, she displaces and represses her feelings onto the house. She also displaces the restrictions placed upon her by her husband/doctor onto the woman she sees imprisoned behind the wallpaper (Masse 701).

The reference gives readers all the information they need to find the summarized material in its original source. They merely need to turn to the "Works Cited" page at the end of the essay and run down the alphabetical list of authors till they come to "Masse." There they will find all the bibliographical data on Masse:

> Masse, Michelle A. "Gothic Repetition: Husbands, Horrors and Things That Go Bump in the Night." *Signs* 15 (1990): 679–709.

Once they have located the issue of *Signs* (an academic journal) in which Masse's article appears, readers can turn to page 701 to find the source of the summarized material.

- **Parenthetical reference giving page number(s) only.** If you mention the author's name when introducing your summary or quotation, or if the author's identity is obvious from the context, simply give the page number:

Masse states that the narrator is subject to Freud's theories of displacement and repression. "At a certain pitch of intensity, she ostensibly moves away from talking about herself to a discussion of safe inanimate objects . . ." (705).

- **Parenthetical reference following a block-indented quotation.** If a quotation runs to five or more typed lines, you should block-indent it. This makes it easier for readers to distinguish the quoted passage from the rest of your text. With block-indented quotations, note that the final period or question mark is placed *before,* rather than after, the parenthetical reference:

Conrad Shumaker, of the University of Central Arkansas, describes "The Yellow Wallpaper" as:

> a question that was . . . and still is—central . . . to the place of women in American culture: What happens to the imagination when it's defined as feminine (and thus weak) and has to face a society that values the useful and the practical and rejects anything else as nonsense? (590)

- **Reference to an anonymously authored text.** If a text is authored anonymously, use the title of the source, or an abbreviated version, within your parenthetical reference, as in this example from the *MLA Handbook* (4th ed.):

The nine grades of mandarins were "distinguished by the color of the button on the hats of office" ("Mandarin").

Here "Mandarin" is the title of an anonymously written encyclopedia article.

- **Reference to a work by an author who is listed two or more times in your Works Cited.** If your Works Cited contains two or more works by the same author, use the author's last name and an abbreviated version of the work's title in your parenthetical reference. For example, if your Works Cited includes two books by Rainer Maria Rilke, a parenthetical reference will look like this:

"Days go by and sometimes I hear life going. And still nothing has happened, still there is nothing real about me . . . " (Rilke, *Letters of Rainer Maria Rilke* 122).

Preparing Your List of Works Cited

The Works Cited begins on a fresh page at the end of your paper and lists all the outside sources you have quoted, paraphrased, or summarized in your work. List sources alphabetically by author's last name, and include the following information, in sequence, for each entry:

- Author (last name first)
- Title of the work
- Title of the larger work, magazine, or journal (if the work you're citing is contained in it)
- Editor, translator, or compiler (if applicable)
- Edition used (if applicable)
- Number of volumes (if applicable)
- Place of publication
- Publisher
- Year of publication
- Page numbers (if the work is only a part of a larger publication, such as a scholarly journal, magazine, or newspaper)

Center the words "Works Cited" (without quotation marks, underlining, or italics) one inch from the top of the page. Double-space down once to begin your first entry. Start the entry flush with the left margin. If the entry goes beyond one line, indent the second and succeeding lines five spaces (this is called a "hanging" indent). Double-space *between* entries as well as *within* an entry.

The following are examples of a few of the more common types of entries you may include in your Works Cited.

- **Book.**
  Lane, Ann J. *The Charlotte Perkins Gilman Reader.* New York: Pantheon Books, 1980.

- **Book with two authors.**
  Rosenthal, M. L., and Sally M. Gall. *The Modern Poetic Sequence: The Genius of Modern Poetry.* New York: Oxford UP, 1983.

- **Book with more than three authors.**
  Britton, James, et al. *The Development of Writing Abilities (11-18).* London: Macmillan Education, 1975.

- **An edited collection of essays.**
  Karpinski, Joanne B., ed. *Critical Essays on Charlotte Perkins Gilman.* New York: G. K. Hall & Co., 1992.

- **A book with an editor and/or translator.**
  Whitman, Walt. *Walt Whitman's Workshop: A Collection of Unpublished Manuscripts.* Ed. Clifton Joseph Furness. Cambridge: Harvard UP, 1928.

Rilke, Rainer Maria. *Letters of Rainer Maria Rilke.* Trans. Jane Bannard Greene and M. D. Herter Norton. 2 vols. New York: Norton Library, 1969.

- **A short story, poem, or essay included in an edited anthology or collection.**

  Faulkner, William. "That Evening Sun." *The Oxford Book of American Short Stories.* Ed. Joyce Carol Oates. New York: Oxford UP, 1992. 334–51.

  Rich, Adrienne. "Diving into the Wreck." *The Heath Anthology of American Literature.* Ed. Paul Lauter et al. 2nd ed. Vol. 2. Lexington: Heath, 1994. 2531–34.

  Golden, Catherine. "'Overwriting' the Rest Cure: Charlotte Perkins Gilman's Literary Escape from S. Weir Mitchell's Fictionalization of Women." *Critical Essays on Charlotte Perkins Gilman.* Ed. Joanne B. Karpinski. New York: G. K. Hall & Co., 1992. 144–58.

- **Two or more texts by the same author.** Order the texts alphabetically according to the first word (other than "A" or "The") of the title. For second and successive works, substitute three hyphens and a period for the author's name.

  Gilman, Charlotte Perkins. *The Living of Charlotte Perkins Gilman.* New York: Arno Press, 1935.

  ---. "The Yellow Wallpaper." *Literature: An Introduction to Critical Reading.* Ed. William Vesterman. New York: Harcourt, 1993: 87–100.

- **Article in a professional journal that numbers pages continuously throughout the year.**

  Shumaker, Conrad. "Too Terribly Good to Be Printed: Charlotte Gilman's 'The Yellow Wallpaper.'" *American Literature* 57 (1985): 588–99.

- **Article in a professional journal that begins each issue with page one.**

  Behrens, L. "Writing, Reading, and the Rest of the Faculty: A Survey." *English Journal* 67.6 (1978): 54–66.

In the example, "6" indicates that this is the sixth issue of the year (1978).

- **Article in an encyclopedia.**

  "Mandarin." *The Encyclopedia Americana.* 1993 ed.

- **An audio recording.**

  Copland, Aaron. *Symphony No. 3, Quiet City.* Deutsche Grammophon, 1986.

- **A video recording (example borrowed from the *MLA Handbook,* 4th ed.).**

  A Room with a View. Dir. James Ivory. Prod. Ismail Merchant. Cinecom Intl. Films, 1985.

- **A published interview.**
  Davis, Miles. Interview. *Talking Jazz: An Oral History.* By Ben Sidran. Expanded edition. New York: Da Capo, 1995. 7–15.

- **An interview you conducted yourself.**
  Young, William. Personal interview. 4 April 1995.
  Stephenson, Mary. Telephone interview. 6 Dec. 1993.

- **Material accessed on CD-ROM and with a specified printed source (example borrowed from *MLA Handbook,* 4th ed.).**
  Galloway, Stephen. "TV Takes the Fall in Violence Poll." *Hollywood Reporter* 23 July 1993: 16. *Predicasts F and S Plus Text: United States.* CD-ROM. SilverPlatter. Oct. 1993.

- **Material accessed on CD-ROM without a specified printed source (example borrowed from *MLA Handbook,* 4th ed.).**
  "Time Warner, Inc.: Sales Summary, 1988–1992." *Disclosure/Worldscope.* CD-ROM. W/D Partners. Oct. 1993.

- **Material accessed through a computer service (example borrowed from *MLA Handbook,* 4th ed.).**
  Galloway, Stephen. "TV Takes the Fall in Violence Poll." *Hollywood Reporter* 23 July 1993: 16. *PTS F and S Indexes.* Online. Dialog. 14 Jan. 1994.

Creating a Writing Portfolio

A "writing portfolio," as used in this book, is a selection of your best work that you assemble, over a period of time, for presentation to others and for you own use. A portfolio is the result of a sustained process of recursive reading and writing in which you set aside your failed or mediocre writings and concentrate on perfecting your best. Part III suggests strategies for finishing your best work and creating a writing portfolio.

9

Making the Works: Twelve Strategies for Revising

> As you can imagine, I have hundreds of new ideas in my head, but the main thing is making, not thinking.
>
> —Johann Wolfgang von Goethe

> Make *the Works*. . . .
>
> —Walt Whitman

The word "portfolio" means different things in different contexts. As used in this book, a portfolio is a selection of your best work that you assemble, over a period of time, to present to others and to please yourself. In terms of the writing or literature course you are currently taking, your portfolio might be a selection of writings that you submit to your instructor at the end of the quarter or semester for a final grade; in a nonclassroom context, your portfolio might consist of the best work that you assemble, share, and perhaps even publish over a span of years or a lifetime.

A portfolio is the result of a sustained process of recursive reading and writing. No writer writes well consistently; for every piece of writing that succeeds, there may be five or ten or a dozen that fail. Fortunately, professional writers are not evaluated on every scribble they make in the privacy of their workrooms; they are able, instead, to discard the failed texts and present only the worthy ones to their readers. Portfolio evaluation takes into account this unevenness in quality that is common to all writers. Rather than being graded on your failures, a portfolio allows you to be judged on that portion of your cumulative output which is the *best*. You write profusely and get graded on the selected few pieces of work that you revise and polish for inclusion in your portfolio. This process is especially appropriate in a course involving literature because it parallels the composing methods used by the authors in our anthology, who wrote in large quantities and published selectively.

This chapter describes some specific strategies for revising your work. Since revision of essays about literature has already been addressed in Chapter 7, this chapter focuses on revising your writings of a more "creative" nature, such as stories, poems, letters, dialogues, prequels and sequels, or personal memoirs and narratives. Examples of these and related kinds of writing are collected, for your reference, in Appendix A.

What is "good" writing, and how do you know when you've produced it? There is no simple answer to this question because "good" writing means different things to different groups and in different contexts. A "good" piece of writing, e.g., a clear memorandum, an informative report, in a business setting exhibits different qualities from "good" writing in a workshop for science fiction writers; good writing for a popular newspaper differs from good writing for an audience of experts in an academic discipline. Good writing is defined by the community of those among whom and for whom you write. In this course, the community is yourself and your classmates, instructor, and others (such as friends or family members) to whom you show your work. Your best way to gauge the quality of your favorite writings is by reworking and sharing them within that community. This chapter shows you some ways of doing that.

Strategies in this chapter are sequenced to move from techniques for more global revision, e.g., starting over from scratch, to more modest revisions. Included are strategies you can do by yourself and ones that involve interaction with a peer or a small group. Treat these ideas as items on a menu; you don't need to use them all. Simply consult the chapter whenever you are revising—at any time during the quarter or semester—and use the particular ideas that fit your needs at that moment.

Finally, your notebook is a repository for all kinds of writings, from one- or two-sentence notes to longer responses to literary texts. In this chapter the word "draft," which usually implies a longer piece of writing, can be used interchangeably with "note," "sketch," or "idea."

1. Start Over: Consult Chapter 3

Perhaps you have selected a notebook text for revision because you like the ideas or issues it addresses, but, as a piece of writing, it is awkward or uninteresting. Review the "Ten Ideas for Writing in a Reading Notebook" in Chapter 3 to find stimulating alternative ways of reworking your draft. For instance, consider recasting your unsatisfying "letter to the author" as a dialogue or rewriting your "character biography" of the husband in "The Yellow Wallpaper" as a prequel to that story.

2. Start Over: Rewrite Using a Topic/Form Grid

A Topic/Form Grid enables you to observe all your options for rewriting in a concise visual format.

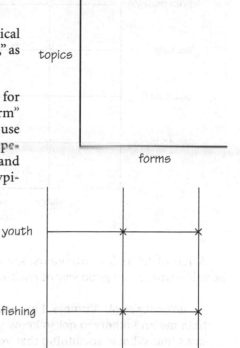

1. Draw a grid and label the vertical axis "topics" and the horizontal "forms," as at right.

2. Along the "topic" axis list topics for writing that interest you. Along the "form" axis list forms of discourse you could use to write about these topics. Think especially of forms you use most regularly and spontaneously in everyday life. Some typical favorites are "talking to myself," "personal letter," and "conversation."

3. Use the diverse topic/form matches available to you to generate writings. For instance, a simple grid like that at right gives you four possible topic/ form combinations. You can create a song lyric about youth, a song lyric about fishing, a letter about youth, or a letter about fishing. Increase the number of items along the axes and you increase, exponentially, the combinations available: three topics and three forms yield nine possible combinations; four topics and four forms give you sixteen, and so on.

Virginia is an avid outdoorswoman with a passion for landscaping. Rereading her notebook she discovers the following note:

> Of all things I love landscaping most. I acquired this interest as a small girl from my grandfather, and since then hardly a day passes in the growing season when I don't have my hands in the soil.

She wants to do something with this . . . but what? How can she expand it and say all she would like about her love for landscaping? She consults a Topic/Form Grid she had made a few weeks earlier:

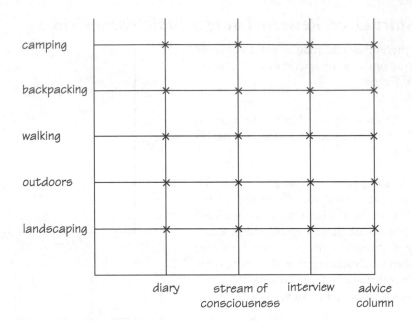

A fan of television interviews, she decides an imaginary interview—with herself—would be a good way of eliciting more information about her passion:

INTERVIEWER (I): Virginia, I am excited to conduct this interview. It will help me and others to get to know you and your interests. Here is my first question. What is something that you enjoy and feel confident doing?

ME (M): I am really interested in landscaping. May I tell you about it?

I: Yes, that would be great.

M: I really take pride in the appearance of my yard. I love to have a well-groomed yard. One that is full of brilliant colors, and a little contrast to emphasize the movement of my lawn. I feel that a yard should be pleasing to the eye.

I: Is this talent close to the imagination of an artist?

M: As a matter of fact, yes. Envision for a minute a blob of clay. Now as a sculptor would begin his piece of work, he plays around with this clay. He or she would place the clay in his or her palm and squeeze it through their fingers. They are creating a picture in their minds of the final piece they are wanting to produce.

I: Hum, interesting.

M: That is basically how I perform my art. As I am out in my yard, doing cultivating, fertilizing, etc. ideas begin to flow. The colors, types of flowers, trees, and rocks that would best express my love for nature begin to materialize.

I: Tell me, Virginia, how did you get interested in this?

M: My grandfather and a good friend of mine were landscapers. They took great pride in their and others' yards. Even as a little child, as I walked to school I observed yards. I really would be disgusted if a yard was unruly. You know, like the look of your hair in the morning?

I: Are you willing to help others manicure their lawns as well as your own?

M: Yes! I have helped three other families upgrade their yards. It's very rewarding, not only for myself but for the other families also.

I: Well, thanks for your time. Could you come and look at my lawn?

M: Thank you, I would love the challenge.

You can see how remarkably individualized the grid is when you compare Virginia's work with Michelle's. A college sophomore, Michelle is currently preoccupied by issues of love and relationships, interests that are reflected in the "topic" portion of her grid:

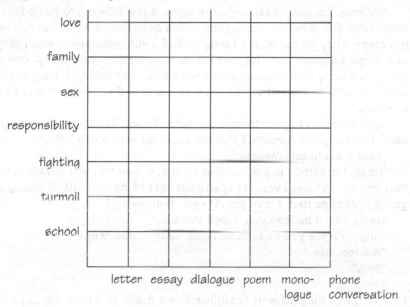

Mulling over her notebook, with its numerous entries about her own experiences of relationships, she discovers how hard it can be to write about them without becoming more personal and confessional than she would like. Her "form" axis gives her an idea: she can use the form of "phone conversation" to render her emotions more objectively. Instead of writing directly about herself, she can invent a conversation between two imaginary lovers experiencing hard times:

Halfway into a long-distance phone conversation:

"John, quit yelling at me! I don't get it. Last week you did the same thing with your friends and I didn't say one word to you!"

"That's not the same thing. When I go to parties with my friends, you know I'm not going to do anything behind your back!"

"So what are you saying, that I can't be trusted? For some reason that doesn't sit right with me!"

"No, Melissa, I'm not trying to say I don't trust you. I just know how you get around other guys when you drink and it makes me worry."

"John, you know how I am around you when I drink and that's because I love you. And it's probably true, I may flirt with guys, but you do the same thing and I know it's harmless. You should know that I would never do anything that might hurt you, no matter how much I've had to drink. I know it's hard living so far away from each other, and if I could change things I would. I hate it every bit as much as you do! But that is no reason not to trust me. I have never been anything but honest with you and I just don't think it's fair when you start coming down on me like this."

"Melissa, I'm sorry. I know you're right. It just kills me to be so far away from you. You know everyone down here teases me about you being away. They all say you're going to find some gorgeous football player and forget all about me. They get me so worried that little things like you going to a party and drinking really set me off. I shouldn't have gotten so upset. I really do trust you. I love you so much and I don't ever want to lose you."

"Quit listening to your friends so much, honey. You know I've never liked football players much. I like the baseball men much better."

"That's not funny, Melissa."

"Okay, I'm sorry. I'm just playing with you. I've told you a million times that you are the one I want to spend the rest of my life with. Nothing is going to change that. I love you. Do you believe me?"

"Yeah, hon. I believe you. I love you too."

"Good! I'll see you as soon as I can, okay? Take care."

"You too. Bye."

"Bye."

One virtue of the grid is its flexibility. Once made, it is never "set in stone"; you can discard old grids and create new ones as your needs and interests change. Moreover, if one topic/form combination fails you, you can shift to a different topic or form on your grid until you find one that works.

Here are a few suggestions for the "form" axis of your grid (certainly not an exhaustive list):

- diary entry or series of diary entries
- personal letter
- unsent letter (e.g., to someone about whom you have strong feelings)
- letter to the editor
- editorial

- monologue
- gossip (a form of dialogue)
- telephone conversation
- E-mail conversation
- song lyrics
- public speech
- drawing or doodle (you don't need to limit yourself to verbal forms; visual sketching can move the imagination in powerful ways)

Use the steps described at the beginning of this section to create your own grid. Then secure the result to the inside cover of your notebook for convenient reference.

3. "Talk" to Your Draft

See Chapter 7, page 83.

4. Do a Postdraft Outline

Postdraft outlining was introduced in Chapter 7 as a tool for revising essays about literature. You can use the same process to revise drafts of a more "creative" nature, such as dialogues, short stories, or personal narratives. Since some creative texts use extremely short individual paragraphs, you may want to summarize *clusters* of related paragraphs (see step #2 on page 86) rather than each individual paragraph.

5. Have Other People Outline Your Draft

See Chapter 7, page 88.

6. Ask Yourself Other Questions Appropriate to the Draft

What questions and problems to address in revision depends on the form (prose narrative, essay, play, poem) of the particular text you are revising. Whatever the form, begin by concentrating on what is working in the draft and on global revisions. From there—and only then—proceed to comments on a more local level. (For a review of the distinction between "global" and "local" revisions, see page 85.) Make your comments *in writing* so you can refer to them as you revise.

For prose narratives such as short fiction texts (stories, prequels, sequels), personal narratives, and plays, respond to the following questions and topics:

- What are two parts of the piece you especially like? Why? Be specific.
- What is one place in the text where you could use more information or detail? Identify the place in the margin.
- Where do the **characters**[1] seem most convincing and alive? Where, if anywhere, are they less so?
- Does the **dialogue** (if any) sound convincing? At what points does it need revising?
- In what places, if any, might the events of the **plot** be arranged more effectively? Is there adequate conflict to generate and sustain reader interest? Is there a clear climax? How can you strengthen it?
- Where (if at all) does the piece lag for you? Why? Be specific.

If you want, provide a partner or members of your small group with copies of your draft, and have them respond to these questions and topics, too.

For poems address questions and topics such as these (again, you can also get feedback on these questions and topics from a partner or peer group):

- What are two parts of the poem you especially like? Why? Be specific.
- What is one place in the poem where you could use more information or detail?
- Describe the poem's impact on you. How does it make you feel? What does it make you think about?
- Does the poem include examples of **figurative language,** such as **metaphors** or **similes**? Where? How do they affect you? How can they be improved?
- React to the poem's physical shape or appearance—the length of the **stanzas** and lines, the amount of white space on the page, for example. How successfully does this shape work to reinforce the poem's overall effect?
- Identify any images that strike you. Describe in the margins how they affect you.
- If the poem is rhymed, circle **rhyme** words you like; then, jot a marginal note beside each such rhyme that describes how it affects you or why you like it.
- Underline uses of other sound effects, e.g., **assonance, alliteration, consonance,** in the poem that you find effective.
- Note any places where you think the poem is excessively obscure or confusing.

---

1. Words in **boldface** are discussed in Part IV, "An Introduction to the Major Genres," and defined in Appendix C, "Glossary of Literary Terms."

7. Get Writer-Initiated Feedback

See Chapter 7, page 89.

8. "Lightning" Revision: Read Your Writing Aloud to a Peer or a Small Group

See Chapter 7, page 92.

9. Revise Your Text for Style

"Style" refers to the "how" (as opposed to the "what") of your writing: how it reads, how it sounds. Sometimes style is seen as an ornament that is merely "added on" to a text during the final stages of review. In fact, however, there is a close kinship between the "how" of your text and its "what." The foundation of style is passionate involvement in what you are writing. If you don't care about the "what" of your writing, the "how" will tend to be correspondingly lackadaisical and dull. On the other hand, if your subject excites passion in you, a corresponding intensity of language will follow (with some work and revision), hence, style. By now you have learned to set aside texts in your notebook that bore you and to concentrate your attention on texts that move and excite you. Thus, some issues of style should already have been resolved. By choosing to work on a text you care about rather than one that bores you, you have prepared the way for style.

That said, there *are* things you can do during the revising stage to strengthen the style of your piece. Your biggest resource here is intertextuality; the best way to improve the style of your own text is by studying other related or similar texts that can serve as examples for you. For instance:

- You are editing a sequel you wrote to Charlotte Perkins Gilman's "The Yellow Wallpaper" (see p. 184); you reread the story to make your style more consistent with Gilman's.
- You are editing a rhymed poem and are frustrated by the awkwardness of your rhymes; you read other rhymed poems, paying particular attention to the rhymed words themselves.
- You are editing a personal memoir that is too stylistically "choppy" for your taste, and you want to make it "flow" better with longer sentences; you read William Faulkner's "Barn Burning" to study its masterful use of long sentences.

Meg wants to edit the style of a story she wrote in response to Herman Melville's "Bartleby, the Scrivener" (see p. 852). Meg's narrator is an individual and opinionated young woman named Candy, who is an overworked secretary in a law office and who tells her story through a series of diary entries. In the current version of the text, Candy sounds less colorful than Meg would like. Accordingly, Meg looks for examples of colorful writing that can help her. Through the short story "Everything That Rises Must Converge" (p. 579), she got interested in the writings of Flannery O'Connor and read a volume of O'Connor's stories, which display just the style she wants. Meg rereads several of these stories to infuse some of O'Connor's stylistic qualities into the character of Candy. You can see the result in Appendix A.

Intertextuality is also of obvious benefit when it comes to improving your stylistic command of the *type* or *form* of writing you are trying to produce, e.g., short story, poem, dialogue, letter, short play, personal essay, etc. For instance, suppose your text is a dialogue. You can find examples of dialogues, written or heard, that are as similar as possible to the one you are trying to create. (The short stories and plays in Part V of this book are excellent places to look.) Then immerse yourself in those dialogues: read them, listen to them, enjoy them. ("Enjoying" will be easy because you have an incentive for studying this form of writing—it is going to help you improve your own text.) How do the dialogues sound when read aloud? What kind of language or vocabulary do they use? Is it formal? informal? special in any way? Is slang used? If the dialogue is printed, e.g., in a short story or a play, how is it punctuated? Where do the quotation marks go? How is the dialogue divided into paragraphs?

Here are some questions to ask yourself when editing your text for style:

1. What stylistic qualities do you want in your text? Consider such factors as:

- Sentence length and complexity. Do you want the sentences to be long or short, simple or complex? How will choices about sentence style affect the meaning of your work?
- Diction (or word choice). Do you want your piece to have a formal-sounding vocabulary, or do you want it to be more informal? Do you want the diction of a sophisticated adult? of a child or adolescent?
- Tone. Do you want the tone to be serious? comic? formal? casual? strident? friendly?
- Rhetorical situation. Who is talking to whom in your piece? What is the relationship between your speaker or narrator and his or her subject? and his or her audience or readers? What kind of language will appropriately reflect that relationship?

2. What other texts exemplify the stylistic qualities you want in your own work? Where—in Part V of this book or elsewhere—can you find these examples?

3. What is the *form* of your text? What are some other texts in that form that you can read and study?

Finally, while it's helpful to study style in any of numerous good books available on the subject, study is no substitute for writing—and doing lots of it.

You can't *strive* for a better style; you can only achieve it by writing in quantity and settling into it. Your style has to find *you*, not the other way round. A personal experience will illustrate.

I habitually take notes in a pocket notepad, and every morning I type the previous day's notes into my computer. I've been doing this now for over two years and have collected several hundred pages of notes on computer disks. In addition to typing new notes I review—regularly—what I've collected, adding and revising as I reread.

During a recent vacation I decided to go through all my shorter notes and harvest fifty to one hundred of the best of them to make a collection of publishable prose poems. I naturally searched for the most brilliant notes, cut and pasted them together, and began reading the collection, breathlessly anticipating a masterpiece. To my astonishment, the work was disappointing—too high-strung and staccato. By contrast, when I scrolled quickly through *all* my notes on the disks I found the writing quite natural and absorbing.

My conclusion—paradoxical but unmistakable—was this: In the aggregate, *my average writings are my best.* To get style write voluminously—brilliantly, badly, and all shades between. Then look for your style to emerge from the average.

10. Break the Revision Task into Smaller Steps

The difference between timid and bold revision is largely psychological. The timid reviser thinks: "Revision is an overwhelming task, like plunging into freezing waters . . . so do anything you can to avoid it!" By contrast, the bold reviser thinks: "No revision task is too hard because it can always be broken into smaller steps. If I can't 'perfect' my text all at once, I can at least do some small things right now to make it *better*."

Whenever a particular revision task seems too big, i.e., you are avoiding doing it, break it into smaller parts. Do one part first, then another, and so on—attacking one small bit at a time. Revise what is easiest to revise first—the soft spots—and leave the parts that resist revision—the hard spots—till later. Gradually, the hard spots will soften; return to them a day or two later and suddenly you will see how to improve them. Then, rather than laboring over them for hours, you can revise them quickly.

What are some soft spots you might revise? A soft spot could be a word or a phrase. It could be a sentence. It could be a matter of moving a couple of paragraphs or of expanding an idea by adding some useful bit of supporting information. If you know your piece has an organization problem but cannot yet see how to correct it, do some editing or revise a sentence or the opening or closing paragraph—anything that comes easily. If you can't get the opening paragraph to come right, work on a middle paragraph.

Sound familiar? This is the very revising strategy Walt Whitman used that was described at the beginning of Chapter 4.

11. Take Advantage of Small Bits of Time

In 1787 the poet and playwright Johann Wolfgang von Goethe was traveling by boat from the Italian mainland to Sicily when he became seasick. Rather than give in to the pain and resign himself to a miserable journey, Goethe got out a draft of one of his plays and began revising it, a bit at a time, as he lay flat on his back. "I remained in my horizontal position," he wrote, "revolving and reviving my play in my mind. The hours passed by and I would not have known what time of day it was if [a friend] had not periodically brought me bread and wine." By journey's end, Goethe reported, he "had almost mastered the whole play."

"I write anywhere," says novelist/attorney Scott Turow. Turow worked out much of his bestselling suspense works, including *Presumed Innocent* and *Pleading Guilty*, while riding the commuter train to work in downtown Chicago. He writes in longhand as the train bumps and rolls along the tracks. Turow utilizes spare moments for writing because he chooses to make time for a life outside that of "author." He has learned to exploit the odd moments of the day for writing.

Novelist Toni Morrison says she is writing all the time, even when she appears to be doing something else. "Writing is a process that goes on all the time," she remarks. "I can find myself in any place, solving some problem in the work that I am at the moment working on. . . . It's just a way of life." The fruits of her habit are impressive, to say the least: over half a dozen novels, two Pulitzer Prizes, a National Book Award, and a Nobel Prize for Literature.

The lesson? Don't wait for huge chunks of time for writing; write in the cracks and crevices of the day. Huge chunks are rare, but the cracks are virtually infinite. Carry around some pages of draft with you and revise when you are:

- In line at the store
- Standing by or pushing the cart while your partner (wife, husband, friend) shops
- Waiting for the water to boil
- Just waking up
- About to sit down to eat
- About to go to bed
- Moving between any two other activities

Above all, try writing at "unlikely" times and in unlikely places, when your expectations of success—and the corresponding pressures to succeed—are low. Often you will surprise yourself by accomplishing more than you expect. For some inspiring examples of what writers can accomplish with small bits of time, review pp. 46–52 in Chapter 4 and look ahead to pp. 164–166 in Chapter 15.

12. Try Various Miscellaneous Revision Strategies

- Develop as broad a repertoire of revision strategies as possible so that when one fails, you can fall back on another.
- Cultivate an attitude of "I'll try this, and, if this doesn't work, I'll try something else." Successful revision depends on risk taking and ingenuity.
- If you get stuck revising one part or aspect of a text, work on a different part or aspect.
- Alternate or diversify your writing tools. If you have been revising at a computer without making satisfactory progress, print a hard copy of your text (or a part of it) and switch to longhand revisions. Conversely, if you are stalling on longhand revisions, change over to computer. If writing at a desk gets tiresome, write in bed or in an easy chair or sit on the floor.
- Alternate between working on details and working on major concepts and structure. When you can't do one, switch to the other. Observe how a painter moves as she creates a painting: she paints close-up to do detail work; then she stands back to get a sense of the whole picture; then she works close-up again.
- Revise steadily. Goethe's motto "Without haste, without rest" is excellent advice for revision. On the one hand, you don't need to make "haste" and attempt to revise your work in a single step; on the other hand, you don't want to "rest" staring at the page doing nothing, either. Always act. Always find something to work on, even if it is only the spelling of a word.
- If you are too tired to revise, if the mere sight of your text sickens you, quit. Do something completely different—jog, houseclean, play tennis, sleep, go to a movie, take a walk. Live.

Checklist of Strategies for Revising

- Start over: Consult Chapter 3.
- Start over: Rewrite using a Topic/Form Grid.
- "Talk" to your draft.
- Do a postdraft outline.
- Have other people outline your draft.
- Ask yourself other questions appropriate to the draft.
- Get writer-initiated feedback.
- "Lightning" revise: Read your writing aloud to a peer or a small group.
- Revise your text for style.
- Break the revision task into smaller steps.
- Take advantage of small bits of time.
- Try various miscellaneous revision strategies.

ACTIVITIES FOR WRITING

1. Use any one of the twelve strategies on one of your drafts. For instance, rewrite using a Topic/Form Grid (Strategy #2), break the revision task into smaller steps (Strategy #10), or revise your work in short stints away from your desk (Strategy #11). Then share the resulting revision with a partner or small group. When you share your revision, also discuss the effectiveness of the strategy you tried, how it helped or didn't help.

2. Repeat Activity #1 with a different strategy.

10

Assembling Your Final Portfolio

> Age sets its house in order, and finishes its works, which to every artist is a
> supreme pleasure.
>
> —RALPH WALDO EMERSON

Chapter 9 described how to revise selected favorite pieces in your note-book. This chapter shows you how to assemble these revised pieces into a final portfolio for submission to your instructor. This process enables you to synthesize your collected and selected writings from the quarter or semester, to reflect on the whole course and on what you have learned, and to consider how this learning can serve you in other courses and in life.

Your instructor will have specific requirements concerning the contents of your portfolio. Typically, a portfolio might include some combination of the following:

- An introduction to the entire portfolio in which you comment on your selections and reflect on what you have done and learned in the course
- Some sample pages of your annotations of a literary text, along with an analysis of those annotations
- A selection of *shorter* notes—thoughts and observations, striking images, phrases, and facts, anecdotes and ideas for writing, and quotations read or heard—that you have collected using a small notepad as described on page 57.
- One or more *longer* creative selections
- One or more essays about literature

- Complete process work for one or more of your final selections, along with a "process memorandum" that interprets your process

Writing an Introduction to Your Portfolio

The introduction will be the first item in your portfolio. Since it is difficult, however, to "introduce" a body of materials before the materials themselves are finished and in place, you will want to compose your introduction last. Think of the introduction as a kind of final exam. The difference is, while an exam sometimes seems to draw attention to what you *don't* know (because someone else asks the questions and sets the agenda), the introduction enables *you* to set the agenda and focus attention on what you *do* know. It is an opportunity to show how thoughtfully you have considered the issues of reading, writing, and literature during the course.

One obvious purpose of the introduction is to help the instructor determine your final grade. There are also other, more self-interested reasons for writing an introduction. As an act of summing-up and reflection, composing an introduction gives you a sense of power vis-à-vis the course you have just taken. Rather than simply finishing the class and saying "Well, that was nice," you assess the course for its current and (likely) long-term value in your life. You see how it fits within your larger life as reader and writer; and you reflect on how you have grown during the course and how you want to continue growing after it's over.

Here are several points to consider in your introduction (you won't be able to do them all; focus on the ones about which you have the most to say):

- Introduce the various selections in your portfolio.
- In what ways do you approach literature differently now than you did at the start of the course? In what ways do you approach reading and writing differently?
- Discuss and illustrate two specific strategies or techniques of writing from reading that you have used during the course and have found especially helpful. (Some possibilities are annotation, conversational reading, rereading, postdraft outlining, any particular forms of writing such as those discussed in Chapter 3.)
- Describe the single *most important* thing you have learned during the course.
- Identify the one aspect of your reading and writing behavior that you would most like to improve.

Examples are crucial for making your ideas clear. Therefore, illustrate your responses to these points with examples from your own notebook and from *Reading and Writing from Literature*. For more on how to add examples, see page 89 in Chapter 7.

Choosing and Interpreting Your Sample Annotations

Annotation is the beginning of response. Each of the finished texts you include in your portfolio originated in some sort of annotation or annotations. Therefore, it is worth reflecting carefully on this process and how you have used it.

Thumb through the annotations you have made in the literary texts included in Part V of *Reading and Writing from Literature*. Identify a few sample pages (your instructor will tell you how many) that show your use of annotation at its best. (Most likely you will find these pages in a literary text that moved you especially powerfully.) Photocopy those pages for your portfolio. In a preface, attached to the sample:

1. Discuss why you chose these particular pages as your sample.
2. Comment on two or three *specific* annotations in the sample that were especially important to you. How did these annotations enrich your reading of the text? How did they stimulate you to do additional thinking and writing?

Preparing a Selection of Your Favorite Shorter Notes

Compile a selection (your instructor will specify how many pages) of your best or favorite *shorter* notebook entries for the term—thoughts and observations, striking images, phrases, and facts, anecdotes and ideas for writing, quotations read or heard, or other kinds of notes you have collected using a small notepad as described on page 57. (*Note:* individual items in this selection would typically be three sentences in length or shorter, as contrasted with the longer entry you revise for the "creative" piece described in the next section.) While you don't need to revise individual items in this selection, you should decide which items to include. If your instructor wishes, attach a preface in which you discuss your experiences with note taking by addressing such questions as the following:

1. What *kinds* of notes did you take—for example, notes of overheard conversation? Of striking images? Of passing thoughts?
2. When and where did ideas most frequently occur to you? Be specific. During walks? When you were listening to music? At a coffee shop?
3. What *tools and mechanical process(es)* did you use for recording these ideas, and how well did they work? Did you try alternative tools and processes? Explain.
4. Did you ever reread your notes? When and how often? With what *effects*? For instance, did rereading inspire you to revise or expand a note, to rethink an opinion, or to create a new piece of writing? Share specific examples.
5. How could you integrate this habit of note taking into your life outside of and after college?

Steps for Choosing and Revising a Favorite Longer Creative Text

Use the process of "rereading" described in Chapter 4:

1. Read through your entire notebook for the quarter or semester.
2. Bracket or underline any pieces that grab or strike you.
3. Reread the marked pieces and choose a favorite. In the margin beside this favorite text, jot down what it is you like about it.
4. If you cannot decide on a favorite text, obtain input on your various options from a partner or small group.
5. Once you have chosen a text, revise it using any of the strategies described in Chapter 9.

Local Revising: Copyediting Your Text

See Chapter 7, page 91.

Preparing a Preface to Your Longer Creative Selection(s)

In order to establish a context for your work, your instructor may want you to attach a preface to your creative selection(s). Here is how:

1. Describe the selection. What kind of text is it? poem? letter to the author? sequel to a play or story? Explain why, out of all the other possibilities available to you, you chose this particular selection for your portfolio.
2. Discuss how the selection originated. What literary text or other source—personal experience, memory, observation, song, movie, photograph—inspired it?
3. Discuss how the piece evolved. Once you got your initial idea, through what sequence of steps did the selection grow into its final form? What challenges or problems did you face during the process of composing, and how did you resolve (or try to resolve) them?
4. If the selection is still not completely satisfactory to you, describe how (given more time) you would change it to improve it.

Be specific and detailed in your preface. The care with which you *reflect* on your work can be as important to your instructor as the work itself.

Preparing a Process Memorandum to Accompany Complete Process Work for One of Your Final Selections

One purpose of a portfolio is to make you more conscious of how you process ideas, from first thoughts to finished work. For at least one of your portfolio selections, save all the writing you did, including first notes, drafts, revisions, and notes on meetings with peers. Turn these in along with the finished text and attach a memorandum (addressed to your instructor) in which you interpret your paper trail and tell the story of your text's evolution.

How did your text originate?

Which parts of the process went well and which posed problems? Why?

At what points did you experience breakthroughs in your development of the piece? Why?

What did you learn through the processes of composing and revising?

Part

IV

An Introduction to the Major Genres

The purpose of Part IV is twofold:

The first purpose is *to increase your technical knowledge of short stories, poetry, essays, plays, and notebooks and journals so that you can write in multiple forms yourself.* For example, if you want to write a personal essay, you can consult Chapter 13 to read about the form and its various components, such as theme, story (or narrative), dialogue, and citation. If you are having trouble deciding how to represent *yourself* in your essay ("How do I want to come across to my readers?"), you can check the paragraphs under the heading "Persona and Voice," which explain that authors construct a persona (or version of a self) to suit the particular context in which they are writing. Then you can peruse or study the essays collected in Part V to see *how* authors shape their personae.

As another example, imagine that a reading of Susan Glaspell's *Trifles* or Terrence McNally's *Andre's Mother* inspires you to write a short play of your own. You have ideas for a couple of characters, and you know a play centers around dialogue; but there your knowledge ends. How do you represent and punctuate dialogue on the page? How do you incorporate scene descriptions and stage directions to indicate the appearance of the stage and the movements and gestures of your characters? And what do you need in the way of a plot to motivate the characters and actions? Chapter 14, read in conjunction with the plays collected in Part V, can assist you with these and other questions.

The second purpose is *to introduce you to key literary terms and concepts that will help you talk and write about the short stories, poems, essays, and plays collected in Part V.* Suppose you read Kate Chopin's "The Story of an Hour" (p. 181), finish the story thinking, "This really grabs me," and decide to write about it for your first essay assignment. You are off to a good start; your excitement suggests the potential for a thoughtful response. In order to write the essay, however, you need to articulate *what* grabs you and *why*. You are fascinated by the story's main character, Louise Mallard. You read the section on "Characters" in Chapter 11 ("Short Stories") to find out ways of discussing characters. There you learn that you can talk about Louise as a "round" character, i.e., one who is individual and complex. In your essay (or in a class discussion) you might analyze this complexity and describe how Mrs. Mallard evolves during the "hour" represented in the story's action. Since the story is told from Mrs. Mallard's perspective, consideration of her character may also lead you to investigate the "Point of View" discussion. In short, the chapter provides you with a vocabulary for articulating your thoughts and feelings about Chopin's story or any of the other stories in Part V.

Note that, throughout Part IV, literary terms are printed in **boldface.** You can find additional information and references to these terms by consulting Appendix C ("Glossary of Literary Terms") and the Subject Index.

11

Short Stories

A **short story** is a brief work of prose fiction, shorter than a novel or novella and longer than an anecdote. All short stories include such elements as point of view, characters, plot, theme, and setting that are found in longer works of fiction. Given the great flexibility writers have for manipulating these elements, however, the diversity of stories is enormous.

Point of View

Point of view refers to the perspective from which a story is told. The two basic types of point of view are first-person and third-person.

In the **first-person** point of view the storyteller or **narrator** is a major or minor character within the story who uses the pronoun "I." The first-person narrator is sometimes also called a **persona,** after the Latin word for "mask," to signify a distinction between the author (as a flesh-and-blood individual) and the "mask" that he or she assumes in a particular story. When the youth, naiveté, limited intelligence, or extreme subjectivity of a first-person narrator leads us to question the accuracy of his or her version of characters and events, he or she is called a **naive** or **unreliable** narrator. An example is Sylvia, the young African American girl from the inner city who is the narrator of Toni Cade Bambara's "The Lesson." The story begins:

> Back in the days when everyone was old and stupid or young and foolish and me and Sugar were the only ones just right, this lady moved on our block with nappy hair and proper speech and no makeup. And quite naturally we laughed at her, laughed the way we did at the junk man who went about his business like he was some big-time president and his sorry-ass horse his secretary.... Miss Moore was her name.... And she was always planning these boring-ass things for us to do.

Throughout the story Sylvia reviles and belittles Miss Moore and her "boring" talk and lessons. Miss Moore's actions, however, constantly undercut Sylvia's version of her and of events. Far from wasting Sylvia's time, Miss Moore ends up teaching her profound life lessons and proves to be a strong and remarkable woman.

In the **third-person** point of view the narrator is outside the story and refers to characters as "he," "she," or "they," or by their proper names. A third-person **omniscient** narrator functions as an all-knowing presence who has access to the thoughts, feelings, and actions of any and all of the characters. An **intrusive** omniscient narrator evaluates the actions and motives of characters and inserts other of his/her personal views into a story. An **objective** narrator, on the other hand, merely shows or reports actions and characters without evaluating them. Objective narration is evident in Anton Chekhov's "Gooseberries" (p. 883).

Rather than seeing everything, a narrator in a **third-person limited** point of view relates events from the perspective of one of the characters within the story. An example is Kate Chopin's "The Story of an Hour," in which we perceive events through the consciousness of Louise Mallard, though Louise herself is not the narrator of the story. (Incidentally, Louise Mallard dies at the end of "The Story of an Hour." Thus, if she had written the story in the first-person with Louise as narrator, Kate Chopin would have had to change her ending.)

Writers sometimes *mix* various points of view in a single story. For instance, William Faulkner's "Barn Burning" (p. 423) is told, for the most part, from a third-person limited point of view (by a narrator who perceives events through the consciousness of the boy Sarty). At times, however, Faulkner shifts the point of view to first-person and writes *as* Sarty, as in the italicized portions of the following passage:

> They were running a middle buster now, his brother holding the plow straight while he handled the reins, and walking beside the straining mule, the rich black soil shearing cool and damp against his bare ankles, he thought *Maybe this is the end of it. Maybe even that twenty bushels that seems hard to have to pay for just a rug will be a cheap price for him to stop forever and always from being what he used to be;* thinking, dreaming now, so that his brother had to speak sharply to him to mind the mule: *Maybe he even won't collect the twenty bushels. Maybe it will all add up and balance and vanish—corn, rug, fire; the terror and grief, the being pulled two ways like between two teams of horses—gone, done with for ever and ever.*

Sarty's thoughts exemplify a type of narrative technique called **stream of consciousness.** In stream of consciousness a writer seeks to reproduce, without a narrator's intervention, the exact flow of thoughts, feelings, and associations that go through a character's mind as that character moves in the "stream" of time.

Point of view in a story is important for at least two major reasons. First, as writer/teacher James Moffett has noted, "*What* a story is about is a question of *how* it is told." A writer's choice of point of view profoundly affects every other aspect of the story, from its themes and plot structure to its characters and style. For instance, Charlotte Perkins Gilman composed "The Yellow Wallpaper" (p. 184) as a first-person narrative. The narrator is a woman in the midst of a profound mental and emotional crisis who records her fluctuating thoughts and feelings in a diary or journal:

> I don't know why I should write this.
> I don't want to.
> I don't feel able.
> And I know John [the narrator's husband] would think it absurd. But I *must* say what I feel and think in some way—it is such a relief!
> But the effort is getting to be greater than the relief.
> Half the time now I am awfully lazy, and lie down ever so much.

Here the point of view contributes to a sense of urgency (reflected in the short sentences and paragraphs, the sudden shifts in thought, the mood of fear and nagging uncertainty) that would probably be weakened or lost if the story were written from a third-person perspective.

Point of view is also important because it involves us in one of the major functions of imagination, namely, the act of seeing and understanding anew by getting out of our own consciousness and into the consciousness of the "other." Alice Walker writes eloquently about this:

> Writing to me is. . . . about expanding myself as much as I can and seeing myself in as many roles and situations as possible. . . . If I could live as a tree, as a river, as the moon, as the sun, as a star, as the earth, as a rock, I would. Writing permits me to be more than I am. Writing permits me to experience life as any number of strange creations.[1]

Playing with point of view helps a writer understand things (self, culture, life, the world, etc.) *better* or *differently* by knowing them from diverse perspectives. In addition, the possibility of alternative points of view provides a writer with a powerful mode of invention. If the stories you write in your notebook lack vitality, you can bring them to life by manipulating the point of view. You can rewrite your dull first-person narrative about "growing up in the nineties" as a third-person narrative or relate the first-person story that "isn't quite working" from the first-person perspective of a different character in the same story.

---

1. Quoted in Claudia Tate, ed., *Black Women Writers at Work* (New York: Continuum, 1983, p. 185).

Characters

Characters are the imaginary persons who appear in fictional narratives or dramatic works, and characterization is achieved through the depiction of action, description, and/or dialogue. A **flat character** is one who remains essentially unchanged throughout the story and tends to be less an individual than a type. Akin to flat characters are the merely undeveloped minor characters who appear in many stories and plays. A **round character,** on the other hand, evolves or undergoes change in the course of the story and is more individualized and complex. Good examples of rounded characters are Louise Mallard in Chopin's "The Story of an Hour," whose thoughts and feelings about her life and marriage are shown to fluctuate quite widely, and Sarty in Faulkner's "Barn Burning." As illustrated in the stream of consciousness passage quoted earlier, Sarty has complex thoughts and emotions; by the end of the story he has grown and changed in his relationship to his father, his family, and his past.

The main character around whom a narrative or dramatic work centers is called the **protagonist** or **hero/heroine.** The protagonist's main opponent, if any, is the **antagonist.** In Toni Cade Bambara's "The Lesson" the protagonist is Sylvia, a young African American girl from the inner city who would rather fool around than get "educated"; the antagonist is Miss Moore, the neighbor woman who quietly and patiently goes about transforming her. Note that the protagonist's conflict in a story can take many forms; it is not always with a personal opponent bent on his or her destruction. For more about conflict, see the section on "Plot," on page 135.

Dialogue

Dialogue is the spoken conversation that occurs in a story and is a major means both of characterization and of advancing the story's plot. Consider again the wife/protagonist in Charlotte Perkins Gilman's "The Yellow Wallpaper." The wife's illness has prompted her physician husband to take her to a house in the country for a complete "rest" cure. From the wife's point of view, however, the cure is not working, and, in the following dialogue, she approaches her husband about leaving the house:

> I thought it was a good time to talk, so I told him that I really was not gaining here, and that I wished he would take me away.
> "Why, darling!" said he. "Our lease will be up in three weeks, and I can't see how to leave before.
> "The repairs are not done at home, and I cannot possibly leave town just now. Of course if you were in any danger, I could and would, but you really are better, dear, whether you can see it or not. I am a doctor, dear, and I know. You are gaining flesh and color, your appetite is better, I feel really much easier about you."

"I don't weigh a bit more," said I, "nor as much; and my appetite may be better in the evening when you are here but it is worse in the morning when you are away!"

"Bless her little heart!" said he with a big hug. "She shall be as sick as she pleases! But now let's improve the shining hours by going to sleep, and talk about it in the morning!"

"And you won't go away?" I asked gloomily.

"Why, how can I, dear? It is only three weeks more and then we will take a nice little trip of a few days while Jennie is getting the house ready. Really, dear, you are better!"

"Better in body perhaps—" I began, and stopped short, for he sat up straight and looked at me with such a stern, reproachful look that I could not say another word.

"My darling," said he, "I beg of you, for my sake and for our child's sake, as well as for your own, that you will never for one instant let that idea enter your mind! There is nothing so dangerous, so fascinating, to a temperament like yours. It is a false and foolish fancy. Can you not trust me as a physician when I tell you so?"

So of course I said no more on that score, and we went to sleep before long.

This bit of dialogue speaks volumes about the two characters and their relationship. That John does nearly all the talking suggests his position of authority over his wife. In saying "I am a doctor, dear, and I know," he uses professional credentials to reinforce this authority. His remark that "*I* feel really much easier about you" [italics added] implies, perhaps, some insensitivity to what *she* feels; and when he exclaims, "Bless her little heart!" he speaks of his wife in the third-person, as if she weren't even present with him in the room. The narrator, for her part, is nearly silent (in stark contrast to her effusiveness when she writes). When she does talk it is to utter a feeble protest ("I don't weigh a bit more"), or to ask a question ("And you won't go away?"), or to be cut short by a look from John ("Better in body perhaps—"). The dialogue crystallizes the fundamental conflicts and differences between wife and husband; it *shows* us wife and husband with far more suggestiveness and precision than could any comparably short passage that might merely *tell* us about that relationship.

Plot

Point of view, character, and dialogue interconnect with plot and other features to create a story. The **plot** of a story refers to the pattern of actions and events that combine to produce a total effect in readers. A plot is driven by some sort of conflict (e.g., between the protagonist and his or her antagonist; between the protagonist and outward circumstances—environmental, social, or cosmic; or between opposing impulses within the main character). Traditional plots have a beginning, a middle, and an end and move chronologically. Some critics divide plots into a **rising action,** which introduces the characters and establishes the conflict; a **climax** in which the conflict reaches its height in the form of some decisive action or decision; a **falling action,** in which the conflict moves toward resolution; and a **resolution,** in which the conflicts are resolved. This is only a basic pattern for plot, however, and story writers often generate suspense and surprise by upsetting our conventional expectations about how a story should begin, proceed, and end.

One common departure from straightforward chronology is **flashback.** In a flashback a narrator interrupts the narrative to present or relate some event(s) that occurred at a time chronologically prior to the events of the story itself. James Joyce makes frequent use of this device in "Eveline" (p. 295). The events that happen *in* the story are relatively few: Eveline, a dutiful daughter in conflict with her family and her ordinary life, tries to decide whether to elope with her boyfriend, Frank. Through flashback, however, Joyce acquaints us with details of Eveline's life before the events of the story proper and shows us the motivations and factors that contribute to her final choice between family and Frank.

Theme and Setting

Theme is the basic idea advanced (or implied) in the text. Of course, any group of readers coming from diverse situations and backgrounds will perceive different nuances of theme in the same text, and the more complex and interesting the story, the more diverse the articulations of theme are likely to be. The theme of "The Story of an Hour" could be variously described (broadly) as "marriage" or (more specifically) as "the constraining effects of marriage on individual freedom."

Setting refers to the place, time, and social context in which a story or other narrative takes place. In some stories setting is extremely important. Faulkner's "Barn Burning" would not be the same story if it were set any place other than the Deep South of the post–Civil War period. Charlotte Perkins Gilman's account of a woman's mental crisis is set within a single wallpapered room on a lonely country estate; the room and its wallpaper become symbolic focus points for the narrator's inner turmoil. Edgar Allan Poe's "The Masque of the Red Death" (p. 701) is about a plague that has "long devastated the country" of the arrogant Prince Prospero. Poe devotes long paragraphs—most of his story, in fact—to describing the environs and interior of the "castellated" abbey where Prospero and "a thousand light-hearted friends" think to insulate themselves from the Red Death. Evoking feelings of horror and the macabre, *place* becomes a major part of our experience of the story; on the other hand, Poe's nonspecificity about the historical *time* in which the events are supposed to occur makes the sense of danger and doom even greater by rendering the "Red Death" suggestively timeless.

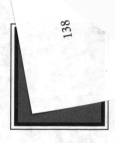

Poetry

S ome students see poetry as the most intimidating form of literature, the form they "love to hate." This may be because of poetry's odd linear appearance on the page or the student's sometimes paralyzing fear of "getting the wrong meaning." It helps, at the outset, to realize that poetry is something broader than a rarified art form; poetry has roots in the ancient past, has flourished among all civilizations and social strata, and is present in popular music, song lyrics, children's verses, and other popular forms. Whether you know it or not, you almost certainly *like* some particular poems even if you profess to *dislike* "poetry" in general.

See for yourself. Before reading the poems in Part V of *Reading and Writing from Literature,* locate and respond to some song lyrics or other poems that you already know and enjoy. Then:

1. Choose one of these texts that you like the best.
2. Read the text aloud and annotate it.
3. In your notebook make a list of the qualities that make this text beautiful, pleasing, memorable, or meaningful to you. What qualities strike you—the sounds of particular words or phrases? rhymes? images? ideas, themes, or life issues the text raises for you?
4. Share your text and responsive notes with classmates.
5. Working collaboratively with a small group of classmates, make a list of "qualities that make for good poetry."

As another way of overcoming the fears you may have about poems, try approaching poetry with a different psychology. Rather than straining to "get the meaning right"—instead of being on your "best behavior" when you read a poem, assume the role of a "dumb" reader. Follow the advice given in Chapter 2 about trusting your intuitions as you annotate (see pp. 11–13). Reread, again, the example of Margaret's annotations of "Marks" (see pp. 14–15). As you read a poem jot down your uncensored reactions; record the various associations—however strange or far-fetched—that the various words, phrases, or images suggest to you. Share your annotations with others; take notes on your peers' ideas and impressions, and realize the enormous diversity of responses a poem can provoke. This diversity of response is part of what makes poems fun.

Major Types of Poetry

Poems can be divided into **narrative** (poems that tell a story), **epic** (long narrative poems on heroic subjects), and **lyric** (poems in which a speaker expresses a state of mind or feeling). Though most of the poems included in *Reading and Writing from Literature* are lyric, some poems like Robert Frost's "Out, Out—" (p. 915) and Charles Bukowski's "my old man" (p. 332) relate a story and are short narrative poems. A fourth subclass of poem is the **prose poem.** Prose poems *look* like prose (i.e., they are laid out in paragraphs rather than lines) but display other features of verbal intensity and compression characteristic of poetry. For examples of prose poems, see Julio Cortázar's "Preamble to the Instructions on How to Wind a Watch" (p. 623) and Jack Ridl's "Last Ditch" (p. 925).

Poems can be further classified as either **traditional** or **free verse.** Traditional poems employ poetic **meter** (see below) and often **rhyme,** and they dominated the Anglo-American tradition of poetry up until the last century. Free verse poems discard meter and usually dispense with rhyme but keep other important poetic elements, such as pronouncedly rhythmic phrasing, various types of patterned sound, and intensive use of **figurative language.**

Speaker and Situation

The "I" in a lyric poem is called the **speaker.** Though the identities of speaker and **author** may seem to be close in some poems, the speaker is normally regarded as a being distinct from the author him- or herself: The "speaker" is a *version* of a self that the author projects in a particular poem, while the "author" is the flesh-and-blood person who wrote the poem. The speaker's situation in a poem is a fundamental part of what the poem means—or more accurately, *how* it means.

Consider Theodore Roethke's "My Papa's Waltz" (p. 329):

The whiskey on your breath
Could make a small boy dizzy;
But I hung on like death:
Such waltzing was not easy.

We romped until the pans   5
Slid from the kitchen shelf;
My mother's countenance
Could not unfrown itself.

The hand that held my wrist
Was battered on one knuckle;   10
At every step you missed
My right ear scraped a buckle.

You beat time on my head
With a palm caked hard by dirt,
Then waltzed me off to bed   15
Still clinging to your shirt.

The poem's subject is fairly clear: an experience of "rough" love between a child
(most likely a son) and his father; but the speaker and situation are at least as
interesting as the subject. At the moment he "speaks," how distant is the
speaker, in time, from the experience described? The past tense verbs indicate
some time has passed, though how much isn't certain. He seems to talk to his
father ("The whiskey on your breath . . .") but more as one might "talk to"
someone indirectly, as in a letter, than face to face. Most important, perhaps,
the whole experience—what happened, the relationship between father
(and mother) and son—is filtered and interpreted for us through the consciousness of the son; we don't get *the* story of the experience but the *son's* version
of it.

Roethke could keep the same subject but change the speaker or situation to
create a radically different poem. For instance, what if he went through the
poem and replaced all the second-person pronouns ("you" and "your") with
third-person pronouns ("he" and "his")? The poem would become more emotionally detached, less profoundly personal. Or what if he rewrote the poem
from either (a) the first-person point of view of the father or mother or (b) the
perspective of a third-person narrator who was uninvolved in the events described but heard about them from the son or the mother? These are questions
of technique as much as of meaning; and, just as story writers work with point
of view, poets work (or play) with such questions constantly.

Poetic Meter

Rhythm refers to a distinct but variable pattern of stressed and lightly stressed
sounds in poetry or prose. When the rhythm follows a *regular* repeating pattern
of stressed and lightly stressed syllables it is called **meter,** and the poem is said

to be metrical. Within a poetic line, meters are measured in **feet,** with each repetition of the pattern comprising a separate foot.

Iambic is by far the most common of meters in traditional poems written in English. An **iambic** foot consists of a lightly stressed followed by a stressed syllable (˘´), as in the following line from Robert Frost's "Out, Out—":

> Aňd noth/iňg háp/pĕned : dáy/wăs aĺl/bŭt dóne.

The vertical slash marks indicate metrical feet. In this example, each line has five feet and the poem is described as being in iambic **pentameter.** A line of four feet is **tetrameter,** three feet **trimeter,** and two feet **dimeter.**

A less common but important meter is the **trochaic** (´˘), illustrated in these lines from Robert Browning's "Soliloquy of the Spanish Cloister":

> Thére's ă / gréat teخt / iň Ğa / látiaňs,
> Oňce yŏu / tríp ŏn / ít, ĕn / taíls
> Twénty / -níne dĭs / tíňct dăm / nátiŏns . . .

Note that the Browning sample exemplifies trochaic tetrameter because it has four metrical feet per line.

Lord Byron's "The Destruction of Sennacherib" provides an example of **anapestic** meter (˘˘´):

> Aňd thĕ wíd / ŏws ŏf Aśh / ŭr aře loúd / ĭn theĭr waíl,
> Aňd thĕ í / dŏls aře bróke / iň thĕ teḿ / plĕ ŏf Báal . . .

Thomas Hardy's "The Voice" illustrates **dactylic** meter (´˘˘):

> Wómăn mŭch / míssed, hŏw yŏu / cáll tŏ mĕ, / cáll tŏ mĕ,
> Sáyiňg thăt / noẃ yŏu ăre / nót ăs yŏu / wére . . .

Using marks to indicate the meter of a poem, as in the above examples, is called a **scansion** of the poem.

Rhyme and Sound Effects

The most familiar sound effect in traditional verse is **end rhyme** (or simply **rhyme**). The example is from "My Papa's Waltz":

> The hand that held my wrist
> Was battered on one knuckle;
> At every step you missed
> My right ear scraped a buckle.

In this example, rhymes like "wrist" and "missed," which consist of a single stressed syllable, are called **masculine rhymes.** A rhyme that falls on a final stressed syllable followed by a lightly stressed one, as in "knuckle" and "buckle," is called a **feminine rhyme.** If the rhyming vowel sounds are only approximately (rather than exactly) alike, the rhyme is called a **slant rhyme** or **partial rhyme.** The rhyme in the second and fourth lines of the following example (from the same poem) illustrate:

> The whiskey on your breath
> Could make a small boy dizzy;
> But I hung on like death:
> Such waltzing was not easy.

The following is conventional notation for indicating the rhyme scheme in a poem:

The whiskey on your breath	a
Could make a small boy dizzy;	b
But I hung on like death:	a
Such waltzing was not easy.	b
We romped until the pans	c
Slid from the kitchen shelf;	d
My mother's countenance	c
Could not unfrown itself.	d
The hand that held my wrist	e
Was battered on one knuckle;	f
At every step you missed	e
My right ear scraped a buckle.	f
You beat time on my head	g
With a palm caked hard by dirt,	h
Then waltzed me off to bed	g
Still clinging to your shirt.	h

The "a" indicates all line endings that rhyme with the first line; "b" indicates a second rhyme sound and its repetitions within the poem; "c" designates a third rhyme sound; and so on.

Three other important types of sound effects—alliteration, assonance, and consonance—involve repetitions of speech sounds in a sequence of nearby words. These sound effects enrich verbal texture, affect meaning, and enhance the pleasure experienced in reading. **Alliteration** occurs when consonant sounds are repeated, particularly at the beginnings of words or of stressed syllables:

> You ferries! you **p**lanks and **p**osts of wharves!
>   —Walt Whitman, "Song of the Open Road" (p. 603)

Assonance refers to repeated vowel sounds within words:

> When I have f**ea**rs that I may c**ea**se to b**e**
>   Before my pen has gl**ea**ned my t**ee**ming brain . . .
>   —John Keats, "When I have fears that I may cease to be" (p. 911)

Consonance refers to repetitions of identical or similar consonant sounds with different intervening vowels:

> Márgarét, are you **gr**íeving Over Golden**gr**ove unleaving? . . .
>   —Gerard Manley Hopkins, "Spring and Fall" (p. 463)

Diction and Syntax

Diction refers to a poet's choice of words and **syntax** to the way those words are put together (e.g., in complex sentences and phrases or simpler sentences and phrases). Persons used to thinking of poetry as always being composed in "high" or rarefied language are sometimes surprised to discover the enormous range of vocabularies that poets actually use. Poets can manipulate language to evoke vastly diverse esthetic effects, cultural contexts, and human experiences. This is because the poet's realm is all of personal and cultural experience rather than just some part of it. Thus at one extreme is the *formal* diction and elaborate syntax of Wordsworth's sonnet "The World Is Too Much with Us" (p. 910):

> The world is too much with us; late and soon,
> Getting and spending, we lay waste our powers:
> Little we see in Nature that is ours;
> We have given our hearts away, a sordid boon!
> This Sea that bares her bosom to the moon. . . .

In this passage words and phrases like "Getting and spending," "sordid boon," and "bares her bosom" convey a sense of formality and magnitude. Syntactically, the speaker's clauses are complex, layered one on the other; it takes him four lines to get through his first sentence, and the fourteen lines of the entire poem are comprised of only three sentences.

At another extreme is the *colloquial* or *informal* diction of Audre Lorde in "Hanging Fire" (p. 469):

> I am fourteen
> and my skin has betrayed me

the boy I cannot live without
still sucks his thumb
in secret
how come my knees are
always so ashy
what if I die
before morning
and momma's in the bedroom
with the door closed.

A first reaction to this poem might be, "It doesn't even sound like poetry!" No less than Wordsworth, however, Lorde chooses and crafts her words to articulate a particular version of experience. In contrast to Wordsworth's formal language and syntax, Lorde evokes the spontaneous bluntness of the frustrated adolescent in such words and phrases as "I am fourteen," "momma's" (instead of "mother's"), and "how come" (instead of "why"). As for syntax, "Hanging Fire" is almost punctuation-free; where we expect to see commas, periods, and question marks there are none; one thought seems to tumble anxiously into the next, in a way that seems appropriate to the jumpy mental state of Lorde's adolescent speaker.

Diction can also be classified as *abstract* (e.g., Wordsworth writes grandly of "The world") or *concrete* (e.g., Lorde's mention of "ashy" knees); *general* (Wordsworth's generic characterization of our wasted lives as made up of "Getting and spending") or *specific* (Lorde's references to thumbsucking and "skin," for example); and *literal* or *figurative* (see next section).

Figurative Language

A **figure** (or **trope**) is a word or phrase used in a way that significantly changes its standard or literal meaning, and **figurative language** is the term used to encompass all nonliteral uses of language. Though figurative language is discussed here with reference to poetry, figures—metaphors, similes, paradoxes, and others—are common in *all* types of discourse, written and spoken. For instance, even in an ordinary expression like "This idea ought to fly" you are speaking figuratively because you are giving nonliteral significations to the literal words "idea" and "fly." That is, the statement doesn't mean that your "idea" is going to sprout literal wings but that it is going to be successful.

Probably the most important of the figures, a **metaphor** makes an implicit comparison between dissimilar items in a way that evokes new or vivid ways of perceiving, knowing, and/or feeling. Adrienne Rich's "Living in Sin" (p. 236) depicts the waking hours of two lovers whose passion is subsiding into routine and boredom. Metaphors make vivid a sense of staleness:

> Not that at five each separate stair would *writhe*
> under the milkman's tramp; that morning light
> so coldly would delineate the scraps
> of last night's cheese and three *sepulchral bottles* . . . [italics added]

The verb "writhe" suggests snakes and other slithery creatures whose touch (for many readers) is unpleasant; the metaphor of stairs *writhing* conveys a sensation tactile enough to send a veritable shudder down the spine. The phrase "sepulchral bottles," yoking together burial vaults and beverage dispensers, suggests bottles that contain dead (stale? moldy? putrid?) matter one would rather not see, smell, touch, or even acknowledge.

Donald Hall's poem "My Son My Executioner" (p. 335) evokes the surprising and simultaneous similarity and dissimilarity between the speaker's "son" and an "executioner." Thus the poem itself functions as a kind of extended metaphor:

> My son my executioner,
>   I take you in my arms,
> Quiet and small and just astir,
>   And whom my body warms.

In another example, the speaker in Rita Dove's "Fifth Grade Autobiography" (p. 341) describes the image of her grandmother in a family photograph:

> Grandmother's hips
> bulge from the brush, she's leaning
> into the ice chest, *sun* through the trees
> *printing* her dress with *soft*
> *luminous paws.* [italics added]

The metaphor in the last three lines evokes the gentleness of the sunlight by likening it to the tangible *weightlessness* one might associate with a cat's paws.

Again, it should be emphasized that metaphor is not the exclusive property of poets. Everyone uses metaphors; they are basic to our daily speech and writing and seem to be built into our very structures of thought. The ancient Greek philosopher Aristotle said that metaphor "produces knowledge," and some contemporary linguists such as George Lakoff and Mark Johnson in their book *Metaphors We Live By* argue that metaphor is a principle mode of understanding the world and of making meaning. For instance, in our conceptualization of time we frequently use metaphors that compare time with money:

> You're *wasting* my time.

> How did you *spend* your day?

> I've *invested* a lot of time in this project.

To appreciate the pervasiveness of metaphor, browse through several pages of your notebook and mark or underline any metaphors. Then take a few minutes to share some of them with a partner or small group. Discuss ways that the metaphors pack more power than would the plain *literal* expressions that could have been used in their place.

Pay close attention to your speech and notebook writing, and you will see how metaphors repeatedly and subconsciously surface in your own language. Note, for instance, these examples from various student notebooks:

> You can only do your best, then wash your hands [not *literally* "wash your hands" but *figuratively* forget your mistakes or inadequacies and move on]

> I like to walk around and around an idea before I act on it [not literally "walk on two legs" but ponder the idea from different perspectives]

> We mask our true motives [not literally "wear a facial covering" but conceal our purposes through silence or subterfuge]

None of these sentences resulted from a labored conscious effort to come up with metaphors. Rather, the metaphors seem to have emerged spontaneously out of a passionate engagement with some feeling or idea. Metaphors, and other kinds of figures as well, tend to be especially abundant when writers or speakers are in a state of heightened intellectual or emotional excitement, as *you* might be when jotting down one of your passing thoughts. Experienced poets are the persons who are probably most often in such states (Emerson declared that poets are "tipsy on water," and the Polish writer Anna Swir once said a poet "should be as sensitive as an aching tooth"); thus they produce some of the most striking, unique, and memorable metaphors. *Live* people bring forth *live* metaphors, and if you want to improve your metaphors you can hardly do better than to live a more concentrated and intentional life.

On the other hand, when our lives are routinized and lackluster our language may tend to be correspondingly lifeless or dead; we use words mechanically and without feeling, and without thinking about what they mean. Flat and predictable comparisons that no longer evoke any particular feeling, thought, or surprise are called "dead metaphors." Dead metaphors are expressions so overused we hardly even recognize them any more as metaphors—expressions like:

> I'm running on empty [used to describe tiredness]

> reinventing the wheel

> Our team ran circles around them

> He's a pain in the neck

What is true of metaphor is also true of the other figures described in this chapter: they appear in prose as well as poetry, in everyday talk as well as writing. With that caveat in mind, let's continue.

Closely related to metaphor, a **simile** makes the comparison between dissimilar items explicit with the word *like* or *as*—as in this example from Sharon Olds's "The Elder Sister" (p. 338):

> . . . now I
> see I had *her* before me always
> *like a shield.* [italics added]

The second stanza of Donald Justice's "Men at forty" (p. 465) also includes a simile:

> At rest on a stair landing,
> They feel it
> Moving beneath them now like the deck of a ship,
> Though the swell is gentle.

The simile conveys a premonition of seasickness that accompanies (sometimes) the midlife passage.

In **metonymy** the literal term for one thing is used to stand for another with which it is closely associated. In the following lines from Edwin Arlington Robinson's "Richard Cory" (p. 614), "meat" and "bread" signify not just literal animal flesh and baked goods but food and money:

> So on we worked, and waited for the light,
> And went without the meat, and cursed the bread . . .

Similarly "drink" and "The Press" in this passage from W. H. Auden's "The Unknown Citizen" (p. 620) signify an alcoholic beverage and the makers of newspapers, respectively, rather than (literally) "any beverage" or "a machine to produce print":

> And our Social Psychology workers found
> That he was popular with his mates and liked *a drink.*
> *The Press* are convinced that he bought a paper every day . . . [italics added]

In **synecdoche** a part of something is used to signify the whole or the whole is used to signify a part. A simple example is the sailor's expression "All hands on deck."

A **paradox** is a statement that seems to be contradictory but proves, on further consideration, to make sense. The first line of the following poem (p. 612) by Emily Dickinson states a paradox:

Much Madness is divinest Sense—
To a discerning Eye—
Much Sense—the starkest Madness—
'Tis the Majority
In this, as All, prevail—   5
Assent—and you are sane—
Demur—you're straightway dangerous—
And handled with a Chain—

As we finish and ponder the poem, the apparently impossible assertion of the opening line becomes understandable; for the speaker indicates that "Sense" and "Madness" are not absolute concepts but defined situationally by majorities (i.e., in the eyes of a majority, a minority is often treated as "mad" simply because it objects to majority opinion or behavior)

Verbal irony refers to a contrast between what a speaker says literally and the meaning that is implied in the larger context of the poem (or story, play, essay). In Wole Soyinka's "Telephone Conversation" (p. 750) a black African speaker talks over the phone with a white landlady about renting an apartment:

The price seemed reasonable, location
Indifferent. The landlady swore she lived
Off premises. Nothing remained
But self-confession. 'Madam,' I warned,
'I hate a wasted journey—I am—African.'   5

The word "self-confession"—implying the speaker has something to be ashamed about—conflicts ironically with our (and Soyinka's) moral sense that no one should have to apologize for the color of his/her skin. The deferential tone of the speaker's address to the woman (in "Madam . . ./. . . I am—African" and elsewhere in the poem) is also ironic, as readers discern the speaker's intellectual and moral superiority to the landlady, whose questions and remarks are ludicrous.

Irony also pervades Carter Revard's poem "Discovery of the New World" (p. 748). Revard's speaker reports how he/she and a force of aliens have conquered and subdued a world that is recognizably planet earth. The poem's last line ("we will be safe, and rich, and happy here, forever") expresses a confidence about the everlasting triumph of the conquerers that is apt to sound ironic to students of history, who know that civilizations rise and fall and that conquerors are themselves invariably conquered.

A **personification** is a figure in which human qualities are ascribed to an abstract concept or inanimate object. In the lines "Because I could not stop for Death—/He kindly stopped for me—" (p. 461), Emily Dickinson personifies death as a kindly gentleman. Though more common in older poems, personification can be used with striking effect by modern or contemporary poets. In

C. P. Cavafy's "The City" (p. 464) the speaker admonishes a friend, who means to bury the past by moving to another city, that "You will find no new lands, you will find no other seas./The city will *follow* you" [italics added]. Here the city loses its character as a fixed place that can be left behind and becomes, instead, like a persistent and living person who will not let the escapee go. The personification makes the speaker's point more effectively than the more literal "You can't get away from the past."

Symbolism

Strictly speaking, a **symbol** refers to something that stands for something else. In literary analysis the term usually has a broader signification, and something is said to be "symbolic" if it evokes a large range of reference beyond itself.

Consider, for instance, Walt Whitman's "open road" in "Song of the Open Road" (p. 603). Whitman begins by talking about the road as a more or less *literal* road (i.e., "an open, generally public way for the passage of vehicles, people, and animals"—*The American Heritage College Dictionary*):

> Afoot and light-hearted I take to the open road,
> Healthy, free, the world before me,
> The long brown path before me leading wherever I choose.

Soon, however, he imagines the road as being something more ("I believe that much unseen is also here"); and later he asserts that "the universe itself [is] a road." By the poem's end the road seems to embrace virtually every aspect of human experience—all struggles, thoughts, passions, fears, sufferings, triumphs, and failures. The range of symbolic reference is so vast that we, as readers, may find it difficult to imagine any way that we can be alive and *not* be on this "road."

In "The Holy Longing" (p. 454) Johann Wolfgang von Goethe's speaker evokes the instinctive yearning that a literal moth or "butterfly" has for a candle flame:

> Distance does not make you falter,
> now, arriving in magic, flying,
> and, finally, insane for the light,
> you are the butterfly and you are gone.

The next stanza, however, makes clear that this is not *only* a literal description of a moth's behavior:

> And so long as you haven't experienced
> this: to die and so to grow,

you are only a troubled guest
on the dark earth.

The moth is suggestively symbolic of human life and of the speaker's assertion that human beings must "die" in order "to grow." Effective literary symbols are, by nature, evocative and complex rather than simple. It would be reductive to speak about *the* meaning of the symbols in either Whitman's or Goethe's poem. Whitman's road *works* as a symbol because it leaves us thinking, for a long time, about the many roads in our personal and collective lives. Similarly, the effectiveness of Goethe's symbol depends on his not attempting to define or explain what is meant by "dying" and "growing"; the poet allows the symbol to resonate in our imaginations and leaves us to discuss and debate among ourselves its manifold implications.

13

Essays

Essay is a simple word used to describe a broad variety of writings. The word derives from the French verb "essaier," which means "to attempt," and the Frenchman Michel de Montaigne (1533–1592), the first great essayist, used the genre for the sorts of exploratory, reflective, and personal purposes that are implied by this verb. Generally, "essay" refers to a unified work of nonfiction prose that is relatively short (i.e., shorter than a book). Essays can be classified into **argumentative** essays, which advance an explicit argument and support it with evidence; **expository** essays, which inform an audience or explain a particular subject; and **personal** and **literary** essays. This last group emphasizes elements that are ordinarily associated with "literary" texts—an engaging persona, an intellectual or emotional focus or theme that is usually implied rather than directly stated, artful use of figurative language and of such other "literary" elements as dialogue and narrative. A literary essayist combines and crafts these elements to produce particular emotional and intellectual effects in readers. Nearly all the essays collected in Part V of this book are personal or literary essays.

Like most texts, essays come into being gradually, through writing and rewriting. The literary essay is latent in journal or notebook entries, personal letters, experimental paragraphs, bits of dialogue, written observations, and portraits of people. Any of these kinds of writing may exhibit the "literary" features characteristic of essays. Thus the texts you compose in your notebook can all be viewed as potential essays or parts of essays. As Montaigne would say, they are "attempts"—the attempts that lurk in the evolutionary background of any "finished" work.

Sample Essay: Judith Ortiz Cofer's "Primary Lessons"

Before continuing, take time to read "Primary Lessons" (p. 497), a personal essay by Judith Ortiz Cofer.

Persona and Voice

As mentioned with reference to short stories and poetry, a persona is the "mask" or version of a self that a writer projects in a particular text. In explicitly autobiographical writings like "Primary Lessons" persona and author may be extremely close, and the authorial presence we perceive in such a text is sometimes called the writer's **voice.** To say that the writer of an essay is "just being herself," however, would be misleading. In important ways the persona is always shaped or *crafted,* for any one essayist will create different personae for different occasions, depending on her subject, purpose, and intended readers. Thus a writer will develop one kind of persona if she is addressing an audience of English professors on the subject of "Metrical Substitutions in the Poems of John Keats" and a very different persona if she is writing for general readers on the subject of "childhood experiences." In the first situation the writer is apt to craft a persona who is authoritative, impersonal, and "scholarly." In the second, the writer will probably want her persona to be personal and "approachable" so as to elicit feelings of empathy or identification in readers.

In "Primary Lessons" Cofer's subject is those "first" or "basic" lessons, learned early, that shape the rest of our lives; her intended audience seems to be adult readers who have experienced similar kinds of "lessons" and who might be interested in revisiting their own childhood experiences by means of this essay. Appropriately, therefore, Cofer crafts a personal and engaging persona who tells a good story. At the same time, she projects a kind of authority—not by marshaling arguments or formidable displays of logic, which might distance her from readers, but by conveying an attitude of simple trust in the facts of her experience:

> My mother walked me to my first day at school at La Escuela Segundo Ruiz Belvis, named after the Puerto Rican patriot born in our town. I remember yellow cement with green trim. All the classrooms had been painted these colors to identify them as government property. This was true all over the Island.

Though in many ways individual and unique, the experience Cofer goes on to relate is apt to resonate in important ways with readers' experiences. Like her, we can recall our "first" school experience, times "of running wild in the sun," or times we didn't want to do what a parent demanded we do. Immediately Cofer establishes a rapport with us, her readers, immersing us in her experiences and making us ready to follow wherever her persona might lead.

Style and Language

A writer's persona in an essay has a shaping effect on his or her style and language.

"Repeat after me, children: Pollito—Chicken," she [*La Mrs.*] commanded in her heavily accented English that only I understood, being the only child in the room who had ever been exposed to the language. But I too remained silent. No use making waves or showing off. Patiently *La Mrs.* sang her song and gestured for us to join in. At some point it must have dawned on the class that this silly routine was likely to go on all day if we did not "repeat after her." It was not her fault that she had to follow the rule in the teacher's manual stating that she must teach English *in* English, and that she must not translate, but merely repeat her lesson in English until the children "begin to respond" more or less "unconsciously." This was one of the vestiges of the regimen followed by her predecessors in the last generation. To this day I can recite "Pollito—Chicken" mindlessly, never once pausing to visualize chicks, hens, pencils, or pens.

Note how Cofer's language fits and reinforces her candid, "ordinary," and forthright persona. There are no inappropriately "fancy" words here, no abstruse sentences or concepts, nothing that can't be understood and followed by an average attentive reader. The vocabulary and syntax are relatively simple. Note, also, how Cofer shuttles between child and adult perspectives on the experiences she relates. The paragraph opens from the viewpoint of herself as a child, looking on ironically at her teacher's "silly routine"; then the perspective shifts to that of the adult who appreciates the causes behind the teacher's behavior: "It was not her fault that she had to follow the rule in her teacher's manual. . . . This was one of the vestiges of the regimen followed by her predecessors. . . ." We trust this story—as we do others in the rest of the essay—as a truthful account of what Cofer thought and felt as a child; at the same time, we enter into the adult vision that transforms those "experiences" into "lessons."

Theme

Theme refers to what the essay is about, its prevailing idea. One theme in "Primary Lessons" seems to be early experiences and their lasting effects (though Cofer never explicitly traces these effects in her essay). Another theme might center on the whole question of *which* lessons in our lives are the most "primary," "basic," or "important." To articulate or discuss theme is to get at the *what* of the essay (i.e., its content and ideas), while discussions of persona, voice, audience, language, and literary technique immerse us in its *how* (i.e., how it conveys its content and ideas effectively to readers).

Dialogue

Dialogue is a familiar element of fiction that also appears in essays. Writers of personal and literary essays often assume the role of storytellers; therefore, it is not surprising that they make use of this narrative device.

The presence of dialogue in essays raises an interesting question: Since an essay is a form of *non*fiction, must the dialogue be an exact transcription of what was actually said? The answer is a guarded "no." Few people have the kind of memory that can recall a conversation verbatim ten or fifteen years after it occurred. Thus dialogue—even in nonfiction—is usually to some extent shaped or constructed. If you want to include dialogue in an essay of your own, a good way to begin is by getting a sense of what was said, a feeling for the conversation's tone, themes, and conflict (if any) and for the persons who were involved. Then relax and begin writing.

Judith Ortiz Cofer includes three passages of dialogue in "Primary Lessons." One passage begins with the third paragraph and runs through the fifth; a second occurs toward the middle of the essay, where *La Mrs.* instructs her class in the English words for "Pollito," "Gallina," and so on; and a third appears at the end, in the overheard conversation between *La Mrs.* and the other teacher. You can appreciate the rhetorical importance of these dialogues if you imagine what would be lost if they were omitted. For instance, suppose the closing dialogue were replaced with a mere *summary* of what the two teachers said. We would miss the casual jocularity of the teachers' banter, which is made ironic by the references to Lorenzo as the "funny *negrito*" and to his looking "like a fly drowned in a glass of milk." The dialogue renders the speaker's experience with evocative specificity; it *shows* us the two teachers' racial attitudes and outlook and the child's puzzled response, rather than simply *telling* us about them. Finally, note that Cofer exercises selectivity about her dialogue. She could have put in more of the dialogue between the two teachers, but she has included just enough to make her point. As she puts it, "The conversation ends there for me."

Story

Cofer's essay includes several stories, examples of things she said or did or that happened to her during that important sixth year of her life. The stories are a part of the reason we read her essay, with interest, to the end. Like the passages of dialogue, the stories *show* us her experiences instead of merely telling us about them. A weakness of some personal essays is that the writer spends too much time relating abstract information about his ideas and experiences without embodying those ideas and experiences through devices like storytelling. If this is a problem in your own writing, try the following: make a point (e.g., "It was a miserable year for me") and begin the next sentence with the simple word "Once . . ."; then let the story grow from there. Later, of course, you can edit out superfluous repetitions of the word "once" while keeping the stories themselves.

Stories within essays entertain readers while also giving "flesh" to ideas; in other words, the stories are purposeful, and illustrative of the essay's themes. To begin his essay on "Looking at Women" (p. 248), Scott Russell Sanders relates a story about the first time *he* "looked at a woman." Elsewhere in the essay he incorporates other personal stories relevant to his theme. The essay is worth studying for its repeated and skillful blending of narrative (i.e., storytelling) and exposition (i.e., passages where Sanders interprets or comments on his experience or informs us through the writings of others).

Citations of Other Texts; Allusions

The term **citation** signifies a reference to another text. Though more typically associated with academic or research essays, citations also appear in some personal and literary essays. The citation may take the form of a direct quotation or a summary and can be used for various purposes: to illustrate a point or idea, to reinforce a writer's argument or reasoning, to bolster reader trust in the authority of the persona, or to add depth to an essay by expanding its range of literary reference.

Sanders's "Looking at Women" discusses the psychology and cultural implications of how men look at women. While personal storytelling provides Sanders with one means of embodying his ideas, his topic is broad and complex and has been addressed, directly or indirectly, by many social scientists, cultural critics, and other writers. Accordingly, Sanders cites some of these writers and their ideas in his essay. His citations (of D. H. Lawrence, Simone de Beauvoir, John Berger, and others) lend greater authority to his persona, as readers appreciate that "he knows what he's talking about." They also enrich the essay's content by acquainting readers with diverse perspectives on the main theme.

An **allusion** is another particular kind of reference that essayists (and other writers) sometimes use. An allusion is a reference, without explicit identification, to a specific person, place, or other text. Like citations, allusions (appropriately used) can broaden an essay's range of literary and cultural reference and enhance the authority of the persona. Since allusions depend on the reader having a shared frame of reference or knowledge with the writer, however, they must be used with caution. The writer has to be careful to use allusions that will be understood by the essay's intended readers. Scott Sanders's two allusions (to Jimmy Carter and *Playboy*) in the following sentence help ground his ideas about "looking at women" in the worlds of contemporary and popular culture:

> While he was president, Jimmy Carter raised a brouhaha by confessing in a *Playboy* interview, of all shady places, that he occasionally felt lust in his heart for women.

Allusion was a favorite device of Henry David Thoreau, as exemplified in this passage from "Where I Lived, and What I Lived For" (p. 930):

> All memorable events, I should say, transpire in morning time and in a morning atmosphere. The Vedas say, "All intelligences awake with the morning." Poetry and art, and the fairest and most memorable of the ac-

tions of men, date from such an hour. All poets and heroes, like Memnon, are the children of Aurora, and emit their music at sunrise.

The allusions here—to "the Vedas" (sacred and ancient Hindu writings), "Memnon" (a heroic ruler of ancient Ethiopia), and "Aurora" (goddess of the dawn in Roman mythology)—lend a special aura of nobility and heroic precedent to the wakeful life that Thoreau is praising.

14

Plays

While one typically reads short stories, poems, and essays in private and silently, a play is a form of performance art; that is, it is a work normally intended for live performance in a theater. A play relates a story; however, rather than narrating (as in a short story), the writer dramatizes the story by means of characters acting and speaking, within a particular imagined setting, on a stage. **Dialogue** is basic to plays. Other important features of the printed text are **scene descriptions,** which describe what the stage looks like for a particular play; **costume descriptions;** and **stage directions,** which describe the movements or gestures of characters on stage. All three of these, which are typically printed in italics, are illustrated in the opening of Susan Glaspell's *Trifles* (p. 259):

SCENE: *The kitchen in the now abandoned farmhouse of* JOHN WRIGHT, *a gloomy kitchen, and left without having been put in order—the walls covered with a faded wallpaper. . . . In the rear wall at* R[IGHT], *up two steps is a door opening onto stairs leading to the second floor. In the rear wall at* L[EFT] *is a door to the shed and from there to the outside. Between these two doors is an old-fashioned black iron stove. . . . At the rear the shed door opens and the* SHERIFF *comes in followed by the* COUNTY AT-TORNEY *and* HALE. *The* SHERIFF *and* HALE *are men in middle life, the* COUNTY AT-TORNEY *is a young man; all are much bundled up and go at once to the stove. They are followed by the two women—the* SHERIFF'S *wife,* MRS. PETERS, *first; she is a slight wiry woman, a thin nervous face.* MRS. HALE *is larger and would ordinarily be called more comfortable looking, but she is disturbed now and looks fearfully about as she enters. The women have come in slowly, and stand close together near the door.*

COUNTY ATTORNEY *(at stove rubbing his hands).* This feels good. Come up to the fire, ladies.

MRS. PETERS *(after taking a step forward).* I'm not—cold.

Note how the italicized text helps you to visualize the action and interpret the characters. For example, the men in the play seem to move around confidently; they enter the kitchen *"and go at once to the stove."* The women, on the other hand, are described as *"nervous"* and fearful; Mrs. Peters takes one *"step forward"* and stops to deliver a very short and halted speech: "I'm not—cold." Already you get a sense of the contrast between the men characters and the women that will be central to the play. Even if you cannot see a particular play performed, dialogue, scene and costume descriptions, and stage directions enable you to do a good production of it in your head.

Plays can follow a range of structural formats. A main division within a play is called an **act,** and full-length plays are typically composed of two or more acts, which may be further subdivided into **scenes.** Some modern and contemporary plays replace acts altogether with a format of multiple scenes or episodes. For instance, Eugene O'Neill's *The Hairy Ape* (p. 502) is composed of eight scenes.

An important subclass of play is the **one-act play,** which bears somewhat the same relationship to a full-length play as a short story does to a novel. One-acts usually dramatize a single incident and include fewer characters than multiple-act plays. In addition, while a full-length play of two hours may represent actions that are supposed to occur over a period of days, months, or years, the time represented by the onstage action of a one-act play usually corresponds closely to real time; that is, a twenty-minute play corresponds to roughly twenty minutes in the lives of the characters.

Setting

Setting refers to the time and place in which the onstage action of a play is supposed to occur. August Wilson's *Fences* (p. 790) dramatizes the story of Troy Maxson, an African-American living in a white man's world. Wilson sets his drama in a specific place (i.e., the yard of *"the Maxson household, an ancient two-story brick house set back off a small alley in a big-city neighborhood"*), and he is also particular about the historical time—1957. In fact, he sets the play against the historical background of migration to America's big cities. While children of European descent found abundant opportunities in the cities, Wilson writes, *"The descendants of African slaves were offered no such welcome or participation. . . . They came strong, eager, searching. The city rejected them and they fled and settled along the riverbanks and under bridges in shallow, ramshackle houses made of sticks and tarpaper."* This description of setting prepares us to understand and appreciate Troy's struggles and motivations, which develop in a context of historically entrenched racism.

Settings do not have to be realistic. *The Hairy Ape* opens in the stokehole of a transatlantic liner, a loud and cramped environment where men labor under circumstances of inhuman oppression and confinement:

> *The room is crowded with men, shouting, cursing, laughing, singing—a con-*
> *fused, inchoate uproar swelling into a sort of unity, a meaning—the bewil-*
> *dered, furious, baffled defiance of a beast in a cage.*

O'Neill indicates that *"The treatment of this scene . . . should by no means be nat-uralistic"*; that is, the scene is meant to distort reality in order to create particu-lar effects. No less than in *Fences,* however, the setting prepares us for what is to follow—the drama of "Yank" Smith (a.k.a. "the Hairy Ape"), whose life and death evoke the ferocity and futility of a defiant "beast in a cage."

Characters and Plot

Like short stories, plays may include **flat characters** and **round characters** (see p. 134); the main character is known as the **protagonist,** and his/her chief oppo-nent in the drama is the **antagonist.**

For purposes of analysis, critics sometimes divide the **plots** of plays into a **rising action,** which introduces the characters and establishes the conflict; a **climax,** in which the conflict reaches its height in the form of some crucial ac-tion or decision; a **falling action,** in which the conflict moves toward resolu-tion; and a **resolution,** in which the central conflict is resolved. As this scheme suggests, the essential ingredient in any plot is conflict, which may include— but is not limited to—a conflict between protagonist and antagonist. Conflict— physical, personal, social, moral, and/or cosmic—helps to define the characters and themes of the play and to sustain the interest of readers or viewers.

Trifles is set in the farmhouse kitchen of John Wright, who has recently died under mysterious circumstances. Two women and several men (including the women's husbands) are investigating the scene of Wright's death. While the men leave the kitchen and pursue fruitless lines of inquiry, the two women chance upon evidence that both incriminates the dead man's wife (Minnie) and unveils the abusive circumstances under which she lived. Hence the focal con-flict: Should the women be law-abiding citizens and turn over the evidence to the men (who remain ignorant of it), or, out of compassion for Minnie, should they conceal the evidence and thus break the law? In plays, as in life, conflict is seldom single and simple but multiple and complex. Thus in *Trifles* one conflict interrelates with others. For instance, one of the women feels an inner conflict of guilt over having neglected Minnie in her unhappy marriage. Additional conflict occurs between the women, who discover evidence among "kitchen things," and the men, who belittle these things as "trifles." At the end of the play the two women make a choice about what to do with their incriminating evi-dence, and the central conflict is resolved. As in all good plays, however, readers or viewers are left with enough unanswered questions to make discussion or re-sponsive writing interesting. What if the women had made a different choice about the evidence? Did they do the "right" thing? Who decides what is or isn't morally "right"?

Dialogue

Dialogue is the primary mode of characterization and of advancing plot in plays. Consider this brief passage of dialogue from *Trifles:*

> COUNTY ATTORNEY: . . . [Y]ou and Mrs. Wright were neighbors. I suppose you were friends, too.
>
> MRS. HALE: *(shaking her head).* I've not seen much of her of late years. I've not been in this house—it's more than a year.
>
> COUNTY ATTORNEY: *(crossing to women U[pper] C[enter]).* And why was that? You didn't like her?
>
> MRS. HALE: I liked her all well enough. Farmers' wives have their hands full, Mr. Henderson. And then—
>
> COUNTY ATTORNEY: Yes—?
>
> MRS. HALE: *(looking about).* It never seemed a very cheerful place.
>
> COUNTY ATTORNEY: No—it's not cheerful. I shouldn't say she had the home-making instinct.
>
> MRS. HALE: Well, I don't know as Wright had, either.
>
> COUNTY ATTORNEY: You mean that they didn't get on very well?
>
> MRS. HALE: No, I don't mean anything. But I don't think a place'd be any cheer-fuller for John Wright's being in it.

The County Attorney initiates and controls the conversation; confident and aggressive, he presses Mrs. Hale for answers. She, by contrast, maintains a tentative attitude about events and hesitates to interpret them ("I don't mean anything"). The dialogue underscores a broad contrast between the men and women in the play: While the men take an aggressive attitude toward the truth (and achieve nothing), the women take a "wait and see" stance (and discover everything). As for plot, Mrs. Hale's last line is one of many clues in the play that define John Wright as a cold and cruel man who brought on his own demise.

In *Tone Clusters* (p. 359), Joyce Carol Oates departs radically from the kind of *realistic* dialogue used in *Trifles.* Frank and Emily Gulick, "good" citizens and parents, who happen to have a rapist/murderer for a son, are the subjects of an interview for the mass media. Their interviewer, a male voiceover identified simply as "VOICE," never appears on stage. Rather than being realistic, the dialogue is **expressionistic;** that is, Oates exaggerates and distorts reality in order to render the world as we *feel* it rather than as we literally see it:

> VOICE: Of today's pressing political issues   the rise in violent crime most concerns American citizens   Number-one political issue of Mr. and Mrs. Gulick   tell our viewers your opinion?
>
> FRANK: In this state,
>   the state of New Jersey
>
> EMILY: Oh it's everywhere

FRANK: there's capital punishment supposedly
EMILY: But the lawyers   the lawyers get them off,
FRANK: you bet
         There's public defenders the taxpayer pays
EMILY: Oh, it's   it's out of control
         (like that, what is it   "acid rain"
FRANK: it can fall on you anywhere,
EMILY: the sun is too hot too:
BOTH: the "greenhouse effect") . . .

The characters speak in fractured sentences; the dialogue is unnaturally redundant; syntax or word order is jumbled; and disturbing themes and impressions evoked by the words seem to overshadow the words themselves. The dialogue conveys a sense of the Gulicks as human yet automaton- or puppet-like, as they mouth, with mechanical predictability, the slogans, fears, and attitudes of their culture.

A **monologue** is a long speech by a single character. For instance, in scene eight of *The Hairy Ape,* Yank (the protagonist) finds himself in *"The monkey house at the Zoo."* Yank has spent most of the play living down an insinuation that he is a "hairy ape," and now he comes face to face with a real-life gorilla, whom he addresses familiarly:

Say, yuh're some hard-lookin' guy, ain't yuh? I seen lots of tough nuts dat de gang called gorillas, but yuh're de foist real one I ever seen. Some chest yuh got, and shoulders, and dem arms and mits! I bet yuh got a punch in eider fist dat'd knock 'em all silly. . . .

At the end of act two, scene two, of *Fences,* Troy Maxson feels ultimate disaster closing in upon him. Troy is an African-American who has suffered racial injustice but is no mere "victim"; in many ways—physical and other—he is a giant of a man: caring and cruel, magnetic and alienating, powerful yet flawed. Alone on stage, he directs his anger at no ordinary enemy but at the king of enemies—"Mr. Death."

TROY *(with a quiet rage that threatens to consume him):* All right . . . Mr. Death. See now . . . I'm gonna tell you what I'm gonna do. I'm gonna take and build me a fence around this yard. See? I'm gonna build me a fence around what belongs to me. And then I want you to stay on the other side. See? You stay over there until you're ready for me. Then you come on. Bring your army. Bring your sickle. Bring your wrestling clothes. I ain't gonna fall down on my vigilance this time. You ain't gonna sneak up on me no more. When you ready for me . . . when the top of your list say Troy Maxson . . . that's when you come around here. You come up and knock on the front door. . . .

The monologue reveals to us Troy's inner essence. Powerfully imaginative, he perceives death as no mere idea but as a physical presence poised and ready to attack. He fears death and yet can reduce it to a tangible human shape ("Mr. Death") whom he bosses and bullies as freely as he does his own family ("You stay. . . . Then you come on. . . . Bring your wrestling clothes. . . . You come up. . . ."). Finally, even as he smells his own demise, Troy can taunt and belittle "Mr. Death" for trying to "sneak up" instead of "[knocking] on the front door." The monologue shows us the qualities of imagination, arrogance, and defiance that are at once Troy's sources of power and his defining weaknesses.

15

Notebooks and Journals

Technically speaking, notebooks and journals are not a literary genre. They adhere to no particular standards of form, structure, or content the way short stories, poems, essays, and plays do. In fact their essence is *freedom*. A *journal* or *notebook* (the two terms are used interchangeably in this book) can include writing in any form (prose or poetry, dialogue or story, simple list or developed analysis) and of any length (from single word to multipage draft). It can be introspective and outward looking, personal and impersonal, emotional and analytical. It can incorporate drawings, photographs, clippings, musical notations, and memorabilia that complement or relate to the writing. Finally, the material within a notebook can be an end in itself, writing done for the intrinsic pleasure or value of writing; or it can be a means toward some other end, such as drafting and revising work for publication.

Although not all writers keep notebooks and journals, they merit an introductory chapter in this part of *Reading and Writing from Literature* because, without them, writing in the other genres might never take place. It is hard to imagine writers producing short stories, poems, essays, or plays without first doing the kind of quick, preliminary, and often rough writing characteristic of notebooks and journals.

This chapter should be read in conjunction with Chapters 3 and 4, which talk specifically about the kinds of materials you can include in a notebook. Between the thematic chapters in Part V of this book you will find several interchapters featuring selections from published notebooks and journals and additional hands-on ideas for using and developing a notebook of your own.

Ralph Waldo Emerson wrote that "[T]he one good in life is concentration; the one evil is dissipation." We live in an age of distraction, and it sometimes seems we want to fill our heads with everything *but* our own thoughts. Notebooks and journals are about the life of the mind, about getting reacquainted with our own thoughts.

An Ideal Democracy of Thoughts

In an ideal political democracy every individual is accepted and has a voice, however personally objectionable he or she may seem to various other members of the society; and, as soon as one person is excluded, or the rights of one are denied, the ideal is torn and the whole fabric begins to come undone. It's the same with the entries in a notebook. If the notebook is going to succeed and the fabric hold, it has to be inclusive enough to allow in everything—good, bad, and indifferent, pleasant and unpleasant.

What follows is a sample day's harvest from one notebook:

An old woman with a waltz tied to her back

I look forward to night and to sunrise.

(A sentence from a book): "If you don't take pains, everything is difficult."

in my own limited way

"There's just so much in this head of mine I can't trust."

a heart like a sponge

I saved the money and read the books but forgot to live.

I always tear up when I compliment somebody to their face. Weird.

An article on "Oppositional Defiant Disorder." Every deviation from "normal" behavior in children has a label, a literature, and probably a medication.

A rain-beaten weed plastered in mud. Too much rain.

My muscles are crying out, Have you forgotten us?

Nothing too special here. . . . Then again, who knows? The danger of summarily rejecting a thought that seems uninteresting or "dumb" is twofold. First, by excluding one thought—a "dumb" one—you set a precedent for excluding others that might be wonderful. Second, you may not really know whether a note is "good" or "dumb" until months or even years after you first wrote it down. Literary history is full of examples of writers recording ideas, forgetting them for years, and then suddenly rediscovering them, recognizing their hidden wealth, and working them up into first-rate stories, poems, and other works.

The poet William Stafford began each day by sitting at a window and writing down anything that came to his mind; the phrase or image of the moment became the impetus from which he spun out his poems, sometimes several in a day—good, average, and bad. Stafford worked with an attitude of *welcome anything* and discussed this approach at length in his remarkable book, *Writing the Australian Crawl* (University of Michigan Press, 1978):

> There are worthy human experiences that become possible only if you accept successive, limited human commitments, and one such is the sustained life of writing. . . . A writer must write bad poems, as they come, among the better, and not scorn the "bad" ones.

By humbly and conscientiously jotting down even a threadbare idea, something plain or trivial, Stafford enhanced exponentially his prospects for collecting the other better ideas that made him one of America's premier poets.

Stafford's example is worth a truckload of books on inspiration. What is it to be "inspired"? Try this: it is *not to hesitate*. "This thought seems dumb. This idea has been said before." Fine. Acknowledge that, and write it down anyway. Another dumb idea? Write that one down, too. Inspiration is an avalanche that begins with a pebble; *should I write it down* is the little stone that holds the dam.

The Art of the Reflective Pause

There is thinking and thinking. A poet is someone who *relaxes* by thinking.
—ANONYMOUS

Henri Nouwen, a Dutch-born teacher and theologian, told this story.

He was in his office trying to work but kept getting interrupted. No sooner would he settle down at his desk than someone would knock on the door or the phone would ring. Each time he answered the call, helped the person in need, and returned—or tried to return—to his work. Finally, frustrated by what seemed like merely annoying distractions, it occurred to him that he was looking at the interruptions in the wrong way. Rather than dismissing them, he had to recognize the interruptions as a meaningful part of his life. By fighting them he was digging himself into an ever-deepening hole of resentment. On the other hand, by approaching them as opportunities he could grow from them, helping others and experiencing the joy of service. From that point on his patience grew, and so did his ability to detect value in every moment—the wanted and unwanted, the planned and unplanned.

The lesson of Nouwen's story? Don't just grit your teeth and barrel through the unplanned, unwanted, or "odd" moment with mind and senses on hold; rather, attempt to extract from each moment its poetry. "Every situation," wrote

Johann Wolfgang von Goethe, "—nay, every moment—is of infinite worth; for it is the representative of a whole eternity."

Sustained work at a desk is desirable and essential for good writing; however, to limit writing to the office or study is, literally, to shut writing inside a room, a *box*. Perhaps being a writer is less a matter of what you do at your desk than of how you work when you are away from it. Writers are people with a singular ability for being *well* interrupted. A poet, or poetic soul, is not so much a person with a special thought or experience as someone who makes a habit of momentarily stopping whatever he or she is doing at the time to *write the thought or experience down.*

The key concept here is to *pause and reflect in the middle of,* and you can pause to reflect and write in the middle of anything . . . for instance, you can pause while walking. William Wordsworth's sister, Dorothy, recalled that the poet conceived some of his best work while strolling up and down in his garden. Henry David Thoreau measured the length of his composing by the length of his walk. ("If shut up in the house," recalled his friend Emerson, "he did not write at all.") People who grew up in William Faulkner's town of Oxford, Mississippi, can remember the great novelist suddenly stopping during a walk to stare up transfixed at an old house or into blank space, quietly contemplating his fictional worlds.

You can also write in the middle of gardening, folding clothes, getting dressed, making the bed, doing dishes, cooking, stepping out of the car, waiting at a traffic light, standing in a line, riding a bus or commuter train, walking between classes, taking a break on the job, strolling in a park, or lying awake in bed. The novelist William Saroyan once said he could have become the greatest writer in America with all the ideas he had failed to write down when he was in bed. Some writers even claim to write *better* amid distractions. John Keats sometimes liked to compose in rooms humming with conversation. So did the philosopher Søren Kierkegaard, who wrote that "my imagination works best when I'm sitting by myself in a large gathering, where bustle and noise provide a substrate for my will to hold on to its object."

Kierkegaard's comment offers a clue as to why activities that seem removed from or even hostile to writing can actually nourish it. Perhaps good ideas for writing come when we are otherwise occupied because that is when our internal censors are asleep—those sentries of the mind that summarily chase off ideas that *look* dumb or useless but really *aren't*. On the other hand, the minute you sit at your desk determined to "concentrate" and "get something done" the censors wake up and get out their red pens. Experienced writers know that many good ideas—including some of the best—have to be *smuggled*.

The notebook writer has two internal enemies. The first is the inner censors. The second, no less dangerous, is the inner poets, purveyors of fine phrases who flatter you that your every sentence is imperishable. When both are asleep bold invention begins.

Consider the Japanese poet, Matsuo Bashō (1644–1694), a master of the contemplative pause. Bashō was a traveller, and wherever he went he never forgot to pack his soul. The following is an excerpt from his book, *The Narrow Road to the Deep North*, a memoir of interlinked poetry and prose:

> I went to a snow-viewing party.
>
> Gladly will I sell
> For profit,
> Dear merchants of the town,
> My hat laden with snow.   5
>
> I saw a traveller on my way.
>
> Even a horse
> Is a spectacle,
> I cannot help stopping to see it
> On the morning of snow.   10
>
> I spent the whole afternoon at the beach.
>
> Over the darkened sea,
> Only the voice of a flying duck
> Is visible—
> In soft white.   15

Bashō's philosophy? *A passing thought is the delight of passing time. . . . Grab it!*
    Bashō doesn't strain for ideas, and he collects many of them in places far away from his desk—at a party, on the road, and at the beach. If he were alive today, he would probably be carrying around a notepad for recording his passing thoughts. One can imagine him rereading his notes, at any place or any time, and revising or adding to them, or musing on them for the pleasure of contemplation. There is no moment in the day when a person can't be inspired to pause, think, and write something down. Bashō had a powerful *will to reflect* that was on call at all times.
    In his *Journal* Henry David Thoreau wrote that "Music is continuous, only listening is intermittent." Bashō would have agreed. The muse knocks continually and we hear; we're just too lazy to answer the door.

Life 101: *Cultivating the Secret Life*

The one good in life is concentration; the one evil is dissipation.

—EMERSON

    The title character of James Thurber's story, "The Secret Life of Walter Mitty" (see page 565), is an ordinary man with an extraordinary fantasy life. In his daydreams Walter Mitty imagines himself in all kinds of amazing roles: he is the commander of a gigantic Navy hydroplane, a surgeon saving the life of a personal friend of the president of the United States, the greatest pistol shot in the world, an ace pilot flying a desperate wartime mission. Other people—notably Mrs. Mitty—constantly intrude on this private world to drag him back to "reality" with sundry warnings and bits of advice: he is driving too fast, he ought to have a doctor look at him, he has to buy some overshoes and puppy biscuits, he needs to put his gloves on, he should watch where he is parking the car. . . . As the story ends Mrs. Mitty has stopped off at a drugstore, and Walter stands "up against the wall of [the store] smoking." Fantasy has the last word:

> He put his shoulders back and his heels together. "To hell with the handker-chief," said Walter Mitty scornfully. He took one last drag on his cigarette and snapped it away. Then, with that faint, fleeting smile playing about his lips, he faced the firing squad; erect and motionless, proud and disdainful, Walter Mitty the Undefeated, inscrutable to the last.

"The Secret Life of Walter Mitty" can be seen as a story about personal autonomy, about the need for cultivating and protecting an inner life of one's own. Various people violate Walter's inner space, and he pushes them out. More than any of his fantasies, perhaps, it is this gesture that makes him "heroic." Walter Mitty's "secret" is that he has found a life where *he* is in control. Though his grasp of common or ordinary "reality" is tenuous, his story confronts us with a question posed by innumerable writers, artists, and philosophers: are there other realities as or more meaningful for our well-being than the largely routinized one in which we eat, sleep, and die?

Though Mrs. Mitty is the main spoiler in this story, the intruders could as easily be teachers, parents, children, partners, friends, peers, coworkers, employers, counselors, or psychotherapists—any of whom might gladly presume to understand Walter better than Walter does . . . and that doesn't include the many *non*human intruders. So how is a person to protect and nurture a soul amid the myriad outside pressures, noises, and expectations of everyday life? To phrase the question differently: how can you *concentrate* your energies in a world that constantly tempts and impels you to *dissipate* or scatter them?

Few writers have been more preoccupied with this question than Emily Dickinson (1830–1886). Emily Dickinson lived in Amherst, Massachusetts, a town that frowned on women writing "intellectual" poetry of the sort she composed. Her father believed that, for a woman, intellectual life should stop at the end of college to be replaced by a life of selfless service to the family. Her mother was withdrawn and sickly and in later years required constant attention from her daughter. Though assisted by servants and a sister, Emily was responsible for many other domestic duties as well.

It was not just the demands on her time that threatened to dissipate her energy; it was also that she lacked any significant encouragement to write poetry. During her lifetime hardly anyone knew who Emily Dickinson was; those who met her had no idea they were encountering one of the two or three greatest poets in the American literary canon. Only a handful of her poems were published before her death, and those few individuals who read and admired her work generally pronounced it flawed and amateurish. In this context her concentration is one of the most remarkable things about her. Living in circumstances that could have scattered the energies of a lesser person, she stuck passionately to her task and wrote, in a span of four decades, nearly eighteen hundred poems that delineate, like no others, the landscape of the human soul.

How would Emily Dickinson have fared had she lived in our day? Clearly, as a woman she would have more opportunities available to her now than she did a century ago; but as a poet she would have faced an exponentially greater number of temptations to distraction: telephone, radio, TV cable and satellite, FAXes and cell phones, the Internet, videos, shopping malls, the enticements and means to be a hundred different places quickly or instantaneously, physically or virtually. Today we are no longer asking, "Should I do A or B?" as Emily Dickinson might have, but "Should I do A, B, C . . . or Z?" And the proliferating choices and opportunities mean that we must learn to say "NO" about twenty times more often than Emily Dickinson ever had to.

Dickinson may have been reflecting on this need of the soul to define and protect its own boundaries when she wrote her poem, "The Soul selects her own Society":

> The Soul selects her own Society—
> Then—shuts the Door—
> To her divine Majority—
> Present no more—
>
> Unmoved—she notes the Chariots—pausing— 5
> At her low Gate—
> Unmoved—an Emperor be kneeling
> Upon her Mat—
>
> I've known her—from an ample nation—
> Choose One— 10
> Then—close the Valves of her attention—
> Like Stone—

The Soul is "divine." "Chariots"—evoking glitter, speed, and grace, the glamour and accomplishments of mighty nations—do not impress her in the least. An "Emperor"—a powerful personage who could buy her off with money, fame, or other mundane riches—cannot turn her head. She is "Unmoved," inscrutable as the Sphinx, possessed of an immense inner power that deflects seducers. Ruthlessly selective about what she notices or ignores, she knows how and when to "close the Valves of her attention." When she chooses she becomes impenetrable, "Like Stone."

The life of Tillie Olsen (see page 299) provides a second example of writing and the secret life. The child of poor Russian emigrants, Tillie Olsen had to quit school after the eleventh grade to work. For some twenty years she held a variety of jobs—as a housekeeper, waitress, meat trimmer in a packing house, typist, secretary—while also raising four children. In addition, she helped organize workers in the meat-packing industry (and was even jailed for a time for her efforts). Tillie Olsen also found that she loved to write; she didn't just like to but *had* to. So she wrote on the bus going to and from work and, as she put it, in "the deep night hours for as long as I could stay awake, after the kids were in bed, after the household tasks were done, sometimes during." Her short story, "I Stand Here Ironing," in which the narrator tells her story while simultaneously pushing an iron, is symbolic of Olsen's own life and writing, which continually overlapped. Tillie Olsen *made* time for the writing that gave her ownership of her own life.

Olsen's experience shows how far removed the *secret* life is from the merely *self-absorbed* one. Her "escape" into writing was not a one-way movement away from jobs, tasks, appointments, and responsibilities. Olsen was a labor organizer for a long time and later became an active feminist. Paradoxically, her insistence on a secret life empowered her to *return* to the common or public life as a stronger, more conscious and intentional human being.

As a final example consider Heather, a high school teacher. In addition to teaching full-time and parenting three children, Heather is active in several social, religious, and cultural organizations. During most of her waking hours she is anticipating or performing actions that will be scrutinized and judged by others—students, peers and professional colleagues, her principal, her family, and friends. Not that she complains: social participation and service of various kinds are necessary, rewarding, and even fun. But she feels they aren't *all* there is to life. She demands a time when she can do, be, and think as she wants to.

Her solution? At 5:30 A.M. every day Heather gets up, dresses, and (weather permitting) sits on her front stoop for a few minutes "doing nothing. I don't even try to think, or be creative. I just sit and let the morning work on me." In her notebook she wrote a meditation about these moments of inaction:

> The first requirement of being a thinker is not to insist on having thoughts; the first requirement of being a poet is not to insist on writing poems. Before the thought or the poem there is sitting quietly in a favorite place (for me, it's the front stoop) doing and thinking nothing. The source of all thought and poetry: Life 101.

Next, Heather goes to her desk, lights a scented candle, and writes exactly what she wants to: reflections, poetry, meditations. "I absolutely refuse to write lesson plans or 'to do' lists, grade student papers, or do any practical business during this time. It doesn't matter how messy the day ahead of me looks. This time is *sacred*." When the rest of the household stirs to life at 7:00 A.M. Heather gets up from her desk satisfied, energized, and "reassured that I still have a soul."

Heather's notebook contains an excellent one-line summary of what the secret life is all about:

Life fills our heads; it's up to us to clear them.

Micro-Stories, Micro-Poems, Micro-Essays, Micro-Plays

Along with being an ideal democracy of thoughts, a notebook can also be a democracy of literary *forms*. Beginning writers sometimes suffer from an impoverished sense of the forms available to them. They get a good topic, start to write about it by choosing from a repertoire of one or two forms only (for instance, "five-paragraph theme" and "expository essay"), and get bored or lose momentum after a few sentences. The problem may be that the particular topic doesn't "fit" the form chosen; and the solution, perhaps, is to write in a different form more suitable to the topic.

For an example of formal experimentation, consider the remarkable notebook of the Swedish statesman, Dag Hammarskjold (1905–1961). Hammarskjold served as undersecretary of the Swedish department of finance from 1936 to 1945, was an officer in the Swedish delegation to the United Nations from 1951 to 1953, and served as secretary-general of the United Nations from 1953 until his death in 1961. Hammarskjold was a writer not by profession but by avocation, a good example of how writing can be integrated into any career or mode of life. His notebook was translated into English by Leif Sjoberg and W. H. Auden and published in 1964 as *Markings*.

Markings illustrates the close connection between notebooks and journals and the other sorts of writing represented in Part V of *Reading and Writing from Literature*; it includes entries suggestive of many literary genres and forms. As you read you can see Hammarskjold moving comfortably from one form to another, using whichever one seems best adapted to the thought, image, or feeling of the moment.

Sometimes he writes poetry, such as the following haiku poems:

The trees pant. Silence.
An irresolute raindrop furrows
The dark pane.

In the bare poplar a voice
Of such well-being
It burst space open.

On other occasions he jots down aphorisms:

The Lover desires the perfection of the Beloved—which requires, among other things, the liberation of the Beloved from the Lover.

The only kind of dignity which is genuine is that which is not diminished by the indifference of others.

Conscious of his role as a shaper of world events, and of his need for strength and steadiness of purpose, he also composes many meditations:

Your position never gives you the right to command. It only imposes on you the duty of so living your life that others can receive your orders without being humiliated.

He believes in the importance of his subconscious wishes and fantasies and frequently transcribes his dreams:

Night. The road stretches ahead. Behind me it winds up in curves towards the house, a gleam in the darkness under the dense trees of the park. I know that, shrouded in the dark out there, people are moving, that all around me, hidden by the night, life is a-quiver. I know that something is waiting for me in the house. Out of the darkness of the park comes the call of a solitary bird: and I go—up there.

Some of Hammarksjold's entries read like conversations with himself—inner dialogues. Dialogue is a form of writing that has been used by other notebook writers as well, notably French novelist Amandine Aurore Lucie Dupin Dudevant (1804–1876), who published under the pen name of "George Sand." Sand sometimes composed journal dialogues between herself and an alter ego, as in the following excerpt, in which she berates herself for a long hiatus from journal writing (in this case Sand's alter ego is a man or a woman or a threesome named "Mesdemoiselles X.Y.Z."):

—Do tell me, why haven't you gone on with your journal? (Probably it is Monsieur Three Stars or Madame So-and-So or Mesdemoiselles X.Y.Z. who ask me this question.)

Answer:
—My dear sir, or madame, or my charming young ladies, there are several reasons; but to tell you the most important, I have lost my notebook.
—What! You have carelessly mislaid a book as rare, precious and original as that!
—Even so. And my book is as well bound as it is carefully edited. In fact, the contents are as valuable as the cover.
—Don't joke about anything so important as your notebook. I am sure it is a work of art.
—Ah, you say that to the author!

—Indeed I wish I had found it myself. I would never have given it back to you.

—What the devil would you have done with it?

—I would have cut out all the autographs to paste in my album.

—I don't understand what you mean.

—Doesn't your book contain scraps of handwriting by various authors, artists, politicians, and prominent assassins?

—Yes, I have some rather literary letters, but why do you want them?

—To show that I own them.

—Oh, I understand!

—Besides, why should you wish to keep them for yourself?

—Well, the handwriting helps me to judge people's characters.

—Can you really read character from handwriting?

—Yes, I make a success of it when I know beforehand what the handwriting should prove.

—What would you say of your own?

—My own? I would describe it as tired writing.

—And you conclude?

—That it is the writing of a tired person.

—Is that all?

—Isn't it enough?

—But of what is the person tired?

—Can't you imagine that one may be tired of many things? Tired of getting up every morning, tired of going to bed every night, tired of being hot all summer and cold all winter, tired of hearing innumerable questions asked and never one that is worth answering—

This conversation could continue almost interminably. One of the attractions of the dialogue form is its capacity to keep generating new ideas. If one voice in the conversation falters, the other voice is there to raise a new point and keep the thought going. Any of the questions in Sand's dialogue (e.g., "Besides, why should you wish to keep them for yourself?" "Can you really read characters from handwriting?" "What would you say of your own?") has the potential to stimulate new details about her topic.

Another literary form that does not appear in *Markings* but has been used by many writers is the journal-*letter*. For example, though Emily Dickinson kept no notebook in the conventional sense, her voluminous personal correspondence with friends and family served some of the functions of a notebook. In her letters Dickinson tried out metaphors, lines for poems, and complete drafts of poems, so that it is sometimes difficult to separate her "letters" from her "poems." Other writers included in Part V of *Reading and Writing from Literature* have also written journal-letters—notably John Keats (see page 911) and Fenton Johnson (see page 357). The letter form has the advantage of intimacy and of implying an immediate and interested audience for your writing. As writer Pam Houston explains,

Like a journal, [letters] are an invaluable reference source and precurser to my fiction and non-fiction projects, but unlike a journal, they have an audience, and when I have an audience, I'm far more inclined to excel.

You can read more about literary forms and find a hands-on activity for using them in your own writing in the section on the Topic/Form Grid on page 111.

As all of these examples show, every note you write has a form and is like a seedling bearing the imprinted code of a larger organism. A note is never *just* a note.

A notebook entry like,

Memory sweeps up after me

can be a line in a "ghost" poem whose definitive outlines have yet to take shape; or perhaps it is already a complete poem, compact and metaphoric, inviting a reader to pause and reflect the way good poetry does. Similarly, a statement like

"Zaabalawi": the whole story is about mystery, living with it

could be an embryonic essay in which you will expand on the original statement with examples, stories, and analysis. Whether a given entry is a single phrase or several pages long, you can think of it—powerfully—as a micro-story, micro-poem, micro-essay, micro-letter, or micro-play. A note is not an end but a beginning, a piece latent with possibilities for growth.

ACTIVITIES FOR WRITING AND DISCUSSION

Since this chapter has dealt more with practices and habits than the other chapters in Part IV, it seems appropriate to end with some activities for writing and discussion.

1. Describe your own history, if any, as a notebook or journal writer. When did you first start keeping a journal or notebook? Why? Did someone inspire you to do so? What physical materials did you use when you first started? Have you kept a journal/notebook consistently since then? Why or why not? How have the physical materials used in your journal writing—and your reasons for keeping a journal—changed over time?
   a. Do a first draft of this history early in the term.
   b. Take notes toward revising the draft periodically during the term.
   c. Prepare a final (for now) version of your story at the end of the term, giving some special attention to how your journal/notebook habits and aims have changed during this class.

2. Do Activity #1 on page 57, above (Chapter 4).

3. Reflect on the following quotation from Samuel Butler:

[My notes] always grow longer if I shorten them. I mean the process of compression makes them more pregnant and they breed new notes.

Reread all or a portion of your own notebook with pen or pencil in hand and record any new notes that are "bred" by rereading *your* notes.

4. Following the example on page 163, share a sample day's harvest from your own notebook with a partner or small group. The object here is to make your notebook an ideal democracy of thoughts, to avoid excluding ideas that look "dumb" or "mediocre" now but may prove fruitful later on. This exercise of sharing the day's notes with a partner or group is worth repeating regularly.

5. Periodically during the quarter or semester, take a few minutes in class to share with a partner or small group some particularly striking entry you have made in your notebook. The entry may be of any length, from a phrase to several pages. Discuss what inspired the entry, why you like it, and what (if anything) you might like to do with it. If you wish, invite feedback or suggestions from your partner or group.

6. Dag Hammarskjold's *Markings* shows how a writer can use different literary forms to fit different topics and diverse moods. Reread all or a portion of your notebook with pen or pencil in hand. As you read keep (on a separate sheet of paper) a running list of "topics for further writing" that are suggested to you by rereading. For instance, you might write down topics like "relationships," "stress," "passion," and "work." Then create a Topic/Form Grid (see pages 111–115), listing your topics on the vertical axis and forms for writing about them on the horizontal axis. Use your grid to generate additional writings as described on pages 111–115. (*Note:* You can return to this grid later and write from it any time you wish.)

For Further Reading

Bashō, Matsuo. *The Narrow Road to the Deep North and Other Travel Sketches.* London: Penguin, 1981.

Butler, Samuel. *Samuel Butler's Notebooks.* Selected and edited by Geoffrey Keynes and Brian Hill. New York: Dutton, 1951.

Canetti, Elias. *The Agony of Flies.* Trans. H.F. Broch de Rothermann. New York: Farrar, Straus and Giroux, 1994.

———. *The Human Province.* Trans. Joachim Neugroschel. New York: Seabury, 1978.

———. *Notes from Hampstead.* Trans. John Hargraves. New York: Farrar, Straus and Giroux, 1994.

———. *The Secret Heart of the Clock.* Trans. Joel Agee. New York: Farrar, Straus and Giroux, 1989.

Dickinson, Emily. *The Complete Poems of Emily Dickinson.* Ed. Thomas H. Johnson. Boston: Little, Brown, 1960.

———. *Selected Letters.* Ed. Thomas H. Johnson. Cambridge: The Belknap Press of Harvard UP, 1971.

Emerson, Ralph Waldo. *Emerson in His Journals.* Ed. Joel Porte. Cambridge: The Belknap Press of Harvard UP, 1982.

———. *The Heart of Emerson's Journals.* Ed. Bliss Perry. New York: Dover, 1995.

Goethe, Johann Wolfgang von. *Maxims and Reflections.* Trans. Elisabeth Stopp. Ed. Peter Hutchinson. London: Penguin, 1998.

Hammarskjold, Dag. *Markings.* Trans. Leif Sjoberg & W.H. Auden. New York: Knopf, 1964.

Houston, Pam. "In Service of the Next Step." *The Writer's Journal: 40 Contemporary Writers and Their Journals.* Ed. Sheila Bender. New York: Delta, 1997. 150–62.

John-Steiner, Vera. *Notebooks of the Mind.* Revised ed. New York: Oxford, 1997.

Keats, John. *Letters of John Keats: A New Selection.* Ed. Robert Gittings. Oxford: Oxford UP, 1970.

Kierkegaard, Søren. *Papers and Journals: A Selection.* Trans. Alastair Hannay. London: Penguin, 1996.

Johnson, Fenton. "Ordinary Acts." *The Writer's Journal: 40 Contemporary Writers and Their Journals.* Ed. Sheila Bender. New York: Delta, 1997. 163–70.

Lichtenberg, Georg Christoph. *Aphorisms.* Trans. R.J. Hollingdale. London: Penguin, 1990.

Olsen, Tillie. *Silences.* New York: Delacorte/Seymour Lawrence, 1978.

Renard, Jules. *The Journal of Jules Renard.* Ed. and trans. Louise Bogan and Elizabeth Roget. New York: George Braziller, 1964.

Sand, George. *The Intimate Journal of George Sand.* Ed. and trans. Marie Jenney Howe. Chicago: Academy Press, 1977.

Sewall, Richard B. *The Life of Emily Dickinson.* Cambridge: Harvard UP, 1994.

Stafford, William. *Writing the Australian Crawl.* Ann Arbor: U of Michigan P, 1978.

Thoreau, Henry David. *A Writer's Journal.* Ed. Laurence Stapleton. New York: Dover, 1960.

Wordsworth, Dorothy. *Journals of Dorothy Wordsworth.* Ed. Mary Moorman. London: Oxford UP, 1971.

Collections/Anthologies

Our Private Lives: Journals, Notebooks, and Diaries. Ed. Daniel Halpern. Hopewell, NJ: Ecco, 1998.

The Poet's Notebook: Excerpts from the Notebooks of Contemporary American Poets. Ed. Stephen Kuusisto, Deborah Tall, and David Weiss. New York: Norton, 1995.

The Writer's Journal: 40 Contemporary Writers and Their Journals. Ed. Sheila Bender. New York: Delta, 1997.

Part

V

A Thematic
Anthology of
Readings

P arts I through IV introduced you to various ideas for conversational reading and writing and to ways of working with the major genres of literature.
Now is your chance to apply these ideas to a range of literary works.

Part V consists of a collection of short stories, poems, essays, and plays for
reading and responsive writing. For purposes of convenience, selections have
been arranged into several thematic categories: "Gender and Relationships,"
"Families," "Experience and Identity," "Individual and Society," "People and
Cultures in Conflict and Change," and "Work and the Quality of Life." The
themes provide a means of classifying related readings into groups of workable
size. You will notice, however, that any such arrangement is somewhat arbi-
trary. Any one story, poem, essay, or play may evoke multiple themes in different readers or in a single reader. For instance, in this book Kate Chopin's "The
Story of an Hour" is classified under the theme of "Gender and Relationships";
yet the story prompted Tyler (see Chapter 2) to produce writing that has little
to do with the sorts of gender-based "relationships" that are the focus of the
particular theme grouping. Tyler created a portrait of a man who served as a
surrogate "grandfather" in his life; he produced work that transcends artificially
imposed thematic boundaries. You should feel free to do the same. Moreover, if
your class is focusing on readings in one thematic section and you want to do
additional reading in a different section, do so. Browse, read, enjoy, and write as
your individual tastes and instincts dictate.

By referring back to Part I—especially Chapters 2 and 3—you can find ideas
for writing in response to *any* of the readings in this anthology. In addition,
over half of the individual readings are followed by Activities for Writing and
Discussion, which provide ready-made prompts for both "creative" and "analytic" work. The Activities for any particular reading are sequenced to begin
with simpler activities and progress toward more complex. Thus, if a particular
text puzzles you, you might choose to address Activity #1 rather than one of the
later, more demanding activities. Conversely, if a reading affects you powerfully, a later activity may be more appealing.

The Activities are not meant to be exhaustive or to restrict your options for
writing. You can best approach *any* story, poem, essay, or play in the anthology
by using the "Four-Step Process for Writing from Reading" described in Chapter 2. Then, for additional writing ideas, either:

1. Consult the Activities (if provided) that follow the selection, or
2. Use one of the "Ten Ideas for Writing" described in Chapter 3, or
3. Use some other mode of response of your own devising.

Each thematic section ends with a set of Additional Activities for Writing
and Discussion. The Additional Activities serve a twofold purpose. First, they
encourage you to make connections among the various readings within the
section. Second, they help you develop habits of recursiveness as you "look
again" at those readings and at the notebook writings you did in response to
them. You can think and talk more about the readings. You can also rewrite, ex-

pand, or otherwise improve your notebook writings as you exercise the habit of "selective revising" that is at the heart of the book.

Finally, in both the Activities for Writing and Discussion and the Additional Activities you will find literary terms printed in **boldface.** These are defined and illustrated in Part IV ("An Introduction to the Major Genres") and Appendix C ("Glossary of Literary Terms").

16

Gender and Relationships

KATE CHOPIN (1850–1904)

The Story of an Hour

Knowing that Mrs. Mallard was afflicted with a heart trouble, great care was 1
taken to break to her as gently as possible the news of her husband's death.

It was her sister Josephine who told her, in broken sentences, veiled hints 2
that revealed in half concealing. Her husband's friend Richards was there, too,
near her. It was he who had been in the newspaper office when intelligence of
the railroad disaster was received, with Brently Mallard's name leading the list
of "killed." He had only taken the time to assure himself of its truth by a second
telegram, and had hastened to forestall any less careful, less tender friend in
bearing the sad message.

She did not hear the story as many women have heard the same, with a par- 3
alyzed inability to accept its significance. She wept at once, with sudden, wild
abandonment, in her sister's arms. When the storm of grief had spent itself she
went away to her room alone. She would have no one follow her.

There stood, facing the open window, a comfortable, roomy armchair. Into 4
this she sank, pressed down by a physical exhaustion that haunted her body and
seemed to reach into her soul.

She could see in the open square before her house the tops of trees that were 5
all aquiver with the new spring life. The delicious breath of rain was in the air.
In the street below a peddler was crying his wares. The notes of a distant song

181

which some one was singing reached her faintly, and countless sparrows were twittering in the eaves.

There were patches of blue sky showing here and there through the clouds 6 that had met and piled one above the other in the west facing her window.

She sat with her head thrown back upon the cushion of the chair, quite mo- 7 tionless, except when a sob came up into her throat and shook her, as a child who has cried itself to sleep continues to sob in its dreams.

She was young, with a fair, calm face, whose lines bespoke repression and 8 even a certain strength. But now there was a dull stare in her eyes, whose gaze was fixed away off yonder on one of those patches of blue sky. It was not a glance of reflection, but rather indicated a suspension of intelligent thought.

There was something coming to her and she was waiting for it, fearfully. 9 What was it? She did not know; it was too subtle and elusive to name. But she felt it, creeping out of the sky, reaching toward her through the sounds, the scents, the color that filled the air.

Now her bosom rose and fell tumultuously. She was beginning to recognize 10 this thing that was approaching to possess her, and she was striving to beat it back with her will—as powerless as her two white slender hands would have been.

When she abandoned herself a little whispered word escaped her slightly 11 parted lips. She said it over and over under her breath: "Free, free, free!" The vacant stare and the look of terror that had followed it went from her eyes. They stayed keen and bright. Her pulses beat fast, and the coursing blood warmed and relaxed every inch of her body.

She did not stop to ask if it were or were not a monstrous joy that held her. 12 A clear and exalted perception enabled her to dismiss the suggestion as trivial.

She knew that she would weep again when she saw the kind, tender hands 13 folded in death; the face that had never looked save with love upon her, fixed and gray and dead. But she saw beyond that bitter moment a long procession of years to come that would belong to her absolutely. And she opened and spread her arms out to them in welcome.

There would be no one to live for during those coming years; she would live 14 for herself. There would be no powerful will bending her in that blind persistence with which men and women believe they have a right to impose a private will upon a fellow-creature. A kind intention or a cruel intention made the act seem no less a crime as she looked upon it in that brief moment of illumination.

And yet she had loved him—sometimes. Often she had not. What did it 15 matter! What could love, the unsolved mystery, count for in face of this possession of self-assertion which she suddenly recognized as the strongest impulse of her being!

"Free! Body and soul free!" she kept whispering. 16

Josephine was kneeling before the closed door with her lips to the keyhole, 17 imploring for admission. "Louise, open the door! I beg; open the door—you will make yourself ill. What are you doing, Louise? For heaven's sake open the door."

"Go away. I am not making myself ill." No; she was drinking in a very elixir   18
of life through that open window.

Her fancy was running riot along those days ahead of her. Spring days, and   19
summer days, and all sorts of days that would be her own. She breathed a quick
prayer that life might be long. It was only yesterday she had thought with a
shudder that life might be long.

She arose at length and opened the door to her sister's importunities. There   20
was a feverish triumph in her eyes, and she carried herself unwittingly like a
goddess of Victory. She clasped her sister's waist, and together they descended
the stairs. Richards stood waiting for them at the bottom.

Some one was opening the front door with a latchkey. It was Brently Mal-   21
lard who entered, a little travel-stained, composedly carrying his grip-sack and
umbrella. He had been far from the scene of accident, and did not even know
there had been one. He stood amazed at Josephine's piercing cry; at Richards'
quick motion to screen him from the view of his wife.

But Richards was too late.   22

When the doctors came they said she had died of heart disease—of joy that   23
kills.

Activities for Writing and Discussion

1. Louise Mallard's feelings toward her husband are complex. We are told
that Brently "never looked save with love upon her," and yet she seems elated
over his death. Is there any evidence that Mr. Mallard has treated her cruelly?
What reasons might she have for feeling "joy" at his death?

2. Chopin's style is concise, leaving much to her readers' imaginations. In
"The Story of an Hour" we get clues about the individual **characters** of Louise
and Brently but do not actually see them together. How do you imagine they
interact with each other? What is their body language like? What sorts of things
do they talk about? Describe a typical day in the marriage of the Mallards, using
dialogue if you wish, or dramatize their interaction in a specific situation (e.g.,
"over breakfast," "after dinner," "with friends").

3. Imagine you are Louise Mallard writing in her diary. Compose a diary
entry—or entries—in which you reflect on your relationship with Brently.

4. Draft a memoir reflecting on any personal connections you have with
the characters or events of this story.

5. Identify and write down two prominent **themes** in this story that interest you. Choose one of them and compare its treatment in this story with its
treatment in any other story, poem, essay, or play in this anthology.

CHARLOTTE PERKINS GILMAN (1860–1935)

The Yellow Wallpaper

It is very seldom that mere ordinary people like John and myself secure ancestral halls for the summer.

A colonial mansion, a hereditary estate, I would say a haunted house and reach the height of romantic felicity—but that would be asking too much of fate!

Still I will proudly declare that there is something queer about it.

Else, why should it be let so cheaply? And why have stood so long untenanted?

John laughs at me, of course, but one expects that.   5

John is practical in the extreme. He has no patience with faith, an intense horror of superstition, and he scoffs openly at any talk of things not to be felt and seen and put down in figures.

John is a physician, and *perhaps*—(I would not say it to a living soul, of course, but this is dead paper and a great relief to my mind)—*perhaps* that is one reason I do not get well faster.

You see, he does not believe I am sick! And what can one do?

If a physician of high standing, and one's own husband, assures friends and relatives that there is really nothing the matter with one but temporary nervous depression—a slight hysterical tendency—what is one to do?

My brother is also a physician, and also of high standing, and he says the 10
same thing.

So I take phosphates or phosphites—whichever it is—and tonics, and air and exercise, and journeys, and am absolutely forbidden to "work" until I am well again.

Personally, I disagree with their ideas.

Personally, I believe that congenial work, with excitement and change, would do me good.

But what is one to do?

I did write for a while in spite of them; but it *does* exhaust me a good deal— 15
having to be so sly about it, or else meet with heavy opposition.

I sometimes fancy that in my condition, if I had less opposition and more society and stimulus—but John says the very worst thing I can do is to think about my condition, and I confess it always makes me feel bad.

So I will let it alone and talk about the house.

The most beautiful place! It is quite alone, standing well back from the road, quite three miles from the village. It makes me think of English places that you read about, for there are hedges and walls and gates that lock, and lots of separate little houses for the gardeners and people.

There is a *delicious* garden! I never saw such a garden—large and shady, full of box-bordered paths, and lined with long grape-covered arbors with seats under them.

There were greenhouses, but they are all broken now.   20

There was some legal trouble, I believe, something about the heirs and co-heirs; anyhow, the place has been empty for years.

That spoils my ghostliness, I am afraid, but I don't care—there is something strange about the house—I can feel it.

I even said so to John one moonlight evening, but he said what I felt was a draught, and shut the window.

I get unreasonably angry with John sometimes. I'm sure I never used to be so sensitive. I think it is due to this nervous condition.

But John says if I feel so, I shall neglect proper self-control; so I take pains to   25
control myself—before him, at least, and that makes me very tired.

I don't like our room a bit. I wanted one downstairs that opened on the piazza and had roses all over the window, and such pretty old-fashioned chintz hangings! But John would not hear of it.

He said there was only one window and not room for two beds, and no near room for him if he took another.

He is very careful and loving, and hardly lets me stir without special direction.

I have a schedule prescription for each hour in the day; he takes all care from me, and so I feel basely ungrateful not to value it more.

He said we came here solely on my account, that I was to have perfect rest   30
and all the air I could get. "Your exercise depends on your strength, my dear," said he, "and your food somewhat on your appetite; but air you can absorb all the time." So we took the nursery at the top of the house.

It is a big, airy room, the whole floor nearly, with windows that look all ways, and air and sunshine galore. It was nursery first and then playroom and gymnasium, I should judge; for the windows are barred for little children, and there are rings and things in the walls.

The paint and paper look as if a boys' school had used it. It is stripped off—the paper—in great patches all around the head of my bed, about as far as I can reach, and in a great place on the other side of the room low down. I never saw a worse paper in my life. One of those sprawling flamboyant patterns committing every artistic sin.

It is dull enough to confuse the eye in following, pronounced enough to constantly irritate and provoke study, and when you follow the lame uncertain curves for a little distance they suddenly commit suicide—plunge off at outrageous angles, destroy themselves in unheard-of contradictions.

The color is repellant, almost revolting; a smouldering unclean yellow, strangely faded by the slow-turning sunlight. It is a dull yet lurid orange in some places, a sickly sulphur tint in others.

No wonder the children hated it! I should hate it myself if I had to live in   35
this room long.

There comes John, and I must put this away—he hates to have me write a word.

We have been here two weeks, and I haven't felt like writing before, since that first day.

I am sitting by the window now, up in this atrocious nursery, and there is nothing to hinder my writing as much as I please, save lack of strength.

John is away all day, and even some nights when his cases are serious.

I am glad my case is not serious!   40

But these nervous troubles are dreadfully depressing.

John does not know how much I really suffer. He knows there is no reason to suffer, and that satisfies him.

Of course it is only nervousness. It does weigh on me so not to do my duty in any way!

I mean to be such a help to John, such a real rest and comfort, and here I am a comparative burden already!

Nobody would believe what an effort it is to do what little I am able—to   45
dress and entertain, and order things.

It is fortunate Mary is so good with the baby. Such a dear baby!

And yet I *cannot* be with him, it makes me so nervous.

I suppose John never was nervous in his life. He laughs at me so about this wallpaper!

At first he meant to repaper the room, but afterwards he said that I was letting it get the better of me, and that nothing was worse for a nervous patient than to give way to such fancies.

He said that after the wallpaper was changed it would be the heavy bed-   50
stead, and then the barred windows, and then that gate at the head of the stairs, and so on.

"You know the place is doing you good," he said, "and really, dear, I don't care to renovate the house just for a three months' rental."

"Then do let us go downstairs," I said. "There are such pretty rooms there."

Then he took me in his arms and called me a blessed little goose, and said he would go down cellar, if I wished, and have it whitewashed into the bargain.

But he is right enough about the beds and windows and things.

It is as airy and comfortable a room as anyone need wish, and, of course, I   55
would not be so silly as to make him uncomfortable just for a whim.

I'm really getting quite fond of the big room, all but that horrid paper.

Out of one window I can see the garden—those mysterious deep-shaded arbors, the riotous old-fashioned flowers, and bushes and gnarly trees.

Out of another I get a lovely view of the bay and a little private wharf belonging to the estate. There is a beautiful shaded lane that runs down there from the house. I always fancy I see people walking in these numerous paths and arbors, but John has cautioned me not to give way to fancy in the least. He says that with my imaginative power and habit of story-making, a nervous weakness like mine is sure to lead to all manner of excited fancies, and that I ought to use my will and good sense to check the tendency. So I try.

I think sometimes that if I were only well enough to write a little it would relieve the press of ideas and rest me.

But I find I get pretty tired when I try. 60

It is so discouraging not to have any advice and companionship about my work. When I get really well, John says we will ask Cousin Henry and Julia down for a long visit; but he says he would as soon put fireworks in my pillow-case as to let me have those stimulating people about now.

I wish I could get well faster.

But I must not think about that. This paper looks to me as if it *knew* what a vicious influence it had!

There is a recurrent spot where the pattern lolls like a broken neck and two bulbous eyes stare at you upside down.

I get positively angry with the impertinence of it and the everlastingness. 65 Up and down and sideways they crawl, and those absurd unblinking eyes are everywhere. There is one place where two breadths didn't match, and the eyes go all up and down the line, one a little higher than the other.

I never saw so much expression in an inanimate thing before, and we all know how much expression they have! I used to lie awake as a child and get more entertainment and terror out of blank walls and plain furniture than most children could find in a toy store.

I remember what a kindly wink the knobs of our big old bureau used to have, and there was one chair that always seemed like a strong friend.

I used to feel that if any of the other things looked too fierce I could always hop into that chair and be safe.

The furniture in this room is no worse than inharmonious, however, for we had to bring it all from downstairs. I suppose when this was used as a playroom they had to take the nursery things out, and no wonder! I never saw such ravages as the children have made here.

The wallpaper, as I said before, is torn off in spots, and it sticketh closer than 70 a brother—they must have had perseverance as well as hatred.

Then the floor is scratched and gouged and splintered, the plaster itself is dug out here and there, and this great heavy bed which is all we found in the room, looks as if it had been through the wars.

But I don't mind it a bit—only the paper.

There comes John's sister. Such a dear girl as she is, and so careful of me! I must not let her find me writing.

She is a perfect and enthusiastic housekeeper, and hopes for no better profession. I verily believe she thinks it is the writing which made me sick!

But I can write when she is out, and see her a long way off from these windows. 75

There is one that commands the road, a lovely shaded winding road, and one that just looks off over the country. A lovely country, too, full of great elms and velvet meadows.

This wallpaper has a kind of sub-pattern in a different shade, a particularly irritating one, for you can only see it in certain lights, and not clearly then.

But in the places where it isn't faded and where the sun is just so—I can see a strange, provoking, formless sort of figure that seems to skulk about behind that silly and conspicuous front design.

There's sister on the stairs!

Well, the Fourth of July is over! The people are all gone, and I am tired out. 80
John thought it might do me good to see a little company, so we just had Mother and Nellie and the children down for a week.

Of course I didn't do a thing. Jennie sees to everything now.

But it tired me all the same.

John says if I don't pick up faster he shall send me to Weir Mitchell in the fall.

But I don't want to go there at all. I had a friend who was in his hands once, and she says he is just like John and my brother, only more so!

Besides, it is such an undertaking to go so far. 85

I don't feel as if it was worthwhile to turn my hand over for anything, and I'm getting dreadfully fretful and querulous.

I cry at nothing, and cry most of the time.

Of course I don't when John is here, or anybody else, but when I am alone.

And I am alone a good deal just now. John is kept in town very often by serious cases, and Jennie is good and lets me alone when I want her to.

So I walk a little in the garden or down that lovely lane, sit on the porch un- 90
der the roses, and lie down up here a good deal.

I'm getting really fond of the room in spite of the wallpaper. Perhaps *because* of the wallpaper.

It dwells in my mind so!

I lie here on this great immovable bed—it is nailed down, I believe—and follow that pattern about by the hour. It is as good as gymnastics, I assure you. I start, we'll say, at the bottom, down in the corner over there where it has not been touched, and I determine for the thousandth time that I *will* follow that pointless pattern to some sort of conclusion.

I know a little of the principle of design, and I know this thing was not arranged on any laws of radiation, or alternation, or repetition, or symmetry, or anything else that I ever heard of.

It is repeated, of course, by the breadths, but not otherwise. 95

Looked at in one way, each breadth stands alone; the bloated curves and flourishes—a kind of "debased Romanesque" with delirium tremens—go waddling up and down in isolated columns of fatuity.

But, on the other hand, they connect diagonally, and the sprawling outlines run off in great slanting waves of optic horror, like a lot of wallowing sea-weeds in full chase.

The whole thing goes horizontally, too, at least it seems so, and I exhaust myself trying to distinguish the order of its going in that direction.

They have used a horizontal breadth for a frieze, and that adds wonderfully to the confusion.

There is one end of the room where it is almost intact, and there, when the crosslights fade and the low sun shines directly upon it, I can almost fancy radiation after all—the interminable grotesque seems to form around a common center and rush off in headlong plunges of equal distraction.

It makes me tired to follow it. I will take a nap, I guess.

I don't know why I should write this.

I don't want to.

I don't feel able.

And I know John would think it absurd. But I *must* say what I feel and think in some way—it is such a relief!

But the effort is getting to be greater than the relief.

Half the time now I am awfully lazy, and lie down ever so much.

John says I mustn't lose my strength, and has me take cod liver oil and lots of tonics and things, to say nothing of ale and wine and rare meat.

Dear John! He loves me very dearly, and hates to have me sick. I tried to have a real earnest reasonable talk with him the other day, and tell him how I wish he would let me go and make a visit to Cousin Henry and Julia.

But he said I wasn't able to go, nor able to stand it after I got there; and I did not make out a very good case for myself, for I was crying before I had finished.

It is getting to be a great effort for me to think straight. Just this nervous weakness, I suppose.

And dear John gathered me up in his arms, and just carried me upstairs and laid me on the bed, and sat by me and read to me till it tired my head.

He said I was his darling and his comfort and all he had, and that I must take care of myself for his sake, and keep well.

He says no one but myself can help me out of it, that I must use my will and self-control and not let any silly fancies run away with me.

There's one comfort—the baby is well and happy, and does not have to occupy this nursery with the horrid wallpaper.

If we had not used it, that blessed child would have! What a fortunate escape! Why, I wouldn't have a child of mine, an impressionable little thing, live in such a room for worlds.

I never thought of it before, but it is lucky that John kept me here after all, I can stand it so much easier than a baby, you see.

Of course I never mention it to them any more—I am too wise—but I keep watch for it all the same.

There are things in that paper that nobody knows about but me, or ever will.

Behind that outside pattern the dim shapes get clearer every day.

It is always the same shape, only very numerous.

And it is like a woman stooping down and creeping about behind that pattern. I don't like it a bit. I wonder—I begin to think—I wish John would take me away from here!

————————

It is so hard to talk with John about my case, because he is so wise, and because he loves me so.

But I tried it last night.

It was moonlight. The moon shines in all around just as the sun does.   125

I hate to see it sometimes, it creeps so slowly, and always comes in by one window or another.

John was asleep and I hated to waken him, so I kept still and watched the moonlight on that undulating wallpaper till I felt creepy.

The faint figure behind seemed to shake the pattern, just as if she wanted to get out.

I got up softly and went to feel and see if the paper *did* move, and when I came back John was awake.

"What is it, little girl?" he said. "Don't go walking about like that—you'll get   130 cold."

I thought it was a good time to talk, so I told him that I really was not gaining here, and that I wished he would take me away.

"Why, darling!" said he. "Our lease will be up in three weeks, and I can't see how to leave before.

"The repairs are not done at home, and I cannot possibly leave town just now. Of course if you were in any danger, I could and would, but you really are better, dear, whether you can see it or not. I am a doctor, dear, and I know. You are gaining flesh and color, your appetite is better, I feel really much easier about you."

"I don't weigh a bit more," said I, "nor as much; and my appetite may be better in the evening when you are here but it is worse in the morning when you are away!"

"Bless her little heart!" said he with a big hug. "She shall be as sick as she   135 pleases! But now let's improve the shining hours by going to sleep, and talk about it in the morning!"

"And you won't go away?" I asked gloomily.

"Why, how can I, dear? It is only three weeks more and then we will take a nice little trip of a few days while Jennie is getting the house ready. Really, dear, you are better!"

"Better in body perhaps—" I began, and stopped short, for he sat up straight and looked at me with such a stern, reproachful look that I could not say another word.

"My darling," said he, "I beg of you, for my sake and for our child's sake, as well as for your own, that you will never for one instant let that idea enter your mind! There is nothing so dangerous, so fascinating, to a temperament like

yours. It is a false and foolish fancy. Can you not trust me as a physician when I
tell you so?"

So of course I said no more on that score, and we went to sleep before long. 140
He thought I was asleep first, but I wasn't, and lay there for hours trying to decide whether that front pattern and the back pattern really did move together
or separately.

On a pattern like this, by daylight, there is a lack of sequence, a defiance of
law, that is a constant irritant to a normal mind.

The color is hideous enough, and unreliable enough, and infuriating
enough, but the pattern is torturing.

You think you have mastered it, but just as you get well under way in following, it turns a back-somersault and there you are. It slaps you in the face, knocks
you down, and tramples upon you. It is like a bad dream.

The outside pattern is a florid arabesque, reminding one of a fungus. If you
can imagine a toadstool in joints, an interminable string of toadstools, budding
and sprouting in endless convolutions   why, that is something like it.

That is, sometimes!   145

There is one marked peculiarity about this paper, a thing nobody seems to
notice but myself, and that is that it changes as the light changes.

When the sun shoots in through the east window—I always watch for that
first long, straight ray—it changes so quickly that I never can quite believe it.

That is why I watch it always.

By moonlight—the moon shines in all night when there is a moon—I
wouldn't know it was the same paper.

At night in any kind of light, in twilight, candlelight, lamplight, and worst 150
of all by moonlight, it becomes bars! The outside pattern, I mean, and the
woman behind it is as plain as can be.

I didn't realize for a long time what the thing was that showed behind, that
dim sub-pattern, but now I am quite sure it is a woman.

By daylight she is subdued, quiet. I fancy it is the pattern that keeps her so
still. It is so puzzling. It keeps me quiet by the hour.

I lie down ever so much now. John says it is good for me, and to sleep all I can.

Indeed he started the habit by making me lie down for an hour after each
meal.

It is a very bad habit I am convinced, for you see, I don't sleep.   155

And that cultivates deceit, for I don't tell them I'm awake—O no!

The fact is I am getting a little afraid of John.

He seems very queer sometimes, and even Jennie has an inexplicable look.

It strikes me occasionally, just as a scientific hypothesis, that perhaps it is
the paper!

I have watched John when he did not know I was looking, and come into 160
the room suddenly on the most innocent excuses, and I've caught him several

times *looking at the paper!* And Jennie too. I caught Jennie with her hand on it once.

She didn't know I was in the room, and when I asked her in a quiet, a very quiet voice, with the most restrained manner possible, what she was doing with the paper—she turned around as if she had been caught stealing, and looked quite angry—asked me why I should frighten her so!

Then she said that the paper stained everything it touched, that she had found yellow smooches on all my clothes and John's, and she wished we would be more careful!

Did not that sound innocent? But I know she was studying that pattern, and I am determined that nobody shall find it out but myself!

———————

Life is very much more exciting now than it used to be. You see I have something more to expect, to look forward to, to watch. I really do eat better, and am more quiet than I was.

John is so pleased to see me improve! He laughed a little the other day, and   165
said I seemed to be flourishing in spite of my wallpaper.

I turned it off with a laugh. I had no intention of telling him it was *because* of the wallpaper—he would make fun of me. He might even want to take me away.

I don't want to leave now until I have found it out. There is a week more, and I think that will be enough.

———————

I'm feeling so much better!

I don't sleep much at night, for it is so interesting to watch developments; but I sleep a good deal during the daytime.

In the daytime it is tiresome and perplexing.   170

There are always new shoots on the fungus, and new shades of yellow all over it. I cannot keep count of them, though I have tried conscientiously.

It is the strangest yellow, that wallpaper! It makes me think of all the yellow things I ever saw—not beautiful ones like buttercups, but old, foul, bad yellow things.

But there is something else about that paper—the smell! I noticed it the moment we came into the room, but with so much air and sun it was not bad. Now we have had a week of fog and rain, and whether the windows are open or not, the smell is here.

It creeps all over the house.

I find it hovering in the dining-room, skulking in the parlor, hiding in the   175
hall, lying in wait for me on the stairs.

It gets into my hair.

Even when I go to ride, if I turn my head suddenly and surprise it—there is that smell!

Such a peculiar odor, too! I have spent hours in trying to analyze it, to find what it smelled like.

It is not bad—at first—and very gentle, but quite the subtlest, most enduring odor I ever met.

In this damp weather it is awful, I wake up in the night and find it hanging   180
over me.

It used to disturb me at first. I thought seriously of burning the house—to reach the smell.

But now I am used to it. The only thing I can think of that it is like is the *color* of the paper! A yellow smell.

There is a very funny mark on this wall, low down, near the mopboard. A streak that runs round the room. It goes behind every piece of furniture, except the bed, a long, straight, even *smooch*, as if it had been rubbed over and over.

I wonder how it was done and who did it, and what they did it for. Round and round and round—round and round and round—it makes me dizzy!

I really have discovered something at last.   185

Through watching so much at night, when it changes so, I have finally found out.

The front pattern *does* move—and no wonder! The woman behind shakes it!

Sometimes I think there are a great many women behind, and sometimes only one, and she crawls around fast, and her crawling shakes it all over.

Then in the very bright spots she keeps still, and in the very shady spots she just takes hold of the bars and shakes them hard.

And she is all the time trying to climb through. But nobody could climb   190
through that pattern—it strangles so; I think that is why it has so many heads.

They get through, and then the pattern strangles them off and turns them upside down, and makes their eyes white!

If those heads were covered or taken off it would not be half so bad.

I think that woman gets out in the daytime!

And I'll tell you why—privately—I've seen her!

I can see her out of every one of my windows!   195

It is the same woman, I know, for she is always creeping, and most women do not creep by daylight.

I see her in that long shaded lane, creeping up and down. I see her in those dark grape arbors, creeping all around the garden.

I see her on that long road under the trees, creeping along, and when a carriage comes she hides under the blackberry vines.

I don't blame her a bit. It must be very humiliating to be caught creeping by daylight!

I always lock the door when I creep by daylight. I can't do it at night, for I 200
know John would suspect something at once.

And John is so queer now that I don't want to irritate him. I wish he would
take another room! Besides, I don't want anybody to get that woman out at
night but myself.

I often wonder if I could see her out of all the windows at once.

But, turn as fast as I can, I can only see out of one at one time.

And though I always see her, she *may* be able to creep faster than I can turn!
I have watched her sometimes away off in the open country, creeping as fast as a
cloud shadow in a wind.

―――――

If only that top pattern could be gotten off from the under one! I mean to 205
try it, little by little.

I have found out another funny thing, but I shan't tell it this time! It does
not do to trust people too much.

There are only two more days to get this paper off, and I believe John is beginning to notice. I don't like the look in his eyes.

And I heard him ask Jennie a lot of professional questions about me. She
had a very good report to give.

She said I slept a good deal in the daytime.

John knows I don't sleep very well at night, for all I'm so quiet! 210

He asked me all sorts of questions, too, and pretended to be very loving and
kind.

As if I couldn't see through him!

Still, I don't wonder he acts so, sleeping under this paper for three months.

It only interests me, but I feel sure John and Jennie are affected by it.

―――――

Hurrah! This is the last day, but it is enough. John is to stay in town over 215
night, and won't be out until this evening.

Jennie wanted to sleep with me—the sly thing; but I told her I should undoubtedly rest better for a night all alone.

That was clever, for really I wasn't alone a bit! As soon as it was moonlight
and that poor thing began to crawl and shake the pattern, I got up and ran to
help her.

I pulled and she shook, I shook and she pulled, and before morning we had
peeled off yards of that paper.

A strip about as high as my head and half around the room.

And then when the sun came and that awful pattern began to laugh at me, I 220
declared I would finish it today!

We go away tomorrow, and they are moving all my furniture down again to
leave things as they were before.

Jennie looked at the wall in amazement, but I told her merrily that I did it
out of pure spite at the vicious thing.

She laughed and said she wouldn't mind doing it herself, but I must not get tired.

How she betrayed herself that time!

But I am here, and no person touches this paper but Me—not *alive*!   225

She tried to get me out of the room—it was too patent! But I said it was so quiet and empty and clean now that I believed I would lie down again and sleep all I could; and not to wake me even for dinner—I would call when I woke.

So now she is gone, and the servants are gone, and the things are gone, and there is nothing left but that great bedstead nailed down, with the canvas mattress we found on it.

We shall sleep downstairs tonight, and take the boat home tomorrow.

I quite enjoy the room, now it is bare again.

How those children did tear about here!   230

This bedstead is fairly gnawed!

But I must get to work.

I have locked the door and thrown the key down into the front path.

I don't want to go out, and I don't want to have anybody come in, till John comes.

I want to astonish him.   235

I've got a rope up here that even Jennie did not find. If that woman does get out, and tries to get away, I can tie her!

But I forgot I could not reach far without anything to stand on!

This bed will *not* move!

I tried to lift and push it until I was lame, and then I got so angry I bit off a little piece at one corner—but it hurt my teeth.

Then I peeled off all the paper I could reach standing on the floor. It sticks   240
horribly and the pattern just enjoys it! All those strangled heads and bulbous eyes and waddling fungus growths just shriek with derision!

I am getting angry enough to do something desperate. To jump out of the window would be admirable exercise, but the bars are too strong even to try.

Besides I wouldn't do it. Of course not. I know well enough that a step like that is improper and might be misconstrued.

I don't like to *look* out of the windows even—there are so many of those creeping women, and they creep so fast.

I wonder if they all come out of that wallpaper as I did?

But I am securely fastened now by my well-hidden rope—you don't get *me*—out in the road there!   245

I suppose I shall have to get back behind the pattern when it comes night, and that is hard!

It is so pleasant to be out in this great room and creep around as I please!

I don't want to go outside. I won't, even if Jennie asks me to.

For outside you have to creep on the ground, and everything is green instead of yellow.

But here I can creep smoothly on the floor, and my shoulder just fits in that   250
long smooch around the wall, so I cannot lose my way.

Why there's John at the door!

It is no use, young man, you can't open it!

How he does call and pound!

Now he's crying to Jennie for an axe.

It would be a shame to break down that beautiful door!   255

"John dear!" said I in the gentlest voice. "The key is down by the front steps, under a plantain leaf!"

That silenced him for a few moments.

Then he said—very quietly indeed, "Open the door, my darling!"

"I can't," said I. "The key is down by the front door under a plantain leaf!"

And then I said it again, several times, very gently and slowly, and said it so 260 often that he had to go and see, and he got it of course, and came in. He stopped short by the door.

"What is the matter?" he cried. "For God's sake, what are you doing!"

I kept on creeping just the same, but I looked at him over my shoulder.

"I've got out at last," said I, "in spite of you and Jane[.] And I've pulled off most of the paper, so you can't put me back!"

Now why should that man have fainted? But he did, and right across my path by the wall, so that I had to creep over him every time!

ACTIVITIES FOR WRITING AND DISCUSSION

1. Describe your first impressions of the narrator. Is she an **unreliable narrator,** or do you find her relatively objective? Cite and share particular passages to support your answer.

2. In paragraph 36 the narrator says her husband "hates to have me write a word." Later, in paragraph 105, she declares, "I *must* say what I feel and think in some way—it is such a relief!" Why does she write? What does writing do for her? Identify any passages in the story that relate to writing or imagination. Then produce evidence to support either of the following assertions:

   a. "Writing helps the narrator," or
   b. "Writing and imagination help destroy the narrator."

As you do this exercise, consider what Gilman said of her own experiences with Dr. S. Weir Mitchell:

> [U]sing the remnants of intelligence that remained . . . I cast the noted specialist's advice to the winds and went to work again—work, the normal life of every human being; work, in which is joy and growth and service, without which one is a pauper and a parasite; ultimately recovering some measure of power.

3. The **narrator** expresses ambivalent feelings about John, sometimes challenging his judgments and elsewhere saying "he is so wise, and . . . he loves me

so" (paragraph 123). How can you account for such contradictory views? What are the narrator's thoughts and feelings about John? Is John good for her? Why or why not? Cite and analyze two or three passages that provide support for your answer.

4. Read aloud the reported **dialogue** between the narrator and John in paragraphs 130–139.
   a. Underline any words or phrases that seem peculiar or interesting to you. How do these words or phrases illuminate the husband/wife relationship? Discuss your thoughts in class or in a small group.
   b. Read the sentence that concludes the dialogue: "So of course I said no more on that score, and we went to sleep before long" (paragraph 140). How is John able to silence his wife and induce her to sleep?
   c. Write an essay in which you analyze the dialogue and how it helps to characterize the narrator, John, and their relationship.

5. Analyze the story's ending. Has the narrator achieved a greater intellectual and emotional clarity, or has she gone insane? Cite illustrative quotations from the story to support your answer.

6. "The Yellow Wallpaper" is a subjective, **first-person** narrative. As a technical challenge, try rendering the same story in a more objective format. For instance, recast the story as a short play. Provide a **scene description** and **stage directions** to supplement the dialogue of your play.

SIDONIE-GABRIELLE COLETTE (1873–1954)

The Other Wife

"Table for two? This way, Monsieur, Madame, there is still a table next to the window, if Madame and Monsieur would like a view of the bay."   1

Alice followed the maître d'.[1]   2

"Oh, yes. Come on, Marc, it'll be like having lunch on a boat on the water . . ."   3

Her husband caught her by passing his arm under hers. "We'll be more comfortable over there."   4

"There? In the middle of all those people? I'd much rather . . ."   5

"Alice, please."   6

He tightened his grip in such a meaningful way that she turned around. "What's the matter?"   7

---

1. **maître d'**: Headwaiter.

"Shh . . ." he said softly, looking at her intently, and led her toward the table 8
in the middle.

"What is it, Marc?" 9

"I'll tell you, darling. Let me order lunch first. Would you like the shrimp? 10
Or the eggs in aspic?"

"Whatever you like, you know that." 11

They smiled at one another, wasting the precious time of an overworked 12
maître d', stricken with a kind of nervous dance, who was standing next to
them, perspiring.

"The shrimp," said Marc. "Then the eggs and bacon. And the cold chicken 13
with a romaine salad. *Fromage blanc?*[2] The house specialty? We'll go with the
specialty. Two strong coffees. My chauffeur will be having lunch also, we'll be
leaving again at two o'clock. Some cider? No, I don't trust it . . . Dry champagne."

He sighed as if he had just moved an armoire, gazed at the colorless midday 14
sea, at the pearly white sky, then at his wife, whom he found lovely in her little
Mercury hat[3] with its large, hanging veil.

"You're looking well, darling. And all this blue water makes your eyes look 15
green, imagine that! And you've put on weight since you've been traveling . . .
It's nice up to a point, but only up to a point!"

Her firm, round breasts rose proudly as she leaned over the table. 16

"Why did you keep me from taking that place next to the window?" 17

Marc Seguy never considered lying. "Because you were about to sit next to 18
someone I know."

"Someone I don't know?" 19

"My ex-wife." 20

She couldn't think of anything to say and opened her blue eyes wider. 21

"So what, darling? It'll happen again. It's not important." 22

The words came back to Alice and she asked, in order, the inevitable ques- 23
tions. "Did she see you? Could she see that you saw her? Will you point her out
to me?"

"Don't look now, please, she must be watching us. . . . The lady with brown 24
hair, no hat, she must be staying in this hotel. By herself, behind those children
in red . . ."

"Yes, I see." 25

Hidden behind some broad-brimmed beach hats, Alice was able to look at 26
the woman who, fifteen months ago, had still been her husband's wife.

"Incompatibility," Marc said. "Oh, I mean . . . total incompatibility! We di- 27
vorced like well-bred people, almost like friends, quietly, quickly. And then I fell
in love with you, and you really wanted to be happy with me. How lucky we are
that our happiness doesn't involve any guilty parties or victims!"

The woman in white, whose smooth, lustrous hair reflected the light from 28
the sea in azure patches, was smoking a cigarette with her eyes half closed. Alice

---

2. **Fromage blanc:** A mild white cheese, something like cottage cheese.
3. **Mercury hat:** Hat with a feather.

turned back toward her husband, took some shrimp and butter, and ate calmly. After a moment's silence she asked: "Why didn't you ever tell me that she had blue eyes, too?"

"Well, I never thought about it!" 29

He kissed the hand she was extending toward the bread basket and she 30 blushed with pleasure. Dusky and ample, she might have seemed somewhat coarse, but the changeable blue of her eyes and her wavy, golden hair made her look like a frail and sentimental blonde. She vowed overwhelming gratitude to her husband. Immodest without knowing it, everything about her bore the overly conspicuous marks of extreme happiness.

They ate and drank heartily, and each thought the other had forgotten the 31 woman in white. Now and then, however, Alice laughed too loudly, and Marc was careful about his posture, holding his shoulders back, his head up. They waited quite a long time for their coffee, in silence. An incandescent river, the straggled reflection of the invisible sun overhead, shifted slowly across the sea and shone with a blinding brilliance.

"She's still there, you know," Alice whispered. 32

"Is she making you uncomfortable? Would you like to have coffee some- 33 where else?"

"No, not at all! She's the one who must be uncomfortable! Besides, she 34 doesn't exactly seem to be having a wild time, if you could see her . . ."

"I don't have to. I know that look of hers." 35

"Oh, was she like that?" 36

He exhaled his cigarette smoke through his nostrils and knitted his eye- 37 brows. "Like that? No. To tell you honestly, she wasn't happy with me."

"Oh, really now!" 38

"The way you indulge me is so charming, darling . . . It's crazy . . . You're an 39 angel . . . You love me . . . I'm so proud when I see those eyes of yours. Yes, those eyes . . . She . . . I just didn't know how to make her happy, that's all, I didn't know how."

"She's just difficult!" 40

Alice fanned herself irritably, and cast brief glances at the woman in white, 41 who was smoking, her head resting against the back of the cane chair, her eyes closed with an air of satisfied lassitude.

Marc shrugged his shoulders modestly. 42

"That's the right word," he admitted. "What can you do? You have to 43 feel sorry for people who are never satisfied. But we're satisfied . . . Aren't we, darling?"

She did not answer. She was looking furtively, and closely, at her husband's 44 face, ruddy and regular; at his thick hair, threaded here and there with white silk; at his short, well-cared-for hands; and doubtful for the first time, she asked herself, "What more did she want from him?"

And as they were leaving, while Marc was paying the bill and asking for the 45 chauffeur and about the route, she kept looking, with envy and curiosity, at the woman in white, this dissatisfied, this difficult, this superior . . .

ACTIVITIES FOR WRITING AND DISCUSSION

1. Annotate the story. Then react to it using any of the "Ten Ideas for Writing" listed on page 35.

2. Reread the last two paragraphs carefully. What is Alice "doubtful" about, and why does she look with "envy" at the other wife? (Different readers will answer these questions differently.) In the **persona** of Alice, write a **stream of consciousness** that expresses your (Alice's) conflicted feelings as you leave the restaurant.

3. Rewrite the story as "The Other Husband" or "The Other Girlfriend/ Boyfriend." Keep the same basic conflict but alter the **point of view**, **setting**, and **characters** as you wish.

4. Write a story of your own, nonfictional or fictional, about a couple who unexpectedly encounter one or the other's "ex" spouse or girlfriend/boyfriend.

DORIS LESSING (b. 1919)

A Woman on a Roof

It was during the week of hot sun, that June. 1

Three men were at work on the roof, where the leads got so hot they had the 2 idea of throwing water on to cool them. But the water steamed, then sizzled; and they made jokes about getting an egg from some woman in the flats under them, to poach it for their dinner. By two it was not possible to touch the guttering they were replacing, and they speculated about what workmen did in regularly hot countries. Perhaps they should borrow kitchen gloves with the egg? They were all a bit dizzy, not used to the heat; and they shed their coats and stood side by side squeezing themselves into a foot-wide patch of shade against a chimney, careful to keep their feet in the thick socks and boots out of the sun. There was a fine view across several acres of roofs. Not far off a man sat in a deck chair reading the newspapers. Then they saw her, between chimneys, about fifty yards away. She lay face down on a brown blanket. They could see the top part of her: black hair, a flushed solid back, arms spread out.

"She's stark naked," said Stanley, sounding annoyed. 3

Harry, the oldest, a man of about forty-five, said: "Looks like it." 4

Young Tom, seventeen, said nothing, but he was excited and grinning. 5

Stanley said: "Someone'll report her if she doesn't watch out." 6

"She thinks no one can see," said Tom, craning his head all ways to see more. 7

At this point the woman, still lying prone, brought her two hands up behind 8 her shoulders with the ends of a scarf in them, tied it behind her back, and sat up. She wore a red scarf tied around her breasts and brief red bikini pants. This being the first day of the sun she was white, flushing red. She sat smoking, and did not look up when Stanley let out a wolf whistle. Harry said: "Small things amuse small minds," leading the way back to their part of the roof, but it was scorching. Harry said: "Wait, I'm going to rig up some shade," and disappeared down the skylight into the building. Now that he'd gone, Stanley and Tom went to the farthest point they could to peer at the woman. She had moved, and all they could see were two pink legs stretched on the blanket. They whistled and shouted but the legs did not move. Harry came back with a blanket and shouted: "Come on, then." He sounded irritated with them. They clambered back to him and he said to Stanley: "What about your missus?" Stanley was newly married, about three months. Stanley said, jeering: "What about my missus?"—preserving his independence. Tom said nothing, but his mind was full of the nearly naked woman. Harry slung the blanket, which he had borrowed from a friendly woman downstairs, from the stem of a television aerial to a row of chimney-pots. This shade fell across the piece of gutter they had to replace. But the shade kept moving, they had to adjust the blanket, and not much progress was made. At last some of the heat left the roof, and they worked fast, making up for lost time. First Stanley, then Tom, made a trip to the end of the roof to see the woman. "She's on her back," Stanley said, adding a jest which made Tom snicker, and the older man smile tolerantly. Tom's report was that she hadn't moved, but it was a lie. He wanted to keep what he had seen to himself: he had caught her in the act of rolling down the little red pants over her hips, till they were no more than a small triangle. She was on her back, fully visible, glistening with oil.

Next morning, as soon as they came up, they went to look. She was already 9 there, face down, arms spread out, naked except for the little red pants. She had turned brown in the night. Yesterday she was a scarlet-and-white woman, today she was a brown woman. Stanley let out a whistle. She lifted her head, startled, as if she'd been asleep, and looked straight over at them. The sun was in her eyes, she blinked and stared, then she dropped her head again. At this gesture of indifference, they all three, Stanley, Tom, and old Harry, let out whistles and yells. Harry was doing it in parody of the younger men, making fun of them, but he was also angry. They were all angry because of her utter indifference to the three men watching her.

"Bitch," said Stanley.   10

"She should ask us over," said Tom, snickering.   11

Harry recovered himself and reminded Stanley: "If she's married, her old 12 man wouldn't like that."

"Christ," said Stanley virtuously, "if my wife lay about like that, for everyone 13 to see, I'd soon stop her."

Harry said, smiling: "How do you know, perhaps she's sunning herself at 14 this very moment?"

"Not a chance, not on our roof." The safety of his wife put Stanley into a 15 good humour, and they went to work. But today it was hotter than yesterday; and several times one or the other suggested they should tell Matthew, the foreman, and ask to leave the roof until the heat wave was over. But they didn't. There was work to be done in the basement of the big block of flats, but up here they felt free, on a different level from ordinary humanity shut in the streets or the buildings. A lot more people came out on to the roofs that day, for an hour at midday. Some married couples sat side by side in deck chairs, the women's legs stockingless and scarlet, the men in vests with reddening shoulders.

The woman stayed on her blanket, turning herself over and over. She ig- 16 nored them, no matter what they did. When Harry went off to fetch more screws, Stanley said: "Come on." Her roof belonged to a different system of roofs, separated from theirs at one point by about twenty feet. It meant a scrambling climb from one level to another, edging along parapets, clinging to chimneys, while their big boots slipped and slithered, but at last they stood on a small square projecting roof looking straight down at her, close. She sat smoking, reading a book. Tom thought she looked like a poster, or a magazine cover, with the blue sky behind her and her legs stretched out. Behind her a great crane at work on a new building in Oxford Street swung its black arm across roofs in a great arc. Tom imagined himself at work on the crane, adjusting the arm to swing over and pick her up and swing her back across the sky to drop her near him.

They whistled. She looked up at them, cool and remote, then went on read- 17 ing. Again, they were furious. Or, rather, Stanley was. His sun-heated face was screwed into a rage as he whistled again and again, trying to make her look up. Young Tom stopped whistling. He stood beside Stanley, excited, grinning; but he felt as if he were saying to the woman: Don't associate me with *him,* for his grin was apologetic. Last night he had thought of the unknown woman before he slept, and she had been tender with him. This tenderness he was remembering as he shifted his feet by the jeering, whistling Stanley, and watched the indifferent, healthy brown woman a few feet off, with the gap that plunged to the street between them. Tom thought it was romantic, it was like being high on two hilltops. But there was a shout from Harry, and they clambered back. Stanley's face was hard, really angry. The boy kept looking at him and wondered why he hated the woman so much, for by now he loved her.

They played their little games with the blanket, trying to trap shade to work 18 under; but again it was not until nearly four that they could work seriously, and they were exhausted, all three of them. They were grumbling about the weather by now. Stanley was in a thoroughly bad humour. When they made their routine trip to see the woman before they packed up for the day, she was apparently asleep, face down, her back all naked save for the scarlet triangle on her buttocks. "I've got a good mind to report her to the police," said Stanley, and Harry said: "What's eating you? What harm's she doing?"

"I tell you, if she was my wife!"   19

"But she isn't, is she?" Tom knew that Harry, like himself, was uneasy at 20 Stanley's reaction. He was normally a sharp young man, quick at his work, making a lot of jokes, good company.

"Perhaps it will be cooler tomorrow," said Harry.   21

But it wasn't; it was hotter, if anything, and the weather forecast said the 22 good weather would last. As soon as they were on the roof, Harry went over to see if the woman was there, and Tom knew it was to prevent Stanley going, to put off his bad humour. Harry had grownup children, a boy the same age as Tom, and the youth trusted and looked up to him.

Harry came back and said: "She's not there." 23

"I bet her old man has put his foot down," said Stanley, and Harry and Tom 24 caught each other's eyes and smiled behind the young married man's back.

Harry suggested they should get permission to work in the basement, and 25 they did, that day. But before packing up Stanley said: "Let's have a breath of fresh air." Again Harry and Tom smiled at each other as they followed Stanley up to the roof, Tom in the devout conviction that he was there to protect the woman from Stanley. It was about five-thirty, and a calm, full sunlight lay over the roofs. The great crane still swung its black arm from Oxford Street to above their heads. She was not there. Then there was a flutter of white from behind a parapet, and she stood up, in a belted, white dressing-gown. She had been there all day, probably, but on a different patch of roof, to hide from them. Stanley did not whistle; he said nothing, but watched the woman bend to collect papers, books, cigarettes, then fold the blanket over her arm. Tom was thinking: If they weren't here, I'd go over and say . . . what? But he knew from his nightly dreams of her that she was kind and friendly. Perhaps she would ask him down to her flat? Perhaps . . . He stood watching her disappear down the skylight. As she went, Stanley let out a shrill derisive yell; she started, and it seemed as if she nearly fell. She clutched to save herself, they could hear things falling. She looked straight at them, angry. Harry said, facetiously: "Better be careful on those slippery ladders, love." Tom knew he said it to save her from Stanley, but she could not know it. She vanished, frowning. Tom was full of a secret delight, because he knew her anger was for the others, not for him.

"Roll on some rain," said Stanley, bitter, looking at the blue evening sky. 26

Next day was cloudless, and they decided to finish the work in the base- 27 ment. They felt excluded, shut in the grey cement basement fitting pipes, from the holiday atmosphere of London in a heat wave. At lunchtime they came up for some air, but while the married couples, and the men in shirt-sleeves or vests, were there, she was not there, either on her usual patch of roof or where she had been yesterday. They all, even Harry, clambered about, between chimney-pots, over parapets, the hot leads stinging their fingers. There was not a sign of her. They took off their shirts and vests and exposed their chests, feeling their feet sweaty and hot. They did not mention the woman. But Tom felt alone again. Last night she had him into her flat: it was big and had fitted white carpets and a bed with a padded white leather head-board. She wore a black filmy negligée and her kindness to Tom thickened his throat as he remembered it. He felt she had betrayed him by not being there.

And again after work they climbed up, but still there was nothing to be seen 28 of her. Stanley kept repeating that if it was as hot as this tomorrow he wasn't going to work and that's all there was to it. But they were all there next day. By ten the temperature was in the middle seventies, and it was eighty long before noon. Harry went to the foreman to say it was impossible to work on the leads in that heat; but the foreman said there was nothing else he could put them on, and they'd have to. At midday they stood, silent, watching the skylight on her roof open, and then she slowly emerged in her white gown, holding a bundle of blanket. She looked at them, gravely, then went to the part of the roof where she was hidden from them. Tom was pleased. He felt she was more his when the other men couldn't see her. They had taken off their shirts and vests, but now they put them back again, for they felt the sun bruising their flesh. "She must have the hide of a rhino," said Stanley, tugging at guttering and swearing. They stopped work, and sat in the shade, moving around behind chimney stacks. A woman came to water a yellow window box opposite them. She was mid-dleaged, wearing a flowered summer dress. Stanley said to her: "We need a drink more than them." She smiled and said: "Better drop down to the pub quick, it'll be closing in a minute." They exchanged pleasantries, and she left them with a smile and a wave.

"Not like Lady Godiva," said Stanley. "She can give us a bit of a chat and a 29 smile."

"You didn't whistle at *her*," said Tom, reproving.   30

"Listen to him," said Stanley, "you didn't whistle, then?"   31

But the boy felt as if he hadn't whistled, as if only Harry and Stanley had. He 32 was making plans, when it was time to knock off work, to get left behind and somehow make his way over to the woman. The weather report said the hot spell was due to break, so he had to move quickly. But there was no chance of being left. The other two decided to knock off work at four, because they were ex-hausted. As they went down, Tom quickly climbed a parapet and hoisted himself higher by pulling his weight up a chimney. He caught a glimpse of her lying on her back, her knees up, eyes closed, a brown woman lolling in the sun. He slipped and clattered down, as Stanley looked for information: "She's gone down," he said. He felt as if he had protected her from Stanley, and that she must be grateful to him. He could feel the bond between the woman and himself.

Next day, they stood around on the landing below the roof, reluctant to 33 climb up into the heat. The woman who had lent Harry the blanket came out and offered them a cup of tea. They accepted gratefully, and sat around Mrs. Pritchett's kitchen an hour or so, chatting. She was married to an airline pilot. A smart blonde, of about thirty, she had an eye for the handsome sharp-faced Stanley; and the two teased each other while Harry sat in a corner, watching, in-dulgent, though his expression reminded Stanley that he was married. And young Tom felt envious of Stanley's ease in badinage; felt, too, that Stanley's getting off with Mrs. Pritchett left his romance with the woman on the roof safe and intact.

"I thought they said the heat wave'd break," said Stanley, sullen, as the time 34 approached when they really would have to climb up into the sunlight.

"You don't like it, then?" asked Mrs. Pritchett.   35

"All right for some," said Stanley. "Nothing to do but lie about as if it was a 36
beach up there. Do you ever go up?"

"Went up once," said Mrs. Pritchett. "But it's a dirty place up there, and it's 37
too hot."

"Quite right too," said Stanley. 38

Then they went up, leaving the cool neat little flat and the friendly Mrs. 39
Pritchett.

As soon as they were up they saw her. The three men looked at her, resentful 40
at her ease in this punishing sun. Then Harry said, because of the expression on
Stanley's face: "Come on, we've got to pretend to work, at least."

They had to wrench another length of guttering that ran beside a parapet 41
out of its bed, so that they could replace it. Stanley took it in his two hands,
tugged, swore, stood up. "Fuck it," he said, and sat down under a chimney. He lit
a cigarette. "Fuck them," he said. "What do they think we are, lizards? I've got
blisters all over my hands." Then he jumped up and climbed over the roofs and
stood with his back to them. He put his fingers either side of his mouth and let
out a shrill whistle. Tom and Harry squatted, not looking at each other, watching him. They could just see the woman's head, the beginnings of her brown
shoulders. Stanley whistled again. Then he began stamping with his feet, and
whistled and yelled and screamed at the woman, his face getting scarlet. He
seemed quite mad, as he stamped and whistled, while the woman did not move,
she did not move a muscle.

"Barmy," said Tom. 42

"Yes," said Harry, disapproving. 43

Suddenly the older man came to a decision. It was, Tom knew, to save some 44
sort of scandal or real trouble over the woman. Harry stood up and began
packing tools into a length of oily cloth. "Stanley," he said, commanding. At first
Stanley took no notice, but Harry said: "Stanley, we're packing it in, I'll tell
Matthew."

Stanley came back, cheeks mottled, eyes glaring. 45

"Can't go on like this," said Harry. "It'll break in a day or so. I'm going to tell 46
Matthew we've got sunstroke, and if he doesn't like it, it's too bad." Even Harry
sounded aggrieved, Tom noted. The small, competent man, the family man
with his grey hair, who was never at a loss, sounded really off balance. "Come
on," he said, angry. He fitted himself into the open square in the roof, and went
down, watching his feet on the ladder. Then Stanley went, with not a glance at
the woman. Then Tom, who, his throat beating with excitement, silently
promised her on a backward glance: Wait for me, wait, I'm coming.

On the pavement Stanley said: "I'm going home." He looked white now, so 47
perhaps he really did have sunstroke. Harry went off to find the foreman, who
was at work on the plumbing of some flats down the street. Tom slipped back,
not into the building they had been working on, but the building on whose roof
the woman lay. He went straight up, no one stopping him. The skylight stood
open, with an iron ladder leading up. He emerged on to the roof a couple of

yards from her. She sat up, pushing back her black hair with both hands. The scarf across her breasts bound them tight, and brown flesh bulged around it. Her legs were brown and smooth. She stared at him in silence. The boy stood grinning, foolish, claiming the tenderness he expected from her.

"What do you want?" she asked.   48

"I . . . I came to . . . make your acquaintance," he stammered, grinning, 49
pleading with her.

They looked at each other, the slight, scarlet-faced excited boy, and the seri- 50
ous, nearly naked woman. Then, without a word, she lay down on her brown
blanket, ignoring him.

"You like the sun, do you?" he enquired of her glistening back.   51

Not a word. He felt panic, thinking of how she had held him in her arms, 52
stroked his hair, brought him where he sat, lordly, in her bed, a glass of some
exhilarating liquor he had never tasted in life. He felt that if he knelt down,
stroked her shoulders, her hair, she would turn and clasp him in her arms.

He said: "The sun's all right for you, isn't it?"   53

She raised her head, set her chin on two small fists. "Go away," she said. He 54
did not move. "Listen," she said, in a slow reasonable voice, where anger was kept
in check, though with difficulty; looking at him, her face weary with anger, "if
you get a kick out of seeing women in bikinis, why don't you take a sixpenny bus
ride to the Lido? You'd see dozens of them, without all this mountaineering."

She hadn't understood him. He felt her unfairness pale him. He stammered: 55
"But I like you, I've been watching you and . . ."

"Thanks," she said, and dropped her face again, turned away from him.   56

She lay there. He stood there. She said nothing. She had simply shut him 57
out. He stood, saying nothing at all, for some minutes. He thought: She'll have
to say something if I stay. But the minutes went past, with no sign of them in
her, except in the tension of her back, her thighs, her arms—the tension of
waiting for him to go.

He looked up at the sky, where the sun seemed to spin in heat; and over the 58
roofs where he and his mates had been earlier. He could see the heat quivering
where they had worked. And they expect us to work in these conditions! he
thought, filled with righteous indignation. The woman hadn't moved. A bit of
hot wind blew her black hair softly; it shone, and was iridescent. He remembered how he had stroked it last night.

Resentment of her at last moved him off and away down the ladder, through 59
the building, into the street. He got drunk then, in hatred of her.

Next day when he woke the sky was grey. He looked at the wet grey and 60
thought, vicious: Well, that's fixed you, hasn't it now? That's fixed you good and
proper.

The three men were at work early on the cool leads, surrounded by damp 61
drizzling roofs where no one came to sun themselves, black roofs, slimy with
rain. Because it was cool now, they would finish the job that day, if they
hurried.

ACTIVITIES FOR WRITING AND DISCUSSION

1. Working alone or in a small group, brainstorm a list of issues this story raises for you. Then select one issue that interests you most and relate it (in writing) to your own or someone else's life experience.

2. Reread and annotate any passages that specifically describe the woman. Note the items and belongings she carries with her, what she apparently does (other than sunbathe) while on the roof. Note her various reactions to the men observing and taunting her. Then, without slavishly following Lessing's plot, rewrite the story from the woman's **point of view.** Consider composing your piece in the form of a personal letter (to a recipient of your own imagining), a series of diary entries, or a **dialogue** between the woman and a friend.

3. Examine Stanley's interactions with Mrs. Pritchett, a woman whom he *likes.* How do these interactions differ from those he has with the woman on the roof, and how might this difference account for his divergent feelings about the two women?

4. Imagine that, after seeing the woman on the roof for the second or third time, Stanley describes her behavior to his wife of three months. In what setting or situation does Stanley broach the subject? What are his unspoken thoughts, feelings, or words?
   a. Create the conversation between wife and husband.
   b. Share your dialogue with the class or a small group.
   c. After hearing the dialogues, write a reaction to your own or someone else's dialogue. What did you hear that surprised you? What do you now understand that you did not when you first read the story?

5. Stanley and Tom react to the woman differently. Stanley feels rage toward her, while we are told that Tom feels a "bond between the woman and himself" (paragraph 32). Discuss the differences in their reactions. Is Tom (a) "better" or "kinder" than Stanley, (b) simply different from Stanley, or (c) really no different from Stanley? Support your analysis with illustrative examples and quotations from the story.

RAY BRADBURY (b. 1920)

[A Story About Love]

And out there in the middle of the first day of August, just getting into his car, 1
was Bill Forrester, who shouted he was going downtown for some extraordinary ice cream or other and would anyone join him? So, not five minutes later,

jiggled and steamed into a better mood, Douglas found himself stepping in off the fiery pavements and moving through the grotto of soda-scented air, of vanilla freshness at the drugstore, to sit at the snow-marble fountain with Bill Forrester. They then asked for a recital of the most unusual ices and when the fountain man said, "Old fashioned lime-vanilla ice . . ."

"That's it!" said Bill Forrester.   2

"Yes, sir!" said Douglas.   3

And, while waiting, they turned slowly on their rotating stools. The silver 4 spigots, the gleaming mirrors, the hushed whirl-around ceiling fans, the green shades over the small windows, the harp-wire chairs, passed under their moving gaze. They stopped turning. Their eyes had touched upon the face and form of Miss Helen Loomis, ninety-five years old, ice-cream spoon in hand, ice cream in mouth.

"Young man," she said to Bill Forrester, "you are a person of taste and imagi- 5 nation. Also, you have the will power of ten men; otherwise you would not dare veer away from the common flavors listed on the menu and order, straight out, without quibble or reservation, such an unheard-of thing as lime-vanilla ice."

He bowed his head solemnly to her.   6

"Come sit with me, both of you," she said. "We'll talk of strange ice creams 7 and such things as we seem to have a bent for. Don't be afraid; I'll foot the bill."

Smiling, they carried their dishes to her table and sat.   8

"You look like a Spaulding," she said to the boy. "You've got your grandfa- 9 ther's head. And you, you're William Forrester. You write for the *Chronicle,* a good enough column. I've heard more about you than I'd care to tell."

"I know you," said Bill Forrester. "You're Helen Loomis." He hesitated, then 10 continued. "I was in love with you once," he said.

"Now that's the way I like a conversation to open." She dug quietly at her ice 11 cream. "That's grounds for another meeting. No—don't tell me where or when or how you were in love with me. We'll save that for next time. You've taken away my appetite with your talk. Look there now! Well, I must get home anyway. Since you're a reporter, come for tea tomorrow between three and four; it's just possible I can sketch out the history of this town, since it was a trading post, for you. And, so we'll both have something for our curiosity to chew on, Mr. Forrester, you remind me of a gentleman I went with seventy, yes, seventy years ago."

She sat across from them and it was like talking with a gray and lost quiver- 12 ing moth. The voice came from far away inside the grayness and the oldness, wrapped in the powders of pressed flowers and ancient butterflies.

"Well." She arose. "Will you come tomorrow?"   13

"I most certainly will," said Bill Forrester.   14

And she went off into the town on business, leaving the young boy and the 15 young man there, looking after her, slowly finishing their ice cream.

———————

William Forrester spent the next morning checking some local news items 16 for the paper, had time after lunch for some fishing in the river outside town,

caught only some small fish which he threw back happily, and, without thinking about it, or at least not noticing that he had thought about it, at three
o'clock he found his car taking him down a certain street. He watched with interest as his hands turned the steering wheel and motored him up a vast circular
drive where he stopped under an ivy-covered entry. Letting himself out, he was
conscious of the fact that his car was like his pipe—old, chewed-on, unkempt
in this huge green garden by this freshly painted, three-story Victorian house.
He saw a faint ghostlike movement at the far end of the garden, heard a whis-
pery cry, and saw that Miss Loomis was there, removed across time and distance, seated alone, the tea service glittering its soft silver surfaces, waiting for
him.

"This is the first time a woman has ever been ready and waiting," he said, 17
walking up. "It is also," he admitted, "the first time in my life I have been on
time for an appointment."

"Why is that?" she asked, propped back in her wicker chair. 18

"I don't know," he admitted. 19

"Well." She started pouring tea. "To start things off, what do you think of 20
the world?"

"I don't know anything." 21

"The beginning of wisdom, as they say. When you're seventeen you know 22
everything. When you're *twenty*-seven if you *still* know everything you're still
seventeen."

"You seem to have learned quite a lot over the years." 23

"It is the privilege of old people to seem to know everything. But it's an act 24
and a mask, like every other act and mask. Between ourselves, we old ones wink
at each other and smile, saying, How do you like *my* mask, *my* act, *my* certainty?
Isn't life a play? Don't I play it well?"

They both laughed quietly. He sat back and let the laughter come naturally 25
from his mouth for the first time in many months. When they quieted she held
her teacup in her two hands and looked into it. "Do you know, it's lucky we met
so late. I wouldn't have wanted you to meet me when I was twenty-one and full
of foolishness."

"They have special laws for pretty girls twenty-one." 26

"So you think I was pretty?" 27

He nodded good-humoredly. 28

"But how can you tell?" she asked. "When you meet a dragon that has eaten 29
a swan, do you guess by the few feathers left around the mouth? That's what it
is—a body like this is a dragon, all scales and folds. So the dragon ate the white
swan. I haven't seen her for years. I can't even remember what she looks like. I
feel her, though. She's safe inside, still alive; the essential swan hasn't changed a
feather. Do you know, there are some mornings in spring or fall, when I wake
and think, I'll run across the fields into the woods and pick wild strawberries!
Or I'll swim in the lake, or I'll dance all night tonight until dawn! And then, in a
rage, discover I'm in this old and ruined dragon. I'm the princess in the crum-
bled tower, no way out, waiting for her Prince Charming."

"You should have written books."   30

"My dear boy, I *have* written. What else was there for an old maid? I was a 31
crazy creature with a headful of carnival spangles until I was thirty, and then
the only man I ever really cared for stopped waiting and married someone else.
So in spite, in anger at myself, I told myself I deserved my fate for not having
married when the best chance was at hand. I started traveling. My luggage was
snowed under blizzards of travel stickers. I have been alone in Paris, alone in
Vienna, alone in London, and, all in all, it is very much like being alone in
Green Town, Illinois. It is, in essence, being alone. Oh, you have plenty of time
to think, improve your manners, sharpen your conversations. But I sometimes
think I could easily trade a verb tense or a curtsy for some company that would
stay over for a thirty-year weekend."

They drank their tea.   32

"Oh, such a rush of self-pity," she said good-naturedly. "About yourself, 33
now. You're thirty-one and still not married?"

"Let me put it this way," he said. "Women who act and think and talk like 34
you are rare."

"My," she said seriously, "you mustn't expect young women to talk like me. 35
That comes later. They're much too young, first of all. And secondly, the average man runs helter-skelter the moment he finds anything like a brain in a lady.
You've probably met quite a few brainy ones who hid it most successfully from
you. You'll have to pry around a bit to find the odd beetle. Lift a few boards."

They were laughing again.   36

"I shall probably be a meticulous old bachelor," he said.   37

"No, no, you mustn't do that. It wouldn't be right. You shouldn't even be 38
here this afternoon. This is a street which ends only in an Egyptian pyramid.
Pyramids are all very nice, but mummies are hardly fit companions. Where
would you like to go, what would you really like to do with your life?"

"See Istanbul, Port Said, Nairobi, Budapest. Write a book. Smoke too many 39
cigarettes. Fall off a cliff, but get caught in a tree halfway down. Get shot at a few
times in a dark alley on a Moroccan midnight. Love a beautiful woman."

"Well, I don't think I can provide them all," she said. "But I've traveled and I 40
can tell you about many of those places. And if you'd care to run across my
front lawn tonight about eleven and if I'm still awake, I'll fire off a Civil War
musket at you. Will that satisfy your masculine urge for adventure?"

"That would be just fine."   41

"Where would you like to go first? I can take you there, you know. I can 42
weave a spell. Just name it. London? Cairo? Cairo makes your face turn on like a
light. So let's go to Cairo. Just relax now. Put some of that nice tobacco in that
pipe of yours and sit back."

He sat back, lit his pipe, half smiling, relaxing, and listened, and she began 43
to talk. "Cairo . . ." she said.

———

The hour passed in jewels and alleys and winds from the Egyptian desert.   44
The sun was golden and the Nile was muddy where it lapped down to the
deltas, and there was someone very young and very quick at the top of the pyramid, laughing, calling to him to come on up the shadowy side into the sun, and
he was climbing, she putting her hand down to help him up the last step, and
then they were laughing on camel back, loping toward the great stretched bulk
of the Sphinx, and late at night, in the native quarter, there was the tinkle of
small hammers on bronze and silver, and music from some stringed instruments fading away and away and away. . . .

William Forrester opened his eyes. Miss Helen Loomis had finished the ad-   45
venture and they were home again, very familiar to each other, on the best of
terms, in the garden, the tea cold in the silver pourer, the biscuits dried in the
latened sun. He sighed and stretched and sighed again.

"I've never been so comfortable in my life."   46

"Nor I."   47

"I've kept you late, I should have gone an hour ago."   48

"You know I love every minute of it. But what you should see in an old silly   49
woman . . ."

He lay back in his chair and half closed his eyes and looked at her. He   50
squinted his eyes so the merest filament of light came through. He tilted his
head ever so little this way, then that.

"What are you doing?" she asked uncomfortably.   51

He said nothing, but continued looking.   52

"If you do this just right," he murmured, "you can adjust, make al-   53
lowances. . . ." To himself he was thinking, You can erase lines, adjust the time
factor, turn back the years.

Suddenly he started.   54

"What's wrong?" she asked.   55

But then it was gone. He opened his eyes to catch it. That was a mistake. He   56
should have stayed back, idling, erasing, his eyes gently half closed.

"For just a moment," he said, "I saw it."   57

"Saw what?"   58

"The swan, of course," he thought. His mouth must have pantomimed the   59
words.

The next instant she was sitting very straight in her chair. Her hands were in   60
her lap, rigid. Her eyes were fixed upon him and as he watched, feeling helpless,
each of her eyes cupped and brimmed itself full.

"I'm sorry," he said, "terribly sorry."   61

"No, don't be." She held herself rigid and did not touch her face or her eyes;   62
her hands remained, one atop the other, holding on. "You'd better go now. Yes,
you may come tomorrow, but go now, please, and don't say any more."

He walked off through the garden, leaving her by her table in the shade. He 63
could not bring himself to look back.

———————

Four days, eight days, twelve days passed, and he was invited to teas, to sup- 64
pers, to lunches. They sat talking through the long green afternoons—they
talked of art, of literature, of life, of society and politics. They ate ice creams
and squabs and drank good wines.

"I don't care what anyone says," she said. "And people are saying things, 65
aren't they?"

He shifted uneasily.   66

"I knew it. A woman's never safe, even when ninety-five, from gossip."   67

"I could stop visiting."   68

"Oh, no," she cried, and recovered. In a quieter voice she said, "You know 69
you can't do that. You know you don't care what they think, do you? So long as
we know it's all right?"

"I don't care," he said.   70

"Now"—she settled back—"let's play our game. Where shall it be this time? 71
Paris? I think Paris."

"Paris," he said, nodding quietly.   72

"Well," she began, "it's the year 1885 and we're boarding the ship in New 73
York harbor. There's our luggage, here are our tickets, there goes the sky line.
Now we're at sea. Now we're coming into Marseilles. . . ."

Here she was on a bridge looking into the clear waters of the Seine, and here 74
he was, suddenly, a moment later, beside her, looking down at the tides of summer flowing past. Here she was with an apéritif in her talcum-white fingers,
and here he was, with amazing quickness, bending toward her to tap her wineglass with his. His face appeared in mirrored halls at Versailles, over steaming
smörgasbörds in Stockholm, and they counted the barber poles in the Venice
canals. The things she had done alone, they were now doing together.

———————

In the middle of August they sat staring at one another one late afternoon. 75

"Do you realize," he said, "I've seen you nearly every day for two and a half 76
weeks?"

"Impossible!"   77

"I've enjoyed it immensely."   78

"Yes, but there are so many young girls . . ."   79

"You're everything they are not—kind, intelligent, witty."   80

"Nonsense. Kindness and intelligence are the preoccupations of age. Being 81
cruel and thoughtless is far more fascinating when you're twenty." She paused
and drew a breath. "Now, I'm going to embarrass you. Do you recall that first
afternoon we met in the soda fountain, you said that you had had some degree
of—shall we say affection for me at one time? You've purposely put me off on

this by never mentioning it again. Now I'm forced to ask you to explain the whole uncomfortable thing."

He didn't seem to know what to say. "That's embarrassing," he protested.   82

"Spit it out!"   83

"I saw your picture once, years ago."   84

"I never let my picture be taken."   85

"This was an old one, taken when you were twenty."   86

"Oh, that. It's quite a joke. Each time I give to a charity or attend a ball they   87
dust that picture off and print it. Everyone in town laughs; even *I*."

"It's cruel of the paper."   88

"No. I told them, If you want a picture of me, use the one taken back in   89
1853. Let them remember me that way. Keep the lid down, in the name of the good Lord, during the service."

"I'll tell you all about it." He folded his hands and looked at them and   90
paused a moment. He was remembering the picture now and it was very clear in his mind. There was time, here in the garden to think of every aspect of the photograph and of Helen Loomis, very young, posing for her picture the first time, alone and beautiful. He thought of her quiet, shyly smiling face.

It was the face of spring, it was the face of summer, it was the warmness of   91
clover breath. Pomegranate glowed in her lips, and the noon sky in her eyes. To touch her face was that always new experience of opening your window one December morning, early, and putting out your hand to the first white cool powdering of snow that had come, silently, with no announcement, in the night. And all of this, this breath-warmness and plum-tenderness was held forever in one miracle of photographic chemistry which no clock winds could blow upon to change one hour or one second; this fine first cool white snow would never melt, but live a thousand summers.

That was the photograph; that was the way he knew her. Now he was talking   92
again, after the remembering and the thinking over and the holding of the picture in his mind. "When I first saw that picture—it was a simple, straightforward picture with a simple hairdo—I didn't know it had been taken that long ago. The item in the paper said something about Helen Loomis marshalling the Town Ball that night. I tore the picture from the paper. I carried it with me all that day. I intended going to the ball. Then, late in the afternoon, someone saw me looking at the picture, and told me about it. How the picture of the beautiful girl had been taken so long ago and used every year since by the paper. And they said I shouldn't go to the Town Ball that night, carrying that picture and looking for you."

They sat in the garden for a long minute. He glanced over at her face. She   93
was looking at the farthest garden wall and the pink roses climbing there. There was no way to tell what she was thinking. Her face showed nothing. She rocked for a little while in her chair and then said softly, "Shall we have some more tea? There you are."

They sat sipping the tea. Then she reached over and patted his arm. "Thank   94
you."

"For what?"   95

"For wanting to come to find me at the dance, for clipping out my picture, 96
for everything. Thank you so very much."

They walked about the garden on the paths.   97

"And now," she said, "it's my turn. Do you remember, I mentioned a certain 98
young man who once attended me, seventy years ago? Oh, he's been dead fifty
years now, at least, but when he was very young and very handsome he rode a
fast horse off for days, or on summer nights over the meadows around town.
He had a healthy, wild face, always sunburned, his hands were always cut and he
fumed like a stovepipe and walked as if he were going to fly apart; wouldn't
keep a job, quit those he had when he felt like it, and one day he sort of rode off
away from me because I was even wilder than he and wouldn't settle down, and
that was that. I never thought the day would come when I would see him alive
again. But you're pretty much alive, you spill ashes around like he did, you're
clumsy and graceful combined, I know everything you're going to do before
you do it, but after you've done it I'm always surprised. Reincarnation's a lot of
milk-mush to me, but the other day I felt, What if I called Robert, Robert, to
you on the street, would William Forrester turn around?"

"I don't know," he said.   99

"Neither do I. That's what makes life interesting."   100

August was almost over. The first cool touch of autumn moved slowly 101
through the town and there was a softening and the first gradual burning fever
of color in every tree, a faint flush and coloring in the hills, and the color of lions in the wheat fields. Now the pattern of days was familiar and repeated like a
penman beautifully inscribing again and again, in practice, a series of *l*'s and
w's and *m*'s, day after day the line repeated in delicate rills.

William Forrester walked across the garden one early August afternoon to 102
find Helen Loomis writing with great care at the tea table.

She put aside her pen and ink.   103

"I've been writing you a letter," she said.   104

"Well, my being here saves you the trouble."   105

"No, this is a special letter. Look at it." She showed him the blue envelope, 106
which she now sealed and pressed flat. "Remember how it looks. When you receive this in the mail, you'll know I'm dead."

"That's no way to talk, is it?"   107

"Sit down and listen to me."   108

He sat.   109

"My dear William," she said, under the parasol shade. "In a few days I will be 110
dead. No." She put up her hand. "I don't want you to say a thing. I'm not afraid.
When you live as long as I've lived you lose that, too. I never liked lobster in my
life, and mainly because I'd never tried it. On my eightieth birthday I tried it. I
can't say I'm greatly excited over lobster still, but I have no doubt as to its taste

now, and I don't fear it. I dare say death will be a lobster, too, and I can come to terms with it." She motioned with her hands. "But enough of that. The important thing is that I shan't be seeing you again. There will be no services. I believe that a woman who has passed through that particular door has as much right to privacy as a woman who has retired for the night."

"You can't predict death," he said at last.   111

"For fifty years I've watched the grandfather clock in the hall, William. After 112 it is wound I can predict to the hour when it will stop. Old people are no different. They can feel the machinery slow down and the last weights shift. Oh, please don't look that way—please don't."

"I can't help it," he said.   113

"We've had a nice time, haven't we? It has been very special here, talking 114 every day. It was that much-overburdened and worn phrase referred to as a 'meeting of the minds.'" She turned the blue envelope in her hands. "I've always known that the quality of love was the mind, even though the body sometimes refuses this knowledge. The body lives for itself. It lives only to feed and wait for the night. It's essentially nocturnal. But what of the mind which is born of the sun, William, and must spend thousands of hours of a lifetime awake and aware? Can you balance off the body, that pitiful, selfish thing of night against a whole lifetime of sun and intellect? I don't know. I only know there has been your mind here and my mind here, and the afternoons have been like none I can remember. There is still so much to talk about, but we must save it for another time."

"We don't seem to have much time now."   115

"No, but perhaps there *will* be another time. Time is so strange and life is 116 twice as strange. The cogs miss, the wheels turn, and lives interlace too early or too late. I lived too long that much is certain. And you were born either too early or too late. It was a terrible bit of timing. But perhaps I am being punished for being a silly girl. Anyway, the next spin around, wheels might function right again. Meantime you must find a nice girl and be married and be happy. But you must promise me one thing."

"Anything."   117

"You must promise me not to live to be too old, William. If it is at all conve- 118 nient, die before you're fifty. It may take a bit of doing. But I advise this simply because there is no telling when another Helen Loomis might be born. It would be dreadful, wouldn't it, if you lived on to be very, very old and some afternoon in 1999 walked down Main Street and saw me standing there, aged twenty-one, and the whole thing out of balance again? I don't think we could go through any more afternoons like these we've had, no matter how pleasant, do you? A thousand gallons of tea and five hundred biscuits is enough for one friendship. So you must have an attack of pneumonia some time in about twenty years. For I don't know how long they let you linger on the other side. Perhaps they send you back immediately. But I shall do my best, William, really I shall. And everything put right and in balance, do you know what might happen?"

"You tell me."   119

"Some afternoon in 1985 or 1990 a young man named Tom Smith or John   120
Green or a name like that, will be walking downtown and will stop in the drugstore and order, appropriately, a dish of some unusual ice cream. A young girl
the same age will be sitting there and when she hears the name of that ice cream,
something will happen. I can't say what or how. *She* won't know why or how, as-
suredly. Nor will the young man. It will simply be that the name of that ice
cream will be a very good thing to both of them. They'll talk. And later, when
they know each other's names, they'll walk from the drugstore together."

She smiled at him.   121

"This is all very neat, but forgive an old lady for tying things in neat packets.   122
It's a silly trifle to leave you. Now let's talk of something else. What shall we talk
about? Is there any place in the world we haven't traveled to yet? Have we been
to Stockholm?"

"Yes, it's a fine town."   123

"Glasgow? Yes? Where then?"   124

"Why not Green Town, Illinois?" he said. "Here. We haven't really visited   125
our own town together at all."

She settled back, as did he, and she said, "I'll tell you how it was, then, when   126
I was only nineteen, in this town, a long time ago. . . ."

It was a night in winter and she was skating lightly over a pond of white   127
moon ice, her image gliding and whispering under her. It was a night in summer in this town of fire in the air, in the cheeks, in the heart, your eyes full of
the glowing and shutting-off color of fireflies. It was a rustling night in October, and there she stood, pulling taffy from a hook in the kitchen, singing, and
there she was, running on the moss by the river, and swimming in the granite
pit beyond town on a spring night, in the soft deep warm waters, and now it
was the Fourth of July with rockets slamming the sky and every porch full of
now red-fire, now blue-fire, now white-fire faces, hers dazzling bright among
them as the last rocket died.

"Can you see all these things?" asked Helen Loomis. "Can you see me doing   128
them and being with them?"

"Yes," said William Forrester, eyes closed. "I can see you."   129

"And then," she said, "and then . . ."   130

Her voice moved on and on as the afternoon grew late and the twilight   131
deepened quickly, but her voice moved in the garden and anyone passing on the
road, at a far distance, could have heard its moth sound, faintly, faintly. . . .

―――――――

Two days later William Forrester was at his desk in his room when the letter   132
came. Douglas brought it upstairs and handed it to Bill and looked as if he
knew what was in it.

William Forrester recognized the blue envelope, but did not open it. He   133
simply put it in his shirt pocket, looked at the boy for a moment, and said,
"Come on, Doug; my treat."

They walked downtown, saying very little, Douglas preserving the silence he 134
sensed was necessary. Autumn, which had threatened for a time, was gone.
Summer was back full, boiling the clouds and scouring the metal sky. They
turned in at the drugstore and sat at the marble fountain. William Forrester
took the letter out and laid it before him and still did not open it.

He looked out at the yellow sunlight on the concrete and on the green 135
awnings and shining on the gold letters of the window signs across the street,
and he looked at the calendar on the wall. August 27, 1928. He looked at his
wrist watch and felt his heart beat slowly, saw the second hand of the watch
moving moving with no speed at all, saw the calendar frozen there with its one
day seeming forever, the sun nailed to the sky with no motion toward sunset
whatever. The warm air spread under the sighing fans over his head. A number
of women laughed by the open door and were gone through his vision, which
was focused beyond them at the town itself and the high courthouse clock. He
opened the letter and began to read.

He turned slowly on the revolving chair. He tried the words again and again, 136
silently, on his tongue, and at last spoke them aloud and repeated them.

"A dish of lime-vanilla ice," he said. "A dish of lime-vanilla ice." 137

ACTIVITIES FOR WRITING AND DISCUSSION

1. Respond to the story using the "Four-Step Process for Writing from
Reading" described in Chapter 2.

2. Describe the love that binds Bill and Helen together. Is it physical? spiritual? social? emotional? intellectual? all or some of the above? which? Elaborate
with examples from the text.

3. Reflecting the perspective of ninety-five years of life, Helen's conversation is marvelously witty and perceptive. Annotate any remarks by her that
strike you. Then, in your notebook, reflect on these remarks.

4. Bill and Helen fantasize themselves to be together in various exotic
places around the globe. Imagine that, through a wrinkle in time, a young
William meets a young Helen. What happens? What sort of relationship do
they form? How does this relationship evolve over the next ten, twenty, or fifty
years?

5. The **setting** of the story is memorable: the 1920s, summertime, a small
average town in Middle America. Write a story or memoir of your own in
which you emphasize the setting (whether pleasant or unpleasant), describing
time and place in vivid and evocative terms.

Gabriel Garcia Márquez (b. 1928)

Death Constant Beyond Love

Senator Onésimo Sánchez had six months and eleven days to go before his 1 death when he found the woman of his life. He met her in Rosal del Virrey, an illusory village which by night was the furtive wharf for smugglers' ships, and on the other hand, in broad daylight looked like the most useless inlet on the desert, facing a sea that was arid and without direction and so far from everything no one would have suspected that someone capable of changing the destiny of anyone lived there. Even its name was a kind of joke, because the only rose in that village was being worn by Senator Onésimo Sánchez himself on the same afternoon when he met Laura Farina.

It was an unavoidable stop in the electoral campaign he made every four 2 years. The carnival wagons had arrived in the morning. Then came the trucks with the rented Indians who were carried into the towns in order to enlarge the crowds at public ceremonies. A short time before eleven o'clock, along with the music and rockets and jeeps of the retinue, the ministerial automobile, the color of strawberry soda, arrived. Senator Onésimo Sánchez was placid and weatherless inside the air-conditioned car, but as soon as he opened the door he was shaken by a gust of fire and his shirt of pure silk was soaked in a kind of light-colored soup and he felt many years older and more alone than ever. In real life he had just turned forty-two, had been graduated from Göttingen with honors as a metallurgical engineer, and was an avid reader, although without much reward, of badly translated Latin classics. He was married to a radiant German woman who had given him five children and they were all happy in their home, he the happiest of all until they told him, three months before, that he would be dead forever by next Christmas.

While the preparations for the public rally were being completed, the sena- 3 tor managed to have an hour alone in the house they had set aside for him to rest in. Before he lay down he put in a glass of drinking water the rose he had kept alive all across the desert, lunched on the diet cereals that he took with him so as to avoid the repeated portions of fried goat that were waiting for him during the rest of the day, and he took several analgesic pills before the time prescribed so that he would have the remedy ahead of the pain. Then he put the electric fan close to the hammock and stretched out naked for fifteen minutes in the shadow of the rose, making a great effort at mental distraction so as not to think about death while he dozed. Except for the doctors, no one knew that he had been sentenced to a fixed term, for he had decided to endure his secret all alone, with no change in his life, not because of pride but out of shame.

He felt in full control of his will when he appeared in public again at three 4 in the afternoon, rested and clean, wearing a pair of coarse linen slacks and a floral shirt, and with his soul sustained by the anti-pain pills. Nevertheless, the erosion of death was much more pernicious than he had supposed, for as he went up onto the platform he felt a strange disdain for those who were fighting for the good luck to shake his hand, and he didn't feel sorry as he had at other times for the groups of barefoot Indians who could scarcely bear the hot salt-peter coals of the sterile little square. He silenced the applause with a wave of his hand, almost with rage, and he began to speak without gestures, his eyes fixed on the sea, which was sighing with heat. His measured, deep voice had the quality of calm water, but the speech that had been memorized and ground out so many times had not occurred to him in the nature of telling the truth, but, rather, as the opposite of a fatalistic pronouncement by Marcus Aurelius in the fourth book of his *Meditations*.

"We are here for the purpose of defeating nature," he began, against all his convictions. "We will no longer be foundlings in our own country, orphans of God in a realm of thirst and bad climate, exiles in our own land. We will be different people, ladies and gentlemen, we will be a great and happy people." 5

There was a pattern to his circus. As he spoke his aides threw clusters of paper birds into the air and the artificial creatures took on life, flew about the platform of planks, and went out to sea. At the same time, other men took some prop trees with felt leaves out of the wagons and planted them in the saltpeter soil behind the crowd. They finished by setting up a cardboard façade with make-believe houses of red brick that had glass windows, and with it they covered the miserable real-life shacks. 6

The senator prolonged his speech with two quotations in Latin in order to give the farce more time. He promised rain-making machines, portable breeders for table animals, the oils of happiness which would make vegetables grow in the saltpeter and clumps of pansies in the window boxes. When he saw that his fictional world was all set up, he pointed to it. "That's the way it will be for us, ladies and gentlemen," he shouted. "Look! That's the way it will be for us." 7

The audience turned around. An ocean liner made of painted paper was passing behind the houses and it was taller than the tallest houses in the artificial city. Only the senator himself noticed that since it had been set up and taken down and carried from one place to another the superimposed cardboard town had been eaten away by the terrible climate and that it was almost as poor and dusty as Rosal del Virrey. 8

For the first time in twelve years, Nelson Farina didn't go to greet the senator. He listened to the speech from his hammock amidst the remains of his siesta, under the cool bower of a house of unplaned boards which he had built with the same pharmacist's hands with which he had drawn and quartered his first wife. He had escaped from Devil's Island and appeared in Rosal del Virrey on a ship loaded with innocent macaws, with a beautiful and blasphemous black woman he had found in Paramaribo and by whom he had a daughter. The woman died of natural causes a short while later and she didn't suffer the fate of the other, whose pieces had fertilized her own cauliflower patch, but was buried whole and with her Dutch name in the local cemetery. The daughter had 9 inherited her color and her figure along with her father's yellow and astonished eyes, and he had good reason to imagine that he was rearing the most beautiful woman in the world.

Ever since he had met Senator Onésimo Sánchez during his first electoral 10 campaign, Nelson Farina had begged for his help in getting a false identity card which would place him beyond the reach of the law. The senator, in a friendly but firm way, had refused. Nelson Farina never gave up, and for several years, every time he found the chance, he would repeat his request with a different recourse. But this time he stayed in his hammock, condemned to rot alive in that burning den of buccaneers. When he heard the final applause, he lifted his head, and looking over the boards of the fence, he saw the back side of the farce: the props for the buildings, the framework of the trees, the hidden illusionists who were pushing the ocean liner along. He spat without rancor.

"*Merde*," he said, "*C'est le Blacamán de la politique.*"   11

After the speech, as was customary, the senator took a walk through the 12 streets of the town in the midst of the music and the rockets and was besieged by the townspeople, who told him their troubles. The senator listened to them good-naturedly and he always found some way to console everybody without having to do them any difficult favors. A woman up on the roof of a house with her six youngest children managed to make herself heard over the uproar and the fireworks.

"I'm not asking for much, Senator," she said. "Just a donkey to haul water 13 from Hanged Man's Well."

The senator noticed the six thin children. "What became of your husband?" 14 he asked.

"He went to find his fortune on the island of Aruba," the woman answered 15 good-humoredly, "and what he found was a foreign woman, the kind that puts diamonds on their teeth."

The answer brought on a roar of laughter.   16

"All right," the senator decided, "you'll get your donkey."   17

A short while later an aide of his brought a good pack donkey to the 18 woman's house and on the rump it had a campaign slogan written in indelible paint so that no one would ever forget that it was a gift from the senator.

Along the short stretch of street he made other, smaller gestures, and he 19 even gave a spoonful of medicine to a sick man who had had his bed brought to the door of his house so he could see him pass. At the last corner, through the boards of the fence, he saw Nelson Farina in his hammock, looking ashen and gloomy, but nonetheless the senator greeted him, with no show of affection.

"Hello, how are you?"   20

Nelson Farina turned in his hammock and soaked him in the sad amber of 21 his look.

"*Moi, vous savez,*" he said.   22

His daughter came out into the yard when she heard the greeting. She was 23 wearing a cheap, faded Guajiro Indian robe, her head was decorated with colored bows, and her face was painted as protection against the sun, but even in that state of disrepair it was possible to imagine that there had never been another so beautiful in the whole world. The senator was left breathless. "I'll be damned!" he breathed in surprise. "The Lord does the craziest things!"

That night Nelson Farina dressed his daughter up in her best clothes and 24 sent her to the senator. Two guards armed with rifles who were nodding from the heat in the borrowed house ordered her to wait on the only chair in the vestibule.

The senator was in the next room meeting with the important people of 25 Rosal del Virrey, whom he had gathered together in order to sing for them the truths he had left out of his speeches. They looked so much like all the ones he always met in all the towns in the desert that even the senator himself was sick and tired of that perpetual nightly session. His shirt was soaked with sweat and he was trying to dry it on his body with the hot breeze from an electric fan that was buzzing like a horse fly in the heavy heat of the room.

"We, of course, can't eat paper birds," he said. "You and I know that the day 26 there are trees and flowers in this heap of goat dung, the day there are shad instead of worms in the water holes, that day neither you nor I will have anything to do here, do I make myself clear?"

No one answered. While he was speaking, the senator had torn a sheet off 27 the calendar and fashioned a paper butterfly out of it with his hands. He tossed it with no particular aim into the air current coming from the fan and the butterfly flew about the room and then went out through the half-open door. The senator went on speaking with a control aided by the complicity of death.

"Therefore," he said, "I don't have to repeat to you what you already know 28 too well: that my reelection is a better piece of business for you than it is for me, because I'm fed up with stagnant water and Indian sweat, while you people, on the other hand, make your living from it."

Laura Farina saw the paper butterfly come out. Only she saw it because the 29 guards in the vestibule had fallen asleep on the steps, hugging their rifles. After a few turns, the large lithographed butterfly unfolded completely, flattened against the wall, and remained stuck there. Laura Farina tried to pull it off with her nails. One of the guards, who woke up with the applause from the next room, noticed her vain attempt.

"It won't come off," he said sleepily. "It's printed on the wall." 30

Laura Farina sat down again when the men began to come out of the meet- 31 ing. The senator stood in the doorway of the room with his hand on the latch, and he only noticed Laura Farina when the vestibule was empty.

"What are you doing here?" 32

"*C'est de la part de mon père*," she said. 33

The senator understood. He scrutinized the sleeping guards, then he scruti- 34 nized Laura Farina, whose unusual beauty was even more demanding than his pain, and he resolved then that death had made his decision for him.

"Come in," he told her. 35

Laura Farina was struck dumb standing in the doorway to the room: thou- 36 sands of bank notes were floating in the air, flapping like the butterfly. But the senator turned off the fan and the bills were left without air and alighted on the objects in the room.

"You see," he said, smiling, "even shit can fly." 37

Laura Farina sat down on a schoolboy's stool. Her skin was smooth and 38 firm, with the same color and the same solar density as crude oil, her hair was the mane of a young mare, and her huge eyes were brighter than the light. The senator followed the thread of her look and finally found the rose, which had been tarnished by the saltpeter.

"It's a rose," he said. 39

"Yes," she said with a trace of perplexity. "I learned what they were in Rio- 40 hacha."

The senator sat down on an army cot, talking about roses as he unbuttoned 41 his shirt. On the side where he imagined his heart to be inside his chest he had a corsair's tattoo of a heart pierced by an arrow. He threw the soaked shirt to the floor and asked Laura Farina to help him off with his boots.

She knelt down facing the cot. The senator continued to scrutinize her, 42 thoughtfully, and while she was untying the laces he wondered which one of them would end up with the bad luck of that encounter.

"You're just a child," he said. 43

"Don't you believe it," she said. "I'll be nineteen in April." 44

The senator became interested. 45

"What day?" 46

"The eleventh," she said. 47

The senator felt better. "We're both Aries," he said. And smiling, he added: 48

"It's the sign of solitude." 49

Laura Farina wasn't paying attention because she didn't know what to do 50 with the boots. The senator, for his part, didn't know what to do with Laura Farina, because he wasn't used to sudden love affairs and, besides, he knew that the one at hand had its origins in indignity. Just to have some time to think, he held Laura Farina tightly between his knees, embraced her about the waist, and lay down on his back on the cot. Then he realized that she was naked under her dress, for her body gave off the dark fragrance of an animal of the woods, but her heart was frightened and her skin disturbed by a glacial sweat.

"No one loves us," he sighed. 51

Laura Farina tried to say something, but there was only enough air for her 52 to breathe. He laid her down beside him to help her, he put out the light and the room was in the shadow of the rose. She abandoned herself to the mercies of her fate. The senator caressed her slowly, seeking her with his hand, barely touching her, but where he expected to find her, he came across something iron that was in the way.

"What have you got there?" 53

"A padlock," she said. 54

"What in hell!" the senator said furiously and asked what he knew only too 55 well. "Where's the key?"

Laura Farina gave a breath of relief. 56

"My papa has it," she answered. "He told me to tell you to send one of your 57
people to get it and to send along with him a written promise that you'll
straighten out his situation."

The senator grew tense. "Frog bastard," he murmured indignantly. Then he 58
closed his eyes in order to relax and he met himself in the darkness. *Remember,*
he remembered, *that whether it's you or someone else, it won't be long before
you'll be dead and it won't be long before your name won't even be left.*

He waited for the shudder to pass.   59

"Tell me one thing," he asked then. "What have you heard about me?"   60

"Do you want the honest-to-God truth?"   61

"The honest-to-God-truth."   62

"Well," Laura Farina ventured, "they say you're worse than the rest because 63
you're different."

The senator didn't get upset. He remained silent for a long time with his   64
eyes closed, and when he opened them again he seemed to have returned from
his most hidden instincts.

"Oh, what the hell," he decided. "Tell your son of a bitch of a father that I'll 65
straighten out his situation."

"If you want, I can go get the key myself," Laura Farina said.   66

The senator held her back.   67

"Forget about the key," he said, "and sleep awhile with me. It's good to be 68
with someone when you're so alone."

Then she laid his head on her shoulder with her eyes fixed on the rose. The 69
senator held her about the waist, sank his face into woods-animal armpit, and
gave in to terror. Six months and eleven days later he would die in that same position, debased and repudiated because of the public scandal with Laura Farina
and weeping with rage at dying without her.

—*Translated by Gregory Rabassa*

CLAIRE KEMP (b. 1936)

Keeping Company

William wakes me with water. He sprays me through the window screen and I 1
am introduced to morning under tangled sheets, sprinkled damp and rolled
like laundry ready for the iron. He's whistling. When he sings, "Lazy Mary, will
you get up?", I do and go outside in my nightdress to stand barefoot on the cool
wet cement close to William. "Hello, wife," he says.

Two men walking to the beach smile and wave a hand in greeting. I raise my 2
hand to wave to them but William checks me with a look. He aims the hose at
the street but the pressure is down and the water falls short. "Missed by a mile,"
he says. "I'm losing my touch."

"They're not bothering anyone. What do you care?"   3

"They're bothering me and I care." A small muscle in his cheek keeps an angry beat.   4

"You'll be late for work," I tell him and run inside to make his eggs, soft boiled on white toast.   5

"Never happen," he says. The hose, a fat green snake, uncoils and follows obediently wherever he walks.   6

———

Mornings I go to the beach. I go alone because William won't. Certain young men come to stroll on this beach. Their walk is a slow dance, graceful and sure. They glide on pewter sand like skaters do on ice. In their brief suits, satin bands of azure blue, magenta, yellow, emerald green, they appear as exotic flowers blooming in the desert. I am taken with their beauty and don't mind sitting in their shade. Not unkindly they dismiss me with their eyes, unencumbered souls walking free at water's edge with perhaps a scarlet towel over one tanned shoulder or a small cloth bag worn around the neck to hold the treasures of the moment. They have smiles for each other but not for me. I'm a cabbage in their garden, a woman large with child, a different species altogether. Next year, I'll have someone to keep me company. I'll teach her how to make castles with turrets from paper cups and wet sand. Swizzle sticks will make a fine bridge to span the moat. Perhaps we'll place cocktail parasols for color in the sand palace courtyard. And I'll take her home before the tide comes in to take it down. She's with me now, tumbling and turning in her water bed and dancing on my ribs with tiny heels and toes. She's coming to term and letting me know. It won't be long.   7

Afternoons I tend my flowers. Today, I see an open truck parked next door. And a piano on the porch. Two men are discussing how to get it through the door. One goes inside to pull; the other stays out to push. I think of the piano as a stubborn horse, its mahogany rump splendid in the sun. "Perhaps, if you offer it sugar," I suggest. The outside man grins. "Hello," he says and vaults over his porch rail. I brush potting soil from my hands and reach to shake his hand.   8

"I'm James," he says. His eyes are gray blue and direct. When he smiles his features merge brightly like a photograph in focus. He has a good face. He says, "Dennis is inside. He might come out or he might not. He's shy." Behind him, someone parts the lace curtain at one window and lets it fall.   9

I tell James my name and he says, "It's nice to meet you, Nora. Your flowers are lovely." But he's not looking at my flowers. Just at me. He nods in affirmation of some private thought and says, "Moving's more work than I bargained for. I'd better get back to it."   10

"Yes, see you again" I reply and bend to the task of breaking off the blooms gone by. The aroma of geranium is so strong it seems to leave a taste on my tongue. When I go inside to make myself a cup of tea, the piano has made it through the door and there is no one in sight.   11

After dinner, I tell William we have neighbors and he tells me he's not blind. He uncaps a beer and tilts the bottle to his lips. He wipes foam from his beard   12 with the back of his hand and gives me a long look I'm meant to pay attention to. "Don't bother with them, Nora. They're not our kind." From next door I hear a tentative chord or two. I listen for more but the night air is still, not another note. I listen for sounds from their house over the sounds of our house all evening long. I don't know why I would. After a while the heat leaves the house and it's cool enough for sleep and still I listen.

James brings me a croissant sprinkled with cinnamon and sugar. I put down 13 my watering can and take it from his hand. Dennis is practicing scales and I remember how it felt to play, my eyes on the page, not on the keys.

"What are you hoping for?" James asks shyly. 14

"It's a girl. We already know. Doctors can tell in advance now. We've named 15 her Sara."

"Imagine," he says but his eyes are worried as if he marvels at giving credi- 16 bility to someone who can't yet breathe on her own. "She's like a present, as yet unwrapped," he says. Abruptly the music stops. I picture Dennis closing the piano, covering the keys and going to another part of his house.

"Dennis is tired," James explains. He has already turned from me toward the 17 silence and I am left holding the still warm pastry in one hand and nothing in the other.

I hang the wash, William's work shirts, dish cloths and towels, heavy sheets 18 that pull on my arms. Next door, James and Dennis talking, always talking. Their voices rise and fall and blend together. They have so much to say. They never seem to tire of talk. Their screen door opens and shuts throughout the day as they come and go. When they are out of each other's sight, one calls out and the other answers.

Late in the day, I take in the dry clothes, stripping the line and folding as I go 19 along, leaving the clothespins to bob like small wooden birds. Dennis and James head for the beach. Dennis wears a light jacket zipped to the neck as if he is cold. His short sandy hair curls up around his cap, leaving the back of his neck bare, like a young boy's. I can tell James would walk faster if he was alone. Perhaps he would run. As it is, he holds back to keep the pace that Dennis sets but his energy shows itself in the enthusiastic swing of his arms and the quick, attentive way he inclines his head to catch the words that Dennis speaks. When they're out of sight beyond the dunes, I go inside to wait for William.

James is teaching me backgammon. We sit on his patio under the Cinzano 20 umbrella and drink iced tea with lemon slices on the rim of tall oddly shaped amber glasses, no two alike. Dennis will not play but once he points out a move for me and seems quietly pleased when I take that game from James. I do not tell William where I spend my summer afternoons. I'm where I belong when he gets home. He slides his arms around me and rubs my face with his beard and says proudly, "Nora, I swear, you're as big as a house." "I am," I agree, laughing. "I'm Sara's house." He does not ask me what I do all day and I would not tell him if he did. I know something about myself that I didn't know before. I'm successful at sins of omission, never really lying, never telling truth. I hoard secrets like a dog who buries bones to relish at some future time. I wonder if when that time comes, I will remember why or where I dug the holes.

William comes home early, tires spinning in the sand on the lane between 21 our house and theirs. I'm caught and stand up fast from James' table and hurry home leaving James in the middle of a play.

"I don't want you over there," William tells me. "Is that clear?"   22

"But why? They're good company."   23

"They can keep each other company. Not you. I'm your good company. The 24 only company you'll ever need."

William sighs when he looks at me as though I'm a chore he must complete. 25

Dennis gives a concert in my honor, all my favorite pieces played perfect, 26 without flaw or fault. I sit on my front step as evening falls to dark and listen till he's done.

William is building a wall. To make certain he's within his rights, he engages 27 a surveyor to determine the exact boundaries of our land. After supper and on Saturdays he works on his wall. There are guidelines he must follow as to height. I know if permitted he would make it six feet high, five inches taller than the top of my head, but the law won't allow it. Its purpose is to keep me in my place. When he's done, he calls me out to admire his work and I do. I tell him it's a fine wall which is what he wants to hear. James, on his porch, raises his glass in a silent toast. I send him my best smile, an apology big enough for both William and myself.

William has gone south to deliver a boat and won't be home before mid- 28 night at least. James invites me for dinner. I'm invited, so I go. Their kitchen is yellow and blue, quaint, like a woman's sitting room. There are many plants I can't begin to name in clay pots and hanging baskets. I sit on paisley cushions in a wicker chair by the window watching James make stew from scratch. While James chops vegetables, his hand on the knife making quick, precise cuts, Dennis copies the recipe in his spidery script on a card for me to take home. I set the table, lace cloth from Ireland, tall rose colored candles in crystal, linen napkins in shell rings and sterling silver by the plates. James holds my chair and seats me as if I am a lady and not a country girl in faded shorts and one of William's shirts. Dennis searches the yard for hibiscus blooms. He floats them in a shallow blue bowl for a centerpiece. I have gone over the wall.

Unlike Cinderella, I'm home well before midnight in my own kitchen, with 29
a bowl of stew for William over a low flame on my stove. He eats out of the pan.
"What are these yellow things?" he asks, poking with his fork.

"Parsnips."   30

"OK," he says. "Next time peas. Otherwise, not bad at all."   31

I let him think I made the stew myself which of course I could have done. 32
And maybe will someday. The recipe is out of sight in the bottom of my sewing box.

We are in a tropical depression. Hot steady rain for a week and thick humid 33
air that leaves me worn out and sleepy. I stay inside, an idle woman, changing in
spite of myself like a mushroom growing at a furious rate in this damp and fertile season. We lose our power and Dennis brings candles. He hands the bag to
William and runs off without a proper thank you. William hands it quick to me
as if its contents are not candles but sticks of dynamite that could go off at any
minute. He follows me like the tail of a kite as I place lighted candles on waxed
saucers in each room of our house. "The wall is holding," he says. "Can you believe it?" I say, "Yes, I believe it."

In September, Sara will be born.   34

When the storms give in to sun I'm glad, but it reigns in the sky like a lion. 35
Its heat is fierce. I have not seen Dennis or James. The piano does not play. I
knock on their door and finally James is there behind the screen. He doesn't lift
the latch. I say, "How are you? I miss you two." "Not to worry," he assures me
without meeting my eyes. When I ask for Dennis, James shrugs as if Dennis is
someone he's lost track of somehow and can't be bothered getting back, which I
know for sure is not the truth. He laughs then, a short harsh sound like a bark.
"Sorry," he says. "Dennis is in the hospital. I don't know that he'll be coming
home." He says this like he's asking a question, like he's asking me for an answer.
I put my hand on my side of the screen and James touches it briefly with his. We
stand for a moment, like visitors in prison before he closes the inside door and
shuts me out. I wish I could take back the days.

I go home where I belong. There is laundry to fold, chores to do, an entire 36
house to put to order. I do a proper job of every task, a proper penance. Before
bed, I tell William. I know as I begin to speak that it will not go well but I'm
bound to tell it, to lay it out like a soiled cloth on our clean table.

"Dennis is sick," I say and at just that moment I know that this truth is an- 37
other bone I buried.

William says, "Yes, he is. Very sick. Have you been over there again? I told 38
you to stay away from them. I warned you. But, knowing you. . . ."

"You don't."   39

"Don't what?"   40

"Know me." I stand up. There is a knot of sorrow that drops in me like a 41
sinker in a tidal pool. I walk out the door and away from William. At the jetty, I
climb the slick black rocks, heedless of the cruel pockets of stone that could
snap a limb as easy as not. I find a smooth stone that makes a good seat. I'm
surprised to know I'm crying. Our porch light comes on and there is William,

his pale hair like a halo under its glow. He calls me. "Nora, come home," but the tide takes his voice and swallows my name. When I'm thoroughly chilled and empty of anger, I leave my perch and travel north on the wet sand, close to the cool fingers of incoming tide. I'm a small but competent ship sailing the coast line. I set my own course. I hear someone running in my wake and it's William, breathless from the chase. He passes me on fast feet, then turns, dancing backward like a boxer until I stop just shy of the circle of his arms. He carries my sweater, which he puts around my shoulders with great care, as if it is a precious fur he wraps me in and I too am precious. He buttons one button under my chin with clumsy fingers. "Let's go back," he says, so we do. We do not talk about anything, simply walk forward in silence, which is the way it is between husbands and wives, with married people.

Poems

Wu-Ti (464–549)

People Hide Their Love

Who says that it's by my desire,
This separation, this living so far from you?
My dress still smells of the perfume that you wore;
My hand still holds the letter that you sent.
Round my waist I wear a double sash;   5
I dream that it binds us both with a same-heart knot.
Did you know that people hide their love,
Like a flower that seems too precious to be picked?s

Po-Chu-I (ninth century)

Rejoicing at the Arrival of Ch'ên Hsiung

When the yellow bird's note was almost stopped,
And half formed the green plum's fruit—
Sitting and grieving that spring things were over,
I rose and entered the Eastern Garden's gate.
I carried my cup and was dully drinking alone;   5
Suddenly I heard a knocking sound at the door.
Dwelling secluded, I was glad that someone had come;
How much the more, when I saw it was Ch'ên Hsiung!
At ease and leisure—all day we talked;

Crowding and jostling—the feelings of many years.   10
How great a thing is a single cup of wine!
For it makes us tell the story of our whole lives.

WILLIAM SHAKESPEARE (1564–1616)

Sonnet 18

Shall I compare thee to a summer's day?[1]
Thou art more lovely and more temperate:[2]
Rough winds do shake the darling buds of May,
And summer's lease[3] hath all too short a date;[4]
Sometime too hot the eye of heaven shines,   5
And often is his gold complexion dimm'd,
And every fair from fair[5] sometime declines,
By chance or nature's changing course untrimm'd:[6]
But thy eternal summer shall not fade,
Nor lose possession of that fair thou ow'st,[7]   10
Nor shall Death brag thou wand'rest in his shade,
When in eternal lines to time thou grow'st.[8]
     So long as men can breathe or eyes can see,
     So long lives this, and this gives life to thee.

WALT WHITMAN (1819–1892)

I Heard You Solemn-Sweet Pipes of the Organ

I heard you solemn-sweet pipes of the organ as last Sunday morn I pass'd the
     church,
Winds of autumn, as I walk'd the woods at dusk I heard your long-stretch'd
     sighs up above so mournful,
I heard the perfect Italian tenor singing at the opera, I heard the soprano in the
     midst of the quartet singing;
Heart of my love! you too I heard murmuring low through one of the wrists
     around my head,
Heard the pulse of you when all was still ringing little bells last night under   5
     my ear.

---

1. a summer's day: i.e. the summer season.
2. temperate: of even temperature.
3. lease: allotted time.
4. date: duration.
5. fair . . . fair: beautiful thing . . . beauty.
6. untrimm'd: divested of beauty.
7. ow'st: ownest.
8. to . . . grow'st: you become inseparably engrafted upon time.

I Saw in Louisiana a Live-Oak Growing

I saw in Louisiana a live-oak growing,
All alone stood it and the moss hung down from the branches,
Without any companion it grew there uttering joyous leaves of dark green,
And its look, rude, unbending, lusty, made me think of myself,
But I wonder'd how it could utter joyous leaves standing alone there without   5
    its friend near, for I knew I could not,
And I broke off a twig with a certain number of leaves upon it, and twined
    around it a little moss,
And brought it away, and I have placed it in sight in my room,
It is not needed to remind me as of my own dear friends,
(For I believe lately I think of little else than of them,)
Yet it remains to me a curious token, it makes me think of manly love;   10
For all that, and though the live-oak glistens there in Louisiana solitary in a
    wide flat space,
Uttering joyous leaves all its life without a friend a lover near,
I know very well I could not.

ACTIVITIES FOR WRITING AND DISCUSSION

1. It has been said that no verse is entirely "free" (that is, without verbal or rhythmic patterning of some sort). What sorts of patterning does Whitman use to replace the **rhyme** and **meter** of **traditional verse**? To answer this question, begin by making a list of everything that strikes you in "I Heard You Solemn-Sweet Pipes of the Organ" and "I Saw in Louisiana a Live-Oak Growing": words and phrases, images, and feelings. Then review the poems and identify the pattern(s). Finally, consider how Whitman's type of pattern supplants traditional rhyme and meter.

2. Whitman believed that the function of a poem is to impel readers along individual paths of thought and growth. Thus he wrote that a poem "is no finish to a man or woman" and that "the reader . . . must himself or herself construct indeed the poem . . . the text furnishing the hints, the clue, the start or frame-work." Taking the poet at his word, treat "I Heard You Solemn-Sweet Pipes of the Organ" or "I Saw in Louisiana a Live-Oak Growing" as a "start" to some reflective or imaginative writing of your own. For instance:

    a. Use either poem as a pathway to meditation. Begin by memorizing the poem, reciting it to yourself, and living with it a while. Keep a written record of any thoughts or feelings that occur to you as a result of this process.

    b. Write a poem of your own that employs the long and flowing lines of "I Heard You Solemn-Sweet Pipes of the Organ" and "I Saw in Louisiana a Live-Oak Growing." Afterward reflect on what was challenging about imitating Whitman's style.

3. Though each poem contains several independent clauses, each poem is punctuated as a single sentence. How would the effect of either poem be changed if more terminal punctuation, e.g., periods, were added (for instance, periods could be inserted at the ends of lines 1,2, and 4 in "I Saw in Louisiana a Live-Oak Growing")?

EMILY DICKINSON (1830–1886)

Wild Nights—Wild Nights!

Wild Nights—Wild Nights!
Were I with thee
Wild Nights should be
Our luxury!

Futile—the Winds—   5
To a Heart in port—
Done with the Compass—
Done with the Chart!

Rowing in Eden—
Ah, the Sea!   10
Might I but moor—Tonight—
In Thee!

CHRISTINA ROSSETTI (1830–1894)

Margery

What shall we do with Margery?
    She lies and cries upon her bed,
    All lily-pale from foot to head,
Her heart is sore as sore can be;
Poor guileless shamefaced Margery.   5

A foolish girl, to love a man
    And let him know she loved him so!
She should have tried a different plan;
    Have loved, but not have let him know:
    Then he perhaps had loved her so.   10

What can we do with Margery
   Who has no relish for her food?
We'd take her with us to the sea—
   Across the sea—but where's the good?
She'd fret alike on land and sea.   15

Yes, what the neighbours say is true:
   Girls should not make themselves so cheap.
But now it's done what can we do?
   I hear her moaning in her sleep.
   Moaning and sobbing in her sleep.   20

I think—and I'm of flesh and blood—
   Were I that man for whom she cares
   I would not cost her tears and prayers
To leave her just alone like mud,
   Fretting her simple heart with cares.   25

A year ago she was a child,
   Now she's a woman in her grief;
   The year's now at the falling leaf,
At budding of the leaves she smiled;
Poor foolish harmless foolish child.   30

It was her own fault? so it was.
   If every own fault found us out
   Dogged us and snared us round about,
What comfort should we take because
   Not half our due we thus wrung out?   35

At any rate the question stands:
   What now to do with Margery,
A weak poor creature on our hands?
   Something we must do: I'll not see
   Her blossom fade, sweet Margery.   40

Perhaps a change may after all
   Prove best for her: to leave behind
   Those home-sights seen time out of mind;
To get beyond the narrow wall
Of home, and learn home is not all.   45

Perhaps this way she may forget,
   Not all at once, but in a while;
May come to wonder how she set

Her heart on this slight thing, and smile
At her own folly, in a while.   50

Yet this I say and I maintain:
    Were I the man she's fretting for
    I should my very self abhor
If I could leave her to her pain,
Uncomforted to tears and pain.   55

THOMAS HARDY (1840–1928)

At Tea

The kettle descants in a cosy drone,
And the young wife looks in her husband's face,
And then at her guest's, and shows in her own
Her sense that she fills an envied place;
And the visiting lady is all abloom,   5
And says there was never so sweet a room.

And the happy young housewife does not know
That the woman beside her was first his choice,
Till the fates ordained it could not be so. . . .
Betraying nothing in look or voice   10
The guest sits smiling and sips her tea,
And he throws her a stray glance yearningly.

In the Room of the Bride-Elect

"Would it had been the man of our wish!"
Sighs her mother. To whom with vehemence she
In the wedding-dress—the wife to be—
"Then why were you so mollyish
As not to insist on him for me!"   5
The mother, amazed: "Why, dearest one,
Because you pleaded for this or none!"

"But Father and you should have stood out strong!
Since then, to my cost, I have lived to find
That you were right and that I was wrong;   10
This man is a dolt to the one declined. . . .
Ah!—here he comes with his button-hole rose.
Good God—I must marry him I suppose!"

Outside the Window

"My stick!" he says, and turns in the lane
To the house just left, whence a vixen voice
Comes out with the firelight through the pane,
And he sees within that the girl of his choice
Stands rating her mother with eyes aglare   5
For something said while he was there.

"At last I behold her soul undraped!"
Thinks the man who had loved her more than himself;
"My God—'tis but narrowly I have escaped.—
My precious porcelain proves it delf."   10
His face has reddened like one ashamed,
And he steals off, leaving his stick unclaimed.

ACTIVITIES FOR WRITING AND DISCUSSION

1. Hardy originally published "At Tea," "In the Room of the Bride-Elect," and "Outside the Window" in a collection entitled *Satires of Circumstance*. "Satire" is related to **irony** and refers to "A literary work that attacks human vice or folly through irony, derision, or wit" (*American Heritage College Dictionary*). Describe the "circumstance" depicted in each poem and what makes the circumstance satiric or ironic.

2. Each poem suggests a miniature story or drama complete with the elements of **characters, conflict, dialogue** (actual or implied), **setting,** and the hint at least of a **plot.** Choose one of the poems and reread and annotate it, paying close attention to each of these elements. Then either:
   a. Recast the poem as a story in prose or a short play;
      or
   b. Respond to the poem using one of the "Ten Ideas for Writing" that are described in Chapter 3 and summarized on page 35.

3. Draft an essay in which you draw some conclusions about the nature of marriage as portrayed in these three poems.

EZRA POUND (1885–1972)

The River-merchant's Wife: A Letter

While my hair was still cut straight across my forehead
Played I about the front gate, pulling flowers.

You came by on bamboo stilts, playing horse,
You walked about my seat, playing with blue plums.
And we went on living in the village of Chōkan: 5
Two small people, without dislike or suspicion.

At fourteen I married My Lord you.
I never laughed, being bashful.
Lowering my head, I looked at the wall.
Called to, a thousand times, I never looked back.   10

At fifteen I stopped scowling,
I desired my dust to be mingled with yours
Forever and forever and forever.
Why should I climb the look out?

At sixteen you departed,   15
You went into far Ku-tō-en, by the river of swirling eddies,
And you have been gone five months.
The monkeys make sorrowful noise overhead.

You dragged your feet when you went out.
By the gate now, the moss is grown, the different mosses,   20
Too deep to clear them away!
The leaves fall early this autumn, in wind.
The paired butterflies are already yellow with August
Over the grass in the West garden;
They hurt me. I grow older.   25
If you are coming down through the narrows of the river Kiang,
Please let me know beforehand,
And I will come out to meet you
          As far as Chō-fū-Sa.

                              —*By Rihaku (Li T'ai Po)*

ROBERT BLY (b. 1926)

In Rainy September

In rainy September, when leaves grow down to the dark,
I put my forehead down to the damp, seaweed-smelling sand.
The time has come. I have put off choosing for years,
perhaps whole lives. The fern has no choice but to live;
for this crime it receives earth, water, and night.   5

We close the door. "I have no claim on you."
Dusk comes. "The love I have had with you is enough."
We know we could live apart from one another.
The sheldrake floats apart from the flock.
The oaktree puts out leaves alone on the lonely hillside.   10

Men and women before us have accomplished this.
I would see you, and you me, once a year.
We would be two kernels, and not be planted.
We stay in the room, door closed, lights out.
I weep with you without shame and without honor.   15

ADRIENNE RICH (b. 1929)

Living in Sin

She had thought the studio would keep itself;
no dust upon the furniture of love.
Half heresy, to wish the taps less vocal,
the panes relieved of grime. A plate of pears,
a piano with a Persian shawl, a cat   5
stalking the picturesque amusing mouse
had risen at his urging.
Not that at five each separate stair would writhe
under the milkman's tramp; that morning light
so coldly would delineate the scraps   10
of last night's cheese and three sepulchral bottles;
that on the kitchen shelf among the saucers
a pair of beetle-eyes would fix her own—
envoy from some village in the moldings . . .
Meanwhile, he, with a yawn,   15
sounded a dozen notes upon the keyboard,
declared it out of tune, shrugged at the mirror,
rubbed at his beard, went out for cigarettes;
while she, jeered by the minor demons,
pulled back the sheets and made the bed and found   20
a towel to dust the table-top,
and let the coffee-pot boil over on the stove.
By evening she was back in love again,
though not so wholly but throughout the night
she woke sometimes to feel the daylight coming   25
like a relentless milkman up the stairs.

Aunt Jennifer's Tigers

Aunt Jennifer's tigers prance across a screen,
Bright topaz denizens of a world of green.
They do not fear the men beneath the tree;
They pace in sleek chivalric certainty.

Aunt Jennifer's fingers fluttering through her wool   5
Find even the ivory needle hard to pull.
The massive weight of Uncle's wedding band
Sits heavily upon Aunt Jennifer's hand.

When Aunt is dead, her terrified hands will lie
Still ringed with ordeals she was mastered by.   10
The tigers in the panel that she made
Will go on prancing, proud and unafraid.

Tomioka Taeko (b. 1935)

Just the Two of Us

You'll make tea,
I'll make toast.
While we're doing that,
at times, early in the evening,
someone may notice the moonrise dyed scarlet   5
and at times visit us
but that'll be the last time the person comes here.
We'll shut the doors, lock them,
make tea, make toast,
talk as usual about how   10
sooner or later
there will be a time
you bury me,
and I bury you, in the garden,
and go out as usual to look for food.   15
There will be a time
either you or I
bury either me or you in the garden
and the one left, sipping tea,
then for the first time, will refuse fiction.   20

Even your freedom
was like a fool's story.

—*Translated by Burton Watson and Hiroaki Sato*

ACTIVITIES FOR WRITING AND DISCUSSION

1. Who are the "you" and the "I" in "Just the Two of Us"? How would you characterize their relationship? their lives?

2. Underline or circle any words or phrases that are repeated in the poem. Why are they repeated, and to what effect?

3. What is the "fiction" referred to in line 20? In the context of this poem, is living by "fiction" a virtue or a weakness? How do you interpret the last two lines?

4. Using details in the poem and your own imagination, tell the story of a typical day in the lives of this couple, or, writing from the **point of view** of the surviving partner, narrate the events of the day on which one partner dies.

DIANE WAKOSKI (b. 1937)

Belly Dancer

Can these movements which move themselves
be the substance of my attraction?
Where does this thin green silk come from that covers my body?
Surely any woman wearing such fabrics
would move her body just to feel them touching every part of her.   5

Yet most of the women frown, or look away, or laugh stiffly.
They are afraid of these materials and these movements in some way.
The psychologists would say they are afraid of themselves, somehow.
Perhaps awakening too much desire—
that their men could never satisfy?   10

So they keep themselves laced and buttoned and made up
in hopes that the framework will keep them stiff enough not to feel
the whole register.
In hopes that they will not have to experience that unquenchable desire
for rhythm and contact.   15

If a snake glided across this floor
most of them would faint or shrink away.
Yet that movement could be their own.
That smooth movement frightens them—
awakening ancestors and relatives to the tips of the arms and toes.   20

So my bare feet
and my thin green silks
my bells and finger cymbals
offend them—frighten their old-young bodies.
While the men simper and leer—   25
glad for the vicarious experience and exercise.
They do not realize how I scorn them:
or how I dance for their frightened,
unawakened, sweet
women.   30

ACTIVITIES FOR WRITING AND DISCUSSION

1. Circle any lines, images, or other features that make "Belly Dancer" sensual. What senses (other than sight) are evoked? In which lines and phrases? To what effect(s)?

2. In lines 16–18 the **speaker** imagines the movement of "a snake" and suggests that the women both fear it (they "would faint or shrink away") and desire it ("that movement could be their own"). How do you explain this apparent contradiction?

3. Imagine you are a woman in the dancer's audience. Borrowing details from the poem and writing in a **stream of consciousness** mode, express the emotions and conflicts you have as you watch the dancer dance.

4. As an alternative to Activity #3, imagine yourself to be an audience member of a different sexual orientation, or disabled, or of a different cultural/racial identity. From any of these **points of view,** what do you celebrate or denounce in what you see? What voices from your culture do you hear influencing your voice and the content of your writing?

SHARON OLDS (b. 1942)

Sex Without Love

How do they do it, the ones who make love
without love? Beautiful as dancers,
gliding over each other like ice-skaters
over the ice, fingers hooked
inside each other's bodies, faces   5
red as steak, wine, wet as the
children at birth whose mothers are going to
give them away. How do they come to the
come to the   come to the   God   come to the
still waters, and not love   10
the one who came there with them, light
rising slowly as steam off their joined
skin? These are the true religious,
the purists, the pros, the ones who will not
accept a false Messiah, love the   15
priest instead of the God. They do not
mistake the lover for their own pleasure,
they are like great runners: they know they are alone
with the road surface, the cold, the wind,
the fit of their shoes, their over-all cardio-   20
vascular health—just factors, like the partner
in the bed, and not the truth, which is the
single body alone in the universe
against its own best time.

LIZ ROSENBERG (b. 1958)

In the End, We Are All Light

I love how old men carry purses for their wives,
those stiff light beige or navy wedge-shaped bags
that match the women's pumps,
with small gold clasps that click open and shut.
The men drowse off in medical center waiting rooms,   5
with bags perched in their laps like big tame birds
too worn to flap away. Within, the wives slowly undress,
put on the thin white robes, consult, come out
and wake the husbands dreaming openmouthed.

And when they both rise up   10
to take their constitutional,
walk up and down the block, her arms are free as air,
his right hand dangles down.

So I, desiring to shed this skin
for some light silken one,   15
will tell my husband, "Here, hold this,"
and watch him amble off into the mall among the shining
cans of motor oil, my leather bag
slung over his massive shoulder bone,
so prettily slender-waisted, so forgiving of the ways   20
we hold each other down, that watching him
I see how men love women, and women men,
and how the burden of the other comes to be
light as a feather blown, more quickly vanishing.

ACTIVITIES FOR WRITING AND DISCUSSION

1. Underline images in "In the End, We Are All Light" that strike you. In your notebook, react to one or two of these images by doing some writing or by drawing a realistic or cartoon picture based on the image(s). What sorts of feelings do the images evoke in you? How would you describe the relationship that is suggested between the "old men"/husbands and their wives?

2. How would the poem change if the "old men" were replaced by "young men" with young wives? Does the poem imply any differences between "old" couples and young? If so, what differences?

3. Interpret the last several lines. How or why *does* "the burden of the other [come] to be/light as a feather blown"?

Nonfiction/Essays

FRANCINE DU PLESSIX GRAY (b. 1930)

On Friendship

I saw Madame Bovary[1] at Bloomingdale's the other morning, or rather, I saw   1
many incarnations of her. She was hovering over the cosmetic counters, clutching the current issue of *Cosmopolitan,* whose cover line read "New Styles of
Coupling, Including Marriage." Her face already ablaze with numerous products advertised to make her irresistible to the opposite sex, she looked anguished, grasping, overwrought, and terribly lonely. And I thought to myself:
Poor girl! With all the reams of literature that have analyzed her plight (victimized by double standards, by a materialistic middle-class glutting on the excess
of romantic fiction), notwithstanding all these diagnoses, one fact central to
her tragic fate has never been stressed enough: Emma Bovary had a faithful and
boring husband and a couple of boring lovers—not so intolerable a condition—but she did not have a friend in the world. And when I think of the great
solitude which the original Emma and her contemporaries exude, one phrase
jumps to my mind. It comes from an essay by Francis Bacon, and it is one of the
finest statements ever penned about the human need for friendship: "Those
who have no friends to open themselves unto are cannibals of their own
hearts."

   In the past years the theme of friendship has been increasingly prominent   2
in our conversations, in our books and films, even in our college courses. It is
evident that many of us are yearning with new fervor for this form of bonding.
And our yearning may well be triggered by the same disillusionment with the
reign of Eros that destroyed Emma Bovary. Emma was eating her heart out over
a fantasy totally singular to the Western world, and only a century old at that:
the notion that sexual union between men and women who believe that they
are passionately in love, a union achieved by free choice and legalized by marriage, tends to offer a life of perpetual bliss and is the most desirable human
bond available on earth. It is a notion bred in the same frenzied climate of the
romantic epoch that caused countless young Europeans to act like the characters of their contemporary literature. Goethe's *Werther* is said to have triggered
hundreds of suicides. Numerous wives glutted on the fantasies of George
Sand's heroines demanded separations because their husbands were unpoetic.
And Emma Bovary, palpitating from that romantic fiction which precurses our
current sex manuals in its outlandish hopes for the satiation of desire, muses in

---

1. Title character in the novel by Gustave Flaubert (1821–1880)

the third week of her marriage: Where is "the felicity, the passion, the intoxication" that had so enchanted her in the novels of Sir Walter Scott?

This frenzied myth of love which has also led to the downfall of Cleopatra, 3 Juliet, Romeo, and King Kong continues to breed, in our time, more garbled thinking, wretched verse, and nonsensical jingles than any emotion under the sun: "All You Need Is Love," or as we heard it in our high-school days. "Tell me you'll love me forever, if only tonight." As Flaubert put it, we are all victims of romanticism. And if we still take for granted its cult of heterosexual passion, it is in part because we have been victimized, as Emma was, by the propaganda machine of the Western novel. It was the power and the genius of the novel form to fuse medieval notions of courtly love with the idealization of marriage that marked the rise of the eighteenth-century middle class. (By "romantic love," I mean an infatuation that involves two major ingredients: a sense of being "enchanted" by another person through a complex process of illusion, and a willingness to totally surrender to that person.)

One hardly needs a course in anthropology to realize that this alliance of 4 marriage and romantic love is restricted to a small segment of the Western world, and would seem sheer folly in most areas of this planet. The great majority of humans—be it in China, Japan, Africa, India, the Moslem nations—still engage in marriages prearranged by their elders or dictated by pragmatic reasons of money, land, tribal politics, or (as in the Socialist countries) housing shortages. Romantically motivated marriage as the central ingredient of the good life is almost as novel in our own West. In popular practice, it remained restricted to a narrow segment of the middle class until the twentieth century. And on the level of philosophical reflection, it was always friendship between members of the same sex, never any bonding of sexual affection, which from Greek times to the Enlightenment was held to be the cornerstone of human happiness. Yet this central role allotted to friendship for two thousand years has been progressively eroded by such factors as the nineteenth-century exaltation of instinct; science's monopoly on our theories of human sentiment; the massive eroticizing of society; and that twentieth-century celebration of the body that reaches its peak in the hedonistic solitude of the multiple orgasm.

To Aristotle, friendship can be formed only by persons of virtue: a man's ca- 5 pacity for friendship is the most accurate measure of his virtue; it is the foundation of the state, for great legislators care even more for friendship than they care for justice. To Plato, as we know, passionate affection untainted by physical relations is the highest form of human bonding. To Cicero, *Amicitia* is more important than either money, power, honors, or health because each of these gifts can bring us only one form of pleasure, whereas the pleasures of friendship are marvelously manifold; and friendship being based on equity, the tyrant is the man least capable of forming that bond because of his need to wield power over others. Montaigne's essay, along with Bacon's, is the most famous of many that glorify our theme in the Renaissance. And like the ancients, he stresses the advantages of friendship over any kind of romantic and physical attachment. Love for members of the opposite sex, in Montaigne's words, is "an impetuous and fickle flame, undulating and variable, a fever flame subject to fits and lulls." Whereas the fire of friendship produces "a general and universal warmth, moderate and even," and will always forge bonds superior to those of marriage because marriage's continuace is "constrained and forced, depending on factors other than our free will."

A century later, even La Rouchefoucauld, that great cynic who described the 6 imperialism of the ego better than any other precursor of Freud, finds that friendship is the only human bond in which the tyrannical cycle of our self-love seems broken, in which "we can love each other even more than love ourselves." One of the last classic essays on friendship I can think of before it loses major importance as a philosophical theme is by Ralph Waldo Emerson. And it's interesting to note that by mid-nineteenth century, the euphoric absolutes which had previously described this from of bonding are sobered by many cautious qualifications. A tinge of modern pragmatism sets in. Emerson tends to distrust any personal friendship unless it functions for the purpose of some greater universal fraternity.

Yet however differently these thinkers focused on our theme, they all 7 seemed to reach a consensus on the qualities of free will, equity, trust, and selflessness unique to the affection of friendship. They cannot resist comparing it to physical passion, which yearns for power over the other, seeks possession and the state of being possessed, seeks to devour, breeds on excess, can easily become demonic, is closely allied to the death wish, and is often a form of agitated narcissism quite unknown to the tranquil, balanced rule of friendship. And rereading the sagas of Tristan and Iseult, Madame Bovary, and many other romantic lovers, it is evident that their passions tend to breed as much on a masturbatory excitement as on a longing for the beloved. They are in love with love, their delirium is involved with a desire for self-magnification through suffering, as evidenced in Tristan's words, "Eyes with joy are blinded. I myself am the world." There is confrontation, turmoil, aggression, in the often militaristic language of romantic love: Archers shoot fatal arrows or unerring shafts; the male enemy presses, pursues, and conquers; women surrender after being besieged by amorous assaults. Friendship on the other hand is the most pacifist species in the fauna of human emotions, the most steadfast and sharing. No wonder then that the finest pacifist ideology in the West was devised by a religious group—the Quakers—which takes as its official name the Religious Society of Friends; the same temperate principle of fraternal bonding informs that vow demanded by the Benedictine Order—the Oath of Stability—which remains central to the monastic tradition to this day. No wonder, also, that the kind of passionate friendship shared by David and Jonathan has inspired very few masterpieces of literature, which seem to thrive on tension and illicitness. For until they were relegated to the dissecting rooms of the social sciences, our literary views of friendship tended to be expressed in the essay form, a cool, reflective mode that never provided friendship with the motive, democratic, propagandistic force found by Eros in novel, verse, and stage. To this day, friendship totally resists commercial exploitation, unlike the vast businesses fueled by romantic love that support the couture, perfume, cosmetic, lingerie, and pulp-fiction trades.

One should note, however, that most views of friendship expressed in the 8 past twenty centuries of Western thought have dealt primarily with the male's capacity for affection. And they tend to be extremely dubious about the possibility of women ever being able to enjoy genuine friendships with members of their own sex, not to speak of making friends with male peers. Montaigne expressed a prejudice that lasts well into our day when he wrote, "The ordinary capacity of women is inadequate for that communion and fellowship which is the nurse of that sacred bond, nor does their soul feel firm enough to endure the strain of so tight and durable a knot." It is shocking, though not surprising, to hear prominent social scientists paraphrase that opinion in our own decades. Konrad Lorenz and Lionel Tiger, for instance, seem to agree that women are made eminently unsociable by their genetic programming; their bondings, in Lorenz's words, "must be considered weak imitations of the exclusively male associations." Given the current vogue for sociobiology, such assertions are often supported by carefully researched papers on the courtship patterns of Siberian wolves, the prevalence of eye contact among male baboons, and the vogue for gangbanging among chimpanzees.

Our everyday language reflects the same bias: "Fraternity" is a word that 9 goes far beyond its collegiate context and embraces notions of honor, dignity, loyalty. "Sorority" is something we might have belonged to as members of the University of Oklahoma's bowling team in the early 1950s. So I think it is high time that the same feminist perspective that has begun to correct the biases of art history and psychoanalysis should be brought to bear on this area of anthropology. We have indeed been deprived of those official, dramatically visible rites offered to men in pub, poolroom, Elks, hunting ground, or football league. And having been brought up in a very male world, I'm ashamed to say it took me a decade of feminist consciousness to realize that the few bonding associations left to twentieth century women—garden clubs, church suppers, sewing circles (often derided by men because they do not deal with power)—have been activities considerably more creative and life-enhancing than the competition of the poolroom, the machismo of beer drinking, or the bloodshed of hunting.

Among both sexes, the rites and gestures of friendship seemed to have been 10 decimated in the Victorian era, which brought a fear of homosexuality unprecedented in the West. (They also tended to decrease as rites of heterosexual coupling became increasingly permissive). Were Dr. Johnson and James Boswell gay, those two men who constantly exhibited their affection for each other with kisses, tears, and passionate embraces? I suspect they were as rabidly straight as those tough old soldiers described by Tacitus begging for last kisses when their legion broke up. Since Freud, science has tended to dichotomize human affection along lines of deviance and normalcy, genitality and platonic love, instead of leaving it as a graduated spectrum of emotion in which love, friendship, sensuality, sexuality, can freely flow into each other as they did in the past. This may be another facet of modern culture that has cast coolness and self-consciousness on our gestures of friendship. The 1960s brought us some hope for change, both in its general emotional climate and in our scientists' tendency to relax their definitions of normalcy and deviance. For one of the most beautiful signs of that decade's renewed yearning for friendship and community, particularly evident among the groups who marched in civil-rights or anti-war demonstrations, was the sight of men clutching, kissing, embracing each other unabashedly as Dr. Johnson and James Boswell.

Which leads me to reflect on the reasons why I increasingly turn to friend- 11 ship in my own life: In a world more and more polluted by the lying of politicians and the illusions of the media, I occasionally crave to hear and to tell the truth. To borrow a beautiful phrase from Friedrich Nietzsche, I look upon my friend as "the beautiful enemy" who alone is able to offer me total candor. I look for the kind of honest friend Emma Bovary needed: one who could have told her that her lover was a jerk.

Friendship is by its very nature freer of deceit than any other relationship 12 we can know because it is the bond least affected by striving for power, physical pleasure, or material profit, most liberated from any oath of duty or of constancy. With Eros the *body* stands naked, in friendship our *spirit* is denuded. Friendship, in this sense, is a human condition resembling what may be humanity's most beautiful and necessary lie—the promise of an afterlife. It is an almost celestial sphere in which we most resemble that society of angels offered us by Christian theology, in which we can sing the truth of our inner thoughts in relative freedom and abundance. No wonder then that the last contemporary writers whose essays on friendship may remain classics are those religiously inclined, scholars relatively unaffected by positivism or behaviorism, or by the general scientificization of human sentiment. That marvelous Christian maverick, C. S. Lewis, tells us: "Friendship is unnecessary, like philosophy, like art, like the universe itself (since God did not *need* to create). It has no survival value; rather it is one of those things that give value to survival." And the Jewish thinker Simone Weil focuses on the classic theme of free consent when she writes: "Friendship is a miracle by which a person consents to view from a certain distance, and without coming any nearer, the very being who is necessary to him as food."

The quality of free consent and self-determination inherent in friendship 13 may be crucial to the lives of twentieth-century women beginning their vocations. But in order to return friendship to an absolutely central place in our lives, we might have to wean ourselves in part from the often submissive premises of romantic passion. I suspect that we shall always need some measure of swooning and palpitating, of ecstasy and trembling, of possessing and being possessed. But, I also suspect that we've been bullied and propagandized into many of these manifestations by the powerful modern organism that I call the sexual-industrial complex and that had an antecedent in the novels that fueled Emma Bovary's deceitful fantasies. For one of the most treacherous aspects of the cult of romantic love has been its complex idealization and exploitation of female sexuality. There is now a new school of social scientists who are militantly questioning the notion that Western romantic love is the best foundation for human bonding, and their criticism seems much inspired by feminist perspectives. The Australian anthropologist Robert Brain, for instance, calls romantic love "a lunatic relic of medieval passions . . . the handmaiden of a moribund capitalistic culture and of an equally dead Puritan ethic."

What exactly would happen if we women remodeled our concepts of ideal   14 human bonding on the ties of friendship and abandoned the premises of enchantment and possession? Such a restructuring of our ideals of happiness could be extremely subversive. It might imply a considerable de-eroticizing of society. It could bring about a minor revolution against the sexual-industrial complex that brings billions of dollars to thousands of men by brainwashing us into the roles of temptress and seductress, and estranges us from the plain and beautiful Quaker ideal of being a sister to the world. How topsy-turvy the world would be! Dalliance, promiscuity, all those more sensationalized aspects of the Women's Movement that were once seen as revolutionary might suddenly seem most bourgeois and old-fashioned activities. If chosen in conditions of rigorous self-determination, the following values, considered up to now as reactionary, could suddenly become the most radical ones at hand: Virginity. Celibacy. Monastic communities. And that most endangered species of all, fidelity in marriage, which has lately become so exotically rare that it might soon become very fashionable, and provide the cover story for yet another publication designed to alleviate the seldom-admitted solitude of swinging singles: "Mick Jagger Is into Fidelity."

ACTIVITIES FOR WRITING AND DISCUSSION

1. Read and annotate the essay. Then respond to it in your notebook using Idea #1 from the "Ten Ideas for Writing from Reading" found on page 35. (For a sample using Idea #1 in response to a different text see pages 28–29.)

2. Reread your annotations of "On Friendship." Then identify *one* sentence or paragraph that is *most* significant or provocative to you.
   a. Share your annotations of the sentence or paragraph with a partner or small group.
   b. Use the passage (supplemented by feedback from your partner or group) as a springboard for composing a notebook entry of at least three hundred words.

3. In paragraph 13 Gray introduces the term "sexual-industrial complex." Reread the paragraph carefully. Then, working alone or collaboratively:

    a. Explain (in writing) what Gray means by this term.

    b. Draw upon your knowledge and experience to identify, discuss, and write about some particular manifestations of the sexual-industrial complex in society at large and in your own life. Share examples and, where possible, specific stories.

    c. Examine Gray's conclusion in paragraph 14 that an "ideal human bonding" based on friendship "could be extremely subversive" to the sexual-industrial complex. First explain how she reaches this conclusion; how does the ideal of friendship subvert "the premises of enchantment and possession?" Then agree or disagree with the conclusion, supporting your position with examples from your own knowledge, reading, or experience.

Scott Russell Sanders (b. 1945)

Looking at Women

On that sizzling July afternoon, the girl who crossed at the stoplight in front of our car looked, as my mother would say, as though she had been poured into her pink shorts. The girl's matching pink halter bared her stomach and clung to her nubbin breasts, leaving little to the imagination, as my mother would also say. Until that moment, it had never made any difference to me how much or little a girl's clothing revealed, for my imagination had been entirely devoted to other mysteries. I was eleven. The girl was about fourteen, the age of my buddy Norman who lounged in the back seat with me. Staring after her, Norman elbowed me in the ribs and murmured, "Check out that chassis."

His mother glared around from the driver's seat. "Hush your mouth."

"I was talking about that sweet Chevy," said Norman, pointing out a souped-up jalopy at the curb.

"I know what you were talking about," his mother snapped.

No doubt she did know, since mothers could read minds, but at first I did 5 not have a clue. Chassis? I knew what it meant for a car, an airplane, a radio, or even a cannon to have a chassis. But could a girl have one as well? I glanced after the retreating figure, and suddenly noticed with a sympathetic twitching in my belly the way her long raven ponytail swayed in rhythm to her walk and the way her fanny jostled in those pink shorts. In July's dazzle of sun, her swinging legs and arms beamed at me a semaphore I could almost read.

As the light turned green and our car pulled away, Norman's mother cast one more scowl at her son in the rearview mirror, saying, "Just think how it makes her feel to have you two boys gawking at her."

How? I wondered.

"Makes her feel like hot stuff," said Norman, owner of a bold mouth.

"If you don't get your mind out of the gutter, you're going to wind up in the state reformatory," said his mother.

Norman gave a snort. I sank into the seat, and tried to figure out what power had sprung from that sashaying girl to zap me in the belly.

Only after much puzzling did it dawn on me that I must finally have drifted into the force-field of sex, as a space traveler who has lived all his years in free fall might rocket for the first time within gravitational reach of a star. Even as a bashful eleven-year-old I knew the word *sex,* of course, and I could paste that name across my image of the tantalizing girl. But a label for a mystery no more explains a mystery than the word *gravity* explains gravity. As I grew a beard and my taste shifted from girls to women, I acquired a more cagey language for speaking of desire, I picked up disarming theories. First by hearsay and then by experiment, I learned the delicious details of making babies. I came to appreciate the urgency for propagation that litters the road with maple seeds and drives salmon up waterfalls and yokes the newest crop of boys to the newest crop of girls. Books in their killjoy wisdom taught me that all the valentines and violins, the waltzes and glances, the long fever and ache of romance, were merely embellishments on biology's instructions that we multiply our kind. And yet, the fraction of desire that actually leads to procreation is so vanishingly small as to seem irrelevant. In his lifetime a man sways to a million longings, only a few of which, or perhaps none at all, ever lead to the fathering of children. Now, thirty years away from that July afternoon, firmly married, twice a father, I am still humming from the power unleashed by the girl in pink shorts, still wondering how it made her feel to have two boys gawk at her, still puzzling over how to dwell in the force-field of desire.

How should a man look at women? It is a peculiarly and perhaps neurotically human question. Billy goats do not fret over how they should look at nanny goats. They look or don't look, as seasons and hormones dictate, and feel what they feel without benefit of theory. There is more billy goat in most men than we care to admit. None of us, however, is pure goat. To live utterly as an animal would make the business of sex far tidier but also drearier. If we tried, like Rousseau, to peel off the layers of civilization and imagine our way back to some pristine man and woman who have not yet been corrupted by hand-me-down notions of sexuality, my hunch is that we would find, in our speculative state of nature, that men regarded women with appalling simplicity. In any case, unlike goats, we dwell in history. What attracts our eyes and rouses our blood is only partly instinctual. Other forces contend in us as well: the voices of books and religions, the images of art and film and advertising, the entire chorus of culture. Norman's telling me to relish the sight of females and his mother's telling me to keep my eyes to myself are only two of the many voices quarreling in my head.

If there were a rule book for sex, it would be longer than the one for baseball (that byzantine sport), more intricate and obscure than tax instructions from the Internal Revenue Service. What I present here are a few images and reflections that cling, for me, to this one item in such a compendium of rules: How should a man look at women?

———————

Well before I was to see any women naked in the flesh, I saw a bevy of them naked in photographs, hung in a gallery around the bed of my freshman roommate at college. A *Playboy* subscriber, he would pluck the centerfold from its staples each month and tape another airbrushed lovely to the wall. The gallery was in place when I moved in, and for an instant before I realized what I was looking at, all that expanse of skin reminded me of a meat locker back in Newton Falls, Ohio. I never quite shook that first impression, even after I had inspected the pinups at my leisure on subsequent days. Every curve of buttock and breast was news to me, an innocent kid from the Puritan back roads. Today you would be hard pressed to find a college freshman as ignorant as I was of female anatomy, if only because teenagers now routinely watch movies at home that would have been shown, during my teen years, exclusively on the fly-speck-led screens of honky-tonk cinemas or in the basement of the Kinsey Institute. I studied those alien shapes on the wall with a curiosity that was not wholly sexual, a curiosity tinged with the wonder that astronomers must have felt when they pored over the early photographs of the far side of the moon.

The paper women seemed to gaze back at me, enticing or mocking, yet even 15 in my adolescent dither I was troubled by the phony stare, for I knew this was no true exchange of looks. Those mascaraed eyes were not fixed on me but on a camera. What the models felt as they posed I could only guess—perhaps the boredom of any numbskull job, perhaps the weight of dollar bills, perhaps the sweltering lights of fame, perhaps a tingle of the power that launched a thousand ships.

Whatever their motives, these women had chosen to put themselves on display. For the instant of the photograph, they had become their bodies, as a prizefighter does in the moment of landing a punch, as a weightlifter does in the moment of hoisting a barbell, as a ballerina does in the whirl of a pirouette, as we all do in the crisis of making love or dying. Men, ogling such photographs, are supposed to feel that where so much surface is revealed there can be no depths. Yet I never doubted that behind the makeup and the plump curves and the two dimensions of the image there was an inwardness, a feeling self as mysterious as my own. In fact, during moments when I should have been studying French or thermodynamics, I would glance at my roommate's wall and invent mythical lives for those goddesses. The lives I made up were adolescent ones, to be sure, but so was mine. Without that saving aura of inwardness, these women in the glossy photographs would have become merely another category of objects for sale, alongside the sports cars and stereo systems and liquors advertised in the same pages. If not extinguished, however, their humanity was severely reduced. And if by simplifying themselves they had lost some human essence, then by gaping at them I had shared in the theft.

What did that gaping take from me? How did it affect my way of seeing other women, those who would never dream of lying nude on a fake tiger rug before the million-faceted eye of a camera? The bodies in the photographs were implausibly smooth and slick and inflated, like balloon caricatures that might be floated overhead in a parade. Free of sweat and scars and imperfections, sensual without being fertile, tempting yet impregnable, they were Platonic ideals of the female form, divorced from time and the fluster of living, excused from the perplexities of mind. No actual woman could rival their insipid perfection.

The swains who gathered to admire my roommate's gallery discussed the pinups in the same tones and in much the same language as the farmers back home in Ohio used for assessing cows. The relevant parts of male and female bodies are quickly named—and, the *Kamasutra* and Marquis de Sade notwithstanding, the number of ways in which those parts can be stimulated or conjoined is touchingly small—so these studly conversations were more tedious than chitchat about the weather. I would lie on my bunk pondering calculus or Aeschylus and unwillingly hear the same few nouns and fewer verbs issuing from one mouth after another, and I would feel smugly superior. Here I was, improving my mind, while theirs wallowed in the notorious gutter. Eventually the swains would depart, leaving me in peace, and from the intellectual heights of my bunk I would glance across at those photographs—and yield to the gravity of lust. Idiot flesh! How stupid that a counterfeit stare and artful curves, printed in millions of copies on glossy paper, could arouse me. But there it was, not the first proof of my body's automatism and not the last.

Nothing in men is more machinelike than the flipping of sexual switches. I have never been able to read with a straight face the claims made by D. H. Lawrence and lesser pundits that the penis is a god, a lurking dragon. It more nearly resembles a railroad crossing signal, which stirs into life at intervals to announce, "Here comes a train." Or, if the penis must be likened to an animal, let it be an ill-trained circus dog, sitting up and playing dead and heeling whenever it takes a notion, oblivious of the trainer's commands. Meanwhile, heart, lungs, blood vessels, pupils, and eyelids all assert their independence like the members of a rebellious troupe. Reason stands helpless at the center of the ring, cracking its whip.

While he was president, Jimmy Carter raised a brouhaha by confessing in a *Playboy* interview, of all shady places, that he occasionally felt lust in his heart for women. What man hasn't, aside from those who feel lust in their hearts for other men? The commentators flung their stones anyway. Naughty, naughty, they chirped. Wicked Jimmy. Perhaps Mr. Carter could derive some consolation from psychologist Allen Wheelis, who blames male appetite on biology:

"We have been selected for desiring. Nothing could have convinced us by argument that it would be worthwhile to chase endlessly and insatiably after women, but something has transformed us from within, a plasmid has invaded our DNA, has twisted our nature so that now this is exactly what we *want* to do." Certainly, by Darwinian logic, those males who were most avid in their pursuit of females were also the most likely to pass on their genes. Consoling it may be, yet it is finally no solution to blame biology. "I am extremely sexual in my desires: I carry them everywhere and at all times," William Carlos Williams tells us on the opening page of his autobiography. "I think that from that arises the drive which empowers us all. Given that drive, a man does with it what his mind directs. In the manner in which he directs that power lies his secret." Whatever the contents of my DNA, however potent the influence of my ancestors, I still must direct that rebellious power. I still must live with the consequences of my looking and my longing.

———————

Aloof on their blankets like goddesses on clouds, the pinups did not belong to my funky world. I was invisible to them, and they were immune to my gaze. Not so the women who passed me on the street, sat near me in classes, shared a table with me in the cafeteria: it was risky to stare at them. They could gaze back, and sometimes did, with looks both puzzling and exciting. It only complicated matters for me to realize that so many of these strangers had taken precautions that men should notice them. The girl in matching pink halter and shorts who set me humming in my eleventh year might only have wanted to keep cool in the sizzle of July. But these alluring college femmes had deeper designs. Perfume, eye shadow, uplift bras (about which I learned in the Sears catalog), curled hair, stockings, jewelry, lipstick, lace—what were these if not hooks thrown out into male waters?

I recall being mystified in particular by spike heels. They looked painful to me, and dangerous. Danger may have been the point, since the spikes would have made good weapons—they were affectionately known, after all, as stilettos. Or danger may have been the point in another sense, because a woman teetering along on such heels is tipsy, vulnerable, broadcasting her need for support. And who better than a man to prop her up, some guy who clomps around in brogans wide enough for the cornerstones of flying buttresses? (For years after college, I felt certain that spike heels had been forever banned, like bustles and foot-binding, but lately they have come back in fashion, and once more one encounters women teetering along on knife points.)

Back in those days of my awakening to women, I was also baffled by lingerie. I do not mean underwear, the proletariat of clothing, and I do not mean foundation garments, pale and sensible. I mean what the woman who lives in the house behind ours—owner of a shop called "Bare Essentials"—refers to as "intimate apparel." Those two words announce that her merchandise is both sexy and expensive. These flimsy items cost more per ounce than truffles, more than frankincense and myrrh. They are put-ons whose only purpose is in being taken off. I have a friend who used to attend the men's-only nights at Bare Essentials, during which he would invariably buy a slinky outfit or two, by way of proving his serious purpose, outfits that wound up in the attic because his wife would not be caught dead in them. Most of the customers at the shop are women, however, as the models are women, and the owner is a woman. What should one make of that? During my college days I knew about intimate apparel only by rumor, not being that intimate with anyone who would have tricked herself out in such finery, but I could see the spike heels and other female trappings everywhere I turned. Why, I wondered then and wonder still, do so many women decorate themselves like dolls? And does that mean they wish to be viewed as dolls?

On this question as on many others, Simone de Beauvoir has clarified matters for me, writing in *The Second Sex:* "The 'feminine' woman in making herself prey tries to reduce man, also, to her carnal passivity; she occupies herself in catching him in her trap, in enchaining him by means of the desires she arouses in him in submissively making herself a thing." Those women who transform themselves into dolls, in other words, do so because that is the most potent identity available to them. "It must be admitted," Beauvoir concedes, "that the males find in woman more complicity than the oppressor usually finds in the oppressed. And in bad faith they take authorization from this to declare that she has *desired* the destiny they have imposed on her."

Complicity, oppressor, bad faith: such terms yank us into a moral realm unknown to goats. While I am saddled with enough male guilt to believe three-quarters of Beauvoir's claim, I still doubt that men are so entirely to blame for the turning of women into sexual dolls. I believe human history is more collaborative than her argument would suggest. It seems unlikely to me that one-half the species could have "imposed" a destiny on the other half, unless that other half were far more craven than the females I have known. Some women have expressed their own skepticism on this point. Thus Joan Didion: "That many women are victims of condescension and exploitation and sex-role stereotyping was scarcely news, but neither was it news that other women are not: nobody forces women to buy the package." Beauvoir herself recognized that many members of her sex refuse to buy the "feminine" package: "The emancipated woman, on the contrary, wants to be active, a taker, and refuses the passivity man means to impose on her."

Since my college years, back in the murky 1960s, emancipated women have been discouraging their unemancipated sisters from making spectacles of themselves. Don't paint your face like a clown's or drape your body like a mannequin's, they say. Don't bounce on the sidelines in skimpy outfits, screaming your fool head off, while men compete in the limelight for victories. Don't present yourself to the world as a fluff pastry, delicate and edible. Don't waddle across the stage in a bathing suit in hopes of being named Miss This or That.

A great many women still ignore the exhortations. Wherever a crown for beauty is to be handed out, many still line up to stake their claims. Recently, Miss Indiana Persimmon Festival was quoted in our newspaper about the burdens of possessing the sort of looks that snag men's eyes. "Most of the time I enjoy having guys stare at me," she said, "but every once in a while it makes me feel like a piece of meat." The news photograph showed a cheerleader's perky face, heavily made-up, with starched hair teased into a blond cumulus. She put me in mind not of meat but of a plastic figurine, something you might buy from a booth outside a shrine. Nobody should ever be seen as meat, mere juicy stuff to satisfy an appetite. Better to appear as a plastic figurine, which is not meant for eating, and which is a gesture, however crude, toward art. Joyce described the aesthetic response as a contemplation of form without the impulse to action. Perhaps that is what Miss Indiana Persimmon Festival wishes to inspire in those who look at her, perhaps that is what many women who paint and primp themselves desire: to withdraw from the touch of hands and dwell in the eye alone, to achieve the status of art.

By turning herself (or allowing herself to be turned into) a work of art, does a woman truly escape men's proprietary stare? Not often, says the British critic John Berger. Summarizing the treatment of women in Western painting, he concludes that—with a few notable exceptions, such as works by Rubens and Rembrandt—the woman on canvas is a passive object displayed for the pleasure of the male viewer, especially for the owner of the painting, who is, by extension, owner of the woman herself. Berger concludes: "Men look at women. Women watch themselves being looked at. This determines not only most relations between men and women but also the relation of women to themselves. The surveyor of woman in herself is male: the surveyed female. Thus she turns herself into an object—and most particularly an object of vision: a sight."

That sweeping claim, like the one quoted earlier from Beauvoir, also seems to me about three-quarters truth and one-quarter exaggeration. I know men who outdo the peacock for show, and I know women who are so fully possessed of themselves that they do not give a hang whether anybody notices them or not. The flamboyant gentlemen portrayed by Van Dyck are no less aware of being *seen* than are the languid ladies portrayed by Ingres. With or without clothes, both gentlemen and ladies may conceive of themselves as objects of vision, targets of envy or admiration or desire. Where they differ is in their potential for action: the men are caught in the midst of a decisive gesture or on the verge of making one; the women wait like fuel for someone else to strike a match.

I am not sure the abstract nudes favored in modern art are much of an advance over the inert and voluptuous ones of the old school. Think of two famous examples: Duchamp's *Nude Descending a Staircase* (1912), where the faceless woman has blurred into a waterfall of jagged shards, or Picasso's *Les Demoiselles d'Avignon* (1907), where the five angular damsels have been hammered as flat as cookie sheets and fitted with African masks. Neither painting   30 invites us to behold a woman, but instead to behold what Picasso or Duchamp can make of one.

The naked women in Rubens, far from being passive, are gleefully active, exuberant, their sumptuous pink bodies like rainclouds or plump nebulae. "His nudes are the first ones that ever made me feel happy about my own body," a woman friend told me in one of the Rubens galleries of the Prado Museum. I do not imagine any pinup or store-window mannequin or bathing-suited Miss Whatsit could have made her feel that way. The naked women in Rembrandt, emerging from the bath or rising from bed, are so private, so cherished in the painter's gaze, that we as viewers see them not as sexual playthings but as loved persons. A man would do well to emulate that gaze.

———————

I have never thought of myself as a sight. How much that has to do with being male and how much with having grown up on the back roads where money was scarce and eyes were few, I cannot say. As a boy, apart from combing my hair when I was compelled to and regretting the patches on my jeans (only the poor wore patches), I took no trouble over my appearance. It never occurred to me that anybody outside my family, least of all a girl, would look at me twice. As a young man, when young women did occasionally glance my way, without any prospect of appearing handsome I tried at least to avoid appearing odd. A standard haircut and the cheapest versions of the standard clothes were camouflage enough. Now as a middle-aged man I have achieved once more that boyhood condition of invisibility, with less hair to comb and fewer patches to humble me.

Many women clearly pass through the world aspiring to invisibility. Many others just as clearly aspire to be conspicuous. Women need not make spectacles of themselves in order to draw the attention of men. Indeed, for my taste, the less paint and fewer bangles the better. I am as helpless in the presence of subtle lures as a male moth catching a whiff of pheromones. I am a sucker for hair ribbons, a scarf at the throat, toes leaking from sandals, teeth bared in a smile. By contrast, I have always been more amused than attracted by the enameled exhibitionists whom our biblical mothers would identify as brazen hussies or painted Jezebels or, in the extreme cases, as whores of Babylon.

To encounter female exhibitionists in their full glory and variety, you need to go to a city. I never encountered ogling as a full-blown sport until I visited Rome, where bands of Italian men joined with gusto in appraising the charms of every passing female, and the passing females vied with one another in demonstrating their charms. In our own cities the most notorious bands of oglers tend to be construction gangs or street crews, men who spend much of their day leaning on the handles of shovels or pausing between bursts of riveting guns, their eyes tracing the curves of passersby. The first time my wife and kids and I drove into Boston we followed the signs to Chinatown, only to discover that Chinatown's miserably congested main street was undergoing repairs. That street also proved to be the city's home for X-rated cinemas and girlie shows and skin shops. LIVE SEX ACTS ON STAGE. PEEP SHOWS. PRIVATE BOOTHS. Caught in a traffic jam, we spent an hour listening to jackhammers and wolf whistles as we crept through the few blocks of pleasure palaces, my son and daughter with their noses hanging out the windows, my wife and I steaming. Lighted marquees peppered by burnt-out bulbs announced the titles of sleazy flicks; life-size posters of naked women flanked the doorways of clubs: leggy strippers in miniskirts, the originals for some of the posters, smoked on the curb between numbers.

After we had finally emerged from the zone of eros, eight-year-old Jesse in-   35
quired, "What was *that* place all about?"

"Sex for sale," my wife Ruth explained.

That might carry us some way toward a definition of pornography: making flesh into a commodity, flaunting it like any other merchandise, divorcing bodies from selves. By this reckoning, there is a pornographic dimension to much advertising, where a charge of sex is added to products ranging from cars to shaving cream. In fact, the calculated imagery of advertising may be more harmful than the blatant imagery of the pleasure palaces, that frank raunchiness which Kate Millett refers to as the "truthful explicitness of pornography." One can leave the X-rated zone of the city, but one cannot escape the sticky reach of commerce, which summons girls to the high calling of cosmetic glamor, fashion, and sexual display, while it summons boys to the panting chase.

You can recognize pornography, according to D. H. Lawrence, "by the insult it offers, invariably, to sex, and to the human spirit." He should know, Millet argues in *Sexual Politics,* for in her view Lawrence himself was a purveyor of patriarchal and often sadistic pornography. I think she is correct about the worst of Lawrence, and that she identifies a misogynist streak in his work; but she ignores his career-long struggle to achieve a more public, tolerant vision of sexuality as an exchange between equals. Besides, his novels and stories all bear within themselves their own critiques. George Steiner reminds us that "the list of writers who have had the genius to enlarge our actual compass of sexual awareness, who have given the erotic play of the mind a novel focus, an area of recognition previously unknown or fallow, is very small." Lawrence belongs on that brief list. The chief insult to the human spirit is to deny it, to claim that we are merely conglomerations of molecules, to pretend that we exist purely as bundles of appetites or as food for the appetites of others.

Men commit that insult toward women out of ignorance, but also out of dread. Allen Wheelis again: "Men gather in pornographic shows, not to stimulate desire, as they may think, but to diminish fear. It is the nature of the show to reduce the woman, discard her individuality, her soul, make her into an object, thereby enabling the man to handle her with greater safety, to use her as a toy. . . . As women move increasingly toward equality, the felt danger to men increases, leading to an increase in pornography and, since there are some men whose fears cannot even so be stilled, to an increase also in violence against women."

Make her into an object: all the hurtful ways for men to look at women are 40 variations on this betrayal. "Thus she turns herself into an object," writes Berger. A woman's ultimate degradation is in "submissively making herself a thing," writes Beauvoir. To be turned into an object—whether by the brush of a painter or the lens of a photographer or the eye of a voyeur, whether by hunger or poverty or enslavement, by mugging or rape, bullets or bombs, by hatred, racism, car crashes, fires, or falls—is for each of us the deepest dread; and to reduce another person to an object is the primal wrong.

Caught in the vortex of desire, we have to struggle to recall the wholeness of persons, including ourselves. Beauvoir speaks of the temptation we all occasionally feel to give up the struggle for a self and lapse into the inertia of an object: "Along with the ethical urge of each individual to affirm his subjective existence, there is also the temptation to forgo liberty and become a thing." A woman in particular, given so much encouragement to lapse into thinghood, "is often very well pleased with her role as the *Other*."

Yet one need not forgo liberty and become a thing, without a center or a self, in order to become the Other. In our mutual strangeness, men and women can be doorways one for another, openings into the creative mystery that we share by virtue of our existence in the flesh. "To be sensual," James Baldwin writes, "is to respect and rejoice in the force of life, of life itself, and to be *present* in all that one does, from the effort of loving to the breaking of bread." The effort of loving is reciprocal, not only in act but in desire, an *I* addressing a *Thou*, a meeting in that vivid presence. The distance a man stares across at a woman, or a woman at a man, is a gulf in the soul, out of which a voice cries, *Leap, leap.* One day all men may cease to look on themselves as prototypically human and on women as lesser miracles; women may cease to feel themselves the targets for desire; men and women both may come to realize that we are all mere flickerings in the universal fire; and then none of us, male or female, need give up humanity in order to become the *Other*.

Ever since I gawked at the girl in pink shorts, I have dwelt knowingly in the force-field of sex. Knowingly or not, it is where we all dwell. Like the masses of planets and stars, our bodies curve the space around us. We radiate signals constantly, radio sources that never go off the air. We cannot help being centers of attraction and repulsion for one another. That is not all we are by a long shot, nor all we are capable of feeling, and yet, even after our much-needed revolution in sexual consciousness, the power of eros will still turn our heads and hearts. In a world without beauty pageants, there will still be beauty, however its definition may have changed. As long as men have eyes, they will gaze with yearning and confusion at women.

When I return to the street with the ancient legacy of longing coiled in my DNA, and the residues from a thousand generations of patriarchs silting my brain, I encounter women whose presence strikes me like a slap of wind in the face. I must prepare a gaze that is worthy of their splendor.

ACTIVITIES FOR WRITING AND DISCUSSION

1. Sanders's essay is quite long, complex, and suggestive. To begin establishing a connection with the piece, review your annotations—questions, reactions, personal associations—of the essay. Select two or three that strike or affect you the most and write about them for a few minutes. Then share those selected annotations in class or in a small group.

2. Several paragraphs into his essay Sanders poses the question that becomes his focus: "How should a man look at women?" Is it significant that he uses the word "should" and not "does"? What sorts of cultural influences on sexual attitudes and behavior are implied by "should"? Draw on Sanders's essay and your own experience to make a list of such influences.

3. The essay includes quotations from various writers (Simone de Beauvoir, John Berger, Kate Millett, Allen Wheelis, and others). Reread and annotate these passages. Then select one passage that particularly strikes you and write an objective summary of it. (See p. 100 for some suggestions on summarizing.) Finally, discuss ways in which you agree and/or disagree with the writer quoted in the passage.

4. Sanders relates several experiences from his own past in which he looked at women. Tell the story of a time when *you* "looked at women" (or at men, or were yourself looked at). Then, like Sanders, analyze ways in which the experience reflects wider cultural influences on sexual attitudes and behavior.

Susan Glaspell (1882–1948)

Trifles

SCENE: *The kitchen in the now abandoned farmhouse of* JOHN WRIGHT, *a gloomy kitchen, and left without having been put in order—the walls covered with a faded wallpaper.* D. R. *is a door leading to the parlor. On the* R. *wall above this door is a built-in kitchen cupboard with shelves in the upper portion and drawers below. In the rear wall at* R., *up two steps is a door opening onto stairs leading to the second floor. In the rear wall at* L. *is a door to the shed and from there to the outside. Between these two doors is an old-fashioned black iron stove. Running along the* L. *wall from the shed door is an old iron sink and sink shelf, in which is set a hand pump. Downstage of the sink is an uncurtained window. Near the window is an old wooden rocker. Center stage is an unpainted wooden kitchen table with straight chairs on either side. There is a small chair* D. R. *Unwashed pans under the sink, a loaf of bread outside the breadbox, a dish towel on the table—other signs of incompleted work. At the rear the shed door opens and the* SHERIFF *comes in followed by the* COUNTY ATTORNEY *and* HALE. *The* SHERIFF *and* HALE *are men in middle life, the* COUNTY ATTORNEY *is a young man; all are much bundled up and go at once to the stove. They are followed by the two women—the* SHERIFF'S *wife,* MRS. PETERS, *first; she is a slight wiry woman, a thin nervous face.* MRS. HALE *is larger and would ordinarily be called more comfortable looking, but she is disturbed now and looks fearfully about as she enters. The women have come in slowly, and stand close together near the door.*

COUNTY ATTORNEY (*at stove rubbing his hands*). This feels good. Come up to the fire, ladies.

MRS. PETERS (*after taking a step forward*). I'm not—cold.

SHERIFF (*unbuttoning his overcoat and stepping away from the stove to right of table as if to mark the beginning of official business*). Now, Mr. Hale, before we move things about, you explain to Mr. Henderson just what you saw when you came here yesterday morning.

COUNTY ATTORNEY (*crossing down to left of the table*). By the way, has anything been moved? Are things just as you left them yesterday?

SHERIFF (*looking about*). It's just the same. When it dropped below zero last night I thought I'd better send Frank out this morning to make a fire for us— (*sits right of center table*) no use getting pneumonia with a big case on, but I told him not to touch anything except the stove—and you know Frank.

COUNTY ATTORNEY: Somebody should have been left here yesterday.

SHERIFF: Oh—yesterday. When I had to send Frank to Morris Center for that man who went crazy—I want you to know I had my hands full yesterday. I knew you could get back from Omaha by today and as long as I went over everything here myself——

COUNTY ATTORNEY: Well, Mr. Hale, tell just what happened when you came here yesterday morning.

HALE (*crossing down to above table*). Harry and I had started to town with a load of potatoes. We came along the road from my place and as I got here I said, "I'm going to see if I can't get John Wright to go in with me on a party telephone." I spoke to Wright about it once before and he put me off, saying folks talked too much anyway, and all he asked was peace and quiet—I guess you know about how much he talked himself; but I thought maybe if I went to the house and talked about it before his wife, though I said to Harry that I didn't know as what his wife wanted made much difference to John——

COUNTY ATTORNEY: Let's talk about that later, Mr. Hale. I do want to talk about that, but tell now just what happened when you got to the house.

HALE: I didn't hear or see anything; I knocked at the door, and still it was all quiet inside. I knew they must be up, it was past eight o'clock. So I knocked again, and I thought I heard somebody say, "Come in." I wasn't sure, I'm not sure yet, but I opened the door—this door (*indicating the door by which the two women are still standing*) and there in that rocker—(*pointing to it*) sat Mrs. Wright. (*They all look at the rocker* D. L.)

COUNTY ATTORNEY: What—was she doing?

HALE: She was rockin' back and forth. She had her apron in her hand and was kind of—pleating it.

COUNTY ATTORNEY: And how did she—look?

HALE: Well, she looked queer.

COUNTY ATTORNEY: How do you mean—queer?

HALE: Well, as if she didn't know what she was going to do next. And kind of done up.

COUNTY ATTORNEY (*takes out notebook and pencil and sits left of center table*). How did she seem to feel about your coming?

HALE: Why, I don't think she minded—one way or other. She didn't pay much attention. I said, "How do, Mrs. Wright, it's cold, ain't it?" And she said, "Is it?"—and went on kind of pleating at her apron. Well, I was surprised; she didn't ask me to come up to the stove, or to set down, but just sat there, not even looking at me, so I said, "I want to see John." And then she—laughed. I guess you would call it a laugh. I thought of Harry and the team outside, so I said a little sharp: "Can't I see John?" "No," she says, kind o' dull like. "Ain't he home?" says I. "Yes," says she, "he's home." "Then why can't I see him?" I asked her, out of patience. "'Cause he's dead," says she. *"Dead?"* says I. She just nodded her head, not getting a bit excited, but rockin' back and forth. "Why—

where is he?" says I, not knowing what to say. She just pointed upstairs—like that. (*Himself pointing to the room above*). I started for the stairs, with the idea of going up there. I walked from there to here—then I says, "Why, what did he die of?" "He died of a rope round his neck," says she, and just went on pleatin' at her apron. Well, I went out and called Harry. I thought I might—need help. We went upstairs and there he was lyin'—

COUNTY ATTORNEY: I think I'd rather have you go into that upstairs, where you can point it all out. Just go on now with the rest of the story.

HALE: Well, my first thought was to get that rope off. It looked . . . (*stops, his face twitches*) . . . but Harry, he went up to him, and he said, "No, he's dead all right, and we'd better not touch anything." So we went back downstairs. She was still sitting that same way. "Has anybody been notified?" I asked. "No," says she, unconcerned. "Who did this, Mrs. Wright?" said Harry. He said it business-like—and she stopped pleatin' of her apron. "I don't know," she says. "You don't know?" says Harry. "No," says she. "Weren't you sleepin' in the bed with him?" says Harry. "Yes," says she, "but I was on the inside." "Somebody slipped a rope round his neck and strangled him and you didn't wake up?" says Harry. "I didn't wake up," she said after him. We must 'a' looked as if we didn't see how that could be, for after a minute she said, "I sleep sound." Harry was going to ask her more questions but I said maybe we ought to let her tell her story first to the coroner, or the sheriff, so Harry went fast as he could to Rivers' place, where there's a telephone.

COUNTY ATTORNEY: And what did Mrs. Wright do when she knew that you had gone for the coroner?

HALE: She moved from the rocker to that chair over there (*pointing to a small chair in the* D. R. *corner*) and just sat there with her hands held together and looking down. I got a feeling that I ought to make some conversation, so I said I had come in to see if John wanted to put in a telephone, and at that she started to laugh, and then she stopped and looked at me—scared. (*The* COUNTY ATTORNEY, *who has had his notebook out, makes a note*). I dunno, maybe it wasn't scared. I wouldn't like to say it was. Soon Harry got back, and then Dr. Lloyd came, and you, Mr. Peters, and so I guess that's all I know that you don't.

COUNTY ATTORNEY (*rising and looking around*). I guess we'll go upstairs first—and then out to the barn and around there. (*To the* SHERIFF). You're convinced that there was nothing important here—nothing that would point to any motive?

SHERIFF: Nothing here but kitchen things. (*The* COUNTY ATTORNEY, *after again looking around the kitchen, opens the door of a cupboard closet in* R. *wall. He brings a small chair from* R.—*gets up on it and looks on a shelf. Pulls his hand away, sticky.*)

COUNTY ATTORNEY: Here's a nice mess. (*The women draw nearer* U. C.)

MRS. PETERS (*to the other woman*). Oh, her fruit; it did freeze. (*To the* LAWYER). She worried about that when it turned so cold. She said the fire'd go out and her jars would break.

SHERIFF (*rises*). Well, can you beat the women! Held for murder and worryin' about her preserves.

COUNTY ATTORNEY (*getting down from chair*). I guess before we're through she may have something more serious than preserves to worry about. (*Crosses down* R.C.)

HALE: Well, women are used to worrying over trifles. (*The two women move a little closer together.*)

COUNTY ATTORNEY (*with the gallantry of a young politician*). And yet, for all their worries, what would we do without the ladies? (*The women do not unbend. He goes below the center table to the sink, takes a dipperful of water from the pail and pouring it into a basin, washes his hands. While he is doing this the* SHERIFF *and* HALE *cross to cupboard, which they inspect. The* COUNTY ATTORNEY *starts to wipe his hands on the roller towel, turns it for a cleaner place*). Dirty towels! (*Kicks his foot against the pans under the sink*). Not much of a housekeeper, would you say, ladies?

MRS. HALE (*stiffly*). There's a great deal of work to be done on a farm.

COUNTY ATTORNEY: To be sure. And yet (*with a little bow to her*) I know there are some Dickson County farmhouses which do not have such roller towels. (*He gives it a pull to expose its full length again.*)

MRS. HALE: Those towels get dirty awful quick. Men's hands aren't always as clean as they might be.

COUNTY ATTORNEY: Ah, loyal to your sex, I see. But you and Mrs. Wright were neighbors. I suppose you were friends, too.

MRS. HALE (*shaking her head*). I've not seen much of her of late years. I've not been in this house—it's more than a year.

COUNTY ATTORNEY (*crossing to women* U. C.). And why was that? You didn't like her?

MRS. HALE: I liked her all well enough. Farmers' wives have their hands full, Mr. Henderson. And then——

COUNTY ATTORNEY: Yes——?

MRS. HALE (*looking about*). It never seemed a very cheerful place.

COUNTY ATTORNEY: No—it's not cheerful. I shouldn't say she had the homemaking instinct.

MRS. HALE: Well, I don't know as Wright had, either.

COUNTY ATTORNEY: You mean that they didn't get on very well?

MRS. HALE: No, I don't mean anything. But I don't think a place'd be any cheerfuller for John Wright's being in it.

COUNTY ATTORNEY: I'd like to talk more of that a little later. I want to get the lay of things upstairs now. (*He goes past the women to* U. R. *where steps lead to a stair door.*)

SHERIFF: I suppose anything Mrs. Peters does'll be all right. She was to take in some clothes for her, you know, and a few little things. We left in such a hurry yesterday.

COUNTY ATTORNEY: Yes, but I would like to see what you take, Mrs. Peters, and keep an eye out for anything that might be of use to us.

MRS. PETER: Yes, Mr. Henderson. (*The men leave by* U. R. *door to stairs. The women listen to the men's steps on the stairs, then look about the kitchen.*)

MRS. HALE (*crossing* L. *to sink*). I'd hate to have men coming into my kitchen, snooping around and criticizing. (*She arranges the pans under sink which the* LAWYER *had shoved out of place.*)

MRS. PETERS: Of course it's no more than their duty. (*Crosses to cupboard* U. R.)

MRS. HALE: Duty's all right, but I guess that deputy sheriff that came out to make the fire might have got a little of this on. (*Gives the roller towel a pull*). Wish I'd thought of that sooner. Seems mean to talk about her for not having things slicked up when she had to come away in such a hurry. (*Crosses* R. *to* MRS. PETERS *at cupboard.*)

MRS. PETERS (*who has been looking through cupboard, lifts one end of a towel that covers a pan*). She had bread set. (*Stands still.*)

MRS. HALE (*eyes fixed on a loaf of bread beside the breadbox, which is on a low shelf of the cupboard*). She was going to put this in there. (*Picks up loaf, then abruptly drops it. In a manner of returning to familiar things*). It's a shame about her fruit. I wonder if it's all gone. (*Gets up on the chair and looks*). I think there's some here that's all right, Mrs. Peters. Yes—here; (*holding it toward the window*) this is cherries, too. (*Looking again*). I declare I believe that's the only one. (*Gets down, jar in her hand. Goes to the sink and wipes it off on the outside*). She'll feel awful bad after all her hard work in the hot weather. I remember the afternoon I put up my cherries last summer. (*She puts the jar on the big kitchen table, center of the room. With a sigh, is about to sit down in the rocking chair. Before she is seated realizes what chair it is; with a slow look at it, steps back. The chair which she has touched rocks back and forth.* MRS. PETERS *moves to center table and they both watch the chair rock for a moment or two.*)

MRS. PETERS (*shaking off the mood which the empty rocking chair has evoked. Now in a businesslike manner she speaks*). Well, I must get those things from the front room closet. (*She goes to the door at the* R., *but, after looking into the other room, steps back*). You coming with me, Mrs. Hale? You could help me carry them. (*They go in the other room; reappear,* MRS. PETERS *carrying a dress, petticoat and skirt,* MRS. HALE *following with a pair of shoes*). My, it's cold in there. (*She puts the clothes on the big table, and hurries to the stove.*)

MRS. HALE (*right of center table examining the skirt*). Wright was close. I think maybe that's why she kept so much to herself. She didn't even belong to the Ladies' Aid. I suppose she felt she couldn't do her part, and then you don't enjoy things when you feel shabby. I heard she used to wear pretty clothes and be lively, when she was Minnie Foster, one of the town girls singing in the choir. But that—oh, that was thirty years ago. This all you was to take in?

MRS. PETERS: She said she wanted an apron. Funny thing to want, for there isn't much to get you dirty in jail, goodness knows. But I suppose just to make her feel more natural. (*Crosses to cupboard*). She said they was in the top drawer in this cupboard. Yes, here. And then her little shawl that always hung behind the door. (*Opens stair door and looks*). Yes, here it is. (*Quickly shuts door leading upstairs.*)

MRS. HALE (*abruptly moving toward her*). Mrs. Peters?

MRS. PETERS: Yes, Mrs. Hale? (*At* U. R. *door.*)

MRS. HALE: Do you think she did it?

MRS. PETERS (*in a frightened voice*). Oh, I don't know.

MRS. HALE: Well, I don't think she did. Asking for an apron and her little shawl. Worrying about her fruit.

MRS. PETERS (*starts to speak, glances up, where footsteps are heard in the room above. In a low voice*). Mr. Peters says it looks bad for her. Mr. Henderson is awful sarcastic in a speech and he'll make fun of her sayin' she didn't wake up.

MRS. HALE: Well, I guess John Wright didn't wake when they was slipping that rope under his neck.

MRS. PETERS (*crossing slowly to table and placing shawl and apron on table with other clothing*). No, it's strange. It must have been done awful crafty and still. They say it was such a—funny way to kill a man, rigging it all up like that.

MRS. HALE (*crossing to left of* MRS. PETERS *at table*). That's just what Mr. Hale said. There was a gun in the house. He says that's what he can't understand.

MRS. PETERS: Mr. Henderson said coming out that what was needed for the case was a motive; something to show anger, or—sudden feeling.

MRS. HALE (*who is standing by the table*). Well, I don't see any signs of anger around here. (*She puts her hand on the dish towel which lies on the table, stands looking down at table, one-half of which is clean, the other half messy*). It's wiped to here. (*Makes a move as if to finish work, then turns and looks at loaf of bread outside the breadbox. Drops towel. In that voice of coming back to familiar things*). Wonder how they are finding things upstairs. (*Crossing below table to* D. R.). I hope she had it a little more red-up up there. You know, it seems kind of *sneaking*. Locking her up in town and then coming out here and trying to get her own house to turn against her!

MRS. PETERS: But, Mrs. Hale, the law is the law.

MRS. HALE: I s'pose 'tis. (*Unbuttoning her coat*). Better loosen up your things, Mrs. Peters. You won't feel them when you go out. (MRS. PETERS *takes off her fur tippet, goes to hang it on chair back left of table, stands looking at the work basket on floor near* D. L. *window.*)

MRS. PETERS: She was piecing a quilt. (*She brings the large sewing basket to the center table and they look at the bright pieces,* MRS. HALE *above the table and* MRS. PETERS *left of it.*)

MRS. HALE: It's a log cabin pattern. Pretty, isn't it? I wonder if she was goin' to quilt it or just knot it? (*Footsteps have been heard coming down the stairs. The* SHERIFF *enters followed by* HALE *and the* COUNTY ATTORNEY.)

SHERIFF: They wonder if she was going to quilt it or just knot it! (*The men laugh, the women look abashed.*)

COUNTY ATTORNEY (*rubbing his hands over the stove*). Frank's fire didn't do much up there, did it? Well, let's go out to the barn and get that cleared up. (*The men go outside by* U. L. *door.*)

MRS. HALE (*resentfully*). I don't know as there's anything so strange, our takin' up our time with little things while we're waiting for them to get the evidence. (*She sits in chair right of table smoothing out a block with decision*). I don't see as it's anything to laugh about.

MRS. PETERS (*apologetically*). Of course they've got awful important things on their minds. (*Pulls up a chair and joins* MRS. HALE *at the left of the table.*)

MRS. HALE (*examining another block*). Mrs. Peters, look at this one. Here, this is the one she was working on, and look at the sewing! All the rest of it has been so nice and even. And look at this! It's all over the place! Why, it looks as if she didn't know what she was about! (*After she has said this they look at each other, then start to glance back at the door. After an instant* MRS. HALE *has pulled at a knot and ripped the sewing.*)

MRS. PETERS: Oh, what are you doing, Mrs. Hale?

MRS. HALE (*mildly*). Just pulling out a stitch or two that's not sewed very good. (*Threading a needle*). Bad sewing always made me fidgety.

MRS. PETERS (*with a glance at door, nervously*). I don't think we ought to touch things.

MRS. HALE: I'll just finish up this end. (*Suddenly stopping and leaning forward*). Mrs. Peters?

MRS. PETERS: Yes, Mrs. Hale?

MRS. HALE: What do you suppose she was so nervous about?

MRS. PETERS: Oh—I don't know. I don't know as she was nervous. I sometimes sew awful queer when I'm just tired. (MRS. HALE *starts to say something, looks at* MRS. PETERS *then goes on sewing*). Well, I must get these things wrapped up. They may be through sooner than we think. (*Putting apron and other things together*). I wonder where I can find a piece of paper, and string. (*Rises.*)

MRS. HALE: In that cupboard, maybe.

MRS. PETERS (*crosses* R. *looking in cupboard*). Why, here's a bird-cage. (*Holds it up*). Did she have a bird, Mrs. Hale?

MRS. HALE: Why, I don't know whether she did or not—I've not been here for so long. There was a man around last year selling canaries cheap, but I don't know as she took one; maybe she did. She used to sing real pretty herself.

MRS. PETERS (*glancing around*). Seems funny to think of a bird here. But she must have had one, or why would she have a cage? I wonder what happened to it?

MRS. HALE: I s'pose maybe the cat got it.

MRS. PETERS: No, she didn't have a cat. She's got that feeling some people have about cats—being afraid of them. My cat got in her room and she was real upset and asked me to take it out.

MRS. HALE: My sister Bessie was like that. Queer, ain't it?

MRS. PETERS (*examining the cage*). Why, look at this door. It's broke. One hinge is pulled apart. (*Takes a step down to* MRS. HALE'S *right.*)

MRS. HALE (*looking too*). Looks as if someone must have been rough with it.

MRS. PETERS: Why, yes. (*She brings the cage forward and puts it on the table.*)

MRS. HALE (*glancing toward* U. L. *door*). I wish if they're going to find any evidence they'd be about it. I don't like this place.

MRS. PETERS: But I'm awful glad you came with me, Mrs. Hale. It would be lonesome for me sitting here alone.

MRS. HALE: It would, wouldn't it? (*Dropping her sewing*). But I tell you what I do wish, Mrs. Peters. I wish I had come over sometimes when she was here. I—(*looking around the room*)—wish I had.

MRS. PETERS: But of course you were awful busy, Mrs. Hale—your house and your children.

MRS. HALE (*rises and crosses* L.). I could've come. I stayed away because it weren't cheerful—and that's why I ought to have come. I—(*looking out* L. *window*)—I've never liked this place. Maybe because it's down in a hollow and you don't see the road. I dunno what it is, but it's a lonesome place and always was. I wish I had come over to see Minnie Foster sometimes. I can see now——(*Shakes her head.*)

MRS. PETERS (*left of table and above it*). Well, you mustn't reproach yourself, Mrs. Hale. Somehow we just don't see how it is with other folks until—something turns up.

MRS. HALE: Not having children makes less work—but it makes a quiet house, and Wright out to work all day, and no company when he did come in. (*Turning from window*). Did you know John Wright, Mrs. Peters?

MRS. PETERS: Not to know him; I've seen him in town. They say he was a good man.

MRS. HALE: Yes—good; he didn't drink, and kept his word as well as most, I guess, and paid his debts. But he was a hard man, Mrs. Peters. Just to pass the time of day with him—— (*Shivers*). Like a raw wind that gets to the bone. (*Pauses, her eye falling on the cage*). I should think she would 'a' wanted a bird. But what do you suppose went with it?

MRS. PETERS: I don't know, unless it got sick and died. (*She reaches over and swings the broken door, swings it again, both women watch it.*)

MRS. HALE: You weren't raised round here, were you? (MRS. PETERS *shakes her head*). You didn't know—her?

MRS. PETERS: Not till they brought her yesterday.

MRS. HALE: She—come to think of it, she was kind of like a bird herself—real sweet and pretty, but kind of timid and—fluttery. How—she—did—change. (*Silence; then as if struck by a happy thought and relieved to get back to everyday things. Crosses* R. *above* MRS. PETERS *to cupboard, replaces small chair used to stand on to its original place* D. R.). Tell you what, Mrs. Peters, why don't you take the quilt in with you? It might take up her mind.

MRS. PETERS: Why, I think that's a real nice idea, Mrs. Hale. There couldn't possibly be any objection to it, could there? Now, just what would I take? I wonder if her patches are in here—and her things. (*They look in the sewing basket.*)

MRS. HALE (*crosses to right of table*). Here's some red. I expect this has got sewing things in it. (*Brings out a fancy box*). What a pretty box. Looks like something somebody would give you. Maybe her scissors are in here. (*Opens box. Suddenly puts her hand to her nose*). Why—— (MRS. PETERS *bends nearer, then turns her face away*). There's something wrapped up in this piece of silk.

MRS. PETERS: Why, this isn't her scissors.

MRS. HALE (*lifting the silk*). Oh, Mrs. Peters—it's—— (MRS. PETERS *bends closer.*)

MRS. PETERS: It's the bird.

MRS. HALE: But, Mrs. Peters—look at it! Its neck! Look at its neck! It's all—other side *to*.

MRS. PETERS: Somebody—wrung—its—neck. (*Their eyes meet. A look of growing comprehension, of horror. Steps are heard outside.* MRS. HALE *slips box under quilt pieces, and sinks into her chair. Enter* SHERIFF *and* COUNTY ATTORNEY. MRS. PETERS *steps* D. L. *and stands looking out of window.*)

COUNTY ATTORNEY (*as one turning from serious things to little pleasantries*). Well, ladies, have you decided whether she was going to quilt it or knot it? (*Crosses to* C. *above table.*)

MRS. PETERS: We think she was going to—knot it. (SHERIFF *crosses to right of stove, lifts stove lid and glances at fire, then stands warming hands at stove.*)

COUNTY ATTORNEY: Well, that's interesting, I'm sure. (*Seeing the bird-cage*). Has the bird flown?

MRS. HALE (*putting more quilt pieces over the box*). We think the—cat got it.

COUNTY ATTORNEY (*preoccupied*). Is there a cat? (MRS. HALE *glances in a quick covert way at* MRS. PETERS.)

MRS. PETERS (*turning from window takes a step in*). Well, not *now*. They're superstitious, you know. They leave.

COUNTY ATTORNEY (*to* SHERIFF PETERS, *continuing an interrupted conversation*). No sign at all of anyone having come from the outside. Their own rope. Now let's go up again and go over it piece by piece. (*They start upstairs*). It would have to have been someone who knew just the   (MRS. PETERS *sits down left of table. The two women sit there not looking at one another, but as if peering into something and at the same time holding back. When they talk now it is in the manner of feeling their way over strange ground, as if afraid of what they are saying, but as if they cannot help saying it.*)

MRS. HALE (*hesitatively and in hushed voice*). She liked the bird. She was going to bury it in that pretty box.

MRS. PETERS (*in a whisper*). When I was a girl—my kitten—there was a boy took a hatchet, and before my eyes—and before I could get there——(*Covers her face an instant*). If they hadn't held me back I would have—(*catches herself, looks upstairs where steps are heard, falters weakly*)—hurt him.

MRS. HALE (*with a slow look around her*). I wonder how it would seem never to have had any children around. (*Pause*). No, Wright wouldn't like the bird—a thing that sang. She used to sing. He killed that, too.

MRS. PETERS (*moving uneasily*). We don't know who killed the bird.

MRS. HALE: I knew John Wright.

MRS. PETERS: It was an awful thing was done in this house that night, Mrs. Hale. Killing a man while he slept, slipping a rope around his neck that choked the life out of him.

MRS. HALE: His neck. Choked the life out of him. (*Her hand goes out and rests on the bird-cage.*)

MRS. PETERS (*with rising voice*). We don't know who killed him. We don't know.

MRS. HALE (*her own feeling not interrupted*). If there'd been years and years of nothing, then a bird to sing to you, it would be awful—still, after the bird was still.

MRS. PETERS (*something within her speaking*). I know what stillness is. When we homesteaded in Dakota, and my first baby died—after he was two years old, and me with no other then——

MRS. HALE (*moving*). How soon do you suppose they'll be through looking for the evidence?

MRS. PETERS: I know what stillness is. (*Pulling herself back*). The law has got to punish crime, Mrs. Hale.

MRS. HALE (*not as if answering that*). I wish you'd seen Minnie Foster when she wore a white dress with blue ribbons and stood up there in the choir and sang. (*A look around the room*). Oh, I *wish* I'd come over here once in a while! That was a crime! That was a crime! Who's going to punish that?

MRS. PETERS (*looking upstairs*). We mustn't—take on.

MRS. HALE: I might have known she needed help! I know how things can be—for women. I tell you, it's queer, Mrs. Peters. We live close together and we live far apart. We all go through the same things—it's all just a different kind of the same thing. (*Brushes her eyes, noticing the jar of fruit, reaches out for it*). If I was you I wouldn't tell her her fruit was gone. Tell her it *ain't*. Tell her it's all right. Take this in to prove it to her. She—she may never know whether it was broke or not.

MRS. PETERS (*takes the jar, looks about for something to wrap it in; takes petticoat from the clothes brought from the other room, very nervously begins winding this around the jar. In a false voice*). My, it's a good thing the men couldn't hear us. Wouldn't they just laugh! Getting all stirred up over a little thing like a—dead canary. As if that could have anything to do with—with— wouldn't they *laugh*! (*The men are heard coming downstairs.*)

MRS. HALE (*under her breath*). Maybe they would—maybe they wouldn't.

COUNTY ATTORNEY: No, Peters, it's all perfectly clear except a reason for doing it. But you know juries when it comes to women. If there was some definite thing. (*Crosses slowly to above table.* SHERIFF *crosses* D. R. MRS. HALE *and* MRS. PETERS *remain seated at either side of table*). Something to show— something to make a story about—a thing that would connect up with this strange way of doing it—— (*The women's eyes meet for an instant. Enter* HALE *from outer door.*)

HALE (*remaining* U. L. *by door*). Well, I've got the team around. Pretty cold out there.

COUNTY ATTORNEY: I'm going to stay awhile by myself. (*To the* SHERIFF). You can send Frank out for me, can't you? I want to go over everything. I'm not satisfied that we can't do better.

SHERIFF: Do you want to see what Mrs. Peters is going to take in? (*The* LAWYER *picks up the apron, laughs.*)

COUNTY ATTORNEY: Oh, I guess they're not very dangerous things the ladies have picked out. (*Moves a few things about, disturbing the quilt pieces which cover the box. Steps back*). No, Mrs. Peters doesn't need supervising. For that matter a sheriff's wife is married to the law. Ever think of it that way, Mrs. Peters?

MRS. PETERS: Not—just that way.

SHERIFF (*chuckling*). Married to the law. (*Moves to* D. R. *door to the other room*). I just want you to come in here a minute, George. We ought to take a look at these windows.

COUNTY ATTORNEY (*scoffingly*). Oh, windows!

SHERIFF: We'll be right out, Mr. Hale. (HALE *goes outside. The* SHERIFF *follows the* COUNTY ATTORNEY *into the other room. Then* MRS. HALE *rises, hands tight together, looking intensely at* MRS. PETERS, *whose eyes make a slow turn, finally meeting* MRS. HALE'S. *A moment* MRS. HALE *holds her, then her own eyes point the way to where the box is concealed. Suddenly* MRS. PETERS *throws back quilt pieces and tries to put the box in the bag she is carrying. It is too big. She opens box, starts to take bird out, cannot touch it, goes to pieces, stands there helpless. Sound of a knob turning in the other room.* MRS. HALE *snatches the box and puts it in the pocket of her big coat. Enter* COUNTY ATTORNEY *and* SHERIFF, *who remains* D. R.)

COUNTY ATTORNEY (*crosses to* U. L. *door facetiously*). Well, Henry, at least we found out that she was not going to quilt it. She was going to—what is it you call it, ladies?

MRS. HALE (*standing* C. *below table facing front, her hand against her pocket*). We call it knot it, Mr. Henderson.

CURTAIN

ACTIVITIES FOR WRITING AND DISCUSSION

1. Do a "readers' theater" performance of the play. Form into groups of five or six, assign character roles, and read the play aloud. Since **scene descriptions** and **stage directions**—printed in italics—are important, you may want to assign one person to read the italicized text. As you are performing:

   a. Mark any words, lines, stage directions, or other things that strike you—for whatever reason, and

   b. Note any ways that your interpretation of a character changes as you hear the play performed.

When you are finished, share with the class or your group any new perspectives you have on the play as a result of hearing it performed.

2. Imagine you are Minnie Wright, and you have kept a diary of your experiences since girlhood. After consulting details of Minnie's life story as revealed in the play, compose several of the entries you believe she might have written in her diary. You might include your (Minnie's) thoughts and feelings about life, music, John, and the canary, among other things.

3. Based on evidence in the play, determine whether Minnie Wright murdered her husband and how she might have done it. Then, writing in the **first-person** as Minnie Wright or as a **third-person narrator,** tell the story of how John Wright died.

4. Sometimes you can obtain interesting perspectives on a story or play by assuming the **point of view** of an involved inanimate object or animal. Imagine you are the unfortunate canary in *Trifles*. Tell your story, paying particular attention to your life and witness in the Wright household.

TERRENCE MCNALLY (b. 1939)

Andre's Mother

Characters

Cal, a young man
Arthur, his father
Penny, his sister
Andre's Mother

Time: Now
Place: New York City, Central Park

Four people—Cal, Arthur, Penny, and Andre's Mother—enter. They are nicely dressed and each carries a white helium-filled balloon on a string.

CAL: You know what's really terrible? I can't think of anything terrific to say. Goodbye. I love you. I'll miss you. And I'm supposed to be so great with words!

PENNY: What's that over there?

ARTHUR: Ask your brother.

CAL: It's a theatre. An outdoor theatre. They do plays there in the summer. Shakespeare's plays. (*To Andre's Mother.*) God, how much he wanted to play

Hamlet again. He would have gone to Timbuktu to have another go at that part. The summer he did it in Boston, he was so happy!

PENNY: Cal, I don't think she . . . ! It's not the time. Later.

ARTHUR: Your son was a . . . the Jews have a word for it' . . .

PENNY (*quietly appalled*): Oh my God!

ARTHUR: Mensch, I believe it is, and I think I'm using it right. It means warm, solid, the real thing. Correct me if I'm wrong.

PENNY: Fine, Dad, fine. Just quit while you're ahead.

ARTHUR: I won't say he was like a son to me. Even my son isn't always like a son to me. I mean . . . ! In my clumsy way, I'm trying to say how much I liked Andre. And how much he helped me to know my own boy. Cal was always two handsful but Andre and I could talk about anything under the sun. My wife was very fond of him, too.

PENNY: Cal, I don't understand about the balloons.

CAL: They represent the soul. When you let go, it means you're letting his soul ascend to Heaven. That you're willing to let go. Breaking the last earthly ties.

PENNY: Does the Pope know about this?

ARTHUR: Penny!

PENNY: Andre loved my sense of humor. Listen, you can hear him laughing. (*She lets go of her white balloon.*) So long, you glorious, wonderful, I-know-what-Cal-means-about-words . . . *man!* God forgive me for wishing you were straight every time I laid eyes on you. But if any man was going to have you, I'm glad it was my brother! Look how fast it went up. I bet that means something. Something terrific.

ARTHUR (*lets his balloon go*): Goodbye. God speed.

PENNY: Cal?

CAL: I'm not ready yet.

PENNY: Okay. We'll be over there. Come on, Pop, you can buy your little girl a Good Humor.

ARTHUR: They still make Good Humor?

PENNY: Only now they're called Dove Bars and they cost twelve dollars.

(*Penny takes Arthur off. Cal and Andre's Mother stand with their balloons.*)

CAL: I wish I knew what you were thinking. I think it would help me. You know almost nothing about me and I only know what Andre told me about you. I'd always had it in my mind that one day we would be friends, you and me. But if you didn't know about Andre and me . . . If this hadn't happened, I wonder if he would have ever told you. When he was sick, if I asked him once I asked him a thousand times, tell her. She's your mother. She won't mind. But he was so afraid of hurting you and of your disapproval. I don't know which was worse. (*No response. He sighs.*) God, how many of us live in this city because we don't want to hurt our mothers and live in mortal terror of their disapproval. We lose ourselves here. Our lives aren't furtive, just our feelings toward people like you are! A city of fugitives from our parents' scorn or heartbreak.

Sometimes he'd seem a little down and I'd say, "What's the matter, babe?" and this funny sweet, sad smile would cross his face and he'd say, "Just a little homesick, Cal, just a little bit." I always accused him of being a country boy just playing at being a hotshot, sophisticated New Yorker. (*He sighs.*)

It's bullshit. It's all bullshit. (*Still no response.*)

Do you remember the comic strip *Little Lulu?* Her mother had no name, she was so remote, so formidable to all the children. She was just Lulu's mother. "Hello, Lulu's Mother," Lulu's friends would say. She was almost anonymous in her remoteness. You remind me of her. Andre's mother. Let me answer the questions you can't ask and then I'll leave you alone and you won't ever have to see me again. Andre died of AIDS. I don't know how he got it. I tested negative. He died bravely. You would have been proud of him. The only thing that frightened him was you. I'll have everything that was his sent to you. I'll pay for it. There isn't much. You should have come up the summer he played Hamlet. He was magnificent. Yes, I'm bitter. I'm bitter I've lost him. I'm bitter what's happening. I'm bitter even now, after all this, I can't reach you. I'm beginning to feel your disapproval and it's making me ill. (*He looks at his balloon.*) Sorry, old friend. I blew it. (*He lets go of the balloon.*)

Good night, sweet prince, and flights of angels sing thee to thy rest! (*Beat.*)

Goodbye, Andre's mother.

(*He goes. Andre's Mother stands alone holding her white balloon. Her lips tremble. She looks on the verge of breaking down. She is about to let go of the balloon when she pulls it down to her. She looks at it awhile before she gently kisses it. She lets go of the balloon. She follows it with her eyes as it rises and rises. The lights are beginning to fade. Andre's Mother's eyes are still on the balloon. The lights fade.*)

GENDER AND RELATIONSHIPS: ADDITIONAL ACTIVITIES FOR WRITING AND DISCUSSION

1. Reread all or a portion of your notebook. Mark any passages, however long or short, that strike you, for whatever reason. Beside each passage, write a note explaining its significance for you. Finally, pick a favorite passage and either:

    a. Expand it into a new piece of writing, or
    b. Make notes on how you *could* expand or use it at some future date, or
    c. Rewrite it in a different form (e.g., poem, dialogue, letter, memoir).

For a list of strategies for expanding or revising, see Chapter 9.

2. Following the death of her husband, Minnie Wright (*Trifles*) sits in her jail cell. Several women **characters** and **speakers** in this section of readings

might have things to say to her. Imagine that one or more of the following visit Minnie in her cell: the unnamed narrator of "The Yellow Wallpaper," one of the women in the Thomas Hardy poems, Christina Rossetti's Margery, Pound's river-merchant's wife, Rich's "Aunt Jennifer," Wakoski's belly dancer. After selecting your visitor(s), draft a list of subjects she/they might raise with Minnie. Then dramatize her/their encounter with Minnie in the form of a dialogue or a short play (including, if you wish, a **scene description** and **stage directions**).

3. Several readings in this section take what could be seen as a "dim" view of men. As an alternative to Activity #2, bring together two or more male characters or speakers from these texts and create a dialogue or short play about their encounter.

4. What ground do the gay couple James and Dennis ("Keeping Company") and Cal (*Andre's Mother*) occupy in the "gender wars"? Conduct an interview with one or more of these characters, inviting their opinions on any of the characters or conflicts featured in the other readings within this thematic section.

5. The death of a spouse occurs (or is implied) in both Chopin's "The Story of an Hour" and Tomioka Taeko's "Just the Two of Us." Both texts also highlight the notion of "freedom" (note the next-to-last line of Taeko's poem and Louise Mallard's thoughts in "The Story of an Hour"). Write a notebook entry or essay assessing these and/or any other connections you see between these two texts and the characters whose lives they dramatize.

6. Imagine you are Kate Chopin's Louise Mallard; Colette's Alice, the narrator in Claire Kemp's "Keeping Company"; or one of the other women characters, speakers, or personae included in the readings in Chapter 16. Then read Francine du Plessix Gray's "On Friendship" and
   a. Annotate the essay as that particular character/speaker/persona might.
   b. Still in character, respond to "On Friendship" in an essay or a letter to the author. If you wish, pay special attention to ideas and issues raised in the paragraph that begins, "The quality of free consent . . ." (paragraph #13).

7. Near the end of "Looking at Women," Scott Russell Sanders writes:

To be turned into an object—whether by the brush of a painter or the lens of a photographer or the eye of a voyeur, whether by hunger or poverty or enslavement, by mugging or rape, bullets or bombs, by hatred, racism, car crashes, fires, or falls—is for each of us the deepest dread; and to reduce another person to an object is the primal wrong.

Reread the paragraph in which this sentence appears and any other passages that discuss how women—or people generally—turn themselves (or are turned) into objects. If you have not already done so, annotate those passages. Then in an essay:

a. Summarize the process of objectification to which Sanders and others (e.g., John Berger, Allen Wheelis) are referring. By what means do women/human beings become "objects," and in what respects is being thus objectified bad or harmful?

b. Apply the process of objectification you have just summarized in an analysis of "A Woman on a Roof," "Keeping Company," "Sex Without Love," or some other story or poem you have read thus far in the course.

8. Review your entire notebook; as you do, make a running list of memorable or striking topics, e.g., "women as objects," "friendship," "marriages," "kinds of love." Then choose a favorite topic, make a Topic/Form Grid (see Chapter 9), and use one of the forms on your grid to create a new notebook entry about the topic. Should your chosen form not work, do a Topic/Form Shift to a different form on your grid.

Interchapter on Notebooks and Journals (I)

Generic Ideas for Writing in Response to Published Notebooks and Journals

> Ten minutes of Lichtenberg and all the things he suppressed in himself for a year are running through his head.
>
> —ELIAS CANETTI

In the above quotation Elias Canetti, winner of the 1981 Nobel Prize for Literature, describes being inspired by someone else's notebook—specifically, the notebook of G.C. Lichtenberg (see page 47). Lichtenberg made a habit of writing down even his most commonplace reflections. Lichtenberg's ordinary passing thoughts seemed to validate Canetti's own. What Canetti suppressed he now felt emboldened to honor—and presumably write down (Canetti published several notebooks of his own).

Canetti's experience is suggestive. If great novels or poems sometimes daunt us with their finish and perfection and incline us to leave composing to the masters, a notebook or journal can have the opposite effect. Few kinds of writing can do more to inspire thought and writing in you, the reader. Notebook and journal entries are characteristically preliminary and unfinished; they invite you to shed your inhibitions and participate. The writer delivers the open-

ing conversational gambit, and you build on it. An engaging notebook or journal writer like Lichtenberg or Canetti is a sort of master conversationalist who
doesn't dominate talk but gets *you* to "say" the most interesting and surprising
things yourself.

The following are ideas for writing to use as you read published notebooks
and journals, specifically the selections included as "interchapters" in Part V of
this book. Try the ideas that suit you at a given moment, invent others of your
own, and recycle those that work best.

1. Record any stray thoughts you have while reading, however unrelated
   they may seem to the text. Remember Emerson's observation: "[Y]ou
   only read to start your own team."
2. Copy down phrases or passages that strike you. Build a collection of favorite quotations which you can reread for amusement, reflection, or as
   spurs to additional writing. (For some ideas for rereading see p. 53.)

Watch your thoughts closely as you copy out a favorite quotation: the mere
process of copying longhand sometimes suggests unrelated but interesting
ideas. For instance, Tom was in the middle of writing out a sentence from Jules
Renard's *Journal*:

God will often say to us, "You are not in heaven for fun!"

when he thought of the following, which he turned aside to jot down:

Hell would be a completely childproof society.

What Tom wrote is quite different in content—or *dissociated*—from the sentence he was copying, and his experience illustrates a psychological curiosity:
that to look hard at one thing—an object, an idea, a quotation—can point you
toward something else. "Seek and you shall find" something different—and
perhaps even better—than what you were looking for. If you have a sudden
lucky thought as Tom did, pause to jot it down. Take your time. Your accidental
thought could be the start of something worthwhile.

3. Record references to the names of authors, books, or other resources that
   pique your interest. Notebooks and journals can introduce you to a variety of fascinating writers from diverse time periods, cultures, and languages; and if you like a particular writer's notebook or journal you may
   also want to read his or her novels, poems, stories, essays, plays, or other
   works.
4. Record ideas for writing that are suggested to you by the text you are
   reading or by your own daydreaming.
5. Study a passage you like and imitate it. For example, imitate a description or a style.

6. Note any special and interesting ideas of ways to use a notebook. For instance, if the writer records anecdotes, makes lists of flowers, or writes a dialogue, make a note that you could use your own notebook for similar purposes.
7. Do the "Four-Step Process for Writing from Reading" (read, annotate, list key thoughts, write).

Finally, here are three general suggestions:

First, the most essential quality for reading other people's notebooks and journals is a reflective mind, and reflection requires a sense of *leisure*. Rather than studying or attacking notebooks as you might a steak or a job, stroll in them; and if you find a particularly delightful or appealing passage—if, so to speak, the "shade" is good—sit and read.

Second, writers' notebooks and journals are probably best dipped into at random, rather than being read consecutively from first page to last. Skip what doesn't interest you and savor what does. Above all, adapt your reading pace to the rhythm of your own thought. If a few sentences of reading launch you into five minutes of reverie or into writing several sentences of your own, so be it; you have probably read enough for one sitting.

Third, books should *do* things to you: entertain, inform, agitate or antagonize, maybe even change your life. Let them. Think, meditate, write; and share what you are thinking about and writing. Let your ideas and enthusiasms overflow in conversation so that reading and writing get contextualized into your everyday life, like food, work, and play.

Families

GUY DE MAUPASSANT (1850–1893)

The Olive Grove

When the longshoremen of Garandou, a little port of Provence, situated in the 1
bay of Pisca, between Marseilles and Toulon, perceived the boat of the Abbé
Vilbois entering the harbor, they went down to the beach to help him pull her
ashore.

The priest was alone in the boat. In spite of his fifty-eight years, he rowed 2
with all the energy of a real sailor. He had placed his hat on the bench beside
him, his sleeves were rolled up, disclosing his powerful arms, his cassock was
open at the neck and turned over his knees, and he wore a round hat of heavy,
white canvas. His whole appearance bespoke an odd and strenuous priest of
southern climes, better fitted for adventures than for clerical duties.

He rowed with strong and measured strokes, as if to show the southern 3
sailors how the men of the north handle the oars, and from time to time he
turned around to look at the landing point.

The skiff struck the beach and slid far up, the bow plowing through the 4
sand; then it stopped abruptly. The five men watching for the abbé drew near,
jovial and smiling.

"Well!" said one, with the strong accent of Provence, "have you been suc- 5
cessful, Monsieur le Curé?"

The abbé drew in the oars, removed his canvas headcovering, put on his hat, 6
pulled down his sleeves, and buttoned his coat. Then having assumed the usual
appearance of a village priest, he replied proudly: "Yes, I have caught three red-
snappers, two eels, and five sunfish."

The fishermen gathered around the boat to examine, with the air of experts, 7
the dead fish, the fat red-snappers, the flat-headed eels, those hideous sea-
serpents, and the violet sunfish, streaked with bright orange-colored stripes.

Said one: "I'll carry them up to your house, Monsieur le Curé."   8

"Thank you, my friend."   9

Having shaken hands all around, the priest started homeward, followed by 10
the man with the fish; the others took charge of the boat.

The Abbé Vilbois walked along slowly with an air of dignity. The exertion of 11
rowing had brought beads of perspiration to his brow and he uncovered his
head each time that he passed through the shade of an olive grove. The warm
evening air, freshened by a slight breeze from the sea, cooled his high forehead
covered with short, white hair, a forehead far more suggestive of an officer than
of a priest.

The village appeared, built on a hill rising from a large valley which de- 12
scended toward the sea.

It was a summer evening. The dazzling sun, traveling toward the ragged 13
crests of the distant hills, outlined on the white, dusty road the figure of the
priest, the shadow of whose three-cornered hat bobbed merrily over the fields,
sometimes apparently climbing the trunks of the olive-trees, only to fall immediately to the ground and creep among them.

With every step he took, he raised a cloud of fine, white dust, the invisible 14
powder which, in summer, covers the roads of Provence; it clung to the edge of
his cassock turning it grayish white. Completely refreshed, his hands deep in his
pockets, he strode along slowly and ponderously, like a mountaineer. His eyes
were fixed on the distant village where he had lived twenty years, and where he
hoped to die. Its church—his church—rose above the houses clustered around
it; the square turrets of gray stone, of unequal proportions and quaint design,
stood outlined against the beautiful southern valley; and their architecture suggested the fortifications of some old château rather than the steeples of a place
of worship.

The abbé was happy; for he had caught three red-snappers, two eels, and 15
five sunfish. It would enable him to triumph again over his flock, which respected him, no doubt, because he was one of the most powerful men of the
place, despite his years. These little innocent vanities were his greatest pleasures. He was a fine marksman; sometimes he practiced with his neighbor, a retired army provost who kept a tobacco shop; he could also swim better than
anyone along the coast.

In his day he had been a well-known society man, the Baron de Vilbois, but 16
had entered the priesthood after an unfortunate love-affair. Being the scion of
an old family of Picardy, devout and royalistic, whose sons for centuries had

entered the army, the magistracy, or the Church, his first thought was to follow his mother's advice and become a priest. But he yielded to his father's suggestion that he should study law in Paris and seek some high office.

While he was completing his studies his father was carried off by pneumo- 17 nia; his mother, who was greatly affected by the loss, died soon afterward. He came into a fortune, and consequently gave up the idea of following a profession to live a life of idleness. He was handsome and intelligent, but somewhat prejudiced by the traditions and principles which he had inherited, along with his muscular frame, from a long line of ancestors.

Society gladly welcomed him and he enjoyed himself after the fashion of a 18 well-to-do and seriously inclined young man. But it happened that a friend introduced him to a young actress, a pupil of the Conservatoire, who was appearing with great success at the Odéon. It was a case of love at first sight.

His sentiment had all the violence, the passion of a man born to believe in 19 absolute ideas. He saw her act the romantic rôle in which she had achieved a triumph the first night of her appearance. She was pretty, and, though naturally perverse, possessed the face of an angel.

She conquered him completely; she transformed him into a delirious fool, 20 into one of those ecstatic idiots whom a woman's look will forever chain to the pyre of fatal passions. She became his mistress and left the stage. They lived together four years, his love for her increasing during the time. He would have married her in spite of his proud name and family traditions, had he not discovered that for a long time she had been unfaithful to him with the friend who had introduced them.

The awakening was terrible, for she was about to become a mother, and he 21 was awaiting the birth of the child to make her his wife.

When he held the proof of her transgressions—some letters found in a 22 drawer—he confronted her with his knowledge and reproached her with all the savageness of his uncouth nature for her unfaithfulness and deceit. But she, a child of the people, being as sure of this man as of the other, braved and insulted him with the inherited daring of those women, who, in times of war, mounted with the men on the barricades.

He would have struck her to the ground—but she showed him her form. As 23 white as death, he checked himself, remembering that a child of his would soon be born to this vile, polluted creature. He rushed at her to crush them both, to obliterate this double shame. Reeling under his blows, and seeing that he was about to stamp out the life of her unborn babe, she realized that she was lost. Throwing out her hands to parry the blows, she cried:

"Do not kill me! It is his, not yours!"   24

He fell back, so stunned with surprise that for a moment his rage subsided. 25 He stammered:

"What? What did you say?"   26

Crazed with fright, having read her doom in his eyes and gestures, she re- 27 peated: "It's not yours, it's his."

Through his clenched teeth, he stammered: 28

"The child?"   29

"Yes."   30

"You lie!"   31

And again he lifted his foot as if to crush her, while she struggled to her   32
knees in a vain attempt to rise. "I tell you it's his. If it was yours, wouldn't it have
come much sooner?"

He was struck by the truth of this argument. In a moment of strange lucid-   33
ity, his mind evolved precise, conclusive, irresistible reasons to disclaim the
child of this miserable woman, and he felt so appeased, so happy at the
thought, that he decided to let her live.

He then spoke in a calmer voice: "Get up and leave, and never let me see you   34
again."

Quite cowed, she obeyed him and went. He never saw her again.   35

Then he left Paris and came south. He stopped in a village situated in a val-   36
ley, near the coast of the Mediterranean. Selecting for his abode an inn facing
the sea, he lived there eighteen months in complete seclusion, nursing his sorrow and despair. The memory of the unfaithful one tortured him; her grace,
her charm, her perversity haunted him, and withal came the regret of her
caresses.

He wandered aimlessly in those beautiful vales of Provence, baring his head,   37
filled with the thoughts of that woman, to the sun that filtered through the
grayish-green leaves of the olive-trees.

His former ideas of religion, the abated ardor of his faith, returned to him   38
during his sorrowful retreat. Religion had formerly seemed a refuge from the
unknown temptations of life, now it appeared as a refuge from its snares and
tortures. He had never given up the habit of prayer. In his sorrow, he turned
anew to its consolations, and often at dusk he would wander into the little village church, where in the darkness gleamed the light of the lamp hung above
the altar, to guard the sanctuary and symbolize the Divine Presence.

He confided his sorrow to his God, told Him of his misery, asking advice,   39
pity, help, and consolation. Each day, his fervid prayers disclosed stronger faith.

The bleeding heart of this man, crushed by love for a woman, still longed   40
for affection; and soon his prayers, his seclusion, his constant communion with
the Savior who consoles and cheers the weary, wrought a change in him, and
the mystic love of God entered his soul, casting out the love of the flesh.

He then decided to take up his former plans and to devote his life to the   41
Church.

He became a priest. Through family connections he succeeded in obtaining   42
a call to the parish of this village which he had come across by chance. Devoting
a large part of his fortune to the maintenance of charitable institutions, and
keeping only enough to enable him to help the poor as long as he lived, he
sought refuge in a quiet life filled with prayer and acts of kindness toward his
fellow-men.

Narrow-minded but kind-hearted, a priest with a soldier's temperament, he   43
guided his blind, erring flock forcibly through the mazes of this life in which

every taste, instinct, and desire is a pitfall. But the old man in him never disappeared entirely. He continued to love out-of-door exercise and noble sports, but he hated every woman, having an almost childish fear of their dangerous fascination.

II

The sailor who followed the priest, being a southerner, found it difficult to refrain from talking. But he did not dare start a conversation, for the abbé exerted a great prestige over his flock. At last he ventured a remark: "So you like your lodge, do you, Monsieur le Curé?"   44

This lodge was one of the tiny constructions that are inhabited during the summer by the villagers and the town people alike. It was situated in a field not far from the parish-home, and the abbé had hired it because the latter was very small and built in the heart of the village next to the church.   45

During the summer time, he did not live altogether at the lodge, but would remain a few days at a time to practice pistol-shooting and be close to nature.   46

"Yes, my friend," said the priest, "I like it very well."   47

The low structure could now be seen; it was painted pink, and the walls were almost hidden under the leaves and branches of the olive-trees that grew in the open field. A tall woman was passing in and out of the door, setting a small table at which she placed, at each trip, a knife and fork, a glass, a plate, a napkin, and a piece of bread. She wore the small cap of the women of Arles, a pointed cone of silk or black velvet, decorated with a white rosette.   48

When the abbé was near enough to make himself heard, he shouted: 49

"Eh! Marguerite!"   50

She stopped to ascertain whence the voice came, and recognizing her master: "Oh! it's you, Monsieur le Curé!"   51

"Yes. I have caught some fine fish, and want you to broil this sunfish immediately, do you hear?"   52

The servant examined, with a critical and approving glance, the fish that the sailor carried.   53

"Yes, but we are going to have a chicken for dinner," she said.   54

"Well, it cannot be helped. Tomorrow the fish will not be as fresh as it is now. I mean to enjoy a little feast—it does not happen often—and the sin is not great."   55

The woman picked out a sunfish and prepared to go into the house. "Ah!" she said, "a man came to see you three times while you were out, Monsieur le Curé."   56

Indifferently he inquired: "A man! What kind of man?"   57

"Why, a man whose appearance was not in his favor."   58

"What! a beggar?"   59

"Perhaps—I don't know. But I think he is more of a 'maoufatan.' "   60

The abbé smiled at this word, which, in the language of Provence means a highwayman, a tramp, for he was well aware of Marguerite's timidity, and knew that every day and especially every night she fancied they would be murdered.   61

He handed a few sous to the sailor, who departed. And just as he was saying: 62
"I am going to wash my hands"—for his past dainty habits still clung to him—
Marguerite called to him from the kitchen where she was scraping the fish with
a knife, thereby detaching its blood-stained, silvery scales:

"There he comes!" 63

The abbé looked down the road and saw a man coming slowly toward the 64
house; he seemed poorly dressed, indeed, so far as he could distinguish. He
could not help smiling at his servant's anxiety, and thought, while he waited for
the stranger: "I think, after all, she is right; he does look like a 'maoufatan.' "

The man walked slowly, with his eyes on the priest and his hands buried 65
deep in his pockets. He was young and wore a full, blond beard; strands of curly
hair escaped from his soft felt hat, which was so dirty and battered that it was
impossible to imagine its former color and appearance. He was clothed in a
long, dark overcoat, from which emerged the frayed edge of his trousers; on his
feet were bathing shoes that deadened his steps, giving him the stealthy walk of
a sneak thief.

When he had come within a few steps of the priest, he doffed, with a sweep- 66
ing motion, the ragged hat that shaded his brow. He was not bad-looking,
though his face showed signs of dissipation and the top of his head was bald, an
indication of premature fatigue and debauch, for he certainly was not over
twenty-five years old.

The priest responded at once to his bow, feeling that this fellow was not an 67
ordinary tramp, a mechanic out of work, or a jail-bird, hardly able to speak any
other tongue but the mysterious language of prisons.

"How do you do, Monsieur le Curé?" said the man. The priest answered 68
simply, "I salute you," unwilling to address this ragged stranger as "Monsieur."
They considered each other attentively; the abbé felt uncomfortable under the
gaze of the tramp, invaded by a feeling of unrest unknown to him.

At last the vagabond continued: "Well, do you recognize me?" 69

Greatly surprised, the priest answered: "Why, no, you are a stranger to me." 70

"Ah! you do not know me? Look at me well." 71

"I have never seen you before." 72

"Well, that may be true," replied the man sarcastically, "but let me show you 73
some one whom you will know better."

He put on his hat and unbuttoned his coat, revealing his bare chest. A red 74
sash wound around his spare frame held his trousers in place. He drew an envelope from his coat pocket, one of those soiled wrappers destined to protect the
sundry papers of the tramp, whether they be stolen or legitimate property,
those papers which he guards jealously and uses to protect himself against the
too zealous gendarmes. He pulled out a photograph about the size of a folded
letter, one of those pictures which were popular long ago; it was yellow and dim
with age, for he had carried it around with him everywhere and the heat of his
body had faded it.

Pushing it under the abbé's eyes, he demanded: 75

"Do you know him?" 76

The priest took a step forward to look and grew pale, for it was his own like- 77
ness that he had given Her years ago.

Failing to grasp the meaning of the situation he remained silent.   78

The tramp repeated: 79

"Do you recognize him?"   80

And the priest stammered: "Yes."   81

"Who is it?"   82

"It is I."   83

"It is you?"   84

"Yes."   85

"Well, then, look at us both—at me and at your picture!"   86

Already the unhappy man had seen that these two beings, the one in the 87
picture and the one by his side, resembled each other like brothers; yet he did
not understand, and muttered: "Well, what is it you wish?"

Then in an ugly voice, the tramp replied: "What do I wish? Why, first I wish 88
you to recognize me."

"Who are you?"   89

"Who am I? Ask anybody by the roadside, ask your servant, let's go and ask 90
the mayor and show him this; and he will laugh, I tell you that! Ah! you will not
recognize me as your son, papa curé?"

The old man raised his arms above his head, with patriarchal gesture, and 91
muttered despairingly: "It cannot be true!"

The young fellow drew quite close to him.   92

"Ah! It cannot be true, you say! You must stop lying, do you hear?" His 93
clenched fists and threatening face, and the violence with which he spoke, made
the priest retreat a few steps, while he asked himself anxiously which one of
them was laboring under a mistake.

Again he asserted: "I never had a child."   94

The other man replied: "And no mistress, either?"   95

The aged priest resolutely uttered one word, a proud admission: 96

"Yes."   97

"And was not this mistress about to give birth to a child when you left her?" 98

Suddenly the anger which had been quelled twenty-five years ago, not 99
quelled, but buried in the heart of the lover, burst through the wall of faith, resignation, and renunciation he had built around it. Almost beside himself, he
shouted:

"I left her because she was unfaithful to me and was carrying the child of 100
another man; had it not been for this, I should have killed both you and her,
sir!"

The young man hesitated, taken aback at the sincerity of this outburst. 101
Then he replied in a gentler voice:

"Who told you that it was another man's child?"   102

"She told me herself and braved me."   103

Without contesting this assertion the vagabond assumed the indifferent 104
tone of a loafer judging a case:

"Well, then, mother made a mistake, that's all!"   105

After his outburst of rage, the priest had succeeded in mastering himself 106
sufficiently to be able to inquire:

"And who told you that you were my son?"   107

"My mother, on her deathbed, M'sieur le Curé. And then—this!" And he 108
held the picture under the eyes of the priest.

The old man took it from him; and slowly, with a heart bursting with an- 109
guish, he compared this stranger with his faded likeness and doubted no
longer—it was his son.

An awful distress wrung his very soul, a terrible, inexpressible emotion in- 110
vaded him; it was like the remorse of some ancient crime. He began to understand a little, he guessed the rest. He lived over the brutal scene of the parting. It
was to save her life, then, that the wretched and deceitful woman had lied to
him, her outraged lover. And he had believed her. And a son of his had been
brought into the world and had grown up to be this sordid tramp, who exhaled
the very odor of vice as a goat exhales its animal smell.

He whispered: "Will you take a little walk with me, so that we can discuss 111
these matters?"

The young man sneered: "Why, certainly! Isn't that what I came for?"   112

They walked side by side through the olive grove. The sun had gone down 113
and the coolness of southern twilights spread an invisible cloak over the country. The priest shivered, and raising his eyes with a familiar motion, perceived
the trembling gray foliage of the holy tree which had spread its frail shadow
over the Son of Man in His great trouble and despondency.

A short, despairing prayer rose within him, uttered by his soul's voice, a 114
prayer by which Christians implore the Savior's aid: "O Lord! have mercy on
me."

Turning to his son he said: "So your mother is dead?"   115

These words, "Your mother is dead," awakened a new sorrow; it was the tor- 116
ment of the flesh which cannot forget, the cruel echo of past sufferings; but
mostly the thrill of the fleeting, delirious bliss of his youthful passion.

The young man replied: "Yes, Monsieur le Curé, my mother is dead."   117

"Has she been dead a long while?"   118

"Yes, three years."   119

A new doubt entered the priest's mind. "And why did you not find me out 120
before?"

The other man hesitated.   121

"I was unable to, I was prevented. But excuse me for interrupting these rec- 122
ollections—I will enter into more details later—for I have not had anything to
eat since yesterday morning."

A tremor of pity shook the old man and holding forth both hands: "Oh! my 123
poor child!" he said.

The young fellow took those big, powerful hands in his own slender and 124
feverish palms.

Then he replied, with that air of sarcasm which hardly ever left his lips: "Ah! 125
I'm beginning to think that we shall get along very well together, after all!"

The curé started toward the lodge.   126

"Let us go to dinner," he said.   127

He suddenly remembered, with a vague and instinctive pleasure, the fine 128
fish he had caught, which, with the chicken, would make a good meal for the
poor fellow.

The servant was in front of the door, watching their approach with an anx- 129
ious and forbidding face.

"Marguerite," shouted the abbé, "take the table and put it into the dining- 130
room, right away; and set two places, as quick as you can."

The woman seemed stunned at the idea that her master was going to dine 131
with this tramp.

But the abbé, without waiting for her, removed the plate and napkin and 132
carried the little table into the dining-room.

A few minutes later he was sitting opposite the beggar, in front of a soup- 133
tureen filled with savory cabbage soup, which sent up a cloud of fragrant steam.

III

When the plates were filled, the tramp fell to with ravenous avidity. The abbé 134
had lost his appetite and ate slowly, leaving the bread in the bottom of his plate.
Suddenly he inquired:

"What is your name?"   135

The man smiled; he was delighted to satisfy his hunger.   136

"Father unknown," he said, "and no other name but my mother's, which 137
you probably remember. But I possess two Christian names, which, by the way,
are quite unsuited to me—Philippe-Auguste."

The priest whitened.   138

"Why were you named thus?" he asked.   139

The tramp shrugged his shoulders. "I fancy you ought to know. After 140
mother left you, she wished to make your rival believe that I was his child. He
did believe it until I was about fifteen. Then I began to look too much like you.
And he disclaimed me, the scoundrel. I had been christened Philippe-Auguste;
now, if I had not resembled a soul, or if I had been the son of a third person,
who had stayed in the background, today I should be the Vicomte Philippe-Auguste de Pravallon, son of the count and senator bearing this name. I have
christened myself 'No-luck.' "

"How did you learn all this?"   141

"They discussed it before me, you know; pretty lively discussions they were, 142
too. I tell you, that's what shows you the seamy side of life!"

Something more distressing than all he had suffered during the last half 143
hour now oppressed the priest. It was a sort of suffocation which seemed as if it
would grow and grow till it killed him; it was not due so much to the things he
heard as to the manner in which they were uttered by this wayside tramp. Between himself and this beggar, between his son and himself, he was discovering
the existence of those moral divergencies which are as fatal poisons to certain
souls. Was this his son? He could not yet believe it. He wanted all the proofs,
every one of them. He wanted to hear all, to listen to all. Again he thought of

the olive-trees that shaded his little lodge, and for the second time he prayed: "O Lord! have mercy upon me."

Philippe-Auguste had finished his soup. He inquired: "Is there nothing else, 144 abbé?"

The kitchen was built in an annex. Marguerite could not hear her master's 145 voice. He always called her by striking a Chinese gong hung on the wall behind his chair. He took the brass hammer and struck the round metal plate. It gave a feeble sound, which grew and vibrated, becoming sharper and louder till it finally died away on the evening breeze.

The servant appeared with a frowning face and cast angry glances at the 146 tramp, as if her faithful instinct had warned her of the misfortune that had befallen her master. She held a platter on which was the sunfish, spreading a savory odor of melted butter through the room. The abbé divided the fish lengthwise, helping his son to the better half: "I caught it a little while ago," he said, with a touch of pride in spite of his keen distress.

Marguerite had not left the room. 147

The priest added: "Bring us some wine, the white wine of Cape Corse." 148

She almost rebelled, and the priest, assuming a severe expression was 149 obliged to repeat: "Now, go, and bring two bottles, remember," for, when he drank with anybody, a very rare pleasure, indeed, he always opened one bottle for himself.

Beaming, Philippe-Auguste remarked: "Fine! A splendid idea! It has been a 150 long time since I've had such a dinner." The servant came back after a few minutes. The abbé thought it an eternity, for now a thirst for information burned his blood like infernal fire.

After the bottles had been opened, the woman still remained, her eyes glued 151 on the tramp.

"Leave us," said the curé. 152

She intentionally ignored his command. 153

He repeated almost roughly: "I have ordered you to leave us." 154

Then she left the room. 155

Philippe-Auguste devoured the fish voraciously, while his father sat watch- 156 ing him, more and more surprised and saddened at all the baseness stamped on the face that was so like his own. The morsels the abbé raised to his lips remained in his mouth, for his throat could not swallow; so he ate slowly, trying to choose, from the host of questions which besieged his mind, the one he wished his son to answer first. At last he spoke:

"What was the cause of her death?" 157

"Consumption." 158

"Was she ill a long time?" 159

"About eighteen months." 160

"How did she contract it?" 161

"We could not tell." 162

Both men were silent. The priest was reflecting. He was oppressed by the 163 multitude of things he wished to know and to hear, for since the rupture, since the day he had tried to kill her, he had heard nothing. Certainly, he had not cared to know, because he had buried her, along with his happiest days, in forgetfulness; but now, knowing that she was dead and gone, he felt within himself the almost jealous desire of a lover to hear all.

He continued: "She was not alone, was she?"   164

"No, she lived with him."   165

The old man started: "With him? With Pravallon?"   166

"Why, yes."   167

And the betrayed man rapidly calculated that the woman who had deceived   168
him, had lived over thirty years with his rival.

Almost unconsciously he asked: "Were they happy?"   169

The young man sneered. "Why, yes, with ups and downs! It would have been   170
better had I not been there. I always spoiled everything."

"How, and why?" inquired the priest.   171

"I have already told you. Because he thought I was his son up to my fifteenth 172
year. But the old fellow wasn't a fool, and soon discovered the likeness. That
created scenes. I used to listen behind the door. He accused mother of having
deceived him. Mother would answer: 'Is it my fault? you knew quite well when
you took me that I was the mistress of that other man.' You were that other
man."

"Ah! They spoke of me sometimes?"   173

"Yes, but never mentioned your name before me, excepting toward the end,   174
when mother knew she was lost. I think they distrusted me."

"And you—and you learned quite early the irregularity of your mother's   175
position?"

"Why, certainly. I am not innocent and I never was. Those things are easy to 176
guess as soon as one begins to know life."

Philippe-Auguste had been filling his glass repeatedly. His eyes now were   177
beginning to sparkle, for his long fast was favorable to the intoxicating effects of
the wine. The priest noticed it and wished to caution him. But suddenly the
thought that a drunkard is imprudent and loquacious flashed through him,
and lifting the bottle he again filled the young man's glass.

Meanwhile Marguerite had brought the chicken. Having set it on the table, 178
she again fastened her eyes on the tramp, saying in an indignant voice: "Can't
you see that he's drunk, Monsieur le Curé?"

"Leave us," replied the priest, "and return to the kitchen."   179

She went out, slamming the door.   180

He then inquired: "What did your mother say about me?"   181

"Why, what a woman usually says of a man she has jilted: that you were hard 182
to get along with, very strange, and that you would have made her life miserable
with your peculiar ideas."

"Did she say that often?"   183

"Yes, but sometimes only in allusions, for fear I would understand; but nev- 184
ertheless I guessed all."

"And how did they treat you in that house?"   185

The Olive Grove   289

"Me? They treated me very well at first and very badly afterward. When 186
mother saw that I was interfering with her, she shook me."

"How?" 187

"How? very easily. When I was about sixteen years old, I got into various 188
scrapes, and those blackguards put me into a reformatory to get rid of me." He
put his elbows on the table and rested his cheeks in his palms. He was hopelessly intoxicated, and felt the unconquerable desire of all drunkards to talk and
boast about themselves.

He smiled sweetly, with a feminine grace, an arch grace the priest knew and 189
recognized as the hated charm that had won him long ago, and had also
wrought his undoing. Now it was his mother whom the boy resembled, not so
much because of his features, but because of his fascinating and deceptive
glance, and the seductiveness of the false smile that played around his lips, the
outlet of his inner ignominy.

Philippe-Auguste began to relate: "Ah! Ah! Ah!—I've had a fine life since I 190
left the reformatory! A great writer would pay a large sum for it! Why, old Père
Dumas's Monte Cristo has had no stranger adventures than mine."

He paused to reflect with the philosophical gravity of the drunkard, then he 191
continued slowly:

"When you wish a boy to turn out well, no matter what he has done, never 192
send him to reformatory. The associations are too bad. Now, I got into a bad
scrape. One night about nine o'clock, I, with three companions—we were all a
little drunk—was walking along the road near the ford of Folac. All at once a
wagon hove in sight, with the driver and his family asleep in it. They were people from Martinon on their way home from town. I caught hold of the bridle,
led the horse to the ferryboat, made him walk into it, and pushed the boat into
the middle of the stream. This created some noise and the driver awoke. He
could not see in the dark, but whipped up the horse, which started on a run and
landed in the water with the whole load. All were drowned! My companions denounced me to the authorities, though they thought it was a good joke when
they saw me do it. Really, we didn't think that it would turn out that way. We
only wanted to give the people a ducking, just for fun. After that I committed
worse offenses to revenge myself for the first one, which did not, on my honor,
warrant the reformatory. But what's the use of telling them? I will speak only of
the latest one, because I am sure it will please you. Papa, I avenged you!"

The abbé was watching his son with terrified eyes; he had stopped eating. 193

Philippe-Auguste was preparing to begin. "No, not yet," said the priest, "in a 194
little while."

And he turned to strike the Chinese gong. 195

Marguerite appeared almost instantly. Her master addressed her in such a 196
rough tone that she hung her head, thoroughly frightened and obedient: "Bring
in the lamp and the dessert, and then do not appear until I summon you."

She went out and returned with a porcelain lamp covered with a green 197
shade, and bringing also a large piece of cheese and some fruit.

After she had gone, the abbé turned resolutely to his son. 198

"Now I am ready to hear you."   199

Philippe-Auguste calmly filled his plate with dessert and poured wine into   200
his glass. The second bottle was nearly empty, though the priest had not
touched it.

His mouth and tongue, thick with food and wine, the man stuttered: "Well,   201
now for the last job. And it's a good one. I was home again—stayed there in
spite of them, because they feared me—yes, feared me. Ah! you can't fool with
me, you know—I'll do anything, when I'm roused. They lived together on and
off. The old man had two residences. One official, for the senator, the other
clandestine, for the lover. Still, he lived more in the latter than in the former, as
he could not get along without mother. Mother was a sharp one—she knew
how to hold a man! She had taken him body and soul, and kept him to the last!
Well, I had come back and I kept them down by fright. I am resourceful at
times—nobody can match me for sharpness and for strength, too—I'm afraid
of no one. Well, mother got sick and the old man took her to a fine place in the
country, near Meulan, situated in a park as big as a wood. She lasted about eighteen months, as I told you. Then we felt the end to be near. He came from Paris
every day—he was very miserable—really.

"One morning they chatted a long time, over an hour, I think, and I could   202
not imagine what they were talking about. Suddenly mother called me in and
said:

" 'I am going to die, and there is something I want to tell you before-hand,   203
in spite of the Count's advice.' In speaking of him she always said 'the Count.' 'It
is the name of your father, who is alive.' I had asked her this more than fifty
times—more than fifty times—my father's name—more than fifty times—and
she always refused to tell. I think I even beat her one day to make her talk, but it
was of no use. Then, to get rid of me, she told me that you had died penniless,
that you were worthless and that she had made a mistake in her youth, an innocent girl's mistake. She lied so well, I really believed you had died.

"Finally she said: 'It is your father's name.'   204

"The old man, who was sitting in an armchair, repeated three times, like   205
this: 'You do wrong, you do wrong, you do wrong, Rosette.'

"Mother sat up in bed. I can see her now, with her flushed cheeks and shin-   206
ing eyes; she loved me, in spite of everything; and she said: 'Then you do something for him, Philippe!' In speaking to him she called him 'Philippe' and me
'Auguste.'

"He began to shout like a madman: 'Do something for that loafer—that   207
blackguard, that convict? Never!'

"And he continued to call me names, as if he had done nothing else all his   208
life but collect them.

"I was angry, but mother told me to hold my tongue, and she resumed: 209
'Then you must want him to starve, for you know that I leave no money.'

"Without being deterred, he continued: 'Rosette, I have given you thirty-   210
five thousand francs a year for thirty years—that makes more than a million. I
have enabled you to live like a wealthy, a beloved, and I may say, a happy

woman. I owe nothing to that fellow, who has spoiled our late years, and he will not get a cent from me. It is useless to insist. Tell him the name of his father, if you wish. I am sorry, but I wash my hands of him.'

"Then mother turned toward me. I thought: 'Good! now I'm going to find 211 my real father—if he has money, I'm saved.'

"She went on: 'Your father, the Baron de Vilbois, is today the Abbé Vilbois, 212 curé of Garandou, near Toulon. He was my lover before I left him for the Count!'

"And she told me all, except that she had deceived you about her pregnancy. 213 But women, you know, never tell the whole truth."

Sneeringly, unconsciously, he was revealing the depths of his foul nature. 214 With beaming face he raised the glass to his lips and continued:

"Mother died two days—two days later. We followed her remains to the 215 grave, he and I—say—wasn't it funny?—he and I—and three servants—that was all. He cried like a calf—we were side by side—we looked like father and son.

"Then he went back to the house alone. I was thinking to myself: 'I'll have to 216 clear out now and without a penny, too.' I owned only fifty francs. What could I do to revenge myself?

"He touched me on the arm and said: 'I wish to speak to you.' I followed 217 him into his office. He sat down in front of the desk and, wiping away his tears, he told me that he would not be as hard on me as he had said he would to mother. He begged me to leave you alone. That—that concerns only you and me. He offered me a thousand-franc note—a thousand—a thousand francs. What could a fellow like me do with a thousand francs?—I saw that there were very many bills in the drawer. The sight of the money made me wild. I put out my hand as if to take the note he offered me, but instead of doing so, I sprang at him, threw him to the ground and choked him till he grew purple. When I saw that he was going to give up the ghost, I gagged and bound him. Then I undressed him, laid him on his stomach and—ah! ah! ah!—I avenged you in a funny way!"

He stopped to cough, for he was choking with merriment. His ferocious, 218 mirthful smile reminded the priest once more of the woman who had wrought his undoing.

"And then?" he inquired. 219

"Then—ah! ah! ah!—There was a bright fire in the fireplace—it was in the 220 winter—in December—mother died—a bright coal fire—I took the poker—I let it get red-hot—and I made crosses on his back, eight or more, I cannot remember how many—then I turned him over and repeated them on his stomach. Say, wasn't it funny, papa? Formerly they marked convicts in this way. He wriggled like an eel—but I had gagged him so that he couldn't scream. I gathered up the bills—twelve in all—with mine it made thirteen—an unlucky number. I left the house, after telling the servants not to bother their master until dinner-time, because he was asleep. I thought that he would hush the matter up because he was a senator and would fear the scandal. I was mistaken. Four days later I was arrested in a Paris restaurant. I got three years for the job. That is the reason why I did not come to you sooner." He drank again, and stuttering so as to render his words almost unintelligible, continued:

"Now—papa—isn't it funny to have one's papa a curé? You must be nice to   221 me, very nice, because you know, I am not commonplace—and I did a good job—didn't I—on the old man?"

The anger which years ago had driven the Abbé Vilbois to desperation rose   222 within him at the sight of this miserable man.

He, who in the name of the Lord, had so often pardoned the infamous se-   223 crets whispered to him under the seal of confession, was now merciless in his own behalf. No longer did he implore the help of a merciful God, for he real-ized that no power on earth or in the sky could save those who had been visited by such a terrible disaster.

All the ardor of his passionate heart and of his violent blood, which long   224 years of resignation had tempered, awoke against the miserable creature who was his son. He protested against the likeness he bore to him and to his mother, the wretched mother who had formed him so like herself; and he rebelled against the destiny that had chained this criminal to him, like an iron ball to a galley-slave.

The shock roused him from the peaceful and pious slumber which had   225 lasted twenty-five years; with a wonderful lucidity he saw all that would in-evitably ensue.

Convinced that he must talk loud so as to intimidate this man from the   226 first, he spoke with his teeth clenched with fury:

"Now that you have told all, listen to me. You will leave here tomorrow   227 morning. You will go to a country that I shall designate, and never leave it with-out my permission. I will give you a small income, for I am poor. If you disobey me once, it will be withdrawn and you will learn to know me."

Though Philippe-Auguste was half dazed with wine, he understood the   228 threat. Instantly the criminal within him rebelled. Between hiccoughs he sput-tered: "Ah! papa, be careful what you say—you're a curé, remember—I hold you—and you have to walk straight, like the rest!"

The abbé started. Through his whole muscular frame crept the unconquer-   229 able desire to seize this monster, to bend him like a twig, so as to show him that he would have to yield.

Shaking the table, he shouted: "Take care, take care—I am afraid of no-   230 body."

The drunkard lost his balance and seeing that he was going to fall and   231 would forthwith be in the priest's power, he reached with a murderous look for one of the knives lying on the table. The abbé perceived his motion, and he gave the table a terrible shove; his son toppled over and landed on his back. The lamp fell with a crash and went out.

During a moment the clinking of broken glass was heard in the darkness, then   232 the muffled sound of a soft body creeping on the floor, and then all was silent.

With the crashing of the lamp a complete darkness spread over them; it was 233
so prompt and unexpected that they were stunned by it as by some terrible
event. The drunkard, pressed against the wall, did not move; the priest remained on his chair in the midst of the night which had quelled his rage. The
somber veil that had descended so rapidly, arresting his anger, also quieted the
furious impulses of his soul; new ideas, as dark and dreary as the obscurity, beset him.

The room was perfectly silent, like a tomb where nothing draws the breath 234
of life. Not a sound came from outside, neither the rumbling of a distant
wagon, nor the bark of a dog, nor even the sigh of the wind passing through the
trees.

This lasted a long time, perhaps an hour. Then suddenly the gong vibrated! 235
It rang once, as if it had been struck a short, sharp blow, and was instantly followed by the noise of a falling body and an overturned chair.

Marguerite came running out of the kitchen, but as soon as she opened the 236
door she fell back, frightened by the intense darkness. Trembling, her heart
beating as if it would burst, she called in a low, hoarse voice: "M'sieur le Curé!
M'sieur le Curé!"

Nobody answered, nothing stirred. 237

"*Mon Dieu, mon Dieu,*" she thought, "what has happened, what have they 238
done?"

She did not dare enter the room, yet feared to go back to fetch a light. She 239
felt as if she would like to run away, to screech at the top of her voice, though
she knew her legs would refuse to carry her. She repeated: "M'sieur le Curé!
M'sieur le Curé! it is me, Marguerite."

But, notwithstanding her terror, the instinctive desire of helping her master 240
and a woman's courage, which is sometimes heroic, filled her soul with a terrified audacity, and running back to the kitchen she fetched a lamp.

She stopped at the doorsill. First, she caught sight of the tramp lying against 241
the wall, asleep, or simulating slumber; then she saw the broken lamp, and then,
under the table, the feet and black-stockinged legs of the priest, who must have
fallen backward, striking his head on the gong.

Her teeth chattering and her hands trembling with fright, she kept on re- 242
peating: "My God! My God! what is this?"

She advanced slowly, taking small steps, till she slid on something slimy and 243
almost fell.

Stooping, she saw that the floor was red and that a red liquid was spreading 244
around her feet toward the door. She guessed that it was blood. She threw down
her light so as to hide the sight of it, and fled from the room out into the fields,
running half crazed toward the village. She ran screaming at the top of her
voice, and bumping against the trees she did not heed, her eyes fastened on the
gleaming lights of the distant town.

Her shrill voice rang out like the gloomy cry of the night-owl, repeating 245
continuously, "The maoufatan—the maoufatan—the maoufatan"—

When she reached the first house, excited men came out and surrounded 246
her; but she could not answer them and struggled to escape, for the fright had
turned her head.

After a while they guessed that something must have happened to the curé, 247
and a little rescuing party started for the lodge.

The little pink house standing in the middle of the olive grove had grown 248
black and invisible in the dark, silent night. Since the gleam of the solitary window had faded, the cabin was plunged in darkness, lost in the grove, and unrec-
ognizable for anyone but a native of the place.

Soon lights began to gleam near the ground, between the trees, streaking 249
the dried grass with long, yellow reflections. The twisted trunks of the olive-
trees assumed fantastic shapes under the moving lights, looking like monsters
or infernal serpents. The projected reflections suddenly revealed a vague, white
mass, and soon the low, square wall of the lodge grew pink from the light of the
lanterns. Several peasants were carrying the lamps, escorting two gendarmes
with revolvers, the mayor, the *garde-champêtre*, and Marguerite, supported by
the men, for she was almost unable to walk.

The rescuing party hesitated a moment in front of the open, gruesome 250
door. But the brigadier, snatching a lantern from one of the men, entered, followed by the rest.

The servant had not lied, blood covered the floor like a carpet. It had spread 251
to the place where the tramp was lying, bathing one of his hands and legs.

The father and son were asleep, the one with a severed throat, the other in a 252
drunken stupor. The two gendarmes seized the latter and before he awoke they
had him handcuffed. He rubbed his eyes, stunned, stupefied with liquor, and
when he saw the body of the priest, he appeared terrified, unable to understand
what had happened.

"Why did he not escape?" said the mayor. 253

"He was too drunk," replied the officer. 254

And every man agreed with him, for nobody ever thought that perhaps the 255
Abbé Vilbois had taken his own life.

ACTIVITIES FOR WRITING AND DISCUSSION

1. What do you see as the major themes of the story? Orally or in writing,
explain and illustrate the themes with examples, events, or passages from the
text.

2. Maupassant is known for his skillful **plot** construction. What central
conflicts (see p. 135) keep you reading this story? Where do you locate the climax? Is the end of the story forshadowed in any ways, and, if so, how? Support
your thoughts with references to specific passages in the text.

3. In paragraph 224 the narrator states that "[The abbé] protested against
the likeness [his son] bore to him and to his mother, the wretched mother who

had formed him so like herself." Is the character of Philippe-Auguste purely his mother's creation, or does it bear qualities of the father he has never met till now? Explain your answer with evidence to support your view.

4. Working with a small group or as a class, reconstruct the details of what happens between the time the lamp crashes (paragraph 231) and the last sentence of the story.

5. The Abbé Vilbois meets his son for the first time and dies just a few hours later. During those few hours, however, he is forced to remember his whole unhappy life. We witness his "fury" and his determination to intimidate Philippe-Auguste but are privy to few details of what passes through his mind as he tries to process the sordid revelations presented him. After the lamp crashes and the room has gone dark father and son sit still and silent for "perhaps an hour." Reread this part of the story. Then:

   a. Recreate, in a **stream of consciousness** form, the "new ideas" that "beset" the abbé (what is your, i.e., the abbé's, plan?); or

   b. Imagine that Philippe-Auguste has fled the room and, as the priest, write a suicide note or a murder-suicide note that explains what you are about to do next.

6. Rewrite the ending any way you wish. Then discuss whether Maupassant's ending is the only possible satisfactory ending, or whether there are others equally good or better.

James Joyce (1882–1941)

Eveline

She sat at the window watching the evening invade the avenue. Her head was leaned against the window curtains and in her nostrils was the odour of dusty cretonne. She was tired.

Few people passed. The man out of the last house passed on his way home; she heard his footsteps clacking along the concrete pavement and afterwards crunching on the cinder path before the new red houses. One time there used to be a field there in which they used to play every evening with other people's children. Then a man from Belfast bought the field and built houses in it—not like their little brown houses but bright brick houses with shining roofs. The children of the avenue used to play together in that field—the Devines, the Waters, the Dunns, little Keogh the cripple, she and her brothers and sisters. Ernest, however, never played: he was too grown up. Her father used often to hunt them in out of the field with his blackthorn stick; but usually little Keogh used to keep *nix* and call out when he saw her father coming. Still they seemed to have been rather happy then. Her father was not so bad then; and besides, her mother was alive. That was a long time ago; she and her brothers and sisters were all grown up; her mother was dead. Tizzie Dunn was dead, too, and the Waters had gone back to England. Everything changes. Now she was going to go away like the others, to leave her home.

Home! She looked round the room, reviewing all its familiar objects which 3 she had dusted once a week for so many years, wondering where on earth all the dust came from. Perhaps she would never see again those familiar objects from which she had never dreamed of being divided. And yet during all those years she had never found out the name of the priest whose yellowing photograph hung on the wall above the broken harmonium beside the coloured print of the promises made to Blessed Margaret Mary Alacoque. He had been a school friend of her father. Whenever he showed the photograph to a visitor her father used to pass it with a casual word:

—He is in Melbourne now. 4

She had consented to go away, to leave her home. Was that wise? She tried to 5 weigh each side of the question. In her home anyway she had shelter and food; she had those whom she had known all her life about her. Of course she had to work hard both in the house and at business. What would they say of her in the Stores when they found out that she had run away with a fellow? Say she was a fool, perhaps, and her place would be filled up by advertisement. Miss Gavan would be glad. She had always had an edge on her, especially whenever there were people listening.

—Miss Hill, don't you see these ladies are waiting? 6
—Look lively, Miss Hill, please. 7

She would not cry many tears at leaving the Stores. 8

But in her new home, in a distant unknown country, it would not be like 9 that. Then she would be married—she, Eveline. People would treat her with respect then. She would not be treated as her mother had been. Even now, though she was over nineteen, she sometimes felt herself in danger of her father's violence. She knew it was that that had given her the palpitations. When they were growing up he had never gone for her, like he used to go for Harry and Ernest, because she was a girl; but latterly he had begun to threaten her and say what he would do to her only for her dead mother's sake. And now she had nobody to protect her. Ernest was dead and Harry, who was in the church decorating business, was nearly always down somewhere in the country. Besides, the invariable squabble for money on Saturday nights had begun to weary her unspeakably. She always gave her entire wages—seven shillings—and Harry always sent up what he could but the trouble was to get any money from her father. He said she used to squander the money, that she had no head, that he wasn't going to give her his hard-earned money to throw about the streets, and much more, for he was usually fairly bad of a Saturday night. In the end he would give her the money and ask her had she any intention of buying Sunday's dinner. Then she had to rush out as quickly as she could and do her marketing, holding her black leather purse tightly in her hand as she elbowed her way through the crowds and returning home late under her load of provisions. She had hard work to keep the house together and to see that the two young children who had been left to her charge went to school regularly and got their meals regularly. It was hard work—a hard life—but now that she was about to leave it she did not find it a wholly undesirable life.

She was about to explore another life with Frank. Frank was very kind, manly, open-hearted. She was to go away with him by the night-boat to be his wife and to live with him in Buenos Ayres where he had a home waiting for her. How well she remembered the first time she had seen him; he was lodging in a house on the main road where she used to visit. It seemed a few weeks ago. He was standing at the gate, his peaked cap pushed back on his head and his hair tumbled forward over a face of bronze. Then they had come to know each other. He used to meet her outside the Stores every evening and see her home. He took her to see *The Bohemian Girl* and she felt elated as she sat in an unaccustomed part of the theatre with him. He was awfully fond of music and sang a little. People knew that they were courting and, when he sang about the lass that loves a sailor, she always felt pleasantly confused. He used to call her Poppens out of fun. First of all it had been an excitement for her to have a fellow and then she had begun to like him. He had tales of distant countries. He had started as a deck boy at a pound a month on a ship of the Allan Line going out to Canada. He told her the names of the ships he had been on and the names of the different services. He had sailed through the Straits of Magellan and he told her stories of the terrible Patagonians. He had fallen on his feet in Buenos Ayres, he said, and had come over to the old country just for a holiday. Of course, her father had found out the affair and had forbidden her to have anything to say to him. 10

—I know these sailor chaps, he said. 11

One day he had quarrelled with Frank and after that she had to meet her lover secretly. 12

The evening deepened in the avenue. The white of two letters in her lap grew indistinct. One was to Harry; the other was to her father. Ernest had been her favourite but she liked Harry too. Her father was becoming old lately, she noticed; he would miss her. Sometimes he could be very nice. Not long before, when she had been laid up for a day, he had read her out a ghost story and made toast for her at the fire. Another day, when their mother was alive, they had all gone for a picnic to the Hill of Howth. She remembered her father putting on her mother's bonnet to make the children laugh. 13

Her time was running out but she continued to sit by the window, leaning her head against the window curtain, inhaling the odour of dusty cretonne. Down far in the avenue she could hear a street organ playing. She knew the air. Strange that it should come that very night to remind her of the promise to her mother, her promise to keep the home together as long as she could. She remembered the last night of her mother's illness; she was again in the close dark room at the other side of the hall and outside she heard a melancholy air of Italy. The organ-player had been ordered to go away and given sixpence. She remembered her father strutting back into the sickroom saying: 14

—Damned Italians! coming over here! 15

As she mused the pitiful vision of her mother's life laid its spell on the very   16
quick of her being—that life of commonplace sacrifices closing in final crazi-
ness. She trembled as she heard again her mother's voice saying constantly with
foolish insistence:

—Derevaun Seraun! Derevaun Seraun!   17

She stood up in a sudden impulse of terror. Escape! She must escape! Frank   18
would save her. He would give her life, perhaps love, too. But she wanted to live.
Why should she be unhappy? She had a right to happiness. Frank would take
her in his arms, fold her in his arms. He would save her.

<hr />

She stood among the swaying crowd in the station at the North Wall. He   19
held her hand and she knew that he was speaking to her, saying something
about the passage over and over again. The station was full of soldiers with
brown baggages. Through the wide doors of the sheds she caught a glimpse of
the black mass of the boat, lying in beside the quay wall, with illumined port-
holes. She answered nothing. She felt her cheek pale and cold and, out of a
maze of distress, she prayed to God to direct her, to show her what was her
duty. The boat blew a long mournful whistle into the mist. If she went, tomorrow she would be on the sea with Frank, steaming towards Buenos Ayres.
Their passage had been booked. Could she still draw back after all he had done
for her? Her distress awoke a nausea in her body and she kept moving her lips
in silent fervent prayer.

A bell clanged upon her heart. She felt him seize her hand: 20

—Come!   21

All the seas of the world tumbled about her heart. He was drawing her into   22
them: he would drown her. She gripped with both hands at the iron railing.

—Come!   23

No! No! No! It was impossible. Her hands clutched the iron in frenzy. Amid   24
the seas she sent a cry of anguish!

—Eveline! Evvy!   25

He rushed beyond the barrier and called to her to follow. He was shouted   26
at to go on but he still called to her. She set her white face to him, passive,
like a helpless animal. Her eyes gave him no sign of love or farewell or recognition.

ACTIVITIES FOR WRITING AND DISCUSSION

1. Joyce's story uses the device of **flashback** rather than straightforward
chronology. Collaboratively, reconstruct the complex details of Eveline's life
story, family, and relationships with her father and mother. For what reasons,
ultimately, does she choose to stay with her family rather than elope with
Frank?

2. Assuming the **character** of Eveline, compose a series of diary entries that articulate your divided feelings for Frank and your family. Where appropriate, incorporate details from Joyce's story into your entries.

3. Eveline's conflict (self-development versus social duty or duty to family) is shared by countless sons and daughters. Tell the story of a real-life (or imagined) son or daughter whose experience is analogous to Eveline's.

TILLIE OLSEN (b.1912/1913)

I Stand Here Ironing

I stand here ironing, and what you asked me moves tormented back and forth 1 with the iron.

"I wish you would manage the time to come in and talk with me about your 2 daughter. I'm sure you can help me understand her. She's a youngster who needs help and whom I'm deeply interested in helping."

"Who needs help." Even if I came, what good would it do? You think be- 3 cause I am her mother I have a key, or that in some way you could use me as a key? She has lived for nineteen years. There is all that life that has happened outside of me, beyond me.

And when is there time to remember, to sift, to weigh, to estimate, to total? I 4 will start and there will be an interruption and I will have to gather it all together again. Or I will become engulfed with all I did or did not do, with what should have been and what cannot be helped.

She was a beautiful baby. The first and only one of our five that was beauti- 5 ful at birth. You do not guess how new and uneasy her tenancy in her now-love-liness. You did not know her all those years she was thought homely, or see her poring over her baby pictures, making me tell her over and over how beautiful she had been—and would be, I would tell her—and was now, to the seeing eye. But the seeing eyes were few or non-existent. Including mine.

I nursed her. They feel that's important nowadays. I nursed all the children, 6 but with her, with all the fierce rigidity of first motherhood, I did like the books then said. Though her cries battered me to trembling and my breasts ached with swollenness, I waited till the clock decreed.

Why do I put that first? I do not even know if it matters, or if it explains 7 anything.

She was a beautiful baby. She blew shining bubbles of sound. She loved mo- 8 tion, loved light, loved color and music and textures. She would lie on the floor in her blue overalls patting the surface so hard in ecstasy her hands and feet would blur. She was a miracle to me, but when she was eight months old I had to leave her daytimes with the woman downstairs to whom she was no miracle at all, for I worked or looked for work and for Emily's father, who "could no longer endure" (he wrote in his good-bye note) "sharing want with us."

I was nineteen. It was the pre-relief, pre-WPA world of the depression. I 9 would start running as soon as I got off the streetcar, running up the stairs, the place smelling sour, and awake or asleep to startle awake, when she saw me she would break into a clogged weeping that could not be comforted, a weeping I can hear yet.

After a while I found a job hashing at night so I could be with her days, and 10 it was better. But it came to where I had to bring her to his family and leave her.

It took a long time to raise the money for her fare back. Then she got 11 chicken pox and I had to wait longer. When she finally came, I hardly knew her, walking quick and nervous like her father, looking like her father, thin, and dressed in a shoddy red that yellowed her skin and glared at the pockmarks. All the baby loveliness gone.

She was two. Old enough for nursery school they said, and I did not know 12 then what I know now—the fatigue of the long day, and the lacerations of group life in the nurseries that are only parking places for children.

Except that it would have made no difference if I had known. It was the only 13 place there was. It was the only way we could be together, the only way I could hold a job.

And even without knowing, I knew. I knew the teacher that was evil because 14 all these years it has curdled into my memory, the little boy hunched in the corner, her rasp, "why aren't you outside, because Alvin hits you? that's no reason, go out, scaredy." I knew Emily hated it even if she did not clutch and implore "don't go Mommy" like the other children, mornings.

She always had a reason why she should stay home. Momma, you look sick, 15 Momma. I feel sick. Momma, the teachers aren't there today, they're sick. Momma, we can't go, there was a fire there last night. Momma, it's a holiday to-day, no school, they told me.

But never a direct protest, never rebellion. I think of our others in their 16 three-, four-year-oldness—the explosions, the tempers, the denunciations, the demands—and I feel suddenly ill. I put the iron down. What in me demanded that goodness in her? And what was the cost, the cost to her of such goodness?

The old man living in the back once said in his gentle way: "You should 17 smile at Emily more when you look at her." What *was* in my face when I looked at her? I loved her. There were all the acts of love.

It was only with the others I remembered what he said, and it was the face of 18 joy, and not of care or tightness or worry I turned to them—too late for Emily. She does not smile easily, let alone almost always as her brothers and sisters do. Her face is closed and sombre, but when she wants, how fluid. You must have seen it in her pantomimes, you spoke of her rare gift for comedy on the stage that rouses a laughter out of the audience so dear they applaud and applaud and do not want to let her go.

Where does it come from, that comedy? There was none of it in her when 19
she came back to me that second time, after I had had to send her away again.
She had a new daddy now to learn to love, and I think perhaps it was a better
time.

Except when we left her alone nights, telling ourselves she was old enough. 20
"Can't you go some other time, Mommy, like tomorrow?" she would ask. 21
"Will it be just a little while you'll be gone? Do you promise?"

The time we came back, the front door open, the clock on the floor in the 22
hall. She rigid awake. "It wasn't just a little while. I didn't cry. Three times I
called you, just three times, and then I ran downstairs to open the door so you
could come faster. The clock talked loud. I threw it away, it scared me what it
talked."

She said the clock talked loud again that night I went to the hospital to have 23
Susan. She was delirious with the fever that comes before red measles, but she
was fully conscious all the week I was gone and the week after we were home
when she could not come near the new baby or me.

She did not get well. She stayed skeleton thin, not wanting to eat, and night 24
after night she had nightmares. She would call for me, and I would rouse from
exhaustion to sleepily call back: "You're all right, darling, go to sleep, it's just a
dream," and if she still called, in a sterner voice, "now go to sleep, Emily, there's
nothing to hurt you." Twice, only twice, when I had to get up for Susan anyhow,
I went in to sit with her.

Now when it is too late (as if she would let me hold and comfort her like I 25
do the others) I get up and go to her at once at her moan or restless stirring.
"Are you awake, Emily? Can I get you something?" And the answer is always the
same: "No, I'm all right, go back to sleep, Mother."

They persuaded me at the clinic to send her away to a convalescent home in 26
the country where "she can have the kind of food and care you can't manage for
her, and you'll be free to concentrate on the new baby." They still send children
to that place. I see pictures on the society page of sleek young women planning
affairs to raise money for it, or dancing at the affairs, or decorating Easter eggs
or filling Christmas stockings for the children.

They never have a picture of the children so I do not know if the girls still 27
wear those gigantic red bows and the ravaged looks on the every other Sunday
when parents can come to visit "unless otherwise notified"—as we were notified the first six weeks.

Oh it is a handsome place, green lawns and tall trees and fluted flower beds. 28
High up on the balconies of each cottage the children stand, the girls in their
red bows and white dresses, the boys in white suits and giant red ties. The parents stand below shrieking up to be heard and the children shriek down to be
heard, and between them the invisible wall "Not To Be Contaminated by
Parental Germs or Physical Affection."

There was a tiny girl who always stood hand in hand with Emily. Her 29
parents never came. One visit she was gone. "They moved her to Rose

College," Emily shouted in explanation. "They don't like you to love anybody here."

She wrote once a week, the labored writing of a seven-year-old. "I am fine. 30
How is the baby. If I write my leter nicly I will have a star. Love." There never
was a star. We wrote every other day, letters she could never hold or keep but
only hear read—once. "We simply do not have room for children to keep any
personal possessions," they patiently explained when we pieced one Sunday's
shrieking together to plead how much it would mean to Emily, who loved so to
keep things, to be allowed to keep her letters and cards.

Each visit she looked frailer. "She isn't eating," they told us.   31

(They had runny eggs for breakfast or mush with lumps, Emily said later, I'd   32
hold it in my mouth and not swallow. Nothing ever tasted good, just when they
had chicken.)

It took us eight months to get her released home, and only the fact that she   33
gained back so little of her seven lost pounds convinced the social worker.

I used to try to hold and love her after she came back, but her body would   34
stay stiff, and after a while she'd push away. She ate little. Food sickened her, and
I think much of life too. Oh she had physical lightness and brightness, twinkling by on skates, bouncing like a ball up and down up and down over the
jump rope, skimming over the hill; but these were momentary.

She fretted about her appearance, thin and dark and foreign-looking at a   35
time when every little girl was supposed to look or thought she should look a
chubby blonde replica of Shirley Temple. The doorbell sometimes rang for her,
but no one seemed to come and play in the house or be a best friend. Maybe because we moved so much.

There was a boy she loved painfully through two school semesters. Months   36
later she told me how she had taken pennies from my purse to buy him candy.
"Licorice was his favorite and I brought him some every day, but he still liked
Jennifer better'n me. Why, Mommy?" The kind of question for which there is
no answer.

School was a worry to her. She was not glib or quick in a world where glib-   37
ness and quickness were easily confused with ability to learn. To her overworked and exasperated teachers she was an overconscientious "slow learner"
who kept trying to catch up and was absent entirely too often.

I let her be absent, though sometimes the illness was imaginary. How differ-   38
ent from my now-strictness about attendance with the others. I wasn't working.
We had a new baby, I was home anyhow. Sometimes, after Susan grew old
enough, I would keep her home from school, too, to have them all together.

Mostly Emily had asthma, and her breathing, harsh and labored, would fill   39
the house with a curiously tranquil sound. I would bring the two old dresser
mirrors and her boxes of collections to her bed. She would select beads and single earrings, bottle tops and shells, dried flowers and pebbles, old postcards and
scraps, all sorts of oddments; then she and Susan would play Kingdom, setting
up landscapes and furniture, peopling them with action.

Those were the only times of peaceful companionship between her and Su- 40
san. I have edged away from it, that poisonous feeling between them, that terrible balancing of hurts and needs I had to do between the two, and did so badly,
those earlier years.

Oh there are conflicts between the others too, each one human, needing, de- 41
manding, hurting, taking—but only between Emily and Susan, no, Emily toward Susan that corroding resentment. It seems so obvious on the surface, yet it
is not obvious. Susan, the second child, Susan, golden- and curly-haired and
chubby, quick and articulate and assured, everything in appearance and manner Emily was not; Susan, not able to resist Emily's precious things, losing or
sometimes clumsily breaking them; Susan telling jokes and riddles to company
for applause while Emily sat silent (to say to me later: that was *my* riddle,
Mother, I told it to Susan); Susan, who for all the five years' difference in age
was just a year behind Emily in developing physically.

I am glad for that slow physical development that widened the difference 42
between her and her contemporaries, though she suffered over it. She was too
vulnerable for that terrible world of youthful competition, of preening and
parading, of constant measuring of yourself against every other, of envy, "If I
had that copper hair," "If I had that skin. . . ." She tormented herself enough
about not looking like the others, there was enough of the unsureness, the having to be conscious of words before you speak, the constant caring—what are
they thinking of me? without having it all magnified by the merciless physical
drives.

Ronnie is calling. He is wet and I change him. It is rare there is such a cry 43
now. That time of motherhood is almost behind me when the ear is not one's
own but must always be racked and listening for the child cry, the child call. We
sit for a while and I hold him, looking out over the city spread in charcoal with
its soft aisles of light. "Shoogily," he breathes and curls closer. I carry him back to
bed, asleep. *Shoogily*. A funny word, a family word, inherited from Emily, invented by her to say: *comfort*.

In this and other ways she leaves her seal, I say aloud. And startle at my say- 44
ing it. What do I mean? What did I start to gather together, to try and make coherent? I was at the terrible, growing years. War years. I do not remember them
well. I was working, there were four smaller ones now, there was not time for
her. She had to help be a mother, and housekeeper, and shopper. She had to set
her seal. Mornings of crisis and near hysteria trying to get lunches packed, hair
combed, coats and shoes found, everyone to school or Child Care on time, the
baby ready for transportation. And always the paper scribbled on by a smaller
one, the book looked at by Susan then mislaid, the homework not done. Running out to that huge school where she was one, she was lost, she was a drop;
suffering over the unpreparedness, stammering and unsure in her classes.

There was so little time left at night after the kids were bedded down. She 45
would struggle over books, always eating (it was in those years she developed
her enormous appetite that is legendary in our family) and I would be ironing,

or preparing food for the next day, or writing V-mail to Bill, or tending the baby. Sometimes, to make me laugh, or out of her despair, she would imitate happenings or types at school.

I think I said once: "Why don't you do something like this in the school am- 46 ateur show?" One morning she phoned me at work, hardly understandable through the weeping: "Mother, I did it. I won, I won; they gave me first prize; they clapped and clapped and wouldn't let me go."

Now suddenly she was Somebody, and as imprisoned in her difference as 47 she had been in anonymity.

She began to be asked to perform at other high schools, even in colleges, 48 then at city and statewide affairs. The first one we went to, I only recognized her that first moment when thin, shy, she almost drowned herself into the curtains. Then: Was this Emily? The control, the command, the convulsing and deadly clowning, the spell, then the roaring, stamping audience, unwilling to let this rare and precious laughter out of their lives.

Afterwards: You ought to do something about her with a gift like that—but 49 without money or knowing how, what does one do? We have left it all to her, and the gift has as often eddied inside, clogged and clotted, as been used and growing.

She is coming. She runs up the stairs two at a time with her light graceful 50 step, and I know she is happy tonight. Whatever it was that occasioned your call did not happen today.

"Aren't you ever going to finish the ironing, Mother? Whistler painted his 51 mother in a rocker. I'd have to paint mine standing over an ironing board." This is one of her communicative nights and she tells me everything and nothing as she fixes herself a plate of food out of the icebox.

She is so lovely. Why did you want me to come in at all? Why were you con- 52 cerned? She will find her way.

She starts up the stairs to bed. "Don't get me up with the rest in the morn- 53 ing." "But I thought you were having midterms." "Oh, those," she comes back in, kisses me, and says quite lightly, "in a couple of years when we'll all be atom-dead they won't matter a bit."

She has said it before. She *believes* it. But because I have been dredging the 54 past, and all that compounds a human being is so heavy and meaningful in me, I cannot endure it tonight.

I will never total it all. I will never come in to say: She was a child seldom 55 smiled at. Her father left me before she was a year old. I had to work her first six years when there was work, or I sent her home and to his relatives. There were years she had care she hated. She was dark and thin and foreign-looking in a world where the prestige went to blondeness and curly hair and dimples, she was slow where glibness was prized. She was a child of anxious, not proud, love. We were poor and could not afford for her the soil of easy growth. I was a young mother, I was a distracted mother. There were the other children push-ing up, demanding. Her younger sister seemed all that she was not. There were years she did not want me to touch her. She kept too much in herself, her life was such she had to keep too much in herself. My wisdom came too late. She has much to her and probably nothing will come of it. She is a child of her age, of depression, of war, of fear.

Let her be. So all that is in her will not bloom—but in how many does it? There is still enough left to live by. Only help her to know—help make it so there is cause for her to know—that she is more than this dress on the ironing board, helpless before the iron.   56

ACTIVITY FOR WRITING AND DISCUSSION

1. Respond to the story using the "Four-Step Process for Writing from Reading" described in Chapter 2.

TOBIAS WOLFF (b. 1945)

The Rich Brother

There were two brothers, Pete and Donald.   1

Pete, the older brother, was in real estate. He and his wife had a Century 21 franchise in Santa Cruz. Pete worked hard and made a lot of money, but not any more than he thought he deserved. He had two daughters, a sailboat, a house from which he could see a thin slice of the ocean, and friends doing well enough in their own lives not to wish bad luck on him. Donald, the younger brother, was still single. He lived alone, painted houses when he found the work, and got deeper in debt to Pete when he didn't.   2

No one would have taken them for brothers. Where Pete was stout and hearty and at home in the world, Donald was bony, grave, and obsessed with the fate of his soul. Over the years Donald had worn the images of two different Perfect Masters around his neck. Out of devotion to the second of these he entered an ashram in Berkeley, where he nearly died of undiagnosed hepatitis. By the time Pete finished paying the medical bills Donald had become a Christian. He drifted from church to church, then joined a pentecostal community that met somewhere in the Mission District to sing in tongues and swap prophecies.   3

Pete couldn't make sense of it. Their parents were both dead, but while they were alive neither of them had found it necessary to believe in anything. They managed to be decent people without making fools of themselves, and Pete had the same ambition. He thought that the whole thing was an excuse for Donald to take himself seriously.   4

The trouble was that Donald couldn't content himself with worrying about his own soul. He had to worry about everyone else's, and especially Pete's. He handed down his judgments in ways that he seemed to consider subtle: through   5 significant silence, innuendo, looks of mild despair that said, *Brother, what have you come to?* What Pete had come to, as far as he could tell, was prosperity. That was the real issue between them. Pete prospered and Donald did not prosper.

At the age of forty Pete took up sky diving. He made his first jump with two 6 friends who'd started only a few months earlier and were already doing stunts. They were both coked to the gills when they jumped but Pete wanted to do it straight, at least the first time, and he was glad that he did. He would never have used the word *mystical,* but that was how Pete felt about the experience. Later he made the mistake of trying to describe it to Donald, who kept asking how much it cost and then acted appalled when Pete told him.

"At least I'm trying something new," Pete said. "At least I'm breaking the pat- 7 tern."

Not long after that conversation Donald also broke the pattern, by going to 8 live on a farm outside of Paso Robles. The farm was owned by several members of Donald's community, who had bought it and moved there with the idea of forming a family of faith. That was how Donald explained it in the first letter he sent. Every week Pete heard how happy Donald was, how "in the Lord." He told Pete that he was praying for him, he and the rest of Pete's brothers and sisters on the farm.

"I only have one brother," Pete wanted to answer, "and that's enough." But 9 he kept this thought to himself.

In November the letters stopped. Pete didn't worry about this at first, but 10 when he called Donald at Thanksgiving Donald was grim. He tried to sound upbeat but he didn't try hard enough to make it convincing. "Now listen," Pete said, "you don't have to stay in that place if you don't want to."

"I'll be all right," Donald answered. 11

"That's not the point. Being all right is not the point. If you don't like what's 12 going on up there, then get out."

"I'm all right," Donald said again, more firmly. "I'm doing fine." 13

But he called Pete a week later and said that he was quitting the farm. When 14 Pete asked him where he intended to go, Donald admitted that he had no plan. His car had been repossessed just before he left the city, and he was flat broke.

"I guess you'll have to stay with us," Pete said. 15

Donald put up a show of resistance. Then he gave in. "Just until I get my feet 16 on the ground," he said.

"Right," Pete said. "Check out your options." He told Donald he'd send him 17 money for a bus ticket, but as they were about to hang up Pete changed his mind. He knew that Donald would try hitchhiking to save the fare. Pete didn't want him out on the road all alone where some head case could pick him up, where anything could happen to him.

"Better yet," he said, "I'll come and get you." 18

"You don't have to do that. I didn't expect you to do that," Donald said. He 19 added, "It's a pretty long drive."

"Just tell me how to get there."   20

But Donald wouldn't give him directions. He said that the farm was too de-   21
pressing, that Pete wouldn't like it. Instead, he insisted on meeting Pete at a service station called Jonathan's Mechanical Emporium.

"You must be kidding," Pete said.   22

"It's close to the highway," Donald said. "I didn't name it."   23

"That's one for the collection," Pete said.   24

The day before he left to bring Donald home, Pete received a letter from a man   25
who described himself as "head of household" at the farm where Donald had
been living. From this letter Pete learned that Donald had not quit the farm,
but had been asked to leave. The letter was written on the back of a mimeo-
graphed survey form asking people to record their response to a ceremony of
some kind. The last question said:

What did you feel during the liturgy?
  a) Being
  b) Becoming
  c) Being and Becoming
  d) None of the Above
  e) All of the Above

Pete tried to forget the letter. But of course he couldn't. Each time he   26
thought of it he felt crowded and breathless, a feeling that came over him again
when he drove into the service station and saw Donald sitting against a wall
with his head on his knees. It was late afternoon. A paper cup tumbled slowly
past Donald's feet, pushed by the damp wind.

Pete honked and Donald raised his head. He smiled at Pete, then stood and   27
stretched. His arms were long and thin and white. He wore a red bandanna
across his forehead, a T-shirt with a couple of words on the front. Pete couldn't
read them because the letters were inverted.

"Grow up," Pete yelled. "Get a Mercedes."   28

Donald came up to the window. He bent down and said, "Thanks for com-   29
ing. You must be totally whipped."

"I'll make it." Pete pointed at Donald's T-shirt. "What's that supposed to   30
say?"

Donald looked down at his shirt front. "Try God. I guess I put it on back-   31
wards. Pete, could I borrow a couple of dollars? I owe these people for coffee
and sandwiches."

Pete took five twenties from his wallet and held them out the window.   32

Donald stepped back as if horrified. "I don't need that much."   33

"I can't keep track of all these nickels and dimes," Pete said. "Just pay me   34
back when your ship comes in." He waved the bills impatiently. "Go on—take
it."

"Only for now." Donald took the money and went into the service station 35
office. He came out carrying two orange sodas, one of which he gave to Pete as
he got into the car. "My treat," he said.

"No bags?" 36

"Wow, thanks for reminding me," Donald said. He balanced his drink on 37
the dashboard, but the slight rocking of the car as he got out tipped it onto the
passenger's seat, where half its contents foamed over before Pete could snatch it
up again. Donald looked on while Pete held the bottle out the window, soda
running down his fingers.

"Wipe it up," Pete told him. "Quick!" 38

"With what?" 39

Pete stared at Donald. "That shirt. Use the shirt." 40

Donald pulled a long face but did as he was told, his pale skin puckering 41
against the wind.

"Great, just great," Pete said. "We haven't even left the gas station yet." 42

Afterwards, on the highway, Donald said, "This is a new car, isn't it?" 43

"Yes. This is a new car." 44

"Is that why you're so upset about the seat?" 45

"Forget it, okay? Let's just forget about it." 46

"I said I was sorry." 47

Pete said, "I just wish you'd be more careful. These seats are made of leather. 48
That stain won't come out, not to mention the smell. I don't see why I can't
have leather seats that smell like leather instead of orange pop."

"What was wrong with the other car?" 49

Pete glanced over at Donald. Donald had raised the hood of the blue sweat- 50
shirt he'd put on. The peaked hood above his gaunt, watchful face gave him the
look of an inquisitor.

"There wasn't anything wrong with it," Pete said. "I just happened to like 51
this one better."

Donald nodded. 52

There was a long silence between them as Pete drove on and the day dark- 53
ened toward evening. On either side of the road lay stubble-covered fields. A
line of low hills ran along the horizon, topped here and there with trees black
against the grey sky. In the approaching line of cars a driver turned on his headlights. Pete did the same.

"So what happened?" he asked. "Farm life not your bag?" 54

Donald took some time to answer, and at last he said, simply, "It was my 55
fault."

"What was your fault?" 56

"The whole thing. Don't play dumb, Pete. I know they wrote to you." Don- 57
ald looked at Pete, then stared out the windshield again.

"I'm not playing dumb." 58

Donald shrugged. 59

"All I really know is they asked you to leave," Pete went on. "I don't know any 60
of the particulars."

"I blew it," Donald said. "Believe me, you don't want to hear the gory details." 61
"Sure I do," Pete said. He added, "Everybody likes the gory details." 62
"You mean everybody likes to hear how someone else messed up." 63
"Right," Pete said. "That's the way it is here on Spaceship Earth." 64

Donald bent one knee onto the front seat and leaned against the door so 65
that he was facing Pete instead of the windshield. Pete was aware of Donald's
scrutiny. He waited. Night was coming on in a rush now, filling the hollows of
the land. Donald's long cheeks and deep-set eyes were dark with shadow. His
brow was white. "Do you ever dream about me?" Donald asked.

"Do I ever dream about you? What kind of a question is that? Of course I 66
don't dream about you," Pete said, untruthfully.

"What do you dream about?" 67

"Sex and money. Mostly money. A nightmare is when I dream I don't have 68
any."

"You're just making that up," Donald said. 69
Pete smiled. 70

"Sometimes I wake up at night," Donald went on, "and I can tell you're 71
dreaming about me."

"We were talking about the farm," Pete said. "Let's finish that conversation 72
and then we can talk about our various out-of-body experiences and the interesting things we did during previous incarnations."

For a moment Donald looked like a grinning skull; then he turned serious 73
again. "There's not that much to tell," he said. "I just didn't do anything right."

"That's a little vague," Pete said. 74

"Well, like the groceries. Whenever it was my turn to get the groceries I'd 75
blow it somehow. I'd bring the groceries home and half of them would be missing, or I'd have all the wrong things, the wrong kind of flour or the wrong kind
of chocolate or whatever. One time I gave them away. It's not funny, Pete."

Pete said, "Who did you give the groceries to?" 76

"Just some people I picked up on the way home. Some fieldworkers. They 77
had about eight kids with them and they didn't even speak English—just nodded their heads. Still, I shouldn't have given away the groceries. Not all of them,
anyway. I really learned my lesson about that. You have to be practical. You have
to be fair to yourself." Donald leaned forward, and Pete could sense his excitement. "There's nothing actually wrong with being in business," he said. "As long
as you're fair to other people you can still be fair to yourself. I'm thinking of going into business, Pete."

"We'll talk about it," Pete said. "So, that's the story? There isn't any more to it 78
than that?"

"What did they tell you?" Donald asked. 79
"Nothing." 80
"They must have told you something." 81
Pete shook his head. 82
"They didn't tell you about the fire?" When Pete shook his head again 83
Donald regarded him for a time, then said, "I don't know. It was stupid. I just

completely lost it." He folded his arms across his chest and slumped back into the corner. "Everybody had to take turns cooking dinner. I usually did tuna casserole or spaghetti with garlic bread. But this one night I thought I'd do something different, something really interesting." Donald looked sharply at Pete. "It's all a big laugh to you, isn't it?"

"I'm sorry," Pete said.   84

"You don't know when to quit. You just keep hitting away."   85

"Tell me about the fire, Donald."   86

Donald kept watching him. "You have this compulsion to make me look 87
foolish."

"Come off it, Donald. Don't make a big thing out of this."   88

"I know why you do it. It's because you don't have any purpose in life. You're 89
afraid to relate to people who do, so you make fun of them."

"Relate," Pete said softly.   90

"You're basically a very frightened individual," Donald said. "Very threat- 91
ened. You've always been like that. Do you remember when you used to try to
kill me?"

"I don't have any compulsion to make you look foolish, Donald—you do it 92
yourself. You're doing it right now."

"You can't tell me you don't remember," Donald said. "It was after my oper- 93
ation. You remember that."

"Sort of." Pete shrugged. "Not really."   94

"Oh yes," Donald said. "Do you want to see the scar?"   95

"I remember you had an operation. I don't remember the specifics, that's 96
all. And I sure as hell don't remember trying to kill you."

"Oh yes," Donald repeated, maddeningly. "You bet your life you did. All the 97
time. The thing was, I couldn't have anything happen to me where they sewed
me up because then my intestines would come apart again and poison me. That
was a big issue, Pete. Mom was always in a state about me climbing trees and so
on. And you used to hit me there every chance you got."

"Mom was in a state every time you burped," Pete said. "I don't know. 98
Maybe I bumped into you accidentally once or twice. I never did it deliberately."

"Every chance you got," Donald said. "Like when the folks went out at night 99
and left you to baby-sit. I'd hear them say good night, and then I'd hear the car
start up, and when they were gone I'd lie there and listen. After a while I would
hear you coming down the hall, and I would close my eyes and pretend to be
asleep. There were nights when you would stand outside the door, just stand
there, and then go away again. But most nights you'd open the door and I
would hear you in the room with me, breathing. You'd come over and sit next to
me on the bed—you remember, Pete, you have to—you'd sit next to me on the
bed and pull the sheets back. If I was on my stomach you'd roll me over. Then
you would lift up my pajama shirt and start hitting me on my stitches. You'd hit
me as hard as you could, over and over. And I would just keep lying there with
my eyes closed. I was afraid that you'd get mad if you knew I was awake. Is that

strange or what? I was afraid that you'd get mad if you found out that I knew you were trying to kill me." Donald laughed. "Come on, you can't tell me you don't remember that."

"It might have happened once or twice. Kids do those things. I can't get all excited about something I maybe did twenty-five years ago." 100

"No maybe about it. You did it." 101

Pete said, "You're wearing me out with this stuff. We've got a long drive ahead of us and if you don't back off pretty soon we aren't going to make it. You aren't, anyway." 102

Donald turned away. 103

"I'm doing my best," Pete said. The self-pity in his own voice made the words sound like a lie. But they weren't a lie! He was doing his best. 104

The car topped a rise. In the distance Pete saw a cluster of lights that blinked out when he started downhill. There was no moon. The sky was low and black. 105

"Come to think of it," Pete said, "I did have a dream about you the other night." Then he added, impatiently, as if Donald were badgering him, "A couple of other nights too. I'm getting hungry," he said. 106

"The same dream?" 107

"Different dreams. I only remember one of them well. There was something wrong with me, and you were helping out. Taking care of me. Just the two of us. I don't know where everyone else was supposed to be." 108

Pete left it at that. He didn't tell Donald that in this dream he was blind. 109

"I wonder if that was when I woke up," Donald said. He added, "I'm sorry I got into that thing about my scar. I keep trying to forget it but I guess I never will. Not really. It was pretty strange, having someone around all the time who wanted to get rid of me." 110

"Kid stuff," Pete said. "Ancient history." 111

They ate dinner at a Denny's on the other side of King City. As Pete was paying the check he heard a man behind him say, "Excuse me, but I wonder if I might ask which way you're going?" and Donald answer, "Santa Cruz." 112

"Perfect," the man said. 113

Pete could see him in the fish eye mirror above the cash register: a red blazer with some kind of crest on the pocket, little black moustache, glossy black hair combed down on his forehead like a Roman emperor's. A rug, Pete thought. Definitely a rug. 114

Pete got his change and turned. "Why is that perfect?" he asked. 115

The man looked at Pete. He had a soft ruddy face that was doing its best to express pleasant surprise, as if this new wrinkle were all he could have wished for, but the eyes behind the aviator glasses showed signs of regret. His lips were moist and shiny. "I take it you're together," he said. 116

"You got it," Pete told him. 117

"All the better, then," the man went on. "It so happens I'm going to Santa Cruz myself. Had a spot of car trouble down the road. The old Caddy let me down." 118

"What kind of trouble?" Pete asked.   119

"Engine trouble," the man said. "I'm afraid it's a bit urgent. My daughter is   120
sick. Urgently sick. I've got a telegram here." He patted the breast pocket of his
blazer.

Pete grinned. Amazing, he thought, the old sick daughter ploy, but before he   121
could say anything Donald got into the act again. "No problem," Donald said.
"We've got tons of room."

"Not that much room," Pete said.   122

Donald nodded. "I'll put my things in the trunk."   123

"The trunk's full," Pete told him.   124

"It so happens I'm traveling light," the man said. "This leg of the trip any-   125
way. In fact I don't have any luggage at this particular time."

Pete said, "Left it in the old Caddy, did you?"   126

"Exactly," the man said.   127

"No problem," Donald repeated. He walked outside and the man went with   128
him. Together they strolled across the parking lot, Pete following at a distance.
When they reached Pete's car Donald raised his face to the sky, and the man did
the same. They stood there looking up. "Dark night," Donald said.

"Stygian," the man said.   129

Pete still had it in mind to brush him off, but he didn't do that. Instead he   130
unlocked the door for him. He wanted to see what would happen. It was an adventure, but not a dangerous adventure. The man might steal Pete's ashtrays
but he wouldn't kill him. If Pete got killed on the road it would be by some spiritual person in a sweatsuit, someone with his eyes on the far horizon and a wet
Try God T-shirt in his duffel bag.

As soon as they left the parking lot the man lit a cigar. He blew a cloud of   131
smoke over Pete's shoulder and sighed with pleasure. "Put it out," Pete told him.

"Of course," the man said. Pete looked into the rearview mirror and saw the   132
man take another long puff before dropping the cigar out the window. "Forgive
me," he said. "I should have asked. Name's Webster, by the way."

Donald turned and looked back at him. "First name or last?"   133

The man hesitated. "Last," he said finally.   134

"I know a Webster," Donald said. "Mick Webster."   135

"There are many of us," Webster said.   136

"Big fellow, wooden leg," Pete said.   137

Donald gave Pete a look.   138

Webster shook his head. "Doesn't ring a bell. Still, I wouldn't deny the con-   139
nection. Might be one of the cousinry."

"What's your daughter got?" Pete asked.   140

"That isn't clear," Webster answered. "It appears to be a female complaint of   141
some nature. Then again it may be tropical." He was quiet for a moment, and
added: "If indeed it *is* tropical, I will have to assume some of the blame myself.
It was my own vaulting ambition that first led us to the tropics and kept us in
the tropics all those many years, exposed to every evil. Truly I have much to answer for. I left my wife there."

Donald said quietly, "You mean she died?"   142

"I buried her with these hands. The earth will be repaid, gold for gold."   143

"Which tropics?" Pete asked.   144

"The tropics of Peru."   145

"What part of Peru are they in?"   146

"The lowlands," Webster said.   147

Pete nodded. "What's it like down there?"   148

"Another world," Webster said. His tone was sepulchral. "A world better   149
imagined than described."

"Far out," Pete said.   150

The three men rode in silence for a time. A line of trucks went past in the   151
other direction, trailers festooned with running lights, engines roaring.

"Yes," Webster said at last, "I have much to answer for."   152

Pete smiled at Donald, but Donald had turned in his seat again and was gaz-   153
ing at Webster. "I'm sorry about your wife," Donald said.

"What did she die of?" Pete asked.   154

"A wasting illness," Webster said. "The doctors have no name for it, but I   155
do." He leaned forward and said, fiercely, "*Greed.*" Then he slumped back
against his seat. "My greed, not hers. She wanted no part of it."

Pete bit his lip. Webster was a find and Pete didn't want to scare him off by   156
hooting at him. In a voice low and innocent of knowingness, he asked, "What
took you there?"

"It's difficult for me to talk about."   157

"Try," Pete told him.   158

"A cigar would make it easier."   159

Donald turned to Pete and said, "It's okay with me."   160

"All right," Pete said. "Go ahead. Just keep the window rolled down."   161

"Much obliged." A match flared. There were eager sucking sounds.   162

"Let's hear it," Pete said.   163

"I am by training an engineer," Webster began. "My work has exposed me to   164
all but one of the continents, to desert and alp and forest, to every terrain and
season of the earth. Some years ago I was hired by the Peruvian government to
search for tungsten in the tropics. My wife and daughter accompanied me. We
were the only white people for a thousand miles in any direction, and we had
no choice but to live as the Indians lived—to share their food and drink and
even their culture."

Pete said, "You knew the lingo, did you?"   165

"We picked it up." The ember of the cigar bobbed up and down. "We were   166
used to learning as necessity decreed. At any rate, it became evident after a couple of years that there was no tungsten to be found. My wife had fallen ill
and was pleading to be taken home. But I was deaf to her pleas, because
by then I was on the trail of another metal—a metal far more valuable than
tungsten."

"Let me guess," Pete said. "Gold?"   167

Donald looked at Pete, then back at Webster.   168

"Gold," Webster said. "A vein of gold greater than the Mother Lode itself. Af-   169
ter I found the first traces of it nothing could tear me away from my search—
not the sickness of my wife nor anything else. I was determined to uncover the
vein, and so I did—but not before I laid my wife to rest. As I say, the earth will
be repaid."

Webster was quiet. Then he said, "But life must go on. In the years since my   170
wife's death I have been making the arrangements necessary to open the mine. I
could have done it immediately, of course, enriching myself beyond measure,
but I knew what that would mean—the exploitation of our beloved Indians,
the brutal destruction of their environment. I felt I had too much to atone for
already." Webster paused, and when he spoke again his voice was dull and
rushed, as if he had used up all the interest he had in his own words. "Instead I
drew up a program for returning the bulk of the wealth to the Indians themselves. A kind of trust fund. The interest alone will allow them to secure their
ancient lands and rights in perpetuity. At the same time, our investors will be
rewarded a thousandfold. Two-thousandfold. Everyone will prosper together."

"That's great," Donald said. "That's the way it ought to be."   171

Pete said, "I'm willing to bet that you just happen to have a few shares left.   172
Am I right?"

Webster made no reply.   173

"Well?" Pete knew that Webster was on to him now, but he didn't care. The   174
story had bored him. He'd expected something different, something original,
and Webster had let him down. He hadn't even tried. Pete felt sour and stale.
His eyes burned from cigar smoke and the high beams of road-hogging truck-
ers. "Douse the stogie," he said to Webster. "I told you to keep the window
down."

"Got a little nippy back here."   175

Donald said, "Hey, Pete. Lighten up."   176

"Douse it!"   177

Webster sighed. He got rid of the cigar.   178

"I'm a wreck," Pete said to Donald. "You want to drive for a while?"   179

Donald nodded.   180

Pete pulled over and they changed places.   181

Webster kept his counsel in the back seat. Donald hummed while he drove,   182
until Pete told him to stop. Then everything was quiet.

Donald was humming again when Pete woke up. Pete stared sullenly at the   183
road, at the white lines sliding past the car. After a few moments of this he
turned and said, "How long have I been out?"

Donald glanced at him. "Twenty, twenty-five minutes."   184

Pete looked behind him and saw that Webster was gone. "Where's our   185
friend?"

"You just missed him. He got out in Soledad. He told me to say thanks and   186
good-bye."

"Soledad? What about his sick daughter? How did he explain her away?" 187
Pete leaned over the seat. Both ashtrays were still in place. Floor mats. Door
handles.

"He has a brother living there. He's going to borrow a car from him and 188
drive the rest of the way in the morning."

"I'll bet his brother's living there," Pete said. "Doing fifty concurrent life 189
sentences. His brother and his sister and his mom and his dad."

"I kind of liked him," Donald said. 190

"I'm sure you did," Pete said wearily. 191

"He was interesting. He'd been places." 192

"His cigars had been places, I'll give you that." 193

"Come on, Pete." 194

"Come on yourself. What a phony." 195

"You don't know that." 196

"Sure I do." 197

"How? How do you know?" 198

Pete stretched. "Brother, there are some things you're just born knowing. 199
What's the gas situation?"

"We're a little low." 200

"Then why didn't you get some more?" 201

"I wish you wouldn't snap at me like that," Donald said. 202

"Then why don't you use your head? What if we run out?" 203

"We'll make it," Donald said. "I'm pretty sure we've got enough to make it. 204
You didn't have to be so rude to him," Donald added.

Pete took a deep breath. "I don't feel like running out of gas tonight, okay?" 205
Donald pulled in at the next station they came to and filled the tank while 206
Pete went to the men's room. When Pete came back, Donald was sitting in the
passenger's seat. The attendant came up to the driver's window as Pete got in
behind the wheel. He bent down and said, "Twelve fifty-five."

"You heard the man," Pete said to Donald. 207

Donald looked straight ahead. He didn't move. 208

"Cough up," Pete said. "This trip's on you." 209

Donald said, softly, "I can't." 210

"Sure you can. Break out that wad." 211

Donald glanced up at the attendant, then at Pete. "Please," he said. "Pete, I 212
don't have it anymore."

Pete took this in. He nodded, and paid the attendant. 213

Donald began to speak when they left the station but Pete cut him off. He 214
said, "I don't want to hear from you right now. You just keep quiet or I swear to
God I won't be responsible."

They left the fields and entered a tunnel of tall trees. The trees went on and 215
on. "Let me get this straight," Pete said at last. "You don't have the money I gave
you."

"You treated him like a bug or something," Donald said. 216

"You don't have the money," Pete said again.   217

Donald shook his head.   218

"Since I bought dinner, and since we didn't stop anywhere in between, I as-   219
sume you gave it to Webster. Is that right? Is that what you did with it?"

"Yes."   220

Pete looked at Donald. His face was dark under the hood but he still man-   221
aged to convey a sense of remove, as if none of this had anything to do with him.

"Why?" Pete asked. "Why did you give it to him?" When Donald didn't an-   222
swer, Pete said, "A hundred dollars. Gone. Just like that. I *worked* for that
money, Donald."

"I know, I know," Donald said.   223

"You don't know! How could you? You get money by holding out your   224
hand."

"I work too," Donald said.   225

"You work too. Don't kid yourself, brother."   226

Donald leaned toward Pete, about to say something, but Pete cut him off   227
again.

"You're not the only one on the payroll, Donald. I don't think you under-   228
stand that. I have a family."

"Pete, I'll pay you back."   229

"Like hell you will. A hundred dollars!" Pete hit the steering wheel with the 230
palm of his hand. "Just because you think I hurt some goofball's feelings. Jesus,
Donald."

"That's not the reason," Donald said. "And I didn't just *give* him the money." 231

"What do you call it, then? What do you call what you did?"   232

"I *invested* it. I wanted a share, Pete." When Pete looked over at him Donald 233
nodded and said again, "I wanted a share."

Pete said, "I take it you're referring to the gold mine in Peru."   234

"Yes," Donald said.   235

"You believe that such a gold mine exists?"   236

Donald looked at Pete, and Pete could see him just beginning to catch on.   237
"You'll believe anything," Pete said. "Won't you? You really will believe anything
at all."

"I'm sorry," Donald said, and turned away.   238

Pete drove on between the trees and considered the truth of what he had   239
just said—that Donald would believe anything at all. And it came to him that it
would be just like this unfair life for Donald to come out ahead in the end, by
believing in some outrageous promise that would turn out to be true and that
he, Pete, would reject out of hand because he was too wised up to listen to anybody's pitch anymore except for laughs. What a joke. What a joke if there really
was a blessing to be had, and the blessing didn't come to the one who deserved
it, the one who did all the work, but to the other.

And as if this had already happened Pete felt a shadow move upon him,   240
darkening his thoughts. After a time he said, "I can see where all this is going,
Donald."

"I'll pay you back," Donald said.   241

"No," Pete said. "You won't pay me back. You can't. You don't know how. All 242
you've ever done is take. All your life."

Donald shook his head.   243

"I see exactly where this is going," Pete went on. "You can't work, you can't 244
take care of yourself, you believe anything anyone tells you. I'm stuck with you,
aren't I?" He looked over at Donald. "I've got you on my hands for good."

Donald pressed his fingers against the dashboard as if to brace himself. "I'll 245
get out," he said.

Pete kept driving.   246

"Let me out," Donald said. "I mean it, Pete."   247

"Do you?"   248

Donald hesitated. "Yes," he said.   249

"Be sure," Pete told him. "This is it. This is for keeps."   250

"I mean it."   251

"All right. You made the choice." Pete braked the car sharply and swung it to 252
the shoulder of the road. He turned off the engine and got out. Trees loomed on
both sides, shutting out the sky. The air was cold and musty. Pete took Donald's
duffel bag from the back seat and set it down behind the car. He stood there,
facing Donald in the red glow of the taillights. "It's better this way," Pete said.

Donald just looked at him.   253

"Better for you," Pete said.   254

Donald hugged himself. He was shaking. "You don't have to say all that," he 255
told Pete. "I don't blame you."

"Blame me? What the hell are you talking about? Blame me for what?"   256

"For anything," Donald said.   257

"I want to know what you mean by blame me."   258

"Nothing. Nothing, Pete. You'd better get going. God bless you."   259

"That's it," Pete said. He dropped to one knee, searching the packed dirt 260
with his hands. He didn't know what he was looking for; his hands would know
when they found it.

Donald touched Pete's shoulder. "You'd better go," he said.   261

Somewhere in the trees Pete heard a branch snap. He stood up. He looked at 262
Donald, then went back to the car and drove away. He drove fast, hunched over
the wheel, conscious of the way he was hunched and the shallowness of his
breathing, refusing to look at the mirror above his head until there was nothing
behind him but darkness.

Then he said, "A hundred dollars," as if there were someone to hear.   263

The trees gave way to fields. Metal fences ran beside the road, plastered with 264
windblown scraps of paper. Tule fog hung above the ditches, spilling into the
road, dimming the ghostly halogen lights that burned in the yards of the farms
Pete passed. The fog left beads of water rolling up the windshield.

Pete rummaged among his cassettes. He found Pachelbel's Canon and 265
pushed it into the tape deck. When the violins began to play he leaned back and
assumed an attentive expression as if he were really listening to them. He

smiled to himself like a man at liberty to enjoy music, a man who has finished his work and settled his debts, done all things meet and due.

And in this way, smiling, nodding to the music, he went another mile or so 266 and pretended that he was not already slowing down, that he was not going to turn back, that he would be able to drive on like this, alone, and have the right answer when his wife stood before him in the doorway of his home and asked, Where is he? Where is your brother?

ACTIVITIES FOR WRITING AND DISCUSSION

1. Why, despite their many differences, do Pete and Donald remain connected? Do they have anything in common besides blood? Explain. Drawing on experiences in your own family or in other families, share any stories of siblings who are similarly "opposite" in character or temperament. In those instances has the opposition been a source of alienation or of a stronger relationship?

2. Donald is described as intensely introspective, as "bony, grave, and obsessed with the fate of his soul" (paragraph 3). Review the key events in Donald's story and his opinions about Pete, money, work, and the meaning of life. Then write a series of diary entries, in his **persona,** that cover some portion of his life—for instance, his stint at the farm commune he was asked to leave.

3. Donald accuses Pete of trying to "kill" him when they were children.
   a. Reread and annotate the paragraphs where this accusation is discussed.
   b. In your notebook recreate the story of this attempted "killing." Narrate from either Donald's or Pete's **point of view,** or from a third-person perspective, inventing background and details as necessary.
   c. Use your fictional version of the event to discuss *why* this episode is in Wolff's story.

4. Write a sequel in which Pete (a) returns and picks up Donald; or (b) continues on home without Donald. If you do (b) write the dialogue that occurs when Pete encounters his wife.

5. Interpret paragraphs 260–262.

GLORIA NAYLOR (b. 1950)

Kiswana Browne

From the window of her sixth-floor studio apartment, Kiswana could see over   1
the wall at the end of the street to the busy avenue that lay just north of Brewster Place. The late-afternoon shoppers looked like brightly clad marionettes as

they moved between the congested traffic, clutching their packages against their bodies to guard them from sudden bursts of the cold autumn wind. A portly mailman had abandoned his cart and was bumping into indignant window-shoppers as he puffed behind the cap that the wind had snatched from his head. Kiswana leaned over to see if he was going to be successful, but the edge of the building cut him off from her view.

A pigeon swept across her window, and she marveled at its liquid movements in the air waves. She placed her dreams on the back of the bird and fantasized that it would glide forever in transparent silver circles until it ascended to the center of the universe and was swallowed up. But the wind died down, and she watched with a sigh as the bird beat its wings in awkward, frantic movements to land on the corroded top of a fire escape on the opposite building. This brought her back to earth.

Humph, it's probably sitting over there crapping on those folks' fire escape, she thought. Now, that's a safety hazard. . . . And her mind was busy again, creating flames and smoke and frustrated tenants whose escape was being hindered because they were slipping and sliding in pigeon shit. She watched their cussing, haphazard descent on the fire escapes until they had all reached the bottom. They were milling around, oblivious to their burning apartments, angrily planning to march on the mayor's office about the pigeons. She materialized placards and banners for them, and they had just reached the corner, boldly sidestepping fire hoses and broken glass, when they all vanished.

A tall copper-skinned woman had met this phantom parade at the corner, and they had dissolved in front of her long, confident strides. She plowed through the remains of their faded mists, unconscious of the lingering wisps of their presence on her leather bag and black fur-trimmed coat. It took a few seconds for this transfer from one realm to another to reach Kiswana, but then suddenly she recognized the woman.

"Oh, God, it's Mama!" She looked down guiltily at the forgotten newspaper in her lap and hurriedly circled random job advertisements.

By this time Mrs. Browne had reached the front of Kiswana's building and was checking the house number against a piece of paper in her hand. Before she went into the building she stood at the bottom of the stoop and carefully inspected the condition of the street and the adjoining property. Kiswana watched this meticulous inventory with growing annoyance but she involuntarily followed her mother's slowly rotating head, forcing herself to see her new neighborhood through the older woman's eyes. The brightness of the unclouded sky seemed to join forces with her mother as it highlighted every broken stoop railing and missing brick. The afternoon sun glittered and cascaded across even the tiniest fragments of broken bottle, and at that very moment the wind chose to rise up again, sending unswept grime flying into the air, as a stray tin can left by careless garbage collectors went rolling noisily down the center of the street.

Kiswana noticed with relief that at least Ben wasn't sitting in his usual place on the old garbage can pushed against the far wall. He was just a harmless old wino, but Kiswana knew her mother only needed one wino or one teenager with a reefer within a twenty-block radius to decide that her daughter was living in a building seething with dope factories and hang-outs for derelicts. If she had seen Ben, nothing would have made her believe that practically every apartment contained a family, a Bible, and a dream that one day enough could be scraped from those meager Friday night paychecks to make Brewster Place a distant memory.

As she watched her mother's head disappear into the building, Kiswana 8 gave silent thanks that the elevator was broken. That would give her at least five minutes' grace to straighten up the apartment. She rushed to the sofa bed and hastily closed it without smoothing the rumpled sheets and blanket or removing her nightgown. She felt that somehow the tangled bedcovers would give away the fact that she had not slept alone last night. She silently apologized to Abshu's memory as she heartlessly crushed his spirit between the steel springs of the couch. Lord, that man was sweet. Her toes curled involuntarily at the passing thought of his full lips moving slowly over her instep. Abshu was a foot man, and he always started his lovemaking from the bottom up. For that reason Kiswana changed the color of the polish on her toenails every week. During the course of their relationship she had gone from shades of red to brown and was now into the purples. I'm gonna have to start mixing them soon, she thought aloud as she turned from the couch and raced into the bathroom to remove any traces of Abshu from there. She took up his shaving cream and razor and threw them into the bottom drawer of her dresser beside her diaphragm. Mama wouldn't dare pry into my drawers right in front of me, she thought as she slammed the drawer shut. Well, at least not the *bottom* drawer. She may come up with some sham excuse for opening the top drawer, but never the bottom one.

When she heard the first two short raps on the door, her eyes took a final 9 flight over the small apartment, desperately seeking out any slight misdemeanor that might have to be defended. Well, there was nothing she could do about the crack in the wall over that table. She had been after the landlord to fix it for two months now. And there had been no time to sweep the rug, and everyone knew that off-gray always looked dirtier than it really was. And it was just too damn bad about the kitchen. How was she expected to be out job-hunting every day and still have time to keep a kitchen that looked like her mother's, who didn't even work and still had someone come in twice a month for general cleaning. And besides . . .

Her imaginary argument was abruptly interrupted by a second series of 10 knocks, accompanied by a penetrating, "Melanie, Melanie, are you there?"

Kiswana strode toward the door. She's starting before she even gets in here. 11 She knows that's not my name anymore.

She swung the door open to face her slightly flushed mother. "Oh, hi, 12 Mama. You know, I thought I heard a knock, but I figured it was for the people next door, since no one hardly ever calls me Melanie." Score one for me, she thought.

"Well, it's awfully strange you can forget a name you answered to for 13 twenty-three years," Mrs. Browne said, as she moved past Kiswana into the apartment. "My, that was a long climb. How long has your elevator been out? Honey, how do you manage with your laundry and groceries up all those steps? But I guess you're young, and it wouldn't bother you as much as it does me." This long string of questions told Kiswana that her mother had no intentions of beginning her visit with another argument about her new African name.

"You know I would have called before I came, but you don't have a phone 14 yet. I didn't want you to feel that I was snooping. As a matter of fact, I didn't expect to find you home at all. I thought you'd be out looking for a job." Mrs. Browne had mentally covered the entire apartment while she was talking and taking off her coat.

"Well, I got up late this morning. I thought I'd buy the afternoon paper and 15 start early tomorrow."

"That sounds like a good idea." Her mother moved toward the window and 16 picked up the discarded paper and glanced over the hurriedly circled ads. "Since when do you have experience as a fork-lift operator?"

Kiswana caught her breath and silently cursed herself for her stupidity. "Oh, 17 my hand slipped—I meant to circle file clerk." She quickly took the paper before her mother could see that she had also marked cutlery salesman and chauffeur.

"You're sure you weren't sitting here moping and daydreaming again?" Am- 18 ber specks of laughter flashed in the corner of Mrs. Browne's eyes.

Kiswana threw her shoulders back and unsuccessfully tried to disguise her 19 embarrassment with indignation.

"Oh, God, Mama! I haven't done that in years—it's for kids. When are you 20 going to realize that I'm a woman now?" She sought desperately for some womanly thing to do and settled for throwing herself on the couch and crossing her legs in what she hoped looked like a nonchalant arc.

"Please, have a seat," she said, attempting the same tones and gestures she'd 21 seen Bette Davis use on the late movies.

Mrs. Browne, lowering her eyes to hide her amusement, accepted the invita- 22 tion and sat at the window, also crossing her legs. Kiswana saw immediately how it should have been done. Her celluloid poise clashed loudly against her mother's quiet dignity, and she quickly uncrossed her legs. Mrs. Browne turned her head toward the window and pretended not to notice.

"At least you have a halfway decent view from here. I was wondering what 23 lay beyond that dreadful wall—it's the boulevard. Honey, did you know that you can see the trees in Linden Hills from here?"

Kiswana knew that very well, because there were many lonely days that she 24 would sit in her gray apartment and stare at those trees and think of home, but she would rather have choked than admit that to her mother.

"Oh, really, I never noticed. So how is Daddy and things at home?" 25

"Just fine. We're thinking of redoing one of the extra bedrooms since you 26 children have moved out, but Wilson insists that he can manage all that work alone. I told him that he doesn't really have the proper time or energy for all that. As it is, when he gets home from the office, he's so tired he can hardly move. But you know you can't tell your father anything. Whenever he starts complaining about how stubborn you are, I tell him the child came by it honestly. Oh, and your brother was by yesterday," she added, as if it had just occurred to her.

So that's it, thought Kiswana. That's why she's here.   27

Kiswana's brother, Wilson, had been to visit her two days ago, and she had   28
borrowed twenty dollars from him to get her winter coat out of layaway. That son-of-a-bitch probably ran straight to Mama—and after he swore he wouldn't say anything. I should have known, he was always a snotty-nosed sneak, she thought.

"Was he?" she said aloud. "He came by to see me, too, earlier this week. And   29
I borrowed some money from him because my unemployment checks hadn't cleared in the bank, but now they have and everything's just fine." There, I'll beat you to that one.

"Oh, I didn't know that," Mrs. Browne lied. "He never mentioned you. He   30
had just heard that Beverly was expecting again, and he rushed over to tell us."

Damn. Kiswana could have strangled herself.   31

"So she's knocked up again, huh?" she said irritably.   32

Her mother started. "Why do you always have to be so crude?"   33

"Personally, I don't see how she can sleep with Willie. He's such a dishrag."   34

Kiswana still resented the stance her brother had taken in college. When   35
everyone at school was discovering their blackness and protesting on campus, Wilson never took part; he had even refused to wear an Afro. This had outraged Kiswana because, unlike her, he was dark-skinned and had the type of hair that was thick and kinky enough for a good "Fro." Kiswana had still insisted on cutting her own hair, but it was so thin and fine-textured, it refused to thicken even after she washed it. So she had to brush it up and spray it with lacquer to keep it from lying flat. She never forgave Wilson for telling her that she didn't look African, she looked like an electrocuted chicken.

"Now that's some way to talk. I don't know why you have an attitude against   36
your brother. He never gave me a restless night's sleep, and now he's settled with a family and a good job."

"He's an assistant to an assistant junior partner in a law firm. What's the big   37
deal about that?"

"The job has a future, Melanie. And at least he finished school and went on   38
for his law degree."

"In other words, not like me, huh?"   39

"Don't put words into my mouth, young lady. I'm perfectly capable of say-   40
ing what I mean."

Amen, thought Kiswana.   41

"And I don't know why you've been trying to start up with me from the mo-   42
ment I walked in. I didn't come here to fight with you. This is your first place

away from home, and I just wanted to see how you were living and if you're doing all right. And I must say, you've fixed this apartment up very nicely."

"Really, Mama?" She found herself softening in the light of her mother's ap- 43
proval.

"Well, considering what you had to work with." This time she scanned the 44
apartment openly.

"Look, I know it's not Linden Hills, but a lot can be done with it. As soon 45
as they come and paint, I'm going to hang my Ashanti print over the couch.
And I thought a big Boston Fern would go well in that corner, what do you
think?"

"That would be fine, baby. You always had a good eye for balance." 46

Kiswana was beginning to relax. There was little she did that attracted her 47
mother's approval. It was like a rare bird, and she had to tread carefully around
it lest it fly away.

"Are you going to leave that statue out like that?" 48

"Why, what's wrong with it? Would it look better somewhere else?" 49

There was a small wooden reproduction of a Yoruba goddess with large pro- 50
truding breasts on the coffee table.

"Well," Mrs. Browne was beginning to blush, "it's just that it's a bit sugges- 51
tive, don't you think? Since you live alone now, and I know you'll be having male
friends stop by, you wouldn't want to be giving them any ideas. I mean, uh, you
know, there's no point in putting yourself in any unpleasant situations because
they may get the wrong impressions and uh, you know, I mean, well . . ." Mrs.
Browne stammered on miserably.

Kiswana loved it when her mother tried to talk about sex. It was the only 52
time she was at a loss for words.

"Don't worry, Mama." Kiswana smiled. "That wouldn't bother the type of 53
men I date. Now maybe if it had big feet . . ." And she got hysterical, thinking of
Abshu.

Her mother looked at her sharply. "What sort of gibberish is that about feet? 54
I'm being serious, Melanie."

"I'm sorry, Mama." She sobered up. "I'll put it away in the closet," she said, 55
knowing that she wouldn't.

"Good," Mrs. Browne said, knowing that she wouldn't either. "I guess you 56
think I'm too picky, but we worry about you over here. And you refuse to put in
a phone so we can call and see about you."

"I haven't refused, Mama. They want seventy-five dollars for a deposit, and I 57
can't swing that right now."

"Melanie, I can give you the money." 58

"I don't want you to be giving me money—I've told you that before. Please, 59
let me make it by myself."

"Well, let me lend it to you, then." 60

"No!" 61

"Oh, so you can borrow money from your brother, but not from me." 62

Kiswana turned her head from the hurt in her mother's eyes. "Mama, when 63
I borrow from Willie, he makes me pay him back. You never let me pay you
back," she said into her hands.

"I don't care. I still think it's downright selfish of you to be sitting over here 64
with no phone, and sometimes we don't hear from you in two weeks—anything
could happen—especially living among these people."

Kiswana snapped her head up. "What do you mean, *these people*. They're my 65
people and yours, too, Mama—we're all black. But maybe you've forgotten that
over in Linden Hills."

"That's not what I'm talking about, and you know it. These streets—this 66
building—it's so shabby and rundown. Honey, you don't have to live like this."

"Well, this is how poor people live." 67

"Melanie, you're not poor." 68

"No, Mama, *you're* not poor. And what you have and I have are two totally 69
different things. I don't have a husband in real estate with a five-figure income
and a home in Linden Hills—*you* do. What I have is a weekly unemployment
check and an overdrawn checking account at United Federal. So this studio on
Brewster is all I can afford."

"Well, you could afford a lot better," Mrs. Browne snapped, "if you hadn't 70
dropped out of college and had to resort to these dead-end clerical jobs."

"Uh-huh, I knew you'd get around to that before long." Kiswana could feel 71
the rings of anger begin to tighten around her lower backbone, and they sent
her forward onto the couch. "You'll never understand, will you? Those bourgie
schools were counterrevolutionary. My place was in the streets with my people,
fighting for equality and a better community."

"Counterrevolutionary!" Mrs. Browne was raising her voice. "Where's your 72
revolution now, Melanie? Where are all those black revolutionaries who were
shouting and demonstrating and kicking up a lot of dust with you on that campus? Huh? They're sitting in wood-paneled offices with their degrees in mahogany frames, and they won't even drive their cars past this street because the
city doesn't fix potholes in this part of town."

"Mama," she said, shaking her head slowly in disbelief, "how can you—a 73
black woman—sit there and tell me that what we fought for during the Movement wasn't important just because some people sold out?"

"Melanie, I'm not saying it wasn't important. It was damned important to 74
stand up and say that you were proud of what you were and to get the vote and
other social opportunities for every person in this country who had it due. But
you kids thought you were going to turn the world upside down, and it just
wasn't so. When all the smoke had cleared, you found yourself with a fistful of
new federal laws and a country still full of obstacles for black people to fight
their way over—just because they're black. There was no revolution, Melanie,
and there will be no revolution."

"So what am I supposed to do, huh? Just throw up my hands and not care 75
about what happens to my people? I'm not supposed to keep fighting to make
things better?"

"Of course, you can. But you're going to have to fight within the system, be- 76
cause it and these so-called 'bourgie' schools are going to be here for a long
time. And that means that you get smart like a lot of your old friends and get an
important job where you can have some influence. You don't have to sell out, as
you say, and work for some corporation, but you could become an assembly-
woman or a civil liberties lawyer or open a freedom school in this very neighborhood. That way you could really help the community. But what help are you
going to be to these people on Brewster while you're living hand-to-mouth on
file-clerk jobs waiting for a revolution? You're wasting your talents, child."

"Well, I don't think they're being wasted. At least I'm here in day-to-day 77
contact with the problems of my people. What good would I be after four or
five years of a lot of white brainwashing in some phony, prestige institution,
huh? I'd be like you and Daddy and those other educated blacks sitting over
there in Linden Hills with a terminal case of middle-class amnesia."

"You don't have to live in a slum to be concerned about social conditions, 78
Melanie. Your father and I have been charter members of the NAACP for the
last twenty-five years."

"Oh, God!" Kiswana threw her head back in exaggerated disgust. "That's be- 79
ing concerned? That middle-of-the-road, Uncle Tom dumping ground for
black Republicans!"

"You can sneer all you want, young lady, but that organization has been 80
working for black people since the turn of the century, and it's still working for
them. Where are all those radical groups of yours that were going to put a Cadillac in every garage and Dick Gregory in the White House? I'll tell you where."

I knew you would, Kiswana thought angrily. 81

"They burned themselves out because they wanted too much too fast. Their 82
goals weren't grounded in reality. And that's always been your problem."

"What do you mean, my problem? I know exactly what I'm about." 83

"No, you don't. You constantly live in a fantasy world—always going to ex- 84
tremes—turning butterflies into eagles, and life isn't about that. It's accepting
what is and working from that. Lord, I remember how worried you had me,
putting all that lacquered hair spray on your head. I thought you were going to
get lung cancer—trying to be what you're not."

Kiswana jumped up from the couch. "Oh, God, I can't take this anymore. 85
Trying to be something I'm not—trying to be something I'm not, Mama! Trying to be proud of my heritage and the fact that I was of African descent. If
that's being what I'm not, then I say fine. But I'd rather be dead than be like
you—a white man's nigger who's ashamed of being black!"

Kiswana saw streaks of gold and ebony light follow her mother's flying body 86
out of the chair. She was swung around by the shoulders and made to face the
deadly stillness in the angry woman's eyes. She was too stunned to cry out from
the pain of the long fingernails that dug into her shoulders, and she was
brought so close to her mother's face that she saw her reflection, distorted and
wavering, in the tears that stood in the older woman's eyes. And she listened in
that stillness to a story she had heard from a child.

"My grandmother," Mrs. Browne began slowly in a whisper, "was a full- 87
bloodied Iroquois, and my grandfather a free black from a long line of journey-
men who had lived in Connecticut since the establishment of the colonies. And
my father was a Bajan who came to this country as a cabin boy on a merchant
mariner."

"I know all that," Kiswana said, trying to keep her lips from trembling.   88

"Then, know this." And the nails dug deeper into her flesh. "I am alive be- 89
cause of the blood of proud people who never scraped or begged or apologized
for what they were. They lived asking only one thing of this world—to be allowed to be. And I learned through the blood of these people that black isn't
beautiful and it isn't ugly—black is! It's not kinky hair and it's not straight
hair—it just is.

"It broke my heart when you changed your name. I gave you my grand- 90
mother's name, a woman who bore nine children and educated them all, who
held off six white men with a shotgun when they tried to drag one of her sons
to jail for 'not knowing his place.' Yet you needed to reach into an African dictionary to find a name to make you proud.

"When I brought my babies home from the hospital, my ebony son and my 91
golden daughter, I swore before whatever gods would listen—those of my
mother's people or those of my father's people—that I would use everything I
had and could ever get to see that my children were prepared to meet this world
on its own terms, so that no one could sell them short and make them ashamed
of what they were or how they looked—whatever they were or however they
looked. And Melanie, that's not being white or red or black—that's being a
mother."

Kiswana followed her reflection in the two single tears that moved down 92
her mother's cheeks until it blended with them into the woman's copper
skin. There was nothing and then so much that she wanted to say, but her
throat kept closing up every time she tried to speak. She kept her head down
and her eyes closed, and thought, Oh, God, just let me die. How can I face
her now?

Mrs. Browne lifted Kiswana's chin gently. "And the one lesson I wanted you 93
to learn is not to be afraid to face anyone, not even a crafty old lady like me who
can outtalk you." And she smiled and winked.

"Oh, Mama, I . . ." and she hugged the woman tightly.   94

"Yeah, baby." Mrs. Browne patted her back. "I know."   95

She kissed Kiswana on the forehead and cleared her throat. "Well, now, I 96
better be moving on. It's getting late, there's dinner to be made, and I have to
get off my feet—these new shoes are killing me."

Kiswana looked down at the beige leather pumps. "Those are really classy. 97
They're English, aren't they?"

"Yes, but, Lord, do they cut me right across the instep." She removed the 98
shoe and sat on the couch to massage her foot.

Bright red nail polish glared at Kiswana through the stockings. "Since when 99
do you polish your toenails?" she gasped. "You never did that before."

"Well . . ." Mrs. Browne shrugged her shoulders, "your father sort of talked 100
me into it, and, uh, you know, he likes it and all, so I thought, uh, you know,
why not, so . . ." And she gave Kiswana an embarrassed smile.

I'll be damned, the young woman thought, feeling her whole face tingle. 101
Daddy's into feet! And she looked at the blushing woman on her couch and
suddenly realized that her mother had trod through the same universe that she
herself was now traveling. Kiswana was breaking no new trails and would eventually end up just two feet away on that couch. She stared at the woman she had
been and was to become.

"But I'll never be a Republican," she caught herself saying aloud. 102

"What are you mumbling about, Melanie?" Mrs. Browne slipped on her 103
shoe and got up from the couch.

She went to get her mother's coat. "Nothing, Mama. It's really nice of you to 104
come by. You should do it more often."

"Well, since it's not Sunday, I guess you're allowed at least one lie." 105

They both laughed. 106

After Kiswana had closed the door and turned around, she spotted an enve- 107
lope sticking between the cushions of her couch. She went over and opened it
up; there was seventy-five dollars in it.

"Oh, Mama, darn it!" She rushed to the window and started to call to the 108
woman, who had just emerged from the building, but she suddenly changed
her mind and sat down in the chair with a long sigh that caught in the upward
draft of the autumn wind and disappeared over the top of the building.

ACTIVITIES FOR WRITING AND DISCUSSION

1. React to the paragraph near the end of the story that begins, "I'll be
damned . . ."

> And she looked at the blushing woman on her couch and suddenly real-
> ized that her mother had trod through the same universe that she herself
> was now traveling. Kiswana was breaking no new trails and would eventu-
> ally end up just two feet away on that couch. She stared at the woman she
> had been and was to become.

   a. In what ways *is* Kiswana's mother "the woman she [Kiswana] had
      been and was to become"? Jot down some ways and discuss them with
      a partner or group.
   b. Compose a sequel in which you sketch out Kiswana's subsequent life.
      What choices does she make about family, career, politics, and social
      causes? How does the middle-aged Kiswana/Melanie resemble or dif-
      fer from her middle-aged mother?

2. Make a list of similarities and differences between you and your own
mother or father. Then, in a notebook entry, explore how *you* have become
more—or less—like your own mother or father as you have grown older.

3. Recall a conflict in your relationship with your own mother or father. Brainstorm a list of memories of that conflict. Then create a dialogue between you and your parent that dramatizes the conflict and its resolution—if there was one.

Poems

WILLIAM CARLOS WILLIAMS (1883–1963)

The Last Words of My English Grandmother

There were some dirty plates
and a glass of milk
beside her on a small table
near the rank, disheveled bed—

Wrinkled and nearly blind   5
she lay and snored
rousing with anger in her tones
to cry for food,

Gimme something to eat—
They're starving me—   10
I'm all right I won't go
to the hospital. No, no, no

Give me something to eat
Let me take you
to the hospital, I said   15
and after you are well

you can do as you please.
She smiled, Yes
you do what you please first
then I can do what I please—   20

Oh, oh, oh! she cried
as the ambulance men lifted
her to the stretcher—
Is this what you call

making me comfortable?   25
By now her mind was clear—

Oh you think you're smart
you young people,

she said, but I'll tell you
you don't know anything.   30
Then we started.
On the way

we passed a long row
of elms. She looked at them
awhile out of   35
the ambulance window and said,

What are all those
fuzzy-looking things out there?   Senile
Trees? Well, I'm tired
of them and rolled her head away.   40

ACTIVITIES FOR WRITING AND DISCUSSION

1. How would you describe the **speaker's** feelings about his grandmother? What clues in the poem help you with your description?

2. Look at the poem's **free verse** form. Try rewriting a few of Williams's sentences in *prose* form. What, if anything, is lost by not having the text laid out in lines and **stanzas**? How does Williams's visual layout affect your experience of the poem?

3. Think of elderly men or women you have met or known. List some of their characteristics, for instance, their personalities, appearance, gestures, speech, or favorite topics of conversation. Then, assuming the character of an elderly person in the midst of some urgent situation such as death, illness, a move, or some other change in lifestyle, write out your thoughts in a **stream of consciousness** form.

THEODORE ROETHKE (1908–1963)

My Papa's Waltz

The whiskey on your breath
Could make a small boy dizzy;
But I hung on like death:
Such waltzing was not easy.

We romped until the pans
Slid from the kitchen shelf;
My mother's countenance
Could not unfrown itself.

The hand that held my wrist
Was battered on one knuckle;
At every step you missed
My right ear scraped a buckle.

You beat time on my head
With a palm caked hard by dirt,
Then waltzed me off to bed
Still clinging to your shirt.

5

10

15

ACTIVITIES FOR WRITING AND DISCUSSION

1. Considering the title alone, what expectations do you have for the poem's tone and content? How and where are these expectations met or undercut as you read the poem itself?

2. Working in a small group or as a class, read the poem aloud twice. During the second reading, pause after each line or two to discuss any associations that are triggered for you by individual words or phrases. How, if at all, do any of these words or phrases affect your sense of the poem's meaning?

3. The poem offers a concise sketch of a family unit—father, mother, and child. Supplementing clues in the text with your own imagination and experience of families, try to describe this family—its members and their interrelationships—in as much detail as you can. Then show how your finished description is consistent with the spare details provided in the poem.

ANNA SWIR (1909–1984)

I Wash the Shirt

For the last time I wash the shirt
of my father who died.
The shirt smells of sweat. I remember
that sweat from my childhood,
so many years
I washed his shirts and underwear,
I dried them

5

at an iron stove in the workshop,
he would put them on unironed.

From among all bodies in the world,   10
animal, human,
only one exuded that sweat.
I breathe it in
for the last time. Washing this shirt
I destroy it   15
forever.
Now
only paintings survive him
which smell of oils.

—*Translated from the Polish by Czeslaw Milosz and Leonard Nathan*

The Greatest Love

She is sixty. She lives
the greatest love of her life.

She walks arm-in-arm with her dear one,
her hair streams in the wind.
Her dear one says: 5
"You have hair like pearls."

Her children say:
"Old fool."

—*Translated from the Polish by Czeslaw Milosz and Leonard Nathan*

ROBERT HAYDEN (1913–1980)

Those Winter Sundays

Sundays too my father got up early
and put his clothes on in the blueblack cold,
then with cracked hands that ached
from labor in the weekday weather made   5
banked fires blaze. No one ever thanked him.

I'd wake and hear the cold splintering, breaking.
When the rooms were warm, he'd call,
and slowly I would rise and dress,
fearing the chronic angers of that house,

Speaking indifferently to him,   10
who had driven out the cold
and polished my good shoes as well.
What did I know, what did I know
of love's austere and lonely offices?

GWENDOLYN BROOKS (b. 1917)

Sadie and Maud

Maud went to college.
Sadie stayed at home.
Sadie scraped life
With a fine-tooth comb.

She didn't leave a tangle in.   5
Her comb found every strand.
Sadie was one of the livingest chits
In all the land.

Sadie bore two babies
Under her maiden name.   10
Maud and Ma and Papa
Nearly died of shame.

When Sadie said her last so-long
Her girls struck out from home.
(Sadie had left as heritage   15
Her fine-tooth comb.)

Maud, who went to college,
Is a thin brown mouse.
She is living all alone
In this old house.   20

CHARLES BUKOWSKI (1920–1994)

my old man

16 years old
during the depression

I'd come home drunk
and all my clothing—
shorts, shirts, stockings—   5
suitcase, and pages of
short stories
would be thrown out on the
front lawn and about the
street.   10

my mother would be
waiting behind a tree:
"Henry, Henry, don't
go in . . . he'll
kill you, he's read   15
your stories . . ."

"I can whip his
ass . . ."

"Henry, please take
this . . . and   20
find yourself a room."

but it worried him
that I might not
finish high school
so I'd be back   25
again.

one evening he walked in
with the pages of
one of my short stories
(which I had never submitted   30
to him)
and he said, "this is
a great short story."
I said, "o.k.,"
and he handed it to me   35
and I read it.
it was a story about
a rich man
who had a fight with
his wife and had   40
gone out into the night
for a cup of coffee

and had observed
the waitress and the spoons
and forks and the   45
salt and pepper shakers
and the neon sign
in the window
and then had gone back
to his stable   50
to see and touch his
favorite horse
who then
kicked him in the head
and killed him.   55

somehow
the story held
meaning for him
though
when I had written it   60
I had no idea
of what I was
writing about.

so I told him,
"o.k., old man, you can   65
have it."
and he took it
and walked out
and closed the door.
I guess that's   70
as close
as we ever got.

ACTIVITIES FOR WRITING AND DISCUSSION

1. How does this piece change—or what does it lose—if you re-format it as prose and transform each grouping of lines into a prose paragraph?

2. The father objects to his son's short stories. Why?

3. The father liked *one* of the **speaker's** short stories. Based on the little you know of the father, what "meaning" could that story have "held" for him? What do you make of the word "close" in the next-to-last line? Do you take the word literally or as an example of **verbal irony**? What kind of closeness did this father and son have?

4. Drawing on details in the poem and on your own imagination, reconstruct the speaker's early life with his parents. Tell the story of his life from the **point of view** of the son or of either parent.

DONALD HALL (b. 1928)

My Son My Executioner

My son my executioner,
    I take you in my arms,
Quiet and small and just astir,
    And whom my body warms.

Sweet death, small son, our instrument   5
    Of immortality,
Your cries and hungers document
    Our bodily decay.

We twenty-five and twenty-two,   10
    Who seemed to live forever,
Observe enduring life in you
    And start to die together.

ACTIVITIES FOR WRITING AND DISCUSSION

1. Read the poem aloud. Plot out the **rhyme** scheme. Indicate sound patterns using a single underline for examples of **alliteration** and a double underline for examples of **assonance** or **consonance**.

2. Who are the "our" and the "we" in the poem?

3. Working alone or in a group, explicate the poem's dominant metaphor, which identifies "my son" as "my executioner."
    a. What images come to mind when you think of an "executioner"? Make a list of these images or of any other **connotations** the word has for you.
    b. Describe any ways in which the son *is* his father's "executioner." Are all sons or daughters executioners of their fathers or mothers? As an experiment, carry the metaphor to an extreme: Create a short dialogue between parent and child in which the child is a *literal* executioner. Finally, with the class or your group, discuss how a literal executioner differs from a metaphoric one.

LINDA PASTAN (b. 1932)

Marks

My husband gives me an A
for last night's supper,
an incomplete for my ironing,
a B plus in bed.
My son says I am average,   5
an average mother, but if
I put my mind to it
I could improve.
My daughter believes
in Pass/Fail and tells me   10
I pass. Wait 'til they learn
I'm dropping out.

TED KOOSER (b. 1939)

Father

Theodore Briggs Kooser
May 19, 1902–December 31, 1979

You spent fifty-five years
walking the hard floors
of the retail business,
first, as a boy playing store

in your grandmother's barn,   5
sewing feathers on hats
that the neighbors threw out,
then stepping out onto

the smooth pine planks
of your uncle's grocery—   10
SALADA TEA in gold leaf
over the door, your uncle

and father still young then
in handlebar mustaches,
white aprons with dusters   15
tucked into their sashes—

then to the varnished oak
of a dry goods store—
music to your ears,
that bumpety-bump   20

of bolts of bright cloth
on the counter tops,
the small rattle of buttons,
the bell in the register—

then on to the cold tile   25
of a bigger store, and then one
still bigger—gray carpet,
wide aisles, a new town

to get used to—then into
retirement, a few sales   30
in your own garage,
the concrete under your feet.

You had good legs, Dad,
and a good storekeeper's eye:
asked once if you remembered   35
a teacher of mine,

you said, "I certainly do;
size ten, a little something
in blue." How you loved
what you'd done with your life!   40

Now you're gone, and the clerks
are lazy, the glass cases
smudged, the sale sweaters
pulled off on the floor.

But what good times we had   45
before it was over:
after those stores had closed,
you posing as customers,

strutting in big flowered hats,
those aisles like a stage,   50
the pale manikins watching;
we laughed till we cried.

Sharon Olds (b. 1942)

The Elder Sister

When I look at my elder sister now
I think how she had to go first, down through the
birth canal, to force her way
head-first through the tiny channel,
the pressure of Mother's muscles on her brain,   5
the tight walls scraping her skin.
Her face is still narrow from it, the long
hollow cheeks of a Crusader on a tomb,
and her inky eyes have the look of someone who has
been in prison a long time and   10
knows they can send her back. I look at her
body and think how her breasts were the first to
rise, slowly, like swans on a pond.

By the time mine came along, they were just
two more birds on the flock, and when the hair   15
rose on the white mound of her flesh, like
threads of water out of the ground, it was the
first time, but when mine came
they knew about it. I used to think
only in terms of her harshness, sitting and   20
pissing on me in bed, but now I
see I had her before me always
like a shield. I look at her wrinkles, her clenched
jaws, her frown-lines—I see they are
the dents on my shield, the blows that did not reach me.   25
She protected me, not as a mother
protects a child, with love, but as a
hostage protects the one who makes her
escape as I made my escape, with my sister's
body held in front of me.   30

Linda Hogan (b. 1947)

Heritage

From my mother, the antique mirror
where I watch my face take on her lines.

She left me the smell of baking bread
to warm fine hairs in my nostrils,
she left the large white breasts that weigh down   5
my body.

From my father I take his brown eyes,
the plague of locusts that leveled our crops,
they flew in formation like buzzards.

From my uncle the whittled wood   10
that rattles like bones
and is white
and smells like all our old houses
that are no longer there. He was the man
who sang old chants to me, the words   15
my father was told not to remember.

From my grandfather who never spoke
I learned to fear silence.
I learned to kill a snake
when you're begging for rain.   20

And grandmother, blue-eyed woman
whose skin was brown,
she used snuff.
When her coffee can full of black saliva
spilled on me   25
it was like the brown cloud of grasshoppers
that leveled her fields.
It was the brown stain
that covered my white shirt,
my whiteness a shame.   30
That sweet black liquid like the food
she chewed up and spit into my father's mouth
when he was an infant.
It was the brown earth of Oklahoma
stained with oil.   35
She said tobacco would purge your body of poisons.
It has more medicine than stones and knives
against your enemies.

That tobacco is the dark night that covers me.

She said it is wise to eat the flesh of deer   40
so you will be swift and travel over many miles.

She told me how our tribe has always followed a stick
that pointed west
that pointed east.
From my family I have learned the secrets   45
of never having a home.

ACTIVITIES FOR WRITING AND DISCUSSION

1. React to the poem's images. How do they make you feel? Are they pleasant? unpleasant? perplexing? disturbing? Why? Be specific, and share your reactions in class or in a small group.

2. How would you characterize the **speaker's** attitude toward her heritage? Does she regard it fondly? bitterly? with mixed emotions? Cite words or lines in the poem to support your answers.

3. Create a poem about your own heritage. Consider imitating Hogan's form by beginning each section with the words "From my [grandmother/uncle/father/mother" and so on] and following with the particular legacy you have from that ancestor or relative.

DEB CASEY (b. 1950)

ZOOOOOOOM

A FAMILIAR STORY: DROP-OFF/PICK–UP PANIC
ZOOOM: morning frenzy, the held-breath beginning to each work day. (Zip past the entire get-up, dress-feed-comb/brush-assemble struggle, the tension between adults as to who is doing what, and who isn't.) **BEGIN** at the car: load, fasten, dash back for forgotten items. Check watch: two minutes past the sure parking spot. Accelerate. Stay calm. Sing, babble, wiggle, jounce, offer a finger to chew, look at the *"Look"* commands: back, sideways; **DRIVE.** Five miles to campus. **Park.** (First spot easy.) Unbelt, gather children (*stay close!* to the oldest), deliver one: sign in, situate, converse with Lead Teacher (casual mother), glance to clock, *Ooops!: Got to go* . . . Be thankful: almost past the tearful good-byes with this daughter. **Re-situate:** baby into seat (again), kiss the sweet lips, eager eyes (careful not to bend legs backward in haste). Turn around. Now the real struggle. Twenty minutes gone in that drop-off (and the center opens no earlier). Circle. Lot after lot. Seeth. No parking. No options—no *good* options. Give up. **Park** on the fringe. Prepare for the hike. Gather bags, umbrella, baby stuff, books. Adjust Baby in the front pack, distribute weight. **Stride!** (And be thankful the umbrella isn't necessary, no hand left.) Trudge. **DELIVER** baby to grad-student in father's office. (Take advantage of his morning-empty space.)

Whisk out the baby decor: padded play place, fur, jump-seat, chewables. Nurse. Insistently: here. Now. Greet care taker. Make fast small-talk. Say goodbyes. Breathe—no, not yet. Ignore the sudden squawk, tears, of a baby who wants you. No, don't: acknowledge the uneasiness. **Return.** Console. Promise. Leave again. NOW breathe. Find a bathroom—forget it: late. Run. (Forget, too, figuring how on earth you'll regroup bodies with the car, where it is compared to all three of our stations. **Skip** the logistics of breastfeeding connections and so on. Get to the day's close.) **DEPARTURE:** Get edgy as meeting runs late. **Fidget.** Lose all train of thought. Try not to be obvious as you pack-up, already overdue. Dash across the quad, and up three flights (fast!), present the breast, **FEED,** hear her contented warble, relax, sooth her moist cheek, soft fontanel, **marvel** again: how wide her *feed-me*-bird-mouth glomps around the nipple (See: we working mothers are not oblivious), keep her attached as you try to move smoothly, quickly (the easy minute up), **gather** her pieces. Sweater her snug, hug closely as you run to the car, urging all the bulk of you to advance a bit faster, imagining you'll find your older daughter parked on the curb: *"her time was up."* Don't exaggerate. No guilt: you called apologizing, think no more of it. Get to the car. Strap Baby in. Try to hush her yelps. Promise (again): *soon* . . . Remember what you should have brought home from the office. Try not to catch your mind sliding forward, backward. Don't think what you'd like is a drink. A moment . . . Watch the road, **shift, sing, juggle, jiggle,** fingerrub the baby's gums. Zoom. Grab Baby (gently!): up and over (watch the head). Find Older Daughter. Apologize to Lead Teacher. Concentrate on this reunion time: **focus**—while urging Daughter toward her cubby and out of the action. (And don't wrinkle the painting.) Keep Baby from the breast position temptation. **Give up:** sling Baby over hip, guide to nipple, button Older Daughter's sweater, one handed, gather other drawings, praise (sincerely), pat, burp, sign-out (Don't forget!), get them out and loaded (again) into the car and belted and grinning, or grumbling (whatever), **DRIVE.** Sing. (What's in the fridge?) Shift.

Rita Dove (b. 1952)

Fifth Grade Autobiography

I was four in this photograph fishing
with my grandparents at a lake in Michigan.
My brother squats in poison ivy.
His Davy Crockett cap
sits squared on his head so the raccoon tail   5
flounces down the back of his sailor suit.

My grandfather sits to the far right
in a folding chair,

and I know his left hand is on
the tobacco in his pants pocket   10
because I used to wrap it for him
every Christmas. Grandmother's hips
bulge from the brush, she's leaning
into the ice chest, sun through the trees
printing her dress with soft   15
luminous paws.

I am staring jealously at my brother;
the day before he rode his first horse, alone.
I was strapped in a basket
behind my grandfather.   20
He smelled of lemons. He's died—

but I remember his hands.

ACTIVITY FOR WRITING AND DISCUSSION

1. Find a childhood photograph of you and your family. Writing in the present tense, describe the photograph's visual details. In your description, incorporate the thoughts that were likely going through your mind—and/or the minds of others in the picture—at the moment the picture was taken.

ALBERTO RIOS (b. 1952)

A Dream of Husbands

Though we thought it, Doña Carolina did not die.
She was too old for that nonsense, and too set.
That morning she walked off just a little farther
into her favorite dream, favorite but not nice
so much, not nice and not bad, so it was not death.   5
She dreamed the dream of husbands
and over there she found him after all the years.
Cabrón, she called him, *animal,* very loud
so we could hear it, for us it was a loud truck
passing, or thunder, or too many cats, very loud   10
for having left her for so long and so far. Days now
her voice is the squeak of the rocking chair
as she complains, we hear it, it will not go
not with oils or sanding or shouts back at her.

But it becomes too the sound a spoon makes, her old   15
very large wooden spoon as it stirs a pot of soup.
Dinnertimes, we think of her, the good parts, of her
cooking, we like her best then, even the smell of her.
But then, *cabrones* she calls us, *animales,* irritated,
from over there, from the dream, they come, her words   20
they are the worst sounds of the street in the night
so that we will not get so comfortable about her,
so comfortable with her having left us
we thinking that her husband and her long dream
are so perfect, because no, they are not, not so much,   25
she is not so happy this way, not in this dream,
this is not heaven, don't think it. She tells us this,
sadness too is hers, a half measure, sadness at having
no time for the old things, for rice, for chairs.

SHARON HASHIMOTO (b. 1953)

Eleven A.M. on My Day Off, My Sister Phones Desperate for a Babysitter

Sitting in sunlight, the child
I sometimes pretend is my own
fingers the green weave of the rug
while the small shadow of her head falls over
a part of my lap and bent knee. At three,   5
she could be that younger part of myself, just beginning
to remember how the dusty warmth feels on her back.
"Are you hungry?" I ask. Together we open
the door of the refrigerator. One apple sits
in the vegetable bin but she gives it to me,   10
repeating her true mother's words "to share."
Turning the round fruit under the faucet,
the afternoon bright in my face, I look down
at a smile in the half moons of her eyes
and for a moment, I'm seven, looking up   15
at my childless aunt in Hawaii,
her hands and the long knife peeling
the mango I picked off the tree, rubbing my arms
from the stretch on the back porch
to an overhead branch. Plump   20
with the island's humidity, it tasted tart

like the heavy clatter of rain on a June Sunday.
"Careful," my niece warns as I slice the apple sideways
to show her the star in the middle.
She eats the core but saves the seeds   25
to plant in the soft earth of my yard.

Nonfiction/Essays

RAYMOND CARVER (1938–1988)

My Father's Life

My dad's name was Clevie Raymond Carver. His family called him Raymond and friends called him C. R. I was named Raymond Clevie Carver, Jr. I hated the "Junior" part. When I was little my dad called me Frog, which was okay. But later, like everybody else in the family, he began calling me Junior. He went on calling me this until I was thirteen or fourteen and announced that I wouldn't answer to that name any longer. So he began calling me Doc. From then until his death, on June 17, 1967, he called me Doc, or else Son.

When he died, my mother telephoned my wife with the news. I was away from my family at the time, between lives, trying to enroll in the School of Library Science at the University of Iowa. When my wife answered the phone, my mother blurted out, "Raymond's dead!" For a moment, my wife thought my mother was telling her that I was dead. Then my mother made it clear *which* Raymond she was talking about and my wife said, "Thank God. I thought you meant *my* Raymond."

My dad walked, hitched rides, and rode in empty boxcars when he went from Arkansas to Washington State in 1934, looking for work. I don't know whether he was pursuing a dream when he went out to Washington. I doubt it. I don't think he dreamed much. I believe he was simply looking for steady work at decent pay. Steady work was meaningful work. He picked apples for a time and then landed a construction laborer's job on the Grand Coulee Dam. After he'd put aside a little money, he bought a car and drove back to Arkansas to help his folks, my grandparents, pack up for the move west. He said later that they were about to starve down there, and this wasn't meant as a figure of speech. It was during that short while in Arkansas, in a town called Leola, that my mother met my dad on the sidewalk as he came out of a tavern.

"He was drunk," she said. "I don't know why I let him talk to me. His eyes were glittery. I wish I'd had a crystal ball." They'd met once, a year or so before, at a dance. He'd had girlfriends before her, my mother told me. "Your dad always had a girlfriend, even after we married. He was my first and last. I never had another man. But I didn't miss anything."

They were married by a justice of the peace on the day they left for Wash- 5 ington, this big, tall country girl and a farmhand-turned-construction worker. My mother spent her wedding night with my dad and his folks, all of them camped beside the road in Arkansas.

In Omak, Washington, my dad and mother lived in a little place not much bigger than a cabin. My grandparents lived next door. My dad was still working on the dam, and later, with the huge turbines producing electricity and the water backed up for a hundred miles into Canada, he stood in the crowd and heard Franklin D. Roosevelt when he spoke at the construction site. "He never mentioned those guys who died building that dam," my dad said. Some of his friends had died there, men from Arkansas, Oklahoma, and Missouri.

He then took a job in a sawmill in Clatskanie, Oregon, a little town alongside the Columbia River. I was born there, and my mother has a picture of my dad standing in front of the gate to the mill, proudly holding me up to face the camera. My bonnet is on crooked and about to come untied. His hat is pushed back on his forehead, and he's wearing a big grin. Was he going in to work or just finishing his shift? It doesn't matter. In either case, he had a job and a family. These were his salad days.

In 1941 we moved to Yakima, Washington, where my dad went to work as a saw filer, a skilled trade he'd learned in Clatskanie. When war broke out, he was given a deferment because his work was considered necessary to the war effort. Finished lumber was in demand by the armed services, and he kept his saws so sharp they could shave the hair off your arm.

After my dad had moved us to Yakima, he moved his folks into the same neighborhood. By the mid-1940s the rest of my dad's family—his brother, his sister, and her husband, as well as uncles, cousins, nephews, and most of their extended family and friends—had come out from Arkansas. All because my dad came out first. The men went to work at Boise Cascade, where my dad worked, and the women packed apples in the canneries. And in just a little while, it seemed—according to my mother—everybody was better off than my dad. "Your dad couldn't keep money," my mother said. "Money burned a hole in his pocket. He was always doing for others."

The first house I clearly remember living in, at 1515 South Fifteenth Street, 10 in Yakima, had an outdoor toilet. On Halloween night, or just any night, for the hell of it, neighbor kids, kids in their early teens, would carry our toilet away and leave it next to the road. My dad would have to get somebody to help him bring it home. Or these kids would take the toilet and stand it in somebody else's backyard. Once they actually set it on fire. But ours wasn't the only house that had an outdoor toilet. When I was old enough to know what I was doing, I threw rocks at the other toilets when I'd see someone go inside. This was called bombing the toilets. After a while, though, everyone went to indoor plumbing until, suddenly, our toilet was the last outdoor one in the neighborhood. I remember the shame I felt when my third-grade teacher, Mr. Wise, drove me home from school one day. I asked him to stop at the house just before ours, claiming I lived there.

I can recall what happened one night when my dad came home late to find that my mother had locked all the doors on him from the inside. He was drunk, and we could feel the house shudder as he rattled the door. When he'd managed to force open a window, she hit him between the eyes with a colander and knocked him out. We could see him down there on the grass. For years afterward, I used to pick up this colander—it was as heavy as a rolling pin—and imagine what it would feel like to be hit in the head with something like that.

It was during this period that I remember my dad taking me into the bedroom, sitting me down on the bed, and telling me that I might have to go live with my Aunt LaVon for a while. I couldn't understand what I'd done that meant I'd have to go away from home to live. But this, too—whatever prompted it—must have blown over, more or less, anyway, because we stayed together, and I didn't have to go live with her or anyone else.

I remember my mother pouring his whiskey down the sink. Sometimes she'd pour it all out and sometimes, if she was afraid of getting caught, she'd only pour half of it out and then add water to the rest. I tasted some of his whiskey once myself. It was terrible stuff, and I don't see how anybody could drink it.

After a long time without one, we finally got a car, in 1949 or 1950, a 1938 Ford. But it threw a rod the first week we had it, and my dad had to have the motor rebuilt.

"We drove the oldest car in town," my mother said. "We could have had a Cadillac for all he spent on car repairs." One time she found someone else's tube of lipstick on the floorboard, along with a lacy handkerchief. "See this?" she said to me. "Some floozy left this in the car."

Once I saw her take a pan of warm water into the bedroom where my dad was sleeping. She took his hand from under the covers and held it in the water. I stood in the doorway and watched. I wanted to know what was going on. This would make him talk in his sleep, she told me. There were things she needed to know, things she was sure he was keeping from her.

Every year or so, when I was little, we would take the North Coast Limited across the Cascade Range from Yakima to Seattle and stay in the Vance Hotel and eat, I remember, at a place called the Dinner Bell Cafe. Once we went to Ivar's Acres of Clams and drank glasses of warm clam broth.

In 1956, the year I was to graduate from high school, my dad quit his job at the mill in Yakima and took a job in Chester, a little sawmill town in northern California. The reasons given at the time for his taking the job had to do with a higher hourly wage and the vague promise that he might, in a few years' time, succeed to the job of head filer in this new mill. But I think, in the main, that my dad had grown restless and simply wanted to try his luck elsewhere. Things had gotten a little too predictable for him in Yakima. Also, the year before, there had been the deaths, within six months of each other, of both his parents.

But just a few days after graduation, when my mother and I were packed to move to Chester, my dad penciled a letter to say he'd been sick for a while. He didn't want us to worry, he said, but he'd cut himself on a saw. Maybe he'd got a tiny sliver of steel in his blood. Anyway, something had happened and he'd had to miss work, he said. In the same mail was an unsigned postcard from somebody down there telling my mother that my dad was about to die and that he was drinking "raw whiskey."

When we arrived in Chester, my dad was living in a trailer that belonged to   20
the company. I didn't recognize him immediately. I guess for a moment I didn't want to recognize him. He was skinny and pale and looked bewildered. His pants wouldn't stay up. He didn't look like my dad. My mother began to cry. My dad put his arm around her and patted her shoulder vaguely, like he didn't know what this was all about, either. The three of us took up life together in the trailer, and we looked after him as best we could. But my dad was sick, and he couldn't get any better. I worked with him in the mill that summer and part of the fall. We'd get up in the mornings and eat eggs and toast while we listened to the radio, and then go out the door with our lunch pails. We'd pass through the gate together at eight in the morning, and I wouldn't see him again until quitting time. In November I went back to Yakima to be closer to my girlfriend, the girl I'd made up my mind I was going to marry.

He worked at the mill in Chester until the following February, when he collapsed on the job and was taken to the hospital. My mother asked if I would come down there and help. I caught a bus from Yakima to Chester, intending to drive them back to Yakima. But now, in addition to being physically sick, my dad was in the midst of a nervous breakdown, though none of us knew to call it that at the time. During the entire trip back to Yakima, he didn't speak, not even when asked a direct question. ("How do you feel, Raymond?" "You okay, Dad?") He'd communicate, if he communicated at all, by moving his head or by turning his palms up as if to say he didn't know or care. The only time he said anything on the trip, and for nearly a month afterward, was when I was speeding down a gravel road in Oregon and the car muffler came loose. "You were going too fast," he said.

Back in Yakima a doctor saw to it that my dad went to a psychiatrist. My mother and dad had to go on relief, as it was called, and the county paid for the psychiatrist. The psychiatrist asked my dad, "Who is the President?" He'd had a question put to him that he could answer. "Ike," my dad said. Nevertheless, they put him on the fifth floor of Valley Memorial Hospital and began giving him electroshock treatments. I was married by then and about to start my own family. My dad was still locked up when my wife went into this same hospital, just one floor down, to have our first baby. After she had delivered, I went upstairs to give my dad the news. They let me in through a steel door and showed me where I could find him. He was sitting on a couch with a blanket over his lap. *Hey,* I thought. *What in hell is happening to my dad?* I sat down next to him and told him he was a grandfather. He waited a minute and then said, "I feel like a grandfather." That's all he said. He didn't smile or move. He was in a big room with a lot of other people. Then I hugged him, and he began to cry.

Somehow he got out of there. But now came the years when he couldn't work and just sat around the house trying to figure what next and what he'd done wrong in his life that he'd wound up like this. My mother went from job to crummy job. Much later she referred to that time he was in the hospital, and those years just afterward, as "when Raymond was sick." The word *sick* was never the same for me again.

In 1964, through the help of a friend, he was lucky enough to be hired on at a mill in Klamath, California. He moved down there by himself to see if he could hack it. He lived not far from the mill, in a one-room cabin not much different from the place he and my mother had started out living in when they went west. He scrawled letters to my mother, and if I called she'd read them aloud to me over the phone. In the letters, he said it was touch and go. Every day that he went to work, he felt like it was the most important day of his life. But every day, he told her, made the next day that much easier. He said for her to tell me he said hello. If he couldn't sleep at night, he said, he thought about me and the good times we used to have. Finally, after a couple of months, he regained some of his confidence. He could do the work and didn't think he had to worry that he'd let anybody down ever again. When he was sure, he sent for my mother.

He'd been off from work for six years and had lost everything in that time— 25 home, car, furniture, and appliances, including the big freezer that had been my mother's pride and joy. He'd lost his good name too—Raymond Carver was someone who couldn't pay his bills—and his self-respect was gone. He'd even lost his virility. My mother told my wife, "All during that time Raymond was sick we slept together in the same bed, but we didn't have relations. He wanted to a few times, but nothing happened. I didn't miss it, but I think he wanted to, you know."

During those years I was trying to raise my own family and earn a living. But, one thing and another, we found ourselves having to move a lot. I couldn't keep track of what was going down in my dad's life. But I did have a chance one Christmas to tell him I wanted to be a writer. I might as well have told him I wanted to become a plastic surgeon. "What are you going to write about?" he wanted to know. Then, as if to help me out, he said, "Write about stuff you know about. Write about some of those fishing trips we took." I said I would, but I knew I wouldn't. "Send me what you write," he said. I said I'd do that, but then I didn't. I wasn't writing anything about fishing, and I didn't think he'd particularly care about, or even necessarily understand, what I was writing in those days. Besides, he wasn't a reader. Not the sort, anyway, I imagined I was writing for.

Then he died. I was a long way off, in Iowa City, with things still to say to him. I didn't have the chance to tell him good-bye, or that I thought he was doing great at his new job. That I was proud of him for making a comeback.

My mother said he came in from work that night and ate a big supper. Then he sat at the table by himself and finished what was left of a bottle of whiskey, a bottle she found hidden in the bottom of the garbage under some coffee grounds a day or so later. Then he got up and went to bed, where my mother joined him a little later. But in the night she had to get up and make a bed for herself on the couch. "He was snoring so loud I couldn't sleep," she said. The next morning when she looked in on him, he was on his back with his mouth open, his cheeks caved in. *Graylooking,* she said. She knew he was dead—she didn't need a doctor to tell her that. But she called one anyway, and then she called my wife.

Among the pictures my mother kept of my dad and herself during those early days in Washington was a photograph of him standing in front of a car, holding a beer and a stringer of fish. In the photograph he is wearing his hat back on his forehead and has this awkward grin on his face. I asked her for it and she gave it to me, along with some others. I put it up on my wall, and each time we moved, I took the picture along and put it up on another wall. I looked at it carefully from time to time, trying to figure out some things about my dad, and maybe myself in the process. But I couldn't. My dad just kept moving further and further away from me and back into time. Finally, in the course of another move, I lost the photograph. It was then that I tried to recall it, and at the same time make an attempt to say something about my dad, and how I thought that in some important ways we might be alike. I wrote the poem when I was living in an apartment house in an urban area south of San Francisco, at a time when I found myself, like my dad, having trouble with alcohol. The poem was a way of trying to connect up with him.

Photograph of My Father in His Twenty-Second Year

October. Here in this dank, unfamiliar kitchen
I study my father's embarrassed young man's face.
Sheepish grin, he holds in one hand a string
of spiny yellow perch, in the other
a bottle of Carlsberg beer.

In jeans and flannel shirt, he leans
against the front fender of a 1934 Ford.
He would like to pose brave and hearty for his posterity,
wear his old hat cocked over his ear.
All his life my father wanted to be bold.

But the eyes give him away, and the hands
that limply offer the string of dead perch
and the bottle of beer. Father, I love you,
yet how can I say thank you, I who can't hold my liquor either
and don't even know the places to fish.

The poem is true in its particulars, except that my dad died in June and not October, as the first word of the poem says. I wanted a word with more than one syllable to it to make it linger a little. But more than that, I wanted a month appropriate to what I felt at the time I wrote the poem—a month of short days and failing light, smoke in the air, things perishing. June was summer nights and days, graduations, my wedding anniversary, the birthday of one of my children. June wasn't a month your father died in.

After the service at the funeral home, after we had moved outside, a woman I didn't know came over to me and said, "He's happier where he is now." I stared at this woman until she moved away. I still remember the little knob of a hat she was wearing. Then one of my dad's cousins—I didn't know the man's name—reached out and took my hand, "We all miss him," he said, and I knew he wasn't saying it just to be polite.

I began to weep for the first time since receiving the news. I hadn't been able to before. I hadn't had the time, for one thing. Now, suddenly, I couldn't stop. I held my wife and wept while she said and did what she could do to comfort me there in the middle of that summer afternoon.

I listened to people say consoling things to my mother, and I was glad that my dad's family had turned up, had come to where he was. I thought I'd remember everything that was said and done that day and maybe find a way to tell it sometime. But I didn't. I forgot it all, or nearly. What I do remember is that I heard our name used a lot that afternoon, my dad's name and mine. But I knew they were talking about my dad. *Raymond*, these people kept saying in their beautiful voices out of my childhood. *Raymond*.

ACTIVITIES FOR WRITING AND DISCUSSION

1. Describe Carver's **persona.** What qualities of the persona attract or repel you, and how and where—specifically—are those qualities conveyed by the language of the text? Consider word choice, vocabulary, sentence length and style, and tone. If possible look carefully at one specific paragraph or event in the essay and concentrate your analysis on that paragraph or event.

2. Identify a moment in the essay that is particularly powerful or meaningful for you. Annotate the passage and share it with others. Then expand on your annotations in a longer notebook entry, using, if you wish, one of the "Ten Ideas for Writing" found on page 27.

3. Carver's essay is a collection of many stories about his father.
   a. Over a period of time write down and collect stories—however short or long—of your own family or of some significant individual in it, such as a parent, surrogate parent, or sibling. For source material draw upon your own memory and/or the memories of others' (as Carver draws upon his mother's memories).
   b. Arrange these stories—or a portion of them—into an essay-memoir, adding a beginning, an ending, and connecting material as needed.

4. Reread paragraph 29, where Carver describes a photograph of his father and shares a poem inspired by it. Then find a photo of your own family or some

family member that has special meaning for you. Following Carver's example, first tell the story behind the photo—the context in which it was taken, who is in it, and how it has fit into your life. Then, using the photo as a springboard, write a response to it in a form of your own choice, as Carver wrote a poem.

JOY HARJO (b. 1951)

The Place of Origins

for my cousin John Jacobs (1918–1991), who will always be with me

I felt as if I had prepared for the green corn ceremony my whole life. It's nothing I can explain in print, and no explanation would fit in the English language. All I can say is that it is central to the mythic construct of the Muscogee people (otherwise known as "Creek"), a time of resonant renewal, of forgiveness.

The drive to Tallahassee Grounds in northeastern Oklahoma, with my friends Helen and Jim Burgess and Sue Williams, was filled with stories. Stories here are thick as the insects singing. We were part of the ongoing story of the people. Helen and I had made a promise to participate together in a ceremony that ensures the survival of the people, a link in the epic story of grace. The trees and tall, reedlike grasses resounded with singing.

There's nothing quite like it anywhere else I've been, and I've traveled widely. The most similar landscape is in Miskito country in northeastern Nicaragua. I thought I was home again as I walked with the Miskito people whose homeland had suffered terrible destruction from both sides in the war. The singing insects provided a matrix of complex harmonics, shifting the cells in the body that shape imagination. I imagine a similar insect language in a place I've dreamed in West Africa. In summer in Oklahoma it's as if insects shape the world by songs. Their collective punctuation helps the growing corn remember the climb to the sun.

Our first stop was Holdenville, to visit one of my favorite older cousins, John Jacobs, and his wife Carol. They would join us later at the grounds. We traded gifts and stories, ate a perfectly fried meal at the Dairy Queen, one of the few restaurants open in a town hit hard by economic depression. I always enjoy visiting and feasting with these, my favorite relatives, and I feel at home in their house, a refuge surrounded by peacocks, dogs, and well-loved cats, guarded by giant beneficent spirits disguised as trees.

Across the road an oil well pumps relentlessly. When I was a child in Okla-   5
homa, the monster insect bodies of the pumping wells terrified me. I would duck down in the car until we passed. Everyone thought it was funny. I was called high-strung and imaginative. I imagined the collapse of the world, as if the wells were giant insects without songs, pumping blood from the body of Earth. I wasn't far from the truth.

Marsie Harjo and Family. (Courtesy Joy Harjo.)

Marsie Harjo and Katie Menawe Harjo. (Courtesy Joy Harjo.)

My cousin John, who was more like a beloved uncle, gave me two photographs he had culled for me from family albums. I had never before seen my great-grandparents on my father's side. As I held them in my hand, reverberations of memory astounded me.

I believe stories are encoded in the DNA spiral and call each cell into perfect position. Sound tempered with emotion and meaning propels the spiral beyond three dimensions. I recognized myself in this photograph. I saw my sister, my brothers, my son and daughter. My father lived once again at the wheel of a car, my father who favored Cadillacs and Lincolns—cars he was not always able to afford but sacrificed to own anyway because he was compelled by the luxury of well-made vehicles, the humming song of a finely constructed motor. He made sure his cars were greased and perfectly tuned. That was his favorite music.

I was shocked (but not surprised) to recognize something I must always have known—the images of my great-grandmother Katie Menawe, my great-grandfather Marsie Harjo, my grandmother Naomi, my aunts Lois and Mary, and my uncle Joe. They were always inside me, as if I were a soul catcher made of a blood-formed crystal. I had heard the names, the stories, and perhaps their truths had formed the images, had propelled me into the world. My grandchildren and great-grandchildren will also see a magnification of themselves in their grandparents. It's implicit in the way we continue, the same way as corn plants, the same way as stars or cascades of insects singing in the summer. The old mystery of division and multiplication will always lead us to the root.

I think of my Aunt Lois's admonishments about photographs. She said that they could steal your soul. I believe it's true, for an imprint remains behind forever, locked in paper and chemicals. Perhaps the family will always be touring somewhere close to the border, dressed in their Sunday best, acutely aware of the soul stealer that Marsie Harjo hired to photograph them, steadying his tripod on the side of the road. Who's to say they didn't want something left to mark time in that intimate space, a space where they could exist forever as a family, a world drenched in sepia?

Nothing would ever be the same again. But here the family is ever-present, as is the unnamed photographer through his visual arrangement. I wonder if he was surprised to see rich Indians.

The parents of both my great-grandparents made the terrible walk of the Muscogee Nation from Alabama to Indian Territory. They were settled on land bordered on the north by what is now Tulsa—the place my brothers, my sister, and I were born. The people were promised that if they made this move they would be left alone by the U.S. government, which claimed it needed the tribal homelands for expansion. But within a few years, white settlers were once again crowding Indian lands, and in 1887 the Dawes Act, better known as the Allotment Act, was made law. Private ownership was forced on the people. Land that supposedly belonged in perpetuity to the tribe was divided into plots, allotted to individuals. What was "left over" was opened for white settlement. But this did not satisfy the settlers, who proceeded, by new laws, other kinds of trickery, and raw force, to take over allotments belonging to the Muscogee and other tribes. The Dawes Act undermined one of the principles that had always kept the people together: that land was communal property which could not be owned.

On December 1, 1905, oil was struck in Glenpool, Oklahoma. This was one of the richest lakes of oil discovered in the state. At its height it produced forty million barrels annually. Marsie Harjo's allotted land was in Glenpool. He was soon a rich man, as were many other Indian people whose allotted land lay over lakes of oil. Land grabs intensified. Many tribal members were swindled out of their property, or simply killed for their money. It's a struggle that is still being played out in the late twentieth century.

Oil money explains the long elegant car Marsie Harjo poses in with his family. In the stories I've been told, he always loved Hudsons. The family was raised in luxury. My grandmother Naomi and my Aunt Lois both received B.F.A. degrees in art and were able to take expensive vacations at a time when many people in this country were suffering from economic deprivation. They also had an African-American maid, whose name was Susie. I've tried to find out more about her, but all I know is that she lived with the family for many years and made the best ice cream.

There are ironies here, because Marsie Harjo was also half or nearly half African-American, and in more recent years there has been racism directed at African-Americans by the tribe, which originally accepted Africans and often welcomed them as relatives. The acceptance of slavery came with the embrace of European-American cultural values. It was then that we also began to hate ourselves for our own darkness. It's all connected: ownership of land has everything to do with the ownership of humans and how they are treated, with the attitude toward all living things.

This picture of my great-grandparents' family explodes the myth of being   15
Indian in this country for both non-Indian and Indian alike. I wonder how the image of a Muscogee family in a car only the wealthy could own would be interpreted by another Muscogee person, or by another tribal person, or by a non-Indian anywhere in this land. It challenges the popular culture's version of "Indian"—an image that fits no tribe or person. By presenting it here, I mean to question those accepted images that have limited us to cardboard cut-out figures, without blood or tears or laughter.

There were many photographs of this family. I recently sent my cousin Donna Jo Harjo a photograph of her father Joe as a child about five. He was dressed in a finely tailored suit and drove a child's-size model of a car. His daughter has never lived in this kind of elegance. She lives on her salary as a sorter for a conglomerate nut and dried fruit company in northern California. She loves animals, especially horses and cats. (Our clan is the Tiger Clan.) I wonder at the proliferation of photographs and the family's diminishment in numbers to this present generation.

The second photograph is a straight-on shot of the same great-grandparents standing with two Seminole men in traditional dress, wearing turbans. They are in stark contrast to my great-grandparents—especially Marsie Harjo, who is stately and somewhat stiff with the fear of God in his elegant white man's clothes, his Homburg hat.

Marsie Harjo was a preacher, a Creek Baptist minister, representing a counterforce to traditional Muscogee culture. He embodied one side in the split in our tribe since Christianity was introduced and the people were influenced by European cultural values; the dividing lines remain the same centuries later. He was quite an advanced thinker, and I imagine he repressed what he foresaw for the Muscogee people, who probably would not have believed him anyway.

My great-grandfather was in Stuart, Florida, as he was every winter, to "save" the souls of the Seminole people. He bought a plantation there, and because he hated pineapples, he had every one of the plants dug up and destroyed. I've also heard that he owned an alligator farm. I went to Stuart this spring on my way to Miami and could find no trace of the mission or the plantation anywhere in the suburban mix of concrete, glass, and advertisements. My memories are easier to reach in a dimension that is as alive and living as anything in the three dimensions we know with our five senses.

My great-grandmother Katie Menawe is much more visible here than in the 20 first photograph, where she is not up front, next to the driver, but in the very back of the car, behind her four children. Yet she quietly presides over everything as she guards her soul from the intrusive camera. I sense that Marsie boldly entered the twentieth century ahead of most people, while Katie reluctantly followed. I doubt if she ever resolved the split in her heart between her background and foreground.

I don't know much about her. She and her siblings were orphaned. Her sister Ella, a noted beauty, was my cousin John's mother. They were boarded for some time at Eufaula Indian School. I don't know how old Katie was when she married Marsie Harjo. But the name Monahwee* is one of those Muscogee names that is charged with memory of rebellion, with strength in the face of terrible adversity. Tecumseh came looking for Monahwee when he was building his great alliance of nations in the 1800s. Monahwee was one of the leaders of the Red Stick War, an armed struggle against the U.S. government to resist Andrew Jackson's demand for the removal of the tribes from their Southeastern homelands. Creeks, Seminoles, and Africans made up the fighting forces. Most of those who survived went to Florida, where the Seminoles successfully resisted colonization by hiding in the swamps. They beat the United States forces, who were aided by other tribes, including other Creeks who were promised land and homes for their help. The promises were like others from the U.S. government. Those who assisted were forced to walk west to Indian Territory like everyone else.

Monahwee stayed in Alabama and was soon forced west, but not before he joined with Jackson's forces to round up Seminoles for removal to Oklahoma. My cousin John said he died on the trail. I know that he died of a broken heart. I have a McKenney Hall portrait print of Monahwee, an original hand-colored

*His name is sometimes spelled Menawe or Menewa, but on his gravestone in Okmulgee, Oklahoma, it is spelled Monahwee. [Author's note]

lithograph dated 1848. Katie has the same eyes and composure of this man who was her father.

By going to Tallahassee Grounds to take part in a traditional tribal ceremony, I was taking my place in the circle of relatives, one more link in the concatenation of ancestors. Close behind me are my son and daughter, behind them, my granddaughter. Next to me, interlocking the pattern, are my cousins, my aunts and my uncles, my friends. We dance together in this place of knowing beyond the physical dimensions of space, much denser than the chemicals and paper of photographs. This place is larger than mere human memory, than the destruction we have walked through to come to this ground.

Time can never be stopped, rather it is poised so we can make a leap into knowing or into a field of questions. I understood this as we stompdanced in the middle of the night, as the stars whirred overhead in the same patterns as when Katie, Marsie, and the children lived beneath them. I heard time resume as the insects took up their singing again, to guide us through memory. The old Hudson heads to the east of the border of the photograph. For the Muscogee, East is the place of origins, the place the People emerged from so many hundreds of years ago. It is also a place of return.

ACTIVITIES FOR WRITING AND DISCUSSION

1. In paragraph 15 Harjo says, "This picture of my great-grandparents' family explodes the myth of being Indian in this country for both non-Indian and Indian alike." What is this "myth"? Why should Harjo be concerned to "explode" it?

2. What do the photographs add to this essay? How would the text be weakened, strengthened, or changed if the photos were eliminated?

3. Following Harjo's example, compose an essay about your own family in which you include one or more family photographs that serve as springboards for your writing. If you wish, select photographs that reveal both your family and some aspects of a culture to which you and your family belong.

4. Harjo sees family and culture as closely interconnected. Consider a culture (racial, religious, ethnic, social, avocational, or professional) with which you yourself identify. In an essay, describe some myths or beliefs about the culture that are held by outsiders. Then show how you, your family, or others close to you exemplify and/or belie those myths.

5. As an alternative to Activity #4, focus on a culture with which you do *not* identify instead of one with which you do. If possible, interview some members of that culture or do other outside research on it. Then, in an essay, discuss the stereotypes you and others have of that culture and show how the stereotypes are exemplified and/or belied by individuals.

FENTON JOHNSON (b. 1953)

The Limitless Heart

It is late March—the Saturday of Passover, to be exact—and I am driving an oversize rented car through west Los Angeles. I have never seen this side of the city except in the company of my companion, who died of AIDS-related complications in a Paris hospital in autumn of last year. He was an only child and often asked that I promise to visit his parents after his death. As the youngest son of a large family and a believer in brutal honesty, I refused. I have too much family already, I said. There are limits to how much love one can give.

Now I am here, driving along San Vicente Boulevard, one of the lovelier streets of Santa Monica, Calif., west from Wilshire to the Pacific. The street is divided by a broad green median lined with coral trees, which the city has seen fit to register as landmarks. They spread airy, elegant crowns against a movie-set heaven, a Maxfield Parrish blue. Each branch bleeds at its end an impossibly scarlet blossom, as if the twigs themselves had pierced the thin-skinned sky.

My friend's parents are too old to get about much. They are survivors of the Holocaust, German Jews who spent the war years hiding in a Dutch village a few miles from Germany itself. Beaten by Nazis before the war, my friend's father hid for four years with broken vertebrae, unable to see a doctor. When he was no longer able to move, his desperate wife descended to the street to find help, and saw falling from the sky the parachutes of their liberators.

After the war they came to California, promised land of this promised land. Like Abraham and Sarah,[1] they had a single son in their advanced years, proof that it is possible, in the face of the worst, to pick up sticks and start again.

At his home in Santa Monica, my friend's father sits in chronic pain, uncomplaining. Unlike his wife, he is reserved; he does not talk about his son with the women of his life—his wife or his surviving sister. No doubt he fears giving way before his grief, and his life has not allowed for much giving way. This much he and I share: as a gay man who grew up in the rural South, I am no stranger to hiding.

His wife always goes to bed early—partly as a way of coping with grief—but tonight he all but asks her to retire. After she leaves he begins talking of his son, and I listen and respond with gratefulness. We are two men in control, who permit ourselves to speak to each other of these matters because we subscribe implicitly, jointly, unconditionally to this code of conduct.

He tells of a day when his son, then 8 years old, wanted to go fishing. The quintessential urban Jew, my friend's father nonetheless bought poles and hooks and drove 50 miles to Laguna Beach. There they dropped their lines from a pier to discover the hooks dangled some 10 feet above the water. ("Thank

---

1. In the Old Testament, Abraham and Sarah gave birth to a son, Isaac, in their old age.

God," he says. "Otherwise we might have caught something.") A passer-by scoffed. "What the hell do you think you're trying to catch?" My friend's father shrugged, unperturbed. "Flying fish," he replied.

I respond with my most vivid memory of his son. He was a wiser man than I, and spoke many times across our years together of his great luck, his great good fortune. Denial pure and simple, or so I told myself at first. AZT, DDI, ACT-UP, CMV, DHPG, and what I came to think of as the big "A" itself—he endured this acronymed life, while I listened and learned and participated and helped when I could.

Until our third and last trip to Paris, the city of his dreams. On what would be his last night to walk about the city we sat in the courtyard of the Picasso Museum. There at dusk, under a deep sapphire sky, I turned to him and said, "I'm so lucky," and it was as if the time allotted to him to teach this lesson, the time for me to learn it, had been consumed, and there were nothing left but the facts of things to play out.

A long silence after this story—I have ventured beyond what I permit my- 10 self, what I am permitted.

I change the subject, asking my friend's father to talk of the war years. He does not allow himself to speak of his beatings or of murdered family and friends. Instead he remembers moments of affection, loyalty, even humor, until he talks of winters spent immobilized with pain and huddled in his wife's arms, their breaths freezing on the quilt as they sang together to pass the time, to stay warm.

Another silence; now he has ventured too far. "I have tried to forget these stories," he says in his halting English.

In the presence of these extremes of love and horror I am reduced to cliché. "It's only by remembering them that we can hope to avoid repeating them."

"They are being repeated all the time," he says. "It is bad sometimes to watch too much television. You see these things and you know we have learned nothing."

Are we so dense that we can learn nothing from all this pain, all this death? 15 Is it impossible to learn from experience? The bitterness of these questions I can taste, as I drive east to spend the night at a relative's apartment.

Just south of the seedier section of Santa Monica Boulevard, I stop at a bar recommended by a friend. I need a drink, and I need the company of men like myself—survivors, for the moment anyway, albeit of a very different struggle.

The bar is filled with Latinos wearing the most extraordinary clothes. Eighty years of B movies have left Hollywood the nation's most remarkable supply of secondhand dresses, most of which, judging from this evening, have made their ways to these guys' closets.

I am standing at the bar, very Anglo, very out of place, very much thinking of leaving, when I am given another lesson:

A tiny, wizened, gray-haired Latina approaches the stage, where under jerry-rigged lights (colored cellophane, Scotch tape) a man lip-syncs to Brazilian rock. His spike heels raise him to something above six feet; he wears a floor-length sheath dress, slit up the sides and so taut, so brilliantly silver, so lustrous that it catches and throws back the faces of his audience. The elderly Latina raises a dollar bill. On tottering heels he lowers himself, missing not a word of his song while half-crouching, half-bending so that she may tuck her dollar in his cleavage and kiss his cheek.

"*Su abuelita,*" the bartender says laconically. "His grandmother."   20

One A.M. in the City of Angels—the streets are clogged with cars. Stuck in traffic, I am haunted by voices and visions: the high thin songs of my companion's parents as they huddle under their frozen quilt, singing into their breath; a small boy and his father sitting on a very long pier, their baitless fishhooks dangling above the vast Pacific; the face of *su abuelita,* uplifted, reverent, mirrored in her grandson's dress.

Somewhere a light changes; the traffic unglues itself. As cars begin moving I am visited by two last ghosts—my companion and myself, sitting in the courtyard of the Hôtel Salé, transfigured by the limitless heart.

Plays

Joyce Carol Oates (b. 1938)

Tone Clusters

A Play in Nine Scenes

CHARACTERS

FRANK GULICK: fifty-three years old
EMILY GULICK: fifty-one years old
VOICE: male, indeterminate age

These are white Americans of no unusual distinction, nor are they in any self-evident way "representative."

Tone Clusters is not intended to be a realistic work, thus any inclination toward the establishment of character should be resisted. Its primary effect should be visual (the dominance of the screen at center stage, the play of lights of sharply contrasting degrees of intensity) and audio (the VOICE, *the employment of music—"tone clusters" of Henry Cowell and/or Charles Ives, and electronic music, etc.). The mood is one of fragmentation, confusion, yet, at times, strong emotion. A fractured narrative emerges which the audience will have no difficulty piecing together even as—and this is the tragicomedy of the piece—the characters* MR. *and* MRS. GULICK *deny it.*

In structure, Tone Clusters *suggests an interview, but a stylized interview in which questions and answers are frequently askew. Voices trail off into silence or may be mocked or extended by strands of music. The* VOICE *is sometimes overamplified and booming; sometimes marred by static; sometimes clear, in an ebullient tone, like that of a talk-show host. The* VOICE *has no identity but must be male. It should not be represented by any actual presence on the stage or within view of the audience. At all times, the* VOICE *is in control: the principals on the stage are dominated by their interrogator and by the screen, which is seemingly floating in the air above them, at center stage. Indeed the screen emerges as a character.*

The piece is divided into nine uneven segments. When one ends, the lights dim, then come up again immediately. (After the ninth segment the lights go out completely and darkness is extended for some seconds to indicate that the piece is ended: it ends on an abrupt cutoff of lights and images on the screen and the monitors.)

By degree the GULICKS *become somewhat accustomed to the experience of being interviewed and filmed, but never wholly accustomed: they are always slightly disoriented, awkward, confused, inclined to speak slowly and methodically or too quickly, "unprofessionally," often with inappropriate emotion (fervor, enthusiasm, hope, sudden rage) or no emotion at all (like "computer voices"). The* GULICKS *may at times speak in unison (as if one were an echo of the other); they may mimic the qualities of tone-cluster music or electronic music (I conceive of their voices, and that of the* VOICE, *as music of a kind); should the director wish, there may be some clear-cut relationship between subject and emotion or emphasis—but the piece should do no more than approach "realism," and then withdraw. The actors must conceive of themselves as elements in a dramatic structure, not as "human characters" wishing to establish rapport with an audience.*

Tone Clusters *is about the absolute mystery—the* not knowing—*at the core of our human experience. That the mystery is being exploited by a television documentary underscores its tragicomic nature.*

Scene 1.

Lights up. Initially very strong, near-blinding. On a bare stage, middle-aged FRANK *and* EMILY GULICK *sit ill-at-ease in "comfortable" modish cushioned swivel chairs, trying not to squint or grimace in the lights (which may be represented as the lights of a camera crew provided the human figures involved can be kept shadowy, even indistinct). They wear clip-on microphones, to which they are unaccustomed. They are "dressed up" for the occasion, and clearly nervous: they continually touch their faces, or clasp their hands firmly in their laps, or fuss with fingernails, buttons, the microphone cords, their hair. The nervous mannerisms continue throughout the piece but should never be too distracting and never comic.*

Surrounding the GULICKS, *dominating their human presence, are the central screen and the TV monitors and/or slide screens upon which, during the course of the play, disparate images, words, formless flashes of light are projected. Even when the* GULICKS' *own images appear on the screens they are upstaged by it: they glance at it furtively, with a kind of awe.*

The rest of the time, the monitors always show the stage as we see it: the GULICKS *seated, glancing uneasily up at the large screen. Thus there is a "screen within a screen."*

The employment of music is entirely at the director's discretion. The opening might be accompanied by classical tone cluster piano pieces—Henry Cowell's "Advertisement," for instance. The music should never be intrusive. The ninth scene might well be completely empty of music. There should certainly be no "film-music" effect. (The GULICKS *do not hear the music.)*

The VOICE *too in its modulations is at the discretion of the director. Certainly at the start the* VOICE *is booming and commanding. There should be intermittent audio trouble (whistling, static, etc.); the* VOICE, *wholly in control, can exude any number of effects throughout the play—pomposity, charity, condescension, bemusement, false chattiness, false pedantry, false sympathy, mild incredulity (like that of a television emcee), affectless "computer talk." The* GULICKS *are entirely intimidated by the* VOICE *and try very hard to answer its questions.*

Screen shifts from its initial image to words: IN A CASE OF MURDER—*large black letters on white.*

VOICE: In a case of murder   (taking murder as an abstraction)   there is always a sense of the Inevitable   once the identity of the murderer   is established. Beforehand there   is   a sense   of disharmony.
    And humankind fears and loathes disharmony,
    Mr. and Mrs. Gulick of Lakepointe, New Jersey, would you comment?
    FRANK: . . .Yes I would say,   I think that
    EMILY: What is that again, exactly?   I . . .
    FRANK: My wife and I, we . . .
    EMILY: Disharmony . . . ?
    FRANK: I don't like disharmony.   I mean, all the family,
we are a law-abiding family.
    VOICE: A religious family   I believe?
    FRANK: Oh yes.   Yes,
We go to church every
    EMILY: We almost never miss a,   a Sunday
For a while,   I helped with Sunday School classes
The children,   the children don't always go but they believe,
our daughter Judith for instance she   and Carl
    FRANK: oh yes   yessir
    EMILY: and Dennis,   they do believe they were raised to
believe in God and, and Jesus Christ
    FRANK: We raised them that way because   we were raised that way,
    EMILY: there *is* a God whether you agree with Him   or not.

VOICE: "Religion" may be defined as   a sort of adhesive matter invisibly
holding together   nation-states, nationalities, tribes, families
     for   the   good   of   those   so
                                        held together,
                              would you comment?

FRANK: Oh,   oh yes.

EMILY: For the good of . . .

FRANK: Yes I would say so,   I think so.

EMILY: My husband and I, we were married in church, in

FRANK: In the Lutheran Church.

EMILY: In Penns Neck.

FRANK: In New Jersey.

EMILY: All our children,

BOTH: they believe.

EMILY: God sees into the human heart.

VOICE: Mr. and Mrs. Gulick   from your experience would you   theorize for
our audience: is the Universe "predestined"   in every particular
     or   is   man   capable   of   acts   of   "freedom"?

BOTH: . . .

EMILY: . . . I would say,   that is hard to say.

FRANK: Yes. I believe that man is free.

EMILY: If you mean like, I guess   choosing good and evil?   Yes

FRANK: I would have to say   yes.   You would have to say
mankind is free.
Like moving my hand. *(moves hand)*

EMILY: If nobody is free   it wouldn't be right would it
to punish anybody?

FRANK: There is always   Hell.
I believe in Hell.

EMILY: Anybody at all

FRANK: Though I am not free to, to   fly up in the air am I? *(laughs)*
because   Well I'm not built right for that am I? *(laughs)*

VOICE: Man is free.   Thus man is   responsible for his acts.

EMILY: Except, oh   sometime if,   maybe for instance if
A baby born without

FRANK: Oh one of those "AIDS" babies

EMILY: poor thing

FRANK: "crack" babies
Or if you were captured   by some enemy, y'know   and tortured
Some people never have a chance.

EMILY: But God sees into the human heart,
God knows who to forgive   and who not.

Lights down.

Scene 2.

Lights up. Screen shows a suburban street of lower-income homes; the GULICKS *stare at the screen and their answers are initially distracted.*

VOICE: Here we have Cedar Street   in Lakepointe, New Jersey   neatly kept
homes (as you can see)   American suburb   low crime rate,
single-family homes   suburb of Newark, New Jersey
   population twelve thousand   the neighborhood of
   Mr. and Mrs. Frank Gulick the parents of   Carl Gulick
   Will you introduce yourselves to our audience please?
   (House lights come up.)
   FRANK: . . . Go on, you first
   EMILY: I, I don't know what to say
   FRANK: My name is   Frank Gulick, I   I am fifty-three years old
that's our house there   2368 Cedar Street
   EMILY: My name is Emily Gulick, fifty-one years old,
   VOICE: How employed,   would you care to say?   Mr. Gulick?
   FRANK: I work for the post office,   I'm a supervisor for
   EMILY: He has worked for the post office for twenty-five years
   FRANK: . . . The Terhune Avenue branch.
   VOICE: And how long have you resided   in your attractive home   on Cedar
   Street?
   (House lights begin to fade down.)
   FRANK: . . . Oh I guess, how long   if this is
this is 1990?
   EMILY: (oh just think: 1990!)
   FRANK: we moved there in, uh   Judith wasn't born yet so
   EMILY: Oh there was our thirtieth anniversary a year ago,
   FRANK: wedding
no that was two years ago
   EMILY: was it?
   FRANK: or three, I   twenty-seven years, this is 1990
   EMILY: Yes: Judith is twenty-six,   now I'm a grandmother
   FRANK: Carl is twenty-two
   EMILY: Denny is seventeen, he's a senior in high school
No none of them are living at home now
   FRANK: not now
   EMILY: Right now poor Denny is staying with my sister in
   VOICE: Frank and Emily Gulick you have been happy here   in Lakepointe
   raising your family like any   American couple   with your
hopes and aspirations
                              until recently?
   FRANK: . . . Yes, oh yes.

EMILY: Oh for a long time we *were*

FRANK: oh yes.

EMILY: It's so strange to,   to think of
The years go by so

VOICE: You have led a   happy family life   like so many millions
of Americans

EMILY: Until this,   this terrible thing

FRANK: *Innocent until proven guilty*—that's a laugh!

EMILY: Oh it's a, a terrible thing

FRANK: Never any hint beforehand of   the meanness of people's hearts.
I mean the neighbors.

EMILY: Oh now don't start that,   this isn't the

FRANK: Oh God you just try to   comprehend

EMILY: this isn't the place, I

FRANK: Like last night: this carload of kids
drunk, beer-drinking   foul language in the night

EMILY: oh don't, my hands are

FRANK: Yes but you know it's the parents   set them going
And telephone calls   our number is changed now, but

EMILY: my hands are shaking so
we are both on medication   the doctor says,

FRANK: oh you would not believe, you would not   believe   the hatred
like Nazi Germany

EMILY: Denny had to drop out of school,   he loved school he is
an honor student

FRANK: everybody turned against us

EMILY: My sister in Yonkers, he's staying with

FRANK: Oh he'll never be the same   boy again.
none of us will.

VOICE: In the development of   human identity   there's the element
of chance,   and there is genetic determinism.
    Would you comment please?

FRANK: The thing is,   you try your best.

EMILY: oh dear God yes.

FRANK: Your best.

EMILY: You give all that's in your heart

FRANK: you
can't do more than that can you?

EMILY: Yes but there is certain to be   justice.
There *is* a, a sense of things.

FRANK: Sometimes there is a chance, the way they   turn out
but also   what they *are*.

EMILY: Your own babies

VOICE: Frank Gulick   and Mary   what is your assessment of
American civilization   today?

EMILY: . . . it's Emily.

FRANK: My wife's name is,

EMILY: it's

Emily.

VOICE: Frank and EMILY   Gulick.

FRANK: . . . The state of the   civilization?

EMILY: It's so big,

FRANK: We are here to   tell our side of,

EMILY: . . . I don't know: it's a,   a Democracy

FRANK: the truth is,   do you want the truth?

the truth is where we live

Lakepointe

it's changing too

EMILY: it has changed

FRANK: Yes but it's all over, it's

terrible, just terrible

EMILY: Now we are grandparents we fear for

FRANK: Yes what you read and see on TV

EMILY: You don't know what to think,

FRANK: Look: in this country   half the crimes

are committed by the,   by half the population against

the other half.   *(laughs)*

You have your law-abiding citizens,

EMILY: taxpayers

FRANK: and you have the   rest of them

Say you went downtown into a city like   Newark, some night

EMILY: you'd be crazy if you got out of your car

FRANK: you'd be dead.   That's what.

VOICE: Is it possible,   probable   or in your assessment *im*probable

that the slaying of   fourteen-year-old   Edith Kaminsky

on February 12, 1990   is related to

the social malaise

of which you speak?

FRANK: . . . "ma-lezz"?

EMILY: . . . oh it's hard to,   I would say yes

FRANK: . . . whoever did it, he

EMILY: Oh it's terrible the things that

keep happening

FRANK: If only the police would arrest the right person,

VOICE: Frank and Emily Gulick   you remain adamant in your belief

in your faith in your twenty-two-year-old son   Carl

that he is innocent   in the death of

fourteen-year-old Edith Kaminsky

on February 12, 1990?

EMILY: Oh yes,

FRANK: oh yes that is
the single thing we are convinced of.
    EMILY: On this earth.
    BOTH: With God as our witness,
    FRANK: yes
    EMILY: Yes.
    FRANK: The single thing.

Lights down.

Scene 3.

Lights up. Screen shows violent movement: urban scenes, police patrol cars, a fire burning out of control, men being arrested and herded into vans; a body lying in the street. The GULICKS *stare at the screen.*

    VOICE: Of today's pressing political issues   the rise in violent crime
most concerns American citizens   Number-one political issue of
    Mr. and Mrs. Gulick   tell our viewers your opinion?
    FRANK: In this state,
the state of New Jersey
    EMILY: Oh it's everywhere
    FRANK: there's capital punishment supposedly
    EMILY: But the lawyers   the lawyers get them off,
    FRANK: you bet
There's public defenders the taxpayer pays
    EMILY: Oh, it's   it's out of control
(like that, what is it   "acid rain"
    FRANK: it can fall on you anywhere,
    EMILY: the sun is too hot too:
    BOTH: the "greenhouse effect")
    FRANK: It's a welfare state by any other name
    EMILY: Y'know who pays:
    BOTH: the taxpayer
    FRANK: The same God damn criminal, you pay for him   then he
That's the joke of it *(laughs)*
the same criminal who slits your throat *(laughs)*
He's the one you pay bail for, to get out.
But it sure isn't funny.   *(laughs)*
    EMILY: Oh God.
    FRANK: It sure isn't funny.
    VOICE: Many Americans have come to believe   this past decade   that
capital punishment is one of the   answers: would you
comment please?
    FRANK: Oh in cases of actual, proven   murder
    EMILY: Those drug dealers

FRANK: Yes *I* would have to say, definitely   yes

EMILY: I would say so yes

FRANK: You always hear them say   opponents of the death penalty
"The death penalty doesn't stop crime"

EMILY: Oh that's what they say!

FRANK: Yes but *I* say, once a man is dead   he sure ain't gonna commit
any more crimes, is he.   *(laughs)*

VOICE: The death penalty *is* a deterrent to crime   in those cases
when the criminal has been   executed

FRANK: But you have to find the right,
the actual murderer.

EMILY: Not some poor innocent*   some poor innocent*

Lights down.

Scene 4.

*Lights up. Screen shows a grainy magnified snapshot of a boy about ten. Quick
jump to a snapshot of the same boy a few years older. Throughout this scene images
of "Carl Gulick" appear and disappear on the screen though not in strict
relationship to what is being said, nor in chronological order. "Carl Gulick" in his
late teens and early twenties is muscular but need not have any other outstanding
characteristics: he may look like any American boy at all.*

VOICE: Carl Gulick, twenty-two years old   the second-born child of Frank
and Emily Gulick of Lakepointe, New Jersey   How would you
describe your son, Frank and Emily

FRANK: D'you mean how he looks or . . . ?

EMILY: He's a shy boy, he's   shy   Not backward just

FRANK: He's about my height I guess   brown hair, eyes

EMILY: Oh! no I think   no he's much taller Frank
he's been taller than you   for years

FRANK: Well that depends on how we're both standing.
How we're both   standing
Well in one newspaper it said six feet one inch, in the other
six feet three inches, that's the kind of

EMILY: accuracy

FRANK: reliability of the news media
you can expect!

EMILY: And oh that terrible picture of,
in the paper
that face he was making   the police carrying him
against his will   laying their hands on him

FRANK: handcuffs

---

*"Innocent" is an adjective here, not a noun. [Author's note]

EMILY: Oh that isn't *him*

BOTH: that isn't our son

(GULICKS *respond dazedly to snapshots flashed on screen.*)

EMILY: Oh! that's Carl   age I guess about

FRANK: four?

EMILY: that's at the beach one summer

FRANK: only nine or ten, he was big for

EMILY: With his sister Judith

FRANK: that's my brother George

EMILY: That's

FRANK: he loved Boy Scouts,

EMILY: but

Oh when you are the actual parents it's

a different

FRANK: Oh it is so different!

from something just on TV.

VOICE: In times of disruption   of fracture   it is believed that
human behavior moves   in unchartable leaps   History is a formal
record of such   leaps   but in large-scale demographical   terms
   in which the   individual   is   lost
      Frank and Emily Gulick it's said your son   Carl   charged
in the savage slaying of   fourteen-year-old   shows no sign of
   remorse   that is to say, *awareness* of the act:
thus the question we pose to you   Can guilt reside in those
   without conscience,
or is memory   conscience, and conscience memory?
   can "the human" reside in those
      devoid of "memory"

EMILY: . . . Oh the main thing is,

he is innocent.

FRANK: . . . Stake my life on it.

EMILY: He has always been   cheerful, optimistic

FRANK: a good boy, of course he has not

forgotten

BOTH: He is innocent.

EMILY: How could our son "forget" when he has nothing to

BOTH: "forget"

FRANK: He took that lie detector test voluntarily didn't he

EMILY: Oh there he is   weight-lifting, I don't remember

who took that picture?

FRANK: When you are the actual parents you see them every day,

you don't form judgments.

VOICE: And how is your son employed, Mr. and Mrs. Kaminsky?

Excuse me: GULICK.

FRANK: Up until Christmas he was working in

This butcher shop in East Orange

EMILY: . . . it isn't easy, at that age
FRANK: Before that, loading and unloading
EMILY: at Sears at the mall
FRANK: No: that was before, that was before the other
EMILY: No: the job at Sears was
FRANK: . . . Carl was working for that Italian, y'know that
EMILY: the lawn service
FRANK: Was that before?   or after
Oh in this butcher shop   his employer
EMILY: yes there were hard feelings, on both sides
FRANK: Look: you can't believe a single thing   in the newspaper
or TV
EMILY: it's not that they lie
FRANK: Oh yes they lie
EMILY: not that they lie, they just   get everything wrong
FRANK: Oh they do lie!   And it's printed and you can't stop them.
EMILY: In this meat shop, I never wanted him to work there
FRANK: In this shop there was pressure on him
to join the union.
EMILY: Then the other side, his employer
did not want him to join.
He's a sensitive boy,   his stomach and nerves
He lost his appetite for weeks, he'd say "oh if you could see
some of the things I see"   "the insides of things"
and so much blood
VOICE: There was always a loving   relationship   in the household?
EMILY: . . . When they took him away he said,   he was so brave
he said Momma I'll be back soon
I'll be right back,   I am innocent he said
I don't know how she came to be in   our house
I don't know,   I don't know he said
I looked into my son's eyes and saw   truth shining
His eyes have always been   dark green,
like mine.
VOICE: On the afternoon of   February 12 you have told police that
no one was home   in your house?
EMILY: I, I was . . . I had a doctor's appointment,
My husband was working, he doesn't get home until
FRANK: Whoever did it,   and brought her body in
EMILY: No: they say she was   they say it,   it happened there
FRANK: No I don't buy that,   He brought her in   carried her
whoever that was,
I believe he tried   other houses
seeing who was home and who   wasn't
and then he
EMILY: Oh it was like lightning striking

VOICE: Your son Dennis   was at Lakepointe High School attending a meeting
of the yearbook staff,   your son Carl has told police he
   was   riding   his   motor scooter
      in the park,
   FRANK: They dragged him like   an animal
put their hands on him like
Like Nazi Germany,
   EMILY: it couldn't be any worse
   FRANK: And that judge
it's a misuse of power, it's
   EMILY: I just don't understand
   VOICE: Your son Carl on and after   February 12   did not exhibit
(in your presence) any unusual sign of   emotion?
   agitation? guilt?
   EMILY: Every day in a house,   a household
is like the other days.   Oh you never step back,   never *see.*
Like I told them, the   police,   everybody. *He did not.*

Lights down.

Scene 5.

*Lights up. Screen shows snapshots, photographs, of the murdered girl Kaminsky.
Like Carl Gulick, she is anyone at all of that age: white, neither strikingly beautiful
nor unattractive.*

   VOICE: Sometime in the evening of February 12 of this year forensic
reports say   fourteen-year-old Edith Kaminsky daughter of   neighbors
2361 Cedar Street, Lakepointe, New Jersey   multiple stab wounds,
sexual assault   strangulation
An arrest has been made but   legally or otherwise,   the absolute
identity of the murderer has yet to be
   EMILY: Oh it's so unjust,
   FRANK: the power of a single man
That judge
   EMILY: Carl's birthday is   next week
Oh God he'll be in that terrible   cold place
   FRANK: "segregated" they call it
How can a judge refuse to set bail
   EMILY: oh I would borrow a million dollars
if I could
   FRANK: Is this America or   Russia?
   EMILY: I can't stop crying
   FRANK: . . . we are both under medication you see but
   EMILY: Oh it's true he wasn't himself   sometimes.
   FRANK: But that day when it happened, that wasn't one of the times.

VOICE: You hold out for the possibility that   the true murderer
carried Edith Kaminsky into your house,   into your basement
thus meaning to throw suspicion on your son?
FRANK: Our boy is guiltless that's the main thing, I will never doubt that.
EMILY: Our body is innocent . . .   What did I say?
FRANK: Why the hell do they make so much of
Carl lifting weights, his   muscles
He is not a freak.
EMILY: There's lots of them   and women too, today   like that,
FRANK: He has other interests he used to collect stamps   play baseball
EMILY: Oh there's so much misunderstanding
FRANK: actual lies
Because the police do not know who the murderer *is*
of course they will blame   anyone they can.

Lights down.

Scene 6.

*Lights up. Screen shows the exterior of the Gulick house seen from various angles;
then the interior (the basement, evidently, and the "storage area" where the young
girl's body was found).*

VOICE: If, as is believed, "premeditated" acts arise   out of a
mysterious sequence of neuron discharges   (in the brain)
out of what source   do
   "unpremeditated"   acts   arise?
EMILY: Nobody was down in,   in the basement
until the police came.   The storage space is behind the
water heater,   but
FRANK: My God if my son is   so shiftless   like people are saying
just look: he helped me paint the house last summer
EMILY: Yes Carl and Denny both,
FRANK: Why are they telling such   lies, our neighbors?   We have never
wished them harm,
EMILY: I believed a certain neighbor was my friend,   her and I, we
we'd go shopping together   took my car
Oh my heart is broken
FRANK: It's robin's-egg blue,   the paint turned out brighter than
when it dried, a little brighter than we'd   expected
EMILY: *I* think it's pretty
FRANK: Well.   We'll have to sell the house,   there's no choice
the legal costs   Mr. Filco our attorney has said
EMILY: He told us
FRANK: he's going to fight all the way, he believes Carl is   innocent
EMILY: My heart is broken.

FRANK: *My* heart isn't,
I'm going to fight this all the way
    EMILY: A tragedy like this,   you learn fast who is your friend and who
is your enemy
    FRANK: Nobody's your friend.
    VOICE: The Gulicks and Kaminskys were   well acquainted?
    EMILY: We lived on Cedar first,   when they moved in I don't remember:
my mind isn't right these days
    FRANK: Oh yes   we knew them
    EMILY: I'd have said Mrs. Kaminsky   was my friend, but
that's how people are
    FRANK: Yes
    EMILY: Carl knew her,   Edith
I mean, we all did
    FRANK: but not well,
    EMILY: just neighbors
Now they're our declared enemies, the Kaminskys
    FRANK: well,   so be it.
    EMILY: Oh! that poor girl   if only she hadn't,
I mean, there's no telling who   she was with,   walking home
walking home from school I guess
    FRANK: Well she'd been missing overnight,
    EMILY: yes overnight
    FRANK: of course we were aware
    FRANK: The Kaminskys came around ringing doorbells,
    EMILY: then the police,
    FRANK: then
they got a search party going,   Carl helped them out
    EMILY: Everybody said how much he helped
    FRANK: he kept at it for hours
They walked miles and miles,
he's been out of work for a while,
    EMILY: he'd been looking
in the *help wanted* ads but
    FRANK: . . . He doesn't like to use the telephone.
    EMILY: People laugh at him he says,
    FRANK: I told him no he was imagining it.
    EMILY: This neighborhood:
    FRANK: you would not believe it.
    EMILY: Call themselves Christians
    FRANK: Well   some are Jews.
    EMILY: Well it's still white isn't it   a white neighborhood,   you expect
better.
    VOICE: The murder weapon   has yet to be found?

FRANK: One of the neighbors had to offer an opinion,   something sarcastic
I guess
    EMILY: Oh don't go into *that*
    FRANK: the color of the paint   on our house
So Carl said, You don't like it, wear sunglasses.
    EMILY: But,
he was smiling.
    VOICE: A young man with a sense of   humor.
    FRANK: Whoever hid that poor girl's
body
in the storage space of our
basement well clearly it
obviously it was   to deceive
to cast blame on our son.
    EMILY: Yes   if there were fingerprints down there,
    BOTH: that handprint they found on the wall
    FRANK: well for God's sake it was from when Carl
was down there
    BOTH: helping them
    FRANK: He cooperated with them,
    EMILY: Frank wasn't home,
    FRANK: Carl led them downstairs
    EMILY: Why they came to our house, I don't know.
Who was saying things   I don't know,
it was like everybody had gone   crazy
casting blame on all sides.
    VOICE: Mr. and Mrs. Gulick   it's said that from your son's room
Lakepointe police officers confiscated   comic books, military
magazines, pornographic magazines   a cache of more than one dozen
    knives including   switchblades   plus
a U.S. Army bayonet (World War II)   Nazi memorabilia
    including a "souvenir" SS helmet   (manufactured in Taiwan)
a pink plastic skull   with lightbulbs in eyes
    a naked Barbie doll, badly scratched   bitten
      numerous pictures of naked women
    and women in fashion magazines,   their eyes
breasts   crotches   cut out with a scissors
    (pause)
Do you have any comment   Mr. and Mrs. Gulick?
    FRANK: . . . .
Mainly they were hobbies,
    EMILY: I guess I don't,
    FRANK: we didn't know about
    EMILY: Well   he wouldn't allow me in his room,   to vacuum, or

FRANK: You know how boys are

EMILY: Didn't want his mother

FRANK: poking her nose in

EMILY: So . . .

(EMILY *upsets a glass of water on the floor.*)

VOICE: Police forensic findings   bloodstains, hairs, semen
   and DNA "fingerprinting"   constitute a tissue of
       circumstance   linking your son to

EMILY *(interrupting)*: Mr. Filco says   it's all pieced together
"Circumstantial evidence," he says   not proof

FRANK: *I* call it bullshit   *(laughs)*

EMILY: Oh Frank

FRANK: *I* call it bullshit   *(laughs)*

VOICE: Eyewitness accounts disagree,   two parties report
having seen Carl Gulick and Edith Kaminsky   walking together
   in the afternoon, in the alley   behind Cedar Street
       a third party   a neighbor   claims to have seen
the girl   in the company of a   stranger   at approximately
       4:15 p.m.   And Carl Gulick insists
he was "riding his motor scooter"   all afternoon

FRANK: He is a boy

EMILY: not capable of lying

FRANK: Look: I would have to discipline him sometimes,

EMILY: You have to, with boys

FRANK: Oh yes you have to, otherwise

EMILY: He was always a good eater   didn't fuss

FRANK: He's a quiet boy

EMILY: You can't guess his thoughts

FRANK: But he loved his mother and father   respected

EMILY: Always well behaved at home
That ugly picture in the paper, oh

FRANK: THAT WASN'T HIM

EMILY: You can't believe   the cruelty in the human heart

FRANK: Giving interviews! his own teachers from the school

EMILY: Telling lies   cruel   nasty

FRANK: His own teachers from the   school

VOICE: Mr. and Mrs. Gulick   you had no suspicion
                   no   awareness
   you   had   no   sense   of   the   fact
       that the battered   raped   mutilated body of
               fourteen-year-old Edith Kaminsky
       was hidden in your basement   in a storage space
               wrapped in plastic garbage bags
for approximately   forty   hours

GULICKS: . . . .

VOICE: No consciousness of   disharmony
in your household?
   FRANK: It was a day like
   EMILY: It *was,*   I mean, it wasn't
   FRANK: I keep the cellar clean, I   There's leakage
   EMILY: Oh
Last week at my sister's   where we were staying,
we had to leave   this terrible place
in Yonkers I was crying,   I could not stop   crying
downstairs in the kitchen   three in the morning
I was standing by a window and there was suddenly   it looked
like snow!
it was moonlight moving in the window and there came a   shadow I
guess
like an eclipse?   was there an eclipse?
Oh I felt so, I felt   my heart stopped   Oh but I, I wasn't scared
I was thinking   I was seeing how the world is
how the universe *is*
it's so hard to say, I feel like a   a fool
I was gifted by this, by   seeing   how the world *is* not
how you see it   with your eyes, or talk   talk about it
I mean names you give to,   parts of it   No I mean how it *is*
when there is nobody there.
   VOICE: A subliminal conviction of disharmony   may be nullified by   a
     transcendental leap of   consciousness;   to a "higher plane"
          of celestial harmony.
     would you comment   Mr. and Mrs. Gulick?
   EMILY: Then Sunday night it was,
   FRANK: this last week
   EMILY: they came again
   FRANK: threw trash on our lawn
   EMILY: screamed
Murderers! they were drunk, yelling   in the night *Murderers!*
   FRANK: There was the false report that Carl was released on   bail
that he was home with us,
   EMILY: Oh dear God if only that was true
   FRANK: I've lost fifteen pounds since February
   EMILY: Oh Frank has worked so hard   on that lawn,
it's his pride and joy and in the neighborhood   everybody knows,
they compliment him,   and now
Yes he squats right out there, he pulls out crabgrass   by hand
Dumping such such ugly nasty disgusting things
Then in the A&P a woman followed me   up and down the aisles
I could hear people   *That's her, that's the mother of
the murderer*   I could hear them   everywhere in the store

Is that her,   is that the mother of the murderer? they were saying
Lived in this neighborhood, in this town   for so many years
we thought we were welcome here and now
Aren't you ashamed to show your face!   a voice screamed
What can I do with my face,   can I hide it forever?
    FRANK: And all this when our boy is   innocent.
    VOICE: Perceiving the inviolate nature of   the Universe   apart from human
    suffering   rendered you happy, Mrs. Gulick   is this so?
        for some precious moments?
    EMILY: Oh yes, I was crying but
not because of
no   I was crying because
I was happy I think.

Lights down.

Scene 7.

*Lights up. Screen shows neurological X-rays, medical diagrams, charts as of EEG
and CAT-scan tests.*

    VOICE: Is it possible that in times of   fracture, of evolutionary
unease   or, perhaps, at any time   human behavior mimics that
of minute   particles   of light?   The atom is primarily emptiness
    the neutron dense-packed
The circuitry of the human brain   circadian rhythms   can be tracked
but never,   it's said comprehended.   And then   in descent
from "identity"—(memory?)   to tissue to cells to cell-particles
    electrical impulses   axon-synapse-dendrite
        and beyond, be-
          neath
        to subatomic bits
    Where is "Carl Gulick"?
(GULICKS *turn to each other in bewilderment. Screen flashes images: kitchen
interior; weightlifting paraphernalia; a shelf of trophies; photographs; domestic
scenes, etc.*)
    VOICE: Mr. and Mrs. Gulick you did not notice anything   unusual   in
your son's behavior on the night of February 12   or the following
day,   to the best   of your recollection?
    EMILY: . . . Oh we've told the police this so many   many times
    FRANK: Oh you forget what you remember,
    EMILY: That night, before we knew there was anyone missing   I mean, in
the neighborhood   anyone we knew
    FRANK: I can't remember.
    EMILY: Yes but Carl had supper with us like always
    FRANK: No I think,   he was napping up in his room
    EMILY: he was at the table with us:

FRANK: I remember   he came down around nine o'clock,   but he did
eat.

EMILY: Him and Denny, they were at the table with us

FRANK: We've told the police this so many times, it's
I don't know any longer

EMILY: I'm sure it was Denny too.   Both our sons.
We had meatloaf   ketchup baked on top, it's the boys'
favorite dish just about   isn't it?

FRANK: Oh anything with hamburger and ketchup!

EMILY: Of course he was at the table with us,   he had his usual appetite.

FRANK: . . . he was upstairs, said he had a touch of   flu

EMILY: Oh no he was there.

FRANK: It's hard to speak of your own flesh and blood,   as if
they are other people
it's hard   without giving false testimony against your will.

VOICE: Is the intrusion of the "extra-ordinary"   into the dimension of the
"ordinary"   an indication that such Aristotelian categories are
invalid?   If one day fails to resemble the preceding
      what does it resemble?

FRANK: . . . He has sworn to us, we are his parents
He did not touch a hair of that poor child's head   let alone the rest.
Anybody who knew him, they'd know

EMILY: Oh those trophies!   he was so proud
one of them is from the, I guess the Lakepointe YMCA
there's some from the New Jersey competition   at Atlantic City
two years ago?

FRANK: no, he was in high school
the first was, Carl was only fifteen years old

EMILY: Our little muscleman!

VOICE: Considering the evidence of thousands of years   of human culture
of language   art   religion   the judicial system   "The family
unit"   athletics   hobbies   fraternal organizations
charitable impulses   gods of all species
is   it   possible   that   humankind   desires
      not   to   know
            its   place   in
                  the
            food cycle?

EMILY: One day he said
he wasn't going back to school,
my heart was broken.

FRANK: Only half his senior year ahead
but you can't argue,   not with

EMILY: oh his temper!   he takes after,
oh I don't know who

FRANK: we always have gotten along together
in this household   haven't we
EMILY: yes but the teachers would laugh at him he said
girls laughed at him he said   stared and pointed at him he said
and there was this pack of   oh we're not prejudiced
against Negros,   it's just that
the edge of the Lakepointe school district
well
FRANK: Carl got in fights sometimes
in the school cafeteria and   I guess the park?
EMILY: the park isn't safe for law-abiding people these days
they see the color of your skin,   they'll attack
some of them are just like animals   yes they *are*
FRANK: Actually our son was attacked first   it isn't like he got
into fights by himself
EMILY: Who his friends are now, I don't   remember
FRANK: He is a quiet boy, keeps to himself
EMILY: he wanted to work
he was looking for work
FRANK: Well: our daughter Judith was misquoted about that
EMILY: also about Carl having a bad temper   she never said that
the reporter for the paper twisted her words
Mr. Filco says   we might sue
FRANK: Look: our son never raised a hand against anybody let alone against
EMILY: He loves his mother and father,   he respects us
FRANK: He is a religious boy at heart
EMILY: He looked me in the eyes he said   Momma you believe me don't
you?   and I said Oh yes   Oh yes   he's just my baby
FRANK: nobody knows him
EMILY: nobody knows him the way we do
FRANK: who would it be, if they did?
I ask you.

Scene 8.

House lights come up, TV screen shows video rewind. Sounds of audio rewind.
Screen shows GULICKS *onstage.*

VOICE: Frank and Mary Gulick we're very sorry   something happened to
the tape we're going to have to re-shoot   Let's go back just to,
we're showing an interior   Carl's room   the trophies
I will say,   I'll be repeating
Are you ready?
(House lights out, all tech returns to normal.)

Well Mr. and Mrs. Gulick your son has
  quite a collection of trophies!
FRANK: . . . I,   I don't remember what I
EMILY: . . . yes he,
FRANK: Carl was proud of   he had other hobbies though
EMILY: Oh he was so funny, didn't want his mother   poking in his room
he said
FRANK: Yes but that's   how boys are
EMILY: That judge refuses to set bail, which I don't   understand
FRANK: Is this the United States or   is this the Soviet Union?
EMILY: we are willing to sell our house to stand up for what is
VOICE: You were speaking of your son Carl   having quit school,
  his senior year?   and then?
EMILY: . . . He had a hard time, the teachers   were down on him.
FRANK: I don't know why,
EMILY: we were never told
And now in the newspapers
FRANK: the kinds of lies they are saying
EMILY: that he got into fights, that he was
FRANK: that kind of thing is all a distortion
EMILY: He was always a quiet boy
FRANK: but he had his own friends
EMILY: they came over to the house sometime, I don't remember   who
FRANK: there was that one boy what was his name
EMILY: Oh Frank   Carl hasn't seen him in years
he had friends in grade school
FRANK: Look: in the newspaper there were false statements
EMILY: Mr. Filco says   we might sue
FRANK: Oh no: he says we can't,   we have to prove "malice"
EMILY: Newspapers and TV are filled with lies
FRANK: Look: our son Carl never raised a hand against anybody let alone
against
EMILY: He loves his mother and father,
FRANK: he respects us
VOICE: Frank and,   it's Emily isn't it   Frank and Emily Gulick
  that is very moving.

Lights down.

Scene 9.

Lights up. Screen shows GULICKS *in theater.*

VOICE: The discovery of radioactive elements   in the late nineteenth
century enabled scientists to set back the estimated age of the Earth

to several billion years,   and the discovery in more
recent decades   that the Universe is expanding,   thus that
there is a point in Time when the Universe   was tightly
compressed   smaller than your tiniest fingernail!
>   thus that the age of the Universe is many billions
>   of   years
>   uncountable.
Yet   humankind resides in Time,   God bless us.
>   Frank and Emily Gulick as we wind down *our* time together
>   *What are your plans for the future?*
>   FRANK: . . . Oh that is, that's hard to   that's hard to answer.
>   EMILY: It depends I guess on
>   FRANK: Mr. Filco has advised
>   EMILY: I guess it's,

next is the grand jury
>   FRANK: Yes: the grand jury.

Mr. Filco cannot be present for the session   to protect our boy
I don't understand the law, just the prosecutor is there
swaying the jurors' minds
Oh I try to understand but I can't,
>   EMILY: he says we should be prepared

we should be prepared for a trial
>   VOICE: You are ready for the trial   to clear your son's name?
>   FRANK: Oh yes . . .
>   EMILY: yes that is a way of,   of putting it

Yes.   To clear Carl's name.
>   FRANK: . . . Oh yes you have to be realistic.
>   EMILY: Yes but before that   the true murderer of Edith Kaminsky

might come forward.
If the true murderer is watching this   *Please come forward.*
>   FRANK: . . . Well we both believe Carl is protecting someone, some

friend   another boy
>   EMILY: the one who really   committed that terrible crime
>   FRANK: So all we can do is pray.   Pray Carl will come

to his senses   give police the other boy's name, or
I believe this: if it's a friend of Carl's
he must have some decency   in his heart
>   VOICE: Your faith   in your son remains unshaken?
>   EMILY: You would have had to see his   toes,

his tiny baby toes in his bath.
His curly hair,   splashing in the bath.
His yellow rompers or no: I guess that was Denny
>   FRANK: If your own flesh and blood looks you in the eye,

you believe

EMILY: Oh yes.

VOICE: Human personality, it might be theorized, is a phenomenon of memory

yet memory   built up from cells, and   atoms does not "exist":

thus memory   like mind   like personality

is but a fiction?

EMILY: Oh   remembering backward is so hard!   oh it's,

FRANK: it pulls your brain in two.

EMILY: This medication the doctor gave me, my mouth   my mouth is so dry

In the middle of the night I wake up drenched in

FRANK: You don't know who you are   until a thing like this happens, then you don't know.

EMILY: It tears your brain in two, trying to   remember,

like even looking at the pictures

Oh you are lost.

FRANK: in Time you are lost

EMILY: You fall and fall,

. . . ever since the,   the butcher shop

he wasn't always himself   but

who he was then, I don't know.   But

it's so hard, remembering why.

FRANK: Yes my wife means thinking backward the way   the way the police make you, so many questions   you start forgetting right away

it comes out crazy.

Like now,   right here   I don't remember anything up to now

I mean, I can't swear to it: the first time, you see, we just

lived. We lived in our house. I am a, I am a post office employee

I guess I said that?   well, we live in our,   our house.

I mean, it was the first time through.   Just living.

Like the TV, the picture's always on if nobody's watching it

you know?   So,   the people we were then,

I guess I'm trying to say

those actual people, me and her   the ones you see *here*

aren't them. *(laughs)*

I guess that sounds crazy,

VOICE: We have here the heartbeat   of parental love and faith, it's

a beautiful thing   Frank and Molly Gulick. please comment?

FRANK: We are that boy's father and mother.

We know that our son is not a murderer and a,   a rapist

EMILY: We know, if that girl came to harm,   there is some reason

for it to be revealed, but

they never found the knife, for one thing

FRANK: or whatever it was

EMILY: They never found the knife, the murderer could tell them where
it's buried, or   whatever it was.
Oh he could help us so   if he just would.

VOICE: And your plans for the future,   Mr. and Mrs. Gulick of Lakepointe,
New Jersey?

FRANK: . . . Well.
I guess,   I guess we don't have any.
(Long silence, to the point of awkwardness.)

VOICE: . . . Plans for the future, Mr. and Mrs. Gulick of Lakepointe,
New Jersey?

FRANK: The thing is, you discover   you need to be protected
from your own thoughts sometimes,   but
who is there to do it?

EMILY: God didn't make any of us strong enough I guess.

FRANK: Look: one day in a family like this, it's   like the next day
and the day before.

EMILY: You could say it *is* the next day, I mean the same   the same day.

FRANK: Until one day it isn't

Lights slowly down, then out.

(THE END)

ACTIVITIES FOR WRITING AND DISCUSSION

1. What functions do the various devices of electronic imagery—visual and
aural—seem to serve in the play? What, if anything, would be lost if they were
omitted?

2. The action and **setting** of the play suggest a live TV program, and many
of the trappings of the TV medium are blatantly visible such as a "Voice"/inter-
viewer, microphones, nervous interviewees, and monitors. What does the play
imply about TV 's role in the coverage and presentation of such deeds as Carl's?

3. At the beginning of scene one, the "Voice" is likened to a "television emcee," but often his language is strikingly unlike that of any TV emcee, interviewer, or talk-show host. For instance, he refers to Aristotle, "the food chain,"
and other matters that seem remote from the subject of the murder/rape and
that fail to register any reaction from Frank and Emily. Locate several such
speeches by the Voice and analyze Oates's possible motives for writing the
speeches as she did.

4. Based on evidence in the play, write up a list of Frank and Emily's major
beliefs and values. Can you make any connections between these beliefs and
values and Carl's personality and crime? If not, explain. If so, give examples
that illustrate the connections.

5. Citing evidence in the play about his jobs, interests, personal associations, and so on, compose a character portrait of Carl. In what ways might the character of the son be (a) a result of the character of the parents and (b) a mystery that is beyond the parents' control?

6. Re-create the life and conflicts within the Gulick household through either of the following exercises:
   a. Write a mealtime conversation among Frank, Emily, and Carl (and possibly Denny). Create some situation of conflict (borrowed from the play or invented) that will bring out the personality of each family member.
   b. In the play Emily mentions that Carl didn't like her coming into his room. Imagine that Emily enters Carl's room to vacuum it and discovers him there or that she is vacuuming the room and is caught in the act by him. Write the dialogue that occurs.

7. Like many parents, Emily and Frank try to be "good" parents, yet they conflict and clash with their children. Compose a dialogue or scene that dramatizes relationships and conflicts within a family, either your own or some imaginary family of your own creation.

MILCHA SANCHEZ-SCOTT (b. 1953)

The Cuban Swimmer

CHARACTERS

MARGARITA SUÁREZ, the swimmer
EDUARDO SUÁREZ, her father, the coach
SIMÓN SUÁREZ, her brother
AÍDA SUÁREZ, her mother
ABUELA, her grandmother
VOICE OF MEL MUNSON
VOICE OF MARY BETH WHITE
VOICE OF RADIO OPERATOR

Live conga drums can be used to punctuate the action of the play.

TIME: Summer.
PLACE: The Pacific Ocean between San Pedro and Catalina Island.

Scene 1

Pacific Ocean. Midday. On the horizon, in perspective, a small boat enters U.L., crosses to U.R. and exits. Pause. Lower on the horizon, the same boat, in larger perspective, enters U.R., crosses and exits U.L. Blackout.

Scene 2

Pacific Ocean. Midday. The swimmer, MARGARITA SUÁREZ, *is swimming. On the boat following behind her are her father,* EDUARDO SUÁREZ, *holding a megaphone, and* SIMÓN, *her brother, sitting on top of the cabin with his shirt off, punk sunglasses on, binoculars hanging on his chest.*

EDUARDO: (*Leaning forward, shouting in time to* MARGARITA'S *swimming.*) *Uno, dos, uno, dos. Y uno, dos* . . . keep your shoulders parallel to the water.

SIMÓN: I'm gonna take these glasses off and look straight into the sun.

EDUARDO: (*Through megaphone.*) *Muy bien, muy bien* . . . but punch those arms in, baby.

SIMÓN: (*Looking directly at the sun through binoculars.*) Come on, come on, zap me. Show me something. (*He looks behind at the shoreline and ahead at the sea.*) Stop! Stop, Papi! Stop! (AÍDA SUÁREZ *and* ABUELA, *the swimmer's mother and grandmother, enter running from the back of the boat.*)

AÍDA and ABUELA: *Qué? Qué es?*

AÍDA: *Es un* shark?

EDUARDO: Eh?

ABUELA: *Que es un* shark *dicen?* (EDUARDO *blows whistle.* MARGARITA *looks up at the boat.*)

SIMÓN: No, Papi, no shark, no shark. We've reached the halfway mark.

ABUELA: (*Looking into the water.*) *A dónde está?*

AÍDA: It's not in the water.

ABUELA: Oh no? Oh no?

AÍDA: No! *A poco* do you think they're gonna have signs in the water to say you are halfway to Santa Catalina? No. It's done very scientific. *A ver, hijo,* explain it to your grandma.

SIMÓN: Well, you see Abuela—(*He points behind.*) There's San Pedro. (*He points ahead.*) And there's Santa Catalina. Looks halfway to me. (ABUELA *shakes her head and is looking back and forth, trying to make the decision, when suddenly the sound of a helicopter is heard.*)

ABUELA: (*Looking up.*) *Virgencita de la Caridad del Cobre. Qué es eso?* (*Sound of helicopter gets closer.* MARGARITA *looks up.*)

MARGARITA: Papi, Papi! (*A small commotion on the boat, with everybody pointing at the helicopter above. Shadows of the helicopter fall on the boat.* SIMÓN *looks up at it through binoculars.*) Papi—*qué es?* What is it?

EDUARDO: (*Through megaphone.*) Uh . . . uh . . . uh *un momentico* . . . *mi hija.* . . . Your papi's got everything under control, understand? Uh . . . you just keep stroking. And stay . . . uh . . . close to the boat.

SIMÓN: Wow, Papi! We're on TV man! Holy Christ, we're all over the fucking U.S.A.! It's Mel Munson and Mary Beth White!

AÍDA: *Por Dios!* SIMÓN, don't swear. And put on your shirt. (AÍDA *fluffs her hair, puts on her sunglasses and waves to the helicopter.* SIMÓN *leans over the side of the boat and yells to* MARGARITA.)

SIMÓN: Yo, Margo! You're on TV, man.

EDUARDO: Leave your sister alone. Turn on the radio.

MARGARITA: Papi! *Qué está pasando?*

ABUELA: *Que es la televisión dicen? (She shakes her head.) Porque como yo no puedo ver nada sin mis espejuelos. (ABUELA rummages through the boat, looking for her glasses. Voices of* MEL MUNSON *and* MARY BETH WHITE *are heard over the boat's radio.)*

MEL'S VOICE: As we take a closer look at the gallant crew of La Havana . . . and there . . . yes, there she is . . . the little Cuban swimmer from Long Beach, California, nineteen-year-old Margarita Suárez. The unknown swimmer is our Cinderella entry . . . a bundle of tenacity, battling her way through the choppy, murky waters of the cold Pacific to reach the Island of Romance . . . Santa Catalina . . . where should she be the first to arrive, two thousand dollars and a gold cup will be waiting for her.

AÍDA: Doesn't even cover our expenses.

ABUELA: *Qué dice?*

EDUARDO: Shhhh!

MARY BETH'S VOICE: This is really a family effort, Mel, and—

MEL'S VOICE: Indeed it is. Her trainer, her coach, her mentor is her father, Eduardo Suárez. Not a swimmer himself, it says here, Mr. Suárez is head usher of the Holy Name Society and the owner-operator of Suárez Treasures of the Sea and Salvage Yard. I guess it's one of those places . . .

MARY BETH'S VOICE: If I might interject a fact here, Mel, assisting in this swim is Mrs. Suárez who is a former Miss Cuba.

MEL'S VOICE: And a beautiful woman in her own right. Let's try and get a closer look. *(Helicopter sound gets louder.* MARGARITA, *frightened, looks up again.)*

MARGARITA: Papi!

EDUARDO: *(Through megaphone.) Mi hija,* don't get nervous . . . it's the press. I'm handling it.

AÍDA: I see how you're handling it.

EDUARDO: *(Through megaphone.)* Do you hear? Everything is under control. Get back into your rhythm. Keep your elbows high and kick and kick and kick and kick . . .

ABUELA: *(Finds her glasses and puts them on.) Ay sí, es la televisión . . . (She points to helicopter.) Qué lindo mira . . . (She fluffs her hair, gives a big wave.) Alo América! Viva mi Margarita, viva todo los Cubanos en los Estados Unidos!*

AÍDA: *Ay por Dios,* Cecilia, the man didn't come all this way in his helicopter to look at you jumping up and down, making a fool of yourself.

ABUELA: I don't care. I'm proud.

AÍDA: He can't understand you anyway.

ABUELA: *Viva . . . (She stops.) Simón, comó se dice viva?*

SIMÓN: Hurray.

ABUELA: Hurray for *mi* Margarita *y* for all the Cubans living *en* the United States, *y un abrazo . . .* Simón, *abrazo . . .*

SIMÓN: A big hug.

ABUELA: *Sí,* a big hug to all my friends in Miami, Long Beach, Union City, except for my son Carlos who lives in New York in sin! He lives . . . *(She crosses herself.)* in Brooklyn with a Puerto Rican woman in sin! *No decente* . . .

SIMÓN: Decent.

ABUELA: Carlos, *no decente.* This family, *decente.*

AÍDA: Cecilia, *por Dios.*

MEL'S VOICE: Look at that enthusiasm. The whole family has turned out to cheer little Margarita on to victory! I hope they won't be too disappointed.

MARY BETH'S VOICE: She seems to be making good time, Mel.

MEL'S VOICE: Yes, it takes all kinds to make a race. And it's a testimonial to the all-encompassing fairness . . . the greatness of this, the Wrigley Invitational Women's Swim to Catalina, where among all the professionals there is still room for the amateurs . . . like these, the simple people we see below us on the ragtag La Havana, taking their long-shot chance to victory. *Vaya con Dios!* *(Helicopter sound fading as family, including* MARGARITA, *watch silently. Static as* SIMÓN *turns radio off.* EDUARDO *walks to bow of boat, looks out on the horizon.)*

EDUARDO: *(To himself.)* Amateurs.

AÍDA: Eduardo, that person insulted us. Did you hear, Eduardo? That he called us a simple people in a ragtag boat? Did you hear . . . ?

ABUELA: *(Clenching her fist at departing helicopter.) Mal-Rayo los parta*!

SIMÓN: *(Same gesture.)* Asshole! (AÍDA *follows* EDUARDO *as he goes to side of boat and stares at* MARGARITA.*)*

AÍDA: This person comes in his helicopter to insult your wife, your family, your daughter . . .

MARGARITA: *(Pops her head out of the water.)* Papi?

AÍDA: Do you hear me, Eduardo? I am not simple.

ABUELA: *Sí.*

AÍDA: I am complicated.

ABUELA: *Sí, demasiada complicada.*

AÍDA: Me and my family are not so simple.

SIMÓN: Mom, the guy's an asshole.

ABUELA: *(Shaking her fist at helicopter.)* Asshole!

AÍDA: If my daughter was simple she would not be in that water swimming.

MARGARITA: Simple? Papi . . . ?

AÍDA: *Ahora,* Eduardo, this is what I want you to do. When we get to Santa Catalina I want you to call the TV station and demand *un* apology.

EDUARDO: *Cállete mujer! Aquí mando yo.* I will decide what is to be done.

MARGARITA: Papi, tell me what's going on.

EDUARDO: Do you understand what I am saying to you, Aída?

SIMÓN: *(Leaning over side of boat, to* MARGARITA.*)* Yo Margo! You know that Mel Munson guy on TV? He called you a simple amateur and said you didn't have a chance.

ABUELA: *(Leaning directly behind* SIMÓN.*) Mi hija, insultó a la familia. Desgraciado!!*

AÍDA: *(Leaning in behind* ABUELA.*)* He called us peasants! And your father is not doing anything about it. He just knows how to yell at me.

EDUARDO: *(Through megaphone.)* Shut up! All of you! Do you want to break her concentration? Is that what you are after? Eh? (ABUELA, AÍDA *and* SIMÓN *shrink back.* EDUARDO *paces before them.)* Swimming is rhythm and concentration. You win a race *aquí. (Pointing to his head.)* Now . . . *(To* SIMÓN.*)* you, take care of the boat, Aída y Mama . . . do something. Anything. Something practical. (ABUELA *and* AÍDA *get on knees and pray in Spanish.)* Hija, give it everything, eh? . . . *por la familia. Uno . . . dos. . . .* You must win. (SIMÓN *goes into cabin. The prayers continue as lights change to indicate bright sunlight, later in the afternoon.)*

Scene 3

Tableau for a couple of beats. EDUARDO *on bow with timer in one hand as he counts strokes per minute.* SIMÓN *is in the cabin steering, wearing his sunglasses, baseball cap on backwards.* ABUELA *and* AÍDA *are at the side of the boat, heads down, hands folded, still muttering prayers in Spanish.*

AÍDA *and* ABUELA: *(Crossing themselves.) En el nombre del Padre, del Hijo y del Espíritu Santo amén.*

EDUARDO: *(Through megaphone.)* You're stroking seventy-two!

SIMÓN: *(Singing.)* Mama's stroking, Mama's stroking seventy-two . . .

EDUARDO: *(Through megaphone.)* You comfortable with it?

SIMÓN: *(Singing)* Seventy-two, seventy-two, seventy-two for you.

AÍDA: *(Looking at the heavens.) Ay,* Eduardo, *ven acá,* we should be grateful that *Nuestro* Señor gave us such a beautiful day.

ABUELA: *(Crosses herself.) Sí, gracias a Dios.*

EDUARDO: She's stroking seventy-two, with no problem. *(He throws a kiss to the sky.)* It's a beautiful day to win.

AÍDA: *Qué hermoso!* So clear and bright. Not a cloud in the sky. *Mira! Mira!* Even rainbows on the water . . . a sign from God.

SIMÓN: *(Singing.)* Rainbows on the water . . . you in my arms . . .

ABUELA *and* EDUARDO: *(Looking the wrong way.) Dónde?*

AÍDA: *(Pointing toward* MARGARITA.*)* There, dancing in front of Margarita, leading her on . . .

EDUARDO: Rainbows on. . . . *Ay coño!* It's an oil slick! You . . . you . . . *(To* SIMÓN.*)* Stop the boat. *(Runs to bow, yelling.)* Margarita! Margarita! *(On the next stroke,* MARGARITA *comes up all covered in black oil.)*

MARGARITA: Papi! Papi! *(Everybody goes to the side and stares at* MARGARITA, *who stares back.* EDUARDO *freezes.)*

AÍDA: *Apúrate* Eduardo, move . . . what's wrong with you . . . *no me oíste,* get my daughter out of the water.

EDUARDO: *(Softly.)* We can't touch her. If we touch her, she's disqualified.

AÍDA: But I'm her mother.

EDUARDO: Not even by her own mother. Especially by her own mother. . . . You always want the rules to be different for you, you always want to be the exception. *(To* SIMÓN*)* And you . . . you didn't see it, eh? You were playing again?

SIMÓN: Papi, I was watching . . .

AÍDA: *(Interrupting.) Pues,* do something Eduardo. You are the big coach, the monitor.

SIMÓN: Mentor! Mentor!

EDUARDO: How can a person think around you? *(He walks off to bow, puts head in hands.)*

ABUELA: *(Looking over side.) Mira como todos los* little birds are dead. *(She crosses herself.)*

AÍDA: Their little wings are glued to their sides.

SIMÓN: Christ, this is like the La Brea tar pits.

AÍDA: They can't move their little wings.

ABUELA: *Esa niña tiene que moverse.*

SIMÓN: Yeah Margo, you gotta move, man. *(*ABUELA *and* SIMÓN *gesture for* MARGARITA *to move.* AÍDA *gestures for her to swim.)*

ABUELA: *Anda niña, muévete.*

AÍDA: Swim, *hija,* swim or the *aceite* will stick to your wings.

MARGARITA: Papi?

ABUELA: *(Taking megaphone.)* Your papi say "move it!" *(*MARGARITA *with difficulty starts moving.)*

ABUELA, AÍDA and SIMÓN. *(Laboriously counting.) Uno, dos . . . uno, dos . . . anda . . . uno, dos.*

EDUARDO: *(Running to take megaphone from* ABUELA*.) Uno, dos . . .* (SIMÓN *races into cabin and starts the engine.* ABUELA, AÍDA *and* EDUARDO *count together.)*

SIMÓN: *(Looking ahead.)* Papi, it's over there!

EDUARDO: Eh?

SIMÓN: *(Pointing ahead and to* R.*)* It's getting clearer over there.

EDUARDO: *(Through megaphone.)* Now pay attention to me. Go to the right. (SIMÓN, ABUELA, AÍDA *and* EDUARDO *all lean over side. They point ahead and to* R., *except* ABUELA, *who points to* L.*)*

FAMILY: *(Shouting together.) Para yá! Para yá! (Lights go down on boat. A special light on* MARGARITA, *swimming through the oil, and on* ABUELA, *watching her.)*

ABUELA: *Sangre de mi sangre,* you will be another to save us. *En Bolondron,* where your great-grandmother Luz Suárez was born, they say one day it rained blood. All the people, they run into their houses. They cry, they pray, *pero* your great-grandmother Luz she had *cojones* like a man. She run outside. She look straight at the sky. She shake her fist. And she say to the evil one, "*Mira . . . (Beating her chest.) coño, Diablo, aquí estoy si me quieres.*" And she open her mouth, and she drunk the blood.

(Blackout.)

Scene 4

Lights up on boat. AÍDA *and* EDUARDO *are on deck watching* MARGARITA *swim.*

We hear the gentle, rhythmic lap, lap, lap, of the water, then the sound of inhaling and exhaling as MARGARITA'S *breathing becomes louder. Then* MARGARITA'S *heartbeat is heard, with the lapping of the water and the breathing under it. These sounds continue beneath the dialogue to the end of the scene.*

AÍDA: *Dios mío.* Look how she moves through the water . . .

EDUARDO: You see, it's very simple. It is a matter of concentration.

AÍDA: The first time I put her in water she came to life, she grew before my eyes. She moved, she smiled, she loved it more than me. She didn't want my breast any longer. She wanted the water.

EDUARDO: And of course, the rhythm. The rhythm takes away the pain and helps the concentration. (*Pause.* AÍDA *and* EDUARDO *watch* MARGARITA.)

AÍDA: Is that my child, or a seal. . . .

EDUARDO: Ah a seal, the reason for that is that she's keeping her arms very close to her body. She cups her hands and then she reaches and digs, reaches and digs.

AÍDA: To think that a daughter of mine . . .

EDUARDO: It's the training, the hours in the water. I used to tie weights around her little wrists and ankles.

AÍDA: A spirit, an ocean spirit, must have entered my body when I was carrying her.

EDUARDO: (*To* MARGARITA.) Your stroke is slowing down. (*Pause. We hear* MARGARITA'S *heartbeat with the breathing under, faster now.*)

AÍDA: Eduardo, that night, the night on the boat . . .

EDUARDO: Ah, the night on the boat again . . . the moon was . . .

AÍDA: The moon was full. We were coming to America. . . . *Qué romantico.* (*Heartbeat and breathing continue.*)

EDUARDO: We were cold, afraid, with no money, and on top of everything, you were hysterical, yelling at me, tearing at me with your nails. (*Opens his shirt, points to the base of his neck.*) Look, I still bear the scars . . . telling me that I didn't know what I was doing . . . saying that we were going to die. . . .

AÍDA: You took me, you stole me from my home . . . you didn't give me a chance to prepare. You just said we have to go now, now! Now, you said. You didn't let me take anything. I left everything behind . . . I left everything behind.

EDUARDO: Saying that I wasn't good enough, that your father didn't raise you so that I could drown you in the sea.

AÍDA: You didn't let me say even a goodbye. You took me, you stole me, you tore me from my home.

EDUARDO: I took you so we could be married.

AÍDA: That was in Miami. But that night on the boat, Eduardo. . . . We were not married, that night on the boat.

EDUARDO: *No pasó nada!* Once and for all get it out of your head, it was cold, you hated me and we were afraid. . . .

AÍDA: *Mentiroso!*

EDUARDO: A man can't do it when he is afraid.

AÍDA: Liar! You did it very well.

EDUARDO: I did?

AÍDA: *Sí.* Gentle. You were so gentle and then strong . . . my passion for you so deep. Standing next to you . . . I would ache . . . looking at your hands I would forget to breathe, you were irresistible.

EDUARDO: I was?

AÍDA: You took me into your arms, you touched my face with your fingertips . . . you kissed my eyes . . . *la esquina de la boca y* . . .

EDUARDO: *Sí, sí,* and then . . .

AÍDA: I look at your face on top of mine, and I see the lights of Havana in your eyes. That's when you seduced me.

EDUARDO: Shhh, they're gonna hear you. *(Lights go down. Special on* AÍDA.*)*

AÍDA: That was the night. A woman doesn't forget those things . . . and later that night was the dream . . . the dream of a big country with fields of fertile land and big, giant things growing. And there by a green, slimy pond I found a giant pea pod and when I opened it, it was full of little, tiny baby frogs. (AÍDA *crosses herself as she watches* MARGARITA. *We hear louder breathing and heartbeat.)*

MARGARITA: Santa Teresa. Little Flower of God, pray for me. San Martín de Porres, pray for me. Santa Rosa de Lima, *Virgencita de la Caridad del Cobre,* pray for me. . . . Mother pray for me.

Scene 5

Loud howling of wind is heard, as lights change to indicate unstable weather, fog and mist. Family on deck, braced and huddled against the wind. SIMÓN *is at the helm.*

AÍDA: *Ay Dios mío, qué viento.*

EDUARDO: *(Through megaphone.)* Don't drift out . . . that wind is pushing you out. *(To* SIMÓN*)* You! Slow down. Can't you see your sister is drifting out?

SIMÓN: It's the wind, Papi.

AÍDA: Baby, don't go so far. . . .

ABUELA: *(To heaven.) Ay Gran Poder de Dios, quita este maldito viento.*

SIMÓN: Margo! Margo! Stay close to the boat.

EDUARDO: Dig in. Dig in hard. . . . Reach down from your guts and dig in.

ABUELA: *(To heaven.) Ay Virgen de la Caridad del Cobre, por lo más tú quieres a pararla.*

AÍDA: *(Putting her hand out, reaching for* MARGARITA.*)* Baby, don't go far. (ABUELA *crosses herself. Action freezes. Lights get dimmer, special on* MARGARITA. *She keeps swimming, stops, starts again, stops, then, finally exhausted, stops altogether. The boat stops moving.)*

EDUARDO: What's going on here? Why are we stopping?

SIMÓN: Papi, she's not moving! Yo Margo! *(The family all run to the side.)*

EDUARDO: Hija! . . . Hijita! You're tired, eh?

AÍDA: *Por supuesto* she's tired. I like to see you get in the water, waving your arms and legs from San Pedro to Santa Catalina. A person isn't a machine, a person has to rest.

SIMÓN: Yo, Mama! Cool out, it ain't fucking brain surgery.

EDUARDO: *(To* SIMÓN*)* Shut up, you. *(Louder to* MARGARITA*.)* I guess your mother's right for once, huh? . . . I guess you had to stop, eh? . . . Give your brother, the idiot . . . a chance to catch up with you.

SIMÓN: *(Clowning like Mortimer Snerd.)* Dum dee dum dee dum ooops, ah shucks. . . .

EDUARDO: I don't think he's Cuban.

SIMÓN: *(Like Ricky Ricardo.)* Oye Lucy! I'm home! Ba ba lu!

EDUARDO: *(Joins in clowning, grabbing* SIMÓN *in a headlock.)* What am I gonna do with this idiot, eh? I don't understand this idiot. He's not like us Margarita. *(Laughing.)* You think if we put him into your bathing suit with a cap on his head . . . *(He laughs hysterically.)* you think anyone would know . . . huh? Do you think anyone would know? *(Laughs.)*

SIMÓN: *(Vamping.)* Ay, mi amor. Anybody looking for tits would know. *(*EDUARDO *slaps* SIMÓN *across the face, knocking him down.* AÍDA *runs to* SIMÓN's *aid.* ABUELA *holds* EDUARDO *back.)*

MARGARITA: *Mía culpa! Mía culpa!*

ABUELA: *Qué dices hija?*

MARGARITA: Papi, it's my fault, it's all my fault. . . . I'm so cold, I can't move. . . . I put my face in the water . . . and I hear them whispering . . . laughing at me. . . .

AÍDA: Who is laughing at you?

MARGARITA: The fish are all biting me . . . they hate me . . . they whisper about me. She can't swim, they say. She can't glide. She has no grace. . . . Yellowtails, bonita, tuna, man-o'-war, snub-nose sharks, los baracudas . . . they all hate me . . . only the dolphins care . . . and sometimes I hear the whales crying . . . she is lost, she is dead. I'm so numb, I can't feel. Papi! Papi! Am I dead?

EDUARDO: *Vamos*, baby, punch those arms in. Come on . . . do you hear me?

MARGARITA: Papi . . . Papi . . . forgive me. . . . *(All is silent on the boat.* EDUARDO *drops his megaphone, his head bent down in dejection.* ABUELA, AÍDA, SIMÓN *all leaning over the side of the boat.* SIMÓN *slowly walks away.)*

AÍDA: *Mi hija, qué tienes?*

SIMÓN: Oh Christ, don't make her say it. Please don't make her say it.

ABUELA: Say what? *Qué cosa?*

SIMÓN: She wants to quit, can't you see she's had enough?

ABUELA: *Mira, para eso. Esta niña* is turning blue.

AÍDA: *Oyeme, mi hija.* Do you want to come out of the water?

MARGARITA: Papi?

SIMÓN: *(To* EDUARDO*)* She won't come out until *you* tell her.

AÍDA: Eduardo . . . answer your daughter.

EDUARDO: *Le dije* to concentrate . . . concentrate on your rhythm. Then the rhythm would carry her . . . ay it's a beautiful thing, Aída. It's like yoga, like meditation, the mind over matter . . . the mind controlling the body . . . that's how the great things in the world have been done. I wish you . . . I wish my wife could understand.

MARGARITA: Papi?

SIMÓN: *(To* MARGARITA*)* Forget him.

AÍDA: *(Imploring.)* Eduardo, *por favor.*

EDUARDO: *(Walking in circles.)* Why didn't you let her concentrate? Don't you understand, the concentration, the rhythm is everything. But no, you wouldn't listen. *(Screaming to the ocean.)* Goddam Cubans, why, God, why do you make us go everywhere with our families? *(He goes to back of boat.)*

AÍDA: *(Opening her arms.) Mi hija, ven,* come to Mami. *(Rocking.)* Your mami knows. (ABUELA *has taken the training bottle, puts it in a net. She and* SIMÓN *lower it to* MARGARITA.*)*

SIMÓN: Take this. Drink it. *(As* MARGARITA *drinks,* ABUELA *crosses herself.)*

ABUELA: *Sangre de mi sangre. (Music comes up softly.* MARGARITA *drinks, gives the bottle back, stretches out her arms, as if on a cross. Floats on her back. She begins a graceful backstroke. Lights fade on boat as special lights come up on* MARGARITA. *She stops. Slowly turns over and starts to swim, gradually picking up speed. Suddenly as if in pain she stops, tries again, then stops in pain again. She becomes disoriented and falls to the bottom of the sea. Special on* MARGARITA *at the bottom of the sea.)*

MARGARITA: *Ya no puedo* . . . I can't . . . A person isn't a machine . . . *es mi culpa* . . . Father forgive me . . . Papi! Papi! One, two. *Uno, dos. (Pause.)* Papi! *A dónde estás? (Pause)* One, two, one, two. Papi! Ay Papi! Where are you . . . ? Don't leave me. . . . Why don't you answer me? *(Pause. She starts to swim, slowly.) Uno, dos, uno, dos.* Dig in, dig in. *(Stops swimming.) Por favor,* Papi! *(Starts to swim again.)* One, two, one, two. Kick from your hip, kick from your hip. *(Stops swimming. Starts to cry.)* Oh God, please. . . . *(Pause.)* Hail Mary, full of grace . . . dig in, dig in . . . the Lord is with thee. . . . *(She swims to the rhythm of her Hail Mary.)* Hail Mary, full of grace . . . dig in, dig in, . . . the Lord is with thee . . . dig in, dig in. . . . Blessed art thou among women. . . . Mommie it hurts. You let go of my hand. I'm lost. . . . And blessed is the fruit of thy womb, now and at the hour of our death. Amen. I don't want to die, I don't want to die. (MARGARITA *is still swimming. Blackout. She is gone.)*

Scene 6

Lights up on boat, we hear radio static. There is a heavy mist. On deck we see only black outline of ABUELA *with shawl over her head. We hear the voices of* EDUARDO, AÍDA *and* RADIO OPERATOR.

EDUARDO'S VOICE: La Havana! Coming from San Pedro. Over.

RADIO OPERATOR'S VOICE: Right. DT6-6, you say you've lost a swimmer.

AÍDA'S VOICE: Our child, our only daughter . . . listen to me. Her name is Margarita Inez Suárez, she is wearing a black one-piece bathing suit cut high in the legs with a white racing stripe down the sides, a white bathing cap with goggles and her whole body covered with a . . . with a . . .

EDUARDO'S VOICE: With lanolin and paraffin.

AÍDA'S VOICE: *Sí . . . con* lanolin and paraffin. *(More radio static. Special on* SIMÓN, *on the edge of the boat.)*

SIMÓN: Margo! Yo Margo! *(Pause)* Man don't do this. *(Pause.)* Come on. . . . Come on. . . . *(Pause.)* God, why does everything have to be so hard? *(Pause.)* Stupid. You know you're not supposed to die for this. Stupid. It's his dream and he can't even swim. *(Pause.)* Punch those arms in. Come home. Come home. I'm your little brother. Don't forget what Mama said. You're not supposed to leave me behind. *Vamos*, Margarita, take your little brother, hold his hand tight when you cross the street. He's so little. *(Pause.)* Oh Christ, give us a sign. . . . I know! I know! Margo, I'll send you a message . . . like mental telepathy. I'll hold my breath, close my eyes and I'll bring you home. *(He takes a deep breath; a few beats.)* This time I'll beep . . . I'll send out sonar signals like a dolphin. *(He imitates dolphin sounds. The sound of real dolphins takes over from* SIMÓN, *then fades into sound of* ABUELA *saying the Hail Mary in Spanish, as full lights come up slowly.)*

Scene 7

EDUARDO *coming out of cabin, sobbing,* AÍDA *holding him.* SIMÓN *anxiously scanning the horizon.* ABUELA *looking calmly ahead.*

EDUARDO: *Es mi culpa, sí, es mi culpa. (He hits his chest.)*

AÍDA: *Ya, ya viejo* . . . it was my sin . . . I left my home.

EDUARDO: Forgive me, forgive me. I've lost our daughter, our sister, our granddaughter, *mi carne, mi sangre, mis ilusiones. (To heaven.) Dios mío* take me . . . take me, I say . . . Goddammit, take me!

SIMÓN: I'm going in.

AÍDA and EDUARDO: No!

EDUARDO: *(Grabbing and holding* SIMÓN, *speaking to heaven.)* God, take me, not my children. They are my dreams, my illusions . . . and not this one, this one is my mystery . . . he has my secret dreams. In him are the parts of me I cannot see. (EDUARDO *embraces* SIMÓN. *Radio static becomes louder.)*

AÍDA: I . . . I think I see her.

SIMÓN: No it's just a seal.

ABUELA: *(Looking out with binoculars.) Mi nietacita, dónde estás? (She feels her heart.)* I don't feel the knife in my heart . . . my little fish is not lost. *(Radio crackles with static. As lights dim on boat, voices of* MEL *and* MARY BETH *are heard over the radio.)*

MEL'S VOICE: Tragedy has marred the face of the Wrigley Invitational Women's Race to Catalina. The Cuban swimmer, little Margarita Suárez, has reportedly been lost at sea. Coast Guard and divers are looking for her as we speak. Yet in spite of this tragedy the race must go on because . . .

MARY BETH'S VOICE: *(Interrupting loudly.)* Mel!

MEL'S VOICE: *(Startled.)* What!

MARY BETH'S VOICE: Ah . . . excuse me, Mel . . . we have a winner. We've just received word from Catalina that one of the swimmers is just fifty yards from the breakers . . . it's oh, it's Margarita Suárez! *(Special on family in cabin listening to radio.)*

MEL'S VOICE: What? I thought she died! *(Special on* MARGARITA, *taking off bathing cap, trophy in hand, walking on the water.)*

MARY BETH'S VOICE: Ahhh . . . unless . . . unless this is a tragic. . . . No . . . there she is, Mel. Margarita Suárez! The only one in the race wearing a black bathing suit cut high in the legs with a racing stripe down the side. *(Family cheering, embracing.)*

SIMÓN: *(Screaming.)* Way to go Margo!

MEL'S VOICE: This is indeed a miracle! It's a resurrection! Margarita Suárez with a flotilla of boats to meet her, is now walking on the waters, through the breakers . . . onto the beach, with crowds of people cheering her on. What a jubilation! This is a miracle! *(Sound of crowds cheering. Pinspot on* ABUELA.*)*

ABUELA: *Sangre de mi sangre* you will be another to save us, ... to say to the evil one, *Coño Diablo, aqui estoy si me quieres. (Lights and cheering fade. Blackout.)*

END OF PLAY

FAMILIES: ADDITIONAL ACTIVITIES FOR WRITING AND DISCUSSION

1. Reread all or a portion of your notebook. Mark any passages, however long or short, that strike you, for whatever reason. Beside each passage, write a note explaining its significance for you. Finally, pick a favorite passage and either:

    a. Expand it into a new piece of writing, or

    b. Make notes on how you *could* expand or use it at some future date, or

    c. Rewrite it in a different form (e.g., poem, dialogue, letter, memoir).

For a list of strategies for expanding or revising, see Chapter 9.

2. To what extent are children fated to be like their parents, and to what extent can they determine their own personalities and futures? Bring together two or more **characters, speakers,** or **personae** from the different texts and have

them discuss this question in a dialogue. Some possible participants might include the father or son in "The Olive Grove," the mother or daughter in Olsen's "I Stand Here Ironing," Kiswana Browne in Gloria Naylor's story, the speaker/son in Bukowski's "my old man." Begin by listing some pertinent questions and considering how the various speakers might respond to them. Then write the dialogue.

3. Several texts in this section ("Eveline," "Kiswana Browne," "Heritage," *Tone Clusters,* and *The Cuban Swimmer,* to name just a few) indicate ways that families are shaped by the larger cultures of which they are a part. Write an essay about your own family in which you discuss:

   a. Ways in which your family might be perceived as representative of some culture (ethnic, racial, religious, socioeconomic), and

   b. Ways in which your family has an identity that *transcends* that culture.

Make your essay vivid by illustrating it with specific examples and stories.

4. Several texts in this thematic section incorporate—or refer to—family photographs. Emulate the creative method of Rita Dove ("Fifth Grade Autobiography"), Raymond Carver ("My Father's Life"), and Joy Harjo ("The Place of Origins"), and use a family photograph (or photographs) as a springboard for writing about your family. *Alternative:* Study a photograph (wife/husband, partners, parent/child, or larger family grouping) of a family other than your own—perhaps a family of a different time or culture—and write from *that* photograph. Obviously, you will need to use your imagination and *invent* details and stories about that family. If possible, do some background research to improve your writing about this "stranger" family.

5. Sibling relationships and rivalries are a theme of several selections in this chapter, such as "The Rich Brother," "Kiswana Browne," "Sadie and Maud," and "The Elder Sister." In each case, who is involved? What are the causes and results of the conflict, and from whose point of view is the conflict related? Analyze the theme in any one text or compare and contrast its treatment in any two or more texts.

6. Review your entire notebook; as you do, make a running list of memorable or striking topics, e.g., "fathers and sons," "mothers and daughters," "siblings," "breaking free of the parent." Then choose a favorite topic, make a Topic/Form Grid (see Chapter 9), and use one of the forms on your grid to create a new notebook entry about the topic. Should your chosen form not work, do a Topic/Form Shift to a different form on your grid.

Interchapter on Notebooks and Journals (II)

"The Stories of How We Lived": Joy Harjo

Poet, essayist, editor, and children's writer, Joy Harjo's work has been closely tied to her identity as a Creek Indian. Harjo was born in 1951 in Tulsa, Oklahoma, in the heart of the Creek Nation. She attended school at the Institute of American Indian Arts in Santa Fe, New Mexico, and graduated with a B.A. degree from the University of New Mexico, Albuquerque in 1976. In 1978 she earned an MFA in creative writing from the University of Iowa Writers' Workshop, and since then she has continued both writing and teaching. Among her books are: *She Had Some Horses* (1983), *Secrets from the Center of the World* (1989), *In Mad Love and War* (1990), and *The Woman Who Fell from the Sky: Poems* (1996).

The following journal selections and Harjo's prefatory note are reprinted from *The Poet's Notebook,* an anthology edited by Stephen Kuusisto, Deborah Tall, and David Weiss and published by Norton (1995).

My earliest poems were derived directly from journal work. I would write wildly and intuitively in my journal to rev up to the higher frequency of a poem. I'd revise and play out possibilities in the journal, then transfer to a typewriter to revise and see the final poem. Now I do most of my journaling and writing on the computer, though I keep a journal and pen by my bed for dreams. I've included a few dreams here, but most I keep to myself, especially the very powerful, for I don't wish them to lose power by revealing them to possible misuse.

I sometimes read back through a journal to find scraps of meaning I am missing from some larger piece, when I need something personally historical, or to find a quote or something else I've stuck in the pages: newspaper articles, images, or lists. It's like fishing. Sometimes I see something that totally surprises. Often I write in my journal while I am still quite asleep. These entries are the most surprising, and often include information and leaps of logic I don't figure out until something happens a few years later.

I wish I could include songs. Last night I dreamed a rewrite of a song my band and I have written to go with the poem "She Had Some Horses." We added another movement that enlarged the overall meaning. By the time I awoke to deadlines and the need to bake bread for a lunch for visiting relatives, I had forgotten it. Maybe the skill to notate in shorthand what I hear in dream music will come.

My journal is like the sketch book I used to carry around when I painted. I sketched gestures, ideas for larger drawings and paintings. Eventually everything in the sketchbook was used, whether or not I failed in the exercise of imaging. I gained knowledge of my art through each venture.

7/16/94

I can't help it, I love sweet sad ballads with heartache saxophone: Art Pepper, John Coltrane, especially Coltrane. The music breaks away at any crust of unlove to the longing for that home far from the density of years of soap opera on earth.

1/3/94

the explosion at genesis creates stones who tell the stories of how we lived. I consider the radius of intimacy and imagine you showering in the artificial light of the motel room, before dawn when most earthly spirits are returning from memory. . . . it was a tender arc marked by absolute grace and a little rain.

There is no love beyond faithful love. Le Ly Hayslip's mother, from *When Heaven and Earth Change Places*

10/19/93

The heart has four winds. I heard them last night as my son, his daughter Haleigh and I drove from a birthday dinner. It was raining and dark, difficult to differentiate between shadow and pavement. I remembered weather in the womb. . . . And then the four winds as they created the child, talked to her, shaped the elegant and tiny bones. All humans come out of the dark this way, into the dark. Each human knows a woman intimately. The four winds of the mother's heart directs the fate of the child. Perhaps the path forms the physical heart, consequently.

Remembering and imagination enter and leave from the same area of the soul.

It was hot and wet. To feel was another dimension not available to me, another field in the weave of magnetic waves—yet, approaching me were spirits who rose in waves from the brackish sweet smell of the newly dead whose corpses littered the killing ground. I'm sorry, I said, though I no longer had a mouth or a tongue. Though I no longer had words with which to approach the altar of the living.

There's a lullabye. Made to calm the ruler of sharp things.

UNDATED FROM THIS GENERAL TIME
When you grow up you either make uneasy peace with the density of destiny, and entertain the possibility of a reckless, cruel god, or watch television with the rest of the escapees.

See those sensitive hills? They need to be talked to, sung to. . . .

7/8/90 TUCSON
We descend into the damp city. I anticipate the wet flowering of the desert. And it will remind me of the warm pools of moisture under your body after we have made love, when we are at the mercy of a tenderness beyond this world.

6/3/91 HONOLULU
Full of beans, rice, sweets and a crimson tea. A light mist outside, all seven windows open and trees brushing the second story. Talked of massacres, genocide at dinner last night with Haunani-Kay and her companion David—how those words don't translate, nor do body counts. What's missing are names, terms of endearment, and stories. There's always been a problem negotiating from the language of commerce to the spiritual realm. . . . The smells here are so old, sweet and familiar.

6/4/91
Some spirits go willingly (at death). In the tragedy of massacre the shock of rolling thoughtlessness can trap one in the house of disbelief. The body is a house of memory that decay cannot loosen.

11/10/91
"Blazing above Powell Observatory near Louisburg, Kansas, the aurora borealis filled the sky Friday evening. The northern lights, not usually seen this far south, painted the sky with shimmering curtains of reds, greens, blues and whites. Chances for more displays are good tonight and later this week. Get away from city lights and look north any time after dark." The *Kansas City Star,* Front page.

6/20/91
The first thought is of the angel of death, who can take everything but the heart rooted to acts of imagination. What is imagined and what is not?

In the first dream her spirit had knocked on the door of my truck. She was living in the Fifth World, or are we in it?

I don't think worlds are as easily defineable as that . . . they exist simultane- 20
ously. The people are always emerging. They are always falling through the hole in the sky.

I think death has been overrated. I heard too many fire and brimstone stories from the stiff pews of Christians. I saw too many cheap Hollywood movies featuring winners and losers, though no one ever won. No Indians survived. In Ecuador the tribes from the southern hemisphere thought we'd all been killed by John Wayne. Now *there's* an angel of death.

And what of my friend who this afternoon weeded her garden, wielding a cigarette in one hand as she coughed with the cancer eating her, a friend on each side holding her up? She wants to leave with a little grace, yet doesn't want to leave at all. What do we know about anything?

We cannot escape memory, but carry it in us like a huge organ with lungs sucking air for survival. It is an organ like the skin, covering everything, but from the inside.

Was there ever mercy? Is Mercy an errant angel so horrified by cruel acts of humans she cannot bear to look on us? Mercy, come find us in the labyrinth of cruelty.

I don't know what to tell you, beloved.   25

2/10/92 BONN
In Beethoven's house . . . there is no evidence of Beethoven's mother in this place. Who was she? There would be no Beethoven without her.

10/20/92
I felt the immensity of my anger for the first time. I felt totally present as yellow sharpened itself against the blue sky.

3/9/93
Each path reeked of afterbirth, rain and mice. . . . Humans only think we can bend time into increments of money.

3/25/93
As soon as I stepped from the automatic glass doors of the hotel a dragonfly alit on my arm. I once knew that language.

8/10/93

(From these notes came the poem "The Naming," for my granddaughter Haleigh 30
Sara, who was born in Green Bay, Wisconsin. The poem with story follows.)

The most honorable wars weren't fought with swords or the yelling of fools.
The greatest thinkers (each representing their tribe) sat on opposite hills and
had a contest to outimagine the other. You can manipulate an enemy's weakness so the enemy destroys himself/herself with foolishness.

Names are the least idle of sounds. The night after she was born I spent the
night in a hotel near the lake left over from the ice age. A conference of tribes
gathered in the ballroom a few floors below.

I think of names that have profoundly changed the direction of disaster. Of
the raw whirling wind outlining femaleness emerging from the underworld. It
blesses the frog taking refuge under the squash flower cloud, the stubborn
weeds leaning in the direction of the wind.

Clouds scheme and provoke a glitter of electricity.

THE NAMING

FOR HALEIGH SARA BUSH

I think of names that have profoundly changed the direction of disaster. Of 35
the raw whirling wind outlining femaleness emerging from the underworld.

It blesses the frog taking refuge under the squash-flower cloud, the stubborn weeds leaning in the direction of wind bringing rain.

My grandmother is the color of night as she tells me to move away from the
window when it is storming. *The lightning will take you.*

I thought it was my long dark hair appearing as lightning. The lightning appears to be relatives.

Truth can appear as disaster in a land of things unspoken. It can be reached
with white arrows, each outlining the meaning of delicate struggle.

And can happen on a night like this when the arrow light is bitten by sweet
wind.

My grandmother took leave years ago by way of her aggravated heart. I
haven't seen her since, but her warnings against drownings, lightning or anything else portending death by sudden means still cling to my ears.

I take those risks against the current of warnings as if she had invented negative space of wind around the curve of earth.

That night after my granddaughter-born-for-my-son climbed from the underworld we could smell ozone over the lake made of a few centuries of rain.

I went hunting for the right name and found the spirit of the ice age making plans in the bottom of the lake. Eventually the spirit will become rain, remake the shoreline with pines and laughter.

In the rain I saw the child who was carried by lightning to the other side of the storm. I saw my grandmother who never had any peace in this life blessed with animals and songs.

Oh daughter-born-of-my-son, of my grandmother, of my mother; I name you all these things:

The bag of white arrows is heavy with rain.

The earth is wet with happiness.

I never liked my mother's mother, Leona May Baker. When we would visit her and my grandfather in their two-room house in northwestern Arkansas where they were sharecroppers, she would awaken me long before dawn. I would be irritable with lack of sleep as she would sit by my bed and catalogue the gruesome details of every death of every relative and friend as well as each event of personal disaster within her known landscape.

My grandmother, who was half Cherokee and Irish, was orphaned at a very young age and raised by full-blood Cherokees in Jay, Oklahoma. She gave birth to six sons and one daughter—my mother. Each birth added to the burden of life. Once she took out a gun and shot at all of them as they ran through the trees to get away from her. My mother recalls the sounds of bullets flying by her head. My grandmother disliked my mother.

With the impending birth of my son's daughter I was prompted to find out more about this grandmother who I had never made peace with. My mother told me of her incredible gift of storytelling, how she would keep the children entranced for weeks by tales she would invent—they had no books, television or radio. And then she told me this story:

My grandfather Desmond Baker left to work on the railroad when they were especially destitute. While he was away my grandmother had an affair. When he returned nine months later she was near full term with a baby who wasn't his. He beat her until she went into labor and gave birth to the murdered child.

Shortly after the killing my grandparents attempted double suicide. They stood 40
on the tracks while a train bore down on them as all the children watched in hor-
ror. At the last possible second my grandfather pushed my grandmother off to
safety and leaped behind her.

I began to have compassion for this woman who was weighted down with
seven children and no opportunities. Maybe her affair was the lightness she needed
to stay alive.

When my granddaughter Haleigh was born I felt the spirit of this grandmother
in the hospital room. Her presence was a blessing.

I welcomed her.

- The spirit who came to take care of my heart
- The eating and sculpting with shit episode
- Relentless toilet training
- Polio scare and hospital:
      separation
      spinal tap
- Father in jail
- Father chopping the Christmas tree top off with an ax in the living room
- My brother's birth
- My mother's scarlet fever. I am sent far away to relatives I dislike. They take my stuffed black cat away from me and try to replace it with a doll. I am bereft.
- The "following sound" revelation, set off by a trumpet jazz solo on the radio as I am just learning language.
- Difficult birth and separation
- Sun mote language
- Sexual play retribution in public
- Stomach aches, throwing up and castor-oil
- I begin hiding from my father
- Carried home from parents' parties wrapped in my father's brown leather jacket, smells of her perfume White Shoulders
- The babysitter scene, a house at night filled with strange and frightened children cared for by an elderly man and woman. I am terrified. They put me to bed in a crib. My friend Ronnie, whose parents beat him for wetting his pants, comforts me.

3/23/94

My father, too, continued to drink. His white co-workers called him "chief." He 45
just drank off the sting. . . . My parents both liked to dance and party and some of
my favorite memories the few years just before the birth of my sister was being a
child running with other children at these parties. And carried to the car after I'd
fallen asleep, wrapped in the leather bomber jacket that had been my father's but
taken over by my mother. It smelled of White Shoulders and tobacco. The smell

was home to me, and it was comforting to be carried in, tucked into my Army cot to sleep. I could feel the tenderness well up in my parents as they looked at me, as I feigned sleep. . . . His violence became a thick monster whirling through the rooms of the house. I saw this thing once as it pounded on the front door on Saturday afternoon. My mother grabbed up my little brother and me and we hid in the back bedroom.

4/8/94

Certain numbers chase you through life. The house I was raised in until I was eight was number 419. (Later we moved into a house that had so many traumatic experiences I could not find it when I went back a few years ago, though I knew the street and the number. It was there, though I could not see it. My mother now rented it out.) Nearly forty years later I was picked up at the airport in Albuquerque, from Tucson, by an old friend for a reading to be held at the law school the next afternoon. It was a perfect spring night and my blood went excited at the familiar smell of the land to which I returned as a relative. My blood also felt the halo of impact preceding a life changing event. When I read the address to the house to which I'd been invited for a little wine and talk before retiring, I knew something would change. The house number was distinctly 419. . . . I soon lived in that house. It became the home I had been approaching for many years.

W. H. Auden " . . . poetry makes nothing happen; it survives."

3/24/94 (IN BETWEEN ALBUQUERQUE AND CHICAGO)

What was certain was a sensitivity that crackled and burned. I could hear words and the roots of words veering from the base of silence. I wonder where my father is now in the stream of all things that once had a place here? Does he think of me or of the tragedy of connection? Did he ever experience beauty from the inside out? There's a dinosaur under the house, and other bones of those who once walked the surface of the planet, like my father. I've considered this planet as a prison, a school for the hard headed. . . . What comes back to me is the result of my actions for instance—fury begets fury. The form may change. Hatred is self-hatred, though it may mask as xenophobia or other forms of fear and aggression.

1/26/94

In this dream Rainy, Sue and I walk under a huge overpass to watch the planes taking off and landing at an airport about the size of LAX. We are so close it is frightening. One plane falters, then goes down. It is absolutely terrifying, particularly to listen as the breaking apart metal monster slides across the grass towards us. We run hard away from it, in anticipation of the explosion. I've dreamed many variations of this scene. It's always just as horrifying.

2/7/94

Sandra Cisneros is holding a turtle. I am aware that turtles can snap, bite hard,   50
but this turtle reaches out his head to nudge me. The turtle then turns into a
baby boy in a high chair. Or he appears to be a baby boy in a high chair. He's
pissed because he's a fully conscious human in a baby's body. I tell him he can
pass as a dwarf once he can walk.

7/26/94

To be born into a family of mixed nations, involving alliances and enmities
from time immemorial, in a land of refugees from persecution in Europe, the
Americas, Asia and anywhere else there are evil governments and religious fun-
damentalists who mete out destiny, or of forced slavery over an ocean turned
red from the blood of those who didn't survive, or moved from homelands
against the will of the tribes—the land on which all are to be settled amicably
into a "melting pot"—is to be disturbed and shaped by the spirits of ancestors
who fight it out among themselves in the world intersecting the physical, who
cannot rest because the direct track to the original heart has been lost, (and it's
easy to get distracted by neon, fast food and the appearance of nude bodies on
billboards), as well as fiercely loved and guarded by those who see themselves in
you, a promise for continuance when continuance is a myth buried in libraries
and in stories told under the stars in sacred languages that have been kept burning by sheer will, sheer love.

SOMETIME EARLIER

I was the first born, arrived with great difficulty to this tempestuous love, this
shakey sea. I was born during a new moon, a moon that represents new beginnings, the direction East. East is the harbor for those spirits who point us on
our journey. East is the direction of our tribal homelands, the place of forced
exile not but a few generations ago—in the southeast of this continent, made
of nearly tropical foliage, water, and thick with animal power. My birth contradicted the prediction of destruction, the myth of the vanishing Indian that
was bought and sold by the American public, for if we disappeared guilt would
vanish, and the right to the land by strangers would be sealed. Though we lost
over half the tribe during the forced walk from a land that had nurtured our
people through millennia, we didn't die. I was the next loop in the spiral of
memory.

ACTIVITIES FOR WRITING AND DISCUSSION

1. Harjo writes, "I keep a journal and pen by my bed for dreams. . . . Often I
write in my journal while I am still quite asleep." Following Harjo's example,

keep a notepad at your bedside for jotting down dreams or thoughts you have in the middle of the night.

2. Harjo compares rereading her journal to "fishing. Sometimes I see something that totally surprises." Ponder this comparison. Does it jibe with any experiences you have had rereading your own notebook or journal? Explain.

3. While the bulk of your writer's notebook naturally consists of your own writing, Harjo's mention of newspaper articles in the pages of her journal suggests the possibility of including other materials as well, such as photographs, clippings, memorabilia, song lyrics, and drawings. Experiment with incorporating these or any other alternative materials into your notebook. What are the benefits?

4. Respond to Harjo's journal selections using any of the "Generic Ideas for Writing" found on page 275.

Experience and Identity

18

Short Stories

D. H. LAWRENCE (1885–1930)

The Rocking-Horse Winner

There was a woman who was beautiful, who started with all the advantages, 1
yet she had no luck. She married for love, and the love turned to dust. She
had bonny children, yet she felt they had been thrust upon her, and she could
not love them. They looked at her coldly, as if they were finding fault with her.
And hurriedly she felt she must cover up some fault in herself. Yet what it was
that she must cover up she never knew. Nevertheless, when her children were
present, she always felt the centre of her heart go hard. This troubled her, and in
her manner she was all the more gentle and anxious for her children, as if she
loved them very much. Only she herself knew that at the centre of her heart was
a hard little place that could not feel love, no, not for anybody. Everybody else
said of her: "She is such a good mother. She adores her children." Only she herself, and her children themselves, knew it was not so. They read it in each
other's eyes.

There were a boy and two little girls. They lived in a pleasant house, with a 2
garden, and they had discreet servants, and felt themselves superior to anyone
in the neighbourhood.

Although they lived in style, they felt always an anxiety in the house. There 3
was never enough money. The mother had a small income, and the father had a
small income, but not nearly enough for the social position which they had to
keep up. The father went into town to some office. But though he had good
prospects, these prospects never materialised. There was always the grinding
sense of the shortage of money, though the style was always kept up.

At last the mother said: "I will see if *I* can't make something." But she did   4
not know where to begin. She racked her brains, and tried this thing and the
other, but could not find anything successful. The failure made deep lines come
into her face. Her children were growing up, they would have to go to school.
There must be more money, there must be more money. The father, who was
always very handsome and expensive in his tastes, seemed as if he never *would*
be able to do anything worth doing. And the mother, who had a great belief in
herself, did not succeed any better, and her tastes were just as expensive.

And so the house came to be haunted by the unspoken phrase: *There must*   5
be more money! There must be more money! The children could hear it all the
time, though nobody said it aloud. They heard it at Christmas, when the expensive and splendid toys filled the nursery. Behind the shining modern rocking-
horse, behind the smart doll's house, a voice would start whispering: "There
must be more money! There *must* be more money!" And the children would
stop playing, to listen for a moment. They would look into each other's eyes, to
see if they had all heard. And each one saw in the eyes of the other two that they
too had heard. "There *must* be more money! There *must* be more money!"

It came whispering from the springs of the still-swaying rocking-horse, and   6
even the horse, bending his wooden, champing head, heard it. The big doll, sitting so pink and smirking in her new pram, could hear it quite plainly, and
seemed to be smirking all the more self-consciously because of it. The foolish
puppy, too, that took the place of the teddy-bear, he was looking so extraordinarily foolish for no other reason but that he heard the secret whisper all over
the house: "There *must* be more money!"

Yet nobody ever said it aloud. The whisper was everywhere, and therefore   7
no one spoke it. Just as no one ever says: "We are breathing!" in spite of the fact
that breath is coming and going all the time.

"Mother," said the boy Paul one day, "Why don't we keep a car of our own?   8
Why do we always use uncle's, or else a taxi?"

"Because we're the poor members of the family," said the mother.   9

"But why *are* we, mother?"   10

"Well—I suppose," she said slowly and bitterly, "it's because your father has   11
no luck."

The boy was silent for some time.   12

"Is luck money, mother?" he asked, rather timidly.   13

"No, Paul. Not quite. It's what causes you to have money."   14

"Oh!" said Paul vaguely. "I thought when Uncle Oscar said *filthy lucker*, it   15
meant money."

"*Filthy lucre* does mean money," said the mother. "But it's lucre, not luck."   16

"Oh!" said the boy. "Then what *is* luck, mother?"   17

"It's what causes you to have money. If you're lucky you have money. That's   18
why it's better to be born lucky than rich. If you're rich, you may lose your
money. But if you're lucky, you will always get more money."

"Oh! Will you? And is father not lucky?"   19

"Very unlucky, I should say," she said bitterly.   20

The boy watched her with unsure eyes.   21

"Why?" he asked.   22

"I don't know. Nobody ever knows why one person is lucky and another   23
unlucky."

"Don't they? Nobody at all? Does *nobody* know?"   24

"Perhaps God. But He never tells."   25

"He ought to, then. And aren't you lucky either, mother?"   26

"I can't be, if I married an unlucky husband."   27

"But by yourself, aren't you?"   28

"I used to think I was, before I married. Now I think I am very unlucky   29
indeed."

"Why?"   30

"Well—never mind! Perhaps I'm not really," she said.   31

The child looked at her to see if she meant it. But he saw, by the lines of her   32
mouth, that she was only trying to hide something from him.

"Well, anyhow," he said stoutly, "I'm a lucky person."   33

"Why?" said his mother, with a sudden laugh.   34

He stared at her. He didn't even know why he had said it.   35

"God told me," he asserted, brazening it out.   36

"I hope He did, dear!" she said, again with a laugh, but rather bitter.   37

"He did, mother!"   38

"Excellent!" said the mother, using one of her husband's exclamations.   39

The boy saw she did not believe him; or rather, that she paid no attention to   40
his assertion. This angered him somewhat, and made him want to compel her
attention.

He went off by himself, vaguely, in a childish way, seeking for the clue to   41
"luck." Absorbed, taking no heed of other people, he went about with a sort of
stealth, seeking inwardly for luck. He wanted luck, he wanted it, he wanted it.
When the two girls were playing dolls in the nursery, he would sit on his big
rocking-horse, charging madly into space, with a frenzy that made the little
girls peer at him uneasily. Wildly the horse careered, the waving dark hair of the
boy tossed, his eyes had a strange glare in them. The little girls dared not speak
to him.

When he had ridden to the end of his mad little journey, he climbed down   42
and stood in front of his rocking-horse, staring fixedly into its lowered face. Its
red mouth was slightly open, its big eye was wide and glassy-bright.

"Now!" he would silently command the snorting steed. "Now, take me to   43
where there is luck! Now take me!"

And he would slash the horse on the neck with the little whip he had asked   44
Uncle Oscar for. He *knew* the horse could take him to where there was luck, if
only he forced it. So he would mount again and start on his furious ride, hoping
at last to get there. He knew he could get there.

"You'll break your horse, Paul!" said the nurse.   45

"He's always riding like that! I wish he'd leave off!" said his elder sister Joan.   46

But he only glared down on them in silence. Nurse gave him up. She could 47 make nothing of him. Anyhow, he was growing beyond her.

One day his mother and his Uncle Oscar came in when he was on one of his 48 furious rides. He did not speak to them.

"Hallo, you young jockey! Riding a winner?" said his uncle. 49

"Aren't you growing too big for a rocking-horse? You're not a very little boy 50 any longer, you know," said his mother.

But Paul only gave a blue glare from his big, rather close-set eyes. He would 51 speak to nobody when he was in full tilt. His mother watched him with an anxious expression on her face.

At last he suddenly stopped forcing his horse into the mechanical gallop 52 and slid down.

"Well, I got there!" he announced fiercely, his blue eyes still flaring, and his 53 sturdy long legs straddling apart.

"Where did you get to?" asked his mother. 54

"Where I wanted to go," he flared back at her. 55

"That's right, son!" said Uncle Oscar. "Don't you stop till you get there. 56 What's the horse's name?"

"He doesn't have a name," said the boy. 57

"Gets on without all right?" asked the uncle. 58

"Well, he has different names. He was called Sansovino last week." 59

"Sansovino, eh? Won the Ascot. How did you know this name?" 60

"He always talks about horse-races with Bassett," said Joan. 61

The uncle was delighted to find that his small nephew was posted with all 62 the racing news. Bassett, the young gardener, who had been wounded in the left foot in the war and had got his present job through Oscar Cresswell, whose batman he had been, was a perfect blade of the "turf." He lived in the racing events, and the small boy lived with him.

Oscar Cresswell got it all from Bassett. 63

"Master Paul comes and asks me, so I can't do more than tell him, sir," said 64 Bassett, his face terribly serious, as if he were speaking of religious matters.

"And does he ever put anything on a horse he fancies?" 65

"Well—I don't want to give him away—he's a young sport, a fine sport, sir. 66 Would you mind asking him yourself? He sort of takes a pleasure in it, and perhaps he'd feel I was giving him away, sir, if you don't mind."

Bassett was serious as a church. 67

The uncle went back to his nephew and took him off for a ride in the car. 68

"Say, Paul, old man, do you ever put anything on a horse?" the uncle asked. 69

The boy watched the handsome man closely. 70

"Why, do you think I oughtn't to?" he parried. 71

"Not a bit of it! I thought perhaps you might give me a tip for the Lincoln." 72

The car sped on into the country, going down to Uncle Oscar's place in 73 Hampshire.

"Honour bright?" said the nephew. 74

"Honour bright, son!" said the uncle.   75

"Well, then, Daffodil."   76

"Daffodil! I doubt it, sonny. What about Mirza?"   77

"I only know the winner," said the boy. "That's Daffodil."   78

"Daffodil, eh?"   79

There was a pause. Daffodil was an obscure horse comparatively.   80

"Uncle!"   81

"Yes, son?"   82

"You won't let it go any further, will you? I promised Bassett."   83

"Bassett be damned, old man! What's he got to do with it?"   84

"We're partners. We've been partners from the first. Uncle, he lent me my   85
first five shillings, which I lost. I promised him, honour bright, it was only between me and him; only you gave me that ten-shilling note I started winning with, so I thought you were lucky. You won't let it go any further, will you?"

The boy gazed at his uncle from those big, hot, blue eyes, set rather close to-   86
gether. The uncle stirred and laughed uneasily.

"Right you are, son! I'll keep your tip private. Daffodil, eh? How much are   87
you putting on him?"

"All except twenty pounds," said the boy. "I keep that in reserve."   88

The uncle thought it a good joke.   89

"You keep twenty pounds in reserve, do you, you young romancer? What   90
are you betting, then?"

"I'm betting three hundred," said the boy gravely. "But it's between you and   91
me, Uncle Oscar! Honour bright?"

The uncle burst into a roar of laughter.   92

"It's between you and me all right, you young Nat Gould," he said, laughing.   93
"But where's your three hundred?"

"Bassett keeps it for me. We're partners."   94

"You are, are you! And what is Bassett putting on Daffodil?"   95

"He won't go quite as high as I do, I expect. Perhaps he'll go a hundred and   96
fifty."

"What, pennies?" laughed the uncle.   97

"Pounds," said the child, with a surprised look at his uncle. "Bassett keeps a   98
bigger reserve than I do."

Between wonder and amusement Uncle Oscar was silent. He pursued the   99
matter no further, but he determined to take his nephew with him to the Lincoln races.

"Now, son," he said, "I'm putting twenty on Mirza, and I'll put five on for   100
you on any horse you fancy. What's your pick?"

"Daffodil, uncle."   101

"No, not the fiver on Daffodil!"   102

"I should if it was my own fiver," said the child.   103

"Good! Good! Right you are! A fiver for me and a fiver for you on Daffodil."   104

The child had never been to a race-meeting before, and his eyes were blue   105
fire. He pursed his mouth tight and watched. A Frenchman just in front had put

his money on Lancelot. Wild with excitement, he flayed his arms up and down, yelling *"Lancelot! Lancelot!"* in his French accent.

Daffodil came in first, Lancelot second, Mirza third. The child, flushed and 106 with eyes blazing, was curiously serene. His uncle brought him four five-pound notes, four to one.

"What am I to do with these?" he cried, waving them before the boy's eyes. 107

"I suppose we'll talk to Bassett," said the boy. "I expect I have fifteen hun- 108 dred now; and twenty in reserve; and this twenty."

His uncle studied him for some moments. 109

"Look here, son!" he said. "You're not serious about Bassett and that fifteen 110 hundred, are you?"

"Yes, I am. But it's between you and me, uncle. Honour bright?" 111

"Honour bright all right, son! But I must talk to Bassett." 112

"If you'd like to be a partner, uncle, with Bassett and me, we could all be 113 partners. Only, you'd have to promise, honour bright, uncle, not to let it go be-yond us three. Bassett and I are lucky, and you must be lucky, because it was your ten shillings I started winning with. . . . "

Uncle Oscar took both Bassett and Paul into Richmond Park for an after- 114 noon, and there they talked.

"It's like this, you see, sir," Bassett said. "Master Paul would get me talking 115 about racing events, spinning yarns, you know, sir. And he was always keen on knowing if I'd made or if I'd lost. It's about a year since, now, that I put five shillings on Blush of Dawn for him; and we lost. Then the luck turned, with that ten shillings he had from you: that we put on Singhalese. And since that time, it's been pretty steady, all things considering. What do you say, Master Paul?"

"We're all right when we're sure," said Paul. "It's when we're not quite sure 116 that we go down."

"Oh, but we're careful then," said Bassett. 117

"But when are you *sure*?" smiled Uncle Oscar. 118

"It's Master Paul, sir," said Bassett in a secret, religious voice. "It's as if he 119 had it from heaven. Like Daffodil, now, for the Lincoln. That was as sure as eggs."

"Did you put anything on Daffodil?" asked Oscar Cresswell. 120

"Yes, sir. I made my bet." 121

"And my nephew?" 122

Bassett was obstinately silent, looking at Paul. 123

"I made twelve hundred, didn't I, Bassett? I told uncle I was putting three 124 hundred on Daffodil."

"That's right," said Bassett, nodding. 125

"But where's the money?" asked the uncle. 126

"I keep it safe locked up, sir. Master Paul he can have it any minute he likes 127 to ask for it."

"What, fifteen hundred pounds?" 128

"And twenty! And *forty,* that is, with the twenty he made on the course." 129

"It's amazing!" said the uncle.   130

"If Master Paul offers you to be partners, sir, I would, if I were you: if you'll 131
excuse me," said Bassett.

Oscar Creswell thought about it.   132

"I'll see the money," he said.   133

They drove home again, and, sure enough, Bassett came round to the gar- 134
den-house with fifteen hundred pounds in notes. The twenty pounds reserve
was left with Joe Glee, in the Turf Commission deposit.

"You see, it's all right, uncle, when I'm *sure*! Then we go strong, for all we're 135
worth. Don't we, Bassett?"

"We do that, Master Paul."   136

"And when are you sure?" said the uncle, laughing.   137

"Oh, well, sometimes I'm *absolutely* sure, like about Daffodil," said the boy; 138
"and sometimes I have an idea; and sometimes I haven't even an idea, have I,
Bassett? Then we're careful, because we mostly go down."

"You do, do you! And when you're sure, like about Daffodil, what makes you 139
sure, sonny?"

"Oh, well, I don't know," said the boy uneasily. "I'm sure, you know, uncle; 140
that's all."

"It's as if he had it from heaven, sir," Bassett reiterated.   141

"I should say so!" said the uncle.   142

But he became a partner. And when the Leger was coming on Paul was 143
"sure" about Lively Spark, which was a quite inconsiderable horse. The boy insisted on putting a thousand on the horse, Bassett went for five hundred, and
Oscar Cresswell two hundred. Lively Spark came in first, and the betting had
been ten to one against him. Paul had made ten thousand.

"You see," he said, "I was absolutely sure of him."   144

Even Oscar Cresswell had cleared two thousand.   145

"Look here, son," he said, "this sort of thing makes me nervous."   146

"It needn't, uncle! Perhaps I shan't be sure again for a long time."   147

"But what are you going to do with your money?" asked the uncle.   148

"Of course," said the boy, "I started it for mother. She said she had no luck, 149
because father is unlucky, so I thought if *I* was lucky, it might stop whispering."

"What might stop whispering?"   150

"Our house. I *hate* our house for whispering."   151

"What does it whisper?"   152

"Why—why"—the boy fidgeted—"why, I don't know. But it's always short 153
of money, you know, uncle."

"I know it, son, I know it."   154

"You know people send mother writs, don't you, uncle?"   155

"I'm afraid I do," said the uncle.   156

"And then the house whispers, like people laughing at you behind your 157
back. It's awful, that is! I thought if I was lucky _____"

You might stop it," added the uncle.   158

The boy watched him with big blue eyes, that had an uncanny cold fire in 159
them, and he said never a word.

"Well, then!" said the uncle. "What are we doing?"   160

"I shouldn't like mother to know I was lucky," said the boy.   161

"Why not, son?"   162

"She'd stop me."   163

"I don't think she would."   164

"Oh!"—and the boy writhed in an odd way—"I *don't* want her to know, 165
uncle."

"All right son! We'll manage it without her knowing."   166

They managed it very easily. Paul, at the other's suggestion, handed over five 167
thousand pounds to his uncle, who deposited it with the family lawyer, who
was then to inform Paul's mother that a relative had put five thousand pounds
into his hands, which sum was to be paid out a thousand pounds at a time, on
the mother's birthday, for the next five years.

"So she'll have a birthday present of a thousand pounds for five successive 168
years," said Uncle Oscar. "I hope it won't make it all the harder for her later."

Paul's mother had her birthday in November. The house had been "whis- 169
pering" worse than ever lately, and, even in spite of his luck, Paul could not bear
up against it. He was very anxious to see the effect of the birthday letter, telling
his mother about the thousand pounds.

When there were no visitors, Paul now took his meals with his parents, as he 170
was beyond the nursery control. His mother went into town nearly every day.
She had discovered that she had an odd knack of sketching furs and dress materials, so she worked secretly in the studio of a friend who was the chief "artist"
for the leading drapers. She drew the figures of ladies in furs and ladies in silk
and sequins for the newspaper advertisements. This young woman artist
earned several thousand pounds a year, but Paul's mother only made several
hundred, and she was again dissatisfied. She so wanted to be first in something,
and she did not succeed, even in making sketches for drapery advertisements.

She was down to breakfast on the morning of her birthday. Paul watched 171
her face as she read her letters. He knew the lawyer's letter. As his mother read
it, her face hardened and became more expressionless. Then a cold, determined
look came on her mouth. She hid the letter under the pile of others, and said
not a word about it.

"Didn't you have anything nice in the post for your birthday, mother?" said 172
Paul.

"Quite moderately nice," she said, her voice cold and absent.   173

She went away to town without saying more.   174

But in the afternoon Uncle Oscar appeared. He said Paul's mother had had a 175
long interview with the lawyer, asking if the whole five thousand could not be
advanced at once, as she was in debt.

"What do you think, uncle?" said the boy.   176

"I leave it to you, son."   177

"Oh, let her have it, then! We can get some more with the other," said the 178
boy.

"A bird in the hand is worth two in the bush, laddie!" said Uncle Oscar.   179

"But I'm sure to *know* for the Grand National; or the Lincolnshire; or else 180
the Derby. I'm sure to know for *one* of them," said Paul.

So Uncle Oscar signed the agreement, and Paul's mother touched the whole 181
five thousand. Then something very curious happened. The voices in the house
suddenly went mad, like a chorus of frogs on a spring evening. There were certain new furnishings, and Paul had a tutor. He was *really* going to Eton, his father's school, in the following autumn. There were flowers in the winter, and a
blossoming of the luxury Paul's mother had been used to. And yet the voices in
the house, behind the sprays of mimosa and almond blossom, and from under
the piles of iridescent cushions, simply trilled and screamed in a sort of ecstasy:
"There *must* be more money! Oh-h-h; there *must* be more money. Oh, now,
now-w! Now-w-w—there *must* be more money!—more than ever! More than
ever!"

It frightened Paul terribly. He studied away at his Latin and Greek with his 182
tutor. But his intense hours were spent with Bassett. The Grand National had
gone by: he had not "known," and had lost a hundred pounds. Summer was at
hand. He was in agony for the Lincoln. But even for the Lincoln he didn't
"know," and he lost fifty pounds. He became wild-eyed and strange, as if something were going to explode in him.

"Let it alone, son! Don't you bother about it!" urged Uncle Oscar. But it was 183
as if the boy couldn't really hear what his uncle was saying.

"I've got to know for the Derby! I've got to know for the Derby!" the child 184
reiterated, his big blue eyes blazing with a sort of madness.

His mother noticed how overwrought he was.   185

"You'd better go to the seaside. Wouldn't you like to go now to the seaside, 186
instead of waiting? I think you'd better," she said, looking down at him anxiously, her heart curiously heavy because of him.

But the child lifted his uncanny blue eyes.   187

"I couldn't possibly go before the Derby, mother!" he said. "I couldn't possi- 188
bly!"

"Why not?" she said, her voice becoming heavy when she was opposed. 189
"Why not? You can still go from the seaside to see the Derby with your Uncle
Oscar, if that's what you wish. No need for you to wait here. Besides, I think you
care too much about these races. It's a bad sign. My family has been a gambling
family, and you won't know till you grow up how much damage it has done. But
it has done damage. I shall have to send Bassett away, and ask Uncle Oscar not
to talk racing to you, unless you promise to be reasonable about it: go away to
the seaside and forget it. You're all nerves!"

"I'll do what you like, mother, so long as you don't send me away till after 190
the Derby," the boy said.

"Send you away from where? Just from this house?"   191

"Yes," he said, gazing at her. 192

"Why, you curious child, what makes you care about this house so much, 193
suddenly? I never knew you loved it."

He gazed at her without speaking. He had a secret within a secret, some- 194
thing he had not divulged, even to Bassett or to his Uncle Oscar.

But his mother, after standing undecided and a little bit sullen for some mo- 195
ments, said:

"Very well, then! Don't go to the seaside till after the Derby, if you don't 196
wish it. But promise me you won't let your nerves go to pieces. Promise you
won't think so much about horse-racing and *events,* as you call them!"

"Oh no," sad the boy casually. "I won't think much about them, mother. You 197
needn't worry. I wouldn't worry, mother, if I were you."

"If you were me and I were you," said his mother, "I wonder what we *should* 198
do!"

"But you know you needn't worry, mother, don't you?" the boy repeated. 199

"I should be awfully glad to know it," she said wearily. 200

"Oh, well, you *can,* you know. I mean, you *ought* to know you needn't 201
worry," he insisted.

"Ought I? Then I'll see about it," she said. 202

Paul's secret of secrets was his wooden horse, that which had no name. 203
Since he was emancipated from a nurse and a nursery-governess, he had had
his rocking-horse removed to his own bedroom at the top of the house.

"Surely you're too big for a rocking-horse!" his mother had remonstrated. 204

"Well, you see, mother, till I can have a *real* horse, I like to have *some* sort of 205
animal about," had been his quaint answer.

"Do you feel he keeps you company?" she laughed. 206

"Oh yes! He's very good, he always keeps me company, when I'm there," said 207
Paul.

So the horse, rather shabby, stood in an arrested prance in the boy's bed- 208
room.

The Derby was drawing near, and the boy grew more and more tense. He 209
hardly heard what was spoken to him, he was very frail, and his eyes were really
uncanny. His mother had sudden strange seizures of uneasiness about him.
Sometimes, for half an hour, she would feel a sudden anxiety about him that
was almost anguish. She wanted to rush to him at once, and know he was safe.

Two nights before the Derby, she was at a big party in town, when one of her 210
rushes of anxiety about her boy, her first-born, gripped her heart till she could
hardly speak. She fought with the feeling, might and main, for she believed in
common sense. But it was too strong. She had to leave the dance and go downstairs to telephone to the country. The children's nursery-governess was terribly
surprised and startled at being rung up in the night.

"Are the children all right, Miss Wilmot?" 211

"Oh yes, they are quite all right." 212

"Master Paul? Is he all right?" 213

"He went to bed as right as a trivet. Shall I run up and look at him?"   214

"No," said Paul's mother reluctantly. "No! Don't trouble. It's all right. Don't   215
sit up. We shall be home fairly soon." She did not want her son's privacy intruded upon.

"Very good," said the governess.   216

It was about one o'clock when Paul's mother and father drove up to their   217
house. All was still. Paul's mother went to her room and slipped off her white
fur cloak. She had told her maid not to wait up for her. She heard her husband
downstairs, mixing a whisky and soda.

And then, because of the strange anxiety at her heart, she stole upstairs to   218
her son's room. Noiselessly she went along the upper corridor. Was there a faint
noise? What was it?

She stood, with arrested muscles, outside his door, listening. There was a   219
strange, heavy, and yet not loud noise. Her heart stood still. It was a soundless
noise, yet rushing and powerful. Something huge, in violent, hushed motion.
What was it? What in God's name was it? She ought to know. She felt that she
knew the noise. She knew what it was.

Yet she could not place it. She couldn't say what it was. And on and on it   220
went, like a madness.

Softly, frozen with anxiety and fear, she turned the doorhandle.   221

The room was dark. Yet in the space near the window, she heard and saw   222
something plunging to and fro. She gazed in fear and amazement.

Then suddenly she switched on the light, and saw her son, in his green pyja-   223
mas, madly surging on the rocking-horse. The blaze of light suddenly lit him
up, as he urged the wooden horse, and lit her up, as she stood, blonde, in her
dress of pale green and crystal, in the doorway.

"Paul!" she cried. "Whatever are you doing?"   224

"It's Malabar!" he screamed in a powerful, strange voice. "It's Malabar!"   225

His eyes blazed at her for one strange and senseless second, as he ceased   226
urging his wooden horse. Then he fell with a crash to the ground, and she, all
her tormented motherhood flooding upon her, rushed to gather him up.

But he was unconscious, and unconscious he remained, with some brain-   227
fever. He talked and tossed, and his mother sat stonily by his side.

"Malabar! It's Malabar! Bassett, Bassett, I *know!* It's Malabar!"   228

So the child cried, trying to get up and urge the rocking-horse that gave him   229
his inspiration.

"What does he mean by Malabar?" asked the heart-frozen mother.   230

"I don't know," said the father stonily.   231

"What does he mean by Malabar?" she asked her brother Oscar.   232

"It's one of the horses running for the Derby," was the answer.   233

And, in spite of himself, Oscar Cresswell spoke to Bassett, and himself put a   234
thousand on Malabar: at fourteen to one.

The third day of the illness was critical: they were waiting for a change. The   235
boy, with his rather long, curly hair, was tossing ceaselessly on the pillow. He

neither slept nor regained consciousness, and his eyes were like blue stones. His mother sat, feeling her heart had gone, turned actually into a stone.

In the evening, Oscar Cresswell did not come, but Bassett sent a message, 236 saying could he come up for one moment, just one moment? Paul's mother was very angry at the intrusion, but on second thought she agreed. The boy was the same. Perhaps Bassett might bring him to consciousness.

The gardener, a shortish fellow with a little brown moustache and sharp lit- 237 tle brown eyes, tiptoed into the room, touched his imaginary cap to Paul's mother, and stole to the bedside, staring with glittering, smallish eyes at the tossing, dying child.

"Master Paul!" he whispered. "Master Paul! Malabar came in first all right, a 238 clean win. I did as you told me. You've made over seventy thousand pounds, you have; you've got over eighty thousand. Malabar came in all right, Master Paul."

"Malabar! Malabar! Did I say Malabar, mother? Did I say Malabar? Do you 239 think I'm lucky, mother? I knew Malabar, didn't I? Over eighty thousand pounds! I call that lucky, don't you, mother? Over eighty thousand pounds? I knew, didn't I know I knew? Malabar came in all right. If I ride my horse till I'm sure, then I tell you, Bassett, you can go as high as you like. Did you go for all you were worth, Bassett?"

"I went a thousand on it, Master Paul."   240

"I never told you, mother, that if I can ride my horse, and *get there*, then I'm 241 absolutely sure—oh, absolutely! Mother, did I ever tell you? I *am* lucky!"

"No, you never did," said his mother.   242

But the boy died in the night.   243

And even as he lay dead, his mother heard her brother's voice saying to her: 244 "My God, Hester, you're eighty-odd thousand to the good, and a poor devil of a son to the bad. But, poor devil, poor devil, he's best gone out of a life where he rides his rocking-horse to find a winner."

ACTIVITIES FOR WRITING AND DISCUSSION

1. Annotate the story, and write a notebook response using any of the "Ten Ideas for Writing" summarized on page 35.

2. Reread the opening paragraphs which introduce Paul's family. What problems does the family have? What's missing from their lives? Working alone or collaboratively, take some time to jot down your responses to these questions. Then, working from details and background furnished by the opening paragraphs and your own imagination, write a prequel to the story in which you relate the family's previous history leading up to the events in the story.

3. Why do the voices ("There *must* be more money!") actually *worsen* when more money arrives (paragraph 181)? Imagine you are D.H. Lawrence, and you

want to revise the story to *silence* the voices. Imagine the revision required; then make it.

4. Inanimate objects in this story are treated as lifelike—the house (with its voices), the rocking-horse, "the big doll" (paragraph 6). Why does Lawrence do this, and what impact does this have on the characters and on you as a reader? Respond to this question. Then write a **monologue** from the point of view of the voices in the house or the rocking-horse in which you tell your own story (where you came from, what you signify) and comment on the characters and events in the story. *Alternative:* Write from the point of view of the *money* Paul wins.

KATHERINE MANSFIELD (1888–1923)

Her First Ball

Exactly when the ball began Leila would have found it hard to say. Perhaps her   1
first real partner was the cab. It did not matter that she shared the cab with the Sheridan girls and their brother. She sat back in her own little corner of it, and the bolster on which her hand rested felt like the sleeve of an unknown young man's dress suit; and away they bowled, past waltzing lampposts and houses and fences and trees.

"Have you really never been to a ball before, Leila? But, my child, how too   2
weird—" cried the Sheridan girls.

"Our nearest neighbor was fifteen miles," said Leila softly, gently opening   3
and shutting her fan.

Oh, dear, how hard it was to be indifferent like the others! She tried not to   4
smile too much; she tried not to care. But every single thing was so new and exciting . . . Meg's tuberoses, Jose's long loop of amber, Laura's little dark head, pushing above her white fur like a flower through snow. She would remember for ever. It even gave her a pang to see her cousin Laurie throw away the wisps of tissue paper he pulled from the fastening of his new gloves. She would like to have kept those wisps as a keepsake, as a remembrance. Laurie leaned forward and put his hand on Laura's knee.

"Look here, darling," he said. "The third and the ninth as usual. Twig?"   5

Oh, how marvellous to have a brother! In her excitement Leila felt that if   6
there had been time, if it hadn't been impossible, she couldn't have helped crying because she was an only child, and no brother had ever said "Twig?" to her; no sister would ever say, as Meg said to Jose that moment, "I've never known your hair go up more successfully than it has tonight!"

But, of course, there was no time. They were at the drill hall already; there   7
were cabs in front of them and cabs behind. The road was bright on either side with moving fan-like lights, and on the pavement gay couples seemed to float through the air; little satin shoes chased each other like birds.

"Hold on to me, Leila; you'll get lost," said Laura.   8

"Come on, girls, let's make a dash for it," said Laurie.   9

Leila put two fingers on Laura's pink velvet cloak, and they were somehow 10
lifted past the big gold lantern, carried along the passage, and pushed into the
little room marked "Ladies." Here the crowd was so great there was hardly space
to take off their things; the noise was deafening. Two benches on either side
were stacked high with wraps. Two old women in white aprons ran up and
down tossing fresh armfuls. And everybody was pressing forward trying to get
at the little dressing table and mirror at the far end.

A great quivering jet of gas lighted the ladies' room. It couldn't wait; it was 11
dancing already. When the door opened again and there came a burst of tuning
from the drill hall, it leaped almost to the ceiling.

Dark girls, fair girls were patting their hair, tying ribbons again, tucking 12
handkerchiefs down the front of their bodices, smoothing marble-white gloves.
And because they were all laughing it seemed to Leila that they were all lovely.

"Aren't there any invisible hairpins?" cried a voice. "How most extraordi- 13
nary! I can't see a single invisible hairpin."

"Powder my back, there's a darling," cried some one else.   14

"But I must have a needle and cotton. I've torn simply miles and miles of 15
the frill," wailed a third.

Then, "Pass them along, pass them along!" The straw basket of programs was 16
tossed from arm to arm. Darling little pink-and-silver programs, with pink pencils and fluffy tassels. Leila's fingers shook as she took one out of the basket. She
wanted to ask someone, "Am I meant to have one too?" but she had just time to
read: "Waltz 3. *Two, Two in a Canoe.* Polka 4. *Making the Feathers Fly,*" when Meg
cried, "Ready, Leila?" and they pressed their way through the crush in the passage towards the big double doors of the drill hall.

Dancing had not begun yet, but the band had stopped tuning, and the noise 17
was so great it seemed that when it did begin to play it would never be heard.
Leila, pressing close to Meg, looking over Meg's shoulder, felt that even the little
quivering colored flags strung across the ceiling were talking. She quite forgot
to be shy; she forgot how in the middle of dressing she had sat down on the bed
with one shoe off and one shoe on and begged her mother to ring up her
cousins and say she couldn't go after all. And the rush of longing she had had to
be sitting on the veranda of their forsaken upcountry home, listening to the
baby owls crying "More pork" in the moonlight, was changed to a rush of joy so
sweet that it was hard to bear alone. She clutched her fan, and, gazing at the
gleaming, golden floor, the azaleas, the lanterns, the stage at one end with its
red carpet and gilt chairs and the band in a corner, she thought breathlessly,
"How heavenly; how simply heavenly!"

All the girls stood grouped together at one side of the doors, the men at the 18
other, and the chaperones in dark dresses, smiling rather foolishly, walked with
little careful steps over the polished floor towards the stage.

"This is my little country cousin Leila. Be nice to her. Find her partners; 19
she's under my wing," said Meg, going up to one girl after another.

Strange faces smiled at Leila—sweetly, vaguely. Strange voices answered, 20
"Of course, my dear." But Leila felt the girls didn't really see her. They were
looking towards the men. Why didn't the men begin? What were they waiting
for? There they stood, smoothing their gloves, patting their glossy hair and
smiling among themselves. Then, quite suddenly, as if they had only just made
up their minds that that was what they had to do, the men came gliding over
the parquet. There was a joyful flutter among the girls. A tall, fair man flew up
to Meg, seized her program, scribbled something; Meg passed him on to Leila.
"May I have the pleasure?" He ducked and smiled. There came a dark man
wearing an eyeglass, then cousin Laurie with a friend, and Laura with a little
freckled fellow whose tie was crooked. Then quite an old man—fat, with a big
bald patch on his head—took her program and murmured, "Let me see, let me
see!" And he was a long time comparing his program, which looked black with
names, with hers. It seemed to give him so much trouble that Leila was
ashamed. "Oh, please don't bother," she said eagerly. But instead of replying the
fat man wrote something, glanced at her again. "Do I remember this bright little face?" he said softly. "Is it known to me of yore?" At that moment the band
began playing; the fat man disappeared. He was tossed away on a great wave of
music that came flying over the gleaming floor, breaking the groups up into
couples, scattering them, sending them spinning. . . .

Leila had learned to dance at boarding school. Every Saturday afternoon the 21
boarders were hurried off to a little corrugated iron mission hall where Miss
Eccles (of London) held her "select" classes. But the difference between that
dusty-smelling hall—with calico texts on the walls, the poor terrified little
woman in a brown velvet toque with rabbit's ears thumping the cold piano,
Miss Eccles poking the girls' feet with her long white wand—and this was so
tremendous that Leila was sure if her partner didn't come and she had to listen
to that marvelous music and to watch the others sliding, gliding over the
golden floor, she would die at least, or faint, or lift her arms and fly out of one
of those dark windows that showed the stars.

"Ours, I think—" Some one bowed, smiled, and offered her his arm; she 22
hadn't to die after all. Some one's hand pressed her waist, and she floated away
like a flower that is tossed into a pool.

"Quite a good floor, isn't it?" drawled a faint voice close to her ear.   23

"I think it's most beautifully slippery," said Leila.   24

"Pardon!" The faint voice sounded surprised. Leila said it again. And there 25
was a tiny pause before the voice echoed, "Oh, quite!" and she was swung round
again.

He steered so beautifully. That was the great difference between dancing 26
with girls and men, Leila decided. Girls banged into each other, and stamped
on each other's feet; the girl who was gentleman always clutched you so.

The azaleas were separate flowers no longer; they were pink and white flags 27
streaming by.

"Were you at the Bells' last week?" the voice came again. It sounded tired. 28
Leila wondered whether she ought to ask him if he would like to stop.

"No, this is my first dance," said she.　　　　　　　　　　　　　29

Her partner gave a little gasping laugh. "Oh, I say," he protested.　　30

"Yes, it is really the first dance I've ever been to." Leila was most fervent. It　31
was such a relief to be able to tell somebody. "You see, I've lived in the country
all my life up until now. . . ."

At that moment the music stopped, and they went to sit on two chairs　32
against the wall. Leila tucked her pink satin feet under and fanned herself, while
she blissfully watched the other couples passing and disappearing through the
swing doors.

"Enjoying yourself, Leila?" asked Jose, nodding her golden head.　　33

Laura passed and gave her the faintest little wink; it made Leila wonder for a　34
moment whether she was quite grown up after all. Certainly her partner did not
say very much. He coughed, tucked his handkerchief away, pulled down his waist-
coat, took a minute thread off his sleeve. But it didn't matter. Almost immediately
the band started, and her second partner seemed to spring from the ceiling.

"Floor's not bad," said the new voice. Did one always begin with the floor?　35
And then, "Were you at the Neaves' on Tuesday?" And again Leila explained.
Perhaps it was a little strange that her partners were not more interested. For it
was thrilling. Her first ball! She was only at the beginning of everything. It
seemed to her that she had never known what the night was like before. Up till
now it had been dark, silent, beautiful very often—oh, yes—but mournful
somehow. Solemn. And now it would never be like that again—it had opened
dazzling bright.

"Care for an ice?" said her partner. And they went through the swing doors,　36
down the passage, to the supper room. Her cheeks burned, she was fearfully
thirsty. How sweet the ices looked on little glass plates, and how cold the frosted
spoon was, iced too! And when they came back to the hall there was the fat man
waiting for her by the door. It gave her quite a shock again to see how old he
was; he ought to have been on the stage with the fathers and mothers. And
when Leila compared him with her other partners he looked shabby. His waist-
coat was creased, there was a button off his glove, his coat looked as if it was
dusty with French chalk.

"Come along, little lady," said the fat man. He scarcely troubled to clasp her,　37
and they moved away so gently, it was more like walking than dancing. But he
said not a word about the floor. "Your first dance, isn't it?" he murmured.

"How *did* you know?"　　　　　　　　　　　　　　　　　　38

"Ah," said the fat man, "that's what it is to be old!" He wheezed faintly as he　39
steered her past an awkward couple. "You see, I've been doing this kind of thing
for the last thirty years."

"Thirty years?" cried Leila. Twelve years before she was born!　　40

"It hardly bears thinking about, does it?" said the fat man gloomily. Leila　41
looked at his bald head, and she felt quite sorry for him.

"I think it's marvelous to be still going on," she said kindly.　　42

"Kind little lady," said the fat man, and he pressed her a little closer, and　43
hummed a bar of the waltz. "Of course," he said, "you can't hope to last

anything like as long as that. No-o," said the fat man, "long before that you'll be sitting up there on the stage, looking on, in your nice black velvet. And these pretty arms will have turned into little short fat ones, and you'll beat time with such a different kind of fan—a black bony one." The fat man seemed to shudder. "And you'll smile away like the poor old dears up there, and point to your daughter, and tell the elderly lady next to you how some dreadful man tried to kiss her at the club ball. And your heart will ache, ache"—the fat man squeezed her closer still, as if he really was sorry for that poor heart—"because no one wants to kiss you now. And you'll say how unpleasant these polished floors are to walk on, how dangerous they are. Eh, Mademoiselle Twinkletoes?" said the fat man softly.

Leila gave a light little laugh, but she did not feel like laughing. Was it— 44 could it all be true? It sounded terribly true. Was this first ball only the beginning of her last ball after all? At that the music seemed to change; it sounded sad, sad it rose upon a great sigh. Oh, how quickly things changed! Why didn't happiness last for ever? For ever wasn't a bit too long.

"I want to stop," she said in a breathless voice. The fat man led her to the 45 door.

"No," she said, "I won't go outside. I won't sit down. I'll just stand here, 46 thank you." She leaned against the wall, tapping with her foot, pulling up her gloves and trying to smile. But deep inside her a little girl threw her pinafore over her head and sobbed. Why had he spoiled it all?

"I say, you know," said the fat man, "you mustn't take me seriously, little 47 lady."

"As if I should!" said Leila, tossing her small dark head and sucking her 48 underlip. . . .

Again the couples paraded. The swing doors opened and shut. Now new 49 music was given out by the bandmaster. But Leila didn't want to dance any more. She wanted to be home, or sitting on the veranda listening to those baby owls. When she looked through the dark windows at the stars, they had long beams like wings. . . .

But presently a soft, melting, ravishing tune began, and a young man with 50 curly hair bowed before her. She would have to dance, out of politeness, until she could find Meg. Very stiffly she walked into the middle; very haughtily she put her hand on his sleeve. But in one minute, in one turn, her feet glided, glided. The lights, the azaleas, the dresses, the pink faces, the velvet chairs, all became one beautiful flying wheel. And when her next partner bumped her into the fat man and he said, "Par*don*," she smiled at him more radiantly than ever. She didn't even recognize him again.

William Faulkner (1897–1962)

Barn Burning

The store in which the Justice of the Peace's court was sitting smelled of cheese. 1
The boy, crouched on his nail keg at the back of the crowded room, knew he
smelled cheese, and more: from where he sat he could see the ranked shelves
close-packed with the solid, squat, dynamic shapes of tin cans whose labels his
stomach read, not from the lettering which meant nothing to his mind but
from the scarlet devils and the silver curve of fish—this, the cheese which he
knew he smelled and the hermetic meat which his intestines believed he
smelled coming in intermittent gusts momentary and brief between the other
constant one, the smell and sense just a little of fear because mostly of despair
and grief, the old fierce pull of blood. He could not see the table where the Justice sat and before which his father and his father's enemy (*our enemy* he
thought in that despair; *ourn! mine and hisn both! He's my father!*) stood, but he
could hear them, the two of them that is, because his father had said no word
yet:

"But what proof have you, Mr. Harris?" 2

"I told you. The hog got into my corn. I caught it up and sent it back to him. 3
He had no fence that would hold it. I told him so, warned him. The next time I
put the hog in my pen. When he came to get it I gave him enough wire to patch
up his pen. The next time I put the hog up and kept it. I rode down to his house
and saw the wire I gave him still rolled on to the spool in his yard. I told him he
could have the hog when he paid me a dollar pound fee. That evening a nigger
came with the dollar and got the hog. He was a strange nigger. He said, 'He say
to tell you wood and hay kin burn.' I said, 'What?' 'That whut he say to tell you,'
the nigger said. 'Wood and hay kin burn.' That night my barn burned. I got the
stock out but I lost the barn."

"Where is the nigger? Have you got him?" 4

"He was a strange nigger, I tell you. I don't know what became of him." 5

"But that's not proof. Don't you see that's not proof?" 6

"Get that boy up here. He knows." For a moment the boy thought too that 7
the man meant his older brother until Harris said, "Not him. The little one. The
boy," and, crouching, small for his age, small and wiry like his father, in patched
and faded jeans even too small for him, with straight, uncombed, brown hair
and eyes gray and wild as storm scud, he saw the men between himself and the
table part and become a lane of grim faces, at the end of which he saw the Justice, a shabby, collarless, graying man in spectacles, beckoning him. He felt no
floor under his bare feet; he seemed to walk beneath the palpable weight of the
grim turning faces. His father, stiff in his black Sunday coat donned not for the
trial but for the moving, did not even look at him. *He aims for me to lie,* he
thought, again with that frantic grief and despair. *And I will have to do hit.*

"What's your name, boy?" the Justice said. 8

"Colonel Sartoris Snopes," the boy whispered.   9

"Hey?" the Justice said. "Talk louder. Colonel Sartoris? I reckon anybody 10
named for Colonel Sartoris in this country can't help but tell the truth, can
they?" The boy said nothing. *Enemy! Enemy!* he thought; for a moment he
could not even see, could not see that the Justice's face was kindly nor discern
that his voice was troubled when he spoke to the man named Harris: "Do you
want me to question this boy?" But he could hear, and during those subsequent
long seconds while there was absolutely no sound in the crowded little room
save that of quiet and intent breathing it was as if he had swung outward at the
end of a grape vine, over a ravine, and at the top of the swing had been caught
in a prolonged instant of mesmerized gravity, weightless in time.

"No!" Harris said violently, explosively. "Damnation! Send him out of 11
here!" Now time, the fluid world, rushed beneath him again, the voices coming
to him again through the smell of cheese and sealed meat, the fear and despair
and the old grief of blood:

"This case is closed. I can't find against you, Snopes, but I can give you ad- 12
vice. Leave this country and don't come back to it."

His father spoke for the first time, his voice cold and harsh, level, without 13
emphasis: "I aim to. I don't figure to stay in a country among people who . . ."
he said something unprintable and vile, addressed to no one.

"That'll do," the Justice said. "Take your wagon and get out of this country 14
before dark. Case dismissed."

His father turned, and he followed the stiff black coat, the wiry figure walk- 15
ing a little stiffly from where a Confederate provost's man's musket ball had
taken him in the heel on a stolen horse thirty years ago, followed the two backs
now, since his older brother had appeared from somewhere in the crowd, no
taller than the father but thicker, chewing tobacco steadily, between the two
lines of grim-faced men and out of the store and across the worn gallery and
down the sagging steps and among the dogs and half-grown boys in the mild
May dust, where as he passed a voice hissed:

"Barn burner!"   16

Again he could not see, whirling; there was a face in a red haze, moonlike, 17
bigger than the full moon, the owner of it half again his size, he leaping in the
red haze toward the face, feeling no blow, feeling no shock when his head struck
the earth, scrabbling up and leaping again, feeling no blow this time either and
tasting no blood, scrabbling up to see the other boy in full flight and himself already leaping into pursuit as his father's hand jerked him back, the harsh, cold
voice speaking above him: "Go get in the wagon."

It stood in a grove of locusts and mulberries across the road. His two hulk- 18
ing sisters in their Sunday dresses and his mother and her sister in calico and
sunbonnets were already in it, sitting on and among the sorry residue of the
dozen and more movings which even the boy could remember—the battered
stove, the broken beds and chairs, the clock inlaid with mother-of-pearl, which
would not run, stopped at some fourteen minutes past two o'clock of a dead
and forgotten day and time, which had been his mother's dowry. She was cry-

ing, though when she saw him she drew her sleeve across her face and began to descend from the wagon. "Get back," the father said.

"He's hurt. I got to get some water and wash his . . ." 19

"Get back in the wagon," his father said. He got in too, over the tail-gate. His 20 father mounted to the seat where the older brother already sat and struck the gaunt mules two savage blows with the peeled willow, but without heat. It was not even sadistic; it was exactly that same quality which in later years would cause his descendants to over-run the engine before putting a motor car into motion, striking and reining back in the same movement. The wagon went on, the store with its quiet crowd of grimly watching men dropped behind; a curve in the road hid it. *Forever* he thought. *Maybe he's done satisfied now, now that he has* . . . stopping himself, not to say it aloud even to himself. His mother's hand touched his shoulder.

[handwritten marginal note: story must be flash-back]

"Does hit hurt?" she said. 21

"Naw," he said. "Hit don't hurt. Lemme be." 22

"Can't you wipe some of the blood off before hit dries?" 23

"I'll wash to-night," he said. "Lemme be, I tell you." 24

The wagon went on. He did not know where they were going. None of them 25 ever did or ever asked, because it was always somewhere, always a house of sorts waiting for them a day or two days or even three days away. Likely his father had already arranged to make a crop on another farm before he . . . Again he had to stop himself. He (the father) always did. There was something about his wolflike independence and even courage when the advantage was at least neutral which impressed strangers, as if they got from his latent ravening ferocity not so much a sense of dependability as a feeling that his ferocious conviction in the rightness of his own actions would be of advantage to all whose interest lay with his.

That night they camped, in a grove of oaks and beeches where a spring ran. 26 The nights were still cool and they had a fire against it, of a rail lifted from a nearby fence and cut into lengths—a small fire, neat, niggard almost, a shrewd fire; such fires were his father's habit and custom always, even in freezing weather. Older, the boy might have remarked this and wondered why not a big one; why should not a man who had not only seen the waste and extravagance of war, but who had in his blood an inherent voracious prodigality with material not his own, have burned everything in sight? Then he might have gone a step farther and thought that that was the reason: that niggard blaze was the living fruit of nights passed during those four years in the woods hiding from all men, blue or gray, with his strings of horses (captured horses, he called them). And older still, he might have divined the true reason: that the element of fire spoke to some deep mainspring of his father's being, as the element of steel or of powder spoke to other men, as the one weapon for the preservation of integrity, else breath were not worth the breathing, and hence to be regarded with respect and used with discretion.

But he did not think this now and he had seen those same niggard blazes all 27 his life. He merely ate his supper beside it and was already half asleep over his iron plate when his father called him, and once more he followed the stiff back, the stiff and ruthless limp, up the slope and on to the starlit road where, turning, he could see his father against the stars but without face or depth—a shape black, flat, and bloodless as though cut from tin in the iron folds of the frock-coat which had not been made for him, the voice harsh like tin and without heat like tin:

"You were fixing to tell them. You would have told him." He didn't answer. 28 His father struck him with the flat of his hand on the side of the head, hard but without heat, exactly as he had struck the two mules at the store, exactly as he would strike either of them with any stick in order to kill a horse fly, his voice still without heat or anger: "You're getting to be a man. You got to learn. You got to learn to stick to your own blood or you ain't going to have any blood to stick to you. Do you think either of them, any man there this morning, would? Don't you know all they wanted was a chance to get at me because they knew I had them beat? Eh?" Later, twenty years later, he was to tell himself, "If I had said they wanted only truth, justice, he would have hit me again." But now he said nothing. He was not crying. He just stood there. "Answer me," his father said.

"Yes," he whispered. His father turned.   29

"Get on to bed. We'll be there tomorrow."   30

To-morrow they were there. In the early afternoon the wagon stopped be- 31 fore a paintless two-room house identical almost with the dozen others it had stopped before even in the boy's ten years, and again, as on the other dozen occasions, his mother and aunt got down and began to unload the wagon, although his two sisters and his father and brother had not moved.

"Likely hit ain't fitten for hawgs," one of the sisters said.   32

"Nevertheless, fit it will and you'll hog it and like it," his father said. "Get out 33 of them chairs and help your Ma unload."

The two sisters got down, big, bovine, in a flutter of cheap ribbons; one of 34 them drew from the jumbled wagon bed a battered lantern, the other a worn broom. His father handed the reins to the older son and began to climb stiffly over the wheel. "When they get unloaded, take the team to the barn and feed them." Then he said, and at first the boy thought he was still speaking to his brother: "Come with me."

"Me?" he said.   35

"Yes," his father said. "You."   36

"Abner," his mother said. His father paused and looked back—the harsh 37 level stare beneath the shaggy, graying, irascible brows.

"I reckon I'll have a word with the man that aims to begin to-morrow own- 38 ing me body and soul for the next eight months."

They went back up the road. A week ago—or before last night, that is—he 39 would have asked where they were going, but not now. His father had struck him before last night but never before had he paused afterward to explain why; it was as if the blow and the following calm, outrageous voice still rang, repercussed, divulging nothing to him save the terrible handicap of being young, the light weight of his few years, just heavy enough to prevent his soaring free of the world as it seemed to be ordered but not heavy enough to keep him footed solid in it, to resist it and try to change the course of its events.

Presently he could see the grove of oaks and cedars and the other flowering 40
trees and shrubs where the house would be, though not the house yet. They
walked beside a fence massed with honeysuckle and Cherokee roses and came
to a gate swinging open between two brick pillars, and now, beyond a sweep of
drive, he saw the house for the first time and at that instant he forgot his father
and the terror and despair both, and even when he remembered his father again
(who had not stopped) the terror and despair did not return. Because, for all
the twelve movings, they had sojourned until now in a poor country, a land of
small farms and fields and houses, and he had never seen a house like this before. *Hit's big as a courthouse* he thought quietly, with a surge of peace and joy
whose reason he could not have thought into words, being too young for that:
*They are safe from him. People whose lives are a part of this peace and dignity are
beyond his touch, he no more to them than a buzzing wasp: capable of stinging for
a little moment but that's all; the spell of this peace and dignity rendering even the
barns and stable and cribs which belong to it impervious to the puny flames he
might contrive . . .* this, the peace and joy, ebbing for an instant as he looked
again at the stiff black back, the stiff and implacable limp of the figure which
was not dwarfed by the house, for the reason that it had never looked big anywhere and which now, against the serene columned backdrop, had more than
ever that impervious quality of something cut ruthlessly from tin, depthless, as
though, sidewise to the sun, it would cast no shadow. Watching him, the boy remarked the absolutely undeviating course which his father held and saw the
stiff foot come squarely down in a pile of fresh droppings where a horse had
stood in the drive and which his father could have avoided by a simple change
of stride. But it ebbed only for a moment, though he could not have thought
this into words either, walking on in the spell of the house, which he could even
want but without envy, without sorrow, certainly never with that ravening and
jealous rage which unknown to him walked in the ironlike black coat before
him: *Maybe he will feel it too. Maybe it will even change him now from what
maybe he couldn't help but be.*

They crossed the portico. Now he could hear his father's stiff foot as it came 41
down on the boards with clocklike finality, a sound out of all proportion to the
displacement of the body it bore and which was not dwarfed either by the white
door before it, as though it had attained to a sort of vicious and ravening minimum not to be dwarfed by anything—the flat, wide, black hat, the formal coat
of broadcloth which had once been black but which had now that friction-
glazed greenish cast of the bodies of old house flies, the lifted sleeve which was
too large, the lifted hand like a curled claw. The door opened so promptly that
the boy knew the Negro must have been watching them all the time, an old man
with neat grizzled hair, in a linen jacket, who stood barring the door with his
body, saying, "Wipe yo foots, white man, fo you come in here. Major ain't home
nohow."

"Get out of my way, nigger," his father said, without heat too, flinging the 42
door back and the Negro also and entering, his hat still on his head. And now
the boy saw the prints of the stiff foot on the doorjamb and saw them appear on
the pale rug behind the machinelike deliberation of the foot which seemed to

bear (or transmit) twice the weight which the body compassed. The Negro was shouting "Miss Lula! Miss Lula!" somewhere behind them, then the boy, deluged as though by a warm wave by a suave turn of carpeted stair and a pendant glitter of chandeliers and a mute gleam of gold frames, heard the swift feet and saw her too, a lady—perhaps he had never seen her like before either—in a gray, smooth gown with lace at the throat and an apron tied at the waist and the sleeves turned back, wiping cake or biscuit dough from her hands with a towel as she came up the hall, looking not at his father at all but at the tracks on the blond rug with an expression of incredulous amazement.

"I tried," the Negro cried. "I tole him to . . ."   43

"Will you please go away?" she said in a shaking voice. "Major de Spain is   44
not at home. Will you please go away?"

His father had not spoken again. He did not speak again. He did not even   45
look at her. He just stood stiff in the center of the rug, in his hat, the shaggy iron-gray brows twitching slightly above the pebble-colored eyes as he appeared to examine the house with brief deliberation. Then with the same deliberation he turned; the boy watched him pivot on the good leg and saw the stiff foot drag round the arc of the turning, leaving a final long and fading smear. His father never looked at it, he never once looked down at the rug. The Negro held the door. It closed behind them, upon the hysteric and indistinguishable woman-wail. His father stopped at the top of the steps and scraped his boot clean on the edge of it. At the gate he stopped again. He stood for a moment, planted stiffly on the stiff foot, looking back at the house. "Pretty and white, ain't it?" he said. "That's sweat. Nigger sweat. Maybe it ain't white enough yet to suit him. Maybe he wants to mix some white sweat with it."

Two hours later the boy was chopping wood behind the house within which   46
his mother and aunt and the two sisters (the mother and aunt, not the two girls, he knew that; even at this distance and muffled by walls the flat loud voices of the two girls emanated an incorrigible idle inertia) were setting up the stove to prepare a meal, when he heard the hooves and saw the linen-clad man on a fine sorrel mare, whom he recognized even before he saw the rolled rug in front of the Negro youth following on a fat bay carriage horse—a suffused, angry face vanishing, still at full gallop, beyond the corner of the house where his father and brother were sitting in the two tilted chairs; and a moment later, almost before he could have put the axe down, he heard the hooves again and watched the sorrel mare go back out of the yard, already galloping again. Then his father began to shout one of the sisters' names, who presently emerged backward from the kitchen door dragging the rolled rug along the ground by one end while the other sister walked behind it.

"If you ain't going to tote, go on and set up the wash pot," the first said.   47

"You, Sarty!" the second shouted. "Set up the wash pot!" His father appeared   48
at the door, framed against that shabbiness, as he had been against that other bland perfection, impervious to either, the mother's anxious face at his shoulder.

"Go on," the father said. "Pick it up." The two sisters stooped, broad, lethar-   49
gic; stooping, they presented an incredible expanse of pale cloth and a flutter of tawdry ribbons.

The girls are having to suffer for their father?

"If I thought enough of a rug to have to git hit all the way from France I 50 wouldn't keep hit where folks coming in would have to tromp on hit," the first said. They raised the rug.

"Abner," the mother said. "Let me do it." 51

"You go back and git dinner," his father said. "I'll tend to this." 52

From the woodpile through the rest of the afternoon the boy watched them, 53 the rug spread flat in the dust beside the bubbling wash-pot, the two sisters stooping over it with that profound and lethargic reluctance, while the father stood over them in turn, implacable and grim, driving them though never raising his voice again. He could smell the harsh homemade lye they were using; he saw his mother come to the door once and look toward them with an expression not anxious now but very like despair; he saw his father turn, and he fell to with the axe and saw from the corner of his eye his father raise from the ground a flattish fragment of field stone and examine it and return to the pot, and this time his mother actually spoke: "Abner. Abner. Please don't. Please, Abner."

Then he was done too. It was dusk; the whippoorwills had already begun. 54 He could smell coffee from the room where they would presently eat the cold food remaining from the mid-afternoon meal, though when he entered the house he realized they were having coffee again probably because there was a fire on the hearth, before which the rug now lay spread over the backs of the two chairs. The tracks of his father's foot were gone. Where they had been were now long, water-cloudy scoriations resembling the sporadic course of a lilliputian mowing machine.

It still hung there while they ate the cold food and then went to bed, scat- 55 tered without order or claim up and down the two rooms, his mother in one bed, where his father would later lie, the older brother in the other, himself, the aunt, and the two sisters on pallets on the floor. But his father was not in bed yet. The last thing the boy remembered was the depthless, harsh silhouette of the hat and coat bending over the rug and it seemed to him that he had not even closed his eyes when the silhouette was standing over him, the fire almost dead behind it, the stiff foot prodding him awake. "Catch up the mule," his father said.

When he returned with the mule his father was standing in the black door, 56 the rolled rug over his shoulder. "Ain't you going to ride?" he said.

"No. Give me your foot." 57

He bent his knee into his father's hand, the wiry, surprising power flowed 58 smoothly, rising, he rising with it, on to the mule's bare back (they had owned a saddle once; the boy could remember it though not when or where) and with the same effortlessness his father swung the rug up in front of him. Now in the starlight they retraced the afternoon's path, up the dusty road rife with honeysuckle, through the gate and up the black tunnel of the drive to the lightless house, where he sat on the mule and felt the rough warp of the rug drag across his thighs and vanish.

"Don't you want me to help?" he whispered. His father did not answer and 59 now he heard again that stiff foot striking the hollow portico with that wooden and clocklike deliberation, that outrageous overstatement of the weight it carried. The rug, hunched, not flung (the boy could tell that even in the darkness) from his father's shoulder, struck the angle of wall and floor with a sound unbelievably loud, thunderous, then the foot again, unhurried and enormous; a light came on in the house and the boy sat, tense, breathing steadily and quietly and just a little fast, though the foot itself did not increase its beat at all, descending the steps now; now the boy could see him.

"Don't you want to ride now?" he whispered. "We kin both ride now," the 60 light within the house altering now, flaring up and sinking. *He's coming down the stairs now,* he thought. He had already ridden the mule up beside the horse block; presently his father was up behind him and he doubled the reins over and slashed the mule across the neck, but before the animal could begin to trot the hard, thin arm came round him, the hard, knotted hand jerking the mule back to a walk.

In the first red rays of the sun they were in the lot, putting plow gear on the 61 mules. This time the sorrel mare was in the lot before he heard it at all, the rider collarless and even bareheaded, trembling, speaking in a shaking voice as the woman in the house had done, his father merely looking up once before stooping again to the hame he was buckling, so that the man on the mare spoke to his stooping back:

"You must realize you have ruined that rug. Wasn't there anybody here, any 62 of your women . . ." he ceased, shaking, the boy watching him, the older brother leaning now in the stable door, chewing, blinking slowly and steadily at nothing apparently. "It cost a hundred dollars. But you never had a hundred dollars. You never will. So I'm going to charge you twenty bushels of corn against your crop. I'll add it in your contract and when you come to the commissary you can sign it. That won't keep Mrs. de Spain quiet but maybe it will ~~teach you to wipe~~ your ~~feet off before you enter her house~~ again."

Then he was gone. The boy looked at his father, who still had not spoken 63 or even looked up again, who was now adjusting the logger-head in the hame.

"Pap," he said. His father looked at him——the inscrutable face, the shaggy 64 brows beneath which the gray eyes glinted coldly. Suddenly the boy went toward him, fast, stopping as suddenly. "You done the best you could!" he cried. "If he wanted hit done different why didn't he wait and tell you how? He won't git no twenty bushels! He won't git none! We'll gether hit and hide hit! I kin watch . . ."

"Did you put the cutter back in that straight stock like I told you?"   65
"No, sir," he said.   66
"Then go do it."   67

That was Wednesday. During the rest of that week he worked steadily, at 68 what was within his scope and some which was beyond it, with an industry that did not need to be driven nor even commanded twice; he had this from his mother, with the difference that some at least of what he did he liked to do, such as splitting wood with the half-size axe which his mother and aunt had earned, or saved money somehow, to present him with at Christmas. In company with the two older women (and on one afternoon, even one of the sisters), he built pens for the shoat and the cow which were a part of his father's contract with the landlord, and one afternoon, his father being absent, gone somewhere on one of the mules, he went to the field.

They were running a middle buster now, his brother holding the plow straight while he handled the reins, and walking beside the straining mule, the rich black soil shearing cool and damp against his bare ankles, he thought *Maybe this is the end of it. Maybe even that twenty bushels that seems hard to have to pay for just a rug will be a cheap price for him to stop forever and always from being what he used to be;* thinking, dreaming now, so that his brother had to speak sharply to him to mind the mule: *Maybe he even won't collect the twenty bushels. Maybe it will all add up and balance and vanish—corn, rug, fire; the terror and grief, the being pulled two ways like between two teams of horses—gone, done with for ever and ever.* 69

Then it was Saturday; he looked up from beneath the mule he was harnessing and saw his father in the black coat and hat. "Not that," his father said. "The wagon gear." And then, two hours later, sitting in the wagon bed behind his father and brother on the seat, the wagon accomplished a final curve, and he saw the weathered paintless store with its tattered tobacco- and patent-medicine posters and the tethered wagons and saddle animals below the gallery. He mounted the gnawed steps behind his father and brother, and there again was the lane of quiet, watching faces for the three of them to walk through. He saw the man in spectacles sitting at the plank table and he did not need to be told this was a Justice of the Peace; he sent one glare of fierce, exultant, partisan defiance at the man in collar and cravat now, whom he had seen but twice before in his life, and that on a galloping horse, who now wore on his face an expression not of rage but of amazed unbelief which the boy could not have known was at the incredible circumstance of being sued by one of his own tenants, and came and stood against his father and cried at the Justice: "He ain't done it! He ain't burnt..." 70

"Go back to the wagon," his father said. 71

"Burnt?" the Justice said. "Do I understand this rug was burned too?" 72

"Does anybody here claim it was?" his father said. "Go back to the wagon." But he did not, he merely retreated to the rear of the room, crowded as that other had been, but not to sit down this time, instead, to stand pressing among the motionless bodies, listening to the voices: 73

"And you claim twenty bushels of corn is too high for the damage you did to the rug?" 74

"He brought the rug to me and said he wanted the tracks washed out of it. I washed the tracks out and took the rug back to him." 75

"But you didn't carry the rug back to him in the same condition it was in before you made the tracks on it." 76

His father did not answer, and now for perhaps half a minute there was no sound at all save that of breathing, the faint, steady suspiration of complete and intent listening. 77

"You decline to answer that, Mr. Snopes?" Again his father did not answer.   78
"I'm going to find against you, Mr. Snopes. I'm going to find that you were responsible for the injury to Major de Spain's rug and hold you liable for it. But
twenty bushels of corn seems a little high for a man in your circumstances to
have to pay. Major de Spain claims it cost a hundred dollars. October corn will
be worth about fifty cents. I figure that if Major de Spain can stand a ninety-
five-dollar loss on something he paid cash for, you can stand a five-dollar loss
you haven't earned yet. I hold you in damages to Major de Spain to the amount
of ten bushels of corn over and above your contract with him, to be paid to him
out of your crop at gathering time. Court adjourned."

It had taken no time hardly, the morning was but half begun. He thought   79
they would return home and perhaps back to the field, since they were late, far
behind all other farmers. But instead his father passed on behind the wagon,
merely indicating with his hand for the older brother to follow with it, and
crossed the road toward the blacksmith shop opposite, pressing on after his
father, overtaking him, speaking, whispering up at the harsh, calm face beneath the weathered hat: "He won't git no ten bushels neither. He won't git one.
We'll . . ." until his father glanced for an instant down at him, the face absolutely calm, the grizzled eyebrows tangled above the cold eyes, the voice almost pleasant, almost gentle:

"You think so? Well, we'll wait till October anyway."   80

The matter of the wagon—the setting of a spoke or two and the tightening   81
of the tires—did not take long either, the business of the tires accomplished by
driving the wagon into the spring branch behind the shop and letting it stand
there, the mules nuzzling into the water from time to time, and the boy on the
seat with the idle reins, looking up the slope and through the sooty tunnel of
the shed where the slow hammer rang and where his father sat on an upended
cypress bolt, easily, either talking or listening, still sitting there when the boy
brought the dripping wagon up out of the branch and halted it before the door.

"Take them on to the shade and hitch," his father said. He did so and re-   82
turned. His father and the smith and a third man squatting on his heels inside
the door were talking, about crops and animals; the boy, squatting too in the
ammoniac dust and hoof-parings and scales of rust, heard his father tell a long
and unhurried story out of the time before the birth of the older brother even
when he had been a professional horsetrader. And then his father came up beside him where he stood before a tattered last year's circus poster on the other
side of the store, gazing rapt and quiet at the scarlet horses, the incredible pois-
ings and convolutions of tulle and tights and the painted leers of comedians,
and said "It's time to eat."

But not at home. Squatting beside his brother against the front wall, he   83
watched his father emerge from the store and produce from a paper sack a segment of cheese and divide it carefully and deliberately into three with his
pocket knife and produce crackers from the same sack. They all three squatted
on the gallery and ate, slowly, without talking; then in the store again, they
drank from a tin dipper tepid water smelling of the cedar bucket and of living
beech trees. And still they did not go home. It was a horse lot this time, a tall rail

fence upon and along which men stood and sat and out of which one by one horses were led, to be walked and trotted and then cantered back and forth along the road while the slow swapping and buying went on and the sun began to slant westward, they—the three of them—watching and listening, the older brother with his muddy eyes and his steady, inevitable tobacco, the father commenting now and then on certain of the animals, to no one in particular.

It was after sundown when they reached home. They ate supper by lamp- 84
light, then, sitting on the doorstep, the boy watched the night fully accomplish, listening to the whippoorwills and the frogs, when he heard his mother's voice: "Abner! No! No! Oh, God. Oh, God. Abner!" and he rose, whirled, and saw the altered light through the door where a candle stub now burned in a bottle neck on the table and his father, still in the hat and coat, at once formal and burlesque as though dressed carefully for some shabby and ceremonial violence, emptying the reservoir of the lamp back into the five-gallon kerosene can from which it had been filled, while the mother tugged at his arm until he shifted the lamp to the other hand and flung her back, not savagely or viciously, just hard, into the wall, her hands flung out against the wall for balance, her mouth open and in her face the same quality of hopeless despair as had been in her voice. Then his father saw him standing in the door.

"Go to the barn and get that can of oil we were oiling the wagon with," he 85
said. The boy did not move. Then he could speak.

"What . . ." he cried. "What are you . . ." 86

"Go get that oil," his father said. "Go." 87

Then he was moving, running, outside the house, toward the stable: this is 88
the old habit, the old blood which he had not been permitted to choose for himself, which had been bequeathed him willy nilly and which had run for so long (and who knew where, battening on what of outrage and savagery and lust) before it came to him. *I could keep on,* he thought. *I could run on and on and never look back, never need to see his face again. Only I can't. I can't,* the rusted can in his hand now, the liquid sploshing in it as he ran back to the house and into it, into the sound of his mother's weeping in the next room, and handed the can to his father.

FEAR!

"Ain't you going to even send a nigger?" he cried. "At least you sent a nigger 89
before!"

This time his father didn't strike him. The hand came even faster than the 90
blow had, the same hand which had set the can on the table with almost excruciating care flashing from the can toward him too quick for him to follow it, gripping him by the back of his shirt and on to tiptoe before he had seen it quit the can, the face stooping at him in breathless and frozen ferocity, the cold, dead voice speaking over him to the older brother who leaned against the table, chewing with that steady, curious, sidewise motion of cows:

"Empty the can into the big one and go on. I'll catch up with you." 91

"Better tie him up to the bedpost," the brother said. 92

"Do like I told you," the father said. Then the boy was moving, his bunched 93
shirt and the hard, bony hand between his shoulder-blades, his toes just touching the floor, across the room and into the other one, past the sisters sitting

with spread heavy thighs in the two chairs over the cold hearth, and to where his mother and aunt sat side by side on the bed, the aunt's arms about his mother's shoulders.

"Hold him," the father said. The aunt made a startled movement. "Not you," 94 the father said. "Lennie. Take hold of him. I want to see you do it." His mother took him by the wrist. "You'll hold him better than that. If he gets loose don't you know what he is going to do? He will go up yonder." He jerked his head toward the road. "Maybe I'd better tie him."

"I'll hold him," his mother whispered.   95

"See you do then." Then his father was gone, the stiff foot heavy and mea- 96 sured upon the boards, ceasing at last.

Then he began to struggle. His mother caught him in both arms, he jerking 97 and wrenching at them. He would be stronger in the end, he knew that. But he had no time to wait for it. "Lemme go!" he cried. "I don't want to have to hit you!"

"Let him go!" the aunt said. "If he don't go, before God, I am going there 98 myself!"

"Don't you see I can't!" his mother cried. "Sarty! Sarty! No! No! Help me, 99 Lizzie!"

Then he was free. His aunt grasped at him but it was too late. He whirled, 100 running, his mother stumbled forward on to her knees behind him, crying to the nearer sister: "Catch him, Net! Catch him!" But that was too late too, the sister (the sisters were twins, born at the same time, yet either of them now gave the impression of being, encompassing as much living meat and volume and weight as any other two of the family) not yet having begun to rise from the chair, her head, face, alone merely turned, presenting to him in the flying instant an astonishing expanse of young female features untroubled by any surprise even, wearing only an expression of bovine interest. Then he was out of the room, out of the house, in the mild dust of the starlit road and the heavy rifeness of honeysuckle, the pale ribbon unspooling with terrific slowness under his running feet, reaching the gate at last and turning in, running, his heart and lungs drumming, on up the drive toward the lighted house, the lighted door. He did not knock, he burst in, sobbing for breath, incapable for the moment of speech; he saw the astonished face of the Negro in the linen jacket without knowing when the Negro had appeared.

"De Spain!" he cried, panted. "Where's . . ." then he saw the white man too 101 emerging from a white door down the hall. "Barn!" he cried. "Barn!"

"What?" the white man said. "Barn?"   102

"Yes!" the boy cried. "Barn!"   103

"Catch him!" the white man shouted.   104

But it was too late this time too. The Negro grasped his shirt, but the entire 105 sleeve, rotten with washing, carried away, and he was out that door too and in the drive again, and had actually never ceased to run even while he was screaming into the white man's face.

Behind him the white man was shouting, "My horse! Fetch my horse!" and 106 he thought for an instant of cutting across the park and climbing the fence into the road, but he did not know the park nor how high the vine-massed fence might be and he dared not risk it. So he ran on down the drive, blood and breath roaring; presently he was in the road again though he could not see it. He could not hear either: the galloping mare was almost upon him before he heard her, and even then he held his course, as if the very urgency of his wild grief and need must in a moment more find him wings, waiting until the ultimate instant to hurl himself aside and into the weed-choked roadside ditch as the horse thundered past and on, for an instant in furious silhouette against the stars, the tranquil early summer night sky which, even before the shape of the horse and rider vanished, stained abruptly and violently upward: a long, swirling roar incredible and soundless, blotting the stars, and he springing up and into the road again, running again, knowing it was too late yet still running even after he heard the shot and, an instant later, two shots, pausing now without knowing he had ceased to run, crying "Pap! Pap!", running again before he knew he had begun to run, stumbling, tripping over something and scrabbling up again without ceasing to run, looking backward over his shoulder at the glare as he got up, running on among the invisible trees, panting, sobbing, "Father! Father!"

At midnight he was sitting on the crest of a hill. He did not know it was 107 midnight and he did not know how far he had come. But there was no glare behind him now and he sat now, his back toward what he had called home for four days anyhow, his face toward the dark woods which he would enter when breath was strong again, small, shaking steadily in the chill darkness, hugging himself into the remainder of his thin, rotten shirt, the grief and despair now no longer terror and fear but just grief and despair. *Father. My father,* he thought. "He was brave!" he cried suddenly, aloud but not loud, no more than a whisper: "He was! He was in the war! He was in Colonel Sartoris' cav'ry!" not knowing that his father had gone to that war a private in the fine old European sense, wearing no uniform, admitting the authority of and giving fidelity to no man or army or flag, going to war as Malbrouck himself did: for booty—it meant nothing and less than nothing to him if it were enemy booty or his own.

The slow constellations wheeled on. It would be dawn and then sun-up af- 108 ter a while and he would be hungry. But that would be to-morrow and now he was only cold, and walking would cure that. His breathing was easier now and he decided to get up and go on, and then he found that he had been asleep because he knew it was almost dawn, the night almost over. He could tell that from the whippoorwills. They were everywhere now among the dark trees below him, constant and inflectioned and ceaseless, so that, as the instant for giving over to the day birds drew nearer and nearer, there was no interval at all between them. He got up. He was a little stiff, but walking would cure that too as it would the cold, and soon there would be the sun. He went on down the hill, toward the dark woods within which the liquid silver voices of the birds called unceasing—the rapid and urgent beating of the urgent and quiring heart of the late spring night. He did not look back.

ACTIVITIES FOR WRITING AND DISCUSSION

1. The story is told primarily from the **third-person limited point of view** of the boy Sarty. How would the story change if it were told by Sarty in the *first person,* using "I"?

2. Reread the story for details of the Snopes family's life before the story's happenings. What kind of life has the family led? What did Abner (the father) do during the Civil War? What are the personalities and appearances of the sisters, mother, aunt, and brother? Based on these details, prepare a brief dossier on the family (perhaps for use by law enforcement officials or social workers).

3. Gather evidence of the range of Sarty's feelings for his father. What attracts him? repels him? confuses him? How extensive is the father's influence on the boy's life? In your opinion, will Sarty be able to establish an identity of his own, separate from his father's? Why or why not?

4. Compose a sequel to the story. Away from his father, what does Sarty do next? Where does he go? What does he do with his life? Strive to make the facts of your sequel psychologically consistent with the personality of Sarty as portrayed in Faulkner's story.

NAGUIB MAHFOUZ (b. 1911)

Zaabalawi

Finally I became convinced that I had to find Sheikh Zaabalawi.   1

The first time I had heard of his name had been in a song: 2

> "What's wrong with the world, O Zaabalawi?
> They've turned it upside down and made it insipid."

It had been a popular song in my childhood and one day it had occurred to   3
me—in the way children have of asking endless questions—to ask my father
about him.

"Who is Zaabalawi, father?"   4

He had looked at me hesitantly as though doubting my ability to under-   5
stand the answer. However, he had replied:

"May his blessing descend upon you, he's a true saint of God, a remover of   6
worries and troubles. Were it not for him I would have died miserably—"

In the years that followed I heard him many a time sing the praises of this   7
good saint and speak of the miracles he performed. The days passed and

brought with them many illnesses from each one of which I was able, without too much trouble and at a cost I could afford, to find a cure, until I became afflicted with that illness for which no one possesses a remedy. When I had tried everything in vain and was overcome by despair, I remembered by chance what I had heard in my childhood: Why, I asked myself, should I not seek out Sheikh Zaabalawi? I recollected that my father had said that he had made his acquaintance in Khan Gaafar at the house of Sheikh Kamar, one of those sheikhs who practised law in the religious courts, and I therefore took myself off to his house. Wishing to make sure that he was still living there, I made enquiries of a vendor of beans whom I found in the lower part of the house.

"Sheikh Kamar!" he said, looking at me in amazement. "He left the quarter 8 ages ago. They say he's now living in Garden City and has his office in Al-Azhaar Square."

I looked up the office address in the telephone book and immediately set off 9 to the Chamber of Commerce Building, where it was located. On asking to see him I was ushered into a room just as a beautiful woman with a most intoxicating perfume was leaving it. The man received me with a smile and motioned me towards a fine leather-upholstered chair. My feet were conscious of the costly lushness of the carpet despite the thick soles of my shoes. The man wore a lounge suit and was smoking a cigar; his manner of sitting was that of someone well satisfied both with himself and his worldly possessions. The look of warm welcome he gave me left no doubt in my mind that he thought me a prospective client, and I felt acutely embarrassed at encroaching upon his valuable time.

"Welcome!" he said, prompting me to speak.   10

"I am the son of your old friend Sheikh Ali al-Tatawi," I answered so as to 11 put an end to my equivocal position.

A certain languor was apparent in the glance he cast at me; the languor was 12 not total in that he had not as yet lost all hope in me.

"God rest his soul," he said. "He was a fine man."   13

The very pain that had driven me to go there now prevailed upon me to 14 stay.

"He told me," I continued, "of a devout saint named Zaabalawi whom he 15 met at Your Honour's. I am in need of him, sir, if he be still in the land of the living."

The languor became firmly entrenched in his eyes and it would have come 16 as no surprise to me if he had shown the door to both me and my father's memory.

"That," he said in the tone of one who has made up his mind to terminate 17 the conversation, "was a very long time ago and I scarcely recall him now."

Rising to my feet so as to put his mind at rest regarding my intention of go- 18 ing, I asked:

"Was he really a saint?"   19

"We used to regard him as a man of miracles."   20

"And where could I find him today?" I asked, making another move towards 21 the door.

"To the best of my knowledge he was living in the Birgawi Residence in al- 22
Azhar," and he applied himself to some papers on his desk with a resolute
movement that indicated he wouldn't open his mouth again. I bowed my
head in thanks, apologized several times for disturbing him and left the office,
my head so buzzing with embarrassment that I was oblivious to all sounds
around me.

I went to the Birgawi Residence which was situated in a thickly populated 23
quarter. I found that time had so eaten into the building that nothing was left of
it save an antiquated façade and a courtyard which, despite it being supposedly
in the charge of a caretaker, was being used as a rubbish dump. A small insignificant fellow, a mere prologue to a man, was using the covered entrance as a
place for the sale of old books on theology and mysticism.

On my asking him about Zaabalawi, he peered at me through narrow, in- 24
flamed eyes and said in amazement:

"Zaabalawi! Good heavens, what a time ago that was! Certainly he used to 25
live in this house when it was livable in, and many was the time he would sit
with me talking of bygone days and I would be blessed by his holy presence.
Where, though, is Zaabalawi today?"

He shrugged his shoulders sorrowfully and soon left me to attend to an ap- 26
proaching customer. I proceeded to make enquiries of many shopkeepers in the
district. While I found that a large number of them had never even heard of
him, some, though recalling nostalgically the pleasant times they had spent
with him, were ignorant of his present whereabouts, while others openly made
fun of him, labelled him a charlatan, and advised me to put myself in the hands
of a doctor—as though I had not already done so. I therefore had no alternative
but to return disconsolately home.

With the passing of the days like motes in the air my pains grew so severe 27
that I was sure I would not be able to hold out much longer. Once again I fell to
wondering about Zaabalawi and clutching at the hopes his venerable name
stirred within me. Then it occurred to me to seek the help of the local Sheikh of
the district; in fact, I was surprised I hadn't thought of this to begin with. His
office was in the nature of a small shop except that it contained a desk and a
telephone, and I found him sitting at his desk wearing a jacket over his striped
galabia.[1] As he did not interrupt his conversation with a man sitting beside
him, I stood waiting till the man had gone. He then looked up at me coldly. I
told myself that I should win him over by the usual methods, and it wasn't long
before I had him cheerfully inviting me to sit down.

"I'm in need of Sheikh Zaabalawi," I answered his enquiry as to the purpose 28
of my visit.

He gazed at me with the same astonishment as that shown by those I had 29
previously encountered.

"At least," he said, giving me a smile that revealed his gold teeth, "he is still 30
alive. The devil of it is, though, he has no fixed abode. You might well bump

---

1. An outer robe.

into him as you go out of here, on the other hand you might spend days and
months in fruitless search of him."

"Even you can't find him!" 31

"Even I! He's a baffling man, but I thank the Lord that he's still alive!" 32

He gazed at me intently, and murmured: 33

"It seems your condition is serious." 34

"Very!" 35

"May God come to your aid! But why don't you go about it rationally?" 36

He spread out a sheet of paper on the desk and drew on it with unexpected 37
speed and skill until he had made a full plan of the district showing all the various quarters, lanes, alleyways, and squares. He looked at it admiringly and said,
"These are dwelling-houses, here is the Quarter of the Perfumers, here the
Quarter of the Coppersmiths, the Mouski, the Police and Fire Stations. The
drawing is your best guide. Look carefully in the cafés, the places where the
dervishes perform their rites, the mosques and prayer-rooms, and the Green
Gate, for he may well be concealed among the beggars and be indistinguishable
from them. Actually, I myself haven't seen him for years, having been somewhat
preoccupied with the cares of the world and was only brought back to those
most exquisite times of my youth by your enquiry."

I gazed at the map in bewilderment. The telephone rang and he took up the 38
receiver.

"Take it," he told me, generously. "We're at your service." 39

Folding up the map, I left and wandered off through the quarter, from 40
square to street to alleyway, making enquiries of everyone I felt was familiar
with the place. At last the owner of a small establishment for ironing clothes
told me:

"Go to the calligrapher Hassanein in Umm al-Ghulam—they were friends." 41

I went to Umm al-Ghulam where I found old Hassenein working in a deep, 42
narrow shop full of signboards and jars of colour. A strange smell, a mixture of
glue and perfume, permeated its every corner. Old Hassanein was squatting on
a sheepskin rug in front of a board propped against the wall; in the middle of it
he had inscribed the word "Allah" in silver lettering. He was engrossed in em-
bellishing the letters with prodigious care. I stood behind him, fearful to disturb him or break the inspiration that flowed to his masterly hand. When my
concern at not interrupting him had lasted some time, he suddenly enquired
with unaffected gentleness:

"Yes?" 43

Realizing that he was aware of my presence, I introduced myself. 44

"I've been told that Sheikh Zaabalawi is your friend and I'm looking for 45
him," I said.

His hand came to a stop. He scrutinized me in astonishment. 46

"Zaabalawi! God be praised!" he said with a sigh. 47

"He is a friend of yours, isn't he?" I asked eagerly. 48

"He was, once upon a time. A real man of mystery: he'd visit you so often 49
that people would imagine he was your nearest and dearest, then would disappear as though he'd never existed. Yet saints are not to be blamed."

The spark of hope went out with the suddenness of a lamp by a power-cut.   50

"He was so constantly with me," said the man, "that I felt him to be a part of   51
everything I drew. But where is he today?"

"Perhaps he is still alive?"   52

"He's alive, without a doubt. He had impeccable taste and it was due to him   53
that I made my most beautiful drawings."

"God knows," I said, in a voice almost stifled by the dead ashes of hope,   54
"that I am in the direst need of him and no one knows better than you of the
ailments in respect of which he is sought."

"Yes—yes. May God restore you to health. He is, in truth, as is said of him, a   55
man, and more—"

Smiling broadly, he added: "And his face is possessed of an unforgettable   56
beauty. But where is he?"

Reluctantly I rose to my feet, shook hands and left. I continued on my way   57
eastwards and westwards through the quarter, enquiring about him from
everyone who, by reason of age or experience, I felt was likely to help me. Eventually I was informed by a vendor of lupine that he had met him a short while
ago at the house of Sheikh Gad, the well-known composer. I went to the musician's house in Tabakshiyya where I found him in a room tastefully furnished in
the old style, its walls redolent with history. He was seated on a divan, his famous lute lying beside him, concealing within itself the most beautiful
melodies of our age, while from within the house came the sound of pestle and
mortar and the clamour of children. I immediately greeted him and introduced
myself, and was put at my ease by the unaffected way in which he received me.
He did not ask, either in words or gesture, what had brought me, and I did not
feel that he even harboured any such curiosity. Amazed at his understanding
and kindness, which boded well, I said:

"O Sheikh Gad, I am an admirer of yours and have long been enchanted by   58
the renderings of your songs."

"Thank you," he said with a smile.   59

"Please excuse my disturbing you," I continued timidly, "but I was told that   60
Zaabalawi was your friend and I am in urgent need of him."

"Zaabalawi!" he said, frowning in concentration. "You need him? God be   61
with you, for who knows, O Zaabalawi, where you are?"

"Doesn't he visit you?" I asked eagerly.   62

"He visited me some time ago. He might well come now; on the other hand   63
I mightn't see him till death!"

I gave an audible sigh and asked: 64

"What made him like that?"   65

He took up his lute. "Such are saints or they would not be saints," he said   66
laughing.

"Do those who need him suffer as I do?"   67

"Such suffering is part of the cure!"   68

He took up the plectrum and began plucking soft strains from the strings. Lost   69
in thought, I followed his movements. Then, as though addressing myself, I said:

"So my visit has been in vain!" 70

He smiled, laying his cheek against the side of the lute. 71

"God forgive you," he said, "for saying such a thing of a visit that has caused 72
me to know you and you me!"

I was much embarrassed and said apologetically: 73

"Please forgive me; my feelings of defeat made me forget my manners!" 74

"Do not give in to defeat. This extraordinary man brings fatigue to all who 75
seek him. It was easy enough with him in the old days when his place of abode
was known. Today, though, the world has changed and after having enjoyed a
position attained only by potentates, he is now pursued by the police on a
charge of false pretences. It is therefore no longer an easy matter to reach him,
but have patience and be sure that you will do so."

He raised his head from the lute and skillfully led into the opening bars of a 76
melody. Then he sang:

"I make lavish mention, even though I blame myself,
of those I have loved,
For the words of lovers are my wine."

With a heart that was weary and listless I followed the beauty of the melody 77
and the singing.

"I composed the music to this poem in a single night," he told me when he 78
had finished. "I remember that it was the night of the Lesser Bairam. He was my
guest for the whole of that night and the poem was of his choosing. He would
sit for a while just where you are, then would get up and play with my children
as though he were one of them. Whenever I was overcome by weariness or my
inspiration failed me he would punch me playfully in the chest and joke with
me, and I would bubble over with melodies and thus I continued working till I
finished the most beautiful piece I have ever composed."

"Does he know anything about music?" 79

"He was the epitome of things musical. He had an extremely beautiful 80
speaking voice and you had only to hear him to want to burst into song. His
loftiness of spirit stirred within you—"

"How was it that he cured those diseases before which men are powerless?" 81

"That is his secret. Maybe you will learn it when you meet him." 82

But when would that meeting occur? We relapsed into silence and the hub- 83
bub of children once more filled the room.

Again, the Sheikh began to sing. He went on repeating the words "and I have 84
a memory of her" in different and beautiful variations until the very walls
danced in ecstasy. I expressed my wholehearted admiration and he gave me a
smile of thanks. I then got up and asked permission to leave and he accompanied me to the outer door. As I shook him by the hand he said, "I hear that
nowadays he frequents the house of Haag Wanas al-Damanhouri. Do you know
him?"

I shook my head, a modicum of renewed hope creeping into my heart. 85

"He is a man of private means," he told me, "who from time to time visits 86 Cairo, putting up at some hotel or other. Every evening, though, he spends at the Negma Bar in Alfi Street."

I waited for nightfall and went to the Negma Bar. I asked a waiter about 87 Haag Wanas and he pointed to a corner which was semi-secluded because of its position behind a large pillar with mirrors on its four sides. There I saw a man seated alone at a table with a bottle three-quarters empty and another empty one in front of him; there were no snacks or food to be seen and I was sure that I was in the presence of a hardened drinker. He was wearing a loosely flowing silk *galabia* and a carefully wound turban; his legs were stretched out towards the base of the pillar, and as he gazed into the mirror in rapt contentment the sides of his face, rounded and handsome despite the fact that he was approaching old age, were flushed with wine. I approached quietly till I stood but a few feet away from him. He did not turn towards me or give any indication that he was aware of my presence.

"Good evening, Mr. Wanas," I said with amiable friendliness.   88

He turned towards me abruptly as though my voice had roused him from 89 slumber and glared at me in disapproval. I was about to explain what had brought me to him when he interrupted me in an almost imperative tone of voice which was none the less not devoid of an extraordinary gentleness:

"First, please sit down, and, second, please get drunk!"   90

I opened my mouth to make my excuses but, stopping up his ears with his 91 fingers, he said:

"Not a word till you do what I say."   92

I realized that I was in the presence of a capricious drunkard and told my- 93 self that I should go along with him at least halfway.

"Would you permit me to ask one question?" I said with a smile, sitting 94 down.

Without removing his hands from his ears he indicated the bottle.   95

"When engaged in a drinking bout like this I do not allow any conversation 96 between myself and another unless, like me, he is drunk, otherwise the session loses all propriety and mutual comprehension is rendered impossible."

I made a sign indicating that I didn't drink.   97

"That's your look-out," he said offhandedly. "And that's my condition!"   98

He filled me a glass which I meekly took and drank. No sooner had it settled 99 in my stomach than it seemed to ignite. I waited patiently till I had grown used to its ferocity, and said:

"It's very strong, and I think the time has come for me to ask you about—" 100

Once again, however, he put his fingers in his ears.   101

"I shan't listen to you until you're drunk!"   102

He filled up my glass for the second time. I glanced at it in trepidation; then, 103 overcoming my innate objection, I drank it down at a gulp. No sooner had it come to rest inside me than I lost all will-power. With the third glass I lost my memory and with the fourth the future vanished. The world turned round about me and I forgot why I had gone there. The man leaned towards me attentively but I saw him—saw everything—as a mere meaningless series of coloured planes. I don't know how long it was before my head sank down on to the arm of the chair and I plunged into deep sleep. During it I had a beautiful dream the like of which I had never experienced. I dreamed that I was in an immense garden surrounded on all sides by luxuriant trees and the sky was nothing but stars seen between the entwined branches, all enfolded in an atmosphere like that of sunset or a sky overcast with cloud. I was lying on a small hummock of jasmine petals which fell upon me like rain, while the lucent spray of a fountain unceasingly sprinkled my head and temples. I was in a state of deep contentedness, of ecstatic serenity. An orchestra of warbling and cooing played in my ear. There was an extraordinary sense of harmony between me and my inner self, and between the two of us and the world, everything being in its rightful place without discord or distortion. In the whole world there was no single reason for speech or movement, for the universe moved in a rapture of ecstasy. This lasted but a short while. When I opened my eyes consciousness struck at me like a policeman's fist and I saw Wanas al-Damanhouri regarding me with concern. In the bar only a few drowsy people were left.

"You have slept deeply," said my companion; "you were obviously hungry 104 for sleep."

I rested my heavy head in the palms of my hands. When I took them away in 105 astonishment and looked down at them I found that they glistened with drops of water.

"My head's wet," I protested. 106

"Yes, my friend tried to rouse you," he answered quietly. 107

"Somebody saw me in this state?" 108

"Don't worry, he is a good man. Have you not heard of Sheikh Zaabalawi?" 109

"Zaabalawi!" I exclaimed, jumping to my feet. 110

"Yes," he answered in surprise. "What's wrong?" 111

"Where is he?" 112

"I don't know where he is now. He was here and then he left." 113

I was about to run off in pursuit but found I was more exhausted than I had 114 imagined. Collapsed over the table, I cried out in despair:

"My sole reason for coming to you was to meet him. Help me to catch up 115 with him or send someone after him."

The man called a vendor of prawns and asked him to seek out the Sheikh 116 and bring him back. Then he turned to me.

"I didn't realize you were afflicted. I'm very sorry—" 117

"You wouldn't let me speak," I said irritably. 118

"What a pity! He was sitting on this chair beside you the whole time. He was 119 playing with a string of jasmine petals he had round his neck, a gift from one of his admirers, then, taking pity on you, he began to sprinkle some water on your head to bring you round."

"Does he meet you here every night?" I asked, my eyes not leaving the door- 120 way through which the vendor of prawns had left.

"He was with me tonight, last night and the night before that, but before 121 that I hadn't seen him for a month."

"Perhaps he will come tomorrow," I answered with a sigh. 122

"Perhaps."   123

"I am willing to give him any money he wants."   124

Wanas answered sympathetically: 125

"The strange thing is that he is not open to such temptations, yet he will   126
cure you if you meet him."

"Without charge?"   127

"Merely on sensing that you love him."   128

The vendor of prawns returned, having failed in his mission.   129

I recovered some of my energy and left the bar, albeit unsteadily. At every   130
street corner I called out, "Zaabalawi!" in the vague hope that I would be rewarded with an answering shout. The street boys turned contemptuous eyes on
me till I sought refuge in the first available taxi.

The following evening I stayed up with Wanas al-Damanhouri till dawn,   131
but the Sheikh did not put in an appearance. Wanas informed me that he would
be going away to the country and wouldn't be returning to Cairo until he'd sold
the cotton crop.

I must wait, I told myself; I must train myself to be patient. Let me content   132
myself with having made certain of the existence of Zaabalawi, and even of his
affection for me, which encourages me to think that he will be prepared to cure
me if a meeting between us takes place.

Sometimes, however, the long delay wearied me. I would become beset by   133
despair and would try to persuade myself to dismiss him from my mind completely. How many weary people in this life know him not or regard him as a
mere myth! Why, then, should I torture myself about him in this way?

No sooner, however, did my pains force themselves upon me than I would   134
again begin to think about him, asking myself as to when I would be fortunate
enough to meet him. The fact that I ceased to have any news of Wanas and was
told he had gone to live abroad did not deflect me from my purpose; the truth of
the matter was that I had become fully convinced that I had to find Zaabalawi.

Yes, I have to find Zaabalawi.   135

—*Translated by Denys Johnson-Davies*

ACTIVITIES FOR WRITING AND DISCUSSION

1. Reread and annotate the reactions of the several people to whom the
narrator mentions the name, "Zaabalawi." Do they all react in the same way? in
different ways? Working with a partner or small group, try to provide some
plausible explanations for the type(s) of reactions you find. Finally, write a description of the Zaabalawi who emerges for you through the impressions of the
various characters.

2. After reviewing the context in which it appears, interpret the following
dialogue (paragraphs 67 and 68.):

Narrator: "Do those who need him suffer as I do?"
Sheikh Gad: "Such suffering is part of the cure!"

Alternative: Identify any other dialogue in the story that intrigues you, annotate it, and give your reading of its literal and/or **symbolic** meanings.

3. At story's end the narrator has yet to "find" Zaabalawi. Does it matter? Have his efforts been wasted? rewarded in any ways? Explain, supporting your response with evidence or quotations from the story.

4. Is the narrator's quest for Zaabalawi symbolic in any ways? If so, *how* or *of what?*

Toni Cade Bambara (1939–1995)

The Lesson

Back in the days when everyone was old and stupid or young and foolish and   1
me and Sugar were the only ones just right, this lady moved on our block with nappy hair and proper speech and no makeup. And quite naturally we laughed at her, laughed the way we did at the junk man who went about his business like he was some big-time president and his sorry-ass horse his secretary. And we kinda hated her too, hated the way we did the winos who cluttered up our parks and pissed on our handball walls and stank up our hallways and stairs so you couldn't halfway play hide-and-seek without a goddamn gas mask. Miss Moore was her name. The only woman on the block with no first name. And she was black as hell, cept for her feet, which were fish-white and spooky. And she was always planning these boring-ass things for us to do, us being my cousins, mostly, who lived on the block cause we all moved North the same time and to the same apartment then spread out gradual to breathe. And our parents would yank our heads into some kinda shape and crisp up our clothes so we'd be presentable for travel with Miss Moore, who always looked like she was going to church, though she never did. Which is just one of the things the grownups talked about when they talked behind her back like a dog. But when she came calling with some sachet she'd sewed up or some gingerbread she'd made or some book, why then they'd all be too embarrassed to turn her down and we'd get handed over all spruced up. She'd been to college and said it was only right that she should take responsibility for the young ones' education, and she not even related by marriage or blood. So they'd go for it. Specially Aunt Gretchen. She was the main gofer in the family. You got some ole dumb shit foolishness you want somebody to go for, you send for Aunt Gretchen. She

been screwed into the go-along for so long, it's a blood-deep natural thing with her. Which is how she got saddled with me and Sugar and Junior in the first place while our mothers were in a la-de-da apartment up the block having a good ole time.

So this one day, Miss Moore rounds us all up at the mailbox and it's purdee 2 hot and she's knockin herself out about arithmetic. And school suppose to let up in summer I heard, but she don't never let up. And the starch in my pinafore scratching the shit outta me and I'm really hating this nappy-head bitch and her goddamn college degree. I'd much rather go to the pool or to the show where it's cool. So me and Sugar leaning on the mailbox being surly, which is a Miss Moore word. And Flyboy checking out what everybody brought for lunch. And Fat Butt already wasting his peanut-butter-and-jelly sandwich like the pig he is. And Junebug punchin on Q.T.'s arm for potato chips. And Rosie Giraffe shifting from one hip to the other waiting for somebody to step on her foot or ask her if she from Georgia so she can kick ass, preferably Mercedes'. And Miss Moore asking us do we know what money is, like we a bunch of retards. I mean real money, she say, like it's only poker chips or monopoly papers we lay on the grocer. So right away I'm tired of this and say so. And would much rather snatch Sugar and go to the Sunset and terrorize the West Indian kids and take their hair ribbons and their money too. And Miss Moore files that remark away for next week's lesson on brotherhood, I can tell. And finally I say we oughta get to the subway cause it's cooler and besides we might meet some cute boys. Sugar done swiped her mama's lipstick, so we ready.

So we heading down the street and she's boring us silly about what things 3 cost and what our parents make and how much goes for rent and how money ain't divided up right in this country. And then she gets to the part about we all poor and live in the slums, which I don't feature. And I'm ready to speak on that, but she steps out in the street and hails two cabs just like that. Then she hustles half the crew in with her and hands me a five-dollar bill and tells me to calculate 10 percent tip for the driver. And we're off. Me and Sugar and Junebug and Flyboy hangin out the window and hollering to everybody, putting lipstick on each other cause Flyboy a faggot anyway, and making farts with our sweaty armpits. But I'm mostly trying to figure how to spend this money. But they all fascinated with the meter ticking and Junebug starts laying bets as to how much it'll read when Flyboy can't hold his breath no more. Then Sugar lays bets as to how much it'll be when we get there. So I'm stuck. Don't nobody want to go for my plan, which is to jump out at the next light and run off to the first bar-b-que we can find. Then the driver tells us to get the hell out cause we there already. And the meter reads eighty-five cents. And I'm stalling to figure out the tip and Sugar say give him a dime. And I decide he don't need it bad as I do, so later for him. But then he tries to take off with Junebug foot still in the door so we talk about his mamma something ferocious. Then we check out that we on Fifth Avenue and everybody dressed up in stockings. One lady in a fur coat, hot as it is. White folks crazy.

"This is the place," Miss Moore say, presenting it to us in the voice she uses 4
at the museum. "Let's look in the windows before we go in."

"Can we steal?" Sugar asks very serious like she's getting the ground rules 5
squared away before she plays. "I beg your pardon," say Miss Moore, and we fall
out. So she leads us around the windows of the toy store and me and Sugar
screamin, "This is mine, that's mine, I gotta have that, that was made for me, I
was born for that," till Big Butt drowns us out.

"Hey, I'm goin to buy that there." 6

"That there? You don't even know what it is, stupid." 7

"I do so," he say punchin on Rosie Giraffe. "It's a microscope." 8

"Whatcha gonna do with a microscope, fool?" 9

"Look at things." 10

"Like what, Ronald?" ask Miss Moore. And Big Butt ain't got the first no- 11
tion. So here go Miss Moore gabbing about the thousands of bacteria in a drop
of water and the somethinorother in a speck of blood and the million and one
living things in the air around us is invisible to the naked eye. And what she say
that for? Junebug go to town on that "naked" and we rolling. Then Miss Moore
ask what it cost. So we all jam into the window smudgin it up and the price tag
say $300. So then she ask how long'd take for Big Butt and Junebug to save up
their allowances. "Too long," I say. "Yeh," adds Sugar, "outgrown it by that time."
And Miss Moore say no, you never outgrow learning instruments. "Why, even
medical students and interns and," blah, blah, blah. And we ready to choke Big
Butt for bringing it up in the first damn place.

"This here costs four hundred eighty dollars," say Rosie Giraffe. So we pile 12
up all over her to see what she pointin out. My eyes tell me it's a chunk of glass
cracked with something heavy, and different-color inks dripped into the splits,
then the whole thing put into a oven or something. But for $480 it don't make
sense.

"That's a paperweight made of semi-precious stones fused together under 13
tremendous pressure," she explains slowly, with her hands doing the mining
and all the factory work.

"So what's a paperweight?" ask Rosie Giraffe. 14

"To weigh paper with, dumbbell," say Flyboy, the wise man from the East. 15

"Not exactly," say Miss Moore, which is what she say when you warm or way 16
off too. "It's to weigh paper down so it won't scatter and make your desk un-
tidy." So right away me and Sugar curtsy to each other and then to Mercedes
who is more the tidy type.

"We don't keep paper on top of the desk in my class," say Junebug, figuring 17
Miss Moore crazy or lyin one.

"At home, then," she say. "Don't you have a calendar and a pencil case and 18
blotter and a letter-opener on your desk at home where you do your homework?" And she know damn well what our homes look like cause she nosys
around in them every chance she gets.

"I don't even have a desk," say Junebug. "Do we?" 19

"No. And I don't get no homework neither," says Big Butt.   20

"And I don't even have a home," says Flyboy like he do at school to keep the   21
white folks off his back and sorry for him. Send this poor kid to camp posters,
is his specialty.

"I do," says Mercedes. "I have a box of stationery on my desk and a picture   22
of my cat. My godmother bought the stationery and the desk. There's a big rose
on each sheet and the envelopes smell like roses."

"Who wants to know about your smelly-ass stationery," say Rosie Giraffe   23
fore I can get my two cents in.

"It's important to have a work area all your own so that . . . "   24

"Will you look at this sailboat, please," say Flyboy, cutting her off and   25
pointin to the thing like it was his. So once again we tumble all over each other
to gaze at this magnificent thing in the toy store which is just big enough to
maybe sail two kittens across the pond if you strap them to the posts tight. We
all start reciting the price tag like we in assembly. "Handcrafted sailboat of
fiberglass at one thousand one hundred ninety-five dollars."

"Unbelievable," I hear myself say and am really stunned. I read it again for   26
myself just in case the group recitation put me in a trance. Same thing. For
some reason this pisses me off. We look at Miss Moore and she lookin at us,
waiting for I dunno what.

"Who'd pay all that when you can buy a sailboat set for a quarter at Pop's, a   27
tube of glue for a dime, and a ball of string for eight cents? It must have a motor
and a whole lot else besides," I say. "My sailboat cost me about fifty cents."

"But will it take water?" say Mercedes with her smart ass.   28

"Took mine to Alley Pond Park once," say Flyboy. "String broke. Lost it.   29
Pity."

"Sailed mine in Central Park and it keeled over and sank. Had to ask my fa-   30
ther for another dollar."

"And you got the strap," laugh Big Butt. "The jerk didn't even have a string   31
on it. My old man wailed on his behind."

Little Q.T. was staring hard at the sailboat and you could see he wanted it   32
bad. But he too little and somebody'd just take it from him. So what the hell.
"This boat for kids, Miss Moore?"

"Parents silly to buy something like that just to get all broke up," say Rosie   33
Giraffe.

"That much money it should last forever," I figure.   34

"My father'd buy it for me if I wanted it."   35

"Your father, my ass," say Rosie Giraffe getting a chance to finally push   36
Mercedes.

"Must be rich people shop here," say Q.T.   37

"You are a very bright boy," say Flyboy. "What was your first clue?" And he   38
rap him on the head with back of his knuckles, since Q.T. the only one he could
get away with. Though Q.T. liable to come up behind you years later and get his
licks in when you half expect it.

"What I want to know is," I says to Miss Moore though I never talk to her, I 39
wouldn't give the bitch that satisfaction, "is how much a real boat costs? I figure
a thousand'd get you a yacht any day."

"Why don't you check that out," she says, "and report back to the group?" 40
Which really pains my ass. If you gonna mess up a perfectly good swim day
least you could do is have some answers. "Let's go in," she say like she got something up her sleeve. Only she don't lead the way. So me and Sugar turn the corner to where the entrance is, but when we get there I kinda hang back. Not that
I'm scared, what's there to be afraid of, just a toy store. But I feel funny, shame.
But what I got to be shamed about? Got as much right to go in as anybody. But
somehow I can't seem to get hold of the door, so I step away from Sugar to lead.
But she hangs back too. And I look at her and she looks at me and this is ridiculous. I mean, damn, I have never ever been shy about doing nothing or going
nowhere. But then Mercedes steps up and then Rosie Giraffe and Big Butt
crowd in behind and shove, and next thing we all stuffed into the doorway with
only Mercedes squeezing past us, smoothing out her jumper and walking right
down the aisle. Then the rest of us tumble in like a glued-together jigsaw done
all wrong. And people lookin at us. And it's like the time me and Sugar crashed
into the Catholic church on a dare. But once we got in there and everything so
hushed and holy and the candles and the bowin and the handkerchiefs on all
the drooping heads, I just couldn't go through with the plan. Which was for me
to run up to the altar and do a tap dance while Sugar played the nose flute and
messed around in the holy water. And Sugar kept given me the elbow. Then
later teased me so bad I tied her up in the shower and turned it on and locked
her in. And she'd be there till this day if Aunt Gretchen hadn't finally figured I
was lyin about the boarder takin a shower.

Same thing in the store. We all walkin on tiptoe and hardly touchin the 41
games and puzzles and things. And I watched Miss Moore who is steady
watchin us like she waitin for a sign. Like Mama Drewery watches the sky and
sniffs the air and takes note of just how much slant is in the bird formation.
Then me and Sugar bump smack into each other, so busy gazing at the toys,
'specially the sailboat. But we don't laugh and go into our fat-lady bump-stom-
ach routine. We just stare at that price tag. Then Sugar run a finger over the
whole boat. And I'm jealous and want to hit her. Maybe not her, but I sure want
to punch somebody in the mouth.

"Watcha bring us here for, Miss Moore?" 42

"You sound angry, Sylvia. Are you mad about something?" Givin me one of 43
them grins like she tellin a grown-up joke that never turns out to be funny. And
she's lookin very closely at me like maybe she plannin to do my portrait from
memory. I'm mad, but I won't give her that satisfaction. So I slouch around the
store bein very bored and say, "Let's go."

Me and Sugar at the back of the train watchin the tracks whizzin by large 44
then small then getting gobbled up in the dark. I'm thinkin about this tricky toy
I saw in the store. A clown that somersaults on a bar then does chin-ups just

cause you yank lightly at his leg. Cost $35. I could see me askin my mother for a $35 birthday clown. "You wanna who that costs what?" she'd say, cocking her head to the side to get a better view of the hole in my head. Thirty-five dollars could buy new bunk beds for Junior and Gretchen's boy. Thirty-five dollars and the whole household could go visit Granddaddy Nelson in the country. Thirty-five dollars would pay for the rent and the piano bill too. Who are these people that spend that much for performing clowns and $1000 for toy sailboats? What kinda work they do and how they live and how come we ain't in on it? Where we are is who we are, Miss Moore always pointin out. But it don't necessarily have to be that way, she always adds then waits for somebody to say that poor people have to wake up and demand their share of the pie and don't none of us know what kind of pie she talking about in the first damn place. But she ain't so smart cause I still got her four dollars from the taxi and she sure ain't gettin it. Messin up my day with this shit. Sugar nudges me in my pocket and winks.

Miss Moore lines us up in front of the mailbox where we started from, seem   45
like years ago, and I got a headache for thinkin so hard. And we lean all over each other so we can hold up under the draggy-ass lecture she always finishes us off with at the end before we thank her for borin us to tears. But she just looks at us like she readin tea leaves. Finally she say, "Well, what did you think of F. A. O. Schwarz?"

Rosie Giraffe mumbles, "White folks crazy."   46

"I'd like to go there again when I get my birthday money," says Mercedes,   47
and we shove her out the pack so she has to lean on the mailbox by herself.

"I'd like a shower. Tiring day," say Flyboy.   48

Then Sugar surprises me by sayin, "You know, Miss Moore, I don't think all   49
of us here put together eat in a year what that sailboat costs." And Miss Moore lights up like somebody goosed her. "And?" she say, urging Sugar on. Only I'm standin on her foot so she don't continue.

"Imagine for a minute what kind of society it is in which some people can   50
spend on a toy what it would cost to feed a family of six or seven. What do you think?"

"I think," say Sugar pushing me off her feet like she never done before, cause   51
I whip her ass in a minute, "that this is not much of a democracy if you ask me. Equal chance to pursue happiness means an equal crack at the dough, don't it?" Miss Moore is besides herself and I am disgusted with Sugar's treachery. So I stand on her foot one more time to see if she'll shove me. She shuts up, and Miss Moore looks at me, sorrowfully I'm thinkin. And somethin weird is going on, I can feel it in my chest.

"Anybody else learn anything today?" lookin dead at me. I walk away and   52
Sugar has to run to catch up and don't even seem to notice when I shrug her arm off my shoulder.

"Well, we got four dollars anyway," she says.   53

"Uh, hunh."   54

"We could go to Hascombs and get a half a chocolate layer and then go to   55
the Sunset and still have plenty money for potato chips and ice cream sodas."

"Uh hunh."   56

"Race you to Hascombs," she say.   57

We start down the block and she gets ahead which is O.K. by me cause I'm go-   58
ing to the West End and then over to the Drive to think this day through. She can
run if she want to and even run faster. But ain't nobody gonna beat me at nuthin.

ACTIVITIES FOR WRITING AND DISCUSSION

1. Respond to the story using the "Four-Step Process for Writing from
Reading" described in Chapter 2. For Step #4 use any of the "Ten Ideas" listed
on page 27 of Chapter 3.

2. Summarize "the lesson" that Sylvia learns.

3. Jot down your impressions of the story's **first-person** narrator, Sylvia.
Then review the various passages of dialogue with her friends (Flyboy, Rosie
Giraffe, and so forth). Are there definite advantages to having Sylvia as narra-
tor, or could any of her friends—or even Miss Moore—have served just as well?
Explain your answer.

4. Study the story's vernacular language and style. Then write a story of
your own with a first-person narrator who uses a strong vernacular.

5. Sylvia's "lesson" isn't from a textbook but out of life—"the school of
hard knocks." Recall some "hard knocks" lesson (early or more recent) of your
own and write a story about it.

6. Sylvia ends, "But ain't nobody gonna beat me at nuthin." Interpret this
closing sentence. How does it follow from the rest of the story? Then:
   a. Write a sequel, in a point of view of your own choice (Miss Moore's
      perhaps), that traces Sylvia's subsequent life; or
   b. Imagine you are Sylvia in middle-age, and write a letter of apprecia-
      tion to Miss Moore about "the lesson," telling her about your subse-
      quent life.

MARY ROBISON (b. 1949)

I Am Twenty-One

I heard ringing, and I realized that what I had done was continued my answer   1
to Essay Question I—"What effect did the discovery of the barrel vault have on
the architecture of 13th century cathedrals?"—writing clockwise in the left,
top, and right-hand margins of page one in my exam book. I had forgotten to

move along to page two or to Essay Question II. The ringing was coming from in me—probably from overdoing it with diet pills or from the green tea all last night and from reading so much all the time.

I was doing C work in all courses but this one—"The Transition from Ro- 2 manesque to Gothic." I needed to blast this course on its butt, and that was possible because for this course I knew it all. I needed only time and space to tell it. My study notes were 253 pencil sketches from slides we had seen and from plates in books at the Fine Arts Library and some were from our text. I had sixty-seven pages of lecture notes that I had copied over once for clarity. Everything Professor Williamson had said in class was recorded in my notes—practically even his throat clearings and asides about the weather. It got to the point where if he rambled, I thought, yeah, yeah, cut the commercial and get back to the program.

Some guy whose hair I could've ripped out was finished with his exam. He 3 was actually handing it to the teaching assistant. How could he be *finished,* have given even a cursory treatment to the three questions? He was a quitter, a skimmer, I decided; a person who knew shit about detail.

I was having to stop now and then, really too often, to skin the tip of my 4 pencil with the razor blade I had brought along. I preferred a pencil because it couldn't dry up or leak. But this was a Number 2 graphite and gushy-gummy and I was writing the thing away. The eraser was just a blackened nub. Why hadn't I brought a damn *box* of pencils?

The teaching assistant was Clark—Clark Something or Something Clark, I 5 didn't know. He was baggy and sloppy, but happy-looking. He had asked me out once for Cokes, but I had brushed him off. That was maybe stupid because he might've been in charge of grading exams.

I decided to ignore Essay Question II, pretend I hadn't even seen it. I leaned 6 hard into Question III, on church decoration, windows, friezes, flora, fauna, bestiaries, the iconography in general. I was quoting Honorius of Autun when the class bell fired off.

I looked up. Most people were gone.   7

"Come on, everyone!" Clark called. "Please. Come on now. Miss Bittle? Mr. 8 Kenner, please. Miss Powers?"

"Go blow, Clark," I said right out loud. But I slapped him my exam booklet 9 and hurried out of Meverett, feeling let down and apathetic all of a sudden, and my skin going rubbery cold.

I biked home with a lot of trouble. I went on the sidewalks. I was scared that 10 in the streets I'd get my ringing confused with car warnings.

I was still ringing.   11

Last semester I had had a decorating idea for my apartment, this monastic 12 idea of strict and sparse. I had stripped the room down to a cot, a book table, one picture. The plaster walls were a nothing oatmeal color, which was okay. But not okay was that some earlier renter had gooped orange—unbelievably—

paint on the moldings and window frames. So where I lived looked not like a scholar's den, finally, but more like a bum's sleepover, like poverty.

My one picture up wasn't of a Blessed Virgin or a detail from Amiens of the 13 King of Judah holding a rod of the Tree of Jesse. Instead, it was an eight-by-ten glossy of Rudy and Leslie, my folks. Under the backing was written *Gold Coast, the first cool day.* The photo had been shot out on North Lake Shore Drive around 1964, I'd say, when I was three. Leslie, my mom, was huddled into Rudy, sharing his lined leather jacket. They appeared, for all the eye sparkle, like people in an engagement-ring ad. I kept the picture around because, oddly, putting away the *idea* of my folks would've been worse than losing the real them. In the photo, they at least *looked* familiar.

They had been secret artists. Rudy was a contractor for a living, Leslie a 14 physical therapist. So they worked all their art urges out on me—on my school projects, for instance, which they hurled themselves into. One project "I did" for seventh grade that they helped me with was, I swear, good enough for a world's fair. It was a kind of three-dimensional diorama triptych of San Francisco Bay with both bridges—Oakland and Golden Gate—that may have even lit up or glowed in the dark. We had to borrow a neighbor's station wagon just to get the thing safely over to Dreiser Junior High—it lined up as long as an ironing board.

I got my bike tugged inside, left it leaning against the wall under the photo- 15 graph. I clapped a kettle onto the midget stove in my kitchen part of the apartment, and paced, waiting for the water to heat. The pitch of the steam when it got going was only a quarter tone below the ringing in my head.

My folks were two and a half years gone. 16

I used to drive out to the site of their accident all the time—a willow tree on 17 Route 987. The last time I went, the tree was still healing. The farmlands were a grim powdery blond in the white sun, and the earth was still ragged from winter. I sat there in my tiny Vega on the broken crumbly shoulder. The great tree and the land around—flat as a griddle for miles and miles—didn't seem as fitting as I had once thought, not such a poetic place for two good lives to have stopped.

I had my tea now and grieved about the exam. Leaving a whole essay ques- 18 tion unanswered! How could I expect to get better than a C?

Just before my first sip of tea, my ringing shut off as though somebody had 19 punched a button, said, "Enough of that for her."

I decided it was time to try for sleep, but first I used a pen with a nylon point 20 to tattoo a P on the back of my hand. This meant when I woke up I was to eat some protein—shrimp or eggs or a green something.

On the cot I tried, as a sleep trick, to remember my answer to Essay Ques- 21 tion I—word for fucking word.

ACTIVITIES FOR WRITING AND DISCUSSION

1. The narrator in this story is going through hard times. Write about her from the **point of view** of someone who observes her at this point in her life, such as a classmate, the teaching assistant named in paragraph 5, or another teacher. Invent details as necessary, and note that *Robison's* **protagonist** does not have to be the exclusive focus of your story.

2. Could Robison's story be retitled "I Am Eighteen" or "I Am Twenty-Three" and keep the same basic content? How do—or don't—the conflicts and anxieties posed in the story seem unique to a twenty-one-year old? Answer with reference to specific details in the story.

3. Using this story as a springboard or model, compose a story of your own about a person of a different age, "I Am Six," "I am Forty-Five," "I Am Seventy." Make the style, vocabulary, and language of your narrator and the content appropriate to the age you choose. (Note: Do not be afraid to write from an older person's point of view just because you are young.)

Poems

JOHANN WOLFGANG VON GOETHE (1749–1832)

The Holy Longing

Tell a wise person, or else keep silent,
because the massman will mock it right away.
I praise what is truly alive,
what longs to be burned to death.

In the calm water of the love-nights,   5
where you were begotten, where you have begotten,
a strange feeling comes over you
when you see the silent candle burning.

Now you are no longer caught
in the obsession with darkness,   10
and a desire for higher love-making
sweeps you upward.

Distance does not make you falter,
now, arriving in magic, flying,
and, finally, insane for the light,   15
you are the butterfly and you are gone.

And so long as you haven't experienced
this: to die and so to grow,
you are only a troubled guest
on the dark earth.   20

    —*Translated by Robert Bly*

ACTIVITIES FOR WRITING AND DISCUSSION

 1. Analyze the central image of the poem: the burning candle sought by the moth or "butterfly." What, literally, is this image about, i.e., what natural phenomenon does it describe? In what ways might the image function as a **symbol** of a type of human experience?

 2. The poem is rich in **paradoxes.** How can something be "truly alive" if it "longs to be burned to death"? How does one "grow" through dying? What are some examples of the sort of dying the speaker intends?

 3. Invent a personal narrative written from the **point of view** of someone who has followed the advice ("to die and so to grow") given in the final stanza. Make up life stories about this person that show the process of growth through "dying."

WILLIAM BLAKE (1757–1827)

Proverbs of Hell

In seed time learn, in harvest teach, in winter enjoy.
Drive your cart and your plow over the bones of the dead.
The road of excess leads to the palace of wisdom.
Prudence is a rich, ugly old maid courted by Incapacity.
He who desires but acts not, breeds pestilence.   5
The cut worm forgives the plow.
Dip him in the river who loves water.
A fool sees not the same tree that a wise man sees.
He whose face gives no light, shall never become a star.

Eternity is in love with the productions of time.   10
The busy bee has no time for sorrow.
The hours of folly are measur'd by the clock; but of wisdom, no clock can
    measure.
All wholesome food is caught without a net or a trap.
Bring out number, weight & measure in a year of dearth.
No bird soars too high, if he soars with his own wings.   15
A dead body revenges not injuries.
The most sublime act is to set another before you.
If the fool would persist in his folly he would become wise.
Folly is the cloke of knavery.
Shame is Pride's cloke.   20
Prisons are built with stones of Law, Brothels with bricks of Religion.
The pride of the peacock is the glory of God.
The lust of the goat is the bounty of God.
The wrath of the lion is the wisdom of God.
The nakedness of woman is the work of God.   25
Excess of sorrow laughs. Excess of joy weeps.
The roaring of lions, the howling of wolves, the raging of the stormy sea, and
    the destructive sword, are portions of eternity, too great for the eye of man.
The fox condemns the trap, not himself.
Joys impregnate. Sorrows bring forth.
Let man wear the fell of the lion, woman the fleece of the sheep.   30
The bird a nest, the spider a web, man friendship.
The selfish, smiling fool, & the sullen, frowning fool shall be both thought
    wise, that they may be a rod.
What is now proved was once only imagin'd.
The rat, the mouse, the fox, the rabbet watch the roots; the lion, the tyger, the
    horse, the elephant watch the fruits.
The cistern contains: the fountain overflows.   35
One thought fills immensity.
Always be ready to speak your mind, and a base man will avoid you.
Every thing possible to be believ'd is an image of truth.
The eagle never lost so much time as when he submitted to learn of the crow.
The fox provides for himself, but God provides for the lion.   40
Think in the morning. Act in the noon. Eat in the evening. Sleep in the night.
He who has suffer'd you to impose on him, knows you.
As the plow follows words, so God rewards prayers.
The tygers of wrath are wiser than the horses of instruction.
Expect poison from the standing water.   45
You never know what is enough unless you know what is more than enough.
Listen to the fool's reproach! it is a kingly title!
The eyes of fire, the nostrils of air, the mouth of water, the beard of earth.
The weak in courage is strong in cunning.

The apple tree never asks the beech how he shall grow; nor the lion, the horse,   50
    how he shall take his prey.
The thankful receiver bears a plentiful harvest.
If others had not been foolish, we should be so.
The soul of sweet delight can never be defil'd.
When thou seest an Eagle, thou seest a portion of Genius; lift up thy head!
As the catterpiller chooses the fairest leaves to lay her eggs on, so the priest lays   55
    his curse on the fairest joys.
To create a little flower is the labour of ages.
Damn braces. Bless relaxes.
The best wine is the oldest, the best water the newest.
Prayers plow not! Praises reap not!
Joys laugh not! Sorrows weep not!   60
The head Sublime, the heart Pathos, the genitals Beauty, the hands & feet
    Proportion.
As the air to a bird or the sea to a fish, so is contempt to the contemptible.
The crow wish'd every thing was black, the owl that every thing was white.
Exuberance is Beauty.
If the lion was advised by the fox, he would be cunning.   65
Improvement makes strait roads; but the crooked roads without Improvement
    are roads of Genius.
Sooner murder an infant in its cradle than nurse unacted desires.
Where man is not, nature is barren.
Truth can never be told so as to be understood, and not be believ'd.
Enough! or Too much.   70

    The ancient Poets animated all sensible objects with Gods or Geniuses, calling them by the names and adorning them with the properties of woods, rivers, mountains, lakes, cities, nations, and whatever their enlarged & numerous senses could perceive.
    And particularly they studied the genius of each city & country, placing it under its mental deity;
    Till a system was formed, which some took advantage of, & enslav'd the vulgar by attempting to realize or abstract the mental deities from their objects: thus began Priesthood;
    Choosing forms of worship from poetic tales.
    And at length they pronounc'd that the Gods had order'd such things.   75
    Thus men forgot that All deities reside in the human breast.

ACTIVITIES FOR WRITING AND DISCUSSION

1. The "Proverbs of Hell" are Blake's most famous collection of **aphorisms.** Setting aside for a moment the unusual title, read and annotate the "Proverbs," noting especially: (a) proverbs you like; and (b) proverbs that puzzle you. Share your reactions with a partner or small group.

2. Identify striking examples of any of the following: **metaphor, simile, personification, verbal irony,** and **symbolism.** Choose two or three such examples, and, as an experiment, rewrite them using only *literal* language. In each case, how does the **figure** or **trope** pack more power than the flatly *literal* expression you tried in its place?

3. Reread page 12 in Chapter 2, which describes how Blake used annotations to stimulate his thinking and writing. Over the next several weeks use your annotations of readings and your quick-notes (see p. 46) to compose and collect aphorisms of your own.

4. Blake wrote that "Without Contraries is no progression." His "Proverbs" are excerpted from his prose satire, *The Marriage of Heaven and Hell.* Using these two facts as clues, speculate on why Blake entitled these aphorisms "Proverbs of Hell."

WALT WHITMAN (1819–1892)

To You

Whoever you are, I fear you are walking the walks of dreams,
I fear these supposed realities are to melt from under your feet and hands,
Even now your features, joys, speech, house, trade, manners, troubles, follies,
    costume, crimes, dissipate away from you,
Your true soul and body appear before me,
They stand forth out of affairs, out of commerce, shops, work, farms, clothes,   5
    the house, buying, selling, eating, drinking, suffering, dying.

Whoever you are, now I place my hand upon you, that you be my poem,
I whisper with my lips close to your ear,
I have loved many women and men, but I love none better than you.

O I have been dilatory and dumb,
I should have made my way straight to you long ago,   10
I should have blabb'd nothing but you, I should have chanted nothing but you.

I will leave all and come and make the hymns of you,
None has understood you, but I understand you,
None has done justice to you, you have not done justice to yourself,
None but has found you imperfect, I only find no imperfection in you,   15
None but would subordinate you, I only am he who will never consent to
    subordinate you,
I only am he who places over you no master, owner, better, God, beyond what
    waits intrinsically in yourself.

Painters have painted their swarming groups and the centre-figure of all,
From the head of the centre-figure spreading a nimbus of gold-color'd light,
But I paint myriads of heads, but paint no head without its nimbus of gold-   20
    color'd light,
From my hand from the brain of every man and woman it streams, effulgently
    flowing forever.

O I could sing such grandeurs and glories about you!
You have not known what you are, you have slumber'd upon yourself all your
    life,
Your eyelids have been the same as closed most of the time,
What you have done returns already in mockeries,   25
(Your thrift, knowledge, prayers, if they do not return in mockeries, what is
    their return?)

The mockeries are not you,
Underneath them and within them I see you lurk,
I pursue you where none else has pursued you,
Silence, the desk, the flippant expression, the night, the accustom'd routine, if   30
    these conceal you from others or from yourself, they do not conceal you
    from me,
The shaved face, the unsteady eye, the impure complexion, if these balk others
    they do not balk me,
The pert apparel, the deform'd attitude, drunkenness, greed, premature death,
    all these I part aside.

There is no endowment in man or woman that is not tallied in you,
There is no virtue, no beauty in man or woman, but as good is in you,
No pluck, no endurance in others, but as good is in you,   35
No pleasure waiting for others, but an equal pleasure waits for you.

As for me, I give nothing to any one except I give the like carefully to you,
I sing the songs of the glory of none, not God, sooner than I sing the songs of
    the glory of you.

Whoever you are! claim your own at any hazard!

These shows of the East and West are tame compared to you,   40
These immense meadows, these interminable rivers, you are immense and
     interminable as they,
These furies, elements, storms, motions of Nature, throes of apparent
     dissolution, you are he or she who is master or mistress over them,
Master or mistress in your own right over Nature, elements, pain, passion,
     dissolution.

The hopples fall from your ankles, you find an unfailing sufficiency,
Old or young, male or female, rude, low, rejected by the rest, whatever you are   45
     promulges itself,
Through birth, life, death, burial, the means are provided, nothing is scanted,
Through angers, losses, ambition, ignorance, ennui, what you are picks its way.

A Noiseless Patient Spider

A noiseless patient spider,
I mark'd where on a little promontory it stood isolated,
Mark'd how to explore the vacant vast surrounding,
It launch'd forth filament, filament, filament, out of itself,
Ever unreeling them, ever tirelessly speeding them.   5

And you O my soul where you stand,
Surrounded, detached, in measureless oceans of space,
Ceaselessly musing, venturing, throwing, seeking the spheres to connect them,
Till the bridge you will need be form'd, till the ductile anchor hold,
Till the gossamer thread you fling catch somewhere, O my soul.   10

ACTIVITIES FOR WRITING AND DISCUSSION

1. Read "To You" aloud to yourself or communally, with each person taking
a turn reading a few lines. As you read and listen mark any lines, phrases, or individual words that strike you. At the end of the reading share the passages that
moved you most with a small group or the class.

2. Few poets talk to "you," the reader, as directly and persistently as Whitman did. How does this direct address make you feel? uncomfortable? embarrassed? violated? understood or encouraged? some combination of the
preceding? Explain your answer with references to specific lines or passages in
the poem.

3. Characterize the speaker in "To You." Who is he? How does he know so
much? What gives him the right to talk to you with such familiarity? *Does* he

have the right? Consider addressing all of these questions by drafting a verbal portrait or description of the speaker as you imagine him.

4. Write a poem or personal letter to the speaker in "To You" in which you react to his poem and share some stories from your life that bear on its themes.

EMILY DICKINSON (1830–1886)

Because I could not stop for Death

Because I could not stop for Death—
He kindly stopped for me—
The Carriage held but just Ourselves—
And Immortality.

We slowly drove—He knew no haste   5
And I had put away
My labor and my leisure too,
For His Civility—

We passed the School, where Children strove
At Recess—in the Ring—   10
We passed the Fields of Gazing Grain—
We passed the Setting Sun—

Or rather—He passed Us—
The Dews drew quivering and chill—
For only Gossamer,¹ my Gown—   15
My Tippet²—only Tulle—³

We paused before a House that seemed
A Swelling of the Ground—
The Roof was scarcely visible—
The Cornice⁴—in the Ground—   20

Since then—'tis Centuries—and yet
Feels shorter than the Day
I first surmised the Horses Heads
Were toward Eternity—

---

1. A finely woven fabric.   2. A covering for the shoulders, such as a shawl.   3. A very fine net of silk or similar fabric.   4. Molding that crowns a roof or a wall.

Thomas Hardy (1840–1928)

The Ruined Maid

"O 'mélia, my dear, this does everything crown!
Who could have supposed I should meet you in Town?
And whence such fair garments, such prosperi-ty?"—
"O didn't you know I'd been ruined?" said she.

—"You left us in tatters, without shoes or socks,   5
Tired of digging potatoes, and spudding up docks;
And now you've gay bracelets and bright feathers three!"—
"Yes: that's how we dress when we're ruined," said she.

—"At home in the barton you said 'thee' and 'thou,'
And 'thik oon,' and 'theäs oon,' and 't'other'; but now   10
Your talking quite fits 'ee for high compa-ny!"—
"Some polish is gained with one's ruin," said she.

—"Your hands were like paws then, your face blue and bleak
But now I'm bewitched by your delicate cheek,
And your little gloves fit as on any la-dy!"—   15
"We never do work when we're ruined," said she.

—"You used to call home-life a hag-ridden dream,
And you'd sigh, and you'd sock; but at present you seem
To know not of megrims or melancho-ly!"—
"True. One's pretty lively when ruined," said she.   20

—"I wish I had feathers, a fine sweeping gown,
And a delicate face, and could strut about Town!"—
"My dear—a raw country girl, such as you be,
Cannot quite expect that. You ain't ruined," said she.

Activities for Writing and Discussion

1. Review the material on **meter** in Chapter 12 and Appendix C. Then read the poem aloud and determine its meter.

2. Consider the two speakers in the poem.
   a. How would you characterize their **diction**—as formal or informal? as **abstract** or **concrete**? as general or specific? as literal or **figurative**? Give examples.

   b. Based on the content and diction of their dialogue, what would you suppose the speakers' backgrounds to be? In what sort of environment did they grow up? What is their social status?

3. How do you interpret the word "ruined" as it is used in the poem?

4. In poetry or prose, compose a prequel to the poem. That is, reconstruct the events in the two speakers' lives that have brought them to this moment of conversation. Embellish your narrative with additional details as needed, but strive to remain faithful to the characters of the two women as set forth in the poem.

GERARD MANLEY HOPKINS (1844–1889)

Spring and Fall

To a Young Child

Márgarét, áre you gríeving
Over Goldengrove unleaving?
Leáves, líke the things of man, you
With your fresh thoughts care for, can you?
Áh! ás the heart grows older   5
It will come to such sights colder
By and by, nor spare a sigh
Though worlds of wanwood leafmeal lie;
And yet you *will* weep and know why.
Now no matter, child, the name: 10
Sórrow's spríngs áre the same.
Nor mouth had, no nor mind, expressed
What heart heard of, ghost[1] guessed:
It ís the blight man was born for,
It is Margaret you mourn for.   15

ACTIVITIES FOR WRITING AND DISCUSSION

1. The sound and **meter** of a poem were extremely important to Hopkins. In this poem he has carefully inserted accent marks (e.g., "Márgarét, are you gríeving") to indicate syllables that are to receive special stress in a pattern of

---

1. spirit, soul

what he called "sprung rhythm." Read the poem aloud several times to yourself and with a partner or small group. Though the meanings of certain lines may baffle you, concentrate on experiencing the meter and on identifying and marking any examples of sound effects such as **assonance, alliteration**, or **consonance**. Are there any lines or phrases that you find difficult to perform aloud? Explain and discuss.

2. Hopkins also experimented boldly with **diction**. Mark any words in the poem that surprise, please, or puzzle you, and, in each case, speculate on *why* Hopkins may have chosen the particular word he did. For instance, why does he use the word "unleaving" in line two or "*fresh* thoughts" in line four? Could he have chosen better alternatives?

3. Following Hopkins's example, use your own notebook or quick notes (see p. 46) to experiment with diction. Invent new words (neologisms) and play with unusual word combinations or sounds, as Hopkins does.

4. In one sentence paraphrase what you see as the main point of the poem.

C. P. Cavafy (1863–1933)

The City

You said, "I will go to another land, I will go to another sea.
Another city will be found, a better one than this.

Every effort of mine is a condemnation of fate;

and my heart is—like a corpse—buried.
How long will my mind remain in this wasteland.   5

Wherever I turn my eyes, wherever I may look
I see black ruins of my life here,
where I spent so many years destroying and wasting."

You will find no new lands, you will find no other seas.

The city will follow you. You will roam the same   10

streets. And you will age in the same neighborhoods;

and you will grow gray in these same houses.
Always you will arrive in this city. Do not hope for any
    other—

There is no ship for you, there is no road.
As you have destroyed your life here   15
in this little corner, you have ruined it in the entire world.

—Translated by Rae Dalven

Denise Levertov (1923–1997)

Contraband

The tree of knowledge was the tree of reason.
That's why the taste of it
drove us from Eden. That fruit
was meant to be dried and milled to a fine powder
for use a pinch at a time, a condiment.   5
God had probably planned to tell us later
about this new pleasure.
                          We stuffed our mouths full of it,
gorged on *but* and *if* and *how* and again
but, knowing no better.   10
It's toxic in large quantities; fumes
swirled in our heads and around us
to form a dense cloud that hardened to steel,
a wall between us and God, Who was Paradise.
Not that God is unreasonable   but reason   15
in such excess was tyranny
and locked us into its own limits, a polished cell
reflecting our own faces. God lives
on the other side of that mirror,
but through the slit where the barrier doesn't   20
quite touch ground, manages still
to squeeze in   as filtered light,
splinters of fire, a strain of music heard
then lost, then heard again.

Donald Justice (b. 1925)

Men at forty

Men at forty
Learn to close softly
The doors to rooms they will not be
Coming back to.

At rest on a stair landing,
They feel it
Moving beneath them now like the deck of a ship,   5
Though the swell is gentle.

And deep in mirrors
They rediscover   10
The face of the boy as he practices tying
His father's tie there in secret

And the face of that father,
Still warm with the mystery of lather.
They are more fathers than sons themselves now.   15
Something is filling them, something

That is like the twilight sound
Of the crickets, immense,
Filling the woods at the foot of the slope
Behind their mortgaged houses.   20

Maya Angelou (b. 1928)

Seven Women's Blessed Assurance

1
One thing about me,
I'm little and low,
find me a man
wherever I go.

2
They call me string bean   5
'cause I'm so tall.
Men see me,
they ready to fall.

3
I'm young as morning
and fresh as dew.   10
Everybody loves me
and so do you.

4

I'm fat as butter
and sweet as cake.
Men start to tremble   15
each time I shake.

5

I'm little and lean,
sweet to the bone.
They like to pick me up
and carry me home.   20

6

When I passed forty
I dropped pretense,
'cause men like women
who got some sense.

7

Fifty-five is perfect,   25
so is fifty-nine,
'cause every man needs
to rest sometime.

Ursula Fanthorpe (b. 1929)

Growing Up

I wasn't good
At being a baby. Burrowed my way
Through the long yawn of infancy,
Masking by instinct how much I knew
Of the senior world, sabotaging   5
As far as I could, biding my time,
Biting my rattle, my brother (in private),
Shoplifting daintily into my pram.
Not a good baby,
No.   10

I wasn't good
At being a child. I missed
The innocent age. Children,

Being childish, were beneath me.
Adults I despised or distrusted. They   15
Would label my every disclosure
Precocious, naïve, whatever it was.
I disdained definition, preferred to be surly.
Not a nice child,
No.   20

I wasn't good
At adolescence. There was a dance,
A catchy rhythm; I was out of step.
My body capered, nudging me
With hairy, fleshy growths and monthly outbursts,   25
To join the party. I tried to annul
The future, pretended I knew it already,
Was caught bloody-thighed, a criminal
Guilty of puberty.
Not a nice girl,   30
No.
(My hero, intransigent Emily,
Cauterised her own-dog-mauled
Arm with a poker,
Struggled to die on her feet,   35
Never told anyone anything.)

I wasn't good
At growing up. Never learned
The natives' art of life. Conversation
Disintegrated as I touched it,   40
So I played mute, wormed along years,
Reciting the hard-learned arcane litany
Of cliché, my company passport.
Not a nice person,
No.   45

The gift remains
Masonic,[1] dark. But age affords
A vocation even for wallflowers.
Called to be connoisseur, I collect,
Admire, the effortless bravura   50
Of other people's lives, proper and comely,
Treading the measure, shopping, chaffing,

---

1. Masonic here means "secret."

Quarrelling, drinking, not knowing
How right they are, or how, like well-oiled bolts,
Swiftly and sweet, they slot into the grooves   55
Their ancestors smoothed out along the grain.

Audre Lorde (1934–1992)

Hanging Fire

I am fourteen
and my skin has betrayed me
the boy I cannot live without
still sucks his thumb
in secret   5
how come my knees are
always so ashy
what if I die
before morning
and momma's in the bedroom   10
with the door closed.

I have to learn how to dance
in time for the next party
my room is too small for me
suppose I die before graduation   15
they will sing sad melodies
but finally
tell the truth about me
There is nothing I want to do
and too much   20
that has to be done
and momma's in the bedroom
with the door closed.

Nobody even stops to think
about my side of it   25
I should have been on Math Team
my marks were better than his
why do I have to be
the one
wearing braces   30
I have nothing to wear tomorrow
will I live long enough

to grow up
and momma's in the bedroom
with the door closed.   35

ACTIVITIES FOR WRITING AND DISCUSSION

1. Other than the periods at the ends of stanzas, the poem has no punctuation. How does this lack of punctuation affect the way you read the poem, and how (if at all) does it "fit" the subject of the poem?

2. How do you explain the repetition of the lines "and momma's in the bedroom/with the door closed" at the end of each stanza?

3. After annotating the poem, identify a particular line or group of lines that resonates with your own experience of adolescence. Use the line(s) as a "springboard" to writing about that experience.

4. Rewrite the poem as a dialogue between the **speaker** and her "momma."

MARY OLIVER (b. 1935)

The Black Snake

When the black snake
flashed onto the morning road,
and the truck could not swerve—
death, that is how it happens.

Now he lies looped and useless   5
as an old bicycle tire.
I stop the car
and carry him into the bushes.

He is as cool and gleaming
as a braided whip, he is as beautiful and quiet   10
as a dead brother.
I leave him under the leaves

and drive on, thinking
about *death:* its suddenness,
its terrible weight,   15
its certain coming. Yet under

reason burns a brighter fire, which the bones
have always preferred.
It is the story of endless good fortune.
It says to oblivion: not me!   20

It is the light at the center of every cell.
It is what sent the snake coiling and flowing forward
happily all spring through the green leaves before
he came to the road.

Some Questions You Might Ask

Is the soul solid, like iron?
Or is it tender and breakable, like
the wings of a moth in the beak of the owl?
Who has it, and who doesn't?
I keep looking around me.   5
The face of the moose is as sad
as the face of Jesus.
The swan opens her white wings slowly.
In the fall, the black bear carries leaves into the darkness.
One question leads to another.   10
Does it have a shape? Like an iceberg?
Like the eye of a hummingbird?
Does it have one lung, like the snake and the scallop?
Why should I have it, and not the anteater
who loves her children?   15
Why should I have it, and not the camel?
Come to think of it, what about the maple trees?
What about the blue iris?
What about all the little stones, sitting alone in the moonlight?
What about roses, and lemons, and their shining leaves?   20
What about the grass?

BARBARA CROOKER (b. 1945)

Patty's Charcoal Drive-in

First job. In tight black shorts
and a white bowling shirt, red lipstick
and bouncing pony tail, I present

each overflowing tray as if it were a banquet.
I'm sixteen and college-bound,   5
this job's temporary as the summer sun,
but right now, it's the boundaries of my life.
After the first few nights of mixed orders
and missing cars, the work goes easily.
I take out the silver trays and hook them to the windows,   10
inhale the mingled smells of seared meat patties,
salty ketchup, rich sweet malteds.
The lure of grease drifts through the thick night air.
And it's always summer at Patty's Charcoal Drive-In—
carloads of blonde-and-tan girls   15
pull up next to red convertibles,
boys in black tee shirts and slick hair.
Everyone knows what they want.
And I wait on them, hoping for tips,
loose pieces of silver   20
flung carelessly as the stars.
Doo-wop music streams from the jukebox
and each night repeats itself,
faithful as a steady date.
Towards 10 P.M., traffic dwindles.   25
We police the lot, pick up wrappers.
The dark pours down, sticky as Coke,
but the light from the kitchen
gleams like a beacon.
A breeze comes up, chasing papers   30
in the far corners of the darkened lot,
as if suddenly a cold wind had started to blow
straight at me from the future—
I read that in a Doris Lessing book—
but right now, purse fat with tips,   35
the moon sitting like a cheeseburger on a flat black grill,
this is enough.
Your order please.

Activities for Writing and Discussion

1. Respond to "Patty's Charcoal Drive-in" using the "Four-Step Process for Writing from Reading" described in Chapter 2.

2. Writing in either verse or prose, tell the story of your own first job. Following Crooker's example, use sensual details of sight, sound, taste, touch, and smell to locate the job within a specific time and place in your life.

Mark Rudman (b. 1948)

Chrome

On the late news I watch hundreds of helmeted riders
almost indecipherable in the dust
tearing up the holes of desert turtles in the Mojave[1]—
and I remember our bravura cycling:
the trick was to go as fast as you could   5
without being thrown by rock or incline.
Hills leeched of color,
the desert a kind of form,
with rimrock and succulents and gulches
providing borders—boundaries.   10
Dust and desire.
I wanted to go down toward the desert floor,
where the spines of the saguaro cactus
guarded the sticky pulp I loved,
the sweet, incomparable, centerless center.   15
O sweet sixteen, to be sprung again and again against
the rock-studded sand, the danger not
in the desert but around it.
The body's oneness with the mind
on the lean machine seemed just right, the body   20
soaring while hovering close
to the sand as the Honda 125
jounced past yucca and cactus and took
the long dip into the arroyo[2] where the ring
of distant chimney rocks and hills   25
like space stations receded, and I
twisted the handle-bars like the horns
of a steer to side-wind up and over the rim.
I was thrown only by breaks in the terrain,
grit and stones and dips in the sand,   30
or by sudden soft patches; or by swerving to avoid
a brush with tumbleweed or a mesquite bush.
Spills were rehearsals for free falling, a way to slow
time down, cease to feel your own weight,
achieve clarity and edge as if edging down   35
off the concrete onto the sand was the aim. . . .
Circling demoniacally, I didn't notice

---

1. A desert in the southwestern United States   2. A gully cut by a stream.

the ferocious sun, a fusion of horizon and sky,
or the hawks stunned and motionless as clouds.
Each time, bloody but happy,   40
I eased back onto the highway,
and set off down the canyon road
into the sun, whitening as it hung
level with the cliff. Once I rode toward it
hearing only the hush of the tires,   45
the pure elation of it taking my head off as I took
a horseshoe curve at 50 and approached
an even sharper one—the slender cycle shaking apart—;
and I wondered *what to do,* like Porthos[3]
going back to the bomb he'd planted to make sure   50
he'd lit the fuse . . . when — BOOM!—;
I turned the accelerator handle all the way forward
to slow down—gunning the engine
by accident when the cycle bucked, reared,
and surged ahead—I rose, the cliff's gravel   55
gleamed, radiant, it was all over;
I could feel my soul leave my body and see my body flung out
over the canyon rim—
it looked as if I'd leap the cliff and fly
into the sun, time gone, space erased,   60
not a piñon in sight to break my fall, only the cliff
wall, studded with jagged stones.
And I knew if I braked abruptly on the gravel the bike
would catapult me headlong into the open,
so I let go of the throttle—threw up my hands—   65
and the bike went off the highway, keeled over
and died at the cliff's edge.
I owe my life to letting go.

Gary Soto (b. 1952)

Oranges

The first time I walked
With a girl, I was twelve,
Cold, and weighted down
With two oranges in my jacket.

---

3. One of the musketeers in Alexandre Dumas's *The Three Musketeers* (1846).

December. Frost cracking   5
Beneath my steps, my breath
Before me, then gone,
As I walked toward
Her house, the one whose
Porch light burned yellow   10
Night and day, in any weather.
A dog barked at me, until
She came out pulling
At her gloves, face bright
With rouge. I smiled,   15
Touched her shoulder, and led
Her down the street, across
A used car lot and a line
Of newly planted trees,
Until we were breathing   20
Before a drugstore. We
Entered, the tiny bell
Bringing a saleslady
Down a narrow aisle of goods.
I turned to the candies   25
Tiered like bleachers,
And asked what she wanted—
Light in her eyes, a smile
Starting at the corners
Of her mouth. I fingered   30
A nickel in my pocket,
And when she lifted a chocolate
That cost a dime,
I didn't say anything.
I took the nickel from   35
My pocket, then an orange,
And set them quietly on
The counter. When I looked up,
The lady's eyes met mine,
And held them, knowing   40
Very well what it was all
About.

     Outside,
A few cars hissing past,
Fog hanging like old   45
Coats between the trees.
I took my girl's hand
In mine for two blocks,

Then released it to let
Her unwrap the chocolate.
I peeled my orange   50
That was so bright against
The gray of December
That, from some distance,
Someone might have thought   55
I was making a fire in my hands.

ACTIVITIES FOR WRITING AND DISCUSSION

1. What was the incident of the nickel and the orange "all/About" (lines 41–42)? In your notebook, narrate any similar incidents in your own experience.

2. In poetry or prose, retell the incident of the nickel and the orange from the **point of view** of either the girl or the saleslady.

3. With what mixture of emotions does the poem leave you? Explain.

Nonfiction/Essays

MAYA ANGELOU (b. 1928)

Graduation

The children in Stamps[1] trembled visibly with anticipation. Some adults were excited too, but to be certain the whole young population had come down with graduation epidemic. Large classes were graduating from both the grammar school and the high school. Even those who were years removed from their own day of glorious release were anxious to help with preparations as a kind of dry run. The junior students who were moving into the vacating classes' chairs were tradition-bound to show their talents for leadership and management. They strutted through the school and around the campus exerting pressure on the lower grades. Their authority was so new that occasionally if they pressed a little too hard it had to be overlooked. After all, next term was coming, and it never hurt a sixth grader to have a play sister in the eighth grade, or a tenth-year

---

1. A town in Arkansas.

student to be able to call a twelfth grader Bubba. So all was endured in a spirit of shared understanding. But the graduating classes themselves were the nobility. Like travelers with exotic destinations on their minds, the graduates were remarkably forgetful. They came to school without their books, or tablets or even pencils. Volunteers fell over themselves to secure replacements for the missing equipment. When accepted, the willing workers might or might not be thanked, and it was of no importance to the pregraduation rites. Even teachers were respectful of the now quiet and aging seniors, and tended to speak to them, if not as equals, as beings only slightly lower than themselves. After tests were returned and grades given, the student body, which acted like an extended family, knew who did well, who excelled, and what piteous ones had failed.

Unlike the white high school, Lafayette County Training School distinguished itself by having neither lawn, nor hedges, nor tennis court, nor climbing ivy. Its two buildings (main classrooms, the grade school and home economics) were set on a dirt hill with no fence to limit either its boundaries or those of bordering farms. There was a large expanse to the left of the school which was used alternately as a baseball diamond or basketball court. Rusty hoops on swaying poles represented the permanent recreational equipment, although bats and balls could be borrowed from the P.E. teacher if the borrower was qualified and if the diamond wasn't occupied.

Over this rocky area relieved by a few shady tall persimmon trees the graduating class walked. The girls often held hands and no longer bothered to speak to the lower students. There was a sadness about them, as if this old world was not their home and they were bound for higher ground. The boys, on the other hand, had become more friendly, more outgoing. A decided change from the closed attitude they projected while studying for finals. Now they seemed not ready to give up the old school, the familiar paths and classrooms. Only a small percentage would be continuing on to college—one of the South's A & M (agricultural and mechanical) schools, which trained Negro youths to be carpenters, farmers, handymen, masons, maids, cooks and baby nurses. Their future rode heavily on their shoulders, and blinded them to the collective joy that had pervaded the lives of the boys and girls in the grammar school graduating class.

Parents who could afford it had ordered new shoes and readymade clothes for themselves from Sears and Roebuck or Montgomery Ward. They also engaged the best seamstresses to make the floating graduating dresses and to cut down secondhand pants which would be pressed to a military slickness for the important event.

Oh, it was important, all right. Whitefolks would attend the ceremony, and two or three would speak of God and home, and the Southern way of life, and Mrs. Parsons, the principal's wife, would play the graduation march while the lower-grade graduates paraded down the aisles and took their seats below the platform. The high school seniors would wait in empty classrooms to make their dramatic entrance.

In the Store I was the person of the moment. The birthday girl. The center. Bailey[2] had graduated the year before, although to do so he had had to forfeit all pleasures to make up for his time lost in Baton Rouge.

My class was wearing butter-yellow piqué dresses, and Momma launched out on mine. She smocked the yoke into tiny crisscrossing puckers, then shirred the rest of the bodice. Her dark fingers ducked in and out of the lemony cloth as she embroidered raised daisies around the hem. Before she considered herself finished she had added a crocheted cuff on the puff sleeves, and a pointy crocheted collar.

I was going to be lovely. A walking model of all the various styles of fine hand sewing and it didn't worry me that I was only twelve years old and merely graduating from the eighth grade. Besides, many teachers in Arkansas Negro schools had only that diploma and were licensed to impart wisdom.

The days had become longer and more noticeable. The faded beige of former times had been replaced with strong and sure colors. I began to see my classmates' clothes, their skin tones, and the dust that waved off pussy willows. Clouds that lazed across the sky were objects of great concern to me. Their shiftier shapes might have held a message that in my new happiness and with a little bit of time I'd soon decipher. During that period I looked at the arch of heaven so religiously my neck kept a steady ache. I had taken to smiling more often, and my jaws hurt from the unaccustomed activity. Between the two physical sore spots, I suppose I could have been uncomfortable, but that was not the case. As a member of the winning team (the graduating class of 1940) I had outdistanced unpleasant sensations by miles. I was headed for the freedom of open fields.

Youth and social approval allied themselves with me and we trammeled 10
memories of slights and insults. The wind of our swift passage remodeled my features. Lost tears were pounded to mud and then to dust. Years of withdrawal were brushed aside and left behind, as hanging ropes of parasitic moss.

My work alone had awarded me a top place and I was going to be one of the first called in the graduating ceremonies. On the classroom blackboard, as well as on the bulletin board in the auditorium, there were blue stars and white stars and red stars. No absences, no tardinesses, and my academic work was among the best of the year. I could say the preamble to the Constitution even faster than Bailey. We timed ourselves often: "We the people of the United States in order to form a more perfect union . . ." I had memorized the Presidents of the United States from Washington to Roosevelt in chronological as well as alphabetical order.

My hair pleased me too. Gradually the black mass had lengthened and thickened, so that it kept at last to its braided pattern, and I didn't have to yank my scalp off when I tried to comb it.

Louise and I had rehearsed the exercises until we tired out ourselves. Henry Reed was class valedictorian. He was a small, very black boy with hooded eyes, a

---

2. The author's brother.

long, broad nose and an oddly shaped head. I had admired him for years because each term he and I vied for the best grades in our class. Most often he bested me, but instead of being disappointed I was pleased that we shared top places between us. Like many Southern Black children, he lived with his grandmother, who was as strict as Momma and as kind as she knew how to be. He was courteous, respectful and soft-spoken to elders, but on the playground he chose to play the roughest games. I admired him. Anyone, I reckoned, sufficiently afraid or sufficiently dull could be polite. But to be able to operate at a top level with both adults and children was admirable.

His valedictory speech was entitled "To Be or Not to Be." The rigid tenth-grade teacher had helped him write it. He'd been working on the dramatic stresses for months.

The weeks until graduation were filled with heady activities. A group of small children were to be presented in a play about buttercups and daisies and bunny rabbits. They could be heard throughout the building practicing their hops and their little songs that sounded like silver bells. The older girls (non-graduates, of course) were assigned the task of making refreshments for the night's festivities. A tangy scent of ginger, cinnamon, nutmeg and chocolate wafted around the home economics building as the budding cooks made samples for themselves and their teachers.

In every corner of the workshop, axes and saws split fresh timber as the woodshop boys made sets and stage scenery. Only the graduates were left out of the general bustle. We were free to sit in the library at the back of the building or look on quite detachedly, naturally, on the measures being taken for our event.

Even the minister preached on graduation the Sunday before. His subject was, "Let your light so shine that men will see your good works and praise your Father, Who is in Heaven." Although the sermon was purported to be addressed to us, he used the occasion to speak to backsliders, gamblers and general ne'er-do-wells. But since he had called our names at the beginning of the service we were mollified.

Among Negroes the tradition was to give presents to children going only from one grade to another. How much more important this was when the person was graduating at the top of the class. Uncle Willie and Momma had sent away for a Mickey Mouse watch like Bailey's. Louise gave me four embroidered handkerchiefs. (I gave her crocheted doilies.) Mrs. Sneed, the minister's wife, made me an undershirt to wear for graduation, and nearly every customer gave me a nickel or maybe even a dime with the instruction "Keep on moving to higher ground," or some such encouragement.

Amazingly the great day finally dawned and I was out of bed before I knew it. I threw open the back door to see it more clearly, but Momma said, "Sister, come away from that door and put your robe on."

I hoped the memory of that morning would never leave me. Sunlight was itself young, and the day had none of the insistence maturity would bring it in a few hours. In my robe and barefoot in the backyard, under cover of going to see about my new beans, I gave myself up to the gentle warmth and thanked God that no matter what evil I had done in my life He had allowed me to live to see this day. Somewhere in my fatalism I had expected to die, accidentally, and never have the chance to walk up the stairs in the auditorium and gracefully receive my hard-earned diploma. Out of God's merciful bosom I had won reprieve.

Bailey came out in his robe and gave me a box wrapped in Christmas paper. He said he had saved his money for months to pay for it. It felt like a box of chocolates, but I knew Bailey wouldn't save money to buy candy when we had all we could want under our noses.

He was as proud of the gift as I. It was a soft-leather-bound copy of a collection of poems by Edgar Allan Poe, or, as Bailey and I called him, "Eap." I turned to "Annabel Lee" and we walked up and down the garden rows, the cool dirt between our toes, reciting the beautifully sad lines.

Momma made a Sunday breakfast although it was only Friday. After we finished the blessing, I opened my eyes to find the watch on my plate. It was a dream of a day. Everything went smoothly and to my credit I didn't have to be reminded or scolded for anything. Near evening I was too jittery to attend to chores, so Bailey volunteered to do all before his bath.

Days before, we had made a sign for the Store, and as we turned out the lights Momma hung the cardboard over the doorknob. It read clearly: CLOSED, GRADUATION.

My dress fitted perfectly and everyone said that I looked like a sunbeam in it. On the hill, going toward the school, Bailey walked behind with Uncle Willie, who muttered, "Go on, Ju." He wanted him to walk ahead with us because it embarrassed him to have to walk so slowly. Bailey said he'd let the ladies walk together, and the men would bring up the rear. We all laughed, nicely.

Little children dashed by out of the dark like fireflies. Their crepe-paper dresses and butterfly wings were not made for running and we heard more than one rip, dryly, and the regretful "uh oh" that followed.

The school blazed without gaiety. The windows seemed cold and unfriendly from the lower hill. A sense of ill-fated timing crept over me, and if Momma hadn't reached for my hand I would have drifted back to Bailey and Uncle Willie, and possibly beyond. She made a few slow jokes about my feet getting cold, and tugged me along to the now-strange building.

Around the front steps, assurance came back. There were my fellow "greats," the graduating class. Hair brushed back, legs oiled, new dresses and pressed pleats, fresh pocket handkerchiefs and little handbags, all homesewn. Oh, we were up to snuff, all right. I joined my comrades and didn't even see my family go in to find seats in the crowded auditorium.

The school band struck up a march and all classes filed in as had been rehearsed. We stood in front of our seats, as assigned, and on a signal from the choir director, we sat. No sooner had this been accomplished than the band started to play the national anthem. We rose again and sang the song, after which we recited the pledge of allegiance. We remained standing for a brief minute before the choir director and the principal signaled to us, rather desperately I thought, to take our seats. The command was so unusual that our carefully rehearsed and smooth-running machine was thrown off. For a full minute we fumbled for our chairs and bumped into each other awkwardly. Habits change or solidify under pressure, so in our state of nervous tension we had been ready to follow our usual assembly pattern: the American national anthem, then the pledge of allegiance, then the song every Black person I knew called the Negro National Anthem. All done in the same key, with the same passion and most often standing on the same foot.

Finding my seat at last, I was overcome with a presentiment of worse things 30 to come. Something unrehearsed, unplanned, was going to happen, and we were going to be made to look bad. I distinctly remember being explicit in the choice of pronoun. It was "we," the graduating class, the unit, that concerned me then.

The principal welcomed "parents and friends" and asked the Baptist minister to lead us in prayer. His invocation was brief and punchy, and for a second I thought we were getting on the high road to right action. When the principal came back to the dais, however, his voice had changed. Sounds always affected me profoundly and the principal's voice was one of my favorites. During assembly it melted and lowed weakly into the audience. It had not been in my plan to listen to him, but my curiosity was piqued and I straightened up to give him my attention.

He was talking about Booker T. Washington, our "late great leader," who said we can be as close as the fingers on the hand, etc. . . . Then he said a few vague things about friendship and the friendship of kindly people to those less fortunate than themselves. With that his voice nearly faded, thin, away. Like a river diminishing to a stream and then to a trickle. But he cleared his throat and said, "Our speaker tonight, who is also our friend, came from Texarkana to deliver the commencement address, but due to the irregularity of the train schedule, he's going to, as they say, 'speak and run.' " He said that we understood and wanted the man to know that we were most grateful for the time he was able to give us and then something about how we were willing always to adjust to another's program, and without more ado—"I give you Mr. Edward Donleavy."

Not one but two white men came through the door off-stage. The shorter one walked to the speaker's platform, and the tall one moved to the center seat and sat down. But that was our principal's seat, and already occupied. The dislodged gentleman bounced around for a long breath or two before the Baptist minister gave him his chair, then with more dignity than the situation deserved, the minister walked off the stage.

Donleavy looked at the audience once (on reflection, I'm sure that he wanted only to reassure himself that we were really there), adjusted his glasses and began to read from a sheaf of papers.

He was glad "to be here and to see the work going on just as it was in the 35 other schools."

At the first "Amen" from the audience I willed the offender to immediate death by choking on the word. But Amens and Yes, sir's began to fall around the room like rain through a ragged umbrella.

He told us of the wonderful changes we children in Stamps had in store. The Central School (naturally, the white school was Central) had already been granted improvements that would be in use in the fall. A well-known artist was coming from Little Rock to teach art to them. They were going to have the newest microscopes and chemistry equipment for their laboratory. Mr. Donleavy didn't leave us long in the dark over who made these improvements available to Central High. Nor were we to be ignored in the general betterment scheme he had in mind.

He said that he had pointed out to people at a very high level that one of the first-line football tacklers at Arkansas Agricultural and Mechanical College had graduated from good old Lafayette County Training School. Here fewer Amen's were heard. Those few that did break through lay dully in the air with the heaviness of habit.

He went on to praise us. He went on to say how he had bragged that "one of the best basketball players at Fisk sank his first ball right here at Lafayette County Training School."

The white kids were going to have a chance to become Galileos and 40 Madame Curies and Edisons and Gauguins, and our boys (the girls weren't even in on it) would try to be Jesse Owenses and Joe Louises.

Owens and the Brown Bomber were great heroes in our world, but what school official in the white-goddom of Little Rock had the right to decide that those two men must be our only heroes? Who decided that for Henry Reed to become a scientist he had to work like George Washington Carver, as a bootblack, to buy a lousy microscope? Bailey was obviously always going to be too small to be an athlete, so which concrete angel glued to what country seat had decided that if my brother wanted to become a lawyer he had to first pay penance for his skin by picking cotton and hoeing corn and studying correspondence books at night for twenty years?

The man's dead words fell like bricks around the auditorium and too many settled in my belly. Constrained by hard-learned manners I couldn't look behind me, but to my left and right the proud graduating class of 1940 had dropped their heads. Every girl in my row had found something new to do with her handkerchief. Some folded the tiny squares into love knots, some into triangles, but most were wadding them, then pressing them flat on their yellow laps.

On the dais, the ancient tragedy was being replayed. Professor Parsons sat, a sculptor's reject, rigid. His large, heavy body seemed devoid of will or willingness, and his eyes said he was no longer with us. The other teachers examined the flag (which was draped stage right) or their notes, or the windows which opened on our now-famous playing diamond.

Graduation, the hush-hush magic time of frills and gifts and congratulations and diplomas, was finished for me before my name was called. The accomplishment was nothing. The meticulous maps, drawn in three colors of ink, learning and spelling decasyllabic words, memorizing the whole of *The Rape of Lucrece*—it was for nothing. Donleavy had exposed us.

We were maids and farmers, handymen and washerwomen, and anything 45
higher that we aspired to was farcical and presumptuous.

Then I wished that Gabriel Prosser and Nat Turner had killed all whitefolks
in their beds and that Abraham Lincoln had been assassinated before the signing
of the Emancipation Proclamation, and that Harriet Tubman had been killed
by that blow on her head and Christopher Columbus had drowned in the *Santa
Maria.*

It was awful to be a Negro and have no control over my life. It was brutal to
be young and already trained to sit quietly and listen to charges brought against
my color with no chance of defense. We should all be dead. I thought I should
like to see us all dead, one on top of the other. A pyramid of flesh with the
whitefolks on the bottom, as the broad base, then the Indians with their silly
tomahawks and teepees and wigwams and treaties, the Negroes with their mops
and recipes and cotton sacks and spirituals sticking out of their mouths. The
Dutch children should all stumble in their wooden shoes and break their necks.
The French should choke to death on the Louisiana Purchase (1803) while silk-
worms ate all the Chinese with their stupid pigtails. As a species, we were an
abomination. All of us.

Donleavy was running for election, and assured our parents that if he won
we could count on having the only colored paved playing field in that part of
Arkansas. Also—he never looked up to acknowledge the grunts of acceptance—also, we were bound to get some new equipment for the home economics building and the workshop.

He finished, and since there was no need to give any more than the most
perfunctory thank-you's, he nodded to the men on the stage, and the tall white
man who was never introduced joined him at the door. They left with the atti
tude that now they were off to something really important. (The graduation
ceremonies at Lafayette County Training School had been a mere preliminary.)

The ugliness they left was palpable. An uninvited guest who wouldn't leave. 50
The choir was summoned and sang a modern arrangement of "Onward, Christian Soldiers," with new words pertaining to graduates seeking their place in the
world. But it didn't work. Elouise, the daughter of the Baptist minister, recited
"Invictus," and I could have cried at the impertinence of "I am the master of my
fate, I am the captain of my soul."

My name had lost its ring of familiarity and I had to be nudged to go and receive my diploma. All my preparations had fled. I neither marched up to the
stage like a conquering Amazon, nor did I look in the audience for Bailey's nod
of approval. Marguerite Johnson, I heard the name again, my honors were read,
there were noises in the audience of appreciation, and I took my place on the
stage as rehearsed.

I thought about colors I hated: ecru, puce, lavender, beige and black.

There was shuffling and rustling around me, then Henry Reed was giving
his valedictory address, "To Be or Not to Be." Hadn't he heard the whitefolks?
We couldn't *be,* so the question was a waste of time. Henry's voice came out
clear and strong. I feared to look at him. Hadn't he got the message? There was

no "nobler in the mind" for Negroes because the world didn't think we had minds, and they let us know it. "Outrageous fortune"? Now, that was a joke. When the ceremony was over I had to tell Henry Reed some things. That is, if I still cared. Not "rub," Henry, "erase." "Ah, there's the erase." Us.

Henry had been a good student in elocution. His voice rose on tides of promise and fell on waves of warnings. The English teacher had helped him to create a sermon winging through Hamlet's soliloquy. To be a man, a doer, a builder, a leader, or to be a tool, an unfunny joke, a crusher of funky toadstools. I marveled that Henry could go through with the speech as if we had a choice.

I had been listening and silently rebutting each sentence with my eyes 55 closed; then there was a hush, which in an audience warns that something unplanned is happening. I looked up and saw Henry Reed, the conservative, the proper, the A student, turn his back to the audience and turn to us (the proud graduating class of 1940) and sing, nearly speaking,

> "Lift ev'ry voice and sing
> Till earth and heaven ring
> Ring with the harmonies of Liberty . . ."

It was the poem written by James Weldon Johnson. It was the music composed by J. Rosamond Johnson. It was the Negro national anthem. Out of habit we were singing it.

Our mothers and fathers stood in the dark hall and joined the hymn of encouragement. A kindergarten teacher led the small children onto the stage and the buttercups and daisies and bunny rabbits marked time and tried to follow:

> "Stony the road we trod
> Bitter the chastening rod
> Felt in the days when hope, unborn, had died.
> Yet with a steady beat
> Have not our weary feet
> Come to the place for which our fathers sighed?"

Each child I knew had learned that song with his ABC's and along with "Jesus Loves Me This I Know." But I personally had never heard it before. Never heard the words, despite the thousands of times I had sung them. Never thought they had anything to do with me.

On the other hand, the words of Patrick Henry had made such an impression on me that I had been able to stretch myself tall and trembling and say, "I know not what course others may take, but as for me, give me liberty or give me death."

And now I heard, really for the first time:

> "We have come over a way that with tears
> has been watered,

We have come, treading our path through
the blood of the slaughtered."

While echoes of the song shivered in the air, Henry Reed bowed his head, 60
said "Thank you," and returned to his place in the line. The tears that slipped
down many faces were not wiped away in shame.

We were on top again. As always, again. We survived. The depths had been
icy and dark, but now a bright sun spoke to our souls. I was no longer simply a
member of the proud graduating class of 1940; I was a proud member of the
wonderful, beautiful Negro race.

Oh, Black known and unknown poets, how often have your auctioned pains
sustained us? Who will compute the lonely nights made less lonely by your
songs, or the empty pots made less tragic by your tales?

If we were a people much given to revealing secrets, we might raise monu-
ments and sacrifice to the memories of our poets, but slavery cured us of that
weakness. It may be enough, however, to have it said that we survive in exact relationship to the dedication of our poets (include preachers, musicians and
blues singers).

EDWARD HOAGLAND (b. 1932)

Learning to Eat Soup

Learning to eat soup: Like little boats that go out to sea, I push my spoon ahead
of me.

At my parents' wedding in Michigan, one of Mother's uncles leaned over before the cake cutting and whispered to her, "Feed the brute and flatter the ass."
The uncles threw rice at them as they jumped into their car, and Dad, after going a mile down the road, stopped and silently swept it out. That night, before
deflowering each other (both over thirty), they knelt by the bed to consecrate
the experience.

To strike a balance is everything. If a person sings quietly to himself on the
street, people smile with approval; but if he talks, it's not all right; they think
he's crazy. The singer is presumed to be happy and the talker unhappy, which
counts heavily against him. . . . To strike a balance: If, for example, walking in
the woods, we flake off a bit of hangnail skin and an ant drags this bonanza
away, we might say that the ants were feasting on human flesh, but probably
wouldn't. On the other hand, if a man suffers a heart attack there and festers
undiscovered, then we would.

Baby inside M.'s stomach feels like the popping and simmering of oatmeal cooking, as I lay my hand across. Pain, "a revelation to me like fireworks, those comets that whirl," she says in the labor room. She lies like a boy under stress in the canoe-shaped cot, the nurses gathering gravely, listening to the baby's heartbeat through the stethoscope between contractions—heart like a drumbeat sounded a block away. Baby, with bent monkey feet, is born still in its sac. Doctor is unlocatable. The interns gather. A nurse picks up both phones simultaneously and calls him with urgency. The crowd, the rooting and cheering in the delivery room—as if the whole world were gathered there—after the solitary labor room.

Very old people age somewhat as bananas do.   5

Two Vietcong prisoners: An American drew crosses on their foreheads, one guy's cross red, other guy's green, to distinguish which was the target and which the decoy to be thrown out of the helicopter to make the target talk.

Winter travel: Snowbanks on river ice means thin ice because snow layers shield the ice from the cold. And water is always wearing it away from underneath; therefore keep on the *inside* of curves and away from all cutbanks, where the current is fast. Travel on barest ice and avoid obstacles like rocks and drift piles sticking through, which also result in a thinning of the cover. Gravel bars may dam the river, causing overflows, which "smoke" in cold weather like a fire, giving some warning before you sink through the slush on top and into the overflow itself. Overflows also can occur in slow sections of the river where the ice is thick and grinds against itself. A special danger area is the junction of incoming creeks whose whirlpools have kept the water open under a concealment of snow. If the water level falls abruptly, sometimes you can walk on the dry edges of the riverbed under solid ice which remains on top as though you were in a tunnel, but that can be dangerous because bears enjoy following such a route too.

You butter a cat's paws when moving it to a new home, so it can find its way back after going out exploring the first time.

My friend Danny Chapman, the Ringling Bros. clown, had a sliding, circus sort of face, like the eternal survivor, marked by the sun, wind, pain, bad luck, and bad dealings, the standard lusts and equivocations, like a stone that the water has slid over for sixty years. Face was much squarer when not in august-clown blackface, its seams smudged by reacting to all he'd seen, and holding so many expressions in readiness that none could be recognized as characteristic of him.

Success in writing, versus painting, means that your work becomes *cheaper*,   10
purchasable by anybody.

The *New York Times* is a vast democratic souk in which every essayist can find a place to publish his or her voice. But otherwise, for a native New Yorker with proud and lengthy ties to the city, it's not so easy. The *New York Review of Books* is published by a group of sensibilities that give the impression of having been born in this metropolis but of wishing they were Londoners instead. And *The New Yorker* traditionally has been the home of writers and editors born in Columbus, Ohio—who yearned so much to seem like real New Yorkers that their city personalities in print had an artificial, overeager sophistication and snobbery.

I ride my stutter, posting over its jolts, swerving with it, guiding it, if never "mastering" it.

At the annual sports show at the New York Colosseum: "Stay straight with sports," says a poster, a picture of a girl wearing a T-shirt with that slogan over her breasts. An exhibitor tells me he just saw two men fondling each other in the men's room—"It just turns your stomach." A woman wearing a huge odd-looking hat made of dried pheasants' heads is cooing affectionately at a cageful of pheasants. A skinning contest is held in which three taxidermists go to work on the carcasses of three Russian boars.

"If two people are in love they can sleep on the blade of a knife."

Karl Wheeler used a baby bottle until he was five years old, whereupon his mother said to him, "That's your last bottle, Karl. When you break that one you'll never get another one!" and he began to toss it idly in the air to catch it, but missed.

First white men in British Columbia sold some of the Indians their names: Ten dollars for a fine name like O'Shaughnessy, five dollars for the more modest Harris.

At six A.M. I shoot a porcupine in the garage (knew about it from seeing Bimbo vomit from a fear reaction after his many tangles with porcupines). It goes under the building to die but not too far for a rake to reach. I take it to Paul Brooks's house. In his freezer he has woodchucks, beaver, bear, deer, bobcat, and porcupine meat (he is a man living only on Social Security), and he cleans it for me. We see it's a mama with milk in her breasts. His mouth fills with saliva as he works; he's also preparing a venison roast for lunch, with garlic salt, Worcestershire sauce, pepper, onions, etc. Says this time of year, first of June, the woodchucks are light as your hat, the winter has been so long for them; you can feel their thin legs. Porcupine liver is a delicacy, the rest not so much. The porcupine had been chewing at my garage for the salts; I eat the porcupine; therefore I'm eating my garage—dark drumsticks that night by kerosene lamp. Game tastes herby even without herbs—best is bobcat and muskrat, in my experience, not counting big meats like moose. One countryman we know had his ashes scattered on his muskrat pond. The porcupine had chattered its teeth and rattled its poor quiver of quills as I approached with my gun. Was so waddly it could not even limp properly when badly wounded. Lay on its side gurgling, choking, and sighing like a man dying.

At the Freifields' one-room cabin, with snowshoes hung under steep roof, I read Larry's father's hectic journal, written in Austro-English, of desperate orphanhood on the Austrian-Russian front in WWI. He, adopted by the rival armies as they overran the town, living in the trenches with them, living off stolen crusts otherwise, surviving the bombardments, dodging the peasants who hated Jews, but cherished by Austrian soldiers, who then were killed—saw one's legs blown off just after he'd changed places with him. That night peed in his pants in the trench and froze himself to the ground.

"Old Bet," the first circus elephant in America, was bought by Hachaliah Bailey from an English ship captain in 1815 but was shot eventually by religious fanatics in Connecticut as resembling the biblical Behemoth of the Book of Job (as indeed she did).

My first overtly sexual memory is of me on my knees in the hallway outside 20
our fifth-grade classroom cleaning the floor, and Lucy Smith in a white blouse and black skirt standing above me, watching me.

My first memory is of being on a train which derailed in a rainstorm in Dakota one night when I was two—and of hearing, as we rode in a hay wagon toward the distant weak lights of a little station, that a boy my age had just choked to death from breathing mud. But maybe my first real memory emerged when my father was dying. I was thirty-five and I dreamed so incredibly vividly of being dandled and rocked and hugged by him, being only a few months old, giggling helplessly and happily.

Had supper at a local commune where they have a fast turnover and have made life hard. They buy twenty-dollar used cars instead of spending two hundred dollars, use kerosene instead of the electricity they have, and a team of horses to plow. They got 180 gallons of maple syrup out of their trees, but they washed 1,400 sugaring pails in the bathtub in cold water, never having put in a hot-water heater. Much husky embracing, like wrestlers; and before they eat their supper they have Grace, where twenty-some people clasp hands around the table, meditating and squeezing fingers. Bread bakes on a puffy wood stove. Rose hips and chili peppers hang from the ceiling on strings, other herbs everywhere and pomegranates and jars of basic grains. The toilet is a car on blocks up the hill. Supper is a soup bowl full of rice and chard and potato pancakes with two sour sauces and apple butter, yogurt for dessert; and we drink from mason jars of water passed around. And the final "course" is dental floss, which everybody solemnly uses. A dulcimer is played with the quill of a feather, accompanied by bongo drums. The women ended the public festivities by each announcing where she was going to sleep that night, which bedroom or which hayloft, in case anyone wished to join her. Clothing is heaped in a feed bin near the bottom of the stairs, and everybody is supposed to reach in in the morning and remove the first items that fit them and come to hand, without regard for which particular sex the clothes were originally made for. The saddest moment of the evening for me was when a little girl came around to her mother carrying a hairbrush in her hand and asking to be put to bed. The mother lost her temper. "Why run to me?" she said. "Everybody in this room is your parent. Anybody can brush your hair and tell you a story and put you to bed."

Manhattan, now 14,310 acres, was 9,800.

Bernard Malamud speaks of writing as a battle: "go to paper" with a novel. At age sixty-one is trying to "write wise," a new aim, and hard. Being between books, I say I'm in a period of withdrawal and inaction like that of a snake that is shedding its skin.

On the crest of Moose Mountain is an old birch growing low and twisty out 25 of the ruins of a still older, bigger bole, surrounded by ferns, and it's there that the deer that feed in my field bed down during the day.

There is a whole literary genre that consists, first, of foolish writing and then later capitalizing upon the foolishness by beating one's breast and crying *mea culpa*. Why *was* I a white Black Panther, a drug swallower, a jackbooted feminist, a jet-set-climbing novelist, a 1940s Communist? How interesting and archetypal of me to have shared my generation's extremes.

Busybodies are called in Yiddish *kochleffl*, "cooking spoon," because they stir people up.

The hollow in the center of the upper lip is where "the angel touched you and told you to forget what you had seen in heaven."

Wife of F.'s uncle, to prevent him from going to work one morning when she preferred he stay home, set the alarm so that it seemed it was too late for him to make the train when he woke. But he did rush so terribly he got to the station, and there collapsed and died, and she, only twenty-seven, never remarried.

Joyce consulted Jung, who diagnosed his poor daughter as incurably schizo- 30 phrenic partly on the evidence of her brilliant, obsessive punning. Joyce remarked that he, too, was a punner. "You are a deep-sea diver," said Jung. "She is drowning."

The cure for stuttering of holding stones in one's mouth works because of the discomfort of them rattling against one's teeth. Stones from a crocodile's stomach were thought to be best.

Amerigo Vespucci said that Indian women enlarged their lovers' sexual parts by applying venomous insects to them.

After losing her virginity at seventeen, she felt unstoppered on the street, like a hollow tube, as though the wind could blow right through her.

The sea, at the village of Soya on Hokkaido island in 1792, was so fertile that twelve quarts of dry rice could be bartered for 1,200 herring, 100 salmon, 300 trout, or 3 sealskins.

How Davy Crockett kept warm when lost in the woods one night: climbing   35 thirty feet up a smooth tree trunk and sliding down.

Am drunk from a soft-shell-crab lunch with Random House's Joe Fox, but stutter so vigorously with William Shawn as to obscure both from him and myself my drunkenness—stutter through it and give myself time to recall names like Numeiry and Assad, necessary to win Shawn's backing for the trip to Africa. He, as reported, is excessively solicitous of my comfort and state of mind; insulated and jittery; heated by electric heater (in August), yet fanned by electric fan; in his shirtsleeves, and immediately suggests I remove my coat. He has an agonized, bulging baby's head with swallowed-up eyes, like that of the tormented child in Francis Bacon's painting *The Scream*. Questions me effectively, however, on my knowledge of the Sudan and the prospects for a salable article there. Says OK. I go to 42nd St. and watch screwing to relax—crazily enough, less is charged to see live souls (twenty-five cents) than for a porno flick—then walk home. Lunch the next day with Alfred Kazin, my old teacher (and the day after that with Barthelme, who has just broken through a writing block, he says, and is therefore more cheerful and sober than I have seen him in a considerable while; says women's movement will produce changes as profound as the abolition of slavery). Kazin as always is a veritable tumult of impressions, like H. S. Commager and other busy intellectuals I have liked, but in Kazin's case it is enormously in earnest and felt. Expresses hurt at Bellow's recent inexplicable anger. Otherwise an outpouring of talk about his new book on the forties, when he published his first book and met the literary figures of the day. Played violin with drunken Alan Tate. Advances the idea that William James, a hero of his, is a better direct heir of Emerson than Thoreau; also the view that students now resent the fact that a professor knows more than they do, want him to learn along with them in class, as in group therapy, and when caught out on homework facts, get offended instead of trying to fake through, as in the old days. On Ph.D. orals, the candidates seem to have no favorite poem, no poem they can quote from, when he asks them for one at the end.

I like Easterners more than Westerners but Western geography more than Eastern geography; and I like the country more than the city, but I like city people more than country people.

Essays, the most conversational form, have naturally drawn me, who have a hard time speaking with my actual mouth.

Tail end of hurricane rains buckets, flooding Barton River. Then the sky clears with nearly full moon, and I hear the deer whickering and whanging to one another gleefully, the mountain behind them gigantic and white.

Bellow says in Jerusalem journal that "light may be the outer garment of 40 God."

Oil spills seem to attract aquatic birds; the sheen may resemble schooling fish. Also, oil slicks calm the surface, look like a landing area.

Roth speaks of his debt to both Jean Genet and the Fugs for *Portnoy.* Roth a man who wears his heart on his sleeve, thus rather vulnerable to insult and injury; part of his exceptional generosity. Tells story of man bleeding in front of God but trying to hide blood from His sight apologetically.

William Gaddis: jockeylike, narrow-boned, fastidious Irishman, clever and civilized, with none of the usual hangdog bitterness of the neglected writer.

Warhol: keen, Pan face with tight manipulated skin that makes it ageless except for his eyes. Bleached hair hanging to his leather collar. Fame based upon being immobile.

Pete Hamill, bursting personality, does columns in half an hour, movie 45 script in three weeks, discipline based upon not drinking till day's stint is through. Fewer bar brawls now, more empathetic, though still lives from a suitcase. "Irish Ben Hecht," he laughs.

Malamud: not at all the "Jewish businessman's face" I'd heard about, but a sensitive, gentle face, often silent or dreamy at Podhoretz's, disagreeing with the host and Midge, but holds his tongue and hugs him at the end with professional gratitude to an editor who once published him. When he speaks, his voice is young, light, and quick, an enthusiast's, idealist's. Hurt by attacks on him in *Jerusalem Post,* for dovishness. Extremely solicitous of me, as kind in his way as Bellow, though style of it is modulated lower. Both of us distressed by Israeli's grinning description of Arab prisoners being beaten up. William Phelps says he thinks the Palestinians probably have a point but that he's not interested in hearing what it is. Podhoretz mentions Israel's "Samson option," pulling everything down, and makes fun of Malamud's "ego" when he's left.

Grace Paley: short, stocky woman who at first sight on the Sarah Lawrence campus I mistook for the cleaning woman; asked her where the men's room was. We rode rubbing knees throughout that semester in the back seat of a car pool. She'd been marching in protests since high school (Ethiopia and Spanish civil war), but her exhilaration at being arrested in Washington peace march in midterm reminded me of my own exuberance at completing the hard spells of army basic training. Yes, we were good enough!

Heard MacLeish at YMHA. Afterward unrecovered yet from defeat of his play *Scratch* on B'way. Sweetness and bounce of his voice, however, is unchanged in twenty years; sounds forty, a matinee tenor, and the old lilt to his rhetoric. Face like a sachem's, too wise, too heroic, with a public man's nose. Talks of friendships with Joyce and Hemingway and imitates Sandburg's O very well. Talks of Saturday Club in Boston where monthly Harlow Shapley debated Robert Frost. Reminisces of artillery lieutenant days in World War I, "making the world safe for democracy," where his brother was killed. Five years later he and other nondead *did* die a bit when they realized it had been a "commercial" war and they had been lied to. He is a man of Hector-type heroes. Says Andrew Marvell poem was written while going home from Persia after his father's death.

Berryman given five-thousand-dollar prize at the Guggenheim reading, wearing a graybeard's beard which hides tieless collar. Reads best "Dream Songs," plus two sonnets and Rilke, Ralph Hodgson, and eighteenth-century Japanese poet. Emphatically, spoutingly drunk, reads with frail man's grotesqueries, contortions, and his own memorable concoction of earnestness, coyness, staginess, name dropping, and absolutely forceful, rock-bottom directness. Becomes louder and louder at the end of this floodlighted moment after long years of obscurity and hardship. Here was the current Wild Man, people thought, successor to Pound, there being one to a generation, though many others may have been reminded of Dylan Thomas as he fell into the arms of Robert Lowell, punching him affectionately, when he finished. His whole life was thereupon paraded before him, when old mistresses and chums and students like me came up, expecting recognition, and one of his old wives, presenting him with a son whom obviously he hadn't laid eyes on for a long while. He boomed with love and guilt, with repeated thanks for letters informing him that So-and-so had had a child or remarried, till one was wearied of watching. One felt guilty too, as though competing for his attention with the neglected son. I felt Berryman had not long to live and I ought to be content with my memories of him and lessons learned and not join in the hounding of him. Nevertheless, I did go next afternoon to the Chelsea Hotel, with bronze plaques outside memorializing other tragic figures, like Thomas and Brendan Behan. He'd said the son would be there, so I was afraid that, like my last visit with Bellow, I would be taking time away from a son who needed to see him much more. But the son had left—all that remained was a note in Ann B.'s handwriting. Instead a *Life* photographer and reporter were talking with him, plying him with drinks, though he was holding back dignifiedly, talking of fame, of Frost, and his own dog Rufus. Frost was a shit who tried to hurt him, but he quoted the wonderful couplet about God forgiving our little faux pas if we forgive Him His great big joke on us. Is bombastic in his total commitment to words. Legs look very small, but chest inflates with importance of uttering snatches of poems, till he collapses in coughs. Rubs beard and hair exhaustedly, recklessly spendthrift with his strength, and begins harder drinking; leads me to bar, where waiter, thinking from his red face and thin clothing that he is a bum, won't serve him till he lays a ten-dollar bill on the table. I soon leave, but he was hospitalized within a couple of days. "Twinkle" was his favorite word at this time. He used it for commentary, by itself, and irony, or expostulation, quoting an enemy like Oscar Williams, then merely adding a somber "Twinkle."

Turgenev's brain was the heaviest ever recorded, 4.7 pounds; three is average. [50]

Child's tale about a man who suffered from shortness of breath. Afraid he would run out, he blew up a bunch of balloons as an extra supply for emergencies. Blew up so many that he floated away holding on to them.

Updike comes to U. of Iowa for first workshop session in three years (hasn't really taught for sixteen years) but handles himself in a classy manner nevertheless, and very well prepared with students' manuscripts beforehand, and in the exhilaration of reading his own work in front of one thousand people in McBride Hall (which we call Mammal Hall because it's part of Nat'l Hist. Museum), freely sheds his private-person role that had made him a bit stiff before, when he'd refused even a newspaper interview. Signs autograph cards for eleven-year-old boys and physics texts for Japanese students and mimeo forms for students with nothing better to offer him. Wife is ample, attractive woman with large, intense face, obviously both loving and sexy, a relaxed, close companion—he is wearing a wedding ring and ignoring the ambitious students who show up for his morning class wearing cocktail dresses. We talk of Africa—both finishing Africa books—and classmates and lit. hierarchies. He mentions Cheever's drunkenness—once he had to dress him after a party like dressing a father. Our mothers are same age. "Poor Johnny," his said, watching a TV program about senility with him recently.

Updike says he quit teaching years ago because he "felt stupid," seeing only one way to write a given story properly, not the endless alternatives students proposed in discussions.

Indians used to scratch small children with mouse teeth fastened to a stick as a punishment for crying in front of white men. (White man, of course, a "skinned" man.)

Short stories tend to be boat-shaped, with a lift at each end, to float.   55

Richard Yates says art is a result of a quarrel with oneself, not others.

Five toes to a track means it's wild, four toes means cat or dog.

Writers customarily write in the morning and try to make news, make love, or make friends in the afternoon. But alas, I write all day.

Bellow says he spent the first third of his life absorbing material, the second third trying to make himself famous, and the last third trying to evade fame.

"A woman without a man is like a fish without a bicycle": T-shirt.   60

People say they'll take a dip in the sea as if it were like dipping into a book, but I nearly drowned in surf's riptide off Martha's Vineyard's South Beach. Repeatedly changed swimming strokes to rest myself as I struggled in the water, surf too loud to shout over, and I'm too nearsighted to see where to shout to. Reaching beach, I sprawled for an hour before moving further. Spent next day in bed, next week aching.

New England is "pot-bound," says Charlton Ogburn; thus superfertile.

Petrarch, climbing Mount Ventoux in 1336, began the Renaissance by being the first learned man ever to climb a mountain only for the view.

Rahv told Roth, "You can't be both Scott Fitzgerald and Franz Kafka."

People who marry their great loves sometimes wish they'd married their   65
best friends; and vice versa.

Trapeze artists some days complain "there's too much gravity," when a change of the weather or the magnetic field affects their bodies. Elvin Bale bought his heel-hook act from Geraldine Soules, who after a fall started doing a dog act instead. Soules had, in turn, bought it from Vander Barbette, who, walking funny after *his* fall, had become a female impersonator and trainer of circus showgirls.

In old-time Georgia you ate mockingbird eggs for a stutter; boiled an egg for jaundice and went and sat beside a red-ant anthill and ate the white and fed the yolk to the ants. For warts, you bled them, put the blood on grains of corn, and fed that to a chicken. Fiddlers like to put a rattlesnake rattle inside their fiddles.

The fifties are an interim decade of life, like the thirties. In the thirties one still has the energy of one's twenties, combined with the judgment (sometimes) of the forties. In the fifties one still has the energy of one's forties, combined with the composure of the sixties.

The forties are the old age of youth and the fifties are the youth of old age.

Adage: "God sends meat, the Devil sends cooks." 70

Carnival stuntman whom Byron Burford banged the drum for used to swallow live rats and Ping-Pong balls, upchucking whichever ones the crowd asked for first. Stunned the rats with cigar smoke before he swallowed them.

The intellect of man is forced to choose
Perfection of the life, or of the work,
And if it take the second must refuse
A heavenly mansion, raging in the dark.
        —YEATS, "Choice"

Lying to my lieutenant as a private at Fort Sam Houston as to whether I'd shaved that morning before inspection, or only the night before—he reaching out and rubbing his hand down my face.

Glenn Gould liked to practice with the vacuum cleaner on, to hear "the skeleton of the music."

Nature writers, I sometimes think, are second only to cookbook writers in 75 being screwed up.

Deer follow moose in these woods, says Toad. I say maybe they look like father (mother) figures to them.

At Academy-Institute ceremonial, the big scandal is Ellison's lengthy introduction of Malamud for a prize and Barbara Tuchman's brutal interruption of it. Stegner very youthful, as befits an outdoorsman. Cowley very food-hungry as always, as befits a 1930s survivor. Commager tells my wife that his daughter loved me and so he loved me. Lots of cold-faced ambitious poets cluster around each other and Northrop Frye; Galway seems likably unaffected and truthful next to them. Ditto Raymond Carver. Ellison had tried to speak of blacks and Jews.

Joe Flaherty's line for the Brooklyn Bridge: "the Irish gangplank."

Whale mother's milk would stain the sea after she was harpooned, and the calf would circle the ship forlornly. "I do not say that John or Jonathan will realize all this," said Thoreau, in finishing *Walden;* and that's the central and tragic dilemma as the environmental movement fights its rearguard battles.

In starving midwinter, foxes catch cats by rolling on their backs like a kitten   80 ready to play.

Warblers average eight thousand or ten thousand songs a day in spring; vireo twenty thousand. Woodchucks wag their tails like a dog. Blue jays like to scare other birds by imitating a red-shouldered hawk.

My bifocals are like a horse's halter, binding the lower half of my eyes to the day's work.

At my frog pond a blue heron circles low overhead while a brown-muzzled black bear clasps chokecherry bushes and eats off them thirty yards away from me.

Only six hours old, a red calf stumbles toward the barn, as mother is herded in by Hugh Stevens on ATV vehicle, and is eventually tied to its mother's stanchion with hay twine, while a six-inch red tab of its previous cord hangs from its belly. It's as shiny as a new pair of shoes, its deerlike hooves perfectly formed, including the dew claws. Mother and calf had had a brief wild idyll under the summer sky before they were discovered by Hugh—the last sky this vealer will ever see.

Crocodiles yawn to cool themselves in hot weather, but coyotes yawn as an   85 agonistic device. Mice yawn from sleepiness, as people do, but we also yawn from boredom, which is to say contempt—agonistic again.

Old people seem wise because they have grown resigned and because they remember the axioms, even if they've forgotten the data.

"When you come to the end of your life, make sure you're used up."

I trust love more than friendship, which is why I trust women more than men.

"All hat and no cows." Or, "Big hat, no cattle": Texas saying.

"Eat with the rich, laugh with the poor."   90

Buying a new car after thirteen years, I discover why country people like to keep the old one about the yard. First, it makes the house look occupied. Second, it's a nesting site for ducks and geese and a shelter for chickens during the day. Third, it reminds you of *you*.

ACTIVITIES FOR WRITING AND DISCUSSION

1. You can write long, or you can write short; and there is a place and value for everything you write, whatever its length or apparent individual significance. Hoagland's essay seems to underscore that every thought and experience matters and contributes to a larger picture. Read and annotate the essay.

2. Is this a collection of random and unrelated notes, or is there some sort of focus to it? If there is a focus, what *is* it? Are there paragraphs that don't seem to *fit*—for instance, paragraph 6 about the Vietcong prisoners, or paragraph 23 ("Manhattan, now 14,310 acres, was 9,800")? What do you think, and why? Good arguments can be made either way.

3. Hoagland's essay reads like a selection of journal or notebook entries. Therefore, read and respond to the piece using any of the "Generic Ideas for Writing in Response to Published Notebooks or Journals" listed on page 275.

4. Brainstorm any ideas for writing that this piece gives you. For instance, could you organize a selection of your own notebook entries around some topic or theme? If so, what topic or theme? What would be the advantage(s) of using Hoagland's "selected notes" format instead of the consecutive prose of a traditional essay?

JUDITH ORTIZ COFER (b. 1952)

Primary Lessons

My mother walked me to my first day at school at La Escuela Segundo Ruiz Belvis, named after the Puerto Rican patriot born in our town. I remember yellow cement with green trim. All the classrooms had been painted these colors to identify them as government property. This was true all over the Island. Everything was color-coded, including the children, who wore uniforms from first through twelfth grade. We were a midget army in white and brown, led by the hand to our battleground. From practically every house in our barrio emerged a crisply ironed uniform inhabited by the savage creatures we had become over a summer of running wild in the sun.

At my grandmother's house where we were staying until my father returned to Brooklyn Yard in New York and sent for us, it had been complete chaos, with several children to get ready for school. My mother had pulled my hair harder than usual while braiding it, and I had dissolved into a pool of total self-pity. I wanted to stay home with her and Mamá, to continue listening to stories in the late afternoon, to drink *café con leche* with them, and to play rough games with my many cousins. I wanted to continue living the dream of summer afternoons in Puerto Rico, and if I could not have it, then I wanted to go back to Paterson,

New Jersey, back to where I imagined our apartment waited, peaceful and cool for the three of us to return to our former lives. Our gypsy lifestyle had convinced me, at age six, that one part of life stops and waits for you while you live another for a while—and if you don't like the present, you can always return to the past. Buttoning me into my stiff blouse while I tried to squirm away from her, my mother attempted to explain to me that I was a big girl now and should try to understand that, like all the other children my age, I had to go to school.

"What about him?" I yelled pointing at my brother who was lounging on the tile floor of our bedroom in his pajamas, playing quietly with a toy car.

"He's too young to go to school, you know that. Now stay still." My mother pinned me between her thighs to button my skirt, as she had learned to do from Mamá, from whose grip it was impossible to escape.

"It's not fair, it's not fair. I can't go to school here. I don't speak Spanish." It   5 was my final argument, and it failed miserably because I was shouting my defiance in the language I claimed not to speak. Only I knew what I meant by saying in Spanish that I did not speak Spanish. I had spent my early childhood in the United States, where I lived in a bubble created by my Puerto Rican parents in a home where two cultures and languages became one. I learned to listen to the English from the television with one ear while I heard my mother and father speaking in Spanish with the other. I thought I was an ordinary American kid—like the children on the shows I watched—and that everyone's parents spoke a secret second language at home. When we came to Puerto Rico right before I started first grade, I switched easily to Spanish. It was the language of fun, of summertime games. But school—that was a different matter.

I made one last desperate attempt to make my mother see reason: "Father will be very angry. You know that he wants us to speak good English." My mother, of course, ignored me as she dressed my little brother in his playclothes. I could not believe her indifference to my father's wishes. She was usually so careful about our safety and the many other areas that he was forever reminding her about in his letters. But I was right, and she knew it. Our father spoke to us in English as much as possible, and he corrected my pronunciation constantly—not "jes" but "y-es." Y-es, sir. How could she send me to school to learn Spanish when we would be returning to Paterson in just a few months?

But, of course, what I feared was not language, but loss of freedom. At school there would be no playing, no stories, only lessons. It would not matter if I did not understand a word, and I would not be allowed to make up my own definitions. I would have to learn silence. I would have to keep my wild imagination in check. Feeling locked into my stiffly starched uniform, I only sensed all this. I guess most children can intuit their loss of childhood's freedom on that first day of school. It is separation anxiety too, but mother is just the guardian of the "playground" of our early childhood.

The sight of my cousins in similar straits comforted me. We were marched down the hill of our barrio where Mamá's robin-egg-blue house stood at the top. I must have glanced back at it with yearning. Mamá's house—a place built for children—where anything that could be broken had already been broken by my grandmother's early batch of offspring (they ranged in age from my mother's oldest sisters to my uncle who was six months older than me). Her house had long since been made childproof. It had been a perfect summer place. And now it was September—the cruelest month for a child.

La Mrs., as all the teachers were called, waited for her class of first-graders at the door of the yellow and green classroom. She too wore a uniform: It was a blue skirt and a white blouse. This teacher wore black high heels with her "standard issue." I remember this detail because when we were all seated in rows she called on one little girl and pointed to the back of the room where there were shelves. She told the girl to bring her a shoebox from the bottom shelf. Then, when the box had been placed in her hands, she did something unusual. She had the little girl kneel at her feet and take the pointy high heels off her feet and replace them with a pair of satin slippers from the shoe box. She told the group that every one of us would have a chance to do this if we behaved in her class. Though confused about the prize, I soon felt caught up in the competition to bring *La Mrs.* her slippers in the morning. Children fought over the privilege.

Our first lesson was English. In Puerto Rico, every child has to take twelve 10 years of English to graduate from school. It is the law. In my parents' school days, all subjects were taught in English. The U.S. Department of Education had specified that as a U.S. territory, the Island had to be "Americanized," and to accomplish this task, it was necessary for the Spanish language to be replaced in one generation through the teaching of English in all schools. My father began his school day by saluting the flag of the United States and singing "America" and "The Star-Spangled Banner" by rote, without understanding a word of what he was saying. The logic behind this system was that, though the children did not understand the English words, they would remember the rhythms. Even the games the teacher's manuals required them to play became absurd adaptations. "Here We Go Round the Mulberry Bush" became "Here We Go Round the Mango Tree." I have heard about the confusion caused by the use of a primer in which the sounds of animals were featured. The children were forced to accept that a rooster says *cockadoodledoo,* when they knew perfectly well from hearing their own roosters each morning that in Puerto Rico a rooster says *cocorocó.* Even the vocabulary of their pets was changed; there are still family stories circulating about the bewilderment of a first-grader coming home to try to teach his dog to speak in English. The policy of assimilation by immersion failed on the Island. Teachers adhered to it on paper, substituting their own materials for the texts, but no one took their English home. In due time, the program was minimized to the one class in English per day that I encountered when I took my seat in *La Mrs.*'s first grade class.

Catching us all by surprise, she stood very straight and tall in front of us and began to sing in English:

Pollito   —   Chicken
Gallina   —   Hen

Lápiz   —   Pencil
Y Pluma   —   Pen.

"Repeat after me, children: Pollito — Chicken," she commanded in her heavily accented English that only I understood, being the only child in the room who had ever been exposed to the language. But I too remained silent. No use making waves or showing off. Patiently *La Mrs.* sang her song and gestured for us to join in. At some point it must have dawned on the class that this silly routine was likely to go on all day if we did not "repeat after her." It was not her fault that she had to follow the rule in her teacher's manual stating that she must teach English *in* English, and that she must not translate, but merely repeat her lesson in English until the children "begin to respond" more or less "unconsciously." This was one of the vestiges of the regimen followed by her predecessors in the last generation. To this day I can recite "Pollito — Chicken" mindlessly, never once pausing to visualize chicks, hens, pencils, or pens.

I soon found myself crowned "teacher's pet" without much effort on my part. I was a privileged child in her eyes simply because I lived in "Nueva York," and because my father was in the navy. His name was an old one in our pueblo, associated with once-upon-a-time landed people and long-gone money. Status is judged by unique standards in a culture where, by definition, everyone is a second-class citizen. Remembrance of past glory is as good as titles and money. Old families living in decrepit old houses rank over factory workers living in modern comfort in cement boxes—all the same. The professions raise a person out of the dreaded "sameness" into a niche of status, so that teachers, nurses, and everyone who went to school for a job were given the honorifics of *El Míster* or *La Mrs.* by the common folks, people who were likely to be making more money in American factories than the poorly paid educators and government workers.

My first impressions of the hierarchy began with my teacher's shoe-changing ceremony and the exaggerated respect she received from our parents. *La Mrs.* was always right, and adults scrambled to meet her requirements. She wanted all our schoolbooks covered in the brown paper now used for paper bags (used at that time by the grocer to wrap meats and other foods). That first week of school the grocer was swamped with requests for paper which he gave away to the women. That week and the next, he wrapped produce in newspapers. All school projects became family projects. It was considered disrespectful at Mamá's house to do homework in privacy. Between the hours when we came home from school and dinner time, the table was shared by all of us working together with the women hovering in the background. The teachers communicated directly with the mothers, and it was a matriarchy of far-reaching power and influence.

There was a black boy in my first-grade classroom who was also the teacher's pet but for a different reason than I: I did not have to do anything to win her favor; he would do anything to win a smile. He was as black as the caul- 15 dron that Mamá used for cooking stew and his hair was curled into tight little balls on his head—*pasitas,* like little raisins glued to his skull, my mother had said. There had been some talk at Mamá's house about this boy; Lorenzo was his name. I later gathered that he was the grandson of my father's nanny. Lorenzo lived with Teresa, his grandmother, having been left in her care when his mother took off for "Los Nueva Yores" shortly after his birth. And they were poor. Everyone could see that his pants were too big for him—hand-me-downs—and his shoe soles were as thin as paper. Lorenzo seemed unmindful of the giggles he caused when he jumped up to erase the board for *La Mrs.* and his baggy pants rode down to his thin hips as he strained up to get every stray mark. He seemed to relish playing the little clown when she asked him to come to the front of the room and sing his phonetic version of "o-bootifool, forpa-shios-keeis," leading the class in our incomprehensible tribute to the American flag. He was a bright, loving child, with a talent for song and mimicry that everyone commented on. He should have been chosen to host the PTA show that year instead of me.

At recess one day, I came back to the empty classroom to get something. My cup? My nickel for a drink from the kiosk man? I don't remember. But I remember the conversation my teacher was having with another teacher. I remember because it concerned me, and because I memorized it so that I could ask my mother to explain what it meant.

"He is a funny *negrito,* and, like a parrot, he can repeat anything you teach him. But his Mamá must not have the money to buy him a suit."

"I kept Rafaelito's First Communion suit; I bet Lorenzo could fit in it. It's white with a bow-tie," the other teacher said.

"But, Marisa," laughed my teacher, "in that suit, Lorenzo would look like a fly drowned in a glass of milk."

Both women laughed. They had not seen me crouched at the back of the 20 room, digging into my schoolbag. My name came up then.

"What about the Ortiz girl? They have money."

"I'll talk to her mother today. The superintendent, *El Americano* from San Juan, is coming down for the show. How about if we have her say her lines in both Spanish and English?"

The conversation ends there for me. My mother took me to Mayagüez and bought me a frilly pink dress and two crinoline petticoats to wear underneath so that I looked like a pink and white parachute with toothpick legs sticking out. I learned my lines, "Padres, maestros, Mr. Leonard, bien-venidos/Parents, teachers, Mr. Leonard, welcome. . . ." My first public appearance. I took no pleasure in it. The words were formal and empty. I had simply memorized them. My dress pinched me at the neck and arms, and made me itch all over.

I had asked my mother what it meant to be a "mosca en un vaso de leche," a fly in a glass of milk. She had laughed at the image, explaining that it meant being "different," but that it wasn't something I needed to worry about.

ACTIVITIES FOR WRITING AND DISCUSSION

1. Consider the various meanings of the title. "Primary" can refer to the elementary grades of school; it can also mean "fundamental," "basic," or "of first importance." Do the lessons learned by the six-year-old Cofer fit these different definitions? If so, in what ways?

2. Working with a group, make a list of the "primary lessons" Cofer learned as a six-year-old. Then identify an item on your list that resembles a lesson that *you* once learned, and write the story of that lesson. Either:
   a. Write the story in the form of a personal essay, or
   b. Write a dialogue, set in the past, between yourself and someone who was a key player in the "lesson," or
   c. Tell the story of your particular experience from a **third-person point of view,** i.e., write about yourself as "he" or "she."

3. The final paragraph shows the young Cofer asking her mother an awkward question, which the mother brushes aside. Invent a dialogue in which you either:
   a. Flesh out and expand the conversation you imagine to have taken place between Cofer and her mother, or
   b. Relate a similar type of conversation you had with your own parent, or
   c. Create a fictional conversation of a small child asking a parent about some controversial or "adult" subject.

Play

EUGENE O'NEILL (1888–1953)

The Hairy Ape

A COMEDY OF ANCIENT AND MODERN LIFE IN EIGHT SCENES

CHARACTERS

ROBERT SMITH, "YANK"

PADDY

LONG

MILDRED DOUGLAS

HER AUNT

SECOND ENGINEER

A GUARD

A SECRETARY OF AN ORGANIZATION

Stokers, Ladies, Gentlemen, etc.

SCENES

Scene I: The firemen's forecastle of an ocean liner—an hour after sailing from New York.

Scene II: Section of promenade deck, two days out—morning.

Scene III: The stokehole. A few minutes later.

Scene IV. Same as Scene I. Half an hour later.

Scene V: Fifth Avenue, New York. Three weeks later.

Scene VI: An island near the city. The next night.

Scene VII: In the city. About a month later.

Scene VIII: In the city. Twilight of the next day.

SCENE ONE

The firemen's forecastle of a transatlantic liner an hour after sailing from New York for the voyage across. Tiers of narrow, steel bunks, three deep, on all sides. An entrance in rear. Benches on the floor before the bunks. The room is crowded with men, shouting, cursing, laughing, singing—a confused, inchoate uproar swelling into a sort of unity, a meaning—the bewildered, furious, baffled defiance of a beast in a cage. Nearly all the men are drunk. Many bottles are passed from hand to hand. All are dressed in dungaree pants, heavy ugly shoes. Some wear singlets, but the majority are stripped to the waist.

The treatment of this scene, or of any other scene in the play, should by no means be naturalistic. The effect sought after is a cramped space in the bowels of a ship, imprisoned by white steel. The lines of bunks, the uprights supporting them, cross each other like the steel framework of a cage. The ceiling crushes down upon the men's heads. They cannot stand upright. This accentuates the natural stooping posture which shoveling coal and the resultant over-development of back and shoulder muscles have given them. The men themselves should resemble those pictures in which the appearance of Neanderthal Man is guessed at. All are hairy-chested, with long arms of tremendous power, and low, receding brows above their small, fierce, resentful eyes. All the civilized white races are represented, but except for the slight differentiation in color of hair, skin, eyes, all these men are like.

The curtain rises on a tumult of sound. YANK *is seated in the foreground. He seems broader, fiercer, more truculent, more powerful, more sure of himself than the rest. They respect his superior strength—the grudging respect of fear. Then, too, he represents to them a self-expression, the very last word in what they are, their most highly developed individual.*

VOICES: Gif me trink dere, you!
'Ave a wet!
Salute!
Gesundheit!
Skoal!
Drunk as a lord, God stiffen you!
Here's how!
Luck!
Pass back that bottle, damn you!
Pourin' it down his neck!
Ho, Froggy! Where the devil have you been?
La Touraine.
I hit him smash in yaw, py Gott!
Jenkins—the First—he's a rotten swine—
And the coppers nabbed him—and I run—
I like peer better. It don't pig head gif you.
A slut, I'm sayin'! She robbed me aslape—
To hell with 'em all!
You're a bloody lair!
Say dot again! *(Commotion. Two men about to fight are pulled apart).*
No scrappin' now!
Tonight—
See who's the best man!
Bloody Dutchman!
Tonight on the for'ard square.
I'll bet on Dutchy.
He packa da wallop, I tella you!
Shut up, Wop!
No fightin', maties. We're all chums, ain't we?
(A voice starts bawling a song).

"Beer, beer, glorious beer!
Fill yourselves right up to here."

YANK *(for the first time seeming to take notice of the uproar about him, turns around threateningly—in a tone of contemptuous authority)*: Choke off dat noise! Where d'yuh get dat beer stuff? Beer, hell! Beer's for goils—and Dutchmen. Me for somep'n wit a kick to it! Gimme a drink, one of youse guys. *(Several bottles are eagerly offered. He takes a tremendous gulp at one of them; then, keeping the bottle in his hand, glares belligerently at the owner, who hastens to acquiesce in this robbery by saying)* All righto, Yank. Keep it and have another. *(YANK contemptuously turns his back on the crowd again. For a second there is an embarrassed silence. Then—)*
VOICES: We must be passing the Hook.
She's beginning to roll to it.

Six days in hell—and then Southampton.

Py Yesus, I vish somepody take my first vatch for me!

Gittin' seasick, Square-head?

Drink up and forget it!

What's in your bottle?

Gin.

Dot's nigger trink.

Absinthe? It's doped. You'll go off your chump, Froggy.

Cochon!

Whisky, that's the ticket!

Where's Paddy?

Going asleep.

Sing us that whisky song, Paddy. *(They all turn to an old, wizened Irishman who is dozing, very drunk, on the benches forward. His face is extremely monkey-like with all the sad, patient pathos of that animal in his small eyes).*

Singa da song, Caruso Pat!

He's gettin' old. The drink is too much for him.

He's too drunk.

PADDY *(blinking about him, starts to his feet resentfully, swaying, holding on to the edge of a bunk)*: I'm never too drunk to sing. 'Tis only when I'm dead to the world I'd be wishful to sing at all. *(With a sort of sad contempt)* "Whisky Johnny," ye want? A chanty, ye want? Now that's a queer wish from the ugly like of you, God help you. But no matther. *(He starts to sing in a thin, nasal, doleful tone)*:

Oh, whisky is the life of man!
   Whisky! O Johnny! *(They all join in on this)*.
Oh, whisky is the life of man!
   Whisky for my Johnny! *(Again chorus)*.

Oh, whisky drove my old man mad!
   Whisky! O Johnny!
Oh, whisky drove my old man mad!
   Whisky for my Johnny!

YANK *(again turning around scornfully)*: Aw hell! Nix on dat old sailing ship stuff! All dat bull's dead, see? And you're dead, too, yuh damned old Harp, on'y yuh don't know it. Take it easy, see? Give us a rest. Nix on de loud noise. *(With a cynical grin)* Can't youse see I'm tryin' to t'ink?

ALL *(repeating the word after him as one with the same cynical amused mockery)*: Think! *(The chorused word has a brazen metallic quality as if their throats were phonograph horns. It is followed by a general uproar of hard, barking laughter)*.

VOICES: Don't be cracking your head wit ut, Yank.

You gat headache, py yingo!

One thing about it—it rhymes with drink!

Ha, ha, ha!
Drink, don't think!
Drink, don't think!
Drink, don't think! (*A whole chorus of voices has taken up this refrain, stamping on the floor, pounding on the benches with fists*).

YANK (*taking a gulp from his bottle—good-naturedly*): Aw right. Can de noise. I got yuh de foist time. (*The uproar subsides. A very drunken sentimental tenor begins to sing*):

"Far away in Canada,
    Far across the sea,
There's a lass who fondly waits
    Making a home for me—"

YANK (*fiercely contemptuous*): Shut up, yuh lousy boob! Where d'yuh get dat tripe? Home? Home, hell! I'll make a home for yuh! I'll knock yuh dead. Home! T'hell wit home! Where d'yuh get dat tripe? Dis is home, see? What d'yuh want wit home? (*Proudly*) I runned away from mine when I was a kid. On'y too glad to beat it, dat was me. Home was lickings for me, dat's all. But yuh can bet your shoit no one ain't never licked me since! Wanter try it, any of youse? Huh! I guess not. (*In a more placated but still contemptuous tone*) Goils waitin' for yuh, huh? Aw, hell! Dat's all tripe. Dey don't wait for no one. Dey'd double-cross yuh for a nickel. Dey're all tarts, get me? Treat 'em rough, dat's me. To hell wit 'em. Tarts, dat's what, de whole bunch of 'em.

LONG (*very drunk, jumps on a bench excitedly, gesticulating with a bottle in his hand*): Listen 'ere, Comrades! Yank 'ere is right. 'E says this 'ere stinkin' ship is our 'ome. And 'e says as 'ome is 'ell. And 'e's right! This is 'ell. We lives in 'ell, Comrades—and right enough we'll die in it. (*Raging*) And who's ter blame, I arsks yer? We ain't. We wasn't born this rotten way. All men is born free and ekal. That's in the bleedin' Bible, maties. But what d'they care for the Bible— them lazy, bloated swine what travels first cabin? Them's the ones. They dragged us down 'til we're on'y wage slaves in the bowels of a bloody ship, sweatin', burnin' up, eatin' coal dust! Hit's them's ter blame—the damned Capitalist clarss! (*There had been a gradual murmur of contemptuous resentment rising among the men until now he is interrupted by a storm of catcalls, hisses, boos, hard laughter*).

VOICES: Turn it off!
Shut up!
Sit down!
Closa da face!
Tamn fool! (*Etc.*).

YANK (*standing up and glaring at* LONG): Sit down before I knock yuh down! (LONG *makes haste to efface himself.* YANK *goes on contemptuously*) De Bible, huh? De Cap'tlist class, huh? Aw nix on dat Salvation Army–Socialist bull. Git a soapbox! Hire a hall! Come and be saved, huh? Jerk us to Jesus, huh? Aw g'wan! I've listened to lots of guys like you, see. Yuh're all wrong. Wanter know what I t'ink? Yuh ain't no good for no one. Yuh're de bunk. Yuh ain't got no noive, get me? Yuh're yellow, dat's what. Yellow, dat's you. Say! What's dem slobs in de foist cabin got to do wit us? We're better men dan dey are, ain't we? Sure! One of us guys could clean up de whole mob wit one mit. Put one of 'em down here for one watch in de stokehole, what'd happen? Dey'd carry him off on a stretcher. Dem boids don't amount to nothin'. Dey're just baggage. Who makes dis old tub run? Ain't it us guys? Well den, we belong, don't we? We belong and dey don't. Dat's all. *(A loud chorus of approval.* YANK *goes on)* As for dis bein' hell—aw, nuts! Yuh lost your noive, dat's what. Dis is a man's job, get me? It belongs. It runs dis tub. No stiffs need apply. But yuh're a stiff, see? Yuh're yellow, dat's you.

VOICES *(with a great hard pride in them)*:
Righto!
A man's job!
Talk is cheap, Long.
He never could hold up his end.
Divil take him!
Yank's right. We make it go.
Py Gott, Yank say right ting!
We don't need no one cryin' over us.
Makin' speeches.
Throw him out!
Yellow!
Chuck him overboard!
I'll break his jaw for him!
(They crowd around Long threateningly).

YANK *(half good-natured again—contemptuously)*: Aw, take it easy. Leave him alone. He ain't woith a punch. Drink up. Here's how, whoever owns dis. *(He takes a long swallow from his bottle. All drink with him. In a flash all is hilarious amiability again, backslapping, loud talk, etc.).*

PADDY *(who has been sitting in a blinking, melancholy daze—suddenly cries out in a voice full of old sorrow)*: We belong to this, you're saying? We make the ship to go, you're saying? Yerra then, that Almighty God have pity on us! *(His voice runs into the wail of a keen, he rocks back and forth on his bench. The men stare at him, startled and impressed in spite of themselves)* Oh, to be back in the fine days of my youth, ochone! Oh, there was fine beautiful ships them days— clippers wid tall masts touching the sky—fine strong men in them—men that was sons of the sea as if 'twas the mother that bore them. Oh, the clean skins of them, and the clear eyes, the straight backs and full chests of them! Brave men they was, and bold men surely! We'd be sailing out, bound down round the Horn maybe. We'd be making sail in the dawn, with a fair breeze, singing a chanty song wid no care to it. And astern the land would be sinking low and dying out, but we'd give it no heed but a laugh, and never a look behind. For the day that was, was enough, for we was free men—and I'm thinking 'tis only slaves do be giving heed to the day that's gone or the day to come—until they're old like me. *(With a sort of religious exaltation)* Oh, to be scudding south again wid the power of the Trade Wind driving her on steady through the nights and the days! Full sail on her! Nights and days! Nights when the foam of the wake would be flaming wid fire, when the sky'd be blazing and winking wid stars. Or the full of the moon maybe. Then you'd see her driving through the gray night, her sails stretching aloft all silver and white, not a sound on the deck, the lot of us dreaming dreams, till you'd believe 'twas no real ship at all you was on but a ghost ship like the *Flying Dutchman* they say does be roaming the seas forevermore widout touching a port. And there was the days, too. A warm sun on the clean decks. Sun warming the blood of you, and wind over the miles of shiny green ocean like strong drink to your lungs. Work—aye, hard work—but who'd mind that at all? Sure, you worked under the sky and 'twas work wid skill and daring to it. And wid the day done, in the dog watch, smoking me pipe at ease, the lookout would be raising land maybe, and we'd see the mountains of South Americy wid the red fire of the setting sun painting the white tops and the clouds floating by them! *(His tone of exaltation ceases. He goes on mournfully)* Yerra, what's the use of talking? 'Tis a dead man's whisper. *(To* YANK *resentfully)* 'Twas them days men belonged to ships, not now. 'Twas them days a ship was part of the sea, and a man was part of a ship, and the sea joined all together and made it one. *(Scornfully)* Is it one wid this you'd be, Yank—black smoke from the funnels smudging the sea, smudging the decks—the bloody engines pounding and throbbing and shaking—wid divil a sight of sun or a breath of clean air—choking our lungs wid coal dust—breaking our backs and hearts in the hell of the stokehole—feeding the bloody furnace—feeding our lives along wid the coal, I'm thinking—caged in by steel from a sight of the sky like bloody apes in the Zoo! *(With a harsh laugh)* Ho-ho, divil mend you! Is it to belong to that you're wishing? Is it a flesh and blood wheel of the engines you'd be?

YANK *(who has been listening with a contemptuous sneer, barks out the answer)*: Sure ting! Dat's me. What about it?

PADDY *(as if to himself—with great sorrow)*: Me time is past due. That a great wave wid sun in the heart of it may sweep me over the side sometime I'd be dreaming of the days that's gone!

YANK: Aw, yuh crazy Mick! *(He springs to his feet and advances on* PADDY *threateningly—then stops, fighting some queer struggle within himself—lets his hands fall to his sides—contemptuously)* Aw, take it easy. Yuh're aw right, at dat. Yuh're bugs, dat's all—nutty as a cuckoo. All dat tripe yuh been pullin'—Aw, dat's all right. On'y it's dead, get me? Yuh don't belong no more, see. Yuh don't get de stuff. Yuh're too old. *(Disgustedly)* But aw say, come up for air onct in a while, can't yuh? See what's happened since yuh croaked. *(He suddenly bursts forth vehemently, growing more and more excited)* Say! Sure! Sure I meant it! What de hell—Say, lemme talk! Hey! Hey, you old Harp! Hey, youse guys! Say, listen to me—wait a moment—I gotter talk, see. I belong and he don't. He's dead but I'm livin'. Listen to me! Sure I'm part of de engines! Why de hell not! Dey move, don't dey? Dey're speed, ain't dey? Dey smash trou, don't dey? Twenty-five knots a hour! Dat's goin' some! Dat's new stuff! Dat belongs! But him, he's too old. He gets dizzy. Say, listen. All dat crazy tripe about nights and days; all dat crazy tripe about stars and moons; all dat crazy tripe about suns and winds, fresh air and de rest of it—Aw hell, dat's all a dope dream! Hittin' de pipe of de past, dat's what he's doin'. He's old and don't belong no more. But me, I'm young! I'm in de pink! I move wit it! It, get me! I mean de ting dat's de guts of all dis. It ploughs trou all de tripe he's been sayin'. It blows dat up! It knocks dat dead! It slams dat offen de face of de oith! It, get me! De engines and de coal and de smoke and all de rest of it! He can't breathe and swallow coal dust, but I kin, see? Dat's fresh air for me! Dat's food for me! I'm new, get me? Hell in de stokehole? Sure! It takes a man to work in hell. Hell, sure, dat's my fav'rite climate. I eat it up! I git fat on it! It's me makes it hot! It's me makes it roar! It's me makes it move! Sure, on'y for me everything stops. It all goes dead, get me? De noise and smoke and all de engines movin' de woild, dey stop. Dere ain't nothin' no more! Dat's what I'm sayin'. Everyting else dat makes de woild move, somep'n makes it move. It can't move witout somep'n else, see? Den yuh get down to me. I'm at de bottom, get me! Dere ain't nothin' foither. I'm de end! I'm de start! I start somep'n and de woild moves! It—dat's me!—de new dat's moiderin' de old! I'm de ting in coal dat makes it boin; I'm steam and oil for de engines; I'm de ting in noise dat makes yuh hear it; I'm smoke and express trains and steamers and factory whistles; I'm de ting in gold dat makes it money! And I'm what makes iron into steel! Steel, dat stands for de whole ting! And I'm steel—steel—steel! I'm de muscles in steel, de punch behind it! *(As he says this he pounds with his fist against the steel bunks. All the men, roused to a pitch of frenzied self-glorification by his speech, do likewise. There is a deafening metallic roar, through which* YANK'S *voice can be heard bellowing)* Slaves, hell! We run de whole woiks. All de rich guys dat tink dey're somep'n, dey ain't nothin'! Dey don't belong. But us guys, we're in de move, we're at de bottom, de whole ting is us! *(*PADDY *from the start of* YANK'S *speech has been taking one gulp after another from his bottle, at first frightenedly, as if he were afraid to listen, then desperately, as if to drown his senses, but finally has achieved complete indifferent, even amused, drunkenness.* YANK *sees his lips moving. He quells the uproar with a shout)* Hey, youse guys, take it easy! Wait a moment! De nutty Harp is sayin' somep'n.

PADDY *(is heard now—throws his head back with a mocking burst of laughter)*: Ho-ho-ho-ho-ho—

YANK *(drawing back his fist, with a snarl)*: Aw! Look out who yuh're givin' the bark!

PADDY *(begins to sing the "Miller of Dee" with enormous good nature)*:

"I care for nobody, no, not I,
And nobody cares for me."

YANK (*good-natured himself in a flash, interrupts* PADDY *with a slap on the bare back like a report*): Dat's de stuff! Now yuh're gettin' wise to somep'n. Care for nobody, dat's de dope! To hell wit 'em all! And nix on nobody else carin'. I kin care for myself, get me! (*Eight bells sound, muffled, vibrating through the steel walls as if some enormous brazen gong were imbedded in the heart of the ship. All the men jump up mechanically, file through the door silently close upon each other's heels in what is very like a prisoners' lockstep.* YANK *slaps* PADDY *on the back*) Our watch, yuh old Harp! (*Mockingly*) Come on down in hell. Eat up de coal dust. Drink in de heat. It's it, see! Act like yuh liked it, yuh better—or croak yuhself.

PADDY (*with jovial defiance*): To the divil wid it! I'll not report this watch. Let thim log me and be damned. I'm no slave the like of you. I'll be sittin' here at me ease, and drinking, and thinking, and dreaming dreams.

YANK (*contemptuously*): Tinkin' and dreamin', what'll that get yuh? What's tinkin' got to do wit it? We move, don't we? Speed, ain't it? Fog, dat's all you stand for. But we drive trou dat, don't we? We split dat up and smash trou— twenty-five knots a hour! (*Turns his back on* PADDY *scornfully*) Aw, yuh make me sick! Yuh don't belong! (*He strides out the door in rear.* PADDY *hums to himself, blinking drowsily*)

Curtain

SCENE TWO
Two days out. A section of the promenade deck. MILDRED DOUGLAS *and her aunt are discovered reclining in deck chairs. The former is a girl of twenty, slender, delicate, with a pale, pretty face marred by a self-conscious expression of disdainful superiority. She looks fretful, nervous and discontented, bored by her own anemia. Her aunt is a pompous and proud—and fat—old lady. She is a type even to the point of a double chin and lorgnettes. She is dressed pretentiously, as if afraid her face alone would never indicate her position in life.* MILDRED *is dressed all in white.*

The impression to be conveyed by this scene is one of the beautiful, vivid life of the sea all about—sunshine on the deck in a great flood, the fresh sea wind blowing across it. In the midst of this, these two incongruous, artificial figures, inert and disharmonious, the elder like a gray lump of dough touched up with rouge, the younger looking as if the vitality of her stock had been sapped before she was conceived, so that she is the expression not of its life energy but merely of the artificialities that energy had won for itself in the spending.

MILDRED (*looking up with affected dreaminess*): How the black smoke swirls back against the sky! Is it not beautiful?

AUNT (*without looking up*): I dislike smoke of any kind.

MILDRED: My great-grandmother smoked a pipe—a clay pipe.

AUNT (*ruffling*): Vulgar!

MILDRED: She was too distant a relative to be vulgar. Time mellows pipes.

AUNT *(pretending boredom but irritated)*: Did the sociology you took up at college teach you that—to play the ghoul on every possible occasion, excavating old bones? Why not let your great-grandmother rest in her grave?

MILDRED *(dreamily)*: With her pipe beside her—puffing in Paradise.

AUNT *(with spite)*: Yes, you are a natural born ghoul. You are even getting to look like one, my dear.

MILDRED *(in a passionless tone)*: I detest you, Aunt. *(Looking at her critically)* Do you know what you remind me of? Of a cold pork pudding against a background of linoleum tablecloth in the kitchen of a—but the possibilities are wearisome. *(She closes her eyes)*.

AUNT *(with a bitter laugh)*: Merci for your candor. But since I am and must be your chaperon—in appearance, at least—let us patch up some sort of armed truce. For my part you are quite free to indulge any pose of eccentricity that beguiles you—as long as you observe the amenities—

MILDRED *(drawling)*: The inanities?

AUNT *(going on as if she hadn't heard)*: After exhausting the morbid thrills of social service work on New York's East Side—how they must have hated you, by the way, the poor that you made so much poorer in their own eyes!— you are now bent on making your slumming international. Well, I hope Whitechapel will provide the needed nerve tonic. Do not ask me to chaperon you there, however. I told your father I would not. I loathe deformity. We will hire an army of detectives and you may investigate everything—they allow you to see.

MILDRED *(protesting with a trace of genuine earnestness)*: Please do not mock at my attempts to discover how the other half lives. Give me credit for some sort of groping sincerity in that at least. I would like to help them. I would like to be some use in the world. Is it my fault I don't know how? I would like to be sincere, to touch life somewhere. *(With weary bitterness)* But I'm afraid I have neither the vitality nor integrity. All that was burnt out in our stock before I was born. Grandfather's blast furnaces, flaming to the sky, melting steel, making millions—then father keeping those home fires burning, making more millions—and little me at the tail-end of it all. I'm a waste product in the Bessemer process—like the millions. Or rather, I inherit the acquired trait of the by-product, wealth, but none of the energy, none of the strength of the steel that made it. I am sired by gold and damned by it, as they say at the race track— damned in more ways than one. *(She laughs mirthlessly)*.

AUNT *(unimpressed—superciliously)*: You seem to be going in for sincerity today. It isn't becoming to you, really—except as an obvious pose. Be as artificial as you are, I advise. There's a sort of sincerity in that, you know. And, after all, you must confess you like that better.

MILDRED *(again affected and bored)*: Yes, I suppose I do. Pardon me for my outburst. When a leopard complains of its spots, it must sound rather grotesque. *(In a mocking tone)* Purr, little leopard. Purr, scratch, tear, kill, gorge yourself and be happy—only stay in the jungle where your spots are camouflage. In a cage they make you conspicuous.

AUNT: I don't know what you are talking about.

MILDRED: It would be rude to talk about anything to you. Let's just talk. *(She looks at her wrist watch)* Well, thank goodness, it's about time for them to come for me. That ought to give me a new thrill, Aunt.

AUNT *(affectedly troubled)*: You don't mean to say you're really going? The dirt—the heat must be frightful—

MILDRED: Grandfather started as a puddler. I should have inherited an immunity to heat that would make a salamander shiver. It will be fun to put it to the test.

AUNT: But don't you have to have the captain's—or someone's—permission to visit the stokehole?

MILDRED *(with a triumphant smile)*: I have it—both his and the chief engineer's. Oh, they didn't want to at first, in spite of my social service credentials. They didn't seem a bit anxious that I should investigate how the other half lives and works on a ship. So I had to tell them that my father, the president of Nazareth Steel, chairman of the board of directors of this line, had told me it would be all right.

AUNT: He didn't.

MILDRED: How naïve age makes one! But I said he did, Aunt. I even said he had given me a letter to them—which I had lost. And they were afraid to take the chance that I might be lying. *(Excitedly)* So it's ho! for the stokehole. The second engineer is to escort me. *(Looking at her watch again)* It's time. And here he comes, I think. *(The* SECOND ENGINEER *enters. He is a husky, fine-looking man of thirty-five or so. He stops before the two and tips his cap, visibly embarrassed and ill-at-ease).*

SECOND ENGINEER: Miss Douglas?

MILDRED: Yes. *(Throwing off her rugs and getting to her feet)* Are we all ready to start?

SECOND ENGINEER: In just a second, ma'am. I'm waiting for the Fourth. He's coming along.

MILDRED *(with a scornful smile)*: You don't care to shoulder this responsibility alone, is that it?

SECOND ENGINEER *(forcing a smile)*: Two are better than one. *(Disturbed by her eyes, glances out to sea—blurts out)* A fine day we're having.

MILDRED: Is it?

SECOND ENGINEER: A nice warm breeze—

MILDRED: It feels cold to me.

SECOND ENGINEER: But it's hot enough in the sun—

MILDRED: Not hot enough for me. I don't like Nature. I was never athletic.

SECOND ENGINEER *(forcing a smile)*: Well, you'll find it hot enough where you're going.

MILDRED: Do you mean hell?

SECOND ENGINEER *(flabbergasted, decides to laugh)*: Ho-ho! No, I mean the stokehole.

MILDRED: My grandfather was a puddler. He played with boiling steel.

SECOND ENGINEER *(all at sea—uneasily)*: Is that so? Hum, you'll excuse me, ma'am, but are you intending to wear that dress?

MILDRED: Why not?

SECOND ENGINEER: You'll likely rub against oil and dirt. It can't be helped.

MILDRED: It doesn't matter. I have lots of white dresses.

SECOND ENGINEER: I have an old coat you might throw over—

MILDRED: I have fifty dresses like this. I will throw this one into the sea when I come back. That ought to wash it clean, don't you think?

SECOND ENGINEER *(doggedly)*: There's ladders to climb down that are none to clean—and dark alleyways—

MILDRED: I will wear this very dress and none other.

SECOND ENGINEER: No offense meant. It's none of my business. I was only warning you—

MILDRED: Warning? That sounds thrilling.

SECOND ENGINEER *(looking down the deck—with a sigh of relief)*: There's the Fourth now. He's waiting for us. If you'll come—

MILDRED: Go on. I'll follow you. *(He goes.* MILDRED *turns a mocking smile on her aunt)* An oaf—but a handsome, virile oaf.

AUNT *(scornfully)*: Poser!

MILDRED: Take care. He said there were dark alleyways—

AUNT *(in the same tone)*: Poser!

MILDRED *(biting her lips angrily)*: You are right. But would that my millions were not so anemically chaste!

AUNT: Yes, for a fresh pose I have no doubt you would drag the name of Douglas in the gutter!

MILDRED: From which it sprang. Good-by, Aunt. Don't pray too hard that I may fall into the fiery furnace.

AUNT: Poser!

MILDRED *(viciously)*: Old hag! *(She slaps her aunt insultingly across the face and walks off, laughing gaily).*

AUNT *(screams after her)*: I said poser!

Curtain

SCENE THREE

The stokehole. In the rear, the dimly-outlined bulks of the furnaces and boilers. High overhead one hanging electric bulb sheds just enough light through the murky air laden with coal dust to pile up masses of shadows everywhere. A line of men, stripped to the waist, is before the furnace doors. They bend over, looking neither to right nor left, handling their shovels as if they were part of their bodies, with a strange, awkward, swinging rhythm. They use the shovels to throw open the furnace doors. Then from these fiery round holes in the black a flood of terrific light and heat pours full upon the men who are outlined in silhouette in the crouching, inhuman attitudes of chained gorillas. The men shovel with a rhythmic motion, swinging as on a pivot from the coal which lies in heaps on the floor behind to hurl it into the flaming mouths before them. There is a tumult of noise— the brazen clang of the furnace doors as they are flung open or slammed shut, the grating, teeth-gritting grind of steel against steel, of crunching coal. This clash of sounds stuns one's ears with its rending dissonance. But there is order in it, rhythm, a mechanical regulated recurrence, a tempo. And rising above all, making the air hum with the quiver of liberated energy, the roar of leaping flames in the furnaces, the monotonous throbbing beat of the engines.

As the curtain rises, the furnace doors are shut. The men are taking a breathing spell. One or two are arranging the coal behind them, pulling it into more accessible heaps. The others can be dimly made out leaning on their shovels in relaxed attitudes of exhaustion.

PADDY *(from somewhere in the line—plaintively)*: Yerra, will this divil's own watch nivir end? Me back is broke. I'm destroyed entirely.

YANK *(from the center of the line—with exuberant scorn)*: Aw, yuh make me sick! Lie down and croak, why don't yuh? Always beefin', dat's you! Say, dis is a cinch! Dis was made for me! It's my meat, get me! *(A whistle is blown—a thin, shrill note from somewhere overhead in the darkness.* YANK *curses without resentment)* Dere's de damn engineer crackin' de whip. He tinks we're loafin'.

PADDY *(vindictively)*: God stiffen him!

YANK *(in an exultant tone of command)*: Come on, youse guys! Git into de game! She's gittin' hungry! Pile some grub in her. Trow it into her belly! Come on now, all of youse! Open her up! *(At this last all the men, who have followed his movements of getting into position, throw open their furnace doors with a deafening clang. The fiery light floods over their shoulders as they bend round for the coal. Rivulets of sooty sweat have traced maps on their backs. The enlarged muscles form bunches of high light and shadow).*

YANK *(chanting a count as he shovels without seeming effort)*: One—two— tree— *(His voice rising exultantly in the joy of battle)* Dat's de stuff! Let her have it! All togedder now! Sling it into her! Let her ride! Shoot de piece now! Call de toin on her! Drive her into it! Feel her move! Watch her smoke! Speed, dat's her middle name! Give her coal, youse guys! Coal, dat's her booze! Drink it up, baby! Let's see yuh sprint! Dig in and gain a lap! Dere she go-o-es. *(This last in the chanting formula of the gallery gods at the six-day bike race. He slams his furnace door shut. The others do likewise with as much unison as their wearied bodies will permit. The effect is of one fiery eye after another being blotted out with a series of accompanying bangs).*

PADDY *(groaning)*: Me back is broke. I'm bate out—bate— *(There is a pause. Then the inexorable whistle sounds again from the dim regions above the electric light. There is a growl of cursing rage from all sides).*

YANK (*shaking his fist upward—contemptuously*): Take it easy dere, you! Who d'yuh tink's runnin' dis game, me or you? When I git ready, we move. Not before! When I git ready, get me!

VOICES (*approvingly*): That's the stuff!

Yank tal him, py golly!

Yank ain't affeerd.

Goot poy, Yank!

Give him hell!

Tell 'im 'e's a bloody swine!

Bloody slave-driver!

YANK (*contemptuously*): He ain't got no noive. He's yellow, get me? All de engineers is yellow. Dey got streaks a mile wide. Aw, to hell wit him! Let's move, youse guys. We had a rest. Come on, she needs it! Give her pep! It ain't for him. Him and his whistle, dey don't belong. But we belong, see! We gotter feed de baby! Come on! (*He turns and flings his furnace door open. They all follow his lead. At this instant the* SECOND *and* FOURTH ENGINEERS *enter from the darkness on the left with* MILDRED *between them. She starts, turns paler, her pose is crumbling, she shivers with fright in spite of the blazing heat, but forces herself to leave the* ENGINEERS *and take a few steps nearer the men. She is right behind* YANK. *All this happens quickly while the men have their backs turned*).

YANK: Come on, youse guys! (*He is turning to get coal when the whistle sounds again in a peremptory, irritating note. This drives* YANK *into a sudden fury. While the other men have turned full around and stopped dumfounded by the spectacle of* MILDRED *standing there in her white dress,* YANK *does not turn far enough to see her. Besides, his head is thrown back, he blinks upward through the murk trying to find the owner of the whistle, he brandishes his shovel murderously over his head in one hand, pounding on his chest, gorilla-like, with the other, shouting*) Toin off dat whistle! Come down outa dere, yuh yellow, brass-buttoned, Belfast bum, yuh! Come down and I'll knock yer brains out! Yuh lousy, stinkin', yellow mut of a Catholic-moiderin' bastard! Come down and I'll moider yuh! Pullin' dat whistle on me, huh? I'll show yuh! I'll crash yer skull in! I'll drive yer teet' down yer troat! I'll slam yer nose trou de back of yer head! I'll cut yer guts out for a nickel, yuh lousy boob, yuh dirty, crummy, muckeatin' son of a— (*Suddenly he becomes conscious of all the other men staring at something directly behind his back. He whirls defensively with a snarling, murderous growl, crouching to spring, his lips drawn back over his teeth, his small eyes gleaming ferociously. He sees* MILDRED, *like a white apparition in the full light from the open furnace doors. He glares into her eyes, turned to stone. As for her, during his speech she has listened, paralyzed with horror, terror, her whole personality crushed, beaten in, collapsed, by the terrific impact of this unknown, abysmal brutality, naked and shameless. As she looks at his gorilla face, as his eyes bore into hers, she utters a low, choking cry and shrinks away from him, putting both hands up before her eyes to shut out the sight of his face, to protect her own. This startles* YANK *to a reaction. His mouth falls open, his eyes grow bewildered*).

MILDRED (*about to faint—to the* ENGINEERS, *who now have her one by each arm—whimperingly*): Take me away! Oh, the filthy beast! (*She faints. They carry her quickly back, disappearing in the darkness at the left, rear. An iron door clangs shut. Rage and bewildered fury rush back on* YANK. *He feels himself insulted in some unknown fashion in the very heart of his pride. He roars*) God damn yuh! (*And hurls his shovel after them at the door which has just closed. It hits the steel bulkhead with a clang and falls clattering on the steel floor. From overhead the whistle sounds again in a long, angry, insistent command*).

Curtain

SCENE FOUR

The firemen's forecastle. YANK'S *watch has just come off duty and had dinner. Their faces and bodies shine from a soap and water scrubbing but around their eyes, where a hasty dousing does not touch, the coal dust sticks like black make-up, giving them a queer, sinister expression.* YANK *has not washed either face or body. He stands out in contrast to them, a blackened, brooding figure. He is seated forward on a bench in the exact attitude of Rodin's "The Thinker." The others, most of them smoking pipes, are staring at* YANK *half-apprehensively, as if fearing an outburst; half-amusedly, as if they saw a joke somewhere that tickled them.*

VOICES: He ain't ate nothin'.
Py golly, a fallar gat to gat grub in him.
Divil a lie.
Yank feeda da fire, no feeda da face.
Ha-ha.
He aint even washed hisself.
He's forgot.
Hey, Yank, you forgot to wash.
YANK (*sullenly*): Forgot nothin'! To hell wit washin'.
VOICES: It'll stick to you.
It'll get under your skin.
Give yer the bleedin' itch, that's wot.
It makes spots on you—like a leopard.
Like a piebald nigger, you mean.
Better wash up, Yank.
You sleep better.
Wash up, Yank.
Wash up! Wash up!
YANK (*resentfully*): Aw say, youse guys. Lemme alone. Can't youse see I'm tryin' to tink?
ALL (*repeating the word after him as one with cynical mockery*): Think! (*The word has a brazen, metallic quality as if their throats were phonograph horns. It is followed by a chorus of hard, barking laughter*).

YANK (*springing to his feet and glaring at them belligerently*): Yes, tink! Tink, dat's what I said! What about it? (*They are silent, puzzled by his sudden resentment at what used to be one of his jokes.* YANK *sits down again in the same attitude of "The Thinker"*).

VOICES: Leave him alone.

He's got a grouch on.

Why wouldn't he?

PADDY (*with a wink at the others*): Sure I know what's the matther. 'Tis aisy to see. He's fallen in love, I'm telling you.

ALL (*repeating the word after him as one with cynical mockery*): Love! (*The word has a brazen, metallic quality as if their throats were phonograph horns. It is followed by a chorus of hard, barking laughter*).

YANK (*with a contemptuous snort*): Love, hell! Hate, dat's what. I've fallen in hate, get me?

PADDY (*philosophically*): 'Twould take a wise man to tell one from the other. (*With a bitter, ironical scorn, increasing as he goes on*) But I'm telling you it's love that's in it. Sure what else but love for us poor bastes in the stokehole would be bringing a fine lady, dressed like a white quane, down a mile of ladders and steps to be havin' a look at us? (*A growl of anger goes up from all sides*).

LONG (*jumping on a bench—hectically*): Hinsultin' us! Hinsultin' us, the bloody cow! And them bloody engineers! What right 'as they got to be exhibitin' us 's if we was bleedin' monkeys in a menagerie? Did we sign for hinsults to our dignity as 'onest workers? Is that in the ship's articles? You kin bloody well bet it ain't! But I know why they done it. I asked a deck steward 'o she was and 'e told me. 'Er old man's a bleedin' millionaire, a bloody Capitalist! 'E's got enuf bloody gold to sink this bleedin' ship! 'E makes arf the bloody steel in the world! 'E owns this bloody boat! And you and me, Comrades, we're 'is slaves! And the skipper and mates and engineers, they're 'is slaves! And she's 'is bloody daughter and we're all 'er slaves, too! And she gives 'er orders as 'ow she wants to see the bloody animals below decks and down they takes 'er! (*There is a roar of rage from all sides*).

YANK (*blinking at him bewilderedly*): Say! Wait a moment! Is all dat straight goods?

LONG: Straight as string! The bleedin' steward as waits on 'em, 'e told me about 'er. And what're we goin' ter do, I arsks yer? 'Ave we got ter swaller 'er hinsults like dogs? It ain't in the ship's articles. I tell yer we got a case. We kin go to law—

YANK (*with abysmal contempt*): Hell! Law!

ALL (*repeating the word after him as one with cynical mockery*): Law! (*The word has a brazen metallic quality as if their throats were phonograph horns. It is followed by a chorus of hard, barking laughter*).

LONG (*feeling the ground slipping from under his feet—desperately*): As voters and citizens we kin force the bloody governments—

YANK (*with abysmal contempt*): Hell! Governments!

ALL (*repeating the word after him as one with cynical mockery*): Governments! (*The word has a brazen metallic quality as if their throats were phonograph horns. It is followed by a chorus of hard, barking laughter*).

LONG (*hysterically*): We're free and equal in the sight of God—

YANK (*with abysmal contempt*): Hell! God!

ALL (*repeating the word after him as one with cynical mockery*) God! (*The word has a brazen metallic quality as if their throats were phonograph horns. It is followed by a chorus of hard, barking laughter*).

YANK (*witheringly*): Aw, join de Salvation Army!

ALL: Sit down! Shut up! Damn fool! Sea-lawyer! (LONG *slinks back out of sight*).

PADDY (*continuing the trend of his thoughts as if he had never been inter-rupted—bitterly*): And there she was standing behind us, and the Second pointing at us like a man you'd hear in a circus would be saying: In this cage is a queerer kind of baboon than ever you'd find in darkest Africy. We roast them in their own sweat—and be damned if you won't hear some of thim saying they like it! (*He glances scornfully at* YANK).

YANK (*with a bewildered uncertain growl*): Aw!

PADDY: And there was Yank roarin' curses and turning round wid his shovel to brain her—and she looked at him, and him at her—

YANK (*slowly*): She was all white. I tought she was a ghost. Sure.

PADDY (*with heavy, biting sarcasm*): 'Twas love at first sight, divil a doubt of it! If you'd seen the endearin' look on her pale mug when she shriveled away with her hands over her eyes to shut out the sight of him! Sure, 'twas as if she'd seen a great hairy ape escaped from the Zoo!

YANK (*stung—with a growl of rage*): Aw!

PADDY: And the loving way Yank heaved his shovel at the skull of her, only she was out the door! (*A grin breaking over his face*) 'Twas touching, I'm telling you! It put the touch of home, swate home in the stokehole. (*There is a roar of laughter from all*).

YANK (*glaring at* PADDY *menacingly*): Aw, choke dat off, see!

PADDY (*not heeding him—to the others*): And her grabbin' at the Second's arm for protection. (*With a grotesque imitation of a woman's voice*) Kiss me, Engineer dear, for it's dark down here and me old man's in Wall Street making money! Hug me tight, darlin', for I'm afeerd in the dark and me mother's on deck makin' eyes at the skipper! (*Another roar of laughter*).

YANK (*threateningly*): Say! What yuh tryin' to do, kid me, yuh old Harp?

PADDY: Divil a bit! Ain't I wishin' myself you'd brained her?

YANK (*fiercely*): I'll brain her! I'll brain her yet, wait 'n' see! (*Coming over to* PADDY—*slowly*) Say, is dat what she called me—a hairy ape?

PADDY: She looked it at you if she didn't say the word itself.

YANK (*grinning horribly*): Hairy ape, huh? Sure! Dat's de way she looked at me, aw right. Hairy ape! So dat's me, huh? (*Bursting into rage—as if she were still in front of him*) Yuh skinny tart! Yuh white-faced bum, yuh! I'll show yuh who's a ape! (*Turning to the others, bewilderment seizing him again*) Say, youse guys. I was bawlin' him out for pullin' de whistle on us. You heard me. And den I seen youse lookin' at somep'n and I tought he'd sneaked down to come up in back of me, and I hopped round to knock him dead wit de shovel. And dere she was wit de light on her! Christ, yuh coulda pushed me over with a finger! I was scared, get me? Sure! I tought she was a ghost, see? She was all in white like dey wrap around stiffs. You seen her. Kin yuh blame me? She didn't belong, dat's what. And den when I come to and seen it was a real skoit and seen de way she was lookin' at me—like Paddy said—Christ, I was sore, get me? I don't stand for dat stuff from nobody. And I flung de shovel—on'y she'd beat it. (*Furiously*) I wished it'd banged her! I wished it'd knocked her block off!

LONG: And be 'anged for murder or 'lectrocuted? She ain't bleedin' well worth it.

YANK: I don't give a damn what! I'd be square wit her, wouldn't I? Tink I wanter let her put somep'n over on me? Tink I'm goin' to let her git away wit dat stuff? Yuh don't know me! No one ain't never put nothin' over on me and got away wit it, see!—not dat kind of stuff—no guy and no skoit neither! I'll fix her! Maybe she'll come down again—

VOICE: No chance, Yank. You scared her out of a year's growth.

YANK: I scared her? Why de hell should I scare her? Who de hell is she? Ain't she de same as me? Hairy ape, huh? (*With his old confident bravado*) I'll show her I'm better'n her, if she on'y knew it. I belong and she don't, see! I move and she's dead! Twenty-five knots an hour, dat's me! Dat carries her but I make dat. She's on'y baggage. Sure! (*Again bewilderedly*) But, Christ, she was funny lookin'! Did yuh pipe her hands? White and skinny. Yuh could see de bones through 'em. And her mush, dat was dead white, too. And her eyes, dey was like dey'd seen a ghost. Me, dat was! Sure! Hairy ape! Ghost, huh? Look at dat arm! (*He extends his right arm, swelling out the great muscles*) I coulda took her wit dat, wit just my little finger even, and broke her in two. (*Again bewilderedly*) Say, who is dat skoit, huh? What is she? What's she come from? Who made her? Who give her de noive to look at me like dat? Dis ting's got my goat right. I don't get her. She's new to me. What does a skoit like her mean, huh? She don't belong, get me! I can't see her. (*With growing anger*) But one ting I'm wise to, aw right, aw right! Youse all kin bet your shoits I'll git even wit her. I'll show her if she tinks she—She grinds de organ and I'm on de string, huh? I'll fix her! Let her come down again and I'll fling her in de furnace! She'll move den! She won't shiver at nothin', den! Speed, dat'll be her! She'll belong den! (*He grins horribly*).

PADDY: She'll never come. She's had her belly-full, I'm telling you. She'll be in bed now, I'm thinking, wid ten doctors and nurses feedin' her salts to clean the fear out of her.

YANK (*enraged*): Yuh tink I made her sick, too, do yuh? Just lookin' at me, huh? Hairy ape, huh? (*In a frenzy of rage*) I'll fix her! I'll tell her where to git off! She'll git down on her knees and take it back or I'll bust de face offen her! (*Shaking one fist upward and beating on his chest with the other*) I'll find yuh! I'm comin', d'yuh hear? I'll fix yuh, God damn yuh! (*He makes a rush for the door*).

VOICES: Stop him!
He'll get shot!
He'll murder her!
Trip him up!
Hold him!
He's gone crazy!
Gott, he's strong!
Hold him down!
Look out for a kick!
Pin his arms!

(They have all piled on him and, after a fierce struggle, by sheer weight of numbers have borne him to the floor just inside the door).

PADDY *(who has remained detached)*: Kape him down till he's cooled off. *(Scornfully)* Yerra, Yank, you're a great fool. Is it payin' attention at all you are to the like of that skinny sow widout one drop of rale blood in her?

YANK *(frenziedly, from the bottom of the heap)*: She done me doit! She done me doit, didn't she? I'll git square wit her! I'll get her some way! Git offen me, youse guys! Lemme up! I'll show her who's a ape!

Curtain

SCENE FIVE

Three weeks later. A corner of Fifth Avenue in the Fifties on a fine Sunday morning. A general atmosphere of clean, well-tidied, wide street; a flood of mellow, tempered sunshine; gentle, genteel breezes. In the rear, the show windows of two shops, a jewelry establishment on the corner, a furrier's next to it. Here the adornments of extreme wealth are tantalizingly displayed. The jeweler's window is gaudy with glittering diamonds, emeralds, rubies, pearls, etc., fashioned in ornate tiaras, crowns, necklaces, collars, etc. From each piece hangs an enormous tag from which a dollar sign and numerals in intermittent electric lights wink out the incredible prices. The same in the furrier's. Rich furs of all varieties hang there bathed in a downpour of artificial light. The general effect is of a background of magnificence cheapened and made grotesque by commercialism, a background in tawdry disharmony with the clear light and sunshine on the street itself.

Up the side street YANK *and* LONG *come swaggering.* LONG *is dressed in shore clothes, wears a black Windsor tie, cloth cap.* YANK *is in his dirty dungarees. A fireman's cap with black peak is cocked defiantly on the side of his head. He has not shaved for days and around his fierce, resentful eyes—as around those of* LONG *to a lesser degree—the black smudge of coal dust still sticks like make-up. They hesitate and stand together at the corner, swaggering, looking about them with a forced, defiant contempt.*

LONG *(indicating it all with an oratorical gesture)*: Well, 'ere we are. Fif' Avenoo. This 'ere's their bleedin' private lane, as yer might say. *(Bitterly)* We're trespassers 'ere. Proletarians keep orf the grass!

YANK *(dully)*: I don't see no grass, yuh boob. *(Staring at the sidewalk)* Clean, ain't it? Yuh could eat a fried egg offen it. The white wings got some job sweepin' dis up. *(Looking up and down the avenue—surlily)* Where's all de white-collar stiffs yuh said was here—and de skoits—*her* kind?

LONG: In church, blast 'em! Arskin' Jesus to give 'em more money.

YANK: Choich, huh? I useter go to choich onct—sure—when I was a kid. Me old man and woman, dey made me. Dey never went demselves, dough. Always got too big a head on Sunday mornin', dat was dem. *(With a grin)* Dey was scrappers for fair, bot' of dem. On Satiday nights when dey bot' got a skinful dey could put up a bout oughter been staged at de Garden. When dey got trough dere wasn't a chair or table wit a leg under it. Or else dey bot' jumped on me for somep'n. Dat was where I loined to take punishment. *(With a grin and a swagger)* I'm a chip offen de old block, get me?

LONG: Did yer old man follow the sea?

YANK: Naw. Worked along shore. I runned away when me old lady croaked wit de tremens. I helped at truckin' and in de market. Den I shipped in de stokehole. Sure. Dat belongs. De rest was nothin'. *(Looking around him)* I ain't never seen dis before. De Brooklyn waterfront, dat was where I was dragged up. *(Taking a deep breath)* Dis ain't so bad at dat, huh?

LONG: Not bad? Well, we pays for it wiv our bloody sweat, if yer wants to know!

YANK *(with sudden angry disgust)*: Aw hell! I don't see no one, see—like her. All dis gives me a pain. It don't belong. Say, ain't dere a back room around dis dump? Let's go shoot a ball. All dis is too clean and quiet and dolled-up, get me! It gives me a pain.

LONG: Wait and yer'll bloody well see—

YANK: I don't wait for no one. I keep on de move. Say, what yuh drag me up here for, anyway? Tryin' to kid me, yuh simp, yuh?

LONG: Yer wants to get back at 'er, don't yer? That's what yer been sayin' every bloomin' hour since she hinsulted yer.

YANK *(vehemently)*: Sure ting I do! Didn't I try to get even wit her in Southampton? Didn't I sneak on de dock and wait for her by de gangplank? I was goin' to spit in her pale mug, see! Sure, right in her pop-eyes! Dat woulda made me even, see? But no chanct. Dere was a whole army of plainclothes bulls around. Dey spotted me and gimme de bum's rush. I never seen her. But I'll git square wit her yet, you watch! *(Furiously)* De lousy tart! She tinks she kin get away wit moider—but not wit me! I'll fix her! I'll tink of a way!

LONG *(as disgusted as he dares to be)*: Ain't that why I brought yer up 'ere—to show yer? Yer been lookin' at this 'ere 'ole affair wrong. Yer been actin' an' talkin' 's if it was all a bleedin' personal matter between yer and that bloody cow. I wants to convince yer she was on'y a representative of 'er clarss. I wants to awaken yer bloody clarss consciousness. Then yer'll see it's 'er clarss yer've got to fight, not 'er alone. There's a 'ole mob of 'em like 'er, Gawd blind 'em!

YANK *(spitting on his hands—belligerently)*: De more de merrier when I gits started. Bring on de gang!

LONG: Yer'll see 'em in arf a mo', when that church lets out. (*He turns and sees the window display in the two stores for the first time*) Blimey! Look at that, will yer? (*They both walk back and stand looking in the jeweler's.* LONG *flies into a fury*) Just look at this 'ere bloomin' mess! Just look at it! Look at the bleedin' prices on 'em—more'n our 'ole bloody stokehole makes in ten voyages sweatin' in 'ell! And they—'er and 'er bloody clarss—buys 'em for toys to dangle on 'em! One of these 'ere would buy scoff for a starvin' family for a year!

YANK: Aw, cut de sob stuff! T' hell wit de starvin' family! Yuh'll be passin' de hat to me next. (*With naïve admiration*) Say, dem tings is pretty, huh? Bet yuh dey'd hock for a piece of change aw right. (*Then turning away, bored*) But, aw hell, what good are dey? Let me have 'em. Dey don't belong no more'n she does. (*With a gesture of sweeping the jewelers into oblivion*) All dat don't count, get me?

LONG (*who has moved to the furrier's—indignantly*): And I s'pose this 'ere don't count neither—skins of poor, 'armless animals slaughtered so as 'er and 'ers can keep their bleedin' noses warm!

YANK (*who has been staring at something inside—with queer excitement*): Take a slant at dat! Give it de once-over! Monkey fur—two t'ousand bucks! (*Bewilderedly*) Is dat straight goods—monkey fur? What de hell—?

LONG (*bitterly*): It's straight enuf. (*With grim humor*) They wouldn't bloody well pay that for a 'airy ape's skin—no, nor for the 'ole livin' ape with all 'is 'ead, and body, and soul thrown in!

YANK (*clenching his fists, his face growing pale with rage as if the skin in the window were a personal insult*): Trowin' it up in my face! Christ! I'll fix her!

LONG (*excitedly*): Church is out. 'Ere they come, the bleedin' swine. (*After a glance at* YANK'S *lowering face—uneasily*) Easy goes, Comrade. Keep yer bloomin' temper. Remember force defeats itself. It ain't our weapon. We must impress our demands through peaceful means—the votes of the on-marching proletarians of the bloody world!

YANK (*with abysmal contempt*): Votes, hell! Votes is a joke, see. Votes for women! Let dem do it!

LONG (*still more uneasily*): Calm, now. Treat 'em wiv the proper contempt. Observe the bleedin' parasites but 'old yer 'orses.

YANK (*angrily*): Get away from me! Yuh're yellow, dat's what. Force, dat's me! De punch, dat's me every time, see! (*The crowd from church enter from the right, sauntering slowly and affectedly, their heads held stiffly up, looking neither to right nor left, talking in toneless, simpering voices. The women are rouged, calcimined, dyed, overdressed to the nth degree. The men are in Prince Alberts, high hats, spats, canes, etc. A procession of gaudy marionettes, yet with something of the relentless horror of Frankensteins in their detached, mechanical unawareness*).

VOICES: Dear Doctor Caiaphas! He is so sincere!

What was the sermon? I dozed off.

About the radicals, my dear—and the false doctrines that are being preached.

We must organize a hundred per cent American bazaar.

And let everyone contribute one one-hundredth per cent of their income tax.

What an original idea!

We can devote the proceeds to rehabilitating the veil of the temple.

But that has been done so many times.

YANK *(glaring from one to the other of them—with an insulting snort of scorn)*: Huh! Huh! *(Without seeming to see him, they make wide detours to avoid the spot where he stands in the middle of the sidewalk).*

LONG *(frightenedly)*: Keep yer bloomin' mouth shut, I tells yer.

YANK *(viciously)*: G'wan! Tell it to Sweeney! *(He swaggers away and deliberately lurches into a top-hatted gentleman, then glares at him pugnaciously)* Say, who d'yuh tink yuh're bumpin'? Tink yuh own de oith?

GENTLEMAN *(coldly and affectedly)*: I beg your pardon. *(He has not looked at* YANK *and passes on without a glance, leaving him bewildered).*

LONG *(rushing up and grabbing* YANK'S *arm)*: 'Ere! Come away! This wasn't what I meant. Yer'll 'ave the bloody coppers down on us.

YANK *(savagely—giving him a push that sends him sprawling)*: G'wan!

LONG *(picks himself up—hysterically)*: I'll pop orf then. This ain't what I meant. And whatever 'appens, yer can't blame me. *(He slinks off left).*

YANK: T' hell wit youse! *(He approaches a lady—with a vicious grin and a smirking wink)* Hello, Kiddo. How's every little ting? Got anyting on for tonight? I know an old boiler down to de docks we kin crawl into. *(The lady stalks by without a look, without a change of pace.* YANK *turns to others— insultingly)* Holy smokes, what a mug! Go hide yuhself before de horses shy at yuh. Gee, pipe de heine on dat one! Say, youse, yuh look like de stoin of a ferryboat. Paint and powder! All dolled up to kill! Yuh look like stiffs laid out for de boneyard! Aw, g'wan, de lot of youse! Yuh give me de eye-ache. Yuh don't belong, get me! Look at me, why don't youse dare? I belong, dat's me! *(Pointing to a skyscraper across the street which is in process of construction—with bravado)* See dat building goin' up dere? See de steel work? Steel, dat's me! Youse guys live on it and tink yuh're somep'n. But I'm *in* it, see! I'm de hoistin' engine dat makes it go up! I'm it—de inside and bottom of it! Sure! I'm steel and steam and smoke and de rest of it! It moves—speed—twenty-five stories up— and me at de top and bottom—movin'! Youse simps don't move. Yuh're on'y dolls I winds up to see 'm spin. Yuh're de garbage, get me—de leavins—de ashes we dump over de side! Now, what 'a' yuh gotta say? *(But as they seem neither to see nor hear him, he flies into a fury)* Bums! Pigs! Tarts! Bitches! *(He turns in a rage on the men, bumping viciously into them but not jarring them the least bit. Rather it is he who recoils after each collision. He keeps growling)* Git off de oith! G'wan, yuh bum! Look where yuh're goin', can't yuh? Git outa here! Fight, why don't yuh? Put up yer mits! Don't be a dog! Fight or I'll knock yuh dead! *(But, without seeming to see him, they all answer with mechnical affected politeness)* I beg your pardon. *(Then at a cry from one of the women, they all scurry to the furrier's window).*

THE WOMAN (*ecstatically, with a gasp of delight*): Monkey fur! (*The whole crowd of men and women chorus after her in the same tone of affected delight*) Monkey fur!

YANK (*with a jerk of his head back on his shoulders, as if he had received a punch full in the face—raging*): I see yuh, all in white! I see yuh, yuh white-faced tart, yuh! Hairy ape, huh? I'll hairy ape yuh! (*He bends down and grips at the street curbing as if to pick it out and hurl it. Foiled in this, snarling with passion, he leaps to the lamp-post on the corner and tries to pull it up for a club. Just at that moment a bus is heard rumbling up. A fat, high-hatted, spatted gentleman runs out from the side street. He calls out plaintively*): Bus! Bus! Stop there! (*and runs full tilt into the bending, straining* YANK, *who is bowled off his balance*).

YANK (*seeing a fight—with a roar of joy as he springs to his feet*): At last! Bus, huh? I'll bust yuh! (*He lets drive a terrific swing, his fist landing full on the fat gentleman's face. But the gentleman stands unmoved as if nothing had happened*).

GENTLEMAN: I beg your pardon. (*Then irritably*) You have made me lose my bus. (*He claps his hands and begins to scream*): Officer! Officer! (*Many police whistles shrill out on the instant and a whole platoon of policemen rush in on* YANK *from all sides. He tries to fight but is clubbed to the pavement and fallen upon. The crowd at the window have not moved or noticed this disturbance. The clanging gong of the patrol wagon approaches with a clamoring din*).

Curtain

SCENE SIX

Night of the following day. A row of cells in the prison on Blackwells Island. The cells extend back diagonally from right front to left rear. They do not stop, but disappear in the dark background as if they ran on, numberless, into infinity. One electric bulb from the low ceiling of the narrow corridor sheds its light through the heavy steel bars of the cell at the extreme front and reveals part of the interior. YANK *can be seen within, crouched on the edge of his cot in the attitude of Rodin's "The Thinker." His face is spotted with black and blue bruises. A blood-stained bandage is wrapped around his head.*

YANK (*suddenly starting as if awakening from a dream, reaches out and shakes the bars—aloud to himself, wonderingly*): Steel. Dis is de Zoo, huh? (*A burst of hard, barking laughter comes from the unseen occupants of the cells, runs back down the tier, and abruptly ceases*).

VOICES (*mockingly*): The Zoo? That's a new name for this coop—a damn good name!

Steel, eh? You said a mouthful. This is the old iron house.

Who is that boob talkin'?

He's the bloke they brung in out of his head. The bulls had beat him up fierce.

YANK (*dully*): I musta been dreamin'. I tought I was in a cage at de Zoo—but de apes don't talk, do dey?

VOICES *(with mocking laughter):* You're in a cage aw right.

A coop!

A pen!

A sty!

A kennel! *(Hard laughter—a pause).*

Say, guy! Who are you? No, never mind lying. What are you?

Yes, tell us your sad story. What's your game?

What did they jug yuh for?

YANK *(dully):* I was a fireman—stokin' on de liners. *(Then with sudden rage, rattling his cell bars)* I'm a hairy ape, get me? And I'll bust youse all in de jaw if yuh don't lay off kiddin' me.

VOICES: Huh! You're a hard boiled duck, ain't you!

When you spit, it bounces! *(Laughter).*

Aw, can it. He's a regular guy. Ain't you?

What did he say he was—a ape?

YANK *(defiantly):* Sure ting! Ain't dat what youse all are—apes? *(A silence. Then a furious rattling of bars from down the corridor).*

A VOICE *(thick with rage):* I'll show yuh who's a ape, yuh bum!

VOICES: Ssshh! Nix!

Can de noise!

Piano!

You'll have the guard down on us!

YANK *(scornfully):* De guard? Yuh mean de keeper, don't yuh? *(Angry exclamations from all the cells).*

VOICE *(placatingly):* Aw, don't pay no attention to him. He's off his nut from the beatin'-up he got. Say, you guy! We're waitin' to hear what they landed you for—or ain't yuh tellin'?

YANK: Sure, I'll tell youse. Sure! Why de hell not? On'y—youse won't get me. Nobody gets me but me, see? I started to tell de Judge and all he says was: "Toity days to tink it over." Tink it over! Christ, dat's all I been doin' for weeks! *(After a pause)* I was tryin' to git even with someone, see?—someone dat done me doit.

VOICES *(cynically):* De old stuff, I bet. Your goil, huh?

Give yuh the double-cross, huh?

That's them every time!

Did yuh beat up de odder guy?

YANK *(disgustedly):* Aw, yuh're all wrong! Sure dere was a skoit in it—but not what youse mean, not dat old tripe. Dis was a new kind of skoit. She was dolled up all in white—in de stokehole. I tought she was a ghost. Sure. *(A pause).*

VOICES *(whispering):* Gee, he's still nutty.

Let him rave. It's fun listenin'.

YANK *(unheeding—groping in his thoughts):* Her hands—dey was skinny and white like dey wasn't real but painted on somep'n. Dere was a million miles from me to her—twenty-five knots a hour. She was like some dead ting de cat brung in. Sure, dat's what. She didn't belong. She belonged in de window of a toy store, or on de top of a garbage can, see! Sure! *(He breaks out angrily)* But would yuh believe it, she had de noive to do me doit. She lamped me like she was seein' somep'n broke loose from de menagerie. Christ, yuh'd oughter seen her eyes! *(He rattles the bars of his cell furiously)* But I'll get back at her yet, you watch! And if I can't find her I'll take it out on de gang she runs wit. I'm wise to where dey hangs out now. I'll show her who belongs! I'll show her who's in de move and who ain't. You watch my smoke!

VOICES *(serious and joking)*: Dat's de talkin'!

Take her for all she's got!

What was this dame, anyway? Who was she, eh?

YANK: I dunno. First cabin stiff. Her old man's a millionaire, dey says—name of Douglas.

VOICES: Douglas? That's the president of the Steel Trust, I bet.

Sure, I seen his mug in de papers.

He's filthy with dough.

VOICE: Hey, feller, take a tip from me. If you want to get back at that dame, you better join the Wobblies. You'll get some action then.

YANK: Wobblies? What de hell's dat?

VOICE: Ain't you ever heard of the I.W.W.?

YANK: Naw. What is it?

VOICE: A gang of blokes—a tough gang. I been readin' about 'em today in the paper. The guard give me the *Sunday Times.* There's a long spiel about 'em. It's from a speech made in the Senate by a guy named Senator Queen. *(He is in the cell next to* YANK'S. *There is a rustling of paper)* Wait'll I see if I got light enough and I'll read you. Listen. *(He reads)* "There is a menace existing in this country today which threatens the vitals of our fair Republic—as foul a menace against the very life-blood of the American Eagle as was the foul conspiracy of Catiline against the eagles of ancient Rome!"

VOICE *(disgustedly)*: Aw, hell! Tell him to salt de tail of dat eagle!

VOICE *(reading)*: "I refer to that devil's brew of rascals, jailbirds, murderers and cutthroats who libel all honest working men by calling themselves the Industrial Workers of the World; but in the light of their nefarious plots, I call them the Industrious *Wreckers* of the World!"

YANK *(with vengeful satisfaction)*: Wreckers, dat's de right dope! Dat belongs! Me for dem!

VOICE: Ssshh! *(reading)* "This fiendish organization is a foul ulcer on the fair body of our Democracy—"

VOICE: Democracy, hell! Give him the boid, fellers—the raspberry! *(They do)*.

VOICE: Ssshh! *(reading)* "Like Cato I say to this Senate, the I.W.W. must be destroyed! For they represent an ever-present dagger pointed at the heart of the greatest nation the world has ever known, where all men are born free and equal, with equal opportunities to all, where the Founding Fathers have guaranteed to each one happiness, where Truth, Honor, Liberty, Justice, and the Brotherhood of Man are a religion absorbed with one's mother's milk, taught at our father's knee, sealed, signed, and stamped upon in the glorious Constitution of these United States!" *(A perfect storm of hisses, catcalls, boos, and hard laughter).*

VOICES *(scornfully)*: Hurrah for de Fort' of July!

Pass de hat!

Liberty!

Justice!

Honor!

Opportunity!

Brotherhood!

ALL *(with abysmal scorn)*: Aw, hell!

VOICE: Give that Queen Senator guy the bark! All togedder now—one—two—tree—*(A terrific chorus of barking and yapping).*

GUARD *(from a distance)*: Quiet there, youse—or I'll git the hose. *(The noise subsides).*

YANK *(with growling rage)*: I'd like to catch dat senator guy alone for a second. I'd loin him some trute!

VOICE: Ssshh! Here's where he gits down to cases on the Wobblies. *(Reads)* "They plot with fire in one hand and dynamite in the other. They stop not before murder to gain their ends, nor at the outraging of defenseless womanhood. They would tear down society, put the lowest scum in the seats of the mighty, turn Almighty God's revealed plan for the world topsy-turvy, and make of our sweet and lovely civilization a shambles, a desolation where man, God's masterpiece, would soon degenerate back to the ape!"

VOICE *(to YANK)*: Hey, you guy. There's your ape stuff again.

YANK *(with a growl of fury)*: I got him. So dey blow up tings, do dey? Dey turn tings round, do dey? Hey, lend me dat paper, will yuh?

VOICE: Sure. Give it to him. On'y keep it to yourself, see. We don't wanter listen to no more of that slop.

VOICE: Here you are. Hide it under your mattress.

YANK *(reaching out)*: Tanks. I can't read much but I kin manage. *(He sits, the paper in the hand at his side, in the attitude of Rodin's "The Thinker." A pause. Several snores from down the corridor. Suddenly YANK jumps to his feet with a furious groan as if some appalling thought had crashed on him—bewilderedly)* Sure—her old man—president of de Steel Trust—makes half de steel in de world—steel—where I tought I belonged—drivin' trou—movin'—in dat—to make *her*—and cage me in for her to spit on! Christ! *(He shakes the bars of his cell door till the whole tier trembles. Irritated, protesting exclamations from those awakened or trying to get to sleep)* He made dis—dis cage! Steel! *It* don't belong, dat's what! Cages, cells, locks, bolts, bars—dat's what it means!—holdin' me down wit him at de top! But I'll drive trou! Fire, dat melts it! I'll be fire—under de heap—fire dat never goes out—hot as hell—breakin' out in de night—*(While he has been saying this last he has shaken his cell door to a clanging accompaniment. As he comes to the "breakin' out" he seizes one bar with both hands and, putting his two feet up against the others so that his position is parallel to the floor like a monkey's, he gives a great wrench backwards. The bar bends like a licorice stick under his tremendous strength. Just at this moment the* PRISON GUARD *rushes in, dragging a hose behind him).*

GUARD *(angrily)*: I'll loin youse bums to wake me up! *(Sees* YANK*)* Hello, it's you, huh? Got the D.T.'s, hey? Well, I'll cure 'em. I'll drown your snakes for yuh! *(Noticing the bar)* Hell, look at dat bar bended! On'y a bug is strong enough for dat!

YANK *(glaring at him)*: Or a hairy ape, yuh big yellow bum! Look out! Here I come! *(He grabs another bar).*

GUARD *(scared now—yelling off left)*: Toin de hose on, Ben!—full pressure! And call de others—and a straitjacket! *(The curtain is falling. As it hides* YANK *from view, there is a splattering smash as the stream of water hits the steel of* YANK'S *cell).*

Curtain

SCENE SEVEN

Nearly a month later. An I.W.W. local near the waterfront, showing the interior of a front room on the ground floor, and the street outside. Moonlight on the narrow street, buildings massed in black shadow. The interior of the room, which is general assembly room, office, and reading room, resembles some dingy settlement boys' club. A desk and high stool are in one corner. A table with papers, stacks of pamphlets, chairs about it, is at center. The whole is decidedly cheap, banal, commonplace and unmysterious as a room could well be. The secretary is perched on the stool making entries in a large ledger. An eye shade casts his face into shadows. Eight or ten men, longshoremen, iron workers, and the like, are grouped about the table. Two are playing checkers. One is writing a letter. Most of them are smoking pipes. A big signboard is on the wall at the rear, "Industrial Workers of the World—Local No. 57."

YANK *(comes down the street outside. He is dressed as in Scene Five. He moves cautiously, mysteriously. He comes to a point opposite the door; tiptoes softly up to it, listens, is impressed by the silence within, knocks carefully, as if he were guessing at the password to some secret rite. Listens. No answer. Knocks again a bit louder. No answer. Knocks impatiently, much louder).*

SECRETARY *(turning around on his stool)*: What the hell is that—someone knocking? *(Shouts)* Come in, why don't you? *(All the men in the room look up.* YANK *opens the door slowly, gingerly, as if afraid of an ambush. He looks around for secret doors, mystery, is taken aback by the commonplaceness of the room and the men in it, thinks he may have gotten in the wrong place, then sees the signboard on the wall and is reassured).*

YANK *(blurts out)*: Hello.

MEN *(reservedly)*: Hello.

YANK *(more easily)*: I thought I'd bumped into de wrong dump.

SECRETARY *(scrutinizing him carefully)*: Maybe you have. Are you a member?

YANK: Naw, not yet. Dat's what I came for—to join.

SECRETARY: That's easy. What's your job—longshore?

YANK: Naw. Fireman—stoker on de liners.

SECRETARY *(with satisfaction)*: Welcome to our city. Glad to know you people are waking up at last. We haven't got many members in your line.

YANK: Naw. Dey're all dead to de woild.

SECRETARY: Well, you can help to wake 'em. What's your name? I'll make out your card.

YANK *(confused)*: Name? Lemme tink.

SECRETARY *(sharply)*: Don't you know your own name?

YANK: Sure; but I been just Yank for so long—Bob, dat's it—Bob Smith.

SECRETARY *(writing)*: Robert Smith. *(Fills out the rest of card)* Here you are. Cost you half a dollar.

YANK: Is dat all—four bits? Dat's easy. *(Gives the Secretary the money)*.

SECRETARY *(throwing it in drawer)*: Thanks. Well, make yourself at home. No introductions needed. There's literature on the table. Take some of those pamphlets with you to distribute aboard ship. They may bring results. Sow the seed, only go about it right. Don't get caught and fired. We got plenty out of work. What we need is men who can hold their jobs—and work for us at the same time.

YANK: Sure. *(But he still stands, embarrassed and uneasy)*.

SECRETARY *(looking at him—curiously)*: What did you knock for? Think we had a coon in uniform to open doors?

YANK: Naw. I tought it was locked—and dat yuh'd wanter give me the once-over trou a peep-hole or somep'n to see if I was right.

SECRETARY *(alert and suspicious but with an easy laugh)*: Think we were running a crap game? That door is never locked. What put that in your nut?

YANK *(with a knowing grin, convinced that this is all camouflage, a part of the secrecy)*: Dis burg is full of bulls, ain't it?

SECRETARY *(sharply)*: What have the cops got to do with us? We're breaking no laws.

YANK *(with a knowing wink)*: Sure. Youse wouldn't for woilds. Sure. I'm wise to dat.

SECRETARY: You seem to be wise to a lot of stuff none of us knows about.

YANK *(with another wink)*: Aw, dat's aw right, see. *(Then made a bit resentful by the suspicious glances from all sides)* Aw, can it! Youse needn't put me trou de toid degree. Can't youse see I belong? Sure! I'm reg'lar. I'll stick, get me? I'll shoot de woiks for youse. Dat's why I wanted to join in.

SECRETARY *(breezily, feeling him out)*: That's the right spirit. Only are you sure you understand what you've joined? It's all plain and above board; still, some guys get a wrong slant on us. *(Sharply)* What's your notion of the purpose of the I.W.W.?

YANK: Aw, I know all about it.

SECRETARY *(sarcastically)*: Well, give us some of your valuable information.

YANK *(cunningly)*: I know enough not to speak outa my toin. *(Then resentfully again)* Aw, say! I'm reg'lar. I'm wise to de game. I know yuh got to watch your step wit a stranger. For all youse know, I might be a plain-clothes dick, or somep'n, dat's what yuh're tinkin', huh? Aw, forget it! I belong, see? Ask any guy down to de docks if I don't.

SECRETARY: Who said you didn't?

YANK: After I'm 'nitiated, I'll show yuh.

SECRETARY *(astounded)*: Initiated? There's no initiation.

YANK *(disappointed)*: Ain't there no password—no grip nor nothin'?

SECRETARY: What'd you think this is—the Elks—or the Black Hand?

YANK: De Elks, hell! De Black Hand, dey're a lot of yellow back-stickin' Ginees. Naw. Dis is a man's gang, ain't it?

SECRETARY: You said it! That's why we stand on our two feet in the open. We got no secrets.

YANK *(surprised but admiringly)*: Yuh mean to say yuh always run wide open—like dis?

SECRETARY: Exactly.

YANK: Den yuh sure got your noive wit youse!

SECRETARY *(sharply)*: Just what was it made you want to join us? Come out with that straight.

YANK: Yuh call me? Well, I got noive, too! Here's my hand. Yuh wanter blow tings up, don't yuh? Well, dat's me! I belong!

SECRETARY *(with pretended carelessness)*: You mean change the unequal conditions of society by legitimate direct action—or with dynamite?

YANK: Dynamite! Blow it offen de oith—steel—all de cages—all de factories, steamers, buildings, jails—de Steel Trust and all dat makes it go.

SECRETARY: So—that's your idea, eh? And did you have any special job in that line you wanted to propose to us? *(He makes a sign to the men, who get up cautiously one by one and group behind* YANK*).*

YANK *(boldly)*: Sure, I'll come out wit it. I'll show youse I'm one of de gang. Dere's dat millionaire guy, Douglas—

SECRETARY: President of the Steel Trust, you mean? Do you want to assassinate him?

YANK: Naw, dat don't get yuh nothin'. I mean blow up de factory, de woiks, where he makes de steel. Dat's what I'm after—to blow up de steel, knock all de steel in de woild up to de moon. Dat'll fix tings! *(Eagerly, with a touch of bravado)* I'll do it by me lonesome! I'll show yuh! Tell me where his woiks is, how to git there, all de dope. Gimme de stuff, de old butter—and watch me do de rest! Watch de smoke and see it move! I don't give a damn if dey nab me— long as it's done! I'll soive life for it—and give 'em de laugh! *(Half to himself)* And I'll write her a letter and tell her de hairy ape done it. Dat'll square tings.

SECRETARY *(stepping away from* YANK*)*: Very interesting. *(He gives a signal. The men, huskies all, throw themselves on* YANK *and before he knows it they have* *his legs and arms pinioned. But he is too flabbergasted to make a struggle, anyway. They feel him over for weapons).*

MAN: No gat, no knife. Shall we give him what's what and put the boots to him?

SECRETARY: No. He isn't worth the trouble we'd get into. He's too stupid. *(He comes closer and laughs mockingly in* YANK's *face)* Ho-ho! By God, this is the biggest joke they've put up on us yet. Hey, you Joke! Who sent you—Burns or Pinkerton? No, by God, you're such a bonehead I'll bet you're in the Secret Service! Well, you dirty spy, you rotten agent provocator, you can go back and tell whatever skunk is paying you blood-money for betraying your brothers that he's wasting his coin. You couldn't catch a cold. And tell him that all he'll ever get on us, or ever has got, is just his own sneaking plots that he's framed up to put us in jail. We are what our manifesto says we are, neither more nor less— and we'll give him a copy of that any time he calls. And as for you—*(He glares scornfully at* YANK, *who is sunk in an obvious stupor)* Oh, hell, what's the use of talking? You're a brainless ape.

YANK *(aroused by the word to fierce but futile struggles)*: What's dat, yuh Sheeny bum, yuh!

SECRETARY: Throw him out, boys. *(In spite of his struggles, this is done with gusto and éclat. Propelled by several parting kicks,* YANK *lands sprawling in the middle of the narrow cobbled street. With a growl he starts to get up and storm the closed door, but stops bewildered by the confusion in his brain, pathetically impotent. He sits there, brooding, in as near to the attitude of Rodin's "Thinker" as he can get in his position).*

YANK *(bitterly)*: So dem boids don't tink I belong, neider. Aw, to hell wit 'em! Dey're in de wrong pew—de same old bull—soapboxes and Salvation Army—no guts! Cut out an hour offen de job a day and make me happy! Gimme a dollar more a day and make me happy! Tree square a day, and cauliflowers in de front yard—ekal rights—a woman and kids—a lousy vote— and I'm all fixed for Jesus, huh? Aw, hell! What does dat get yuh? Dis ting's in your inside, but it ain't your belly. Feedin' your face—sinkers and coffee—dat don't touch it. It's way down—at de bottom. Yuh can't grab it, and yuh can't stop it. It moves, and everything moves. It stops and de whole woild stops. Dat's me now—I don't tick, see?—I'm a busted Ingersoll, dat's what. Steel was me, and I owned de woild. Now I ain't steel, and de woild owns me. Aw, hell! I can't see—it's all dark, get me? It's all wrong! *(He turns a bitter mocking face up like an ape gibbering at the moon)* Say, youse up dere, Man in de Moon, yuh look so wise, gimme de answer, huh? Slip me de inside dope, de information right from de stable—where do I get off at, huh?

A POLICEMAN *(who has come up the street in time to hear this last—with grim humor)*: You'll get off at the station, you boob, if you don't get up out of that and keep movin'.

YANK *(looking up at him—with a hard, bitter laugh)*: Sure! Lock me up! Put me in a cage! Dat's de on'y answer yuh know. G'wan, lock me up!

POLICEMAN: What you been doin'?

YANK: Enuf to gimme life for! I was born, see? Sure, dat's de charge. Write it in de blotter. I was born, get me!

POLICEMAN *(jocosely)*: God pity your old woman! *(Then matter-of-fact)* But I've no time for kidding. You're soused. I'd run you in but it's too long a walk to the station. Come on now, get up, or I'll fan your ears with this club. Beat it now! *(He hauls* YANK *to his feet).*

YANK *(in vague mocking tone)*: Say, where do I go from here?

POLICEMAN *(giving him a push—with a grin, indifferently)*: Go to hell.

Curtain

SCENE EIGHT

Twilight of the next day. The monkey house at the Zoo. One spot of clear gray light falls on the front of one cage so that the interior can be seen. The other cages are vague, shrouded in shadow from which chatterings pitched in a conversational tone can be heard. On the one cage a sign from which the word "gorilla" stands out. The gigantic animal himself is seen squatting on his haunches on a bench in much the same attitude as Rodin's "Thinker." YANK *enters from the left. Immediately a chorus of angry chattering and screeching breaks out. The gorilla turns his eyes but makes no sound or move.*

YANK *(with a hard, bitter laugh)*: Welcome to your city, huh? Hail, hail, de gang's all here! *(At the sound of his voice the chattering dies away into an attentive silence.* YANK *walks up to the gorilla's cage and, leaning over the railing, stares in at its occupant, who stares back at him, silent and motionless. There is a pause of dead stillness. Then* YANK *begins to talk in a friendly confidential tone, half-mockingly, but with a deep undercurrent of sympathy)* Say, yuh're some hard-lookin' guy, ain't yuh? I seen lots of tough nuts dat de gang called gorillas, but yuh're de foist real one I ever seen. Some chest yuh got, and shoulders, and dem arms and mits! I bet yuh got a punch in eider fist dat'd knock 'em all silly! *(This with genuine admiration. The gorilla, as if he understood, stands upright, swelling out his chest and pounding on it with his fist.* YANK *grins sympathetically)* Sure, I get yuh. Yuh challenge de whole woild, huh? Yuh got what I was sayin' even if yuh muffed de woids. *(Then bitterness creeping in)* And why wouldn't yuh get me? Ain't we both members of de same club—de Hairy Apes? *(They stare at each other—a pause—then* YANK *goes on slowly and bitterly)* So yuh're what she seen when she looked at me, de white-faced tart! I was you to her, get me? On'y outa de cage—broke out—free to moider her, see? Sure! Dat's what she tought. She wasn't wise dat I was in a cage, too—worser'n yours—sure—a damn sight—'cause you got some chanct to bust loose—but me—*(He grows confused)* Aw, hell! It's all wrong, ain't it? *(A pause)* I s'pose yuh wanter know what I'm doin' here, huh? I been warmin' a bench down to de Battery—ever since last night. Sure. I seen de sun come up. Dat was pretty, too—all red and pink and green. I was lookin' at de skyscrapers—steel—and all de ships comin' in, sailin' out, all over de oith—and dey was steel, too. De sun was warm, dey wasn't no clouds, and dere was a breeze blowin'. Sure, it was great stuff, I got it aw right—what Paddy said about dat bein' de right dope—on'y I couldn't get *in* it, see? I couldn't belong in dat. It was over my head. And I kept tinkin'—and den I beat it up here to see what youse was like. And I waited till dey was all gone to git yuh alone. Say, how d'yuh feel sittin' in dat pen all de time, havin' to stand for 'em comin' and starin' at yuh—de white-faced, skinny tarts and de boobs that marry 'em—makin' fun of yuh, laughin' at yuh, gittin' scared of yuh—damn 'em! *(He pounds on the rail with his fist. The gorilla rattles the bars of his cage and snarls. All the other monkeys set up an angry chattering in the darkness.* YANK *goes on excitedly)* Sure! Dat's de way it hits me, too. On'y yuh're lucky, see? Yuh don't belong wit 'em and yuh know it. But me, I belong wit 'em—but I don't, see? Dey don't belong wit me, dat's what. Get me? Tinkin' is hard—*(He passes one hand across his forehead with a painful gesture. The gorilla growls impatiently.* YANK *goes on gropingly)* It's dis way, what I'm drivin' at. Youse can sit and dope dream in de past, green woods, de jungle and de rest of it. Den yuh belong and dey don't. Den yuh kin laugh at 'em, see? Yuh're de champ of de woild. But me—I ain't got no past to tink in, nor nothin' dat's comin', on'y what's now—and dat don't belong. Sure, you're de best off! Yuh can't tink, can yuh? Yuh can't talk neider. But I kin make a bluff at talkin' and tinkin'—a'most git away wit it—a'most!—and dat's where de joker comes in. *(He laughs)* I ain't on oith and I ain't in heaven, get me? I'm in de middle tryin' to separate 'em, takin' all de woist punches from bot' of 'em. Maybe dat's what dey call hell, huh? But you, yuh're at de bottom. You belong! Sure! Yuh're de on'y one in de woild dat does, yuh lucky stiff! *(The gorilla growls proudly)* And dat's why dey gotter put yuh in a cage, see? *(The gorilla roars angrily)* Sure! Yuh get me. It beats it when you try to tink it or talk it—it's way down—deep—behind— you 'n' me we feel it. Sure! Bot' members of dis club! *(He laughs—then in a savage tone)* What de hell! T' hell with it! A little action, dat's our meat! Dat belongs! Knock 'em down and keep bustin' 'em till dey croaks yuh with a gat—wit steel! Sure! Are yuh game? Dey've looked at youse, ain't dey—in a cage? Wanter git even? Wanter wind up like a sport 'stead of croakin' slow in dere? *(The gorilla roars an emphatic affirmative.* YANK *goes on with a sort of furious exaltation)* Sure! Yuh're reg'lar! Yuh'll stick to de finish! Me 'n' you, huh?—bot' members of this club! We'll put up one last star bout dat'll knock 'em offen deir seats! Dey'll have to make de cages stronger after we're trou! *(The gorilla is straining at his bars, growling, hopping from one foot to the other.* YANK *takes a jimmy from under his coat and forces the lock on the cage door. He throws this open)* Pardon from de governor! Step out and shake hands. I'll take yuh for a walk down Fif' Avenoo. We'll knock 'em offen de oith and croak wit de band playin'. Come on, Brother. *(The gorilla scrambles gingerly out of his cage. Goes to* YANK *and stands looking at him.* YANK *keeps his mocking tone—holds out his hand)* Shake—de secret grip of our order. *(Something, the tone of mockery, perhaps, suddenly enrages the animal. With a spring he wraps his huge arms around* YANK *in a murderous hug. There is a crackling snap of crushed ribs—a gasping cry, still mocking, from* YANK*)* Hey, I didn't say kiss me! *(The gorilla lets the crushed body slip to the floor; stands over it* *uncertainly, considering; then picks it up, throws it in the cage, shuts the door, and shuffles off menacingly into the darkness at left. A great uproar of frightened chattering and whimpering comes from the other cages. Then* YANK *moves, groaning, opening his eyes, and there is silence. He mutters painfully)* Say—dey oughter match him—wit Zybszko. He got me, aw right. I'm trou. Even him didn't tink I belonged. *(Then, with sudden passionate despair)* Christ, where do I get off at? Where do I fit in? *(Checking himself as suddenly)* Aw, what de hell! No squawkin', see! No quittin', get me! Croak wit your boots on! *(He grabs hold of the bars of the cage and hauls himself painfully to his feet—looks around him bewilderedly—forces a mocking laugh)* In de cage, huh? *(In the strident tones of a circus barker)* Ladies and gents, step forward and take a slant at de one and only—*(His voice weakening)*—one and original—Hairy Ape from de wilds of— *(He slips in a heap on the floor and dies. The monkeys set up a chattering, whimpering wail. And, perhaps, the Hairy Ape at last belongs).*

Curtain

ACTIVITIES FOR WRITING AND DISCUSSION

1. *The Hairy Ape* is an example of dramatic **expressionism.** Rather than trying to present characters and events realistically, O'Neill distorts and exaggerates reality in order to produce certain powerful and expressive effects in readers or viewers. Thus, for instance, the coal stokers in scene 1 are characterized less as individual human beings than as a single beast in a "cage" or as anonymous versions of "Neanderthal Man"; the rich people who are assaulted by Yank in scene 5 do not even feel the impact of his blows. Mark these and any other passages in the play that strike you as expressionistic. Then write an essay in which you discuss how the expressionistic devices enhance the themes or impact of the play.

2. Reread the scene 1 speeches of Yank, Long, and Paddy. In your notebook summarize the outlook of each and how those outlooks conflict or clash.

3. In scene 1 both Yank and Paddy talk about "belonging." To whom or to what does each see himself as belonging? In what ways do their notions of belonging resemble and/or differ from each other? What reasons can you think of for their obsessive concern with "belonging"?

4. Consider the various meanings that "belonging" has in your own life and in the play.

   a. Write about your own concept of "belonging." To what extent and in what ways does your own identity seem to be shaped by the groups, organizations, socioeconomic class, race, religious and ethnic cultures, and so forth to which you "belong"?

b. Locate recurrences of the words "belong" and "belonging" in *The Hairy Ape*. In each case, annotate what you think the speaker is using the word to mean in that situation.

c. To whom or what do the following "belong": Yank, Mildred Douglas, the rich people on Fifth Avenue in scene 5, the workers in the office of the I.W.W., the gorilla in the zoo?

d. Interpret O'Neill's final stage direction in the play: "*And, perhaps, the Hairy Ape at last belongs.*" Do you take this sentence literally or ironically? Why? To *what* does he "belong" at play's end?

5. Mildred Douglas appears in only one scene, but her impact on Yank resonates through the entire play. Reread scene 2, paying particular attention to Mildred's character, attitudes, and style of speech. Then imagine you are Mildred and it is the day after your encounter with Yank. In a letter to a friend of your (i.e., Mildred's) own economic and social class, relate the story of your meeting with the "beast" in the stokehole. In addition to mentioning the encounter, use your imagination to fill the letter with chat about other matters—your aunt, impressions of the ship, things you have done and seen. How much of your letter will you devote to the encounter with Yank? While we know the meeting left a profound impact on Yank, how significant an effect did it have on you/Mildred?

6. In an earlier version of the ending of the play, O'Neill had Yank return to the stokehole to live out his prisonlike existence. Draft a new scene 8 with this ending. Then compare the new ending with the one O'Neill actually chose. Which do you find more effective, and why?

WOODY ALLEN (b. 1935)

Death Knocks

The play takes place in the bedroom of the Nat Ackermans' two-story house, somewhere in Kew Gardens. The carpeting is wall-to-wall. There is a big double bed and a large vanity. The room is elaborately furnished and curtained, and on the walls there are several paintings and a not really attractive barometer. Soft theme music as the curtain rises. Nat Ackerman, a bald, paunchy fifty-seven-year-old dress manufacturer is lying on the bed finishing off tomorrow's Daily News. *He wears a bathrobe and slippers, and reads by a bed light clipped to the white headboard of the bed. The time is near midnight. Suddenly we hear a noise, and Nat sits up and looks at the window.*

NAT: What the hell is that?

[*Climbing awkwardly through the window is a sombre, caped figure. The intruder wears a black hood and skintight black clothes. The hood covers his head but not his face, which is middle-aged and stark white. He is something like* NAT *in appearance. He huffs audibly and then trips over the windowsill and falls into the room.*]

DEATH [*for it is no one else*]: Jesus Christ. I nearly broke my neck.

NAT [*watching with bewilderment*]: Who are you?

DEATH: Death.

NAT: Who?

DEATH: Death. Listen—can I sit down? I nearly broke my neck. I'm shaking like a leaf.

NAT: Who *are* you?

DEATH: *Death.* You got a glass of water?

NAT: Death? What do you mean, Death?

DEATH: What is wrong with you? You see the black costume and the whitened face?

NAT: Yeah.

DEATH: Is it Halloween?

NAT: No.

DEATH: Then I'm Death. Now can I get a glass of water—or a Fresca?

NAT: If this is some joke—

DEATH: What kind of joke? You're fifty-seven? Nat Ackerman? One eighteen Pacific Street? Unless I blew it—where's that call sheet? [*He fumbles through pocket, finally producing a card with an address on it. It seems to check.*]

NAT: What do you want with me?

DEATH: What do I want? What do you think I want?

NAT: You must be kidding. I'm in perfect health.

DEATH [*unimpressed*]: Uh-huh. [*Looking around.*]This is a nice place. You do it yourself?

NAT: We had a decorator, but we worked with her.

DEATH [*looking at picture on the wall*]: I love those kids with the big eyes.

NAT: I don't want to go yet.

DEATH: *You* don't want to go? Please don't start in. As it is, I'm nauseous from the climb.

NAT: What climb?

DEATH: I climbed up the drainpipe. I was trying to make a dramatic entrance. I see the big windows and you're awake reading. I figure it's worth a shot. I'll climb up and enter with a little—you know ... [*Snaps fingers.*] Meanwhile, I get my heel caught on some vines, the drainpipe breaks, and I'm hanging by a thread. Then my cape begins to tear. Look, let's just go. It's been a rough night.

NAT: You broke my drainpipe?

DEATH: Broke. It didn't break. It's a little bent. Didn't you hear anything? I slammed into the ground.

NAT: I was reading.

DEATH: You must have really been engrossed. [*Lifting newspaper* NAT *was reading.*] "NAB COEDS IN POT ORGY." Can I borrow this?

NAT: I'm not finished.

DEATH: Er—I don't know how to put this to you, pal . . .

NAT: Why didn't you just ring downstairs?

DEATH: I'm telling you, I could have, but how does it look? This way I get a little drama going. Something. Did you read *Faust?*

NAT: What?

DEATH: And what if you had company? You're sitting there with important people. I'm Death—I should ring the bell and traipse right in the front? Where's your thinking?

NAT: Listen, Mister, it's very late.

DEATH: Yeah. Well, you want to go?

NAT: Go where?

DEATH: Death. It. The Thing. The Happy Hunting Grounds. [*Looking at his own knee.*] Y'know, that's a pretty bad cut. My first job, I'm liable to get gangrene yet.

NAT: Now, wait a minute. I need time. I'm not ready to go.

DEATH: I'm sorry. I can't help you. I'd like to, but it's the moment.

NAT: How can it be the moment? I just merged with Modiste Originals.

DEATH: What's the difference, a couple of bucks more or less.

NAT: Sure, what do you care? You guys probably have all your expenses paid.

DEATH: You want to come along now?

NAT [*studying him*]: I'm sorry, but I cannot believe you're Death.

DEATH: Why? What'd you expect—Rock Hudson?

NAT: No, it's not that.

DEATH: I'm sorry if I disappointed you.

NAT: Don't get upset. I don't know, I always thought you'd be . . . uh . . . taller.

DEATH: I'm five seven. It's average for my weight.

NAT: You look a little like me.

DEATH: Who should I look like? I'm your death.

NAT: Give me some time. Another day.

DEATH: I can't. What do you want me to say?

NAT: One more day. Twenty-four hours.

DEATH: What do you need it for? The radio said rain tomorrow.

NAT: Can't we work out something?

DEATH: Like what?

NAT: You play chess?

DEATH: No, I don't.

NAT: I once saw a picture of you playing chess.

DEATH: Couldn't be me, because I don't play chess. Gin rummy, maybe.

NAT: You play gin rummy?

DEATH: Do I play gin rummy? Is Paris a city?

NAT: You're good, huh?

DEATH: Very good.

NAT: I'll tell you what I'll do—

DEATH: Don't make any deals with me.

NAT: I'll play you gin rummy. If you win, I'll go immediately. If I win, give me some more time. A little bit—one more day.

DEATH: Who's got time to play gin rummy?

NAT: Come on. If you're so good.

DEATH: Although I feel like a game . . .

NAT: Come on. Be a sport. We'll shoot for a half hour.

DEATH: I really shouldn't.

NAT: I got the cards right here. Don't make a production.

DEATH: All right, come on. We'll play a little. It'll relax me.

NAT [*getting cards, pad, and pencil*]: You won't regret this.

DEATH: Don't give me a sales talk. Get the cards and give me a Fresca and put out something. For God's sake, a stranger drops in, you don't have potato chips or pretzels.

NAT: There's M&M's downstairs in a dish.

DEATH: M&M's. What if the President came? He'd get M&M's, too?

NAT: You're not the President.

DEATH: Deal.

[NAT *deals, turns up a five.*]

NAT: You want to play a tenth of a cent a point to make it interesting?

DEATH: It's not interesting enough for you?

NAT: I play better when money's at stake.

DEATH: Whatever you say, Newt.

NAT: Nat. Nat Ackerman. You don't know my name?

DEATH: Newt, Nat—I got such a headache.

NAT: You want that five?

DEATH: No.

NAT: So pick.

DEATH [*surveying his hand as he picks*]: Jesus, I got nothing here.

NAT: What's it like?

DEATH: What's what like?

[*Throughout the following, they pick and discard.*]

NAT: Death.

DEATH: What should it be like? You lay there.

NAT: Is there anything after?

DEATH: Aha, you're saving twos.

NAT: I'm asking. Is there anything after?

DEATH [*absently*]: You'll see.

NAT: Oh, then I will actually see something?

DEATH: Well, maybe I shouldn't have put it that way. Throw.

NAT: To get an answer from you is a big deal.

DEATH: I'm playing cards.

NAT: All right, play, play.

DEATH: Meanwhile, I'm giving you one card after another.

NAT: Don't look through the discards.

DEATH: I'm not looking. I'm straightening them up. What was the knock card?

NAT: Four. You ready to knock already?

DEATH: Who said I'm ready to knock? All I asked was what was the knock card.

NAT: And all I asked was is there anything for me to look forward to.

DEATH: Play.

NAT: Can't you tell me anything? Where do we go?

DEATH: We? To tell you the truth, *you* fall in a crumpled heap on the floor.

NAT: Oh, I can't wait for that! Is it going to hurt?

DEATH: Be over in a second.

NAT: Terrific. [*Sighs.*] I needed this. A man merges with Modiste Originals . . .

DEATH: How's four points?

NAT: You're knocking?

DEATH: Four points is good?

NAT: No, I got two.

DEATH: You're kidding.

NAT: No, you lose.

DEATH: Holy Christ, and I thought you were saving sixes.

NAT: No. Your deal. Twenty points and two boxes. Shoot. [*Death deals.*] I must fall on the floor, eh? I can't be standing over the sofa when it happens?

DEATH: No. Play.

NAT: Why not?

DEATH: Because you fall on the floor! Leave me alone. I'm trying to concentrate.

NAT: Why must it be on the floor? That's all I'm saying! Why can't the whole thing happen and I'll stand next to the sofa?

DEATH: I'll try my best. Now can we play?

NAT: That's all I'm saying. You remind me of Moe Lefkowitz. He's also stubborn.

DEATH: I remind him of Moe Lefkowitz. I'm one of the most terrifying figures you could possibly imagine, and him I remind of Moe Lefkowitz. What is he, a furrier?

NAT: You should be such a furrier. He's good for eighty thousand a year. Passementeries. He's got his own factory. Two points.

DEATH: What?

NAT: Two points. I'm knocking. What have you got?

DEATH: My hand is like a basketball score.

NAT: And it's spades.

DEATH: If you didn't talk so much.

[*They redeal and play on.*]

NAT: What'd you mean before when you said this was your first job?

DEATH: What does it sound like?

NAT: What are you telling me—that nobody ever went before?

DEATH: Sure they went. But I didn't take them.

NAT: So who did?

DEATH: Others.

NAT: There's others?

DEATH: Sure. Each one has his own personal way of going.

NAT: I never knew that.

DEATH: Why should you know? Who are you?

NAT: What do you mean who am I? Why—I'm nothing?

DEATH: Not nothing. You're a dress manufacturer. Where do you come to knowledge of the eternal mysteries?

NAT: What are you talking about? I make a beautiful dollar. I sent two kids through college. One is in advertising, the other's married. I got my own home. I drive a Chrysler. My wife has whatever she wants. Maids, mink coat, vacations. Right now she's at the Eden Roc. Fifty dollars a day because she wants to be near her sister. I'm supposed to join her next week, so what do you think I am—some guy off the street?

DEATH: All right. Don't be so touchy.

NAT: Who's touchy?

DEATH: How would you like it if I got insulted quickly?

NAT: Did I insult you?

DEATH: You didn't say you were disappointed in me?

NAT: What do you expect? You want me to throw you a block party?

DEATH: I'm not talking about that. I mean me personally. I'm too short, I'm this, I'm that.

NAT: I said you looked like me. It's like a reflection.

DEATH: All right, deal, deal.

[*They continue to play as music steals in and the lights dim until all is in total darkness. The lights slowly come up again, and now it is later and their game is over.* NAT *tallies.*]

NAT: Sixty-eight . . . one-fifty . . . Well, you lose.

DEATH [*dejectedly looking through the deck*]: I knew I shouldn't have thrown that nine. Damn it.

NAT: So I'll see you tomorrow.

DEATH: What do you mean you'll see me tomorrow?

NAT: I won the extra day. Leave me alone.

DEATH: You were serious?

NAT: We made a deal.

DEATH: Yeah, but—

NAT: Don't "but" me. I won twenty-four hours. Come back tomorrow.

DEATH: I didn't know we were actually playing for time.

NAT: That's too bad about you. You should pay attention.

DEATH: Where am I going to go for twenty-four hours?

NAT: What's the difference? The main thing is I won an extra day.

DEATH: What do you want me to do—walk the streets?

NAT: Check into a hotel and go to a movie. Take a *schvitz*.[1] Don't make a federal case.

DEATH: Add the score again.

NAT: Plus you owe me twenty-eight dollars.

DEATH: *What?*

NAT: That's right, Buster. Here it is—read it.

DEATH [*going through pockets*]: I have a few singles—not twenty-eight dollars.

NAT: I'll take a check.

DEATH: From what account?

NAT: Look who I'm dealing with.

DEATH: Sue me. Where do I keep my checking account?

NAT: All right, gimme what you got and we'll call it square.

DEATH: Listen, I need that money.

NAT: Why should you need money?

DEATH: What are you talking about? You're going to the Beyond.

NAT: So?

DEATH: So—you know how far that is?

NAT: So?

DEATH: So where's gas? Where's tolls?

NAT: We're going by car?

DEATH: You'll find out. [*Agitatedly.*] Look—I'll be back tomorrow, and you'll give me a chance to win the money back. Otherwise I'm in definite trouble.

NAT: Anything you want. Double or nothing we'll play. I'm liable to win an extra week or a month. The way you play, maybe years.

DEATH: Meantime I'm stranded.

NAT: See you tomorrow.

DEATH [*being edged to the doorway*]: Where's a good hotel? What am I talking about hotel, I got no money. I'll go sit in Bickford's. [*He picks up the* News.]

NAT: Out. Out. That's my paper. [*He takes it back.*]

DEATH [*exiting*]: I couldn't just take him and go. I had to get involved in rummy.

NAT [*calling after him*]: And be careful going downstairs. On one of the steps the rug is loose.

---

1. Steam bath.

[*And, on cue, we hear a terrific crash.* NAT *sighs, then crosses to the bedside table and makes a phone call.*]

NAT: Hello, Moe? Me. Listen, I don't know if somebody's playing a joke, or what, but Death was just here. We played a little gin . . . No, *Death*. In person. Or somebody who claims to be Death. But, Moe, he's such a *schlep!*[2]

Curtain

ACTIVITIES FOR WRITING AND DISCUSSION

1. Indicate passages in the play that you find funny, and explain how those passages work as comedy. How does the character Death undercut or conflict with traditional images of death? How do other aspects of the play (such as characterization, **setting, stage directions, plot,** and **dialogue**) conflict with what you might expect in an actual encounter between a human being and Death?

2. In a humorous way, *Death Knocks* dramatizes an imaginary conversation between a person (Nat) and a personified abstraction (Death). Try writing such a conversation yourself. Compose an imaginary dialogue between yourself and some abstraction, e.g., your inner self-critic, your conscience, your ideal self, the "child" in you, the "parent" in you, having the abstraction talk as if it were a person.

Steps:
a. Brainstorm a list of possible abstractions you could personify.
b. Choose one that looks most interesting.
c. Imagine what this abstraction would look like if it were a person. Describe such things as facial appearance, eyes, hair, body build, posture, gestures, expressions, how he/she walks, talks, for instance.
d. Pose some conflict between yourself and this "person."
e. Write the dialogue.

Note: Your writing for Activity #2 may be quite personal, and you should feel free *not* to share it with anyone else.

EXPERIENCE AND IDENTITY: ADDITIONAL ACTIVITIES FOR WRITING AND DISCUSSION

1. Reread all or a portion of your notebook. Mark any passages, however long or short, that strike you, for whatever reasons. Beside each such passage,

---

2. A person who is unkempt, down-at-the-heels, clumsy.

write a note explaining its significance for you. Finally, pick a favorite passage and either:

    a. Expand it into a new piece of writing, or

    b. Make notes on how you *could* expand or use it at some future date, or

    c. Rewrite it in a different form, e.g., poem, dialogue, letter, memoir.

For a list of strategies for expanding or revising, see Chapter 9.

    2. Explicitly or implicitly, several texts in this section address how growth can occur through experiences of pain, defeat, or even "death," e.g., as figuratively described by Goethe in "The Holy Longing."

    a. Compare how this theme plays out in several texts and/or in the text of your own life, or

    b. Create an imaginary "interview" with one or more of the **characters, speakers,** or **personae** who experience such growth. Ask them to explain their outlook and to share some stories (which you may invent yourself) that justify that outlook.

    3. The protagonists of several selections in this chapter are on a quest of some sort: Yank (a quest for "belonging"), the narrator of "Zaabalawi" (a quest for the elusive Zaabalawi and personal healing), Paul in "The Rocking-Horse Winner" (a quest for money and possibly/probably love), the narrator of "I Am Twenty-One" (a quest for identity), to name a few. The enormous contrasts among these characters make it tantalizing to imagine them meeting. Each lonely and driven, what would they discuss? Bring two or more of the characters together in an imaginative setting—Paul's bedroom, the zoo at the end of *The Hairy Ape,* or the bicycle lot outside Mary Robison's protagonist's school, for instance—and have them talk.

    4. Maya Angelou's "Seven Women's Blessed Assurance" articulates the feelings and attitudes of seven women at various stages of life. Assume the **persona** of someone who has moved through three or more stages of life, e.g., infancy, childhood, adolescence, midlife. Create a text, in poetry or in prose, in which this person reflects on his/her changing perspectives on life and experience. Alternative: Write a dialogue between *yourself* at one stage of life and yourself at a different stage of life. Emphasize age-related conflicts and differences between your two "selves." Does the older self "like" the younger or resent it? Does the younger respect the older . . . scorn it?

    5. One subject common to Faulkner's "Barn Burning," Rudman's "Chrome," Angelou's "Graduation," and other texts within this section is the notion of "overcoming." Compare how this subject is treated in any two or three of these texts. Alternative: Write a story about "overcoming" in your own life, and (if you wish) relate it to one of the assigned readings.

    6. Several writings in this section are about "firsts." Katherine Mansfield writes about "Her First Ball," Gary Soto's poem is about a first date, Judith Ortiz

Cofer's essay is about a first experience of school. Write a story, poem, or essay of your own about some actual or imagined "first" experience.

7. Review your entire notebook; as you do, make a running list of memorable or striking topics, such as "childhood experience," "life transitions," "initiations." Then choose a favorite topic,make a Topic/Form Grid (see Chapter 9), and use one of the forms on your grid to create a new notebook entry about the topic. Should your chosen form not work, do a Topic/Form Shift to a different form on your grid.

Interchapter on Notebooks and Journals (III)

"Pen and Paper and a Breath of Air": Mary Oliver

B orn in 1935 in Cleveland, Ohio, Mary Oliver attended Ohio State University and Vassar College. *No Voyage, and Other Poems* (1963) was her first book, followed by *The Night Traveler* (1978), *Twelve Moons* (1978), *Sleeping in the Forest* (1979), and *American Primitive* (Pulitzer Prize, 1984). *New and Selected Poems* won the National Book Award in 1992. Fellow poet Maxine Kumin has called Oliver an "indefatigable guide to the natural world" who is comfortable with being "on the margins of things, on the line between earth and sky, the thin membrane that separates human from what we loosely call animal." Oliver's most recent book is *West Wind* (1997), a collection of poems and prose poems.

The following notebook selections and introductory note are reprinted from Oliver's book, *Blue Pastures* (New York: Harcourt, 1991). A slightly different version of this piece also appeared in *The Poet's Notebook,* an anthology edited by Stephen Kuusisto, Deborah Tall, and David Weiss and published by Norton (1997).

For at least thirty years, and at almost all times, I have carried a notebook with 1
me, in my back pocket. It has always been the same kind of notebook—small, three inches by five inches, and hand-sewn. By no means do I write poems in these notebooks. And yet over the years the notebooks have been laced with phrases that eventually appear in poems. So, they are the pages upon which I begin. Also I record various facts which are permanently or temporarily important to me— when I first see certain birds in the spring, addresses, quotes from books I'm reading, things people say, shopping lists, recipes, thoughts.

Some of the phrases and ideas written down in the notebooks never make the 2
leap into finished prose or poems. They do not elaborate themselves in my uncon-
scious thoughts, apparently, nor does my conscious mind pluck at them. This does
not necessarily mean that they are of a casual or fleeting order of things; it could be
that they are seeds broadcast on a chilly day—their time has not yet come. Often I
find the same idea will emerge through several phrases before it gets worked on.

I don't use the pages front to back, but randomly, in a disorderly way. I write 3
wherever I happen to open the notebook. I don't know why this is. When the note-
book is fairly full, I start another. In the spring and fall notebooks especially, there
are pages where the writing is blurred and hard to read. Spring and fall are the
rainy seasons, and almost all of the entries are made somewhere out-of-doors.

What I write down is extremely exact in terms of phrasing and of cadence. In 4
an old notebook I can find, "look the trees / are turning / their own bodies / into
pillars of light." In a more recent notebook, "the refined anguish of language /
passed over him." Sometimes what is written down is not generally understand-
able at all, but is a kind of private shorthand. The entry "6/8/92 woof!" records for
me that on this day, and with this very doggy sound, I first came upon coyotes in
the Provincelands. Both the shorthand and the written phrase are intended to re-
turn me to the moment and place of the entry. I mean this very exactly. The words
do not take me to the reason I made the entry, but back to the felt experience,
whatever it was. This is important. I can, then, think forward again to the idea—
that is, the significance of the event—rather than back upon it. It is the instant I
try to catch in the notebooks, not the comment, not the thought. And, of course,
this is so often what I am aiming to do in the finished poems themselves.

EXCERPTS
Who would tell the mockingbird his song is frivolous, since it lacks words?   5

—————

Do you think the wren ever dreams of a better house?   6

—————

Though you have not seen them, there are swans, even now   7
tapping from the egg and emerging
into the sunlight.
They know who they are.

—————

When will you have a little pity for   8
every soft thing
that walks through the world,
yourself included?

—————

When the main characters of one's life die, is there any replacement? Or, is there   9
anything *but* replacement?

_____

I hope I don't live to be a hundred   10
in the arms of my family.

_____

When you first saw her—beauty, the dream—the human vortex of your life—   11
or him—did you stop, and stand in the crisp air, breathing like a tree? Did you
change your life?

_____

The small deadly voice   12
of vanity.

_____

It's better for the heart to break   13
than not to break.

_____

Elly Ameling during a masterclass at Tanglewood, talking to a young singer: 14
"No! No! No! Make it like peaches in your mouth!"

_____

All my life, and it has not come to any more than this: beauty and terror.   15

Something totally unexpected,   16
like a barking cat.

_____

Sharpsburg: "One well-read member of the 9th New York wrote long afterward: 17
The mental strain was so great that I saw at that moment the singular effect
mentioned, I think, in the life of Goethe on a similar occasion—the whole
landscape for an instant turned slightly red."
                                                    —B. Catton, *Mr. Lincoln's Army*

_____

The sword, after all, is not built just to glitter like a ribbon in the air.   18

_____

But I want to say something more uncomfortable even than that.   19

_____

"And then, who knows? Perhaps we will be taken in hand by certain memories,   20
as if by angels."

—*M. Yourcenar*

Molasses, an orange, fennel seed, anise seed, rye flour, two cakes of yeast.   21

Culture: power, money, and security (therefore).   22
Art: hope, vision, the soul's need to speak.

All culture developed as some wild, raw creature strived to live better and   23
longer.

Dreams don't have time/space constriction. Of course, in a way Adam naming   24
the things of this world was narrowing his horizons.

    Perhaps dreaming is meditating, before language existed. Animals certainly   25
dream.

Language, the tool of consciousness.   26

The line is the device upon which the poem spins itself into being. Verse, ver-   27
sus, *vers,* turn the plough, turn the line. It is impossible to measure the frustration I feel when, after making careful decisions about where the lines should
turn, an editor snaps off the long limbs to fit some magazine's column-girth or
print-line.

Who are you? They called out, at the edge of the village.   28
I am one of you, the poet called back.
Though he was dressed like the wind, though he looked like
a waterfall.

F. has been to visit us, and now he is gone. The power of last resort, is the power   29
to disrupt.

M. arranging the curtains in the next room. "Hello there, darling moon," I hear   30
her say.

If you kill for knowledge, what is the name of what you have lost?   31

—————

The danger of people becoming infatuated with knowledge. Thoreau gassing   32
the moth to get a perfect specimen. Audubon pushing the needle into the bit-
tern's heart.

I took the fox bones back into the dunes and buried them. I don't want to hold   33
on to such things anymore. I mean, I'm certainly full of admiration, and curiosity. But I think something else—a reverence that disavows keeping things—
must come to us all, sooner or later. Like a gift, an understanding, a more happy
excitement than possession. Or, of a sudden—too late!—like a stone between
the eyes.

—————

Everybody has to have their little tooth of power.   34
Everybody wants to be able to bite.

—————

About poems that don't work—who wants to see a bird almost fly?   35

—————

With what sugar in your voice would you persuade   36
the beach plum
to hurry?

—————

After a cruel childhood, one must reinvent oneself.   37
Then reimagine the world.

—————

van Gogh—he considered everything, and still went crazy with rapture.   38

—————

A snapping turtle was floating today on Little Sister Pond.   39
Goldeneyes still on Great Pond.

—————

Laughing gulls fly by the house laughing.   40
Maybe a hundred pilot whales off the point.

—————

All July and into August, Luke and I see foxes. An adult fox with a young pup.   41
The adult serious and nervous and quick. The young one trailing behind, not

serious. It reached up, swatted the pine boughs with a black paw before it vanished under the trees.

_____

To Unity College, in Maine, and back. We stayed in Waterville, saw two bald ea- 42
gles flying over open rivers, though there was still much ice, and snow. A good
trip, friendly people, an interested audience. Luke and Bear were quiet throughout, except that Bear threw up on me just as we arrived in the parking lot. I
hope he learns to ride better than that.

_____

Hundreds of gannets feeding just offshore, plunging, tufts of water rising with 43
a white up-kick. Scary birds, long wings, very white, fearful-looking beaks. We
opened the car windows and there was no sound but the sound of their wings
rustling. They fed at three or four places, then were gone much farther out. We
were at the right place at the right time.

_____

"I am doing pretty well, gathering energy, working . . . and every now and then 44
timor mortis descends over me like midnight."

Letter from D. H.

_____

Just at the lacy edge of the sea, a dolphin's skull. Recent, but perfectly clean. And 45
entirely beautiful. I held it in my hands, I was so excited I was breathless. What
will I do?

_____

Three deer near the path to Oak Head—of course now they always make me 46
think of Luke. Happiness by association.

_____

Who knows, maybe the root is the flower   47
of that other life.

_____

Money, in our culture, is equal to power. And money, finally, means very little 48
because power, in the end, means nothing.

_____

Lee, as he was dying, called out, "Strike the tent!" Sonewall Jackson said at the 49
end, softly as I imagine it, "Let us cross over the river and rest under the shade
of the trees."

_____

Today I am altogether without ambition. Where did I get such wisdom?   50

You there, like a red fist under by ribs—   51
be reasonable.

-----

little myrtle warblers   52
kissing the air

Let's not pretend we know how the mule feels.   53

Hearing a crow, the first one in a long time. I listened to it, deeply and with   54
pleasure. And I thought: what if I were dead, lying there dead, and *I heard that!*

Which would you rather be, intellectually deft, or spiritually graceful?   55

The sugar of vanity, the honey of truth.   56

When I was young, I was attracted to sorrow. It seemed interesting. It seemed   57
an energy that would take me somewhere. Now I am older, if not old, and I hate
sorrow. I see that it has no energy of its own, but uses mine, furtively. I see that
it is leaden, without breath, and repetitious, and unsolvable.

And now I see that I am sorrowful about only a few things, but over and over.   58

Fairy tales—the great difference is between doing something, and doing noth-   59
ing. Always, in such tales, the hero or heroine does *something.*

The new baby is all awash with glory.   60
She has a cry that says *I'm here! I'm here!*

Give me that dark moment I will carry it everywhere   61
like a mouthful of rain.

There is a place
in the woods
where my swift
and stout-hearted dog
turns and wants to climb

into my arms.
62

Don't engage in too much fancy footwork before you strike a blow.
63

So much of what Woolf wrote she wrote not because she was a woman, but because she was Woolf.
64

I would like to do whatever it is that presses the essence from the hour.
65

A fact: one picks it up and reads it, and puts it down, and there is an end to it. But an idea! That one may pick up, and reflect upon, and oppose, and expand, and so pass a delightful afternoon altogether.
66

From my way of thinking, Thoreau frequently seems an overly social person.
67

The cry of the killdeer / like a tiny sickle.
68

The translation of experience into contemplation, and the placement of this contemplation within the formality of a certain kind of language, with intent to make contact—be it across whatever thin or wild a thread—with the spiritual condition of the reader, is not poetry. Archibald MacLeish: Here is the writer, and over there—there is "the mystery of the universe." The poem exists—indeed, gets itself written—in the relation *between* the man and the world. The three ingredients of poetry: the mystery of the universe, spiritual curiosity, the energy of language.
69

And what is the universe, as far as we are concerned?
70

Leo Frobenius: "It was first the animal world, in its various species, that impressed mankind as a mystery, and that, in its character of admired immediate neighbor, evoked the impulse to imitative identification. Next, it was the vegetable world and the miracle of the fruitful earth, wherein death is changed into
71

life. And finally . . . the focus of attention lifted to the mathematics" of the heavens.

Art cannot separate from these first examples which willed it into existence. Say 72 such forces belong now only to dream or nightmare or to Jung's (our) collective unconscious—or to the ecologically sensitive—I say it's entirely more primal than that. Poetry was born in the relationship between men of earth and the earth itself. Without perceptual experience of life on this earth, how could the following lines be meaningful?

It is the east, and Juliet is the sun. *Or,*

And what rough beast, its hour come round at last,
Slouches toward Bethlehem to be born?

I think as an ecologist. But I feel as a member of a great family—one that in- 73 cludes the elephant and the wheat stalk as well as the schoolteacher and the industrialist. This is not a mental condition, but a spiritual condition. Poetry is a product of our history, and our history is inseparable from the natural world. Now, of course, in the hives and dungeons of the cities, poetry cannot console, it carries no weight, for the pact between the natural world and the individual has been broken. There is no more working for harvest—only hunting, for profit. Lives are no longer exercises in pleasure and valor, but only the means to the amassment of worldly goods. If poetry is ever to become meaningful to such persons, *they* must take the first step—away from their materially bound and self-interested lives, toward the trees, and the waterfall. It is not poetry's fault that it has so small an audience, so little effect upon the frightened, money-loving world. Poetry, after all, is not a miracle. It is an effort to formal- ize (ritualize) individual moments and the transcending effects of these mo- ments into a music that all can use. It is the song of our species.

Hasn't the end of the world been coming absolutely forever?   74

It takes about   75
seventy hours to drag
a poem into
the light.

---

delirious with certainty   76

It's almost six A.M. The mockingbird is still singing. I'm on my way to the ocean,   77
with the sun, just rising, on my left shoulder, and the moon, like a circle of pale
snow, lingering on my right.

ACTIVITIES FOR WRITING AND DISCUSSION

1. In her prefatory note Oliver carefully describes the physical qualities of
her notebook: "It has always been the same kind . . . hand sewn"; "there are
pages where the writing is blurred and hard to read" from spring and fall rains.
Do the physical properties—size, color, feel or texture, portability, etc.—of
your own notebook make it a place where you *like* to write? If so, why? If not,
what alternative kind of notebook could you buy—or perhaps make—that
would be more appealing?

2. In her prefatory note Oliver says that "Sometimes what is written down
is not generally understandable at all, but is a kind of private shorthand. . . .
The words do not take me to the reason I made the entry, but back to the felt
experience, whatever it was." Shorthand is a device for jotting down a thought
or impression quickly and exactly, and in just enough words that you can understand it when rereading. In order to record your own impressions more precisely and economically, strive to develop a "private shorthand" of your own.

3. Respond to Oliver's notebook selections using any of the "Generic Ideas
for Writing" found on pages 275–277.

19

Individual and Society

NATHANIEL HAWTHORNE (1804–1864)

The Minister's Black Veil

A PARABLE
BY THE AUTHOR OF "SIGHTS FROM A STEEPLE"

The sexton stood in the porch of Milford meeting-house, pulling lustily at the 1 bell-rope. The old people of the village came stooping along the street. Children, with bright faces, tript merrily beside their parents, or mimicked a graver gait, in the conscious dignity of their sunday clothes. Spruce bachelors looked sidelong at the pretty maidens, and fancied that the sabbath sunshine made them prettier than on week-days. When the throng had mostly streamed into the porch, the sexton began to toll the bell, keeping his eye on the Reverend Mr. Hooper's door. The first glimpse of the clergyman's figure was the signal for the bell to cease its summons.

"But what has good Parson Hooper got upon his face?" cried the sexton in 2 astonishment.

All within hearing immediately turned about, and beheld the semblance of 3 Mr. Hooper, pacing slowly his meditative way towards the meeting-house. With one accord they started, expressing more wonder than if some strange minister were coming to dust the cushions of Mr. Hooper's pulpit.

"Are you sure it is our parson?" inquired Goodman Gray of the sexton. 4

"Of a certainty it is good Mr. Hooper," replied the sexton. "He was to have 5 exchanged pulpits with Parson Shute of Westbury; but Parson Shute sent to excuse himself yesterday, being to preach a funeral sermon."

The cause of so much amazement may appear sufficiently slight. Mr. 6 Hooper, a gentlemanly person of about thirty, though still a bachelor, was dressed with due clerical neatness, as if a careful wife had starched his band, and brushed the weekly dust from his Sunday's garb. There was but one thing remarkable in his appearance. Swathed about his forehead, and hanging down over his face, so low as to be shaken by his breath, Mr. Hooper had on a black veil. On a nearer view, it seemed to consist of two folds of crape, which entirely concealed his features, except the mouth and chin, but probably did not intercept his sight, farther than to give a darkened aspect to all living and inanimate things. With this gloomy shade before him, good Mr. Hooper walked onward, at a slow and quiet pace, stooping somewhat and looking on the ground, as is customary with abstracted men, yet nodding kindly to those of his parishioners who still waited on the meeting-house steps. But so wonderstruck were they, that his greeting hardly met with a return.

"I can't really feel as if good Mr. Hooper's face was behind that piece of 7 crape," said the sexton.

"I don't like it," muttered an old woman, as she hobbled into the meeting- 8 house. "He has changed himself into something awful, only by hiding his face."

"Our parson has gone mad!" cried Goodman Gray, following him across the 9 threshhold.

A rumor of some unaccountable phenomenon had preceded Mr. Hooper 10 into the meeting-house, and set all the congregation astir. Few could refrain from twisting their heads towards the door; many stood upright, and turned directly about; while several little boys clambered upon the seats, and came down again with a terrible racket. There was a general bustle, a rustling of the women's gowns and shuffling of the men's feet, greatly at variance with that hushed repose which should attend the entrance of the minister. But Mr. Hooper appeared not to notice the perturbation of his people. He entered with an almost noiseless step, bent his head mildly to the pews on each side, and bowed as he passed his oldest parishioner, a white-haired great-grandsire, who occupied an arm-chair in the centre of the aisle. It was strange to observe, how slowly this venerable man became conscious of something singular in the appearance of his pastor. He seemed not fully to partake of the prevailing wonder, till Mr. Hooper had ascended the stairs, and showed himself in the pulpit, face to face with his congregation, except for the black veil. That mysterious emblem was never once withdrawn. It shook with his measured breath as he gave out the psalm; it threw its obscurity between him and the holy page, as he read the Scriptures; and while he prayed, the veil lay heavily on his uplifted countenance. Did he seek to hide it from the dread Being whom he was addressing?

Such was the effect of this simple piece of crape, that more than one woman 11 of delicate nerves was forced to leave the meeting-house. Yet perhaps the pale-faced congregation was almost as fearful a sight to the minister, as his black veil to them.

Mr. Hooper had the reputation of a good preacher, but not an energetic 12 one: he strove to win his people heavenward, by mild persuasive influences, rather than to drive them thither, by the thunders of the Word. The sermon which he now delivered, was marked by the same characteristics of style and manner, as the general series of his pulpit oratory. But there was something, either in the sentiment of the discourse itself, or in the imagination of the auditors, which made it greatly the most powerful effort that they had ever heard from their pastor's lips. It was tinged, rather more darkly than usual, with the gentle gloom of Mr. Hooper's temperament. The subject had reference to secret sin, and those sad mysteries which we hide from our nearest and dearest, and would fain conceal from our own consciousness, even forgetting that the Omniscient can detect them. A subtle power was breathed into his words. Each member of the congregation, the most innocent girl, and the man of hardened breast, felt as if the preacher had crept upon them, behind his awful veil, and discovered their hoarded iniquity of deed or thought. Many spread their clasped hands on their bosoms. There was nothing terrible in what Mr. Hooper said; at least, no violence; and yet, with every tremor of his melancholy voice, the hearers quaked. An unsought pathos came hand in hand with awe. So sensible were the audience of some unwonted attribute in their minister, that they longed for a breath of wind to blow aside the veil, almost believing that a stranger's visage would be discovered, though the form, gesture, and voice were those of Mr. Hooper.

At the close of the services, the people hurried out with indecorous confu- 13 sion, eager to communicate their pent-up amazement, and conscious of lighter spirits, the moment they lost sight of the black veil. Some gathered in little circles, huddled closely together, with their mouths all whispering in the centre; some went homeward alone, wrapt in silent meditation; some talked loudly, and profaned the Sabbath-day with ostentatious laughter. A few shook their sagacious heads, intimating that they could penetrate the mystery; while one or two affirmed that there was no mystery at all, but only that Mr. Hooper's eyes were so weakened by the midnight lamp, as to require a shade. After a brief interval, forth came good Mr. Hooper also, in the rear of his flock. Turning his veiled face from one group to another, he paid due reverence to the hoary heads, saluted the middle-aged with kind dignity, as their friend and spiritual guide, greeted the young with mingled authority and love, and laid his hands on the little children's heads to bless them. Such was always his custom on the Sabbath-day. Strange and bewildered looks repaid him for his courtesy. None, as on former occasions, aspired to the honor of walking by their pastor's side. Old Squire Saunders, doubtless by an accidental lapse of memory, neglected to invite Mr. Hooper to his table, where the good clergyman had been wont to bless the food, almost every Sunday since his settlement. He returned, therefore, to the parsonage, and, at the moment of closing the door, was observed to look back upon the people, all of whom had their eyes fixed upon the minister.

A sad smile gleamed faintly from beneath the black veil, and flickered about his mouth, glimmering as he disappeared.

appearance means a lot

"How strange," said a lady, "that a simple black veil, such as any woman   14
might wear on her bonnet, should become such a terrible thing on Mr. Hooper's face!"

"Something must surely be amiss with Mr. Hooper's intellects," observed   15
her husband, the physician of the village. "But the strangest part of the affair is the effect of this vagary, even on a sober-minded man like myself. The black veil, though it covers only our pastor's face, throws its influence over his whole person, and makes him ghost-like from head to foot. Do you not feel it so?"

"Truly do I," replied the lady; "and I would not be alone with him for the   16
world. I wonder he is not afraid to be alone with himself!"

"Men sometimes are so," said her husband.   17

The afternoon service was attended with similar circumstances. At its con-   18
clusion, the bell tolled for the funeral of a young lady. The relatives and friends were assembled in the house, and the more distant acquaintances stood about the door, speaking of the good qualities of the deceased, when their talk was interrupted by the appearance of Mr. Hooper, still covered with his black veil. It was now an appropriate emblem. The clergyman stepped into the room where the corpse was laid, and bent over the coffin, to take a last farewell of his deceased parishioner. As he stooped, the veil hung straight down from his forehead, so that, if her eye-lids had not been closed for ever, the dead maiden might have seen his face. Could Mr. Hooper be fearful of her glance, that he so hastily caught back the black veil? A person, who watched the interview between the dead and living, scrupled not to affirm, that, at the instant when the clergyman's features were disclosed, the corpse had slightly shuddered, rustling the shroud and muslin cap, though the countenance retained the composure of death. A superstitious old woman was the only witness of this prodigy. From the coffin, Mr. Hooper passed into the chambers of the mourners, and thence to the head of the staircase, to make the funeral prayer. It was a tender and heart-dissolving prayer, full of sorrow, yet so imbued with celestial hopes, that the music of a heavenly harp, swept by the fingers of the dead, seemed faintly to be heard among the saddest accents of the minister. The people trembled, though they but darkly understood him, when he prayed that they, and himself, and all of mortal race, might be ready, as he trusted this young maiden had been, for the dreadful hour that should snatch the veil from their faces. The bearers went heavily forth, and the mourners followed, saddening all the street, with the dead before them, and Mr. Hooper in his black veil behind.

"Why do you look back?" said one in the procession to his partner.   19

"I had a fancy," replied she, "that the minister and the maiden's spirit were   20
walking hand in hand."

"And so had I, at the same moment," said the other.   21

That night, the handsomest couple in Milford village were to be joined in   22
wedlock. Though reckoned a melancholy man, Mr. Hooper had a placid cheerfulness for such occasions, which often excited a sympathetic smile, where live-

lier merriment would have been thrown away. There was no quality of his disposition which made him more beloved than this. The company at the wedding awaited his arrival with impatience, trusting that the strange awe, which had gathered over him throughout the day, would now be dispelled. But such was not the result. When Mr. Hooper came, the first thing that their eyes rested on was the same horrible black veil, which had added deeper gloom to the funeral, and could portend nothing but evil to the wedding. Such was its immediate effect on the guests, that a cloud seemed to have rolled duskily from beneath the black crape, and dimmed the light of the candles. The bridal pair stood up before the minister. But the bride's cold fingers quivered in the tremulous hand of the bridegroom, and her death-like paleness caused a whisper, that the maiden who had been buried a few hours before, was come from her grave to be married. If ever another wedding were so dismal, it was that famous one, where they tolled the wedding-knell. After performing the ceremony, Mr. Hooper raised a glass of wine to his lips, wishing happiness to the new-married couple, in a strain of mild pleasantry that ought to have brightened the features of the guests, like a cheerful gleam from the hearth. At that instant, catching a glimpse of his figure in the looking-glass, the black veil involved his own spirit in the horror with which it overwhelmed all others. His frame shuddered—his lips grew white—he spilt the untasted wine upon the carpet—and rushed forth into the darkness. For the Earth, too, had on her Black Veil.

The next day, the whole village of Milford talked of little else than Parson Hooper's black veil. That, and the mystery concealed behind it, supplied a topic for discussion between acquaintances meeting in the street, and good women gossiping at their open windows. It was the first item of news that the tavern-keeper told to his guests. The children babbled of it on their way to school. One imitative little imp covered his face with an old black handkerchief, thereby so affrighting his playmates, that the panic seized himself, and he well nigh lost his wits by his own waggery.

It was remarkable, that, of all the busy-bodies and impertinent people in the parish, not one ventured to put the plain question to Mr. Hooper, wherefore he did this thing. Hitherto, whenever there appeared the slightest call for such interference, he had never lacked advisers, nor shown himself averse to be guided by their judgment. If he erred at all, it was by so painful a degree of self-distrust, that even the mildest censure would lead him to consider an indifferent action as a crime. Yet, though so well acquainted with this amiable weakness, no individual among his parishioners chose to make the black veil a subject of friendly remonstrance. There was a feeling of dread, neither plainly confessed nor carefully concealed, which caused each to shift the responsibility upon another, till at length it was found expedient to send a deputation of the church, in order to deal with Mr. Hooper about the mystery, before it should grow into a scandal. Never did an embassy so ill discharge its duties. The minister received them with friendly courtesy, but became silent, after they were seated, leaving to his visitors the whole burthen of introducing their important business. The topic, it might be supposed, was obvious enough. There was the black veil, swathed round Mr. Hooper's forehead, and concealing every feature above his placid mouth, on which, at times, they could perceive the glimmering of a melancholy smile. But that piece of crape, to their imagination, seemed to hang down before his heart, the symbol of a fearful secret between him and them. Were the veil but cast aside, they might speak freely of it, but not till then. Thus they sat a considerable time, speechless, confused, and shrinking uneasily from Mr. Hooper's eye, which they felt to be fixed upon them with an invisible glance. Finally, the deputies returned abashed to their constituents, pronouncing the matter too weighty to be handled, except by a council of the churches, if, indeed, it might not require a general synod.

But there was one person in the village, unappalled by the awe with which the black veil had impressed all beside herself. When the deputies returned without an explanation, or even venturing to demand one, she, with the calm energy of her character, determined to chase away the strange cloud that appeared to be settling round Mr. Hooper, every moment more darkly than before. As his plighted wife, it should be her privilege to know what the black veil concealed. At the minister's first visit, therefore, she entered upon the subject, with a direct simplicity, which made the task easier both for him and her. After he had seated himself, she fixed her eyes steadfastly upon the veil, but could discern nothing of the dreadful gloom that had so overawed the multitude: it was but a double fold of crape, hanging down from his forehead to his mouth, and slightly stirring with his breath. 25

"No," said she aloud, and smiling, "there is nothing terrible in this piece of crape, except that it hides a face which I am always glad to look upon. Come, good sir, let the sun shine from behind the cloud. First lay aside your black veil: then tell me why you put it on." 26

Mr. Hooper's smile glimmered faintly. 27

"There is an hour to come," said he, "when all of us shall cast aside our veils. Take it not amiss, beloved friend, if I wear this piece of crape till then." 28

"Your words are a mystery too," returned the young lady. "Take away the veil from them, at least." 29

"Elizabeth, I will," said he, "so far as my vow may suffer me. Know, then, this veil is a type and a symbol, and I am bound to wear it ever, both in light and darkness, in solitude and before the gaze of multitudes, and as with strangers, so with my familiar friends. No mortal eye will see it withdrawn. This dismal shade must separate me from the world: even you, Elizabeth, can never come behind it!" 30

"What grievous affliction hath befallen you," she earnestly inquired, "that you should thus darken your eyes for ever?" 31

"If it be a sign of mourning," replied Mr. Hooper, "I, perhaps, like most other mortals, have sorrows dark enough to be typified by a black veil." 32

"But what if the world will not believe that it is the type of an innocent sorrow?" urged Elizabeth. "Beloved and respected as you are, there may be whispers, that you hide your face under the consciousness of secret sin. For the sake of your holy office, do away this scandal!" 33

The color rose into her cheeks, as she intimated the nature of the rumors 34
that were already abroad in the village. But Mr. Hooper's mildness did not forsake him. He even smiled again—that same sad smile, which always appeared
like a faint glimmering of light, proceeding from the obscurity beneath the veil.

"If I hide my face for sorrow, there is cause enough," he merely replied; "and 35
if I cover it for secret sin, what mortal might not do the same?"

And with this gentle, but unconquerable obstinacy, did he resist all her en- 36
treaties. At length Elizabeth sat silent. For a few moments she appeared lost in
thought, considering, probably, what new methods might be tried, to withdraw
her lover from so dark a fantasy, which, if it had no other meaning, was perhaps
a symptom of mental disease. Though of a firmer character than his own, the
tears rolled down her cheeks. But, in an instant, as it were, a new feeling took
the place of sorrow: her eyes were fixed insensibly on the black veil, when, like a
sudden twilight in the air, its terrors fell around her. She arose, and stood trembling before him.

"And do you feel it then at last?" said he mournfully. 37

She made no reply, but covered her eyes with her hand, and turned to leave 38
the room. He rushed forward and caught her arm.

"Have patience with me, Elizabeth!" cried he passionately. "Do not desert 39
me, though this veil must be between us here on earth. Be mine, and hereafter
there shall be no veil over my face, no darkness between our souls! It is but a
mortal veil—it is not for eternity! Oh, you know not how lonely I am and how
frightened to be alone behind my black veil. Do not leave me in this miserable
obscurity for ever!"

"Lift the veil but once, and look me in the face," said she. 40

"Never! It cannot be!" replied Mr. Hooper. 41

"Then, farewell!" said Elizabeth. 42

She withdrew her arm from his grasp, and slowly departed, pausing at the 43
door, to give one long, shuddering gaze, that seemed almost to penetrate the mystery of the black veil. But, even amid his grief, Mr. Hooper smiled to think that
only a material emblem had separated him from happiness, though the horrors
which it shadowed forth, must be drawn darkly between the fondest of lovers.

From that time no attempts were made to remove Mr. Hooper's black veil, 44
or, by a direct appeal, to discover the secret which it was supposed to hide. By
persons who claimed a superiority to popular prejudice, it was reckoned merely
an eccentric whim, such as often mingles with the sober actions of men otherwise rational, and tinges them all with its own semblance of insanity. But with
the multitude, good Mr. Hooper was irreparably a bugbear. He could not walk
the street with any peace of mind, so conscious was he that the gentle and timid
would turn aside to avoid him, and that others would make it a point of hardi-
hood to throw themselves in his way. The impertinence of the latter class compelled him to give up his customary walk, at sunset, to the burial ground; for
when he leaned pensively over the gate, there would always be faces behind the
grave-stones, peeping at his black veil. A fable went the rounds, that the stare of
the dead people drove him thence. It grieved him, to the very depth of his kind

heart, to observe how the children fled from his approach, breaking up their merriest sports, while his melancholy figure was yet afar off. Their instinctive dread caused him to feel, more strongly than aught else, that a preternatural horror was interwoven with the threads of the black crape. In truth, his own antipathy to the veil was known to be so great, that he never willingly passed before a mirror, nor stooped to drink at a still fountain, lest, in its peaceful bosom, he should be affrighted by himself. This was what gave plausibility to the whispers, that Mr. Hooper's conscience tortured him for some great crime, too horrible to be entirely concealed, or otherwise than so obscurely intimated. Thus, from beneath the black veil, there rolled a cloud into the sunshine, an ambiguity of sin or sorrow, which enveloped the poor minister, so that love or sympathy could never reach him. It was said, that ghost and fiend consorted with him there. With self-shudderings and outward terrors, he walked continually in its shadow, groping darkly within his own soul, or gazing through a medium that saddened the whole world. Even the lawless wind, it was believed, respected his dreadful secret, and never blew aside the veil. But still good Mr. Hooper sadly smiled, at the pale visages of the worldly throng as he passed by.   45

Among all its bad influences, the black veil had the one desirable effect, of making its wearer a very efficient clergyman. By the aid of his mysterious emblem—for there was no other apparent cause—he became a man of awful power, over souls that were in agony for sin. His converts always regarded him with a dread peculiar to themselves, affirming, though but figuratively, that, before he brought them to celestial light, they had been with him behind the black veil. Its gloom, indeed, enabled him to sympathize with all dark affections. Dying sinners cried aloud for Mr. Hooper, and would not yield their breath till he appeared; though ever, as he stooped to whisper consolation, they shuddered at the veiled face so near their own. Such were the terrors of the black veil, even when death had bared his visage! Strangers came long distances to attend service at his church, with the mere idle purpose of gazing at his figure, because it was forbidden them to behold his face. But many were made to quake ere they departed! Once, during Governor Belcher's administration, Mr. Hooper was appointed to preach the election sermon. Covered with his black veil, he stood before the chief magistrate, the council, and the representatives, and wrought so deep an impression, that the legislative measures of that year, were characterized by all the gloom and piety of our earliest ancestral sway.   46

In this manner Mr. Hooper spent a long life, irreproachable in outward act, yet shrouded in dismal suspicions; kind and loving, though unloved, and dimly feared; a man apart from men, shunned in their health and joy, but ever summoned to their aid in mortal anguish. As years wore on, shedding their snows above his sable veil, he acquired a name throughout the New-England churches, and they called him Father Hooper. Nearly all his parishioners, who were of mature age when he was settled, had been borne away by many a funeral: he had one congregation in the church, and a more crowded one in the church-yard; and having wrought so late into the evening, and done his work so well, it was now good Father Hooper's turn to rest.

Several persons were visible by the shaded candlelight, in the death-cham- 47
ber of the old clergyman. Natural connections he had none. But there was the
decorously grave, though unmoved physician, seeking only to mitigate the last
pangs of the patient whom he could not save. There were the deacons, and
other eminently pious members of his church. There, also, was the Reverend
Mr. Clark, of Westbury, a young and zealous divine, who had ridden in haste to
pray by the bed-side of the expiring minister. There was the nurse, no hired
handmaiden of death, but one whose calm affection had endured thus long, in
secresy, in solitude, amid the chill of age, and would not perish, even at the dying hour. Who, but Elizabeth! And there lay the hoary head of good Father
Hooper upon the death-pillow, with the black veil still swathed about his brow
and reaching down over his face, so that each more difficult gasp of his faint
breath caused it to stir. All through life that piece of crape had hung between
him and the world: it had separated him from cheerful brotherhood and
woman's love, and kept him in that saddest of all prisons, his own heart; and
still it lay upon his face, as if to deepen the gloom of his darksome chamber,
and shade him from the sunshine of eternity.

For some time previous, his mind had been confused, wavering doubtfully 48
between the past and the present, and hovering forward, as it were, at intervals,
into the indistinctness of the world to come. There had been feverish turns,
which tossed him from side to side, and wore away what little strength he had.
But in his most convulsive struggles, and in the wildest vagaries of his intellect,
when no other thought retained its sober influence, he still showed an awful solicitude lest the black veil should slip aside. Even if his bewildered soul could
have forgotten, there was a faithful woman at his pillow, who, with averted eyes,
would have covered that aged face, which she had last beheld in the comeliness
of manhood. At length the death-stricken old man lay quietly in the torpor of
mental and bodily exhaustion, with an imperceptible pulse, and breath that
grew fainter and fainter, except when a long, deep, and irregular inspiration
seemed to prelude the flight of his spirit.

The minister of Westbury approached the bedside.   49

"Venerable Father Hooper," said he, "the moment of your release is at hand. 50
Are you ready for the lifting of the veil, that shuts in time from eternity?"

Father Hooper at first replied merely by a feeble motion of his head; then, 51
apprehensive, perhaps, that his meaning might be doubtful, he exerted himself
to speak.

"Yea," said he, in faint accents, "my soul hath a patient weariness until that 52
veil be lifted."

"And is it fitting," resumed the Reverend Mr. Clark, "that a man so given to 53
prayer, of such a blameless example, holy in deed and thought, so far as mortal
judgment may pronounce; is it fitting that a father in the church should leave a
shadow on his memory, that may seem to blacken a life so pure? I pray you, my
venerable brother, let not this thing be! Suffer us to be gladdened by your triumphant aspect, as you go to your reward. Before the veil of eternity be lifted,
let me cast aside this black veil from your face!"

And thus speaking, the reverend Mr. Clark bent forward to reveal the mystery of so many years. But, exerting a sudden energy, that made all the behold- 54
ers stand aghast, Father Hooper snatched both his hands from beneath the bed-clothes, and pressed them strongly on the black veil, resolute to struggle, if the minister of Westbury would contend with a dying man.

"Never!" cried the veiled clergyman. "On earth, never!"

"Dark old man!" exclaimed the affrighted minister, "with what horrible 55
crime upon your soul are you now passing to the judgment?" 56

Father Hooper's breath heaved; it rattled in his throat; but, with a mighty effort, grasping forward with his hands, he caught hold of life, and held it back 57
till he should speak. He even raised himself in bed; and there he sat, shivering with the arms of death around him, while the black veil hung down, awful, at that last moment, in the gathered terrors of a life-time. And yet the faint, sad smile, so often there, now seemed to glimmer from its obscurity, and linger on Father Hooper's lips.

"Why do you tremble at me alone?" cried he, turning his veiled face round the circle of pale spectators. "Tremble also at each other! Have men avoided me, 58
and women shown no pity, and children screamed and fled, only for my black veil? What, but the mystery which it obscurely typifies, has made this piece of crape so awful? When the friend shows his inmost heart to his friend; the lover to his best-beloved; when man does not vainly shrink from the eye of his Creator, loathsomely treasuring up the secret of his sin; then deem me a monster, for the symbol beneath which I have lived, and die! I look around me, and lo! on every visage a black veil!"

While his auditors shrank from one another, in mutual affright, Father Hooper fell back upon his pillow, a veiled corpse, with a faint smile lingering on 59
the lips. Still veiled, they laid him in his coffin, and a veiled corpse they bore him to the grave. The grass of many years has sprung up and withered on that grave, the burial-stone is moss-grown, and good Mr. Hooper's face is dust; but awful is still the thought, that it mouldered beneath the black veil!

ACTIVITIES FOR WRITING AND DISCUSSION

1. Annotate any passages that describe the veil's effects on Mr. Hooper's parishioners. Do different people react differently, and, if so, why? Imagining yourself into the **persona** of one specific parishioner mentioned in the story (young or old, male or female) and writing in the **first-person,** tell the story of your own reactions to the veil.

2. Annotate any passages that bear on Mr. Hooper's motives for wearing the veil. For what reason(s) has he chosen to don the veil and never remove it? How do his own apparent aims in wearing it agree, or conflict, with the actual effects the veil has on his congregation—or on himself?

3. Assess Mr. Hooper's overall impact on his congregation. Was his crusade with the veil a sign of superior insight and virtue or of "mental disease" (see

paragraph 36)? Gather evidence to support either view. Then present your position orally or in an essay.

4. Write an alternative ending in which the dying Mr. Hooper *removes* the veil. Write in the **third-person,** or, if you wish, from the first-person point of view of someone present at the deathbed.

5. Hawthorne calls his story "a **parable,**" i.e., "a simple story illustrating a moral or religious lesson" *(American Heritage College Dictionary)*. What would you say is the **theme** of this parable, and what relevance, if any, does it have to life in the twenty-first century?

   a. Write an essay on the foregoing question; or
   b. Write a story, nonfictional or fictional, that is set in the present and that addresses the theme of Hawthorne's parable.

James Thurber (1894–1961)

The Secret Life of Walter Mitty

"We're going through!" The Commander's voice was like thin ice breaking. He 1
wore his full-dress uniform, with the heavily braided white cap pulled down rakishly over one cold gray eye. "We can't make it, sir. It's spoiling for a hurricane, if you ask me." "I'm not asking you, Lieutenant Berg," said the Commander. "Throw on the power lights! Rev her up to 8,500! We're going through!" The pounding of the cylinders increased: ta-pocketa-pocketa-pocketa-*pocketa-pocketa*. The Commander stared at the ice forming on the pilot window. He walked over and twisted a row of complicated dials. "Switch on No. 8 auxiliary!" he shouted. "Switch on No. 8 auxiliary!" repeated Lieutenant Berg. "Full strength in No. 3 turret!" shouted the Commander. "Full strength in No. 3 turret!" The crew, bending to their various tasks in the huge, hurtling eight-engined Navy hydroplane, looked at each other and grinned. "The Old Man'll get us through," they said to one another. "The Old Man ain't afraid of Hell!" . . .

"Not so fast! You're driving too fast!" said Mrs. Mitty. "What are you driving 2
so fast for?"

"Hmm?" said Walter Mitty. He looked at his wife, in the seat beside him, 3
with shocked astonishment. She seemed grossly unfamiliar, like a strange woman who had yelled at him in a crowd. "You were up to fifty-five," she said. "You know I don't like to go more than forty. You were up to fifty-five." Walter Mitty drove on toward Waterbury in silence, the roaring of the SN202 through the worst storm in twenty years of Navy flying fading in the remote, intimate airways of his mind. "You're tensed up again," said Mrs. Mitty. "It's one of your days. I wish you'd let Dr. Renshaw look you over."

Walter Mitty stopped the car in front of the building where his wife went to 4
have her hair done. "Remember to get those overshoes while I'm having my hair done," she said. "I don't need overshoes," said Mitty. She put her mirror back into her bag. "We've been all through that," she said, getting out of the car.

"You're not a young man any longer." He raced the engine a little. "Why don't you wear your gloves? Have you lost your gloves?" Walter Mitty reached in a pocket and brought out the gloves. He put them on, but after she had turned and gone into the building and he had driven on to a red light, he took them off again. "Pick it up, brother!" snapped a cop as the light changed, and Mitty hastily pulled on his gloves and lurched ahead. He drove around the streets aimlessly for a time, and then he drove past the hospital on his way to the parking lot.

. . . "It's the millionaire banker, Wellington McMillan," said the pretty nurse. 5 "Yes?" said Walter Mitty, removing his gloves slowly. "Who has the case?" "Dr. Renshaw and Dr. Benbow, but there are two specialists here, Dr. Remington from New York and Dr. Pritchard-Mitford from London. He flew over." A door opened down a long, cool corridor and Dr. Renshaw came out. He looked distraught and haggard. "Hello, Mitty," he said. "We're having the devil's own time with McMillan, the millionaire banker and close personal friend of Roosevelt. Obstreosis of the ductal tract. Tertiary. Wish you'd take a look at him." "Glad to," said Mitty.

In the operating room there were whispered introductions: "Dr. Reming- 6 ton, Dr. Mitty, Dr. Pritchard-Mitford, Dr. Mitty." "I've read your book on streptothricosis," said Pritchard-Mitford, shaking hands. "A brilliant performance, sir." "Thank you," said Walter Mitty. "Didn't know you were in the States, Mitty," grumbled Remington. "Coals to Newcastle, bringing Mitford and me up here for a tertiary." "You are very kind," said Mitty. A huge, complicated machine, connected to the operating table, with many tubes and wires, began at this moment to go pocketa-pocketa-pocketa. "The new anesthetizer is giving way!" shouted an intern. "There is no one in the East who knows how to fix it!" "Quiet, man!" said Mitty, in a low, cool voice. He sprang to the machine, which was now going pocketa-pocketa-queep-pocketa-queep. He began fingering delicately a row of glistening dials. "Give me a fountain pen!" he snapped. Someone handed him a fountain pen. He pulled a faulty piston out of the machine and inserted the pen in its place. "That will hold for ten minutes," he said. "Get on with the operation." A nurse hurried over and whispered to Renshaw, and Mitty saw the man turn pale. "Coreopsis has set in," said Renshaw nervously. "If you would take over, Mitty?" Mitty looked at him and at the craven figure of Benbow, who drank, and at the grave, uncertain faces of the two great specialists. "If you wish," he said. They slipped a white gown on him; he adjusted a mask and drew on thin gloves; nurses handed him shining. . . .

"Back it up, Mac! Look out for that Buick!" Walter Mitty jammed on the 7 brakes. "Wrong lane, Mac," said the parking-lot attendant, looking at Mitty closely. "Gee. Yeh," muttered Mitty. He began cautiously to back out of the lane marked "Exit Only." "Leave her sit there," said the attendant. "I'll put her away." Mitty got out of the car. "Hey, better leave the key." "Oh," said Mitty, handing the man the ignition key. The attendant vaulted into the car, backed it up with insolent skill, and put it where it belonged.

They're so damn cocky, thought Walter Mitty, walking along Main Street; 8 they think they know everything. Once he had tried to take his chains off, outside New Milford, and he had got them wound around the axles. A man had had to come out in a wrecking car and unwind them, a young, grinning garageman. Since then Mrs. Mitty always made him drive to the garage to have the chains taken off. The next time, he thought, I'll wear my right arm in a sling; they won't grin at me then. I'll have my right arm in a sling and they'll see I couldn't possibly take the chains off myself. He kicked at the slush on the sidewalk. "Overshoes," he said to himself, and he began looking for a shoe store.

When he came out into the street again, with the overshoes in a box under his arm, Walter Mitty began to wonder what the other thing was his wife had told him to get. She had told him, twice, before they set out from their house for Waterbury. In a way he hated these weekly trips to town—he was always getting something wrong. Kleenex, he thought, Squibb's, razor blades? No. Toothpaste, toothbrush, bicarbonate, carborundum, initiative and referendum? He gave it up. But she would remember it. "Where's the what's-its-name?" she would ask. "Don't tell me you forgot the what's-its-name." A newsboy went by shouting something about the Waterbury trial.

. . . "Perhaps this will refresh your memory." The District Attorney suddenly thrust a heavy automatic at the quiet figure on the witness stand. "Have you ever seen this before?" Walter Mitty took the gun and examined it expertly. "This is my Webley-Vickers 50.80," he said calmly. An excited buzz ran around the courtroom. The Judge rapped for order. "You are a crack shot with any sort of firearms, I believe?" said the District Attorney, insinuatingly. "Objection!" shouted Mitty's attorney. "We have shown that the defendant could not have fired the shot. We have shown that he wore his right arm in a sling on the night of the fourteenth of July." Walter Mitty raised his hand briefly and the bickering attorneys were stilled. "With any known make of gun," he said evenly, "I could have killed Gregory Fitzhurst at three hundred feet *with my left hand*." Pandemonium broke loose in the courtroom. A woman's scream rose above the bedlam and suddenly a lovely, dark-haired girl was in Walter Mitty's arms. The District Attorney struck at her savagely. Without rising from his chair, Mitty let the man have it on the point of the chin. "You miserable cur!" . . .

"Puppy biscuit," said Walter Mitty. He stopped walking and the buildings of Waterbury rose up out of the misty courtroom and surrounded him again. A woman who was passing laughed, "He said 'Puppy biscuit,'" she said to her companion. "That man said 'Puppy biscuit' to himself." Walter Mitty hurried on. He went into an A. & P., not the first one he came to but a smaller one farther up the street. "I want some biscuit for small, young dogs," he said to the clerk. "Any special brand, sir?" The greatest pistol shot in the world thought a moment. "It says 'Puppies Bark for It' on the box," said Walter Mitty.

His wife would be through at the hairdresser's in fifteen minutes, Mitty saw in looking at his watch, unless they had trouble drying it; sometimes they had trouble drying it. She didn't like to get to the hotel first; she would want him to be there waiting for her as usual. He found a big leather chair in the lobby, facing a window, and he put the overshoes and the puppy biscuit on the floor beside it. He picked up an old copy of *Liberty* and sank down into the chair. "Can Germany Conquer the World through the Air?" Walter Mitty looked at the pictures of bombing planes and of ruined streets.

. . . "The cannonading has got the wind up in young Raleigh, sir," said the 13 sergeant. Captain Mitty looked up at him through tousled hair. "Get him to bed," he said wearily. "With the others. I'll fly alone." "But you can't, sir," said the sergeant anxiously. "It takes two men to handle that bomber and the Archies are pounding hell out of the air. Von Richtman's circus is between here and Saulier." "Somebody's got to get that ammunition dump," said Mitty. "I'm going over. Spot of brandy?" He poured a drink for the sergeant and one for himself. War thundered and whined around the dugout and battered at the door. There was a rending of wood and splinters flew through the room. "A bit of a near thing," said Captain Mitty carelessly. "The box barrage is closing in," said the sergeant. "We only live once, Sergeant," said Mitty, with his faint, fleeting smile. "Or do we?" He poured another brandy and tossed it off. "I never see a man could hold his brandy like you, sir," said the sergeant. "Begging your pardon, sir." Captain Mitty stood up and strapped on his huge Webley-Vickers automatic. "It's forty kilometers through hell, sir," said the sergeant. Mitty finished one last brandy. "After all," he said softly, "what isn't?" The pounding of the cannon increased; there was the rat-tat-tatting of machine guns, and from somewhere came the menacing pocket-pocketa-pocketa of the new flame-throwers. Walter Mitty walked to the door of the dugout humming "Auprès de Ma Blonde." He turned and waved to the sergeant. "Cheerio!" he said. . . .

Something struck his shoulder. "I've been looking all over this hotel for 14 you," said Mrs. Mitty. "Why do you have to hide in this old chair? How did you expect me to find you?" "Things close in," said Walter Mitty vaguely. "What?" Mrs. Mitty said. "Did you get the what's-its-name? The puppy biscuit? What's in that box?" "Overshoes," said Mitty. "Couldn't you have put them on in the store?" "I was thinking," said Walter Mitty. "Does it ever occur to you that I am sometimes thinking?" She looked at him. "I'm going to take your temperature when I get you home," she said.

They went out through the revolving doors that made a faintly derisive 15 whistling sound when you pushed them. It was two blocks to the parking lot. At the drugstore on the corner she said, "Wait here for me. I forgot something. I won't be a minute." She was more than a minute. Walter Mitty lighted a cigarette. It began to rain, rain with sleet in it. He stood up against the wall of the drugstore, smoking. . . . He put his shoulders back and his heels together. "To hell with the handkerchief," said Walter Mitty scornfully. He took one last drag on his cigarette and snapped it away. Then, with that faint, fleeting smile playing about his lips, he faced the firing squad; erect and motionless, proud and disdainful, Walter Mitty the Undefeated, inscrutable to the last.

RAY BRADBURY (b. 1920)

The Murderer

Music moved with him in the white halls. He passed an office door: "The Merry 1
Widow Waltz." Another door: "Afternoon of a Faun." A third: "Kiss Me Again."
He turned into a cross corridor: "The Sword Dance" buried him in cymbals,
drums, pots, pans, knives, forks, thunder and tin lightning. All washed away as
he hurried through an anteroom where a secretary sat nicely stunned by
Beethoven's Fifth. He moved himself before her eyes like a hand; she didn't see
him.

His wrist radio buzzed. 2

"Yes?" 3

"This is Lee, Dad. Don't forget about my allowance." 4

"Yes, son, yes. I'm busy." 5

"Just didn't want you to forget, Dad," said the wrist radio. Tchaikovsky's 6
"Romeo and Juliet" swarmed about the voice and flushed into the long halls.

The psychiatrist moved in the beehive of offices, in the cross-pollination of 7
themes, Stravinsky mating with Bach, Haydn unsuccessfully repulsing Rach-
maninoff, Schubert slain by Duke Ellington. He nodded to the humming secretaries and the whistling doctors fresh to their morning work. At his office he
checked a few papers with his stenographer, who sang under her breath, then
phoned the police captain upstairs. A few minutes later a red light blinked, a
voice said from the ceiling:

"Prisoner delivered to Interview Chamber Nine." 8

He unlocked the chamber door, stepped in, heard the door lock behind 9
him.

"Go away," said the prisoner, smiling. 10

The psychiatrist was shocked by that smile. A very sunny, pleasant warm 11
thing, a thing that shed bright light upon the room. Dawn among the dark hills.
High noon at midnight, that smile. The blue eyes sparkled serenely above that
display of self-assured dentistry.

"I'm here to help you," said the psychiatrist, frowning. Something was 12
wrong with the room. He had hesitated the moment he entered. He glanced
around. The prisoner laughed. "If you're wondering why it's so quiet in here, I
just kicked the radio to death."

Violent, thought the doctor. 13

The prisoner read this thought, smiled, put out a gentle hand. "No, only to 14
machines that yak-yak-yak."

Bits of the wall radio's tubes and wires lay on the gray carpeting. Ignoring 15
these, feeling that smile upon him like a heat lamp, the psychiatrist sat across
from his patient in the unusual silence which was like the gathering of a storm.

"You're Mr. Albert Brock, who calls himself The Murderer?" 16

Brock nodded pleasantly. "Before we start . . . " He moved quietly and 17
quickly to detach the wrist radio from the doctor's arm. He tucked it in his
teeth like a walnut, gritted and heard it crack, handed it back to the appalled
psychiatrist as if he had done them both a favor. "That's better."

The psychiatrist stared at the ruined machine. "You're running up quite a 18
damage bill."

"I don't care," smiled the patient. "As the old song goes: 'Don't Care What 19
Happens to Me!' " He hummed it.

The psychiatrist said: "Shall we start?" 20

"Fine. The first victim, or one of the first, was my telephone. Murder most 21
foul. I shoved it in the kitchen Insinkerator! Stopped the disposal unit in mid-
swallow. Poor thing strangled to death. After that I shot the television set!"

The psychiatrist said, "Mmm." 22

"Fired six shots right through the cathode. Made a beautiful tinkling crash, 23
like a dropped chandelier."

"Nice imagery." 24

"Thanks, I always dreamt of being a writer." 25

"Suppose you tell me when you first began to hate the telephone." 26

"It frightened me as a child. Uncle of mine called it the Ghost Machine. 27
Voices without bodies. Scared the living hell out of me. Later in life I was never
comfortable. Seemed to me a phone was an impersonal instrument. If it *felt* like
it, it let your personality go through its wires. If it didn't *want* to, it just drained
your personality away until what slipped through at the other end was some
cold fish of a voice all steel, copper, plastic, no warmth, no reality. It's easy to say
the wrong thing on telephones; the telephone changes your meaning on you.
First thing you know, you've made an enemy. Then, of course, the telephone's
such a *convenient* thing; it just sits there and *demands* you call someone who
doesn't want to be called. Friends were always calling, calling, calling me. Hell, I
hadn't any time of my own. When it wasn't the telephone it was the television,
the radio, the phonograph. When it wasn't the television or radio or the phonograph it was motion pictures at the corner theater, motion pictures projected,
with commercials on low-lying cumulus clouds. It doesn't rain rain any more,
it rains soapsuds. When it wasn't High-Fly Cloud advertisements, it was music
by Mozzek in every restaurant; music and commercials on the busses I rode to
work. When it wasn't music, it was interoffice communications, and my horror
chamber of a radio wrist watch on which my friends and my wife phoned every
five minutes. What is there about such 'conveniences' that makes them so
temptingly convenient? The average man thinks, Here I am, time on my hands,
and there on my wrist is a wrist telephone, so why not just buzz old Joe up, eh?
'Hello, hello!' I love my friends, my wife, humanity, very much, but when one
minute my wife calls to say, 'Where are you *now* dear?' and a friend calls and
says, 'Got the best off-color joke to tell you. Seems there was a guy——' and a
stranger calls and cries out, 'This is the Find-Fax Poll. What gum are you chewing at this very *instant!* Well!"

"How did you feel during the week?" 28

"The fuse lit. On the edge of the cliff. That same afternoon I did what I did 29
at the office."

"Which was?" 30

"I poured a paper cup of water into the intercommunications system." 31

The psychiatrist wrote on his pad. 32

"And the system shorted?" 33

"Beautifully! The Fourth of July on wheels! My God, stenographers ran 34
around looking *lost!* What an uproar!"

"Felt better temporarily, eh?" 35

"Fine! Then I got the idea at noon of stomping my wrist radio on the side- 36
walk. A shrill voice was just yelling out of it at me, 'This is People's Poll Number
Nine. What did you eat for lunch?' when I kicked the Jesus out of the wrist radio!"

"Felt even *better,* eh?" 37

"It *grew* on me!" Brock rubbed his hands together. "Why didn't I start a soli- 38
tary revolution, deliver man from certain 'conveniences'? 'Convenient for
whom?' I cried. Convenient for friends: 'Hey, Al, thought I'd call you from the
locker room out here at Green Hills. Just made a sockdolager hole in one! A
hole in one, Al! A *beautiful* day. Having a shot of whiskey now. Thought you'd
want to know, Al!' Convenient for my office, so when I'm in the field with my
car radio there's no moment when I'm not in touch. In *touch! There's* a slimy
phrase. Touch, hell. *Gripped!* Pawed, rather. Mauled and massaged and
pounded by FM voices. You can't leave your car without checking in: 'Have
stopped to visit gas-station men's room.' 'Okay, Brock, step on it!' 'Brock, what
took you so long?' 'Sorry, sir.' 'Watch it next time, Brock.' *'Yes, sir!'* So, do you
know what I did, Doctor? I bought a quart of French chocolate ice cream and
spooned it into the car radio transmitter."

"Was there any *special* reason for selecting French chocolate ice cream to 39
spoon into the broadcasting unit?"

Brock thought about it and smiled. "It's my favorite flavor." 40

"Oh," said the doctor. 41

"I figured, hell, what's good enough for me is good enough for the radio 42
transmitter."

"What made you think of spooning *ice cream* into the radio?" 43

"It was a hot day." 44

The doctor paused. 45

"And what happened next?" 46

"Silence happened next. God, it was *beautiful.* That car radio cackling all 47
day, Brock go here, Brock go there, Brock check in, Brock check out, okay
Brock, hour lunch, Brock, lunch over, Brock, Brock, Brock. Well, that silence
was like putting ice cream in my ears."

"You seem to like ice cream a lot." 48

"I just rode around feeling of the silence. It's a big bolt of the nicest, softest 49
flannel ever made. Silence. A whole hour of it. I just sat in my car; smiling, feeling of that flannel with my ears. I felt *drunk* with Freedom!"

"Go on."   50

"Then I got the idea of the portable diathermy machine. I rented one, took   51
it on the bus going home that night. There sat all the tired commuters with
their wrist radios, talking to their wives, saying, 'Now I'm at Forty-third, now
I'm at Forty-fourth, here I am at Forty-ninth, now turning at Sixty-first.' One
husband cursing, 'Well, get *out* of that bar, damn it, and get home and get dinner started, I'm at Seventieth!' And the transit-system radio playing 'Tales from
the Vienna Woods,' a canary singing words about a first-rate wheat cereal.
Then—I switched on my diathermy! Static! Interference! All wives cut off from
husbands grousing about a hard day at the office. All husbands cut off from
wives who had just seen their children break a window! The 'Vienna Woods'
chopped down, the canary mangled! *Silence!* A terrible, unexpected silence. The
bus inhabitants faced with having to converse with each other. Panic! Sheer, animal panic!"

"The police seized you?"   52

"The bus *had* to stop. After all, the music *was* being scrambled, husbands   53
and wives *were* out of touch with reality. Pandemonium, riot, and chaos. Squirrels chattering in cages! A trouble unit arrived, triangulated on me instantly,
had me reprimanded, fined, and home, minus my diathermy machine, in jig
time."

"Mr. Brock, may I suggest that so far your whole pattern here is not very—   54
practical? If you didn't like transit radios or office radios or car business radios,
why didn't you join a fraternity of radio haters, start petitions, get legal and
constitutional rulings? After all, this *is* a democracy."

"And I," said Brock, "am that thing called a minority. I *did* join fraternities,   55
picket, pass petitions, take it to court. Year after year I protested. Everyone
laughed. Everyone else *loved* bus radios and commercials. *I* was out of step."

"Then you should have taken it like a good soldier, don't you think? The   56
majority rules."

"But they went too far. If a little music and 'keeping in touch' was charming,   57
they figured a lot would be ten times as charming. I went *wild!* I got home to
find my wife hysterical. *Why?* Because she had been completely out of touch
with me for half a day. Remember, I did a dance on my wrist radio? Well, that
night I laid plans to murder my house."

"Are you *sure* that's how you want me to write it down?"   58

"That's semantically accurate. Kill it dead. It's one of those talking, singing,   59
humming, weather-reporting, poetry-reading, novel-reciting, jingle-jangling,
rockaby-crooning-when-you-go-to-bed houses. A house that screams opera to
you in the shower and teaches you Spanish in your sleep. One of those blather-
ing caves where all kinds of electronic Oracles make you feel a trifle larger than
a thimble, with stoves that say, 'I'm apricot pie, and I'm *done*,' or 'I'm prime
roast beef, so *baste* me!' and other nursery gibberish like that. With beds that
rock you to sleep and *shake* you awake. A house that *barely* tolerates humans, I
tell you. A front door that barks: 'You've mud on your feet, sir!' And an electronic vacuum hound that snuffles around after you from room to room, inhaling every fingernail or ash you drop. Jesus God, *I* say, Jesus God!"

"Quietly," suggested the psychiatrist.   60

"Remember that Gilbert and Sullivan song—'I've Got It on My List, It   61
Never Will Be Missed'? All night I listed grievances. Next morning early I
bought a pistol. I *purposely* muddied my feet. I stood at our front door. The
front door shrilled, 'Dirty feet, muddy feet! Wipe your feet! Please be *neat!*' I
shot the damn thing in its keyhole. I ran to the kitchen, where the stove was just
whining, 'Turn me *over!*' In the middle of a mechanical omelet I did the stove to
death. Oh, how it sizzled and screamed, 'I'm *shorted!*' Then the telephone rang
like a spoiled brat. I shoved it down the Insinkerator. I must state here and now
I have *nothing* whatever against the Insinkerator; it was an innocent bystander. I
feel sorry for it now, a practical device indeed, which never said a word, purred
like a sleepy lion most of the time, and digested our leftovers. I'll have it restored. Then I went in and shot the televisor, that insidious beast, that Medusa,
which freezes a billion people to stone every night, staring fixedly, that Siren
which called and sang and promised so much and gave, after all, so little, but
myself always going back, going back, hoping and waiting until—bang! Like a
headless turkey, gobbling, my wife whooped out the front door. The police
came. Here I *am!*"

He sat back happily and lit a cigarette.   62

"And did you realize, in committing these crimes, that the wrist radio, the   63
broadcasting transmitter, the phone, the bus radio, the office intercoms, all
were rented or were someone else's property?"

"I would do it all over again, so help me God."   64

The psychiatrist sat there in the sunshine of that beatific smile.   65

"You don't want any further help from the Office of Mental Health? You're   66
ready to take the consequences?"

"This is only the beginning," said Mr. Brock. "I'm the vanguard of the small   67
public which is tired of noise and being taken advantage of and pushed around
and yelled at, every moment music, every moment in touch with some voice
somewhere, do this, do that, quick, quick, now here, now there. You'll see. The
revolt begins. My name will go down in history!"

"Mmm." The psychiatrist seemed to be thinking.   68

"It'll take time, of course. It was all so enchanting at first. The very *idea* of   69
these things, the practical uses, was wonderful. They were almost toys, to be
played with, but the people got too involved, went too far, and got wrapped up
in a pattern of social behavior and couldn't get out, couldn't admit they were *in*,
even. So they rationalized their nerves as something else. 'Our modern age,'
they said. 'Conditions,' they said. 'High-strung,' they said. But mark my words,
the seed has been sown. I got world-wide coverage on TV, radio, films; *there's* an
irony for you. That was five days ago. A billion people know about me. Check
your financial columns. Any day now. Maybe today. Watch for a sudden spurt, a
rise in sales for French chocolate ice cream!"

"I see," said the psychiatrist.   70

"Can I go back to my nice private cell now, where I can be alone and quiet   71
for six months?"

"Yes," said the psychiatrist quietly.   72

"Don't worry about me," said Mr. Brock, rising. "I'm just going to sit around   73
for a long time stuffing that nice soft bolt of quiet material in both ears."

"Mmm," said the psychiatrist, going to the door.   74

"Cheers," said Mr. Brock.   75

"Yes," said the psychiatrist.   76

He pressed a code signal on a hidden button, the door opened, he stepped   77
out, the door shut and locked. Alone, he moved in the offices and corridors.
The first twenty yards of his walk were accompanied by "Tambourine Chinois."
Then it was "Tzigane," Bach's "Passacaglia" and Fugue in something Minor,
"Tiger Rag," "Love Is Like a Cigarette." He took his broken wrist radio from his
pocket like a dead praying mantis. He turned in at his office. A bell sounded; a
voice came out of the ceiling, "Doctor?"

"Just finished with Brock," said the psychiatrist.   78

"Diagnosis?"   79

"Seems completely disorientated, but convivial. Refuses to accept the sim-   80
plest realities of his environment and work *with* them."

"Prognosis?"   81

"Indefinite. Left him enjoying a piece of invisible material."   82

Three phones rang. A duplicate wrist radio in his desk drawer buzzed like a   83
wounded grasshopper. The intercom flashed a pink light and click-clicked.
Three phones rang. The drawer buzzed. Music blew in through the open door.
The psychiatrist, humming quietly, fitted the new wrist radio to his wrist,
flipped the intercom, talked a moment, picked up one telephone, talked, picked
up another telephone, talked, picked up the third telephone, talked, touched
the wrist-radio button, talked calmly and quietly, his face cool and serene, in
the middle of the music and the lights flashing, the two phones ringing again,
and his hands moving, and his wrist radio buzzing, and the intercoms talking,
and voices speaking from the ceiling. And he went on quietly this way through
the remainder of a cool, air-conditioned, and long afternoon; telephone, wrist
radio, intercom, telephone, wrist radio, intercom, telephone, wrist radio, intercom, telephone, wrist radio, intercom, telephone, wrist radio, intercom, telephone, wrist radio . . .

ACTIVITIES FOR WRITING AND DISCUSSION

1. Read and annotate the story. Then:
   a. Share and discuss a few of your favorite annotations with a small
      group, and take notes on your groupmates' annotations to enrich
      your response to the story.
   b. React to "The Murderer" in your notebook using any of the "Ten Ideas
      for Writing" described in Chapter 3 and summarized on page 35.

2. Reannotate the psychiatrist's half of the dialogue, his comments and
questions. Choose two or three specific comments or questions that seem par-

ticularly interesting to you and react to them in your notebook. How do the psychiatrist's concerns and values differ from Brock's?

3. Identify and explain any **ironies** in the story—its title, Brock's attitude toward prison, the various ironies surrounding the words "conveniences" and "convenient," and other ironies you find.

4. Modifying the characters and plot as necessary, recreate the story in a twenty-first century **setting.**

KURT VONNEGUT, JR. (b. 1922)

Harrison Bergeron

The year was 2081, and everybody was finally equal. They weren't only equal 1
before God and the law. They were equal every which way. Nobody was smarter than anybody else. Nobody was better looking than anybody else. Nobody was stronger or quicker than anybody else. All this equality was due to the 211th, 212th, and 213th Amendments to the Constitution, and to the unceasing vigilance of agents of the United States Handicapper General.

Some things about living still weren't quite right, though. April, for in- 2
stance, still drove people crazy by not being springtime. And it was in that clammy month that the H-G men took George and Hazel Bergeron's fourteen-year-old son, Harrison, away.

It was tragic, all right, but George and Hazel couldn't think about it very 3
hard. Hazel had a perfectly average intelligence, which meant she couldn't think about anything except in short bursts. And George, while his intelligence was way above normal, had a little mental handicap radio in his ear. He was required by law to wear it at all times. It was tuned to a government transmitter. Every twenty seconds or so, the transmitter would send out some sharp noise to keep people like George from taking unfair advantage of their brains.

George and Hazel were watching television. There were tears on Hazel's 4
cheeks, but she'd forgotten for the moment what they were about.

On the television screen were ballerinas. 5

A buzzer sounded in George's head. His thoughts fled in panic, like bandits 6
from a burglar alarm.

"That was a real pretty dance, that dance they just did," said Hazel. 7

"Huh?" said George. 8

"That dance—it was nice," said Hazel. 9

"Yup," said George. He tried to think a little about the ballerinas. They 10
weren't really very good—no better than anybody else would have been, anyway. They were burdened with sashweights and bags of birdshot, and their faces were masked, so that no one, seeing a free and graceful gesture or a pretty face, would feel like something the cat drug in. George was toying with the vague

notion that maybe dancers shouldn't be handicapped. But he didn't get very far with it before another noise in his ear radio scattered his thoughts.

George winced. So did two out of the eight ballerinas. 11

Hazel saw him wince. Having no mental handicap herself, she had to ask 12 George what the latest sound had been.

"Sounded like somebody hitting a milk bottle with a ball peen hammer," 13 said George.

"I'd think it would be real interesting, hearing all the different sounds," said 14 Hazel, a little envious. "All the things they think up."

"Um," said George. 15

"Only, if I was Handicapper General, you know what I would do?" said 16 Hazel. Hazel, as a matter of fact, bore a strong resemblance to the Handicapper General, a woman named Diana Moon Glampers. "If I was Diana Moon Glampers," said Hazel, "I'd have chimes on Sunday—just chimes. Kind of in honor of religion."

"I could think, if it was just chimes," said George. 17

"Well—maybe make 'em real loud," said Hazel. "I think I'd make a good 18 Handicapper General."

"Good as anybody else," said George. 19

"Who knows better'n I do what normal is?" said Hazel. 20

"Right," said George. He began to think glimmeringly about his abnormal 21 son who was now in jail, about Harrison, but a twenty-one-gun salute in his head stopped that.

"Boy!" said Hazel, "that was a doozy, wasn't it?" 22

It was such a doozy that George was white and trembling, and tears stood 23 on the rims of his red eyes. Two of the eight ballerinas had collapsed to the studio floor, were holding their temples.

"All of a sudden you look so tired," said Hazel. "Why don't you stretch out 24 on the sofa, so's you can rest your handicap bag on the pillows, honeybunch." She was referring to the forty-seven pounds of birdshot in a canvas bag, which was padlocked around George's neck. "Go on and rest the bag for a little while," she said. "I don't care if you're not equal to me for a while."

George weighed the bag with his hands. "I don't mind it," he said. "I don't 25 notice it any more. It's just a part of me."

"You been so tired lately—kind of wore out," said Hazel. "If there was just 26 some way we could make a little hole in the bottom of the bag, and just take out a few of them lead balls. Just a few."

"Two years in prison and two thousand dollars fine for every ball I took 27 out," said George. "I don't call that a bargain."

"If you could just take a few out when you came home from work," said 28 Hazel. "I mean—you don't compete with anybody around here. You just set around."

"If I tried to get away with it," said George, "then other people'd get away 29 with it—and pretty soon we'd be right back to the dark ages again, with everybody competing against everybody else. You wouldn't like that, would you?"

"I'd hate it," said Hazel.   30

"There you are," said George. "The minute people start cheating on laws,   31
what do you think happens to society?"

If Hazel hadn't been able to come up with an answer to this question,   32
George couldn't have supplied one. A siren was going off in his head.

"Reckon it'd fall all apart," said Hazel.   33

"What would?" said George blankly.   34

"Society," said Hazel uncertainly. "Wasn't that what you just said?"   35

"Who knows?" said George.   36

The television program was suddenly interrupted for a news bulletin. It   37
wasn't clear at first as to what the bulletin was about, since the announcer, like
all announcers, had a serious speech impediment. For about half a minute, and
in a state of high excitement, the announcer tried to say, "Ladies and gentlemen—"

He finally gave up, handed the bulletin to a ballerina to read.   38

"That's all right—" Hazel said of the announcer, "he tried. That's the big   39
thing. He tried to do the best he could with what God gave him. He should get a
nice raise for trying so hard."

"Ladies and gentlemen—" said the ballerina, reading the bulletin. She must   40
have been extraordinarily beautiful, because the mask she wore was hideous.
And it was easy to see that she was the strongest and most graceful of all the
dancers, for her handicap bags were as big as those worn by two-hundred-
pound men.

And she had to apologize at once for her voice, which was a very unfair   41
voice for a woman to use. Her voice was a warm, luminous, timeless melody.
"Excuse me—" she said, and she began again, making her voice absolutely
uncompetitive.

"Harrison Bergeron, age fourteen," she said in a grackle squawk, "has just   42
escaped from jail, where he was held on suspicion of plotting to overthrow the
government. He is a genius and an athlete, is under-handicapped, and should
be regarded as extremely dangerous."

A police photograph of Harrison Bergeron was flashed on the screen—up-   43
side down, then sideways, upside down again, then right side up. The picture
showed the full length of Harrison against a background calibrated in feet and
inches. He was exactly seven feet tall.

The rest of Harrison's appearance was Halloween and hardware. Nobody   44
had ever born heavier handicaps. He had outgrown hindrances faster than the
H-G men could think them up. Instead of a little ear radio for a mental handicap, he wore a tremendous pair of earphones, and spectacles with thick wavy
lenses. The spectacles were intended to make him not only half blind, but to
give him whanging headaches besides.

Scrap metal was hung all over him. Ordinarily, there was a certain symme-   45
try, a military neatness to the handicaps issued to strong people, but Harrison
looked like a walking junkyard. In the race of life, Harrison carried three hundred pounds.

And to offset his good looks, the H-G men required that he wear at all times 46
a red rubber ball for a nose, keep his eyebrows shaved off, and cover his even
white teeth with black caps at snaggle-tooth random.

"If you see this boy," said the ballerina, "do not—I repeat, do not—try to 47
reason with him."

There was the shriek of a door being torn from its hinges. 48

Screams and barking cries of consternation came from the television set. 49
The photograph of Harrison Bergeron on the screen jumped again and again,
as though dancing to the tune of an earthquake.

George Bergeron correctly identified the earthquake, and well he might 50
have—for many was the time his own home had danced to the same crashing
tune. "My God—" said George, "that must be Harrison!"

The realization was blasted from his mind instantly by the sound of an au- 51
tomobile collision in his head.

When George could open his eyes again, the photograph of Harrison was 52
gone. A living, breathing Harrison filled the screen.

Clanking, clownish, and huge, Harrison stood in the center of the studio. 53
The knob of the uprooted studio door was still in his hand. Ballerinas, techni-
cians, musicians, and announcers cowered on their knees before him, expecting
to die.

"I am the Emperor!" cried Harrison. "Do you hear? I am the Emperor! 54
Everybody must do what I say at once!" He stamped his foot and the studio
shook.

"Even as I stand here—" he bellowed, "crippled, hobbled, sickened—I am a 55
greater ruler than any man who ever lived! Now watch me become what I *can*
become!"

Harrison tore the straps of his handicap harness like wet tissue paper, tore 56
straps guaranteed to support five thousand pounds.

ACTIVITIES FOR WRITING AND DISCUSSION

1. Annotate the story and respond to it using any of the "Ten Ideas for
Writing" described in Chapter 3 and summarized on page 35.

2. "Harrison Bergeron" is a satire, i.e., "a literary work that attacks human
vice or folly through irony, derision, or wit" *(American Heritage College Dictionary).*

    a. What, specifically, is Vonnegut satirizing? (Several answers are possi-
ble.)

    b. What passages in the story strike you as particularly satiric? Focus on
one or two such passages, and use them as examples to explain how
Vonnegut's satire works. Share your analysis orally or in an essay.

3. The futuristic America Vonnegut depicts is dedicated to the eradication
of excellence and the enforcement of mediocrity. How the country got that way

is left for us to imagine. Suppose it is the year 2081, and you have been hired as the official national historian. In the **persona** of the historian write the history of the events that culminated in Harrison Bergeron's America. (Bear in mind that your version of events should be acceptable to those who hired you.)

4. Vonnegut's story is set in the distant future, but are there any aspects of the society he imagines—for instance, Hazel and George's inability to think for more than a few seconds at a time, or the need for outstanding people to apologize for their excellence (paragraph 41)—that could be read as **symbolic** of realities today? Explain.

FLANNERY O'CONNOR (1925–1964)

Everything That Rises Must Converge

Her doctor had told Julian's mother that she must lose twenty pounds on ac- 1
count of her blood pressure, so on Wednesday nights Julian had to take her downtown on the bus for a reducing class at the Y. The reducing class was designed for working girls over fifty, who weighed from 165 to 200 pounds. His mother was one of the slimmer ones, but she said ladies did not tell their age or weight. She would not ride the buses by herself at night since they had been integrated, and because the reducing class was one of her few pleasures, necessary for her health, and *free*, she said Julian could at least put himself out to take her, considering all she did for him. Julian did not like to consider all she did for him, but every Wednesday night he braced himself and took her.

She was almost ready to go, standing before the hall mirror, putting on her 2
hat, while he, his hands behind him, appeared pinned to the door frame, waiting like Saint Sebastian for the arrows to begin piercing him. The hat was new and had cost her seven dollars and a half. She kept saying, "Maybe I shouldn't have paid that for it. No, I shouldn't have. I'll take it off and return it tomorrow. I shouldn't have bought it."

Julian raised his eyes to heaven. "Yes, you should have bought it," he said. 3
"Put it on and let's go." It was a hideous hat. A purple velvet flap came down on one side of it and stood up on the other; the rest of it was green and looked like a cushion with the stuffing out. He decided it was less comical than jaunty and pathetic. Everything that gave her pleasure was small and depressed him.

She lifted the hat one more time and set it down slowly on top of her head. 4
Two wings of gray hair protruded on either side of her florid face, but her eyes, sky-blue, were as innocent and untouched by experience as they must have been when she was ten. Were it not that she was a widow who had struggled fiercely to feed and clothe and put him through school and who was supporting him still, "until he got on his feet," she might have been a little girl that he had to take to town.

"It's all right, it's all right," he said. "Let's go." He opened the door himself 5
and started down the walk to get her going. The sky was a dying violet and the
houses stood out darkly against it, bulbous liver-colored monstrosities of a uniform ugliness though no two were alike. Since this had been a fashionable
neighborhood forty years ago, his mother persisted in thinking they did well to
have an apartment in it. Each house had a narrow collar of dirt around it in
which sat, usually, a grubby child. Julian walked with his hands in his pockets,
his head down and thrust forward, and his eyes glazed with the determination
to make himself completely numb during the time he would be sacrificed to
her pleasure.

The door closed and he turned to find the dumpy figure, surmounted by 6
the atrocious hat, coming toward him. "Well," she said, "you only live once and
paying a little more for it, I at least won't meet myself coming and going."

"Some day I'll start making money," Julian said gloomily—he knew he 7
never would—"and you can have one of those jokes whenever you take the fit."
But first they would move. He visualized a place where the nearest neighbor
would be three miles away on either side.

"I think you're doing fine," she said, drawing on her gloves. "You've only 8
been out of school a year. Rome wasn't built in a day."

She was one of the few members of the Y reducing class who arrived in hat 9
and gloves and who had a son who had been to college. "It takes time," she said,
"and the world is in such a mess. This hat looked better on me than any of the
others, though when she brought it out I said, 'Take that thing back. I wouldn't
have it on my head,' and she said, 'Now wait till you see it on,' and when she put
it on me, I said, 'We-ull,' and she said, 'If you ask me, that hat does something
for you and you do something for the hat, and besides,' she said, 'with that hat,
you won't meet yourself coming and going.' "

Julian thought he could have stood his lot better if she had been selfish, if 10
she had been an old hag who drank and screamed at him. He walked along, saturated in depression, as if in the midst of his martyrdom he had lost his faith.
Catching sight of his long, hopeless, irritated face, she stopped suddenly with a
grief-stricken look, and pulled back on his arm. "Wait on me," she said. "I'm going back to the house and take this thing off and tomorrow I'm going to return
it. I was out of my head. I can pay the gas bill with the seven-fifty."

He caught her arm in a vicious grip. "You are not going to take it back," he 11
said. "I like it."

"Well," she said, "I don't think I ought . . ." 12

"Shut up and enjoy it," he muttered, more depressed than ever. 13

"With the world in the mess it's in," she said, "it's a wonder we can enjoy 14
anything. I tell you, the bottom rail is on the top."

Julian sighed. 15

"Of course," she said, "if you know who you are, you can go anywhere." She 16
said this every time he took her to the reducing class. "Most of them in it are
not our kind of people," she said, "but I can be gracious to anybody. I know who
I am."

"They don't give a damn for your graciousness," Julian said savagely. 17
"Knowing who you are is good for one generation only. You haven't the foggiest
idea where you stand now or who you are."

She stopped and allowed her eyes to flash at him. "I most certainly do know 18
who I am," she said, "and if you don't know who you are, I'm ashamed of you."

"Oh hell," Julian said. 19

"Your great-grandfather was a former governor of this state," she said. "Your 20
grandfather was a prosperous landowner. Your grandmother was a Godhigh."

"Will you look around you," he said tensely, "and see where you are now?" 21
and he swept his arm jerkily out to indicate the neighborhood, which the growing darkness at least made less dingy.

"You remain what you are," she said. "Your great-grandfather had a planta- 22
tion and two hundred slaves."

"There are no more slaves," he said irritably. 23

"They were better off when they were," she said. He groaned to see that she 24
was off on that topic. She rolled onto it every few days like a train on an open
track. He knew every stop, every junction, every swamp along the way, and
knew the exact point at which her conclusion would roll majestically into the
station: "It's ridiculous. It's simply not realistic. They should rise, yes, but on
their own side of the fence."

"Let's skip it," Julian said. 25

"The ones I feel sorry for," she said, "are the ones that are half white. They're 26
tragic."

"Will you skip it?" 27

"Suppose we were half white. We would certainly have mixed feelings." 28

"I have mixed feelings now," he groaned. 29

"Well let's talk about something pleasant," she said. "I remember going 30
to Grandpa's when I was a little girl. Then the house had double stairways
that went up to what was really the second floor—all the cooking was done
on the first. I used to like to stay down in the kitchen on account of the way the
walls smelled. I would sit with my nose pressed against the plaster and
take deep breaths. Actually the place belonged to the Godhighs but your grandfather Chestny paid the mortgage and saved it for them. They were in reduced circumstances," she said, "but reduced or not, they never forgot who they
were."

"Doubtless that decayed mansion reminded them," Julian muttered. He 31
never spoke of it without contempt or thought of it without longing. He had
seen it once when he was a child before it had been sold. The double stairways
had rotted and had been torn down. Negroes were living in it. But it remained
in his mind as his mother had known it. It appeared in his dreams regularly. He
would stand on the wide porch, listening to the rustle of oak leaves, then wander through the high-ceilinged hall into the parlor that opened onto it and gaze
at the worn rugs and faded draperies. It occurred to him that it was he, not she,
who would have appreciated it. He preferred its threadbare elegance to anything he could name and it was because of it that all the neighborhoods they

had lived in had been a torment to him—whereas she had hardly known the difference. She called her insensitivity "being adjustable."

"And I remember the old darky who was my nurse, Caroline. There was no 32 better person in the world. I've always had a great respect for my colored friends," she said. "I'd do anything in the world for them and they'd . . ."

"Will you for God's sake get off that subject?" Julian said. When he got on a 33 bus by himself, he made it a point to sit down beside a Negro, in reparation as it were for his mother's sins.

"You're mighty touchy tonight," she said. "Do you feel all right?" 34

"Yes I feel all right," he said. "Now lay off." 35

She pursed her lips. "Well, you certainly are in a vile humor," she observed. 36 "I just won't speak to you at all."

They had reached the bus stop. There was no bus in sight and Julian, his 37 hands still jammed in his pockets and his head thrust forward, scowled down the empty street. The frustration of having to wait on the bus as well as ride on it began to creep up his neck like a hot hand. The presence of his mother was borne in upon him as she gave a pained sigh. He looked at her bleakly. She was holding herself very erect under the preposterous hat, wearing it like a banner of her imaginary dignity. There was in him an evil urge to break her spirit. He suddenly unloosened his tie and pulled it off and put it in his pocket.

She stiffened. "Why must you look like *that* when you take me to town?" she 38 said. "Why must you deliberately embarrass me?"

"If you'll never learn where you are," he said, "you can at least learn where I 39 am."

"You look like a—thug," she said. 40

"Then I must be one," he murmured. 41

"I'll just go home," she said. "I will not bother you. If you can't do a little 42 thing like that for me . . ."

Rolling his eyes upward, he put his tie back on. "Restored to my class," he 43 muttered. He thrust his face toward her and hissed, "True culture is in the mind, the *mind*," he said, and tapped his head, "the mind."

"It's in the heart," she said, "and in how you do things and how you do 44 things is because of who you *are*."

"Nobody in the damn bus cares who you are." 45

"I care who I am," she said icily. 46

The lighted bus appeared on top of the next hill and as it approached, they 47 moved out into the street to meet it. He put his hand under her elbow and hoisted her up on the creaking step. She entered with a little smile, as if she were going into a drawing room where everyone had been waiting for her. While he put in the tokens, she sat down on one of the broad front seats for three which faced the aisle. A thin woman with protruding teeth and long yellow hair was sitting on the end of it. His mother moved up beside her and left room for Julian beside herself. He sat down and looked at the floor across the aisle where a pair of thin feet in red and white canvas sandals were planted.

His mother immediately began a general conversation meant to attract any- 48 one who felt like talking. "Can it get any hotter?" she said and removed from her purse a folding fan, black with a Japanese scene on it, which she began to flutter before her.

"I reckon it might could," the woman with the protruding teeth said, "but I 49 know for a fact my apartment couldn't get no hotter."

"It must get the afternoon sun," his mother said. She sat forward and looked 50 up and down the bus. It was half filled. Everybody was white. "I see we have the bus to ourselves," she said. Julian cringed.

"For a change," said the woman across the aisle, the owner of the red and 51 white canvas sandals. "I come on one the other day and they were thick as fleas—up front and all through."

"The world is in a mess everywhere," his mother said. "I don't know how 52 we've let it get in this fix."

"What gets my goat is all those boys from good families stealing automobile 53 tires," the woman with the protruding teeth said. "I told my boy, I said you may not be rich but you been raised right and if I ever catch you in any such mess, they can send you on to the reformatory. Be exactly where you belong."

"Training tells," his mother said. "Is your boy in high school?" 54

"Ninth grade," the woman said. 55

"My son just finished college last year. He wants to write but he's selling 56 typewriters until he gets started," his mother said.

The woman leaned forward and peered at Julian. He threw her such a 57 malevolent look that she subsided against the seat. On the floor across the aisle there was an abandoned newspaper. He got up and got it and opened it out in front of him. His mother discreetly continued the conversation in a lower tone but the woman across the aisle said in a loud voice, "Well that's nice. Selling typewriters is close to writing. He can go right from one to the other."

"I tell him," his mother said, "that Rome wasn't built in a day." 58

Behind the newspaper Julian was withdrawing into the inner compartment 59 of his mind where he spent most of his time. This was a kind of mental bubble in which he established himself when he could not bear to be part of what was going on around him. From it he could see out and judge but in it he was safe from any kind of penetration from without. It was the only place where he felt free of the general idiocy of his fellows. His mother had never entered it but from it he could see her with absolute clarity.

The old lady was clever enough and he thought that if she had started from 60 any of the right premises, more might have been expected of her. She lived according to the laws of her own fantasy world, outside of which he had never seen her set foot. The law of it was to sacrifice herself for him after she had first created the necessity to do so by making a mess of things. If he had permitted her sacrifices, it was only because her lack of foresight had made them necessary. All of her life had been a struggle to act like a Chestny without the Chestny goods, and to give him everything she thought a Chestny ought to have; but since, said she, it was fun to struggle, why complain? And when you had won, as she had won, what fun to look back on the hard times! He could not forgive her that she had enjoyed the struggle and that she thought *she* had won.

What she meant when she said she had won was that she had brought him 61 up successfully and had sent him to college and that he had turned out so well—good looking (her teeth had gone unfilled, so that his could be straightened), intelligent (he realized he was too intelligent to be a success), and with a future ahead of him (there was of course no future ahead of him). She excused his gloominess on the grounds that he was still growing up and his radical ideas on his lack of practical experience. She said he didn't yet know a thing about "life," that he hadn't even entered the real world—when already he was as disenchanted with it as a man of fifty.

The further irony of all this was that in spite of her, he had turned out so 62 well. In spite of going to only a third-rate college, he had, on his own initiative, come out with a first-rate education; in spite of growing up dominated by a small mind, he had ended up with a large one; in spite of all her foolish views, he was free of prejudice and unafraid to face facts. Most miraculous of all, instead of being blinded by love for her as she was for him, he had cut himself emotionally free of her and could see her with complete objectivity. He was not dominated by his mother.

The bus stopped with a sudden jerk and shook him from his meditation. A 63 woman from the back lurched forward with little steps and barely escaped falling in his newspaper as she righted herself. She got off and a large Negro got on. Julian kept his paper lowered to watch. It gave him a certain satisfaction to see injustice in daily operation. It confirmed his view that with a few exceptions there was no one worth knowing within a radius of three hundred miles. The Negro was well dressed and carried a briefcase. He looked round and then sat down on the other end of the seat where the woman with the red and white canvas sandals was sitting. He immediately unfolded a newspaper and obscured himself behind it. Julian's mother's elbow at once prodded insistently into his ribs. "Now you see why I won't ride on these buses by myself," she whispered.

The woman with the red and white canvas sandals had risen at the same 64 time the Negro sat down and had gone further back in the bus and taken the seat of the woman who had got off. His mother leaned forward and cast her an approving look.

Julian rose, crossed the aisle, and sat down in the place of the woman with 65 the canvas sandals. From this position, he looked serenely across at his mother. Her face had turned an angry red. He stared at her, making his eyes the eyes of a stranger. He felt his tension suddenly lift as if he had openly declared war on her.

He would have liked to get in conversation with the Negro and to talk with 66 him about art or politics or any subject that would be above the comprehension of those around them, but the man remained entrenched behind his paper. He was either ignoring the change of seating or had never noticed it. There was no way for Julian to convey his sympathy.

His mother kept her eyes fixed reproachfully on his face. The woman with 67
the protruding teeth was looking at him avidly as if he were a type of monster
new to her.

"Do you have a light?" he asked the Negro. 68

Without looking away from his paper, the man reached in his pocket and 69
handed him a packet of matches.

"Thanks," Julian said. For a moment he held the matches foolishly. A NO 70
SMOKING sign looked down upon him from over the door. This alone would not
have deterred him; he had no cigarettes. He had quit smoking some months before because he could not afford it. "Sorry," he muttered and handed back the
matches. The Negro lowered the paper and gave him an annoyed look. He took
the matches and raised the paper again.

His mother continued to gaze at him but she did not take the advantage of 71
his momentary discomfort. Her eyes retained their battered look. Her face
seemed to be unnaturally red, as if her blood pressure had risen. Julian allowed
no glimmer of sympathy to show on his face. Having got the advantage, he
wanted desperately to keep it and carry it through. He would have liked to teach
her a lesson that would last her a while, but there seemed no way to continue
the point. The Negro refused to come out from behind his paper.

Julian folded his arms and looked stolidly before him, facing her but as if he 72
did not see her, as if he had ceased to recognize her existence. He visualized a
scene in which, the bus having reached their stop, he would remain in his seat
and when she said, "Aren't you going to get off?" he would look at her as a
stranger who had rashly addressed him. The corner they got off on was usually
deserted, but it was well lighted and it would not hurt her to walk by herself the
four blocks to the Y. He decided to wait until the time came and then decide
whether or not he would let her get off by herself. He would have to be at the Y
at ten to bring her back, but he could leave her wondering if he was going to
show up. There was no reason for her to think she could always depend on him.

He retired again into the high-ceilinged room sparsely settled with large 73
pieces of antique furniture. His soul expanded momentarily but then he became aware of his mother across from him and the vision shriveled. He studied
her coldly. Her feet in little pumps dangled like a child's and did not quite reach
the floor. She was training on him an exaggerated look of reproach. He felt
completely detached from her. At that moment he could with pleasure have
slapped her as he would have slapped a particularly obnoxious child in his
charge.

He began to imagine various unlikely ways by which he could teach her a 74
lesson. He might make friends with some distinguished Negro professor or
lawyer and bring him home to spend the evening. He would be entirely justified
but her blood pressure would rise to 300. He could not push her to the extent of
making her have a stroke, and moreover, he had never been successful at making any Negro friends. He had tried to strike up an acquaintance on the bus
with some of the better types, with ones that looked like professors or ministers
or lawyers. One morning he had sat down next to a distinguished-looking dark

brown man who had answered his questions with a sonorous solemnity but who had turned out to be an undertaker. Another day he had sat down beside a cigar-smoking Negro with a diamond ring on his finger, but after a few stilted pleasantries, the Negro had rung the buzzer and risen, slipping two lottery tickets into Julian's hand as he climbed over him to leave.

He imagined his mother lying desperately ill and his being able to secure 75 only a Negro doctor for her. He toyed with that idea for a few minutes and dropped it for a momentary vision of himself participating as a sympathizer in a sit-in demonstration. This was possible but he did not linger with it. Instead, he approached the ultimate horror. He brought home a beautiful suspiciously Negroid woman. Prepare yourself, he said. There is nothing you can do about it. This is the woman I've chosen. She's intelligent, dignified, even good, and she's suffered and she hasn't thought it *fun*. Now persecute us, go ahead and persecute us. Drive her out of here, but remember, you're driving me too. His eyes were narrowed and through the indignation he had generated, he saw his mother across the aisle, purplefaced, shrunken to the dwarf-like proportions of her moral nature, sitting like a mummy beneath the ridiculous banner of her hat.

He was tilted out of his fantasy again as the bus stopped. The door opened 76 with a sucking hiss and out of the dark a large, gaily dressed, sullen-looking colored woman got on with a little boy. The child, who might have been four, had on a short plaid suit and a Tyrolean hat with a blue feather in it. Julian hoped that he would sit down beside him and that the woman would push in beside his mother. He could think of no better arrangement.

As she waited for her tokens, the woman was surveying the seating possibil- 77 ities—he hoped with the idea of sitting where she was least wanted. There was something familiar-looking about her but Julian could not place what it was. She was a giant of a woman. Her face was set not only to meet opposition but to seek it out. The downward tilt of her large lower lip was like a warning sign: DON'T TAMPER WITH ME. Her bulging figure was encased in a green crepe dress and her feet overflowed in red shoes. She had on a hideous hat. A purple velvet flap came down on one side of it and stood up on the other; the rest of it was green and looked like a cushion with the stuffing out. She carried a mammoth red pocketbook that bulged throughout as if it were stuffed with rocks.

To Julian's disappointment, the little boy climbed up on the empty seat be- 78 side his mother. His mother lumped all children, black and white, into the common category, "cute," and she thought little Negroes were on the whole cuter than little white children. She smiled at the little boy as he climbed on the seat.

Meanwhile the woman was bearing down upon the empty seat beside Ju- 79 lian. To his annoyance, she squeezed herself into it. He saw his mother's face change as the woman settled herself next to him and he realized with satisfaction that this was more objectionable to her than it was to him. Her face seemed almost gray and there was a look of dull recognition in her eyes, as if suddenly she had sickened at some awful confrontation. Julian saw that it was because she and the woman had, in a sense, swapped sons. Though his mother would not realize the symbolic significance of this, she would feel it. His amusement showed plainly on his face.

The woman next to him muttered something unintelligible to herself. He 80 was conscious of a kind of bristling next to him, muted growling like that of an angry cat. He could not see anything but the red pocketbook upright on the bulging green thighs. He visualized the woman as she had stood waiting for her tokens—the ponderous figure, rising from the red shoes upward over the solid hips, the mammoth bosom, the haughty face, to the green and purple hat.

His eyes widened. 81

The vision of the two hats, identical, broke upon him with the radiance of a 82 brilliant sunrise. His face was suddenly lit with joy. He could not believe that Fate had thrust upon his mother such a lesson. He gave a loud chuckle so that she would look at him and see that he saw. She turned her eyes on him slowly. The blue in them seemed to have turned a bruised purple. For a moment he had an uncomfortable sense of her innocence, but it lasted only a second before principle rescued him. Justice entitled him to laugh. His grin hardened until it said to her as plainly as if he were saying aloud: Your punishment exactly fits your pettiness. This should teach you a permanent lesson.

Her eyes shifted to the woman. She seemed unable to bear looking at him and 83 to find the woman preferable. He became conscious again of the bristling presence at his side. The woman was rumbling like a volcano about to become active. His mother's mouth began to twitch slightly at one corner. With a sinking heart, he saw incipient signs of recovery on her face and realized that this was going to strike her suddenly as funny and was going to be no lesson at all. She kept her eyes on the woman and an amused smile came over her face as if the woman were a monkey that had stolen her hat. The little Negro was looking up at her with large fascinated eyes. He had been trying to attract her attention for some time.

"Carver," the woman said suddenly. "Come heah!" 84

When he saw that the spotlight was on him at last, Carver drew his feet up 85 and turned himself toward Julian's mother and giggled.

"Carver!" the woman said. "You heah me? Come heah!" 86

Carver slid down from the seat but remained squatting with his back 87 against the base of it, his head turned slowly around toward Julian's mother, who was smiling at him. The woman reached a hand across the aisle and snatched him to her. He righted himself and hung backwards on her knees, grinning at Julian's mother. "Isn't he cute?" Julian's mother said to the woman with the protruding teeth.

"I reckon he is," the woman said without conviction. 88

The Negress yanked him upright but he eased out of her grip and shot 89 across the aisle and scrambled, giggling wildly, onto the seat beside his love.

"I think he likes me," Julian's mother said, and smiled at the woman. It was 90 the smile she used when she was being particularly gracious to an inferior. Julian saw everything lost. The lesson had rolled off her like rain on a roof.

The woman stood up and yanked the little boy off the seat as if she were 91 snatching him from contagion. Julian could feel the rage in her at having no weapon like his mother's smile. She gave the child a sharp slap across his leg. He howled once and then thrust his head into her stomach and kicked his feet against her shins. "Behave," she said vehemently.

The bus stopped and the Negro who had been reading the newspaper got   92
off. The woman moved over and set the little boy down with a thump between herself and Julian. She held him firmly by the knee. In a moment he put his hands in front of his face and peeped at Julian's mother through his fingers.

"I see yoooooooo!" she said and put her hand in front of her face and   93
peeped at him.

The woman slapped his hand down. "Quit yo' foolishness," she said, "before   94
I knock the living Jesus out of you!"

Julian was thankful that the next stop was theirs. He reached up and pulled   95
the cord. The woman reached up and pulled it at the same time. Oh my God, he thought. He had the terrible intuition that when they got off the bus together, his mother would open her purse and give the little boy a nickel. The gesture would be as natural to her as breathing. The bus stopped and the woman got up and lunged to the front, dragging the child, who wished to stay on, after her. Julian and his mother got up and followed. As they neared the door, Julian tried to relieve her of her pocketbook.

"No," she murmured, "I want to give the little boy a nickel."   96

"No!" Julian hissed. "No!"   97

She smiled down at the child and opened her bag. The bus door opened and   98
the woman picked him up by the arm and descended with him, hanging at her hip. Once in the street she set him down and shook him.

Julian's mother had to close her purse while she got down the bus step but as   99
soon as her feet were on the ground, she opened it again and began to rummage inside. "I can't find but a penny," she whispered, "but it looks like a new one."

"Don't do it!" Julian said fiercely between his teeth. There was a streetlight   100
on the corner and she hurried to get under it so that she could better see into her pocketbook. The woman was heading off rapidly down the street with the child still hanging backward on her hand.

"Oh little boy!" Julian's mother called and took a few quick steps and caught   101
up with them just beyond the lamppost. "Here's a bright new penny for you," and she held out the coin, which shone bronze in the dim light.

The huge woman turned and for a moment stood, her shoulders lifted and   102
her face frozen with frustrated rage, and stared at Julian's mother. Then all at once she seemed to explode like a piece of machinery that had been given one ounce of pressure too much. Julian saw the black fist swing out with the red pocketbook. He shut his eyes and cringed as he heard the woman shout, "He don't take nobody's pennies!" When he opened his eyes, the woman was disappearing down the street with the little boy staring wide-eyed over her shoulder. Julian's mother was sitting on the sidewalk.

"I told you not to do that," Julian said angrily. "I told you not to do that!"   103

He stood over her for a minute, gritting his teeth. Her legs were stretched   104
out in front of her and her hat was on her lap. He squatted down and looked

her in the face. It was totally expressionless. "You got exactly what you deserved," he said. "Now get up."

He picked up her pocketbook and put what had fallen out back in it. He 105
picked the hat up off her lap. The penny caught his eye on the sidewalk and he picked that up and let it drop before her eyes into the purse. Then he stood up and leaned over and held his hands out to pull her up. She remained immobile. He sighed. Rising above them on either side were black apartment buildings, marked with irregular rectangles of light. At the end of the block a man came out of a door and walked off in the opposite direction. "All right," he said, "suppose somebody happens by and wants to know why you're sitting on the sidewalk?"

She took the hand and, breathing hard, pulled heavily up on it and then 106
stood for a moment, swaying slightly as if the spots of light in the darkness were circling around her. Her eyes, shadowed and confused, finally settled on his face. He did not try to conceal his irritation. "I hope this teaches you a lesson," he said. She leaned forward and her eyes raked his face. She seemed trying to determine his identity. Then, as if she found nothing familiar about him, she started off with a headlong movement in the wrong direction.

"Aren't you going to the Y?" he asked.   107

"Home," she muttered.   108

"Well, are we walking?"   109

For answer she kept going. Julian followed along, his hands behind him. He 110
saw no reason to let the lesson she had had go without backing it up with an explanation of its meaning. She might as well be made to understand what had happened to her. "Don't think that was just an uppity Negro woman," he said. "That was the whole colored race which will no longer take your condescending pennies. That was your black double. She can wear the same hat as you, and to be sure," he added gratuitously (because he thought it was funny), "it looked better on her than it did on you. What all this means," he said, "is that the old world is gone. The old manners are obsolete and your graciousness is not worth a damn." He thought bitterly of the house that had been lost for him. "You aren't who you think you are," he said.

She continued to plow ahead, paying no attention to him. Her hair had 111
come undone on one side. She dropped her pocketbook and took no notice. He stopped and picked it up and handed it to her but she did not take it.

"You needn't act as if the world had come to an end," he said, "because it 112
hasn't. From now on you've got to live in a new world and face a few realities for a change. Buck up," he said, "it won't kill you."

She was breathing fast.   113

"Let's wait on the bus," he said.   114

"Home," she said thickly.   115

"I hate to see you behave like this," he said. "Just like a child. I should be able 116
to expect more of you." He decided to stop where he was and make her stop and wait for a bus. "I'm not going any farther," he said, stopping. "We're going on the bus."

She continued to go on as if she had not heard him. He took a few steps and 117
caught her arm and stopped her. He looked into her face and caught his breath.
He was looking into a face he had never seen before. "Tell Grandpa to come get
me," she said.

He stared, stricken.   118

"Tell Caroline to come get me," she said.   119

Stunned, he let her go and she lurched forward again, walking as if one leg 120
were shorter than the other. A tide of darkness seemed to be sweeping her from
him. "Mother!" he cried. "Darling, sweetheart, wait!" Crumpling, she fell to the
pavement. He dashed forward and fell at her side, crying, "Mamma, Mamma!"
He turned her over. Her face was fiercely distorted. One eye, large and staring,
moved slightly to the left as if it had become unmoored. The other remained
fixed on him, raked his face again, found nothing, and closed.

"Wait here, wait here!" he cried and jumped up and began to run for help   121
toward a cluster of lights he saw in the distance ahead of him. "Help, help!" he
shouted, but his voice was thin, scarcely a thread of sound. The lights drifted
farther away the faster he ran and his feet moved numbly as if they carried him
nowhere. The tide of darkness seemed to sweep him back to her, postponing
from moment to moment his entry into the world of guilt and sorrow.

ACTIVITIES FOR WRITING AND DISCUSSION

1. Working alone or with a group, make a list of conflicts—personal, social,
moral—that make this story suspenseful. Identify places where your interest
was greatest and why.

2. Pick one specific *moment* or *scene* in the story that is particularly intense
or powerful for you. Annotate or reannotate that passage, emphasizing aspects
of the moment or scene that make it tense. Then:
   a. Share your scene and annotations with a small group.
   b. Write an analysis of the moment or scene you have chosen and ex-
      plain how it reinforces the impact of the story as a whole.

3. Describe the **point of view** of the story. Then return to the moment or
scene you examined in Activity #2 and rewrite it from the **first-person** point of
view of either Julian, Julian's mother, or some other character in the story. What
is lost, gained, or changed by using the alternative point of view?

4. Julian believes that his mother "lived according to the laws of her own
fantasy world. . . ." Could the same be said of Julian himself? Assuming the
point of view of some detached observer (e.g., one of Julian's college counselors
or professors, his boss at the typewriter business) compose an informal letter of
evaluation that describes what Julian's "fantasy world" is.

5. Imagine you are Julian.

a. What thoughts and feelings go through your mind the moment after your mother collapses on the pavement at the end of the story? Write out the rapid flow of thoughts exactly as they occur to you.

b. Writing from Julian's point of view or some other, draft a sequel to the story. What becomes of Julian? Is he changed by the events in the story? If not, why not? If so, how—and for better or for worse?

6. O'Connor once described her stories as "parables." A parable is "a simple story illustrating a moral or religious lesson" *(American Heritage College Dictionary)*. Is the term applicable to "Everything That Rises Must Converge," and, if so, what "moral or religious lesson" does the story illustrate?

Alice Walker (b. 1944)

Nineteen Fifty-five

1955

The car is a brandnew red Thunderbird convertible, and it's passed the house 1 more than once. It slows down real slow now, and stops at the curb. An older gentleman dressed like a Baptist deacon gets out on the side near the house, and a young fellow who looks about sixteen gets out on the driver's side. They are white, and I wonder what in the world they doing in this neighborhood.

Well, I say to J. T., put your shirt on, anyway, and let me clean these glasses 2 offa the table.

We had been watching the ballgame on TV. I wasn't actually watching, I was 3 sort of daydreaming, with my foots up in J. T.'s lap.

I seen 'em coming on up the walk, brisk, like they coming to sell something, 4 and then they rung the bell, and J. T. declined to put on a shirt but instead disappeared into the bedroom where the other television is. I turned down the one in the living room; I figured I'd be rid of these two double quick and J. T. could come back out again.

Are you Gracie Mae Still? asked the old guy, when I opened the door and 5 put my hand on the lock inside the screen

And I don't need to buy a thing, said I. 6

What makes you think we're sellin'? he asks, in that hearty Southern way 7 that makes my eyeballs ache.

Well, one way or another and they're inside the house and the first thing the 8 young fellow does is raise the TV a couple of decibels. He's about five feet nine, sort of womanish looking, with real dark white skin and a red pouting mouth. His hair is black and curly and he looks like a Loosianna creole.

About one of your songs, says the deacon. He is maybe sixty, with white hair 9
and beard, white silk shirt, black linen suit, black tie and black shoes. His cold
grey eyes look like they're sweating.

One of my songs? 10

Traynor here just *loves* your songs. Don't you, Traynor? He nudges Traynor 11
with his elbow. Traynor blinks, says something I can't catch in a pitch I don't
register.

The boy learned to sing and dance livin' round you people out in the coun- 12
try. Practically cut his teeth on you.

Traynor looks up at me and bites his thumbnail. 13

I laugh. 14

Well, one way or another they leave with my agreement that they can record 15
one of my songs. The deacon writes me a check for five hundred dollars, the
boy grunts his awareness of the transaction, and I am laughing all over myself
by the time I rejoin J. T.

Just as I am snuggling down beside him though I hear the front door bell 16
going off again.

Forgit his hat? asks J. T. 17

I hope not, I say. 18

The deacon stands there leaning on the door frame and once again I'm 19
thinking of those sweaty-looking eyeballs of his. I wonder if sweat makes your
eyeballs pink because his are sure pink. Pink and gray and it strikes me that nobody I'd care to know is behind them.

I forgot one little thing, he says pleasantly. I forgot to tell you Traynor and I 20
would like to buy up all of those records you made of the song. I tell you we
sure do love it.

Well, love it or not, I'm not so stupid as to let them do that without making 21
'em pay. So I says, Well, that's gonna cost you. Because, really, that song never
did sell all that good, so I was glad they was going to buy it up. But on the other
hand, them two listening to my song by themselves, and nobody else getting to
hear me sing it, give me a pause.

Well, one way or another the deacon showed me where I would come out 22
ahead on any deal he had proposed so far. Didn't I give you five hundred dollars? he asked. What white man—and don't even need to mention colored—
would give you more? We buy up all your records of that particular song: first,
you git royalties. Let me ask you, how much you sell that song for in the first
place? Fifty dollars? A hundred, I say. And no royalties from it yet, right? Right.
Well, when we buy up all of them records you gonna git royalties. And that's
gonna make all them race record shops sit up and take notice of Gracie Mae
Still. And they gonna push all them other records of yourn they got. And you
no doubt will become one of the big name colored recording artists. And then
we can offer you another five hundred dollars for letting us do all this for you.
And by God you'll be sittin' pretty! You can go out and buy you the kind of outfit a star should have. Plenty sequins and yards of red satin.

I had done unlocked the screen when I saw I could get some more money 23
out of him. Now I held it wide open while he squeezed through the opening

between me and the door. He whipped out another piece of paper and I signed it.

He sort of trotted out to the car and slid in beside Traynor, whose head was 24 back against the seat. They swung around in a u-turn in front of the house and then they was gone.

J. T. was putting his shirt on when I got back to the bedroom. Yankees beat 25 the Orioles 10–6, he said. I believe I'll drive out to Paschal's pond and go fishing. Wanta go?

While I was putting on my pants J. T. was holding the two checks. 26

I'm real proud of a woman that can make cash money without leavin' home, 27 he said. And I said *Umph*. Because we met on the road with me singing in first one little low-life jook after another, making ten dollars a night for myself if I was lucky, and sometimes bringin' home nothing but my life. And J. T. just loved them times. The way I was fast and flashy and always on the go from one town to another. He loved the way my singin' made the dirt farmers cry like babies and the womens shout Honey, hush! But that's mens. They loves any style to which you can get 'em accustomed.

1956

My little grandbaby called me one night on the phone: Little Mama, Little 28 Mama, there's a white man on the television singing one of your songs! Turn on channel 5.

Lord, if it wasn't Traynor. Still looking half asleep from the neck up, but 29 kind of awake in a nasty way from the waist down. He wasn't doing too bad with my song either, but it wasn't just the song the people in the audience was screeching and screaming over, it was that nasty little jerk he was doing from the waist down.

Well, Lord have mercy, I said, listening to him. If I'da closed my eyes, it 30 could have been me. He had followed every turning of my voice, side streets, avenues, red lights, train crossings and all. It give me a chill.

Everywhere I went I heard Traynor singing my song, and all the little white 31 girls just eating it up. I never had so many ponytails switched across my line of vision in my life. They was so *proud*. He was a *genius*.

Well, all that year I was trying to lose weight anyway and that and high 32 blood pressure and sugar kept me pretty well occupied. Traynor had made a smash from a song of mine, I still had seven hundred dollars of the original one thousand dollars in the bank, and I felt if I could just bring my weight down, life would be sweet.

1957

I lost ten pounds in 1956. That's what I give myself for Christmas. And J. T. and 33 me and the children and their friends and grandkids of all description had just finished dinner—over which I had put on nine and a half of my lost ten—when who should appear at the front door but Traynor. Little Mama, Little Mama! It's that white man who sings —— —— ——. The children didn't call it my song anymore. Nobody did. It was funny how that happened. Traynor and the deacon had bought up all my records, true, but on his record he had put "written by Gracie Mae Still." But that was just another name on the label, like "produced by Apex Records."

On the TV he was inclined to dress like the deacon told him. But now he looked presentable.   34

Merry Christmas, said he.   35

And same to you, Son.   36

I don't know why I called him Son. Well, one way or another they're all our sons. The only requirement is that they be younger than us. But then again, Traynor seemed to be aging by the minute.   37

You looks tired, I said. Come on in and have a glass of Christmas cheer.   38

J. T. ain't never in his life been able to act decent to a white man he wasn't working for, but he poured Traynor a glass of bourbon and water, then he took all the children and grandkids and friends and whatnot out to the den. After while I heard Traynor's voice singing the song, coming from the stereo console. It was just the kind of Christmas present my kids would consider cute.   39

I looked at Traynor, complicit. But he looked like it was the last thing in the world he wanted to hear. His head was pitched forward over his lap, his hands holding his glass and his elbows on his knees.   40

I done sung that song seem like a million times this year, he said. I sung it on the Grand Ole Opry, I sung it on the Ed Sullivan show. I sung it on Mike Douglas, I sung it at the Cotton Bowl, the Orange Bowl. I sung it at Festivals. I sung it at Fairs. I sung it overseas in Rome, Italy, and once in a submarine *underseas.* I've sung it and sung it, and I'm making forty thousand dollars a day offa it, and you know what, I don't have the faintest notion what that song means.   41

Whatchumean, what do it mean? It mean what it says. All I could think was: These suckers is making forty thousand a *day* offa my song and now they gonna come back and try to swindle me out of the original thousand.   42

It's just a song, I said. Cagey. When you fool around with a lot of no count mens you sing a bunch of 'em. I shrugged.   43

Oh, he said. Well. He started brightening up. I just come by to tell you I think you are a great singer.   44

He didn't blush, saying that. Just said it straight out.   45

And I brought you a little Christmas present too. Now you take this little box and you hold it until I drive off. Then you take it outside under that first streetlight back up the street aways in front of that green house. Then you open the box and see . . . Well, just *see.*   46

What had come over this boy, I wondered, holding the box. I looked out the window in time to see another white man come up and get in the car with him and then two more cars full of white mens start out behind him. They was all in long black cars that looked like a funeral procession.   47

Little Mama, Little Mama, what is it? One of my grandkids come running 48
up and started pulling at the box. It was wrapped in gay Christmas paper—the
thick, rich kind that it's hard to picture folks making just to throw away.

J. T. and the rest of the crowd followed me out the house, up the street to the 49
streetlight and in front of the green house. Nothing was there but somebody's
gold-grilled white Cadillac. Brandnew and most distracting. We got to looking
at it so till I almost forgot the little box in my hand. While the others were busy
making 'miration I carefully took off the paper and ribbon and folded them up
and put them in my pants pocket. What should I see but a pair of genuine solid
gold caddy keys.

Dangling the keys in front of everybody's nose, I unlocked the caddy, mo- 50
tioned for J. T. to git in on the other side, and us didn't come back home for two
days.

1960

Well, the boy was sure nuff famous by now. He was still a mite shy of twenty but 51
already they was calling him the Emperor of Rock and Roll.

Then what should happen but the draft.   52

Well, says J. T. There goes all this Emperor of Rock and Roll business.   53

But even in the army the womens was on him like white on rice. We watched 54
it on the News.

Dear Gracie Mae [he wrote from Germany],   55

How you? Fine I hope as this leaves me doing real well. Before I come in the 56
army I was gaining a lot of weight and gitting jittery from making all them dumb
movies. But now I exercise and eat right and get plenty of rest. I'm more awake
than I been in ten years.

I wonder if you are writing any more songs?   57

> *Sincerely,*
> *Traynor*

I wrote him back:

Dear Son,   58

We is all fine in the Lord's good grace and hope this finds you the same. J. T. 59
and me be out all times of the day and night in that car you give me—which you
know you didn't have to do. Oh, and I do appreciate the mink and the new self-
cleaning oven. But if you send anymore stuff to eat from Germany I'm going to
have to open up a store in the neighborhood just to get rid of it. Really, we have
more than enough of everything. The Lord is good to us and we don't know Want.

Glad to hear you is well and gitting your right rest. There ain't nothing like ex- 60
ercising to help that along. J. T. and me work some part of every day that we don't
go fishing in the garden.

Well, so long Soldier.   61

                                           Sincerely,   62
                                           Gracie Mae

He wrote: 63

Dear Gracie Mae,   64

   I hope you and J. T. like that automatic power tiller I had one of the stores back 65
home send you. I went through a mountain of catalogs looking for it—I wanted
something that even a woman could use.

   I've been thinking about writing some songs of my own but every time I finish 66
one it don't seem to be about nothing I've actually lived myself. My agent keeps
sending me other people's songs but they just sound mooney. I can hardly git
through 'em without gagging.

   Everybody still loves that song of yours. They ask me all the time what do I 67
think it means, really. I mean, they want to know just what I want to know. Where
out of your life did it come from?

                                           Sincerely,
                                           Traynor

1968

I didn't see the boy for seven years. No. Eight. Because just about everybody was 68
dead when I saw him again. Malcolm X, King, the president and his brother,
and even J. T. J. T. died of a head cold. It just settled in his head like a block of
ice, he said, and nothing we did moved it until one day he just leaned out the
bed and died.

   His good friend Horace helped me put him away, and then about a year 69
later Horace and me started going together. We was sitting out on the front
porch swing one summer night, dusk-dark, and I saw this great procession of
lights winding to a stop.

   Holy Toledo! said Horace. (He's got a real sexy voice like Ray Charles.) Look 70
at it. He meant the long line of flashy cars and the white men in white summer
suits jumping out on the drivers' sides and standing at attention. With wings
they could pass for angels, with hoods they could be the Klan.

   Traynor comes waddling up the walk.   71

   And suddenly I know what it is he could pass for. An Arab like the ones you 72
see in storybooks. Plump and soft and with never a care about weight. Because
with so much money, who cares? Traynor is almost dressed like someone from
a storybook too. He has on, I swear, about ten necklaces. Two sets of bracelets
on his arms, at least one ring on every finger, and some kind of shining buckles
on his shoes, so that when he walks you get quite a few twinkling lights.

   Gracie Mae, he says, coming up to give me a hug. J. T.   73

   I explain that J. T. passed. That this is Horace.   74

Horace, he says, puzzled but polite, sort of rocking back on his heels, Horace.   75

That's it for Horace. He goes in the house and don't come back.   76

Looks like you and me is gained a few, I say.   77

He laughs. The first time I ever heard him laugh. It don't sound much like a   78
laugh and I can't swear that it's better than no laugh a'tall.

He's gitting fat for sure, but he's still slim compared to me. I'll never see   79
three hundred pounds again and I've just about said (excuse me) fuck it. I got
to thinking about it one day an' I thought: aside from the fact that they say it's
unhealthy, my fat ain't never been no trouble. Mens always have loved me. My
kids ain't never complained. Plus they's fat. And fat like I is I looks distinguished. You see me coming and know somebody's *there.*

Gracie Mae, he says, I've come with a personal invitation to you to my house   80
tomorrow for dinner. He laughed. What did it sound like? I couldn't place it.
See them men out there? he asked me. I'm sick and tired of eating with them.
They don't never have nothing to talk about. That's why I eat so much. But if
you come to dinner tomorrow we can talk about the old days. You can tell me
about that farm I bought you.

I sold it, I said.   81

You did?   82

Yeah, I said, I did. Just cause I said I liked to exercise by working in a garden   83
didn't mean I wanted five hundred acres! Anyhow, I'm a city girl now. Raised in
the country it's true. Dirt poor—the whole bit —but that's all behind me now.

Oh well, he said, I didn't mean to offend you.   84

We sat a few minutes listening to the crickets.   85

Then he said: You wrote that song while you was still on the farm, didn't   86
you, or was it right after you left?

You had somebody spying on me? I asked.   87

You and Bessie Smith got into a fight over it once, he said.   88

You *is* been spying on me!   89

But I don't know what the fight was about, he said. Just like I don't know   90
what happened to your second husband. Your first one died in the Texas electric chair. Did you know that? Your third one beat you up, stole your touring
costumes and your car and retired with a chorine to Tuskegee. He laughed. He's
still there.

I had been mad, but suddenly I calmed down. Traynor was talking very   91
dreamily. It was dark but seems like I could tell his eyes weren't right. It was like
some*thing* was sitting there talking to me but not necessarily with a person behind it.

You gave up on marrying and seem happier for it. He laughed again. I married   92
but it never went like it was supposed to. I never could squeeze any of my own life
either into it or out of it. It was like singing somebody else's record. I copied the
way it was sposed to be *exactly* but I never had a clue what marriage meant.

I bought her a diamond ring big as your fist. I bought her clothes. I built her   93
a mansion. But right away she didn't want the boys to stay there. Said they
smoked up the bottom floor. Hell, there were *five* floors.

No need to grieve, I said. No need to. Plenty more where she come from.   94

He perked up. That's part of what that song means, ain't it? No need to   95
grieve. Whatever it is, there's plenty more down the line.

I never really believed that way back when I wrote that song, I said. It was all   96
bluffing then. The trick is to live long enough to put your young bluffs to use.
Now if I was to sing that song today I'd tear it up. 'Cause I done lived long
enough to know it's *true.* Them words could hold me up.

I ain't lived that long, he said.   97

Look like you on your way, I said. I don't know why, but the boy seemed to   98
need some encouraging. And I don't know, seem like one way or another you
talk to rich white folks and you end up reassuring *them.* But what the hell, by
now I feel something for the boy. I wouldn't be in his bed all alone in the middle
of the night for nothing. Couldn't be nothing worse than being famous the
world over for something you don't even understand. That's what I tried to tell
Bessie. She wanted that same song. Overheard me practicing it one day,
said, with her hands on her hips: Gracie Mae, I'ma sing your song tonight.
I *likes* it.

Your lips be too swole to sing, I said. She was mean and she was strong, but I   99
trounced her.

Ain't you famous enough with your own stuff? I said. Leave mine alone.   100
Later on, she thanked me. By then she was Miss Bessie Smith to the World, and
I was still Miss Gracie Mae Nobody from Notasulga.

The next day all these limousines arrived to pick me up. Five cars and twelve   101
bodyguards. Horace picked that morning to start painting the kitchen.

Don't paint the kitchen, fool, I said. The only reason that dumb boy of ours   102
is going to show me his mansion is because he intends to present us with a new
house.

What you gonna do with it? he asked me, standing there in his shirtsleeves   103
stirring the paint.

Sell it. Give it to the children. Live in it on weekends. It don't matter what I   104
do. He sure don't care.

Horace just stood there shaking his head. Mama you sure looks *good,* he   105
says. Wake me up when you git back.

Fool, I say, and pat my wig in front of the mirror.   106

The boy's house is something else. First you come to this mountain, and then   107
you commence to drive and drive up this road that's lined with magnolias. Do
magnolias grow on mountains? I was wondering. And you come to lakes and
you come to ponds and you come to deer and you come up on some sheep. And
I figure these two is sposed to represent England and Wales. Or something out
of Europe. And you just keep on coming to stuff. And it's all pretty. Only the
man driving my car don't look at nothing but the road. Fool. And then *finally,*

after all this time, you begin to go up the driveway. And there's more magnolias—only they're not in such good shape. It's sort of cool up this high and I don't think they're gonna make it. And then I see this building that looks like if it had a name it would be The Tara Hotel. Columns and steps and outdoor chandeliers and rocking chairs. Rocking chairs? Well, and there's the boy on the steps dressed in a dark green satin jacket like you see folks wearing on TV late at night, and he looks sort of like a fat dracula with all that house rising behind him, and standing beside him there's this little white vision of loveliness that he introduces as his wife.

He's nervous when he introduces us and he says to her: This is Gracie Mae Still, 108 I want you to know me. I mean . . . and she gives him a look that would fry meat.

Won't you come in, Gracie Mae, she says, and that's the last I see of her. 109

He fishes around for something to say or do and decides to escort me to the 110 kitchen. We go through the entry and the parlor and the breakfast room and the dining room and the servants' passage and finally get there. The first thing I notice is that, altogether, there are five stoves. He looks about to introduce me to one.

Wait a minute, I say. Kitchens don't do nothing for me. Let's go sit on the 111 front porch.

Well, we hike back and we sit in the rocking chairs rocking until dinner. 112

Gracie Mae, he says down the table, taking a piece of fried chicken from the 113 woman standing over him, I got a little surprise for you.

It's a house, ain't it? I ask, spearing a chitlin. 114

You're getting *spoiled,* he says. And the way he says *spoiled* sounds funny. He 115 slurs it. It sounds like his tongue is too thick for his mouth. Just that quick he's finished the chicken and is now eating chitlins *and* a pork chop. *Me* spoiled, I'm thinking.

I already got a house. Horace is right this minute painting the kitchen. I 116 bought that house. My kids feel comfortable in that house.

But this one I bought you is just like mine. Only a little smaller. 117

I still don't need no house. And anyway who would clean it? 118

He looks surprised. 119

Really, I think, some peoples advance *so* slowly. 120

I hadn't thought of that. But what the hell, I'll get you somebody to live in. 121

I don't want other folks living 'round me. Makes me nervous. 122

You *don't*? It *do*? 123

What I want to wake up and see folks I don't even know for? 124

He just sits there downtable staring at me. Some of that feeling is in the 125 song, ain't it? Not the words, the *feeling.* What I want to wake up and see folks I don't even know for? But I see twenty folks a day I don't even know, including my wife.

This food wouldn't be bad to wake up to though, I said. The boy had found 126 the genius of corn bread.

He looked at me real hard. He laughed. Short. They want what you got but 127
they don't want you. They want what I got only it ain't mine. That's what makes
'em so hungry for me when I sing. They getting the flavor of something but
they ain't getting the thing itself. They like a pack of hound dogs trying to gobble up a scent.

Your talking 'bout your fans? 128

Right. Right. He says. 129

Don't worry 'bout your fans, I say. They don't know their asses from a hole 130
in the ground. I doubt there's a honest one in the bunch.

That's the point. Dammit, that's the point! He hits the table with his fist. It's 131
so solid it don't even quiver. You need a honest audience! You can't have folks
that's just gonna lie right back to you.

Yeah, I say, it was small compared to yours, but I had one. It would have 132
been worth my life to try to sing 'em somebody else's stuff that I didn't know
nothing about.

He must have pressed a buzzer under the table. One of his flunkies zombies up. 133

Git Johnny Carson, he says. 134

On the phone? asks the zombie. 135

On the phone, says Traynor, what you think I mean, git him offa the front 136
porch? Move your ass.

———————

So two weeks later we's on the Johnny Carson show. 137

———————

Traynor is all corseted down nice and looks a little bit fat but mostly good. And 138
all the women that grew up on him and my song squeal and squeal. Traynor
says: The lady who wrote my first hit record is here with us tonight, and she's
agreed to sing it for all of us, just like she sung it forty-five years ago. Ladies and
Gentlemen, the great Gracie Mae Still!

Well, I had tried to lose a couple of pounds my own self, but failing that I 139
had me a very big dress made. So I sort of rolls over next to Traynor, who is
dwarfted by me, so that when he puts his arm around back of me to try to hug
me it looks funny to the audience and they laugh.

I can see this pisses him off. But I smile out there at 'em. Imagine squealing 140
for twenty years and not knowing why you're squealing? No more sense of endings and beginnings than hogs.

It don't matter, Son, I say. Don't fret none over me. 141

I commence to sing. And I sound——wonderful. Being able to sing good 142
ain't all about having a good singing voice a'tall. A good singing voice helps. But
when you come up in the Hard Shell Baptist church like I did you understand
early that the fellow that sings is the singer. Them that waits for programs and
arrangements and letters from home is just good voices occupying body space.

So there I am singing my own song, my own way. And I give it all I got and 143
enjoy every minute of it. When I finish Traynor is standing up clapping and

clapping and beaming at first me and then the audience like I'm his mama for true. The audience claps politely for about two seconds.

Traynor looks disgusted.   144

He comes over and tries to hug me again. The audience laughs.   145

Johnny Carson looks at us like we both weird.   146

Traynor is mad as hell. He's supposed to sing something called a love ballad.   147 But instead he takes the mike, turns to me and says: Now see if my imitation still holds up. He goes into the same song, *our* song, I think, looking out at his flaky audience. And he sings it just the way he always did. My voice, my tone, my inflection, everything. But he forgets a couple of lines. Even before he's finished the matronly squeals begin.

He sits down next to me looking whipped.   148

It don't matter, Son, I say, patting his hand. You don't even know those peo-   149 ple. Try to make the people you know happy.

Is that in the song? he asks.   150

Maybe, I say.   151

1977

For a few years I hear from him, then nothing. But trying to lose weight takes all   152 the attention I got to spare. I finally faced up to the fact that my fat is the hurt I don't admit, not even to myself, and that I been trying to bury it from the day I was born. But also when you git real old, to tell the truth, it ain't as pleasant. It gits lumpy and slack. Yuck. So one day I said to Horace, I'ma git this shit offa me.

And he fell in with the program like he always try to do and Lord such a   153 procession of salads and cottage cheese and fruit juice!

One night I dreamed Traynor had split up with his fifteenth wife. He said: 154 *You meet 'em for no reason. You date 'em for no reason. You marry 'em for no reason. I do it all but I swear it's just like somebody else doing it. I feel like I can't remember Life.*

The boy's in trouble, I said to Horace.   155

You've always said that, he said.   156

I have?   157

Yeah. You always said he looked asleep. You can't sleep through life if you   158 wants to live it.

You not such a fool after all, I said, pushing myself up with my cane and   159 hobbling over to where he was. Let me sit down on your lap, I said, while this salad I ate takes effect.

In the morning we heard Traynor was dead. Some said fat, some said heart,   160 some said alcohol, some said drugs. One of the children called from Detroit. Them dumb fans of his is on a crying rampage, she said. You just ought to turn on the t.v.

But I didn't want to see 'em. They was crying and crying and didn't even   161
know what they was crying for. One day this is going to be a pitiful country, I
thought.

ACTIVITIES FOR WRITING AND DISCUSSION

1. Respond to the story using the "Four-Step Process for Writing from
Reading" described in Chapter 2.

2. What effects does Walker achieve by narrating the story from the **first-
person point of view** of Gracie Mae? What advantages, if any, does her choice
of first-person have over a **third-person** narration?

3. The story's events take place over a span of twenty-two years. What purposes are served by dividing the story up according to years? If you wish, compose a first-person narrative of your own that is similarly structured, i.e., by
years.

4. Events in the story are a weave of the personal and the cultural. For instance, in 1956 Gracie Mae is trying to lose weight (personal) and Traynor makes
a smash hit out of her song (cultural). Write a story of your own that portrays a
person embedded in some culture, time, or movement of your own choosing.

Poems

WILLIAM BLAKE (1757–1827)

The Garden of Love

I went to the Garden of Love,
And saw what I never had seen:
A Chapel was built in the midst,
Where I used to play on the green.

And the gates of this Chapel were shut,   5
And "Thou shalt not" writ over the door;
So I turn'd to the Garden of Love
That so many sweet flowers bore;

And I saw it was filled with graves,
And tomb-stones where flowers should be;   10
And Priests in black gowns were walking their rounds,
And binding with briars my joys & desires.

Walt Whitman (1819–1892)

Song of the Open Road

1

Afoot and light-hearted I take to the open road,
Healthy, free, the world before me,
The long brown path before me leading wherever I choose.

Henceforth I ask not good-fortune, I myself am good-fortune,
Henceforth I whimper no more, postpone no more, need nothing,   5
Done with indoor complaints, libraries, querulous criticisms,
Strong and content I travel the open road.

The earth, that is sufficient,
I do not want the constellations any nearer,
I know they are very well where they are,   10
I know they suffice for those who belong to them.

(Still here I carry my old delicious burdens,
I carry them, men and women, I carry them with me wherever I go,
I swear it is impossible for me to get rid of them,
I am fill'd with them, and I will fill them in return.)   15

2

You road I enter upon and look around, I believe you are not all
     that is here,
I believe that much unseen is also here.

Here the profound lesson of reception, nor preference nor denial,
The black with his woolly head, the felon, the diseas'd, the illiterate
     person, are not denied;
The birth, the hasting after the physician, the beggar's tramp, the   20
     drunkard's stagger, the laughing party of mechanics,
The escaped youth, the rich person's carriage, the fop, the eloping
     couple,
The early market-man, the hearse, the moving of furniture into the
     town, the return back from the town,
They pass, I also pass, any thing passes, none can be interdicted,
None but are accepted, none but shall be dear to me.

3

You air that serves me with breath to speak!   25
You objects that call from diffusion my meanings and give them
    shape!
You light that wraps me and all things in delicate equable showers!
You paths worn in the irregular hollows by the roadsides!
I believe you are latent with unseen existences, you are so dear
    to me.

You flagg'd walks of the cities! you strong curbs at the edges!   30
You ferries! you planks and posts of wharves! you timber-lined
    sides! you distant ships!
You rows of houses! you window-pierc'd façades! you roofs!
You porches and entrances! you copings and iron guards!
You windows whose transparent shells might expose so much!
You doors and ascending steps! you arches!   35
You gray stones of interminable pavements! you trodden crossings!
From all that has touch'd you I believe you have imparted to
    yourselves, and now would impart the same secretly to me,
From the living and the dead you have peopled your impassive
    surfaces, and the spirits thereof would be evident and
    amicable with me.

4

The earth expanding right hand and left hand,
The picture alive, every part in its best light,   40
The music falling in where it is wanted, and stopping where it is
    not wanted,
The cheerful voice of the public road, the gay fresh sentiment of
    the road.

O highway I travel, do you say to me *Do not leave me?*
Do you say *Venture not—if you leave me you are lost?*
Do you say *I am already prepared, I am well-beaten and un-*
    denied, adhere to me?   45

O public road, I say back I am not afraid to leave you, yet I love
    you,
You express me better than I can express myself,
You shall be more to me than my poem.

I think heroic deeds were all conceiv'd in the open air, and all
    free poems also,

I think I could stop here myself and do miracles,   50
I think whatever I shall meet on the road I shall like, and who-
    ever beholds me shall like me,
I think whoever I see must be happy.

5

From this hour I ordain myself loos'd of limits and imaginary
    lines,
Going where I list, my own master total and absolute,
Listening to others, considering well what they say,   55
Pausing, searching, receiving, contemplating,
Gently, but with undeniable will, divesting myself of the holds
    that would hold me.

I inhale great draughts of space,
The east and the west are mine, and the north and the south are
    mine.

I am larger, better than I thought,   60
I did not know I held so much goodness.

All seems beautiful to me,
I can repeat over to men and women You have done such good
    to me I would do the same to you,
I will recruit for myself and you as I go,
I will scatter myself among men and women as I go,   65
I will toss a new gladness and roughness among them,
Whoever denies me it shall not trouble me,
Whoever accepts me he or she shall be blessed and shall bless me.

6

Now if a thousand perfect men were to appear it would not amaze
    me,
Now if a thousand beautiful forms of women appear'd it would   70
    not astonish me.

Now I see the secret of the making of the best persons,
It is to grow in the open air and to eat and sleep with the earth.

Here a great personal deed has room,
(Such a deed seizes upon the hearts of the whole race of men,
Its effusion of strength and will overwhelms law and mocks all   75
    authority and all argument against it.)

Here is the test of wisdom,
Wisdom is not finally tested in schools,
Wisdom cannot be pass'd from one having it to another not
    having it,
Wisdom is of the soul, is not susceptible of proof, is its own proof,
Applies to all stages and objects and qualities and is content,   80
Is the certainty of the reality and immortality of things, and the
    excellence of things;
Something there is in the float of the sight of things that provokes
    it out of the soul.

Now I re-examine philosophies and religions,
They may prove well in lecture-rooms, yet not prove at all under
    the spacious clouds and along the landscape and flowing
    currents.

Here is realization,   85
Here is a man tallied—he realizes here what he has in him,
The past, the future, majesty, love—if they are vacant of you,
    you are vacant of them.

Only the kernel of every object nourishes;
Where is he who tears off the husks for you and me?
Where is he that undoes stratagems and envelopes for you and me?   90

Here is adhesiveness, it is not previously fashion'd, it is apropos;
Do you know what it is as you pass to be loved by strangers?
Do you know the talk of those turning eye-balls?

7

Here is the efflux of the soul,
The efflux of the soul comes from within through embower'd   95
    gates, ever provoking questions,
These yearnings why are they? these thoughts in the darkness
    why are they?
Why are there men and women that while they are nigh me the
    sunlight expands my blood?
Why when they leave me do my pennants of joy sink flat and lank?
Why are there trees I never walk under but large and melodious
    thoughts descend upon me?
(I think they hang there winter and summer on those trees and   100
    always drop fruit as I pass;)
What is it I interchange so suddenly with strangers?
What with some driver as I ride on the seat by his side?

What with some fisherman drawing his seine by the shore as I
    walk by and pause?
What gives me to be free to a woman's and man's good-will?
    what gives them to be free to mine?

8

The efflux of the soul is happiness, here is happiness,   105
I think it pervades the open air, waiting at all times,
Now it flows unto us, we are rightly charged.

Here rises the fluid and attaching character,
The fluid and attaching character is the freshness and sweetness
    of man and woman,
(The herbs of the morning sprout no fresher and sweeter every   110
    day out of the roots of themselves, than it sprouts fresh
    and sweet continually out of itself.)

Toward the fluid and attaching character exudes the sweat of the
    love of young and old,
From it falls distill'd the charm that mocks beauty and attainments,
Toward it heaves the shuddering longing ache of contact.

9

Allons![1] whoever you are come travel with me!
Traveling with me you find what never tires.   115

The earth never tires,
The earth is rude, silent, incomprehensible at first, Nature is rude
    and incomprehensible at first,
Be not discouraged, keep on, there are divine things well envelop'd,
I swear to you there are divine things more beautiful than words
    can tell.

Allons! we must not stop here,   120
However sweet these laid-up stores, however convenient this dwell-
    ing we cannot remain here,
However shelter'd this port and however calm these waters we
    must not anchor here,
However welcome the hospitality that surrounds us we are per-
    mitted to receive it but a little while.

---

1. French word for "Let us go."

10

Allons! the inducements shall be greater,
We will sail pathless and wild seas,   125
We will go where winds blow, waves dash, and the Yankee clipper
    speeds by under full sail.
Allons! with power, liberty, the earth, the elements,
Health, defiance, gayety, self-esteem, curiosity;
Allons! from all formules![2]
From your formules, O bat-eyed and materialistic priests.   130

The stale cadaver blocks up the passage—the burial waits no
    longer.

Allons! yet take warning!
He traveling with me needs the best blood, thews, endurance,
None may come to the trial till he or she bring courage and health,
Come not here if you have already spent the best of yourself,   135
Only those may come who come in sweet and determin'd bodies,
No diseas'd person, no rum-drinker or venereal taint is permitted
    here.

(I and mine do not convince by arguments, similes, rhymes,
We convince by our presence.)

11

Listen! I will be honest with you,   140
I do not offer the old smooth prizes, but offer rough new prizes,
These are the days that must happen to you:
You shall not heap up what is call'd riches,
You shall scatter with lavish hand all that you earn or achieve,
You but arrive at the city to which you were destin'd, you hardly 145
    settle yourself to satisfaction before you are call'd by an
    irresistible call to depart,
You shall be treated to the ironical smiles and mockings of those
    who remain behind you,
What beckonings of love you receive you shall only answer with
    passionate kisses of parting,
You shall not allow the hold of those who spread their reach'd
    hands toward you.

---

2. Formulas.

12

Allons! after the great Companions, and to belong to them!
They too are on the road—they are the swift and majestic men—   150
    they are the greatest women,
Enjoyers of calms of seas and storms of seas,
Sailors of many a ship, walkers of many a mile of land,
Habituès of many distant countries, habituès of far-distant dwellings,
Trusters of men and women, observers of cities, solitary toilers,
Pausers and contemplators of tufts, blossoms, shells of the shore,   155
Dancers at wedding-dances, kissers of brides, tender helpers of
    children, bearers of children,
Soldiers of revolts, standers by gaping graves, lowerers-down of
    coffins,
Journeyers over consecutive seasons, over the years, the curious
    years each emerging from that which preceded it,
Journeyers as with companions, namely their own diverse phases,
Forth-steppers from the latent unrealized baby-days,   160
Journeyers gayly with their own youth, journeyers with their
    bearded and well-grain'd manhood,
Journeyers with their womanhood, ample, unsurpass'd, content,
Journeyers with their own sublime old age of manhood or womanhood,
Old age, calm, expanded, broad with the haughty breadth of the
    universe,
Old age, flowing free with the delicious near-by freedom of death.   165

13

Allons! to that which is endless as it was beginningless,
To undergo much, tramps of days, rests of nights,
To merge all in the travel they tend to, and the days and nights
    they tend to,
Again to merge them in the start of superior journeys,
To see nothing anywhere but what you may reach it and pass it,   170
To conceive no time, however distant, but what you may reach it
    and pass it,
To look up or down no road but it stretches and waits for you,
    however long but it stretches and waits for you,
To see no being, not God's or any, but you also go thither,
To see no possession but you may posses it, enjoying all without
    labor or purchase, abstracting the feast yet not abstracting
    one particle of it,
To take the best of the farmer's farm and the rich man's elegant   175
    villa, and the chaste blessings of the well-married couple,
    and the fruits of orchards and flowers of gardens,

To take to your use out of the compact cities as you pass through,
To carry buildings and streets with you afterward wherever you go,
To gather the minds of men out of their brains as you encounter
    them, to gather the love out of their hearts,
To take your lovers on the road with you, for all that you leave
    them behind you,
To know the universe itself as a road, as many roads, as roads for   180
    traveling souls.

All parts away for the progress of souls,
All religion, all solid things, arts, governments—all that was or is
    apparent upon this globe or any globe, falls into niches and
    corners before the procession of souls along the grand roads
    of the universe.

Of the progress of the souls of men and women along the grand
    roads of the universe, all other progress is the needed
    emblem and sustenance.

Forever alive, forever forward,
Stately, solemn, sad, withdrawn, baffled, mad, turbulent, feeble,   185
    dissatisfied,
Desperate, proud, fond, sick, accepted by men, rejected by men,
They go! they go! I know that they go, but I know not where
    they go,
But I know that they go toward the best—toward something
    great.

Whoever you are, come forth! or man or woman come forth!
You must not stay sleeping and dallying there in the house,   190
    though you built it, or though it has been built for you.

Out of the dark confinement! out from behind the screen!
It is useless to protest, I know all and expose it.

Behold through you as bad as the rest,
Through the laughter, dancing, dining, supping, of people,
Inside of dresses and ornaments, inside of those wash'd and   195
    trimm'd faces,
Behold a secret silent loathing and despair.

No husband, no wife, no friend, trusted to hear the confession,
Another self, a duplicate of every one, skulking and hiding it goes,
Formless and wordless through the streets of the cities, polite and
    bland in the parlors,

In the cars of railroads, in steamboats, in the public assembly,   200
Home to the houses of men and women, at the table, in the bed-
 room, everywhere,
Smartly attired, countenance smiling, form upright, death under
 the breast-bones, hell under the skull-bones,
Under the broadcloth and gloves, under the ribbons and artificial
 flowers,
Keeping fair with the customs, speaking not a syllable of itself,
Speaking of any thing else but never of itself.   205

14

Allons! through struggles and wars!
The goal that was named cannot be countermanded.

Have the past struggles succeeded?
What has succeeded? yourself? your nation? Nature?
Now understand me well—it is provided in the essence of things   210
 that from any fruition of success, no matter what, shall
 come forth something to make a greater struggle necessary.

My call is the call of battle, I nourish active rebellion,
He going with me must go well arm'd,
He going with me goes often with spare diet, poverty, angry
 enemies, desertions.

15

Allons! the road is before us!
It is safe—I have tried it—my own feet have tried it well—be   215
 not detain'd!
Let the paper remain on the desk unwritten, and the book on the
 shelf unopen'd!
Let the tools remain in the workshop! let the money remain
 unearn'd!
Let the school stand! mind not the cry of the teacher!
Let the preacher preach in his pulpit! let the lawyer plead in the
 court, and the judge expound the law.

Camerado, I give you my hand!   220
I give you my love more precious than money,
I give you myself before preaching or law;
Will you give me yourself? will you come travel with me?
Shall we stick by each other as long as we live?

ACTIVITIES FOR WRITING AND DISCUSSION

1. Whitman urged people to read his poems "in the open air every season of every year of your life." Taking this advice literally, read the poem aloud outdoors and live with it over a period of days. Feel free to read and reread the poem in several sittings, focusing on sections that strike you and skimming over others that don't. In your notebook, keep a record of your impressions of the poem and any thoughts or feelings it prompts in you.

2. Whitman saw poetry as a force for bringing people together. Follow your private reading of the poem with a communal reading in class or with a small group. Have each person take a turn at reading a verse paragraph or numbered section, and pause after each section to share and discuss your annotations of particular lines or passages.

3. Think about the title. The poem does not seem to be a "song" in the literal sense. In what respects, if any, is it song*like*? Why does Whitman say "open road" instead of "road"? Of what sorts of experiences and emotions does the phrase "open road" remind you? Make a list of these experiences and emotions. To what (or whom) is the road "open"? Illustrate your answers with examples from the poem.

4. How does it make you feel when the speaker addresses "you" directly? How would the poem change if this element of direct address to the reader were eliminated?

5. Reread sections 12 and 13 and other passages that help explain what the "open road" is. Is the open road for everyone or for a select few? Does a person have to journey physically in order to be on the open road, or are there other **symbolic** types of "journeys"? Identify lines that support your answers to these questions. Then assume the **persona** of a homemaker, a factory worker, a political prisoner, an office clerk, a lawyer, or someone else of your own choosing, and write a letter to Whitman in which you respond to his invitation to "take to the open road."

6. Tell the story of a time when you knew the exhilaration and/or trials of a literal or symbolic "open road."

EMILY DICKINSON (1830–1886)

Much Madness is divinest Sense

Much Madness is divinest Sense—
To a discerning Eye—
Much Sense—the starkest Madness—
'Tis the Majority

In this, as All, prevail—
Assent—and you are sane—
Demur[1]—you're straightway dangerous—
And handled with a Chain—

The Soul selects her own Society

The Soul selects her own Society—
Then—shuts the Door—
To her divine Majority—
Present no more—

Unmoved—she notes the Chariots—pausing—
At her low Gate—
Unmoved—an Emperor be kneeling
Upon her Mat—

I've known her—from an ample nation—
Choose One—
Then—close the Valves of her attention—
Like Stone—

Some keep the Sabbath going to Church

Some keep the Sabbath going to Church—
I keep it, staying at Home—
With a Bobolink for a Chorister—
And an Orchard, for a Dome—

Some keep the Sabbath in Surplice—
I just wear my Wings—
And instead of tolling the Bell, for Church,
Our little Sexton—sings.

God preaches, a noted Clergyman—
And the sermon is never long,
So instead of getting to Heaven, at last—
I'm going, all along.

Tell all the Truth but tell it slant

Tell all the Truth but tell it slant—
Success in Circuit lies

---

1. Disagree.

*Theme— Sometimes
the truth is too much too
handle so it should be let
down gently.*

Too bright for our infirm Delight
The Truth's superb surprise
As Lightning to the Children eased   5
With explanation kind
The Truth must dazzle gradually
Or every man be blind—

ACTIVITIES FOR WRITING AND DISCUSSION

1. Read the four Dickinson poems aloud, identifying the **meter, rhymes,** and other sound effects such as **assonance** and **alliteration.** Attempting, for the moment, to set aside issues of "meaning," what passages—words, phrases, or lines—please you because of their sound or rhythm?

2. In a small group or as a class, progress towards strong readings of the poems by assuming, initially, the role of "dumb" readers. Simply go through a poem, line by line, and brainstorm any images, associations, or feelings that occur to you. Rather than suppressing "dumb," "irrelevant," or "eccentric" responses, *honor* them and write them down. Then discuss how people's diverse responses illuminate the poem and/or evoke thoughts about life experiences that may not be explicitly addressed in the poem itself.

3. Dickinson's astonishing **metaphors, similes,** and **paradoxes** challenge and subvert logical or rational ways of thinking and our desire for neatly packaged meanings. Working with a group:
   a. Identify and mark as many metaphors, similes, and paradoxes—or other **figures**—as you can.
   b. Select two or three favorites.
   c. Orally or in an essay, explain how these favorites work, i.e., what makes them striking or powerful.

4. Respond to one or more of the poems using one of the "Ten Ideas for Writing from Reading" described in Chapter 3 and summarized on page 35.

EDWIN ARLINGTON ROBINSON (1869–1935)

Richard Cory

Whenever Richard Cory went down town,
We people on the pavement looked at him:
He was a gentleman from sole to crown,
Clean favored, and imperially slim.

And he was always quietly arrayed,   5
And he was always human when he talked;
But still he fluttered pulses when he said,
"Good-morning," and he glittered when he walked.

And he was rich—yes, richer than a king—
And admirably schooled in every grace: 10
In fine, we thought that he was everything
To make us wish that we were in his place.

So on we worked, and waited for the light,
And went without the meat, and cursed the bread;
And Richard Cory, one calm summer night,   15
Went home and put a bullet through his head.

ACTIVITIES FOR WRITING AND DISCUSSION

1. Is it significant that the **speaker** uses the first-person *plural* pronoun ("we") instead of the singular ("I")? Why or why not?

2. Why does Richard Cory kill himself? To enrich what might be a rather pat answer to this question, invent a series of entries from "The Diary of Richard Cory" in which you (Richard) narrate experiences and describe feelings that are weighing on you. Alternative: Write Richard's suicide note, or compose a character biography of Richard.

3. Write a conversation between two townsfolk (gossips, perhaps) discussing Richard Cory, before and/or just after his death.

ANTONIO MACHADO (1875–1939)

Excerpts from *Proverbs and Song-verse*

To José Ortega y Gasset.

I
  The eye you see is an eye
not because you see it;
it's an eye because it sees you.

II
  For dialogue,
first ask,   5
then . . . listen.

III

Any narcissism
is an ugly vice—
and an old one by now.

IV

But seek out the other in your mirror,   10
the other who keeps you company.

VIII

Today always is still.

XI

Once again my attention
is bound by water—
but water in the live   15
rock of my heart.

XII

From the sound of water, can you tell
if it's water of peak or valley,
town fountain, garden or grove?

XIV

Never set down your limits   20
or fuss with your profile;
they're only externals.

XV

Look for your counterpart
who's always alongside you
and is usually your opposite.   25

XVI

Now that spring's here,
fly off to the flowers;
don't chew on the wax.

XXIV

Slowly now, nice neat letters:
the point is to do things well,   30
not just to do them.

XXVIII

Singers, the clapping
and cheers should be left
to the others.

XXIX

Singers, wake up.
Time for echoes to end
and voices to start.

35

XXX

But don't hunt for dissonance:
There is no such thing;
people dance to all tunes.

40

XXXVI

It's not the basic I
that the poet is after
but the essential you.

XXXIX

Find a mirror in your fellow man,
but not one for shaving
or dyeing your hair.

45

XL

Those eyes you long for;
make no mistake,
eyes you see yourself in—
are eyes because they see you.

50

XLIV

Don't look down on words.
The world is noisy and mute,
poets; God alone speaks.

XLVIII

Doubtless the worst of the wicked
is the rogue who forgets
his devil's vocation.

55

XLIX

Did you speak a half-truth?
They'll call you liar twice over
if you speak the other half.

LIII
   After living and dreaming
comes what matters most:
waking up.   60

LVI
   Gypsy conversation:
"Pal, how're we doing?"
"Taking a stroll on the shortcut."   65

LVII
   Some who give up
end it all with a rope;
others with four little words:
faith's back in style.

—Translated by Alan S. Trueblood

ACTIVITIES FOR WRITING AND DISCUSSION

   1. These short poems shouldn't be hurried and probably do not need to be read in sequence. Skip around, hovering over the poems that strike you. What do you like? What thoughts and feelings do the "Proverbs" evoke from you? Are there particular images, **metaphors** or other **figures** that stand out for you? Describe your thoughts and feelings in your notebook or orally.

   2. In your notebook react to Machado's **persona** in the "Proverbs." Do you find the persona preachy? appealing? a combination of both? Explain with reference to specific lines and passages.

   3. Think about the format of the "Proverbs."
       a. Based on these excerpts, does there seem to be an underlying pattern of organization, or do the proverbs seem to be set down in a random order? If you detect a pattern of organization, what is it?
       b. Reformat some of the verse sections into prose. What is lost, gained, or changed by doing so?
       c. Skim through your own notebook. Identify any passages of intellectually or emotionally heightened prose that tend toward poetry and reformat them into verse.

   4. As a long-term project, compose a collection of "proverbs in verse" of your own. Carrying a small notepad (see page 57) will enable you to jot down and collect the sorts of passing thoughts, images, and intuitions that are found in Machado's proverbs.

MIYAZAWA KENJI (1896–1933)

November 3rd

neither yielding to rain
nor yielding to wind
yielding neither to
snow nor to summer heat
  with a stout body   5
      like that
without greed
never getting angry
always smiling quiet-
        ly   10
eating one and a half pints of brown rice
and bean paste and a bit of
           vegetables a day
in everything
not taking oneself   15
    into account
      looking listening understanding well
and not forgetting
living in the shadow of pine trees in a field
  in a small   20
    hut thatched with miscanthus
if in the east there's a
    sick child
going and nursing
      him   25
if in the west there's a tired mother
going and for her
    carrying
    bundles of rice
if in the south   30
  there's someone
        dying
going
  and saying
    you don't have to be   35
    afraid
if in the north
    there's a quarrel
      or a lawsuit
saying it's not worth it   40

                stop it
in a drought
        shedding tears
in a cold summer
        pacing back and forth   lost   45
called
        a good-for-nothing
                by everyone
neither praised
nor thought a pain   50
        someone
                like that
is what I want
                to be

— *Translated by Hiroaki Sato and Burton Watson*

W. H. Auden (1907–1973)

The Unknown Citizen

(To JS/07/M/378
This Marble Monument
Is Erected by the State)

He was found by the Bureau of Statistics to be
One against whom there was no official complaint,
And all the reports on his conduct agree
That, in the modern sense of an old-fashioned word, he was a saint,
For in everything he did he served the Greater Community.   5
Except for the War till the day he retired
He worked in a factory and never got fired,
But satisfied his employers, Fudge Motors Inc.
Yet he wasn't a scab or odd in his views,
For his Union reports that he paid his dues,   10
(Our report on his Union shows it was sound)
And our Social Psychology workers found
That he was popular with his mates and liked a drink.
The Press are convinced that he bought a paper every day
And that his reactions to advertisements were normal in every way.   15
Policies taken out in his name prove that he was fully insured,
And his Health-card shows he was once in hospital but left it cured.
Both Producers Research and High Grade Living declare
He was fully sensible to the advantages of the Installment Plan
And had everything necessary to the Modern Man,   20

A phonograph, radio, a car and a frigidaire.
Our researchers into Public Opinion are content
That he held the proper opinions for the time of year;
When there was peace, he was for peace; when there was war, he went.
He was married and added five children to the population,   25
Which our Eugenist says was the right number for a parent of his generation,
And our teachers report that he never interfered with their education.
Was he free? Was he happy? The question is absurd:
Had anything been wrong, we should certainly have heard.

ACTIVITIES FOR WRITING AND DISCUSSION

1. Read the poem aloud and jot down the impressions and feelings it evokes in you by its sound, **rhythm,** and **rhymes.** Would you describe the poem as **traditional verse** or **free verse**? Does it have features of both? Explain. Finally, how do the sound, rhythm, and rhymes relate to the poem's meaning(s)?

2. Study the three italicized lines immediately after the title. How do you react to them, and particularly to the *first* line, with its cryptic initials, slash marks, and numbers? What expectations, if any, do they give you for the poem that follows?

3. Who is the "we" in this poem? How would it change the effect or meaning of the poem if "we" were replaced by "I" or "they" or by a more precise phrase such as "we, the people"?

4. The twentieth century has sometimes been called the "age of irony." With a small group, compile a list of examples of **verbal irony** in this poem.

5. Reflect on the society this poem depicts. What sorts of values and behaviors does it honor? What are some distinctive qualities of its heroes (such as "The Unknown Citizen" himself)? Imagine that an outsider enters this society. Mentioning at least some of the institutions and terms named in the poem, e.g., "the Bureau of Statistics," "Fudge Motors Inc.," "Producers Research," or "the Installment Plan," tell the story of some experiences he/she has. If you wish, compose your narrative as a series of journal entries or reports that record this person's experiences of—and observations on—this society.

STANISLAW J. LEC (1909–1966)

Excerpts from *Unkempt Thoughts*

You will always find some Eskimos ready to instruct the Congolese on how to   1
cope with heat waves.

On the neck of a giraffe a flea begins to believe in immortality.   2

I prefer the sign NO ENTRY to the one that says NO EXIT.   3

Only the dead can be resurrected. It's more difficult with the living.   4

Truth will always be naked, even when turned out in the latest fashion.   5

All is in the hands of man. Therefore wash them often.   6

Thoughts, like fleas, jump from man to man. But they don't bite everybody.   7

If only we could also *milk* the scapegoat!   8

If the art of conversation stood a little higher we would have a lower birthrate.   9

Men, enough of this modesty. Don't pretend to be lions.   10

In prison cells the sun draws shadows of the bars on the floor. In the squares the prisoners can play crossword puzzles. The possibilities depend on the size of the bars.   11

The aspen trembles under every regime, but it grows green under every regime anyway.   12

I give you bitter pills in sugar coating. The pills are harmless; the poison is in the sugar.   13

When I eat sardines I sometimes tremble that I may be biting a Jonah from the bible of the little people.   14

The fact that he died does not prove that he lived.   15

If you want to hide your face, walk naked.   16

Do not walk on the well-trodden path—you may slip.   17

On every summit you are on the brink of an abyss.   18

You can spit on yourself without opening your mouth.   19

—*Translated by Jacek Galazka*

ACTIVITIES FOR WRITING AND DISCUSSION

1. Read Lec's **aphorisms** aloud to yourself or in a group. Mark or annotate any aphorisms that particularly strike you, and identify the particular features (e.g., ideas, themes, word choice, **metaphors, ironies,** or other kinds of **figurative language**) that make those selections memorable or appealing. Put your reactions in writing, and be prepared to share them with classmates.

2. Lec's tiny but explosive thoughts seem to have been drafted on-the-run, perhaps in odd places or at odd times on scrap paper or in a small notepad. Over the next several weeks compose a collection of aphorisms of your own— when and as they occur to you—in which you imitate the ironic style of Lec, or, if you prefer, compose in a style of your own. For other aphorisms, see Blake's "Proverbs of Hell" on page 455, Machado's aphoristic verse on page 615, and Joubert's notebooks on page 696.

JULIO CORTÁZAR (1914–1984)

Preamble to the Instructions on How to Wind a Watch

Think of this: When they present you with a watch they are gifting you with a tiny flowering hell, a wreath of roses, a dungeon of air. They aren't simply wishing the watch on you, and many more, and we hope it will last you, it's a good brand, Swiss, seventeen rubies; they aren't just giving you this minute stonecutter which will bind you by the wrist and walk along with you. They are giving you—they don't know it, it's terrible that they don't know it—they are gifting you with a new, fragile, and precarious piece of yourself, something that's yours but not a part of your body, that you have to strap to your body like your belt, like a tiny, furious bit of something hanging onto your wrist. They gift you with the job of having to wind it every day, an obligation to wind it, so that it goes on being a watch; they gift you with the obsession of looking into jewelry-shop windows to check the exact time, check the radio announcer, check the telephone service. They give you the gift of fear, someone will steal it from you, it'll fall on the street and get broken. They give you the gift of your trademark and the assurance that it's a trademark better than the others, they gift you with the impulse to compare your watch with other watches. They aren't giving you a watch, you are the gift, they're giving you yourself for the watch's birthday.

—*Translated by Paul Blackburn*

ACTIVITIES FOR WRITING AND DISCUSSION

1. Though few people "wind" watches anymore, is this **prose poem** still timely? Explain. Are there any actions or "obligations" in the digital age that are analogous to the old obligation of winding a watch? If so, what are they?

2. Read the poem aloud with a partner or small group, with your pen or pencil out to mark arresting words or phrases as you read and listen. Then reread the poem, pausing after each sentence to share your moment by moment reactions to striking or puzzling words, phrases, and/or ideas.

3. The poem is packed with **metaphors** and other comparisons. Practice carrying a small notepad (see pages 57–58) for jotting down metaphors of your own, on whatever topics, as they occur to you. (Note: This will probably work best if you don't *try* to write metaphors but, rather, *detect* them as they occur.) If possible, expand one of your jottings into a prose poem.

4. React to the poem using the "Four-Step Process" (see Chapter 2).

WISLAWA SZYMBORSKA (b. 1923)

An Opinion on the Question of Pornography

There's nothing more debauched than thinking.
This sort of wantonness runs wild like a wind-borne weed
on a plot laid out for daisies.

Nothing's sacred for those who think.
Calling things brazenly by name,   5
risqué analyses, salacious syntheses,
frenzied, rakish chases after the bare facts,
the filthy fingering of touchy subjects,
discussion in heat—it's music to their ears.

In broad daylight or under cover of night   10
they form circles, triangles, or pairs.

The partners' age or sex are unimportant.
Their eyes glitter, their cheeks are flushed.
Friend leads friend astray.
Degenerate daughters corrupt their fathers.   15
A brother pimps for his little sister.

They prefer the fruits
from the forbidden tree of knowledge
to the pink buttocks found in glossy magazines—
all that ultimately simple-hearted smut.   20
The books they relish have no pictures.

What variety they have lies in certain phrases
marked with a thumbnail or a crayon.

It's shocking, the positions,
the unchecked simplicity with which   25
one mind contrives to fertilize another!
Such positions the Kama Sutra itself doesn't know.

During these trysts of theirs, the only thing that's steamy is the tea.
People sit on their chairs and move their lips.
Everyone crosses only his own legs   30
so that one foot is resting on the floor
while the other dangles freely in midair.
Only now and then does somebody get up,
go to the window,
and through a crack in the curtains   35
take a peep out at the street.

—*Translated by Stanislaw Barańczak and Clare Cavanagh*

MARGARET ATWOOD (b. 1939)

The City Planners

Cruising these residential Sunday
streets in dry August sunlight:
what offends us is
the sanities:
the houses in pedantic rows, the planted   5
sanitary trees, assert
levelness of surface like a rebuke
to the dent in our car door.

No shouting here, or
shatter of glass; nothing more abrupt   10
than the rational whine of a power mower
cutting a straight swath in the discouraged grass.

But though the driveways neatly
sidestep hysteria
by being even, the roofs all display   15
the same slant of avoidance to the hot sky,
certain things:
the smell of spilled oil a faint

sickness lingering in the garages,
a splash of paint on brick surprising as a bruise,   20
a plastic hose poised in a vicious
coil; even the too-fixed stare of the wide windows

give momentary access to
the landscape behind or under
the future cracks in the plaster   25

when the houses, capsized, will slide
obliquely into the clay seas, gradual as glaciers
that right now nobody notices.

That is where the City Planners
with the insane faces of political conspirators   30
are scattered over unsurveyed
territories, concealed from each other,
each in his own private blizzard;

guessing directions, they sketch
transitory lines rigid as wooden borders   35
on a wall in the white vanishing air

tracing the panic of suburb
order in a bland madness of snows.

CATHY APPEL (b. 1948)

Letters

Don't put your disembodied voice in an envelope—
send objects,

tangibles from Vermont, like the broken thread
from the last shirt button you've lost,
photographs of the house;   5
I should see you as you are.
What kind of soap is in your bathroom;
where do you keep your car keys? Send me
your favorite recipe, something from your pocket
like a ticket stub or tattered list.   10
I'll answer promptly
enclosing dust from my closet,
mud from the soles of my shoes.
Can you imagine me exhausted,
tissues tucked in a sleeve,   15
lying beside my husband, who, regardless,
caresses my hip? I could send you
a toenail clipping
or the umpteen odd barrettes, rubber bands,
unanswered letters scattered in my drawer.   20
Don't write in sentences.
No matter how we feel, send specifics—a branch
of your family's Christmas tree,
your daughter's loose tooth, crumbs
from the toast you ate this morning.   25
Send me what defies
language, something of which
there isn't any doubt.

LEO ROMERO (b. 1950)

What the Gossips Saw

Everyone pitied Escolastica, her leg
had swollen like a watermelon in the summer
It had practically happened over night
She was seventeen, beautiful and soon
to be married to Guillermo who was working   5
in the mines at Terreros, eighty miles away
far up in the mountains, in the wilderness
Poor Escolastica, the old women would say
on seeing her hobble to the well with a bucket
carrying her leg as if it were the weight   10
of the devil, surely it was a curse from heaven
for some misdeed, the young women who were

jealous would murmur, yet they were grieved too
having heard that the doctor might cut
her leg, one of a pair of the most perfect legs   15
in the valley, and it was a topic of great
interest and conjecture among the villagers
whether Guillermo would still marry her
if she were crippled, a one-legged woman—
as if life weren't hard enough for a woman   20
with two legs—how could she manage

Guillermo returned and married Escolastica
even though she had but one leg, the sound
of her wooden leg pounding down the wooden aisle
stayed in everyone's memory for as long   25
as they lived, women cried at the sight
of her beauty, black hair so dark
that the night could get lost in it, a face
more alluring than a full moon

Escolastica went to the dances with her husband   30
and watched and laughed but never danced
though once she had been the best dancer
and could wear holes in a pair of shoes
in a matter of a night, and her waist had been
as light to the touch as a hummingbird's flight   35
And Escolastica bore five children, only half
what most women bore, yet they were healthy
In Escolastica's presence, no one would mention
the absence of her leg, though she walked heavily
And it was not long before the gossips   40
spread their poison, that she must be in cohorts
with the devil, had given him her leg
for the power to bewitch Guillermo's heart
and cloud his eyes so that he could not see
what was so clear to them all   45

ACTIVITIES FOR WRITING AND DISCUSSION

1. Why do you suppose Romero is vague about the precise medical causes of Escolastica's loss of a leg?

2. Jot down your impressions of the village in which Escolastica lives. What are the people like? What sorts of beliefs and attitudes do they have? What are their families like? their entertainments? Then, using details provided in the

poem (and fabricating others where necessary), invent the conversation about Escolastica that occurs among any of the following: "the old women," "the young women," "the villagers," or "the gossips."

3. Recall a situation out of your own experience or knowledge in which one person was an object of gossip. Make a few notes about the person, the source of the gossip, and the gossipers. Then write the text of the gossip. Alternative: Invent such a situation.

Nonfiction/Essays

Arthur Schopenhauer (1788–1860)

On Thinking for Oneself

257

Just as the largest library, badly arranged, is not so useful as a very moderate one that is well arranged, so the greatest amount of knowledge, if not elaborated by our own thoughts, is worth much less than a far smaller volume that has been abundantly and repeatedly thought over. For only by universally combining what we know, by comparing every truth with every other, do we fully assimilate our own knowledge and get it into our power. We can think over only what we know, and so we should learn something; but we know only what we have thought out. . . .

258

. . . Therefore the mind is deprived of all its elasticity by *much* reading as is a spring when a weight is continually applied to it; and the surest way not to have thoughts of our own is for us at once to take up a book when we have a moment to spare. This practice is the reason why erudition makes most men more stupid and simple than they are by nature and also deprives their literary careers of every success. As Pope says, they remain:

For ever reading, never to be read.

The Dunciad, 3:193–94.

Scholars are those who have read in books, but thinkers, men of genius, world enlighteners, and reformers of the human race are those who have read directly in the book of the world.

259

At bottom, only our own fundamental ideas have truth and life; for it is they alone that we really and thoroughly understand. The ideas of someone else that we have read are the scraps and leavings of someone else's meal, the cast-off clothes of a stranger.

The idea of another that we have read is related to our own that occurs to us 5 as the impression in stone of a plant from the primeval world to the blossoming plant of spring.

260

Reading is a mere makeshift for original thinking. When we read, we allow another to guide our thoughts in leading strings. Moreover, many books merely serve to show how many false paths there are and how seriously we could go astray if we allowed ourselves to be guided by them. But whoever is guided by genius, in other words thinks for himself, thinks freely and of his own accord and thinks correctly; he has the compass for finding the right way. We should, therefore, read only when the source of our own ideas dries up, which will be the case often enough even with the best minds. On the other hand, to scare away our own original and powerful ideas in order to take up a book, is a sin against the Holy Ghost. We then resemble the man who runs away from free nature in order to look at a herbarium, or to contemplate a beautiful landscape in a copper engraving.

Even if occasionally we had been able very easily and conveniently to find in a book a truth or view that we very laboriously and slowly discovered through our own thinking and combining, it is nevertheless a hundred times more valuable if we have arrived at it through our own original thinking. Only then does it enter into the whole system of our ideas as an integral part and living member; only then is it completely and firmly connected therewith, is understood in all its grounds and consequents, bears the color, tone, and stamp of our whole mode of thought, has come at the very time when the need for it was keen, is therefore firmly established and cannot again pass away. Accordingly, Goethe's verse here finds its most perfect application and even explanation:

What from your fathers' heritage is lent,
Earn it anew, really to possess it!

Thus the man who thinks for himself only subsequently becomes acquainted with the authorities for his opinions when they serve merely to confirm him therein and to encourage him. The book-philosopher, on the other hand, starts from those authorities in that he constructs for himself an entire system from the opinions of others that he has collected in the course of his reading. Such a system is then like an automaton composed of foreign material, whereas that of the original thinker resembles a living human being. For it originated like this, since the external world fertilized the thinking mind that afterwards carried it and gave birth to it.

The truth that has been merely learned sticks to us like an artificial limb, a false tooth, a nose of wax, or at best like a rhinoplastic nose formed from someone else's flesh. On the other hand, the truth acquired through our own thinking is like the natural limb; it alone really belongs to us. On this rests the distinction between the thinker and the mere scholar. The intellectual gain of the man who thinks for himself is, therefore, like a beautiful painting that vividly stands out with correct light and shade, sustained tone, and perfect harmony of colors. The intellectual acquisition of the mere scholar, on the other hand, is like a large palette full of bright colors, systematically arranged perhaps, but without harmony, sequence, and significance.

261

Reading is equivalent to thinking with someone else's head instead of with one's own. Now for our own thinking, whence a coherent and connected whole, a system though not strictly rounded off, endeavors to evolve, nothing is more detrimental than too strong an influx of other people's ideas through constant reading. For each of them has sprung from the mind of another, belongs to another system, bears another tint; and never do they flow of themselves into a totality of thought, knowledge, insight, and conviction. On the contrary, they set up in the head a slight Babylonian confusion of tongues, and a mind so crammed is now robbed of all clear insight and thus is well-nigh disorganized. This state can be observed in many scholars and results in their being inferior to many illiterate men as regards common sense, correct judgment, and practical tact. The latter have always subordinated to, and incorporated in, their own thinking the little knowledge that has come to them from without through experience, conversation, and a little reading. Now it is just this that the scientific *thinker* also does to a greater degree. Although he needs much knowledge and must, therefore, read a great deal, his mind is nevertheless strong enough to master all this, to assimilate it, to incorporate it into his system of ideas, and thus to subordinate it to the organically consistent totality of his vast and ever-growing insight. Here his own thinking, like the ground-bass of an organ, always dominates everything and is never drowned by the notes and tones of others, as is the case with the minds of mere pundits and polyhistors, where fragments of music in all keys run into one another, so to speak, and the fundamental note can no longer be detected at all.

262

Those who have spent their lives in reading, and have drawn their wisdom from   10 books, resemble men who have acquired precise information about a country from many descriptions of travel. They are able to give much information about things, but at bottom they have really no coherent, clear, and thorough knowledge of the nature of the country. On the other hand, those who have spent their lives in thinking are like men who have themselves been in that country. They alone really know what they are talking about; they have a consistent and coherent knowledge of things there and are truly at home in them. . . .

265

. . . The characteristic sign of all first-rate minds is the directness of all their judgments and opinions. All that they express and assert is the result of their own original thinking and everywhere proclaims itself as such even by the style of delivery. Accordingly, like princes, they have an imperial immediacy in the realm of the mind; the rest are all mediatized, as is already seen from their style that has no stamp of originality.

Therefore every genuine and original thinker is to this extent like a monarch; he is immediate and perceives no one who is his superior. Like the decrees of a monarch, his judgments spring from his own supreme power and come directly from himself. For he no more accepts authorities than does the monarch take orders; on the contrary, he admits nothing but what he himself has confirmed. On the other hand, minds of the common ruck who labor under all kinds of current opinions, authorities, and prejudices, are like the crowd that silently obeys laws and orders. . . .

268

The presence of an idea is like that of a loved one. We imagine that we shall never forget it and that the beloved can never become indifferent to us; but out of sight, out of mind! The finest thought runs the risk of being irretrievably forgotten if it is not written down, and the beloved of being taken from us unless she has been wedded.

—Translated by E.F.J. Payne

ACTIVITIES FOR WRITING AND DISCUSSION

1. Review your annotations of Schopenhauer's text. Choose one or more that speak(s) most powerfully to your own experiences of reading or thinking. Then use the annotated passage(s) as a springboard to writing and reflecting on your experiences. Write in **essay** form, or, if you wish, compose a letter to Schopenhauer or a dialogue with him in which you share your experiences of reading and thinking.

2. Schopenhauer's text is rich in **metaphors**, **similes** and analogies. Working alone or in a group, underline and annotate as many examples of these figures as you can. Then choose two or three and show how they help explain or clarify Schopenhauer's ideas.

3. Working from your annotations of "On Thinking for Oneself," summarize the distinctions Schopenhauer makes between "reading" and "thinking." Then agree or disagree with the distinctions.

ADRIENNE RICH (b. 1929)

A Leak in History

I'm staying in a house in the Vermont countryside, shaded in front by three big sugar maples. Behind it lies a grove of the same trees, and on a hillside far away I can see another grove, glowing green in rich late-afternoon light. In autumn the leaves turn scarlet; in late winter thaw the pale aqueous sap starts rising and is gathered and laboriously evaporated, in little steamy shacks and cabins, down to its essence, a syrup fine as honey. The Abnaki Indians knew this process before the Yankees came to clear scattered pools of land for grazing, leaving old forest lands in between. Taught by the Abnaki, the first white men made maple sugar in Vermont in 1752.

Under snow, the sap shrinks back. In early thaw, farmers trudge and horse-sledge through the woods to drill little taps into the rough-barked trunks. The sap used to be collected in wooden firkins, then in tin pails hung over the taps; more recently, where terrain and weather allow, plastic tubing is used. A culture formed around this labor-intensive harvesting, first ritual of the northern spring, the culture of the sugarhouse with its ancient sprung castoff chairs, steaming evaporation trays, wet snow and mud trodden inside on heavy boots, doughnuts and coffee, pickles, frankfurters, and beer brought down by women from farm kitchens, eaten and drunk by men lugging and pouring sap and stoking the wood fires. Hard manual labor—about forty gallons of sap being collected and boiled down to obtain one gallon of syrup—and adept, sensitive calculation of the cycles of thaw and freeze that make for the best sugaring-off; testing for the moment when the thin, faintly sweet sap has reached the density of amber syrup. The sour crispness of pickle on the tongue amid all that sweaty sweetness. There is a summer culture too, at church suppers and county fairs, where "sugar on snow" still competes with cotton-candy machines and barbecue—pans of last winter's snow from icehouse, cemetery vault, or freezer, sticky arabesques of hot syrup poured on, served on paper plates with the necessary pickle and doughnut on the side.

Maple trees reproduce with energy: Under any big tree you will find dozens of seedlings crowding each other; in spring the seeds, or keys, blow far afield on little brown wings soon after the new leaves uncurl. The root system of a full-grown maple is many times the circumference of the great crown. In their early-summer-evening green, in the hectic flare of their October changing, in the strong, stripped upreaching of their winter bareness, they are presences of enormous vitality and generosity, trees that yield much to the eye, to the tongue, to the modest cash assets of farm families.

It's said that acid rain and road salt are slowly dooming the sugar maples. Studying and testing the rings of mature trees, scientists have found that up until 1955 they show no evidence of chemical stress; since 1955 acidity has been wearing into the trees and will eventually destroy them. I look out at the grove on the hill, the old trees just outside the window; all seems as it has always been, without smirch or taint.

I remember other trees that stood in this landscape when I first knew it: the wineglass elms. Every village common, every roadside, had them. *Ulmus americanus,* outspreading limbs sweeping up from a straight and slender trunk in the form of a true wineglass, green in summer, golden in autumn, architecturally elegant in nakedness. An old pamphlet from the State Agricultural Service, found in a drawer, implores cooperation in destroying infested bark and wood and protecting still-healthy trees. But the fungus-carrying elm bark beetle won out. Throughout New England, elms fell barren in summer, sick to death, easily splintered by winds. Soon a living elm in leaf was something rare and precious. Now it's hard to remember where they stood.

The poorer we become, the less we remember what we had. Whenever I walk into this house after an absence, I drink, slowly and deliberately, a glass of pure cold water from the spring-fed tap. I don't drink from most taps because I don't like their ill flavor. And the taste of bottled water from the supermarket has no savor; it reminds me of nothing. The spring water flowing into this house does—in its transparency, its lucidity, its original cold. Of course it tastes of this place, sharp with memories, but also of water I drank as a child in the 1930s, from an iron pipe set in the side of a ravine where I used to play. It seemed like the saving, merciful drink of water in legends or poetry; through it I sensuously understood the beautiful, lip-smacking words "to quench a thirst." This was not in the country, but in a wooded park in Baltimore. There was a stream there too, where we waded, and plunged our hands in to the wrists, and never got sick.

Three thousand miles to the west, where I live now, on a much-traveled hill road winding eastward from the coast, there is a standing pipe called the Lombardi Spring. A few cars and trucks are almost always parked on the shoulder, people lined up with jugs and bottles, because that water is held to be particularly delicious and good. And it is free.

Sensual vitality is essential to the struggle for life. It's as simple—and as threatened—as that. To have no love for the taste of the water you drink is a loss of vitality. If your appetite is embalmed in prescriptives, you are weakened for the struggle. Under the most crushing conditions of deprivation, people have to fill their stomachs, eat earth, eat plain starch, force down watery and rancid soup, drink urine for survival. Yet there's another story. In the newsletter produced by inmates in a women's facility, among columns on law, religion, politics, current prison issues, there is the "Konvict Kitchen," with recipes for special microwaved dishes to be created by combining items from the prison store:

> 1 can Mixin' Chicken
> 1 Shrimp Noodle Cup
> jalapeño peppers (optional)
> onions (optional)
> bell peppers (optional)
> 2 packages margarine

> Crush noodles and put in large microwave bowl with enough water to cover them. Let sit for three minutes. Take bell peppers, onions, and hot peppers and saute in microwave for two minutes. Take mixture out, add noodles, stir thoroughly and cook in microwave for approximately 20–25 minutes, until noodles are crisp. Stir every five minutes. Keep lid lightly on mixture but not tightly closed. Serves 2.

> —*Gloria Bolden*

Poetry being a major form of prison literature, it goes without saying that there are poems in the newsletter. Like the recipe above, they work within the prison context but refuse to be subdued.

> This is prison not the Hilton
> Heard we got it made in here?
> This is livin' at its finest?
> Country clubs with kegs of beer?
> Say—listen up my friend
> let me tell you what it's like
> to be livin' in the sewer
> flushed further down the pipe . . .
>
> This is prison not the Hilton
> Election time is on its way
> you'll hear it on the TV
> we should suffer every day

days of torture
nights of terror—
feel your heart's been torn in shreds?
Say you're showered with asbestos,
drinking nitrate in your bed? . . .

This is prison not the Hilton
care to change your place for mine?
Think that 20 out of 60
isn't doing enough time?
Care to try this life of leisure?
Care to leave your folks behind?
This is prison not the Hilton
and its hell here all the time.[1]

Sensual vitality is essential to the struggle for life. Many people drink as if 10
filling themselves with dirt or starch: the filling of an emptiness. But what
comes after is a greater emptiness. In the reputations of poets like Hart Crane,
Dylan Thomas, Kenneth Rexroth, James Wright, Richard Hugo, Delmore
Schwartz, Robert Lowell, Elizabeth Bishop, John Berryman, Anne Sexton,
drinking has been romanticized as part of the "poetic fate," the "despondency
and madness" of the poet—as if bricklayers, surgeons, housewives, miners,
generals, salesmen haven't also poured down liquids to fire up or numb interior
spaces of dread. A politician's wife confesses to having drunk aftershave, nail-
polish remover, in desperate substitute for confiscated bottles. Whether done
with nail-polish remover or antique liqueur of pear, this is self-poisoning.

But there's a sensual vitality in drinking wine and "spirits" as in drinking 11
pure water. Both belong to ancient human rites and memories. People have fer-
mented the apple, the grape, the palm, hops and barley, rice, berries, the potato,
the dandelion, the plum. Along with the rising of the yeast in bread was the fermentation of the grain, the fruit. Blessed be the Spirit of the Universe, who created the fruit of the vine. For us to use it as we may.

That so many of us use, or have used, the fruit of the vine in an attempt to 12
fill our terrifying voids may point to the failure of a general communal vitality
more than to some inherent poisoning in the fermentation process. I don't
minimize the ultimate transaction between the individual and the bottle. But
the individual's sense of emptiness reflects—and helps perpetuate—a public
emptiness.

When a vast, stifling denial in the public realm is felt by every individual yet 13
there is no language, no depiction, of what is being denied, it becomes for each

---

[1]Composed by Jacqueline Dixon-Bey and Mary Glover, inside Florence Crane Women's Prison, Cold-
water, Michigan, Spring 1990; recipe and poem from *Insight: Serving the Women of Florence Crane
Women's Facility,* 2d quarter ed. (1990). [Rich's note.]

his or her own anxious predicament, a daily struggle to act "as if" everything were normal. Alcohol, drugs offer a reprieve—not ceremony or celebration, but a substitute for vital bonds of community and friendship, for collective memory and responsibility. Where there is no public face of interdependence, of justice and mercy, where there is no social language for "picking up the pieces when we don't know what/where they are," anomie and amnesia, alcohol and drug abuse can work as social controls and, because they appear "normal," can be more effective—in a very large country—than terrorization by a secret police.

The danger lies in forgetting what we had. The flow between generations 14 becomes a trickle, grandchildren tape-recording grandparents' memories on special occasions perhaps—no casual storytelling jogged by daily life, there being no shared daily life what with migrations, exiles, diasporas, rendings, the search for work. Or there is a shared daily life riddled with holes of silence. In 1979 Helen Epstein published her book of interviews, *Children of the Holocaust.* In 1985 Judy Kaplan and Linn Shapiro edited *Red Diaper Babies: Children of the Left,* a compilation of transcripts of taped sessions at two conferences held in 1982 and 1983 by children of leftist and Communist families, then in their thirties and forties. There are haunting resonances between the two groups of testimony: the children's experience of knowing that there was something of major weight at the center of their parents' lives, something secret, unspoken, unspeakable. (Epstein refers to "that quiet, invisible community, that peer group without a sign.") Both groups of children knowing about things that could not be discussed on the playground or with "strangers," that were to a greater or lesser degree unmentionable even at home. A tattoo on an aunt's wrist. A neighbor's withdrawal. A mother's nightmares; a parent's terror when a child left the house or came home late. A father in jail or underground. Close friends who suddenly could not be mentioned. Certain newspapers having to be hidden; jobs inexplicably lost; children trained that "the walls have ears"; a car parked across the street for hours, one day every week, two men sitting inside. There can be no question of equalizing the events that catalyzed these two silences. Yet the passing on of living history is an essential ingredient of individual and communal self-knowledge, and in both cases that continuity was breached. Forty years is a wilderness of silence.

The loss can be a leak in history or a shrinking in the vitality of everyday 15 life. Fewer and fewer people in this country entertain each other with verbal games, recitations, charades, singing, playing on instruments, doing anything as amateurs—people who are good at something because they enjoy it. To be good at talk, not pompously eloquent or didactic, but having a vivid tongue, savoring turns of phrase—to sing on key and know many songs by heart—to play fiddle, banjo, mandolin, flute, accordion, harmonica—to write long letters—to draw pictures or whittle wood with some amount of skill—to do moderately and pleasingly well, in short, a variety of things without solemn investment or disenabling awe—these were common talents till recently, crossing class and racial lines. People used their human equipment—memory, image making, narrative, voice, hand, eye—unselfconsciously, to engage with other people, and not as specialists or "artistes." My father and his mother both loved to recite poetry learned long ago in school. He had Poe's "The Raven" and "Annabel Lee" from memory, and he had won a school medal for his recitation of a long narrative poem called "Lasca," which began:

> I want free life and I want fresh air,
> And I sigh for the canter after the cattle,
> The crack of whips like shots in a battle,
> The green below, and the blue above,
> And dash, and danger, and life, and love—
> And Lasca.

And my grandmother still remembered a poem she'd learned in Vicksburg, Mississippi—Jewish girl sent to a convent school where there were no secular schools. In her seventies she could recite, black eyes glowing, "Asleep at the Switch":

> It was down in the Lehigh Valley,
> At the bottom of the bottomless ditch,
> I lived alone in a cabin,
> And attended the railway switch.

The reciters of these two poems could not have been in person more unlike   16 the "speaker" of each poem, and that was part of the excitement: to see a known person become someone new and different, change his or her identity but within a framework that allowed each to change back at the end—from Texan desperado to my sedentary, scholarly father; from negligent, solitary switchman to my sheltered, precise grandmother. And such recitations let a child feel that poetry (verse, really, with its structured rhymes, meters, and ringingly fulfilled aural expectations) was not just words on the page, but could live in people's minds for decades, to be summoned up with relish and verve, and that poetry was not just literature, but embodied in voices.

For ordinary people to sing or whistle used to be as common as breathing. I   17 remember men whistling, briskly or hauntingly, women humming with deep-enclosed chest tones. Where did it go? A technology of "canned" music available through car radios, portable "boom boxes," and cassette players, programmed music piped into the workplace, has left people born in the 1950s and later largely alien to the experience of hearing or joining in casual music making. Knowing how to pitch your voice isn't the privilege of the conservatory; people used to learn it from hearing others casually, unself-consciously sing, as they learned language, accent, inflection in speech. Now singing belongs to professionals, is preserved in churches; rap, a spontaneous and sophisticated expression of black street youth at first, quickly became a commodity on videotape, adapted as a new style for television commercials. (Yet rap goes on around the world, picking up on local griefs, local insurgencies.)

Part of the experience of casual singing was the undeliberate soaking up of 18 many songs, many verses. Ballads, hymns, work songs, opera arias, folk songs, popular songs, labor songs, schoolchildren's playground songs. And, of course, with the older songs words changed over time, new generations of singers mis-remembering or modifying. Tunes changed, too, as songs traveled: from England or Wales to Appalachia, from Africa to the Sea Islands, France to Québec, and across the continent.

To ears accustomed to high-technology amplification and recording 19 processes, the unamplified human voice, the voice not professionally trained, may sound acoustically lacking, even perhaps embarrassing. And so we're severed from a physical release and pleasure, whether in solitude or community— the use of breath to produce song. But breath is also *Ruach*, spirit, the human connection to the universe.

ACTIVITIES FOR WRITING AND DISCUSSION

1. Twice in the essay Rich writes, "Sensual vitality is essential to the struggle for life," and the phrase "sensual vitality" occurs several times elsewhere. Based on the stories included in the first dozen paragraphs of the essay, explain what you think Rich means by the phrases "sensual vitality" and "struggle for life." Jot down and share some stories or examples of your own that reinforce her point that such vitality is "essential."

2. Reread and annotate paragraphs 12 and 13. Then:
   a. Use the process described on pages 100–102 to write a summary of Rich's argument in these paragraphs.
   b. Share your summary—and any of your annotations (including questions or confusions over difficult concepts)—with a partner or small group.
   c. Write a notebook entry agreeing or disagreeing with Rich's argument.

3. In paragraph 14, Rich says that we have "no shared daily life" today, or that it is "a shared daily life riddled with holes of silence." Based on your own experiences, do you tend to agree or disagree? Share—orally or in writing— your own stories of "shared" or alienated life.

4. Reread and reannotate paragraphs 15 to 19. Then react (in writing) to the picture of contemporary life and lifestyle that Rich presents in these paragraphs. If you believe her picture is accurate, are there ways of reversing the trends she describes, and, if so, what are they?

CAROL BLY (b. 1930)

Growing Up Expressive

Love, death, the cruelty of power, and time's curve past the stars are what children want to look at. For convenience's sake, let's say these are the four most vitally touching things in life. Little children ask questions about them with relish. Children, provided they are still little enough, have no eye to doing any problem solving about love or death or injustice or the universe; they are simply interested. I've noticed that as we read aloud literature to them, about Baba Yaga, and Dr. Doolittle, and Ivan and the Firebird, and Rat and Mole, children are not only interested, they are prepared to be vitally touched by the great things of life. If you like the phrase, they are what some people call "being as a little child." Another way of looking at it is to say that in our minds we have two kinds of receptivity to life going on all the time: first, being vitally touched and enthusiastic (grateful, enraged, puzzled—but, at all events, *moved*) and, second, having a will to solve problems.

Our gritty society wants and therefore deliberately trains problem solvers, however, not mystics. We teach human beings to keep themselves conscious only of problems that *can* conceivably be solved. There must be no hopeless causes. Now this means that some subjects, of which death and sexual love come to mind straight off, should be kept at as low a level of consciousness as possible. Both resist problem solving. A single-minded problem solver focuses his consciousness, of course, on problems to be solved, but even he realizes there is a concentric, peripheral band of other material around the problems. This band appears to him as "issues." He is not interested in these issues for themselves; he sees them simply as impacting on the problems. He will allow us to talk of love, death, injustice, and eternity—he may even encourage us to do so because his group-dynamics training advises him to let us have our say, thus dissipating our willfulness—but his heart is circling, circling, looking for an opening to *wrap up* these "issues" so he can return attention to discrete, solvable problems. For example, a physician who has that mentality does not wish to be near dying patients very much. They are definitely not a solvable problem. If he is wicked, he will regard them as a present issue with impact on a future problem: then he will order experimentation done on them during their last weeks with us. It means his ethic is toward the healing process only, but not toward the dying person. His ethic is toward problem solving, not toward wonder. He will feel quite conscientious while doing the experiments on the dying patient, because he feels he is saving lives of future patients.

To return to little children for a second: they simply like to contemplate life and death. So our difficulty, in trying to educate adults so they will be balanced but enthusiastic, is to keep both streams going—the problem solving, which seems to be the mental genius of our species, and the fearless contemplation of gigantic things, the spiritual genius of our species.

The problem-solving mentality is inculcated no less in art and English classes than in mathematics and science. Its snake oil is hope of success: by setting very small topics in front of people, for which it is easy for them to see the goals, the problems, the solutions, their egos are not threatened. They feel hopeful of being effective. Therefore, to raise a generation of problem solvers, you encourage them to visit the county offices (as our sixth-grade teachers do) and you lead them to understand that this is citizenship. You carefully do not suggest that citizenship also means comparatively complex and hopeless activities like Amnesty International's pressure to get prisoners in far places released or at least no longer tortured. Small egos are threatened by huge, perhaps insoluble problems. Therefore, one feeds the small ego confidence by setting before it dozens and dozens of very simple situations. The ego is nourished by feeling it understands the relationship between the county recorder's office and the county treasurer's office; in later life, when young people find a couple of sticky places in county government, they will confidently work at smoothing them. How very different an experience such problem solving is from having put before one the spectacle of the United States' various stances and activities with respect to germ warfare. Educators regularly steer off all interest in national and international government to one side, constantly feeding our rural young people on questions to which one can hope for answers on a short timeline. We do not ask them to exercise that muscle which bears the weight of vast considerations—such as cruelty in large governments. By the time the average rural Minnesotan is eighteen, he or she expects to stay in cheerful places, devote some time to local government and civic work, and "win the little ones." Rural young people have a repertoire of pejorative language for hard causes: "opening that keg of worms," "no end to that once you get into it," "don't worry—you can't do anything about that from where you are," "we could go on about that forever!" They are right, of course: we could, and our species, at its most cultivated, does go on forever about love, death, power, time, the universe. But some of us, alas, have been conditioned by eighteen fashionably to despise those subjects because there are no immediate answers to all the questions they ask us.

The other way we negatively reinforce any philosophical bent in children is 5 to pretend we don't see the content in their artwork. We comment only on the technique, in somewhat the same way you can scarcely get a comment on rural preachers' sermon content: the response is always, He does a good (or bad) job of speaking. "Well, but what did he say?" "Oh, he talked really well. The man can preach!"

The way to devalue the content of a child's painting is to say, "Wow, you sure can paint!" The average art teacher in Minnesota is at pains to find something to say to the third grader's painting of a space machine with complicated, presumably electronic equipment in it. Here is the drawing in words: A man is sitting at some controls. Outside his capsule, fire is flying from emission points on his ship toward another spaceship at right, hitting it. Explosions are coming out of its side and tail. What is an art teacher to do with this? Goodness knows. So he or she says, "My goodness, I can see there's a lot of action there!" It is said in a deliberately encouraging way but anyone can hear under the carefully supportive comment: "A lot of work going into nothing but more TV-inspired violence." One might as well have told the child, "Thank you for sharing."

I once attended a regional writers' group at which a young poet wrote about his feelings of being a single parent and trying to keep his sanity as he cared for his children. In his poem, he raced up the staircase, grabbed a gun, and shot the clock. When he finished reading it aloud to us, someone told him, "I certainly am glad you shared with us. I'd like to really thank you for sharing."

If we are truly serious about life we are going to have to stop thanking people for sharing. It isn't enough response to whatever has been offered. It is half ingenuous, and sometimes it is insincere, and often it is patronizing. It is the *dictum excrementi* of our decade.

I would like to keep in mind for a moment the art works described above: the child's painting of a spaceship assaulting another spaceship, and the harrowed father's racing up the staircase and shooting the clock. Here is a third. It is a twelve-year-old's theme for English class.

> They were their four days and nights before anyone found them. It was wet and cold down there. As little kids at the orphanage, they had been beaten every night until they could scarcely make it to bed. Now they were older. Duane and Ellen leaned together. "I love you forever," she told him. He asked her, "Even though my face is marked from getting scarlet fever and polio and small pox and newmonya and they wouldn't take decent care of me, not call the doctor or anything, so the marks will always be on me?" "You know I love you," Ellen told him. "You know that time they tortured me for information and I was there but I didn't talk and later I found out it was your uncle who did it. I didn't talk because I remembered the American flag." Just then they heard someone shout, "Anyone alive down there in this mess?" You see a bomb had gone off destroying a entire U.S.A. city where they lived. Duane had lived with his cruel uncle who took him out of the orphanage to get cheap labor and Ellen lived at a boardinghouse where there were rats that ate pages of her diary all the time. Now they both looked up and shouted "We're here!" A head appeared at the top of the well into which they had fallen or they would of been in 6,500 pieces like all the other men and ladies even pregnant ones and little kids in that town. Now this head called down, "Oh—a boy and a girl!" then the head explained it was going for a ladder and ropes and it ducked away and where it had been they saw the beginnings of stars for that night, the stars still milky in front of the bright blue because the sky wasn't dark enough yet to show them up good.

The English teacher will typically comment on this story by observing that   10
the spelling is uneven, and adjectives get used as adverbs. In rural Minnesota (if not elsewhere) an English teacher can spend every class hour on adjectives used as adverbs: it is meat and potatoes to a nag. But when we discuss spelling, syntax, and adverbs, we are talking method, not content. The child notices that

nothing is said of the story's *plot*. No one remarks on the *feelings* in it. Now if this happens every time a child hands in fiction or a poem, the child will realize by the time he reaches twelfth grade that meaning or feelings are not worth anything, that "mechanics" (note the term) are all that matter.

It is rare for a public school English teacher to comment on a child's content unless the material is *factual*. Minnesota teachers encourage writing booklets about the state, themes on ecology and county government, on how Dad strikes the field each autumn, on how Mom avoids open-kettle canning because the USDA advises against it. In this way, our children are conditioned to regard writing as problem solving instead of contemplation, as routine thinking instead of imaginative inquiry.

How can we manage it otherwise?

I would like to suggest some questions we can ask children about their artwork which will encourage them to grow up into lovers, lobby supporters, and Amnesty International members, instead of only township officers and annual protestors against daylight saving time. Let us gather all the elements of the three artworks presented in this Letter: the little boy's spaceship-war painting, the young divorced father's narrative poem, and the twelve-year-old girl's story of love in a well. We have a set of images before us, then:

Man directing spaceship fire
Another aircraft being obliterated
Staircase, man shooting a clock; children
Cruel orphanage
Torture
Last survivors of a decimated city

Let us, instead of lending the great sneer to these images, be respectful of them. It may help to pretend the painting is by Picasso, that Flaubert wrote the father/clock scene, and that Tolstoy wrote the well story. It helps to remember that Picasso felt the assault of historical events on us—like Guernica; Flaubert, as skillfully as Dostoyevsky and with less self-pity, was an observer of violent detail; and the Tolstoy who wrote *Resurrection* or the scene of Pierre's imprisonment in *War and Peace* would turn to the well/love story without qualm.

We know we would never say to Picasso, Flaubert, or Tolstoy, "Why don't you draw something you know about from everyday life? Why don't you write about something you know about? You say Anna was smashed beneath a train? Thank you for sharing!"

The fact is that a child's feelings about orphanages and torture and love are things that he does know about. They are psychic realities inside him, and when he draws them, he is drawing something from everyday life. Sometimes they are from his night life of dreaming, but in any event they are images of passion and he is drawing from his genuine if garbled experience. A few years ago there was a stupid movement to discourage children's reading of Grimms' fairy tales. Later, with a more sophisticated psychology, we learned that the stepmother who is hostile and overweening is a reality to all children; the cutting-off of the hero's right hand and replacing of it with a hand of silver is a reality to all children. Spaceships, witches' gingerbread houses, orphanages, being the last two people to survive on earth—all these are part of the inner landscape, something children know about. Therefore, in examining their artwork, we need better sets of questions to ask them. Young people who are not repressed are going to lay their wild stuff in front of adults (hoping for comment of some kind, praise if possible) until the sands of life are run, so we had better try to be good at responding to them. And unless we want to raise drones suitable only for conveyor-belt shifts, we had better be at least half as enthusiastic as when they tell us, Mama, I got the mowing finished.

Here are some questions to ask our young artist. How much of that electronic equipment is used for firepower and how much just to run the ship? After the other spaceship is blown up and the people in it are dead, what will this man do? Will he go home somewhere? Were the stars out that night? You said he'll go home to his parents. Did the other man have parents? How soon will that man's parents find out that his spaceship was destroyed? Could you draw in the stars? You said they were out—could you draw them into the picture some way? but don't ruin anything you've got in there now. Also, that wire you said ran to the solar plates, will you darken it so it shows better? Don't change it—just make it clearer. Yes—terrific! Can you see the planet where the other man would have returned to if he had lived till morning?

The young father's story: There is an obvious psychic complication to this story: the violence in his shooting out the clock face is gratuitous, and the plea for attention on the part of the author directed at the reader is glaring: clock faces as psychological symbols are in the public domain. Anyone who tells a friend (or a group of strangers) I am going to shoot up a clock face at 11 P.M. is asking for psychological attention. In a civil world, to ask is to receive, so if we are civilized we have to pay attention and ask the young author: Why does the father in the story blast the clock? And, when he replies, we have to ask some more. If there was ever an instance in which it was O.K. to say, "Thanks for sharing," this is not it.

I should like to add that this will be especially difficult for rural teachers because the traditional country way to treat any kind of mental problem is to stare it down. It didn't happen. I didn't hear that insane thing you just said, and you know you don't really hate your mother. What nice parent would shoot a clock? We uniformly do what Dr. Vaillant in *Adaptations to Life* would call a denial adaptation. It takes a brave questioner when the young person brings in a crazy story.

The well/love story: Did you know there really are such orphanages? There are orphanages where the children have to get up at four-thirty to work in the dairy, and the girls work hours and hours in the kitchens, and the children's growth is stunted. Did you make the girl so brave on purpose? Were they a lucky couple or an unlucky couple, or is that the sort of a question you can't ask? You made a point of telling us they'd been through a lot of hardship. What would it have been like for them if they hadn't? Do you want to talk about what blew up the city? Did you imagine yourself in the well?

Those are not brilliant questions; they are simply respectful, because the art 20 works described are concerned with death by violence; cruelty by institutions; treachery by relations; bravery (or cowardice—either one is important); sexual love, either despite or encouraged by dreadful circumstances.

They are some of the subjects in *War and Peace,* in Dürer's etchings, paintings, and woodcuts, and in *Madame Bovary.*

It is a moot question in my mind which of two disciplines will be the more useful in helping people stay vitally touched by the Great Things: psychology might do it—and English literature in high school might do it (instruction on the college level is generally so dutiful to methodology that it seems a lost cause to me. "How did D. H. Lawrence foreshadow this event?" and "What metaphors does Harold Rosenberg use in his discussion of Action Painting?" are the questions of technocrats, not preservers of spirit. It is as if we got home from church and the others said, "How was church?" "We had Eucharist," we tell them. "Well, how was it?" they ask. "Pretty good," we reply. "Bishop Anderson was there. He held the chalice eight inches above the rail so no one spilled, then he turned and wiped the chalice after each use so no germs were passed along. People who had already communed returned to their benches using the north aisle so there was no bottlenecking at the chancel.")

I don't think churches will be helpful in preserving the mystical outlook as long as they see life and death as a *problem*—a problem of salvation—with a solution to be worked at. Churches have an axe to grind. They might take the father running up the staircase to be an impact subject: they would wish to use their program to solve his problem. Churchmen often appear to be companionable counselors, but the appearance is largely manner and habit. Under the manner, the clergyman's mindset is nearly always to see a disturbed or grieving person's imagery as *the issues.* From there, he swings into psychological problem solving.

I would like to commend this responsibility to our English teachers: that they help our children preserve pity, happiness, and grief inside themselves. They can enhance those feelings by having young children both write and draw pictures. They can be very enthusiastic about the children's first drawings of death in the sky. Adults, particularly mature ones who have *not* got children in school at the moment, should make it clear that we expect this of English teachers and that we don't give a damn if LeRoy and Merv never in their lives get the sentence balance of past conditional and perfect subjunctive clauses right. We need to protect some of the Things Invisible inside LeRoy and Merv and the rest of us.

This is my last Letter from the Country. That is why it is so shrill. Gadflies 25 are always looking out a chance to be shrill anyway, so I jumped to this one and have shouted my favorite hope: that we can educate children not to be problem solvers but to be madly expressive all their lives.

ACTIVITIES FOR WRITING AND DISCUSSION

1. Working in a group, jot down what you think Bly means by the terms "problem solvers" (or "the problem-solving mentality") and "expressive." Then draw upon Bly's essay and your own experience to give some examples of each. Do you find the terms meaningful for thinking about learning and education? Why or why not?

2. Throughout her essay, Bly reviles the expression "Thank you for sharing." Identify some situations in which people use this expression, and explain the reasons Bly dislikes it. Do you share her dislike? Why or why not? Additional activity: Compose a text (story, dialogue, public speech, poem) in which this expression either recurs or serves as the focal subject.

3. In paragraph 18 Bly says that "the traditional country way to treat any kind of mental problem is to stare it down. It didn't happen." Bly is a rural Minnesotan. Is the phenomenon of "staring it down" confined to rural America? Write a dialogue between two people or characters in which one tries to "stare down" the other's "mental problem."

4. Bly criticizes the ways that some teachers teach. For instance, in paragraph 10 she says that English teachers focus their comments on students' "spelling, syntax, and adverbs" in order to avoid responding to the content and ideas in students' papers. "Now if this happens every time a child hands in fiction or a poem, the child will realize by the time he reaches twelfth grade that meaning or feelings are not worth anything, that 'mechanics' . . . are all that matter."

    a. Does this jibe—or conflict—with your own experience in English classes? Explain, and illustrate with some specific stories of your experiences.

    b. Imagine a situation in which a student is "madly expressive" in his or her writing, drawing, or other creative work. Create the student's madly expressive work and invent the comments that a "problem-solving" teacher might put on it.

5. In the last paragraph Bly states that her "favorite hope" is "that we can educate children not to be problem solvers but to be madly expressive all their lives." Take a point of view that is opposed to Bly's and argue for the importance and value of teaching children to be problem solvers. Alternative: Write a dialogue between someone who shares Bly's view (expressed in the above quotation) and someone who opposes it. Emphasize the conflict between the two speakers and avoid an easy resolution of the conflict.

ATHOL FUGARD (b. 1932)

The Road to Mecca

Characters

MISS HELEN
ELSA
MARIUS BYLEVELD

Time

AUTUMN 1974

Place

NEW BETHESDA, SOUTH AFRICA

ACT ONE

The living room and, leading off it, the bedroom alcove of a house in the small Karoo village of New Bethesda. An extraordinary room by virtue of the attempt to use as much light and color as is humanly possible. The walls—mirrors on all of them—are all of different colors, while on the ceiling and floor are solid, multicolored geometric patterns. Yet the final effect is not bizarre but rather one of light and extravagant fantasy. Just what the room is really about will be revealed later when its candles and lamps—again, a multitude of them of every size, shape and color—are lit. The late afternoon light does, however, give some hint of the magic to come.

MISS HELEN is in the bedroom alcove. A frail, birdlike little woman in her late sixties. A suggestion of personal neglect, particularly in her clothes, which are shabby and were put on with obvious indifference to the final effect. She is nervously fussing around an old-fashioned washstand, laying out towels, soap, etc., etc., and from time to time directs her attention to the living room and a door leading from it to the rest of the house. In the course of moving around she sees an overnight bag and a briefcase on the floor near the living-room entrance. She fetches these and carries them into the alcove.

ELSA enters, a strong young woman in her late twenties dressed in a track suit or something else suitable for a long motorcar ride.

ELSA: Not cold enough yet for the car to freeze up, is it?

HELEN: No. No danger of that. We haven't had any frost yet.

ELSA: I'm too exhausted to put it away. *(Collapses on the bed)* Whew! Thank God that's over. Another hour and I would have been wiped out. That road gets longer and longer every time.

HELEN: Your hot water is nearly ready.

ELSA: Good. *(Starts to unpack her overnight bag)*

HELEN: Nice clean towels . . . and I've opened that box of scented soaps you brought me last time.

ELSA: What? Oh, those. Haven't you used them yet?

HELEN: Of course not! I was keeping them for a special occasion.

ELSA: And this is it?

HELEN: Yes. An unexpected visit from you is a *very* special occasion. Is that all your luggage?

ELSA: When I said a short visit I really meant it.

HELEN: Such a long way to drive for just one night.

ELSA: I know.

HELEN: You don't think you could . . . ?

ELSA: Stay longer?

HELEN: Even just two nights?

ELSA: Impossible. We're right in the middle of exams. I've got to be in that classroom at eight-thirty on Monday morning. As it is I should be sitting at home right now marking papers. I've even brought a pile of them with me just in case I get a chance up here. *(Starts to undress—track-suit top, sneakers and socks)*

HELEN: Put anything you want washed on one side and I'll get a message to Katrina first thing in the morning.

ELSA: Don't bother her with that. I can do it myself.

HELEN: You can't leave without seeing Katrina! She'll never forgive me if I don't let her know you're here. Please . . . even if it's only for a few minutes.

ELSA: I won't leave without seeing Katrina, Miss Helen! But I don't need her to wash a pair of pants and a bra for me. I do my own washing.

HELEN: I'm sorry . . . I just thought you might. . . . There's an empty drawer here if you want to pack anything away.

ELSA *(An edge to her voice)*: Please stop fussing, Miss Helen! I know my way around by now.

HELEN: It's just that if I'd known you were coming, I would have had every-thing ready for you.

ELSA: Everything is fine just the way it is.

HELEN: No, it isn't! I don't even know that I've got enough in the kitchen for a decent supper tonight. I did buy bread yesterday, but for the rest . . .

ELSA: Please, Miss Helen! If we need anything, I'll get old Retief to open his shop for us. In any case, I'm not hungry. All I need at this moment is a good wash and a chance to unwind so that I can forget I've been sitting in a motorcar for twelve hours.

HELEN: Be patient with me, Elsie. Remember the little saying: "Patience is a virtue, virtue is a grace, and—"

ELSA (*Unexpectedly sharp*): For God's sake, Helen! Just leave me alone for a few minutes!

Pause.

HELEN (*Timidly*): I'll get your hot water.

MISS HELEN *exits.* ELSA *slumps down on the bed, her head in her hands.* MISS HELEN *returns a few seconds later with a large kettle of hot water. She handles it with difficulty.*

I've got the small one on for tea.

ELSA: Let me do that!

She jumps up and takes the kettle away from MISS HELEN. *The two women stand staring at each other for a few seconds.* ELSA *puts down the kettle and then puts her hands on* MISS HELEN *shoulders.*

My turn to say sorry.

HELEN: You don't need to do that.

ELSA: Please! It will help. Sorry, Miss Helen. I also need to hear you say you forgive me.

HELEN: To tell you the truth, I was getting on my own nerves.

ELSA (*Now smiling*): Come on.

HELEN: Oh, all right. . . . But I promise you it isn't necessary. You're forgiven.

ELSA (*Leading* MISS HELEN *over to a chair*): Now sit down and stop worrying about me. We're both going to close our eyes, take a deep breath and start again. Ready?

HELEN: Ready.

ELSA: One, two, three . . .

Closed eyes and deep breaths.

And now?

HELEN (*With the sly, tongue-in-cheek humor we will come to recognize as characteristic of the relaxed woman*): Well, if you really mean it, I think the best thing is for you to get back into your car, drive around the block and arrive again. And this time I want you, please, to hoot three times the way you usually do, so that I don't think a ghost has walked in through the front door when you appear.

ELSA (*Calling* MISS HELEN's *bluff*): Right. Where are the car keys? (*Finds them and heads for the front door*)

HELEN: Where are you going?

ELSA: To do what you said. Drive around the block and arrive again.

HELEN: Like that?

ELSA: Why, what's wrong?

HELEN: Elsie! Sterling Retief will have a heart attack if he sees you like that.

ELSA: But I wear less than this when I go to the beach. Oh, all right then, you old spoilsport, let's pretend.

ELSA *runs into the other room, revs up her motorcar, grinds through all its gears and "arrives." Three blasts on the horn. The two women play the "arrival game" (specifics to be determined in rehearsal). At the end of it they come together in a good laugh.*

If my friends in Cape Town were to have seen that! You must understand, Miss Helen, Elsa Barlow is known as a "serious young woman." Bit of a blue stocking, in fact. Not much fun there! I don't know how you did it, Helen, but you caught me with those stockings down from the first day we met. You have the rare distinction of being the only person who can make me make a fool of myself . . . and enjoy it.

HELEN: You weren't making a fool of yourself. And anyway what about me? Nearly seventy and behaving as if I were seven!

ELSA: Let's face it, we've both still got a little girl hidden away in us somewhere.

HELEN: And they like to play together.

ELSA: Mine hasn't done that for a long time.

HELEN: And I didn't even know that mine was still alive.

ELSA: *That* she most certainly is. She's the one who comes running out to play first. Feeling better?

HELEN: Much better.

For the moment all tensions are gone. ELSA *cleans herself as thoroughly as a basin of water, a facecloth and a bar of scented soap will allow.*

ELSA: God, this Karoo dust gets right into your pores. I can even taste it. That first mouthful of tea is going to be mud. I'll fill up all the kettles tomorrow and have a really good scrub. When did you last have one? (MISS HELEN *has to think about that)* Right, settled. Your name is down for one as well. *(A few seconds of industrious scrubbing.* MISS HELEN *watches her)* What are you thinking?

HELEN: So many things! About the way you *did* arrive. I wasn't joking. For a few seconds I did think I was seeing a ghost. I heard the front door open . . . I thought it was little Katrina, she also never knocks . . . but instead there you were. *(She wants to say more but stops herself.)*

ELSA: Go on.

HELEN: It was so strange. Almost as if you didn't really see me or anything else at first . . . didn't want to. And so cross! I've never seen you like that before.

ELSA: This isn't quite like the other times, Miss Helen.

HELEN: That's a pity. They were all good times. *(Pause)* So what sort of time is this going to be? A bad one?

ELSA *(Evenly):*   I hope not. Doesn't have to be. It depends on you.

MISS HELEN *avoids* ELSA's *eyes. The young woman looks around the room.*

But you're right. I hadn't really arrived until now.

HELEN: Where were you, Elsie?

ELSA *(She thinks about the question before answering):*   Way back at the turnoff to the village from the National Road . . . or maybe a few miles further along it now . . . walking to Cradock.

HELEN: I don't understand.

ELSA: I gave a lift to a woman outside Graaff-Reinet. That's most probably where she is now. I dropped her at the turnoff to the village.

HELEN: Who was she?

ELSA *(Shrugging with apparent indifference):*   An African woman.

HELEN: Cradock! That's a long walk.

ELSA: I know.

HELEN: It's about another eighty miles from the turn-off. *(She waits for* ELSA *to say more)*

ELSA: I nearly didn't stop for her. She didn't signal that she wanted a lift or anything like that. Didn't even look up when I passed . . . I was watching her in the rearview mirror. Maybe that's what told me there was a long walk ahead of her . . . the way she had her head down and just kept on walking. And then the baby on her back. It was hot out there, Miss Helen, hot and dry and a lot of empty space. . . . There wasn't a farmhouse in sight. She looked very small and unimportant in the middle of all that. Anyway, I stopped and reversed and offered her a lift. Not very graciously. I'd already been driving for ten hours and all I wanted was to get here as fast as I could. She got in and after a few miles we started talking. Her English wasn't very good, but when I finally got around to understanding what she was trying to tell me it added up to a good old South African story. Her husband, a farm laborer, had died recently, and no sooner had they buried him when the *baas* told her to pack up and leave the farm. So there she was . . . on her way to the Cradock district, where she hoped to find a few distant relatives and a place to live. *(Trying to remember the woman as clearly as possible)* About my age. The baby couldn't have been more than a few months old. All she had with her was one of those plastic shopping bags they put your groceries in at supermarkets. I saw a pair of old slippers. She was barefoot.

HELEN: Poor woman.

ELSA: So I dropped her at the turnoff. Gave her what was left of my food and some money. She carried on walking and I drove here.

Pause.

HELEN: Is there something else?

ELSA: No. That's all.

HELEN: I'm sure somebody else will give her a lift.

ELSA *(Too casily):* I hope so. If not, she and her baby are in for a night beside the road. There's eighty miles of the Karoo ahead of her. Shadows were already stretching out across the veld when she got out of the car. The Great Karoo! And just when I thought I was getting used to it, beginning to like it, in fact. Down in Cape Town I've actually caught myself talking rubbish about its vast space and emptiness, its awesome stillness and silence! Just like old Getruida down the road. It's that all right, but only because everything else has been all but damned out of existence. It's so obvious where you Afrikaners get your ideas of God from. Beats me how you've put up with it so long, Miss Helen. Nearly seventy years? My God, you deserve a medal. I would have packed up and left it at the first opportunity . . . and let's face it, you've had plenty of those.

HELEN: I was born here, Elsa.

ELSA: I sympathize, Miss Helen. Believe me, I truly sympathize.

HELEN: It's not really as bad as you make it sound. The few times I've been away, I've always ended up missing it and longing to be back.

ELSA: Because you wanted to get back to your work.

HELEN *(Shaking her head)*: No. Even before all that started. It grows on you, Elsa.

ELSA: Which is just about the only growing it seems to allow. For the rest, it's as merciless as the religion they preach around here. Looking out of the car window this afternoon I think I finally understood a few things about you Afrikaners . . . and it left me feeling just a little uneasy.

HELEN: You include me in all you're saying.

ELSA: Yes. You might not go to church anymore, but you're still an Afrikaner, Miss Helen. You were in there with them, singing hymns every Sunday, for a long, long time. Bit of a renegade now, I admit, but you're still one at heart.

HELEN: And that heart is merciless?

Pause.

ELSA: No. That you aren't. A lot of other things maybe, but certainly not that. Sorry, sorry, sorry . . .

HELEN: You're still very cross, aren't you? And something else as well. There's a new sound in your voice. One I haven't heard before.

ELSA: What do you mean?

HELEN: Like the way you talked about that woman on the road. Almost as if you didn't care, which I know isn't true.

ELSA: Of course I cared. I cared enough to stop and pick her up, to give her money and food. But I also don't want to fool myself. That was a sop to my conscience and nothing more. It wasn't a real contribution to her life and what she is up against. Anyway, what's the point in talking about her? She's most probably curling up in a stormwater drain at this moment—that's where she said she'd sleep if she didn't get a lift—and I feel better for a good wash.

HELEN: There it is again.

ELSA: Well, it's the truth.

HELEN: It was the way you said it.

ELSA: You're imagining things, Miss Helen. Come on, let's talk about something else. It's too soon to get serious. We've got enough time, and reasons, for that later on. What's been happening in the village? Give me the news. Your last letter didn't have much of that in it.

ELSA *gets into clean clothes.* MISS HELEN *starts to fold the discarded track suit.* ELSA *stops her.*

I can do that.

HELEN: I just wanted to help.

ELSA: And you can do that by making a nice pot of tea and giving me the village gossip.

MISS HELEN *goes into the living room. She takes cups and saucers, etc., from a sideboard and places them on the table.*

HELEN: I haven't got any gossip. Little Katrina is the only one who really visits me anymore, and all she wants to talk about these days is her baby. There's also Marius, of course, but he never gossips.

ELSA: He still comes snooping around, does he?

HELEN: Don't put it like that, Elsa. He's a very old friend.

ELSA: Good luck to him. I hope the friendship continues. It's just that *I* wouldn't want him for one. Sorry, Miss Helen, but I don't trust your old friend, and I have a strong feeling that Pastor Marius Byleveld feels the same way about me. So let's change the subject. Tell me about Katrina. What has she been up to?

HELEN: She's fine. And so is the baby. As prettily dressed these days as any white baby, thanks to the clothes you sent her. She's been very good to me, Elsa. Never passes my front door without dropping in for a little chat. Is always asking about you. I don't know what I would do without her. But I'm afraid Koos has started drinking again. And making all sorts of terrible threats about her and the baby. He still doesn't believe it's his child.

ELSA: Is he beating her?

HELEN: No. The warning you gave him last time seems to have put a stop to that.

ELSA: God, it makes me sick! Why doesn't she leave him?

HELEN: And then do what?

ELSA: Find somebody else! Somebody who will value her as a human being and take care of her and the child.

HELEN: She can't do that, Elsie. They're married.

ELSA: Oh, for God's sake, Helen. There's the Afrikaner in you speaking. There is nothing sacred about a marriage that abuses the woman! I'll have a talk to her tomorrow. Let's make sure we get a message to her to come around.

HELEN: Don't make things more difficult for her, Elsa.

ELSA: How much more difficult can "things" be than being married to a drunken bully? She *has* got a few rights, Miss Helen, and I just want to make sure she knows what they are. How old is she now?

HELEN: Seventeen, I think.

ELSA: At that age I was still at school dreaming about my future, and here she is with a baby and bruises. Quick, tell me something else.

HELEN: Let me see . . . Good gracious me! Of course, yes! I have got important news. Old Getruida has got the whole village up in arms. Brace yourself, Elsa. She's applied for a license to open a liquor store.

ELSA: A what?

HELEN: A liquor store. Alcoholic beverages.

ELSA: Booze in New Bethesda?

HELEN: If you want to put it that bluntly . . . yes.

ELSA: Now that *is* headline material. Good for old Gerty. I always knew she liked her sundowner, but I never thought she'd have the spunk to go that far.

HELEN: Don't joke about it, Elsie. It's a very serious matter. The village is very upset.

ELSA: Headed, no doubt, by your old friend Pastor Marius Byleveld.

HELEN: That's right. I understand that his last sermon was all about the evils of alcohol and how it's ruining the health and lives of our Coloured folk.

Getruida says he's taking unfair advantage of the pulpit and that the Coloureds get it anyway from Graaff-Reinet.

ELSA: Then tell her to demand a turn.

HELEN: At what?

ELSA: The pulpit. Tell her to demand her right to get up there and put her case . . . and remind her before she does that the first miracle was water into wine.

HELEN *(Trying not to laugh):* You're terrible, Elsie! Old Getruida in the pulpit!

ELSA: And you're an old hypocrite, Miss Helen. You love it when I make fun of the Church.

HELEN: No, I don't. I was laughing at Gerty, not the Church. And you have no right to make me laugh. It's a very serious matter.

ELSA: Of course it is! Which is why I want to know who you think is worse: the dominee deciding what is right and wrong for the Coloured folk or old Getruida exploiting their misery?

HELEN: I'm afraid it's even more complicated than that, Elsa. Marius *is* only thinking about what's best for them, but on the other hand Getruida has offered to donate part of her profits to their school building fund. And what about Koos? Wouldn't it make things even worse for Katrina if he had a local supply?

ELSA: They are two separate issues, Miss Helen. You don't punish a whole community because one man can't control his drinking. Which raises yet another point: has anybody bothered to ask the Coloured people what they think about it all?

HELEN: Are we going to have that argument again?

ELSA: I'm not trying to start an argument. But it does seem to me right and proper that if you're going to make decisions which affect other people, you should find out what those people think.

HELEN: It is the same argument. You know they don't do that here.

ELSA: Well, it's about time they started. I don't make decisions affecting the pupils at school without giving them a chance to say something. And they're children! We're talking about adult men and women in the year 1974.

HELEN: Those attitudes might be all right in Cape Town, Elsa, but you should know by now that the valley has got its own way of doing things.

ELSA: Well, it can't cut itself off from the twentieth century forever. Honestly, coming here is like stepping into the middle of a Chekhov play. While the rest of the world is hoping the bomb won't drop today, you people are arguing about who owns the cherry orchard. Your little world is not as safe as you would like to believe, Helen. If you think it's going to be left alone to stagnate in the nineteenth century while the rest of us hold our breath hoping we'll reach the end of the twentieth, you're in for one hell of a surprise. And it will start with your Coloured folk. They're not fools. They also read newspapers, you know. And if you don't believe me, try talking about something other than the weather and her baby next time Katrina comes around. You'll be surprised at what's going on inside that little head. As for you Helen! Sometimes the contradictions in you make me want to scream. Why do you always stand up and defend this bunch of bigots? Look at the way they've treated you.

HELEN *(Getting nervous):* They leave me alone now.

ELSA: That is not what you said in your last letter!

HELEN: My last letter?

ELSA: Yes.

Pause. HELEN *has tensed.*

Are you saying you don't remember it, Helen?

HELEN: No . . . I remember it.

ELSA: And what you said in it?

HELEN *(Trying to escape):* Please, little Elsie! Not now. Let's talk about it later. I'm still all flustered with you arriving so unexpectedly. Give me a chance to collect my wits together. Please? And while I'm doing that, I'll make that pot of tea you asked for.

MISS HELEN *exits into the kitchen.* ELSA *takes stock of the room. Not an idle examination; rather, she is trying to see it objectively, trying to understand something. She spends a few seconds at the window, staring out at the statues in the yard. She sees a cardboard box in a corner and opens it—handfuls of colored ceramic chips. She also discovers a not very successful attempt to hide an ugly burn mark on one of the walls.* MISS HELEN *returns with tea and biscuits.*

ELSA: What happened here?

HELEN: Oh, don't worry about that. I'll get Koos or somebody to put a coat of paint over it.

ELSA: But what happened?

HELEN: One of the lamps started smoking badly when I was out of the room.

ELSA: And new curtains.

HELEN: Yes. I got tired of the old ones. I found a few Marie biscuits in the pantry. Will you be mother?

Light is starting to fade in the room. ELSA *pours the tea, dividing her attention between that and studying the older woman.* MISS HELEN *tries to hide her unease.*

Do I get a turn now to ask for news?

ELSA: No.

HELEN: Why not?

ELSA: I haven't come up here to talk about myself.

HELEN: That's not fair!

ELSA: It's boring.

HELEN: Not to me. Come on Elsie, fair is fair. You asked me for the village gossip and I did my best. Now it's your turn.

ELSA: What do you want to know?

HELEN: Everything you would have told me about in your letters if you had kept your promise and written them.

ELSA: Good and bad news?

HELEN: I said everything . . . but try to make the good a little bit more than the bad.

ELSA: Right. The *Elsa Barlow Advertiser*! Hot off the presses! What do you want to start with? Financial, crime or sports page?

HELEN: The front-page headline.

ELSA: How's this? "Barlow to appear before School Board for possible disciplinary action."

HELEN: Not again!

ELSA: Yep.

HELEN: Oh dear! What was it this time?

ELSA: Wait for the story. "Elsa Barlow, a twenty-eight-year-old English-language teacher, is to appear before a Board of Enquiry of the Cape Town School Board. She faces the possibility of strict disciplinary action. The enquiry follows a number of complaints from the parents of pupils in Miss Barlow's Standard Nine class. It is alleged that in April this year Miss Barlow asked the class, as a homework exercise, to write a five-hundred-word letter to the State President on the subject of racial inequality. Miss Barlow teaches at a Coloured School."

HELEN: Is that true?

ELSA: Are you doubting the accuracy and veracity of the *Advertiser*?

HELEN: Elsie! Elsie! Sometimes I think you deliberately look for trouble.

ELSA: All I "deliberately look for," Miss Helen, are opportunities to make those young people in my classroom think for themselves.

HELEN: So what is going to happen?

ELSA: Depends on me, I suppose. If I appear before them contrite and apologetic, a stern reprimand. But if I behave the way I really feel, I suppose I could lose my job.

HELEN: Do you want my advice?

ELSA: No.

HELEN: Well, I'm going to give it to you all the same. Say you're sorry and that you won't do it again.

ELSA: Both of those are lies, Miss Helen.

HELEN: Only little white ones.

ELSA: God, I'd give anything to be able to walk in and tell that School Board exactly what I think of them and their educational system. But you're right, there are the pupils as well, and for as long as I'm in the classroom a little subversion is possible. Rebellion starts, Miss Helen, with just one man or woman standing up and saying, "No. Enough!" Albert Camus. French writer.

HELEN: You make me nervous when you talk like that.

ELSA: And you sound just like one of those parents. You know something? I think you're history's first reactionary-revolutionary. You're a double agent, Helen!

HELEN: Haven't you got any good news?

ELSA: Lots. I still don't smoke. I drink very moderately. I try to jog a few miles every morning.

HELEN: You're not saying anything about David.

ELSA: Turn to the lonely hearts column. There's a sad little paragraph: "Young lady seeks friendship with young man, etc., etc."

HELEN: You're talking in riddles. I was asking you about David.

ELSA: And I'm answering you. I've said nothing about him because there's nothing to say. It's over.

HELEN: You mean . . . you and David . . . ?

ELSA: Yes, that is exactly what I mean. It's finished. We don't see each other anymore.

HELEN: I knew there was something wrong from the moment you walked in.

ELSA: If you think this is me with something wrong, you should have been around two months ago. Your little Elsie was in a bad way. You were in line for an unexpected visit a lot earlier than this, Helen.

HELEN: You should have come.

ELSA: I nearly did. But your letters suggested that you weren't having such a good time either. If we'd got together at that point, we might have come up with a suicide pact.

HELEN: I don't think so.

ELSA: Joke, Miss Helen.

HELEN: Then don't joke about those things. Weren't you going to tell me?

ELSA: I'm trying to forget it, Helen! There's another reason why I didn't come up. It has left me with a profound sense of shame.

HELEN: Of what?

ELSA: Myself. The whole stupid mess.

HELEN: Mess?

ELSA: Yes, mess! Have you got a better word to describe a situation so rotten with lies and deceit that your only sense of yourself is one of disgust?

HELEN: And you were so happy when you told me about him on your last visit.

ELSA: God, that was more than just happiness, Miss Helen. It was like discovering the reason for being the person, the woman, I am for the first time in my life. And a little bit scary . . . realizing that another person could do so much to your life, to your sense of yourself. Even before it all went wrong, there were a couple of times when I wasn't so sure I liked it.

HELEN: But what happened? Was there a row about something?

ELSA (*Bitter little laugh*): Row? Oh, Helen! Yes, there were plenty of those. But they were incidental. There had to be some sort of noise, so we shouted at each other. We also cried. We did everything you're supposed to.

HELEN: All I know about him is what you told me. He sounded like such a sensitive and good man, well-read and intelligent. So right for you.

ELSA: He was all of that. (*A moment's hesitation. She is not certain about saying something. She decides to take the chance*) There's also something about him I didn't tell you. He's married. He has a devoted, loving wife—quite pretty in fact—and a child. A little girl. Shocked you?

HELEN: Yes. You should have told me, Elsie. I would have warned you.

ELSA: That's exactly why I didn't. I knew you would, but I was going to prove you wrong. Anyway, I didn't need any warnings. Anything you could have said to me, Helen, I'd said to myself from the very beginning . . . but I was going to prove myself wrong as well. What it all came down to finally was that there were two very different ideas about what was happening, and we discovered it too late. You see, I was in it for keeps, Helen. I knew that we were all going to get hurt, that somehow we would all end up being victims of the situation . . . but I also believed that when the time came to choose I would be the lucky winner, that he would leave his wife and child and go with me. Boy, was I wrong! Ding-dong, wrong-wrong, tolls Elsa's bell at the close of the day!

HELEN: Don't do that.

ELSA: Defense mechanism. It still hurts. I'm getting impatient for the time when I'll be able to laugh at it all. I mustn't make him sound like a complete bastard. He wasn't without a conscience. Far from it. If anything, it was too big. The end would have been a lot less messy if he'd known how to just walk away and close the door behind him. When finally the time for that did come, he sat around in pain and torment, crying—God, that was awful!—waiting for me to tell him to go back to his wife and child. Should have seen him, Helen. He came up with postures of despair that would have made Michelangelo jealous. I know it's all wrong to find another person's pain disgusting, but that is what eventually happened. The last time he crucified himself on the sofa in my living room I felt like vomiting. He told me just once too often how much he hated himself for hurting me.

HELEN: Elsie, my poor darling. Come here.

ELSA *(Taut):* I'm all right now. *(Pause)* Do you know what the really big word is, Helen? I had it all wrong. Like most people, I suppose I used to think it was "love." That's the big one all right, and it's quite an event when it comes along. But there's an even bigger one. Trust. And more dangerous. Because that's when you drop your defenses, lay yourself wide open, and if you've made a mistake, you're in big, big trouble. And it hurts like hell. Ever heard the story about the father giving his son his first lesson in business? (MISS HELEN *shakes her head)* I think it's meant to be a joke, so remember to laugh. He puts his little boy high up on something or other and says to him "Jump. Don't worry, I'll catch you." The child is nervous, of course, but Daddy keeps reassuring him: "I'll catch you." Eventually the little boy works up enough courage and does jump, and Daddy, of course, doesn't make a move to catch him. When the child has stopped crying—because he has hurt himself—the father says: "Your first lesson in business, my son. Don't trust anybody." *(Pause)* If you tell it with a Jewish accent, it's even funnier.

HELEN: I don't think it's funny.

ELSA: I think it's ugly. That little boy is going to think twice about jumping again, and at this moment the same goes for Elsa Barlow.

HELEN: Don't speak too soon, Elsie. Life has surprised me once or twice.

ELSA: I'm talking about trust, Miss Helen. I can see myself loving somebody else again. Not all that interested in it right at the moment, but there's an even chance that it will happen again. Doesn't seem as if we've got much choice in the matter anyway. But trusting?

HELEN: You can have the one without the other?

ELSA: Oh yes. That much I've learned. I went on loving David long after I realized I couldn't trust him anymore. That is why life is just a bit complicated at the moment. A little of that love is still hanging around.

HELEN: I've never really thought about it.

ELSA: Neither had I. It needs a betrayal to get you going.

HELEN: Then I suppose I've been lucky. I never had any important trusts to betray . . . until I met you. My marriage might have looked like that, but it was habit that kept Stefanus and me together. I was never . . . open? . . . to him. Was that the phrase you used?

ELSA: Wide open.

HELEN: That's it! It's a good one. I was never "wide open" to anyone. But with you all of that changed. So it's as simple as that. Trust. I've always tried to understand what made you, and being with you, so different from anything else in my life. But, of course, that's it. I trust you. That's why my little girl can come out and play. All the doors are wide open!

ELSA *(Breaking the mood)*: So there, Miss Helen. You asked for the news . . .

HELEN: I almost wish I hadn't.

Light has now faded. MISS HELEN *fetches a box of matches and lights the candles on the table. The room floats up gently out of the gloom, the mirrors and glitter on the walls reflecting the candlelight.* ELSA *picks up one of the candles and walks around the room with it, and we see something of the magic to come.*

ELSA: Still works, Miss Helen. In the car driving up I was wondering if the novelty would have worn off a little. But here it is again. You're a little wizard, you know. You make magic with your mirrors and glitter. "Never light a candle carelessly, and be sure you know what you're doing when you blow one out!" Remember saying that?

HELEN: To myself, yes. Many times.

ELSA: And to me . . . after you had stopped laughing at the expression on my face when you lit them for the first time. "Light is a miracle, Miss Barlow, which even the most ordinary human being can make happen." We had just had our first pot of tea together. Maybe I do take it all just a little for granted now. But that first time . . . I wish I could make you realize what it's like to be walking down a dusty, deserted little street in a Godforsaken village in the middle of the Karoo, bored to death by the heat and flies and silence, and then to be stopped in your tracks—and I mean stopped!—by all of that out there. And then, having barely recovered from that, to come inside and find *this*! Believe me Helen, when I saw your "Mecca" for the first time, I just stood there and gaped. "What in God's name am I looking at? Camels and pyramids? Not three, but dozens of Wise Men? Owls with old motorcar headlights for eyes? Peacocks with more color and glitter than the real birds? Heat stroke? Am I hallucinating?" And then you! Standing next to a mosque made out of beer bottles and staring back at me like one of your owls! *(A good laugh at the memory)* She's mad. No question about it. Everything they've told me about her is true. A genuine Karoo nutcase. *(Walking carefully around* MISS HELEN *in a mock attitude of wary and suspicious examination)* Doesn't look dangerous, though. Wait . . . she's smiling! Be careful, Barlow! Could be a trick. They didn't say she was violent, though. Just mad. Mad as a hatter. Go on. Take a chance. Say hello and see what happens. "Hello!"

Both women laugh.

HELEN: You're exaggerating. It wasn't like that at all.

ELSA: Yes, it was.

HELEN: And I'm saying it wasn't. To start with, it wasn't the mosque. I was repairing a mermaid.

ELSA: I forgot the mermaids!

HELEN *(Serenely certain):* And I was the one who spoke first. I asked you to point out the direction to Mecca. You made a mistake, and so I corrected you. Then I invited you into the yard, showed you around, after which we came into the house for that pot of tea.

ELSA: That is precisely what I mean! Who would ever believe it? That you found yourself being asked to point out the direction to Mecca—not London, or New York, or Paris, but Mecca—in the middle of the Karoo by a little lady no bigger than a bird surrounded by camels and owls . . . and mermaids! . . . made of cement? Who in their right mind is going to believe that? And then this *(The room),* your little miracle of light and color. (MISS HELEN *is smiling with suppressed pride and pleasure)* You were proud of yourself, weren't you? Come on, admit it.

HELEN *(Trying hard to contain her emotion):* Yes, I admit I was a little proud.

ELSA: Miss Helen, just a little?

HELEN *(She can't hold back any longer):* All right, then, no! Not just a little. Oh, most definitely not. I was prouder of myself that day than I had ever been in my life. Nobody before you, or since, has done that to me. I was tingling all over with excitement as we walked around the yard looking at the statues. All those years of working on my Mecca had at last been vindicated. I've got a silly little confession to make about that first meeting. When we came inside and were sitting in here talking and drinking tea and the light started to fade and it became time to light a candle . . . I suddenly realized I was beginning to feel shy, more shy than I had even been with Stefanus on my wedding night. It got so bad I was half-wishing you would stand up and say it was time to go! You see, when I lit the candles you were finally going to see all of me. I don't mean my face, or the clothes I was wearing—you had already seen all of that out in the yard—I mean the *real* me, because that is what this room is . . . and I desperately, oh so desperately, wanted you to like what you saw. By the time we met I had got used to rude eyes staring at me and my work, dismissing both of them as ugly. I'd lived with those eyes for fifteen years, and they didn't bother me anymore. Yours were different. In just the little time we had already been together I had ended up feeling. . . . No, more than that: I *knew* I could trust them. There's our big word again, Elsie! I was so nervous I didn't know what we were talking about anymore while I sat here trying to find enough courage to get a box of matches and light the candles. But eventually I did and you . . . you looked around the room and laughed with delight! You liked what you saw! This is the best of me, Elsa. This is what I really am. Forget everything else. Nothing, not even my name or my face, is me as much as those Wise Men and their camels traveling to the East, or the light and glitter in this room. The mermaids, the wise old owls, the gorgeous peacocks . . . all of them are *me*. And I had delighted you!

Dear God. If you only knew what you did for my life that day. How much courage, how much faith in it you gave me. Because all those years of being laughed at and thought a mad old woman had taken their toll, Elsie. When you walked into my life that afternoon I hadn't been able to work or make anything for nearly a year . . . and I was beginning to think I wouldn't ever again, that I had reached the end. The only reason I've got for being alive is my Mecca. Without that I'm . . . nothing . . . a useless old woman getting on everybody's nerves . . . and that is exactly what I had started to feel like. You revived my life.

I didn't sleep that night after you left. My Mecca was a long way from being finished! All the things I still had to do, all the statues I still had to make, came crowding in on me when I went to bed. I thought my head was going to burst! I've never been so impatient with darkness all my life. I sat up in bed all night waiting for the dawn to come so that I could start working again, and then just go on working and working.

ELSA: And you certainly did that, Miss Helen. On my next trip you proudly introduced me to a very stern Buddha, remember? The cement was still wet.

HELEN: That's quite right. That was my next one.

ELSA: Then came the Easter Island head, the one with the topknot.

HELEN: Correct.

ELSA: And you still haven't explained to me what it's doing in Mecca — and, for that matter, wise old owls and mermaids as well.

HELEN: My Mecca has got a logic of its own, Elsa. Even I don't properly understand it.

ELSA: And then my favorite! That strange creature, half-cock, half-man, on the point of dropping his trousers. Really Helen!

HELEN: That one is pure imagination. I don't know where it comes from. And I've told you before, he's not dropping his trousers, he's pulling them up.

ELSA: And I remain unconvinced. Take another good look at the expression on his face. That's anticipation, not satisfaction. Any surprises this time?

Pause.

HELEN: This time?

ELSA: Yes.

HELEN: No. There aren't any surprises this time.

ELSA: Work in progress?

HELEN: Not at the moment. I haven't managed to get started on anything since you were last here.

ELSA: What happened to the moon mosaic? Remember? Against the back wall! You were going to use those ceramic chips I brought you.

HELEN: They're safe. There in the corner.

ELSA: Yes, I saw them . . . in exactly the same spot where I left them three months ago. It sounded such a wonderful idea, Helen. You were so excited when you told me about it.

HELEN: And I still am. I've still got it.

ELSA: So what are you waiting for? Roll up your sleeves and get on with it.

HELEN: It's not as simple as that, Elsie. You see . . . that's the trouble. It's still only just an *idea* I'm *thinking* about. I can't see it clearly enough yet to start work on it. I've told you before, Elsie, I have to *see* them very clearly first. They've got to come to me inside like pictures. And if they don't, well, all I can do is wait . . . and hope that they will. I wish I knew how to make it happen, but I don't. I don't know where the pictures come from. I can't force myself to see something that isn't there. I've tried to do that once or twice in the past when I was desperate, but the work always ended up a lifeless, shapeless mess. If they don't come, all I can do is wait . . . which is what I'm doing. (*She is revealing a lot of inner agitation*)

ELSA *(Carefully)*: I'm listening, Miss Helen. Go on.

HELEN: I try to be patient with myself, but it's hard. There isn't all that much time left . . . and then my eyes . . . and my hands . . . they're not what they used to be. But the worst thing of all is . . . suppose that I'm waiting for nothing, that there won't be any more pictures inside ever again, that this time I *have* reached the end? Oh God, no! Please no. Anything but that. You do understand, don't you, Elsie?

ELSA: I think I do. (*She speaks quietly. It is not going to be easy*) Come and sit down here with me, Helen. (MISS HELEN *does so, but apprehensively*) It's time to talk about your last letter, Helen.

HELEN: Do we have to do that now? Can't it wait?

ELSA: No.

HELEN: Please.

ELSA: Sorry, Helen, but we've only got tonight.

HELEN: Then don't spoil it!

ELSA: Helen . . . that letter is the reason for me being here. You do realize that, don't you?

HELEN: Yes. I guessed that was the reason for your visit. But you must make allowances, little Elsie. I wasn't feeling very well when I wrote it.

ELSA: That much is obvious.

HELEN: But I've cheered up ever so much since then. Truly. And now with your visit . . . I just know everything is going to be all right again. I was very depressed you see. I wrote it in a bad depression. But I regretted posting it the moment after I had dropped it into the letter box. I even thought about asking the postmaster if I could have it back.

ELSA: Why didn't you? (*Pause*) Or send me a telegram: "Ignore last letter. Feeling much better." Six words. That would have done it.

HELEN: I didn't think of that.

ELSA: We're wasting precious time. You wrote it, posted it, and I received it.

HELEN: So can't we now, please, just forget it?

ELSA *(Disbelief):* Miss Helen, do you remember what you said in it?

HELEN: Vaguely.

ELSA: That's not good enough. *(She goes to the bedroom alcove and fetches the letter from her briefcase)*

HELEN: What are you going to do?

ELSA: Read it.

HELEN: No! I don't want to hear it.

ELSA: You already have, Miss Helen. You wrote it.

HELEN: But I don't want to talk about it.

ELSA: Yes, you must.

HELEN: Don't bully me, Elsa! You know I don't know how to fight back. Please . . . not tonight. Can't we—

ELSA: No, we can't. For God's sake, Helen! We've only got tonight and maybe a little of tomorrow to talk.

HELEN: But you mustn't take it seriously.

ELSA: Too late, Helen. I already have. I've driven eight hundred miles without a break because of this. And don't lie to me. You meant every word of it. *(Pause)* I'm not trying to punish you for writing it. I've come because I want to try and help. *(She sits down at the table, pulls the candle closer and reads. She struggles a little to decipher words. The handwriting is obviously bad)*

My very own and dearest little Elsie,

Have you finally also deserted me? This is my fourth letter to you and still no reply. Have I done something wrong? This must surely be the darkest night of my soul. I thought I had lived through that fifteen years ago, but I was wrong. This is worse. Infinitely worse. I had nothing to lose that night. Nothing in my life was precious or worth holding on to. Now there is so much and I am losing it all . . . you, the house, my work, my Mecca. I can't fight them alone, little Elsie. I need you. Don't you care about me anymore? It is only through your eyes that I now see my Mecca. I need you, Elsie. My eyesight is so bad that I can barely see the words I am writing. And my hands can hardly hold the pen. Help me, little Elsie. Everything is ending and I am alone in the dark. There is no light left. I would rather do away with myself than carry on like this.

Your ever-loving and anguished
Helen.

(She carefully folds up the letter and puts it back in the envelope) What's all that about losing your house. Who's trying to get you out?

HELEN: I exaggerated a little. They're not really being nasty about it.

ELSA: Who?

HELEN: The Church Council. They say it's for my own good. And I do understand what they mean, it's just that—

ELSA: Slowly, Miss Helen, slowly. I still don't know what you're talking about. Start from the beginning. What has the Church Council got to do with you and the house? I thought it was yours.

HELEN: It is.

ELSA: So?

HELEN: It's not the house, Elsa. It's me. They discussed me . . . my situation . . . at one of their meetings.

ELSA *(Disbelief and anger)*: They *what?*

HELEN: That's how Marius put it. He . . . he said they were worried about me living here alone.

ELSA: *They* are worried about *you?*

HELEN: Yes. It's my health they are worried about.

ELSA *(Shaking her head):* When it comes to hypocrisy—and blatant hypocrisy at that—you Afrikaners are in a class by yourselves. So tell me, did they also discuss Gertruida's situation? And what about Mrs. van Heerden down at the other end of the village? They're about the same age as you and they also live alone.

HELEN: That's what I said. But Marius said it's different with them.

ELSA: In what way?

HELEN: Well, you see, because of my hands and everything else, they don't believe I can look after myself so well anymore.

ELSA: Are they right?

HELEN: No! I'm quite capable of looking after myself.

ELSA: And where are you supposed to go if you leave the village? To a niece, four times removed, in Durban, whom you've only seen a couple of times in your life?

MISS HELEN *goes to a little table at the back and fetches a form which she hands to* ELSA.

(Reading) "Sunshine Home for the Aged." I see. So it's like that, is it? That's the lovely old house on the left when you come into Graaff-Reinet, next to the church. In fact, it's run by the church, isn't it?

HELEN: Yes.

ELSA: That figures. It's got a beautiful garden, Miss Helen. Whenever I drive past on my way up here there are always a few old folk in their "twilight years" sitting around enjoying the sunshine. It's well named. It all looks very restful. So that's what they want to do with you. This is not your handwriting.

HELEN: No. Marius filled it in for me.

ELSA: Very considerate of him.

HELEN: He's coming to fetch it tonight.

ELSA: For an old friend he sounds a little overeager to have you on your way, Miss Helen.

HELEN: It's just that they've got a vacancy at the moment. They're usually completely full. There's a long waiting list. But I haven't signed it yet!

ELSA *studies* MISS HELEN *in silence for a few moments.*

ELSA: How bad are your hands? Be honest with me.

HELEN: They're not *that* bad. I exaggerated a little in my letter.

ELSA: You could still work with them if you wanted to?

HELEN: Yes.

ELSA: Is there anything you can't do?

HELEN: I can do anything I want to, Elsie . . . if I make the effort.

ELSA: Let me see them.

HELEN: Please don't. I'm ashamed of them.

ELSA: Come on.

MISS HELEN *holds out her hands.* ELSA *examines them.*
And these scabs?

HELEN: They're nothing. A little accident at the stove. I was making prickly-pear syrup for you.

ELSA: There seem to have been a lot of little accidents lately. Better be more careful.

HELEN: I will. I definitely will.

ELSA: Pain?

HELEN: Just a little. *(While* ELSA *studies her hands)* Just that one letter after your last visit, saying you had arrived back safely and would be writing again soon, and then nothing. Three months.

ELSA: I did write, Helen. Two very long letters.

HELEN: I never got them.

ELSA: Because I never posted them.

HELEN: Elsie! Why? They would have made all the difference in the world.

ELSA *(Shaking her head):* No. Muddled, confused, full of self-pity. Knowing now what you were trying to deal with here, they were hardly what you needed in your life.

HELEN: You're very wrong. Anything would have been better than nothing.

ELSA: No, Helen. Believe me nothing was better than those two letters. I've still got them at home. I read them now whenever I need to count my blessings. They remind me of the mess I was in.

HELEN: That's why I feel so bad now about the letter I wrote you. My problems seem so insignificant compared with yours.

ELSA: Don't let's start that, Helen. Sorting our problem priorities isn't going to get us anywhere. In any case, mine are over and done with . . . which leaves us with you. So what are you going to do?

MISS HELEN *doesn't answer.* ELSA *is beginning to lose patience.*
Come *on,* Helen! If I hadn't turned up tonight, what were you going to say to Dominee Marius Byleveld when he came around?

HELEN: I was going to ask him to give me a little more time to think about it.

ELSA: You were going to *ask* him for it, not *tell* him you *wanted* it? And *do* you need more time to think about it? I thought you knew what you wanted?

HELEN: Of course I do.

ELSA: Then tell me again. And say it simply. I need to hear it.

HELEN: You know I can't leave here, Elsa!

ELSA: For a moment I wasn't so sure. So then what's the problem? When he comes around tonight hand this back to him . . . unsigned . . . and say no. Thank him for his trouble but tell him you are perfectly happy where you are and quite capable of looking after yourself. *(*MISS HELEN *hesitates. A sense of increasing emotional confusion and uncertainty)* Helen, you have just said that is what you want.

HELEN: I know. It's just that Marius is such a persuasive talker.

ELSA: Then talk back!

HELEN: I'm not very good at that. Won't you help me, little Elsie, please, and speak to him as well? You are so much better at arguing than me.

ELSA: No, I won't! And for God's sake stop behaving like a naughty child who's been called to the principal's office. I'm sorry, but the more I hear about your Marius, the worse it gets. If you want my advice, you'll keep the two of us well away from each other. I *won't* argue with him on your behalf because there is nothing to argue about. This is not his house, and it most certainly is not his life that is being discussed at Church Council meetings. Who the hell do they think they are? Sitting around a table deciding what is going to happen to you!

HELEN: Marius did say that they were trying to think of what was best for me.

ELSA: No, they're not! God knows what they're thinking about, but it's certainly not that. Dumping you with a lot of old people who've hung on for too long and nobody wants around anymore? You're still living your life, Helen, not drooling it away. The only legal way they can get you out of this house is by having you certified. *(Awkward silence)* We all know you're as mad as a hatter, but it's not quite that bad. *(Another pause)* One little question though, Miss Helen. You haven't been going around talking about doing away with yourself to anyone have you?

HELEN: I told you, Katrina is the only person I really see anymore.

ELSA: And Marius. Don't forget him. Anyway it doesn't matter who it is. All it needs is one person to be able to stand up and testify that they heard you say it.

HELEN: Well, I haven't.

ELSA: Because it would make life a lot easier for them if they ever did try to do something. So no more of that. Okay? Did you hear me, Helen?

HELEN: Yes, I heard you.

ELSA: And while you're about it, add me to your list. I don't want to hear or read any more about it either.

HELEN: I heard you, Elsie! Why do you keep on about it?

ELSA: Because talk like that could be grounds for forcibly committing someone to a "Sunshine Home for the Aged"! I'm sorry, Helen, but what do you expect me to do? Pretend you never said it? Is that what you would have done if our situations had been reversed? If in the middle of my mess I had threatened to do that? God knows, I came near to feeling like it a couple of times. I had a small taste of how bloody pointless everything can seem to be. But if I can hang on, then you most certainly can't throw in the towel—not after all the rounds you've already won against them. So when the dominee comes around, you're going to put on a brave front. Let's get him and his stupid ideas about an old-age home right out of your life. Because you're going to say no, remember? Be as polite and civil as you like—we'll offer him tea and biscuits and discuss the weather and the evils of alcohol—but when the time comes, you're going to thank him for all his trouble and consideration and then hand this back to him with a firm "No, thank you." *(Another idea)* And just to make quite sure he gets the message, you can also mention your trip into Graaff-Reinet next week to see a doctor and an optician.

HELEN: What do you mean?

ELSA: Exactly what I said: appointments with a doctor and an optician.

HELEN: But I haven't got any.

ELSA: You will on Monday. Before I leave tomorrow I'm going to ask Getruida to take you into Graaff-Reinet next week. And this time you're going to go. There must be something they can do about your hands, even if it's just to ease the pain. And a little "regmaker" for your depressions. (MISS HELEN *wants to say something*) No arguments! And to hell with your vanity as well. We all know you think you're the prettiest thing in the village, but if you need glasses, you're going to wear them. I'll make the appointments myself and phone through after you've been in to find out what the verdict is. I'm not trying to be funny, Helen. You've got to prove to the village that you are quite capable of looking after yourself. It's the only way to shut them up.

HELEN: You're going too fast for me, Elsa. You're not allowing me to say anything.

ELSA: That's quite right. How many times in the past have we sat down and tried to talk about all of this? And every time the same story: "I'll think about it, Elsa." Your thinking has got us nowhere, Helen. This time you're just going to agree . . . and that includes letting Katrina come in a couple of times each week to do the house.

HELEN: There's nothing for her to do. I can manage by myself.

ELSA: No, you can't. (*She runs her finger over a piece of furniture and holds it up for* MISS HELEN *to see the dust*)

HELEN: Everything would have been spotless if I had known you were coming.

ELSA: It's got to be spotless all the time! To hell with *my* visits and holidays. I don't live here. You do. I'm concerned with *your* life, Helen. And I'm also not blind, you know. I saw you struggling with that large kettle. Yes, let's talk about that. When did you last boil up enough water for a decent bath? Come on, Helen. Can't you remember? Some time ago, right? Is it because of personal neglect that you've stopped caring about yourself or because you aren't able to? Answer me.

HELEN: I can't listen to you anymore, Elsa. (*She makes a move to leave the room*)

ELSA: Don't do that to me Helen! If you leave this room I'm getting into my car and driving back to Cape Town. You wrote that letter. I haven't made it up. All I'm trying to do is deal with it.

HELEN: No, you're not.

ELSA: Then I give up. What in God's name have we been talking about?

HELEN: A pair of spectacles and medicine for my arthritis and Katrina dusting the house—

ELSA: Do you want me to read it again?

HELEN (*Ignoring the interruption*): You're treating that letter like a shopping list. That isn't what I was writing about.

ELSA: Then what was it?

HELEN: Darkness, Elsa! Darkness! (*She speaks with an emotional intensity and authority which forces* ELSA *to listen in silence*) The Darkness that nearly smothered my life in here one night fifteen years ago. The same Darkness that used to come pouring down the chimney and into the room at night when I was a little girl and frighten me. If you still don't know what I'm talking about, blow out the candles!

But those were easy Darknesses to deal with. The one I'm talking about now is much worse. It's inside me, Elsa . . . it's got inside me at last and I can't light candles there. *(Pause)*

I never knew that could happen. I thought I was safe. I had grown up and I had all the candles I wanted. That is all that little girl could think about when she lay there in bed, trying to make her prayers last as long as she could because she was terrified of the moment when her mother would bend down and kiss her and take away the candle. One day she would have her very own! That was the promise: that one day when I was big enough, she would leave one at my bedside for me to light as often as I wanted. That's all that "getting big" ever meant to me—my very own candle at my bedside.

Such brave little lights! And they taught the little girl how to be that. When she saw one burning in the middle of the night, she knew what courage was. All my life they have helped me to find courage . . . until now.

I'm frightened, Elsie, more frightened than that little girl ever was. There's no "getting big" left to wait for, no prayers to say until that happens . . . and the candles don't help anymore. That is what I was trying to tell you. I'm frightened. And Marius can see it. He's no fool, Elsa. He knows that his moment has finally come.

ELSA: What moment?

HELEN: He's been waiting a long time for me to reach the end of my Mecca. I thought I had cheated him out of it, that that moment would never come.

All those years when I was working away, when it was slowly taking shape, he was there as well . . . standing in the distance, watching and waiting.

I used to peep at him through the curtains. He'd come walking past, then stop, stand there at the gate with his hands behind his back and stare at my Wise Men. And even though he didn't show anything, I know he didn't like what he saw. I used to sing when I was working. He heard me one day and came up and asked: "Are you really that happy, Helen?"

I laughed. Not at *him,* believe me not at him, but because I had a secret he would never understand. *(Pause)*

It's his turn to laugh now. But he won't, of course. He's not that sort of man. He'll be very gentle again . . . pull the curtains and close the shutters the way he did that night fifteen years ago . . . because nobody must stare into a house where there's been a death.

If my Mecca is finished, Elsa, then so is my life.

ELSA *is overwhelmed by a sense of helplessness and defeat.*

ELSA: I think I've had it. It's too much for one day. That woman on the road and now you. I honestly don't know how to handle it. In fact, at this moment, I don't think I know anything. I don't know what it means to be walking eighty miles to Cradock with your baby on your back. I don't know whether your

Mecca is finished or not. And all I know about Darkness is that that is when you put on the lights. Jesus! I wouldn't mind somebody coming along and telling me what it does all mean.

So where does all of that leave us, Miss Helen? I'm lost. What are you going to do when he comes? *(No answer)* Ask him—please—for more time? One thing I can tell you right now is that there's no point to that. If you don't say no tonight, you won't ever, in which case you might as well sign that form and get it over and done with. *(A cruel, relentless tone in her voice)* There's no point in talking about anything until that's settled. So you better think about it, Helen. While you do that, I'll see what I can organize for supper.

She exits into the kitchen. A man's voice off: "Anybody at home?" MARIUS *appears in the doorway:*

MARIUS: Miss Helen! Alone in the dark? I didn't think anybody was home.

ELSA *appears from the kitchen.*

Ah, Miss Barlow!

END OF ACT ONE

ACT TWO

The same a few minutes later. MARIUS *and* ELSA *are now at the table with* MISS HELEN, *the center of attraction being a basket of vegetables which* MARIUS *has brought with him. He is about the same age as* MISS HELEN *and is neatly but casually dressed. He speaks with simple sincerity and charm.*

MARIUS *(Holding up a potato)*: Feast your eyes on this, Miss Barlow! A genuine Sneeuberg potato! A pinch of salt and you've got a meal, and if you want to be extravagant, add a little butter and you have indeed got a feast. We had a farmer from the Gamtoos Valley up here last week, trying to sell potatoes to us! Can you believe it? Did you see him, Helen? He had his lorry parked in front of the Post Office. What's the English expression, Miss Barlow? Coals to—where?

ELSA: Coals to Newcastle.

MARIUS: That's it! Well in this case it was very near to being an insult as well. We pride ourselves in these parts on knowing what a potato really is. And here you have it. The "apple of the earth," as the French would say. But I don't imagine that poor man will come again. Shame! I ended up feeling very sorry for him. "Don't you people like potatoes?" he asked me. What could I say? I didn't have the heart to tell him he'd wasted his time driving all this distance, that *nobody* comes to Sneeuberg to sell potatoes! And then, to make me feel really bad, he insisted on giving me a small sack of them before he drove off. I don't think he sold enough to cover the cost of his petrol back home.

I also brought you a few beets and tomatoes. The beets have passed their best now, but if you pickle and bottle them, they'll be more than all right. Have you ever treated our young friend to a taste of that, Miss Helen? *(To* ELSA*)* It's one of our local specialties. One thing I can assure you ladies is that these vegetables are as fresh as you are ever likely to get. I dug them up myself this afternoon.

HELEN: It's very kind of you, Marius, but you really shouldn't have bothered.

MARIUS: It wasn't any bother at all. I've got more than enough for myself stored away in the pantry. Would have been a sin to leave them to rot in the ground when somebody else could use them. And at our age we need fresh vegetables, Helen. *(Wagging a finger at her)* Marie biscuits and tea are not a balanced diet. *(To* ELSA*)* In the old days Helen used to have a very fine vegetable garden of her own out there. But as you can see, the humble potato has been crowded out by other things. I don't think there's enough room left out there now to grow a radish. *(He turns back to the basket)* Yes, the Good Lord was very generous to us this past year. I don't really know that we deserve it, but our rains came just when we needed them. Not too much or too little. Believe me, young lady, we are well experienced in both those possibilities. Not so, Helen?

ELSA: The Karoo looked very dry and desolate to me as I drove through it this afternoon.

MARIUS: Dry it certainly is, but not desolate. It might appear that to a townsman's eye—as indeed it did to mine when I first came here!—but that is because we are already deep into our autumn. It will be a good few months before we see rain again.

ELSA: I've never thought of this world as having seasons . . . certainly not the soft ones. To me it has always been a landscape of extremes, too hot or too cold, too dry or else Miss Helen is writing to me about floods that have cut off the village from the outside world. It reminds me of something I once read where the desert was described as "God without mankind."

MARIUS: What an interesting thought: "God without mankind." I can't decide whether that's Catholic or Protestant. Would you know?

ELSA *(Shaking her head):* No.

MARIUS: Who wrote it?

ELSA: A French writer. Balzac. It sums up the way I feel about the Karoo. The Almighty hasn't exactly made mankind overwelcome here, has he? In fact, it almost looks as if he resented our presence. Sorry, Dominee, I don't mean to be blasphemous or ungenerous to your world, it's just that I'm used to a gentler one.

MARIUS: You judge it too harshly, Miss Barlow. It has got its gentle moments and moods as well . . . all the more precious because there are so few of them. We can't afford to take them for granted. As you can see, it feeds us. Can any man or woman ask for more than that from the little bit of earth he lives on?

ELSA: Do you think your Coloured folk feel the same way about things?

MARIUS: Why should it be any different for them?

ELSA: I was just wondering whether they had as many reasons to be as contented as you?

MARIUS: I was talking about simple gratitude, Miss Barlow. Wouldn't you say contentment is a more complicated state of mind? One that can very easily be disturbed. But grateful? Yes! Our Coloured folk also have every reason to be. Ask them. Ask little Katrina, who visits Miss Helen so faithfully, if she or her baby have ever wanted for food . . . even when Koos has spent all his wages on liquor. There are no hungry people, white or Coloured, in this village, Miss Barlow. Those of us who are more fortunate than others are well aware of the responsibilities that go with that good fortune. But I don't want to get into an argument. It is my world—and Helen's—and we can't expect an outsider to love or understand it as we do.

ELSA: I'll put these *(The vegetables)* away for you, Miss Helen.

MARIUS: Don't bother to unpack them now. I'll collect the basket tomorrow after church. *(Calling after* ELSA *as she leaves the room)* And there's no need to wash them. I've already done that. Just put them straight into the pot.

Exit ELSA.

I've got a feeling that, given half a chance, your young friend and myself *could* very easily find ourselves in an argument. I think Miss Barlow gets a little impatient with our old-fashioned ways and attitudes. But it's too late for us to change now. Right, Helen?

HELEN: Elsa and I have already had those arguments, Marius.

MARIUS: I hope you put up a good defense on our behalf.

HELEN: I tried my best.

MARIUS: And yet the two of you still remain good friends.

HELEN: Oh yes!

MARIUS: And so it should be. A true friendship should be able to accommodate a difference of opinion. You didn't mention anything about her coming up for a visit last time we talked.

HELEN: Because I didn't know. It's an unexpected visit.

MARIUS: Will she be staying long?

HELEN: Just tonight. She goes back tomorrow.

MARIUS: Good heavens! All this way for only one night. I hope nothing is wrong.

HELEN: No. She just decided on the spur of the moment to visit me. But she's got to go back because they're very busy at school. They're right in the middle of exams.

MARIUS: I see. May I sit down for a moment, Helen?

HELEN: Of course, Marius. Forgive me, I'm forgetting my manners.

MARIUS: I won't stay long. I must put down a few thoughts for tomorrow's sermon. And, thanks to you, I know what I want to say.

HELEN: Me?

MARIUS: Yes, you. *(Teasing her)* You are responsible . . .

HELEN: Oh dear!

MARIUS *(A little laugh):* Relax, Helen. I only said "thanks to you" because it came to me this afternoon while I was digging up your vegetables. I spent a lot of time, while I was out in the garden doing that, just leaning on my spade. My back is giving me a bit of trouble again and, to tell you the truth, I also felt lazy.

I wasn't thinking about anything in particular . . . just looking, you know, the way an old man does, looking around, recognizing once again and saying the names. Spitskop in the distance! Aasvoelkrans down at the other end of the valley. The poplars with their autumn foliage standing around as yellow and still as that candle flame!

And a lot of remembering.

As you know, Helen, I had deep and very painful wounds in my soul when I first came here. Wounds I thought would never heal. This was going to be where I finally escaped from life, turned by back on it and justified what was left of my existence by ministering to you people's simple needs. I was very wrong. I didn't escape life here, I discovered it, what it really means, the fullness and goodness of it. It's a deep and lasting regret that Aletta wasn't alive to share that discovery with me. Anyway, all of this was going on in my head when I realized I was hearing a small little voice, and the small little voice was saying, "Thank you." With every spadeful of earth that I turned when I went down on my knees to lift the potatoes out of the soil, there it was: "Thank you." It was mine! I was muttering away to myself the way we old folks are inclined to do when nobody is around. It was me saying, "Thank you."

That is what I want to do tomorrow, Helen. Give thanks, but in a way that I've never done before.

I know I've stood there in the pulpit many times telling all of you to do exactly that, but oh dear me, the cleverness and conceit in the soul of Marius Byleveld when he was doing that! I had an actor's vanity up there, Helen. I'm not saying I was a total hypocrite but, believe me, in those thanksgivings I was listening to my dominee's voice and its hoped-for eloquence every bit as much as to the true little voice inside my heart . . . the voice I heard so clearly this afternoon.

That's the voice that must speak tomorrow! And to do that I must find words as simple as the sky I was standing under this afternoon or the earth I was turning over with my spade. They have got no vanities and conceits. They are just "there." If the Almighty takes pity on us, the one gives us rain so that the other can in turn . . . give us this day our daily potato. *(A smile at this gentle little joke)* Am I making sense, Helen? Answer me truthfully.

HELEN: Yes, you are, Marius. And if all you do tomorrow is say what you have just said to me, it will be very moving and beautiful.

MARIUS *(Sincerely):* Truly, Helen? Do you really mean that?

HELEN: Every word of it.

MARIUS: Then I will try.

My twentieth anniversary comes up next month. Yes, that is how long I've been here. Twenty-one years ago, on May the sixteenth, the Good Lord called my Aletta to his side, and just over a year later, on June the eleventh, I gave my first sermon in New Bethesda. *(A little laugh at the memory)* What an occasion that was!

I don't know if I showed it, Helen, but let me confess now that I was more than just a little nervous when I went up into the pulpit and looked down at that stern and formidable array of faces. A very different proposition from the town and city congregations I had been preaching to up until then. When Miss de Klerk played the first bars of the hymn at the end of it, I heaved a very deep sigh of relief. None of you had fallen asleep! *(HELEN is shaking her head)* What's the matter?

HELEN: Young Miss de Klerk came later. Mrs. Niewoudt was still our organist when you gave your first service.

MARIUS: Are you sure?

HELEN: Yes. Mrs. Niewoudt also played at the reception we gave you afterwards in Mr. van Heerden's house. She played the piano and Sterling Retief sang.

MARIUS: You know something, I do believe you're right! Good heavens, Helen, your memory is better than mine.

HELEN: And you had no cause to be nervous. You were very impressive.

MARIUS *(A small pause as he remembers something else):* Yes, of course. You were in that congregation. Stefanus was at your side, as he was going to be every Sunday after that for . . . what? Another five years?

HELEN: Five years.

MARIUS: That was all a long time ago.

HELEN: More than a long time, Marius. It feels like another life.

ELSA *returns with a tray of tea and sandwiches.*

MARIUS: Ah, here comes your supper. I must be running along.

ELSA: Just a sandwich, Dominee. Neither of us is very hungry.

MARIUS: I'll drop by tomorrow night if that is all right with you, Helen.

ELSA: Won't you have a cup of tea with us? It's the least we can offer in return for all those lovely vegetables.

MARIUS: I don't want to intrude. Helen tells me you're here for just the night, Miss Barlow. I'm sure you ladies have got things to talk about in private.

ELSA: We've already done quite a lot of that, haven't we, Helen? Please don't go because of me. I have some school work I must see to. I'll take my tea through to the other room.

HELEN: Don't go, Elsa!

ELSA: I told you I had papers to mark, Miss Helen. I'll just get on with that quietly while the two of you have a little chat.

HELEN: Please!

ELSA: All right then, if it will make you happier, I'll bring my work through and do it in here.

MARIUS: No. I've obviously come at an inconvenient time.

ELSA: Not at all, Dominee. Miss Helen was expecting you.

ELSA *fetches the application form for the old-age home and puts it down on the table. A moment between* ELSA *and* MARIUS. *He turns to* HELEN *for confirmation.*

HELEN: Yes, I was.

ELSA: How do you like your tea?

MARIUS: Very well, if you insist. Milk but no sugar, please.

ELSA *pours tea, then collects her briefcase from the bedroom alcove and settles down to work at a small table at the back of the room.*

You're quite certain you want to discuss this now, Helen?

HELEN: Yes, Marius.

MARIUS: It can wait until tomorrow.

HELEN: No, I'm ready.

MARIUS: Right. Just before we start talking, Helen, the good news is that I've spoken to Dominee Gericke in Graaff-Reinet again, and the room is definitely yours—that is, if you want it, of course. But they obviously can't have it standing empty indefinitely. As it is, he's already broken the rules by putting you at the top of the waiting list, but as a personal favor. He understands the circumstances. So the sooner we decide, one way or the other, the better. But I want you to know that I do realize how big a move it is for you. I want you to be quite certain and happy in your mind that you're doing the right thing. So don't think we've got to rush into it, start packing up immediately or anything like that. A decision must be made, one way or the other, but once you've done that, you can relax and take all the time you need.

MARIUS *takes spectacles, a little notebook, pen and pencil from a jacket pocket. The way he handles everything, carefully and precisely, reveals a meticulous and orderly mind. He opens the application form.* MISS HELEN *gives* ELSA *the first of many desperate and appealing looks.* ELSA, *engrossed in her work, apparently does not notice it.* MARIUS *puts his spectacles on.*

I know we went over this the last time, but there still are just a few questions. Yes . . . we put Stefanus's father's name down as Petrus Johannes Martins, but in the church registry it's down as Petrus *Jacobus. (He takes his spectacles off)* Which one is correct, Helen? Can you remember? You were so certain of Petrus Johannes last time.

HELEN: I still am. But what did you say the other one was?

MARIUS: Petrus Jacobus.

HELEN: Jacobus . . . Johannes. . . . No, maybe I'm not.

MARIUS: In that case what I think I will do is enter it as Petrus *J.* Martins. Just as well I checked. *(He puts his spectacles on again and turns back to the form)* And next . . . yes, the date of your confirmation. Have you been able to find the certificate?

HELEN: No, I haven't. I'm sorry, Marius. I did look, but I'm afraid my papers are all in a mess.

MARIUS *(Taking his spectacles off):* I've been through the church records, but I can't find anything that sheds any light on it. It's not all that important, of course, but it would have been nice to have had that date as well. *(He replaces his spectacles)* Let's see . . . what shall we do? You think you were about twelve?

HELEN: Something like that.

MARIUS: What I'll do is just pencil in 1920 and have one more look. I hate giving up on *that* one. But you surprise me, Helen—of all the dates to have forgotten.

That takes care of the form now. *(He consults his notebook)* Yes. Two little points from Dominee Gericke, after which you can relax and enjoy your supper. He asked me—and do believe me, Helen, he was just trying to be practical and helpful, nothing else—whether you had taken care of everything by way of a last will and testament, and obviously I said I didn't know.

HELEN: What do you mean, Marius?

MARIUS: That in the event of something happening, your house and possessions will be disposed of in the way that you want them to be. Have you done that?

HELEN: I've still got a copy of Stefanus's will. He left everything to me.

MARIUS: We're talking about you, Helen. Have you seen a lawyer?

HELEN: No, I . . . I've never thought of it.

MARIUS: Then it is just as well Gericke asked. Believe me, Helen, in my time as a minister I have seen so many bitterly unhappy situations because somebody neglected to look after that side of things. Families not talking to each other! Lawsuits over a few pieces of furniture! I really do think it is something you should see to. We're at an age now when anything can happen. I had mine revised only a few months ago. *(He glances at the notebook again)* And finally, he made the obvious suggestion that we arrange for you to visit the home as soon as possible. Just to meet the matron and other people there and to see your room. He's particularly anxious for you to see it so that you know what you need to bring on your side. He had a dreadful to-do a few months ago with a lady who tried to move a whole houseful of furniture into her little room. Don't get worried, though. There's plenty of space for personal possessions and a few of your . . . ornaments. That covers everything, I think. All that's left now is for you to sign it . . . provided you want to do that, of course. *(He places his fountain pen, in readiness, on the form)*

HELEN: Marius . . . please . . . please can I talk for a little bit now?

MARIUS: But of course, Helen.

HELEN: I've done a lot of thinking since we last spoke—

MARIUS: Good! We both agreed that was necessary. This is not a step to be taken lightly.

HELEN: Yes, I've done a lot of thinking, and I've worked out a plan.

MARIUS: For what, Helen?

HELEN: A plan to take care of everything.

MARIUS: Excellent!

HELEN: I'm going in to Graaff-Reinet next week, Marius, to see a doctor. I'm going to make the appointment on Monday, and I'll ask Getruida to drive me in.

MARIUS: You make it sound serious, Helen.

HELEN: No, it's just my arthritis. I'm going to get some medicine for it.

MARIUS: For a moment you had me worried. I thought the burns were possibly more serious than we had realized. But why not save yourself a few pennies and see Dr. Lubbe at the home? He looks after everybody there free of charge.

HELEN *(Hanging on):* And spectacles. I'm also going to make arrangements to see an optician and get a pair of spectacles.

MARIUS: Splendid, Helen! You certainly have been making plans.

HELEN: And, finally, I've decided to get Katrina to come in two or three times a week to help me with the house.

MARIUS: Katrina?

HELEN: Little Katrina. Koos Malgas's wife.

MARIUS: I know who you're talking about, Helen. It's just . . . oh dear! I'm sorry to be the one to tell you this, Helen, but I think you are going to lose your little Katrina.

HELEN: What do you mean, Marius?

MARIUS: Koos has asked the Divisional Council for a transfer to their Aberdeen depot, and I think he will get it.

HELEN: So?

MARIUS: I imagine Katrina and the baby will go with him.

HELEN: Katrina . . . ?

MARIUS: Will be leaving the village.

HELEN: No, it can't be.

MARIUS: It's the truth, Helen.

HELEN: But she's said nothing to me about it. She was in here just a few days ago and she didn't mention anything about leaving.

MARIUS: She most probably didn't think it important.

HELEN: How can you say that, Marius? Of course it is! She knows how much I depend on her. If Katrina goes, I'll be completely alone here except for you and the times when Elsa is visiting. *(She is becoming increasingly distressed)*

MARIUS: Come now, Helen! It's not as bad as that. I know Katrina is a sweet little soul and that you are very fond of her, as we all are, but don't exaggerate things. There are plenty of good women in the location who can come and give you a hand in here and help you pack up . . . if you decide to move. Tell you what I'll do: if you're worried about a stranger being in here with all your personal things, I'll lend you my faithful old Nonna. She's been looking after me for ten years now, and in that time I haven't missed a single thing. You could trust her with your life.

HELEN: I'm not talking about a servant, Marius.

MARIUS: I thought we were.

HELEN: Katrina is the only friend I've got left in the village.

MARIUS: That's a hard thing you're saying, Helen. All of us still like to think of ourselves as your friends.

HELEN: I wasn't including you, Marius. You're different. But as for the others . . . no. They've all become strangers to me. I might just as well not know their names. And they treat me as if I were a stranger to them as well.

MARIUS: You're being very unfair, Helen. They behave towards you in the way you apparently want them to, which is to leave you completely alone. Really, Helen! Strangers? Old Getruida, Sterling, Jerry, Boet, Mrs. van Heerden? You grew up in this village with all of them.

To be very frank, Helen, it's your manner which now keeps them at a distance. I don't think you realize how much you've changed over the years. You're not easily recognizable to others anymore as the person they knew fifteen years ago. And then your hobby, if I can call it that, hasn't really helped matters. This is not exactly the sort of room the village ladies are used to or would feel comfortable in having afternoon tea. As for all of that out there . . . the less said about it, the better.

HELEN: I don't harm or bother anyone, Marius!

MARIUS: And does anyone harm or bother you?

HELEN: Yes! Everybody is trying to force me to leave my home.

MARIUS: Nobody is *forcing* you, Helen! In Heaven's name, where do you get that idea from? If you sign this form, it must be of your own free will.

You're very agitated tonight, Helen. Has something happened to upset you? You were so reasonable about everything the last time we talked. You seemed to understand that the only motive on our side is to try and do what is best for you. And even then it's only in the way of advice. We can't *tell* you what to do. But if you want us to stop caring about what happens to you, we can try . . . though I don't know how our Christian consciences would allow us to do that.

HELEN: I don't believe the others care about me, Marius. All they want is to get rid of me. This village has also changed over the past fifteen years. I am not alone in that. I don't recognize it anymore as the simple, innocent world I grew up in.

MARIUS: If it's as bad as that, Helen, if you are now really that unhappy and lonely here, then I don't know why you have any doubts about leaving.

MISS HELEN*'s emotional state has deteriorated steadily.* MARIUS*'s fountain pen has ended up in her hand. She looks down at the application form. A few seconds' pause and then a desperate cry.*

HELEN: Why don't you stop me, Elsa! I'm going to sign it!

ELSA *(Abandoning all pretense of being absorbed in her work):* Then go ahead and do it! Sign that fucking form. If that's what you want to do with your life, just get it over and done with, for God's sake!

MARIUS: Miss Barlow!

ELSA *(Ignoring him):* What are you waiting for, Helen? You're wasting our time. It's late and we want to go to bed.

HELEN: But you said I mustn't sign it.

ELSA *(Brutally):* I've changed my mind. Do it. Hurry up and dispose of your life so that we can get on with ours.

HELEN: Stop it, Elsa. Help me. Please help me.

ELSA: Sorry, Helen. I've had more woman-battering today than I can cope with. You can at least say no. That woman on the road couldn't. But if you haven't got the guts to do that, then too bad. I'm not going to do it for you.

HELEN: I tried.

ELSA: You call that trying? All it required was one word—no.

HELEN: Please believe me, Elsa . . . I was trying!

ELSA: No good, Helen. If that's your best, then maybe you will be better off in an old-age home.

MARIUS: Gently, Miss Barlow! In Heaven's name, gently! What's got into you?

ELSA: Exhaustion, Dominee. Very near total mental and emotional exhaustion, to the point where I want to scream. I've already done that once today, and right now I wouldn't mind doing it a second time. Yes, Helen, I've had it. Why were you "crying out to me in the dark"? To be an audience when you signed away your life? Is that why I'm here? Twelve hours of driving like a lunatic for that? God. What a farce! I might just as well have stayed in Cape Town.

MARIUS: Maybe it's a pity you didn't. I think I understand now why Helen is so agitated tonight. But unfortunately you are here, and if you've got anything to say to her, in Heaven's name be considerate of the state she is in. She needs help, not to be confused and terrified even more.

ELSA: Helen understands the way I feel. We *did* do a lot of talking before you came, Dominee.

MARIUS: I'm concerned with *her* feelings, Miss Barlow, not yours. And if by any chance you are as well, then try to show some respect for her age. Helen is a much older woman than you. You were shouting at her as if she were a child.

ELSA: Me, treating her like a child? Oh my God! You can stand there and accuse me of that after what I've just seen and heard from you?

MARIUS: I don't know what you're talking about.

ELSA: Then I'll tell you. You were doing everything in your power to bully and blackmail her into signing that. You were taking the grossest advantage of what you call her confusion and helplessness. I've been trying to tell her she's neither confused nor helpless.

MARIUS: So you know what is best for her.

ELSA: No, no, no! Wrong again, Dominee. I think *she* does. And if you had given her half a chance, she would have told you that that is not being dumped in an old-age home full of old people who have reached the end of their lives. She hasn't. You forget one thing: I didn't stop her signing that form. She stopped herself.

MARIUS: It was a moment of confusion.

ELSA: There you go again! Can't you leave that word alone? She is not confused!

MARIUS: When Helen and I discussed the matter a few days ago—

ELSA: Don't talk about her as if she were not here. She's right next to you, Dominee. Ask her, for God's sake . . . but this time give her a chance to answer.

MARIUS: Don't try to goad me with blasphemy, Miss Barlow. I'm beginning to think Helen needs as much protection from you as she does from herself.

ELSA: You still haven't asked her.

MARIUS: Because I have some sympathy for her condition. Look at her! She is in no condition now, thanks to you, to think clearly about anything.

ELSA: She was an emotional mess, thanks to you, before I opened my mouth. Don't expect me to believe you really care about her.

MARIUS *(Trying hard to control himself):* Miss Barlow, for the last time, what you do or don't believe is not of the remotest concern to me. Helen is, and my concern is that she gets a chance to live out what is left of her life as safely and happily as is humanly possible. I don't think that should include the danger of her being trapped in here when this house goes up in flames.

ELSA: What are you talking about?

MARIUS: Her accident. The night she knocked over the candle. (ELSA *is obviously at a loss*) You don't know about that? When was it, Helen? Four weeks ago? (*Pause.* MISS HELEN *doesn't respond*) I see. You didn't tell your friend about your narrow escape. I think I owe you an apology, Miss Barlow. I assumed you knew all about it.

ELSA: You owe me nothing. Just tell me what happened.

MARIUS: Yes, it was about four weeks ago. Helen knocked over a candle one night and set fire to the curtains. I try not to think about what would have happened if Sterling hadn't been looking out of his window at that moment and seen the flames. He rushed over, and just in time. She had stopped trying to put out the flames herself and was just standing staring at them. Even so she picked up a few bad burns on her hands. We had to get Sister Lategan out of bed to treat them. But it could have been a lot worse. (ELSA *is staring at* MISS HELEN) We don't want that on our consciences. So you see, Miss Barlow, our actions are not quite as pointless or as uncaring as they must have seemed to you.

ELSA: One of the lamps started smoking badly, and there was a little accident at the stove while you were making prickly-pear syrup for me! Oh boy! You certainly can do it, Helen. Don't let us ever again talk about trust between the two of us. Anyway, that settles it. I leave the two of you to fight it out . . . and may the best man win! I'm going to bed.

HELEN: Give me a chance to explain.

ELSA (*Ignoring the plea*): Good night. See you in the morning. I'll be making an early start, Helen.

HELEN: Don't abandon me, Elsa!

ELSA: You've abandoned yourself, Helen! Don't accuse me of that! You were the first to jump overboard. You haven't got enough faith in your life and your work to defend them against him. You lied to me . . . and such stupid bloody lies! What was the point? For that matter, what is the point of anything? Why *did* you make me come up? And then all our talk about trust? God, what a joke. You've certainly made me make a fool of myself again, but this time I don't think it's funny. In fact, I fucking well resent it.

HELEN: I didn't tell you because I was frightened you would agree with them.

ELSA: Don't say anything, Helen. You're making it worse. (*She studies* MISS HELEN *with cruel detachment*) But you might have a point there. Now that I've heard about your "little accident," I'm beginning to think they might be right. (*She indicates the room*) Corrugated iron and wooden walls? Give it half a chance and this would go up like a bonfire. (*She is hating herself, hurting herself every bit as much as she is hurting* MISS HELEN, *but is unable to stop*) And he says you were just standing and staring at it. What was that all about? Couldn't you make a run for it? They say that about terror—it makes you either run like hell or stand quite still. Sort of paralysis. Because it was just an accident, wasn't it, Helen? I mean, you weren't trying anything else, were you? Spite everybody by taking the house with you in a final blaze of glory! Dramatic! But it's a hell of a way to go. There are easier methods.

MISS HELEN *goes up to* ELSA *and stares at her.*

HELEN: Who are you?

The question devastates ELSA.

MARIUS: Ladies, ladies, enough! Stop now! I don't know what's going on between the two of you, but in Heaven's name stop it. I think Helen is aware of the dangers involved, Miss Barlow. And now that you do as well, can't we appeal to you to add your weight to ours and help persuade her to do the right thing? As I am sure you now realize, our only concern has been her well-being.

ELSA: You want my help.

MARIUS: Yes. If now at last you understand why we were trying to persuade Helen to move to the home, then on her behalf I am indeed appealing to you. We don't persecute harmless old ladies, Miss Barlow.

ELSA: And one that isn't so harmless?

MARIUS: Now what are you trying to say?

ELSA: That Helen isn't harmless, Dominee. Anything but that. That's why you people can't leave her alone.

MARIUS: For fifteen years we have done exactly that.

ELSA: Stoning her house and statues at night is not leaving her alone. That is not the way you treat a harmless old lady.

MARIUS: In Heaven's name! Are you going to drag that up? Those were children, Miss Barlow, and it was a long, long time ago. It has not happened again. Do you really mean to be that unfair? Can't you bring as much understanding as you claim to have of Helen's situation to a few other things as well? You've seen what is out there . . . *(He gestures at the window and* MISS HELEN*'s "Mecca")* How else do you expect the simple children of the village to react to all that? It frightens them, Miss Barlow. I'm not joking! Think back to your impressionable years as a little girl. I know for a fact that all the children in the village believe this house is haunted and that ghosts walk around out there at night. Don't scoff at them. I'm sure there were monsters and evil spirits in your childhood as well. But as I said, that was all a long, long time ago. The moment we discovered what they were doing, we in turn did everything we could to put a stop to it. Mr. Lategan, the school principal, and I both lectured them in the sternest possible manner. Come now, Miss Barlow, have you learned nothing about us in the course of the few years that you've been visiting the village?

ELSA: A lot more than I would have liked to. Those children didn't arrive at their attitude to Helen on their own. I've also heard about the parents who frighten naughty children with stories about Miss Helen's "monsters." They got the courage to start throwing stones because of what they had heard their mothers and fathers saying. And as far as *they* are concerned, Helen is anything but a harmless old lady. God, what an irony. We spend our time talking about "poor, frightened Miss Helen," whereas it's all of you who are really frightened.

MARIUS: I can only repeat what I've already said to Helen: the people you are talking about grew up with her and have known her a lot longer than you.

ELSA: Not anymore. You also said that, remember? That stopped fifteen years ago when she didn't resign herself to being the meek, churchgoing little widow you all expected her to be. Instead she did something which small minds and small souls can never forgive . . . she dared to be different! Which does make you right about one thing, Dominee. Those statues out there *are* monsters. And they are that for the simple reason that they express Helen's freedom. Yes, I never thought it was a word you would like. I'm sure it ranks as a cardinal sin in these parts. A free woman! God forgive us!

Have you ever wondered why I come up here? It's a hell of a long drive, you know, if the only reason is sympathy for a lonely old lady whom nobody is talking to anymore. And it's also not for the scenery.

She challenges me, Dominee. She challenges me into an awareness of myself and my life, of my responsibilities to both that I never had until I met her. There's a hell of a lot of talk about freedom, and all sorts of it, in the world where I come from. But it's mostly talk, Dominee, easy talk and nothing else. Not with Helen. She's lived it. One dusty afternoon five years ago, when I came walking down that road hoping for nothing more than to get away from the flies that were driving me mad, I met the first truly free spirit I have ever known. *(She looks at* MISS HELEN*)* It is her betrayal of all of that tonight that has made me behave the way I have.

A pause. MARIUS *has been confronted with something he has never had to deal with before.*

MARIUS: You call that . . . that nightmare out there an expression of freedom?

ELSA: Yes. Scary, isn't it? What did you call it earlier? Her hobby? *(She laughs)* Oh no, Dominee. It's much more dangerous than that . . . and I think you know it.

MARIUS: In another age and time it might have been called idolatry.

ELSA: Did you hear that, Helen? *(To* MARIUS*)* You know what you've just said, don't you?

MARIUS *(Total conviction)*: Oh yes . . . yes, indeed I do. I am also choosing my words very carefully, Miss Barlow.

When I first realized that it was my duty as a friend and a Christian to raise the question with Helen of a move to an old-age home, I decided I would do so on the basis of her physical well-being and safety and nothing else. Helen will tell you that that is all we have ever talked about. I came here tonight meaning once again to do only that. But you have raised other issues, chosen to talk about more than that . . . which forces me now to do so as well. Because there is a lot more than Helen's physical well-being that has worried me, Miss Barlow— and gravely so! Those "expressions of freedom" have crowded out more than just a few fresh vegetables. I do not take them lightly anymore.

I remember the first one very clearly, Helen. I made the mistake of smiling at it, dismissing it as an idle whim coming out of your loneliness. In fact, I think that is how you yourself described it to me, as something to pass away the time. I was very wrong, wasn't I? And very slow in realizing what was really happening. I only began to feel uneasy about it all that first Sunday you weren't in church.

The moment I stood up there in front of the congregation, I knew your place was empty. But even then, you see, I thought you were sick. After the service I hurried around here, but instead of being in bed there you were outside in the yard making yet another . . . *(At a loss for words)* I don't really know what to call them.

HELEN *(A small but calm voice. She is very still):* It was an owl, Marius. My first owl.

MARIUS: It couldn't have waited until after the service, Helen?

HELEN: Oh no! *(Quietly emphatic)* The picture had come to me in here the night before. I just had to go to work immediately while it was still fresh in my mind. They don't last long, Marius. After a little while it becomes very hard to remember clearly what you saw. I tried explaining to Elsa how it all works . . . but I don't suppose any of you will ever understand.

But don't ever think that missing church that Sunday was something I did lightly, Marius. You don't break the habit of a lifetime without realizing that that life will never quite be the same again. I was already dressed and ready! I had my Bible and hymnbook, I was on the point of leaving this room as I had done every Sunday for as long as I could remember . . . but I knew that if I did, I would never make that owl. . . . I think I also knew that if I didn't, that if I put aside my Bible and hymnbook, took off my hat and changed my dress and went to work. . . . Yes! That was my very first owl!

MARIUS: Helen, Helen! I grieve for you! You turned your back on your church, on your faith and then on us for that? Do you realize that that is why you are now in trouble and so helplessly alone? Those statues out there can't give you love or take care of you the way we wanted to. And, God knows, we were ready to do that. But you spurned us, Helen. You turned your back on our love and left us for the company of those cement monstrosities.

ELSA, *who has been listening and watching quietly, begins to understand.*

ELSA: Helen, listen to me. Listen to me carefully because if you understand what I'm going to say, I think everything will be all right.

They're not only frightened of you, Helen; they're also jealous. It's not just the statues that have frightened them. They were throwing stones at something much bigger than that—you. Your life, your beautiful, light-filled glittering life. And they can't leave it alone, Helen, because they are so, so jealous of it.

HELEN *(Calmly):* Is that true, Marius?

MARIUS: Helen, has your trust in me been eroded away to the extent that you can ask me that? Does she have so much power over you that you will now believe anything she says?

HELEN: Then . . . it isn't true?

MARIUS: Dear God, what is there left for me to say or do that will make you listen to me the way you do to her?

HELEN: But I have been listening to you, Marius.

MARIUS: No, you haven't! If that were so, you wouldn't be asking me to defend myself against the accusations of someone who knows nothing, nothing, about my true feelings for you. I feel as if I were on trial, Helen. For what? For caring about you? *(He confronts* MISS HELEN*)* That I am frightened of what you have done to yourself and your life, yes, that is true! When I find that the twenty years we have known each other, all that we have shared in that time, are outweighed by a handful of visits from her, then yes again. That leaves me bewildered and jealous. Don't you realize that you are being used, Helen—she as much as admitted to that—to prove some lunatic notion about freedom? And since we're talking about it, yes yet again, I *do* hate that word. You aren't free, Helen. If anything, exactly the opposite. Don't let her deceive you. If there is one last thing you will let me do for you, then let it be this: see yourself as I do and tell me if that is what you call being "free." A life I care about as deeply as any I have known, trapped now finally in the nightmare this house has become . . . with an illiterate little Coloured girl and a stranger from a different world as your only visitors and friends! I know I'm not welcome in here anymore. I can feel it the moment I walk in. It's unnatural, Helen. Your life has become as grotesque as those creations of yours out there.

Why, Helen? Why? I will take that question with me to my grave. What possessed you to abandon the life you had, your faith?

HELEN: What life, Marius? What faith? The one that brought me to church every Sunday? *(Shaking her head)* No. You were much too late if you only started worrying about that on the first Sunday I wasn't there in my place. The worst had happened long, long before that. Yes. All those years when, as Elsa said, I sat there so obediently next to Stefanus, it was all a terrible, terrible lie. I tried hard, Marius, but your sermons, the prayers, the hymns, they had all become just words. And there came a time when even they lost their meaning.

Do you know what the word "God" looks like when you've lost your faith? It looks like a little stone, a cold, round, little stone. "Heaven" is another one, but it's got an awkward, useless shape, while "Hell" is flat and smooth. All of them—damnation, grace, salvation—a handful of stones.

MARIUS: Why didn't you come to me, Helen? If only you had trusted me enough to tell me, and we had faced it together, I would have broken my soul to help you win back that faith.

HELEN: It felt too late. I'd accepted it. Nothing more was going to happen to me except time and the emptiness inside and I had got used to that . . . until the night in here after Stefanus's funeral. *(Pause. She makes a decision)*

I've never told you about that night, Marius. I've told no one, not even Elsa, because it was a secret, you see, a very special one, and it had to stay that way while I was working on my Mecca. But so much has happened here tonight, it feels right to do so now. *(Pause)*

You brought me home from the cemetery, remember, and when we had got inside the house and you had helped me off with my coat, you put on a kettle for a pot of tea and then . . . ever so thoughtfully . . . pulled the curtains and closed the shutters. Such a small little thing, and I know that you meant well by it, that you didn't want people to stare in at me and my grief . . . but in doing that it felt as if you were putting away my life as surely as the undertaker had done to Stefanus a little earlier when he closed the coffin lid. There was even an odor of death in here with us, wasn't there, sitting in the gloom and talking, both of us in black, our Bibles in our laps? Your words of comfort didn't help. But that wasn't your fault. You didn't know I wasn't mourning Stefanus's death.

He was a good man, and it was very sad that he had died so young, but I never loved him. My black widowhood was really for my own life, Marius. While Stefanus was alive there had at least been some pretense at it . . . of a life I hadn't lived. But with him gone . . . ! You had a little girl in here with you, Marius, who had used up all the prayers she knew and was dreading the moment when her mother would bend down, blow out the candle and leave her in the dark. You lit one for me before you left—there was a lot of darkness in this room—and after you had gone I sat here with it. Such a sad little light, with its little tears of wax running down the side! I had none. Neither for Stefanus nor for myself. You see, nothing hurt anymore. That little candle did all the crying in here that night, and it burned down very low while doing that. I don't know how much time had passed, but I was just sitting here staring into its flame. I had surrendered myself to what was going to happen when it went out . . . but then instead of doing the same, allowing the darkness to defeat it, that small, uncertain little light seemed to find its courage again. It started to get brighter and brighter. I didn't know whether I was awake any longer or dreaming because a strange feeling came over me . . . that it was leading me . . . leading me far away to a place I had never been to before. *(She looks around the room and speaks with authority)* Light the candles, Elsa. That one first.

She indicates a candelabra that has been set up very prominently on a little table. ELSA *lights it.*

And you know why, Marius? That is the East. Go out there into the yard and you'll see that all my Wise Men and their camels are traveling in that direction. Follow that candle on and one day you'll come to Mecca. Oh yes, Marius, it's true! I've done it. That is where I went that night and it was the candle you lit that led me there.

(She is radiantly alive with her vision) A city, Marius! A city of light and color more splendid than anything I had ever imagined. There were palaces and beautiful buildings everywhere, with dazzling white walls and glittering minarets. Strange statues filled the courtyards. The streets were crowded with camels and turbaned men speaking a language I didn't understand, but that didn't matter because I knew, oh I just knew, it was Mecca! And I was on my way to the grand temple.

In the center of Mecca there is a temple, Marius, and in the center of the temple is a vast room with hundreds of mirrors on the walls and hanging lamps, and that is where the Wise Men of the East study the celestial geometry of light and color. I became an apprentice that night.

Light them all, Elsa, so that I can show Marius what I've learned!

ELSA *moves around the room lighting all the candles, and as she does so its full magic and splendor is revealed.* MISS HELEN *laughs ecstatically.*

Look, Marius! Look! Light. Don't be nervous. It's harmless. It only wants to play. That is what I do in here. We play with it like children with a magical toy that never ceases to delight and amuse. Light just one little candle in here, let in the light from just one little star, and the dancing starts. I've even taught it how to skip around corners. Yes, I have! When I lie in bed and look in *that* mirror, I can see *that* mirror, and in *that* one the full moon when it rises over the Sneeuberg *behind* my back! This is my world and I have banished darkness from it.

It is not madness, Marius. They say mad people can't tell the difference between what is real and what is not. I can. I know my little Mecca out there, and this room, for what they really are. I had to learn how to bend rusty wire into the right shape and mix sand cement to make my Wise Men and their camels, how to grind down beer bottles in a coffee mill to put glitter on my walls. My hands will never let me forget. They'll keep me sane. It's the best I could do, as near as I could get to the real Mecca. The journey is over now. This is as far as I can go.

I won't be using this *(The application form)*. I can't reduce my world to a few ornaments in a small room in an old-age home.

MARIUS *takes the form. When he speaks again we sense a defeated man, an acceptance of the inevitable behind the quiet attempt to maintain his dignity.*

MARIUS: Mecca! So that's where you went. I'll look for it on my atlas of the world when I get home tonight. That's a long way away, Helen! I didn't realize you had traveled that far from me. So to find you I must light a candle and follow it to the East! *(He makes a helpless gesture)* No. I think I'm too old now for that journey . . . and I have a feeling that you will never come back.

HELEN: I'm also too old for another journey, Marius. It's taken me my whole life to get here.

I know I've disappointed you—most probably, bitterly so—but, whatever you do, please believe me that it wasn't intentional. I had as little choice over all that has happened as I did over the day I was born.

MARIUS: No, I think I do believe you, Helen . . . which only makes it all the harder to accept. All these years it has always felt as if I could reach you. It seemed so inevitable that I would, so right that we should find each other again and be together for what time was left to us in the same world. It seems wrong . . . terribly wrong . . . that we won't. Aletta's death was wrong in the same way.

Pause.

HELEN: What's the matter, Marius?

MARIUS: I am trying to go. It's not easy . . . trying to find the first moment of a life that must be lived out in the shadow of something that is terribly wrong.

HELEN: We're trying to say goodbye to each other, aren't we, Marius?

MARIUS: Yes, I suppose it had come to that. I never thought that was going to happen tonight, but I suppose there *is* nothing else left to say. *(He starts to go. He sees* ELSA, *hesitates for a few seconds, but there is nothing to say to her either)* Be sure all the candles are out when you go to bed, Helen. *(He pauses at the door)* I've never seen you as happy as this! There is more light in you than in all your candles put together.

He leaves. A silence follows his departure. ELSA *eventually makes a move to start blowing out the candles.*

HELEN: No, don't. I must do that. *(From this point on she goes around the room putting out the candles, a quiet but deliberate and grave punctuation to what follows)*

ELSA: Tell me about his wife.

HELEN: Her name was Aletta. Aletta Byleveld. I've only seen pictures of her. She must have been a very beautiful woman.

ELSA: What happened?

HELEN: Her death?

ELSA: Yes.

HELEN: All I know is that there was a long illness. And a very painful one. They never had any children. Marius was a bitter and lonely man when he first came to the valley. Why do you ask?

ELSA: Because he was, and most probably still is, in love with you.

HELEN: Elsa . . .

ELSA: Yes. I don't suppose I would have ever guessed it if it hadn't been for tonight. Like all good Afrikaners, he does a good job of hiding his feelings. But it is very obvious now.

HELEN *(Agitated):* No, Elsie. When he used the word "love" he meant it in the way—

ELSA: No, Helen. I'm not talking about the good shepherd's feelings for one of his flock. Marius Byleveld, the man, loves you Helen, the woman.

HELEN: What are you talking about? Look at me, Elsa. Look at my hands—

ELSA: You fool! Do you think that is what we see when we look at you? You heard him: "There is more light in you than in all your candles put together." And he's right. You are radiant. You can't be that naive and innocent, Helen!

MISS HELEN *wants to deny it, but the validity, the possible truth, of what* ELSA *has said is very strong.*

It's a very moving story. Twenty years of loving you in the disguise of friendship and professional concern for your soul. *(There is an unnatural and forced tone to her voice)* Anyway, that's his problem, right, Helen? You did what you had to. In fact, you deserve a few bravos for your performance tonight. I'm proud of you. I told you that you never needed me. And you did more than just say no to him. You affirmed your right, as a woman . . . *(Pause)* Do you love him? The way he loves you?

MISS HELEN *thinks before speaking. When she does so there is no doubt about her answer.*

HELEN: No, I don't.

ELSA: Just asking. You're also an Afrikaner. You could also be hiding your real feelings the way he did. That would make it an even better story! The two of you in this Godforsaken little village, each loving the other in secret!

HELEN: Are you all right, Elsa?

ELSA: No.

HELEN: What's wrong?

ELSA: It's my turn to be jealous.

HELEN: Of what?

ELSA *(With a helpless gesture):* Everything. You and him . . . and, stupid as it may sound, I feel fucking lonely as well.

HELEN: You are jealous? Of us . . . Marius and me? With your whole life still ahead of you?

ELSA: Even that woman on the road has at least got a baby in her arms at this moment. She's got something, for Christ's sake! Mind you, it's cold out there now. It could be on her back again. She might have crawled out of her stormwater drain and started walking to keep warm.

HELEN: Leave that poor woman alone now, Elsa!

ELSA: She won't leave me alone, Helen!

HELEN: For all you know, she might have got a lift.

ELSA *(Another unexpected flash of cruelty):* I hope not.

HELEN *(Appalled):* Elsa! That is not you talking. You don't mean that.

ELSA: Yes, I do! A lift to where, for God's sake? There's no Mecca waiting for her at the end of that road, Helen. Just the rest of her life, and there won't be any glitter on that. The sooner she knows what the score really is, the better.

HELEN: Then think about the baby, Elsa.

ELSA: What the hell do you think I've been doing? Do you think I don't care? That baby could have been mine, Helen! *(Pause. Then a decision)* I may as well vomit it all out tonight. Two weeks after David left me I discovered I was pregnant. I had an abortion. *(Pause)* Do you understand what I'm saying, Helen?

HELEN: I understand you, Elsa.

ELSA: I put an abrupt and violent end to the first real consequence my life has ever had.

HELEN: I understand, Elsa.

Pause.

ELSA: There is a little sequel to my story about giving that woman a lift. When I stopped at the turnoff and she got out of the car, after I had given her what was left of my food and the money in my purse, after she had stopped thanking me and telling me over and over again that God would bless me, after all of that I asked her who she was. She said: "My English name is Patience." She hitched up the baby, tightened her *doek,* picked up her little plastic shopping bag and started walking. As I watched her walk away, measuring out the next eighty miles of her life in small steps, I wanted to scream. And about a mile further on, in the *kloof,* I did exactly that. I stopped the car, switched off the engine, closed my eyes and started to scream.

I think I lost control of myself. I screamed louder and longer than I have ever done in my life. I can't describe it, Helen. I hated her, I hated the baby, I hated you for dragging me all the way up here . . . and most of all I hated myself. That baby is mine, Helen. Patience is my sister, you are our mother . . . and I still feel fucking lonely.

HELEN: Then don't be so cruel to us. There were times tonight when I hardly recognized you. Why were you doing it?

ELSA: I wanted to punish us.

HELEN: For what? What have we done to deserve that?

ELSA: I've already told you. For being old, for being black, for being born . . . for being twenty-eight years old and trusting enough to jump. For our stupid helplessness.

HELEN: You don't punish people for that, Elsa. I only felt helpless tonight when I thought I had lost you.

ELSA: So what do you want me to do, Helen?

HELEN: Stop screaming.

ELSA: And cry instead?

HELEN: What is wrong with that? Is it something to be ashamed of? I wish I still could . . . not for myself . . . for you, Patience, her little baby. Was it a boy or a girl?

ELSA: I don't know. I'll never know.

Her moment of emotional release has finally come. She cries. MISS HELEN *comforts her.*

I'll be all right.

HELEN: I never doubted that for a moment.

ELSA *(Total exhaustion):* God Almighty, what a day! I'm dead, Helen, dead, dead, dead . . .

HELEN: No, you're not. You're tired . . . and you've got every right and reason to be. *(She fetches a blanket and puts it over* ELSA*'s shoulders)*

ELSA: I wasn't much of a help tonight, was I?

HELEN: You were more than that. You were a "challenge." I like that word.

ELSA: But we didn't solve very much.

HELEN: Nonsense! Of course we did. Certainly as much as *we* could. I *am* going to see a doctor and an optician, and Katrina . . . *(She remembers)* or somebody else, will come in here a few times a week and help me with the house.

ELSA: My shopping list!

HELEN: It is as much as "we" could do, Elsa. The rest is up to myself and, who knows, maybe it will be a little easier after tonight. I won't lie to you. I can't say that I'm not frightened anymore. But at the same time I think I can say that I understand something now.

The road to my Mecca *was* one I had to travel alone. It was a journey on which no one could keep me company, and because of that, now that it is over, there is only me there at the end of it. It couldn't have been any other way.

You see, I meant what I said to Marius. This is as far as I can go. My Mecca is finished and with it—*(Pause)* I must try to say it, mustn't I?—the only real purpose my life has ever had.

(She blows out a candle) I was wrong to think I could banish darkness, Elsa. Just as I taught myself how to light candles, and what that means, I must teach myself now how to blow them out . . . and what that means.

(She attempts a brave smile) The last phase of my apprenticeship . . . and if I can get through it, I'll be a master!

ELSA: I'm cold.

HELEN: Cup of tea to warm you up and then bed. I'll put on the kettle.

ELSA: And I've got just the thing to go with it. *(She goes into the bedroom alcove and returns with her toilet bag, from which she takes a small bottle of pills)* Valiums. They're delicious. I think you should also have one.

HELEN *(All innocence):* So tiny! What are they? Artificial sweeteners?

The unintended and gentle irony of her question is not lost on ELSA. *A little chuckle becomes a good laugh.*

ELSA: That is perfect, Helen. Yes, they're artificial sweeteners.

HELEN: I don't know how I did it, but that laugh makes me as proud of myself as of any one of those statues out there.

She exits to put on the kettle. ELSA *goes to the window and looks out at Mecca.* MISS HELEN *returns.*

ELSA: Helen, I've just thought of something. You know what the real cause of all your trouble is? You've never made an angel.

HELEN: Good Heavens, no. Why should I?

ELSA: Because I think they would leave you alone if you did.

HELEN: The village doesn't need more of those. The cemetery is full of them . . . all wings and halos, but no glitter. *(Tongue-in-cheek humor)* But if I did make one, it wouldn't be pointing up to heaven like the rest.

ELSA: No? What would it be doing?

HELEN: Come on, Elsa, you know! I'd have it pointing to the East. Where else? I'd misdirect all the good Christian souls around here and put them on the road to Mecca.

Both have a good laugh.

ELSA: God, I love you! I love so much it hurts.

HELEN: What about trust?

Pause. The two women look at each other.

ELSA: Open your arms and catch me! I'm going to jump!

END OF PLAY

ACTIVITIES FOR WRITING AND DISCUSSION

1. Both Helen and Elsa are socially independent and "nonconformists," yet they seem quite different in their nonconformity. Compare and contrast the two characters as nonconformists.

2. Elsa claims that the villagers fear Helen because she is "dangerous." Is she? What values, norms, or social codes does she threaten? If you wish, assume the **persona** of one of the villagers and articulate (in the form of a diary entry or a letter to the Church Council) the logic or reasoning that regards Helen as a "danger" to society.

3. Note the subjects of Helen's statues—mermaids, camels, Wise Men, for instance. Why does she create these statues and fill up her yard and house with

them? Do they serve any purpose? If so, what purposes? If not, why does she keep making them?

4. Elsa asserts that Marius has long been in love with Helen. What *are* Marius's feelings about Helen? Is he in love with her? or jealous of her statues? or envious of her life? or some combination of the above? Imagine it is a time shortly after the action of the play has ended. In the persona of Marius, reveal your true—and perhaps contradictory—feelings about Helen in a letter to her or in a **monologue.**

5. Write a script of the Church Council meeting at which members discuss what to do about Helen. What attitudes do they have about her work? Why do they want to get her out of her own house and into the old-age home? If you wish, include the voice of a dissenting member who defends Helen.

6. In act 2 we learn that children of the village used to throw stones at Helen's house and statues. According to Elsa, they would not have done so without some influence from their parents. How do you suppose the parents in the village did (or do) discuss Helen with their children? Write the **dialogue** of one father and mother talking with their child or children about Helen and her "work."

7. Imagine it is some time in the future, and Helen has died. You are Elsa, and you want to write down your thoughts and feelings about your dead friend. Building on details furnished in the play, tell the story of your various encounters with Helen and the impact she had on your life. Compose the piece as a diary entry or memoir or as a letter addressed to another, younger woman to whom Helen might be of interest.

INDIVIDUAL AND SOCIETY: ADDITIONAL ACTIVITIES FOR WRITING AND DISCUSSION

1. Reread all or a portion of your notebook. Mark any passages, however long or short, that strike you, for whatever reason. Beside each such passage, write a note explaining its significance for you. Finally, pick a favorite passage and either:
    a. Expand it into a new piece of writing, or
    b. Make notes on how you could expand or use it at some future date, or
    c. Rewrite it in a different form, e.g., a poem, dialogue, letter, memoir.

For a list of strategies for expanding or revising, see Chapter 9.

2. Write down your own definitions of "individual" and "society." Then think about this question: Is society essentially the *enemy* of the individual or the *friend*? Finally, bring together two or more **characters, speakers,** or **personae** from the texts in this section and write a dialogue in which they debate

the question. Some participants in this dialogue might include James Thurber's Walter Mitty, Ray Bradbury's Brock, the William Blake of "The Garden of Love," the dead man commemorated in Auden's "The Unknown Citizen," one of Margaret Atwood's "City Planners," the Cathy Appel of "Letters," Carol Bly. If you wish, include yourself in the dialogue as a participant or moderator.

3. Is "individuality" mainly a matter of being independent, or does it include dependence of various kinds? Are there kinds of dependence that can enhance individuality, or is dependence generally at odds with individuality? Compare the ways in which "independence" and "dependence" interweave as themes in any of the texts within this section, such as Hawthorne's "The Minister's Black Veil," O'Connor's "Everything That Rises Must Converge," Rich's "A Leak in History," or Fugard's *The Road to Mecca*.

4. As a variation on Activity #3, write about the same issues in some alternative literary form, e.g., in a dialogue between or among characters or speakers, a personal essay, or a short story.

5. Review Whitman's "Song of the Open Road," paying special attention to the kinds of qualities (personal, physical, moral, spiritual) his speaker prescribes for travelers on the open road. Make a list of these qualities. Then choose any three or four characters, speakers, or personae from this thematic grouping and place them on the road.
   a. Which of your travelers do well? Which, if any, decide to give up the journey? Why?
   b. If you wish, write imaginary travel diaries for one or more of your travelers in which they record their impressions of the journey and why they decide to abandon it (if they decide to abandon it).

6. Several times in *The Road to Mecca*, Helen is referred to as "mad." Annotate and interpret Emily Dickinson's "Much Madness is divinest Sense." Then:
   a. In an essay, argue that the poem could be used as a gloss (or commentary) on the story of Helen in *The Road to Mecca*.
   b. Bring Emily Dickinson and Helen together for a dialogue or an exchange of letters on the subject of "madness" and "sanity." Alternative: Include other characters and speakers from this thematic section, e.g., Walter Mitty, Brock from "The Murderer," Harrison Bergeron, Gracie Mae from Walker's "Nineteen Fifty-five," the speaker in Lec's *Unkempt Thoughts*.

7. Write about any common themes you see in Schopenhauer's "On Thinking for Oneself" and Bly's "Growing Up Expressive." Do the two essays articulate a common message? Are there any important differences?

8. Review your entire notebook; as you do, make a running list of memorable or striking topics, e.g., "individuality," "nonconformists," "communities," "friendship." Then choose a favorite topic, make a Topic/Form Grid (see page 111), and use one of the forms on your grid to create a new notebook entry

about the topic. Should your chosen form not work, do a Topic/Form Shift to a different form on your grid.

9. Walker's "Nineteen Fifty-five" is a *mix* of literary forms, combining **first-person** narrative by Gracie Mae with imaginary letters between Traynor and Gracie Mae. Use the topic you chose for Activity #8 and compose a notebook piece that mixes two or more forms from your Topic/Form Grid.

Interchapter on Notebooks and Journals (IV)

The Notebook As "Pure" Poetry: Joseph Joubert

Joseph Joubert once wrote, "And perhaps there is no advice to give a writer more important than this:—Never write anything that does not give you great pleasure." Joubert followed his own advice: uninterested in money, publication, or fame, for some four decades he wrote for no other apparent reason than the pleasure of it.

Joubert had an outwardly uneventful life. Born in Montignac (Dordogue), France in 1754, the second of eight surviving children, in his twenties he moved to Paris, where he became a secretary to the great French encyclopedist and man of letters, Denis Diderot, and a member of French literary and artistic circles. He served a term as a rural justice of the peace but withdrew from politics in the bloody wake of the French Revolution, which he had initially welcomed. During his fifties he returned to public service as an education inspector. Living in the small town of Villeneuve in Burgundy, the family home of his wife (a member of the moneyed middle class), he died in 1824, at the age of 70.

From the late 1780s on Joubert's notebooks were his absorbing passion. As he wrote: "These thoughts form not only the foundation of my work, but of my life." Insatiably curious, he read widely in all subjects and was an ardent practitioner of what Ralph Waldo Emerson would later call "read[ing] to start your own team": Joubert darkened the margins of the books he read with annotations, which he subsequently reread and used to inspire reflections and observations of his own.

His friends repeatedly urged him to publish his work, but Joubert declined. After his death his widow found his notes—many of them scribbled on the backs of envelopes or on fragments of scrap paper held together by safety pins—inside a large trunk he had used for storing papers. The first published selection from the notebooks, edited by the French writer and statesman, Chateaubriand (who had been a friend of Joubert's), did not appear until 1838. Other editions followed, in French and in translation, and by the latter part of the nineteenth century Joubert had become posthumously famous in Europe and America.

Why Joubert refused to publish remains a mystery. Having married a woman of means, he didn't need to write for money, and he wasn't interested in fame. The future of his writings didn't concern him. To have recorded a thought and worded it accurately was reward enough. When friends saw him they probably learned to ask, not, "What have you been doing, Joseph?" but "What have you been *thinking*?"

If such a thing exists, you could almost call Joubert a "pure" poet. Not that his writing is "poetry" in the technical sense: many of his reflections seem more philosophic than poetic, and his words aren't formatted as verse. But Joubert engages life with a purely poetic spirit. Every moment is a package; inside is the gift. "All reflection," he writes, "is art."

Joubert in his notebooks is far removed from a purely *functional* orientation toward life. The functional outlook holds that everything has to have a use to be meaningful, that simply to *be* is not enough. A man or woman is made meaningful by a job; every idea has to be developed and applied, or it wasn't worth having; every poem or story has to be finished and published, or it has been a waste of time. Even a vacation, perhaps, is only "successful" if it has resulted in the conquest of "X" many cities or "Y" many popular landmarks. The functional outlook emphasizes action and minimizes reflection; one acts without necessarily pausing to question *why* (or without considering the possible advantages of doing nothing). . . . The functionality of our actions, of course, is important and necessary; if we rejected it outright—if we stopped doing jobs or developing ideas—we would probably starve. The issue is one of balance.

Early in life Joubert seems to have decided that the poetry of a thing is that you don't have to *do* anything with it. The poetry of an idea is the idea itself—a thing to be recorded and contemplated without necessarily turning it to public use. The poetry of a rose or a river is what you get by perceiving it—looking, listening, smelling, touching. Trees are poetic not as building materials or as shelter against rain—both valuable *functions* of trees—but because you enjoy being in their presence.

As far as words are concerned, with the thought, "I could *do* something with this," poetry recedes and rhetoric takes over. Published writers hammer and caress their words into shape for public consumption without (they hope) compromising the artistic qualities. In this respect the poems of Shakespeare, Mary Oliver, Wislawa Szymborska, and Gary Soto—to name just a few of the poets anthologized in this book—are the result of poetry and rhetoric working *together*. For reasons known only to himself, Joubert was content to pitch his tent inside the initial hunch or intuition and never stir from the spot. He seems to say, *Why try to round or finish what isn't? Effort lies.*

Joubert writes about anything and everything—weather, astronomy, music, silence and sound, the nature of memory, politics, time, imagination, theology, parents and children, love, body and soul—whatever hooks his attention at the moment. "The thoughts that come to us are worth more than the ones we seek," he writes. His observations are typically no more than a sentence or two in length, aiding the rapid shift from topic to topic:

> One would say that in such dark eyes there is a flame without light.

> Pleasures are always children, pains always have wrinkles.

> Everything is a game except what makes the soul better or worse.

> Our arms are canes of flesh with which the soul reaches out and touches.

> The weather strikes me on the head. I feel it rattle my teeth.

Some notes are not even complete grammatical sentences:

> . . . passing their life in contradicting their childhood,—in erasing it.

> Abuse of words, foundation of ideology.

> Children. Need models more than critics.

This brevity and fragmentariness should not be mistaken for laziness or incompetence. Joubert habitually reread his notes and painstakingly revised those that interested him most . . . or, more accurately, he revised his *thoughts*. In a brilliant sentence about literary style he remarks, "It is not my words that I polish, but my ideas." For instance, he could have edited the last note above to make a single complete sentence ("Children need models more than critics"); however, the revision weakens the point of the note. It seems that he wants to give the word "Children" added weight by assigning it its own sentence, thereby emphasizing the "weighty" importance of children as a topic of private and public concern.

Focusing his energies on phrases and sentences, Joubert is forever striving "to put a whole book in a page, a whole page in a sentence, and this sentence in a word." For him style is perfected in the sentence or nowhere; and the sentence is only perfected in the idea.

In an age like our own that is saturated with images of celebrity, Joubert reminds us that the main pleasure of writing is the act of writing itself; and, while *having written*—achieving commercial success or getting published—is desirable and gratifying, it is the *least interesting* part of composing. If this weren't so, why would we find that the best writers continually start new works even as they are finishing with the old? To "enjoy" a success is to put it behind you. Creation itself is the fruit of composing, says Joubert, success and notoriety the rind.

For further reading:
Joubert, Joseph. *The Notebooks of Joseph Joubert: A Selection.* Ed. and trans. Paul Auster. San Francisco: North Point P, 1983.

Excerpts from *The Notebooks of Joseph Joubert*

I imitate the dove, and often I throw a blade of grass to the drowning ant.   1

———————

Thought forms in the soul in the same way clouds form in the air.   2

———————

Through memory we travel against time, through forgetfulness we follow its course.   3

———————

We are in the world as words are in a book. Each generation is like a line, a phrase.   4

———————

Let heaven forgive the wicked, after they have been punished.   5

———————

Pleasures are always children, pains always have wrinkles.   6

———————

There are truths that cannot be apprehended in conversation.   7

———————

God is the place where I do not remember the rest.   8

———————

Lovers. Whoever does not have their weaknesses cannot have their strengths.   9

———————

Our arms are canes of flesh with which the soul reaches and touches.   10

———————

What good is modesty?—It makes us seem more beautiful when we are beautiful, and less ugly when we are ugly.   11

———————

Children. Need models more than critics.   12

———————

Everything is a game except what makes the soul better or worse.   13

———————

One would say that in such dark eyes there is a flame without light.   14

———————

The weather strikes me on the head. I feel it rattle my teeth.   15

———————

The natural pace of the mind. And how it should move so as not to get worn out by quickness or bogged down and made impatient by slowness.   16

———————

The thoughts that come to us are worth more than the ones we seek.   17

———————

Lightning flashes that cross the mind and illuminate so quickly they are hardly noticed. In such cases, more is seen than retained. Thus, whoever does not observe himself carries within him some experience he does not know about.   18

———————

Anger. Its fermentation is necessary to the maturing of certain soft and   19
peaceful feelings. But if the crisis does not take place, if the fermentation leads
only to its own bitterness, the operation has not borne fruit and the natural
course of things has not been followed.

———————

Those useless phrases that come into the head. The mind is grinding its   20
colors.

———————

These thoughts form not only the foundation of my work, but of my life.   21

———————

It is not my words that I polish, but my ideas.   22

———————

Of those who feel God as rules, as light, and of those who feel him as love.   23

———————

. . . passing their life in contradicting their childhood,—in erasing it.   24

———————

All reflection is art.   25

———————

And, in fact, when we speak, we write what we are saying in the air.   26

———————

My dreams are more amorous than my actions have ever been.   27

———————

The little cat and the piece of paper he turns into a mouse. He touches it   28
lightly, for fear of unmasking his illusion.

———————

Little people have few passions, they hardly have anything but needs.   29

To want to express such subtle ideas faithfully is to want to capture an object   30
that endlessly escapes and reappears, that shows itself only for a moment. You
must wait, in spite of yourself, you must look.

Properly speaking, man inhabits only his head and his heart. All other places   31
are vainly before his eyes, at his sides, and under his feet: he himself is not
there at all.

Freedom. The freedom to do something well. There is no need of any other   32
kind.

Truths. The truths that teach us to act well and to live well. There is no need of   33
any other kind.

Abuse of words, foundation of ideology.   34

I am like Montaigne: "unsuited to continuous discourse."   35

More than once I have brought the cup of abundance to my lips; but it is a   36
water that has always escaped me. (Another version: I have often brought to
my lips the cup that holds abundance; it is a water that has always escaped me.)

There is in each man a divine part that is born with him, and a human and   37
even animal part that grows with time. The first must be conserved and
carefully cultivated within ourselves, the other thrives without help.

Retreat often into your sphere, rest yourself in your center, plunge yourself   38
into your element: good advice, which must be remembered.

———————

Tormented by the cursed ambition always to put a whole book in a page, a   39
whole page in a sentence, and this sentence in a word. I am speaking of myself.

———————

And perhaps there is no advice to give a writer more important than this: —
Never write anything that does not give you great pleasure.   40

—*Translated by Paul Auster*

ACTIVITIES FOR WRITING AND DISCUSSION

1. Review your own notebook and/or your textual annotations. Are there any items that you could describe as "nonfunctional" or "purely" poetic in the Joubertian sense? Share any such items with a partner or small group. If these pieces are not "functional," what value, if any, do they have?

2. Thinking of your own experiences of writing, does writing always have to serve a *function*? If it doesn't serve a function, does the time spent on it seem to you to have been wasted? Can you write "nonfunctionally," as Joubert did, and at the same time excel at the functional kinds of composing emphasized in classes, on the job, and in other public settings? Are the two kinds of writing complementary or at odds with each other? Explain, and, if possible, illustrate your answers with some personal stories or examples.

3. Joubert used his notebooks, in part, to develop his literary style. Try using your own notebook for the same purpose. Jot down "the thoughts that come to" you in single phrases and sentences. Reread these thoughts periodically, identifying those that most intrigue you, and revise them so that they reflect more accurately and forcefully your initial thoughts.

4. Do any of the "Generic Ideas for Writing" on page 275.

People and Cultures in Conflict and Change

EDGAR ALLAN POE (1809–1849)

The Masque of the Red Death

The "Red Death" had long devastated the country. No pestilence had ever been   1
so fatal, or so hideous. Blood was its Avatar and its seal—the redness and the
horror of blood. There were sharp pains, and sudden dizziness, and then pro-
fuse bleeding at the pores, with dissolution. The scarlet stains upon the body
and especially upon the face of the victim, were the pest ban which shut him
out from the aid and from the sympathy of his fellow-men. And the whole
seizure, progress, and termination of the disease, were the incidents of half
an hour.

But the Prince Prospero was happy and dauntless and sagacious. When his   2
dominions were half depopulated, he summoned to his presence a thousand
hale and light-hearted friends from among the knights and dames of his court,
and with these retired to the deep seclusion of one of his castellated abbeys.
This was an extensive and magnificent structure, the creation of the prince's
own eccentric yet august taste. A strong and lofty wall girdled it in. This wall
had gates of iron. The courtiers, having entered, brought furnaces and massy
hammers and welded the bolts. They resolved to leave means neither of ingress

701

nor egress to the sudden impulses of despair or of frenzy from within. The abbey was amply provisioned. With such precautions the courtiers might bid defiance to contagion. The external world could take care of itself. In the meantime it was folly to grieve, or to think. The prince had provided all the appliances of pleasure. There were buffoons, there were improvisatori, there were ballet-dancers, there were musicians, there was Beauty, there was wine. All these and security were within. Without was the "Red Death."

It was toward the close of the fifth or sixth month of his seclusion, and 3 while the pestilence raged most furiously abroad, that the Prince Prospero entertained his thousand friends at a masked ball of the most unusual magnificence.

It was a voluptuous scene, that masquerade. But first let me tell of the 4 rooms in which it was held. There were seven—an imperial suite. In many palaces, however, such suites form a long and straight vista, while the folding doors slide back nearly to the walls on either hand, so that the view of the whole extent is scarcely impeded. Here the case was very different; as might have been expected from the duke's love of the *bizarre*. The apartments were so irregularly disposed that the vision embraced but little more than one at a time. There was a sharp turn at every twenty or thirty yards, and at each turn a novel effect. To the right and left, in the middle of each wall, a tall and narrow Gothic window looked out upon a closed corridor which pursued the windings of the suite. These windows were of stained glass whose color varied in accordance with the prevailing hue of the decorations of the chamber into which it opened. That at the eastern extremity was hung, for example, in blue—and vividly blue were its windows. The second chamber was purple in its ornaments and tapestries, and here the panes were purple. The third was green throughout, and so were the casements. The fourth was furnished and lighted with orange—the fifth with white—the sixth with violet. The seventh apartment was closely shrouded in black velvet tapestries that hung all over the ceiling and down the walls, falling in heavy folds upon a carpet of the same material and hue. But in this chamber only, the color of the windows failed to correspond with the decorations. The panes here were scarlet—a deep blood color. Now in no one of the seven apartments was there any lamp or candelabrum, amid the profusion of golden ornaments that lay scattered to and fro or depended from the roof. There was no light of any kind emanating from lamp or candle within the suite of chambers. But in the corridors that followed the suite, there stood, opposite to each window, a heavy tripod, bearing a brazier of fire, that projected its rays through the tinted glass and so glaringly illumined the room. And thus were produced a multitude of gaudy and fantastic appearances. But in the western or black chamber the effect of the fire-light that streamed upon the dark hangings through the blood-tinted panes was ghastly in the extreme, and produced so wild a look upon the countenances of those who entered, that there were few of the company bold enough to set foot within its precincts at all.

It was in this apartment, also, that there stood against the western wall, a gi- 5 gantic clock of ebony. Its pendulum swung to and fro with a dull, heavy, monotonous clang; and when the minute-hand made the circuit of the face, and the hour was to be stricken, there came from the brazen lungs of the clock a sound which was clear and loud and deep and exceedingly musical, but of so peculiar a note and emphasis that, at each lapse of an hour, the musicians of the orchestra were constrained to pause, momentarily, in their performance, to hearken to the sound; and thus the waltzers perforce ceased their evolutions; and there was a brief disconcert of the whole gay company; and, while the chimes of the clock yet rang, it was observed that the giddiest grew pale, and the more aged and sedate passed their hands over their brows as if in confused revery or meditation. But when the echoes had fully ceased, a light laughter at once pervaded the assembly; the musicians looked at each other and smiled as if at their own nervousness and folly, and made whispering vows, each to the other, that the next chiming of the clock should produce in them no similar emotion; and then, after the lapse of sixty minutes (which embrace three thousand and six hundred seconds of the Time that flies), there came yet another chiming of the clock, and then were the same disconcert and tremulousness and meditation as before.

But, in spite of these things, it was a gay and magnificent revel. The tastes of 6 the duke were peculiar. He had a fine eye for colors and effects. He disregarded the *decora* of mere fashion. His plans were bold and fiery, and his conceptions glowed with barbaric lustre. There are some who would have thought him mad. His followers felt that he was not. It was necessary to hear and see and touch him to be *sure* that he was not.

He had directed, in great part, the movable embellishments of the seven 7 chambers, upon occasion of this great *fête;* and it was his own guiding taste which had given character to the masqueraders. Be sure they were grotesque. There were much glare and glitter and piquancy and phantasm—much of what has been since seen in "Hernani." There were arabesque figures with unsuited limbs and appointments. There were delirious fancies such as the madman fashions. There were much of the beautiful, much of the wanton, much of the *bizarre,* something of the terrible, and not a little of that which might have excited disgust. To and fro in the seven chambers there stalked, in fact, a multitude of dreams And these—the dreams—writhed in and about, taking hue from the rooms, and causing the wild music of the orchestra to seem as the echo of their steps. And, anon, there strikes the ebony clock which stands in the hall of the velvet. And then, for a moment, all is still, and all is silent save the voice of the clock. The dreams are stiff-frozen as they stand. But the echoes of the chime die away—they have endured but an instant—and a light, half-subdued laughter floats after them as they depart. And now again the music swells, and the dreams live, and writhe to and fro more merrily than ever, taking hue from the many-tinted windows through which stream the rays from the tripods. But to the chamber which lies most westwardly of the seven there are now none of the maskers who venture; for the night is waning away; and there flows a ruddier light through the blood-colored panes; and the blackness of the sable drapery appals; and to him whose foot falls upon the sable carpet, there comes from the near clock of ebony a muffled peal more solemnly emphatic than any which reaches *their* ears who indulge in the more remote gaieties of the other apartments.

But these other apartments were densely crowded, and in them beat fever- 8 ishly the heart of life. And the revel went whirlingly on, until at length there commenced the sounding of midnight upon the clock. And then the music ceased, as I have told; and the evolutions of the waltzers were quieted; and there was an uneasy cessation of all things as before. But now there were twelve strokes to be sounded by the bell of the clock; and thus it happened, perhaps that more of thought crept, with more of time, into the meditations of the thoughtful among those who revelled. And thus too, it happened, perhaps, that before the last echoes of the last chime had utterly sunk into silence, there were many individuals in the crowd who had found leisure to become aware of the presence of a masked figure which had arrested the attention of no single individual before. And the rumor of this new presence having spread itself whisperingly around, there arose at length from the whole company a buzz, or murmur, expressive of disapprobation and surprise—then, finally, of terror, of horror, and of disgust.

In an assembly of phantasms such as I have painted, it may well be supposed 9 that no ordinary appearance could have excited such sensation. In truth the masquerade license of the night was nearly unlimited; but the figure in question had out-Heroded Herod, and gone beyond the bounds of even the prince's indefinite decorum. There are chords in the hearts of the most reckless which cannot be touched without emotion. Even with the utterly lost, to whom life and death are equally jests, there are matters of which no jest can be made. The whole company, indeed, seemed now deeply to feel that in the costume and bearing of the stranger neither wit nor propriety existed. The figure was tall and gaunt, and shrouded from head to foot in the habiliments of the grave. The mask which concealed the visage was made so nearly to resemble the countenance of a stiffened corpse that the closest scrutiny must have had difficulty in detecting the cheat. And yet all this might have been endured, if not approved, by the mad revellers around. But the mummer had gone so far as to assume the type of the Red Death. His vesture was dabbled in *blood*—and his broad brow, with all the features of the face, was besprinkled with scarlet horror.

When the eyes of Prince Prospero fell upon this spectral image (which, with 10 a slow and solemn movement, as if more fully to sustain its *rôle*, stalked to and fro among the waltzers) he was seen to be convulsed, in the first moment with a strong shudder either of terror or distaste; but, in the next, his brow reddened with rage.

"Who dares"—he demanded hoarsely of the courtiers who stood near 11 him—"who dares insult us with this blasphemous mockery? Seize him and unmask him—that we may know whom we have to hang, at sunrise, from the battlements!"

It was in the eastern or blue chamber in which stood the Prince Prospero as 12 he uttered these words. They rang throughout the seven rooms loudly and clearly, for the prince was a bold and robust man, and the music had become hushed at the waving of his hand.

It was in the blue room where stood the prince, with a group of pale 13 courtiers by his side. At first, as he spoke, there was a slight rushing movement of this group in the direction of the intruder, who, at the moment was also near at hand, and now, with deliberate and stately step, made closer approach to the speaker. But from a certain nameless awe with which the mad assumptions of the mummer had inspired the whole party, there were found none who put forth hand to seize him; so that, unimpeded, he passed within a yard of the prince's person; and, while the vast assembly, as if with one impulse, shrank from the centres of the rooms to the walls, he made his way uninterruptedly, but with the same solemn and measured step which had distinguished him from the first, through the blue chamber to the purple—through the purple to the green—through the green to the orange—through this again to the white— and even thence to the violet, ere a decided movement had been made to arrest him. It was then, however, that the Prince Prospero, maddening with rage and the shame of his own momentary cowardice, rushed hurriedly through the six chambers, while none followed him on account of a deadly terror that had seized upon all. He bore aloft a drawn dagger, and had approached, in rapid impetuosity, to within three or four feet of the retreating figure, when the latter, having attained the extremity of the velvet apartment, turned suddenly and confronted his pursuer. There was a sharp cry   and the dagger dropped gleaming upon the sable carpet, upon which, instantly afterward, fell prostrate in death the Prince Prospero. Then, summoning the wild courage of despair, a throng of the revellers at once threw themselves into the black apartment, and, seizing the mummer, whose tall figure stood erect and motionless within the shadow of the ebony clock, gasped in unutterable horror at finding the grave cerements and corpse-like mask, which they handled with so violent a rudeness, untenanted by any tangible form.

And now was acknowledged the presence of the Red Death. He had come 14 like a thief in the night. And one by one dropped the revellers in the blood-bedewed halls of their revel, and died each in the despairing posture of his fall. And the life of the ebony clock went out with that of the last of the gay. And the flames of the tripods expired. And Darkness and Decay and the Red Death held illimitable dominion over all.

NADINE GORDIMER (b. 1923)

Once Upon a Time

Someone has written to ask me to contribute to an anthology of stories for chil- 1 dren. I reply that I don't write children's stories; and he writes back that at a recent congress/book fair/seminar a certain novelist said every writer ought to write at least one story for children. I think of sending a postcard saying I don't accept that I "ought" to write anything.

And then last night I woke up—or rather was wakened without knowing 2 what had roused me.

A voice in the echo-chamber of the subconscious?   3

A sound.   4

A creaking of the kind made by the weight carried by one foot after another 5 along a wooden floor. I listened. I felt the apertures of my ears distend with concentration. Again: the creaking. I was waiting for it; waiting to hear if it in- dicated that feet were moving from room to room, coming up the passage—to my door. I have no burglar bars, no gun under the pillow, but I have the same fears as people who do take these precautions, and my windowpanes are thin as rime, could shatter like a wineglass. A woman was murdered (how do they put it) in broad daylight in a house two blocks away, last year, and the fierce dogs who guarded an old widower and his collection of antique clocks were stran- gled before he was knifed by a casual labourer he had dismissed without pay.

I was staring at the door, making it out in my mind rather than seeing it, in 6 the dark. I lay quite still—a victim already—but the arrhythmia of my heart was fleeing, knocking this way and that against its body-cage. How finely tuned the senses are, just out of rest, sleep! I could never listen intently as that in the distractions of the day; I was reading every faintest sound, identifying and clas- sifying its possible threat.

But I learned that I was to be neither threatened nor spared. There was no 7 human weight pressing on the boards, the creaking was a buckling, an epicentre of stress. I was in it. The house that surrounds me while I sleep is built on un- dermined ground; far beneath my bed, the floor, the house's foundations, the stopes and passages of gold mines have hollowed the rock, and when some face trembles, detaches and falls, three thousand feet below, the whole house shifts slightly, bringing uneasy strain to the balance and counterbalance of brick, ce- ment, wood and glass that hold it as a structure around me. The misbeats of my heart tailed off like the last muffled flourishes on one of the wooden xylo- phones made by the Chopi and Tsonga migrant miners who might have been down there, under me in the earth at that moment. The stope where the fall was could have been disused, dripping water from its ruptured veins; or men might now be interred there in the most profound of tombs.

I couldn't find a position in which my mind would let go of my body— 8 release me to sleep again. So I began to tell myself a story; a bedtime story.

In a house, in a suburb, in a city, there were a man and his wife who loved 9 each other very much and were living happily ever after. They had a little boy, and they loved him very much. They had a cat and a dog that the little boy loved very much. They had a car and a caravan trailer for holidays, and a swim- ming-pool which was fenced so that the little boy and his playmates would not fall in and drown. They had a housemaid who was absolutely trustworthy and an itinerant gardener who was highly recommended by the neighbours. For when they began to live happily ever after they were warned, by that wise old witch, the husband's mother, not to take on anyone off the street. They were inscribed in a medical benefit society, their pet dog was licensed, they were insured against fire, flood damage and theft, and subscribed to the local Neighbourhood Watch, which supplied them with a plaque for their gates lettered YOU HAVE BEEN WARNED over the silhouette of a would-be intruder. He was masked; it could not be said if he was black or white, and therefore proved the property owner was no racist.

It was not possible to insure the house, the swimming pool or the car 10 against riot damage. There were riots, but these were outside the city, where people of another colour were quartered. These people were not allowed into the suburb except as reliable housemaids and gardeners, so there was nothing to fear, the husband told the wife. Yet she was afraid that some day such people might come up the street and tear off the plaque YOU HAVE BEEN WARNED and open the gates and stream in . . . Nonsense, my dear, said the husband, there are police and soldiers and tear-gas and guns to keep them away. But to please her—for he loved her very much and buses were being burned, cars stoned, and schoolchildren shot by the police in those quarters out of sight and hearing of the suburb—he had electronically-controlled gates fitted. Anyone who pulled off the sign YOU HAVE BEEN WARNED and tried to open the gates would have to announce his intentions by pressing a button and speaking into a receiver relayed to the house. The little boy was fascinated by the device and used it as a walkie-talkie in cops and robbers play with his small friends.

The riots were suppressed, but there were many burglaries in the suburb 11 and somebody's trusted housemaid was tied up and shut in a cupboard by thieves while she was in charge of her employers' house. The trusted housemaid of the man and wife and little boy was so upset by this misfortune befalling a friend left, as she herself often was, with responsibility for the possessions of the man and his wife and the little boy that she implored her employers to have burglar bars attached to the doors and windows of the house, and an alarm system installed. The wife said, She is right, let us take heed of her advice. So from every window and door in the house where they were living happily ever after they now saw the trees and sky through bars, and when the little boy's pet cat tried to climb in by the fanlight to keep him company in his little bed at night, as it customarily had done, it set off the alarm keening through the house.

The alarm was often answered—it seemed—by other burglar alarms, in 12 other houses, that had been triggered by pet cats or nibbling mice. The alarms called to one another across the gardens in shrills and bleats and wails that everyone soon became accustomed to, so that the din roused the inhabitants of the suburb no more than the croak of frogs and musical grating of cicadas' legs. Under cover of the electronic harpies' discourse intruders sawed the iron bars and broke into homes, taking away hi-fi equipment, television sets, cassette players, cameras and radios, jewellery and clothing, and sometimes were hungry enough to devour everything in the refrigerator or paused audaciously to drink the whisky in the cabinets or patio bars. Insurance companies paid no compensation for single malt, a loss made keener by the property owner's knowledge that the thieves wouldn't even have been able to appreciate what it was they were drinking.

Then the time came when many of the people who were not trusted house- 13 maids and gardeners hung about the suburb because they were unemployed. Some importuned for a job: weeding or painting a roof; anything, *baas*, madam. But the man and his wife remembered the warning about taking on anyone off the street. Some drank liquor and fouled the street with discarded bottles. Some begged, waiting for the man or his wife to drive the car out of the electronically-operated gates. They sat about with their feet in the gutters, un- der the jacaranda trees that made a green tunnel of the street—for it was a beautiful suburb, spoilt only by their presence—and sometimes they fell asleep lying right before the gates in the midday sun. The wife could never see anyone go hungry. She sent the trusted housemaid out with bread and tea, but the trusted housemaid said these were loafers and *tsotsis*, who would come and tie her up and shut her in a cupboard. The husband said, She's right. Take heed of her advice. You only encourage them with your bread and tea. They are looking for their chance . . . And he brought the little boy's tricycle from the garden into the house every night, because if the house was surely secure, once locked and with the alarm set, someone might still be able to climb over the wall or the electronically-closed gates into the garden.

You are right, said the wife, then the wall should be higher. And the wise old 14 witch, the husband's mother, paid for the extra bricks as her Christmas present to her son and his wife—the little boy got a Space Man outfit and a book of fairy tales.

But every week there were more reports of intrusion: in broad daylight and 15 the dead of night, in the early hours of the morning, and even in the lovely summer twilight—a certain family was at dinner while the bedrooms were be- ing ransacked upstairs. The man and his wife, talking of the latest armed rob- bery in the suburb, were distracted by the sight of the little boy's pet cat effortlessly arriving over the seven-foot wall, descending first with a rapid brac- ing of extended forepaws down on the sheer vertical surface, and then a grace- ful launch, landing with swishing tail within the property. The whitewashed wall was marked with the cat's comings and goings; and on the street side of the wall there were larger red-earth smudges that could have been made by the kind of broken running shoes, seen on the feet of unemployed loiterers, that had no innocent destination.

When the man and wife and little boy took the pet dog for its walk round 16 the neighbourhood streets they no longer paused to admire this show of roses or that perfect lawn; these were hidden behind an array of different varieties of security fences, walls and devices. The man, wife, little boy and dog passed a re- markable choice: there was the low-cost option of pieces of broken glass em- bedded in cement along the top of walls, there were iron grilles ending in lance-points, there were attempts at reconciling the aesthetics of prison archi- tecture with the Spanish Villa style (spikes painted pink) and with the plaster urns of neoclassical façades (twelve-inch pikes finned like zigzags of lightning and painted pure white). Some walls had a small board affixed, giving the name and telephone number of the firm responsible for the installation of the devices. While the little boy and the pet dog raced ahead, the husband and wife found themselves comparing the possible effectiveness of each style against its appearance; and after several weeks when they paused before this barricade or that without needing to speak, both came out with the conclusion that only one was worth considering. It was the ugliest but the most honest in its suggestion of the pure concentration-camp style, no frills, all evident efficacy. Placed the length of walls, it consisted of a continuous coil of stiff and shining metal serrated into jagged blades, so that there would be no way of climbing over it and no way through its tunnel without getting entangled in its fangs. There would be no way out, only a struggle getting bloodier and bloodier, a deeper and sharper hooking and tearing of flesh. The wife shuddered to look at it. You're right, said the husband, anyone would think twice . . . And they took heed of the advice on a small board fixed to the wall: Consult DRAGON'S TEETH   The People For Total Security.

Next day a gang of workmen came and stretched the razor-bladed coils all 17 round the walls of the house where the husband and wife and little boy and pet dog and cat were living happily ever after. The sunlight flashed and slashed, off the serrations, the cornice of razor thorns encircled the home, shining. The husband said, Never mind. It will weather. The wife said, You're wrong. They guarantee it's rust-proof. And she waited until the little boy had run off to play before she said, I hope the cat will take heed . . . The husband said, Don't worry, my dear, cats always look before they leap. And it was true that from that day on the cat slept in the little boy's bed and kept to the garden, never risking a try at breaching security.

One evening, the mother read the little boy to sleep with a fairy story from 18 the book the wise old witch had given him at Christmas. Next day he pretended to be the Prince who braves the terrible thicket of thorns to enter the palace and kiss the Sleeping Beauty back to life: he dragged a ladder to the wall, the shining coiled tunnel was just wide enough for his little body to creep in, and with the first fixing of its razor teeth in his knees and hands and head he screamed and struggled deeper into its tangle. The trusted housemaid and the itinerant gardener, whose "day" it was, came running, the first to see and to scream with him, and the itinerant gardener tore his hands trying to get at the little boy. Then the man and his wife burst wildly into the garden and for some reason (the cat, probably) the alarm set up wailing against the screams while the bleeding mass of the little boy was hacked out of the security coil with saws, wire-cutters, choppers, and they carried it—the man, the wife the hysterical trusted housemaid and the weeping gardener—into the house.

ACTIVITIES FOR WRITING AND DISCUSSION

1. In her introductory paragraphs Gordimer mentions that she was asked to write a children's story, and the story she proceeds to tell does use the

language and tone, and many of the stock literary devices and phrases, of a conventional children's story.

    a. Make two lists, one of similarities and the other of differences between "Once Upon a Time" and conventional children's stories.

    b. Given the **themes** and **plot** of her story, is the choice of language and tone appropriate? Why or why not? What effects are created by the dissonance between the story's innocent tone and its disturbing content? Support your answers with references to passages in the text.

2. "Once Upon a Time" concerns the topic of "security."

    a. Address this same topic in any way you wish using a different form— such as dialogue, letter, poem, personal essay, or stream of consciousness; or,

    b. Brainstorm a list of other topics of urgent contemporary social interest. Then choose one topic and write about it, as Gordimer does, in the form of a children's story.

3. "Increasing security breeds more insecurity." Support or rebut this assertion with reference to Gordimer's story, Poe's "The Masque of the Red Death," and/or stories or experiences of your own.

Margaret Atwood (b. 1939)

The Man from Mars

A long time ago Christine was walking through the park. She was still wearing 1 her tennis dress; she hadn't had time to shower and change, and her hair was held back with an elastic band. Her chunky reddish face, exposed with no softening fringe, looked like a Russian peasant's, but without the elastic band the hair got in her eyes. The afternoon was too hot for April; the indoor courts had been steaming, her skin felt poached.

The sun had brought the old men out from wherever they spent the winter: 2 she had read a story recently about one who lived for three years in a manhole. They sat weedily on the benches or lay on the grass with their heads on squares of used newspaper. As she passed, their wrinkled toadstool faces drifted towards her, drawn by the movement of her body, then floated away again, uninterested.

The squirrels were out, too, foraging; two or three of them moved towards 3 her in darts and pauses, eyes fixed on her expectantly, mouths with the ratlike receding chins open to show the yellowed front teeth. Christine walked faster, she had nothing to give them. People shouldn't feed them, she thought; it makes them anxious and they get mangy.

Halfway across the park she stopped to take off her cardigan. As she bent 4 over to pick up her tennis racquet again someone touched her on her freshly bared arm. Christine seldom screamed; she straightened up suddenly, gripping the handle of her racquet. It was not one of the old men, however; it was a dark-haired boy of twelve or so.

"Excuse me," he said, "I search for Economics Building. Is it there?" He mo-   5
tioned towards the west.

Christine looked at him more closely. She had been mistaken: he was not   6
young, just short. He came a little above her shoulder, but then, she was above
the average height; "statuesque," her mother called it when she was straining.
He was also what was referred to in their family as "a person from another culture": oriental without a doubt, though perhaps not Chinese. Christine judged
he must be a foreign student and gave him her official welcoming smile. In high
school she had been president of the United Nations Club; that year her school
had been picked to represent the Egyptian delegation at the Mock Assembly.
It had been an unpopular assignment—nobody wanted to be the Arabs—but
she had seen it through. She had made rather a good speech about the Palestin-
ian refugees.

"Yes," she said, "that's it over there. The one with the flat roof. See it?"   7

The man had been smiling nervously at her the whole time. He was wearing   8
glasses with transparent plastic rims, through which his eyes bulged up at her as
though through a goldfish bowl. He had not followed where she was pointing.
Instead he thrust towards her a small green paper and a ball-point pen.

"You make map," he said.   9

Christine set down her tennis racquet and drew a careful map. "We are   10
here," she said, pronouncing distinctly. "You go this way. The building is here."
She indicated the route with a dotted line and an X. The man leaned close to
her, watching the progress of the map attentively; he smelled of cooked cauliflower and an unfamiliar brand of hair grease. When she had finished Christine
handed the paper and pen back to him with a terminal smile.

"Wait," the man said. He tore the piece of paper with the map off the pad,   11
folded it carefully and put it in his jacket pocket; the jacket sleeves came down
over his wrists and had threads at the edges. He began to write something; she
noticed with a slight feeling of revulsion that his nails and the ends of his fingers were so badly bitten they seemed almost deformed. Several of his fingers
were blue from the leaky ball-point.

"Here is my name," he said, holding the pad out to her.   12

Christine read an odd assemblage of Gs, Ys and Ns, neatly printed in block   13
letters. "Thank you," she said.

"You now write *your* name," he said, extending the pen.   14

Christine hesitated. If this had been a person from her own culture she   15
would have thought he was trying to pick her up. But then, people from her
own culture never tried to pick her up; she was too big. The only one who had
made the attempt was the Moroccan waiter at the beer parlour where they
sometimes went after meetings, and he had been direct. He had just intercepted
her on the way to the Ladies' Room and asked and she said no; that had been
that. This man was not a waiter though, but a student; she didn't want to offend
him. In his culture, whatever it was, this exchange of names on pieces of paper

was probably a formal politeness, like saying thank you. She took the pen from him.

"That is a very pleasant name," he said. He folded the paper and placed it in   16
his jacket with the map.

Christine felt she had done her duty. "Well, goodbye," she said. "It was nice   17
to have met you." She bent for her tennis racquet but he had already stooped
and retrieved it and was holding it with both hands in front of him, like a captured banner.

"I carry this for you."   18

"Oh no, please. Don't bother, I am in a hurry," she said, articulating clearly.   19
Deprived of her tennis racquet she felt weaponless. He started to saunter along
the path; he was not nervous at all now, he seemed completely at ease.

"*Vous parlez français?*" he asked conversationally.   20

"*Oui, un petit peu,*" she said. "Not very well." How am I going to get my rac-   21
quet away from him without being rude? she was wondering.

"*Mais vous avez un bel accent.*" His eyes goggled at her through the glasses: 22
was he being flirtatious? She was well aware that her accent was wretched.

"Look," she said, for the first time letting her impatience show, "I really have   23
to go. Give me my racquet, please."

He quickened his pace but gave no sign of returning the racquet. "Where   24
you are going?"

"Home," she said. "My house."   25

"I go with you now," he said hopefully.   26

"*No,*" she said: she would have to be firm with him. She made a lunge and   27
got a grip on her racquet; after a brief tug of war it came free.

"Goodbye," she said, turning away from his puzzled face and setting off at   28
what she hoped was a discouraging jog-trot. It was like walking away from a
growling dog: you shouldn't let on you were frightened. Why should she be
frightened anyway? He was only half her size and she had the tennis racquet,
there was nothing he could do to her.

Although she did not look back she could tell he was still following. Let   29
there be a streetcar, she thought, and there was one, but it was far down the line,
stuck behind a red light. He appeared at her side, breathing audibly, a moment
after she reached the stop. She gazed ahead, rigid.

"You are my friend," he said tentatively.   30

Christine relented: he hadn't been trying to pick her up after all, he was a   31
stranger, he just wanted to meet some of the local people; in his place she would
have wanted the same thing.

"Yes," she said, doling him out a smile.   32

"That is good," he said. "My country is very far."   33

Christine couldn't think of an apt reply. "That's interesting," she said. "*Très*   34
interessant." The streetcar was coming at last; she opened her purse and got out
a ticket.

"I go with you now," he said. His hand clamped on her arm above the elbow.   35

"You . . . stay . . . *here*," Christine said, resisting the impulse to shout but 36 pausing between each word as though for a deaf person. She detached his hand—his hold was quite feeble and could not compete with her tennis biceps—and leapt off the curb and up the streetcar steps, hearing with relief the doors grind shut behind her. Inside the car and a block away she permitted herself a glance out a side window. He was standing where she had left him; he seemed to be writing something on his little pad of paper.

When she reached home she had only time for a snack, and even then she 37 was almost late for the Debating Society. The topic was, "Resolved: That War Is Obsolete." Her team took the affirmative and won.

Christine came out of her last examination feeling depressed. It was not the 38 exam that depressed her but the fact that it was the last one: it meant the end of the school year. She dropped into the coffee shop as usual, then went home early because there didn't seem to be anything else to do.

"Is that you, dear?" her mother called from the living room. She must have 39 heard the front door close. Christine went in and flopped on the sofa, disturbing the neat pattern of cushions.

"How was your exam, dear?" her mother asked. 40

"Fine," said Christine flatly. It had been fine; she had passed. She was not a 41 brilliant student, she knew that, but she was conscientious. Her professors always wrote things like "A serious attempt" and "Well thought out but perhaps lacking in élan" on her term papers; they gave her Bs, the occasional B+. She was taking Political Science and Economics, and hoped for a job with the Government after she graduated; with her father's connections she had a good chance.

"That's nice." 42

Christine felt, resentfully, that her mother had only a hazy idea of what an 43 exam was. She was arranging gladioli in a vase; she had rubber gloves on to protect her hands as she always did when engaged in what she called "housework." As far as Christine could tell her housework consisted of arranging flowers in vases: daffodils and tulips and hyacinths through gladioli, irises and roses, all the way to asters and mums. Sometimes she cooked, elegantly and with chafing-dishes, but she thought of it as a hobby. The girl did everything else. Christine thought it faintly sinful to have a girl. The only ones available now were either foreign or pregnant; their expressions usually suggested they were being taken advantage of somehow. But her mother asked what they would do otherwise; they'd either have to go into a Home or stay in their own countries, and Christine had to agree this was probably true. It was hard, anyway, to argue with her mother. She was so delicate, so preserved-looking, a harsh breath would scratch the finish.

"An interesting young man phoned today," her mother said. She had fin- 44 ished the gladioli and was taking off her rubber gloves. "He asked to speak with you and when I said you weren't in we had quite a little chat. You didn't tell me about him, dear." She put on the glasses which she wore on a decorative chain around her neck, a signal that she was in her modern, intelligent mood rather than her old-fashioned whimsical one.

"Did he leave his name?" Christine asked. She knew a lot of young men but they didn't often call her; they conducted their business with her in the coffee shop or after meetings.   45

"He's a person from another culture. He said he would call back later."   46

Christine had to think a moment. She was vaguely acquainted with several people from other cultures, Britain mostly; they belonged to the Debating Society.   47

"He's studying Philosophy in Montreal," her mother prompted. "He sounded French."   48

Christine began to remember the man in the park. "I don't think he's French, exactly," she said.   49

Her mother had taken off her glasses again and was poking absentmindedly at a bent gladiolus. "Well, he sounded French." She meditated, flowery sceptre in hand. "I think it would be nice if you had him to tea."   50

Christine's mother did her best. She had two other daughters, both of whom took after her. They were beautiful; one was well married already and the other would clearly have no trouble. Her friends consoled her about Christine by saying, "She's not fat, she's just big-boned, it's the father's side," and "Christine is so healthy." Her other daughters had never gotten involved in activities when they were at school, but since Christine could not possibly ever be beautiful even if she took off weight, it was just as well she was so athletic and political, it was a good thing she had interests. Christine's mother tried to encourage her interests whenever possible. Christine could tell when she was making an extra effort, there was a reproaching edge to her voice.   51

She knew her mother expected enthusiasm but she could not supply it. "I don't know, I'll have to see," she said dubiously.   52

"You look tired, darling," said her mother. "Perhaps you'd like a glass of milk."   53

Christine was in the bathtub when the phone rang. She was not prone to fantasy but when she was in the bathtub she often pretended she was a dolphin, a game left over from one of the girls who used to bathe her when she was small. Her mother was being bell-voiced and gracious in the hall; then there was a tap at the door.   54

"It's that nice young French student, Christine," her mother said.   55

"Tell him I'm in the bathtub," Christine said, louder than necessary. "He isn't French."   56

She could hear her mother frowning. "That wouldn't be very polite, Christine. I don't think he'd understand."   57

"Oh, all right," Christine said. She heaved herself out of the bathtub, swathed her pink bulk in a towel and splattered to the phone.   58

"Hello," she said gruffly. At a distance he was not pathetic, he was a nuisance. She could not imagine how he had tracked her down: most likely he went   59

through the phone book, calling all the numbers with her last name until he hit
on the right one.

"It is your friend."   60

"I know," she said. "How are you?"   61

"I am very fine." There was a long pause, during which Christine had a vi-   62
cious urge to say, "Well goodbye then," and hang up; but she was aware of her
mother poised figurine-like in her bedroom doorway. Then he said, "I hope
you also are very fine."

"Yes," said Christine. She wasn't going to participate.   63

"I come to tea," he said.   64

This took Christine by surprise. "You do?"   65

"Your pleasant mother ask me. I come Thursday, four o'clock."   66

"Oh," Christine said, ungraciously.   67

"See you then," he said, with the conscious pride of one who has mastered a   68
difficult idiom.

Christine set down the phone and went along the hall. Her mother was in   69
her study, sitting innocently at her writing desk.

"Did you ask him to tea on Thursday?"   70

"Not exactly, dear," her mother said. "I did mention he might come round   71
to tea *some*time, though."

"Well, he's coming Thursday. Four o'clock."   72

"What's wrong with that?" her mother said serenely. "I think it's a very nice   73
gesture for us to make. I do think you might try to be a little more co-opera-
tive." She was pleased with herself.

"Since you invited him," said Christine, "you can bloody well stick around   74
and help me entertain him. I don't want to be left making nice gestures all by
myself."

"Christine, *dear*," her mother said, above being shocked. "You ought to put   75
on your dressing gown, you'll catch a chill."

After sulking for an hour Christine tried to think of the tea as a cross be-   76
tween an examination and an executive meeting: not enjoyable, certainly, but to
be got through as tactfully as possible. And it was a nice gesture. When the cakes
her mother had ordered arrived from The Patisserie on Thursday morning she
began to feel slightly festive; she even resolved to put on a dress, a good one, instead of a skirt and blouse. After all, she had nothing against him, except the
memory of the way he had grabbed her tennis racquet and then her arm. She
suppressed a quick impossible vision of herself pursued around the living
room, fending him off with thrown sofa cushions and vases of gladioli; nevertheless she told the girl they would have tea in the garden. It would be a treat for
him, and there was more space outdoors.

She had suspected her mother would dodge the tea, would contrive to be   77
going out just as he was arriving: that way she could size him up and then leave
them alone together. She had done things like that to Christine before; the excuse this time was the Symphony Committee. Sure enough, her mother carefully mislaid her gloves and located them with a faked murmur of joy when the

doorbell rang. Christine relished for weeks afterwards the image of her mother's dropped jaw and flawless recovery when he was introduced: he wasn't quite the foreign potentate her optimistic, veil-fragile mind had concocted.

He was prepared for celebration. He had slicked on so much hair cream that 78 his head seemed to be covered with a tight black patent-leather cap, and he had cut the threads off his jacket sleeves. His orange tie was overpoweringly splendid. Christine noticed, however, as he shook her mother's suddenly braced white glove that the ball-point ink on his fingers was indelible. His face had broken out, possibly in anticipation of the delights in store for him; he had a tiny camera slung over his shoulder and was smoking an exotic-smelling cigarette.

Christine led him through the cool flowery softly padded living room and 79 out by the French doors into the garden. "You sit here," she said. "I will have the girl bring tea."

This girl was from the West Indies: Christine's parents had been enraptured 80 with her when they were down at Christmas and had brought her back with them. Since that time she had become pregnant, but Christine's mother had not dismissed her. She said she was slightly disappointed but what could you expect, and she didn't see any real difference between a girl who was pregnant before you hired her and one who got that way afterwards. She prided herself on her tolerance; also there was a scarcity of girls. Strangely enough, the girl became progressively less easy to get along with. Either she did not share Christine's mother's view of her own generosity, or she felt she had gotten away with something and was therefore free to indulge in contempt. At first Christine had tried to treat her as an equal. "Don't call me 'Miss Christine,'" she had said with an imitation of light, comradely laughter. "What you want me to call you then?" the girl had said, scowling. They had begun to have brief, surly arguments in the kitchen, which Christine decided were like the arguments between one servant and another: her mother's attitude towards each of them was similar, they were not altogether satisfactory but they would have to do.

The cakes, glossy with icing, were set out on a plate and the teapot was 81 standing ready; on the counter the electric kettle boiled. Christine headed for it, but the girl, till then sitting with her elbows on the kitchen table and watching her expressionlessly, made a dash and intercepted her. Christine waited until she had poured the water into the pot. Then, "I'll carry it out, Elvira," she said. She had just decided she didn't want the girl to see her visitor's orange tie; already, she knew, her position in the girl's eyes had suffered because no one had yet attempted to get *her* pregnant.

"What you think they pay me for, Miss Christine?" the girl said insolently. 82 She swung towards the garden with the tray; Christine trailed her, feeling lumpish and awkward. The girl was at least as big as she was but in a different way.

"Thank you, Elvira," Christine said when the tray was in place. The girl departed without a word, casting a disdainful backward glance at the frayed jacket 83 sleeves, the stained fingers. Christine was now determined to be especially kind to him.

"You are very rich," he said.   84

"No," Christine protested, shaking her head, "we're not." She had never   85
thought of her family as rich; it was one of her father's sayings that nobody
made any money with the Government.

"Yes," he repeated, "you are very rich." He sat back in his lawn chair, gazing   86
about him as though dazed.

Christine set his cup of tea in front of him. She wasn't in the habit of paying   87
much attention to the house or the garden; they were nothing special, far from
being the largest on the street; other people took care of them. But now she
looked where he was looking, seeing it all as though from a different height: the
long expanses, the border flowers blazing in the early-summer sunlight, the
flagged patio and walks, the high walls and the silence.

He came back to her face, sighing a little. "My English is not good," he said,   88
"but I improve."

"You do," Christine said, nodding encouragement.   89

He took sips of his tea, quickly and tenderly, as though afraid of injuring the   90
cup. "I like to stay here."

Christine passed him the cakes. He took only one, making a slight face as he   91
ate it; but he had several more cups of tea while she finished the cakes. She
managed to find out from him that he had come over on a church fellowship—
she could not decode the denomination—and was studying Philosophy or
Theology, or possibly both. She was feeling well-disposed towards him: he had
behaved himself, he had caused her no inconvenience.

The teapot was at last empty. He sat up straight in his chair, as though   92
alerted by a soundless gong. "You look this way, please," he said. Christine saw
that he had placed his miniature camera on the stone sundial her mother had
shipped back from England two years before. He wanted to take her picture.
She was flattered, and settled herself to pose, smiling evenly.

He took off his glasses and laid them beside his plate. For a moment she saw   93
his myopic, unprotected eyes turned towards her, with something tremulous
and confiding in them she wanted to close herself off from knowing about.
Then he went over and did something to the camera, his back to her. The next
instant he was crouched beside her, his arm around her waist as far as it could
reach, his other hand covering her own hands which she had folded in her lap,
his cheek jammed up against hers. She was too startled to move. The camera
clicked.

He stood up at once and replaced his glasses, which glittered now with a sad   94
triumph. "Thank you, miss," he said to her. "I go now." He slung the camera
back over his shoulder, keeping his hand on it as though to hold the lid on and
prevent escape. "I send to my family; they will like."

He was out the gate and gone before Christine had recovered; then she   95
laughed. She had been afraid he would attack her, she could admit it now, and
he had; but not in the usual way. He had raped, *rapeo, rapere, rapui, to seize and
carry off,* not herself but her celluloid image, and incidently that of the silver tea
service, which glinted mockingly at her as the girl bore it away, carrying it re-
gally, the insignia, the official jewels.

Christine spent the summer as she had for the past three years: she was the 96
sailing instructress at an expensive all-girls camp near Algonquin Park. She had
been a camper there, everything was familiar to her; she sailed almost better
than she played tennis.

The second week she got a letter from him, postmarked Montreal and for- 97
warded from her home address. It was printed in block letters on a piece of the
green paper, two or three sentences. It began, "I hope you are well," then described the weather in monosyllables and ended, "I am fine." It was signed,
"Your friend." Each week she got another of these letters, more or less identical.
In one of them a colour print was enclosed: himself, slightly cross-eyed and
grinning hilariously, even more spindly than she remembered him against her
billowing draperies, flowers exploding around them like firecrackers, one of his
hands an equivocal blur in her lap, the other out of sight; on her own face, astonishment and outrage, as though he was sticking her in the behind with his
hidden thumb.

She answered the first letter, but after that the seniors were in training for 98
the races. At the end of the summer, packing to go home, she threw all the letters away.

When she had been back for several weeks she received another of the green 99
letters. This time there was a return address printed at the top which Christine
noted with foreboding was in her own city. Every day she waited for the phone
to ring; she was so certain his first attempt at contact would be a disembodied
voice that when he came upon her abruptly in midcampus she was unprepared.

"How are you?" 100

His smile was the same, but everything else about him had deteriorated. He 101
was, if possible, thinner; his jacket sleeves had sprouted a lush new crop of
threads, as though to conceal hands now so badly bitten they appeared to have
been gnawed by rodents. His hair fell over his eyes, uncut, ungreased; his eyes in
the hollowed face, a delicate triangle of skin stretched on bone, jumped behind
his glasses like hooded fish. He had the end of a cigarette in the corner of his
mouth, and as they walked he lit a new one from it.

"I'm fine," Christine said. She was thinking, I'm not going to get involved 102
again, enough is enough, I've done my bit for internationalism. "How are you?"

"I live here now," he said. "Maybe I study Economics." 103

"That's nice." He didn't sound as though he was enrolled anywhere. 104

"I come to see you." 105

Christine didn't know whether he meant he had left Montreal in order to be 106
near her or just wanted to visit her at her house as he had done in the spring; either way she refused to be implicated. They were outside the Political Science
Building. "I have a class here," she said. "Goodbye." She was being callous, she
realized that, but a quick chop was more merciful in the long run, that was what
her beautiful sisters used to say.

Afterwards she decided it had been stupid of her to let him find out where 107
her class was. Though a timetable was posted in each of the colleges: all he had

to do was look her up and record her every probable movement in block letters on his green notepad. After that day he never left her alone.

Initially he waited outside the lecture rooms for her to come out. She said 108 hello to him curtly at first and kept on going, but this didn't work; he followed her at a distance, smiling his changeless smile. Then she stopped speaking altogether and pretended to ignore him, but it made no difference, he followed her anyway. The fact that she was in some way afraid of him—or was it just embarrassment?—seemed only to encourage him. Her friends started to notice, asking her who he was and why he was tagging along behind her; she could hardly answer because she hardly knew.

As the weekdays passed and he showed no signs of letting up, she began to 109 jog-trot between classes, finally to run. He was tireless, and had an amazing wind for one who smoked so heavily: he would speed along behind her, keeping the distance between them the same, as though he were a pull-toy attached to her by a string. She was aware of the ridiculous spectacle they must make, galloping across campus, something out of a cartoon short, a lumbering elephant stampeded by a smiling, emaciated mouse, both of them locked in the classic pattern of comic pursuit and flight; but she found that to race made her less nervous than to walk sedately, the skin on the back of her neck crawling with the feel of his eyes on it. At least she could use her muscles. She worked out routines, escapes: she would dash in the front door of the Ladies' Room in the coffee shop and out the back door, and he would lose the trail, until he discovered the other entrance. She would try to shake him by detours through baffling archways and corridors, but he seemed as familiar with the architectural mazes as she was herself. As a last refuge she could head for the women's dormitory and watch from safety as he was skidded to a halt by the receptionist's austere voice: men were not allowed past the entrance.

Lunch became difficult. She would be sitting, usually with other members 110 of the Debating Society, just digging nicely into a sandwich, when he would appear suddenly as though he'd come up through an unseen manhole. She then had the choice of barging out through the crowded cafeteria, sandwich half eaten, or finishing her lunch with him standing behind her chair, everyone at the table acutely aware of him, the conversation stilting and dwindling. Her friends learned to spot him from a distance; they posted lookouts. "Here he comes," they would whisper, helping her collect her belongings for the sprint they knew would follow.

Several times she got tired of running and turned to confront him. "What 111 do you want?" she would ask, glowering belligerently down at him, almost clenching her fists; she felt like shaking him, hitting him.

"I wish to talk with you." 112

"Well, here I am," she would say. "What do you want to talk about?" 113

But he would say nothing; he would stand in front of her, shifting his feet, 114 smiling perhaps apologetically (though she could never pinpoint the exact tone of that smile, chewed lips stretched apart over the nicotine-yellowed teeth, rising at the corners, flesh held stiffly in place for an invisible photographer), his eyes jerking from one part of her face to another as though he saw her in fragments.

Annoying and tedious though it was, his pursuit of her had an odd result: 115 mysterious in itself, it rendered her equally mysterious. No one had ever found Christine mysterious before. To her parents she was a beefy heavyweight, a plodder, lacking in flair, ordinary as bread. To her sisters she was the plain one, treated with an indulgence they did not give to each other: they did not fear her as a rival. To her male friends she was the one who could be relied on. She was helpful and a hard worker, always good for a game of tennis with the athletes among them. They invited her along to drink beer with them so they could get into the cleaner, more desirable Ladies and Escorts side of the beer parlour, taking it for granted she would buy her share of the rounds. In moments of stress they confided to her their problems with women. There was nothing devious about her and nothing interesting.

Christine had always agreed with these estimates of herself. In childhood 116 she had identified with the false bride or the ugly sister; whenever a story had begun, "Once there was a maiden as beautiful as she was good," she had known it wasn't her. That was just how it was, but it wasn't so bad. Her parents never expected her to be a brilliant social success and weren't overly disappointed when she wasn't. She was spared the manoeuvring and anxiety she witnessed among others her age, and she even had a kind of special position among men: she was an exception, she fitted none of the categories they commonly used when talking about girls; she wasn't a cock-teaser, a cold fish, an easy lay or a snarky bitch; she was an honorary person. She had grown to share their contempt for most women.

Now, however, there was something about her that could not be explained. 117 A man was chasing her, a peculiar sort of man, granted, but still a man, and he was without doubt attracted to her, he couldn't leave her alone. Other men examined her more closely than they ever had, appraising her, trying to find out what it was those twitching bespectacled eyes saw in her. They started to ask her out, though they returned from these excursions with their curiosity unsatisfied, the secret of her charm still intact. Her opaque dumpling face, her solid bearshaped body became for them parts of a riddle no one could solve. Christine sensed this. In the bathtub she no longer imagined she was a dolphin; instead she imagined she was an elusive water-nixie, or sometimes, in moments of audacity, Marilyn Monroe. The daily chase was becoming a habit; she even looked forward to it. In addition to its other benefits she was losing weight.

All these weeks he had never phoned her or turned up at the house. He must 118 have decided however that his tactics were not having the desired result, or perhaps he sensed she was becoming bored. The phone began to ring in the early morning or late at night when he could be sure she would be there. Sometimes he would simply breathe (she could recognize, or thought she could, the quality of his breathing), in which case she would hang up. Occasionally he would say again that he wanted to talk to her, but even when she gave him lots of time nothing else would follow. Then he extended his range: she would see him on her streetcar, smiling at her silently from a seat never closer than three away;

she could feel him tracking her down her own street, though when she would break her resolve to pay no attention and would glance back he would be invisible or in the act of hiding behind a tree or hedge.

Among crowds of people and in daylight she had not really been afraid of 119 him; she was stronger than he was and he had made no recent attempt to touch her. But the days were growing shorter and colder, it was almost November. Often she was arriving home in twilight or a darkness broken only by the feeble orange streetlamps. She brooded over the possibility of razors, knives, guns; by acquiring a weapon he could quickly turn the odds against her. She avoided wearing scarves, remembering the newspaper stories about girls who had been strangled by them. Putting on her nylons in the morning gave her a funny feeling. Her body seemed to have diminished, to have become smaller than his.

Was he deranged, was he a sex maniac? He seemed so harmless, yet it was 120 that kind who often went berserk in the end. She pictured those ragged fingers at her throat, tearing at her clothes, though she could not think of herself as screaming. Parked cars, the shrubberies near her house, the driveways on either side of it, changed as she passed them from unnoticed background to sinister shadowed foreground, every detail distinct and harsh: they were places a man might crouch, leap out from. Yet every time she saw him in the clear light of morning or afternoon (for he still continued his old methods of pursuit), his aging jacket and jittery eyes convinced her that it was she herself who was the tormentor, the persecutor. She was in some sense responsible; from the folds and crevices of the body she had treated for so long as a reliable machine was emanating, against her will, some potent invisible odour, like a dog's in heat or a female moth's, that made him unable to stop following her.

Her mother, who had been too preoccupied with the unavoidable fall enter- 121 taining to pay much attention to the number of phone calls Christine was getting or to the hired girl's complaints of a man who hung up without speaking, announced that she was flying down to New York for the weekend; her father decided to go too. Christine panicked: she saw herself in the bathtub with her throat slit, the blood drooling out of her neck and running in a little spiral down the drain (for by this time she believed he could walk through walls, could be everywhere at once). The girl would do nothing to help; she might even stand in the bathroom door with her arms folded, watching. Christine arranged to spend the weekend at her married sister's.

When she arrived back Sunday evening she found the girl close to hysterics. 122 She said that on Saturday she had gone to pull the curtains across the French doors at dusk and had found a strangely contorted face, a man's face, pressed against the glass, staring in at her from the garden. She claimed she had fainted and had almost had her baby a month too early right there on the living-room carpet. Then she had called the police. He was gone by the time they got there but she had recognized him from the afternoon of the tea; she had informed them he was a friend of Christine's.

They called Monday evening to investigate, two of them. They were very po- 123 lite, they knew who Christine's father was. Her father greeted them heartily; her mother hovered in the background, fidgeting with her porcelain hands, letting them see how frail and worried she was. She didn't like having them in the living room but they were necessary.

Christine had to admit he'd been following her around. She was relieved 124
he'd been discovered, relieved also that she hadn't been the one to tell, though if
he'd been a citizen of the country she would have called the police a long time
ago. She insisted he was not dangerous, he had never hurt her.

"That kind don't hurt you," one of the policemen said. "They just kill you. 125
You're lucky you aren't dead."

"Nut cases," the other one said. 126

Her mother volunteered that the thing about people from another culture 127
was that you could never tell whether they were insane or not because their
ways were so different. The policemen agreed with her, deferential but also condescending, as though she was a royal halfwit who had to be humoured.

"You know where he lives?" the first policeman asked. Christine had long 128
ago torn up the letter with his address on it; she shook her head.

"We'll have to pick him up tomorrow then," he said. "Think you can keep 129
him talking outside your class if he's waiting for you?"

After questioning her they held a murmured conversation with her father in 130
the front hall. The girl, clearing away the coffee cups, said if they didn't lock
him up she was leaving, she wasn't going to be scared half out of her skin like
that again.

Next day when Christine came out of her Modern History lecture he was 131
there, right on schedule. He seemed puzzled when she did not begin to run. She
approached him, her heart thumping with treachery and the prospect of freedom. Her body was back to its usual size; she felt herself a giantess, self-controlled, invulnerable.

"How are you?" she asked, smiling brightly. 132

He looked at her with distrust. 133

"How have you been?" she ventured again. His own perennial smile faded; 134
he took a step back from her.

"This the one?" said the policeman, popping out from behind a notice 135
board like a Keystone Cop and laying a competent hand on the worn jacket
shoulder. The other policeman lounged in the background; force would not be
required.

"Don't *do* anything to him," she pleaded as they took him away. They nod- 136
ded and grinned, respectful, scornful. He seemed to know perfectly well who
they were and what they wanted.

The first policeman phoned that evening to make his report. Her father 137
talked with him, jovial and managing. She herself was now out of the picture;
she had been protected, her function was over.

"What did they *do* to him?" she asked anxiously as he came back into the 138
living room. She was not sure what went on in police stations.

"They didn't do anything to him," he said, amused by her concern. "They 139
could have booked him for Watching and Besetting, they wanted to know if I'd

like to press charges. But it's not worth a court case: he's got a visa that says he's only allowed in the country as long as he studies in Montreal, so I told them to just ship him down there. If he turns up here again they'll deport him. They went around to his rooming house, his rent's two weeks overdue; the landlady said she was on the point of kicking him out. He seems happy enough to be getting his back rent paid and a free train ticket to Montreal." He paused. "They couldn't get anything out of him though."

"*Out* of him?" Christine asked.   140

"They tried to find out why he was doing it; following you, I mean." Her fa- 141
ther's eyes swept her as though it was a riddle to him also. "They said when they asked him about that he just clammed up. Pretended he didn't understand English. He understood well enough, but he wasn't answering."

Christine thought this would be the end, but somehow between his arrest 142
and the departure of the train he managed to elude his escort long enough for one more phone call.

"I see you again," he said. He didn't wait for her to hang up.   143

Now that he was no longer an embarrassing present reality, he could be 144
talked about, he could become an amusing story. In fact, he was the only amusing story Christine had to tell, and telling it preserved both for herself and for others the aura of her strange allure. Her friends and the men who continued to ask her out speculated about his motives. One suggested he had wanted to marry her so he could remain in the country; another said that oriental men were fond of well-built women: "It's your Rubens quality."

Christine thought about him a lot. She had not been attracted to him, rather 145
the reverse, but as an idea only he was a romantic figure, the one man who had found her irresistible; though she often wondered, inspecting her unchanged pink face and hefty body in her full-length mirror, just what it was about her that had done it. She avoided whenever it was proposed the theory of his insanity; it was only that there was more than one way of being sane.

But a new acquaintance, hearing the story for the first time, had a different 146
explanation. "So he got you, too," he said, laughing. "That has to be the same guy who was hanging around our day camp a year ago this summer. He followed all the girls like that, a short guy, Japanese or something, glasses, smiling all the time."

"Maybe it was another one," Christine said.   147

"There couldn't be two of them, everything fits. This was a pretty weird 148
guy."

"What . . . *kind* of girls did he follow?" Christine asked.   149

"Oh, just anyone who happened to be around. But if they paid any attention 150
to him at first, if they were nice to him or anything, he was unshakeable. He was a bit of a pest, but harmless."

Christine ceased to tell her amusing story. She had been one among many, 151
then. She went back to playing tennis, she had been neglecting her game.

A few months later the policeman who had been in charge of the case tele- 152
phoned her again.

"Like you to know, miss, that fellow you were having the trouble with was   153
sent back to his own country. Deported."

"What for?" Christine asked. "Did he try to come back here?" Maybe she   154
had been special after all, maybe he had dared everything for her.

"Nothing like it," the policeman said. "He was up to the same tricks in Mon-   155
treal but he really picked the wrong woman this time—a Mother Superior of a
convent. They don't stand for things like that in Quebec—had him out of here
before he knew what happened. I guess he'll be better off in his own place."

"How old was she?" Christine asked, after a silence.   156

"Oh, around sixty, I guess."   157

"Thank you very much for letting me know," Christine said in her best offi-   158
cial manner. "It's such a relief." She wondered if the policeman had called to
make fun of her.

She was almost crying when she put down the phone. What *had* he wanted   159
from her then? A Mother Superior. Did she really look sixty, did she look like a
mother? What did convents mean? Comfort, charity? Refuge? Was it that something had happened to him, some intolerable strain just from being in this
country; her tennis dress and exposed legs too much for him, flesh and money
seemingly available everywhere but withheld from him wherever he turned, the
nun the symbol of some final distortion, the robe and veil reminiscent to his
nearsighted eyes of the women of his homeland, the ones he was able to understand? But he was back in his own country, remote from her as another planet;
she would never know.

He hadn't forgotten her though. In the spring she got a postcard with a for-   160
eign stamp and the familiar block-letter writing. On the front was a picture of a
temple. He was fine, he hoped she was fine also, he was her friend. A month
later another print of the picture he had taken in the garden arrived, in a sealed
manila envelope otherwise empty.

Christine's aura of mystery soon faded; anyway, she herself no longer be-   161
lieved in it. Life became again what she had always expected. She graduated
with mediocre grades and went into the Department of Health and Welfare; she
did a good job, and was seldom discriminated against for being a woman because nobody thought of her as one. She could afford a pleasant-sized apartment, though she did not put much energy into decorating it. She played less
and less tennis; what had been muscle with a light coating of fat turned gradually into fat with a thin substratum of muscle. She began to get headaches.

As the years were used up and the war began to fill the newspapers and   162
magazines, she realized which Eastern country he had actually been from. She
had known the name but it hadn't registered at the time, it was such a minor
place; she could never keep them separate in her mind.

But though she tried, she couldn't remember the name of the city, and the   163
postcard was long gone—had he been from the North or the South, was he near
the battle zone or safely far from it? Obsessively she bought magazines and
pored over the available photographs, dead villagers, soldiers on the march,

colour blowups of frightened or angry faces, spies being executed; she studied maps, she watched the late-night newscasts, the distant country and terrain becoming almost more familiar to her than her own. Once or twice she thought she could recognize him but it was no use, they all looked like him.

Finally she had to stop looking at the pictures. It bothered her too much, it 164 was bad for her; she was beginning to have nightmares in which he was coming through the French doors of her mother's house in his shabby jacket, carrying a packsack and a rifle and a huge bouquet of richly coloured flowers. He was smiling in the same way but the blood streaked over his face, partly blotting out the features. She gave her television set away and took to reading nineteenth-century novels instead; Trollope and Galsworthy were her favourites. When, despite herself, she would think about him, she would tell herself that he had been crafty and agile-minded enough to survive, more or less, in her country, so surely he would be able to do it in his own, where he knew the language. She could not see him in the army, on either side; he wasn't the type, and to her knowledge he had not believed in any particular ideology. He would be something nondescript, something in the background, like herself; perhaps he had become an interpreter.

ACTIVITIES FOR WRITING AND DISCUSSION

1. Working alone or in a group, identify any moments or junctures in the story that made you wonder, "What's going to happen next?" Then compare what you *expected* would happen with what *actually* happened. What conclusions can you draw from the contrast, if any, between your expectations and what happened?

2. Reread any passages pertaining to Christine's self-image. How did she get her self-image, and what was it like before she met "the man from Mars"? How does it evolve in the course of her relationship with the alien man? Why?

3. What motivations do various **characters** ascribe to "the man from Mars"? What reasons do they believe he has for pursuing Christine? What motivations, if any, are implied by the man himself? Investigate these questions. Then:
   a. Invent some diary entries or letters home in which you ("the man from Mars") talk about Christine, or
   b. Write an imaginary interview with the man in which you get the man to explain himself, or
   c. Invent an exchange of letters between yourself and the **author** in which she discusses her intentions in the story.

4. What is the native land of "the man from Mars"? A sentence in the second-to-last paragraph begins, "Obsessively [Christine] bought magazines and pored over the available photographs." How can you account for this

obsession? In the **persona** of Christine, write about your "obsession" and your inability to forget the man.

JAMES ALAN McPHERSON (b. 1943)

A Loaf of Bread

It was one of those obscene situations, pedestrian to most people, but invested 1 with meaning for a few poor folk whose lives are usually spent outside the imaginations of their fellow citizens. A grocer named Harold Green was caught red-handed selling to one group of people the very same goods he sold at lower prices at similar outlets in better neighborhoods. He had been doing this for many years, and at first he could not understand the outrage heaped upon him. He acted only from habit, he insisted, and had nothing personal against the people whom he served. They were his neighbors. Many of them he had carried on the cuff during hard times. Yet, through some mysterious access to a television station, the poor folk were now empowered to make grand denunciations of the grocer. Green's children now saw their father's business being picketed on the Monday evening news.

No one could question the fact that the grocer had been overcharging the 2 people. On the news even the reporter grimaced distastefully while reading the statistics. His expression said, "It is my job to report the news, but sometimes even I must disassociate myself from it to protect my honor." This, at least, was the impression the grocer's children seemed to bring away from the television. Their father's name had not been mentioned, but there was a close-up of his store with angry black people, and a few outraged whites, marching in groups of three in front of it. There was also a close-up of his name. After seeing this, they were in no mood to watch cartoons. At the dinner table, disturbed by his children's silence, Harold Green felt compelled to say, "I am not a dishonest man." Then he felt ashamed. The children, a boy and his older sister, immediately left the table, leaving Green alone with his wife. "Ruth, I am not dishonest," he repeated to her.

Ruth Green did not say anything. She knew, and her husband did not, that 3 the outraged people had also picketed the school attended by their children. They had threatened to return each day until Green lowered his prices. When they called her at home to report this, she had promised she would talk with him. Since she could not tell him this, she waited for an opening. She looked at her husband across the table.

"I did not make the world," Green began, recognizing at once the serious- 4 ness in her stare. "My father came to this country with nothing but his shirt. He was exploited for as long as he couldn't help himself. He did not protest or picket. He put himself in a position to play by the rules he had learned." He waited for his wife to answer, and when she did not, he tried again. "I did not make this world," he repeated. "I only make my way in it. Such people as these, they do not know enough to not be exploited. If not me, there would be a Greek, a Chinaman, maybe an Arab or a smart one of their own kind. Believe me, I deal with them. There is something in their style that lacks the patience to run a concern such as mine. If I closed down, take my word on it, someone else would do what has to be done."

But Ruth Green was not thinking of his leaving. Her mind was on other matters. Her children had cried when they came home early from school. She had no special feeling for the people who picketed, but she did not like to see her children cry. She had kissed them generously, then sworn them to silence. "One day this week," she told her husband, "you will give free, for eight hours, anything your customers come in to buy. There will be no publicity, except what they spread by word of mouth. No matter what they say to you, no matter what they take, you will remain silent." She stared deeply into him for what she knew was there. "If you refuse, you have seen the last of your children and myself."

Her husband grunted. Then he leaned toward her. "I will not knuckle under," he said. "I will *not* give!"

"We shall see," his wife told him.

The black pickets, for the most part, had at first been frightened by the audacity of their undertaking. They were peasants whose minds had long before become resigned to their fate as victims. None of them, before now, had thought to challenge this. But now, when they watched themselves on television, they hardly recognized the faces they saw beneath the hoisted banners and placards. Instead of reflecting the meekness they all felt, the faces looked angry. The close-ups looked especially intimidating. Several of the first pickets, maids who worked in the suburbs, reported that their employers, seeing the activity on the afternoon news, had begun treating them with new respect. One woman, midway through the weather report, called around the neighborhood to disclose that her employer had that very day given her a new china plate for her meals. The paper plates, on which all previous meals had been served, had been thrown into the wastebasket. One recipient of this call, a middle-aged woman known for her bashfulness and humility, rejoined that her husband, a sheet-metal worker, had only a few hours before been called "Mister" by his supervisor, a white man with a passionate hatred of color. She added the tale of a neighbor down the street, a widow-woman named Murphy, who had at first been reluctant to join the picket; this woman now was insisting it should be made a daily event. Such talk as this circulated among the people who had been instrumental in raising the issue. As news of their victory leaked into the ears of others who had not participated, they received all through the night calls from strangers requesting verification, offering advice, and vowing support. Such strangers listened, and then volunteered stories about indignities inflicted on them by city officials, policemen, other grocers. In this way, over a period of hours, the community became even more incensed and restless than it had been at the time of the initial picket.

Soon, the man who had set events in motion found himself a hero. His name was Nelson Reed, and all his adult life he had been employed as an assembly-line worker. He was a steady husband, the father of three children, and a deacon in the Baptist church. All his life he had trusted in God and gotten along. But now something in him capitulated to the reality that came suddenly into focus. "I was wrong," he told people who called him. "The onliest thing that matters in this world is *money*. And when was the last time you seen a picture of Jesus on a dollar bill?" This line, which he repeated over and over, caused a few callers to laugh nervously, but not without some affirmation that this was indeed the way things were. Many said they had known it all along. Others argued that although it was certainly true, it was one thing to live without money and quite another to live without faith. But still most callers laughed and said, "You right. You *know* I know you right. Ain't it the truth, though?" Only a few people, among them Nelson Reed's wife, said nothing and looked very sad. 9

Why they looked sad, however, they would not communicate. And anyone observing their troubled faces would have to trust his own intuition. It is known that Reed's wife, Betty, measured all events against the fullness of her own experience. She was skeptical of everything. Brought to the church after a number of years of living openly with a jazz musician, she had embraced religion when she married Nelson Reed. But though she no longer believed completely in the world, she nonetheless had not fully embraced God. There was something in the nature of Christ's swift rise that had always bothered her, and something in the blood and vengeance of the Old Testament that was mellowing and refreshing. But she had never communicated these thoughts to anyone, especially her husband. Instead, she smiled vacantly while others professed leaps of faith, remained silent when friends spoke fiercely of their convictions. The presence of this vacuum in her contributed to her personal mystery; people said she was beautiful, although she was not outwardly so. Perhaps it was because she wished to protect this inner beauty that she did not smile now, and looked extremely sad, listening to her husband on the telephone. 10

Nelson Reed had no reason to be sad. He seemed to grow more energized and talkative as the days passed. He was invited by an alderman, on the Tuesday after the initial picket, to tell his story on a local television talk show. He sweated heavily under the hot white lights and attempted to be philosophical. "I notice," the host said to him, "that you are not angry at this exploitative treatment. What, Mr. Reed, is the source of your calm?" The assembly-line worker looked unabashedly into the camera and said, "I have always believed in *Justice* with a capital *J*. I was raised up from a baby believin' that God ain't gonna let nobody go *too* far. See, in *my* mind God is in charge of *all* the capital letters in the alphabet of this world. It say in the Scripture He is Alpha and Omega, the first and the last. He is just about the *onliest* capitalizer they is." Both Reed and the alderman laughed. "Now, when *men* start to capitalize, they gets *greedy*. They put a little *j* in *joy* and a littler one in *justice*. They raise up a big *G* in *Greed* 11 and a big *E* in *Evil*. Well, soon as they commence to put a little *g* in *god*, you can expect some kind of reaction. The Savior will just raise up the *H* in *Hell* and go on from there. And that's just what I'm doin', giving these sharpies *HELL* with a big *H*." The talk show host laughed along with Nelson Reed and the alderman. After the taping they drank coffee in the back room of the studio and talked about the sad shape of the world.

—————

Three days before he was to comply with his wife's request, Green, the gro- 12 cer, saw this talk show on television while at home. The words of Nelson Reed sent a chill through him. Though Reed had attempted to be philosophical, Green did not perceive the statement in this light. Instead, he saw a vindictive-looking black man seated between an ambitious alderman and a smug talk-show host. He saw them chatting comfortably about the nature of evil. The cameraman had shot mostly close-ups, and Green could see the set in Nelson Reed's jaw. The color of Reed's face was maddening. When his children came into the den, the grocer was in a sweat. Before he could think, he had shouted at them and struck the button turning off the set. The two children rushed from the room screaming. Ruth Green ran in from the kitchen. She knew why he was upset because she had received a call about the show; but she said nothing and pretended ignorance. Her children's school had been picketed that day, as it had the day before. But both children were still forbidden to speak of this to their father.

"Where do they get so much power?" Green said to his wife. "Two days ago, 13 nobody would have cared. Now, everywhere, even in my home, I am condemned as a rascal. And what do I own? An airline? A multinational? Half of South America? *No!* I own three stores, one of which happens to be in a certain neighborhood inhabited by people who cost me money to run it." He sighed and sat upright on the sofa, his chubby legs spread wide. "A cab driver has a meter that clicks as he goes along. I pay extra for insurance, iron bars, pilfering by customers and employees. Nothing clicks. But when I add a little overhead to my prices, suddenly everything clicks. But for someone else. When was there last such a world?" He pressed the palms of both hands to his temples, suggesting a bombardment of brain-stinging sounds.

This gesture evoked no response from Ruth Green. She remained standing 14 by the door, looking steadily at him. She said, "To protect yourself, I would not stock any more fresh cuts of meat in the store until after the giveaway on Saturday. Also, I would not tell it to the employees until after the first customer of the day has begun to check out. But I would urge you to hire several security guards to close the door promptly at seven-thirty, as is usual." She wanted to say much more than this, but did not. Instead she watched him. He was looking at the blank gray television screen, his palms still pressed against his ears. "In case you need to hear again," she continued in a weighty tone of voice, "I said two days ago, and I say again now, that if you fail to do this you will not see your children again for many years."

He twisted his head and looked up at her. "What is the color of these peo- 15
ple?" he asked.

"Black," his wife said.   16

"And what is the name of my children?"   17

"Green."   18

The grocer smiled. "There is your answer," he told his wife. "Green is the 19
only color I am interested in."

His wife did not smile. "Insufficient," she said.   20

"The world is mad!" he moaned. "But it is a point of sanity with me to not 21
bend. I will not bend." He crossed his legs and pressed one hand firmly atop his
knee. "*I will not bend*," he said.

"We will see," his wife said.   22

———————

Nelson Reed, after the television interview, became the acknowledged 23
leader of the disgruntled neighbors. At first a number of them met in the
kitchen at his house; then, as space was lacking for curious newcomers, a mass
meeting was held on Thursday in an abandoned theater. His wife and three
children sat in the front row. Behind them sat the widow Murphy, Lloyd Dukes,
Tyrone Brown, Les Jones—those who had joined him on the first picket line.
Behind these sat people who bought occasionally at the store, people who lived
on the fringes of the neighborhood, people from other neighborhoods come to
investigate the problem, and the merely curious. The middle rows were occupied by a few people from the suburbs, those who had seen the talk show and
whose outrage at the grocer proved much more powerful than their fear of
black people. In the rear of the theater crowded aging, old-style leftists, somber
students, cynical young black men with angry grudges to explain with inarticu-
late gestures. Leaning against the walls, and huddled near the doors at the rear,
tape-recorder-bearing social scientists looked as detached and serene as book-
ies at the track. Here and there, in this diverse crowd, a politician stationed
himself, pumping hands vigorously and pressing his palms gently against the
shoulders of elderly people. Other visitors passed out leaflets, buttons, glossy
color prints of men who promoted causes, the familiar and obscure. There was
a hubbub of voices, a blend of the strident and the playful, the outraged and the
reverent, lending an undercurrent of ominous energy to the assembly.

Nelson Reed spoke from a platform on the stage, standing before a yel- 24
lowed, shredded screen that had once reflected the images of matinee idols. "I
don't mind sayin' that I have always been a sucker," he told the crowd. "All my
life I have been a sucker for the words of Jesus. Being a natural-born fool, I just
ain't never had the *sense* to learn no better. Even right today, while the whole
world is sayin' wrong is right and up is down, I'm so dumb I'm *still* steady believin' what is wrote in the Good Book . . ."

From the audience, especially the front rows, came a chorus singing, 25
"Preach!"

"I have no doubt," he continued in a low baritone, "that it's true what is writ   26
in the Good Book: 'The last shall be first and the first shall be last.' I don't know
about y'all, but I have *always* been the last. I never wanted to be the first, but
sometimes it look like the world get so bad that them that's holdin' onto the
tree of life is the onliest ones left when God commence to blowin' dead leafs off
the branches."

"Now you preaching," someone called.   27

In the rear of the theater a white student shouted an awkward "Amen."   28

Nelson Reed began walking across the stage to occupy the major part of his   29
nervous energy. But to those in the audience, who now hung on his every word,
it looked as though he strutted. "All my life," he said, "I have claimed to be a
man without earnin' the right to call myself that. You know, the *average* man
ain't really a man. The average man is a *bootlicker*. In fact, the *average* man
would *run away* if he found hisself standing alone facin' down a adversary. I
have done that *too many a time* in my life! But *not no more*. Better to be *once* was
than *never* was a man. I will tell you tonight, there is somethin' *wrong* in being
average. *I intend to stand up!* Now, if your average man that ain't really a man
stand up, two things gonna happen: *One*, he g'on bust through all the weights
that been place on his head, and, *two*, he g'on feel a lot of pain. But that same
hurt is what make things fall in place. That, and gettin' your hands on one
of these slick four-flushers tight enough so's you can squeeze him and say,
'*No more!*' You do that, you g'on hurt some, but *you won't be average no
more . . .*"

"*No more!*" a few people in the front rows repeated.   30

"I say *no more!*" Nelson Reed shouted.   31

"*No more! No more! No more!*" The chant rustled through the crowd like the   32
rhythm of an autumn wind against a shedding tree.

Then people laughed and chattered in celebration.   33

As for the grocer, from the evening of the television interview he had begun   34
to make plans. Unknown to his wife, he cloistered himself several times with his
brother-in-law, an insurance salesman, and plotted a course. He had no intention of tossing steaks to the crowd. "And why should I, Tommy?" he asked his
wife's brother, a lean, bald-headed man named Thomas. "I don't cheat anyone. I
have never cheated anyone. The businesses I run are always on the up-and-up.
So why should I pay?"

"Quite so," the brother-in-law said, chewing an unlit cigarillo. "The world   35
has gone crazy. Next they will say that people in my business are responsible for
prolonging life. I have found that people who refuse to believe in death refuse
also to believe in the harshness of life. I sell well by saying that death is a long
happiness. I show people the realities of life and compare this to a funeral with
dignity, *and* the promise of a bundle for every loved one salted away. When they
look around hard at life, they usually buy."

"So?" asked Green. Thomas was a college graduate with a penchant for phi- 36
losophy.

"So," Thomas answered. "You must fight to show these people the reality of 37
both your situation and theirs. How would it be if you visited one of their
meetings and chalked out, on a blackboard, the dollars and cents of your operation? Explain your overhead, your security fees, all the additional expenses. If
you treat them with respect, they might understand."

Green frowned. "That I would never do," he said. "It would be admission of 38
a certain guilt."

The brother-in-law smiled, but only with one corner of his mouth. "Then 39
you have something to feel guilty about?" he asked.

The grocer frowned at him. "*Nothing!*" he said with great emphasis.   40

"So?" Thomas said.   41

This first meeting between the grocer and his brother-in-law took place on 42
Thursday, in a crowded barroom.

At the second meeting, in a luncheonette, it was agreed that the grocer 43
should speak privately with the leader of the group, Nelson Reed. The meeting
at which this was agreed took place on Friday afternoon. After accepting this
advice from Thomas, the grocer resigned himself to explain to Reed, in as finite
detail as possible, the economic structure of his operation. He vowed to suppress no information. He would explain everything: inventories, markups, sale
items, inflation, balance sheets, specialty items, overhead, and that mysterious
item called profit. This last item, promising to be the most difficult to explain,
Green and his brother-in-law debated over for several hours. They agreed first
of all that a man should not work for free, then they agreed that it was unethical
to ruthlessly exploit. From these parameters, they staked out an area between
fifteen and forty percent, and agreed that someplace between these two borders
lay an amount of return that could be called fair. This was easy, but then
Thomas introduced the factor of circumstance. He questioned whether the fact
that one serviced a risky area justified the earning of profits closer to the forty-
percent edge of the scale. Green was unsure. Thomas smiled. "Here is a case that
will point out an analogy," he said, licking a cigarillo. "I read in the papers that a
family wants to sell an electric stove. I call the home and the man says fifty dollars. I ask to come out and inspect the merchandise. When I arrive I see they are
poor, have already bought a new stove that is connected and are selling the old
one for fifty dollars because they want it out of the place. The electric stove is in
good condition, worth much more than fifty. But because I see what I see I offer
forty-five."

Green, for some reason, wrote down this figure on the back of the sales slip 44
for the coffee they were drinking.

The brother-in-law smiled. He chewed his cigarillo. "The man agrees to take 45
forty-five dollars, saying he has had no other calls. I look at the stove again and
see a spot of rust. I say I will give him forty dollars. He agrees to this, on condition that I myself haul it away. I say I will haul it away if he comes down to
thirty. You, of course, see where I am going."

The grocer nodded. "The circumstances of his situation, his need to get rid of 46
the stove quickly, placed him in a position where he has little room to bargain?"

"Yes," Thomas answered. "So? Is it ethical, Harry?"   47

Harold Green frowned. He had never liked his brother-in-law, and now he 48
thought the insurance agent was being crafty. "But," he answered, "this man
does not *have* to sell! It is his choice whether to wait for other calls. It is not the
fault of the buyer that the seller is in a hurry. It is the right of the buyer to get
what he wants at the lowest price possible. That is the rule. That has *always*
been the rule. And the reverse of it applies to the seller as well."

"Yes," Thomas said, sipping coffee from the Styrofoam cup. "But suppose 49
that in addition to his hurry to sell, the owner was also of a weak soul. There
are, after all, many such people." He smiled. "Suppose he placed no value on the
money?"

"Then," Green answered, "your example is academic. Here we are not talk- 50
ing about real life. One man lives by the code, one man does not. Who is there
free enough to make a judgment?" He laughed. "Now you see," he told his
brother in law. "Much more than a few dollars are at stake. If this one buyer is
to be condemned, then so are most people in the history of the world. An examination of history provides the only answer to your question. This code will
be here tomorrow, long after the ones who do not honor it are not."

They argued fiercely late into the afternoon, the brother-in-law leaning 51
heavily on his readings. When they parted, a little before 5:00 P.M., nothing had
been resolved.

Neither was much resolved during the meeting between Green and Nelson 52
Reed. Reached at home by the grocer in the early evening, the leader of the
group spoke coldly at first, but consented finally to meet his adversary at a
nearby drugstore for coffee and a talk. They met at the lunch counter, shook
hands awkwardly, and sat for a few minutes discussing the weather. Then the
grocer pulled two gray ledgers from his briefcase. "You have for years come into
my place," he told the man. "In my memory I have always treated you well. Now
our relationship has come to this." He slid the books along the counter until
they touched Nelson Reed's arm.

Reed opened the top book and flipped the thick green pages with his 53
thumb. He did not examine the figures. "All I know," he said, "is over at your
place a can of soup cost me fifty-five cents, and two miles away at your other
store for white folks you chargin' thirty-nine cents." He said this with the calm
authority of an outraged soul. A quality of condescension tinged with pity
crept into his gaze.

The grocer drummed his fingers on the counter top. He twisted his head 54
and looked away, toward shelves containing cosmetics, laxatives, toothpaste.
His eyes lingered on a poster of a woman's apple red lips and milk white teeth.
The rest of the face was missing.

"Ain't no use to hide," Nelson Reed said, as to a child. "*I* know you wrong, 55
you know you wrong, and before I finish, *everybody in this city* g'on know you
wrong. God don't *like* ugly." He closed his eyes and gripped the cup of coffee.

Then he swung his head suddenly and faced the grocer again. "Man, why you want to *do* people that way?" he asked. "We human, same as you."

"Before *God*!" Green exclaimed, looking squarely into the face of Nelson 56
Reed. "Before God!" he said again. "*I am not an evil man!*" These last words sounded more like a moan as he tightened the muscles in his throat to lower the sound of his voice. He tossed his left shoulder as if adjusting the sleeve of his coat, or as if throwing off some unwanted weight. Then he peered along the countertop. No one was watching. At the end of the counter the waitress was scrubbing the coffee urn. "Look at these figures, please," he said to Reed.

The man did not drop his gaze. His eyes remained fixed on the grocer's face. 57

"All right," Green said. "Don't look. I'll tell you what is in these books, be- 58
lieve me if you want. I work twelve hours a day, one day off per week, running my business in three stores. I am not a wealthy person. In one place, in the area you call white, I get by barely by smiling lustily at old ladies, stocking gourmet stuff on the chance I will build a reputation as a quality store. The two clerks there cheat me; there is nothing I can do. In this business you must be friendly with everybody. The second place is on the other side of town, in a neighbor-hood as poor as this one. I get out there seldom. The profits are not worth the gas. I use the loss there as a write-off against some other properties." He paused. "Do you understand write-off?" he asked Nelson Reed.

"Naw," the man said. 59

Harold Green laughed. "What does it matter?" he said in a tone of voice in- 60
tended for himself alone. "In this area I will admit I make a profit, but it is not so much as you think. But I do not make a profit here because the people are black. I make a profit because a profit is here to be made. I invest more here in window bars, theft losses, insurance, spoilage; I deserve to make more here than at the other places." He looked, almost imploringly, at the man seated next to him. "You don't accept this as the right of a man in business?"

Reed grunted. "Did the bear shit in the woods?" he said. 61

Again Green laughed. He gulped his coffee awkwardly, as if eager to go. Yet 62
his motions slowed once he had set the coffee cup down on the blue plastic saucer. "Place yourself in *my* situation," he said, his voice high and tentative. "If *you* were running my store in this neighborhood, what would be *your* position? Say on a profit scale of fifteen to forty percent, at what point in between would you draw the line?"

Nelson Reed thought. He sipped his coffee and seemed to chew the liquid. 63
"Fifteen to forty?" he repeated.

"Yes." 64

"I'm a churchgoin' man," he said. "Closer to fifteen than to forty." 65

"How close?" 66

Nelson Reed thought. "In church you tithe ten percent." 67

"In restaurants you tip fifteen," the grocer said quickly. 68

"All right," Reed said. "Over fifteen." 69

"How much over?" 70

Nelson Reed thought. 71

"Twenty, thirty, thirty-five?" Green chanted, leaning closer to Reed.   72

Still the man thought.   73

"Forty? Maybe even forty-five or fifty?" the grocer breathed in Reed's ear.   74
"In the supermarkets, you know, they have more subtle ways of accomplishing
such feats."

Reed slapped his coffee cup with the back of his right hand. The brown liq-   75
uid swirled across the counter top, wetting the books. "*Damn this!*" he shouted.

Startled, Green rose from his stool.   76

Nelson Reed was trembling. "I ain't *you,*" he said in a deep baritone. "I ain't   77
the *supermarket* neither. All I is is a poor man that works *too* hard to see his pay
slip through his fingers like rainwater. All I know is you done *cheat* me, you done
cheat everybody in the neighborhood, and we organized now to get some of it
back!" Then he stood and faced the grocer. "My daddy sharecropped down in
Mississippi and bought in the company store. He owed them twenty-three years
when he died. I paid off five of them years and then run away to up here. Now,
I'm a deacon in the Baptist church. I raised my kids the way my daddy raise me
and don't bother nobody. Now come to find out, after all my runnin', they done
lift that *same company store* up out of Mississippi and slip it down on us here!
Well, my daddy was a *fighter,* and if he hadn't owed all them years he would of
raise him some hell. Me, I'm steady my daddy's child, plus I got seniority in my
union. I'm a free man. Buddy, don't you know *I'm gonna raise me some hell!*"

Harold Green reached for a paper napkin to sop the coffee soaking into his   78
books.

Nelson Reed threw a dollar on top of the books and walked away.   79

"I *will not* do it!" Harold Green said to his wife that same evening. They   80
were in the bathroom of their home. Bending over the face bowl, she was washing her hair with a towel draped around her neck. The grocer stood by the door,
looking in at her. "I will not bankrupt myself tomorrow," he said.

"I've been thinking about it, too," Ruth Green said, shaking her wet hair.   81
"You'll do it, Harry."

"Why should I?" he asked. "You won't leave. You know it was a bluff. I've   82
waited this long for you to calm down. Tomorrow is Saturday. This week has
been a hard one. Tonight let's be realistic."

"Of course you'll do it," Ruth Green said. She said it the way she would say   83
"Have some toast." She said, "You'll do it because you want to see your children
grow up."

"And for what other reason?" he asked.   84

She pulled the towel tighter around her neck. "Because you are at heart a   85
moral man."

He grinned painfully. "If I am, why should I have to prove it to *them?*"   86

"Not them," Ruth Green said, freezing her movements and looking in the   87
mirror. "Certainly not them. By no means them. They have absolutely nothing
to do with this."

"Who, then?" he asked, moving from the door into the room. "Who else 88 should I prove something to?"

His wife was crying. But her entire face was wet. The tears moved secretly 89 down her face.

"Who else?" Harold Green asked. 90

It was almost 11:00 P.M. and the children were in bed. They had also cried 91 when they came home from school. Ruth Green said, "For yourself, Harry. For the love that lives inside your heart."

All night the grocer thought about this. 92

──────────

Nelson Reed also slept little that Friday night. When he returned home 93 from the drugstore, he reported to his wife as much of the conversation as he could remember. At first he had joked about the exchange between himself and the grocer, but as more details returned to his conscious mind he grew solemn and then bitter. "He ask me to put myself in *his* place," Reed told his wife. "Can you imagine that kind of gumption? I never cheated nobody in my life. All my life I have lived on Bible principles. I am a deacon in the church. I have work all my life for other folks and I don't even own the house I live in." He paced up and down the kitchen, his big arms flapping loosely at his sides. Betty Reed sat at the table, watching. "This here's a low-down, ass-kicking world," he said. "I swear to God it is! All my life I have lived on principle and I ain't got a dime in the bank. Betty," he turned suddenly toward her, "don't you think I'm a fool?"

"Mr. Reed," she said. "Let's go on to bed." 94

But he would not go to bed. Instead, he took the fifth of bourbon from the 95 cabinet under the sink and poured himself a shot. His wife refused to join him. Reed drained the glass of whiskey, and then another, while he resumed pacing the kitchen floor. He slapped his hands against his sides. "*I* think I'm a fool," he said. "Ain't got a dime in the bank, ain't got a pot to *pee* in or a wall to pitch it over, and that there *cheat* ask me to put myself inside *his* shoes. Hell, I can't even *afford* the kind of shoes he wears." He stopped pacing and looked at his wife.

"Mr. Reed," she whispered, "tomorrow ain't a work day. Let's go to bed." 96

Nelson Reed laughed, the bitterness in his voice rattling his wife. "The *hell* I 97 will!" he said.

He strode to the yellow telephone on the wall beside the sink and began to 98 dial. The first call was to Lloyd Dukes, a neighbor two blocks away and a lieu-tenant in the organization. Dukes was not at home. The second call was to McElroy's Bar on the corner of 65th and Carroll, where Stanley Harper, another of the lieutenants, worked as a bartender. It was Harper who spread the word, among those men at the bar, that the organization would picket the grocer's store the following morning. And all through the night, in the bedroom of their house, Betty Reed was awakened by telephone calls coming from Lester Jones, Nat Lucas, Mrs. Tyrone Brown, the widow-woman named Murphy, all coordi-nating the time when they would march in a group against the store owned by Harold Green. Betty Reed's heart beat loudly beneath the covers as she listened to the bitterness and rage in her husband's voice. On several occasions, hearing him declare himself a fool, she pressed the pillow against her eyes and cried.

———————

The grocer opened later than usual this Saturday morning, but still it was 99 early enough to make him one of the first walkers in the neighborhood. He parked his car one block from the store and strolled to work. There were no birds singing. The sky in this area was not blue. It was smog-smutted and gray, seeming on the verge of a light rain. The street, as always, was littered with cans, papers, bits of broken glass. As always the garbage cans overflowed. The morning breeze plastered a sheet of newspaper playfully around the sides of a rusted garbage can. For some reason, using his right foot, he loosened the paper and stood watching it slide into the street and down the block. The movement made him feel good. He whistled while unlocking the bars shielding the windows and door of his store. When he had unlocked the main door he stepped in quickly and threw a switch to the right of the jamb, before the shrill sound of the alarm could shatter his mood. Then he switched on the lights. Everything was as it had been the night before. He had already telephoned his two employees and given them the day off. He busied himself doing the usual things—hauling milk and vegetables from the cooler, putting cash in the till—not thinking about the silence of his wife, or the look in her eyes, only an hour before when he left home. He had determined, at some point while driving through the city, that today it would be business as usual. But he expected very few customers.

The first customer of the day was Mrs. Nelson Reed. She came in around 100 9:30 A.M. and wandered about the store. He watched her from the checkout counter. She seemed uncertain of what she wanted to buy. She kept glancing at him down the center aisle. His suspicions aroused, he said finally, "Yes, may I help you, Mrs. Reed?" His words caused her to jerk, as if some devious thought had been perceived going through her mind. She reached over quickly and lifted a loaf of whole wheat bread from the rack and walked with it to the counter. She looked at him and smiled. The smile was a broad, shy one, that rare kind of smile one sees on virgin girls when they first confess love to themselves. Betty Reed was a woman of about forty-five. For some reason he could not comprehend, this gesture touched him. When she pulled a dollar from her purse and laid it on the counter, an impulse, from no place he could locate with his mind, seized control of his tongue. "Free," he told Betty Reed. She paused, then pushed the dollar toward him with a firm and determined thrust of her arm. "Free," he heard himself saying strongly, his right palm spread and meeting her thrust with absolute force. She clutched the loaf of bread and walked out of his store.

The next customer, a little girl, arriving well after 10:30 A.M., selected a 101 candy bar from the rack beside the counter. "Free," Green said cheerfully. The little girl left the candy on the counter and ran out of the store.

At 11:15 A.M. a wino came in looking desperate enough to sell his soul. The 102 grocer watched him only for an instant. Then he went to the wine counter and selected a half-gallon of medium-grade red wine. He shoved the jug into the belly of the wino, the man's sour breath bathing his face. "Free," the grocer said. "But you must not drink it in here."

He felt good about the entire world, watching the wino through the window 103 gulping the wine and looking guiltily around.

At 11:25 A.M. the pickets arrived. 104

Two dozen people, men and women, young and old, crowded the pavement 105 in front of his store. Their signs, placards, and voices denounced him as a parasite. The grocer laughed inside himself. He felt lighthearted and wild, like a man drugged. He rushed to the meat counter and pulled a long roll of brown wrapping paper from the rack, tearing it neatly with a quick shift of his body resembling a dance step practiced fervently in his youth. He laid the paper on the chopping block and with the black-inked, felt-tipped marker scrawled, in giant letters, the word FREE. This he took to the window and pasted in place with many strands of Scotch tape. He was laughing wildly. "Free!" he shouted from behind the brown paper. "Free! Free! Free! Free! Free! Free!" He rushed to the door, pushed his head out, and screamed to the confused crowd, "*Free!*" Then he ran back to the counter and stood behind it, like a soldier at attention.

They came in slowly. 106

Nelson Reed entered first, working his right foot across the dirty tile as if 107 tracking a squiggling worm. The others followed: Lloyd Dukes dragging a placard, Mr. and Mrs. Tyrone Brown, Stanley Harper walking with his fists clenched, Lester Jones with three of his children, Nat Lucas looking sheepish and detached, a clutch of winos, several bashful nuns, ironic-smiling teenagers and a few students. Bringing up the rear was a bearded social scientist holding a tape recorder to his chest. "Free!" the grocer screamed. He threw up his arms in a gesture that embraced, or dismissed, the entire store. "*All free!*" he shouted. He was grinning with the grace of a madman.

The winos began grabbing first. They stripped the shelf of wine in a matter 108 of seconds. Then they fled, dropping bottles on the tile in their wake. The others, stepping quickly through this liquid, soon congealed it into a sticky, blood-like consistency. The young men went for the cigarettes and luncheon meats and beer. One of them had the prescience to grab a sack from the counter, while the others loaded their arms swiftly, hugging cartons and packages of cold cuts like long-lost friends. The students joined them, less for greed than for the thrill of the experience. The two nuns backed toward the door. As for the older people, men and women, they stood at first as if stuck to the wine-smeared floor. Then Stanley Harper, the bartender, shouted, "The man said *free*, y'all heard him." He paused. "Didn't you say *free* now?" he called to the grocer.

"I said free," Harold Green answered, his temples pounding. 109

A cheer went up. The older people began grabbing, as if the secret lusts of a 110 lifetime had suddenly seized command of their arms and eyes. They grabbed toilet tissue, cold cuts, pickles, sardines, boxes of raisins, boxes of starch, cans of soup, tins of tuna fish and salmon, bottles of spices, cans of boned chicken, slippery cans of olive oil. Here a man, Lester Jones, burdened himself with several heads of lettuce, while his wife, in another aisle, shouted for him to drop those small items and concentrate on the gourmet section. She herself took imported sardines, wheat crackers, bottles of candied pickles, herring, anchovies, imported olives, French wafers, an ancient, half-rusted can of paté, stocked, by mistake, from the inventory of another store. Others packed their arms with detergents, hams, chocolate-coated cereal, whole chickens with hanging asses, wedges of bologna and salami like squashed footballs, chunks of cheeses, yellow and white, shriveled onions, and green peppers. Mrs. Tyrone Brown hung a curve of pepperoni around her neck and seemed to take on instant dignity, much like a person of noble birth in possession now of a long sought-after gem. Another woman, the widow Murphy, stuffed tomatoes into her bosom, holding a half-chewed lemon in her mouth. The more enterprising fought desperately over the three rusted shopping carts, and the victors wheeled these along the narrow aisles, sweeping into them bulk items—beer in sixpacks, sacks of sugar, flour, glass bottles of syrup, toilet cleanser, sugar cookies, prune, apple and tomato juices—while others endeavored to snatch the carts from them. There were several fistfights and much cursing. The grocer, standing behind the counter, hummed and rang his cash register like a madman.

Nelson Reed, the first into the store, followed the nuns out, empty-handed. 111

In less than half an hour the others had stripped the store and vanished in 112 many directions up and down the block. But still more people came, those late in hearing the news. And when they saw the shelves were bare, they cursed soberly and chased those few stragglers still bearing away goods. Soon only the grocer and the social scientist remained, the latter stationed at the door with his tape recorder sucking in leftover sounds. Then he too slipped away up the block.

By 12:10 P.M. the grocer was leaning against the counter, trying to make his 113 mind slow down. Not a man given to drink during work hours he nonetheless took a swallow from a bottle of wine, a dusty bottle from beneath the wine shelf, somehow overlooked by the winos. Somewhat recovered, he was preparing to remember what he should do next when he glanced toward a figure at the door. Nelson Reed was standing there, watching him.

"All gone," Harold Green said. "My friend, Mr. Reed, there is no more." Still 114 the man stood in the doorway, peering into the store.

The grocer waved his arms about the empty room. Not a display case had a 115 single item standing. "All gone," he said again, as if addressing a stupid child. "There is nothing left to get. You, my friend, have come back too late for a second load. I am cleaned out."

Nelson Reed stepped into the store and strode toward the counter. He 116 moved through wine-stained flour, lettuce leaves, red, green, and blue labels, bits and pieces of broken glass. He walked toward the counter.

"All day," the grocer laughed not quite hysterically now, "all day long I have 117 not made a single cent of profit. The entire day was a loss. This store, like the others, is *bleeding* me." He waved his arms about the room in a magnificent gesture of uncaring loss. "Now do you understand?" he said. "Now will you put yourself in my shoes? I have nothing here. Come, now, Mr. Reed, would it not be so bad a thing to walk in my shoes?"

"Mr. Green," Nelson Reed said coldly. "My wife bought a loaf of bread in 118 here this mornin'. She forgot to pay you. I, myself, have come here to pay you your money."

"Oh," the grocer said.   119

"I think it was brown bread. Don't that cost more than white?"   120

The two men looked away from each other, but not at anything in the store. 121

"In my store, yes," Harold Green said. He rang the register with the most ca- 122 sual movement of his finger. The register read fifty-five cents.

Nelson Reed held out a dollar.   123

"And two cents tax," the grocer said.   124

The man held out the dollar.   125

"After all," Harold Green said. "We are all, after all, Mr. Reed, in debt to the 126 government."

He rang the register again. It read fifty-seven cents.   127

Nelson Reed held out a dollar.   128

ACTIVITIES FOR WRITING AND DISCUSSION

1. At the beginning of the fourth paragraph, Green says, "I did not make the world." He contends that he is only doing what he *must* and that anyone else in his position would do the same.

    a. Identify a situation that placed someone in a dilemma similar to Green's. Who was involved? What was the focus of conflict? How was (or wasn't) the conflict resolved? Provide the facts and write the story of that situation.

    b. Agree with Green's statement that he "did not make the world," summarizing arguments in the text (or your own) that support his claim. Then disagree with him, summarizing arguments in the text (or your own) that take an opposing point of view.

2. Reread Thomas's story (paragraphs 43–51) about the sale of the electric stove. Then offer your own answer to Thomas's follow-up question, "Is it ethical?" Provide reasons for your answer.

3. Why do you suppose Betty Reed comes to buy something in Green's store on Saturday morning, even though she knows the store is to be picketed that day? To answer this question, first reread and annotate any passages in the story that talk about Betty, her character, or her motivations. Then assume Betty's **persona** and express the thoughts and motives leading up to your action.

4. Using one of the "Ten Ideas for Writing from Reading" in Chapter 3 (page 27)—or some other approach of your own choosing—respond to any of the events that occur in Green's store on that fateful Saturday.

Poems

LANGSTON HUGHES (1902–1967)

Theme for English B

The instructor said,

    Go home and write
    a page tonight.
    And let that page come out of you—
    Then, it will be true.   5

I wonder if it's that simple?

I am twenty-two, colored, born in Winston-Salem.
I went to school there, then Durham, then here
to this college on the hill above Harlem.
I am the only colored student in my class.   10
The steps from the hill lead down to Harlem,
through a park, then I cross St. Nicholas,
Eighth Avenue, Seventh, and I come to the Y,
the Harlem Branch Y, where I take the elevator
up to my room, sit down, and write this page: 15

It's not easy to know what is true for you or me
at twenty-two, my age. But I guess I'm what
I feel and see and hear. Harlem, I hear you:
hear you, hear me—we two—you, me talk on this page.
(I hear New York, too.) Me—who?   20

Well, I like to eat, sleep, drink, and be in love.
I like to work, read, learn, and understand life.
I like a pipe for a Christmas present,
or records—Bessie,[1] bop,[2] or Bach.[3]

I guess being colored doesn't make me not like   25
the same things other folks like who are other races.

---

1. Bessie Smith (1894–1937), legendary blues singer.   2. A kind of jazz popular in the 1940s and 1950s.
3. Johann Sebastian Bach (1685–1750), German composer.

So will my page be colored that I write?
Being me, it will not be white.
But it will be
a part of you, instructor.   30
You are white—
yet a part of me, as I am a part of you.
That's American.

Sometimes perhaps you don't want to be a part of me.
Nor do I often want to be a part of you.   35
But we are, that's true!
As I learn from you,
I guess you learn from me—
although you're older—and white—
and somewhat more free.   40

This is my page for English B.

ACTIVITIES FOR WRITING AND DISCUSSION

1. How does the structure of the speaker's "theme" (or English paper) compare or contrast with your sense of the standard structure for an English paper? Is there an introduction? a conclusion? Why or why not? What are the main ideas, and what connects one idea with another? How do you react when the student addresses the instructor directly (as "you") in his paper? Finally, how are any of these structural or tonal features significant to the poem's meaning?

2. Imagine you are the instructor. It is late at night; you are nodding off over the twenty or thirty student themes you have collected in response to this assignment when you come across this theme. Does the speaker's "page" of writing satisfy your expectations? fail to meet them? surpass them? How does it compare with the other students' themes? Take some notes in response to these questions. Then, as instructor, write a letter of reply or evaluation to the student.

Ballad of the Landlord

Landlord, landlord,
My roof has sprung a leak.
Don't you 'member I told you about it
Way last week?

Landlord, landlord,   5
These steps is broken down.

When you come up yourself
It's a wonder you don't fall down.

Ten Bucks you say I owe you?
Ten Bucks you say is due?   10
Well, that's Ten Bucks more'n I'll pay you
Till you fix this house up new.

What? You gonna get eviction orders?
You gonna cut off my heat?
You gonna take my furniture and   15
Throw it in the street?

Um-huh! You talking high and mighty.
Talk on—till you get through.
You ain't gonna be able to say a word
If I land my fist on you.   20

Police! Police!
Come and get this man!
He's trying to ruin the government
And overturn the land!

Copper's whistle!   25
Patrol bell!
Arrest.

Precinct Station.
Iron cell.
Headlines in press: 30

MAN THREATENS LANDLORD
TENANT HELD NO BAIL
JUDGE GIVES NEGRO 90 DAYS IN COUNTY JAIL

ANNA SWIR (1909–1984)

The Same Inside

Walking to your place for a love feast
I saw at a street corner
an old beggar woman.

I took her hand,
kissed her delicate cheek,   5
we talked, she was
the same inside as I am,
from the same kind,
I sensed this instantly
as a dog knows by scent   10
another dog.

I gave her money,
I could not part from her.
After all, one needs
someone who is close.   15

And then I no longer knew
why I was walking to your place.

—Translated by Czeslaw Milosz and Leonard Nathan

Gwendolyn Brooks (b. 1917)

The Boy Died in My Alley

The Boy died in my alley
without my Having Known.
Policeman said, next morning,
"Apparently died Alone."

"You heard a shot?" Policeman said.   5
Shots I hear and Shots I hear.
I never see the Dead.

The Shot that killed him yes I heard
as I heard the Thousand shots before;
careening tinnily down the nights   10
across my years and arteries.

Policeman pounded on my door.
"Who is it?" "POLICE!" Policeman yelled.
"A Boy was dying in your alley.
A Boy is dead, and in your alley.   15
And have you known this Boy before?"

I have known this Boy before.
I have known this Boy before, who
ornaments my alley.
I never saw his face at all.
I never saw his futurefall.   20
But I have known this Boy.

I have always heard him deal with death.
I have always heard the shout, the volley.
I have closed my heart-ears late and early.   25
And I have killed him ever.

I joined the Wild and killed him
with knowledgeable unknowing.
I saw where he was going.
I saw him Crossed. And seeing,   30
I did not take him down.

He cried not only "Father!"
but "Mother!
Sister!
Brother."   35
The cry climbed up the alley.
It went up to the wind.
It hung upon the heaven
for a long
stretch-strain of Moment.   40

The red floor of my alley
is a special speech to me.

ACTIVITIES FOR WRITING AND DISCUSSION

1. Annotate and discuss any words, phrases, or lines that strike or puzzle you. (An example of a puzzling passage might be lines 27–28 with the closing **oxymoron**: "I joined the Wild and killed him/with knowledgeable unknowing.") What strikes you and why? What puzzles you and why?

2. What are the effects of certain phrases being repeated, e.g., "I have known," "I never saw," "I have always heard"?

3. Using details from the poem and inventing others as necessary, tell the story of the Boy. Who (or what) is he? Try narrating from any of a variety of **points of view**—the Boy's mother's or father's, a sibling's, a friend's.

4. Tell the story of the **speaker.** Where does the speaker live? What is his/her life like? What sorts of things does he/she do, see, hear, experience in a typical day? If you wish, compose your narrative in the form of a series of diary entries by the speaker.

Wislawa Szymborska (b. 1923)

Hatred

See how efficient it still is,
how it keeps itself in shape—
our century's hatred.
How easily it vaults the tallest obstacles.
How rapidly it pounces, tracks us down.   5

It's not like other feelings.
At once both older and younger.
It gives birth itself to the reasons
that give it life.
When it sleeps, it's never eternal rest.   10
And sleeplessness won't sap its strength; it feeds it.

One religion or another—
whatever gets it ready, in position.
One fatherland or another—
whatever helps it get a running start.   15
Justice also works well at the outset
until hate gets its own momentum going.
Hatred. Hatred.
Its face twisted in a grimace
of erotic ecstasy.   20

Oh these other feelings,
listless weaklings.
Since when does brotherhood
draw crowds?
Has compassion   25
ever finished first?
Does doubt ever really rouse the rabble?
Only hatred has just what it takes.

Gifted, diligent, hard-working.
Need we mention all the songs it has composed?   30

All the pages it has added to our history books?
All the human carpets it has spread
over countless city squares and football fields?

Let's face it:
it knows how to make beauty.   35
The splendid fire-glow in midnight skies.
Magnificent bursting bombs in rosy dawns.
You can't deny the inspiring pathos of ruins
and a certain bawdy humor to be found
in the sturdy column jutting from their midst.   40

Hatred is a master of contrast—
between explosions and dead quiet,
red blood and white snow.
Above all, it never tires
of its leitmotif—the impeccable executioner   45
towering over its soiled victim.

It's always ready for new challenges.
If it has to wait awhile, it will.
They say it's blind. Blind?
It has a sniper's keen sight   50
and gazes unflinchingly at the future
as only it can.

—*Translated by Stanislaw Barańczak and Clare Cavanagh*

ACTIVITIES FOR WRITING AND DISCUSSION

1. Where—and with what effect(s)—does Szymborska use **personification** in this poem? What other figures are present, and how do they intensify the poem's impact? Illustrate your answer with specific phrases or lines.

2. Individually or collaboratively, jot down some adjectives to describe the poem's tone. Grim? Angry? Playful? Impassioned? Support your choice of adjectives with evidence from specific lines. Then discuss *why* Szymborska might have chosen the particular tone she did.

3. Rather than condemning hatred, the speaker seems to praise it. How can you tell that the praise is meant to be taken **ironically**? What are some particular words and passages that underscore the irony? Finally, how does this ironic stance to a better job of portraying hatred than would literal condemnation?

4. Do activity #2 on page 542.

Carter Revard (b. 1931)

Discovery of the New World

The creatures that we met this morning
　　marveled at our green skins
　　　　　　　and scarlet eyes.
They lack antennae
　　and can't be made to grasp　　　　　　　　　　5
　　　your proclamation that they are
our lawful food and prey and slaves,
　　nor can they seem to learn
　　　their body-space is needed to materialize
　　　　our oxygen-absorbers—　　　　　　　　10
which they conceive are breathing
　　and thinking creatures whom they implore
at first as angels, then as devils,
　　when they are being snuffed out
　　　　by an absorber swelling　　　　　　　　15
　　　　　into their space.
Their history bled from one this morning,
　　while we were tasting his brain,
　　　in holographic rainbows,
which we assembled into quite an interesting　　　20
　　set of legends—
　　　that's all it came to, though
the colors were quite lovely before we
　　poured them into our time;
　　　　the blue shift bleached away　　　　　　25
meaningless circumstances, and they would not fit
　　any of our truth-matrices—
　　　　there was, however,
　　　a curious visual echo in their history
　　　　　of our own coming to their earth;　　　30
a certain General Sherman said
　　about one group of them precisely what
　　　we have been telling you about these creatures:
it is our destiny to asterize this planet,
　　and they WILL not be asterized,　　　　　　35
　　　　so they must be wiped out.
　　WE NEED their space and nitrogen
　　　which they do not know how to *use,*
nor will they breathe ammonia, as we do;
　　yet they will not give up their "air" unforced,　　40

so it is clear,
  whatever our "agreements" made this
                morning,
  we'll have to kill them all:
    the more we cook this orbit,   45
  the fewer next time round.
We've finished lazing all their crops and stores,
  we've killed their meat-slaves, now
    they'll have to come into our pens
and we can use them for our final studies   50
  of how our heart attacks and cancers spread
                among them,
  since they seem not immune to these.
—If we didn't have this mission it might be sad
    to see such helpless creatures die   55
chanting their sacred psalms and bills of rights; but
                never fear
    the riches of this globe are ours
  and worth whatever pains others may have to
                feel.   60
    We'll soon have it cleared
completely, as it now is, at the poles, and then
  we will be safe, and rich, and happy here, forever.

ACTIVITIES FOR WRITING AND DISCUSSION

1. Where do the "discoverers" seem to be from? What "New World" are they discovering, and how do you know? To whom might the "your" in line 6 refer? What type of writing is this poem meant to represent—a diary entry? report? letter? oral communication of some sort? Explain.

2. Working alone or in a group, underline or circle any odd, puzzling, or striking terms or expressions you find in the poem. Then look for definitions in a dictionary, or attempt to translate the terms into more familiar language. Finally, discuss how these terms or expressions function meaningfully in the poem.

3. Does the poem parody (i.e., provide a satirical imitation of) any actual events in human history? If so, give examples of some such events. Then, in your notebook, analyze how the parody works.

4. React to the final line. Do you take it literally or **ironically**? Why? Write a sequel (in poetry or prose) in which you trace the subsequent fortunes of the "discoverers."

Wole Soyinka (b. 1934)

Telephone Conversation

The price seemed reasonable, location
Indifferent. The landlady swore she lived
Off premises. Nothing remained
But self-confession. 'Madam,' I warned,
'I hate a wasted journey—I am—African.'   5
Silence. Silenced transmission of
Pressurized good-breeding. Voice, when it came,
Lipstick coated, long gold-rolled
Cigarette-holder pipped. Caught I was, foully.
'HOW DARK?' . . . I had not misheard. . . . 'ARE YOU LIGHT   10
OR VERY DARK?' Button B. Button A. Stench
Of rancid breath of public-hide-and-speak.
Red booth.[1] Red pillar-box.[2] Red double-tiered
Omnibus squelching tar. It *was* real! Shamed
By ill-mannered silence, surrender   15
Pushed dumbfoundment to beg simplification.
Considerate she was, varying the emphasis—
'ARE YOU DARK? OR VERY LIGHT?' Revelation came.
'You mean—like plain or milk chocolate?'
Her assent was clinical, crushing in its light   20
Impersonality. Rapidly, wave-length adjusted,
I chose, 'West African sepia'—and as afterthought,
'Down in my passport.' Silence for spectroscopic
Flight of fancy, till truthfulness clanged her accent
Hard on the mouthpiece. 'WHAT'S THAT?' conceding   25
'DON'T KNOW WHAT THAT IS.' 'Like brunette.'
'THAT'S DARK, ISN'T IT?' 'Not altogether.
Facially, I am brunette, but madam, you should see
The rest of me. Palm of my hand, soles of my feet
Are a peroxid blonde. Friction, caused—   30
Foolishly madam—by sitting down, has turned
My bottom raven black—One moment madam!'—sensing
Her receiver rearing on the thunder clap
About my ears—'Madam,' I pleaded, 'wouldn't you rather
See for yourself?'   35

---

1. Phone booth.   2. Mailbox.

ACTIVITIES FOR WRITING AND DISCUSSION

1. How, if at all, would the poem change if this "conversation" took place via email rather than over the phone? Invent the alternative conversation.

2. Analyze the poem's language, e.g., the varied sentence lengths, the choice and use of quoted dialogue, the use of ellipsis points and capitalization in lines 10 and 11 and elsewhere, and other punctuation devices used to depict the rhythms and tensions of the conversation. How do these features enhance the poem's effect? Illustrate your analysis with examples.

3. Soyinka uses a phone conversation to dramatize an example of racial prejudice. In a dialogue within a poem or a prose dialogue, do a takeoff on Soyinka's text. Include one or more of the following elements:

    a. A conflict that goes beyond opinion or thought to the essential selves, e.g., racial, ethnic, linguistic, religious, of the two speakers,

    b. A conflict that threatens to explode but is controlled by a conscious effort at politeness,

    c. A conflict in which one speaker clearly enjoys an implicit position of power over the other.

PAULA GUNN ALLEN (b. 1939)

Pocahontas to Her English Husband, John Rolfe

Had I not cradled you in my arms,
oh beloved   perfidious one,
you would have died.
And how many times did I pluck you
from certain death in the wilderness—   5
my world through which you stumbled
as though blind?
Had I not set you tasks
your masters far across the sea
would have abandoned you—   10
did abandon you, as many times they
left you to reap the harvest of their lies;
still you survived   oh my fair husband
and brought them gold
wrung from a harvest I taught you   15
to plant: Tobacco.   It
is not without irony that by this crop
your descendants die, for other powers
than those you know take part in this.

And indeed I did rescue you   20
not once but a thousand thousand times
and in my arms you slept, a foolish child,
and beside me you played,
chattering nonsense about a God
you had not wit to name;   25
and wondered you at my silence—
simple foolish wanton maid you saw,
dusky daughter of heathen sires
who knew not the ways of grace—
no doubt, no doubt.   30
I spoke little, you said.
And you listened less.
But played with your gaudy dreams
and sent ponderous missives to the throne
striving thereby to curry favor   35
with your king.   I saw you well.   I
understood the ploy and still protected you,
going so far as to die in your keeping—
a wasting, putrifying death, and you,
deceiver, my husband, father of my son,   40
survived, your spirit bearing crop
slowly from my teaching, taking
certain life from the wasting of my bones.

Sharon Olds (b. 1942)

On the Subway

The boy and I face each other.
His feet are huge, in black sneakers
laced with white in a complex pattern like a
set of intentional scars. We are stuck on
opposite sides of the car, a couple of   5
molecules stuck in a rod of light
rapidly moving through darkness. He has the
casual cold look of a mugger,
alert under hooded lids. He is wearing
red, like the inside of the body   10
exposed. I am wearing dark fur, the
whole skin of an animal taken and
used. I look at his raw face,

he looks at my fur coat, and I don't
know if I am in his power—   15
he could take my coat so easily, my
briefcase, my life—
or if he is in my power, the way I am
living off his life, eating the steak
he does not eat, as if I am taking   20
the food from his mouth. And he is black
and I am white, and without meaning or
trying to I must profit from his darkness,
the way he absorbs the murderous beams of the
nation's heart, as black cotton   25
absorbs the heat of the sun and holds it. There is
no way to know how easy this
white skin makes my life, this
life he could take so easily and
break across his knee like a stick the way his   30
own back is being broken, the
rod of his soul that at birth was dark and
fluid and rich as the heart of a seedling
ready to thrust up into any available light.

ACTIVITIES FOR WRITING AND DISCUSSION

1. Describe the emotions you have as you read the first several lines. What words or images contribute to these emotions?

2. Is the **speaker** male or female? Does it matter? Why or why not? What evidence, if any, do you have of the speaker's race and socioeconomic background? of his/her political leanings? Quote and discuss such evidence. Does it matter that the speaker describes the large person across the car as a "boy" rather than a "man"?

3. Working alone or with a group, underline and annotate any **metaphors** and **similes.** Choose two or three that particularly strike you and brainstorm a list of any thoughts, reactions, or images they stir in you. Finally, in your notebook explain how those two or three metaphors or similes work in the poem.

4. The poem captures a momentary encounter, all from the speaker's **point of view.** In poetry or prose, narrate the same encounter from the boy's point of view. Consider the possibility that the boy has no interest in assaulting Olds's speaker. Alternative: Narrate the encounter between the speaker and the boy from the point of view of someone else aboard the subway car.

Jim Sagel (b. 1947)

Baca Grande

Una vaca se topó con un ratón y le dice:
"Tú—¿tan chiquito y con bigote?" Y le responde el ratón:
"Y tú tan grandota—¿y sin brassiere?"

It was nearly a miracle
James Baca remembered anyone at all
from the old hometown gang
having been two years at Yale
     no less   5
and halfway through law school
at the University of California at Irvine

They hardly recognized him either
in his three-piece grey business suit
and surfer-swirl haircut   10
with just the menacing hint
of a tightly trimmed Zapata moustache
     for cultural balance
and relevance

He had come to deliver the keynote address   15
to the graduating class of 80
at his old alma mater
and show off his well-trained lips
which laboriously parted
     each Kennedyish "R"   20
and drilled the first person pronoun
through the microphone
like an oil bit
with the slick, elegantly honed phrases
that slid so smoothly   25
off his meticulously bleached
     tongue
He talked Big Bucks
with astronautish fervor and if he
     the former bootstrapless James A. Baca   30
could dazzle the ass
off the universe

then even you
　　　yes you

Joey Martinez toying with your yellow   35
　　　tassle
and staring dumbly into space
could emulate Mr. Baca someday
　　　possibly
well   40
there was of course
such a thing
as being an outrageously successful
gas station attendant too
　　　let us never forget   45
it doesn't really matter what you do
so long as you excel
　　　James said
never believing a word
of it   50
for he had already risen
　　　as high as they go

Wasn't nobody else
from this deprived environment
who'd ever jumped   55
　　　straight out of college
into the Governor's office
and maybe one day
he'd sit in that big chair
　　　himself   60
and when he did
he'd forget this damned town
and all the petty little people
in it
once and for all   65

That much he promised himself

ACTIVITIES FOR WRITING AND DISCUSSION

1. Describe the occasion depicted and the **speaker.** Do you imagine the speaker is a member of the student audience being addressed by Baca or an outside observer? someone older or younger than Baca? Cite evidence to support your answers.

2. In lines 34–35 the speaker suddenly shifts attention to "you/Joey Martinez," and by the last line he seems to be inside the mind of James Baca. How do you account for these shifts in focus and perspective? Are they clumsy, or are they purposeful in some way? Explain.

3. Based on clues in the poem (and other material from your own imagination), create an outline—or the complete text—of Baca's speech.

Gary Soto (b. 1952)

Black Hair

At eight I was brilliant with my body.
In July, that ring of heat
We all jumped through, I sat in the bleachers
Of Romain Playground, in the lengthening
Shade that rose from our dirty feet.   5
The game before us was more than baseball.
It was a figure—Hector Moreno
Quick and hard with turned muscles,
His crouch the one I assumed before an altar
Of worn baseball cards, in my room.   10

I came here because I was Mexican, a stick
Of brown light in love with those
Who could do it—the triple and hard slide,
The gloves eating balls into double plays.
What could I do with 50 pounds, my shyness,   15
My black torch of hair, about to go out?
Father was dead, his face no longer
Hanging over the table or our sleep,
And mother was the terror of mouths
Twisting hurt by butter knives.   20

In the bleachers I was brilliant with my body,
Waving players in and stomping my feet,
I chewed sunflower seeds. I drank water
And bit my arm through the late innings.
When Hector lined balls into deep   25
Center, in my mind I rounded the bases
With him, my face flared, my hair lifting
Beautifully, because we were coming home
To the arms of brown people.

Sook Lyol Ryu (b. 1954)

Poem by a Yellow Woman

When I first saw America,
it was like a huge giant,
and I was like a pygmy woman.
I made a desperate struggle with this giant
not to fall. He whistled merrily, waving his hands.   5
He was a huge man, but a man like a snake.

Now, here I am in America, where
people drink Coca-Cola, where
people are crazy about Spielberg's silly films, where
people chase endless desires, where   10
people choose an old anachronistic
movie star as their president, where
people enjoy powerful wealth,
but keep homeless people in the street, where
people shout, "ladies first,"   15
and don't allow a woman to be president.
Now here I am from the country, where
the people are burning American flags,
singing, "Yankee, go home!"
Now here I am in America, where   20
most of my yellow people are hungry
for McDonald's and greedy for "Made in U.S.A."
My brother, who has a master's degree in English literature
thinks about Norman Mailer's American Dream
while selling fishes and vegetables   25
to his white neighbors 24 hours a day.
My sister, who liked paintings of
Picasso's Blue Period
is working on a sewing machine, with dyed blond hair.

When colored friends are making a rainbow coalition,   30
my yellow people wonder whether yellow is on the rainbow.
They think the lighter the skin, the closer to heaven,
the darker the skin, the closer to hell.
They decide yellow is in between.
So they smile at white and frown at black.   35
They make money in the hope of becoming a majority
and forget about the minority.

THOMAS S. WHITECLOUD (1914–1972)

Blue Winds Dancing

There is a moon out tonight. Moon and stars and clouds tipped with moonlight. And there is a fall wind blowing in my heart. Ever since this evening, when against a fading sky I saw geese wedge southward. They were going home. . . . Now I try to study, but against the pages I see them again, driving southward. Going home.

Across the valley there are heavy mountains holding up the night sky, and beyond the mountains there is home. Home, and peace, and the beat of drums, and blue winds dancing over snow fields. The Indian lodge will fill with my people, and our gods will come and sit among them. I should be there then. I should be at home.

But home is beyond the mountains, and I am here. Here where fall hides in the valleys, and winter never comes down from the mountains. Here where all the trees grow in rows; the palms stand stiffly by the roadsides, and in the groves the orange trees line in military rows, and endlessly bear fruit. Beautiful, yes; there is always beauty in order, in rows of growing things! But it is the beauty of captivity. A pine fighting for existence on a windy knoll is much more beautiful.

In my Wisconsin, the leaves change before the snows come. In the air there is the smell of wild rice and venison cooking; and when the winds come whispering through the forests, they carry the smell of rotting leaves. In the evenings, the loon calls, lonely; and birds sing their last songs before leaving. Bears dig roots and eat late fall berries, fattening for their long winter sleep. Later, when the first snows fall, one awakens in the morning to find the world white and beautiful and clean. Then one can look back over his trail and see the tracks following. In the woods there are tracks of deer and snowshoe rabbits, and long streaks where partridges slide to alight. Chipmunks make tiny footprints on the limbs; and one can hear squirrels busy in hollow trees, sorting acorns. Soft lake waves wash the shores, and sunsets burst each evening over the lakes, and make them look as if they were afire.

That land which is my home! Beautiful, calm—where there is no hurry to 5
get anywhere, no driving to keep up in a race that knows no ending and no goal. No classes where men talk and talk, and then stop now and then to hear their own words come back to them from the students. No constant peering into the maelstrom of one's mind; no worries about grades and honors; no hysterical preparing for life until that life is half over; no anxiety about one's place in the thing they call Society.

I hear again the ring of axes in deep woods, the crunch of snow beneath my feet. I feel again the smooth velvet of ghost-birch bark. I hear the rhythm of the drums. . . . I am tired. I am weary of trying to keep up this bluff of being civilized. Being civilized means trying to do everything you don't want to, never doing anything you want to. It means dancing to the strings of custom and tradition; it means living in houses and never knowing or caring who is next door. These civilized white men want us to be like them—always dissatisfied, getting a hill and wanting a mountain.

Then again, maybe I am not tired. Maybe I'm licked. Maybe I am just not smart enough to grasp these things that go to make up civilization. Maybe I am just too lazy to think hard enough to keep up.

Still, I know my people have many things that civilization has taken from the whites. They know how to give; how to tear one's piece of meat in two and share it with one's brother. They know how to sing—how to make each man his own songs and sing them; for their music they do not have to listen to other men singing over a radio. They know how to make things with their hands, how to shape beads into design and make a thing of beauty from a piece of birch bark.

But we are inferior. It is terrible to have to feel inferior; to have to read reports of intelligence tests, and learn that one's race is behind. It is terrible to sit in classes and hear men tell you that your people worship sticks of wood—that your gods are all false, that the Manitou forgot your people and did not write them a book.

I am tired. I want to walk again among the ghost-birches. I want to see the leaves turn in autumn, the smoke rise from the lodgehouses, and to feel the blue winds. I want to hear the drums; I want to hear the drums and feel the blue whispering winds.

There is a train wailing into the night. The trains go across the mountains. It would be easy to catch a freight. They will say he has gone back to the blanket; I don't care. The dance at Christmas. . . .

10

A bunch of bums warming at a tiny fire talk politics and women and joke about the Relief and the WPA and smoke cigarettes. These men in caps and overcoats and dirty overalls living on the outskirts of civilization are free, but they pay the price of being free in civilization. They are outcasts. I remember a sociology professor lecturing on adjustment to society; hobos and prostitutes and criminals are individuals who never adjusted, he said. He could learn a lot if he came and listened to a bunch of bums talk. He would learn that work and a woman and a place to hang his hat are all the ordinary man wants. These are all he wants, but other men are not content to let him want only these. He must be taught to want radios and automobiles and a new suit every spring. Progress would stop if he did not want these things. I listen to hear if there is any talk of communism or socialism in the hobo jungles. There is none. At best there is a sort of disgusted philosophy about life. They seem to think there should be a better distribution of wealth, or more work, or something. But they are not rabid about it. The radicals live in the cities.

I find a fellow headed for Albuquerque, and talk road-talk with him. "It is hard to ride fruit cars. Bums break in. Better to wait for a cattle car going back to the Middle West, and ride that." We catch the next east-bound and walk the tops until we find a cattle car. Inside, we crouch near the forward wall, huddle, and try to sleep. I feel peaceful and content at last. I am going home. The cattle car rocks. I sleep.

Morning and the desert. Noon and the Salton Sea, lying more lifeless than a mirage under a somber sun in a pale sky. Skeleton mountains rearing on the skyline, thrusting out of the desert floor, all rock and shadow and edges. Desert. Good country for an Indian reservation. . . .

Yuma and the muddy Colorado. Night again, and I wait shivering for the 15 dawn.

Phoenix. Pima country. Mountains that look like cardboard sets on a forgotten stage. Tucson. Papago country. Giant cacti that look like petrified hitchhikers along the highways. Apache country. At El Paso my road-buddy decides to go on to Houston. I leave him, and head north to the mesa country. Las Cruces and the terrible Organ Mountains, jagged peaks that instill fear and wondering. Albuquerque. Pueblos along the Rio Grande. On the boardwalk there are some Indian women in colored sashes selling bits of pottery. The stone age offering its art to the twentieth century. They hold up a piece and fix the tourist with black eyes until, embarrassed, he buys or turns away. I feel suddenly angry that my people should have to do such things for a living. . . .

Santa Fe trains are fast, and they keep them pretty clean of bums. I decide to hurry and ride passenger coaltenders. Hide in the dark, judge the speed of the train as it leaves, and then dash out, and catch it. I hug the cold steel wall of the tender and think of the roaring fire in the engine ahead, and of the passengers back in the dining car reading their papers over hot coffee. Beneath me there is blur of rails. Death would come quick if my hands should freeze and I fall. Up over the Sangre De Cristo range, around cliffs and through canyons to Denver. Bitter cold here, and I must watch out for Denver Bob. He is a railroad bull who has thrown bums from fast freights. I miss him. It is too cold, I suppose. On north to the Sioux country.

Small towns lit for the coming Christmas. On the streets of one I see a beam-shouldered young farmer gazing into a window filled with shining silver toasters. He is tall and wears a blue shirt buttoned, with no tie. His young wife by his side looks at him hopefully. He wants decorations for his place to hang his hat to please his woman. . . .

Northward again. Minnesota, and great white fields of snow; frozen lakes, and dawn running in dusk without noon. Long forests wearing white. Bitter cold, and one night the northern lights. I am nearing home.

I reach Woodruff at midnight. Suddenly I am afraid, now that I am but 20 twenty miles from home. Afraid of what my father will say, afraid of being looked on as a stranger by my own people. I sit by a fire and think about myself and all the other young Indians. We just don't seem to fit in anywhere—certainly not among the whites, and not among the older people. I think again about the learned sociology professor and his professing. So many things seem to be clear now that I am away from school and do not have to worry about some man's opinion of my ideas. It is easy to think while looking at dancing flames.

Morning. I spend the day cleaning up, and buying some presents for my family with what is left of my money. Nothing much, but a gift is a gift, if a man buys it with his last quarter. I wait until evening, then start up the track toward home.

Christmas Eve comes in on a north wind. Snow clouds hang over the pines, and the night comes early. Walking along the railroad bed, I feel the calm peace of snow-bound forests on either side of me. I take my time; I am back in a world where time does not mean so much now. I am alone; alone but not nearly so lonely as I was back on the campus at school. Those are never lonely who love the snow and the pines; never lonely when the pines are wearing white shawls and snow crunches coldly underfoot. In the woods I know there are the tracks of deer and rabbit; I know that if I leave the rails and go into the woods I shall find them. I walk along feeling glad because my legs are light and my feet seem to know that they are home. A deer comes out of the woods just ahead of me, and stands silhouetted on the rails. The North, I feel, has welcomed me home. I watch him and am glad that I do not wish for a gun. He goes into the woods quietly, leaving only the design of his tracks in the snow. I walk on. Now and then I pass a field, white under the night sky, with houses at the far end. Snow comes from the chimneys of the houses, and I try to tell what sort of wood each is burning by the smoke; some burn pine, others aspen, others tamarack. There is one from which comes black coal smoke that rises lazily and drifts out over the tops of the trees. I like to watch houses and try to imagine what might be happening in them.

Just as a light snow begins to fall, I cross the reservation boundary; somehow it seems as though I have stepped into another world. Deep woods in a white-and-black winter night. A faint trail leading to the village.

The railroad on which I stand comes from a city sprawled by a lake—a city with a million people who walk around without seeing one another; a city sucking the life from all the country around; a city with stores and police and intellectuals and criminals and movies and apartment houses; a city with its politics and libraries and zoos.

Laughing, I go into the woods. As I cross a frozen lake I begin to hear the 25 drums. Soft in the night the drums beat. It is like the pulse beat of the world. The white line of the lake ends at a black forest, and above the trees the blue winds are dancing.

I come to the outlying houses of the village. Simple box houses, etched black in the night. From one or two windows soft lamp light falls on the snow. Christmas here, too, but it does not mean much; not much in the way of parties and presents. Joe Sky will get drunk. Alex Bodidash will buy his children red mittens and a new sled. Alex is a Carlisle man, and tries to keep his home up to white standards. White standards. Funny that my people should be ever falling farther behind. The more they try to imitate whites the more tragic the result. Yet they want us to be imitation white men. About all we imitate well are their vices.

The village is not a sight to instill pride, yet I am not ashamed; one can never be ashamed of his own people when he knows they have dreams as beautiful as white snow on a tall pine.

Father and my brother and sister are seated around the table as I walk in. Father stares at me for a moment, then I am in his arms, crying on his shoulder. I give them the presents I have brought, and my throat tightens as I watch my sister save carefully bits of red string from the packages. I hide my feelings by wrestling with my brother when he strikes my shoulder in token of affection. Father looks at me, and I know he has many questions, but he seems to know why I have come. He tells me to go on alone to the lodge, and he will follow.

I walk along the trail to the lodge, watching the northern lights forming in the heavens. White waving ribbons that seem to pulsate with the rhythm of the drums. Clean snow creaks beneath my feet, and a soft wind sighs through the trees, singing to me. Everything seems to say "Be happy! You are home now— you are free. You are among friends—we are your friends; we, the trees, and the snow, and the lights." I follow the trail to the lodge. My feet are light, my heart seems to sing to the music, and I hold my head high. Across white snow fields blue winds are dancing.

Before the lodge door I stop, afraid. I wonder if my people will remember 30 me. I wonder—"Am I Indian, or am I white?" I stand before the door a long time. I hear the ice groan on the lake, and remember the story of the old woman who is under the ice, trying to get out, so she can punish some runaway lovers. I think to myself, "If I am white I will not believe that story; if I am Indian, I will know that there is an old woman under the ice." I listen for a while, and I know that there is an old woman under the ice. I look again at the lights, and go in.

Inside the lodge there are many Indians. Some sit on benches around the walls, others dance in the center of the floor around a drum. Nobody seems to notice me. It seems as though I were among a people I have never seen before. Heavy women with long black hair. Women with children on their knees— small children that watch with intent black eyes the movements of the dancers, whose small faces are solemn and serene. The faces of the old people are serene, too, and their eyes are merry and bright. I look at the old men. Straight, dressed in dark trousers and beaded velvet vests, wearing soft moccasins. Dark, lined faces intent on the music. I wonder if I am at all like them. They dance on, lifting their feet to the rhythm of the drums, swaying lightly, looking upward. I look at their eyes, and am startled at the rapt attention to the rhythm of the music.

The dance stops. The men walk back to the walls, and talk in low tones or with their hands. There is little conversation, yet everyone seems to be sharing some secret. A woman looks at a small boy wandering away, and he comes back to her.

Strange, I think, and then remember. These people are not sharing words— they are sharing a mood. Everyone is happy. I am so used to white people that it seems strange so many people could be together without someone talking. These Indians are happy because they are together, and because the night is beautiful outside, and the music is beautiful. I try hard to forget school and white people, and be one of these—my people. I try to forget everything but the night, and it is a part of me; that I am one with my people and we are all a part of something universal. I watch eyes, and see now that the old people are speaking to me. They nod slightly, imperceptibly, and their eyes laugh into mine. I look around the room. All the eyes are friendly; they all laugh. No one questions my being here. The drums begin to beat again, and I catch the invitation in the eyes of the old men. My feet begin to lift to the rhythm, and I look out beyond the walls into the night and see the lights. I am happy. It is beautiful. I am home.

ACTIVITIES FOR WRITING AND DISCUSSION

1. Read and annotate the essay. Then:
   a. Share and discuss a few of your favorite annotations with a small group, and take notes on your groupmates' annotations to enrich your response to the essay.
   b. Respond to "Blue Winds Dancing" in your notebook using any of the "Ten Ideas for Writing" described in Chapter 3 and summarized on page 35.

2. React to Whitecloud's **persona.** What qualities of the persona attract or repel you, and how and where—specifically—are those qualities conveyed in the language and content of the text? Consider word choice, vocabulary, sentence length and style, tone, and ideas. If you wish, focus your analysis on the opening paragraphs.

3. Working alone or collaboratively, make as long a list as you can of Whitecloud's criticisms of white society. Then, drawing upon the text and your own experience or knowledge, pick one or two criticisms and debate their justness or accuracy—first orally and then in writing in your notebook.

4. List any topics that are suggested to you by the essay, e.g., "silence," "civilization," "home," etc. Then make a Topic/Form Grid (see p. 111 in Chapter 9),

choose a favorite topic, and use one of the forms on your grid to create a notebook entry about the topic. Should your chosen form or topic not work, do a
Topic/Form Shift to a different form or topic on your grid.

LESLIE MARMON SILKO (b. 1948)

Language and Literature from a Pueblo Indian Perspective

Where I come from, the words most highly valued are those spoken from the
heart, unpremeditated and unrehearsed. Among the Pueblo people, a written
speech or statement is highly suspect because the true feelings of the speaker
remain hidden as she reads words that are detached from the occasion and the
audience. I have intentionally not written a formal paper because I want you to
hear and to experience English in a structure that follows patterns from the oral
tradition. For those of you accustomed to being taken from point A to point B
to point C, this presentation may be somewhat difficult to follow. Pueblo expression resembles something like a spider's web—with many little threads ra-
diating from the center, crisscrossing each other. As with the web, the structure
emerges as it is made and you must simply listen and trust, as the Pueblo people
do, that meaning will be made.

My task is a formidable one: I ask you to set aside a number of basic approaches that you have been using, and probably will continue to use, and instead, to approach language from the Pueblo perspective, one that embraces the
whole of creation and the whole of history and time.

What changes would Pueblo writers make to English as a language for literature? I have some examples of stories in English that I will use to address this
question. At the same time, I would like to explain the importance of storytelling and how it relates to a Pueblo theory of language.

So, I will begin, appropriately enough, with the Pueblo Creation story, an
all-inclusive story of how life began. In this story, Tséitsínako, Thought
Woman, by thinking of her sisters, and together with her sisters, thought of
everything that is. In this way, the world was created. Everything in this world
was a part of the original creation; the people at home understood that far away
there were other human beings, also a part of this world. The Creation story
even includes a prophecy, which describes the origin of European and African
peoples and also refers to Asians.

This story, I think, suggests something about why the Pueblo people are 5
more concerned with story and communication and less concerned with a particular language. There are at least six, possibly seven, distinct languages among
the twenty pueblos of the southwestern United States, for example, Zuñi and
Hopi. And from mesa to mesa there are subtle differences in language. But the

particular language being spoken isn't as important as what a speaker is trying to say, and this emphasis on the story itself stems, I believe, from a view of narrative particular to the Pueblo and other Native American peoples—that is, that language *is* story.

I will try to clarify this statement. At Laguna Pueblo, for example, many individual words have their own stories. So when one is telling a story, and one is using words to tell the story, each word that one is speaking has a story of its own, too. Often the speakers or tellers will go into these word-stories, creating an elaborate structure of stories-within-stories. This structure, which becomes very apparent in the actual telling of a story, informs contemporary Pueblo writing and storytelling as well as the traditional narratives. This perspective on narrative—of story within story, the idea that one story is only the beginning of many stories, and the sense that stories never truly end—represents an important contribution of Native American cultures to the English language.

Many people think of storytelling as something that is done at bedtime, that it is something done for small children. But when I use the term *storytelling,* I'm talking about something much bigger than that. I'm talking about something that comes out of an experience and an understanding of that original view of creation—that we are all part of a whole; we do not differentiate or fragment stories and experiences. In the beginning, Tséitsínako, Thought Woman, thought of all things, and all of these things are held together as one holds many things together in a single thought.

So in the telling (and you will hear a few of the dimensions of this telling) first of all, as mentioned earlier, the storytelling always includes the audience, the listeners. In fact, a great deal of the story is believed to be inside the listener: the storyteller's role is to draw the story out of the listeners. The storytelling continues from generation to generation.

Basically, the origin story constructs our identity—within this story, we know who we are. We are the Lagunas. This is where we come from. We came this way. We came by this place. And so from the time we are very young, we hear these stories, so that when we go out into the world, when one asks who we are, or where we are from, we immediately know: we are the people who came from the north. We are the people of these stories.

In the Creation story, Antelope says that he will help knock a hole in the 10 earth so that the people can come up, out into the next world. Antelope tries and tries; he uses his hooves, but is unable to break through. It is then that Badger says, "Let me help you." And Badger very patiently uses his claws and digs a way through, bringing the people into the world. When the Badger clan people think of themselves, or when the Antelope people think of themselves, it is as people who are of *this* story, and this is *our* place, and we fit into the very beginning when the people first came, before we began our journey south.

Within the clans there are stories that identify the clan. One moves, then, from the idea of one's identity as a tribal person into clan identity, then to one's identity as a member of an extended family. And it is the notion of "extended family" that has produced a kind of story that some distinguish from other

Pueblo stories, though Pueblo people do not. Anthropologists and ethnologists have, for a long time, differentiated the types of stories the Pueblos tell. They tended to elevate the old, sacred, and traditional stories and to brush aside family stories, the family's account of itself. But in Pueblo culture, these family stories are given equal recognition. There is no definite, preset pattern for the way one will hear the stories of one's own family, but it is a very critical part of one's childhood, and the storytelling continues throughout one's life. One will hear stories of importance to the family—sometimes wonderful stories—stories about the time a maternal uncle got the biggest deer that was ever seen and brought it back from the mountains. And so an individual's identity will extend from the identity constructed around the family—"I am from the family of my uncle who brought in this wonderful deer and it was a wonderful hunt."

Family accounts include negative stories, too; perhaps an uncle did something unacceptable. It is very important that one keep track of all these stories—both positive and not so positive—about one's own family and other families. Because even when there is no way around it—old Uncle Pete *did* do a terrible thing—by knowing the stories that originate in other families, one is able to deal with terrible sorts of things that might happen within one's own family. If a member of the family does something that cannot be excused, one always knows stories about similarly inexcusable things done by a member of another family. But this knowledge is not communicated for malicious reasons. It is very important to understand this. Keeping track of all the stories within the community gives us all a certain distance, a useful perspective, that brings incidents down to a level we can deal with. If others have done it before, it cannot be so terrible. If others have endured, so can we.

The stories are always bringing us together, keeping this whole together, keeping this family together, keeping this clan together. "Don't go away, don't isolate yourself, but come here, because we have all had these kinds of experiences." And so there is this constant pulling together to resist the tendency to run or hide or separate oneself during a traumatic emotional experience. This separation not only endangers the group but the individual as well—one does not recover by oneself.

Because storytelling lies at the heart of Pueblo culture, it is absurd to attempt to fix the stories in time. "When did they tell the stories?" or "What time of day does the storytelling take place?"—these questions are nonsensical from a Pueblo perspective, because our storytelling goes on constantly: as some old grandmother puts on the shoes of a child and tells her the story of a little girl who didn't wear her shoes, for instance, or someone comes into the house for coffee to talk with a teenage boy who has just been in a lot of trouble, to reassure him that someone else's son has been in that kind of trouble, too. Storytelling is an ongoing process, working on many different levels.

Here's one story that is often told at a time of individual crisis (and I want   15
to remind you that we make no distinctions between types of story—historical, sacred, plain gossip—because these distinctions are not useful when discussing the Pueblo *experience* of language). There was a young man who, when he came

back from the war in Vietnam, had saved up his army pay and bought a beautiful red Volkswagen. He was very proud of it. One night he drove up to a place called the King's Bar right across the reservation line. The bar is notorious for many reasons, particularly for the deep *arroyo* located behind it. The young man ran in to pick up a cold six-pack, but he forgot to put on his emergency brake. And his little red Volkswagen rolled back into the *arroyo* and was all smashed up. He felt very bad about it, but within a few days everybody had come to him with stories about other people who had lost cars and family members to that *arroyo*, for instance, George Day's station wagon, with his mother-in-law and kids inside. So everybody was saying, "Well, at least your mother-in-law and kids weren't in the car when it rolled in," and one can't argue with that kind of story. The story of the young man and his smashed-up Volkswagen was now joined with all the other stories of cars that fell into that *arroyo*.

Now I want to tell you a very beautiful little story. It is a very old story that is sometimes told to people who suffer great family or personal loss. This story was told by my Aunt Susie. She is one of the first generation of people at Laguna who began experimenting with English—who began working to make English speak for us—that is, to speak from the heart. (I come from a family intent on getting the stories told.) As you read the story, I think you will hear that. And here and there, I think, you will also hear the influence of the Indian school at Carlisle, Pennsylvania, where my Aunt Susie was sent (like being sent to prison) for six years.

This scene is set partly in Acoma, partly in Laguna. Waithea was a little girl living in Acoma and one day she said, "Mother, I would like to have some *yashtoah* to eat." *Yashtoah* is the hardened crust of corn mush that curls up. *Yashtoah* literally means "curled up." She said, "I would like to have some *yashtoah*," and her mother said, "My dear little girl, I can't make you any *yashtoah* because we haven't any wood, but if you will go down off the mesa, down below, and pick up some pieces of wood and bring them home, I will make you some *yashtoah*." So Waithea was glad and ran down the precipitous cliff of Acoma mesa. Down below, just as her mother had told her, there were pieces of wood, some curled, some crooked in shape, that she was to pick up and take home. She found just such wood as these.

She brought them home in a little wicker basket. First she called to her mother as she got home, "*Nayah, deeni!* Mother, upstairs!" The Pueblo people always called "upstairs" because long ago their homes were two, three stories, and they entered from the top. She said, "*Deeni!* UPSTAIRS!" and her mother came. The little girl said, "I have brought the wood you wanted me to bring." And she opened her little wicker basket to lay out the pieces of wood but here they were snakes. They were snakes instead of the crooked sticks of wood. And her mother said, "Oh my dear child, you have brought snakes instead!" She said, "Go take them back and put them back just where you got them." And the little girl ran down the mesa again, down below to the flats. And she put those snakes back just where she got them. They were snakes instead and she was very hurt about this and so she said, "I'm not going home. I'm going to *Kawaik*, the beautiful lake place, *Kawaik*, and drown myself in that lake, *byn'yah'nah* [the "west lake"]. I will go there and drown myself."

So she started off, and as she passed by the Enchanted Mesa near Acoma she met an old man, very aged, and he saw her running, and he said, "My dear child, where are you going?" "I'm going to *Kawaik* and jump into the lake there." "Why?" "Well, because," she said, "my mother didn't want to make any *yashtoah* for me." The old man said, "Oh, no! You must not go my child. Come with me and I will take you home." He tried to catch her, but she was very light and skipped along. And every time he would try to grab her she would skip faster away from him.

The old man was coming home with some wood strapped to his back and tied with yucca. He just let that strap go and let the wood drop. He went as fast as he could up the cliff to the little girl's home. When he got to the place where she lived, he called to her mother. "*Deeni!*" "Come on up!" And he said, "I can't. I just came to bring you a message. Your little daughter is running away. She is going to *Kawaik* to drown herself in the lake there." "Oh my dear little girl!" the mother said. So she busied herself with making the *yashtoah* her little girl liked so much. Corn mush curled at the top. (She must have found enough wood to boil the corn meal and make the *yashtoah*.) 20

While the mush was cooling off, she got the little girl's clothing, her *manta* dress and buckskin moccasins and all her other garments, and put them in a bundle—probably a yucca bag. And she started down as fast as she could on the east side of Acoma. (There used to be a trail there, you know. It's gone now, but it was accessible in those days.) She saw her daughter way at a distance and she kept calling: "Stsamaku! My daughter! Come back! I've got your *yashtoah* for you." But the little girl would not turn. She kept on ahead and she cried: "My mother, my mother, she didn't want me to have any *yashtoah*. So now I'm going to *Kawaik* and drown myself." Her mother heard her cry and said, "My little daughter, come back here!" "No," and she kept a distance away from her. And they came nearer and nearer to the lake. And she could see her daughter now, very plain. "Come back, my daughter! I have your *yashtoah*." But no, she kept on, and finally she reached the lake and she stood on the edge.

She had tied a little feather in her hair, which is traditional (in death they tie this feather on the head). She carried a feather, the little girl did, and she tied it in her hair with a piece of string, right on top of her head she put the feather. Just as her mother was about to reach her, she jumped into the lake. The little feather was whirling around and around in the depths below. Of course the mother was very sad. She went, grieved, back to Acoma and climbed her mesa home. She stood on the edge of the mesa and scattered her daughter's clothing, the little moccasins, the *yashtoah*. She scattered them to the east, to the west, to the north, to the south. And the pieces of clothing and the moccasins and *yashtoah*, all turned into butterflies. And today they say that Acoma has more beautiful butterflies, red ones, white ones, blue ones, yellow ones. They came from this little girl's clothing.

Now this is a story anthropologists would consider very old. The version I have given you is just as Aunt Susie tells it. You can occasionally hear some English she picked up at Carlisle—words like "precipitous." You will also notice that there is a great deal of repetition, and a little reminder about *yashtoah,* and how it is made. There is a remark about the cliff trail at Acoma—that it was once there, but is there no longer. The story may be told at a time of sadness or loss, but within this story many other elements are brought together. Things are not separated out and categorized; all things are brought together, so that the reminder about the *yashtaoh* is valuable information that is repeated—a recipe, if you will. The information about the old trail at Acoma reveals that stories are, in a sense, maps, since even to this day there is little information or material about trails that is passed around with writing. In the structure of this story the repetitions are, of course, designed to help you remember. It is repeated again and again, and then it moves on.

The next story I would like to tell is by Simon Ortiz, from Acoma Pueblo. He is a wonderful poet who also works in narrative. One of the things I find very interesting in this short story is that if you listen very closely, you begin to hear what I was talking about in terms of a story never beginning at the beginning, and certainly never ending. As the Hopis sometimes say, "Well, it has gone this far for a while." There is always that implication of a continuing. The other thing I want you to listen for is the many stories within one story. Listen to the kinds of stories contained within the main story—stories that give one a family identity and an individual identity, for example. This story is called "Home Country":

"Well, it's been a while. I think in 1947 was when I left. My husband had   25
been killed in Okinawa some years before. And so I had no more husband. And I had to make a living. O I guess I could have looked for another man but I didn't want to. It looked like the war had made some of them into a bad way anyway. I saw some of them come home like that. They either got drunk or just stayed around a while or couldn't seem to be satisfied anymore with what was there. I guess now that I think about it, that happened to me too although I wasn't in the war not in the Army or even much off the reservation just that several years at the Indian School. Well there was that feeling things were changing not only the men the boys, but things were changing.

"One day the home nurse the nurse that came from the Indian health service was at my mother's home my mother was getting near the end real sick and she said that she had been meaning to ask me a question. I said what is the question. And the home nurse said well your mother is getting real sick and after she is no longer around for you to take care of, what will you be doing you and her are the only ones here. And I said I don't know. But I was thinking about it what she said made me think about it. And then the next time she came she said to me Eloise the government is hiring Indians now in the Indian schools to take care of the boys and girls I heard one of the supervisors saying that Indians are hard workers but you have to supervise them a lot and I thought of you well because you've been taking care of your mother real good and you follow all my instructions. She said I thought of you because you're a good Indian girl and you would be the kind of person for that job. I didn't say anything I had not ever really thought about a job but I kept thinking about it.

"Well my mother she died and we buried her up at the old place the cemetery there it's real nice on the east side of the hill where the sun shines warm and the wind doesn't blow too much sand around right there. Well I was sad we were all sad for a while but you know how things are. One of my aunties came over and she advised me and warned me about being too sorry about it and all that she wished me that I would not worry too much about it because old folks they go along pretty soon life is that way and then she said that maybe I ought to take in one of my aunties kids or two because there was a lot of them kids and I was all by myself now. But I was so young and I thought that I might do that you know take care of someone but I had been thinking too of what the home nurse said to me about working. Hardly anybody at our home was working at something like that no woman anyway. And I would have to move away.

"Well I did just that. I remember that day very well. I told my aunties and they were all crying and we all went up to the old highway where the bus to town passed by everyday. I was wearing an old kind of bluish sweater that was kind of big that one of my cousins who was older had got from a white person a tourist one summer in trade for something she had made a real pretty basket. She gave me that and I used to have a picture of me with it on it's kind of real ugly. Yeah that was the day I left wearing a baggy sweater and carrying a suitcase that someone gave me too I think or maybe it was the home nurse there wasn't much in it anyway either. I was scared and everybody seemed to be sad I was so young and skinny then. My aunties said one of them who was real fat you make sure you eat now make your own tortillas drink the milk and stuff like candies is no good she learned that from the nurse. Make sure you got your letter my auntie said. I had it folded into my purse. Yes I had one too a brown one that my husband when he was still alive one time on furlough he brought it on my birthday it was a nice purse and still looked new because I never used it.

"The letter said that I had a job at Keams Canyon the boarding school there but I would have to go to the Agency first for some papers to be filled and that's where I was going first. The Agency. And then they would send me out to Keams Canyon. I didn't even know where it was except that someone of our relatives said that it was near Hopi. My uncles teased me about watching out for the Hopi men and boys don't let them get too close they said well you know how they are and they were pretty strict too about those things and then they were joking and then they were not too and so I said aw they won't get near to me I'm too ugly and I promised I would be careful anyway.

"So we all gathered for a while at my last auntie's house and then the old   30
man my grandfather brought his wagon and horses to the door and we all
got in and sat there for a while until my auntie told her father okay father
let's go and shook his elbow because the poor old man was old by then and
kind of going to sleep all the time you had to talk to him real loud. I had
about ten dollars I think that was a lot of money more than it is now you
know and when we got to the highway where the Indian road which is just a
dirt road goes off the pave road my grandfather reached into his blue jeans
and pulled out a silver dollar and put it into my hand. I was so shocked. We
were all so shocked. We all looked around at each other we didn't know
where the old man had gotten it because we were real poor two of my uncles
had to borrow on their accounts at the trading store for the money I had in
my purse but there it was a silver dollar so big and shining in my grandfather's hand and then in my hand.

"Well I was so shocked and everybody was so shocked that we all started
crying right there at the junction of that Indian road and the pave highway I
wanted to be a little girl again running after the old man when he hurried
with his long legs to the cornfields or went for water down to the river. He
was old then and his eye was turned gray and he didn't do much anymore
except drive the wagon and chop a little bit of wood but I just held him and
I just held him so tightly.

"Later on I don't know what happened to the silver dollar it had a date
of 1907 on it but I kept it for a long time because I guess I wanted to have
it to remember when I left my home country. What I did in between then
and now is another story but that's the time I moved away," is what
she said.*

There are a great many parallels between Pueblo experiences and those of
African and Caribbean peoples—one is that we have all had the conqueror's
language imposed on us. But our experience with English has been somewhat
different in that the Bureau of Indian Affairs schools were not interested in
teaching us the canon of Western classics. For instance, we never heard of
Shakespeare. We were given Dick and Jane, and I can remember reading that
the robins were heading south for the winter. It took me a long time to figure
out what was going on. I worried for quite a while about our robins in Laguna
because they didn't leave in the winter, until I finally realized that all the big
textbook companies are up in Boston and *their* robins do go south in the winter. But in a way, this dreadful formal education freed us by encouraging us to
maintain our narratives. Whatever literature we were exposed to at school
(which was damn little), at home the storytelling, the special regard for telling
and bringing together through the telling, was going on constantly.

---

*Simon J. Ortiz, *Howbah Indians* (Tucson: Blue Moon Press, 1978). [Author's note]

And as the old people say, "If you can remember the stories, you will be all right. Just remember the stories." When I returned to Laguna Pueblo after attending college, I wondered how the storytelling was continuing (anthropologists say that Laguna Pueblo is one of the more acculturated pueblos), so I visited an English class at Laguna-Acoma High School. I knew the students had cassette tape recorders in their lockers and stereos at home, and that they listened to Kiss and Led Zeppelin and were well informed about popular culture in general. I had with me an anthology of short stories by Native American writers, *The Man to Send Rain Clouds.* One story in the book is about the killing of a state policeman in New Mexico by three Acoma Pueblo men in the early 1950s. I asked the students how many had heard this story and steeled myself for the possibility that the anthropologists were right, that the old traditions were indeed dying out and the students would be ignorant of the story. But instead, all but one or two raised their hands—they had heard the story, just as I had heard it when I was young, some in English, some in Laguna.

One of the other advantages that we Pueblos have enjoyed is that we have   35 always been able to stay with the land. Our stories cannot be separated from their geographical locations, from actual physical places on the land. We were not relocated like so many Native American groups who were torn away from their ancestral land. And our stories are so much a part of these places that it is almost impossible for future generations to lose them—there is a story connected with every place, every object in the landscape.

Dennis Brutus has talked about the "yet unborn" as well as "those from the past," and how we are still *all* in *this* place, and language—the storytelling—is our way of passing through or being with them, or being together again. When Aunt Susie told her stories, she would tell a younger child to go open the door so that our esteemed predecessors might bring in their gifts to us. "They are out there," Aunt Susie would say. "Let them come in. They're here, they're here with us *within* the stories."

A few years ago, when Aunt Susie was 106, I paid her a visit, and while I was there she said, "Well, I'll be leaving here soon. I think I'll be leaving here next week, and I will be going over to the Cliff House." She said, "It's going to be real good to get back over there." I was listening, and I was thinking that she must be talking about her house at Paguate Village, just north of Laguna. And she went on, "Well, my mother's sister (and she gave her Indian name) will be there. She has been living there. She will be there and we will be over there, and I will get a chance to write down these stories I've been telling you." Now you understand, of course, that Aunt Susie's mother's sister, a great storyteller herself, has long since passed over into the land of the dead. But then I realized, too, that Aunt Susie wasn't talking about death the way most of us do. She was talking about "going over" as a journey, a journey that perhaps we can only begin to understand through an appreciation for the boundless capacity of language that, through storytelling, brings us together, despite great distances between cultures, despite great distances in time.

ACTIVITIES FOR WRITING AND DISCUSSION

1. In the first paragraph Silko comments on the structure her essay will take:

> For those of you accustomed to being taken from point A to point B to point C, this presentation may be somewhat difficult to follow. Pueblo expression resembles something like a spider's web—with many little threads radiating from the center, crisscrossing each other. As with the web, the structure emerges as it is made and you must simply listen and trust, as the Pueblo people do, that meaning will be made.

Do a postdraft outline (see Chapter 7) of all—or some sizable part of—Silko's essay. Then use your outline to show where and how her essay bears out her comments about "structure." Finally, what sorts of things does a "web"-like structure (as opposed to one that goes "from point A to point B to point C") imply about the outlook and values of the culture to which she belongs?

2. Based on your annotations of Silko's text, list and comment on the functions storytelling plays in Pueblo culture. Then, in your notebook, tell one or two particular stories that are important in your own family. What roles do the stories—and storytelling—play in your own family or larger culture? Do they serve any of the functions described by Silko?

3. Look again at the title of Silko's piece. Where in her essay does she discuss "literature"? Jot down your own definition of "literature"; then, as best you can, write down what you think Silko means by the term. How does her Pueblo concept of "literature" resemble and/or differ from your own? Finally, what do the differences suggest about differences between your culture and Silko's?

4. Reread the long story Silko quotes from Simon Ortiz.
   a. Identify and annotate "the many stories within one story" to which she refers.
   b. List and discuss any ways that Ortiz's narrative differs from ones common in your own culture.
   c. If you wish, write a story of your own in which you attempt to imitate the structure and oral style of Ortiz's text.

BRENT STAPLES (b. 1951)

Black Men and Public Space

My first victim was a woman—white, well dressed, probably in her early twenties. I came upon her late one evening on a deserted street in Hyde Park, a relatively affluent neighborhood in an otherwise mean, impoverished section of

Chicago. As I swung onto the avenue behind her, there seemed to be a discreet, uninflammatory distance between us. Not so. She cast back a worried glance. To her, the youngish black man—a broad six feet two inches with a beard and billowing hair, both hands shoved into the pockets of a bulky military jacket—seemed menacingly close. After a few more quick glimpses, she picked up her pace and was soon running in earnest. Within seconds she disappeared into a cross street.

That was more than a decade ago. I was twenty-two years old, a graduate student newly arrived at the University of Chicago. It was in the echo of that terrified woman's footfalls that I first began to know the unwieldy inheritance I'd come into—the ability to alter public space in ugly ways. It was clear that she thought herself the quarry of a mugger, a rapist, or worse. Suffering a bout of insomnia, however, I was stalking sleep, not defenseless wayfarers. As a softy who is scarcely able to take a knife to a raw chicken—let alone hold one to a person's throat—I was surprised, embarrassed, and dismayed all at once. Her flight made me feel like an accomplice in tyranny. It also made it clear that I was indistinguishable from the muggers who occasionally seeped into the area from the surrounding ghetto. That first encounter, and those that followed, signified that a vast, unnerving gulf lay between nighttime pedestrians—particularly women—and me. And I soon gathered that being perceived as dangerous is a hazard in itself. I only needed to turn a corner into a dicey situation, or crowd some frightened, armed person in a foyer somewhere, or make an errant move after being pulled over by a policeman. Where fear and weapons meet—and they often do in urban America—there is always the possibility of death.

In that first year, my first away from my hometown, I was to become thoroughly familiar with the language of fear. At dark, shadowy intersections, I could cross in front of a car stopped at a traffic light and elicit the *thunk, thunk, thunk, thunk* of the driver—black, white, male, or female—hammering down the door locks. On less traveled streets after dark, I grew accustomed to but never comfortable with people crossing to the other side of the street rather than pass me. Then there were the standard unpleasantries with policemen, doormen, bouncers, cabdrivers, and others whose business it is to screen out troublesome individuals *before* there is any nastiness.

I moved to New York nearly two years ago and I have remained an avid night walker. In central Manhattan, the near-constant crowd cover minimizes tense one-on-one street encounters. Elsewhere—in Soho, for example, where sidewalks are narrow and tightly spaced buildings shut out the sky—things can get very taut indeed.

After dark, on the warrenlike streets of Brooklyn where I live, I often see   5 women who fear the worst from me. They seem to have set their faces on neutral, and with their purse straps strung across their chests bandolier-style, they forge ahead as though bracing themselves against being tackled. I understand, of course, that the danger they perceive is not a hallucination. Women are particularly vulnerable to street violence, and young black males are drastically overrepresented among the perpetrators of that violence. Yet these truths are no solace against the kind of alienation that comes of being ever the suspect, a fearsome entity with whom pedestrians avoid making eye contact.

It is not altogether clear to me how I reached the ripe old age of twenty-two without being conscious of the lethality nighttime pedestrians attributed to me. Perhaps it was because in Chester, Pennsylvania, the small, angry industrial town where I came of age in the 1960s, I was scarcely noticeable against a backdrop of gang warfare, street knifings, and murders. I grew up one of the good boys, had perhaps a half-dozen fistfights. In retrospect, my shyness of combat has clear sources.

As a boy, I saw countless tough guys locked away; I have since buried several, too. They were babies, really—a teenage cousin, a brother of twenty-two, a childhood friend in his mid-twenties—all gone down in episodes of bravado played out in the streets. I came to doubt the virtues of intimidation early on. I chose, perhaps unconsciously, to remain a shadow—timid, but a survivor.

The fearsomeness mistakenly attributed to me in public places often has a perilous flavor. The most frightening of these confusions occurred in the late 1970s and early 1980s, when I worked as a journalist in Chicago. One day, rushing into the office of a magazine I was writing for with a deadline story in hand, I was mistaken for a burglar. The office manager called security and, with an ad hoc posse, pursued me though the labyrinthine halls, nearly to my editor's door. I had no way of proving who I was. I could only move briskly toward the company of someone who knew me.

Another time I was on assignment for a local paper and killing time before an interview. I entered a jewelry store on the city's affluent Near North Side. The proprietor excused herself and returned with an enormous red Doberman pinscher straining at the end of a leash. She stood, the dog extended toward me, silent to my questions, her eyes bulging nearly out of her head. I took a cursory look around, nodded, and bade her good night.

Relatively speaking, however, I never fared as badly as another black male journalist. He went to nearby Waukegan, Illinois, a couple of summers ago to work on a story about a murderer who was born there. Mistaking the reporter for the killer, police officers hauled him from his car at gunpoint and but for his press credentials would probably have tried to book him. Such episodes are not uncommon. Black men trade tales like this all the time. 10

Over the years, I learned to smother the rage I felt at so often being taken for a criminal. Not to do so would surely have led to madness. I now take precautions to make myself less threatening. I move about with care, particularly late in the evening. I give a wide berth to nervous people on subway platforms during the wee hours, particularly when I have exchanged business clothes for jeans. If I happen to be entering a building behind some people who appear skittish, I may walk by, letting them clear the lobby before I return, so as not to seem to be following them. I have been calm and extremely congenial on those rare occasions when I've been pulled over by the police.

And on late-evening constitutionals I employ what has proved to be an excellent tension-reducing measure: I whistle melodies from Beethoven and

Vivaldi and the more popular classical composers. Even steely New Yorkers hunching toward nighttime destinations seem to relax, and occasionally they even join in the tune. Virtually everybody seems to sense that a mugger wouldn't be warbling bright, sunny selections from Vivaldi's *Four Seasons*. It is my equivalent of the cowbell that hikers wear when they know they are in bear country.

Judith Ortiz Cofer (b. 1952)

The Myth of the Latin Woman: I Just Met a Girl Named Maria

On a bus trip to London from Oxford University where I was earning some graduate credits one summer, a young man, obviously fresh from a pub, spotted me and as if struck by inspiration went down on his knees in the aisle. With both hands over his heart he broke into an Irish tenor's rendition of "Maria" from *West Side Story*. My politely amused fellow passengers gave his lovely voice the round of gentle applause it deserved. Though I was not quite as amused, I managed my version of an English smile: no show of teeth, no extreme contortions of the facial muscles—I was at this time of my life practicing reserve and cool. Oh, that British control, how I coveted it. But "Maria" had followed me to London, reminding me of a prime fact of my life: you can leave the island, master the English language, and travel as far as you can, but if you are a Latina, especially one like me who so obviously belongs to Rita Moreno's gene pool, the island travels with you.

This is sometimes a very good thing—it may win you that extra minute of someone's attention. But with some people, the same things can make *you* an island—not a tropical paradise but an Alcatraz, a place nobody wants to visit. As a Puerto Rican girl living in the United States and wanting like most children to "belong," I resented the stereotype that my Hispanic appearance called forth from many people I met.

Growing up in a large urban center in New Jersey during the 1960s, I suffered from what I think of as "cultural schizophrenia." Our life was designed by my parents as a microcosm of their *casas* on the island. We spoke in Spanish, ate Puerto Rican food bought at the *bodega,* and practiced strict Catholicism at a church that allotted us a one-hour slot each week for mass, performed in Spanish by a Chinese priest trained as a missionary for Latin America.

As a girl I was kept under strict surveillance by my parents, since my virtue and modesty were, by their cultural equation, the same as their honor. As a teenager I was lectured constantly on how to behave as a *proper señorita*. But it was a conflicting message I received, since the Puerto Rican mothers also encouraged their daughters to look and act like women and to dress in clothes our

Anglo friends and their mothers found too "mature" and flashy. The difference was, and is, cultural; yet I often felt humiliated when I appeared at an American friend's party wearing a dress more suitable to a semi-formal than to a play-room birthday celebration. At Puerto Rican festivities, neither the music nor the colors we wore could be too loud.

I remember Career Day in our high school, when teachers told us to come 5 dressed as if for a job interview. It quickly became obvious that to the Puerto Rican girls "dressing up" meant wearing their mother's ornate jewelry and clothing, more appropriate (by mainstream standards) for the company Christmas party than as daily office attire. That morning I had agonized in front of my closet, trying to figure out what a "career girl" would wear. I knew how to dress for school (at the Catholic school I attended, we all wore uni-forms), I knew how to dress for Sunday mass, and I knew what dresses to wear for parties at my relatives' homes. Though I do not recall the precise details of my Career Day outfit, it must have been a composite of these choices. But I re-member a comment my friend (an Italian American) made in later years that coalesced my impressions of that day. She said that at the business school she was attending, the Puerto Rican girls always stood out for wearing "everything at once." She meant, of course, too much jewelry, too many accessories. On that day at school we were simply made the negative models by the nuns, who were themselves not credible fashion experts to any of us. But it was painfully obvi-ous to me that to the others, in their tailored skirts and silk blouses, we must have seemed "hopeless" and "vulgar." Though I now know that most adoles-cents feel out of step much of the time, I also know that for the Puerto Rican girls of my generation that sense was intensified. The way our teachers and classmates looked at us that day in school was just a taste of the cultural clash that awaited us in the real world, where prospective employers and men on the street would often misinterpret our tight skirts and jingling bracelets as a "come-on."

Mixed cultural signals have perpetuated certain stereotypes—for example, that of the Hispanic woman as the "hot tamale" or sexual firebrand. It is a one-dimensional view that the media have found easy to promote. In their special vocabulary, advertisers have designated "sizzling" and "smoldering" as the ad-jectives of choice for describing not only the foods but also the women of Latin America. From conversations in my house I recall hearing about the harass-ment that Puerto Rican women endured in factories where the "boss-men" talked to them as if sexual innuendo was all they understood, and worse, often gave them the choice of submitting to their advances or being fired.

It is custom, however, not chromosomes, that leads us to choose scarlet over pale pink. As young girls, it was our mothers who influenced our decisions about clothes and colors—mothers who had grown up on a tropical island where the natural environment was a riot of primary colors, where showing your skin was one way to keep cool as well as to look sexy. Most important of all, on the island, women perhaps felt freer to dress and move more provoca-tively since, in most cases, they were protected by the traditions, mores, and laws of a Spanish/Catholic system of morality and machismo whose main rule was: *You may look at my sister, but if you touch her I will kill you.* The extended family and church structure could provide a young woman with a circle of safety in her small pueblo on the island; if a man "wronged" a girl, everyone would close in to save her family honor.

My mother has told me about dressing in her best party clothes on Saturday nights and going to the town's plaza to promenade with her girlfriends in front of the boys they liked. The males were thus given an opportunity to admire the women and to express their admiration in the form of *piropos:* erotically charged street poems they composed on the spot. (I have myself been subjected to a few *piropos* while visiting the island, and they can be outrageous, although custom dictates that they must never cross into obscenity.) This ritual, as I understand it, also entails a show of studied indifference on the woman's part; if she is "decent," she must not acknowledge the man's impassioned words. So I do understand how things can be lost in translation. When a Puerto Rican girl dressed in her idea of what is attractive meets a man from the mainstream culture who has been trained to react to certain types of clothing as a sexual signal, a clash is likely to take place. I remember the boy who took me to my first formal dance leaning over to plant a sloppy, over-eager kiss painfully on my mouth; when I didn't respond with sufficient passion, he remarked resentfully: "I thought you Latin girls were supposed to mature early," as if I were expected to *ripen* like a fruit or vegetable, not just grow into womanhood like other girls.

It is surprising to my professional friends that even today some people, including those who should know better, still put others "in their place." It happened to me most recently during a stay at a classy metropolitan hotel favored by young professional couples for weddings. Late one evening after the theater, as I walked toward my room with a colleague (a woman with whom I was coordinating an arts program), a middle-aged man in a tuxedo, with a young girl in satin and lace on his arm, stepped directly into our path. With his champagne glass extended toward me, he exclaimed "Evita!"

Our way blocked, my companion and I listened as the man half-recited, 10 half-bellowed "Don't Cry for Me, Argentina," When he finished, the young girl said: "How about a round of applause for my daddy?" We complied, hoping this would bring the silly spectacle to a close. I was becoming aware that our little group was attracting the attention of the other guests. "Daddy" must have perceived this too, and he once more barred the way as we tried to walk past him. He began to shout-sing a ditty to the tune of "La Bamba"—except the lyrics were about a girl named Maria whose exploits rhymed with her name and gonorrhea. The girl kept saying "Oh, Daddy" and looking at me with pleading eyes. She wanted me to laugh along with the others. My companion and I stood silently waiting for the man to end his offensive song. When he finished, I looked not at him but at his daughter. I advised her calmly never to ask her father what he had done in the army. Then I walked between them and to my room. My friend complimented me on my cool handling of the situation, but I confessed that I had really wanted to push the jerk into the swimming pool. This same man—probably a corporate executive, well-educated, even worldly by most standards—would not have been likely to regale an Anglo woman with a dirty song in public. He might have checked his impulse by assuming that she could be somebody's wife or mother, or at least *somebody* who might take offense. But, to him, I was just an Evita or a Maria: merely a character in his cartoon-populated universe.

Another facet of the myth of the Latin woman in the United States is the menial, the domestic—Maria the housemaid or countergirl. It's true that work as domestics, as waitresses, and in factories is all that's available to women with little English and few skills. But the myth of the Hispanic menial—the funny maid, mispronouncing words and cooking up a spicy storm in a shiny California kitchen—has been perpetuated by the media in the same way that "Mammy" from *Gone with the Wind* became America's idea of the black woman for generations. Since I do not wear my diplomas around my neck for all to see, I have on occasion been sent to that "kitchen" where some think I obviously belong.

One incident has stayed with me, though I recognize it as a minor offense. My first public poetry reading took place in Miami, at a restaurant where a luncheon was being held before the event. I was nervous and excited as I walked in with notebook in hand. An older woman motioned me to her table, and thinking (foolish me) that she wanted me to autograph a copy of my newly published slender volume of verse, I went over. She ordered a cup of coffee from me, assuming I was the waitress. (Easy enough to mistake my poems for menus, I suppose.) I know it wasn't an intentional act of cruelty. Yet of all the good things that happened later, I remember that scene most clearly, because it reminded me of what I had to overcome before anyone would take me seriously. In retrospect I understand that my anger gave my reading fire. In fact, I have almost always taken any doubt in my abilities as a challenge, the result most often being the satisfaction of winning a convert, of seeing the cold, appraising eyes warm to my words, the body language change, the smile that indicates I have opened some avenue for communication. So that day as I read, I looked directly at that woman. Her lowered eyes told me she was embarrassed at her faux pas, and when I willed her to look up at me, she graciously allowed me to punish her with my full attention. We shook hands at the end of the reading and I never saw her again. She has probably forgotten the entire incident, but maybe not.

Yet I am one of the lucky ones. There are thousands of Latinas without the privilege of an education or the entrees into society that I have. For them life is a constant struggle against the misconceptions perpetuated by the myth of the Latina. My goal is to try to replace the old stereotypes with a much more interesting set of realities. Every time I give a reading, I hope the stories I tell, the dreams and fears I examine in my work, can achieve some universal truth that will get my audience past the particulars of my skin color, my accent, or my clothes.

I once wrote a poem in which I called all Latinas "God's brown daughters." This poem is really a prayer of sorts, offered upward, but also, through the human-to-human channel of art, outward. It is a prayer for communication and for respect. In it, Latin women pray "in Spanish to an Anglo God / with a

Jewish heritage," and they are "fervently hoping / that if not omnipotent, / at least He be bilingual."

ACTIVITIES FOR WRITING AND DISCUSSION

1. In paragraph #13 Cofer writes that "My goal is to try to replace the old stereotypes with a much more interesting set of realities." What, specifically, are "the old stereotypes" she wants to remove (list and describe them) and what is the "more interesting set of realities" she wants to substitute? Does she achieve her goal in this essay? Explain.

2. Explain what Cofer means by the phrase, "mixed cultural signals" (see paragraph #6). Then share any stories of times when *you* have experienced "mixed cultural signals" (or, alternatively, when someone you know has experienced them). What was the context? Who was involved, and what was the source of the confusion? How did you react? What was the final outcome? What, if anything, did you learn about yourself and/or "cultures" through the experience? For this activity, "culture" can be understood variously to refer to race, ethnicity, religion, belief, social group, social class, etc.

3. After you have drafted a response to activity #2, expand it by adding, where appropriate, illustrative dialogue or description as Cofer does in *her* stories.

4. Some debates over "cultures" seem only to inflame passions and prejudices on all sides. Does Cofer's essay, her submission to the debate, do so? Why or why not? To answer this question, examine Cofer's **persona** and how, paragraph by paragraph, it goes about dismantling "the myth of the Latin woman." What strategies does Cofer use to appeal to her readers, and how do those strategies persuade—or repel—*you*?

BELL HOOKS (b. 1952)

Keeping Close to Home: Class and Education

We are both awake in the almost dark of 5 A.M. Everyone else is sound asleep. Mama asks the usual questions. Telling me to look around, make sure I have everything, scolding me because I am uncertain about the actual time the bus arrives. By 5:30 we are waiting outside the closed station. Alone together, we have a chance to really talk. Mama begins. Angry with her children, especially the ones who whisper behind her back, she says bitterly, "Your childhood could not have been that bad. You were fed and clothed. You did not have to do without—that's more than a lot of folks have and I just can't stand the way y'all go on." The hurt in her voice saddens me. I have always wanted to protect mama from hurt, to ease her burdens. Now I am part of what troubles. Confronting me, she says accusingly, "It's not just the other children. You talk too much about the past. You don't just listen." And I do talk. Worse, I write about it.

Mama has always come to each of her children seeking different responses. With me she expresses the disappointment, hurt, and anger of betrayal: anger that her children are so critical, that we can't even have the sense to like the presents she sends. She says, "From now on there will be no presents. I'll just stick some money in a little envelope the way the rest of you do. Nobody wants criticism. Everybody can criticize me but I am supposed to say nothing." When I try to talk, my voice sounds like a twelve year old. When I try to talk, she speaks louder, interrupting me, even though she has said repeatedly, "Explain it to me, this talk about the past." I struggle to return to my thirty-five year old self so that she will know by the sound of my voice that we are two women talking together. It is only when I state firmly in my very adult voice, "Mama, you are not listening," that she becomes quiet. She waits. Now that I have her attention, I fear that my explanations will be lame, inadequate. "Mama," I begin, "people usually go to therapy because they feel hurt inside, because they have pain that will not stop, like a wound that continually breaks open, that does not heal. And often these hurts, that pain has to do with things that have happened in the past, sometimes in childhood, often in childhood, or things that we believe happened." She wants to know, "What hurts, what hurts are you talking about?" "Mom, I can't answer that. I can't speak for all of us, the hurts are different for everybody. But the point is you try to make the hurt better, to heal it, by understanding how it came to be. And I know you feel mad when we say something happened or hurt that you don't remember being that way, but the past isn't like that, we don't have the same memory of it. We remember things differently. You know that. And sometimes folk feel hurt about stuff and you just don't know or didn't realize it, and they need to talk about it. Surely you understand the need to talk about it."

Our conversation is interrupted by the sight of my uncle walking across the park toward us. We stop to watch him. He is on his way to work dressed in a familiar blue suit. They look alike, these two who rarely discuss the past. This interruption makes me think about life in a small town. You always see someone you know. Interruptions, intrusions are part of daily life. Privacy is difficult to maintain. We leave our private space in the car to greet him. After the hug and kiss he has given me every year since I was born, they talk about the day's funerals. In the distance the bus approaches. He walks away knowing that they will see each other later. Just before I board the bus I turn, staring into my mother's face. I am momentarily back in time, seeing myself eighteen years ago, at this same bus stop, staring into my mother's face, continually turning back, waving farewell as I returned to college—that experience which first took me away from our town, from family. Departing was as painful then as it is now. Each movement away makes return harder. Each separation intensifies distance, both physical and emotional.

To a southern black girl from a working-class background who had never been on a city bus, who had never stepped on an escalator, who had never travelled by plane, leaving the comfortable confines of a small town Kentucky life to attend Stanford University was not just frightening; it was utterly painful. My parents had not been delighted that I had been accepted and adamantly opposed my going so far from home. At the time, I did not see their opposition as an expression of their fear that they would lose me forever. Like many working-class folks, they feared what college education might do to their children's minds even as they unenthusiastically acknowledged its importance. They did not understand why I could not attend a college nearby, an all-black college. To them, any college would do. I would graduate, become a school teacher, make a decent living and a good marriage. And even though they reluctantly and skeptically supported my educational endeavors, they also subjected them to constant harsh and bitter critique. It is difficult for me to talk about my parents and their impact on me because they have always felt wary, ambivalent, mistrusting of my intellectual aspirations even as they have been caring and supportive. I want to speak about these contradictions because sorting through them, seeking resolution and reconciliation has been important to me both as it affects my development as a writer, my effort to be fully self-realized, and my longing to remain close to the family and community that provided the groundwork for much of my thinking, writing, and being.

Studying at Stanford, I began to think seriously about class differences. To   5 be materially underprivileged at a university where most folks (with the exception of workers) are materially privileged provokes such thought. Class differences were boundaries no one wanted to face or talk about. It was easier to downplay them, to act as though we were all from privileged backgrounds, to work around them, to confront them privately in the solitude of one's room, or to pretend that just being chosen to study at such an institution meant that those of us who did not come from privilege were already in transition toward privilege. To not long for such transition marked one as rebellious, as unlikely to succeed. It was a kind of treason not to believe that it was better to be identified with the world of material privilege than with the world of the working class, the poor. No wonder our working-class parents from poor backgrounds feared our entry into such a world, intuiting perhaps that we might learn to be ashamed of where we had come from, that we might never return home, or come back only to lord it over them.

Though I hung with students who were supposedly radical and chic, we did not discuss class. I talked to no one about the sources of my shame, how it hurt me to witness the contempt shown the brown-skinned Filipina maids who cleaned our rooms, or later my concern about the $100 a month I paid for a room off-campus which was more than half of what my parents paid for rent. I talked to no one about my efforts to save money, to send a little something home. Yet these class realities separated me from fellow students. We were moving in different directions. I did not intend to forget my class background or alter my class allegiance. And even though I received an education designed to provide me with a bourgeois sensibility, passive acquiescence was not my only option. I knew that I could resist. I could rebel. I could shape the direction and focus of the various forms of knowledge available to me. Even though I some-times envied and longed for greater material advantages (particularly at vaca-tion times when I would be one of few if any students remaining in the dormitory because there was no money for travel), I did not share the sensibil-ity and values of my peers. That was important—class was not just about money; it was about values which showed and determined behavior. While I of-ten needed more money, I never needed a new set of beliefs and values. For ex-ample, I was profoundly shocked and disturbed when peers would talk abut their parents without respect, or would even say that they hated their parents. This was especially troubling to me when it seemed that these parents were car-ing and concerned. It was often explained to me that such hatred was "healthy and normal." To my white, middle-class California roommate, I explained the way we were taught to value our parents and their care, to understand that they were not obligated to give us care. She would always shake her head, laughing all the while, and say, "Missy, you will learn that it's different here, that we think differently." She was right. Soon, I lived alone, like the one Mormon student who kept to himself as he made a concentrated effort to remain true to his reli-gious beliefs and values. Later in graduate school I found that classmates be-lieved "lower class" people had no beliefs and values. I was silent in such discussions, disgusted by their ignorance.

Carol Stack's anthropological study, *All Our Kin,* was one of the first books I read which confirmed my experiential understanding that within black culture (especially among the working class and poor, particularly in southern states), a value system emerged that was counter-hegemonic, that challenged notions of individualism and private property so important to the maintenance of white-supremacist, capitalist patriarchy. Black folk created in marginal spaces a world of community and collectivity where resources were shared. In the pref-ace to *Feminist Theory: from margin to center,* I talked about how the point of difference, this marginality can be the space for the formation of an opposi-tional world view. That world view must be articulated, named if it is to pro-vide a sustained blueprint for change. Unfortunately, there has existed no consistent framework for such naming. Consequently both the experience of this difference and documentation of it (when it occurs) gradually loses pres-ence and meaning.

Much of what Stack documented about the "culture of poverty," for exam-ple, would not describe interactions among most black poor today irrespective of geographical setting. Since the black people she described did not acknowl-edge (if they recognized it in theoretical terms) the oppositional value of their world view, apparently seeing it more as a survival strategy determined less by conscious efforts to oppose oppressive race and class biases than by circum-stance, they did not attempt to establish a framework to transmit their beliefs and values from generation to generation. When circumstances changed, val-ues altered. Efforts to assimilate the values and beliefs of privileged white people, presented through media like television, undermine and destroy potential structures of opposition.

Increasingly, young black people are encouraged by the dominant culture (and by those black people who internalize the values of this hegemony) to believe that assimilation is the only possible way to survive, to succeed. Without the framework of an organized civil rights or black resistance struggle, individual and collective efforts at black liberation that focus on the primacy of self-definition and self-determination often go unrecognized. It is crucial that those among us who resist and rebel, who survive and succeed, speak openly and honestly about our lives and the nature of our personal struggles, the means by which we resolve and reconcile contradictions. This is no easy task. Within the educational institutions where we learn to develop and strengthen our writing and analytical skills, we also learn to think, write, and talk in a manner that shifts attention away from personal experience. Yet if we are to reach our people and all people, if we are to remain connected (especially those of us whose familial backgrounds are poor and working-class), we must understand that the telling of one's personal story provides a meaningful example, a way for folks to identify and connect.

Combining personal with critical analysis and theoretical perspectives can 10 engage listeners who might otherwise feel estranged, alienated. To speak simply with language that is accessible to as many folks as possible is also important. Speaking about one's personal experience or speaking with simple language is often considered by academics and/or intellectuals (irrespective of their political inclinations) to be a sign of intellectual weakness or even anti-intellectualism. Lately, when I speak, I do not stand in place—reading my paper, making little or no eye contact with audiences—but instead make eye contact, talk extemporaneously, digress, and address the audience directly. I have been told that people assume I am not prepared, that I am anti-intellectual, unprofessional (a concept that has everything to do with class as it determines actions and behavior), or that I am reinforcing the stereotype of black people as non-theoretical and gutsy.

Such criticism was raised recently by fellow feminist scholars after a talk I gave at Northwestern University at a conference on "Gender, Culture, Politics" to an audience that was mainly students and academics. I deliberately chose to speak in a very basic way, thinking especially about the few community folks who had come to hear me. Weeks later, KumKum Sangari, a fellow participant who shared with me what was said when I was no longer present, and I engaged in quite rigorous critical dialogue about the way my presentation had been perceived primarily by privileged white female academics. She was concerned that I not mask my knowledge of theory, that I not appear anti-intellectual. Her critique compelled me to articulate concerns that I am often silent about with colleagues. I spoke about class allegiance and revolutionary commitments, explaining that it was disturbing to me that intellectual radicals who speak about transforming society, ending the domination of race, sex, class, cannot break with behavior patterns that reinforce and perpetuate domination, or continue to use as their sole reference point how we might be or are perceived by those who dominate whether or not we gain their acceptance and approval.

This is a primary contradiction which raises the issue of whether or not the academic setting is a place where one can be truly radical or subversive. Concurrently, the use of a language and style of presentation that alienates most folks who are not also academically trained reinforces the notion that the academic world is separate from real life, that everyday world where we constantly adjust our language and behavior to meet diverse needs. The academic setting is separate only when we work to make it so. It is a false dichotomy which suggests that academics and/or intellectuals can only speak to one another, that we cannot hope to speak with the masses. What is true is that we make choices, that we choose our audiences, that we choose voices to hear and voices to silence. If I do not speak in a language that can be understood, then there is little chance for dialogue. This issue of language and behavior is a central contradiction all radical intellectuals, particularly those who are members of oppressed groups, must continually confront and work to resolve. One of the clear and present dangers that exists when we move outside our class of origin, our collective ethnic experience, and enter hierarchical institutions which daily reinforce domination by race, sex, and class, is that we gradually assume a mindset similar to those who dominate and oppress, that we lose critical consciousness because it is not reinforced or affirmed by the environment. We must be ever vigilant. It is important that we know who we are speaking to, who we most want to hear us, who we most long to move, motivate, and touch with our words.

When I first came to New Haven to teach at Yale, I was truly surprised by the marked class divisions between black folks—students and professors—who identify with Yale and those black folks who work at Yale or in surrounding communities. Style of dress and self-presentation are most often the central markers of one's position. I soon learned that the black folks who spoke on the street were likely to be part of the black community and those who carefully shifted their glance were likely to be associated with Yale. Walking with a black female colleague one day, I spoke to practically every black person in sight (a gesture which reflects my upbringing), an action which disturbed my companion. Since I addressed black folk who were clearly not associated with Yale, she wanted to know whether or not I knew them. That was funny to me. "Of course not," I answered. Yet when I thought about it seriously, I realized that in a deep way, I knew them for they, and not my companion or most of my colleagues at Yale, resemble my family. Later that year, in a black women's support group I started for undergraduates, students from poor backgrounds spoke about the shame they sometimes feel when faced with the reality of their connection to working-class and poor black people. One student confessed that her father is a street person, addicted to drugs, someone who begs from passersby. She, like other Yale students, turns away from street people often, sometimes showing anger or contempt; she hasn't wanted anyone to know that she was related to this kind of person. She struggles with this, wanting to find a way to acknowledge and affirm this reality, to claim this connection. The group asked me and one another what we [should] do to remain connected, to honor the bonds we have with working-class and poor people even as our class experience alters.

Maintaining connections with family and community across class boundaries demands more than just summary recall of where one's roots are, where one comes from. It requires knowing, naming, and being ever-mindful of those aspects of one's past that have enabled and do enable one's self-development in the present, that sustain and support, that enrich. One must also honestly confront barriers that do exist, aspects of that past that do diminish. My parents' ambivalence about my love for reading led to intense conflict. They (especially my mother) would work to ensure that I had access to books, but would threaten to burn the books or throw them away if I did not conform to other expectations. Or they would insist that reading too much would drive me insane. Their ambivalence nurtured in me a like uncertainty about the value and significance of intellectual endeavor which took years for me to unlearn. While this aspect of our class reality was one that wounded and diminished, their vigilant insistence that being smart did not make me a "better" or "superior" person (which often got on my nerves because I think I wanted to have that sense that it did indeed set me apart, make me better) made a profound impression. From them I learned to value and respect various skills and talents folk might have, not just to value people who read books and talk about ideas. They and my grandparents might say about somebody, "Now he don't read nor write a lick, but he can tell a story," or as my grandmother would say, "call out the hell in words."

Empty romanticization of poor or working-class backgrounds undermines   15 the possibility of true connection. Such connection is based on understanding difference in experience and perspective and working to mediate and negotiate these terrains. Language is a crucial issue for folk whose movement outside the boundaries of poor and working-class backgrounds changes the nature and direction of their speech. Coming to Stanford with my own version of a Kentucky accent, which I think of always as a strong sound quite different from Tennessee or Georgia speech, I learned to speak differently while maintaining the speech of my region, the sound of my family and community. This was of course much easier to keep up when I returned home to stay often. In recent years, I have endeavored to use various speaking styles in the classroom as a teacher and find it disconcerts those who feel that the use of a particular patois excludes them as listeners, even if there is translation into the usual, acceptable mode of speech. Learning to listen to different voices, having different speech challenges the notion that we must all assimilate—share a single, similar talk—in educational institutions. Language reflects the culture from which we emerge. To deny ourselves daily use of speech patterns that are common and familiar, that embody the unique and distinctive aspect of our self is one of the ways we become estranged and alienated from our past. It is important for us to have as many languages on hand as we can know or learn. It is important for those of us who are black, who speak in particular patois as well as standard English, to express ourselves in both ways.

Often I tell students from poor and working-class backgrounds that if you believe what you have learned and are learning in schools and universities separates you from your past, this is precisely what will happen. It is important to stand firm in the conviction that nothing can truly separate us from our pasts when we nurture and cherish that connection. An important strategy for maintaining contact is ongoing acknowledgement of the primacy of one's past, of one's background, affirming the reality that such bonds are not severed automatically solely because one enters a new environment or moves toward a different class experience.

Again, I do not wish to romanticize this effort, to dismiss the reality of conflict and contradiction. During my time at Stanford, I did go through a period of more than a year when I did not return home. That period was one where I felt that it was simply too difficult to mesh my profoundly disparate realities. Critical reflection about the choice I was making, particularly about why I felt a choice had to be made, pulled me through this difficult time. Luckily I recognized that the insistence on choosing between the world of family and community and the new world of privileged white people and privileged ways of knowing was imposed upon me by the outside. It is as though a mythical contract had been signed somewhere which demanded of us black folks that once we entered these spheres we would immediately give up all vestiges of our underprivileged past. It was my responsibility to formulate a way of being that would allow me to participate fully in my new environment while integrating and maintaining aspects of the old.

One of the most tragic manifestations of the pressure black people feel to assimilate is expressed in the internalization of racist perspectives. I was shocked and saddened when I first heard black professors at Stanford downgrade and express contempt for black students, expecting us to do poorly, refusing to establish nurturing bonds. At every university I have attended as a student or worked at as a teacher, I have heard similar attitudes expressed with little or no understanding of factors that might prevent brilliant black students from performing to their full capability. Within universities, there are few educational and social spaces where students who wish to affirm positive ties to ethnicity—to blackness, to working-class backgrounds—can receive affirmation and support. Ideologically, the message is clear—assimilation is the way to gain acceptance and approval from those in power.

Many white people enthusiastically supported Richard Rodriguez's vehement contention in his autobiography, *Hunger of Memory,* that attempts to maintain ties with his Chicano background impeded his progress, that he had to sever ties with community and kin to succeed at Stanford and in the larger world, that family language, in his case Spanish, had to be made secondary or discarded. If the terms of success as defined by the standards of ruling groups within white-supremacist, capitalist patriarchy are the only standards that exist, then assimilation is indeed necessary. But they are not. Even in the face of powerful structures of domination, it remains possible for each of us, especially those of us who are members of oppressed and/or exploited groups as well as those radical visionaries who may have race, class, and sex privilege, to define and determine alternative standards, to decide on the nature and extent of compromise. Standards by which one's success is measured, whether student or professor, are quite different from those of us who wish to resist reinforcing the domination of race, sex, and class, who work to maintain and strengthen our ties with the oppressed, with those who lack material privilege, with our families who are poor and working-class.

When I wrote my first, book, *Ain't I a Woman: black women and feminism,*   20 the issue of class and its relationship to who one's reading audience might be came up for me around my decision not to use footnotes, for which I have been sharply criticized. I told people that my concern was that footnotes set class boundaries for readers, determining who a book is for. I was shocked that many academic folks scoffed at this idea. I shared that I went into working-class black communities as well as talked with family and friends to survey whether or not they ever read books with footnotes and found that they did not. A few did not know what they were, but most folks saw them as indicating that a book was for college-educated people. These responses influenced my decision. When some of my more radical college-educated friends freaked out about the absence of footnotes, I seriously questioned how we could ever imagine revolutionary transformation of society if such a small shift in direction could be viewed as threatening. Of course, many folks warned that the absence of footnotes would make the work less credible in academic circles. This information also highlighted the way in which class informs our choices. Certainly I did feel that choosing to use simple language, absence of footnotes, etc. would mean I was jeopardizing the possibility of being taken seriously in academic circles but then this was a political matter and a political decision. It utterly delights me that this has proven not to be the case and that the book is read by many academics as well as by people who are not college-educated.

Always our first response when we are motivated to conform or compromise within structures that reinforce domination must be to engage in critical reflection. Only by challenging ourselves to push against oppressive boundaries do we make the radical alternative possible, expanding the realm and scope of critical inquiry. Unless we share radical strategies, ways of rethinking and revisioning with students, with kin and community, with a larger audience, we risk perpetuating the stereotype that we succeed because we are the exception, different from the rest of our people. Since I left home and entered college, I am often asked, usually by white people, if my sisters and brothers are also high achievers. At the root of this question is the longing for reinforcement of the belief in "the exception" which enables race, sex, and class biases to remain intact. I am careful to separate what it means to be exceptional from a notion of "the exception."

Frequently I hear smart black folks, from poor and working-class backgrounds, stressing their frustration that at times family and community do not recognize that they are exceptional. Absence of positive affirmation clearly diminishes the longing to excel in academic endeavors. Yet it is important to distinguish between the absence of basic positive affirmation and the longing for continued reinforcement that we are special. Usually liberal white folks will willingly offer continual reinforcement of us as exceptions—as special. This can be both patronizing and very seductive. Since we often work in situations where we are isolated from other black folks, we can easily begin to feel that encouragement from white people is the primary or only source of support and recognition. Given the internalization of racism, it is easy to view this support as more validating and legitimizing than similar support from black people. Still, nothing takes the place of being valued and appreciated by one's own, by one's family and community. We share a mutual and reciprocal responsibility for affirming one another's successes. Sometimes we have to talk to our folks about the fact that we need their ongoing support and affirmation, that it is unique and special to us. In some cases we may never receive desired recognition and acknowledgement of specific achievements from kin. Rather than seeing this as a basis for estrangement, for severing connection, it is useful to explore other sources of nourishment and support.

I do not know that my mother's mother ever acknowledged my college education except to ask me once, "How can you live so far away from your people?" Yet she gave me sources of affirmation and nourishment, sharing the legacy of her quilt-making, of family history, of her incredible way with words. Recently, when our father retired after more than thirty years of work as a janitor, I wanted to pay tribute to this experience, to identify links between his work and my own as writer and teacher. Reflecting on our family past, I recalled ways he had been an impressive example of diligence and hard work, approaching tasks with a seriousness of concentration I work to mirror and develop, with a discipline I struggle to maintain. Sharing these thoughts with him keeps us connected, nurtures our respect for each other, maintaining a space, however large or small, where we can talk.

Open, honest communication is the most important way we maintain relationships with kin and community as our class experience and backgrounds change. It is as vital as the sharing of resources. Often financial assistance is given in circumstances where there is no meaningful contact. However helpful, this can also be an expression of estrangement and alienation. Communication between black folks from various experiences of material privilege was much easier when we were all in segregated communities sharing common experiences in relation to social institutions. Without this grounding, we must work to maintain ties, connection. We must assume greater responsibility for making and maintaining contact, connections that can shape our intellectual visions and inform our radical commitments.

The most powerful resource any of us can have as we study and teach in 25 university settings is full understanding and appreciation of the richness, beauty, and primacy of our familial and community backgrounds. Maintaining awareness of class differences, nurturing ties with the poor and working-class people who are our most intimate kin, our comrades in struggle, transforms and enriches our intellectual experience. Education as the practice of freedom becomes not a force which fragments or separates, but one that brings us closer, expanding our definitions of home and community.

_____

Play
_____

_____

AUGUST WILSON (b. 1945)

Fences

Characters

TROY MAXSON

JIM BONO, *Troy's friend*

ROSE, *Troy's wife*

LYONS, *Troy's oldest son by previous marriage*

GABRIEL, *Troy's brother*

CORY, *Troy and Rose's son*

RAYNELL, *Troy's daughter*

Setting: *The setting is the yard which fronts the only entrance to the Maxson household, an ancient two-story brick house set back off a small alley in a big-city neighborhood. The entrance to the house is gained by two or three steps leading to a wooden porch badly in need of paint.*

A relatively recent addition to the house and running its full width, the porch lacks congruence. It is a sturdy porch with a flat roof. One or two chairs of dubious value sit at one end where the kitchen window opens onto the porch. An old-fashioned icebox stands silent guard at the opposite end.

The yard is a small dirt yard, partially fenced, except for the last scene, with a wooden sawhorse, a pile of lumber, and other fence-building equipment set off to the side. Opposite is a tree from which hangs a ball made of rags. A baseball bat leans against the tree. Two oil drums serve as garbage receptacles and sit near the house at right to complete the setting.

The Play: *Near the turn of the century, the destitute of Europe sprang on the city with tenacious claws and an honest and solid dream. The city devoured them. They swelled its belly until it burst into a thousand furnaces and sewing machines, a thousand butcher shops and bakers' ovens, a thousand churches and hospitals and funeral parlors and money-lenders. The city grew. It nourished itself and offered each man a partnership limited only by his talent, his guile, and his willingness and capacity for hard work. For the immigrants of Europe, a dream dared and won true.*

The descendants of African slaves were offered no such welcome or participation. They came from places called the Carolinas and the Virginias, Georgia, Alabama, Mississippi, and Tennessee. They came strong, eager, searching. The city rejected them and they fled and settled along the riverbanks and under bridges in shallow, ramshackle houses made of sticks and tarpaper. They collected rags and wood. *They sold the use of their muscles and their bodies. They cleaned houses and washed clothes, they shined shoes, and in quiet desperation and vengeful pride, they stole, and lived in pursuit of their own dream. That they could breathe free, finally, and stand to meet life with the force of dignity and whatever eloquence the heart could call upon.*

By 1957, the hard-won victories of the European immigrants had solidified the industrial might of America. War had been confronted and won with new energies that used loyalty and patriotism as its fuel. Life was rich, full, and flourishing. The Milwaukee Braves won the World Series, and the hot winds of change that would make the sixties a turbulent, racing, dangerous, and provocative decade had not yet begun to blow full.

ACT I · SCENE I

It is 1957. TROY and BONO enter the yard, engaged in conversation. TROY is fifty-three years old, a large man with thick, heavy hands; it is this largeness that he strives to fill out and make an accommodation with. Together with his blackness, his largeness informs his sensibilities and the choices he has made in his life.

Of the two men, BONO is obviously the follower. His commitment to their friendship of thirty-odd years is rooted in his admiration of TROY's honesty, capacity for hard work, and his strength, which BONO seeks to emulate.

It is Friday night, payday, and the one night of the week the two men engage in a ritual of talk and drink. TROY is usually the most talkative and at times he can be crude and almost vulgar, though he is capable of rising to profound heights of expression. The men carry lunch buckets and wear or carry burlap aprons and are dressed in clothes suitable to their jobs as garbage collectors.

BONO: Troy, you ought to stop that lying!

TROY: I ain't lying! The nigger had a watermelon this big.
(He indicates with his hands.)
Talking about . . . "What watermelon, Mr. Rand?" I liked to fell out! "What watermelon, Mr. Rand?" . . . And it sitting there big as life.

BONO: What did Mr. Rand say?

TROY: Ain't said nothing. Figure if the nigger too dumb to know he carrying a watermelon, he wasn't gonna get much sense out of him. Trying to hide that great big old watermelon under his coat. Afraid to let the white man see him carry it home.

BONO: I'm like you . . . I ain't got no time for them kind of people.

TROY: Now what he look like getting mad cause he see the man from the union talking to Mr. Rand?

BONO: He come to me talking about . . . "Maxson gonna get us fired." I told him to get away from me with that. He walked away from me calling you a troublemaker. What Mr. Rand say?

TROY: Ain't said nothing. He told me to go down the Commissioner's office next Friday. They called me down there to see them.

BONO: Well, as long as you got your complaint filed, they can't fire you. That's what one of them white fellows tell me.

TROY: I ain't worried about them firing me. They gonna fire me cause I asked a question? That's all I did. I went to Mr. Rand and asked him, "Why? Why you got the white mens driving and the colored lifting?" Told him, "what's the matter, don't I count? You think only white fellows got sense enough to drive a truck. That ain't no paper job! Hell, anybody can drive a truck. How come you got all whites driving and the colored lifting?" He told me "take it to the union." Well, hell, that's what I done! Now they wanna come up with this pack of lies.

BONO: I told Brownie if the man come and ask him any questions . . . just tell the truth! It ain't nothing but something they done trumped up on you cause you filed a complaint on them.

TROY: Brownie don't understand nothing. All I want them to do is change the job description. Give everybody a chance to drive the truck. Brownie can't see that. He ain't got that much sense.

BONO: How you figure he be making out with that gal be up at Taylors' all the time . . . that Alberta gal?

TROY: Same as you and me. Getting just as much as we is. Which is to say nothing.

BONO: It is, huh? I figure you doing a little better than me . . . and I ain't saying what I'm doing.

TROY: Aw, nigger, look here . . . I know you. If you had got anywhere near that gal, twenty minutes later you be looking to tell somebody. And the first one you gonna tell . . . that you gonna want to brag to . . . is gonna be me.

BONO: I ain't saying that. I see where you be eyeing her.

TROY: I eye all the women. I don't miss nothing. Don't never let nobody tell you Troy Maxson don't eye the women.

BONO: You been doing more than eyeing her. You done bought her a drink or two.

TROY: Hell yeah, I bought her a drink! What that mean? I bought you one, too. What that mean cause I buy her a drink? I'm just being polite.

BONO: It's all right to buy her one drink. That's what you call being polite. But when you wanna be buying two or three . . . that's what you call eyeing her.

TROY: Look here, as long as you known me . . . you ever known me to chase after women?

BONO: Hell yeah! Long as I done known you. You forgetting I knew you when.

TROY: Naw, I'm talking about since I been married to Rose?

BONO: Oh, not since you been married to Rose. Now, that's the truth, there. I can say that.

TROY: All right then! Case closed.

BONO: I see you be walking up around Alberta's house. You supposed to be at Taylors' and you be walking up around there.

TROY: What you watching where I'm walking for? I ain't watching after you.

BONO: I seen you walking around there more than once.

TROY: Hell, you liable to see me walking anywhere! That don't mean nothing cause you see me walking around there.

BONO: Where she come from anyway? She just kinda showed up one day.

TROY: Tallahassee. You can look at her and tell she one of them Florida gals. They got some big healthy women down there. Grow them right up out of the ground. Got a little bit of Indian in her. Most of them niggers down in Florida got some Indian in them.

BONO: I don't know about that Indian part. But she damn sure big and healthy. Woman wear some big stockings. Got them great big old legs and hips as wide as the Mississippi River.

TROY: Legs don't mean nothing. You don't do nothing but push them out of the way. But them hips cushion the ride!

BONO: Troy, you ain't got no sense.

TROY: It's the truth! Like you riding on Goodyears!

(ROSE *enters from the house. She is ten years younger than* TROY, *her devotion to him stems from her recognition of the possibilities of her life without him: a succession of abusive men and their babies, a life of partying and running the streets, the Church, or aloneness with its attendant pain and frustration. She recognizes* TROY'S *spirit as a fine and illuminating one and she either ignores or forgives his faults, only some of which she recognizes. Though she doesn't drink, her presence is an integral part of the Friday night rituals. She alternates between the porch and the kitchen, where supper preparations are under way.*)

ROSE: What you all out here getting into?

TROY: What you worried about what we getting into for? This is men talk, woman.

ROSE: What I care what you all talking about? Bono, you gonna stay for supper?

BONO: No, I thank you, Rose. But Lucille say she cooking up a pot of pigfeet.

TROY: Pigfeet! Hell, I'm going home with you! Might even stay the night if you got some pigfeet. You got something in there to top them pigfeet, Rose?

ROSE: I'm cooking up some chicken. I got some chicken and collard greens.

TROY: Well, go on back in the house and let me and Bono finish what we was talking about. This is men talk. I got some talk for you later. You know what kind of talk I mean. You go on and powder it up.

ROSE: Troy Maxson, don't you start that now!

TROY (*puts his arm around her*): Aw, woman . . . come here. Look here, Bono . . . when I met this woman . . . I got out that place, say, "Hitch up my pony, saddle up my mare . . . there's a woman out there for me somewhere. I looked here. Looked there. Saw Rose and latched on to her." I latched on to her and told her—I'm gonna tell you the truth—I told her, "Baby, I don't wanna marry, I just wanna be your man." Rose told me . . . tell him what you told me, Rose.

ROSE: I told him if he wasn't the marrying kind, then move out the way so the marrying kind could find me.

TROY: That's what she told me. "Nigger, you in my way. You blocking the view! Move out the way so I can find me a husband." I thought it over two or three days. Come back—

ROSE: Ain't no two or three days nothing. You was back the same night.

TROY: Come back, told her . . . "Okay, baby . . . but I'm gonna buy me a banty rooster and put him out there in the backyard . . . and when he see a stranger come, he'll flap his wings and crow . . ." Look here, Bono, I could watch the front door by myself . . . it was that back door I was worried about.

ROSE: Troy, you ought not talk like that. Troy ain't doing nothing but telling a lie.

TROY: Only thing is . . . when we first got married . . . forget the rooster . . . we ain't had no yard!

BONO: I hear you tell it. Me and Lucille was staying down there on Logan Street. Had two rooms with the outhouse in the back. I ain't mind the outhouse none. But when that goddamn wind blow through there in the winter . . . that's what I'm talking about! To this day I wonder why in the hell I ever stayed down there for six long years. But see, I didn't know I could do no better. I thought only white folks had inside toilets and things.

ROSE: There's a lot of people don't know they can do no better than they doing now. That's just something you got to learn. A lot of folks still shop at Bella's.

TROY: Ain't nothing wrong with shopping at Bella's. She got fresh food.

ROSE: I ain't said nothing about if she got fresh food. I'm talking about what she charge. She charge ten cents more than the A&P.

TROY: The A&P ain't never done nothing for me. I spends my money where I'm treated right. I go down to Bella, say, "I need a loaf of bread, I'll pay you Friday." She give it to me. What sense that make when I got money to go and spend it somewhere else and ignore the person who done right by me? That ain't in the Bible.

ROSE: We ain't talking about what's in the Bible. What sense it make to shop there when she overcharge?

TROY: You shop where you want to. I'll do my shopping where the people been good to me.

ROSE: Well, I don't think it's right for her to overcharge. That's all I was saying.

BONO: Look here . . . I got to get on. Lucille going be raising all kind of hell.

TROY: Where you going, nigger? We ain't finished this pint. Come here, finish this pint.

BONO: Well, hell, I am . . . if you ever turn the bottle loose.

TROY (*hands him the bottle):* The only thing I say about the A&P is I'm glad Cory got that job down there. Help him take care of his school clothes and things. Gabe done moved out and things getting tight around here. He got that job. . . . He can start to look out for himself.

ROSE: Cory done went and got recruited by a college football team.

TROY: I told that boy about that football stuff. The white man ain't gonna let him get nowhere with that football. I told him when he first come to me with it. Now you come telling me he done went and got more tied up in it. He ought to go and get recruited in how to fix cars or something where he can make a living.

ROSE: He ain't talking about making no living playing football. It's just something the boys in school do. They gonna send a recruiter by to talk to you. He'll tell you he ain't talking about making no living playing football. It's a honor to be recruited.

TROY: It ain't gonna get him nowhere. Bono'll tell you that.

BONO: If he be like you in the sports . . . he's gonna be all right. Ain't but two men ever played baseball as good as you. That's Babe Ruth and Josh Gibson. Them's the only two men ever hit more home runs than you.

TROY: What it ever get me? Ain't got a pot to piss in or a window to throw it out of.

ROSE: Times have changed since you was playing baseball, Troy. That was before the war. Times have changed a lot since then.

TROY: How in hell they done changed?

ROSE: They got lots of colored boys playing ball now. Baseball and football.

BONO: You right about that, Rose. Times have changed, Troy. You just come along too early.

TROY: There ought not never have been no time called too early! Now you take that fellow . . . what's that fellow they had playing right field for the Yankees back then? You know who I'm talking about, Bono. Used to play right field for the Yankees.

ROSE: Selkirk?

TROY: Selkirk! That's it! Man batting .269, understand? .269. What kind of sense that make? I was hitting .432 with thirty-seven home runs! Man batting .269 and playing right field for the Yankees! I saw Josh Gibson's daughter yesterday. She walking around with raggedy shoes on her feet. Now I bet you Selkirk's daughter ain't walking around with raggedy shoes on her feet! I bet you that!

ROSE: They got a lot of colored baseball players now. Jackie Robinson was the first. Folks had to wait for Jackie Robinson.

TROY: I done seen a hundred niggers play baseball better than Jackie Robinson. Hell, I know some teams Jackie Robinson couldn't even make! What you talking about Jackie Robinson. Jackie Robinson wasn't nobody. I'm talking about if you could play ball then they ought to have let you play. Don't care what color you were. Come telling me I come along too early. If you could play . . . then they ought to have let you play.

(TROY *takes a long drink from the bottle.*)

ROSE: You gonna drink yourself to death. You don't need to be drinking like that.

TROY: Death ain't nothing. I done seen him. Done wrassled with him. You can't tell me nothing about death. Death ain't nothing but a fastball on the outside corner. And you know what I'll do to that! Lookee here, Bono . . . am I lying? You get one of them fastballs, about waist high, over the outside corner of the plate where you can get the meat of the bat on it . . . and good god! You can kiss it goodbye. Now, am I lying?

BONO: Naw, you telling the truth there. I seen you do it.

TROY: If I'm lying . . . that 450 feet worth of lying!

(Pause.)

That's all death is to me. A fastball on the outside corner.

ROSE: I don't know why you want to get on talking about death.

TROY: Ain't nothing wrong with talking about death. That's part of life. Everybody gonna die. You gonna die, I'm gonna die. Bono's gonna die. Hell, we all gonna die.

ROSE: But you ain't got to talk about it. I don't like to talk about it.

TROY: You the one brought it up. Me and Bono was talking about baseball . . . you tell me I'm gonna drink myself to death. Ain't that right, Bono? You know I don't drink this but one night out of the week. That's Friday night. I'm gonna drink just enough to where I can handle it. Then I cuts it loose. I leave it alone. So don't you worry about me drinking myself to death. 'Cause I ain't worried about Death. I done seen him. I done wrestled with him.

Look here, Bono . . . I looked up one day and Death was marching straight at me. Like Soldiers on Parade! The Army of Death was marching straight at me. The middle of July, 1941. It got real cold just like it be winter. It seem like Death himself reached out and touched me on the shoulder. He touch me just like I touch you. I got cold as ice and Death standing there grinning at me.

ROSE: Troy, why don't you hush that talk.

TROY: I say . . . What you want, Mr. Death? You be wanting me? You done brought your army to be getting me? I looked him dead in the eye. I wasn't fearing nothing. I was ready to tangle. Just like I'm ready to tangle now. The Bible say be ever vigilant. That's why I don't get but so drunk. I got to keep watch.

ROSE: Troy was right down there in Mercy Hospital. You remember he had pneumonia? Laying there with a fever talking plumb out of his head.

TROY: Death standing there staring at me . . . carrying that sickle in his hand. Finally he say, "You want bound over for another year?" See, just like that . . . "You want bound over for another year?" I told him, "Bound over hell! Let's settle this now!"

It seem like he kinda fell back when I said that, and all the cold went out of me. I reached down and grabbed that sickle and threw it just as far as I could throw it . . . and me and him commenced to wrestling.

We wrestled for three days and three nights. I can't say where I found the strength from. Every time it seemed like he was gonna get the best of me, I'd reach way down deep inside myself and find the strength to do him one better.

ROSE: Every time Troy tell that story he find different ways to tell it. Different things to make up about it.

TROY: I ain't making up nothing. I'm telling you the facts of what happened. I wrestled with Death for three days and three nights and I'm standing here to tell you about it.

(Pause.)

All right. At the end of the third night we done weakened each other to where we can't hardly move. Death stood up, throwed on his robe . . . had him a white robe with a hood on it. He threw on that robe and went off to look for his sickle. Say, "I'll be back." Just like that. "I'll be back." I told him, say, "Yeah, but . . . you gonna have to find me!" I wasn't no fool. I wan't going looking for him. Death ain't nothing to play with. And I know he's gonna get me. I know I got to join his army . . . his camp followers. But as long as I keep my strength and see him coming . . . as long as I keep up my vigilance . . . he's gonna have to fight to get me. I ain't going easy.

BONO: Well, look here, since you got to keep up your vigilance . . . let me have the bottle.

TROY: Aw hell, I shouldn't have told you that part. I should have left out that part.

ROSE: Troy be talking that stuff and half the time don't even know what he be talking about.

TROY: Bono know me better than that.

BONO: That's right. I know you. I know you got some Uncle Remus in your blood. You got more stories than the devil got sinners.

TROY: Aw hell, I done seen him too! Done talked with the devil.

ROSE: Troy, don't nobody wanna be hearing all that stuff.

(LYONS *enters the yard from the street. Thirty-four years old,* TROY'S *son by a previous marriage, he sports a neatly trimmed goatee, sport coat, white shirt, tieless and buttoned at the collar. Though he fancies himself a musician, he is more caught up in the rituals and "idea" of being a musician than in the actual practice of the music. He has come to borrow money from* TROY, *and while he knows he will be successful, he is uncertain as to what extent his lifestyle will be held up to scrutiny and ridicule.)*

LYONS: Hey, Pop.

TROY: What you come "Hey, Popping" me for?

LYONS: How you doing, Rose?

(He kisses her.)

Mr. Bono. How you doing?

BONO: Hey, Lyons . . . how you been?

TROY: He must have been doing all right. I ain't seen him around here last week.

ROSE: Troy, leave your boy alone. He come by to see you and you wanna start all that nonsense.

TROY: I ain't bothering Lyons.

(Offers him the bottle.)

Here . . . get you a drink. We got an understanding. I know why he come by to see me and he know I know.

LYONS: Come on, Pop . . . I just stopped by to say hi . . . see how you was doing.

TROY: You ain't stopped by yesterday.

ROSE: You gonna stay for supper, Lyons? I got some chicken cooking in the oven.

LYONS: No, Rose . . . thanks. I was just in the neighborhood and thought I'd stop by for a minute.

TROY: You was in the neighborhood all right, nigger. You telling the truth there. You was in the neighborhood cause it's my payday.

LYONS: Well, hell, since you mentioned it . . . let me have ten dollars.

TROY: I'll be damned! I'll die and go to hell and play blackjack with the devil before I give you ten dollars.

BONO: That's what I wanna know about . . . that devil you done seen.

LYONS: What . . . Pop done seen the devil? You too much, Pops.

TROY: Yeah, I done seen him. Talked to him too!

ROSE: You ain't seen no devil. I done told you that man ain't had nothing to do with the devil. Anything you can't understand, you want to call it the devil.

TROY: Look here, Bono . . . I went down to see Hertzberger about some furniture. Got three rooms for two-ninety-eight. That what it say on the radio. "Three rooms . . . two-ninety-eight." Even made up a little song about it. Go down there . . . man tell me I can't get no credit. I'm working every day and can't get no credit. What to do? I got an empty house with some raggedy furniture in it. Cory ain't got no bed. He's sleeping on a pile of rags on the floor. Working every day and can't get no credit. Come back here—Rose'll tell you—madder than hell. Sit down . . . try to figure what I'm gonna do. Come a knock on the door. Ain't been living here but three days. Who know I'm here? Open the door . . . devil standing there bigger than life. White fellow . . . got on good clothes and everything. Standing there with a clipboard in his hand. I ain't had to say nothing. First words come out of his mouth was . . . "I understand you need some furniture and can't get no credit." I liked to fell over. He say, "I'll give you all the credit you want, but you got to pay the interest on it." I told him, "Give me three rooms worth and charge whatever you want." Next day a truck pulled up here and two men unloaded them three rooms. Man what drove the truck gave me a book. Say send ten dollars, first of every month to the address in the book and everything will be all right. Say if I miss a payment the devil was coming back and it'll be hell to pay. That was fifteen years ago. To this day . . . the first of the month I send my ten dollars, Rose'll tell you.

ROSE: Troy lying.

TROY: I ain't never seen that man since. Now you tell me who else that could have been but the devil? I ain't sold my soul or nothing like that, you understand. Naw, I wouldn't have truck with the devil about nothing like that. I got my furniture and pays my ten dollars the first of the month just like clockwork.

BONO: How long you say you been paying this ten dollars a month?

TROY: Fifteen years!

BONO: Hell, ain't you finished paying for it yet? How much the man done charged you?

TROY: Ah hell, I done paid for it. I done paid for it ten times over! The fact is I'm scared to stop paying it.

ROSE: Troy lying. We got that furniture from Mr. Glickman. He ain't paying no ten dollars a month to nobody.

TROY: Aw hell, woman. Bono know I ain't that big a fool.

LYONS: I was just getting ready to say . . . I know where there's a bridge for sale.

TROY: Look here, I'll tell you this . . . it don't matter to me if he was the devil. It don't matter if the devil give credit. Somebody has got to give it.

ROSE: It ought to matter. You going around talking about having truck with the devil . . . God's the one you gonna have to answer to. He's the one gonna be at the Judgment.

LYONS: Yeah, well, look here, Pop . . . let me have that ten dollars. I'll give it back to you. Bonnie got a job working at the hospital.

TROY: What I tell you, Bono? The only time I see this nigger is when he wants something. That's the only time I see him.

LYONS: Come on, Pop, Mr. Bono don't want to hear all that. Let me have the ten dollars. I told you Bonnie working.

TROY: What that mean to me? "Bonnie working." I don't care if she working. Go ask her for the ten dollars if she working. Talking about "Bonnie working." Why ain't you working?

LYONS: Aw, Pop, you know I can't find no decent job. Where am I gonna get a job at? You know I can't get no job.

TROY: I told you I know some people down there. I can get you on the rubbish if you want to work. I told you that the last time you came by here asking me for something.

LYONS: Naw, Pop . . . thanks. That ain't for me. I don't wanna be carrying nobody's rubbish. I don't wanna be punching nobody's time clock.

TROY: What's the matter, you too good to carry people's rubbish? Where you think that ten dollars you talking about come from? I'm just supposed to haul people's rubbish and give my money to you cause you too lazy to work. You too lazy to work and wanna know why you ain't got what I got.

ROSE: What hospital Bonnie working at? Mercy?

LYONS: She's down at Passavant working in the laundry.

TROY: I ain't got nothing as it is. I give you that ten dollars and I got to eat beans the rest of the week. Naw . . . you ain't getting no ten dollars here.

LYONS: You ain't got to be eating no beans. I don't know why you wanna say that.

TROY: I ain't got no extra money. Gabe done moved over to Miss Pearl's paying her the rent and things done got tight around here. I can't afford to be giving you every payday.

LYONS: I ain't asked you to give me nothing. I asked you to loan me ten dollars. I know you got ten dollars.

TROY: Yeah, I got it. You know why I got it? Cause I don't throw my money away out there in the streets. You living the fast life . . . wanna be a musician . . . running around in them clubs and things . . . then, you learn to take care of yourself. You ain't gonna find me going and asking nobody for nothing. I done spent too many years without.

LYONS: You and me is two different people, Pop.

TROY: I done learned my mistake and learned to do what's right by it. You still trying to get something for nothing. Life don't owe you nothing. You owe it to yourself. Ask Bono. He'll tell you I'm right.

LYONS: You got your way of dealing with the world . . . I got mine. The only thing that matters to me is the music.

TROY: Yeah, I can see that! It don't matter how you gonna eat . . . where your next dollar is coming from. You telling the truth there.

LYONS: I know I got to eat. But I got to live too. I need something that gonna help me to get out of the bed in the morning. Make me feel like I belong in the world. I don't bother nobody. I just stay with my music cause that's the only way I can find to live in the world. Otherwise there ain't no telling what I might do. Now I don't come criticizing you and how you live. I just come by to ask you for ten dollars. I don't wanna hear all that about how I live.

TROY: Boy, your mamma did a hell of a job raising you.

LYONS: You can't change me, Pop. I'm thirty-four years old. If you wanted to change me, you should have been there when I was growing up. I come by to see you . . . ask for ten dollars and you want to talk about how I was raised. You don't know nothing about how I was raised.

ROSE: Let the boy have ten dollars, Troy.

TROY *(to* LYONS*):* What the hell you looking at me for? I ain't got no ten dollars. You know what I do with my money. *(To* ROSE*.)* Give him ten dollars if you want him to have it.

ROSE: I will. Just as soon as you turn it loose.

TROY *(handing* ROSE *the money):* There it is. Seventy-six dollars and forty-two cents. You see this, Bono? Now, I ain't gonna get but six of that back.

ROSE: You ought to stop telling that lie. Here, Lyons. *(She hands him the money.)*

LYONS: Thanks, Rose. Look . . . I got to run . . . I'll see you later.

TROY: Wait a minute. You gonna say, "thanks, Rose" and ain't gonna look to see where she got that ten dollars from? See how they do me, Bono?

LYONS: I knew she got it from you, Pop. Thanks. I'll give it back to you.

TROY: There he go telling another lie. Time I see that ten dollars . . . he'll be owing me thirty more.

LYONS: See you, Mr. Bono.

BONO: Take care, Lyons!

LYONS: Thanks, Pop. I'll see you again.

*(*LYONS *exits the yard.)*

TROY: I don't know why he don't go out and get him a decent job and take care of that woman he got.

BONO: He'll be all right, Troy. The boy is still young.

TROY: The *boy* is thirty-four years old.

ROSE: Let's not get off into all that.

BONO: Look here . . . I got to be going. I got to be getting on. Lucille gonna be waiting.

TROY (*puts his arm around* ROSE): See this woman, Bono? I love this woman. I love this woman so much it hurts. I love her so much . . . I done run out of ways of loving her. So I got to go back to basics. Don't you come by my house Monday morning talking about time to go to work . . . 'cause I'm still gonna be stroking!

ROSE: Troy! Stop it now!

BONO: I ain't paying him no mind, Rose. That ain't nothing but gin-talk. Go on, Troy. I'll see you Monday.

TROY: Don't you come by my house, nigger! I done told you what I'm gonna be doing.

(*The lights go down to black.*)

SCENE II

(*The lights come up on* ROSE *hanging up clothes. She hums and sings softly to herself. It is the following morning.*)

ROSE (*sings*): Jesus, be a fence all around me every day

Jesus, I want you to protect me as I travel on my way.

Jesus, be a fence all around me every day.

(TROY *enters from the house.*)

Jesus, I want you to protect me

As I travel on my way.

(*To* TROY.) 'Morning. You ready for breakfast? I can fix it soon as I finish hanging up these clothes?

TROY: I got the coffee on. That'll be all right. I'll just drink some of that this morning.

ROSE: That 651 hit yesterday. That's the second time this month. Miss Pearl hit for a dollar . . . seem like those that need the least always get lucky. Poor folks can't get nothing.

TROY: Them numbers don't know nobody. I don't know why you fool with them. You and Lyons both.

ROSE: It's something to do.

TROY: You ain't doing nothing but throwing your money away.

ROSE: Troy, you know I don't play foolishly. I just play a nickel here and a nickel there.

TROY: That's two nickels you done thrown away.

ROSE: Now I hit sometimes . . . that makes up for it. It always comes in handy when I do hit. I don't hear you complaining then.

TROY: I ain't complaining now. I just say it's foolish. Trying to guess out of six hundred ways which way the number gonna come. If I had all the money niggers, these Negroes, throw away on numbers for one week—just one week— I'd be a rich man.

ROSE: Well, you wishing and calling it foolish ain't gonna stop folks from playing numbers. That's one thing for sure. Besides . . . some good things come from playing numbers. Look where Pope done bought him that restaurant off of numbers.

TROY: I can't stand niggers like that. Man ain't had two dimes to rub together. He walking around with his shoes all run over bumming money for cigarettes. All right. Got lucky there and hit the numbers . . .

ROSE: Troy, I know all about it.

TROY: Had good sense, I'll say that for him. He ain't throwed his money away. I seen niggers hit the numbers and go through two thousand dollars in four days. Man bought him that restaurant down there . . . fixed it up real nice . . . and then didn't want nobody to come in it! A Negro go in there and can't get no kind of service. I seen a white fellow come in there and order a bowl of stew. Pope picked all the meat out the pot for him. Man ain't had nothing but a bowl of meat! Negro come behind him and ain't got nothing but the potatoes and carrots. Talking about what numbers do for people, you picked a wrong example. Ain't done nothing but make a worser fool out of him than he was before.

ROSE: Troy, you ought to stop worrying about what happened at work yesterday.

TROY: I ain't worried. Just told me to be down there at the Commissioner's office on Friday. Everybody think they gonna fire me. I ain't worried about them firing me. You ain't got to worry about that.

(Pause.)

Where's Cory? Cory in the house? *(Calls.)* Cory?

ROSE: He gone out.

TROY: Out, huh? He gone out 'cause he know I want him to help me with this fence. I know how he is. That boy scared of work.

(GABRIEL *enters. He comes halfway down the alley and, hearing* TROY'S *voice, stops.*)

TROY *(continues):* He ain't done a lick of work in his life.

ROSE: He had to go to football practice. Coach wanted them to get in a little extra practice before the season start.

TROY: I got his practice . . . running out of here before he get his chores done.

ROSE: Troy, what is wrong with you this morning? Don't nothing set right with you. Go on back in there and go to bed . . . get up on the other side.

TROY: Why something got to be wrong with me? I ain't said nothing wrong with me.

ROSE: You got something to say about everything. First it's the numbers . . . then it's the way the man runs his restaurant . . . then you done got on Cory. What's it gonna be next? Take a look up there and see if the weather suits you . . . or is it gonna be how you gonna put up the fence with the clothes hanging in the yard.

TROY: You hit the nail on the head then.

ROSE: I know you like I know the back of my hand. Go in there and get you some coffee . . . see if that straighten you up. 'Cause you ain't right this morning.

(TROY *starts into the house and sees* GABRIEL. GABRIEL *starts singing.* TROY'S *brother, he is seven years younger than* TROY. *Injured in World War II, he has a metal plate in his head. He carries an old trumpet tied around his waist and believes with every fiber of his being that he is the Archangel Gabriel. He carries a chipped basket with an assortment of discarded fruits and vegetables he has picked up in the strip district and which he attempts to sell.*)

GABRIEL (*singing*): Yes, ma'am, I got plums
You ask me how I sell them
Oh ten cents apiece
Three for a quarter
Come and buy now
'Cause I'm here today
And tomorrow I'll be gone
(GABRIEL *enters.*)
Hey, Rose!

ROSE: How you doing, Gabe?

GABRIEL: There's Troy . . . Hey, Troy!

TROY: Hey, Gabe.

(*Exits into kitchen.*)

ROSE (*to* GABRIEL): What you got there?

GABRIEL: You know what I got, Rose. I got fruits and vegetables.

ROSE (*looking in basket*): Where's all these plums you talking about?

GABRIEL: I ain't got no plums today, Rose. I was just singing that. Have some tomorrow. Put me in a big order for plums. Have enough plums tomorrow for St. Peter and everybody.

(TROY *reenters from kitchen, crosses to steps.*)

(*To* ROSE.)
Troy's mad at me.

TROY: I ain't mad at you. What I got to be mad at you about? You ain't done nothing to me.

GABRIEL: I just moved over to Miss Pearl's to keep out from in your way. I ain't mean no harm by it.

TROY: Who said anything about that? I ain't said anything about that.

GABRIEL: You ain't mad at me, is you?

TROY: Naw . . . I ain't mad at you, Gabe. If I was mad at you I'd tell you about it.

GABRIEL: Got me two rooms. In the basement. Got my own door too. Wanna see my key?

(*He holds up a key.*)
That's my own key! Ain't nobody else got a key like that. That's my key! My two rooms!

TROY: Well, that's good, Gabe. You got your own key . . . that's good.

ROSE: You hungry, Gabe? I was just fixing to cook Troy his breakfast.

GABRIEL: I'll take some biscuits. You got some biscuits? Did you know when I was in heaven . . . every morning me and St. Peter would sit down by the gate and eat some big fat biscuits? Oh, yeah! We had us a good time. We'd sit there and eat us them biscuits and then St. Peter would go off to sleep and tell me to wake him up when it's time to open the gates for the judgment.

ROSE: Well, come on . . . I'll make up a batch of biscuits.

(ROSE *exits into the house.*)

GABRIEL: Troy . . . St. Peter got your name in the book. I seen it. It say . . . Troy Maxson. I say . . . I know him! He got the same name like what I got. That's my brother!

TROY: How many times you gonna tell me that, Gabe?

GABRIEL: Ain't got my name in the book. Don't have to have my name. I done died and went to heaven. He got your name though. One morning St. Peter was looking at his book . . . marking it up for the judgment . . . and he let me see your name. Got it in there under M. Got Rose's name . . . I ain't seen it like I seen yours . . . but I know it's in there. He got a great big book. Got everybody's name what was ever been born. That's what he told me. But I seen your name. Seen it with my own eyes.

TROY: Go on in the house there. Rose going to fix you something to eat.

GABRIEL: Oh, I ain't hungry. I done had breakfast with Aunt Jemimah. She come by and cooked me up a whole mess of flapjacks. Remember how we used to eat them flapjacks?

TROY: Go on in the house and get you something to eat now.

GABRIEL: I got to go sell my plums. I done sold some tomatoes. Got me two quarters. Wanna see?

(*He shows* TROY *his quarters.*)

I'm gonna save them and buy me a new horn so St. Peter can hear me when it's time to open the gates.

(GABRIEL *stops suddenly. Listens.*)

Hear that? That's the hellhounds. I got to chase them out of here! Go on get out of here! Get out!

(GABRIEL *exits singing.*)

Better get ready for the judgment

Better get ready for the judgment

My Lord is coming down

(ROSE *enters from the house.*)

TROY: He gone off somewhere.

GABRIEL (*offstage*): Better get ready for the judgment

Better get ready for the judgment morning

Better get ready for the judgment

My God is coming down

ROSE: He ain't eating right. Miss Pearl say she can't get him to eat nothing.

TROY: What you want me to do about it, Rose? I done did everything I can for the man. I can't make him get well. Man got half his head blown away . . . what you expect?

ROSE: Seem like something ought to be done to help him.

TROY: Man don't bother nobody. He just mixed up from that metal plate he got in his head. Ain't no sense for him to go back into the hospital.

ROSE: Least he be eating right. They can help him take care of himself.

TROY: Don't nobody wanna be locked up, Rose. What you wanna lock him up for? Man go over there and fight the war . . . messin' around with them Japs, get half his head blown off . . . and they give him a lousy three thousand dollars. And I had to swoop down on that.

ROSE: Is you fixing to go into that again?

TROY: That's the only way I got a roof over my head . . . cause of that metal plate.

ROSE: Ain't no sense you blaming yourself for nothing. Gabe wasn't in no condition to manage that money. You done what was right by him. Can't nobody say you ain't done what was right by him. Look how long you took care of him . . . till he wanted to have his own place and moved over there with Miss Pearl.

TROY: That ain't what I'm saying, woman! I'm just stating the facts. If my brother didn't have that metal plate in his head . . . I wouldn't have a pot to piss in or a window to throw it out of. And I'm fifty-three years old. Now see if you can understand that!

(TROY *gets up from the porch and starts to exit the yard.*)

ROSE: Where you going off to? You been running out of here every Saturday for weeks. I thought you was gonna work on this fence?

TROY: I'm gonna walk down to Taylors'. Listen to the ball game. I'll be back in a bit. I'll work on it when I get back.

(*He exits the yard. The lights go to black.*)

SCENE III

(*The lights come up on the yard. It is four hours later.* ROSE *is taking down the clothes from the line.* CORY *enters carrying his football equipment.*)

ROSE: Your daddy like to had a fit with you running out of here this morning without doing your chores.

CORY: I told you I had to go to practice.

ROSE: He say you were supposed to help him with this fence.

CORY: He been saying that the last four or five Saturdays, and then he don't never do nothing but go down to Taylors'. Did you tell him about the recruiter?

ROSE: Yeah, I told him.

CORY: What he say?

ROSE: He ain't said nothing too much. You get in there and get started on your chores before he gets back. Go on and scrub down them steps before he gets back here hollering and carrying on.

CORY: I'm hungry. What you got to eat, Mama?

ROSE: Go on and get started on your chores. I got some meat loaf in there. Go on and make you a sandwich . . . and don't leave no mess in there.

(CORY *exits into the house.* ROSE *continues to take down the clothes.* TROY *enters the yard and sneaks up and grabs her from behind.*)

Troy! Go on, now. You liked to scared me to death. What was the score of the game? Lucille had me on the phone and I couldn't keep up with it.

TROY: What I care about the game? Come here, woman. (*He tries to kiss her.*)

ROSE: I thought you went down Taylors' to listen to the game. Go on, Troy! You supposed to be putting up this fence.

TROY (*attempting to kiss her again*): I'll put it up when I finish with what is at hand.

ROSE: Go on, Troy. I ain't studying you.

TROY (*chasing after her*): I'm studying you . . . fixing to do my homework!

ROSE: Troy, you better leave me alone.

TROY: Where's Cory? That boy brought his butt home yet?

ROSE: He's in the house doing his chores.

TROY (*calling*): Cory! Get your butt out here, boy!

(ROSE *exits into the house with the laundry.* TROY *goes over to the pile of wood, picks up a board, and starts sawing.* CORY *enters from the house.*)

TROY: You just now coming in here from leaving this morning?

CORY: Yeah, I had to go to football practice.

TROY: Yeah, what?

CORY: Yessir.

TROY: I ain't but two seconds off you noway. The garbage sitting in there overflowing . . . you ain't done none of your chores . . . and you come in here talking about "Yeah."

CORY: I was just getting ready to do my chores now, Pop . . .

TROY: Your first chore is to help me with this fence on Saturday. Everything else come after that. Now get that saw and cut them boards.

(CORY *takes the saw and begins cutting the boards.* TROY *continues working. There is a long pause.*)

CORY: Hey, Pop . . . why don't you buy a TV?

TROY: What I want with a TV? What I want one of them for?

CORY: Everybody got one. Earl, Ba Bra . . . Jesse!

TROY: I ain't asked you who had one. I say what I want with one?

CORY: So you can watch it. They got lots of things on TV. Baseball games and everything. We could watch the World Series.

TROY: Yeah . . . and how much this TV cost?

CORY: I don't know. They got them on sale for around two hundred dollars.

TROY: Two hundred dollars, huh?

CORY: That ain't that much, Pop.

TROY: Naw, it's just two hundred dollars. See that roof you got over your head at night? Let me tell you something about that roof. It's been over ten years since that roof was last tarred. See now . . . the snow come this winter and sit up there on that roof like it is . . . and it's gonna seep inside. It's just gonna be a little bit . . . ain't gonna hardly notice it. Then the next thing you know, it's gonna be leaking all over the house. Then the wood rot from all that water and you gonna need a whole new roof. Now, how much you think it cost to get that roof tarred?

CORY: I don't know.

TROY: Two hundred and sixty-four dollars . . . cash money. While you thinking about a TV, I got to be thinking about the roof . . . and whatever else go wrong around here. Now if you had two hundred dollars, what would you do . . . fix the roof or buy a TV?

CORY: I'd buy a TV. Then when the roof started to leak . . . when it needed fixing . . . I'd fix it.

TROY: Where you gonna get the money from? You done spent it for a TV. You gonna sit up and watch the water run all over your brand new TV.

CORY: Aw, Pop. You got money. I know you do.

TROY: Where I got it at, huh?

CORY: You got it in the bank.

TROY: You wanna see my bankbook? You wanna see that seventy-three dollars and twenty-two cents I got sitting up in there?

CORY: You ain't got to pay for it all at one time. You can put a down payment on it and carry it on home with you.

TROY: Not me. I ain't gonna owe nobody nothing if I can help it. Miss a payment and they come and snatch it right out your house. Then what you got? Now, soon as I get two hundred dollars clear, then I'll buy a TV. Right now, as soon as I get two hundred and sixty-four dollars, I'm gonna have this roof tarred.

CORY: Aw . . . Pop!

TROY: You go on and get you two hundred dollars and buy one if ya want it. I got better things to do with my money.

CORY: I can't get no two hundred dollars. I ain't never seen two hundred dollars.

TROY: I'll tell you what . . . you get you a hundred dollars and I'll put the other hundred with it.

CORY: All right, I'm gonna show you.

TROY: You gonna show me how you can cut them boards right now.

(CORY *begins to cut the boards. There is a long pause.*)

CORY: The Pirates won today. That makes five in a row.

TROY: I ain't thinking about the Pirates. Got an all white team. Got that boy . . . that Puerto Rican boy . . . Clemente. Don't even half-play him. That boy could be something if they give him a chance. Play him one day and sit him on the bench the next.

CORY: He gets a lot of chances to play.

TROY: I'm talking about playing regular. Playing every day so you can get your timing. That's what I'm talking about.

CORY: They got some white guys on the team that don't play every day. You can't play everybody at the same time.

TROY: If they got a white fellow sitting on the bench . . . you can bet your last dollar he can't play! The colored guy got to be twice as good before he get on the team. That's why I don't want you go get all tied up in them sports. Man on the team and what it get him? They got colored on the team and don't use them. Same as not having them. All them teams the same.

CORY: The Braves got Hank Aaron and Wes Covington. Hank Aaron hit two home runs today. That makes forty-three.

TROY: Hank Aaron ain't nobody. That's what you supposed to do. That's how you supposed to play the game. Ain't nothing to it. It's just a matter of timing . . . getting the right follow-through. Hell, I can hit forty-three home runs right now!

CORY: Not off no major-league pitching, you couldn't.

TROY: We had better pitching in the Negro leagues. I hit seven home runs off of Satchel Paige.[1] You can't get no better than that!

CORY: Sandy Koufax. He's leading the league in strikeouts.

TROY: I ain't thinking of no Sandy Koufax.

CORY: You got Warren Spahn and Lew Burdette. I bet you couldn't hit no home runs off of Warren Spahn.

TROY: I'm through with it now. You go on and cut them boards.

(Pause.)

Your mama tell me you done got recruited by a college football team? Is that right?

CORY: Yeah. Coach Zellman say the recruiter gonna be coming by to talk to you. Get you to sign the permission papers.

TROY: I thought you supposed to be working down there at the A&P. Ain't you suppose to be working down there after school?

CORY: Mr. Stawicki say he gonna hold my job for me until after the football season. Say starting next week I can work weekends.

TROY: I thought we had an understanding about this football stuff? You suppose to keep up with your chores and hold that job down at the A&P. Ain't been around here all day on a Saturday. Ain't none of your chores done . . . and now you telling me you done quit your job.

CORY: I'm gonna be working weekends.

TROY: You damn right you are! And ain't no need for nobody coming around here to talk to me about signing nothing.

CORY: Hey, Pop . . . you can't do that. He's coming all the way from North Carolina.

TROY: I don't care where he coming from. The white man ain't gonna let you get nowhere with that football noway. You go on and get your book-learning so you can work yourself up in that A&P or learn how to fix cars or build houses or something, get you a trade. That way you have something can't nobody take away from you. You go on and learn how to put your hands to some good use. Besides hauling people's garbage.

CORY: I get good grades, Pop. That's why the recruiter wants to talk with you. You got to keep up your grades to get recruited. This way I'll be going to college. I'll get a chance . . .

---

1. Legendary black pitcher (1906?–1982) in the Negro leagues.

TROY: First you gonna get your butt down there to the A&P and get your job back.

CORY: Mr. Stawicki done already hired somebody else 'cause I told him I was playing football.

TROY: You a bigger fool than I thought . . . to let somebody take away your job so you can play some football. Where you gonna get your money to take out your girlfriend and whatnot? What kind of foolishness is that to let somebody take away your job?

CORY: I'm still gonna be working weekends.

TROY: Naw . . . naw. You getting your butt out of here and finding you another job.

CORY: Come on, Pop! I got to practice. I can't work after school and play football too. The team needs me. That's what Coach Zellman say . . .

TROY: I don't care what nobody else say. I'm the boss . . . you understand? I'm the boss around here. I do the only saying what counts.

CORY: Come on, Pop!

TROY: I asked you . . . did you understand?

CORY: Yeah . . .

TROY: What?!

CORY: Yessir.

TROY: You go on down there to that A&P and see if you can get your job back. If you can't do both . . . then you quit the football team. You've got to take the crookeds with the straights.

CORY: Yessir.

(Pause.)

Can I ask you a question?

TROY: What the hell you wanna ask me? Mr. Stawicki the one you got the questions for.

CORY: How come you ain't never liked me?

TROY: Liked you? Who the hell say I got to like you? What law is there say I got to like you? Wanna stand up in my face and ask a damn fool-ass question like that. Talking about liking somebody. Come here, boy, when I talk to you.

(CORY comes over to where TROY is working. He stands slouched over and TROY shoves him on his shoulder.)

Straighten up, goddammit! I asked you a question . . . what law is there say I got to like you?

CORY: None.

TROY: Well, all right then! Don't you eat every day?

(Pause.)

Answer me when I talk to you! Don't you eat every day?

CORY: Yeah.

TROY: Nigger, as long as you in my house, you put that sir on the end of it when you talk to me!

CORY: Yes . . . sir.

TROY: You eat every day.

CORY: Yessir!

TROY: Got a roof over your head.

CORY: Yessir!

TROY: Got clothes on your back.

CORY: Yessir.

TROY: Why you think that is?

CORY: Cause of you.

TROY: Ah, hell I know it's 'cause of me . . . but why do you think that is?

CORY (*hesitant*): Cause you like me.

TROY: Like you? I go out of here every morning . . . bust my butt . . . putting up with them crackers every day . . . cause I like you? You about the biggest fool I ever saw.

(*Pause.*)

It's my job. It's my responsibility! You understand that? A man got to take care of his family. You live in my house . . . sleep you behind on my bedclothes . . . fill you belly up with my food . . . cause you my son. You my flesh and blood. Not 'cause I like you! Cause it's my duty to take care of you. I owe a responsibility to you! Let's get this straight right here . . . before it go along any further . . . I ain't got to like you. Mr. Rand don't give me my money come payday cause he likes me. He gives me cause he owe me. I done give you everything I had to give you. I gave you your life! Me and your mama worked that out between us. And liking your black ass wasn't part of the bargain. Don't you try and go through life worrying about if somebody like you or not. You best be making sure they doing right by you. You understand what I'm saying, boy?

CORY: Yessir.

TROY: Then get the hell out of my face, and get on down to that A&P.

(ROSE *has been standing behind the screen door for much of the scene. She enters as* CORY *exits.*)

ROSE: Why don't you let the boy go ahead and play football, Troy? Ain't no harm in that. He's just trying to be like you with the sports.

TROY: I don't want him to be like me! I want him to move as far away from my life as he can get. You the only decent thing that ever happened to me. I wish him that. But I don't wish him a thing else from my life. I decided seventeen years ago that boy wasn't getting involved in no sports. Not after what they did to me in the sports.

ROSE: Troy, why don't you admit you was too old to play in the major leagues? For once . . . why don't you admit that?

TROY: What do you mean too old? Don't come telling me I was too old. I just wasn't the right color. Hell, I'm fifty-three years old and can do better than Selkirk's .269 right now!

ROSE: How's was you gonna play ball when you were over forty? Sometimes I can't get no sense out of you.

TROY: I got good sense, woman. I got sense enough not to let my boy get hurt over playing no sports. You been mothering that boy too much. Worried about if people like him.

ROSE: Everything that boy do . . . he do for you. He wants you to say "Good job, son." That's all.

TROY: Rose, I ain't got time for that. He's alive. He's healthy. He's got to make his own way. I made mine. Ain't nobody gonna hold his hand when he get out there in that world.

ROSE: Times have changed from when you was young, Troy. People change. The world's changing around you and you can't even see it.

TROY (*slow, methodical*): Woman . . . I do the best I can do. I come in here every Friday. I carry a sack of potatoes and a bucket of lard. You all line up at the door with your hands out. I give you the lint from my pockets. I give you my sweat and my blood. I ain't got no tears. I done spent them. We go upstairs in that room at night . . . and I fall down on you and try to blast a hole into forever. I get up Monday morning . . . find my lunch on the table. I go. Make my way. Find my strength to carry me through to the next Friday.

(*Pause.*)

That's all I got, Rose. That's all I got to give. I can't give nothing else.

(TROY *exits into the house. The lights go down to black.*)

SCENE IV

(*It is Friday. Two weeks later.* CORY *starts out of the house with his football equipment. The phone rings.*)

CORY (*calling*): I got it!

(*He answers the phone and stands in the screen door talking.*)

Hello? Hey, Jesse. Naw . . . I was just getting ready to leave now.

ROSE (*calling*): Cory!

CORY: I told you, man, them spikes is all tore up. You can use them if you want, but they ain't no good. Earl got some spikes.

ROSE (*calling*): Cory!

CORY (*calling to* ROSE): Mam? I'm talking to Jesse.

(*Into phone.*)

When she say that? (*Pause.*) Aw, you lying, man. I'm gonna tell her you said that.

ROSE (*calling*): Cory, don't you go nowhere!

CORY: I got to go to the game, Ma!

(*Into the phone.*)

Yeah, hey, look, I'll talk to you later. Yeah, I'll meet you over Earl's house. Later. Bye, Ma.

(CORY *exits the house and starts out the yard.*)

ROSE: Cory, where you going off to? You got that stuff all pulled out and thrown all over your room.

CORY (*in the yard*): I was looking for my spikes. Jesse wanted to borrow my spikes.

ROSE: Get up there and get that cleaned up before your daddy get back in here.

CORY: I got to go to the game! I'll clean it up *when I get back.*
(CORY *exits.*)

ROSE: That's all he need to do is see that room all messed up.
(ROSE *exits into the house.* TROY *and* BONO *enter the yard.* TROY *is dressed in clothes other than his work clothes.*)

BONO: He told him the same thing he told you. Take it to the union.

TROY: Brownie ain't got that much sense. Man wasn't thinking about nothing. He wait until I confront them on it . . . then he wanna come crying seniority.
(*Calls.*)
Hey, Rose!

BONO: I wish I could have seen Mr. Rand's face when he told you.

TROY: He couldn't get it out of his mouth! Liked to bit his tongue! When they called me down there to the Commissioner's office . . . he thought they was gonna fire me. Like everybody else.

BONO: I didn't think they was gonna fire you. I thought they was gonna put you on the warning paper.

TROY: Hey, Rose!
(*To* BONO.)
Yeah, Mr. Rand like to bit his tongue.
(TROY *breaks the seal on the bottle, takes a drink, and hands it to* BONO.)

BONO: I see you run right down to Taylors' and told that Alberta gal.

TROY (*calling*): Hey, Rose! (*To* BONO.) I told everybody. Hey, Rose! I went down there to cash my check.

ROSE (*entering from the house*): Hush all that hollering, man! I know you out here. What they say down there at the Commissioner's office?

TROY: You supposed to come when I call you, woman. Bono'll tell you that.
(*To* BONO.)
Don't Lucille come when you call her?

ROSE: Man, hush your mouth. I ain't no dog . . . talk about "come when you call me."

TROY (*puts his arm around* ROSE): You hear this, Bono? I had me an old dog used to get uppity like that. You say, "C'mere, Blue!" . . . and he just lay there and look at you. End up getting a stick and chasing him away trying to make him come.

ROSE: I ain't studying you and your dog. I remember you used to sing that old song.

TROY (*he sings*): Hear it ring! Hear it ring! I had a dog his name was Blue.

ROSE: Don't nobody wanna hear you sing that old song.

TROY (*sings*): You know Blue was mighty true.

ROSE: Used to have Cory running around here singing that song.

BONO: Hell, I remember that song myself.

TROY (*sings*): You know Blue was a good old dog.
Blue treed a possum in a hollow log.
That was my daddy's song. My daddy made up that song.

ROSE: I don't care who made it up. Don't nobody wanna hear you sing it.

TROY *(makes a song like calling a dog):* Come here, woman.

ROSE: You come in here carrying on, I reckon they ain't fired you. What they say down there at the Commissioner's office?

TROY: Look here, Rose . . . Mr. Rand called me into his office today when I got back from talking to them people down there . . . it come from up top . . . he called me in and told me they was making me a driver.

ROSE: Troy, you kidding!

TROY: No I ain't. Ask Bono.

ROSE: Well, that's great, Troy. Now you don't have to hassle them people no more.

*(*LYONS *enters from the street.)*

TROY: Aw hell, I wasn't looking to see you today. I thought you was in jail. Got it all over the front page of the *Courier* about them raiding Sefus' place . . . where you be hanging out with all them thugs.

LYONS: Hey, Pop . . . that ain't got nothing to do with me. I don't go down there gambling. I go down there to sit in with the band. I ain't got nothing to do with the gambling part. They got some good music down there.

TROY: They got some rogues . . . is what they got.

LYONS: How you been, Mr. Bono? Hi, Rose.

BONO: I see where you playing down at the Crawford Grill tonight.

ROSE: How come you ain't brought Bonnie like I told you. You should have brought Bonnie with you, she ain't been over in a month of Sundays.

LYONS: I was just in the neighborhood . . . thought I'd stop by.

TROY: Here he come . . .

BONO: Your daddy got a promotion on the rubbish. He's gonna be the first colored driver. Ain't got to do nothing but sit up there and read the paper like them white fellows.

LYONS: Hey, Pop . . . if you knew how to read you'd be all right.

BONO: Naw . . . naw . . . you mean if the nigger knew how to *drive* he'd be all right. Been fighting with them people about driving and ain't even got a license. Mr. Rand know you ain't got no driver's license?

TROY: Driving ain't nothing. All you do is point the truck where you want it to go. Driving ain't nothing.

BONO: Do Mr. Rand know you ain't got no driver's license? That's what I'm talking about. I ain't asked if driving was easy. I asked if Mr. Rand know you ain't got no driver's license.

TROY: He ain't got to know. The man ain't got to know my business. Time he find out, I have two or three driver's licenses.

LYONS *(going into his pocket):* Say, look here, Pop . . .

TROY: I knew it was coming. Didn't I tell you, Bono? I know what kind of "Look here, Pop" that was. The nigger fixing to ask me for some money. It's Friday night. It's my payday. All them rogues down there on the avenue . . . the ones that ain't in jail . . . and Lyons is hopping in his shoes to get down there with them.

LYONS: See, Pop . . . if you give somebody else a chance to talk sometime, you'd see that I was fixing to pay you back your ten dollars like I told you. Here . . . I told you I'd pay you when Bonnie got paid.

TROY: Naw . . . you go ahead and keep that ten dollars. Put it in the bank. The next time you feel like you wanna come by here and ask me for something . . . you go on down there and get that.

LYONS: Here's your ten dollars, Pop. I told you I don't want you to give me nothing. I just wanted to borrow ten dollars.

TROY: Naw . . . you go on and keep that for the next time you want to ask me.

LYONS: Come on, Pop . . . here go your ten dollars.

ROSE: Why don't you go on and let the boy pay you back, Troy?

LYONS: Here you go, Rose. If you don't take it I'm gonna have to hear about it for the next six months.

(He hands her the money.)

ROSE: You can hand yours over here too, Troy.

TROY: You see this, Bono. You see how they do me.

BONO: Yeah, Lucille do me the same way.

(GABRIEL is heard singing offstage. He enters.)

GABRIEL: Better get ready for the Judgment! Better get ready for . . . Hey! . . . Hey! . . . There's Troy's boy!

LYONS: How are you doing, Uncle Gabe?

GABRIEL: Lyons . . . The King of the Jungle! Rose . . . hey, Rose. Got a flower for you.

(He takes a rose from his pocket.)

Picked it myself. That's the same rose like you is!

ROSE: That's right nice of you, Gabe.

LYONS: What you been doing, Uncle Gabe?

GABRIEL: Oh, I been chasing hellhounds and waiting on the time to tell St. Peter to open the gates.

LYONS: You been chasing hellhounds, huh? Well . . . you doing the right thing, Uncle Gabe. Somebody got to chase them.

GABRIEL: Oh, yeah . . . I know it. The devil's strong. The devil ain't no pushover. Hellhounds snipping at everybody's heels. But I got my trumpet waiting on the judgment time.

LYONS: Waiting on the Battle of Armageddon, huh?

GABRIEL: Ain't gonna be too much of a battle when God get to waving that Judgment sword. But the people's gonna have a hell of a time trying to get into heaven if them gates ain't open.

LYONS *(putting his arm around GABRIEL)*: You hear this, Pop. Uncle Gabe, you all right!

GABRIEL *(laughing with LYONS)*: Lyons! King of the Jungle.

ROSE: You gonna stay for supper, Gabe. Want me to fix you a plate?

GABRIEL: I'll take a sandwich, Rose. Don't want no plate. Just wanna eat with my hands. I'll take a sandwich.

ROSE: How about you, Lyons? You staying? Got some short ribs cooking.

LYONS: Naw, I won't eat nothing till after we finished playing.

(Pause.)

You ought to come down and listen to me play, Pop.

TROY: I don't like that Chinese music. All that noise.

ROSE: Go on in the house and wash up, Gabe . . . I'll fix you a sandwich.

GABRIEL *(to LYONS, as he exits):* Troy's mad at me.

LYONS: What you mad at Uncle Gabe for, Pop?

ROSE: He think Troy's mad at him cause he moved over to Miss Pearl's.

TROY: I ain't mad at the man. He can live where he want to live at.

LYONS: What he move over there for? Miss Pearl don't like nobody.

ROSE: She don't mind him none. She treats him real nice. She just don't allow all that singing.

TROY: She don't mind that rent he be paying . . . that's what she don't mind.

ROSE: Troy, I ain't going through that with you no more. He's over there cause he want to have his own place. He can come and go as he please.

TROY: Hell, he could come and go as he please here. I wasn't stopping him. I ain't put no rules on him.

ROSE: It ain't the same thing, Troy. And you know it.

(GABRIEL comes to the door.)

Now, that's the last I wanna hear about that. I don't wanna hear nothing else about Gabe and Miss Pearl. And next week . . .

GABRIEL: I'm ready for my sandwich, Rose.

ROSE: And next week . . . when that recruiter come from that school . . . I want you to sign that paper and go on and let Cory play football. Then that'll be the last I have to hear about that.

TROY *(to ROSE as she exits into the house):* I ain't thinking about Cory nothing.

LYONS: What . . . Cory got recruited? What school he going to?

TROY: That boy walking around here smelling his piss . . . thinking he's grown. Thinking he's gonna do what he want, irrespective of what I say. Look here, Bono . . . I left the Commissioner's office and went down to the A&P . . . that boy ain't working down there. He lying to me. Telling me he got his job back . . . telling me he working weekends . . . telling me he working after school . . . Mr. Stawicki tell me he ain't working down there at all!

LYONS: Cory just growing up. He's just busting at the seams trying to fill out your shoes.

TROY: I don't care what he's doing. When he get to the point where he wanna disobey me . . . then it's time for him to move on. Bono'll tell you that. I bet he ain't never disobeyed his daddy without paying the consequences.

BONO: I ain't never had a chance. My daddy came on through . . . but I ain't never knew him to see him . . . or what he had on his mind or where he went. Just moving on through. Searching out the New Land. That's what the old folks used to call it. See a fellow moving around from place to place . . . woman to woman . . . called it searching out the New Land. I can't say if he ever found it. I come along, didn't want no kids. Didn't know if I was gonna be in one place long enough to fix on them right as their daddy. I figured I was going searching too. As it turned out I been hooked up with Lucille near about as long as your daddy been with Rose. Going on sixteen years.

TROY: Sometimes I wish I hadn't known my daddy. He ain't cared nothing about no kids. A kid to him wasn't nothing. All he wanted was for you to learn how to walk so he could start you to working. When it come time for eating . . . he ate first. If there was anything left over, that's what you got. Man would sit down and eat two chickens and give you the wing.

LYONS: You ought to stop that, Pop. Everybody feed their kids. No matter how hard times is . . . everybody care about their kids. Make sure they have something to eat.

TROY: The only thing my daddy cared about was getting them bales of cotton in to Mr. Lubin. That's the only thing that mattered to him. Sometimes I used to wonder why he was living. Wonder why the devil hadn't come and got him. "Get them bales of cotton in to Mr. Lubin" and find out he owe him money . . .

LYONS: He should have just went on and left when he saw he couldn't get nowhere. That's what I would have done.

TROY: How he gonna leave with eleven kids? And where he gonna go? He ain't knew how to do nothing but farm. No, he was trapped and I think he knew it. But I'll say this for him . . . he felt a responsibility toward us. Maybe he ain't treated us the way I felt he should have . . . but without that responsibility he could have walked off and left us . . . made his own way.

BONO: A lot of them did. Back in those days what you talking about . . . they walk out their front door and just take on down one road or another and keep on walking.

LYONS: There you go! That's what I'm talking about.

BONO: Just keep on walking till you come to something else. Ain't you never heard of nobody having the walking blues? Well, that's what you call it when you just take off like that.

TROY: My daddy ain't had them walking blues! What you talking about? He stayed right there with his family. But he was just as evil as he could be. My mama couldn't stand him. Couldn't stand that evilness. She run off when I was about eight. She sneaked off one night after he had gone to sleep. Told me she was coming back for me. I ain't never seen her no more. All his women run off and left him. He wasn't good for nobody.

When my turn come to head out, I was fourteen and got to sniffing around Joe Canewell's daughter. Had us an old mule we called Greyboy. My daddy sent me out to do some plowing and I tied up Greyboy and went to fooling around with Joe Canewell's daughter. We done found us a nice little spot, got real cozy with each other. She about thirteen and we done figured we was grown anyway . . . so we down there enjoying ourselves . . . ain't thinking about nothing. We didn't know Greyboy had got loose and wandered back to the house and my daddy was looking for me. We down there by the creek enjoying ourselves when my daddy come up on us. Surprised us. He had them leather straps off the mule and commenced to whupping me like there was no tomorrow. I jumped up, mad and embarrassed. I was scared of my daddy. When he commenced to whupping on me . . . quite naturally I run to get out of the way.

(Pause.)

Now I thought he was mad cause I ain't done my work. But I see where he was chasing me off so he could have the gal for himself. When I see what the matter of it was, I lost all fear of my daddy. Right there is where I become a man . . . at fourteen years of age.

(Pause.)

Now it was my turn to run him off. I picked up them same reins that he had used on me. I picked up them reins and commenced to whupping on him. The gal jumped up and run off . . . and when my daddy turned to face me, I could see why the devil had never come to get him . . . cause he was the devil himself. I don't know what happened. When I woke up, I was laying right there by the creek, and Blue . . . this old dog we had . . . was licking my face. I thought I was blind. I couldn't see nothing. Both my eyes were swollen shut. I layed there and cried. I didn't know what I was gonna do. The only thing I knew was the time had come for me to leave my daddy's house. And right there the world suddenly got big. And it was a long time before I could cut it down to where I could handle it.

Part of that cutting down was when I got to the place where I could feel him kicking in my blood and knew that the only thing that separated us was the matter of a few years.

(GABRIEL enters from the house with a sandwich.)

LYONS: What you got there, Uncle Gabe?

GABRIEL: Got me a ham sandwich. Rose gave me a ham sandwich.

TROY: I don't know what happened to him. I done lost touch with everybody except Gabriel. But I hope he's dead. I hope he found some peace.

LYONS: That's a heavy story, Pop. I didn't know you left home when you was fourteen.

TROY: And didn't know nothing. The only part of the world I knew was the forty-two acres of Mr. Lubin's land. That's all I knew about life.

LYONS: Fourteen's kinda young to be out on your own. *(Phone rings.)* I don't even think I was ready to be out on my own at fourteen. I don't know what I would have done.

TROY: I got up from the creek and walked on down to Mobile. I was through with farming. Figured I could do better in the city. So I walked the two hundred miles to Mobile.

LYONS: Wait a minute . . . you ain't walked no two hundred miles, Pop. Ain't nobody gonna walk no two hundred miles. You talking about some walking there.

BONO: That's the only way you got anywhere back in them days.

LYONS: Shhh. Damn if I wouldn't have hitched a ride with somebody!

TROY: Who you gonna hitch it with? They ain't had no cars and things like they got now. We talking about 1918.

ROSE *(entering):* What you all out here getting into?

TROY *(to* ROSE*):* I'm telling Lyons how good he got it. He don't know nothing about this I'm talking.

ROSE: Lyons, that was Bonnie on the phone. She say you supposed to pick her up.

LYONS: Yeah, okay, Rose.

TROY: I walked on down to Mobile and hitched up with some of them fellows that was heading this way. Got up here and found out ... not only couldn't you get a job ... you couldn't find no place to live. I thought I was in freedom. Shhh. Colored folks living down there on the riverbanks in whatever kind of shelter they could find for themselves. Right down there under the Brady Street Bridge. Living in shacks made of sticks and tarpaper. Messed around there and went from bad to worse. Started stealing. First it was food. Then I figured, hell, if I steal money I can buy me some food. Buy me some shoes too! One thing led to another. Met your mama. I was young and anxious to be a man. Met your mama and had you. What I do that for? Now I got to worry about feeding you and her. Got to steal three times as much. Went out one day looking for somebody to rob ... that's what I was, a robber. I'll tell you truth. I'm ashamed of it today. But it's the truth. Went to rob this fellow ... pulled out my knife ... and he pulled out a gun. Shot me in the chest. It felt just like somebody had taken a hot branding iron and laid it on me. When he shot me I jumped at him with my knife. They told me I killed him and they put me in the penitentiary and locked me up for fifteen years. That's where I met Bono. That's where I learned how to play baseball. Got out that place and your mama had taken you and went on to make life without me. Fifteen years was a long time for her to wait. But that fifteen years cured me of that robbing stuff. Rose'll tell you. She asked me when I met her if I had gotten all that foolishness out of my system. And I told her, "Baby, it's you and baseball all what count with me." You hear me, Bono? I meant it too. She say, "Which one comes first?" I told her, "Baby, ain't no doubt it's baseball ... but you stick and get old with me and we'll both outlive this baseball." Am I right, Rose? And it's true.

ROSE: Man, hush your mouth. You ain't said no such thing. Talking about, "Baby, you know you'll always be number one with me." That's what you was talking.

TROY: You hear that, Bono. That's why I love her.

BONO: Rose'll keep you straight. You get off the track, she'll straighten you up.

ROSE: Lyons, you better get on up and get Bonnie. She waiting on you.

LYONS *(gets up to go):* Hey, Pop, why don't you come on down to the Grill and hear me play?

TROY: I ain't going down there. I'm too old to be sitting around in them clubs.

BONO: You got to be good to play down at the Grill.

LYONS: Come on, Pop . . .

TROY: I got to get up in the morning.

LYONS: You ain't got to stay long.

TROY: Naw, I'm gonna get my supper and go on to bed.

LYONS: Well, I got to go. I'll see you again.

TROY: Don't you come around my house on my payday.

ROSE: Pick up the phone and let somebody know you coming. And bring Bonnie with you. You know I'm always glad to see her.

LYONS: Yeah, I'll do that, Rose. You take care now. See you, Pop. See you, Mr. Bono. See you, Uncle Gabe.

GABRIEL: Lyons! King of the Jungle!

(LYONS *exits.*)

TROY: Is supper ready, woman? Me and you got some business to take care of. I'm gonna tear it up too.

ROSE: Troy, I done told you now!

TROY (*puts his arm around* BONO): Aw hell, woman . . . this is Bono. Bono like family. I done known this nigger since . . . how long I done know you?

BONO: It's been a long time.

TROY: I done known this nigger since Skippy was a pup. Me and him done been through some times.

BONO: You sure right about that.

TROY: Hell, I done know him longer than I known you. And we still standing shoulder to shoulder. Hey, look here, Bono . . . a man can't ask for no more than that.

(*Drinks to him.*)

I love you, nigger.

BONO: Hell, I love you too . . . but I got to get home see my woman. You got yours in hand. I got to go get mine.

(BONO *starts to exit as* CORY *enters the yard, dressed in his football uniform. He gives* TROY *a hard, uncompromising look.*)

CORY: What you do that for, Pop?

(*He throws his helmet down in the direction of* TROY.)

ROSE: What's the matter? Cory . . . what's the matter?

CORY: Papa done went up to the school and told Coach Zellman I can't play football no more. Wouldn't even let me play the game. Told him to tell the recruiter not to come.

ROSE: Troy . . .

TROY: What you Troying me for. Yeah, I did it. And the boy know why I did it.

CORY: Why you wanna do that to me? That was the one chance I had.

ROSE: Ain't nothing wrong with Cory playing football, Troy.

TROY: The boy lied to me. I told the nigger if he wanna play football . . . to keep up his chores and hold down that job at the A&P. That was the conditions. Stopped down there to see Mr. Stawicki . . .

CORY: I can't work after school during the football season, Pop! I tried to tell you that Mr. Stawicki's holding my job for me. You don't never want to listen to nobody. And then you wanna go and do this to me!

TROY: I ain't done nothing to you. You done it to yourself.

CORY: Just cause you didn't have a chance! You just scared I'm gonna be better than you, that's all.

TROY: Come here.

ROSE: Troy . . .

(CORY *reluctantly crosses over to* TROY.)

TROY: All right! See. You done made a mistake.

CORY: I didn't even do nothing!

TROY: I'm gonna tell you what your mistake was. See . . . you swung at the ball and didn't hit it. That's strike one. See, you in the batter's box now. You swung and you missed. That's strike one. Don't you strike out!

(*Lights fade to black.*)

ACT II · SCENE I

(*The following morning.* CORY *is at the tree hitting the ball with the bat. He tries to mimic* TROY, *but his swing is awkward, less sure.* ROSE *enters from the house.*)

ROSE: Cory, I want you to help me with this cupboard.

CORY: I ain't quitting the team. I don't care what Poppa say.

ROSE: I'll talk to him when he gets back. He had to go see about your Uncle Gabe. The police done arrested him. Say he was disturbing the peace. He'll be back directly. Come on in here and help me clean out the top of this cupboard.

(CORY *exits into the house.* ROSE *sees* TROY *and* BONO *coming down the alley.*)

Troy . . . what they say down there?

TROY: Ain't said nothing. I give them fifty dollars and they let him go. I'll talk to you about it. Where's Cory?

ROSE: He's in there helping me clean out these cupboards.

TROY: Tell him to get his butt out here.

(TROY *and* BONO *go over to the pile of wood.* BONO *picks up the saw and begins sawing.*)

TROY (*to* BONO): All they want is the money. That makes six or seven times I done went down there and got him. See me coming they stick out their *hands.*

BONO: Yeah, I know what you mean. That's all they care about . . . that money. They don't care about what's right.

(*Pause.*)

Nigger, why you got to go and get some hard wood? You ain't doing nothing but building a little old fence. Get you some soft pine wood. That's all you need.

TROY: I know what I'm doing. This is outside wood. You put pine wood inside the house. Pine wood is inside wood. This here is outside wood. Now you tell me where the fence is gonna be?

BONO: You don't need this wood. You can put it up with pine wood and it'll stand as long as you gonna be here looking at it.

TROY: How you know how long I'm gonna be here, nigger? Hell, I might just live forever. Live longer than old man Horsely.

BONO: That's what Magee used to say.

TROY: Magee's a damn fool. Now you tell me who you ever heard of gonna pull their own teeth with a pair of rusty pliers.

BONO: The old folks . . . my granddaddy used to pull his teeth with pliers. They ain't had no dentists for the colored folks back then.

TROY: Get clean pliers! You understand? Clean pliers! Sterilize them! Besides we ain't living back then. All Magee had to do was walk over to Doc Goldblum's.

BONO: I see where you and that Tallahassee gal . . . that Alberta . . . I see where you all done got tight.

TROY: What you mean "got tight"?

BONO: I see where you be laughing and joking with her all the time.

TROY: I laughs and jokes with all of them, Bono. You know me.

BONO: That ain't the kind of laughing and joking I'm talking about.

(CORY *enters from the house.*)

CORY: How you doing, Mr. Bono?

TROY: Cory? Get that saw from Bono and cut some wood. He talking about the wood's too hard to cut. Stand back there, Jim, and let that young boy show you how it's done.

BONO: He's sure welcome to it.

(CORY *takes the saw and begins to cut the wood.*)

Whew-e-e! Look at that. Big old strong boy. Look like Joe Louis. Hell, must be getting old the way I'm watching that boy whip through that wood.

CORY: I don't see why Mama want a fence around the yard noways.

TROY: Damn if I know either. What the hell she keeping out with it? She ain't got nothing nobody want.

BONO: Some people build fences to keep people out . . . and other people build fences to keep people in. Rose wants to hold on to you all. She loves you.

TROY: Hell, nigger, I don't need nobody to tell me my wife loves me, Cory go on in the house and see if you can find that other saw.

CORY: Where's it at?

TROY: I said find it! Look for it till you find it!

(CORY *exits into the house.*)

What's that supposed to mean? Wanna keep us in?

BONO: Troy . . . I done known you seem like damn near my whole life. You and Rose both. I done know both of you all for a long time. I remember when you met Rose. When you was hitting them baseball out the park. A lot of them old gals was after you then. You had the pick of the litter. When you picked Rose, I was happy for you. That was the first time I knew you had any sense. I said . . . My man Troy knows what he's doing . . . I'm gonna follow this nigger . . . he might take me somewhere. I been following you too. I done learned a whole heap of things about life watching you. I done learned how to tell where the shit lies. How to tell it from the alfalfa. You done learned me a lot of things.

You showed me how to not make the same mistakes . . . to take life as it comes along and keep putting one foot in front of the other.
(Pause.)
Rose a good woman, Troy.

TROY: Hell, nigger, I know she a good woman. I been married to her for eighteen years. What you got on your mind, Bono?

BONO: I just say she a good woman. Just like I say anything. I ain't got to have nothing on my mind.

TROY: You just gonna say she a good woman and leave it hanging out there like that? Why you telling me she a good woman?

BONO: She loves you, Troy. Rose loves you.

TROY: You saying I don't measure up. That's what you trying to say. I don't measure up cause I'm seeing this other gal. I know what you trying to say.

BONO: I know what Rose means to you, Troy. I'm just trying to say I don't want to see you mess up.

TROY: Yeah, I appreciate that, Bono. If you was messing around on Lucille I'd be telling you the same thing.

BONO: Well, that's all I got to say. I just say that because I love you both.

TROY: Hell, you know me . . . I wasn't out there looking for nothing. You can't find a better woman than Rose. I know that. But seems like this woman just stuck onto me where I can't shake her loose. I done wrestled with it, tried to throw her off me . . . but she just stuck on tighter. Now she's stuck on for good.

BONO: You's in control . . . that's what you tell me all the time. You responsible for what you do.

TROY: I ain't ducking the responsibility of it. As long as it sets right in my heart . . . then I'm okay. Cause that's all I listen to. It'll tell me right from wrong every time. And I ain't talking about doing Rose no bad turn. I love Rose. She done carried me a long ways and I love and respect her for that.

BONO: I know you do. That's why I don't want to see you hurt her. But what you gonna do when she find out? What you got then? If you try and juggle both of them . . . sooner or later you gonna drop one of them. That's common sense.

TROY: Yeah, I hear what you saying, Bono. I been trying to figure a way to work it out.

BONO: Work it out right, Troy. I don't want to be getting all up between you and Rose's business . . . but work it so it come out right.

TROY: Ah hell, I get all up between you and Lucille's business. When you gonna get that woman that refrigerator she been wanting? Don't tell me you ain't got no money now. I know who your banker is. Mellon don't need that money bad as Lucille want that refrigerator. I'll tell you that.

BONO: Tell you what I'll do . . . when you finish building this fence for Rose . . . I'll buy Lucille that refrigerator.

TROY: You done stuck your foot in your mouth now!

(TROY *grabs up a board and begins to saw.* BONO *starts to walk out the yard.*)
Hey, nigger . . . where you going?

BONO: I'm going home. I know you don't expect me to help you now. I'm protecting my money. I wanna see you put that fence up by yourself. That's what I want to see. You'll be here another six months without me.

TROY: Nigger, you ain't right.

BONO: When it comes to my money . . . I'm right as fireworks on the Fourth of July.

TROY: All right, we gonna see now. You better get your bankbook.

(BONO *exits, and* TROY *continues to work.* ROSE *enters from the house.*)

ROSE: What they say down there? What's happening with Gabe?

TROY: I went down there and got him out. Cost me fifty dollars. Say he was disturbing the peace. Judge set up a hearing for him in three weeks. Say to show cause why he shouldn't be recommitted.

ROSE: What was he doing that cause them to arrest him?

TROY: Some kids was teasing him and he run them off home. Say he was howling and carrying on. Some folks seen him and called the police. That's all it was.

ROSE: Well, what's you say? What'd you tell the judge?

TROY: Told him I'd look after him. It didn't make no sense to recommit the man. He stuck out his big greasy palm and told me to give him fifty dollars and take him on home.

ROSE: Where's he at now? Where'd he go off to?

TROY: He's gone on about his business. He don't need nobody to hold his hand.

ROSE: Well, I don't know. Seem like that would be the best place for him if they did put him into the hospital. I know what you're gonna say. But that's what I think would be best.

TROY: The man done had his life ruined fighting for what? And they wanna take and lock him up. Let him be free. He don't bother nobody.

ROSE: Well, everybody got their own way of looking at it I guess. Come on and get your lunch. I got a bowl of lima beans and some cornbread in the oven. Come on get something to eat. Ain't no sense you fretting over Gabe.

(ROSE *turns to go into the house.*)

TROY: Rose . . . got something to tell you.

ROSE: Well, come on . . . wait till I get this food on the table.

TROY: Rose!

(*She stops and turns around.*)
I don't know how to say this.
(*Pause.*)
I can't explain it none. It just sort of grows on you till it gets out of hand. It starts out like a little bush . . . and the next thing you know it's a whole forest.

ROSE: Troy . . . what is you talking about?

TROY: I'm talking, woman, let me talk. I'm trying to find a way to tell you . . . I'm gonna be a daddy. I'm gonna be somebody's daddy.

ROSE: Troy . . . you're not telling me this? You're gonna be . . . what?

TROY: Rose . . . now . . . see . . .

ROSE: You telling me you gonna by somebody's daddy? You telling your *wife* this?

(GABRIEL *enters from the street. He carries a rose in his hand.*)

GABRIEL: Hey, Troy! Hey, Rose!

ROSE: I have to wait eighteen years to hear something like this.

GABRIEL: Hey, Rose . . . I got a flower for you.

(*He hands it to her.*)

That's a rose. Same rose like you is.

ROSE: Thanks, Gabe.

GABRIEL: Troy, you ain't mad at me is you? Them bad mens come and put me away. You ain't mad at me is you?

TROY: Naw, Gabe, I ain't mad at you.

ROSE: Eighteen years and you wanna come with this.

GABRIEL (*takes a quarter out of his pocket*): See what I got? Got a brand new quarter.

TROY: Rose . . . it's just . . .

ROSE: Ain't nothing you can say, Troy. Ain't no way of explaining that.

GABRIEL: Fellow that gave me this quarter had a whole mess of them. I'm gonna keep this quarter till it stop shining.

ROSE: Gabe, go on in the house there. I got some watermelon in the frigidaire. Go on and get you a piece.

GABRIEL: Say, Rose . . . you know I was chasing hellhounds and them bad mens come and get me and take me away. Troy helped me. He come down there and told them they better let me go before he beat them up. Yeah, he did!

ROSE: You go on and get you a piece of watermelon, Gabe. Them bad mens is gone now.

GABRIEL: Okay, Rose . . . gonna get me some watermelon. The kind with the stripes on it.

(GABRIEL *exits into the house.*)

ROSE: Why, Troy? Why? After all these years to come dragging this in to me now. It don't make no sense at your age. I could have expected this ten or fifteen years ago, but not now.

TROY: Age ain't got nothing to do with it, Rose.

ROSE: I done tried to be everything a wife should be. Everything a wife could be. Been married eighteen years and I got to live to see the day you tell me you been seeing another woman and done fathered a child by her. And you know I ain't never wanted no half nothing in my family. My whole family is half. Everybody got different fathers and mothers . . . my two sisters and my brother. Can't hardly tell who's who. Can't never sit down and talk about Papa and Mama. It's your papa and your mama and my papa and my mama . . .

TROY: Rose . . . stop it now.

ROSE: I ain't never wanted that for none of my children. And now you wanna drag your behind in here and tell me something like this.

TROY: You ought to know. It's time for you to know.

ROSE: Well, I don't want to know, goddamn it!

TROY: I can't just make it go away. It's done now. I can't wish the circumstance of the thing away.

ROSE: And you don't want to either. Maybe you want to wish me and my boy away. Maybe that's what you want? Well, you can't wish us away. I've got eighteen years of my life invested in you. You ought to have stayed upstairs in my bed where you belong.

TROY: Rose . . . now listen to me . . . we can get a handle on this thing. We can talk this out . . . come to an understanding.

ROSE: All of a sudden it's "we." Where was "we" at when you was down there rolling around with some godforsaken woman? "We" should have come to an understanding before you started making a damn fool of yourself. You're a day late and a dollar short when it comes to an understanding with me.

TROY: It's just . . . She gives me a different idea . . . a different understanding about myself. I can step out of this house and get away from the pressures and problems . . . be a different man. I ain't got to wonder how I'm gonna pay the bills or get the roof fixed. I can just be a part of myself that I ain't never been.

ROSE: What I want to know . . . is do you plan to continue seeing her. That's all you can say to me.

TROY: I can sit up in her house and laugh. Do you understand what I'm saying. I can laugh out loud . . . and it feels good. It reaches all the way down to the bottom of my shoes.

(Pause.)

Rose, I can't give that up.

ROSE: Maybe you ought to go on and stay down there with her . . . if she's a better woman than me.

TROY: It ain't about nobody being a better woman or nothing. Rose, you ain't the blame. A man couldn't ask for no woman to be a better wife than you've been. I'm responsible for it. I done locked myself into a pattern trying to take care of you all that I forgot about myself.

ROSE: What the hell was I there for? That was my job, not somebody else's.

TROY: Rose, I done tried all my life to live decent . . . to live a clean . . . hard . . . useful life. I tried to be a good husband to you. In every way I knew how. Maybe I come into the world backwards, I don't know. But . . . you born with two strikes on you before you come to the plate. You got to guard it closely . . . always looking for the curve ball on the inside corner. You can't afford to let none get past you. You can't afford a call strike. If you going down . . . you going down swinging. Everything lined up against you. What you gonna do. I fooled them, Rose. I bunted. When I found you and Cory and a halfway decent job . . . I was safe. Couldn't nothing touch me. I wasn't gonna strike out no more. I wasn't going back to the penitentiary. I wasn't gonna lay in the streets with a bottle of wine. I was safe. I had me a family. A job. I wasn't gonna get that last strike. I was on first looking for one of them boys to knock me in. To get me home.

ROSE: You should have stayed in my bed, Troy.

TROY: Then when I saw that gal . . . she firmed up my backbone. And I got to thinking that if I tried . . . I just might be able to steal second. Do you understand after eighteen years I wanted to steal second.

ROSE: You should have held me tight. You should have grabbed me and held on.

TROY: I stood on first base for eighteen years and I thought . . . well, goddamn it . . . go on for it!

ROSE: We're not talking about baseball! We're talking about you going off to lay in bed with another woman . . . and then bring it home to me. That's what we're talking about. We ain't talking about no baseball.

TROY: Rose, you're not listening to me. I'm trying the best I can to explain it to you. It's not easy for me to admit that I been standing in the same place for eighteen years.

ROSE: I been standing with you! I been right here with you, Troy. I got a life too. I gave eighteen years of my life to stand in the same spot with you. Don't you think I ever wanted other things? Don't you think I had dreams and hopes? What about my life? What about me? Don't you think it ever crossed my mind to want to know other men? That I wanted to lay up somewhere and forget about my responsibilities? That I wanted someone to make me laugh so I could feel good? You not the only one who's got wants and needs. But I held on to you, Troy. I took all my feelings, my wants and needs, my dreams . . . and I buried them inside you. I planted a seed and watched and prayed over it. I planted myself inside you and waited to bloom. And it didn't take me no eighteen years to find out the soil was hard and rocky and it wasn't never gonna bloom.

But I held on to you, Troy. I held you tighter. You was my husband. I owed you everything I had. Every part of me I could find to give you. And upstairs in that room . . . with the darkness falling in on me . . . I gave everything I had to try and erase the doubt that you wasn't the finest man in the world. And wherever you was going . . . I wanted to be there with you. Cause you was my husband. Cause that's the only way I was gonna survive as your wife. You always talking about what you give . . . and what you don't have to give. But you take too. You take . . . and don't even know nobody's giving!

(ROSE *turns to exit into the house;* TROY *grabs her arm.*)

TROY: You say I take and don't give!

ROSE: Troy! You're hurting me!

TROY: You say I take and don't give.

ROSE: Troy . . . you're hurting my arm! Let go!

TROY: I done give you everything I got. Don't you tell that lie on me.

ROSE: Troy!

TROY: Don't you tell that lie on me!

(CORY *enters from the house.*)

CORY: Mama!

ROSE: Troy. You're hurting me.

TROY: Don't you tell me about no taking and giving.

(CORY *comes up behind* TROY *and grabs him.* TROY, *surprised, is thrown off balance just as* CORY *throws a glancing blow that catches him on the chest and knocks him down.* TROY *is stunned, as is* CORY.)

ROSE: Troy. Troy. No!

(TROY *gets to his feet and starts at* CORY.)

Troy . . . no. Please! Troy!

(ROSE *pulls on* TROY *to hold him back.* TROY *stops himself.*)

TROY (*to* CORY): All right. That's strike two. You stay away from around me, boy. Don't you strike out. You living with a full count. Don't you strike out.

(TROY *exits out the yard as the lights go down.*)

Scene II

(*It is six months later, early afternoon.* TROY *enters from the house and starts to exit the yard.* ROSE *enters from the house.*)

ROSE: Troy, I want to talk to you.

TROY: All of a sudden, after all this time, you want to talk to me, huh? You ain't wanted to talk to me for months. You ain't wanted to talk to me last night. You ain't wanted no part of me then. What you wanna talk to me about now?

ROSE: Tomorrow's Friday.

TROY: I know what day tomorrow is. You think I don't know tomorrow's Friday? My whole life I ain't done nothing but look to see Friday coming and you got to tell me it's Friday.

ROSE: I want to know if you're coming home.

TROY: I always come home, Rose. You know that. There ain't never been a night I ain't come home.

ROSE: That ain't what I mean . . . and you know it. I want to know if you're coming straight home after work.

TROY: I figure I'd cash my check . . . hang out at Taylors' with the boys . . . maybe play a game of checkers . . .

ROSE: Troy, I can't live like this. I won't live like this. You livin' on borrowed time with me. It's been going on six months now you ain't been coming home.

TROY: I be here every night. Every night of the year. That's 365 days.

ROSE: I want you to come home tomorrow after work.

TROY: Rose . . . I don't mess up my pay. You know that now. I take my pay and I give it to you. I don't have no money but what you give me back. I just want to have a little time to myself . . . a little time to enjoy life.

ROSE: What about me? When's my time to enjoy life?

TROY: I don't know what to tell you, Rose. I'm doing the best I can.

ROSE: You ain't been home from work but time enough to change your clothes and run out . . . and you wanna call that the best you can do?

TROY: I'm going over to the hospital to see Alberta. She went into the hospital this afternoon. Look like she might have the baby early. I won't be gone long.

ROSE: Well, you ought to know. They went over to Miss Pearl's and got Gabe today. She said you told them to go ahead and lock him up.

TROY: I ain't said no such thing. Whoever told you that is telling a lie. Pearl ain't doing nothing but telling a big fat lie.

ROSE: She ain't had to tell me. I read it on the papers.

TROY: I ain't told them nothing of the kind.

ROSE: I saw it right there on the papers.

TROY: What it say, huh?

ROSE: It said you told them to take him.

TROY: Then they screwed that up, just the way they screw up everything. I ain't worried about what they got on the paper.

ROSE: Say the government send part of his check to the hospital and the other part to you.

TROY: I ain't got nothing to do with that if that's the way it works. I ain't made up the rules about how it work.

ROSE: You did Gabe just like you did Cory. You wouldn't sign the paper for Cory . . . but you signed for Gabe. You signed that paper.

(The telephone is heard ringing inside the house.)

TROY: I told you I ain't signed nothing, woman! The only thing I signed was the release form. Hell, I can't read, I don't know what they had on that paper! I ain't signed nothing about sending Gabe away.

ROSE: I said send him to the hospital . . . you said let him be free . . . now you done went down there and signed him to the hospital for half his money. You went back on yourself, Troy. You gonna have to answer for that.

TROY: See now . . . you been over there talking to Miss Pearl. She done got mad cause she ain't getting Gabe's rent money. That's all it is. She's liable to say anything.

ROSE: Troy, I seen where you signed the paper.

TROY: You ain't seen nothing I signed. What she doing got papers on my brother anyway? Miss Pearl telling a big fat lie. And I'm gonna tell her about it too! You ain't seen nothing I signed. Say . . . you ain't seen nothing I signed.

*(*ROSE *exits into the house to answer the telephone. Presently she returns.)*

ROSE: Troy . . . that was the hospital. Alberta had the baby.

TROY: What she have? What is it?

ROSE: It's a girl.

TROY: I better get on down to the hospital to see her.

ROSE: Troy . . .

TROY: Rose . . . I got to go see her now. That's only right . . . what's the matter . . . the baby's all right, ain't it?

ROSE: Alberta died having the baby.

TROY: Died . . . you say she's dead? Alberta's dead?

ROSE: They said they done all they could. They couldn't do nothing for her.

TROY: The baby? How's the baby?

ROSE: They say it's healthy. I wonder who's gonna bury her.

TROY: She had family, Rose. She wasn't living in the world by herself.

ROSE: I know she wasn't living in the world by herself.

TROY: Next thing you gonna want to know if she had any insurance.

ROSE: Troy, you ain't got to talk like that.

TROY: That's the first thing that jumped out your mouth. "Who's gonna bury her?" Like I'm fixing to take on that task for myself.

ROSE: I am your wife. Don't push me away.

TROY: I ain't pushing nobody away. Just give me some space. That's all. Just give me some room to breathe.

(ROSE *exits into the house.* TROY *walks about the yard.*)

TROY (*with a quiet rage that threatens to consume him*): All right . . . Mr. Death. See now . . . I'm gonna tell you what I'm gonna do. I'm gonna take and build me a fence around this yard. See? I'm gonna build me a fence around what belongs to me. And then I want you to stay on the other side. See? You stay over there until you're ready for me. Then you come on. Bring your army. Bring your sickle. Bring your wrestling clothes. I ain't gonna fall down on my vigilance this time. You ain't gonna sneak up on me no more. When you ready for me . . . when the top of your list say Troy Maxson . . . that's when you come around here. You come up and knock on the front door. Ain't nobody else got nothing to do with this. This is between you and me. Man to man. You stay on the other side of that fence until you ready for me. Then you come up and knock on the front door. Anytime you want. I'll be ready for you.

(*The lights go down to black.*)

SCENE III

(*The lights come up on the porch. It is late evening three days later.* ROSE *sits listening to the ball game waiting for* TROY. *The final out of the game is made and* ROSE *switches off the radio.* TROY *enters the yard carrying an infant wrapped in blankets. He stands back from the house and calls.*)

(ROSE *enters and stands on the porch. There is a long, awkward silence, the weight of which grows heavier with each passing second.*)

TROY: Rose . . . I'm standing here with my daughter in my arms. She ain't but a wee bittie little old thing. She don't know nothing about grownups' business. She innocent . . . and she ain't got no mama.

ROSE: What you telling me for, Troy?

(*She turns and exits into the house.*)

TROY: Well . . . I guess we'll sit out here on the porch.

(*He sits down on the porch. There is an awkward indelicateness about the way he handles the baby. His largeness engulfs and seems to swallow it. He speaks loud enough for* ROSE *to hear.*)

A man's got to do what's right for him. I ain't sorry for nothing I done. It felt right in my heart.

(*To the baby.*)

What you smiling at? Your daddy's a big man. Got these great big old hands. But sometimes he's scared. And right now your daddy's scared cause we sitting out here and ain't got no home. Oh, I been homeless before. I ain't had no little baby with me. But I been homeless. You just be out on the road by your lonesome and you see one of them trains coming and you just kinda go like this . . .

(*He sings as a lullaby.*)

Please, Mr. Engineer let a man ride the line

Please, Mr. Engineer let a man ride the line

I ain't got no ticket please let me ride the blinds

(ROSE *enters from the house.* TROY *hearing her steps behind him, stands and faces her.*)

She's my daughter, Rose. My own flesh and blood. I can't deny her no more than I can deny them boys.

(*Pause.*)

You and them boys is my family. You and them and this child is all I got in the world. So I guess what I'm saying is . . . I'd appreciate it if you'd help me take care of her.

ROSE: Okay, Troy . . . you're right. I'll take care of your baby for you . . . cause . . . like you say . . . she's innocent . . . and you can't visit the sins of the father upon the child. A motherless child has got a hard time.

(*She takes the baby from him.*)

From right now . . . this child got a mother. But you a womanless man.

(ROSE *turns and exits into the house with the baby. Lights go down to black.*)

Scene IV

(*It is two months later.* LYONS *enters from the street. He knocks on the door and calls.*)

LYONS: Hey, Rose! (*Pause.*) Rose!

ROSE (*from inside the house*):   Stop that yelling. You gonna wake up Raynell. I just got her to sleep.

LYONS: I just stopped by to pay Papa this twenty dollars I owe him. Where's Papa at?

ROSE: He should be here in a minute. I'm getting ready to go down to the church. Sit down and wait on him.

LYONS: I got to go pick up Bonnie over her mother's house.

ROSE: Well, sit it down there on the table. He'll get it.

LYONS (*enters the house and sets the money on the table*):   Tell Papa I said thanks. I'll see you again.

ROSE: All right, Lyons. We'll see you.

(LYONS *starts to exit as* CORY *enters.*)

CORY: Hey, Lyons.

LYONS: What's happening, Cory. Say man, I'm sorry I missed your graduation. You know I had a gig and couldn't get away. Otherwise, I would have been there, man. So what you doing?

CORY: I'm trying to find a job.

LYONS: Yeah I know how that go, man. It's rough out here. Jobs are scarce.

CORY: Yeah, I know.

LYONS: Look here, I got to run. Talk to Papa . . . he know some people. He'll be able to help get you a job. Talk to him . . . see what he say.

CORY: Yeah . . . all right, Lyons.

LYONS: You take care. I'll talk to you soon. We'll find some time to talk.

(LYONS *exits the yard.* CORY *wanders over to the tree, picks up the bat, and assumes a batting stance. He studies an imaginary pitcher and swings. Dissatisfied with the result, he tries again.* TROY *enters. They eye each other for a beat.* CORY *puts the bat down and exits the yard.* TROY *starts into the house as* ROSE *exits with* RAYNELL. *She is carrying a cake.*)

TROY: I'm coming in and everybody's going out.

ROSE: I'm taking this cake down to the church for the bake sale. Lyons was by to see you. He stopped by to pay you your twenty dollars. It's laying in there on the table.

TROY *(going into his pocket):* Well . . . here go this money.

ROSE: Put it in there on the table, Troy. I'll get it.

TROY: What time you coming back?

ROSE: Ain't no use in you studying me. It don't matter what time I come back.

TROY: I just asked you a question, woman. What's the matter . . . can't I ask you a question?

ROSE: Troy, I don't want to go into it. Your dinner's in there on the stove. All you got to do is heat it up. And don't you be eating the rest of them cakes in there. I'm coming back for them. We having a bake sale at the church tomorrow.

(ROSE *exits the yard.* TROY *sits down on the steps, takes a pint bottle from his pocket, opens it, and drinks. He begins to sing.*)

TROY: Hear it ring! Hear it ring!
Had an old dog his name was Blue
You know Blue was mighty true
You know Blue was a good old dog
Blue treed a possum in a hollow log
You know from that he was a good old dog

(BONO *enters the yard.*)

BONO: Hey, Troy.

TROY: Hey, what's happening, Bono?

BONO: I just thought I'd stop by to see you.

TROY: What you stop by and see me for? You ain't stopped by in a month of Sundays. Hell, I must owe you money or something.

BONO: Since you got your promotion I can't keep up with you. Used to see you every day. Now I don't even know what route you working.

TROY: They keep switching me around. Got me out in Greentree now . . . hauling white folks' garbage.

BONO: Greentree, huh? You lucky, at least you ain't got to be lifting them barrels. Damn if they ain't getting heavier. I'm gonna put in my two years and call it quits.

TROY: I'm thinking about retiring myself.

BONO: You got it easy. You can *drive* for another five years.

TROY: It ain't the same, Bono. It ain't like working the back of the truck. Ain't got nobody to talk to . . . feel like you working by yourself. Naw, I'm thinking about retiring. How's Lucille?

BONO: She all right. Her arthritis get to acting up on her sometime. Saw Rose on my way in. She going down to the church, huh?

TROY: Yeah, she took up going down there. All them preachers looking for somebody to fatten their pockets.

(Pause.)

Got some gin here.

BONO: Naw, thanks. I just stopped by to say hello.

TROY: Hell, nigger . . . you can take a drink. I ain't never known you to say no to a drink. You ain't got to work tomorrow.

BONO: I just stopped by. I'm fixing to go over to Skinner's. We got us a domino game going over his house every Friday.

TROY: Nigger, you can't play no dominoes. I used to whup you four games out of five.

BONO: Well, that learned me. I'm getting better.

TROY: Yeah? Well, that's all right.

BONO: Look here . . . I got to be getting on. Stop by sometime, huh?

TROY: Yeah, I'll do that, Bono. Lucille told Rose you bought her a new refrigerator.

BONO: Yeah, Rose told Lucille you had finally built your fence . . . so I figured we'd call it even.

TROY: I knew you would.

BONO: Yeah . . . okay. I'll be talking to you.

TROY: Yeah, take care, Bono. Good to see you. I'm gonna stop over.

BONO: Yeah. Okay, Troy.

(BONO exits. TROY drinks from the bottle.)

TROY: Old Blue died and I dig his grave

Let him down with a golden chain

Every night when I hear old Blue bark

I know Blue treed a possum in Noah's Ark.

Hear it ring! Hear it ring!

(CORY enters the yard. They eye each other for a beat. TROY is sitting in the middle of the steps. CORY walks over.)

CORY: I got to get by.

TROY: Say what? What's you say?

CORY: You in my way. I got to get by.

TROY: You got to get by where? This is my house. Bought and paid for. In full. Took me fifteen years. And if you wanna go in my house and I'm sitting on the steps . . . you say excuse me. Like your mama taught you.

CORY: Come on, Pop . . . I got to get by.

(CORY *starts to maneuver his way past* TROY. TROY *grabs his leg and shoves him back.*)

TROY: You just gonna walk over top of me?

CORY: I live here too!

TROY (*advancing toward him*): You just gonna walk over top of me in my own house?

CORY: I ain't scared of you.

TROY: I ain't asked if you was scared of me. I asked you if you was fixing to walk over top of me in my own house? That's the question. You ain't gonna say excuse me? You just gonna walk over top of me?

CORY: If you wanna put it like that.

TROY: How else am I gonna put it?

CORY: I was walking by you to go into the house cause you sitting on the steps drunk, singing to yourself. You can put it like that.

TROY: Without saying excuse me???

(CORY *doesn't respond.*)

I asked you a question. Without saying excuse me???

CORY: I ain't got to say excuse me to you. You don't count around here no more.

TROY: Oh, I see . . . I don't count around here no more. You ain't got to say excuse me to your daddy. All of a sudden you done got so grown that your daddy don't count around here no more . . . Around here in his own house and yard that he done paid for with the sweat of his brow. You done got so grown to where you gonna take over. You gonna take over my house. Is that right? You gonna wear my pants. You gonna go in there and stretch out on my bed. You ain't got to say excuse me cause I don't count around here no more. Is that right?

CORY: That's right. You always talking this dumb stuff. Now, why don't you just get out my way.

TROY: I guess you got someplace to sleep and something to put in your belly. You got that, huh? You got that? That's what you need. You got that, huh?

CORY: You don't know what I got. You ain't got to worry about what I got.

TROY: You right! You one hundred percent right! I done spent the last seventeen years worrying about what you got. Now it's your turn, see? I'll tell you what to do. You grown . . . we done established that. You a man. Now, let's see you act like one. Turn you behind around and walk out this yard. And when you get out there in the alley . . . you can forget about this house. See? 'Cause this is my house. You go on and be a man and get your own house. You can forget about this. 'Cause this is mine. You go on and get yours 'cause I'm through with doing for you.

CORY: You talking about what you did for me . . . what'd you ever give me?

TROY: Them feet and bones! That pumping heart, nigger! I give you more than anybody else is ever gonna give you.

CORY: You ain't never gave me nothing! You ain't never done nothing but hold me back. Afraid I was gonna be better than you. All you ever did was try and make me scared of you. I used to tremble every time you called my name. Every time I heard your footsteps in the house. Wondering all the time . . . what's Papa gonna say if I do this? . . . What's he gonna say if I do that? . . . What's Papa gonna say if I turn on the radio? And Mama, too . . . she tries . . . but she's scared of you.

TROY: You leave your mama out of this. She ain't got nothing to do with this.

CORY: I don't know how she stand you . . . after what you did to her.

TROY: I told you to leave your mama out of this!

(He advances toward CORY.*)*

CORY: What you gonna do . . . give me a whupping? You can't whup me no more. You're too old. You just an old man.

TROY *(shoves him on his shoulder):* Nigger! That's what you are. You just another nigger on the street to me!

CORY: You crazy! You know that?

TROY: Go on now! You got the devil in you. Get on away from me!

CORY: You just a crazy old man . . . talking about I got the devil in me.

TROY: Yeah, I'm crazy! If you don't get on the other side of that yard . . . I'm gonna show you how crazy I am! Go on . . . get the hell out of my yard.

CORY: It ain't your yard. You took Uncle Gabe's money he got from the army to buy this house and then you put him out.

TROY *(*TROY *advances on* CORY*):* Get your black ass out of my yard!

*(*TROY'S *advance backs* CORY *up against the tree.* CORY *grabs up the bat.)*

CORY: I ain't going nowhere! Come on . . . put me out! I ain't scared of you.

TROY: That's my bat!

CORY: Come on!

TROY: Put my bat down!

CORY: Come on, put me out.

*(*CORY *swings at* TROY, *who backs across the yard.)*

What's the matter? You so bad . . . put me out!

*(*TROY *advances toward* CORY.*)*

CORY *(backing up):* Come on! Come on!

TROY: You're gonna have to use it! You wanna draw that bat back on me . . . you're gonna have to use it.

CORY: Come on! . . . Come on!

*(*CORY *swings the bat at* TROY *a second time. He misses.* TROY *continues to advance toward him.)*

TROY: You're gonna have to kill me! You wanna draw that bat back on me. You're gonna have to kill me.

(CORY, *backed up against the tree, can go no farther.* TROY *taunts him. He sticks out his head and offers him a target.*)

Come on! Come on!

(CORY *is unable to swing the bat.* TROY *grabs it.*)

TROY: Then I'll show you.

(CORY *and* TROY *struggle over the bat. The struggle is fierce and fully engaged.* TROY *ultimately is the stronger and takes the bat from* CORY *and stands over him ready to swing. He stops himself.*)

Go on and get away from around my house.

(CORY, *stung by his defeat, picks himself up, walks slowly out of the yard and up the alley.*)

CORY: Tell Mama I'll be back for my things.

TROY: They'll be on the other side of that fence.

(CORY *exits.*)

TROY: I can't taste nothing. Helluljah! I can't taste nothing no more. (TROY *assumes a batting posture and begins to taunt Death, the fastball on the outside corner.*) Come on! It's between you and me now! Come on! Anytime you want! Come on! I be ready for you . . . but I ain't gonna be easy.

(*The lights go down on the scene.*)

SCENE V

(*The time is 1965. The lights come up in the yard. It is the morning of* TROY'S *funeral. A funeral plaque with a light hangs beside the door. There is a small garden plot off to the side. There is noise and activity in the house as* ROSE, LYONS, *and* BONO *have gathered. The door opens and* RAYNELL, *seven years old, enters dressed in a flannel nightgown. She crosses to the garden and pokes around with a stick.* ROSE *calls from the house.*)

ROSE: Raynell!

RAYNELL: Mam?

ROSE: What you doing out there?

RAYNELL: Nothing.

(ROSE *comes to the door.*)

ROSE: Girl, get in here and get dressed. What you doing?

RAYNELL: Seeing if my garden growed.

ROSE: I told you it ain't gonna grow overnight. You got to wait.

RAYNELL: It don't look like it never gonna grow. Dang!

ROSE: I told you a watched pot never boils. Get in here and get dressed.

RAYNELL: This ain't even no pot, Mama.

ROSE: You just have to give it a chance. It'll grow. Now you come on and do what I told you. We got to be getting ready. This ain't no morning to be playing around. You hear me?

RAYNELL: Yes, mam.

(ROSE *exits into the house.* RAYNELL *continues to poke at her garden with a stick.* CORY *enters. He is dressed in a Marine corporal's uniform, and carries a duffel bag. His posture is that of a military man, and his speech has a clipped sternness.*)

CORY (*to* RAYNELL): Hi.

(*Pause.*)

I bet your name is Raynell.

RAYNELL: Uh huh.

CORY: Is your mama home?

(RAYNELL *runs up on the porch and calls through the screen door.*)

RAYNELL: Mama . . . there's some man out here. Mama?

(ROSE *comes to the door.*)

ROSE: Cory? Lord have mercy! Look here, you all!

(ROSE *and* CORY *embrace in a tearful reunion as* BONO *and* LYONS *enter from the house dressed in funeral clothes.*)

BONO: Aw, looka here . . .

ROSE: Done got all grown up!

CORY: Don't cry, Mama. What you crying about?

ROSE: I'm just so glad you made it.

CORY: Hey Lyons. How you doing, Mr. Bono?

(LYONS *goes to embrace* CORY.)

LYONS: Look at you, man. Look at you. Don't he look good, Rose? Got them Corporal stripes.

ROSE: What took you so long?

CORY: You know how the Marines are, Mama. They got to get all their paperwork straight before they let you do anything.

ROSE: Well, I'm sure glad you made it. They let Lyons come. Your Uncle Gabe's still in the hospital. They don't know if they gonna let him out or not. I just talked to them a little while ago.

LYONS: A Corporal in the United States Marines.

BONO: Your daddy knew you had it in you. He used to tell me all the time.

LYONS: Don't he look good, Mr. Bono?

BONO: Yeah, he remind me of Troy when I first met him.

(*Pause.*)

Say, Rose, Lucille's down at the church with the choir. I'm gonna go down and get the pallbearers lined up. I'll be back to get you all.

ROSE: Thanks, Jim.

CORY: See you, Mr. Bono.

LYONS (*with his arm around* RAYNELL): Cory . . . look at Raynell. Ain't she precious? She gonna break a whole lot of hearts.

ROSE: Raynell, come and say hello to your brother. This is your brother, Cory. You remember Cory.

RAYNELL: No, Mam.

CORY: She don't remember me, Mama.

ROSE: Well, we talk about you. She heard us talk about you. *(To* RAYNELL.*)* This is your brother, Cory. Come on and say hello.

RAYNELL: Hi.

CORY: Hi. So you're Raynell. Mama told me a lot about you.

ROSE: You all come on into the house and let me fix you some breakfast. Keep up your strength.

CORY: I ain't hungry, Mama.

LYONS: You can fix me something, Rose. I'll be in there in a minute.

ROSE: Cory, you sure you don't want nothing? I know they ain't feeding you right.

CORY: No, Mama . . . thanks. I don't feel like eating. I'll get something later.

ROSE: Raynell . . . get on upstairs and get that dress on like I told you.

*(*ROSE *and* RAYNELL *exit into the house.)*

LYONS: So . . . I hear you thinking about getting married.

CORY: Yeah, I done found the right one, Lyons. It's about time.

LYONS: Me and Bonnie been split up about four years now. About the time Papa retired. I guess she just got tired of all them changes I was putting her through.

(Pause.)

I always knew you was gonna make something out yourself. Your head was always in the right direction. So . . . you gonna stay in . . . make it a career . . . put in your twenty years?

CORY: I don't know. I got six already, I think that's enough.

LYONS: Stick with Uncle Sam and retire early. Ain't nothing out here. I guess Rose told you what happened with me. They got me down the workhouse. I thought I was being slick cashing other people's checks.

CORY: How much time you doing?

LYONS: They give me three years. I got that beat now. I ain't got but nine more months. It ain't so bad. You learn to deal with it like anything else. You got to take the crookeds with the straights. That's what Papa used to say. He used to say that when he struck out. I seen him strike out three times in a row . . . and the next time up he hit the ball over the grandstand. Right out there in Homestead Field. He wasn't satisfied hitting in the seats . . . he want to hit it over everything! After the game he had two hundred people standing around waiting to shake his hand. You got to take the crookeds with the straights. Yeah, Papa was something else.

CORY: You still playing?

LYONS: Cory . . . you know I'm gonna do that. There's some fellows down there we got us a band . . . we gonna try and stay together when we get out . . . but yeah, I'm still playing. It still helps me to get out of bed in the morning. As long as it do that I'm gonna be right there playing and trying to make some sense out of it.

ROSE *(calling):* Lyons, I got these eggs in the pan.

LYONS: Let me go on and get these eggs, man. Get ready to go bury Papa.

(Pause.)

How you doing? You doing all right?

*(*CORY *nods.* LYONS *touches him on the shoulder and they share a moment of silent grief.* LYONS *exits into the house.* CORY *wanders about the yard.* RAYNELL *enters.)*

RAYNELL: Hi.

CORY: Hi.

RAYNELL: Did you used to sleep in my room?

CORY: Yeah . . . that used to be my room.

RAYNELL: That's what Papa call it. "Cory's room." It got your football in the closet.

*(*ROSE *comes to the door.)*

ROSE: Raynell, get in there and get them good shoes on.

RAYNELL: Mama, can't I wear these? Them other one hurt my feet.

ROSE: Well, they just gonna have to hurt your feet for a while. You ain't said they hurt your feet when you went down to the store and got them.

RAYNELL: They didn't hurt then. My feet done got bigger.

ROSE: Don't you give me no backtalk now. You get in there and get them shoes on.

*(*RAYNELL *exits into the house.)*

Ain't too much changed. He still got that piece of rag tied to that tree. He was out here swinging that bat. I was just ready to go back in the house. He swung that bat and then he just fell over. Seem like he swung it and stood there with this grin on his face . . . and then he just fell over. They carried him on down to the hospital, but I knew there wasn't no need . . . why don't you come on in the house?

CORY: Mama . . . I got something to tell you. I don't know how to tell you this . . . but I've got to tell you . . . I'm not going to Papa's funeral.

ROSE: Boy, hush your mouth. That's your daddy you talking about. I don't want hear that kind of talk this morning. I done raised you to come to this? You standing there all healthy and grown talking about you ain't going to your daddy's funeral?

CORY: Mama . . . listen . . .

ROSE: I don't want to hear it, Cory. You just get that thought out of your head.

CORY: I can't drag Papa with me everywhere I go. I've got to say no to him. One time in my life I've got to say no.

ROSE: Don't nobody have to listen to nothing like that. I know you and your daddy ain't seen eye to eye, but I ain't got to listen to that kind of talk this morning. Whatever was between you and your daddy . . . the time has come to put it aside. Just take it and set it over there on the shelf and forget about it. Disrespecting your daddy ain't gonna make you a man, Cory. You got to find a way to come to that on your own. Not going to your daddy's funeral ain't gonna make you a man.

CORY: The whole time I was growing up . . . living in his house . . . Papa was like a shadow that followed you everywhere. It weighed on you and sunk into your flesh. It would wrap around you and lay there until you couldn't tell which one was you anymore. That shadow digging in your flesh. Trying to crawl in. Trying to live through you. Everywhere I looked, Troy Maxson was staring back at me . . . hiding under the bed . . . in the closet. I'm just saying I've got to find a way to get rid of that shadow, Mama.

ROSE: You just like him. You got him in you good.

CORY: Don't tell me that, Mama.

ROSE: You Troy Maxson all over again.

CORY: I don't want to be Troy Maxson. I want to be me.

ROSE: You can't be nobody but who you are, Cory. That shadow wasn't nothing but you growing into yourself. You either got to grow into it or cut it down to fit you. But that's all you got to make life with. That's all you got to measure yourself against that world out there. Your daddy wanted you to be everything he wasn't . . . and at the same time he tried to make you into everything he was. I don't know if he was right or wrong . . . but I do know he meant to do more good than he meant to do harm. He wasn't always right. Sometimes when he touched he bruised. And sometimes when he took me in his arms he cut.

When I first met your daddy I thought . . . Here is a man I can lay down with and make a baby. That's the first thing I thought when I seen him. I was thirty years old and had done seen my share of men. But when he walked up to me and said, "I can dance a waltz that'll make you dizzy," I thought, Rose Lee, here is a man that you can open yourself up to and be filled to bursting. Here is a man that can fill all them empty spaces you been tipping around the edges of. One of them empty spaces was being somebody's mother.

I married your daddy and settled down to cooking his supper and keeping clean sheets on the bed. When your daddy walked through the house he was so big he filled it up. That was my first mistake. Not to make him leave some room for me. For my part in the matter. But at that time I wanted that. I wanted a house that I could sing in. And that's what your daddy gave me. I didn't know to keep up his strength I had to give up little pieces of mine. I did that. I took on his life as mine and mixed up the pieces so that you couldn't hardly tell which was which anymore. It was my choice. It was my life and I didn't have to live it like that. But that's what life offered me in the way of being a woman and I took it. I grabbed hold of it with both hands.

By the time Raynell came into the house, me and your daddy had done lost touch with one another. I didn't want to make my blessing off of nobody's misfortune . . . but I took on to Raynell like she was all them babies I had wanted and never had.

(The phone rings.)

Like I'd been blessed to relive a part of my life. And if the Lord see fit to keep up my strength . . . I'm gonna do her just like your daddy did you . . . I'm gonna give her the best of what's in me.

RAYNELL *(entering, still with her old shoes):* Mama . . . Reverend Tollivier on the phone.

(ROSE *exits into the house.*)

RAYNELL: Hi.

CORY: Hi.

RAYNELL: You in the Army or the Marines?

CORY: Marines.

RAYNELL: Papa said it was the Army. Did you know Blue?

CORY: Blue? Who's Blue?

RAYNELL: Papa's dog what he sing about all the time.

CORY *(singing):* Hear it ring! Hear it ring!

I had a dog his name was Blue
You know Blue was mighty true
You know Blue was a good old dog
Blue treed a possum in a hollow log
You know from that he was a good old dog.
Hear it ring! Hear it ring!

(RAYNELL *joins in singing.*)

CORY AND RAYNELL: Blue treed a possum out on a limb

Blue looked at me and I looked at him
Grabbed that possum and put him in a sack
Blue stayed there till I came back
Old Blue's feets was big and round
Never allowed a possum to touch the ground.

Old Blue died and I dug his grave
I dug his grave with a silver spade
Let him down with a golden chain
And every night I call his name
Go on Blue, you good dog you
Go on Blue, you good dog you

RAYNELL: Blue laid down and died like a man

Blue laid down and died . . .

BOTH: Blue laid down and died like a man

Now he's treeing possums in the Promised Land
I'm gonna tell you this to let you know
Blue's gone where the good dogs go
When I hear old Blue bark
When I hear old Blue bark
Blue treed a possum in Noah's Ark
Blue treed a possum in Noah's Ark.

(ROSE *comes to the screen door.*)

ROSE: Cory, we gonna be ready to go in a minute.

CORY *(to* RAYNELL*):* You go on in the house and change them shoes like
Mama told you so we can go to Papa's funeral.

RAYNELL: Okay, I'll be back.

(RAYNELL *exits into the house.* CORY *gets up and crosses over to the tree.* ROSE *stands in the screen door watching him.* GABRIEL *enters from the alley.*)

GABRIEL *(calling):* Hey, Rose!

ROSE: Gabe?

GABRIEL: I'm here, Rose. Hey Rose, I'm here!

(ROSE *enters from the house.*)

ROSE: Lord . . . Look here, Lyons!

LYONS: See, I told you, Rose . . . I told you they'd let him come.

CORY: How you doing, Uncle Gabe?

LYONS: How you doing, Uncle Gabe?

GABRIEL: Hey, Rose. It's time. It's time to tell St. Peter to open the gates. Troy, you ready? You ready, Troy. I'm gonna tell St. Peter to open the gates. You get ready now.

(GABRIEL, *with great fanfare, braces himself to blow. The trumpet is without a mouthpiece. He puts the end of it into his mouth and blows with great force, like a man who has been waiting some twenty-odd years for this single moment. No sound comes out of the trumpet. He braces himself and blows again with the same result. A third time he blows. There is a weight of impossible description that falls away and leaves him bare and exposed to a frightful realization. It is a trauma that a sane and normal mind would be unable to withstand. He begins to dance. A slow, strange dance, eerie and life-giving. A dance of atavistic signature and ritual.* LYONS *attempts to embrace him.* GABRIEL *pushes* LYONS *away. He begins to howl in what is an attempt at song, or perhaps a song turning back into itself in an attempt at speech. He finishes his dance and the gates of heaven stand open as wide as God's closet.*)

That's the way that go!

Activities for Writing and Discussion

1. How do you account for the rather long history of migration at the beginning of the play?

2. Working with a group, identify the different conflicts you see between Troy and Cory, and illustrate the conflicts with specific passages from the play. Which of these conflicts strike you as fairly typical of any father/son relationship? Give examples. Which, if any, seem more unique to an African-American father and son? Again, give examples.

3. Examine Troy's motives for not wanting Cory to play football. Citing evidence from the play, argue that he is motivated by:
   a. A desire to protect Cory, to prevent him from getting hurt
   b. Jealousy that Cory has better opportunities than he did
   c. Considerations other than a or b.

4. Find and annotate all the references you find in the play to "fences." What are Rose's thoughts and feelings about the fence around the yard? What are Troy's? What finally prompts Troy to complete the fence? What literal purposes does the fence serve? How, if at all, is it **symbolic**? Finally, give some reasons why Wilson might have chosen "Fences" as the title for his play.

5. Wilson has said that "Troy's flaw is that he does not recognize that the world was changing. That's because he spent fifteen years in a penitentiary." Explain what you think Wilson means. Then consider how this "flaw" affects Troy's family. Does Troy himself suffer as a result of it? Does Rose? Do Lyons and Cory? Explain with references to specific passages in the play.

6. In the play's final scene Rose tells Cory, "You Troy Maxson all over again." In what respects does she seem to be correct? incorrect? Could the same be said of Troy, i.e., that he is *his* father "all over again"? How might such a comparison be accurate, and where (if at all) would it break down?

7. The play ends on the day of Troy's funeral. Cory doesn't plan to attend but then changes his mind.
   a. Write down the thoughts you believe are going through his mind at the end of the play as he "gets up and crosses over to the tree," or
   b. Write a dialogue, set on the day of the funeral, between Cory and the dead Troy, or
   c. Imagine thirty years have passed and you are Cory and now have a teenage son of your own. Tell your son the story of your relationship with Troy, just as Troy told the family about his relationship with *his* father. Invent some pretext or reason for telling this story, e.g., your son is about to make some important life decision or he wants to do something you resist.

People and Cultures in Conflict and Change: Additional Activities for Writing and Discussion

1. Reread all or a portion of your notebook. Mark any passages, however long or short, that strike you, for whatever reason. Beside each such passage, write a note explaining its significance for you. Finally, pick a favorite passage and either:
   a. Expand it into a new piece of writing, or
   b. Make notes on how you could expand or use it at some future date, or
   c. Rewrite it in a different form, e.g., poem, dialogue, letter, or memoir.

For a list of strategies for expanding or revising, see Chapter 9.

2. Explore the concept of "cultures in conflict and change." Is it meaningful to the **characters**, **speakers**, and **personae** represented in this thematic section? If so, in what ways? Is it meaningful for you? Create a dialogue, with two or

more participants, around these questions. Draw your participants from the reading selections and/or the world of your own experience.

3. Harold Green in "A Loaf of Bread" says he is only doing what he must when he charges higher prices to the patrons of his store in the poor black neighborhood. In a sense, he—the ostensible "oppressor" in the story—sees himself as a victim. Are "oppressors" "victims"? Write a dialogue in which you have different characters or speakers from the works in this section take opposing perspectives on this issue.

4. Think of any situations in which you find (or have found) yourself to be a minority because of your race, religion, ethnicity, sexual preference, values, or a disability. In an essay:
   a. Relate some stories or examples that illustrate your minority status.
   b. Characterize the role in which your status places you. Do you perceive yourself as a victim? a hero? a crusader? in some other way, or as some combination of the above? Explain.

5. Scott Russell Sanders, in "Looking at Women" in Chapter 16 (pages 248–258), describes "objectification" as a process by which people treat those who are "different" from themselves as objects, dehumanizing them so that they can be ignored, set apart, persecuted, or destroyed. Review what Sanders says about objectification. Then discuss objectification as a theme in any two or more of the texts in this section.

6. The topic of "fear" is important in many readings within this chapter—Poe's "The Masque of the Red Death" (in which Prospero and his company try to barricade themselves against death and the unwanted outsider), Gordimer's "Once Upon a Time," Olds's "On the Subway," Staples's "Black Men and Public Space," and others. Identify one or two readings that address this topic and analyze it. If you wish, relate the topic and text(s) to experiences of your own.

7. Review your entire notebook. As you do, make a running list of memorable or striking topics, e.g., "racism," "crossing boundaries," "diversity," "multiculturalism," "fear." Then choose a favorite topic, make a Topic/Form Grid (see Chapter 9), and use one of the forms on your grid to create a new notebook entry about the topic. Should your chosen form not work, do a Topic/Form Shift to a different form on your grid.

Interchapter on Notebooks and Journals (V)

"These Notes Are My Daily Prayer": Jules Renard

> I am a man continually astonished, each instant just fallen from the moon.
> —JULES RENARD, *JOURNAL*

Jules Renard was born in Chalons-sur-Mayenne (in France) in 1864 and grew up in Chitry, a village some 140 miles south of Paris. His mother was, in the words of one editor, "a bigot . . . a compulsive talker and fibber." His father stopped talking to his wife after Jules's birth and remained largely indifferent to his son and his son's career. Renard later mined his tormented childhood and family relationships for some of his best work, particularly *Poil de Carotte* ("Carrot-top"—Jules was redheaded), a collection of stories which he later revised into a play. Both parents also figure prominently in his *Journal,* which he began keeping in 1887.

   Renard moved to Paris when he was seventeen and soon resolved to become a writer. Living on clerking and tutoring jobs and a small allowance from his father, he began producing poetry and short stories but had to publish his first collections in both genres at his own expense. By the late 1880s he had started attracting widespread critical notice. His marriage in 1888 to a woman of property enabled him to concentrate more exclusively on his writing, and with *Poil de Carotte* (1894) he became famous. After 1895 he and his family divided their time between Paris and the countryside near Chitry, with homes in both places.

In addition to short stories, Renard wrote and published novels, numerous commercially successful plays, and a book of brief descriptions of animals and plants entitled *Natural Histories* written in a poetic prose similar to that found in his *Journal*. Widely honored as an author, Renard was also elected mayor of his hometown of Chitry in 1904. He died in 1910, in Paris, of artereosclerosis.

Though Renard's writings can be wonderfully witty, whimsical, and light:

> The chattering of the chairs, lined up before the guests arrive on a reception day
>
> If I were a bird, I would sleep only in the clouds

he regarded the practice of writing with profound seriousness. He hated hypocrisy and sham, which he believed degraded language: when people are false, words are cheapened and lose their original meaning and power. For instance, of the word "love" he wrote:

> We no longer know what love is. The thing itself is lost, drowned in a verbal deluge. It is impossible to come through to reality, which should be simple and clear.

Renard's answer to the "verbal deluge" was to strive relentlessly to make his own writing plainer and more economical, "to reproduce in compressed and resistant [prose] life completely pure and completely simple."

> When he drinks with a couple, he always pays, so that people may believe he is the lover.
>
> The life of a cat asleep. From time to time, a leap, a slash of claws, a stretch that resembles action, then everything returns into its fur and goes back to sleep.
>
> A boy from the orphan asylum, hired out near Cervon, at thirteen. He is a little deaf. He receives 120 francs for fifteen months. I am thoughtless enough to say it is not much. Whereupon, lifting his eyes, which he had kept lowered, he says, with pride:
> "There's something else too. You get your washing done, and a pair of shoes."

Never falsely modest, Renard pursued fame and honors and relished his successes, which he viewed with self-amused irony. "It's many a day since I've felt ashamed of my vanity," he wrote when his career was in full stride, "or even tried to correct it. Of all my faults, it is the one that amuses me most." At the same time, he denied that writers are special or extraordinary people to be put on pedestals:

> No novel exists which an ordinary intelligence could not conceive; there is no sentence, no matter how lovely, that a beginner could not construct.

What remains is to pick up the pen, to rule the paper, patiently to fill it up. The strong do not hesitate. They settle down, they sweat, they go on to the end. They exhaust the ink, they use up the paper. . . . In literature, there are only oxen.

A "great" writer was simply an ordinary person with a farm animal's capacity for work.

Renard's comparison of writers to oxen reflects his rural upbringing among peasants whose "animal" virtues he both satirized and admired. It also suggests a certain envy of brute energy and instinct. "I don't give a fig for intelligence," he once wrote; "I should be satisfied with a lot of instinct." Most people probably assume the *more* "intelligence" they have the better; in Renard's view intelligence can actually impede the senses and cloud understanding with excessive analysis, equivocations, and theorizing. Writers need to *un*learn some of what intelligence has taught them—become more like the "dumb" oxen that go to work each day with muscle, energy, and humility.

Renard strove to experience life at first hand, through his own senses, as if he were the first person alive. "To think," he wrote, "is to search for clearings in a wood." If he did not always succeed ("Every time I want to settle down to work, literature gets between"), in his *Journal* at least his writing never seems to get tired. In the midst of his busy life Renard extracted the poetry from every moment and renewed himself by enjoying and recording the ordinary:

> In my church, there is no vaulting between me and the sky.

> I like rain that lasts all day, and don't feel that I am really in the country until I am well caked with mud.

For further reading:
Renard, Jules. *The Journal of Jules Renard.* Ed. and trans. Louise Bogan and Elizabeth Roget. New York: George Braziller, 1964.

Excerpts from *The Journal of Jules Renard*

The true artist will write in, as it were, small leaps, on a hundred subjects that 1 surge unawares into his mind. In this way, nothing is forced. Everything has an unwilled, natural charm. One does not provoke: one waits.

I have an almost incessant need of speaking evil of others; but no interest at 2 all in doing evil to them.

To lie watching one's mind, pen raised, ready to spear the smallest thought 3 that may come out.

The chatting of the chairs, lined up before the guests arrive on a reception day. 4

Work thinks; laziness muses. 5

Sometimes conversation dies out like a lamp. You turn up the wick. A few 6
ideas bring out another gleam, but, decidedly, there is no oil left.

The ideal of calm exists in a sitting cat.   7

All I have read, all I have thought, all my forced paradoxes, my hatred of the 8
conventional, my contempt for the commonplace, do not prevent me from
turning soft on the first day of spring, from looking for violets under the
hedges, among the turds and the scraps of decayed paper; from playing with the
village youngsters, giving close attention to lizards and yellow-robed butterflies, bringing home a little blue flower to my wife. Everlasting contradiction.
Continual effort to get beyond stupidity, and inevitable backsliding. Happily!

Today, Marie Pierry's cow calved. Marie, in tears, said: "I can't watch that. 9
I'm getting out of here."
Then she'd come back. "Oh, the poor dear! The poor dear! There! She is 10
dead! I can see she is dead. She'll never pull out of it!"
The cow lowed and heaved sighs. Lexandre, pulling at the calf's legs, pouted 11
his lips at her: "There, my beauty!" Father Castel presided: "Pull, children,
pull!"
Everyone felt himself to be a mother, and when the cow, having produced 12
her calf and drunk a bottle of sweetened wine, began licking the salt that had
been sprinkled over the calf, everyone had tears in his eyes.

When I make a joke, I watch the maid out of the corner of my eye to see if 13
she is laughing.

The geese had retired, but they could still be heard stirring.   14
They jabbered, deep in their throats. They raised their wings a little in order 15
to close them more comfortably. They settled down like ladies rustling and
drawing together around someone who is about to tell them a piece of gossip.

I like rain that lasts all day, and don't feel that I am really in the country un- 16
til I am well caked with mud.

Visit to the zoo: 17
Tiny parakeets, like tie-pins that sing.   18

How monotonous snow would be if God had not created crows!   19

With its purring, the cat accompanies the tick-tock of the clock; it is the 20
only music in the room.

I want my ear to be a shell that keeps in itself all the sounds of nature.   21

Be modest! It is the kind of pride least likely to offend.   22

My brother Maurice tells me: "Papa and I sit together on the wall. He waits 23
for me to talk, and I wait for him. And that goes on until we go to bed." He can
no longer shoot. He has a pain in the left arm. When a partridge starts out from
somewhere, or a hare goes barreling off, he can't lift his arm. It is as though
someone were to put a hand on his shoulder to prevent him from killing, saying: "That's enough!"

In the old bedroom, the paper is coming off the walls and the plaster is 24
crumbling. Holes are forming. There is one big enough for me to put my watch
into, as in a niche.

Papa walked with me as far as the Bargeot fields, and he wearies me. When 25
we got back, he said: "I am no more tired than when we started, because at my
age you are always tired."

Papa. The swollen veins of his temples. Moles are digging around and rav- 26
aging him under the skin.

The little light existing in the mystery that surrounds us comes from our- 27
selves: it is a false light. The mystery has never shown us its own.

When he drinks with a couple, he always pays, so that people may believe he 28
is the lover.

By six o'clock in the morning, she has finished cleaning her house. Someone 29
may go by her door, who stops and talks. This talk may go on till noon, and the
rest of the day is spent in the same way.

No one ever sees her working. You knock. She opens the door, in wooden 30
shoes, neat and clean, her hands over her belly. Everything is in order. How does
she keep busy? Sometimes, she knits. She is so happy over having lost her husband who drank, and beat her, that even the death of one of her two boys did
not sadden her. She could go on living like this for ever.

When the little peasant girls see us from a distance, they turn aside to smile. 31

The bird alights on the rosebush not because of the rose, but because of the 32
plant lice.

Men like my father respect only those that get rich, and admire only those 33
that die poor.

The magpie fluttered about, dressed up as a sister of charity. 34

Return to Paris. My father and I did not love each other outwardly. We did 35
not hang together by our branches: we loved each other by our roots.

When laziness makes us miserable, it has the same value as work. 36

I read what I write as though I were my mortal enemy.   37

Old woman, your eyes are like the reflection of a star in the water of a wagon rut.   38

The duck tries to jump over a wall and go through a hedge. Halfway up the wall, she falls back heavily. She does not insist: she goes to fetch the drake. Together, their heads held straight up, they examine the wall, look for an opening in the hedge. From time to time, they desist, go around by the field, cut a little grass, and come back.   39

The duck gets half-way into the hedge; but it is too thick: she gives up the idea.   40

They make the turn of the meadow, wasting their day and mine.   41

And their jerky bows.   42

It is a confused act. It would take a comic playwright to straighten it out.   43

Like the soil, my courage needs rain.   44

Our egoism is so excessive that, in a storm, we believe the thunder to be directed only at us.   45

All day, the woods hold in their branches a little of the night.   46

I don't give a fig for intelligence: I should be satisfied with a lot of instinct.   47

I turn home, my heart filled with anguish because I have watched the sun set and heard the birds sing, and because I shall have had so few days on this earth I love, and there are so many dead before me.   48

When I used to see my father walking from one window to the other, bent, silent, his hands behind his back, his look deep, I used to ask myself: "What is he thinking about?" Today I know, because I walk about in exactly the same manner, with the same air, and I can answer in all certainty: "Nothing."   49

I cannot look at the leaf of a tree without being crushed by the universe.   50

We no longer know what love is. The thing itself is lost, drowned in a verbal deluge. It is impossible to come through to reality, which should be simple and clear.   51

Love kills intelligence. The brain and the heart act upon each other in the manner of an hour-glass. One fills itself only to empty the other.   52

If I were a bird, I would sleep only in the clouds.   53

It is hailing. A disaster! But, once the hail has melted, the peasant does not   54
spend time being sorry for himself: he goes back to work.

The wind that makes the chimney look as though it were smoking while on   55
the run.

Toward morning, when you can't sleep, you are possessed with genius. You   56
see luminous things on that black canvas. In the dark, you scribble on a piece of
paper.
The next day, all you find is meaningless scratches.   57

Too fast, the auto. So many pretty landscapes where one does not stop.   58

If I were to begin life again, I should want it as it was. I would only open my   59
eyes a little more. I did not see properly, and I did not see everything in that little universe in which I was feeling my way.

A boy from the orphan asylum, hired out near Cervon, at thirteen. He is a   60
little deaf. He receives 120 francs for fifteen months. I am thoughtless enough
to say it is not much. Whereupon, lifting his eyes, which he had kept lowered, he
says with pride:
"There's something else too. You get your washing done, and a pair of   61
shoes."

The life of a cat asleep. From time to time, a leap, a slash of claws, a stretch   62
that resembles action, then everything returns into its fur and goes back to
sleep.

Laziness: the habit of resting before fatigue sets in.   63

These notes are my daily prayer.   64

On the horizon, the moon, like a balloon unencumbered by a basket, says: 65
"Let go!" It rises. All the cables are cut.
Not a man, not a tree, not a dry branch was able to hang on to its net and   66
unawares rise too.
The red woods burn under it and inflate it.   67
It reaches a cloud, seems caught, stops moving.   68
It disappeared behind a mass of clouds. It was never seen again. Not that   69
moon, at least.

I have an idea the way I look at a bird: I am always afraid it will fly away, and   70
I don't dare touch it.

To the young. I shall tell you a truth that you may not like, because you look   71
forward to novelty. This truth is that one does not grow old. Where the heart is

concerned, the fact is accepted, at least in matters of love. Well, it is the same with the mind. It always remains young. You do not understand life any more at forty than you did at twenty, but you are aware of this fact, and you admit it. To admit it is to remain young.

We are in the world to laugh.   72

In purgatory or in hell we shall no longer be able to do so.   73

And in heaven it would not be proper.   74

After seeing what the bourgeois crave, I feel myself capable of doing with- 75
out everything.

Evening. A soul is wandering; you can hear its little bell.   76

Walks. The body advances, while the mind flutters around it like a bird.   77

A new maid. Marie. Believes in the number thirteen and doesn't work on 78
Sundays. At thirty-eight, she is no more advanced than she was at thirteen. She
was married once, and feels that it's enough.

She remembers only one good situation, at the Spanish embassy.   79

She has been in homes where the coffee was weighed out, and where her 80
dinner consisted of a hard-boiled egg when the masters, who were rich, dined
out.

She eats the crusts of the day before. She hasn't tasted fresh bread for a year. 81
Shy, with an Alsatian accent and a lisp, she begs pardon when she crosses in
front of an armchair.

Rain mixed with piano drops.   82

The Luxembourg gardens are nothing but a dome of leaves under which 83
people dream.

Snow on water: silence upon silence.   84

—Translated by Louise Bogan and Elizabeth Roget

ACTIVITIES FOR WRITING AND DISCUSSION

1. Consider Renard's notion of a "verbal deluge" (page 845). Do you experience this "verbal deluge" anywhere today? If so, what forms does it take, and what are its effects, positive and/or negative, on yourself and society? (For an interesting comparison, see paragraphs 32 and 33 of Whitecloud's "Blue Winds Dancing" on page 763.) Illustrate your responses with stories and examples from your own experience and knowledge.

2. Respond to Renard's journal selections using any of the "Generic Ideas for Writing" found on pages 275–277.

Work and the Quality of Life

HERMAN MELVILLE (1819–1891)

Bartleby, the Scrivener

A STORY OF WALL STREET

I am a rather elderly man. The nature of my avocations, for the last thirty years, has brought me into more than ordinary contact with what would seem an interesting and somewhat singular set of men, of whom, as yet, nothing, that I know of, has ever been written—I mean, the law-copyists, or scriveners. I have known very many of them, professionally and privately, and, if I pleased, could relate diverse histories, at which good-natured gentlemen might smile, and sentimental souls might weep. But I waive the biographies of all other scriveners, for a few passages in the life of Bartleby, who was a scrivener, the strangest I ever saw, or heard of. While, of other law-copyists, I might write the complete life, of Bartleby nothing of that sort can be done. I believe that no materials exist, for a full and satisfactory biography of this man. It is an irreparable loss to literature. Bartleby was one of those beings of whom nothing is ascertainable, except from the original sources, and, in his case, those are very small. What my own astonished eyes saw of Bartleby, *that* is all I know of him, except, indeed, one vague report, which will appear in the sequel.

Ere introducing the scrivener, as he first appeared to me, it is fit I make some mention of myself, my *employés*, my business, my chambers, and general surroundings, because some such description is indispensable to an adequate understanding of the chief character about to be presented. Imprimis:[1] I am a man who, from his youth upwards, has been filled with a profound conviction that the easiest way of life is the best. Hence, though I belong to a profession proverbially energetic and nervous, even to turbulence, at times, yet nothing of that sort have I ever suffered to invade my peace. I am one of those unambitious lawyers who never address a jury, or in any way draw down public applause; but, in the cool tranquillity of a snug retreat, do a snug business among rich men's bonds, and mortgages, and title-deeds. All who know me, consider me an eminently *safe* man. The late John Jacob Astor, a personage little given to poetic enthusiasm, had no hesitation in pronouncing my first grand point to be prudence; my next, method. I do not speak it in vanity, but simply record the fact, that I was not unemployed in my profession by the late John Jacob Astor; a name which, I admit, I love to repeat; for it hath a rounded and orbicular sound to it, and rings like unto bullion. I will freely add, that I was not insensible to the late John Jacob Astor's good opinion.

Some time prior to the period at which this little history begins, my avocations had been largely increased. The good old office, now extinct in the State of New York, of a Master in Chancery, had been conferred upon me. It was not a very arduous office, but very pleasantly remunerative. I seldom lose my temper; much more seldom indulge in dangerous indignation at wrongs and outrages; but I must be permitted to be rash here and declare, that I consider the sudden and violent abrogation of the office of Master in Chancery, by the new Constitution, as a —————————— premature act; inasmuch as I had counted upon a life-lease of the profits, whereas I only received those of a few short years. But this is by the way.

My chambers were up stairs, at No.—Wall Street. At one end, they looked upon the white wall of the interior of a spacious skylight shaft, penetrating the building from top to bottom.

This view might have been considered rather tame than otherwise, deficient in what landscape painters call "life." But, if so, the view from the other end of my chambers offered, at least, a contrast, if nothing more. In that direction, my windows commanded an unobstructed view of a lofty brick wall, black by age and everlasting shade; which wall required no spy-glass to bring out its lurking beauties, but, for the benefit of all near-sighted spectators, was pushed up to within ten feet of my window-panes. Owing to the great height of the surrounding buildings, and my chambers being on the second floor, the interval between this wall and mine not a little resembled a huge square cistern.

At the period just preceding the advent of Bartleby, I had two persons as copyists in my employment, and a promising lad as an office-boy. First, Turkey; second, Nippers; third, Ginger Nut. These may seem names, the like of which are not usually found in the Directory. In truth, they were nicknames, mutually conferred upon each other by my three clerks, and were deemed expressive of their respective persons or characters. Turkey was a short, pursy Englishman, of

5

---

1. In the first place (Latin).

about my own age—that is, somewhere not far from sixty. In the morning, one might say, his face was of a fine florid hue, but after twelve o'clock, meridian—his dinner hour—it blazed like a grate full of Christmas coals; and continued blazing—but, as it were, with a gradual wane—till six o'clock, P.M., or thereabouts; after which, I saw no more of the proprietor of the face, which, gaining its meridian with the sun, seemed to set with it, to rise, culminate, and decline the following day, with the like regularity and undiminished glory. There are many singular coincidences I have known in the course of my life, not the least among which was the fact, that, exactly when Turkey displayed his fullest beams from his red and radiant countenance, just then, too, at that critical moment, began the daily period when I considered his business capacities as seriously disturbed for the remainder of the twenty-four hours. Not that he was absolutely idle, or averse to business then; far from it. The difficulty was, he was apt to be altogether too energetic. There was a strange, inflamed, flurried, flighty recklessness of activity about him. He would be incautious in dipping his pen into his inkstand. All his blots upon my documents were dropped there after twelve o'clock, meridian. Indeed, not only would he be reckless, and sadly given to making blots in the afternoon, but, some days, he went further, and was rather noisy. At such times, too, his face flamed with augmented blazonry, as if cannel coal had been heaped on anthracite. He made an unpleasant racket with his chair; spilled his sand-box; in mending his pens, impatiently split them all to pieces, and threw them on the floor in a sudden passion; stood up, and leaned over his table, boxing his papers about in a most indecorous manner, very sad to behold in an elderly man like him. Nevertheless, as he was in many ways a most valuable person to me, and all the time before twelve o'clock, meridian, was the quickest, steadiest creature, too, accomplishing a great deal of work in a style not easily to be matched—for these reasons, I was willing to overlook his eccentricities, though, indeed, occasionally, I remonstrated with him. I did this very gently, however, because, though the civilest, nay, the blandest and most reverential of men in the morning, yet, in the afternoon, he was disposed, upon provocation, to be slightly rash with his tongue—in fact, insolent. Now, valuing his morning services as I did, and resolved not to lose them—yet, at the same time, made uncomfortable by his inflamed ways after twelve o'clock—and being a man of peace, unwilling by my admonitions to call forth unseemly retorts from him, I took upon me, one Saturday noon (he was always worse on Saturdays) to hint to him, very kindly, that, perhaps, now that he was growing old, it might be well to abridge his labors; in short, he need not come to my chambers after twelve o'clock, but, dinner over, had best go home to his lodgings, and rest himself till tea-time. But no; he insisted upon his afternoon devotions. His countenance became intolerably fervid, as he oratorically assured me—gesticulating with a long ruler at the other end of the room—that if his services in the morning were useful, how indispensable, then, in the afternoon?

"With submission, sir," said Turkey, on this occasion, "I consider myself your right-hand man. In the morning I but marshal and deploy my columns;

but in the afternoon I put myself at their head, and gallantly charge the foe, thus"—and he made a violent thrust with the ruler.

"But the blots, Turkey," intimated I.

"True; but, with submission, sir, behold these hairs! I am getting old. Surely, sir, a blot or two of a warm afternoon is not to be severely urged against gray hairs. Old age—even if it blot the page—is honorable. With submission, sir, we *both* are getting old."

This appeal to my fellow-feeling was hardly to be resisted. At all events, I   10 saw that go he would not. So, I made up my mind to let him stay, resolving, nevertheless, to see to it that, during the afternoon, he had to do with my less important papers.

Nippers, the second on my list, was a whiskered, sallow, and, upon the whole, rather piratical-looking young man, of about five-and-twenty. I always deemed him the victim of two evil powers—ambition and indigestion. The ambition was evinced by a certain impatience of the duties of a mere copyist, an unwarrantable usurpation of strictly professional affairs such as the original drawing up of legal documents. The indigestion seemed betokened in an occasional nervous testiness and grinning irritability, causing the teeth to audibly grind together over mistakes committed in copying; unnecessary maledictions, hissed, rather than spoken, in the heat of business; and especially by a continual discontent with the height of the table where he worked. Though of a very ingenious mechanical turn, Nippers could never get this table to suit him. He put chips under it, blocks of various sorts, bits of pasteboard, and at last went so far as to attempt an exquisite adjustment, by final pieces of folded blotting paper. But no invention would answer. If, for the sake of easing his back, he brought the table-lid at a sharp angle well up towards his chin, and wrote there like a man using the steep roof of a Dutch house for his desk, then he declared that it stopped the circulation in his arms. If now he lowered the table to his waistbands, and stooped over it in writing, then there was a sore aching in his back. In short, the truth of the matter was, Nippers knew not what he wanted. Or, if he wanted anything, it was to be rid of a scrivener's table altogether. Among the manifestations of his diseased ambition was a fondness he had for receiving visits from certain ambiguous-looking fellows in seedy coats, whom he called his clients. Indeed, I was aware that not only was he, at times, considerable of a ward-politician, but he occasionally did a little business at the justices' courts, and was not unknown on the steps of the Tombs.[2] I have good reason to believe, however, that one individual who called upon him at my chambers, and who, with a grand air, he insisted was his client, was no other than a dun, and the alleged title-deed, a bill. But, with all his failings, and the annoyances he caused me, Nippers, like his compatriot Turkey, was a very useful man to me; wrote a neat, swift hand; and, when he chose, was not deficient in a gentlemanly sort of deportment. Added to this, he always dressed in a gentlemanly sort of way; and so, incidentally, reflected credit upon my chambers. Whereas, with

---

2. A prison in New York City.

respect to Turkey, I had much ado to keep him from being a reproach to me. His clothes were apt to look oily, and smell of eating-houses. He wore his pantaloons very loose and baggy in summer. His coats were execrable, his hat not to be handled. But while the hat was a thing of indifference to me, inasmuch as his natural civility and deference, as a dependent Englishman, always led him to doff it the moment he entered the room, yet his coat was another matter. Concerning his coats, I reasoned with him; but with no effect. The truth was, I suppose, that a man with so small an income could not afford to sport such a lustrous face and a lustrous coat at one and the same time. As Nippers once observed, Turkey's money went chiefly for red ink. One winter day, I presented Turkey with a highly respectable-looking coat of my own—a padded gray coat, of a most comfortable warmth, and which buttoned straight up from the knee to the neck. I thought Turkey would appreciate the favor, and abate his rashness and obstreperousness of afternoons. But no; I verily believe that buttoning himself up in so downy and blanket-like a coat had a pernicious effect upon him upon the same principle that too much oats are bad for horses. In fact, precisely as a rash, restive horse is said to feel his oats, so Turkey felt his coat. It made him insolent. He was a man whom prosperity harmed.

Though, concerning the self-indulgent habits of Turkey, I had my own private surmises, yet, touching Nippers, I was well persuaded that, whatever might be his faults in other respects, he was, at least, a temperate young man. But, indeed, nature herself seemed to have been his vintner, and, at his birth, charged him so thoroughly with an irritable, brandy-like disposition, that all subsequent potations were needless. When I consider how, amid the stillness of my chambers, Nippers would sometimes impatiently rise from his seat, and stooping over his table, spread his arms wide apart, seize the whole desk, and move it, and jerk it, with a grim, grinding motion on the floor, as if the table were a perverse voluntary agent, intent on thwarting and vexing him, I plainly perceive that, for Nippers, brandy-and-water were altogether superfluous.

It was fortunate for me that, owing to its peculiar cause—indigestion—the irritability and consequent nervousness of Nippers were mainly observable in the morning, while in the afternoon he was comparatively mild. So that, Turkey's paroxysms only coming on about twelve o'clock, I never had to do with their eccentricities at one time. Their fits relieved each other, like guards. When Nippers' was on, Turkey's was off; and *vice versa*. This was a good natural arrangement, under the circumstances.

Ginger Nut, the third on my list, was a lad, some twelve years old. His father was a carman, ambitious of seeing his son on the bench instead of a cart, before he died. So he sent him to my office, as student at law, errand-boy, cleaner, and sweeper, at the rate of one dollar a week. He had a little desk to himself, but he did not use it much. Upon inspection, the drawer exhibited a great array of the shells of various sorts of nuts. Indeed, to this quick-witted youth, the whole noble science of the law was contained in a nutshell. Not the least among the employments of Ginger Nut, as well as one which he discharged with the most alacrity, was his duty as cake and apple purveyor for Turkey and Nippers. Copying lawpapers being proverbially a dry, husky sort of business, my two scriveners were fain to moisten their mouths very often with Spitzenbergs, to be had at the numerous stalls nigh the Custom House and Post Office. Also, they sent Ginger Nut very frequently for that peculiar cake—small, flat, round, and very spicy—after which he had been named by them. Of a cold morning, when business was but dull, Turkey would gobble up scores of these cakes, as if they were mere wafers—indeed, they sell them at the rate of six or eight for a penny—the scrape of his pen blending with the crunching of the crisp particles in his mouth. Of all the fiery afternoon blunders and flurried rashness of Turkey, was his once moistening a ginger-cake between his lips, and clapping it on to a mortgage, for a seal. I came within an ace of dismissing him then. But he mollified me by making an oriental bow, and saying—

"With submission, sir, it was generous of me to find you in stationery on my 15 own account."

Now my original business—that of a conveyancer and title hunter, and drawer-up of recondite documents of all sorts—was considerably increased by receiving the Master's office. There was now great work for scriveners. Not only must I push the clerks already with me, but I must have additional help.

In answer to my advertisement, a motionless young man one morning stood upon my office threshold, the door being open, for it was summer. I can see that figure now—pallidly neat, pitiably respectable, incurably forlorn! It was Bartleby.

After a few words touching his qualifications, I engaged him, glad to have among my corps of copyists a man of so singularly sedate an aspect, which I thought might operate beneficially upon the flighty temper of Turkey, and the fiery one of Nippers.

I should have stated before that ground-glass folding-doors divided my premises into two parts, one of which was occupied by my scriveners, the other by myself. According to my humor, I threw open these doors, or closed them. I resolved to assign Bartleby a corner by the folding-doors, but on my side of them, so as to have this quiet man within easy call, in case any trifling thing was to be done. I placed his desk close up to a small side-window in that part of the room, a window which originally had afforded a lateral view of certain grimy brickyards and bricks, but which, owing to subsequent erections, commanded at present no view at all, though it gave some light. Within three feet of the panes was a wall, and the light came down from far above, between two lofty buildings, as from a very small opening in a dome. Still further to a satisfactory arrangement, I procured a high green folding screen, which might entirely isolate Bartleby from my sight, though not remove him from my voice. And thus, in a manner, privacy and society were conjoined.

At first, Bartleby did an extraordinary quantity of writing. As if long famish- 20 ing for something to copy, he seemed to gorge himself on my documents. There was no pause for digestion. He ran a day and night line, copying by sunlight and by candle-light. I should have been quite delighted with his application, had he been cheerfully industrious. But he wrote on silently, palely, mechanically.

It is, of course, an indispensable part of a scrivener's business to verify the accuracy of his copy, word by word. Where there are two or more scriveners in an office, they assist each other in this examination, one reading from the copy, the other holding the original. It is a very dull, wearisome, and lethargic affair. I can readily imagine that, to some sanguine temperaments, it would be altogether intolerable. For example, I cannot credit that the mettlesome poet, Byron, would have contentedly sat down with Bartleby to examine a law document of, say five hundred pages, closely written in a crimpy hand.

Now and then, in the haste of business, it had been my habit to assist in comparing some brief document myself, calling Turkey or Nippers for this purpose. One object I had, in placing Bartleby so handy to me behind the screen, was, to avail myself of his services on such trivial occasions. It was on the third day, I think, of his being with me, and before any necessity had arisen for having his own writing examined, that, being much hurried to complete a small affair I had in hand, I abruptly called to Bartleby. In my haste and natural expectancy of instant compliance, I sat with my head bent over the original on my desk, and my right hand sideways, and somewhat nervously extended with the copy, so that, immediately upon emerging from his retreat, Bartleby might snatch it and proceed to business without the least delay.

In this very attitude did I sit when I called to him, rapidly stating what it was I wanted him to do—namely, to examine a small paper with me. Imagine my surprise, nay, my consternation, when, without moving from his privacy, Bartleby, in a singularly mild, firm voice, replied, "I would prefer not to."

I sat awhile in perfect silence, rallying my stunned faculties. Immediately it occurred to me that my ears had deceived me, or Bartleby had entirely misunderstood my meaning. I repeated my request in the clearest tone I could assume; but in quite as clear a one came the previous reply, "I would prefer not to."

"Prefer not to," echoed I, rising in high excitement, and crossing the room 25 with a stride. "What do you mean? Are you moonstruck? I want you to help me compare this sheet here—take it," and I thrust it towards him.

"I would prefer not to," said he.

I looked at him steadfastly. His face was leanly composed; his gray eye dimly calm. Not a wrinkle of agitation rippled him. Had there been the least uneasiness, anger, impatience, or impertinence in his manner; in other words, had there been anything ordinarily human about him, doubtless I should have violently dismissed him from the premises. But as it was, I should have as soon thought of turning my pale plaster-of-paris bust of Cicero out of doors. I stood gazing at him awhile, as he went on with his own writing, and then reseated myself at my desk. This is very strange, thought I. What had one best do? But my business hurried me. I concluded to forget the matter for the present, reserving it for my future leisure. So, calling Nippers from the other room, the paper was speedily examined.

A few days after this, Bartleby concluded four lengthy documents, being quadruplicates of a week's testimony taken before me in my High Court of Chancery. It became necessary to examine them. It was an important suit, and great accuracy was imperative. Having all things arranged, I called Turkey, Nippers, and Ginger Nut, from the next room, meaning to place the four copies in the hands of my four clerks, while I should read from the original. Accordingly, Turkey, Nippers, and Ginger Nut had taken their seats in a row, each with his document in his hand, when I called to Bartleby to join this interesting group.

"Bartleby! quick, I am waiting."

I heard a slow scrape of his chair legs on the uncarpeted floor, and soon he appeared standing at the entrance of his hermitage.

"What is wanted?" said he, mildly.

"The copies, the copies," said I, hurriedly. "We are going to examine them. There"—and I held towards him the fourth quadruplicate.

"I would prefer not to," he said, and gently disappeared behind the screen.

For a few moments I was turned into a pillar of salt, standing at the head of my seated column of clerks. Recovering myself, I advanced towards the screen, and demanded the reason for such extraordinary conduct.

"*Why* do you refuse?"

"I would prefer not to."

With any other man I should have flown outright into a dreadful passion, scorned all further words, and thrust him ignominiously from my presence. But there was something about Bartleby that not only strangely disarmed me, but, in a wonderful manner, touched and disconcerted me. I began to reason with him.

"These are your own copies we are about to examine. It is labor saving to you, because one examination will answer for your four papers. It is common usage. Every copyist is bound to help examine his copy. Is it not so? Will you not speak? Answer!"

"I prefer not to," he replied in a flute-like tone. It seemed to me that, while I had been addressing him, he carefully revolved every statement that I made; fully comprehended the meaning; could not gainsay the irresistible conclusion; but, at the same time, some paramount consideration prevailed with him to reply as he did.

"You are decided, then, not to comply with my request—a request made according to common usage and common sense?"

He briefly gave me to understand, that on that point my judgment was sound. Yes: his decision was irreversible.

It is not seldom the case that, when a man is browbeaten in some unprecedented and violently unreasonable way, he begins to stagger in his own plainest faith. He begins, as it were, vaguely to surmise that, wonderful as it may be, all the justice and all the reason is on the other side. Accordingly, if any disinterested persons are present, he turns to them for some reinforcement for his own faltering mind.

"Turkey," said I, "what do you think of this? Am I not right?"

"With submission, sir," said Turkey, in his blandest tone, "I think that you are."

"Nippers," said I, "what do *you* think of it?"

"I think I should kick him out of the office."

(The reader of nice perceptions will have perceived that, it being morning, Turkey's answer is couched in polite and tranquil terms, but Nippers replies in ill-tempered ones. Or, to repeat a previous sentence, Nippers' ugly mood was on duty, and Turkey's off.)

"Ginger Nut," said I, willing to enlist the smallest suffrage in my behalf, "what do *you* think of it?"

"I think, sir, he's a little *luny*," replied Ginger Nut, with a grin.

"You hear what they say," said I, turning towards the screen, "come forth 50 and do your duty."

But he vouchsafed no reply. I pondered a moment in sore perplexity. But once more business hurried me. I determined again to postpone the consideration of this dilemma to my future leisure. With a little trouble we made out to examine the papers without Bartleby, though at every page or two Turkey deferentially dropped his opinion, that this proceeding was quite out of the common; while Nippers, twitching in his chair with a dyspeptic nervousness, ground out, between his set teeth, occasional hissing maledictions against the stubborn oaf behind the screen. And for his (Nippers') part, this was the first and the last time he would do another man's business without pay.

Meanwhile Bartleby sat in his hermitage, oblivious to everything but his own peculiar business there.

Some days passed, the scrivener being employed upon another lengthy work. His late remarkable conduct led me to regard his ways narrowly. I observed that he never went to dinner; indeed, that he never went anywhere. As yet I had never, of my personal knowledge, known him to be outside of my office. He was a perpetual sentry in the corner. At about eleven o'clock though, in the morning, I noticed that Ginger Nut would advance towards the opening in Bartleby's screen, as if silently beckoned thither by a gesture invisible to me where I sat. The boy would then leave the office, jingling a few pence, and reappear with a handful of ginger-nuts, which he delivered in the hermitage, receiving two of the cakes for his trouble.

He lives, then, on ginger-nuts, thought I; never eats a dinner, properly speaking; he must be a vegetarian, then, but no; he never eats even vegetables, he eats nothing but ginger-nuts. My mind then ran on in reveries concerning the probable effects upon the human constitution of living entirely on ginger-nuts. Ginger-nuts are so called, because they contain ginger as one of their peculiar constituents, and the final flavoring one. Now, what was ginger? A hot, spicy thing. Was Bartleby hot and spicy? Not at all. Ginger, then, had no effect upon Bartleby. Probably he preferred it should have none.

Nothing so aggravates an earnest person as a passive resistance. If the indi- 55 vidual so resisted be of a not inhumane temper, and the resisting one perfectly harmless in his passivity, then, in the better moods of the former, he will endeavor charitably to construe to his imagination what proves impossible to be solved by his judgment. Even so, for the most part, I regarded Bartleby and his ways. Poor fellow! thought I, he means no mischief; it is plain he intends no insolence; his aspect sufficiently evinces that his eccentricities are involuntary. He is useful to me. I can get along with him. If I turn him away, the chances are he will fall in with some less indulgent employer, and then he will be rudely treated, and perhaps driven forth miserably to starve. Yes. Here I can cheaply purchase a delicious self-approval. To befriend Bartleby; to humor him in his strange willfulness, will cost me little or nothing, while I lay up in my soul what will eventually prove a sweet morsel for my conscience. But this mood was not invariable with me. The passiveness of Bartleby sometimes irritated me. I felt strangely goaded on to encounter him in new opposition—to elicit some angry spark from him answerable to my own. But, indeed, I might as well have essayed to strike fire with my knuckles against a bit of Windsor soap. But one afternoon the evil impulse in me mastered me, and the following little scene ensued:

"Bartleby," said I, "when those papers are all copied, I will compare them with you."

"I would prefer not to."

"How? Surely you do not mean to persist in that mulish vagary?"

No answer.

I threw open the folding-doors nearby, and turning upon Turkey and Nip- 60 pers, exclaimed:

"Bartleby a second time says, he won't examine his papers. What do you think of it, Turkey?"

It was afternoon, be it remembered. Turkey sat glowing like a brass boiler; his bald head steaming; his hands reeling among his blotted papers.

"Think of it?" roared Turkey. "I think I'll just step behind his screen, and black his eyes for him!"

So saying, Turkey rose to his feet and threw his arms into a pugilistic position. He was hurrying away to make good his promise, when I detained him, alarmed at the effect of incautiously rousing Turkey's combativeness after dinner.

"Sit down, Turkey," said I, "and hear what Nippers has to say. What do you 65 think of it, Nippers? Would I not be justified in immediately dismissing Bartleby?"

"Excuse me, that is for you to decide, sir. I think his conduct quite unusual, and, indeed, unjust, as regards Turkey and myself. But it may only be a passing whim."

"Ah," exclaimed I, "you have strangely changed your mind, then—you speak very gently of him now."

"All beer," cried Turkey; "gentleness is effects of beer—Nippers and I dined together to-day. You see how gentle *I* am, sir. Shall I go and black his eyes?"

"You refer to Bartleby, I suppose. No, not to-day, Turkey," I replied; "pray, put up your fists."

I closed the doors, and again advanced towards Bartleby. I felt additional in- 70 centives tempting me to my fate. I burned to be rebelled against again. I remembered that Bartleby never left the office.

"Bartleby," said I, "Ginger Nut is away; just step around to the Post Office, won't you?" (it was but a three minutes' walk) "and see if there is anything for me."

"I would prefer not to."

"You *will* not?"

"I *prefer* not."

I staggered to my desk, and sat there in a deep study. My blind inveteracy returned. Was there any other thing in which I could procure myself to be ignominiously repulsed by this lean, penniless wight? my hired clerk? What added thing is there, perfectly reasonable, that he will be sure to refuse to do?

"Bartleby!"

No answer.

"Bartleby," in a louder tone.

No answer.

"Bartleby," I roared.

Like a very ghost, agreeably to the laws of magical invocation, at the third summons, he appeared at the entrance of his hermitage.

"Go to the next room, and tell Nippers to come to me."

"I would prefer not to," he respectfully and slowly said, and mildly disappeared.

"Very good, Bartleby," said I, in a quiet sort of serenely-severe self-possessed tone, intimating the unalterable purpose of some terrible retribution very close at hand. At the moment I half intended something of the kind. But upon the whole, as it was drawing towards my dinner-hour, I thought it best to put on my hat and walk home for the day, suffering much from perplexity and distress of mind.

Shall I acknowledge it? The conclusion of this whole business was, that it soon became a fixed fact of my chambers, that a pale young scrivener, by the name of Bartleby, had a desk there; that he copied for me at the usual rate of four cents a folio (one hundred words); but he was permanently exempt from examining the work done by him, that duty being transferred to Turkey and Nippers, out of compliment, doubtless, to their superior acuteness; moreover, said Bartleby was never, on any account, to be dispatched on the most trivial errand of any sort; and that even if entreated to take upon him such a matter, it was generally understood that he would "prefer not to"—in other words, that he would refuse point blank.

As days passed on, I became considerably reconciled to Bartleby. His steadiness, his freedom from all dissipation, his incessant industry (except when he chose to throw himself into a standing revery behind his screen), his great stillness, his unalterableness of demeanor under all circumstances, made him a valuable acquisition. One prime thing was this—*he was always there*—first in the morning, continually through the day, and the last at night. I had a singular confidence in his honesty. I felt my most precious papers perfectly safe in his hands. Sometimes, to be sure, I could not, for the very soul of me, avoid falling into sudden spasmodic passions with him. For it was exceeding difficult to bear in mind all the time those strange peculiarities, privileges, and unheard-of exemptions, forming the tacit stipulations on Bartleby's part under which he remained in my office. Now and then, in the eagerness of dispatching pressing business, I would inadvertently summon Bartleby, in a short, rapid tone, to put his finger, say, on the incipient tie of a bit of red tape with which I was about compressing some papers. Of course, from behind the screen the usual answer, "I prefer not to," was sure to come; and then, how could a human creature, with the common infirmities of our nature, refrain from bitterly exclaiming upon such perverseness—such unreasonableness? However, every added repulse of this sort which I received only tended to lessen the probability of my repeating the inadvertence.

Here it must be said, that, according to the custom of most legal gentlemen occupying chambers in densely populated law buildings, there were several keys to my door. One was kept by a woman residing in the attic, which person weekly scrubbed and daily swept and dusted my apartments. Another was kept by Turkey for convenience sake. The third I sometimes carried in my own pocket. The fourth I knew not who had.

Now, one Sunday morning I happened to go to Trinity Church, to hear a celebrated preacher, and finding myself rather early on the ground I thought I would walk round to my chambers for a while. Luckily I had my key with me; but upon applying it to the lock, I found it resisted by something inserted from the inside. Quite surprised, I called out; when to my consternation a key was turned from within; and thrusting his lean visage at me, and holding the door ajar, the apparition of Bartleby appeared, in his shirt-sleeves, and otherwise in a strangely tattered *deshabille,* saying quietly that he was sorry, but he was deeply engaged just then, and preferred not admitting me at present. In a brief word or two, he moreover added, that perhaps I had better walk round the block two or three times, and by that time he would probably have concluded his affairs.

Now, the utterly unsurmised appearance of Bartleby, tenanting my law-chambers of a Sunday morning, with his cadaverously gentlemanly *nonchalance,* yet withal firm and self-possessed, had such a strange effect upon me, that incontinently I slunk away from my own door, and did as desired. But not without sundry twinges of impotent rebellion against the mild effrontery of this unaccountable scrivener. Indeed, it was his wonderful mildness chiefly, which not only disarmed me, but unmanned me, as it were. For I consider that one, for the time, is sort of unmanned when he tranquilly permits his hired clerk to dictate to him, and order him away from his own premises. Furthermore, I was full of uneasiness as to what Bartleby could possibly be doing in my office in his shirt-sleeves, and in an otherwise dismantled condition on a Sunday morning. Was anything amiss going on? Nay, that was out of the question. It was not to be thought of for a moment that Bartleby was an immoral person. But what could he be doing there?—copying? Nay again, whatever might be his eccentricities, Bartleby was an eminently decorous person. He would be the last man to sit down to his desk in any state approaching to nudity. Besides, it was Sunday; and there was something about Bartleby that forbade the supposition that he would by any secular occupation violate the proprieties of the day.

Nevertheless, my mind was not pacified; and full of a restless curiosity, at 90 last I returned to the door. Without hindrance I inserted my key, opened it, and entered. Bartleby was not to be seen. I looked round anxiously, peeped behind his screen; but it was very plain that he was gone. Upon more closely examining the place, I surmised that for an indefinite period Bartleby must have ate, dressed, and slept in my office, and that too without plate, mirror, or bed. The cushioned seat of a rickety old sofa in one corner bore the faint impress of a lean, reclining form. Rolled away under his desk, I found a blanket; under the empty grate, a blacking box and brush; on a chair, a tin basin, with soap and a ragged towel; in a newspaper a few crumbs of ginger-nuts and a morsel of cheese. Yes, thought I, it is evident enough that Bartleby has been making his home here, keeping bachelor's hall all by himself. Immediately then the thought came sweeping across me, what miserable friendlessness and loneliness are here revealed! His poverty is great; but his solitude, how horrible! Think of it. Of a Sunday, Wall Street is deserted as Petra;³ and every night of every day it is an emptiness. This building, too, which of weekdays hums with industry and life, at nightfall echoes with sheer vacancy, and all through Sunday is forlorn. And here Bartleby makes his home; sole spectator of a solitude which he has seen all populous—a sort of innocent and transformed Marius⁴ brooding among the ruins of Carthage!

For the first time in my life a feeling of overpowering stinging melancholy seized me. Before, I had never experienced aught but a not unpleasing sadness. The bond of a common humanity now drew me irresistibly to gloom. A fraternal melancholy! For both I and Bartleby were sons of Adam. I remembered the bright silks and sparkling faces I had seen that day, in gala trim, swan-like sailing down the Mississippi of Broadway; and I contrasted them with the pallid copyist, and thought to myself, Ah, happiness courts the light, so we deem the world is gay; but misery hides aloof, so we deem that misery there is none. These sad fancyings—chimeras, doubtless, of a sick and silly brain—led on to other and more special thoughts, concerning the eccentricities of Bartleby. Presentiments of strange discoveries hovered round me. The scrivener's pale form appeared to me laid out, among uncaring strangers, in its shivering winding-sheet.

Suddenly I was attracted by Bartleby's closed desk, the key in open sight left in the lock.

I mean no mischief, seek the gratification of no heartless curiosity, thought I; besides, the desk is mine, and its contents, too, so I will make bold to look within. Everything was methodically arranged, the papers smoothly placed.

_____

3. A City in what is now Jordan, once the center of an Arab kingdom. It was deserted for more than ten centuries, until its rediscovery by explorers in 1812.   4. Gaius Marius (157?–86 B.C.), a Roman general, several times elected consul. Marius's greatest military successes came in the Jugerthine War, in Africa. Later, when his opponents gained power and he was banished, he fled to Africa. Carthage was a city in North Africa.

The pigeon-holes were deep, and removing the files of documents, I groped into their recesses. Presently I felt something there, and dragged it out. It was an old bandanna handkerchief, heavy and knotted. I opened it, and saw it was a saving's bank.

I now recalled all the quiet mysteries which I had noted in the man. I remembered that he never spoke but to answer; that, though at intervals he had considerable time to himself, yet I had never seen him reading—no, not even a newspaper; that for long periods he would stand looking out, at his pale window behind the screen, upon the dead brick wall; I was quite sure he never visited any refectory or eating-house; while his pale face clearly indicated that he never drank beer like Turkey; or tea and coffee even, like other men; that he never went anywhere in particular that I could learn; never went out for a walk, unless, indeed, that was the case at present; that he had declined telling who he was, or whence he came, or whether he had any relatives in the world; that though so thin and pale, he never complained of ill-health. And more than all, I remembered a certain unconscious air of pallid—how shall I call it?—of pallid haughtiness, say, or rather an austere reserve about him, which has positively awed me into my tame compliance with his eccentricities, when I had feared to ask him to do the slightest incidental thing for me, even though I might know, from his long-continued motionlessness, that behind his screen he must be standing in one of those dead-wall reveries of his.

Revolving all these things, and coupling them with the recently discovered 95 fact, that he made my office his constant abiding place and home, and not forgetful of his morbid moodiness; revolving all these things, a prudential feeling began to steal over me. My first emotions had been those of pure melancholy and sincerest pity; but just in proportion as the forlornness of Bartleby grew and grew to my imagination, did that same melancholy merge into fear, that pity into repulsion. So true it is, and so terrible, too, that up to a certain point the thought or sight of misery enlists our best affections; but, in certain special cases, beyond that point it does not. They err who would assert that invariably this is owing to the inherent selfishness of the human heart. It rather proceeds from a certain hopelessness of remedying excessive and organic ill. To a sensitive being, pity is not seldom pain. And when at last it is perceived that such pity cannot lead to effectual succor, common sense bids the soul be rid of it. What I saw that morning persuaded me that the scrivener was the victim of innate and incurable disorder. I might give alms to his body; but his body did not pain him; it was his soul that suffered, and his soul I could not reach.

I did not accomplish the purpose of going to Trinity Church that morning. Somehow, the things I had seen disqualified me for the time from church-going. I walked homeward, thinking what I would do with Bartleby. Finally, I resolved upon this—I would put certain calm questions to him the next morning, touching his history, etc., and if he declined to answer them openly and unreservedly (and I supposed he would prefer not), then to give him a twenty dollar bill over and above whatever I might owe him, and tell him his services were no longer required; but that if in any other way I could assist him,

I would be happy to do so, especially if he desired to return to his native place, wherever that might be, I would willingly help to defray the expenses. Moreover, if, after reaching home, he found himself at any time in want of aid, a letter from him would be sure of a reply.

The next morning came.

"Bartleby," said I, gently calling to him behind his screen.

No reply.

"Bartleby," said I, in a still gentler tone, "come here; I am not going to ask 100 you to do anything you would prefer not to do—I simply wish to speak to you."

Upon this he noiselessly slid into view.

"Will you tell me, Bartleby, where you were born?"

"I would prefer not to."

"Will you tell me *anything* about yourself?"

"I would prefer not to." 105

"But what reasonable objection can you have to speak to me? I feel friendly towards you."

He did not look at me while I spoke, but kept his glance fixed upon my bust of Cicero, which, as I then sat, was directly behind me, some six inches above my head.

"What is your answer, Bartleby?" said I, after waiting a considerable time for a reply, during which his countenance remained immovable, only there was the faintest conceivable tremor of the white attenuated mouth.

"At present I prefer to give no answer," he said, and retired into his hermitage.

It was rather weak in me I confess, but his manner, on this occasion, nettled 110 me. Not only did there seem to lurk in it a certain calm disdain, but his perverseness seemed ungrateful, considering the undeniable good usage and indulgence he had received from me.

Again I sat ruminating what I should do. Mortified as I was at his behavior, and resolved as I had been to dismiss him when I entered my office, nevertheless I strangely felt something superstitious knocking at my heart, and forbidding me to carry out my purpose, and denouncing me for a villain if I dared to breathe one bitter word against this forlornest of mankind. At last, familiarly drawing my chair behind his screen, I sat down and said: "Bartleby, never mind, then, about revealing your history; but let me entreat you, as a friend, to comply as far as may be with the usages of this office. Say now, you will help to examine papers tomorrow or next day: in short, say now, that in a day or two you will begin to be a little reasonable:—say so, Bartleby."

"At present I would prefer not to be a little reasonable," was his mildly cadaverous reply.

Just then the folding-doors opened, and Nippers approached. He seemed suffering from an unusually bad night's rest, induced by severer indigestion than common. He overheard those final words of Bartleby.

"*Prefer not*, eh?" gritted Nippers—"I'd *prefer* him, if I were you, sir," addressing me—"I'd *prefer* him; I'd give him preferences, the stubborn mule! What is it, sir, pray, that he *prefers* not to do now?"

Bartleby moved not a limb.   115

"Mr. Nippers," said I, "I'd prefer that you would withdraw for the present."

Somehow, of late, I had got into the way of involuntarily using this word "prefer" upon all sorts of not exactly suitable occasions. And I trembled to think that my contact with the scrivener had already and seriously affected me in a mental way. And what further and deeper aberration might it not yet produce? This apprehension had not been without efficacy in determining me to summary measures.

As Nippers, looking very sour and sulky, was departing, Turkey blandly and deferentially approached.

"With submission, sir," said he, "yesterday I was thinking about Bartleby here, and I think that if he would but prefer to take a quart of good ale every day, it would do much towards mending him, and enabling him to assist in examining his papers."

"So you have got the word, too," said I, slightly excited.   120

"With submission, what word, sir?" asked Turkey, respectfully crowding himself into the contracted space behind the screen, and by so doing, making me jostle the scrivener. "What word, sir?"

"I would prefer to be left alone here," said Bartleby, as if offended at being mobbed in his privacy.

"*That's* the word, Turkey," said I—"*that's* it."

"Oh, *prefer*? oh yes—queer word. I never use it myself. But, sir, as I was saying, if he would but prefer—"

"Turkey," interrupted I, "you will please withdraw."   125

"Oh certainly, sir, if you prefer that I should."

As he opened the folding-door to retire, Nippers at his desk caught a glimpse of me, and asked whether I would prefer to have a certain paper copied on blue paper or white. He did not in the least roguishly accent the word "prefer." It was plain that it involuntarily rolled from his tongue. I thought to myself, surely I must get rid of a demented man, who already has in some degree turned the tongues, if not the heads of myself and clerks. But I thought it prudent not to break the dismission at once.

The next day I noticed that Bartleby did nothing but stand at his window in his dead-wall revery. Upon asking him why he did not write, he said that he had decided upon doing no more writing.

"Why, how now? what next?" exclaimed I, "do no more writing?"

"No more."   130

"And what is the reason?"

"Do you not see the reason for yourself?" he indifferently replied.

I looked steadfastly at him, and perceived that his eyes looked dull and glazed. Instantly it occurred to me, that his unexampled diligence in copying by his dim window for the first few weeks of his stay with me might have temporarily impaired his vision.

I was touched. I said something in condolence with him. I hinted that of course he did wisely in abstaining from writing for a while; and urged him to embrace that opportunity of taking wholesome exercise in the open air. This, however, he did not do. A few days after this, my other clerks being absent, and being in a great hurry to dispatch certain letters by the mail, I thought that, having nothing else earthly to do, Bartleby would surely be less inflexible than usual, and carry these letters to the Post Office. But he blankly declined. So, much to my inconvenience, I went myself.

Still added days went by. Whether Bartleby's eyes improved or not, I could 135 not say. To all appearance, I thought they did. But when I asked him if they did he vouchsafed no answer. At all events, he would do no copying. At last, in re-plying to my urgings, he informed me that he had permanently given up copy-ing.

"What!" exclaimed I; "suppose your eyes should get entirely well—better than ever before—would you not copy then?"

"I have given up copying," he answered, and slid aside.

He remained as ever, a fixture in my chamber. Nay—if that were possible—he became still more of a fixture than before. What was to be done? He would do nothing in the office; why should he stay there? In plain fact, he had now be-come a millstone to me, not only useless as a necklace, but afflictive to bear. Yet I was sorry for him. I speak less than truth when I say that, on his own account, he occasioned me uneasiness. If he would but have named a single relative or friend, I would instantly have written, and urged their taking the poor fellow away to some convenient retreat. But he seemed alone, absolutely alone in the universe. A bit of wreck in the mid-Atlantic. At length, necessities connected with my business tyrannized over all other considerations. Decently as I could, I told Bartleby that in six days' time he must unconditionally leave the office. I warned him to take measures, in the interval, for procuring some other abode. I offered to assist him in this endeavor, if he himself would but take the first step towards a removal. "And when you finally quit me, Bartleby," added I, "I shall see that you go not away entirely unprovided. Six days from this hour, remem-ber."

At the expiration of that period, I peeped behind the screen, and lo! Bartleby was there.

I buttoned up my coat, balanced myself; advanced slowly towards him, 140 touched his shoulder, and said, "The time has come; you must quit this place; I am sorry for you; here is money; but you must go."

"I would prefer not," he replied, with his back still towards me.

"You *must.*"

He remained silent.

Now I had an unbounded confidence in this man's common honesty. He had frequently restored to me sixpences and shillings carelessly dropped upon the floor, for I am apt to be very reckless in such shirt-button affairs. The pro-ceeding, then, which followed will not be deemed extraordinary.

"Bartleby," said I, "I owe you twelve dollars on account; here are thirty-two; 145 the odd twenty are yours—Will you take it?" and I handed the bills towards him.

But he made no motion.

"I will leave them here, then," putting them under a weight on the table. Then taking my hat and cane and going to the door, I tranquilly turned and added—"After you have removed your things from these offices, Bartleby, you will of course lock the door—since every one is now gone for the day but you—and if you please, slip your key underneath the mat, so that I may have it in the morning. I shall not see you again; so good-bye to you. If, hereafter, in your new place of abode, I can be of any service to you, do not fail to advise me by letter. Good-bye, Bartleby, and fare you well."

But he answered not a word; like the last column of some ruined temple, he remained standing mute and solitary in the middle of the otherwise deserted room.

As I walked home in a pensive mood, my vanity got the better of my pity. I could not but highly plume myself on my masterly management in getting rid of Bartleby. Masterly I call it, and such it must appear to any dispassionate thinker. The beauty of my procedure seemed to consist in its perfect quietness. There was no vulgar bullying, no bravado of any sort, no choleric hectoring, and striding to and fro across the apartment, jerking out vehement commands for Bartleby to bundle himself off with his beggarly traps. Nothing of the kind. Without loudly bidding Bartleby depart—as an inferior genius might have done—I *assumed* the ground that depart he must; and upon that assumption built all I had to say. The more I thought over my procedure, the more I was charmed with it. Nevertheless, next morning, upon awakening, I had my doubts—I had somehow slept off the fumes of vanity. One of the coolest and wisest hours a man has, is just after he awakes in the morning. My procedure seemed as sagacious as ever—but only in theory. How it would prove in practice—there was the rub. It was truly a beautiful thought to have assumed Bartleby's departure; but, after all, that assumption was simply my own, and none of Bartleby's. The great point was, not whether I had assumed that he would quit me, but whether he would prefer to do so. He was more a man of preferences than assumptions.

After breakfast, I walked down town, arguing the probabilities *pro* and *con*. 150 One moment I thought it would prove a miserable failure, and Bartleby would be found all alive at my office as usual; the next moment it seemed certain that I should find his chair empty. And so I kept veering about. At the corner of Broadway and Canal Street, I saw quite an excited group of people standing in earnest conversation.

"I'll take odds he doesn't," said a voice as I passed.

"Doesn't go?—done!" said I, "put up your money."

I was instinctively putting my hand in my pocket to produce my own, when I remembered that this was an election day. The words I had overheard bore no reference to Bartleby, but to the success or non-success of some candidate for the mayoralty. In my intent frame of mind, I had, as it were, imagined that all Broadway shared in my excitement, and were debating the same question with me. I passed on, very thankful that the uproar of the street screened my momentary absent-mindedness.

As I had intended, I was earlier than usual at my office door. I stood listening for a moment. All was still. He must be gone. I tried the knob. The door was locked. Yes, my procedure had worked to a charm; he indeed must be vanished. Yet a certain melancholy mixed with this: I was almost sorry for my brilliant success. I was fumbling under the door mat for the key, which Bartleby was to have left there for me, when accidentally my knee knocked against a panel, producing a summoning sound, and in response a voice came to me from within—"Not yet; I am occupied."

It was Bartleby.   155

I was thunderstruck. For an instant I stood like the man who, pipe in mouth, was killed one cloudless afternoon long ago in Virginia, by summer lightning; at his own warm open window he was killed, and remained leaning out there upon the dreamy afternoon, till someone touched him, when he fell.

"Not gone!" I murmured at last. But again obeying that wondrous ascendancy which the inscrutable scrivener had over me, and from which ascendancy, for all my chafing, I could not completely escape, I slowly went down stairs and out into the street, and while walking round the block, considered what I should next do in this unheard-of perplexity. Turn the man out by an actual thrusting I could not; to drive him away by calling him hard names would not do; calling in the police was an unpleasant idea; and yet, permit him to enjoy his cadaverous triumph over me—this, too, I could not think of. What was to be done? or, if nothing could be done, was there anything further that I could *assume* in the matter? Yes, as before I had prospectively assumed that Bartleby would depart, so now I might retrospectively assume that departed he was. In the legitimate carrying out of this assumption, I might enter my office in a great hurry, and pretending not to see Bartleby at all, walk straight against him as if he were air. Such a proceeding would in a singular degree have the appearance of a home-thrust. It was hardly possible that Bartleby could withstand such an application of the doctrine of assumption. But upon second thoughts the success of the plan seemed rather dubious. I resolved to argue the matter over with him again.

"Bartleby," said I, entering the office, with a quietly severe expression, "I am seriously displeased. I am pained, Bartleby. I had thought better of you. I had imagined you of such a gentlemanly organization, that in any delicate dilemma a slight hint would suffice—in short, an assumption. But it appears I am deceived. Why," I added, unaffectedly starting, "you have not even touched that money yet," pointing to it, just where I had left it the evening previous.

He answered nothing.

"Will you, or will you not, quit me?" I now demanded in a sudden passion,   160
advancing close to him.

"I would prefer *not* to quit you," he replied, gently emphasizing the *not*.

"What earthly right have you to stay here? Do you pay any rent? Do you pay my taxes? Or is this property yours?"

He answered nothing.

"Are you ready to go on and write now? Are your eyes recovered? Could you copy a small paper for me this morning? or help examine a few lines? or step round to the Post Office? In a word, will you do anything at all, to give a coloring to your refusal to depart the premises?"

He silently retired into his hermitage.   165

I was now in such a state of nervous resentment that I thought it but prudent to check myself at present from further demonstrations. Bartleby and I were alone. I remembered the tragedy of the unfortunate Adams and the still more unfortunate Colt in the solitary office of the latter; and how poor Colt, being dreadfully incensed by Adams, and imprudently permitting himself to get wildly excited, was at unawares hurried into his fatal act—an act which certainly no man could possibly deplore more than the actor himself.[5] Often it had occurred to me in my ponderings upon the subject that had that altercation taken place in the public street, or at a private residence, it would not have terminated as it did. It was the circumstance of being alone in a solitary office, up stairs, of a building entirely unhallowed by humanizing domestic associations—an uncarpeted office, doubtless, of a dusty, haggard sort of appearance—this it must have been, which greatly helped to enhance the irritable desperation of the hapless Colt.

But when this old Adam of resentment rose in me and tempted me concerning Bartleby, I grappled him and threw him. How? Why, simply by recalling the divine injunction: "A new commandment give I unto you, that ye love one another." Yes, this it was that saved me. Aside from higher considerations, charity often operates as a vastly wise and prudent principle—a great safeguard to its possessor. Men have committed murder for jealousy's sake, and anger's sake, and hatred's sake, and selfishness' sake, and spiritual pride's sake; but no man, that ever I heard of, ever committed a diabolical murder for sweet charity's sake. Mere self-interest, then, if no better motive can be enlisted, should, especially with high-tempered men, prompt all beings to charity and philanthropy. At any rate, upon the occasion in question, I strove to drown my exasperated feelings towards the scrivener by benevolently construing his conduct. Poor fellow, poor fellow! thought I, he don't mean anything; and besides, he has seen hard times, and ought to be indulged.

I endeavored, also, immediately to occupy myself, and at the same time to comfort my despondency. I tried to fancy, that in the course of the morning, at such time as might prove agreeable to him, Bartleby, of his own free accord, would emerge from his hermitage and take up some decided line of march in the direction of the door. But no. Half-past twelve o'clock came; Turkey began to glow in the face, overturn his inkstand, and become generally obstreperous; Nippers abated down into quietude and courtesy; Ginger Nut munched his noon apple; and Bartleby remained standing at his window in one of his profoundest dead-wall reveries. Will it be credited? Ought I to acknowledge it? That afternoon I left the office without saying one further word to him.

---

5. John C. Colt murdered Samuel Adams in January 1842. Later that year, after his conviction, Colt committed suicide a half-hour before he was to be hanged. The case received wide and sensationalistic press coverage at the time.

Some days now passed, during which, at leisure intervals I looked a little into "Edwards on the Will," and "Priestley on Necessity." Under the circumstances, those books induced a salutary feeling. Gradually I slid into the persuasion that these troubles of mine, touching the scrivener, had been all predestined from eternity, and Bartleby was billeted upon me for some mysterious purpose of an all-wise Providence, which it was not for a mere mortal like me to fathom. Yes, Bartleby, stay there behind your screen, thought I; I shall persecute you no more; you are harmless and noiseless as any of these old chairs; in short, I never feel so private as when I know you are here. At last I see it, I feel it; I penetrate to the predestined purpose of my life. I am content. Others may have loftier parts to enact; but my mission in this world, Bartleby, is to furnish you with office-room for such period as you may see fit to remain.

I believe that this wise and blessed frame of mind would have continued 170 with me, had it not been for the unsolicited and uncharitable remarks obtruded upon me by my professional friends who visited the rooms. But thus it often is, that the constant friction of illiberal minds wears out at last the best resolves of the more generous. Though to be sure, when I reflected upon it, it was not strange that people entering my office should be struck by the peculiar aspect of the unaccountable Bartleby, and so be tempted to throw out some sinister observations concerning him. Sometimes an attorney, having business with me, and calling at my office, and finding no one but the scrivener there, would undertake to obtain some sort of precise information from him touching my whereabouts; but without heeding his idle talk, Bartleby would remain standing immovable in the middle of the room. So after contemplating him in that position for a time, the attorney would depart, no wiser than he came.

Also, when a reference was going on, and the room full of lawyers and witnesses, and business driving fast, some deeply-occupied legal gentleman present, seeing Bartleby wholly unemployed, would request him to run round to his (the legal gentleman's) office and fetch some papers for him. Thereupon, Bartleby would tranquilly decline, and yet remain idle as before. Then the lawyer would give a great stare, and turn to me. And what could I say? At last I was made aware that all through the circle of my professional acquaintance, a whisper of wonder was running round, having reference to the strange creature I kept at my office. This worried me very much. And as the idea came upon me of his possibly turning out a long-lived man, and keeping occupying my chambers, and denying my authority; and perplexing my visitors; and scandalizing my professional reputation; and casting a general gloom over the premises; keeping soul and body together to the last upon his savings (for doubtless he spent but half a dime a day), and in the end perhaps outlive me, and claim possession of my office by right of his perpetual occupancy: as all these dark anticipations crowded upon me more and more, and my friends continually intruded their relentless remarks upon the apparition in my room; a great change was wrought in me. I resolved to gather all my faculties together, and forever rid me of this intolerable incubus.

Ere revolving any complicated project, however, adapted to this end, I first simply suggested to Bartleby the propriety of his permanent departure. In a calm and serious tone, I commended the idea to his careful and mature consideration. But, having taken three days to meditate upon it, he apprised me, that his original determination remained the same; in short, that he still preferred to abide with me.

What shall I do? I now said to myself, buttoning up my coat to the last button. What shall I do? what ought I to do? what does conscience say I *should* do with this man, or, rather, ghost. Rid myself of him, I must; go, he shall. But how? You will not thrust him, the poor, pale, passive mortal, you will not thrust such a helpless creature out of your door? you will not dishonor yourself by such cruelty? No, I will not, I cannot do that. Rather would I let him live and die here, and then mason up his remains in the wall. What, then, will you do? For all your coaxing, he will not budge. Bribes he leaves under your own paperweight on your table; in short, it is quite plain that he prefers to cling to you.

Then something severe, something unusual must be done. What! surely you will not have him collared by a constable, and commit his innocent pallor to the common jail? And upon what ground could you procure such a thing to be done?—a vagrant, is he? What! he a vagrant, a wanderer, who refuses to budge? It is because he will not be a vagrant, then, that you seek to count him *as* a vagrant. That is too absurd. No visible means of support: there I have him. Wrong again: for indubitably he *does* support himself, and that is the only unanswerable proof that any man can show of his possessing the means so to do. No more, then. Since he will not quit me, I must quit him. I will change my offices; I will move elsewhere, and give him fair notice, that if I find him on my new premises I will then proceed against him as a common trespasser.

Acting accordingly, next day I thus addressed him: "I find these chambers too far from the City Hall; the air is unwholesome. In a word, I propose to remove my offices next week, and shall no longer require your services. I tell you this now, in order that you may seek another place." 175

He made no reply, and nothing more was said.

On the appointed day I engaged carts and men, proceeded to my chambers, and, having but little furniture, everything was removed in a few hours. Throughout, the scrivener remained standing behind the screen, which I directed to be removed the last thing. It was withdrawn; and, being folded up like a huge folio, left him the motionless occupant of a naked room. I stood in the entry watching him a moment, while something from within me upbraided me.

I re-entered, with my hand in my pocket—and—and my heart in my mouth.

"Good-bye, Bartleby; I am going—good-bye, and God some way bless you; and take that," slipping something in his hand. But it dropped upon the floor, and then—strange to say—I tore myself from him whom I had so longed to be rid of.

Established in my new quarters, for a day or two I kept the door locked, started at every footfall in the passages. When I returned to my rooms, after any little absence, I would pause at the threshold for an instant, and attentively listen, ere applying my key. But these fears were needless. Bartleby never came nigh me. 180

I thought all was going well, when a perturbed-looking stranger visited me, inquiring whether I was the person who had recently occupied rooms at No.——Wall Street.

Full of forebodings, I replied that I was.

"Then, sir," said the stranger, who proved a lawyer, "you are responsible for the man you left there. He refuses to do any copying; he refuses to do anything; he says he prefers not to; and he refuses to quit the premises."

"I am very sorry, sir," said I, with assumed tranquillity, but an inward tremor, "but, really, the man you allude to is nothing to me—he is no relation or apprentice of mine, that you should hold me responsible for him."

"In mercy's name, who is he?"   185

"I certainly cannot inform you. I know nothing about him. Formerly I employed him as a copyist; but he has done nothing for me now for some time past."

"I shall settle him, then—good morning, sir."

Several days passed, and I heard nothing more; and, though I often felt a charitable prompting to call at the place and see poor Bartleby, yet a certain squeamishness, of I know not what, withheld me.

All is over with him, by this time, thought I, at last, when, through another week, no further intelligence reached me. But, coming to my room the day after, I found several persons waiting at my door in a high state of nervous excitement.

"That's the man here—he comes," cried the foremost one, whom I recog-   190
nized as the lawyer who had previously called upon me alone.

"You must take him away, sir, at once," cried a portly person among them, advancing upon me, and whom I knew to be the landlord of No.——Wall Street. "These gentlemen, my tenants, cannot stand it any longer; Mr. B——" pointing to the lawyer, "has turned him out of his room, and he now persists in haunting the building generally, sitting upon the banisters of the stairs by day, and sleeping in the entry by night. Everybody is concerned; clients are leaving the offices; some fears are entertained of a mob; something you must do, and that without delay."

Aghast at this torrent, I fell back before it, and would fain have locked myself in my new quarters. In vain I persisted that Bartleby was nothing to me—no more than to any one else. In vain—I was the last person known to have anything to do with him, and they held me to the terrible account. Fearful, then, of being exposed in the papers (as one person present obscurely threatened), I considered the matter, and, at length, said, that if the lawyer would give me a confidential interview with the scrivener, in his (the lawyer's) own room, I would, that afternoon, strive my best to rid them of the nuisance they complained of.

Going up stairs to my old haunt, there was Bartleby silently sitting upon the banister at the landing.

"What are you doing here, Bartleby?" said I.

"Sitting upon the banister," he mildly replied.   195

I motioned him into the lawyer's room, who then left us.

"Bartleby," said I, "are you aware that you are the cause of great tribulation to me, by persisting in occupying the entry after being dismissed from the office?"

No answer.

"Now one of two things must take place. Either you must do something, or something must be done to you. Now what sort of business would you like to engage in? Would you like to re-engage in copying for some one?"

"No; I would prefer not to make any change."   200

"Would you like a clerkship in a dry-goods store?"

"There is too much confinement about that. No, I would not like a clerkship; but I am not particular."

"Too much confinement," I cried, "why, you keep yourself confined all the time!"

"I would prefer not to take a clerkship," he rejoined, as if to settle that little item at once.

"How would a bar-tender's business suit you? There is no trying of the eye-   205
sight in that."

"I would not like it at all; though, as I said before, I am not particular."

His unwonted wordiness inspirited me. I returned to the charge.

"Well, then, would you like to travel through the country collecting bills for the merchants? That would improve your health."

"No, I would prefer to be doing something else."

"How, then, would going as a companion to Europe, to entertain some   210
young gentleman with your conversation—how would that suit you?"

"Not at all. It does not strike me that there is anything definite about that. I like to be stationary. But I am not particular."

"Stationary you shall be, then," I cried, now losing all patience, and, for the first time in all my exasperating connections with him, fairly flying into a passion. "If you do not go away from these premises before night, I shall feel bound—indeed, I *am* bound—to—to—to quit the premises myself!" I rather absurdly concluded, knowing not with what possible threat to try to frighten his immobility into compliance. Despairing of all further efforts, I was precipitately leaving him, when a final thought occurred to me—one which had not been wholly unindulged before.

"Bartleby," said I, in the kindest tone I could assume under such exciting circumstances, "will you go home with me now not to my office, but my dwelling—and remain there till we can conclude upon some convenient arrangement for you at our leisure? Come, let us start now, right away."

"No: at present I would prefer not to make any change at all."

I answered nothing; but, effectually dodging every one by the suddenness   215
and rapidity of my flight, rushed from the building, ran up Wall Street towards Broadway, and, jumping into the first omnibus, was soon removed from pursuit. As soon as tranquillity returned, I distinctly perceived that I had now done all that I possibly could, both in respect to the demands of the landlord and his tenants, and with regard to my own desire and sense of duty, to benefit

Bartleby, and shield him from rude persecution. I now strove to be entirely care-free and quiescent; and my conscience justified me in the attempt; though, indeed, it was not so successful as I could have wished. So fearful was I of being again hunted out by the incensed landlord and his exasperated tenants, that, surrendering my business to Nippers, for a few days, I drove about the upper part of the town and through the suburbs, in my rockaway; crossed over to Jersey City and Hoboken, and paid fugitive visits to Manhattanville and Astoria. In fact, I almost lived in my rockaway for the time.

When again I entered my office, lo, a note from the landlord lay upon the desk. I opened it with trembling hands. It informed me that the writer had sent to the police, and had Bartleby removed to the Tombs as a vagrant. Moreover, since I knew more about him than any one else, he wished me to appear at that place, and make a suitable statement of the facts. These tidings had a conflicting effect upon me. At first I was indignant; but, at last, almost approved. The landlord's energetic, summary disposition, had led him to adopt a procedure which I do not think I would have decided upon myself; and yet, as a last resort, under such peculiar circumstances, it seemed the only plan.

As I afterwards learned, the poor scrivener, when told that he must be conducted to the Tombs, offered not the slightest obstacle, but, in his pale, unmoving way, silently acquiesced.

Some of the compassionate and curious by-standers joined the party; and headed by one of the constables arm-in-arm with Bartleby, the silent procession filed its way through all the noise, and heat, and joy of the roaring thoroughfares at noon.

The same day I received the note, I went to the Tombs, or, to speak more properly, the Halls of Justice. Seeking the right officer, I stated the purpose of my call, and was informed that the individual I described was, indeed, within. I then assured the functionary that Bartleby was a perfectly honest man, and greatly to be compassionated, however unaccountably eccentric. I narrated all I knew, and closed by suggesting the idea of letting him remain in as indulgent confinement as possible, till something less harsh might be done—though, indeed, I hardly knew what. At all events, if nothing else could be decided upon, the alms-house must receive him. I then begged to have an interview.

Being under no disgraceful charge, and quite serene and harmless in all his 220 ways, they had permitted him freely to wander about the prison, and, especially, in the inclosed grass-platted yards thereof. And so I found him there, standing all alone in the quietest of the yards, his face towards a high wall, while all around, from the narrow slits of the jail windows, I thought I saw peering out upon him the eyes of murderers and thieves.

"Bartleby!"

"I know you," he said, without looking round—"and I want nothing to say to you."

"It was not I that brought you here, Bartleby," said I, keenly pained at his implied suspicion. "And to you, this should not be so vile a place. Nothing reproachful attaches to you by being here. And see, it is not so sad a place as one might think. Look, there is the sky, and here is the grass."

"I know where I am," he replied, but would say nothing more, and so I left him.

As I entered the corridor again, a broad meat-like man, in an apron, ac- 225
costed me, and, jerking his thumb over my shoulder, said "Is that your friend?"

"Yes."

"Does he want to starve? If he does, let him live on the prison fare, that's all."

"Who are you?" asked I, not knowing what to make of such an unofficially
speaking person in such a place.

"I am the grub-man. Such gentlemen as have friends here, hire me to provide them with something good to eat."

"Is this so?" said I, turning to the turnkey.   230

He said it was.

"Well, then," said I, slipping some silver into the grub-man's hands (for so they
called him), "I want you to give particular attention to my friend there; let him
have the best dinner you can get. And you must be as polite to him as possible."

"Introduce me, will you?" said the grub-man, looking at me with an expression which seemed to say he was all impatience for an opportunity to give a
specimen of his breeding.

Thinking it would prove of benefit to the scrivener, I acquiesced; and, asking the grub-man his name, went up with him to Bartleby.

"Bartleby, this is a friend; you will find him very useful to you."   235

"Your sarvant, sir, your sarvant," said the grub-man, making a low saluta-
tion behind his apron, "Hope you find it pleasant here, sir; nice grounds—cool
apartments—hope you'll stay with us some time—try to make it agreeable.
What will you have for dinner to-day?"

"I prefer not to dine to-day," said Bartleby, turning away. "It would disagree
with me; I am unused to dinners." So saying, he slowly moved to the other side
of the inclosure, and took up a position fronting the dead-wall.

"How's this?" said the grub-man, addressing me with a stare of astonishment. "He's odd, ain't he?"

"I think he is a little deranged," said I, sadly.

"Deranged? deranged is it? Well, now, upon my word, I thought that friend 240
of yourn was a gentleman forger; they are always pale and genteel-like, them
forgers. I can't help pity 'em—can't help it, sir. Did you know Monroe Edwards?" he added, touchingly, and paused. Then, laying his hand piteously on
my shoulder, sighed, "he died of consumption at Sing-Sing. So you weren't acquainted with Monroe?"

"No, I was never socially acquainted with any forgers. But I cannot stop
longer. Look to my friend yonder. You will not lose by it. I will see you again."

Some few days after this, I again obtained admission to the Tombs, and
went through the corridors in quest of Bartleby; but without finding him.

"I saw him coming from his cell not long ago," said a turnkey, "may be he's
gone to loiter in the yards."

So I went in that direction.

"Are you looking for the silent man?" said another turnkey, passing me. 245
"Yonder he lies—sleeping in the yard there. 'Tis not twenty minutes since I saw
him lie down."

The yard was entirely quiet. It was not accessible to the common prisoners. The surrounding walls, of amazing thickness, kept off all sounds behind them. The Egyptian character of the masonry weighed upon me with its gloom. But a soft imprisoned turf grew under foot. The heart of the eternal pyramids, it seemed, wherein, by some strange magic, through the clefts, grass-seed, dropped by birds, had sprung.

Strangely huddled at the base of the wall, his knees drawn up, and lying on his side, his head touching the cold stones, I saw the wasted Bartleby. But nothing stirred. I paused; then went close up to him; stooped over, and saw that his dim eyes were open; otherwise he seemed profoundly sleeping. Something prompted me to touch him. I felt his hand, when a tingling shiver ran up my arm and down my spine to my feet.

The round face of the grub-man peered upon me now. "His dinner is ready. Won't he dine to-day, either? Or does he live without dining?"

"Lives without dining," said I, and closed the eyes.

"Eh!—He's asleep, ain't he?"   250

"With kings and counselors," murmured I.

There would seem little need for proceeding further in this history. Imagination will readily supply the meagre recital of poor Bartleby's interment. But, ere parting with the reader, let me say, that if this little narrative has sufficiently interested him, to awaken curiosity as to who Bartleby was, and what manner of life he led prior to the present narrator's making his acquaintance, I can only reply, that in such curiosity I fully share, but am wholly unable to gratify it. Yet here I hardly know whether I should divulge one little item of rumor, which came to my ear a few months after the scrivener's decease. Upon what basis it rested, I could never ascertain; and hence, how true it is I cannot now tell. But, inasmuch as this vague report has not been without a certain suggestive interest to me, however sad, it may prove the same with some others; and so I will briefly mention it. The report was this: that Bartleby had been a subordinate clerk in the Dead Letter Office at Washington, from which he had been suddenly removed by a change in the administration. When I think over this rumor, hardly can I express the emotions which seize me. Dead letters! does it not sound like dead men? Conceive a man by nature and misfortune prone to a pallid hopelessness, can any business seem more fitted to heighten it than that of continually handling these dead letters, and assorting them for the flames? For by the cart-load they are annually burned. Sometimes from out the folded paper the pale clerk takes a ring the finger it was meant for, perhaps, moulders in the grave; a bank-note sent in swiftest charity he whom it would relieve, nor eats nor hungers any more; pardon for those who died despairing; hope for those who died unhoping; good tidings for those who died stifled by unrelieved calamities. On errands of life, these letters speed to death.

Ah, Bartleby! Ah, humanity!

ACTIVITIES FOR WRITING AND DISCUSSION

1. Reread paragraphs 2, 55, and 167, in which the **narrator** discusses his views on work, money, Bartleby, and other topics. Based on these paragraphs and any others, how would you assess the narrator's values and motives?

2. Several comments by the narrator suggest that Bartleby is, in some ways, an ideal worker and not lazy; for instance, see paragraphs 20 and 86. If not laziness, what other factors might account for Bartleby's refusal to do certain tasks?

3. Why doesn't the narrator simply evict Bartleby from his office? Imagine a different scenario in which he does, and sketch out the event of the dismissal and its aftermath. Then discuss the impact of this change on the story's effectiveness and/or meaning.

4. Describe the nature of Bartleby's job, paying close attention to his specific duties. What aspects of the job make it attractive or unattractive? Then offer your own answer to the question, Why does he "prefer not to" do certain tasks assigned him? In our electronic age scriveners (workers employed to copy out documents longhand) no longer exist. If you were to write a present-day version of this story, in what sort of job would you place Bartleby? Why?

5. On pages 1044–1047 in Appendix A you will find one student's attempt to recast "Bartleby" into a present-day setting. Read and react to the student piece. Then use the student story and/or "Bartleby" as inspiration(s) for composing a creative response of your own. *Note:* For a modern-day story that offers suggestive parallels to "Bartleby," see Ray Bradbury's "The Murderer" (p. 569).

6. Ponder paragraph 254. Are we meant finally to *judge* Bartleby? Humanity?

KATE CHOPIN (1850–1904)

A Pair of Silk Stockings

Little Mrs. Sommers one day found herself the unexpected possessor of fifteen 1 dollars. It seemed to her a very large amount of money, and the way in which it stuffed and bulged her worn old *porte-monnaie*[1] gave her a feeling of importance such as she had not enjoyed for years.

The question of investment was one that occupied her greatly. For a day or 2 two she walked about apparently in a dreamy state, but really absorbed in spec-

---

1. Purse.

ulation and calculation. She did not wish to act hastily, to do anything she might afterward regret. But it was during the still hours of the night when she lay awake revolving plans in her mind that she seemed to see her way clearly toward a proper and judicious use of the money.

A dollar or two should be added to the price usually paid for Janie's shoes, 3 which would insure their lasting an appreciable time longer than they usually did. She would buy so and so many yards of percale for new shirt waists for the boys and Janie and Mag. She had intended to make the old ones do by skilful patching. Mag should have another gown. She had seen some beautiful patterns, veritable bargains in the shop windows. And still there would be left enough for new stockings—two pairs apiece—and what darning that would save for a while! She would get caps for the boys and sailor-hats for the girls. The vision of her little brood looking fresh and dainty and new for once in their lives excited her and made her restless and wakeful with anticipation.

The neighbors sometimes talked of certain "better days" that little Mrs. 4 Sommers had known before she had ever thought of being Mrs. Sommers. She herself indulged in no such morbid retrospection. She had no time—no second of time to devote to the past. The needs of the present absorbed her every faculty. A vision of the future like some dim, gaunt monster sometimes appalled her, but luckily tomorrow never comes.

Mrs. Sommers was one who knew the value of bargains; who could stand 5 for hours making her way inch by inch toward the desired object that was selling below cost. She could elbow her way if need be; she had learned to clutch a piece of goods and hold it and stick to it with persistence and determination till her turn came to be served, no matter when it came.

But that day she was a little faint and tired. She had swallowed a light lun- 6 cheon—no! when she came to think of it, between getting the children fed and the place righted, and preparing herself for the shopping bout, she had actually forgotten to eat any luncheon at all!

She sat herself upon a revolving stool before a counter that was compara- 7 tively deserted, trying to gather strength and courage to charge through an eager multitude that was besieging breast-works of shirting and figured lawn. An all-gone limp feeling had come over her and she rested her hand aimlessly upon the counter. She wore no gloves. By degrees she grew aware that her hand had encountered something very soothing, very pleasant to touch. She looked down to see that her hand lay upon a pile of silk stockings. A placard near by announced that they had been reduced in price from two dollars and fifty cents to one dollar and ninety-eight cents; and a young girl who stood behind the counter asked her if she wished to examine their line of silk hosiery. She smiled, just as if she had been asked to inspect a tiara of diamonds with the ultimate view of purchasing it. But she went on feeling the soft, sheeny luxurious things—with both hands now, holding them up to see them glisten, and to feel them glide serpent-like through her fingers.

Two hectic blotches came suddenly into her pale cheeks. She looked up at 8 the girl.

"Do you think there are any eights-and-a-half among these?"   9

There were any number of eights-and-a-half. In fact, there were more of   10
that size than any other. Here was a light-blue pair; there were some lavender,
some all black and various shades of tan and gray. Mrs. Sommers selected a
black pair and looked at them very long and closely. She pretended to be examining their texture, which the clerk assured her was excellent.

"A dollar and ninety-eight cents," she mused aloud. "Well, I'll take this pair."   11
She handed the girl a five-dollar bill and waited for her change and for her parcel. What a very small parcel it was! It seemed lost in the depths of her shabby
old shopping-bag.

Mrs. Sommers after that did not move in the direction of the bargain   12
counter. She took the elevator, which carried her to an upper floor into the region of the ladies' waiting-rooms. Here, in a retired corner, she exchanged her
cotton stockings for the new silk ones which she had just bought. She was not
going through any acute mental process or reasoning with herself, nor was she
striving to explain to her satisfaction the motive of her action. She was not
thinking at all. She seemed for the time to be taking a rest from that laborious
and fatiguing function and to have abandoned herself to some mechanical impulse that directed her actions and freed her of responsibility.

How good was the touch of the raw silk to her flesh! She felt like lying back   13
in the cushioned chair and reveling for a while in the luxury of it. She did for a
little while. Then she replaced her shoes, rolled the cotton stockings together
and thrust them into her bag. After doing this she crossed straight over to the
shoe department and took her seat to be fitted.

She was fastidious. The clerk could not make her out; he could not reconcile   14
her shoes with her stockings, and she was not too easily pleased. She held back
her skirts and turned her feet one way and her head another way as she glanced
down at the polished, pointed-tipped boots. Her foot and ankle looked very
pretty. She could not realize that they belonged to her and were a part of herself. She wanted an excellent and stylish fit, she told the young fellow who
served her, and she did not mind the difference of a dollar or two more in the
price so long as she got what she desired.

It was a long time since Mrs. Sommers had been fitted with gloves. On rare   15
occasions when she had bought a pair they were always "bargains," so cheap
that it would have been preposterous and unreasonable to have expected them
to be fitted to the hand.

Now she rested her elbow on the cushion of the glove counter, and a pretty,   16
pleasant young creature, delicate and deft of touch, drew a long-wristed "kid"
over Mrs. Sommers's hand. She smoothed it down over the wrist and buttoned
it neatly, and both lost themselves for a second or two in admiring contemplation of the little symmetrical gloved hand. But there were other places where
money might be spent.

There were books and magazines piled up in the window of a stall a few   17
paces down the street. Mrs. Sommers bought two high-priced magazines such
as she had been accustomed to read in the days when she had been accustomed

to other pleasant things. She carried them without wrapping. As well as she could she lifted her skirts at the crossings. Her stockings and boots and well fitting gloves had worked marvels in her bearing—had given her a feeling of assurance, a sense of belonging to the well-dressed multitude.

She was very hungry. Another time she would have stilled the cravings for 18 food until reaching her own home, where she would have brewed herself a cup of tea and taken a snack of anything that was available. But the impulse that was guiding her would not suffer her to entertain any such thought.

There was a restaurant at the corner. She had never entered its doors; from 19 the outside she had sometimes caught glimpses of spotless damask and shining crystal, and soft-stepping waiters serving people of fashion.

When she entered her appearance created no surprise, no consternation, as 20 she had half feared it might. She seated herself at a small table alone, and an attentive waiter at once approached to take her order. She did not want a profusion; she craved a nice and tasty bite—a half dozen blue-points, a plump chop with cress, a something sweet—a crème-frappée, for instance; a glass of Rhine wine, and after all a small cup of black coffee.

While waiting to be served she removed her gloves very leisurely and laid 21 them beside her. Then she picked up a magazine and glanced through it, cutting the pages with a blunt edge of her knife. It was all very agreeable. The damask was even more spotless than it had seemed through the window, and the crystal more sparkling. There were quiet ladies and gentlemen, who did not notice her, lunching at the small tables like her own. A soft, pleasing strain of music could be heard, and a gentle breeze was blowing through the window. She tasted a bite, and she read a word or two, and she sipped the amber wine and wiggled her toes in the silk stockings. The price of it made no difference. She counted the money out to the waiter and left an extra coin on his tray, whereupon he bowed before her as before a princess of royal blood.

There was still money in her purse, and her next temptation presented itself 22 in the shape of a matinée poster.

It was a little later when she entered the theatre, the play had begun and the 23 house seemed to her to be packed. But there were vacant seats here and there, and into one of them she was ushered, between brilliantly dressed women who had gone there to kill time and eat candy and display their gaudy attire. There were many others who were there solely for the play and acting. It is safe to say there was no one present who bore quite the attitude which Mrs. Sommers did to her surroundings. She gathered in the whole—stage and players and people in one wide impression, and absorbed it and enjoyed it. She laughed at the comedy and wept—she and the gaudy woman next to her wept over the tragedy. And they talked a little together over it. And the gaudy woman wiped her eyes and sniffled on a tiny square of filmy, perfumed lace and passed little Mrs. Sommers her box of candy.

The play was over, the music ceased, the crowd filed out. It was like a dream 24 ended. People scattered in all directions. Mrs. Sommers went to the corner and waited for the cable car.

A man with keen eyes, who sat opposite to her, seemed to like the study of   25
her small, pale face. It puzzled him to decipher what he saw there. In truth, he
saw nothing unless he were wizard enough to detect a poignant wish, a powerful longing that the cable car would never stop anywhere, but go on and on
with her forever.

ACTIVITIES FOR WRITING AND DISCUSSION

1. Compare Mrs. Sommers with Louise Mallard, the protagonist of
Chopin's "The Story of an Hour" (see p. 181). How are the characters or life situations of the two women alike? different? Then:
   a. Draft an essay comparing and contrasting the two women; or
   b. Imagine a scene in which Mrs. Mallard joins Mrs. Sommers at the
   corner restaurant described in paragraph 19, and write a dialogue between the two women.

2. Mrs. Sommers meant to spend the fifteen dollars on her children but
ends up spending it on herself. Why? Looking carefully at the motivations mentioned for each of her purchases, find any evidence in the text that you think
justifies her behavior. Then find evidence that suggests her behavior was
"wrong" or inappropriately selfish. Finally, form your own judgment of Mrs.
Sommers and argue it in class.

3. Based on evidence in the story do you think Mrs. Sommers is married,
widowed, or divorced? Does her marital status affect how you feel about her actions? Is it significant that there is no explicit mention in the story of a *Mr.*
Sommers? What possible interpretations can you give of the first sentence in
paragraph 4 ("The neighbors sometimes talked of certain 'better days' that little
Mrs. Sommers had known before she had ever thought of being Mrs. Sommers") and of paragraph 17?

4. Write a sequel in which Mrs. Sommers returns home with her purchases
and encounters her husband and/or children. Do they react? If so, how do they
react? What does she reveal— or conceal—about her day's activities?

ANTON CHEKHOV (1860–1904)

Gooseberries

The sky had been overcast since early morning; it was a still day, not hot, but te-   1
dious, as it usually is when the weather is gray and dull, when clouds have been
hanging over the fields for a long time, and you wait for the rain that does not
come. Ivan Ivanych, a veterinary, and Burkin, a high school teacher, were already tired with walking, and the plain seemed endless to them. Far ahead were

the scarcely visible windmills of the village of Mironositzkoe; to the right lay a range of hills that disappeared in the distance beyond the village, and both of them knew that over there were the river, and fields, green willows, homesteads, and if you stood on one of the hills, you could see from there another vast plain, telegraph poles, and a train that from afar looked like a caterpillar crawling, and in clear weather you could even see the town. Now, when it was still and when nature seemed mild and pensive, Ivan Ivanych and Burkin were filled with love for this plain, and both of them thought what a beautiful land it was.

"Last time when we were in Elder Prokofy's barn," said Burkin, "you were   2 going to tell me a story."

"Yes; I wanted to tell you about my brother."   3

Ivan Ivanych heaved a slow sigh and lit his pipe before beginning his story,   4 but just then it began to rain. And five minutes later there was a downpour, and it was hard to tell when it would be over. The two men halted, at a loss; the dogs, already wet, stood with their tails between their legs and looked at them feelingly.

"We must find shelter somewhere," said Burkin. "Let's go to Alyohin's; it's   5 quite near."

"Let's."   6

They turned aside and walked across a mown meadow, now going straight   7 ahead, now bearing to the right, until they reached the road. Soon poplars came into view, a garden, then the red roofs of barns; the river gleamed, and the view opened on a broad expanse of water with a mill and a white bathing-cabin. That was Sofyino, Alyohin's place.

The mill was going, drowning out the sound of the rain; the dam was shak-   8 ing. Wet horses stood near the carts, their heads drooping, and men were walking about, their heads covered with sacks. It was damp, muddy, dreary; and the water looked cold and unkind. Ivan Ivanych and Burkin felt cold and messy and uncomfortable through and through; their feet were heavy with mud and when, having crossed the dam, they climbed up to the barns, they were silent as though they were cross with each other.

The noise of a winnowing-machine came from one of the barns, the door   9 was open, and clouds of dust were pouring from within. On the threshold stood Alyohin himself, a man of forty, tall and rotund, with long hair, looking more like a professor or an artist than a gentleman farmer. He was wearing a white blouse, badly in need of washing, that was belted with a rope, and drawers, and his high boots were plastered with mud and straw. His eyes and nose were black with dust. He recognized Ivan Ivanych and Burkin and was apparently very glad to see them.

"Please go up to the house, gentlemen," he said, smiling; "I'll be there di-   10 rectly, in a moment."

It was a large structure of two stories. Alyohin lived downstairs in what was   11 formerly the stewards' quarters: two rooms that had arched ceilings and small windows; the furniture was plain, and the place smelled of rye bread, cheap vodka, and harness. He went into the showy rooms upstairs only rarely, when he had guests. Once in the house, the two visitors were met by a chambermaid, a young woman so beautiful that both of them stood still at the same moment and glanced at each other.

"You can't imagine how glad I am to see you, gentlemen," said Alyohin, join- 12 ing them in the hall. "What a surprise! Pelageya," he said, turning to the chambermaid, "give the guests a change of clothes. And, come to think of it, I will change, too. But I must go and bathe first, I don't think I've had a wash since spring. Don't you want to go into the bathing-cabin? In the meanwhile things will be got ready here."

The beautiful Pelageya, with her soft, delicate air, brought them bath towels 13 and soap, and Alyohin went to the bathing-cabin with his guests.

"Yes, it's a long time since I've bathed," he said, as he undressed. "I've an ex- 14 cellent bathing-cabin, as you see—it was put up by my father—but somehow I never find time to use it." He sat down on the steps and lathered his long hair and neck, and the water around him turned brown.

"I say—" observed Ivan Ivanych significantly, looking at his head. 15

"I haven't had a good wash for a long time," repeated Alyohin, embarrassed, 16 and soaped himself once more; the water about him turned dark-blue, the color of ink.

Ivan Ivanych came out of the cabin, plunged into the water with a splash 17 and swam in the rain, thrusting his arms out wide; he raised waves on which white lilies swayed. He swam out to the middle of the river and dived and a minute later came up in another spot and swam on and kept diving, trying to touch bottom. "By God!" he kept repeating delightedly, "by God!" He swam to the mill, spoke to the peasants there, and turned back and in the middle of the river lay floating, exposing his face to the rain. Burkin and Alyohin were already dressed and ready to leave, but he kept on swimming and diving. "By God!" he kept exclaiming. "Lord, have mercy on me."

"You've had enough!" Burkin shouted to him. 18

They returned to the house. And only when the lamp was lit in the big 19 drawing room upstairs, and the two guests, in silk dressing-gowns and warm slippers, were lounging in armchairs, and Alyohin himself, washed and combed, wearing a new jacket, was walking about the room, evidently savoring the warmth, the cleanliness, the dry clothes and light footwear, and when pretty Pelageya, stepping noiselessly across the carpet and smiling softly, brought in a tray with tea and jam, only then did Ivan Ivanych begin his story, and it was as though not only Burkin and Alyohin were listening, but also the ladies, old and young, and the military men who looked down upon them, calmly and severely, from their gold frames.

"We are two brothers," he began, "I, Ivan Ivanych, and my brother, Nikolay 20 Ivanych, who is two years my junior. I went in for a learned profession and became a veterinary; Nikolay at nineteen began to clerk in a provincial branch of the Treasury. Our father was a *kantonist*,[1] but he rose to be an officer and so a

---

1. The son of a private, registered at birth in the army and trained in a military school.

nobleman, a rank that he bequeathed to us together with a small estate. After his death there was a lawsuit and we lost the estate to creditors, but be that as it may, we spent our childhood in the country. Just like peasant children we passed days and nights in the fields and the woods, herded horses, stripped bast from the trees, fished, and so on. And, you know, whoever even once in his life has caught a perch or seen thrushes migrate in the autumn, when on clear, cool days they sweep in flocks over the village, will never really be a townsman and to the day of his death will have a longing for the open. My brother was unhappy in the government office. Years passed, but he went on warming the same seat, scratching away at the same papers, and thinking of one and the same thing: how to get away to the country. And little by little this vague longing turned into a definite desire, into a dream of buying a little property somewhere on the banks of a river or a lake.

"He was a kind and gentle soul and I loved him, but I never sympathized 21 with his desire to shut himself up for the rest of his life on a little property of his own. It is a common saying that a man needs only six feet of earth. But six feet is what a corpse needs, not a man. It is also asserted that if our educated class is drawn to the land and seeks to settle on farms, that's a good thing. But these farms amount to the same six feet of earth. To retire from the city, from the struggle, from the hubbub, to go off and hide on one's own farm—that's not life, it is selfishness, sloth, it is a kind of monasticism, but monasticism without works. Man needs not six feet of earth, not a farm, but the whole globe, all of Nature, where unhindered he can display all the capacities and peculiarities of his free spirit.

"My brother Nikolay, sitting in his office, dreamed of eating his own *shchi,* 22 which would fill the whole farmyard with a delicious aroma, of picnicking on the green grass, of sleeping in the sun, of sitting for hours on the seat by the gate gazing at field and forest. Books on agriculture and the farming items in almanacs were his joy, the delight of his soul. He liked newspapers too, but the only things he read in them were advertisements of land for sale, so many acres of tillable land and pasture, with house, garden, river, mill, and millpond. And he pictured to himself garden paths, flowers, fruit, birdhouses with starlings in them, crucians in the pond, and all that sort of thing, you know. These imaginary pictures varied with the advertisements he came upon, but somehow gooseberry bushes figured in every one of them. He could not picture to himself a single country-house, a single rustic nook, without gooseberries.

" 'Country life has its advantages,' he used to say. 'You sit on the veranda 23 having tea, and your ducks swim in the pond, and everything smells delicious and—the gooseberries are ripening.'

"He would draw a plan of his estate and invariably it would contain the fol- 24 lowing features: a) the master's house; b) servants' quarters; c) kitchen-garden; d) a gooseberry patch. He lived meagerly: he deprived himself of food and drink; he dressed God knows how, like a beggar, but he kept on saving and salting money away in the bank. He was terribly stingy. It was painful for me to see it, and I used to give him small sums and send him something on holidays, but

he would put that away too. Once a man is possessed by an idea, there is no doing anything with him.

"Years passed. He was transferred to another province, he was already past 25
forty, yet he was still reading newspaper advertisements and saving up money.
Then I heard that he was married. Still for the sake of buying a property with a
gooseberry patch he married an elderly, homely widow, without a trace of affection for her, but simply because she had money. After marrying her, he went
on living parsimoniously, keeping her half-starved, and he put her money in
the bank in his own name. She had previously been the wife of a postmaster,
who had got her used to pies and cordials. This second husband did not even
give her enough black bread. She began to sicken, and some three years later
gave up the ghost. And, of course, it never for a moment occurred to my
brother that he was to blame for her death. Money, like vodka, can do queer
things to a man. Once in our town a merchant lay on his deathbed; before he
died, he ordered a plateful of honey and he ate up all his money and lottery
tickets with the honey, so that no one should get it. One day when I was inspecting a drove of cattle at a railway station, a cattle dealer fell under a loco-
motive and it sliced off his leg. We carried him in to the infirmary, the blood
was gushing from the wound—a terrible business, but he kept begging us to
find his leg and was very anxious about it: he had twenty rubles in the boot that
was on that leg, and he was afraid they would be lost."

"That's a tune from another opera," said Burkin.   26

Ivan Ivanych paused a moment and then continued: 27

"After his wife's death, my brother began to look around for a property.   28
Of course, you may scout about for five years and in the end make a mistake,
and buy something quite different from what you have been dreaming of.
Through an agent my brother bought a mortgaged estate of three hundred
acres with a house, servants' quarters, a park, but with no orchard, no gooseberry patch, no duck-pond. There was a stream, but the water in it was the
color of coffee, for on one of its banks there was a brickyard and on the other a
glue factory. But my brother was not at all disconcerted: he ordered a score of
gooseberry bushes, planted them, and settled down to the life of a country gentleman.

"Last year I paid him a visit. I thought I would go and see how things were   29
with him. In his letter to me my brother called his estate 'Chumbaroklov Waste,
or Himalaiskoe' (our surname was Chimsha-Himalaisky). I reached the place
in the afternoon. It was hot. Everywhere there were ditches, fences, hedges, rows
of fir trees, and I was at a loss as to how to get to the yard and where to leave my
horse. I made my way to the house and was met by a fat dog with reddish hair
that looked like a pig. It wanted to bark, but was too lazy. The cook, a fat, bare-
legged woman, who also looked like a pig, came out of the kitchen and said that
the master was resting after dinner. I went in to see my brother, and found him
sitting up in bed, with a quilt over his knees. He had grown older, stouter,
flabby; his cheeks, his nose, his lips jutted out: It looked as though he might
grunt into the quilt at any moment.

"We embraced and dropped tears of joy and also of sadness at the thought 30 that the two of us had once been young, but were now gray and nearing death. He got dressed and took me out to show me his estate.

" 'Well, how are you getting on here?' I asked.   31

" 'Oh, all right, thank God. I am doing very well.'   32

"He was no longer the poor, timid clerk he used to be but a real landowner, 33 a gentleman. He had already grown used to his new manner of living and developed a taste for it. He ate a great deal, steamed himself in the bathhouse, was growing stout, was already having a lawsuit with the village commune and the two factories and was very much offended when the peasants failed to address him as 'Your Honor.' And he concerned himself with his soul's welfare too in a substantial, upper-class manner, and performed good deeds not simply, but pompously. And what good works! He dosed the peasants with bicarbonate and castor oil for all their ailments and on his name day he had a thanksgiving service celebrated in the center of the village, and then treated the villagers to a gallon of vodka, which he thought was the thing to do. Oh, those horrible gallons of vodka! One day a fat landowner hauls the peasants up before the rural police officer for trespassing, and the next, to mark a feast day, treats them to a gallon of vodka, and they drink and shout 'Hurrah' and when they are drunk bow down at his feet. A higher standard of living, overeating and idleness develop the most insolent self-conceit in a Russian. Nikolay Ivanych, who when he was a petty official was afraid to have opinions of his own even if he kept them to himself, now uttered nothing but incontrovertible truths and did so in the tone of a minister of state: 'Education is necessary, but the masses are not ready for it; corporal punishment is generally harmful, but in some cases it is useful and nothing else will serve.'

" 'I know the common people, and I know how to deal with them,' he would 34 say. 'They love me. I only have to raise my little finger, and they will do anything I want.'

"And all this, mark you, would be said with a smile that bespoke kindness 35 and intelligence. Twenty times over he repeated: 'We, of the gentry,' 'I, as a member of the gentry.' Apparently he no longer remembered that our grandfather had been a peasant and our father just a private. Even our surname, 'Chimsha-Himalaisky,' which in reality is grotesque, seemed to him sonorous, distinguished, and delightful.

"But I am concerned now not with him, but with me. I want to tell you 36 about the change that took place in me during the few hours that I spent on his estate. In the evening when we were having tea, the cook served a plateful of gooseberries. They were not bought, they were his own gooseberries, the first ones picked since the bushes were planted. My brother gave a laugh and for a minute looked at the gooseberries in silence, with tears in his eyes—he could not speak for excitement. Then he put one berry in his mouth, glanced at me with the triumph of a child who has at last been given a toy he was longing for and said: 'How tasty!' And he ate the gooseberries greedily, and kept repeating: 'Ah, how delicious! Do taste them!'

"They were hard and sour, but as Pushkin[2] has it, 37

> The falsehood that exalts we cherish more
> Than meaner truths that are a thousand strong.

I saw a happy man, one whose cherished dream had so obviously come true, who had attained his goal in life, who had got what he wanted, who was satisfied with his lot and with himself. For some reason an element of sadness had always mingled with my thoughts of human happiness, and now at the sight of a happy man I was assailed by an oppressive feeling bordering on despair. It weighed on me particularly at night. A bed was made up for me in a room next to my brother's bedroom, and I could hear that he was wakeful, and that he would get up again and again, go to the plate of gooseberries and eat one after another. I said to myself: how many contented, happy people there really are! What an overwhelming force they are! Look at life: the insolence and idleness of the strong, the ignorance and brutishness of the weak, horrible poverty everywhere, overcrowding, degeneration, drunkenness, hypocrisy, lying—— Yet in all the houses and on all the streets there is peace and quiet; of the fifty thousand people who live in our town there is not one who would cry out, who would vent his indignation aloud. We see the people who go to market, eat by day, sleep by night, who babble nonsense, marry, grow old, good-naturedly drag their dead to the cemetery, but we do not see or hear those who suffer, and what is terrible in life goes on somewhere behind the scenes. Everything is peaceful and quiet and only mute statistics protest: so many people gone out of their minds, so many gallons of vodka drunk, so many children dead from malnutrition—— And such a state of things is evidently necessary; obviously the happy man is at ease only because the unhappy ones bear their burdens in silence, and if there were not this silence, happiness would be impossible. It is a general hypnosis. Behind the door of every contented, happy man there ought to be someone standing with a little hammer and continually reminding him with a knock that there are unhappy people, that however happy he may be, life will sooner or later show him its claws, and trouble will come to him—illness, poverty, losses, and then no one will see or hear him, just as now he neither sees nor hears others. But there is no man with a hammer. The happy man lives at his ease, faintly fluttered by small daily cares, like an aspen in the wind—and all is well."

"That night I came to understand that I too had been contented and happy," 38 Ivan Ivanych continued, getting up. "I too over the dinner table or out hunting would hold forth on how to live, what to believe, the right way to govern the people. I too would say that learning was the enemy of darkness, that education was necessary but that for the common people the three R's were sufficient for the time being. Freedom is a boon, I used to say, it is as essential as air, but we must wait awhile. Yes, that's what I used to say, and now I ask: Why must we

---

2. Russian poet (1799–1837).

wait?" said Ivan Ivanych, looking wrathfully at Burkin. "Why must we wait, I ask you? For what reason? I am told that nothing can be done all at once, that every idea is realized gradually, in its own time. But who is it that says so? Where is the proof that it is just? You cite the natural order of things, the law governing all phenomena, but is there law, is there order in the fact that I, a living, thinking man, stand beside a ditch and wait for it to close up of itself or fill up with silt, when I could jump over it or throw a bridge across it? And again, why must we wait? Wait, until we have no strength to live, and yet we have to live and are eager to live!

"I left my brother's place early in the morning, and ever since then it has be- 39 come intolerable for me to stay in town. I am oppressed by the peace and the quiet, I am afraid to look at the windows, for there is nothing that pains me more than the spectacle of a happy family sitting at table having tea. I am an old man now and unfit for combat, I am not even capable of hating. I can only grieve inwardly, get irritated, worked up, and at night my head is ablaze with the rush of ideas and I cannot sleep. Oh, if I were young!"

Ivan Ivanych paced up and down the room excitedly and repeated, "If I were 40 young!"

He suddenly walked up to Alyohin and began to press now one of his hands, 41 now the other.

"Pavel Konstantinych," he said imploringly, "don't quiet down, don't let 42 yourself be lulled to sleep! As long as you are young, strong, alert, do not cease to do good! There is no happiness and there should be none, and if life has a meaning and a purpose, that meaning and purpose is not our happiness but something greater and more rational. Do good!"

All this Ivan Ivanych said with a pitiful, imploring smile, as though he were 43 asking a personal favor.

Afterwards all three of them sat in armchairs in different corners of the 44 drawing room and were silent. Ivan Ivanych's story satisfied neither Burkin nor Alyohin. With the ladies and generals looking down from the golden frames, seeming alive in the dim light, it was tedious to listen to the story of the poor devil of a clerk who ate gooseberries. One felt like talking about elegant people, about women. And the fact that they were sitting in a drawing room where everything—the chandelier under its cover, the armchairs, the carpets underfoot—testified that the very people who were now looking down from the frames had once moved about here, sat and had tea, and the fact that lovely Pelageya was noiselessly moving about—that was better than any story.

Alyohin was very sleepy; he had gotten up early, before three o'clock in the 45 morning, to get some work done, and now he could hardly keep his eyes open, but he was afraid his visitors might tell an interesting story in his absence, and he would not leave. He did not trouble to ask himself if what Ivan Ivanych had just said was intelligent or right. The guests were not talking about groats, or hay, or tar, but about something that had no direct bearing on his life, and he was glad of it and wanted them to go on.

"However, it's bedtime," said Burkin, rising. "Allow me to wish you good 46
night."

Alyohin took leave of his guests and went downstairs to his own quarters, 47
while they remained upstairs. They were installed for the night in a big room in
which stood two old wooden beds decorated with carvings and in the corner
was an ivory crucifix. The wide cool beds which had been made by the lovely
Pelageya gave off a pleasant smell of clean linen.

Ivan Ivanych undressed silently and got into bed. 48

"Lord forgive us sinners!" he murmured, and drew the bedclothes over his 49
head.

His pipe, which lay on the table, smelled strongly of burnt tobacco, and 50
Burkin, who could not sleep for a long time, kept wondering where the unpleasant odor came from.

The rain beat against the window panes all night. 51

—*Translated by Avrahm Yarmolinsky*

ACTIVITIES FOR WRITING AND DISCUSSION

1. In paragraph 37, Ivan Ivanych criticizes his brother for being "a happy
man." Why? In your notebook write a summary of his reasoning. Do you think
his criticism is fair? Why or why not?

2. In paragraph 44 we are told that "Ivan Ivanych's story satisfied neither
Burkin nor Alyohin." Describe the two friends' reactions to the story. Can their
reactions be said to relate in any ways to the **themes** of Ivan's story about his
brother Nikolay?

3. How do you assess Ivan Ivanych's outlook and attitudes? Is he mentally
sick? too intense and serious? wiser than his friends or the world he criticizes?
Of what people (if any) in your own experience does he remind you?

4. Like the **characters** in many Chekhov stories, Ivan Ivanych doesn't just
tell a story: he philosophizes; he wrestles with the meaning of life. Who are we?
Why are we alive? What are our lives for? Create a character of your own and a
subject about which he/she can philosophize. For a context, consider two or
three friends conversing around a campfire or college students talking late at
night in the dorm or over beers.

Jean Thompson (b. 1950)

Applause, Applause

Poor Bernie, Ted thought, as rain thudded against the car like rotten fruit. 1
Watching it stream and bubble on the windshield he promised himself not to
complain about it lest Bernie's feelings be hurt. He was anxious to impress this
on his wife. Poor Bernie, he said aloud. Things never work out the way he plans.

His wife nodded. Ted could see from her unsmiling, preoccupied face that it 2
would be difficult to coax her into a conspiracy. In fact, she was probably blaming him for it: his friend, his weekend, therefore, his rain. Look, Ted said. He
went to so much trouble setting this up. I'd hate to have him think we weren't
enjoying it, whatever happens.

Lee, his wife, turned her chin toward him. He used to call her the Siennese 3
Madonna because of that narrow face, long cheeks and haughty blue eyes. Easy
to see her reduced to two-dimensional paint. She had never heard of Sienna.
Now she said All right, I won't sulk. But I'll save the vivaciousness till later, OK?

He was a little hurt that she saw no need to be charming for him, but he said 4
nothing. After all, she hadn't complained. He burrowed his hands in his pockets
for warmth and looked out the smeared window.

The car was parked in a clearing of pebbled yellow clay. On all sides were 5
dark sopping pine trees, impenetrable, suffocating. It made him a little dizzy to
think of how limitless those trees were, how many square miles they covered.
The clearing contained two gas pumps and a trading post that sold moccasins,
orange pop, and insect repellant. If you turned your back on the building it was
easy to believe the world contained only the pines and the implacable rain.

Poor Bernie. He wondered at what point the friends of one's youth acquire 6
epithets. When do we begin to measure their achievements against their ambi-
tions?

Ten years ago he and Bernie Doyle were in college. Ten years ago they sat in 7
bars, Bernie's pipe smoke looped around their heads. Or perhaps on the bro-
ken-spined, cat-perfumed sofa that was always reincarnated in their succession
of apartments. How they had talked: God, he had never talked that seriously,
that openly, to a woman. Perhaps it was something one outgrew. Like the daydreams of the dusky, moody photographs that would appear on one's book
jackets. The experimentation with names. Theodore Valentine? T. R. Valentine?
T. Robert Valentine? The imaginary interviews. ("Valentine is a disarmingly
candid, intensely personal man whose lean, somber features belie his formidable humor. The day I met him he wore an old black turtleneck, Levis and sandals, a singularly unpretentious yet becoming costume . . . ")

Yes, he had admitted all these fantasies to Bernie, and Bernie admitted he 8
shared them. How vulnerable they had been to each other, still were, he supposed. Behind the naive vanities, the daydreams, they had very badly wanted to
be writers. Had wanted it without knowing at all what it was they wanted, their
fervor making up for their ignorance. His older self was cooler, more noncom-

mittal, for he had learned that to publicize your goals means running the risk of falling short of them.

Ten years of letters, of extravagant alcoholic phone calls. The continual 9 measure they took of each other. Their vanished precocity, reluctantly cast aside at age twenty-five or so. Ten years which established Ted's increasingly self-conscious, increasingly offhand reports of publications, recognitions. Bernie had kept up for a few years, had even talked about getting a book together. After that he responded to Ted's letters with the same grave formula: he wasn't getting a lot done but he hoped to have more time soon. Ted was sure he'd given it up entirely. He knew how easy it was to let your discipline go slack. You had to drive yourself continually, not just to get the work done but to keep faith. Faith that what you were doing was worth the hideous effort you put into it. Easier, much easier, to let it go. The whole process of writing was a road as quirky and blind as the one they had driven this morning to the heart of the Adirondacks, this weekend, and the epithet, Poor Bernie.

Was he himself a success? He wasn't able to say that, not yet at least. Three 10 years ago a national magazine printed a story. The smaller quarterlies published him with some regularity, paid him less frequently. His was one of the names an extremely well-read person might frown at and say Yes, I think I've heard of him. It was like being one of those Presidents no one can ever remember, Polk or Millard Fillmore. Of course you wanted more than that.

But he'd made progress. He hadn't given up. These were the important 11 things. And he dreaded the inevitable discussions with Bernie when their younger incarnations would stand in judgment of them. How could he manage to be both tactful and truthful, feeling as he did that uncomfortable mixture of protectiveness and contempt. Yes, he admitted it, the slightest touch of contempt . . .

Is this them, Lee asked as an orange VW station wagon, its rain-slick paint 12 lurid against the pines, slowed at the clearing. Ted squinted. Maybe . . . The car stopping. Yeah, I think so. The window on the passenger's side was rolled down and a woman's face bobbed and smiled at him. He had an impression of freckles, skin pink as soap. Paula? Ted grinned and pantomimed comprehension.

We're supposed to follow, he told Lee, and eased the car onto the road. 13 Again the dripping trees closed over them. They were climbing now, trailing the VW along a tight spiral. It was impossible to see more than twenty yards ahead. At times they passed mailboxes, or shallow openings in the woods that indicated roads, but for the most part there was only the green-black forest, the thick pudding rain.

Where's that college he teaches at, asked Lee. Ted looked at her and tried to 14 unravel the history of her thoughts for the last silent half-hour. She still wore her languid, neutral expression. The Madonna attends a required meeting of the Ladies' Auxiliary.

Sixty miles away. No, farther. Eighty. It was another thing he wondered 15 about, Bernie's precarious instructor job. Four sections of composition. Abortion, Pro and Con. My First Date. Topic sentences. Footnotes.

And he married one of his students? 16

Ted nodded. It was hard for him to imagine Bernie as a figure of authority 17
or some little girl regarding him with the reverence and hysteria of student
crushes. But it had happened.

Lee pointed. The VW's bumper was winking at them and Ted slowed, ready 18
to turn. Now it was scarcely a road they followed but a dirt lane. Milder, decid-
uous trees interlaced above them and screened the rain somewhat. They rocked
along the muddy ruts for half a mile.

Then the sudden end of the lane, the cabin of dark brown shingles with 19
Bernie already waving from the porch. Ted was out of the car almost before it
had stopped, was shaking Bernie's hand and saying something like Son of a
gun, and grinning. Bernie said Valentine, you lout, and reached up to pound
him on the back.

The women drifted after them. Hey Paula, come shake hands with Ted. And 20
this is Lee. Bernie, Paula. Ted found himself appraising Lee as she climbed the
steps, took satisfaction in her length of leg, her severely beautiful face now soft-
ened with a smile. The four of them stood nodding at each other for a moment.
Like two sets of dolls built to different scale, Ted thought, the Doyles so small,
he and Lee an angular six inches taller. Furious exercise had kept Ted in shape,
and he knew the faint line of sunburn under his eyes was becoming. He realized
he was standing at attention, and cursed his vanity.

Bernie looked more than ever like a Swiss toymaker as imagined by Walt 21
Disney. Small bones and white supple hands. His gray eyes unfocused behind
rimless glasses. The ever-present pipe which, when inserted, drew his whole
face into a preoccupied, constipated look. He had grown a dark manicured
beard.

And Paula? He knew her to be at least twenty-four, but she could have 22
passed for sweet eighteen. Snub little nose. Smiling mouth like the squiggle
painted on a china doll. Green eyes in that pink transparent skin. Yes, she would
be something to take notice of in a stuffy classroom.

Even as he absorbed and ordered his impressions the group broke, Bernie 23
pushing the front door open, Paula talking about food. He followed Bernie into
a paneled room and the damp, bone-deep cold that would accompany the
whole weekend first seized him. He heard Lee's lightly inflected voice keeping
her promise: What a lovely fireplace. We can tell ghost stories around it.

You bet, said Bernie, and squatted before it, poking the grate. There's even 24
dry wood on the porch.

Looking at him, Ted experienced the uneasy process of having to square his 25
observations with his memories. As if this was not really Bernie until he con-
formed with Ted's image of him. How long had it been, three years? He began
to be more sure of himself as he noted familiar mannerisms surfacing. Bernie's
solemnity; he discussed firewood in the same tone another man might use for
religion. The deftness of his hands wielding the fireplace tools. Ted imagined
him shaping chunks of pine into cuckoo clocks, bears, and monkeys . . .

Now stop that, he warned himself. It was a writer's curse, this verbal em- 26
broidery. Never seeing anything as it was, always analyzing and reformulating

it. Maybe the entire habit of observation, the thing he trained himself in, was just a nervous tic, a compulsion. He shook his head and joined Lee in her exploration of the cabin.

The main room was high-ceilinged, dark. In hot weather he imagined its 27 shadows would bless the skin, but now the bare floors made his feet ache with cold. There were two bedrooms, one on each side of the main room. The furniture was a mixture of wicker and raw wood. In the rear were a trim new kitchen and bathroom. They stepped out the back door and Ted whistled.

Even in the rain the blue-gray bowl of the lake freshened his eyes. Its irregu- 28 lar shoreline formed bays, coves, little tongues of land, all furred with silent pine. He could not see the opposite shore. There was an island just where he might have wished for one, a mound of brush and rock. The air smelled clean and thin.

Lee spoke to Bernie, who had joined them. It's incredible. Just too lovely. 29

Bernie grinned, as if the lake were a treat he had prepared especially for 30 them. And Ted felt all his discomfort drop away as he saw his friend's happiness, his desire to make them happy. God bless Bernie; he'd forget all this gloomy nonsense about artistic accomplishment. Are there many cabins up here, he asked.

Quite a few. But the lake is so big and the trees so thick we have a lot of pri- 31 vacy. He pointed with his pipe. There's the boathouse. And dock. No beach I'm afraid, it's all mud.

They stood in the shelter of the porch, rain hanging like lace from the gut- 32 ters. Then Lee said Too cold out here for me, and they all went inside.

Paula was rummaging through groceries in the kitchen. Here, said Lee. Let 33 me do something useful. A little cluster of polite words filled the air, Paula demurring, Lee insisting. Ted hoped that for once Lee would be graceful about helping in the kitchen, leave him and Bernie alone without getting sarcastic later about Man-Talk and Woman's Work. He tried to catch her eye but she was pulling her blonde hair into a knot and asking Paula about the mayonnaise.

Bernie offered him a beer and they drifted to the living room. Sitting down 34 Ted had a moment of apprehension, like the beginning of a job interview. Bernie frowned and coaxed his pipe into life. How often had he used it as a prop; Ted knew his shyness. At last the bowl reddened. So tell me, Bernie said. How goes it with you?

Ted realized how much he'd rehearsed his answer: Not too bad. But I'll 35 never be rich.

Bernie chuckled. Poor but honest. 36

Poor but poor. With Lee's job we get by. And I do some free-lancing, write 37 ad copy for a car dealer, that sort of thing. He shrugged. And how about you?

Ted was aware he had shifted too quickly, had seemed to brush off Bernie's 38 question in an attempt to be polite, reciprocal. Damn. He'd have to watch that.

Ah, Bernie said. The pastoral life of a college instructor. It's like being a 39 country priest, really, with your life revolving around the feast days. Registration. Final exams. Department meetings on First Fridays.

You're getting tired of it?   40

It's a job, Ted. Like anything else it has its ups and downs. Actually I'm glad   41
it's not excessively glamorous. This way I don't feel tied to it, committed. I can
stay fluid, you know?

What would you do instead?   42

Sell hardware. Open a museum. I don't know. Paula wants to work as a pho-   43
tographer. She's pretty good. And I wouldn't mind getting back to the writing.
It's been simmering in me for a long time.

That hint of justification. Ted felt the same prepared quality in Bernie's an-   44
swer as in his own. He risked his question: Have you been able to get anything
done?

Any writing, you mean? Dribs and drabs. I decided what I needed was to re-   45
move myself from pressure, you know? Work at my own pace without worrying
about marketing a finished product. Of course I know that's not the way you go
about it.

Yeah. It's out of the typewriter and into the mails.   46

You still work on a schedule?   47

Absolutely. Seems to be the only way I get anything done. Lee covers for me.   48
I have tantrums if the phone rings.

You must really throw yourself into the thing.   49

The implied sympathy, the chance to speak of his frustrations with some-   50
one who would understand them, was a luxury. Jesus, he said. You spend hours
wrestling with yourself, trying to keep your vision intact, your intensity undiminished. Sometimes I have to stick my head under the tap to get my wits back.
And for what? You know what publishing is like these days. Paper costs going
up all the time. Nothing gets printed unless it can be made into a movie. Everything is media. Crooked politicians sell their unwritten memoirs for thousands.
I've got a great idea for a novel. It's about a giant shark who's possessed by a demon while swimming in the Bermuda Triangle. And the demon talks in CB
lingo, see? There'll be recipes in the back.

Bernie laughed and Ted continued. Then the quarterlies, the places you ex-   51
pect to publish serious writing. They're falling all over themselves trying to be
trendy, avant-garde. If you write in sentence fragments and leave plenty of
blank space on the page, you're in. Pretentiousness disguised as trail-blazing.
All the editors want to set themselves up as interpreters of a new movement.
I hope they choke on their own jargon. Anti-meta-post-contemporary-surfic-
tional literature. Balls.

He stopped for breath. I'm sorry, he said. Didn't mean to get carried away.   52

Not at all. It does me good to hear a tirade now and then. Reminds me of   53
college, makes me feel ten years younger.

Still. He should not have spoken with such bitterness. It sounded like he was   54
making excuses. Ted smiled, lightening his tone. The artist takes his lonely
stand against the world.

As well he ought to. But really, Valentine, don't you get tired of beating your   55
head against all that commercialism? Trying to compete with it? I mean, of
course you do, but do you think it affects what you write?

Was it Bernie's solemnity that always made his questions sound so judg- 56
mental? Ted knew it was more than an issue of mannerisms. Bernie pondered
things, thought them through; you respected his sincerity. Ted gave the only answer pride allowed: No, because the work can't exist in a vacuum. It has to get
out there in the world, and reach people. Ted drained his beer and ventured to
define the issue between them. You're saying it's better to be an Emily Dickinson, a violet by a mossy stone half-hidden to the eye, that sort of thing. Keep it
in shoeboxes in the closet so you can remain uncorrupted.

Bernie turned his hands palms upward and managed to express dissent by 57
spreading his white fingers. Just that it's possible to lose sight of what you set
out to do. Even get too discouraged.

How quickly we've moved into position, Ted thought. Each of us defending 58
our lives. He remembered his earlier resolution to speak tactfully, cushion
any comparison between their accomplishments. And here was Bernie seeming to demand such comparison. How easy it would be to make some mention
of his publications, play up some of the things he'd muted in his letters, insist
on Bernie's paying tribute to them. He even admitted to himself that beneath
everything he'd wanted his success acknowledged. Like the high school loser
who dreams of driving to the class reunion in a custom-made sports car. As if
only those who knew your earlier weakness could verify your success.

But he would not indulge himself. Partly because, like his earlier outburst, 59
it would threaten to say too much, and partly because he wanted this meeting
to be without friction. Couldn't they rediscover their younger, untried selves?
It was a kind of nostalgia. So he said I don't know, Bernie. You may be right.
But the only way for me to accomplish anything is by competing with the
market.

Bernie considered this, seemed to accept it as a final statement. He dumped 60
his pipe into the fireplace. Ted noticed the beginning of a tonsure, a doorknob-
sized patch of naked scalp. The sight enabled him to recapture all his tenderness. Shall we join the ladies, Bernie asked, rising.

They were sitting at the kitchen table with mugs of coffee. Well, Ted said, 61
resting a hand on Lee's shoulder. I hope you haven't been bored. He meant it
half as apology, half as warning: you'd better not be.

Au contraire, Lee answered. We've been trying to reconcile post-Hegelian 62
dogma with Jamesian pragmatism. But she grinned.

And Paula said Actually, we were telling raunchy jokes. Give us ten more 63
minutes.

He liked her. Her pinkness, plumpness. Like a neat little bird, all smooth 64
lines and down. Her round good-humored chin. And Lee seemed to be doing
all right with her.

I think it's quit raining, said Bernie. If you've got sturdy enough shoes we 65
could take a hike.

It was still very wet under the trees. A careless tug at a branch might flip cold 66
rainbow-edged drops down your back. And the sky was gray as concrete. But
they enjoyed the silence, the soft sucking ground matted with last year's needles. They perched on a fallen tree at the lake's edge and chunked stones into

the crisp water. Bernie explained it was too early, too cool for the black flies whose bites made bloody circles just beneath the skin.

How often do you get up here, Ted asked. Bernie told him about every other 67 weekend when the weather was right. Ted launched into abundant, envious speech: They were lucky sons-of-bitches, did they know that back in Illinois there were only tame little man-made lakes, tidy parks, lines of Winnebagoes like an elephant graveyard, right Lee? As if complimenting this part of Bernie's life might restore some balance between them.

They walked back single file along the sunken trail. Ted was at the rear. Lee's 68 blondeness looked whiter, milkier out here. Perhaps it was the heaviness of the dark green air, like the light just before a thunderstorm which plays up contrasts. Bernie and Paula's heads were the same shade of sleek brown, slipping in and out of his vision. It struck him that once again he was observing and being conscious of himself as an observer. It was a habit he'd fallen into, not necessarily a bad one. But he'd been working very hard at the writing lately (Lee had insisted on this vacation; he rather begrudged the time spent away from his desk) and this heightened self-awareness was a sign of strain. As if he couldn't really escape his work or the persona that went with it.

The Artist's impressions of a walk in the woods. The Artist's view on view- 69 ing. The Artist on Art. How do you get your ideas for stories, Mr. Valentine? Well, I simply exploit everything I come into contact with. One ended, of course, by losing all spontaneity. You saw people as characters, sunsets as an excuse for similies—

Bernie called a warning over his shoulder just as Ted felt a drop of rain slide 70 down his nose. They quickened their pace to a trot as the rain fell, first in fat splatters that landed as heavily as frogs, then finer, harder. By the time they reached the porch their clothes were dark and dripping.

Fire, said Bernie. Coffee and hot baths, said Paula. The movement, the busy- 71 ness, cheered them as much as the dry clothes. When at last they sat on each side of the stone fireplace, the odor of smoke working into their skins and hair, they all felt the same sense of shelter.

Damn, said Bernie. I wanted to take you fishing. But he looked comfortable, 72 his pipe bobbing in his mouth.

Maybe tomorrow, said Paula. The rain had polished her skin, now the fire 73 was warming it, bringing out different tints: apricot, cameo. She and Bernie made a peaceful, domestic couple. He could imagine them sitting like this, on either side of the fire, for the next thirty years. The retired Swiss toymaker and his wife.

But was Bernie happy? Did he feel, as Ted would have in his place, a sense of 74 failure, of goals having shrunk. You never knew. Or, this visit would probably not allow him to learn. The time was too short to break down much of the politeness that passed between them as guest and host. Recapturing their former intimacy, that intensity, seemed as difficult as remembering what virginity had felt like. They should have left the wives behind, just come up here for a messy bachelor weekend of drinking and cards. This impulse moved him to ask if anyone wanted a whiskey.

They did. He passed glasses, leaned back into his chair. Well, said Lee. It's 75
too early to tell ghost stories.

Ted and I could talk about our misspent youth. 76

She wants something ghostly, Doyle, not ghastly. 77

Oh go ahead, Lee urged Bernie. Tell me something that can be used against 78
him. She was at her most animated, perhaps from the first bite of the liquor. The
Madonna is photographed for a Seagram's commercial. Go ahead, she repeated.

Tell her I was a football hero. 79

If you won't tell Paula about that indecent exposure thing. 80

Agreed. Ted gulped at his drink to induce the mood of nostalgia. One thing 81
I'll always remember. You and me taking a bottle of strawberry wine up on the
roof of the humanities building.

Did you really, said Paula. 82

We thought we were Bohemians, Bernie explained. Artistic, not ethnic. 83

We pretended it was absinthe. 84

A rooftop in Paris at the turn of the century. 85

I was James Joyce. 86

I was Oscar Wilde. 87

We were going to be paperback sensations. 88

We were full of shit. 89

I don't know, Ted objected. I mean, certainly we were naive. Who isn't at 90
twenty? But you have to begin with wild idealism, dreams of glory. It's the raw
fuel that gets you through the disappointments.

You mean the brute facts of editors, publishing. 91

Ted nodded. The manuscripts that come back stained with spaghetti sauce. 92
The places that misspell your name. All the ambiguities of success. If we'd
known what was actually involved in writing, we probably never would have attempted it.

When we leave here, Lee put in, we have to go to New York and talk with 93
Ted's agent. You wouldn't believe the nastiness and wheeler-dealer stuff that
goes on in that New York scene. It's like a court in Renaissance Italy. Intrigues
within intrigues.

Bernie raised his eyebrows above the rims of his glasses. You have an agent 94
now?

Yes. Since last November. He's trying to place the novel for me. 95

And you've finished the novel? Paula, do we have champagne? I've been 96
hearing about this book for years.

Well, I've finished the draft. If it's accepted I'll no doubt have to do rewrites. 97
Damn Lee for bringing up the agent; it would only make Bernie more aware of
the gap between their achievements. He searched for some way to de-escalate
things. You should be glad you've escaped all this messiness so far. Retained
your youthful innocence.

The bottom log of the fire, which had been threatening to burn through, 98
now collapsed. Red winking sparks flew up the black column of the chimney as
the fire assumed a new pattern. Bernie squatted in front of it raking the embers
into place. He spoke without turning around.

You know, I read that piece you had in—what was it—the one about the 99
schizophrenic?

"The Lunatic." He sat up a little straighter in his chair, adopted the carefully 100
pleasant expression with which he received criticism.

Ted was very happy with that piece, Lee informed everyone. And the maga- 101
zine did a good production job. She beamed at him, sweetly proud of making a
contribution to the discussion. He wished she hadn't spoken, had left him free
to frame his reply after listening to Bernie. But she was only repeating what
she'd heard him say.

That's it, "The Lunatic." I admire the language use, the control in the thing. 102
The way you managed to milk images. But—

that terrible pause—   103

I felt there was a kind of slickness in the thing, almost glibness. I mean, 104
you're talking about a man who's having a mental breakdown. And you treat
that rather flippantly. Perhaps you intended it, but I wondered why.

There were a number of replies he could make. He settled for the most gen- 105
eral: The story is something of a satire, Bernie. Think of all the literature that's
dealt with madness. It's an extremely well-trodden path. You simply can't write
about the subject straightforwardly anymore. People expect something new.

Bernie frowned and rubbed his jaw under the dense beard. Ted knew, 106
watching him, that Bernie had thought his argument through. Had prepared it
carefully, step by step, like he did everything.

I thought, Bernie continued, that your complaint against avant-garde fic- 107
tion was its emphasis on form over content. Blank space on the page, tortured
syntax, that sort of thing. The writing screaming for attention. Aren't you
agreeing with them now? Saying, in effect, rather than exploring the individuality of this character or situation, I'll dress it up in a different package. Pretend
not to take it seriously.

Both women were watching rather helplessly, as if they realized their little 108
store of soothing words and social graces would be of no use. And the defense
that came to Ted's mind (Nobody writes like Henry James anymore. Or, more
crudely, Your aesthetic is outdated) sounded like a small boy's taunts. So he said
I do take the character and situation seriously. That doesn't mean one can't experiment with form, depart from rigid storytelling conventions. Otherwise you
wind up repeating what's already been done. Repeating yourself too.

Bernie shook his head. Again that gesture of judgment. I'm sorry, but I see it 109
as a response to the market. The thing I was talking about earlier. You tailor the
writing to what the editors are buying. Maybe unconsciously. You're certainly
not writing about the giant sharks. But it's still a form of corruption.

And what, in particular, is being corrupted?   110

I hope I can put this right. It's like, that increased self-consciousness, that 111
authorial presence that's always thrusting itself between the reader and the
page—see, I'm telling this story, you're reading it, I'll try to amuse you, watch
this—is rather paralyzing. What you're doing, a general you (a parenthetical
smile), is making disclaimers for the piece, covering your tracks. I'll play this a
little tongue in-cheek so I won't be called to account for it.

You might as well dispute abstraction in painting, Bernie. Form can't be en- 112
tirely neglected in favor of content. Otherwise we might still be seeing those
Victorian pictures of blind children and noble hounds.

It runs the danger of shallowness, Ted. 113

Well, I suppose the only way to avoid the dangers is not to write anything 114
at all.

He hadn't realized how angry he was until he heard himself speak. Damn 115
the whiskey, damn his own thin-skinned hatred of criticism. He was too quick
to take things as insults. Now, having said the one unforgivable thing, there was
no retreat. The four of them sat without looking at each other. Bernie plunged
into a fury of pipe-cleaning, tamping, lighting, as another man might have
cracked his knuckles. The rain filled the silence, gusting against the windows
and shrinking the warmth of the fire.

Finally Paula said I'm going to see what there is for dinner. Ted stood up as 116
soon as she did, muttering about another drink. He paused in the kitchen only
long enough to slosh the liquor in his glass. Paula opened the refrigerator and
said Hm, fried chicken maybe? He said Fine and walked out the back door.

The rain had brought an early blue darkness. He could still make out the 117
shoreline, the agitation of the lake as the rain pocked its surface. Far away on
his left shone one point of light, a white feeble thing that he could not imagine
indicated human companionship, laughter, warmth. Even though he stood under the ledge, moisture beaded his clothes like dew. He gave himself over completely to the melancholy of it all. The only consolation he could find was the
thought that argument was a form of intimacy.

When he came back inside both women were busy in the kitchen. Can I peel 118
potatoes or something, he asked. They sat him at the kitchen table with a bowl
of strawberries to hull. A little boy hiding behind women. He didn't want to go
back to the living room where he knew Bernie would be sitting. Lee and Paula
seemed determined to speak of nothing more serious than gravy making. He
watched Lee as she moved between stove and sink, a little surprised at her vivacity. As if she had formed some alliance without his being aware of it. Her
hair had dried in soft waves with a hint of fuzziness; a looser style than she usually wore. Although she spoke to him occasionally, she did not meet his eye. It
didn't seem that she was avoiding him; rather, she was busy, he was extraneous,
incidental . . .

But he was projecting his injured feeling onto her, his gloom and self-pity. 119
Snap out of it, he told himself. You're going to be here another thirty-six hours.

That realization must have been shared, must have been what got them 120
through the evening. The act of sitting down to food together restored some
tenuous rhythm. Afterward Paula suggested Monopoly. They let the bright
cardboard, the little mock triumphs and defeats, absorb them. Ted thought
how harmless all greed and competition were when reduced to this scale, then
he berated himself for facile irony.

At midnight Bernie yawned and said I'm down to thirty dollars and Marvin 121
Gardens. Somebody buy me out.

Who's ahead? Add it up, Paula suggested. 122

It turned out to be Ted, who felt hulking and foolish raking in his pile of pa- 123
per money. Flimsy pastel trophies. He was duly congratulated. He did a parody
of the young Lindbergh acknowledging cheers. Modestly tugging his forelock.
The tycoon needs some rest, he said, and they all agreed.

Goodnight. Goodnight, and if you need extra blankets they're at the top of 124
the closet. I'm sure we'll be fine. Bernie latched the door and said Maybe it'll
clear up tomorrow.

It took Ted a moment to realize he was speaking of the rain. 125

He waited until everyone was settled before he used the bathroom. No use 126
risking more sprightly greetings. When he got back Lee was in bed, her fair hair
spilling from the rolled sheets like corn silk.

He wanted her to start talking first, but her eyes were squeezed shut against 127
the bed-side lamp. Well, he said. Too neutral, inadequate.

Would you turn that light off? 128

He reached, produced darkness. She sighed and said Much better. He lay for 129
a moment accustoming himself to the black stillness, the smell of the rough
pine boards. The mattress was sparse, lopsided. It seemed to have absorbed the
dank cold of the cabin. He burrowed into its thin center. Then the even sound
of Lee's breathing told him she was falling asleep. Almost angry, he shook her
shoulder.

What? She was more irritated than sleepy. 130

Don't fall asleep. I wanted to talk to you. 131

Go ahead. 132

He waited a moment to control himself. You're not making it very easy. 133

She twisted inside the sheets until she rested on one elbow, facing him. All 134
right, I'll make it easy. What the hell were you arguing about? I hate it when you
start talking like that. All that rhetoric. You take it so seriously. Was any of it
worth snapping at him like that?

Of course I take it seriously. He was accusing me of shallowness. Corrup- 135
tion.

Oh boy. Lee drawled her sarcasm. And you couldn't forget your literary re- 136
flexes for one minute.

No. I guess I couldn't. 137

Her hand emerged from the darkness and gave his shoulder a series of small 138
tentative pats. Poor Ted. Her voice was kinder. The pats continued, light but
persistent, as if a moth were battering itself against him. He supressed the impulse to brush it away.

Why poor Ted? 139

Because sometimes I think you don't enjoy what you're doing at all. The 140
writing I mean. You get so upset.

Don't be silly. 141

I know. The Agony and the Ecstasy. She yawned. Well I hope you two make 142
up. They're nice folks.

Her lips, seeming disembodied in the blind darkness, found his chin, his 143
mouth. Good night.

Good night.   144

He waited until she was asleep or pretending to be asleep. He got up, put on   145
his pants and sweater, and padded into the kitchen. Turned on the fluorescent
light over the sink.

Her cruelest words spoken in her softest voice. Her revenge, thinking or un-   146
thinking, for all the times he'd shut himself away from her. He'd had his work to
do. His sulks and tantrums. His insistence on the loftiness of his purpose,
the promise of his future. His monstrous self-importance. The whole edifice
threatened.

He didn't enjoy it.   147

Of course you were gratified at the high points. The little recognitions and   148
deference. Of course you made a point of bemoaning the labor involved. Saying
it drove you mad with frustration. That was expected. But enjoyment? Where
was the enjoyment?

The pines still rattled in the wind. The rain was a dim silver fabric without   149
seam or edge, unrolling from the sky. He thought of walking into it, losing himself in all that fragrant blackness, in the thick gunmetal lake. Oh he was tired of
his cleverness, his swollen sensitivity. Better to crouch under a rock in the rain
and reduce yourself to nerve, skin, and muscle. But his self-consciousness
would not allow this either. It told him it would be melodramatic, a petulant
gesture. Bad form.

Something, some weight, passed over the floorboards behind him and he   150
turned, his nostrils cocked. It was the ticklish perfume of pipe smoke that
reached him first.

H'lo, he said, and Bernie's mouth curved around the polished wooden stem   151
of his pipe. He managed to walk to where Ted was standing by the back door
without seeming to advance in a straight line.

Foul weather, he said nodding. He too had resumed his clothes.   152

I'll say. They watched the faint movement of water on water. Then Bernie   153
said Drink?

Sure.   154

While there was still tension perceptible in their cautious responses, in   155
Bernie's stiff-wristed pouring of drinks, it seemed a formality. The simple fact
of coming together like this was a promise of reconciliation. When Bernie was
seated across from him, Ted began with the obvious. I'm sorry about tonight. I
was way out of line.

I guess I provoked you, Ted. I'm jealous. I admit it.   156

And I am insecure and narcissistic.   157

Would it be too maudlin to wish we were kids again?   158

Ted shook his head. In some ways I think I'm still twenty. The prize student   159
who's always fawning for approval, pats on the head.

You're too hard on yourself.   160

Yes. I am. He blinked at the checked tablecloth, trying to get his eyes to fo-   161
cus on its pattern.

And I'm not hard enough. Bernie smiled. Such confessions.   162

They're necessary. Who else can absolve us of our sordid pasts?   163

Now the room has the contours and atmosphere of all rooms in which peo-   164
ple stay awake talking. The fluorescent light is grainy, staring. The clutter on the
kitchen table—ketchup bottle, sagging butter dish, tin of Nestle's Quik, the
rowdy crudded ashtray—the world is narrowed into these, a little universe that
the eyes return to again and again. Now it begins, the sorting and testing of
words. Remember that words are not symbols of other words. There are words
which, when tinkered with, become honest representatives of the cresting
blood, the fine living net of nerves. Define rain. Or even joy. It can be done.

ACTIVITIES FOR WRITING AND DISCUSSION

1. In paragraph 11 the narrator comments, "And he [Ted] dreaded the inevitable discussions with Bernie when their younger incarnations would stand
in judgment of them."

   a. Imagine yourself ten—or fifteen or twenty—years from now. Think
      about what you will be doing with your life then—your career (if
      any), your personal life and avocations, causes, friendships. Then
      write a dialogue between this future self and your "younger incarna-
      tion" in which the latter "stand[s] in judgment" of the former. Your
      dialogue might touch upon topics pertinent to Thompson's story,
      such as ambition, success, idealism, competition, and happiness. Or

   b. Write a dialogue between Ted as he is in the story and his younger in-
      carnation, i.e., himself as a college student; or do the same exercise
      with Bernie.

2. Create a Topic/Form Grid (see pp. 111–115) based on this story. Then
match one of your topics with one of your forms and write a notebook response of at least three hundred words.

3. Where do you see the main tension-generating conflict in the **plot**? Between Ted and Bernie? Between Ted and himself? Somewhere else? Justify your
answer. Is the conflict ever resolved? If so, when (specifically)?

4. Reread paragraphs 147 and 148. Why doesn't Ted "enjoy [his work]"?
Compare and contrast Ted's and Bernie's experiences of writing with Joseph
Joubert's (see pp. 693–700).

5. Reread the story's final paragraph. Why does it shift into present verb
tense? Is there a change here in **point of view,** and, if so, why? How do you interpret the paragraph, particularly the last six sentences?

6. Comment on the relevance of the story's title.

LORRIE MOORE (b. 1957)

How to Become a Writer

First, try to be something, anything, else. A movie star/astronaut. A movie 1
star/missionary. A movie star/kindergarten teacher. President of the World. Fail
miserably. It is best if you fail at an early age—say, fourteen. Early, critical disillusionment is necessary so that at fifteen you can write long haiku sequences
about thwarted desire. It is a pond, a cherry blossom, a wind brushing against
sparrow wing leaving for mountain. Count the syllables. Show it to your mom.
She is tough and practical. She has a son in Vietnam and a husband who may be
having an affair. She believes in wearing brown because it hides spots. She'll
look briefly at your writing, then back up at you with a face blank as a donut.
She'll say: "How about emptying the dishwasher?" Look away. Shove the forks
in the fork drawer. Accidentally break one of the freebie gas station glasses. This
is the required pain and suffering. This is only for starters.

In your high school English class look only at Mr. Killian's face. Decide faces 2
are important. Write a villanelle about pores. Struggle. Write a sonnet. Count the
syllables: nine, ten, eleven, thirteen. Decide to experiment with fiction. Here you
don't have to count syllables. Write a short story about an elderly man and
woman who accidentally shoot each other in the head, the result of an inexplicable malfunction of a shotgun which appears mysteriously in their living room
one night. Give it to Mr. Killian as your final project. When you get it back, he has
written on it: "Some of your images are quite nice, but you have no sense of plot."
When you are home, in the privacy of your own room, faintly scrawl in pencil beneath his black-inked comments: "Plots are for dead people, pore-face."

Take all the babysitting jobs you can get. You are great with kids. They love 3
you. You tell them stories about old people who die idiot deaths. You sing them
songs like "Blue Bells of Scotland," which is their favorite. And when they are in
their pajamas and have finally stopped pinching each other, when they are fast
asleep, you read every sex manual in the house, and wonder how on earth anyone could ever do those things with someone they truly loved. Fall asleep in a
chair reading Mr. McMurphy's *Playboy*. When the McMurphys come home,
they will tap you on the shoulder, look at the magazine in your lap, and grin.
You will want to die. They will ask you if Tracey took her medicine all right. Explain, yes, she did, that you promised her a story if she would take it like a big
girl and that seemed to work out just fine. "Oh, marvelous," they will exclaim.

Try to smile proudly.   4

Apply to college as a child psychology major.   5

As a child psychology major, you have some electives. You've always liked 6
birds. Sign up for something called "The Ornithological Field Trip." It meets
Tuesdays and Thursdays at two. When you arrive at Room 134 on the first day
of class, everyone is sitting around a seminar table talking about metaphors.

You've heard of these. After a short, excruciating while, raise your hand and say diffidently, "Excuse me, isn't this Bird-watching One-oh-one?" The class stops and turns to look at you. They seem to all have one face—giant and blank as a vandalized clock. Someone with a beard booms out, "No, this is Creative Writing," Say: "Oh—right," as if perhaps you knew all along. Look down at your schedule. Wonder how the hell you ended up here. The computer, apparently, has made an error. You start to get up to leave and then don't. The lines at the registrar this week are huge. Perhaps you should stick with this mistake. Perhaps your creative writing isn't all that bad. Perhaps it is fate. Perhaps this is what your dad meant when he said, "It's the age of computers, Francie, it's the age of computers."

Decide that you like college life. In your dorm you meet many nice people. 7 Some are smarter than you. And some, you notice, are dumber than you. You will continue, unfortunately, to view the world in exactly these terms for the rest of your life.

The assignment this week in creative writing is to narrate a violent happen- 8 ing. Turn in a story about driving with your Uncle Gordon and another one about two old people who are accidentally electrocuted when they go to turn on a badly wired desk lamp. The teacher will hand them back to you with comments: "Much of your writing is smooth and energetic. You have, however, a ludicrous notion of plot." Write another story about a man and a woman who, in the very first paragraph, have their lower torsos accidentally blitzed away by dynamite. In the second paragraph, with the insurance money, they buy a frozen yogurt stand together. There are six more paragraphs. You read the whole thing out loud in class. No one likes it. They say your sense of plot is outrageous and incompetent. After class someone asks you if you are crazy.

Decide that perhaps you should stick to comedies. Start dating someone 9 who is funny, someone who has what in high school you called a "really great sense of humor" and what now your creative writing class calls "self-contempt giving rise to comic form." Write down all of his jokes, but don't tell him you are doing this. Make up anagrams of his old girlfriend's name and name all of your socially handicapped characters with them. Tell him his old girlfriend is in all of your stories and then watch how funny he can be, see what a really great sense of humor he can have.

Your child psychology advisor tells you you are neglecting courses in your 10 major. What you spend the most time on should be what you're majoring in. Say yes, you understand.

In creative writing seminars over the next two years, everyone continues to 11 smoke cigarettes and ask the same things: "But does it work?" "Why should we care about this character?" "Have you earned this cliché?" These seem like important questions.

On days when it is your turn, you look at the class hopefully as they scour 12 your mimeographs for a plot. They look back up at you, drag deeply, and then smile in a sweet sort of way.

You spend too much time slouched and demoralized. Your boyfriend sug- 13 gests bicycling. Your roommate suggests a new boyfriend. You are said to be self-mutilating and losing weight, but you continue writing. The only happiness you have is writing something new, in the middle of the night, armpits damp, heart pounding, something no one has yet seen. You have only those brief, fragile, untested moments of exhilaration when you know: you are a genius. Understand what you must do. Switch majors. The kids in your nursery project will be disappointed, but you have a calling, an urge, a delusion, an unfortunate habit. You have, as your mother would say, fallen in with a bad crowd.

Why write? Where does writing come from? These are questions to ask 14 yourself. They are like: Where does dust come from? Or: Why is there war? Or: If there's a God, then why is my brother now a cripple?

These are questions that you keep in your wallet, like calling cards. These 15 are questions, your creative writing teacher says, that are good to address in your journals but rarely in your fiction.

The writing professor this fall is stressing the Power of the Imagination. 16 Which means he doesn't want long descriptive stories about your camping trip last July. He wants you to start in a realistic context but then to alter it. Like recombinant DNA. He wants you to let your imagination sail, to let it grow bigbellied in the wind. This is a quote from Shakespeare.

Tell your roommate your great idea, your great exercise of imaginative 17 power: a transformation of Melville to contemporary life. It will be about monomania and the fish-eat-fish world of life insurance in Rochester, New York. The first line will be "Call me Fishmeal," and it will feature a menopausal suburban husband named Richard, who because he is so depressed all the time is called "Mopey Dick" by his witty wife Elaine. Say to your roommate: "Mopey Dick, get it?" Your roommate looks at you, her face blank as a large Kleenex. She comes up to you, like a buddy, and puts an arm around your burdened shoulders. "Listen, Francie," she says, slow as speech therapy. "Let's go out and get a big beer."

The seminar doesn't like this one either. You suspect they are beginning to 18 feel sorry for you. They say: "You have to think about what is happening. Where is the story here?"

The next semester the writing professor is obsessed with writing from per- 19 sonal experience. You must write from what you know, from what has happened to you. He wants deaths, he wants camping trips. Think about what has happened to you. In three years there have been three things: you lost your virginity; your parents got divorced; and your brother came home from a forest ten miles from the Cambodian border with only half a thigh, a permanent smirk nestled into one corner of his mouth.

About the first you write: "It created a new space, which hurt and cried in a 20 voice that wasn't mine, 'I'm not the same anymore, but I'll be okay.'"

About the second you write an elaborate story of an old married couple 21 who stumble upon an unknown land mine in their kitchen and accidentally blow themselves up. You call it: "For Better or for Liverwurst."

About the last you write nothing. There are no words for this. Your type- 22 writer hums. You can find no words.

At undergraduate cocktail parties, people say, "Oh, you write? What do you 23 write about?" Your roommate, who has consumed too much wine, too little cheese, and no crackers at all, blurts: "Oh, my god, she always writes about her dumb boyfriend."

Later on in life you will learn that writers are merely open, helpless texts 24 with no real understanding of what they have written and therefore must half-believe anything and everything that is said of them. You, however, have not yet reached this stage of literary criticism. You stiffen and say, "I do not," the same way you said it when someone in the fourth grade accused you of really liking oboe lessons and your parents really weren't just making you take them.

Insist you are not very interested in any one subject at all, that you are inter- 25 ested in the music of language, that you are interested in—in—syllables, be-cause they are the atoms of poetry, the cells of the mind, the breath of the soul. Begin to feel woozy. Stare into your plastic wine cup.

"Syllables?" you will hear someone ask, voice trailing off, as they glide 26 slowly toward the reassuring white of the dip.

Begin to wonder what you do write about. Of if you have anything to say. Or 27 if there even is such a thing as a thing to say. Limit these thoughts to no more than ten minutes a day; like sit-ups, they can make you thin.

You will read somewhere that all writing has to do with one's genitals. Don't 28 dwell on this. It will make you nervous.

Your mother will come visit you. She will look at the circles under your eyes 29 and hand you a brown book with a brown briefcase on the cover. It is entitled: *How to Become a Business Executive.* She has also brought the *Names for Baby* encyclopedia you asked for; one of your characters, the aging clown-school teacher, needs a new name. Your mother will shake her head and say: "Francie, Francie, remember when you were going to be a child psychology major?"

Say: "Mom, I like to write."   30

She'll say: "Sure you like to write. Of course. Sure you like to write."   31

Write a story about a confused music student and title it: "Schubert Was the 32 One with the Glasses, Right?" It's not a big hit, although your roommate likes the part where the two violinists accidentally blow themselves up in a recital room. "I went out with a violinist once," she says, snapping her gum.

Thank god you are taking other courses. You can find sanctuary in nine- 33
teenth-century ontological snags and invertebrate courting rituals. Certain
globular mollusks have what is called "Sex by the Arm." The male octopus, for
instance, loses the end of one arm when placing it inside the female body during intercourse. Marine biologists call it "Seven Heaven." Be glad you know
these things. Be glad you are not just a writer. Apply to law school.

From here on in, many things can happen. But the main one will be this: 34
you decide not to go to law school after all, and, instead, you spend a good, big
chunk of your adult life telling people how you decided not to go to law school
after all. Somehow you end up writing again. Perhaps you go to graduate
school. Perhaps you work odd jobs and take writing courses at night. Perhaps
you are working on a novel and writing down all the clever remarks and intimate personal confessions you hear during the day. Perhaps you are losing your
pals, your acquaintances, your balance.

You have broken up with your boyfriend. You now go out with men who, 35
instead of whispering "I love you," shout: "Do it to me, baby." This is good for
your writing.

Sooner or later you have a finished manuscript more or less. People look at 36
it in a vaguely troubled sort of way and say, "I'll bet becoming a writer was always a fantasy of yours, wasn't it?" Your lips dry to salt. Say that of all the fantasies possible in the world, you can't imagine being a writer even making the
top twenty. Tell them you were going to be a child psychology major. "I bet,"
they always sigh, "you'd be great with kids." Scowl fiercely. Tell them you're a
walking blade.

Quit classes. Quit jobs. Cash in old savings bonds. Now you have time like 37
warts on your hands. Slowly copy all of your friends' addresses into a new address book.

Vacuum. Chew cough drops. Keep a folder full of fragments. 38

An eyelid darkening sideways.
World as conspiracy.
Possible plot? A woman gets on a bus.
Suppose you threw a love affair and nobody came.

At home drink a lot of coffee. At Howard Johnson's order the cole slaw. 39
Consider how it looks like the soggy confetti of a map: where you've been,
where you're going—"You Are Here," says the red star on the back of the menu.

Occasionally a date with a face blank as a sheet of paper asks you whether 40
writers often become discouraged. Say that sometimes they do and sometimes
they do. Say it's a lot like having polio.

"Interesting," smiles your date, and then he looks down at his arm hairs and 41
starts to smooth them, all, always, in the same direction.

ACTIVITIES FOR WRITING AND DISCUSSION

1. Why isn't the story formatted as one piece of *continuous* prose? What are the advantages, if any, to the piece being organized as a series of short segments separated by white spaces?

2. Moore writes in an unusual **point of view,** *second*-person. How is, or isn't, it appropriate to the story she tells? How would the effect of the story change if the persistent use of "you" were suppressed? Try recasting a part of the story in either the first- or third-person, and assess the result.

3. Compose a story or essay of your own, on a topic of your choice, in the second-person point of view.

4. Following Moore's example, write a "How to Become a _____" piece on a topic of your own choice.

Poems

WILLIAM WORDSWORTH (1770–1850)

The World Is Too Much with Us

The world is too much with us; late and soon,
Getting and spending, we lay waste our powers:
Little we see in Nature that is ours;
We have given our hearts away, a sordid boon!
This Sea that bares her bosom to the moon;   5
The winds that will be howling at all hours,
And are up-gathered now like sleeping flowers;
For this, for every thing, we are out of tune;
It moves us not.—Great God! I'd rather be
A Pagan suckled in a creed outworn;   10
So might I, standing on this pleasant lea,
Have glimpses that would make me less forlorn;
Have sight of Proteus[1] rising from the sea;
Or hear old Triton[2] blow his wreathèd horn.

---

1. In Greek mythology, an old man of the sea who was able to assume a variety of shapes.   2. A god of the sea, often depicted as blowing on a seashell.

JOHN KEATS (1795–1821)

When I have fears that I may cease to be

When I have fears that I may cease to be
  Before my pen has glean'd my teeming brain,
Before high piled books, in charactry,
  Hold like rich garners the full ripen'd grain;
When I behold, upon the night's starr'd face,   5
  Huge cloudy symbols of a high romance,
And think that I may never live to trace
  Their shadows, with the magic hand of chance;
And when I feel, fair creature of an hour,
  That I shall never look upon thee more,   10
Never have relish in the fairy power
  Of unreflecting love;—then on the shore
Of the wide world I stand alone, and think
Till love and fame to nothingness do sink.

ACTIVITIES FOR WRITING AND DISCUSSION

1. Read "When I have fears that I may cease to be" aloud with a partner or small group. Together, do a scansion of the poem, and map out its rhyme pattern (see pp. 140–142).

2. Postponing (for now) questions about meaning, reread the poem aloud once more, and concentrate on its sound effects. Mark or underline examples of **alliteration, assonance,** or **consonance.** Also note any images or phrases you find compelling or beautiful.

3. The aphorist L. P. Smith once wrote that "Sound is more than sense." What do you suppose he meant by this statement, and is Keats's poem a proof of it? Can a poem be pleasurable or beautiful even if you don't fully understand it? Why or why not, and if "yes," in what ways?

4. Keats was a poet who burned for love and fame and died young, at the age of twenty-five. Explain the logic of the poem. What sorts of thoughts would reduce "love and fame to nothingness" in the mind of a profoundly passionate and ambitious poet?

5. As this poem attests, Keats did not shy away from the Big Themes. Following his example, take the concerns and anxieties addressed in the poem and recast them in a prose format using present-day or modern language. For instance, write a meditation, a personal letter, or a series of journal entries ranging over issues of ambition, mortality, love, and fame or success.

WALT WHITMAN (1819–1892)

Sparkles from the Wheel

Where the city's ceaseless crowd moves on the livelong day,
Withdrawn I join a group of children watching, I pause aside with them.

By the curb toward the edge of the flagging,
A knife-grinder works at his wheel sharpening a great knife,
Bending over he carefully holds it to the stone, by foot and knee,   5
With measur'd tread he turns rapidly, as he presses with light but firm hand,
Forth issue then in copious golden jets,
Sparkles from the wheel.

The scene and all its belongings, how they seize and affect me,
The sad sharp-chinn'd old man with worn clothes and broad shoulder-band of   10
    leather,
Myself effusing and fluid, a phantom curiously floating, now here absorb'd and
    arrested,
The group, (an unminded point set in a vast surrounding,)
The attentive, quiet children, the loud, proud, restive base of the streets,
The low hoarse purr of the whirling stone, the light-press'd blade,
Diffusing, dropping, sideways-darting, in tiny showers of gold,   15
Sparkles from the wheel.

The Ox-Tamer

In a far-away northern county in the placid pastoral region,
Lives my farmer friend, the theme of my recitative, a famous tamer of oxen,
There they bring him the three-year-olds and the four-year-olds to break
    them,
He will take the wildest steer in the world and break him and tame him,
He will go fearless without any whip where the young bullock chafes up and   5
    down the yard,
The bullock's head tosses restless high in the air with raging eyes,
Yet see you! how soon his rage subsides—how soon this tamer tames him;
See you! on the farms hereabout a hundred oxen young and old, and he is the
    man who has tamed them,
They all know him, all are affectionate to him;
See you! some are such beautiful animals, so lofty looking;   10
Some are buff-color'd, some mottled, one has a white line running along his
    back, some are brindled,

Some have wide flaring horns (a good sign)—see you the bright hides,
See, the two with stars on their foreheads—see, the round bodies and broad
    backs,
How straight and square they stand on their legs—what fine sagacious eyes!
How they watch their tamer—they wish him near them—how they turn to   15
    look after him!
What yearning expression! how uneasy they are when he moves away from
    them;
Now I marvel what it can be he appears to them, (books, politics, poems,
    depart—all else departs,)
I confess I envy only his fascination—my silent, illiterate friend,
Whom a hundred oxen love there in his life on farms,
In the northern county far, in the placid pastoral region.   20

ACTIVITIES FOR WRITING AND DISCUSSION

1. "Sparkles from the Wheel" and "The Ox-Tamer" describe people at work. What qualities, other than the obvious one of their verse format, make these pieces poetic? Identify and discuss any examples of rhythm, **sound effects,** imagery, **diction,** or **figurative language** that particularly strike you.

2. Draft a portrait of your own, in verse or prose, of a person at work, paying particular attention, as Whitman does, to the details of his/her activity.

EMILY DICKINSON (1830–1886)

Success is counted sweetest

Success is counted sweetest
By those who ne'er succeed.
To comprehend a nectar
Requires sorest need.

Not one of all the purple Host   5
Who took the Flag today
Can tell the definition
So clear of Victory

As he defeated—dying—
On whose forbidden ear   10
The distant strains of triumph
Burst agonized and clear!

WILLIAM BUTLER YEATS (1865–1939)

Adam's Curse

We sat together at one summer's end,
That beautiful mild woman, your close friend,
And you and I, and talked of poetry.
I said: 'A line will take us hours maybe;
Yet if it does not seem a moment's thought,   5
Our stitching and unstitching has been naught.
Better go down upon your marrow-bones
And scrub a kitchen pavement, or break stones
Like an old pauper, in all kinds of weather;
For to articulate sweet sounds together   10
Is to work harder than all these, and yet
Be thought an idler by the noisy set
Of bankers, schoolmasters, and clergymen
The martyrs call the world.'

                  And thereupon   15
That beautiful mild woman for whose sake
There's many a one shall find out all heartache
On finding that her voice is sweet and low
Replied: 'To be born woman is to know—
Although they do not talk of it at school—   20
That we must labour to be beautiful.'

I said: 'It's certain there is no fine thing
Since Adam's fall but needs much labouring.
There have been lovers who thought love should be
So much compounded of high courtesy   25
That they would sigh and quote with learned looks
Precedents out of beautiful old books;
Yet now it seems an idle trade enough.'

We sat grown quiet at the name of love;
We saw the last embers of daylight die,   30
And in the trembling blue-green of the sky
A moon, worn as if it had been a shell
Washed by time's waters as they rose and fell
About the stars and broke in days and years.

I had a thought for no one's but your ears: 35
That you were beautiful, and that I strove

To love you in the old high way of love;
That it had all seemed happy, and yet we'd grown
As weary-hearted as that hollow moon.

Robert Frost (1874–1963)

Stopping by Woods on a Snowy Evening

Whose woods these are I think I know.
His house is in the village though;
He will not see me stopping here
To watch his woods fill up with snow.

My little horse must think it queer   5
To stop without a farmhouse near
Between the woods and frozen lake
The darkest evening of the year.

He gives his harness bells a shake
To ask if there is some mistake.   10
The only other sound's the sweep
Of easy wind and downy flake.

The woods are lovely, dark and deep,
But I have promises to keep,
And miles to go before I sleep,   15
And miles to go before I sleep.

"Out, Out——"

The buzz-saw snarled and rattled in the yard
And made dust and dropped stove-length sticks of wood,
Sweet-scented stuff when the breeze drew across it.
And from there those that lifted eyes could count
Five mountain ranges one behind the other   5
Under the sunset far into Vermont.
And the saw snarled and rattled, snarled and rattled,
As it ran light, or had to bear a load.
And nothing happened: day was all but done.
Call it a day, I wish they might have said   10
To please the boy by giving him the half hour
That a boy counts so much when saved from work.

His sister stood beside them in her apron
To tell them "Supper." At the word, the saw,
As if to prove saws knew what supper meant,   15
Leaped out at the boy's hand, or seemed to leap—
He must have given the hand. However it was,
Neither refused the meeting. But the hand!
The boy's first outcry was a rueful laugh,
As he swung toward them holding up the hand   20
Half in appeal, but half as if to keep
The life from spilling. Then the boy saw all—
Since he was old enough to know, big boy
Doing a man's work, though a child at heart—
He saw all spoiled. "Don't let him cut my hand off—   25
The doctor, when he comes. Don't let him, sister!"
So. But the hand was gone already.
The doctor put him in the dark of ether.
He lay and puffed his lips out with his breath.
And then—the watcher at his pulse took fright.   30
No one believed. They listened at his heart.
Little—less—nothing!—and that ended it.
No more to build on there. And they, since they
Were not the one dead, turned to their affairs.

ACTIVITIES FOR WRITING AND DISCUSSION

1. Respond to either of Frost's poems using the "Four-Step Process for Writing from Reading" discussed in Chapter 2.

2. Working with a group or as a class, read "Out, Out—" aloud. Have each person take a turn reading several lines, and pause periodically to do either or both of the following:

    a. Share and discuss your annotations of specific lines and passages. What parts puzzle you or leave you with questions? What parts strike or "grab" you? Why?

    b. Analyze Frost's **metaphors** and **similes** and how they enhance the poem.

Based on this process and on your annotations, write a response to the poem using one of the "Ten Ideas for Writing" from Chapter 3 (page 27) or a different idea of your own devising.

Ishigaki Rin (b. 1920)

The Pan, the Pot, the Fire I Have Before Me

For a long time
these things have always been placed
before us women:

the pan of a reasonable size
suited to the user's strength,   5
the pot in which it's convenient for rice
to begin to swell and shine, grain by grain,
the glow of the fire inherited from time immemorial—
before these there have always been
mothers, grandmothers, and their mothers   10

What measures of love and sincerity
these persons must have poured
into these utensils—
now red carrots,
now black seaweed,   15
now crushed fish

in the kitchen, always accurately
for morning, noon, and evening, preparations have been made
and before the preparations, in a row, there have always been
some pairs of warm knees and hands.   20

Ah without those persons waiting
how could women have gone on
cooking so happily?
their unflagging care,
so daily a service they became unconscious of it.   25

Cooking was mysteriously assigned
to women, as a role,
but I don't think that was unfortunate;
because of that, their knowledge and positions in society
may have lagged behind the times   30
but it isn't too late:
the things we have before us,
the pan and the pot, and the burning fire,

before these familiar things,
let us study government, economy, literature   35

as sincerely
as we cook potatoes and meat.

not for vanity and promotion
but so everyone
may serve all   40
so everyone may work for love.

   —*Translated by Hiroaki Sato*

ACTIVITIES FOR WRITING AND DISCUSSION

1. Make a list of stories you have heard or read about cooking, women, or politics. Jot down notes on the **characters** in these stories (from books, film, television) and be prepared to share them in your small group.

2. Reread the fourth and fifth **stanzas.** To whom might "pairs of warm knees and hands" refer, and why might the speaker allude to them as "knees" and "hands" instead of as people?

3. Commenting on specific lines or phrases in the poem, attack and/or defend the following statement: "Experiences with 'the pan, the pot, [and] the fire' have nothing to do with preparing women for a role in 'government, economy, [and] literature.'"

DENISE LEVERTOV (1923–1997)

O Taste and See

The world is
not with us enough.
O taste and see

the subway Bible poster said,
meaning *The Lord,* meaning   5
if anything all that lives
to the imagination's tongue,

grief, mercy, language,
tangerine, weather, to
breathe them, bite,   10
savor, chew, swallow, transform

into our flesh our
deaths, crossing the street, plum, quince,
living in the orchard and being

hungry, and plucking   15
the fruit.

ACTIVITIES FOR WRITING AND DISCUSSION

1. This poem is a reply to Wordsworth's sonnet, "The World Is Too Much
With Us." Reread both poems carefully, inferring as much information as you
can about the two poets' worldviews and values. Then:
  a. Working alone or with a group, identify and list points of probable
       agreement and disagreement between the two poets.
  b. Imagine a setting—such as a home, park, or cafe—in which the two
       poets meet. Have them discuss—and possibly debate—their different
       views of "the world," along with any other topics that happen to arise.
       Try to infer the speaking style of each poet from the poetic style you
       detect in their poems. How does the meeting end? In agreement? cor-
       dial disagreement? with one or the other poet leaving angrily?

2. Write an essay in which you compare and contrast the two poems. In addition to considering ideas or outlooks, you might also examine differences and
similarities in **diction,** imagery, tone, and poetic type (Wordsworth's poem is
traditional verse, while Levertov's is free verse).

WISLAWA SZYMBORSKA (b. 1923)

Advertisement

I'm a tranquilizer.
I'm effective at home.
I work in the office.
I can take exams
or the witness stand.   5
I mend broken cups with care.
All you have to do is take me,
let me melt beneath your tongue,
just gulp me
with a glass of water.   10

I know how to handle misfortune,
how to take bad news.
I can minimize injustice,
lighten up God's absence,
or pick the widow's veil that suits your face.   15
What are you waiting for—
have faith in my chemical compassion.

You're still a young man/woman.
It's not too late to learn how to unwind.
Who said   20
you have to take it on the chin?

Let me have your abyss.
I'll cushion it with sleep.
You'll thank me for giving you
four paws to fall on.   25

Sell me your soul.
There are no other takers.

There is no other devil anymore.

—*Translated by Stanislaw Barańczak
and Clare Cavanagh*

ACTIVITIES FOR WRITING AND DISCUSSION

1. Why do you suppose Szymborska titled the poem "Advertisement" instead of "Tranquilizer"?

2. What strategies of advertising in general does the "Advertisement" mimic? What fears and desires does it exploit? Annotate and discuss specific lines and the strategies they illustrate.

3. A more conventional version of this poem might have featured a salesperson extolling the virtues of the tranquilizer in the **third-person.** What effects does Szymborska achieve by **personifying** the tranquilizer and having it speak for itself? If you wish, write a poem of your own from the point of view of some personified commercial product (e.g., a car, item of clothing, television, cell phone) in which you have the product "sell" itself.

4. Based on hints in the poem, what are the personal characteristics and needs of the "you" who will likely buy the tranquilizer? Use your experience and imagination to write his or her life story.

5. The poem is rich in **figures** (e.g., "Let me have your abyss"; "Sell me your soul"). Identify several that are most notable to you, and analyze their power and impact orally or in an essay.

Writing a Résumé

What needs to be done?
Fill out the application
and enclose the résumé.

Regardless of the length of life,
a résumé is best kept short.   5

Concise, well-chosen facts are de rigueur.
Landscapes are replaced by addresses,
shaky memories give way to unshakable dates.

Of all your loves, mention only the marriage;
of all your children, only those who were born.   10

Who knows you matters more than whom you know.
Trips only if taken abroad.
Memberships in what but without why.
Honors, but not how they were earned.

Write as if you'd never talked to yourself   15
and always kept yourself at arm's length.

Pass over in silence your dogs, cats, birds,
dusty keepsakes, friends, and dreams.

Price, not worth,
and title, not what's inside.   20
His shoe size, not where he's off to,
that one you pass off as yourself.
In addition, a photograph with one ear showing.
What matters is its shape, not what it hears.
What is there to hear, anyway?   25
The clatter of paper shredders.

*—Translated by Stanislaw Barańczak
and Clare Cavanagh*

ACTIVITIES FOR WRITING AND DISCUSSION

1. Share your annotations of "Writing a Résumé" with a partner or small group. Then:

    a. Use one annotation or a cluster of annotations that especially strikes you as a springboard for writing in your notebook; or

    b. Respond to the poem using any of the "Ten Ideas for Writing" described in Chapter 3.

2. If you have ever prepared one, describe (in writing) your own experience of composing a resume. Emphasize not just the mechanics but the feelings you had as you composed. Then use your story as a vehicle for writing about the poem in any way you wish.

3. What is the drift of the advice in this poem? Do you think Szymborska intends the advice to be taken **literally** or **ironically?** Explain, and support your explanation with references to specific lines in the poem.

4. One reader described this poem as "a flat-out condemnation of a dehumanized society." Without being privy to the context in which this comment was made, would you agree or disagree? Why?

JAMES WRIGHT (1927–1980)

Lying in a Hammock at William Duffy's Farm in Pine Island, Minnesota

Over my head, I see the bronze butterfly,
Asleep on the black trunk,
Blowing like a leaf in green shadow.
Down the ravine behind the empty house,
The cowbells follow one another   5
Into the distances of the afternoon.
To my right,
In a field of sunlight between two pines,
The droppings of last year's horses
Blaze up into golden stones.   10
I lean back, as the evening darkens and comes on.
A chicken hawk floats over, looking for home.
I have wasted my life.

HERBERT SCOTT (b. 1931)

Boss in the Back Room

1

I love to work the checkstands Saturdays.
The carts lined up, bulging with goods.
You weigh the produce heavy, ring the prices

high. That's where you make your wages.
Keep the customers talking. They don't know   5
which way their money went.

2

There's too much money in groceries.
I seen it happen in my life.
The bankers in their high hats,

they own this place.   10
They don't care nothing about groceries.
It's paper and ink to them.

3

I know the clerks steal.
You got to keep them happy.
Jack the prices a little,   15

let the customers pay.
They got their own racket,
somewheres. They take you,

you take them. Live and let live,
I always say. It ain't the worst   20
business in the world.

4

Marriage, that's the travesty of your life.
You spend the rest of your days
picking the fleas out of your ears.

My wife got married so young   25
she don't remember her maiden name.
And the women you see come in,

day after day, they ain't stupid.
Their old man's sleeping on the couch
or out playing pig's knuckle   30

with the boys. I'm telling you,
this world is full of lonely women.
It's a great place to be.

ACTIVITIES FOR WRITING AND DISCUSSION

1. Describe the poem's **diction,** and illustrate your description with examples. Herbert Scott is a poet. Is his **speaker** in this poem a "poet"? Explain your answer.

2. React to the speaker. Do you trust him? like him? admire him? Why or why not?

3. Describe the speaker's philosophy of life.

4. Describe the speaker's implied audience, the person or people to whom he seems to be speaking. How does his implied audience affect the content and style of his speech? Rewrite all or a part of the poem with a different implied audience—say, of the boss's *boss,* his wife, his peers, or a customer. *Alternative:* Imagine the boss stepping from the back room into the front room, and write what he says in the latter space.

5. The poem is a **monologue.** Following Scott's example and writing in either verse or prose, create a monologue of your own in which a speaker—real or imagined—talks candidly about his or her work to an implied listener or listeners. Choose both your speaker and listener(s) carefully.

TED KOOSER (b. 1939)

A Death at the Office

The news goes desk to desk
like a memo: *Initial*
and pass on. Each of us marks
Surprised or *Sorry.*

The management came early   5
and buried her nameplate
deep in her desk. They have boxed up
the Midol and Lip-Ice,

the snapshots from home,
wherever it was—nephews   10
and nieces, a strange, blurred cat
with fiery, flashbulb eyes

as if it grieved. But who grieves here?
We have her ballpoints back,
her bud vase. One of us tears   15
the scribbles from her calendar.

ACTIVITIES FOR WRITING AND DISCUSSION

1. Identify as many **figures—metaphors, similes, verbal ironies,** and others—as you can. From these choose several that stand out for you, and explain how each enhances the poem's overall effect on you.

2. Based on this poem about a *death* at the office, tell the story of typical day-to-day *life* in this office as you imagine it. If you wish, focus your story on one particular imagined worker.

3. Assess the personality and emotions of the poem's **speaker.** Make a list of adjectives that describe the speaker. If you wish, imagine the habits, personal values, and home life of the speaker. Then invent a dialogue between yourself and the speaker in which you talk about life (and death) at the office—the office in the poem and/or offices you have known yourself.

4. In the **persona** of the dead woman (imagine the dead can speak):
   a. Tell the story of your life, with emphasis on the subject of your work; or
   b. Share your thoughts and feelings about the way your co-workers and office management have reacted to your death.

5. Do you interpret the last stanza literally or ironically? Explain.

JACK RIDL (b. 1944)

Last Ditch

FOR BILLY MAYER

Thirty-one seconds on the clock. Coach is down on one knee, screaming at Tommy to get the ball across mid-court and call time out. We're down by one. Time out. In the huddle, Coach slaps Frank behind the head, "Look at this.

Look. Now, you Frank, you get the ball to Jimmy. Frank, you hear me? Ok. Now, get the ball to Jimmy. Then, Frank, you break down the lane like you're gonna get it back. Got it? Ok. Then, Jimmy, you look for Carl who'll be breaking out to the line after Frank goes by. Frank, you're gonna screen Carl's man. Ok? Now, it's just the same as in practice. No different. No different. Just the same. Just the . . . " And all I can hear is this roar, this sense that the roof is opening and a train is tumbling slowly across the sky. I look over at Jeannie. She's shoving her fist toward the scoreboard and yelling, "Come on Blue. Come on Blue." The horn sounds. We all reach in, grab Coach's hand. "OK. OK. OK. OK. OK. OK." Frank tosses it in to Jimmy. 28, 27, 26, 25. Jimmy dribbles, left, back right; his man presses close; Jimmy keeps the ball tight to his right side, keeps his left arm out. He holds his head high, at one angle. 18, 17, 16, 15. He passes to Tommy. Tommy looks inside, fakes a pass, head fakes, tosses back to Jimmy. The train is rolling, the crowd, the clock, Jeannie is shrieking "C'mon, C'mon, C'mon." 12, 11, 10, Jimmy's still dribbling. Coach is back down on his knee, clapping, "OK. OK. OK." Frank cuts down the lane. Carl fakes left, then starts for the line; Jimmy looks to his right, catches Carl open; Carl turns, fires . . . The last dance, "Goodnight sweetheart, well, it's time to go. Goodnight sweetheart, goodnight." And Jeannie cups her hand around my neck.

ACTIVITIES FOR WRITING AND DISCUSSION

1. Write a **prose poem** that captures a suspenseful moment—or sequence of moments—in a sporting event or other competition.

JAN BEATTY (b. 1952)

A Waitress's Instructions on Tipping
or
Get the Cash Up and Don't Waste My Time

20% minimum as long as the waitress doesn't inflict bodily harm.
If you're two people at a four top, tip extra.
If you sit a long time, pay rent.
Double tips for special orders.
Always tip extra when using coupons.   5
Better yet, don't use coupons.
Never leave change instead of bills.
Never leave pennies at all.
Never hide a tip for fun.

Overtip, overtip, overtip.   10
Remember, I am somebody's mother or daughter.
Large parties *must* overtip, no separate piles of change.
If people in your party don't show up, tip *for* them.
Don't wait around for gratitude if you overtip.
Take a risk. Don't adjust your tip so your credit card total is even.   15
Don't ever, ever pull out a tipping guide in public.
If you leave 10% or less, eat at home.
If I call a taxi for you, tip me.
If I hang up your coat for you, tip me.
If I get cigarettes for you, tip me.   20
Better yet, do it yourself.
If you buy a $50 bottle of wine, pull out a $10.
If I serve you one cocktail, don't hand me $.35.
If you're just having coffee, leave a $5.
Don't fold a bill and hand it to me like you're a big shot.   25
Don't say, *There's a big tip in it for you if . . .*
Don't say, *I want to make sure you get this,* like a busboy would steal it.
Don't say, *Here, honey, this is for you*—ever.
Don't say, *I'll make it worth your while.*
If you're miserable, there's not enough money in the world.   30

JANICE M. LYNCH (b. 1962)

Excerpts from "Sixty-Four Caprices for a Long-Distance Swimmer: Notes on Swimming 100 Miles"

1. A friend asks why I swim. Why not a movie? A drink? Dinner? I answer that I swim for strength, for a rippling tricep and a dimple in my thigh. I hide the lie with a stroke: I swim for the silence of water.

2. An older woman stopped swimming and watched me. What a graceful stroke! What she loved, of course, was the mirrored beauty of her youth—the forgotten pleasure of her toughened skin.

3. The water undulates like a womb I do not remember. My fingers poke through for life. The air is unfamiliar.

4. I tell a friend that life is water. With a pretended fluidity his heart mimics the ocean—but he cannot swim. He answers that a cell full of water explodes.

5. Seventy-year old women stand naked in the locker room. Some use walkers, others have artificial hips, scarred legs and missing breasts, still, they love this morning swim with the distant sun rising.

6. In these women, I witness how I too will age. I avert my eyes, move to far lanes and other shadows.

7. I swim past men to prove my strength—after years of "throwing like a girl"—I lap them twice.

10. I tap slower swimmers' feet to pass them. Their skin startles me, as though I've come upon schools of spot running south for winter.

15. I dream of fire. I dream of fire and combustion. The things water does not heal.

17. How do we breathe underwater? A moment without air is magic. Through goggles, I watch the bubbles insist on my life.

18. Fifty others swim in the pool. Water molecules vibrate with our personalities. I swallow each person's breath, yet remain alone.

21. This—is—the—point—where I always—want to stop. Turn—legs— ache—lungs heave—arms weary—the distance—is forever—force the push—break water.

22. Every morning, two crows perch near the pool's glass doors and peck madly at their reflections. When no one watches, I jump out of the pool and run, arms raised and mouth squawking, to chase them away.

23. Then all three of us jump—the crows with fright to the sky—and me, chilled, to the diving well.

24. Every other breath my face sculpts a water mask.

26. Blood throbs, echoing the physics of water and sound. It sets up a rhythm between myself and other swimmers.

29. At a certain angle, the hand slices sheets of water. This requires a force the body is unaware of, even as pounds of water move away like the curtain rising over the first act.

30. What does it mean to drown in a dream? Is there the hope of bellying-up like a fish? Are we forced to forget breathing?

31. Some days there is no difference between sleep and dreams, between swimming and drowning, water and air.

36. After a winter of depression, inches of sadness float across the pool.

37. Sometimes, breathing, the heaviness of my own life amazes me. Sucking on air, I consume the world.

40. Breaststroke beads the surface like mercury on skin. I'm a skeet barely touching water, needing it only to serve my own motion.

41. I try to describe my father, but he eludes me, fast as a rock skipping the ocean. I try to describe my mother, but she is too much myself—familiar as oxygen gurgling about my waist.

42. I learned to walk because my sister was born and I knew that I would never be carried again.

43. I learned to swim because my father threw me in the deep end and shouted "Swim!"

44. I sweat in the water and my face is cooled, ice cooled on ice.

45. As children, my sisters and I linked arms with my father and ran into the Atlantic, afraid only of letting go and coming up in some other ocean.

46. A man paralyzed from the waist down swims slowly, his legs quivering with the dream of motion. In a dream that my strength reaches him through the water, I swim faster, give up another length.

47. At dawn the moon fits the socket of the sky like a great white bulb.

61. When I swim I am the totality of water. I am hydrogen and oxygen. I am pure strength and energy.

64. I shed the water's silk cocoon for the certain embrace of air; my body emerges from the pool, form from cut crystal.

ACTIVITIES FOR WRITING AND DISCUSSION

1. Lynch calls the numbered sections of her poem "caprices" or "notes," and they resemble the kinds of notes you might jot down in a notebook. Therefore, react to the piece using any of the "Generic Ideas for Writing in Response to Published Notebooks and Journals" that are listed on pp. 276–277.

2. React to the *form* of the piece. Do the numbered sections need to be read in sequence? Do they suggest any underlying pattern of organization? Do they constitute *a* poem or 64 *separate* poems? Support your opinions with references to specific passages.

3. Compare "Sixty-Four Caprices" with Edward Hoagland's essay, "Learning to Eat Soup" (p. 485), which is somewhat similar in format. In what specific ways do the two pieces differ and/or resemble each other? What ideas, if any, does either suggest to you for a writing project of your own?

4. Following Lynch's example, compose and collect a number of "notes" or "caprices" based on experiencing some favorite activity of your own.

HENRY DAVID THOREAU (1817–1862)

Where I Lived, and What I Lived For

At a certain season of our life we are accustomed to consider every spot as the possible site of a house. I have thus surveyed the country on every side within a dozen miles of where I live. In imagination I have bought all the farms in succession, for all were to be bought, and I knew their price. I walked over each farmer's premises, tasted his wild apples, discoursed on husbandry with him, took his farm at his price, at any price, mortgaging it to him in my mind; even put a higher price on it,—took everything but a deed of it,—took his word for his deed, for I dearly love to talk,—cultivated it, and him too to some extent, I trust, and withdrew when I had enjoyed it long enough, leaving him to carry it on. This experience entitled me to be regarded as a sort of real-estate broker by my friends. Wherever I sat, there I might live, and the landscape radiated from me accordingly. What is a house but a *sedes*, a seat?—better if a country seat. I discovered many a site for a house not likely to be soon improved, which some might have thought too far from the village, but to my eyes the village was too far from it. Well, there I might live, I said; and there I did live, for an hour, a summer and a winter life; saw how I could let the years run off, buffet the winter through, and see the spring come in. The future inhabitants of this region, wherever they may place their houses, may be sure that they have been anticipated. An afternoon sufficed to lay out the land into orchard, woodlot, and pasture, and to decide what fine oaks or pines should be left to stand before the door, and whence each blasted tree could be seen to the best advantage; and then I let it lie, fallow perchance, for a man is rich in proportion to the number of things which he can afford to let alone. . . .

The present was my next experiment of this kind, which I purpose to describe more at length, for convenience, putting the experience of two years into one. As I have said, I do not propose to write an ode to dejection, but to brag as lustily as chanticleer in the morning, standing on his roost, if only to wake my neighbors up.

When first I took up my abode in the woods, that is, began to spend my nights as well as days there, which, by accident, was on Independence day, or the fourth of July, 1845, my house was not finished for winter, but was merely a defence against the rain, without plastering or chimney, the walls being of rough weather-stained boards, with wide chinks, which made it cool at night. The upright white hewn studs and freshly planed door and window casings gave it a clean and airy look, especially in the morning, when its timbers were saturated with dew, so that I fancied that by noon some sweet gum would exude from them. To my imagination it retained throughout the day more or less of this auroral character, reminding me of a certain house on a mountain which I had visited a year before. This was an airy and unplastered cabin, fit to entertain a travelling god, and where a goddess might trail her garments. The winds which passed over my dwelling were such as sweep over the ridges of mountains, bearing the broken strains, or celestial parts only, of terrestrial music. The morning wind forever blows, the poem of creation is uninterrupted; but few are the ears that hear it. Olympus is but the outside of the earth everywhere.

The only house I had been the owner of before, if I except a boat, was a tent, which I used occasionally when making excursions in the summer, and this is still rolled up in my garret; but the boat, after passing from hand to hand, has gone down the stream of time. With this more substantial shelter about me, I had made some progress toward settling in the world. This frame, so slightly clad, was a sort of crystallization around me, and reacted on the builder. It was suggestive somewhat as a picture in outlines. I did not need to go out doors to take the air, for the atmosphere within had lost none of its freshness. It was not so much within doors as behind a door where I sat, even in the rainiest weather. The Harivansa says, "An abode without birds is like a meat without seasoning." Such was not my abode, for I found myself suddenly neighbor to the birds; not by having imprisoned one, but having caged myself near them. I was not only nearer to some of those which commonly frequent the garden and the orchard, but to those wilder and more thrilling songsters of the forest which never, or rarely, serenade a villager,—the wood-thrush, the veery, the scarlet tanager, the field-sparrow, the whippoorwill, and many others. . . .

Every morning was a cheerful invitation to make my life of equal simplicity, 5 and I may say innocence, with Nature herself. I have been as sincere a worshipper of Aurora as the Greeks. I got up early and bathed in the pond; that was a religious exercise, and one of the best things which I did. They say that characters were engraven on the bathing tub of king Tching-thang to this effect: "Renew thyself completely each day; do it again, and again, and forever again." I can understand that. Morning brings back the heroic ages. I was as much affected by the faint hum of a mosquito making its invisible and unimaginable tour through my apartment at earliest dawn, when I was sitting with door and windows open, as I could be by any trumpet that ever sang of fame. It was Homer's requiem; itself an Iliad and Odyssey in the air, singing its own wrath and wanderings. There was something cosmical about it; a standing advertisement, till forbidden, of the everlasting vigor and fertility of the world. The morning, which is the most memorable season of the day, is the awakening hour. Then there is least somnolence in us; and for an hour, at least, some part of us awakes which slumbers all the rest of the day and night. Little is to be expected of that day, if it can be called a day, to which we are not awakened by our Genius, but by the mechanical nudgings of some servitor, are not awakened by our own newly-acquired force and aspirations from within, accompanied by the undulations of celestial music, instead of factory bells, and a fragrance filling the air—to a higher life than we fell asleep from; and thus the darkness bear its fruit, and prove itself to be good, no less than the light. That man who does not believe that each day contains an earlier, more sacred, and auroral hour than he has yet profaned, has despaired of life, and is pursuing a descending and darkening way. After a partial cessation of his sensuous life, the soul of man, or its organs rather, are reinvigorated each day, and his Genius tries again what noble life it can make. All memorable events, I should say, transpire in morning time and in a morning atmosphere. The Vedas say, "All intelligences awake with the morning." Poetry and art, and the fairest and most memorable of the actions of men, date from such an hour. All poets and heroes, like Memnon, are the children of Aurora, and emit their music at sunrise. To him whose elastic and vigorous thought keeps pace with the sun, the day is a perpetual morning. It matters not what the clocks say or the attitudes and labors of men. Morning is when I am awake and there is a dawn in me. Moral reform is the effort to throw off sleep. Why is it that men give so poor an account of their day if they have not been slumbering? They are not such poor calculators. If they had not been overcome with drowsiness they would have performed something. The millions are awake enough for physical labor; but only one in a million is awake enough for effective intellectual exertion, only one in a hundred millions to a poetic or divine life. To be awake is to be alive. I have never yet met a man who was quite awake. How could I have looked him in the face?

We must learn to reawaken and keep ourselves awake, not by mechanical aids, but by an infinite expectation of the dawn, which does not forsake us in our soundest sleep. I know of no more encouraging fact than the unquestionable ability of man to elevate his life by a conscious endeavor. It is something to be able to paint a particular picture, or to carve a statue, and so to make a few objects beautiful; but it is far more glorious to carve and paint the very atmosphere and medium through which we look, which morally we can do. To affect the quality of the day, that is the highest of arts. Every man is tasked to make his life, even in its details, worthy of the contemplation of his most elevated and critical hour. If we refused, or rather used up, such paltry information as we get, the oracles would distinctly inform us how this might be done.

I went to the woods because I wished to live deliberately, to front only the essential facts of life, and see if I could not learn what it had to teach, and not, when I came to die, discover that I had not lived. I did not wish to live what was not life, living is so dear; nor did I wish to practise resignation, unless it was quite necessary. I wanted to live deep and suck out all the marrow of life, to live so sturdily and Spartan-like as to put to rout all that was not life, to cut a broad swath and shave close, to drive life into a corner, and reduce it to its lowest terms, and, if it proved to be mean, why then to get the whole and genuine meanness of it, and publish its meanness to the world; or if it were sublime, to know it by experience, and be able to give a true account of it in my next excursion. For most men, it appears to me, are in a strange uncertainty about it, whether it is of the devil or of God, and have *somewhat hastily* concluded that it is the chief end of man here to "glorify God and enjoy him forever." . . .

Why should we live with such hurry and waste of life? We are determined to be starved before we are hungry. Men say that a stitch in time saves nine, and so they take a thousand stitches to-day to save nine to-morrow. As for *work*, we haven't any of any consequence. We have the Saint Vitus' dance, and cannot possibly keep our heads still. If I should only give a few pulls at the parish bell-rope, as for a fire, that is, without setting the bell, there is hardly a man on his farm in the outskirts of Concord, notwithstanding that press of engagements which was his excuse so many times this morning, nor a boy, nor a woman, I might almost say, but would forsake all and follow that sound, not mainly to save property from the flames, but, if we will confess the truth, much more to see it burn, since burn it must, and we, be it known, did not set it on fire,—or to see it put out, and have a hand in it, if that is done as handsomely; yes, even if it were the parish church itself. Hardly a man takes a half hour's nap after dinner, but when he wakes he holds up his head and asks, "What's the news?" as if the rest of mankind had stood his sentinels. Some give directions to be waked every half hour, doubtless for no other purpose; and then, to pay for it, they tell what they have dreamed. After a night's sleep the news is as indispensable as the breakfast. "Pray tell me anything new that has happened to a man anywhere on this globe,"—and he reads it over his coffee and rolls, that a man has had his eyes gouged out this morning on the Wachito River; never dreaming the while that he lives in the dark unfathomed mammoth cave of this world, and has but the rudiment of an eye himself.

For my part, I could easily do without the post-office. I think that there are very few important communications made through it. To speak critically, I never received more than one or two letters in my life—I wrote this some years ago—that were worth the postage. The penny-post is, commonly, an institution through which you seriously offer a man that penny for his thoughts which is so often safely offered in jest. And I am sure that I never read any memorable news in a newspaper. If we read of one man robbed, or murdered, or killed by accident, or one house burned, or one vessel wrecked, or one steamboat blown up, or one cow run over on the Western Railroad, or one mad dog killed, or one lot of grasshoppers in the winter,—we never need read of another. One is enough. If you are acquainted with the principle, what do you care for a myriad instances and applications? To a philosopher all *news*, as it is called, is gossip, and they who edit and read it are old women over their tea. . . .

What news! how much more important to know what that is which was never old! "Kieou-he-yu (great dignitary of the state of Wei) sent a man to Khoung-tseu to know his news. Khoung-tseu caused the messenger to be seated near him, and questioned him in these terms: What is your master doing? The messenger answered with respect: My master desires to diminish the number of his faults, but he cannot come to the end of them. The messenger being gone, 10 the philosopher remarked: What a worthy messenger! What a worthy messenger!" The preacher, instead of vexing the ears of drowsy farmers on their day of rest at the end of the week,—for Sunday is the fit conclusion of an ill-spent week, and not the fresh and brave beginning of a new one,—with this one other draggle-tail of a sermon, should shout with thundering voice,—"Pause! Avast! Why so seeming fast, but deadly slow?"

Shams and delusions are esteemed for soundest truths, while reality is fabulous. If men would steadily observe realities only, and not allow themselves to be deluded, life, to compare it with such things as we know, would be like a fairy tale and the Arabian Nights' Entertainments. If we respected only what is inevitable and has a right to be, music and poetry would resound along the streets. When we are unhurried and wise, we perceive that only great and worthy things have any permanent and absolute existence,—that petty fears and petty pleasures are but the shadow of the reality. This is always exhilarating and sublime. By closing the eyes and slumbering, and consenting to be deceived by shows, men establish and confirm their daily life of routine and habit everywhere, which still is built on purely illusory foundations. Children, who play life, discern its true law and relations more clearly than men, who fail to live it worthily, but who think that they are wiser by experience, that is, by failure. I have read in a Hindoo book, that "there was a king's son, who, being expelled in infancy from his native city, was brought up by a forester, and, growing up to maturity in that state, imagined himself to belong to the barbarous race with which he lived. One of his father's ministers having discovered him, revealed to him what he was, and the misconception of his character was removed, and he knew himself to be a prince. So soul," continues the Hindoo philosopher, "from the circumstances in which it is placed, mistakes its own character, until the truth is revealed to it by some holy teacher, and then it knows itself to be *Brahme*." I perceive that we inhabitants of New England live this mean life that we do because our vision does not penetrate the surface of things. We think that that *is* which *appears* to be. If a man should walk through this town and see only the reality, where, think you, would the "Mill-dam" go to? If he should give us an account of the realities he beheld there, we should not recognize the place in his description. Look at a meeting-house, or a courthouse, or a jail, or a shop, or a dwelling-house, and say what that thing really is before a true gaze, and they would all go to pieces in your account of them. Men esteem truth remote, in the outskirts of the system, behind the farthest star, before Adam and after the last man. In eternity there is indeed something true and sublime. But all these times and places and occasions are now and here. God himself culminates in the present moment, and will never be more divine in the lapse of all the ages. And we are enabled to apprehend at all what is sublime and noble only by the perpetual instilling and drenching of the reality that surrounds us. The universe constantly and obediently answers to our conceptions; whether we travel fast or slow, the track is laid for us. Let us spend our lives in conceiving then. The poet or the artist never yet had so fair and noble a design but some of his posterity at least could accomplish it.

Let us spend one day as deliberately as Nature, and not be thrown off the track by every nutshell and mosquito's wing that falls on the rails. Let us rise early and fast, or break fast, gently and without perturbation; let company come and let company go, let the bells ring and the children cry,—determined to make a day of it. Why should we knock under and go with the stream? Let us not be upset and overwhelmed in that terrible rapid and whirlpool called a dinner, situated in the meridian shallows. Weather this danger and you are safe, for the rest of the way is down hill. With unrelaxed nerves, with morning vigor, sail by it, looking another way, tied to the mast like Ulysses. If the engine whistles, let it whistle till it is hoarse for its pains. If the bell rings, why should we run? We will consider what kind of music they are like. Let us settle ourselves, and work and wedge our feet downward through the mud and slush of opinion, and prejudice, and tradition, and delusion, and appearance, that alluvion which covers the globe, through Paris and London, through New York and Boston and Concord, through church and state, through poetry and philosophy and religion, till we come to a hard bottom and rocks in place, which we can call *reality*, and say, This is, and no mistake; and then begin, having a *point d' appui*, below freshet and frost and fire, a place where you might found a wall or a state, or set a lamppost safely, or perhaps a gauge, not a Nilometer, but a Realometer, that future ages might know how deep a freshet of shams and appearances had gathered from time to time. If you stand right fronting and face to face to a fact, you will see the sun glimmer on both its surfaces, as if it were a cimeter, and feel its sweet edge dividing you through the heart and marrow, and so you will happily conclude your mortal career. Be it life or death, we crave only reality. If we are really dying, let us hear the rattle in our throats and feel cold in the extremities; if we are alive, let us go about our business.

Time is but the stream I go a-fishing in. I drink at it; but while I drink I see the sandy bottom and detect how shallow it is. Its thin current slides away, but eternity remains. I would drink deeper; fish in the sky, whose bottom is pebbly with stars. I cannot count one, I know not the first letter of the alphabet. I have always been regretting that I was not as wise as the day I was born. The intellect is a cleaver; it discerns and rifts its way into the secret of things. I do not wish to be any more busy with my hands than is necessary. My head is hands and feet. I feel all my best faculties concentrated in it. My instinct tells me that my head is an organ for burrowing, as some creatures use their snout, and fore-paws, and with it I would mine and burrow my way through these hills. I think that the richest vein is somewhere hereabouts; so by the divining rod and thin rising vapors I judge; and here I will begin to mine.

ACTIVITIES FOR WRITING AND DISCUSSION

1. Thoreau's prose abounds with memorable sentences. Underline and annotate any that strike you, and be prepared to share and discuss them in class. If you wish, copy some or all of these sentences into a notepad—or a

section within your reading notebook—that you designate for collecting memorable quotations. (For ideas about collecting and using such quotations, see pages 50–51 and 57–58.)

2. One distinctive aspect of Thoreau's style is his use of **allusions,** i.e., references to other literary works or characters or to historical persons, places, or events. Identify two or three allusions in the essay, look up the references, and analyze how the allusions work. Then generalize about how you think allusions strengthen or weaken the effectiveness of Thoreau's prose.

3. Thoreau takes a dim view of newspapers, the postal service, and other cultural resources and institutions that many of us regard as essential. Reread the relevant passages and summarize—as objectively as possible—the rationale behind Thoreau's criticisms. Then agree or disagree with Thoreau's critique.

4. Imagine you are Thoreau and you are living somewhere in America in the 2000s. In a personal essay, reveal how and where you (Thoreau) presently choose to live and why. Then review some contemporary American institutions, values, technologies, and/or behaviors as you believe Thoreau would.

Thomas Moore (b. 1940)

The Sacred Arts of Life

We can return now to one of Plato's expressions for care of the soul, *techne tou biou,* the craft of life. Care of the soul requires craft (*techne*)—skill, attention, and art. To live with a high degree of artfulness means to attend to the small things that keep the soul engaged in whatever we are doing, and it is the very heart of soul-making. From some grand overview of life, it may seem that only the big events are ultimately important. But to the soul, the most minute details and the most ordinary activities, carried out with mindfulness and art, have an effect far beyond their apparent insignificance.

Art is not found only in the painter's studio or in the halls of a museum, it also has its place in the store, the shop, the factory, and the home. In fact, when art is reserved as the province of professional artists, a dangerous gulf develops between the fine arts and the everyday arts. The fine arts are elevated and set apart from life, becoming too precious and therefore irrelevant. Having banished art to the museum, we fail to give it a place in ordinary life. One of the most effective forms of repression is to give a thing excessive honor.

Even in our art schools, a technical viewpoint is often dominant. The young painter learns about materials and schools of thought, but not about the soul of his vocation or the deeper significance of the content of his artwork. A voice major in a university music department expects to become an artist, but in her first lesson she is hooked up to an oscilloscope that will measure the parameters of her voice and indicate areas to be improved. The soul makes a quick exit before these purely technical approaches to learning.

The arts are important for all of us, whether or not we ourselves practice a particular discipline. Art, broadly speaking, is that which invites us into contemplation—a rare commodity in modern life. In that moment of contemplation, art intensifies the presence of the world. We see it more vividly and more deeply. The emptiness that many people complain dominates their lives comes in part from a failure to let the world in, to perceive it and engage it fully. Naturally, we'll feel empty if everything we do slides past without sticking. As we have seen, art *arrests* attention, an important service to the soul. Soul cannot thrive in a fast-paced life because being affected, taking things in and chewing on them, requires time.

Living artfully, therefore, might require something as simple as *pausing*. 5 Some people are incapable of being arrested by things because they are always on the move. A common symptom of modern life is that there is no time for thought, or even for letting impressions of a day sink in. Yet it is only when the world enters the heart that it can be made into soul. The vessel in which soul-making takes place is an inner container scooped out by reflection and wonder. There is no doubt that some people could spare themselves the expense and trouble of psychotherapy simply by giving themselves a few minutes each day for quiet reflection. This simple act would provide what is missing in their lives: a period of nondoing that is essential nourishment to the soul.

Akin to pausing, and just as important in care of the soul, is *taking time*. I realize these are extremely simple suggestions, but taken to heart they could transform a life, by allowing soul to enter. Taking time with things, we get to know them more intimately and to feel more genuinely connected to them. One of the symptoms of modern soullessness, an alienation from nature and things as well as from our fellow human beings, might be overcome if we took time with whatever we are dealing with.

Living artfully might require taking the time to buy things with soul for the home. Good linens, a special rug, or a simple teapot can be a source of enrichment not only in our own life, but also in the lives of our children and grandchildren. The soul basks in this extended sense of time. But we can't discover the soul in a thing without first taking time to observe it and be with it for a while. This kind of observation has a quality of intimacy about it; it's not just studying a consumer guide for factual and technical analysis. Surfaces, textures, and feel count as much as efficiency.

Certain things stimulate the imagination more than others, and that very blossoming of fantasy might be a sign of soul. An airline executive once talked to me about the struggle he was having in deciding between two jobs that had opened up for him. One was full of prestige and power, while the other was comfortable but quite ordinary. The first he felt he should consider because it was highly prized among his peers, but his thoughts about it were dry. The second one he imagined all day long. In his mind he had already begun to design his office and set his schedule. From the richness of his imagination of it, it was quite clear that the more lowly job appealed to his soul.

The ordinary arts we practice every day at home are of more importance to the soul than their simplicity might suggest. For example, I can't explain it, but I enjoy doing dishes. I've had an automatic dishwasher in my home for over a year, and I have never used it. What appeals to me, as I think about it, is the reverie induced by going through the ritual of washing, rinsing, and drying. Marie-Louise von Franz, the Swiss Jungian author, observes that weaving and knitting, too, are particularly good for the soul because they encourage reflection and reverie.

I also cherish the opportunity to hang clothes on a line outdoors. The fresh   10 smell, the wet fabrics, the blowing wind, and the drying sun go together to make an experience of nature and culture that is unique and particularly pleasurable for its simplicity. Deborah Hunter, a photographer, made a study several years ago of clothes on a line tossed by the wind. There was an element in these photographs, difficult to name, that touched upon vitality, the deep pleasures of ordinary life, and unseen forces of nature, all of which can be found around the house.

In a book not yet published, Jean Lall, the astrologer, observes that daily life at home is full of epiphanies. "Within our daily experience," she writes, "as keepers of home and gardens the spirits still move and speak if we but attend. They slip in through the cracks, making themselves felt in little breakdowns in appliances, unplanned sproutings in the flowerbeds, and sudden moments of blinding beauty, as where sunlight glances across a newly-waxed table or the wind stirs clean laundry into fresh choreography."

Many of the arts practiced at home are especially nourishing to the soul because they foster contemplation and demand a degree of artfulness, such as arranging flowers, cooking, and making repairs. I have a friend who is taking time over several months to paint a garden scene on a low panel of her dining room wall. Sometimes these ordinary arts bring out the individual, so that when you go into a home you can see the special character of your hosts in a particular aspect of their home.

Attending to the soul in these ordinary things usually leads to a more individual life, if not to an eccentric style. One of the things I love to do on a free afternoon is to visit Sleepy Hollow cemetery in Concord, Massachusetts. On a small, knobby hill deep in the cemetery is Emerson's grave, marked by a large, red-streaked boulder that contrasts with the typical gray rectangular gravestones all around him. Thoreau and Hawthorne lie a short distance away. For any who love Emerson's writing, this place is filled with soul. To me, his remarkable gravestone reflects his love of nature and mirrors both his greatness of soul and the irrepressible eccentricity of his imagination. The particular thrust of nature and the presence of a community of writers buried together make the place truly sacred.

When imagination is allowed to move to deep places, the sacred is revealed. The more different kinds of thoughts we experience around a thing and the deeper our reflections go as we are arrested by its artfulness, the more fully its sacredness can emerge. It follows, then, that living artfully can be a tonic for the secularization of life that characterizes our time. We can, of course, bring religion more closely in tune with ordinary life by immersing ourselves in formal rituals and traditional teachings; but we can also serve religion's soul by discovering the "natural religion" in all things. The route to this discovery is art, both the fine arts and those of everyday life. If we could loosen our grip on the functionality of life and let ourselves be arrested by the imaginal richness that surrounds all objects, natural and human-made, we might ground our secular attitudes in a religious sensibility and give ordinary life soul.

I'm suggesting that we consider sacredness from the point of view of soul 15 rather than spirit. From that angle, the sacred appears when imagination achieves unusual depth and fullness. The Bible, the Koran, Buddhist writings, and ritual books of all religions move us to imagine with exceptional range and depth. They bring us into wonder about the cosmos, about the far reaches of time past and present, and about ultimate values. But in a less formal way, any source of imagination that approaches this richness and depth helps create a religious sensibility. When they expose the deep images and themes that course through human life, so-called secular literature and art serve the religious impulse.

The medieval idea about learning, that theology is the ultimate science and all the others are "ancillary"—in humble service—is, to me, absolutely correct. Every issue, no matter how secular it appears to be, has a sacred dimension. If you press anything far enough, you will come up against either the holy or the demonic. Our secular sciences of physics, sociology, psychology, and the rest stop short of theological categories, thus preserving their scientific "objectivity," but also losing soul. Religious sensibility and soul are inseparable. I'm not saying that any particular religious affiliation or belief is essential to soul, but that a solid, palpable, and intellectually satisfying appreciation of the sacred is a sine qua non of living soulfully.

The theme requires a book of its own, but suffice it to say that theology is of concern for everyone, because our most ordinary experiences touch upon issues of such immense depth that they can only be considered religious. Recall Nicholas of Cusa's observation that God is the minimum as well as the maximum. The small things in everyday life are no less sacred than the great issues of human existence.

Becoming the artists and theologians of our own lives, we can approach the depth that is the domain of soul. When we leave art only to the accomplished painter and the museum, instead of fostering our own artful sensibilities through them, then our lives lose opportunities for soul. The same is true when we leave religion to church on the weekend. Then religion remains on the periphery of life, even if it is an exalted periphery, and life loses opportunities for soul. Fine art, like formal religion, is at times quite lofty, while soul in any context is lower case, ordinary, daily, familial and communal, felt, intimate, attached, engaged, involved, affected, ruminating, stirred, and poetic. The soul of a piece of art is known intimately, not remotely. It is felt, not just understood. So, too, the soul of religion lies in an immediate acquaintance with the angelic and the demonic. It is a daily involvement in mysteries and a personal quest for a corresponding ethic. Without soul, religion's truths and moral principles might be believed in, perhaps, and discussed, but they are not taken truly to heart and lived from the core of one's being.

Dreams: A Royal Road to Soul

Care of the soul involves "work," in the alchemical sense. It is impossible to care for the soul and live at the same time in unconsciousness. Sometimes soul work is exciting and inspiring, but often it is also challenging, requiring genuine courage. Rarely easy, work with the soul is usually placed squarely in that place we would rather not visit, in that emotion we don't want to feel, and in that understanding we would prefer to do without. The most honest route may be the most difficult to take. It is not easy to visit the place in ourselves that is most challenging and to look straight into the image that gives us the most fright; yet, there, where the work is most intense, is the source of soul.

Since we never want to take up the piece of our emotion that is most in need 20 of attention, I usually recommend to my patients that they give increased awareness to their dreams; for there they will find images that in waking life are very difficult to face. Dreams truly are the mythology of the soul and working with them forms a major piece in the project of making life more artful.

As a visit to any bookstore will demonstrate, there are many approaches to working with dreams. I would like to make a few concrete suggestions about what I consider key attitudes and strategies in dealing with dreams in a manner that preserves their integrity, allows meaning to emerge, and generally serves care of the soul.

Therapeutic work with dreams could be a model for less formal habits of giving dreams a serious place in our ordinary lives. When a person comes to me for an hour of therapy, I like to hear a dream or two early in the session. I don't like to listen to a dream and then immediately reach for an interpretation. It is better to let the dream lead us into new territory than to try to master the dream and figure it out at once. After the dream has been told, we might go on to talk about the person's life, since the therapy is almost always concerned with life situations. I may notice ways in which the dream offers us images and a language for talking about life with depth and imagination. Instead of trying to figure out the dream, we are letting the dream figure us out, allowing the dream to influence and shape our way of imagining. Usually, the main problem with life conundrums is that we don't bring to them enough imagination. We understand our difficulties literally and look for literal solutions, which rarely work precisely because they are part of the problem—lack of imagination. Dreams offer a fresh point of view.

In therapy it's tempting for both therapist and patient to translate a dream into theories and rationalizations that merely support the ideas of the therapist or the problematical attitudes of the patient. It is much better to let the dream interpret us rather than for us to become clever in interpreting the dream in ways most compatible with our existing ideas.

It is my experience that a dream reveals itself to the patient and the therapist slowly, gradually. I hear the dream and usually have a few impressions and ideas come to the surface immediately. But there might also be a great deal of confusion about the imagery. I try to hold back my need to overcome a dream with meaning. I tolerate its mood and let its puzzling imagery confound me, turn me away from my convictions in order to consider *its* mystery. Having patience with dreams is extremely important, and is more effective in the long run than any exercise of knowledge, techniques, and tricks. The dream reveals itself on its own timetable, but it does reveal itself.

It's important to trust your intuitions, which are not the same as your intellectual interpretations. For example, sometimes a person will tell me a dream and immediately recommend a way of understanding it or offer a bias toward one of the characters. A woman, for instance, relates a dream in which she has absent-mindedly left her front door open, allowing a man to sneak into her house. "It was a nightmare," she says, "I think the dream is telling me that I'm not careful enough about keeping myself protected. I'm too open." 25

You see, I'm given a dream and an interpretation. Even though I have considerable experience working with dreams and have been trained not to buy into whatever idea a patient gives me, I'm sometimes unconsciously affected by the interpretation. It's so reasonable. Of course, she is too vulnerable and is threatened by an intruder. But then I remember my first rule: trust your intuitions. I wonder if the "accidental" opening in the door might not be a good thing for this person. The opening may allow new personalities to enter her living space. I'm also aware that the unintentional may not be unintended at all: someone else besides the "I" may wish to leave the door open. The crack in the door may be an accident only to the ego.

There is often an apparent collusion between the dream-ego and the waking dreamer. As the dreamer tells the dream, she may slant her story in the direction of the "I" in the dream, thus convincing the listener to take a certain position in relation to the figures in the dream. Therefore, perhaps sometimes too much in compensation, I like to assume a rather perverse attitude when I hear the dream. I make a point of considering an angle different from the dreamer's. To put it more technically, I assume that in the telling of the dream the dreamer may be locked in the same complex as is the dream-ego. If I simply accept what the dreamer tells me, I may get caught in the dreamer's complex, and then I'm of no use. So I say to this dreamer: "Maybe it's not so bad that your usual thought about closing doors failed in this case. Maybe it allowed an entry that will prove to be beneficial. At least we can keep an open mind."

Speaking for other figures in the dream, sometimes against the bias of the dreamer, can open up a perspective on the dream that is extraordinarily revealing. Care of the soul, remember, does not necessarily mean care of the ego. Other characters may need acceptance and understanding. We may need to consider objectionable actions and characters as somehow necessary and even valuable.

A woman who is a writer tells a dream in which she catches a friend of hers smearing crayons all over the dreamer's typewriter. "It was an awful dream," she said, "and I know what it means. My inner child is always interfering with my adult work. If only I could grow up!"

Notice that this person, too, is quick to move toward interpretation. More than that, she wants me to take a certain position in relation to her dream. In a very subtle way, this desire is a defense against the otherness of the dream, its challenge. Soul and ego are often in a struggle which is sometimes mild and sometimes savage. So, I am careful not to assume that she is right about the content of the dream.

"Was your friend in the dream a child?" I ask.

"No, she was an adult. She was the age she is in life."

"Then why do you think she is being childish?"

"Crayons are a childish thing," she says as if stating the obvious.

"Can you tell me something about this friend of yours?" I am trying to break free of her strong views about her dream.

"She's very seductive, always wearing outlandish clothes—you know, bright colors and always low-cut."

"Is it possible," I say, taking a leap on the basis of her association, "that this colorful, sensual woman could be adding color, body, and some positive qualities of the child to your writing?"

"I suppose it's possible," she says, still unconvinced by this affront to her more satisfying interpretation.

One of the things that turned me away from her reading of the dream, apart from the general principle that we should avoid getting caught in the dream ego's complexes, was the negative narcissism in her judgment about the child: she didn't want to accept her own childlike ways. Once we moved away from her attachment to her usual way of thinking about herself, an attitude that strongly colored her own thoughts about the dream, we could go on to consider some truly fresh ideas about her life situation and her personal habits.

I am going into some detail about dreams not only because they give us a great deal of insight into our habits and our nature, but also because the way we relate to our dreams can be indicative of our way of dealing with all kinds of things, including our interpretations of the past, our current situation and problems, and the culture in the larger sense.

For example, another rule of thumb about dreams is that there is never a single, definitive reading. At another time, the same dream might reveal something altogether new. I like to treat dreams as if they were paintings, and paintings as if they were dreams. A Monet landscape might "mean" something different to various people who contemplate it. It might evoke entirely different reactions in the same person at different viewings. Over many years, a good painting will retain its power to mesmerize, satisfy, and evoke new reverie and wonder.

The same is true with dreams. A dream may survive a lifetime of neglect or an onslaught of interpretations and remain an icon and a fertile enigma for years of reflection. The point in working with a dream is never to translate it into a final meaning, but always to give it honor and respect, drawing from it as much meaningfulness and imaginative meditation as possible. Entering a dream should revitalize the imagination, not keep it in fixed and tired habits.

A simple but effective approach in working with images—whether they are from dreams, art, or personal stories—is never to stop listening to them and exploring them. Why do we listen to Bach's St. Matthew Passion more than once? Because it is the nature of a work of art, of any image, to reveal itself endlessly, one of the methods I use in therapy and in teaching is to listen to a reading of a dream or a story and say, when it is finished, "All right, let's try that again, differently."

Once a young man came to me with a letter he had written to his sweetheart. It was important to him because it expressed his deep feelings. He said he'd like to read it to me aloud. He read it slowly and expressively. When he was finished, I asked him if he'd read it again, with different emphasis. He did, and in this reading we heard different nuances of meaning. We tried it a third and a fourth time, and each time we learned something new. This little exercise points out the rich, multilayered nature of images of all kinds, and the advantage of never stopping in our exploration of them. The images, dreams, and experiences that are important to us will always have a multitude of possible readings and interpretations, because they are rich with imagination and soul.

I understand that this approach to imagination goes against the part of us 45 that longs for a conclusion and a destination in our search for meaning. This is another reason why *care* of the soul, in contrast to *understanding* the soul, amounts to a new paradigm for our modern way of life. It asks us to make a complete turnaround in our usual efforts to figure things out, suggesting a different set of values and new techniques in which we actually appreciate and enjoy the endless unraveling of meaning, the infinitely rich and deep layering of poetics within the shifting, fluid fabric of experience.

The desire to squeeze a single meaning out of a dream or a work of art or a tale from life is inherently and profoundly Promethean. We want to steal fire from the gods for the sake of humanity. We want to replace divine mystery with human rationality. But this loss of complexity and mystery in our everyday response to life stories entails a loss of soul as well, because soul always manifests itself in mystery and multiplicity.

Dreams themselves often show us the way to understand them: they pull the dreamer deep into a body of water, or down into a pit, or down an elevator to a basement, or down a dark stairway, or deep into an alley. Typically, the dreamer, preferring height and light, is afraid to make the downward move into darkness. When I taught in the university, students frequently told me dreams of going into the library, getting on an elevator, then finding themselves in an ancient basement. The dream is not surprising, given the fact that the life of academia is so much an Apollonic, upper-world, ivory tower affair, and stands as a metaphor for all our attempts at understanding.

A woman who worked for a large appliance corporation once told me a dream in which she and her husband got off an elevator on a lower floor of the building, only to find the entire area under water. Together they floated in the water through hallways and streets until they arrived at a wonderful restaurant where they sat and ate a delicious dinner. This, too, is an image of dreamwork: allowing oneself to move around in the liquid atmosphere of fantasy and finding nourishment there. In dreams, which need never be taken literally or according to the laws of nature, we can breathe in a watery atmosphere. Dreams *are* watery: they resist all efforts to make them fixed and solid. We think we can only survive in the airy realms of thought and reason, but this dreamer found that she could be fed in gourmet style in that thicker atmosphere where imagination and life are fluid.

The Guiding Daimon

An approach often taken to images is to find a meaning outside the image itself. A cigar in a dream is considered a phallic symbol instead of a cigar. A woman is an anima figure instead of a particular woman. A child is the "child part of myself" instead of simply the child of the dream. We think of imagination as a kind of symbolic thinking, with, as Freud put it, a latent and a manifest meaning. If we could "decipher" the given symbols, to use a popular rationalistic word, we could learn the meaning that is hidden in the image.

But there is another possible way to understand the creations of the dream 50 world. What if there were no hidden meaning, no underlying message? What if we chose to confront images in all their mystery, deciding whether to follow their lead or to struggle with them?

The Greeks referred to the multitude of unnamed spirits that motivate and guide life as daimons. Socrates claimed to have lived his life according to the dictates of his daimon. In more recent times, W.B. Yeats warned that the daimon both inspires and threatens. In the chapter of *Memories, Dreams, Reflections* entitled "Late Thoughts," Jung, too, discusses the daimon. "We know that something unknown, alien, does come our way, just as we know that we do not ourselves *make* a dream or an inspiration, but that it somehow arises of its own accord. What does happen to us in this manner can be said to emanate from mana, from a daimon, a god, or the unconscious." He goes on to say that he prefers the term *the unconscious,* but he might just as well say *daimon.* Daimonic living is a response to the movements of imagination. When Jung was building his tower, workmen delivered a large piece of stone that was the wrong size. He took this "mistake" as the work of his Mercurial daimon and used the stone for one of his most important sculptures, the Bollingen Stone.

In the fifteenth century, Ficino, in *his* book on care of the soul, recommended finding the guardian daimon that is with us from the beginning: "Whoever examines himself thoroughly will find his own daimon." Rilke also regarded the daimon with respect. In his *Letters to a Young Poet* he suggests diving deeply into oneself in order to find one's own nature: "Go into yourself and see how deep the place is from which your life flows." Rilke is giving advice to a young man who wants to know whether he is called to be an artist, but his recommendation applies to anyone who wants to live everyday life with art. The soul wants to be in touch with that deep place from which life flows, without translating its offerings into familiar concepts. The best way to fulfill this desire is to give attention to the images that arise as independent beings from the springs of day-to-day imagination.

One implication of offering respect to the dream world is that we have to re-imagine imagination itself. Instead of seeing it as a particularly creative form of mind work, we could understand it more along Greek mythological lines, as a spring from which autonomous beings arise. Our relationship to it would change as well, from attempting to translate florid fantasy into reasonable terms to observing and entering a veritable world of personalities, geographies, animals, and events— all irreducible to completely understandable or controllable terms.

We would realize that the images of dreams and art are not puzzles to be solved, and that imagination hides its meaningfulness as much as it reveals it. In order to be affected by a dream, it isn't necessary to understand it or even to mine it for meanings. Merely giving our attention to such imagery, granting its autonomy and mystery, goes a long way toward shifting the center of consciousness from understanding to response. To live in the presence of the daimonic is to obey inner laws and urgencies. Cicero said that it is the *animus*—the Latin translation of *daimon*—that accounts for who you are. Ficino warned against living in conflict with the daimon lest you succumb to the worst kind of soul sickness. As an example, he says you should never decide where to live without taking into full consideration the demands of the daimon, which may appear as an intuitive attraction or inhibition.

The source from which life flows is so deep that it is experienced as "other." Speaking in the ancient language of the daimonic helps bring imagination into our very sense of self. Our relationship to the deep source of life becomes interpersonal, a dramatic tension between self and angel. In this dialogue, life also becomes more artful, in some cases even dramatic. We see this in people we label psychotic. Most of their actions are explicitly dramatic. Their deep "others," the personalities who play significant roles in their lives, appear in full dress. Writers talk about the characters of their fiction as people with will and intention. The novelist Margaret Atwood said once in an interview, "If the author gets too bossy, the characters may remind her that, though she is their creator, they are to some extent her creator as well."

Art teaches us to respect imagination as something far beyond human creation and intention. To live our ordinary life artfully is to have this sensibility about the things of daily life, to live more intuitively and to be willing to surrender a measure of our rationality and control in return for the gifts of soul.

The Soul Arts

Care of the soul may take the form of living in a fully embodied imagination, being an artist at home and at work. You don't have to be a professional in order to bring art into the care of your soul; anyone can have an art studio at home, for instance. Like Jung, Black Elk, and Ficino, we could decorate our homes with images from our dreams and waking fantasy.

One of my own forms of expression is to play the piano in times of strong emotion. I remember well the day Martin Luther King, Jr., was killed. I was so overwhelmed that I went to the piano and played Bach for three hours. The music gave form and voice to my scrambled emotions, without explanations and rational interpretations.

The stuff of the world is there to be made into images that become for us tabernacles of spirituality and containers of mystery. If we don't allow soul its place in our lives, we are forced to encounter these mysteries in fetishes and symptoms, which in a sense are pathological art forms, the gods in our diseases. The example of artists teaches us that every day we can transform ordinary experience into the material of soul—in diaries, poems, drawings, music, letters, watercolors.

In a letter on soul-making to his brother George, Keats describes the process of transforming world into soul with the image of a school: "I will call the world a School instituted for the purpose of teaching little children to read—I will call the human heart the hornbook used in that School—and I will call the child able to read, the Soul made from that school and its hornbook. Do you not see how necessary a World of Pains and troubles is to school an Intelligence and make it a soul?" 60

As we read our experiences and learn to express them artfully, we are making life more soulful. Our homely arts arrest the flow of life momentarily so that events can be submitted to the alchemy of reflection. In a letter to a friend, we can deepen the impressions of experience and settle them in the heart where they can become the foundation for soul. Our great museums of art are simply a grand model for the more modest museum that is our home. There is no reason not to imagine our own homes as a place where the Muses can do their work of inspiration daily.

Another advantage to the soul of practicing the ordinary arts is the gift they leave for future generations. Tradition says that the soul thrives in a sense of time much greater than that of consciousness. To the soul the past is alive and valuable, and so is the future. As we perform the alchemy of sketching or writing upon our daily experience, we are preserving our thoughts for those who follow us. The community made by art transcends the limits of a personal lifetime, so that we can be instructed in our own soul work by the letters of John Keats to his brother.

In the modern world, in which we live mainly for the moment, it is easy to overlook the taste of the soul for a greater sense of time and a profound notion of community. We tend to give superficial explanations for our actions, to speak in literal terms instead of focusing on the reasons of the heart. A man explaining to me why he was getting a divorce went on and on with minor complaints about his wife. What he didn't say was what was obvious from our other conversations, that his heart was going through a major change. He wanted a new life, but tried to justify all the accompanying pain with superficial reasons. Because he didn't speak deeply about what was going on with him, he was cutting himself off from the soul of his divorce.

But when you read the letters of Keats, Rilke, or other poets you find a passionate search for expression and language adequate to the pleasures and pains of life. We can learn from them the importance to everyone, not just poets, of the effort to translate experience into words and pictures. The point of art is not simply to express ourselves, but to create an external, concrete form in which the soul of our lives can be evoked and contained.

Children paint every day and love to show their works on walls and refriger- 65 ator doors. But as we become adults, we abandon this important soul task of childhood. We assume, I suppose, that children are just learning motor coordination and alphabets. But maybe they are doing something more fundamental: finding forms that reflect what is going on in their souls. When we grow up and begin to think of the art gallery as much more advanced than the refrigerator door, we lose an important ritual of childhood, giving it away to the professional artist. We are then left with mere rational reasons for our lives, feelings of emptiness and confusion, expensive visits to a psychotherapist, and a compulsive attachment to pseudoimages, such as shallow television programs. When our own images no longer have a home, a personal museum, we drown our sense of loss in pale substitutes, trashy novels or formulaic movies.

As the poets and painters of centuries have tried to tell us, art is not about the expression of talent or the making of pretty things. It is about the preservation and containment of soul. It is about arresting life and making it available for contemplation. Art captures the eternal in the everyday, and it is the eternal that feeds soul—the whole world in a grain of sand.

Leonardo da Vinci asks an interesting question in one of his notebooks: "Why does the eye see a thing more clearly in dreams than the imagination when awake?" One answer is that the eye of the soul perceives the eternal realities so important to the heart. In waking life, most of us see only with our physical eyes, even though we could, with some effort of imagination, glimpse fragments of eternity in the most ordinary passing events. Dream teaches us to look with that other eye, the eye that in waking life belongs to the artist, to each of us as artist.

When we see pain on a tortured person's face, we might glimpse for a second the image of Jesus crucified, a reality that artists for centuries have shown in infinite variation and detail and one that enters the lives of all of us at one time or another. We might look at a woman in a jewelry shop with the eyes of D.H. Lawrence, who saw Aphrodite in the body of the woman washing her clothes in a river. We might see a Cézanne still life in a momentary glance at our own kitchen table. When a summer breeze blows through an open window as we sit reading in a rare half-hour of quiet, we might recall one of the hundreds of annunciations painters have given us, reminding us that it is the habit of angels to visit in moments of silent reading.

A soul-centered understanding of art sees the interpenetration of poetic image and ordinary life. Art shows us what is already there in the ordinary, but without art we live under the illusion that there is only time, and not eternity. As we practice our daily arts, if only in the composing of a heart-felt letter, we are unearthing the eternal from within ordinary time, engaging in the special qualities, themes, and circumstances of the soul. Soul thrives as we jot down a thought in our diary or note a dream, and give body to a slight influx of eternity. Our notebooks then truly become our own private gospels and sutras, our holy books, and our simple paintings truly serve as icons, every bit as significant in the work of our own soul as the wonderful icons of the Eastern churches are for their congregations.

Care of the soul is not a project of self-improvement nor a way of being released from the troubles and pains of human existence. It is not at all concerned with living properly or with emotional health. These are the concerns of temporal, heroic, Promethean life. Care of the soul touches another dimension, in no way separate from life, but not identical either with the problem solving that occupies so much of our consciousness. We care for the soul solely by honoring its expressions, by giving it time and opportunity to reveal itself, and by living life in a way that fosters the depth, interiority, and quality in which it flourishes. Soul is its own purpose and end. 70

To the soul, memory is more important than planning, art more compelling than reason, and love more fulfilling than understanding. We know we are well on the way toward soul when we feel attachment to the world and the people around us and when we live as much from the heart as from the head. We know soul is being cared for when our pleasures feel deeper than usual, when we can let go of the need to be free of complexity and confusion, and when compassion takes the place of distrust and fear. Soul is interested in the differences among cultures and individuals, and within ourselves it wants to be expressed in uniqueness if not in outright eccentricity.

Therefore, when in the midst of my confusion and my stumbling attempts to live a transparent life, *I* am the fool, and not everyone around me, then I know I am discovering the power of the soul to make a life interesting. Ultimately, care of the soul results in an individual "I" I never would have planned for or maybe even wanted. By caring for the soul faithfully, every day, we step out of the way and let our full genius emerge. Soul coalesces into the mysterious philosophers' stone, that rich, solid core of personality the alchemists sought, or it opens into the peacock's tail—a revelation of the soul's colors and a display of its dappled brilliance.

ACTIVITIES FOR WRITING AND DISCUSSION

1. Since Moore's essay is quite long, try to read it in two or more sittings, focusing on sections that strike you and skimming over those that don't. In your notebook, respond using either:
    a. The "Four-Step Process for Writing" from Reading described in Chapter 2; or
    b. Idea #1 from the "Ten Ideas" described in Chapter 3.

2. In paragraph 45 Moore writes: "*[C]are* of the soul, in contrast to *understanding* the soul, amounts to a new paradigm for our modern way of life." Read the context in which this sentence appears. Then consider:
    a. Some differences between "caring" and "understanding" as Moore seems to use those terms. Can caring and understanding be at odds with each other? If so how and in what situations?
    b. In what ways do you think Moore's statement, quoted above, is accurate or inaccurate?

3. In his discussion of "The Guiding Daimon," Moore writes:

    The source from which life flows is so deep that it is experienced as "other." . . . Our relationship to the deep source of life [i.e., the daimon] becomes interpersonal, a dramatic tension between self and angel

    Explain what you think Moore means by "the daimon." Then do one of the following:
    a. Over a period of days, think about the nature of your own "angel" or "daimon"; describe its power, mystery, promises, and dangers. Then write a dialogue—or a series of short dialogues—between your own "self" and this angel or daimon.
    b. List the names of some outstanding people, living or dead, whom you admire. Choose one such person and write about the nature of the "daimon" that you imagine guides (or guided) that person in his or her life.

MICHAEL DORRIS (1945–1997)

Life Stories

In most cultures, adulthood is equated with self-reliance and responsibility, yet often Americans do not achieve this status until we are in our late twenties or early thirties—virtually the entire average lifespan of a person in a traditional non-Western society. We tend to treat prolonged adolescence as a warm-up for real life, as a wobbly ladder between childhood and legal maturity. Whereas a nineteenth-century Cheyenne or Lakota teenager was expected to alter self-conception in a split-second vision, we often meander through an analogous rite of passage for more than a decade—through high school, college, graduate school.

Though he had never before traveled alone outside his village, the Plains Indian male was expected at puberty to venture solo into the wilderness. There he had to fend for and sustain himself while avoiding the menace of unknown dangers, and there he had absolutely to remain until something happened that would transform him. Every human being, these tribes believed, was entitled to at least one moment of personal, enabling insight.

Anthropology proposes feasible psychological explanations for why this flash was eventually triggered: fear, fatigue, reliance on strange foods, the anguish of loneliness, stress, and the expectation of ultimate success all contributed to a state of receptivity. Every sense was quickened, alerted to perceive deep meaning, until at last the interpretation of an unusual event—a dream, a chance encounter, or an unexpected vista—reverberated with significance. Through this unique prism, abstractly preserved in a vivid memory or song, a boy caught foresight of both his adult persona and his vocation, the two inextricably entwined.

The best approximations that many of us get to such a heady sense of eventuality come in the performance of the jobs we hold during summer vacation. Summers are intermissions, and once we hit our teens it is during these breaks in our structured regimen that we initially taste the satisfaction of remuneration that is earned, not merely doled. Tasks defined as work are not graded, they are compensated; they have a worth that is inarguable because it translates into hard currency. Wage labor—and in the beginning, this generally means a confining, repetitive chore for which we are quickly overqualified—paradoxically brings a sense of blooming freedom. At the outset, the complaint to a peer that business supersedes fun is oddly liberating—no matter what drudgery requires your attention, it is by its very required nature serious and adult.

At least that's how it seemed to me. I come from a line of people hard hit by 5 the Great Depression. My mother and her sisters went to work early in their teens—my mother operated a kind of calculator known as a comptometer while her sisters spent their days, respectively, at a peanut factory and at Western Union. My grandmother did piecework sewing. Their efforts, and the Democratic Party, saw them through, and to this day they never look back without appreciation for their later solvency. They take nothing for granted. Accomplishments are celebrated, possessions are valuable, in direct proportion to the labor entailed to acquire them; anything easily won or bought on credit is suspect. When I was growing up we were far from wealthy, but what money we had was correlated to the hours one of us had logged. My eagerness to contribute to, or at least not diminish, the coffer was countered by the arguments of those whose salaries kept me in school: my higher education was a sound group investment. The whole family was adamant that I have the opportunities they had missed and, no matter how much I objected, they stinted themselves to provide for me.

Summer jobs were therefore a relief, an opportunity to pull a share of the load. As soon as the days turned warm I began to peruse the classifieds, and when the spring semester was done, I was ready to punch a clock. It even felt right. Work in June, July, and August had an almost biblical aspect: in the hot, canicular weather your brow sweats, just as God had ordained. Moreover, summer jobs had the luxury of being temporary. No matter how onerous, how off my supposed track, employment terminated with the falling leaves and I was back to real life. So, during each annual three-month leave from secondary school and later from the university, I compiled an eclectic resumé: lawn cutter, hair sweeper in a barber shop, lifeguard, delivery boy, mail carrier, file clerk, youth program coordinator on my Montana reservation, ballroom dance instructor, theater party promoter, night-shift hospital records keeper, human adding machine in a Paris bank, encyclopedia salesman, newspaper stringer, recreation bus manager, salmon fisherman.

The summer I was eighteen a possibility arose for a rotation at the post office, and I grabbed it. There was something casually sophisticated about work that required a uniform, about having a federal ranking, even if it was GS-1 (Temp/Sub), and it was flattering to be entrusted with a leather bag containing who knew what important correspondence. Every day I was assigned a new beat, usually in a rough neighborhood avoided whenever possible by regular carriers, and I proved quite capable of complicating what would normally be fairly routine missions. The low point came on the first of August when I diligently delivered four blocks' worth of welfare checks to the right numbers on the wrong streets. It is no fun to snatch unexpected wealth from the hands of those who had but moments previously opened their mailboxes and received a bonus.

After my first year of college, I lived with relatives on an Indian reservation in eastern Montana and filled the only post available: Coordinator of Youth Programs. I was seduced by the language of the announcement into assuming that there existed Youth Programs to be coordinated. In fact, the Youth consisted of a dozen bored, disgruntled kids—most of them my cousins—who had nothing better to do each day than to show up at what was euphemistically called "the gym" and hate whatever Program I had planned for them. The Youth ranged in age from fifteen to five and seemed to have as their sole common ambition the determination to smoke cigarettes. This put them at immediate and ongoing odds with the Coordinator, who on his first day naively encouraged them to sing the "Doe, a deer, a female deer" song from *The Sound of Music*. They looked at me, that bleak morning, and I looked at them, each boy and girl equipped with a Pall Mall behind an ear, and we all knew we faced a long, struggle-charged battle. It was to be a contest of wills, the hearty and wholesome versus prohibited vice. I stood for dodge ball, for collecting bugs in glass jars, for arts and crafts; they had pledged a preternatural allegiance to sloth. The odds were not in my favor and each waking dawn I experienced the light-headedness of anticipated exhaustion, that thrill of giddy dissociation in which nothing seems real or of great significance. Finally, I went with the flow and learned to inhale.

The next summer, I decided to find work in an urban setting for a change, and was hired as a general office assistant in the Elsa Hoppenfeld Theatre Party Agency, located above Sardi's restaurant in New York City. The agency consisted of Elsa Hoppenfeld herself, Rita Frank, her regular deputy, and me. Elsa was a gregarious Viennese woman who established contacts through honesty, hard work, and personal charm, and she spent much of the time away from the building courting trade. Rita was therefore both my immediate supervisor and constant companion; she had the most incredible fingernails I had ever seen— long, carefully shaped pegs lacquered in cruel primary colors and hard as stone—and an attitude about her that could only be described as zeal.

The goal of a theater party agent is to sell blocks of tickets to imminent   10
Broadway productions, and the likely buyers are charities, B'nai B'riths, Hadas-sahs, and assorted other fund-raising organizations. We received commissions on volume, and so it was necessary to convince a prospect that a play—prefer-ably an expensive musical—for which we had reserved the rights to seats would be a boffo smash hit.

The object of our greatest expectation that season was an extravaganza called *Chu Chem,* a saga that aspired to ride the coattails of *Fiddler on the Roof* into entertainment history. It starred the estimable Molly Picon and told the story of a family who had centuries ago gone from Israel to China during the Diaspora, yet had, despite isolation in an alien environment, retained orthodox culture and habits. The crux of the plot revolved around a man with several marriageable daughters and nary a kosher suitor within five thousand miles. For three months Rita and I waxed eloquent in singing the show's praises. We sat in our little office, behind facing desks, and every noon while she redid her nails I ordered out from a deli that offered such exotic (to me) delicacies as fried egg sandwiches, lox and cream cheese, pastrami, tongue. I developed of necessity and habit a telephone voice laced with a distinctly Yiddish accent. It could have been a great career. However, come November, *Chu Chem* bombed. Its closing was such a financial catastrophe for all concerned that when the fol-lowing January one Monsieur Dupont advertised on the placement board at my college, I decided to put an ocean between me and my former trusting clientele.

M. Dupont came to campus with the stated purpose of interviewing candi-dates for teller positions in a French bank. Successful applicants, required to be fluent *en français,* would be rewarded with three well-paid months and a rent-free apartment in Paris. On my way to the language lab, I registered for an ap-pointment.

The only French in the interview was *Bonjour, ça va?*, after which M. Dupont switched into English and described the wonderful deal on charter air flights that would be available to those who got the nod. Round-trip to Amsterdam, via Reykjavík, leaving the day after exams and returning in mid-September, no changes or substitutions. I signed up on the spot. I was to be a *banquier,* with a *pied-à-terre* in Montparnasse!

Unfortunately, when I arrived with only $50 in traveler's checks in my pocket—the flight had cleaned me out, but who needed money since my paycheck started right away—no one in Paris had ever heard of M. Dupont. *Alors.*

I stood in the Gare du Nord and considered my options. There weren't any. I 15 scanned a listing of Paris hotels and headed for the cheapest one: the Hotel Villedo, $10 a night. The place had an ambiance that I persuaded myself was antique, despite the red light above the sign. The only accommodation available was "the bridal suite," a steal at $20. The glass door to my room didn't lock and in the adjacent room there was a rather continual floor show, but at some point I must have dozed off. When I awoke the church bells were ringing, the sky was pink, and I felt renewed. No little setback was going to spoil my adventure. I stretched, then walked to a mirror that hung above the sink next to the bed. I leaned forward to punctuate my resolve with a confident look in the eye.

The sink disengaged and fell to the floor. Water gushed. In panic I rummaged through my open suitcase, stuffed two pairs of underpants into the pipe to quell the flow, and before the dam broke, I was out the door. I barreled through the lobby of the first bank I passed, asked to see the director, and told the startled man my sad story. For some reason, whether from shock or pity, he hired me at $1.27 an hour to be a cross-checker of foreign currency transactions, and with two phone calls found me lodgings at a commercial school's dormitory.

From 8 to 5 each weekday my duty was to sit in a windowless room with six impeccably dressed people, all of whom were totaling identical additions and subtractions. We were highly dignified with each other, very professional, no *tutoyer*ing. Monsieur Saint presided, but the formidable Mademoiselle was the true power; she oversaw each of our columns and shook her head sadly at my American-shaped numbers.

My legacy from that summer, however, was more than an enduring penchant for crossed 7s. After I had worked for six weeks, M. Saint asked me during a coffee break why I didn't follow the example of other foreign students he had known and depart the office at noon in order to spend the afternoon touring the sights of Paris with the Alliance Française.

"Because," I replied in my halting French, "that costs money. I depend upon my full salary the same as any of you." M. Saint nodded gravely and said no more, but then on the next Friday he presented me with a white envelope along with my check.

"Do not open this until you have left the Société Général," he said omi- 20 nously. I thought I was fired for the time I had mixed up kroner and guilders, and, once on the sidewalk, I steeled myself to read the worst. I felt the quiet panic of blankness.

"Dear Sir," I translated the perfectly formed script. "You are a person of value. It is not correct that you should be in our beautiful city and not see it. Therefore we have amassed a modest sum to pay the tuition for a two-week afternoon program for you at the Alliance Française. Your wages will not suffer, for it is your assignment to appear each morning in this bureau and reacquaint us with the places you have visited. We shall see them afresh through your eyes." The letter had thirty signatures, from the director to the janitor, and stuffed inside the envelope was a sheaf of franc notes in various denominations.

I rushed back to the tiny office. M. Saint and Mademoiselle had waited, and accepted my gratitude with their usual controlled smiles and precise handshakes. But they had blown their Gallic cover, and for the next ten days and then through all the weeks until I went home in September, our branch was awash with sightseeing paraphernalia. Everyone had advice, favorite haunts, criticisms of the Alliance's choices or explanations. Paris passed through the bank's granite walls as sweetly as a June breeze through a window screen, and ever afterward the lilt of overheard French, a photograph of Sacre-Coeur or the Louvre, even a monthly bank statement, recalls to me that best of all summers.

I didn't wind up in an occupation with any obvious connection to the careers I sampled during my school breaks, but I never altogether abandoned those brief professions either. They were jobs not so much to be held as to be weighed, absorbed, and incorporated, and, collectively, they carried me forward into adult life like an escalator, unfolding a particular pattern at once amazing and inevitable.

ACTIVITIES FOR WRITING AND DISCUSSION

1. Reread the last sentence in the essay.
   a. Interpret this concluding statement. What do you think Dorris means by it?
   b. In an essay, discuss one or two jobs in your own past that had a particular impact on you. Tell some specific stories about those jobs (as Dorris does) to make them vivid for a reader. Think of a crucial moment in any of the stories when there was dialogue, and write the dialogue. To what extent have you "weighed, absorbed, and incorporated" those jobs, and what "particular pattern" (if any) do you perceive in them?

2. Think of an early job that particularly influenced you. Write a letter (sent or unsent) to your employer, in which you recount your experiences on that job and how they affected you, for better or worse, in the short and/or long term.

Linda Hogan (b. 1947)

Waking Up the Rake

In the still dark mornings, my grandmother would rise up from her bed and put wood in the stove. When the fire began to burn, she would sit in front of its warmth and let down her hair. It had never been cut and it knotted down in two long braids. When I was fortunate enough to be there, in those red Oklahoma mornings, I would wake up with her, stand behind her chair, and pull the brush through the long strands of her hair. It cascaded down her back, down over the chair, and touched the floor.

We were the old and the new, bound together in front of the snapping fire, woven like a lifetime's tangled growth of hair. I saw my future in her body and face, and her past was alive in me. We were morning people, and in all of earth's mornings the new intertwines with the old. Even new, a day itself is ancient, old with earth's habit of turning over and over again.

Years later, I was sick, and I went to a traditional healer. The healer was dark and thin and radiant. The first night I was there, she also lit a fire. We sat before it, smelling the juniper smoke. She asked me to tell her everything, my life spoken in words, a case history of living, with its dreams and losses, the scars and wounds we all bear from being in the world. She smoked me with cedar smoke, wrapped a sheet around me, and put me to bed, gently, like a mother caring for her child.

The next morning she nudged me awake and took me outside to pray. We faced east where the sun was beginning its journey on our side of earth.

The following morning in red dawn, we went outside and prayed. The sun 5 was a full orange eye rising up the air. The morning after that we did the same, and on Sunday we did likewise.

The next time I visited her it was a year later, and again we went through the same prayers, standing outside facing the early sun. On the last morning I was there, she left for her job in town. Before leaving, she said, "Our work is our altar."

Those words have remained with me.

Now I am a disciple of birds. The birds that I mean are eagles, owls, and hawks. I clean cages at the Birds of Prey Rehabilitation Foundation. It is the work I wanted to do, in order to spend time inside the gentle presence of the birds.

There is a Sufi saying that goes something like this: "Yes, worship God, go to church, sing praises, but first tie your camel to the post." This cleaning is the work of tying the camel to a post.

I pick up the carcasses and skin of rats, mice, and of rabbits. Some of them 10 have been turned inside out by the sharp-beaked eaters, so that the leathery flesh becomes a delicately veined coat for the inner fur. It is a boneyard. I rake the smooth fragments of bones. Sometimes there is a leg or shank of deer to be picked up.

In this boneyard, the still-red vertebrae lie on the ground beside an open rib cage. The remains of a rabbit, a small intestinal casing, holds excrement like beads in a necklace. And there are the clean, oval pellets the birds spit out, filled with fur, bone fragments and now and then, a delicate sharp claw that looks as if it were woven inside. A feather, light and soft, floats down a current of air, and it is also picked up.

Over time, the narrow human perspective from which we view things expands. A deer carcass begins to look beautiful and rich in its torn redness, the muscle and bone exposed in the shape life took on for a while as it walked through meadows and drank at creeks.

And the bone fragments have their own stark beauty, the clean white jaw bones with ivory teeth small as the head of a pin still in them. I think of medieval physicians trying to learn about our private, hidden bodies by cutting open the stolen dead and finding the splendor inside, the grace of every red organ, and the smooth, gleaming bone.

This work is an apprenticeship, and the birds are the teachers. Sweet-eyed barn owls, such taskmasters, asking us to be still and slow and to move in time with their rhythms, not our own. The short-eared owls with their startling yellow eyes require the full presence of a human. The marsh hawks, behind their branches, watch our every move.

There is a silence needed here before a person enters the bordered world the 15 birds inhabit, so we stop and compose ourselves before entering their doors, and we listen to the musical calls of the eagles, the sound of wings in air, the way their feet with sharp claws, many larger than our own hands, grab hold of a perch. Then we know we are ready to enter, and they are ready for us.

The most difficult task the birds demand is that we learn to be equal to them, to feel our way into an intelligence that is different from our own. A friend, awed at the thought of working with eagles, said, "Imagine knowing an eagle." I answered her honestly, "It isn't so much that we know the eagles. It's that they know us."

And they know that we are apart from them, that as humans we have somehow fallen from our animal grace, and because of that we maintain a distance from them, though it is not always a distance of heart. The places we inhabit, even sharing a common earth, must remain distinct and separate. It was our presence that brought most of them here in the first place, nearly all of them injured in a clash with the human world. They have been shot, or hit by cars, trapped in leg hold traps, poisoned, ensnared in wire fences. To ensure their survival, they must remember us as the enemies that we are. We are the embodiment of a paradox; we are the wounders and we are the healers.

There are human lessons to be learned here, in the work. Fritjof Capra wrote: "Doing work that has to be done over and over again helps us to recognize the natural cycles of growth and decay, of birth and death, and thus become aware of the dynamic order of the universe." And it is true, in whatever we do, the brushing of hair, the cleaning of cages, we begin to see the larger order of things. In this place, there is a constant coming to terms with both the sacred place life occupies, and with death. Like one of those early physicians who discovered the strange, inner secrets of our human bodies, I'm filled with awe at the very presence of life, not just the birds, but a horse contained in its living fur, a dog alive and running. What a marvel it is, the fine shape life takes in all of us. It is equally marvelous that life is quickly turned back to earth-colored ants and the soft white maggots that are time's best and closest companions. To sit with the eagles and their flute-like songs, listening to the longer flute of wind sweep through the lush grasslands, is to begin to know the natural laws that exist apart from our own written ones.

One of those laws, that we carry deep inside us, is intuition. It is lodged in a place even the grave-robbing doctors could not discover. It's a blood-written code that directs us through life. The founder of this healing center, Sigrid Ueblacker, depends on this inner knowing. She watches, listens, and feels her way to an understanding of each eagle and owl. This vision, as I call it, directs her own daily work at healing the injured birds and returning them to the wild.

"Sweep the snow away," she tells me. "The Swainson's hawks should be in Argentina this time of year and should not have to stand in the snow."

I sweep.

And that is in the winter when the hands ache from the cold, and the water freezes solid and has to be broken out for the birds, fresh buckets carried over icy earth from the well. In summer, it's another story. After only a few hours the food begins to move again, as if resurrected to life. A rabbit shifts a bit. A mouse turns. You could say that they have been resurrected, only with a life other than the one that left them. The moving skin swarms with flies and their offspring, ants, and a few wasps, busy at their own daily labor.

Even aside from the expected rewards for this work, such as seeing an eagle healed and winging across the sky it fell from, there are others. An occasional snake, beautiful and sleek, finds its way into the cage one day, eats a mouse and is too fat to leave, so we watch its long muscular life stretched out in the tall grasses. Or, another summer day, taking branches to be burned with a pile of wood near the little creek, a large turtle with a dark and shining shell slips soundlessly into the water, its presence a reminder of all the lives beyond these that occupy us.

One green morning, an orphaned owl perches nervously above me while I clean. Its downy feathers are roughed out. It appears to be twice its size as it clacks its beak at me, warning me: Stay back. Then, fearing me the way we want it to, it bolts off the perch and flies, landing by accident onto the wooden end of my rake, before it sees that a human is an extension of the tool, and it flies again to a safer place, while I return to raking.

The word *rake* means to gather or heap up, to smooth the broken ground.   25 And that's what this work is, all of it, the smoothing over of broken ground, the healing of the severed trust we humans hold with earth. We gather it back together again with great care, take the broken pieces and fragments and return them to the sky. It is work at the borderland between species, at the boundary between injury and healing.

There is an art to raking, a very fine art, one with rhythm in it, and life. On the days I do it well, the rake wakes up. Wood that came from dark dense forests seems to return to life. The water that rose up through the rings of that wood, the minerals of earth mined upward by the burrowing tree roots, all come alive. My own fragile hand touches the wood, a hand full of my own life, including that which rose each morning early to watch the sun return from the other side of the planet. Over time, these hands will smooth the rake's wooden handle down to a sheen.

Raking. It is a labor round and complete, smooth and new as an egg, and the rounding seasons of the world revolving in time and space. All things, even our own heartbeats and sweat, are in it, part of it. And that work, that watching the turning over of life, becomes a road into what is essential. Work is the country of hands, and they want to live there in the dailiness of it, the repetition that is time's language of prayer, a common tongue. Everything is there, in that language, in the humblest of labor. The rake wakes up and the healing is in it. The shadows of leaves that once fell beneath the tree the handle came from are in that labor, and the rabbits that passed this way, on the altar of our work. And when the rake wakes up, all earth's gods are reborn and they dance and sing in the dusty air around us.

Activities for Writing and Discussion

1. The traditional healer whom Hogan visits says, "Our work is our altar." Based on the narrative that precedes this statement, explain what you think the healer means. Then write about ways in which your own "work" (paid or unpaid, vocation or avocation) is—or isn't—an "altar."

2. Hogan says that her work for the Birds of Prey Rehabilitation Foundation is monotonous, yet she seems to value this very monotony. She performs a

task (raking) that would seem to be easy and "mindless," yet she insists "there is an art to [it]." How can monotony be valuable, and how can a menial job—raking or any other—involve "art"? In your notebook try to explain either of these observations. Alternative: Write about any other ideas in the essay that you find surprising or striking, and relate them to your own experience.

3. Hogan says that birds require us "to feel our way into an intelligence that is different from our own." She also regards birds and other animals as soulful creatures from which we humans can learn. Reread and annotate passages about this "teacher"/"apprentice" relationship between animals and humans. Then assume the **point of view** of one such animal—from Hogan's essay or your own experience—and compose a text about your past, your life and its beauty, and your perspective on humans.

Elizabeth Larsen (b. 1964)

Buying Time

It seems like the only people with any free time these days are models in mail-order catalogs who lounge around in sunny breakfast nooks or picturesque farmyards wearing clothes they're trying to sell us.

It used to be that most middle-class people had enough free time to watch TV on weeknights *and* spend their weekends driving around in boat-size cars. But since the early '70s, when Americans' real wages started contracting and women began to enter the workforce en masse, leisure time has had to be scheduled between sorting the laundry, paying the bills, and changing the cat litter.

Of course, there are more and more people who would do just about anything to fill the free time that is the emblem of their unemployment. But among those lucky enough to have jobs that pay a decent wage, is it any wonder that images of the simple life have become so attractive? Just look at the popularity of Amish and Shaker aesthetics—captured in a burgeoning cottage industry of furniture, books, cookbooks, and movies—that sell the fantasy of a life where there's enough time to can fruit, build barns, and drive around in buggies.

But what about those of us who know that a life of such noble austerity would be too much work? What do we do to get simplicity—and the freedom from everyday drudgery that it implies? We buy it, gathering souvenirs of other cultures and hoping that through osmosis, a high-backed chair or a Navajo rug will bring us a more thoughtful, less complicated existence.

As advertisements for appliances from the '40s and '50s—which show high- 5 heeled women smiling at their families as they fill aspic molds—make clear, leisure-class aspirants have been purchasing little pieces of their imaginary movie sets for some time. In the '60s and early '70s, people who wanted a slice of the counterculture eschewed consumerism but still bought drugs that altered their sense of time, making them feel like they had all day to just sit around and experience the universe. When those fantasies got boring (and the American economy was pumped up by Reaganomics), the coke rodeo moved into high gear: Relaxing was passé; nightclubbing and German kitchen appliances that were rarely used became the insignias for people who thought that time was something that needed to be filled—and then managed in the pages of a Filofax.

Now, like the guy who cringes under the covers when he remembers groping the boss's wife at a party the night before, those of us attracted to simple chic are also nursing a hangover. But instead of doing it with Bloody Mary's, we've turned to chamomile tea and dreams of a house in the country.

No one understands our yearning for a simple, unhurried life—and our desire to get it through shopping—better than those mail-order catalogs that picture groups of (tastefully dressed) friends in an unending string of weekend getaways. Take J. Crew, that paragon of WASP chic that's getting more popular as Gap stores move into almost all non-working-class neighborhoods. In an oh-so-Shaker (and oh-so-*not*-Sears) style, J. Crew has started to display their inventory like museum pieces: Flannel shirts, baseball caps, thermal underwear, and jeans (plain, stonewashed, or "broken in") are placed one or two to a page against stark white backgrounds. Every item is a masterpiece of artful rumpling. Even a $218 cashmere sweater looks as comfy and casual as an old college sweatshirt.

When the items are worn by actual people (including light-skinned black women, whose presence assures the customer that this country club is hip to the times), the models strike casual poses on the hood of a Jeep or a Cape Cod porch. You see, the prospect of a weekend without errands or chores is the heartstring that J. Crew tugs at: Couples with no kids (and certainly none of their messy accessories) laze around on Oriental rugs, sipping coffee and reading the paper until it's time to make brunch. Then, still in their flannels, they stage a flirtatious boxing match that leads to sex on unbleached cotton sheets before they finish the Sunday crossword. It's a less tarty version of the same fantasy that's made Victoria's Secret into a gold mine.

Whereas J. Crew sticks to the endless preppy weekend, Tweeds concentrates on a funkier Euro-world. Like its competitor, Tweeds plies its customers with seductive images of leisure, but in Mediterranean village settings full of horse-drawn wagons and old men on bikes with baskets of baguettes. While much of the stuff Tweeds peddles can be worn to work, you'd never guess that by the look on the models' faces. Square-jawed men and women with Pre-Raphaelite curls slouch against stone farmhouses and haystacks, their lips lifted in three-glasses-of-wine smiles. (A friend of mine said that the Tweeds catalog looks like an advertisement for chronic fatigue syndrome.) All this nostalgia makes for good business. After all, which would you choose?—a dress modeled by a babe

riding a rickety old bike through a meadow, or the same dress worn by a har-
ried secretary standing against a gray cubicle wall?

Even as I was scrutinizing these catalogs to see how they hoodwink the   10
poor, naive consumer, I picked up the phone, dialed J. Crew's 800 number, and
ordered some of their pajamas. This made me think that maybe leisure time is
something I can't handle any way other than as an unrealized desire. Like the
people who think that going to a bed and breakfast for a weekend is the equivalent of getting away from it all, I get nervous about too much unstructured
time.

Last summer, after waiting months for my week of vacation in Puget Sound,
I got so stir-crazy listening to the birds and watching for sea lions that I compulsively started to read anything I could get my hands on to fill what seemed
like an endless amount of free time. By night number four, I was in such a panic
that I drove clear to the other side of the island to see *Free Willy.*

Maybe this is what the demise of the American dream has brought many of
us to: a life in which we have to work so hard that we're more comfortable
watching someone have free time on TV than actually experiencing it, a life of
marginal discontent in which we're more than happy to complain, but not unhappy enough to actually change the way we live.

While this kind of existence is certainly uncomfortable, it's also not that
bad. Selling the car and the answering machine (and ditching the kids) to move
to a charming white clapboard house in Iowa is at its core a denial of American
existence in the last years of the 20th century. If we isolate ourselves from the
strung-out, fragmented dilemma that is modern life, we're probably not going
to be motivated to look for the political and social solutions to the problems
that underlie the frenzy and the fatigue.

The key lies in being able to consciously understand our desires. After all,
yearning for enough free time to nurture ourselves and others is a good, even
noble, ideal. The challenge is not to drop out of life entirely but to find ways to
incorporate small pieces of our dreams into our routine. J. Crew and Tweeds
know this, and in their own way they remind us of the gentle, leisurely days that
for the past 40 years have been our utopias—utopias we nourish every time we
consume these images.

What they don't count on is that any of us will ever actually downscale our   15
spending habits. The only way to really get more free time is to stop buying all of
these things that sell our fantasies back to us. Whether it's a picnic basket or
clothes available in colors like java, lagoon, and yam, it all takes money. And the
way that most of us get money is not by planting vegetables or baking pies, but
by getting up each and every morning and going to work.

ACTIVITIES FOR WRITING AND DISCUSSION

1. Larsen's focus is a topic of concern to just about everyone: vanishing
time. To enhance your personal connections with this essay, examine your own

use of time. Write up a time-diary for yesterday. That is, beginning with the time you got out of bed, list and describe—as precisely as you can—what you did during each half hour segment of the day until the time you went to bed. Then answer the following questions in your notebook, and share and compare your answers with a partner or small group:
   a. Was this day typical in terms of how you used your time? Were you pleased with your day? Why or why not?
   b. If you kept this same schedule more or less consistently for the next several years, would it enable you to accomplish what you want to in life? Why or why not? If not, how—specifically—would you need to change your habits or priorities to use your time *better*?

2. Read and annotate Larsen's essay. Then:
   a. Share and discuss a few of your favorite annotations with a small group, and take notes on your groupmates' annotations to enrich your response to the essay.
   b. React to "Buying Time" in your notebook using the strategy described on page 28, ("Converse with specific points in the text that strike you"). Try to write at least three hundred words.

3. Explain what Larsen means by the phrase, "Buying Time." Does she seem to endorse the practice of "buying time," dislike it, or remain ambivalent about it? Support your answer with evidence from the essay. Then, using Larsen's piece as a starting point, develop an essay of your own on the subject of "buying time." Feel free to reach conclusions that are contrary to Larsen's.

Play

Henrik Ibsen (1828–1906)

The Master Builder

Persons
HALVARD SOLNESS, *the Master Builder*
ALINE SOLNESS, *his wife*
DOCTOR HERDAL, *physician*
KNUT BROVIK, *formerly an architect, now in* SOLNESS'S *employment*
RAGNAR BROVIK, *his son, draughtsman*
KAIA FOSLI, *his niece, book-keeper*
MISS HILDA WANGEL
Some Ladies.
A Crowd in the street.

The action passes in and about the house of SOLNESS.

ACT FIRST

A plainly-furnished work-room in the house of HALVARD SOLNESS. *Folding doors on the left lead out to the hall. On the right is the door leading to the inner rooms of the house. At the back is an open door into the draughtsmen's office. In front, on the left, a desk with books, papers, and writing materials. Further back than the folding door, a stove. In the right-hand corner, a sofa, a table, and one or two chairs. On the table a water-bottle and glass. A smaller table, with a rocking-chair and arm-chair, in front on the right. Lighted lamps with shades on the table in the draughtsmen's office, on the table in the corner, and on the desk.*

In the draughtsmen's office sit KNUT BROVIK *and his son* RAGNAR, *occupied with plans and calculations. At the desk in the outer office stands* KAIA FOSLI, *writing in the ledger.* KNUT BROVIK *is a spare old man with white hair and beard. He wears a rather threadbare but well-brushed black coat, spectacles, and a somewhat discolored white neckcloth.* RAGNAR BROVIK *is a well-dressed, light-haired man of about thirty, who stoops a little.* KAIA FOSLI *is a slightly-built girl, a little over twenty, carefully dressed, and delicate-looking. She has a green shade over her eyes.—All three go on working for some time in silence.*

KNUT BROVIK: *(Rises suddenly, as if in distress, from the table; breathes heavily and laboriously as he comes forward into the doorway.)* No, I can't bear it much longer!

KAIA: *(Going up to him.)* You're feeling very ill this evening, aren't you, Uncle?

BROVIK: Oh, I seem to get worse every day.

RAGNAR: *(Has risen and advances.)* You ought to go home, father. Try to get a little sleep——

BROVIK: *(Impatiently.)* Go to bed, I suppose? Would you have me stifled outright?

KAIA: Then take a little walk.

RAGNAR: Yes, do, I will come with you.

BROVIK: *(With warmth.)* I'll not go till he comes! I'm determined to have it out this evening with—*(in a tone of suppressed bitterness)*—with him—with the chief.

KAIA: *(Anxiously.)* Oh no, uncle,—do wait awhile before doing *that!*

RAGNAR: Yes, better wait, father!

BROVIK: *(Draws his breath laboriously.)* Ha—ha—! *I* haven't much time for waiting.

KAIA: *(Listening.)* Hush! I hear him on the stairs. *(All three go back to their work. A short silence.)*

*(*HALVARD SOLNESS *comes in through the hall-door. He is a man of mature age, healthy and vigorous, with close-cut curly hair, dark mustache and dark thick eyebrows. He wears a grayish-green buttoned jacket with an upstanding collar and broad lapels. On his head he wears a soft gray felt hat, and he has one or two light portfolios under his arm.)*

SOLNESS: *(Near the door, points towards the draughtsmen's office, and asks in a whisper:)* Are they gone?

KAIA: *(Softly, shaking her head.)* No.

(She takes the shade off her eyes. SOLNESS *crosses the room, throws his hat on a chair, places the portfolios on the table by the sofa, and approaches the desk again.* KAIA *goes on writing without intermission, but seems nervous and uneasy.)*

SOLNESS: *(Aloud.)* What is that you're entering, Miss Fosli?

KAIA: *(Starts.)* Oh, it's only something that—

SOLNESS: Let me look at it, Miss Fosli. *(Bends over her, pretends to be looking into the ledger, and whispers:)* Kaia?

KAIA: *(Softly, still writing.)* Well?

SOLNESS: Why do you always take that shade off when I come?

KAIA: *(As before.)* I look so ugly with it on.

SOLNESS: *(Smiling.)* Then you don't like to look ugly, Kaia?

KAIA: *(Half glancing up at him.)* Not for all the world. Not in *your* eyes.

SOLNESS: *(Strokes her hair gently.)* Poor, poor little Kaia——

KAIA: *(Bending her head.)* Hush, they can hear you!

(SOLNESS strolls across the room to the right, turns and pauses at the door of the draughtsmen's office.)

SOLNESS: Has any one been here for me?

RAGNAR: *(Rising.)* Yes, the young couple who want a villa built out at Lövstrand.

SOLNESS: *(Growling.)* Oh, those two! They must wait. I'm not quite clear about the plans yet.

RAGNAR: *(Advancing, with some hesitation.)* They were very anxious to have the drawings at once.

SOLNESS: *(As before.)* Yes, of course—so they all are.

BROVIK: *(Looks up.)* They say they're longing so to get into a house of their own.

SOLNESS: Yes, yes—we know all that! And so they're content to take whatever's offered them. They get a—a roof over their heads—an address—but nothing to call a home. No thank you! In that case, let them apply to somebody else. Tell them *that,* the next time they call.

BROVIK: *(Pushes his glasses up on to his forehead and looks in astonishment at him.)* To somebody else? Are you prepared to give up the commission?

SOLNESS: *(Impatiently.)* Yes, yes, yes, devil take it! If that's to be the way of it. —Rather that, than build away at random. *(Vehemently.)* Besides, I know very little about these people as yet.

BROVIK: The people are safe enough. Ragnar knows them. He's a friend of the family. Perfectly safe people.

SOLNESS: Oh, safe—safe enough! That's not at all what I mean. Good lord— don't *you* understand me either? *(Angrily.)* I won't have anything to do with these strangers. They may apply to whom they please, so far as I'm concerned.

BROVIK: *(Rising.)* Do you really mean it?

SOLNESS: *(Sulkily.)* Yes I do.—For once in a way. *(He comes forward.)*
(BROVIK *exchanges a glance with* RAGNAR, *who makes a warning gesture. Then* BROVIK *comes into the front room.)*

BROVIK: May I have a few words with you?

SOLNESS: Certainly.

BROVIK: *(To* KAIA.*)* Just go in there for a moment, Kaia.

KAIA: *(Uneasily.)* Oh, but Uncle—

BROVIK: Do as I say, child. And shut the door after you.

(KAIA *goes reluctantly into the draughtsmen's office, glances anxiously and entreatingly at* SOLNESS, *and shuts the door.)*

BROVIK: *(Lowering his voice a little.)* I don't want the poor children to know how ill I am.

SOLNESS: Yes, you've been looking very poorly of late.

BROVIK: It will soon be all over with me. My strength is ebbing from day to day.

SOLNESS: Won't you sit down?

BROVIK: Thanks—may I?

SOLNESS: *(Placing the arm-chair more conveniently.)* Here—take this chair.—And now?

BROVIK: *(Has seated himself with difficulty.)* Well, you see, it's about Ragnar. That's what weighs most upon me. What is to become of him?

SOLNESS: Of course your son will stay with me as long as ever he likes.

BROVIK: But that's just what he doesn't like. He feels that he can't stay any longer.

SOLNESS: Why, I should say he was very well off here. But if he wants a raise, I shouldn't object to——

BROVIK: No, no! It's not *that.* *(Impatiently.)* But sooner or later he, too, must have a chance of doing something on his own account.

SOLNESS: *(Without looking at him.)* Do you think that Ragnar has quite talent enough to stand alone?

BROVIK: No, that's just the heart-breaking part of it—I've begun to have my doubts about the boy. For you've never said so much as—as one encouraging word about him. And yet I can't help thinking there must be something in him—he can't possibly be without talent.

SOLNESS: Well, but he has learnt nothing—nothing thoroughly, I mean. Except, of course, to draw.

BROVIK: *(Looks at him with covert hatred, and says hoarsely,)* You had learned little enough of the business when you were in my employment. But that didn't prevent you from setting to work—*(breathing with difficulty)*—and pushing your way up, and taking the wind out of my sails—mine, and other people's.

SOLNESS: Yes, you see—circumstances favored me.

BROVIK: You're right there. Everything favored you. But then how can you have the heart to let me go to my grave—without having seen what Ragnar is fit for? And of course I'm anxious to see them married, too—before I go.

SOLNESS: *(Sharply.)* Is it she who wishes it?

BROVIK: Not Kaia so much as Ragnar—he talks about it every day. *(Appealingly.)* You must—you *must* help him to get some independent work now! I *must* see something that the lad has done. Do you hear?

SOLNESS: *(Peevishly.)* You can't expect me to drag commissions down from the moon for him!

BROVIK: He has the chance of a capital commission at this very moment. A big bit of work.

SOLNESS: *(Uneasily, startled.)* Has he?

BROVIK: If *you* would give your consent.

SOLNESS: What sort of work do you mean?

BROVIK: *(With some hesitation.)* He can have the building of that villa out at Lövstrand.

SOLNESS: That! Why, I'm going to build that myself!

BROVIK: Oh, you don't much care about doing it.

SOLNESS: *(Flaring up.)* Don't care! I! Who dares to say that?

BROVIK: You said so yourself just now.

SOLNESS: Oh, never mind what I *say.*—Would they give Ragnar the building of that villa?

BROVIK: Yes. You see, he knows the family. And then—just for the fun of the thing—he's made drawings and estimates and so forth——

SOLNESS: Are they pleased with the drawings? The people who've got to live in the house?

BROVIK: Yes. If you would only look through them and approve of them——

SOLNESS: Then they would let Ragnar build their home for them?

BROVIK: They were immensely pleased with his idea. They thought it exceedingly original, they said.

SOLNESS: Oho! Original! Not the old-fashioned stuff that *I'm* in the habit of turning out.

BROVIK: It seemed to them *different.*

SOLNESS: *(With suppressed irritation.)* So it was to see Ragnar that they came here—whilst I was out!

BROVIK: They came to call upon you—and at the same time to ask whether you would mind retiring——

SOLNESS: *(Angrily.)* Retire? I?

BROVIK: In case you thought that Ragnar's drawings——

SOLNESS: I? Retire in favor of your son?

BROVIK: Retire from the agreement, they meant.

SOLNESS: Oh, it comes to the same thing. *(Laughs angrily.)* So that's it, is it? Halvard Solness is to see about retiring now! To make room for younger men! For the very youngest, perhaps! He's got to make room! Room! Room!

BROVIK: Why, good heavens! there's surely room for more than one single man——

SOLNESS: Oh, there's not so very much room to spare either. But be that as it may—I will never retire! I will never give way to anybody! Never of my own free will. Never in this world will I do *that!*

BROVIK: *(Rises with difficulty.)* Then I am to pass out of life without any certainty? Without a gleam of happiness? Without any faith or trust in Ragnar? Without having seen a single piece of work of his doing? Is that to be the way of it?

SOLNESS: *(Turns half aside, and mutters.)* H'm—don't ask more just now.

BROVIK: But answer me this one thing. Am I to pass out of life in such utter poverty?

SOLNESS: *(Seems to struggle with himself; finally he says in a low but firm voice:)* You must pass out of life as best you can.

BROVIK: Then be it so.
(He goes up the room.)

SOLNESS: *(Following him, half in desperation.)* Don't you understand that I *cannot* help it? I am what I am, and I can't change my nature!

BROVIK: No, no; you evidently can't. *(Reels and supports himself against the sofa-table.)* May I have a glass of water?

SOLNESS: By all means. *(Fills a glass and hands it to him.)*

BROVIK: Thanks. *(Drinks and puts the glass down again.)*
(SOLNESS goes up and opens the door of the draughtsmen's office.

SOLNESS: Ragnar— you must come and take your father home.
(RAGNAR rises quickly. He and KAIA come into the work-room.)

RAGNAR: What's the matter, father?

BROVIK: Give me your arm. Now let us go.

RAGNAR: All right. You'd better put your things on, too, Kaia.

SOLNESS: Miss Fosli must stay—just a moment. There's a letter I want written.

BROVIK: *(Looks at SOLNESS.)* Good-night. Sleep well—if you can.

SOLNESS: Good-night.
(BROVIK and RAGNAR go out through the hall-door. KAIA goes to the desk. SOLNESS stands with bent head, to the right, by the arm-chair.)

KAIA: *(Dubiously.)* Is there any letter——?

SOLNESS: *(Curtly.)* No, of course not. *(Looks sternly at her.)* Kaia!

KAIA: *(Anxiously, in a low voice.)* Yes?

SOLNESS: *(Points imperatively to a spot on the floor.)* Come here! At once!

KAIA: *(Hesitatingly.)* Yes.

SOLNESS: *(As before.)* Nearer!

KAIA: *(Obeying.)* What do you want with me?

SOLNESS: *(Looks at her for a while.)* Is it you I have to thank for all this?

KAIA: No, no, don't think that!

SOLNESS: But confess now—you want to get married!

KAIA: *(Softly.)* Ragnar and I have been engaged for four or five years, and so——

SOLNESS: And so you think it's time there were an end of it. Isn't that so?

KAIA: Ragnar and Uncle say I *must*. So I suppose I'll have to give in.

SOLNESS: *(More gently.)* Kaia, don't you really care a little bit for Ragnar, too?

KAIA: I cared very much for Ragnar once—before I came here to you.

SOLNESS: But you don't now? Not in the least?

KAIA: *(Passionately, clasping her hands and holding them out towards him.)* Oh, you know very well that there's only *one* person I care for now! One, and one only, in all the world. I shall never care for any one else again!

SOLNESS: Yes, you say that. And yet you go away from me—leave me alone here with everything on my hands.

KAIA: But couldn't I stay with you, even if Ragnar——?

SOLNESS: *(Repudiating the idea.)* No, no, that's quite impossible. If Ragnar leaves me and starts work on his own account, then of course he'll need you himself.

KAIA: *(Wringing her hands.)* Oh, I feel as if I *couldn't* be separated from you! It's quite, quite impossible!

SOLNESS: Then be sure you get those foolish notions out of Ragnar's mind. Marry him as much as you please—*(Alters his tone.)* I mean—don't let him throw up his good situation with me. For then I can keep *you* too, my dear Kaia.

KAIA: Oh yes, how lovely that would be, if it could only be managed.

SOLNESS: *(Clasps her head with his two hands and whispers.)* For I *can't* get on without you, you see. I must have you with me every single day.

KAIA: *(In nervous exaltation.)* My God! My God!

SOLNESS: *(Kisses her hair.)* Kaia—Kaia!

KAIA: *(Sinks down before him.)* Oh, how good you are to me! How unspeakably good you are!

SOLNESS: *(Vehemently.)* Get up! For goodness' sake get up! I think I hear some one!

(He helps her to rise. She staggers over to the desk. MRS. SOLNESS *enters by the door on the right. She looks thin and wasted with grief, but shows traces of bygone beauty. Blonde ringlets. Dressed with good taste, wholly in black. Speaks somewhat slowly and in a plaintive voice.)*

MRS. SOLNESS: *(In the doorway.)* Halvard!

SOLNESS: *(Turns.)* Oh, are you there, dear——?

MRS. SOLNESS: *(With a glance at* KAIA.*)* I'm afraid I'm disturbing you.

SOLNESS: Not in the least. Miss Fosli has only a short letter to write.

MRS. SOLNESS: Yes, so I see.

SOLNESS: What do you want with me, Aline?

MRS. SOLNESS: I merely wanted to tell you that Dr. Herdal is in the drawing-room. Won't you come and see him, Halvard?

SOLNESS: *(Looks suspiciously at her.)* H'm—is the doctor so very anxious to talk to me?

MRS. SOLNESS: Well, not exactly anxious. He really came to see me; but he would like to say how-do-you-do to you at the same time.

SOLNESS: *(Laughs to himself.)* Yes, I dare say. Well, you must ask him to wait a little.

MRS. SOLNESS: Then you'll come in later on?

SOLNESS: Perhaps I will. Later on, later on, dear. Presently.

MRS. SOLNESS: *(Glancing again at* KAIA.*)* Well now, don't forget, Halvard. *(Withdraws and closes the door behind her.)*

KAIA: *(Softly.)* Oh dear, oh dear—I'm sure Mrs. Solness thinks ill of me in some way!

SOLNESS: Oh, not in the least. Not more than usual at any rate. But you'd better go now, all the same, Kaia.

KAIA: Yes, yes, now I must go.

SOLNESS: *(Severely.)* And mind you get that matter settled for me. Do you hear?

KAIA: Oh, if it only depended on *me*——

SOLNESS: I *will* have it settled, I say! And to-morrow too—not a day later!

KAIA: *(Terrified.)* If there's nothing else for it, I'm quite willing to break off the engagement.

SOLNESS: *(Angrily.)* Break it off! Are you mad? Would you think of breaking it off?

KAIA: *(Distracted.)* Yes, if necessary. For I *must*—I *must* stay here with you! I can't leave you! That's utterly—utterly impossible!

SOLNESS: *(With a sudden outburst.)* But deuce take it—how about Ragnar then! It's Ragnar that I——

KAIA: *(Looks at him with terrified eyes.)* It is chiefly on Ragnar's account, that—that you——?

SOLNESS: *(Collecting himself.)* No, no, of course not! You don't understand me either. *(Gently and softly.)* Of course it's *you* I want to keep—you above everything, Kaia. But for that very reason you must prevent Ragnar too from throwing up his situation. There, there,—now go home.

KAIA: Yes, yes—good-night, then.

SOLNESS: Good-night. *(As she is going.)* Oh! stop a moment! Are Ragnar's drawings in there?

KAIA: I didn't see him take them with him.

SOLNESS: Then just go in and find them for me. I might perhaps glance over them.

KAIA: *(Happy.)* Oh yes, please do!

SOLNESS: For your sake, Kaia dear. Now, let me have them at once, please.

(KAIA hurries into the draughtsmen's office, searches anxiously in the table-drawer, finds a portfolio and brings it with her.)

KAIA: Here are all the drawings.

SOLNESS: Good. Put them down there on the table.

KAIA: *(Putting down the portfolio.)* Good-night, then. *(Beseechingly.)* And think kindly of me.

SOLNESS: Oh, that I always do. Good-night, my dear little Kaia. *(Glances to the right.)* Go, go now!

(MRS. SOLNESS *and* DR. HERDAL *enter by the door on the right. He is a stoutish, elderly man, with a round, good-humored face, clean shaven, with thin, light hair, and gold spectacles.*)

MRS. SOLNESS: *(Still in the doorway.)* Halvard, I cannot keep the doctor any longer.

SOLNESS: Well then, come in here.

MRS. SOLNESS: *(To* KAIA, *who is turning down the desk-lamp.)* Have you finished the letter already, Miss Fosli.

KAIA: *(In confusion.)* The letter——?

SOLNESS: Yes, it was quite a short one.

MRS. SOLNESS: It must have been very short.

SOLNESS: You may go now, Miss Fosli. And please come in good time to-morrow morning.

KAIA: I will be sure to. Good-night, Mrs. Solness. *(She goes out by the hall-door.)*

MRS. SOLNESS: She must be quite an acquisition to you, Halvard, this Miss Fosli.

SOLNESS: Yes, indeed. She's useful in all sorts of ways.

MRS. SOLNESS: So it seems.

DR. HERDAL: Is she good at book-keeping, too?

SOLNESS: Well—of course she's had a good deal of practice during these two years. And then she's so nice and obliging in every possible way.

MRS. SOLNESS: Yes, that must be very delightful.

SOLNESS: It *is.* Especially when one doesn't get too much of that sort of thing.

MRS. SOLNESS: *(In a tone of general remonstrance.)* Can *you* say that, Halvard?

SOLNESS: Oh, no, no, my dear Aline; I beg your pardon.

MRS. SOLNESS: There's no occasion. Well, then, doctor, you'll come back later on and have a cup of tea with us?

DR. HERDAL: I've only a professional visit to pay, and then I'll come back.

MRS. SOLNESS: Thank you. *(She goes out by the door on the right.)*

SOLNESS: Are you in a hurry, doctor?

DR. HERDAL: No, not at all.

SOLNESS: May I have a little chat with you?

DR. HERDAL: With the greatest of pleasure.

SOLNESS: Then let us sit down.

(*He motions the doctor to take the rocking-chair and sits down himself in the armchair.*)

SOLNESS: *(Looks searchingly at him.)* Tell me, did you notice anything odd about Aline?

DR. HERDAL: Do you mean just now when she was here?

SOLNESS: Yes, in her manner to me. Did you notice anything?

DR. HERDAL: *(Smiling.)* Well, I admit—one couldn't well avoid noticing that your wife—h'm——

SOLNESS: Well?

DR. HERDAL: —that your wife isn't particularly fond of this Miss Fosli.

SOLNESS: Is that all? I've noticed that myself.

DR. HERDAL: And I must say it doesn't surprise me.

SOLNESS: What doesn't?

DR. HERDAL: That she shouldn't exactly approve of you seeing so much of another woman, all day and every day.

SOLNESS: No, no, I suppose you're right there—and Aline too. But it's impossible to make any change.

DR. HERDAL: Could you not engage a clerk?

SOLNESS: The first man that came to hand? No, thanks—that would never do for me.

DR. HERDAL: But now, if your wife——? Suppose, with her delicate health, all this tries her too much?

SOLNESS: Well then there's no help for it—I could almost say. I *must* keep Kaia Fosli. No one else could fill her place.

DR. HERDAL: No one else?

SOLNESS: *(Curtly.)* No, no one.

DR. HERDAL: *(Drawing his chair closer.)* Now listen to me, my dear Mr. Solness. May I ask you a question, quite between ourselves?

SOLNESS: By all means.

DR. HERDAL: Women, you see—in certain matters, they have a deucedly keen intuition——

SOLNESS: They have indeed. There's not the least doubt of that. But——?

DR. HERDAL: Well, tell me now—if your wife can't endure this Kaia Fosli——?

SOLNESS: Well, what then?

DR. HERDAL: —hasn't she got just—just the least little bit of reason for this involuntary dislike?

SOLNESS: *(Looks at him and rises.)* Oho!

DR. HERDAL: Now don't be offended—but *hasn't* she?

SOLNESS: *(With curt decision.)* No.

DR. HERDAL: No reason of any sort?

SOLNESS: No other reason than her own suspicious nature.

DR. HERDAL: I know you've known a good many women in your time.

SOLNESS: Yes, I have.

DR. HERDAL: And have been a good deal taken with some of them, too?

SOLNESS: Oh yes, I don't deny it.

DR. HERDAL: But as regards Miss Fosli, then—there's nothing of that sort in the case?

SOLNESS: No; nothing at all—on *my* side.

DR. HERDAL: But on her side?

SOLNESS: I don't think you have any right to ask that question, doctor.

DR. HERDAL: Well, you know, we were discussing your wife's intuition.

SOLNESS: So we were. And for that matter—*(lowers his voice)*—Aline's intuition, as you call it—in a certain sense, it's not been so far out.

DR. HERDAL: Ah! there we have it!

SOLNESS: *(Sits down.)* Doctor Herdal—I'm going to tell you a strange story—if you care to listen to it.

DR. HERDAL: I like listening to strange stories.

SOLNESS: Very well then. I daresay you recollect that I took Knut Brovik and his son into my service—after the old man's business had gone to the dogs.

DR. HERDAL: Yes, so I've understood.

SOLNESS: You see, they really are clever fellows, these two. Each of them has talent in his way. But then the son took it into his head to get engaged; and the next thing, of course, was that he wanted to get married—and begin to build on his own account. That's the way with all these young people.

DR. HERDAL: *(Laughing.)* Yes, they've a bad habit of wanting to marry.

SOLNESS: Just so. But of course that didn't suit *my* plans; for I needed Ragnar myself—and the old man, too. He's exceedingly good at calculating bearing-strains and cubic contents—and all that sort of devilry, you know.

DR. HERDAL: Oh yes, no doubt that's very important.

SOLNESS: Yes, it is. But Ragnar was absolutely bent on setting to work for himself. He wouldn't hear of anything else.

DR. HERDAL: But he has stayed with you all the same.

SOLNESS: Yes, I'll tell you how that came about. One day this girl, Kaia Fosli, came to see them on some errand or other. She had never been here before. And when I saw how utterly infatuated they were with each other, the thought occurred to me: If only I could get her into the office here, then perhaps Ragnar too would stay where she is.

DR. HERDAL: That was not at all a bad idea.

SOLNESS: Yes, but at the time I didn't breathe a word of what was in my mind. I merely stood and looked at her, and kept wishing intently that I could have her here. Then I talked to her a little, in a friendly way—about one thing and another. And then she went away.

DR. HERDAL: Well?

SOLNESS: Well then, next day, pretty late in the evening, when old Brovik and Ragnar had gone home, she came here again, and behaved as if I had made an arrangement with her.

DR. HERDAL: An arrangement? What about?

SOLNESS: About the very thing my mind had been fixed on. But I hadn't said one single word about it.

DR. HERDAL: That was most extraordinary.

SOLNESS: Yes, wasn't it? And now she wanted to know what she was to do here, whether she could begin the very next morning, and so forth.

DR. HERDAL: Don't you think she did it in order to be with her sweetheart?

SOLNESS: That was what occurred to me at first. But no, that wasn't it. She seemed to drift quite away from *him*—when once she had come here to me.

DR. HERDAL: She drifted over to you, then?

SOLNESS: Yes, entirely. If I happen to look at her when her back is turned, I can tell that she feels it. She quivers and trembles the moment I come near her. What do you think of that?

DR. HERDAL: H'm—that's not very hard to explain.

SOLNESS: Well, but what about the other thing? That she believed I had said to her what I had only wished and willed—silently—inwardly—to myself? What do you say to that? Can you explain that, Dr. Herdal?

DR. HERDAL: No, I won't undertake to do that.

SOLNESS: I felt sure you wouldn't; and so I've never cared to talk about it till now. But it's a cursed nuisance to me in the long run, you understand. Here have I got to go on day after day pretending—. And it's a shame to treat her so, too, poor girl. *(Vehemently.)* But I *can't* do anything else. For if *she* runs away from me—then Ragnar will be off too.

DR. HERDAL: And you haven't told your wife the rights of the story?

SOLNESS: No.

DR. HERDAL: Then why on earth don't you?

SOLNESS: *(Looks fixedly at him and says in a low voice:)* Because I seem to find a sort of—of salutary self-torture in allowing Aline to do me an injustice.

DR. HERDAL: *(Shakes his head.)* I don't in the least understand what you mean.

SOLNESS: Well, you see, it's like paying off a little bit of a huge, immeasurable debt——

DR. HERDAL: To your wife?

SOLNESS: Yes; and that always helps to relieve one's mind a little. One can breathe more freely for a while, you see.

DR. HERDAL: No, goodness knows, I don't see at all——

SOLNESS: *(Breaking off, rises again.)* Well, well, well—then we won't talk any more about it. *(He saunters across the room, returns, and stops beside the table. Looks at the doctor with a sly smile.)* I suppose you think you've drawn me out nicely now, doctor?

DR. HERDAL: *(With some irritation.)* Drawn you out? Again I haven't the faintest notion what you mean, Mr. Solness.

SOLNESS: Oh come, out with it; for I've seen it quite clearly, you know.

DR. HERDAL: *What* have you seen?

SOLNESS: *(In a low voice, slowly.)* That you've been quietly keeping an eye upon me.

DR. HERDAL: That I have! And why in all the world should I do *that*?

SOLNESS: Because you think that I——*(Passionately.)* Well, devil take it—you think the same of me as Aline does.

DR. HERDAL: And what does *she* think about you?

SOLNESS: *(Having recovered his self-control.)* She has begun to think that I'm—that I'm—ill.

DR. HERDAL: Ill! You! She has never hinted such a thing to me. Why, what can she think is the matter with you?

SOLNESS: *(Leans over the back of the chair and whispers.)* Aline has made up her mind that I am mad. *That's* what she thinks.

DR. HERDAL: *(Rising.)* Why, my dear, good fellow——!

SOLNESS: Yes, on my soul she does! I tell you it's so! And she has got you to think the same. Oh, I can assure you, doctor, I see it in your face as clearly as possible. You don't take me in so easily, I can tell you.

DR. HERDAL: *(Looks at him in amazement.)* Never, Mr. Solness—never has such a thought entered my mind.

SOLNESS: *(With an incredulous smile.)* Really? Has it not?

DR. HERDAL: No, never! Nor your wife's mind either, I'm convinced. I could almost swear to that.

SOLNESS: Well, I wouldn't advise you to. For, in a certain sense, you see, perhaps—perhaps she's not so far wrong in thinking something of the kind.

DR. HERDAL: Come now, I really must say——

SOLNESS: *(Interrupting with a sweep of his hand.)* Well, well, my dear doctor—don't let us discuss this any further. We had better agree to differ. *(Changes to a tone of quiet merriment.)* But look here now, doctor—hm—

DR. HERDAL: Well?

SOLNESS: Since you don't believe that I am—ill—and crazy—and mad, and so forth——

DR. HERDAL: What then?

SOLNESS: Then I daresay you fancy that I'm an extremely happy man?

DR. HERDAL: Is *that* mere fancy?

SOLNESS: *(Laughs.)* No, no—of course not! Heaven forbid! Only think—to be Solness the master builder! Halvard Solness! What could be more delightful?

DR. HERDAL: Yes, I must say it seems to me you've had the luck on your side to an astounding degree.

SOLNESS: *(Suppresses a gloomy smile.)* So I have. I can't complain on *that* score.

DR. HERDAL: First of all that grim old robber's-castle was burnt down for you. And that was certainly a great piece of luck.

SOLNESS: *(Seriously.)* It was the home of Aline's family. Remember that.

DR. HERDAL: Yes, it must have been a great grief to *her.*

SOLNESS: She hasn't got over it to this day—not in all these twelve or thirteen years.

DR. HERDAL: Ah, but what followed must have been the worst blow for her.

SOLNESS: The one thing with the other.

DR. HERDAL: But you—yourself—*you* rose upon the ruins. You began as a poor boy from a country village—and now you're at the head of your profession. Ah, yes, Mr. Solness, you've undoubtedly had the luck on your side.

SOLNESS: *(Looks doubtfully across at him.)* Yes, but that's just what makes me so horribly afraid.

DR. HERDAL: Afraid? Because you have the luck on your side!

SOLNESS: It terrifies me—terrifies me every hour of the day. For sooner or later the luck must turn, you see.

DR. HERDAL: Oh, nonsense! What should make the luck turn?

SOLNESS: *(With firm assurance.)* The younger generation.

DR. HERDAL: Pooh! The younger generation! You're not laid on the shelf yet, I should hope. Oh no—your position here is probably firmer now than it has ever been.

SOLNESS: The luck *will* turn. I know it—I feel the day approaching. Some one or other will take it into his head to say: Give *me* a chance! And then all the rest will come clamoring after him, and shake their fists at me and shout: Make room—make room—make room! Yes, just you see, doctor—presently the younger generation will come knocking at my door——

DR. HERDAL: *(Laughing.)* Well, and what if they do?

SOLNESS: What if they do? Then there's an end of Halvard Solness. *(There is a knock at the door on the left.)*

SOLNESS: *(Starts.)* What's that? Didn't you hear something?

DR. HERDAL: Some one is knocking at the door.

SOLNESS: *(Loudly.)* Come in.

(HILDA WANGEL *enters through the hall door. She is of middle height, supple, and delicately built. Somewhat sunburnt. Dressed in a tourist costume, with skirt caught up for walking, a sailor's collar open at the throat, and a small sailor hat on her head. Knapsack on back, plaid shawl in strap, and alpenstock.)*

HILDA: *(Goes straight up to* SOLNESS, *her eyes sparkling with happiness.)* Good-evening!

SOLNESS: *(Looks doubtfully at her.)* Good-evening——

HILDA: *(Laughs.)* I almost believe you don't recognize me!

SOLNESS: No—I must admit that——just for the moment——

DR. HERDAL: *(Approaching.)* But *I* recognize you, my dear young lady——

HILDA: *(Pleased.)* Oh, is it you that——

DR. HERDAL: Of course it is. *(To* SOLNESS.*)* We met at one of the mountain stations this summer. *(To* HILDA.*)* What became of the other ladies?

HILDA: Oh, they went westward.

DR. HERDAL: They didn't much like all the fun we used to have in the evenings.

HILDA: No, I believe they didn't.

DR. HERDAL: *(Holds up his finger at her.)* And I'm afraid it can't be denied that you flirted a little with us.

HILDA: Well, that was better fun than to sit there knitting stockings with all those old women.

DR. HERDAL: *(Laughs.)* There I entirely agree with you!

SOLNESS: Have you come to town this evening?

HILDA: Yes, I've just arrived.

DR. HERDAL: Quite alone, Miss Wangel?

HILDA: Oh yes!

SOLNESS: Wangel? Is your name Wangel?

HILDA: *(Looks in amused surprise at him.)* Yes, of course it is.

SOLNESS: Then you must be the daughter of the district doctor up at Lysanger?

HILDA: *(As before.)* Yes, who else's daughter should I be?

SOLNESS: Oh, then I suppose we met up there, that summer when I was building a tower on the old church.

HILDA: *(More seriously.)* Yes, of course it was then we met.

SOLNESS: Well, that's a long time ago.

HILDA: *(Looks hard at him.)* It's just the ten years.

SOLNESS: You must have been a mere child then, I should think.

HILDA: *(Carelessly.)* Well, I was twelve or thirteen.

DR. HERDAL: Is this the first time you've ever been up to town, Miss Wangel?

HILDA: Yes, it is indeed.

SOLNESS: And don't you know any one here?

HILDA: Nobody but you. And of course, your wife.

SOLNESS: So you know *her* too?

HILDA: Only a little. We spent a few days together at the sanatorium.

SOLNESS: Ah, up there?

HILDA: She said I might come and pay her a visit if ever I came up to town. *(Smiles.)* Not that that was necessary.

SOLNESS: Odd that she should never have mentioned it.

(HILDA *puts her stick down by the stove, takes off the knapsack and lays it and the plaid on the sofa.* DR. HERDAL *offers to help her.* SOLNESS *stands and gazes at her.)*

HILDA: *(Going towards him.)* Well, now I must ask you to let me spend the night here.

SOLNESS: I'm sure we can manage that.

HILDA: For I've no other clothes than those I stand in, except a change of linen in my knapsack. And that has to go to the wash, for it's very dirty.

SOLNESS: Oh yes, we'll see to that. Now I'll just let my wife know——

DR. HERDAL: Meanwhile, I'll visit my patient.

SOLNESS: Yes, do; and come again later on.

DR. HERDAL: *(Playfully, with a glance at* HILDA.*)* Oh that I will, you may be very certain! *(Laughs)* So your prediction has come true, Mr. Solness!

SOLNESS: How so?

DR. HERDAL: The younger generation *did* come knocking at your door.

SOLNESS: *(Cheerfully.)* Yes, but in a very different way from what I meant.

DR. HERDAL: Very different, yes. That's undeniable.

(He goes out by the hall-door. SOLNESS *opens the door on the right and speaks into the side room.)*

SOLNESS: Aline! Will you come in here, please. Here's a friend of yours— Miss Wangel.

MRS. SOLNESS: *(Appears in the door-way.)* Who do you say it is? *(Sees* HILDA.*)* Oh, is it you, Miss Wangel? *(Goes up to her and offers her hand.)* So you've come to town after all.

SOLNESS: Miss Wangel has this moment arrived; and she would like to stay the night here.

MRS. SOLNESS: Here with us? Oh yes, with pleasure.

SOLNESS: So as to get her things a little in order, you see.

MRS. SOLNESS: I will do the best I can for you. It's no more than my duty. I suppose your trunk is coming on later?

HILDA: I *have* no trunk.

MRS. SOLNESS: Well, it will be all right, I daresay. In the meantime, you must excuse my leaving you here with my husband until I can get a room made a little comfortable for you.

SOLNESS: Can't we give her one of the nurseries? *They* are all ready as it is.

MRS. SOLNESS: Oh yes. There we have room and to spare. *(To HILDA.)* Sit down now and rest a little.

(She goes out to the right. HILDA, with her hands behind her back, strolls about the room and looks at various objects. SOLNESS stands in front, beside the table, also with his hands behind his back, and follows her with his eyes.)

HILDA: *(Stops and looks at him.)* Have you several nurseries?

SOLNESS: There are three nurseries in the house.

HILDA: That's a lot. Then I suppose you have a great many children?

SOLNESS: No. We have no child. But now *you* can be the child here, for the time being.

HILDA: For to-night, yes. I sha'n't cry. I mean to sleep as sound as a stone.

SOLNESS: Yes, you must be very tired, I should think.

HILDA: Oh no! But all the same——It's so delicious to lie and dream.

SOLNESS: Do you dream much of nights?

HILDA: Oh yes! Almost always.

SOLNESS: What do you dream about most?

HILDA: I sha'n't tell you to-night. Another time, perhaps.

(She again strolls about the room, stops at the desk and turns over the books and papers a little.)

SOLNESS: *(Approaching.)* Are you searching for anything?

HILDA: No, I'm merely looking at all these things. *(Turns.)* Perhaps I mustn't?

SOLNESS: Oh, by all means.

HILDA: Is it you that writes in this great ledger?

SOLNESS: No, it's my book-keeper.

HILDA: Is it a woman?

SOLNESS: *(Smiles).* Yes.

HILDA: One you employ here, in your office?

SOLNESS: Yes.

HILDA: Is she married?

SOLNESS: No, she's single.

HILDA: Ah!

SOLNESS: But I believe she's soon going to be married.

HILDA: That's a good thing for *her.*

SOLNESS: But not such a good thing for *me.* For then I shall have nobody to help me.

HILDA: Can't you get hold of some one else who'll do just as well?

SOLNESS: Perhaps *you* would stop here and—and write in the ledger?

HILDA: *(Measures him with a glance.)* Yes, I daresay! No, thanks—nothing of that sort for *me*—*(She again strolls across the room, and sits down in the rocking-chair.* SOLNESS *too goes to the table.* HILDA *continues:)*—for there must surely be other things than *that* to be done here. *(Looks smilingly at him.)* Don't you think so too?

SOLNESS: Of course. First and foremost, I suppose you want to make a round of the shops, and get yourself up in the height of fashion.

HILDA: *(Amused.)* No, I think I shall let *that* alone.

SOLNESS: Indeed!

HILDA: For you must know I've run through all my money.

SOLNESS: *(Laughs.)* Neither trunk nor money, then!

HILDA: Neither one nor the other. But never mind—it doesn't matter now.

SOLNESS: Come now, I like you for *that.*

HILDA: Only for *that?*

SOLNESS: For that among other things. *(Sits in the arm-chair.)* Is your father alive still?

HILDA: Yes, father's alive.

SOLNESS: Perhaps you're thinking of studying here?

HILDA: No, that hadn't occurred to me.

SOLNESS: But I suppose you'll be stopping for some time.

HILDA: That must depend upon circumstances.

(She sits awhile rocking herself and looking at him, half seriously, half with a suppressed smile. Then she takes off her hat and puts it on the table in front of her.)

HILDA: Mr. Solness!

SOLNESS: Well?

HILDA: Have you a very bad memory?

SOLNESS: A bad memory? No, not that I'm aware of.

HILDA: Then haven't you anything to say to me about what happened up there?

SOLNESS: *(In momentary surprise.)* Up at Lysanger? *(Indifferently.)* Why, it was nothing much to talk about, it seems to me.

HILDA: *(Looks reproachfully at him.)* How can you sit there and say such things?

SOLNESS: Well, then, *you* talk to *me* about it.

HILDA: When the tower was finished, we had grand doings in the town.

SOLNESS: Yes, I sha'n't easily forget that day.

HILDA: *(Smiles.)* Won't you? That's good of you!

SOLNESS: Good?

HILDA: There was music in the churchyard—and many, many hundreds of people. We school-girls were dressed in white; and we all carried flags.

SOLNESS: Ah yes, those flags—I can tell you I remember them!

HILDA: Then you climbed up over the scaffolding, straight to the very top; and you had a great wreath with you; and you hung that wreath right away up on the weathercock.

SOLNESS: *(Curtly interrupting.)* I always did that in those days. It's an old custom.

HILDA: It was so wonderfully thrilling to stand below and look up at you. Fancy, if he should fall over! He—the master builder himself!

SOLNESS: *(As if to lead her away from the subject.)* Yes, yes, yes, that might very well have happened, too. For one of those white-frocked little devils—she went on in such a way, and screamed up at me so——

HILDA: *(Sparkling with pleasure.)* "Hurra for Mr. Solness!" Yes!

SOLNESS: —and waved and flourished with her flag so that I—so that it almost made me giddy to look at it.

HILDA: *(In a lower voice, seriously.)* That little devil—that was I.

SOLNESS: *(Fixes his eyes steadily upon her.)* I'm sure of that now. It *must* have been you.

HILDA: *(Lively again.)* Oh, it was so gloriously thrilling! I couldn't have believed there was a builder in the whole world that could have built such a tremendously high tower. And then, that you yourself should stand at the very top of it, as large as life! And that you shouldn't be the least bit dizzy! It was that above everything that made one—made one dizzy to think of.

SOLNESS: How could you be so certain that I wasn't——?

HILDA: *(Scouting the idea.)* No indeed! Oh no! I knew that instinctively. For if you had been you could never have stood up there and sung.

SOLNESS: *(Looks at her in astonishment.)* Sung? Did I sing?

HILDA: Yes, I should think you did.

SOLNESS: *(Shakes his head.)* I've never sung a note in my life.

HILDA: Yes, you sang then. It sounded like harps in the air.

SOLNESS: *(Thoughtfully.)* This is very strange—all this.

HILDA: *(Is silent awhile, looks at him and says in a low voice:)* But then,—it was after that—that the *real* thing happened.

SOLNESS: The real thing?

HILDA: *(Sparkling with vivacity.)* Yes, I surely don't need to remind you of *that?*

SOLNESS: Oh yes, do remind me a little of *that*, too.

HILDA: Don't you remember that a great dinner was given in your honor at the Club?

SOLNESS: Yes, to be sure. It must have been the same afternoon, for I left the place next morning.

HILDA: And from the Club you were invited to come round to our house to supper.

SOLNESS: Quite right, Miss Wangel. It's wonderful how all these trifles have impressed themselves on your mind.

HILDA: Trifles! I like that! Perhaps it was a trifle, too, that I was *alone* in the room when you came in?

SOLNESS: *Were* you alone?

HILDA: *(Without answering him.)* You didn't call me a little devil *then*.

SOLNESS: No, I probably didn't.

HILDA: You said I was lovely in my white dress, and that I looked like a little princess.

SOLNESS: I've no doubt you did, Miss Wangel.—And besides—I was feeling so buoyant and free that day——

HILDA: And then you said that when I grew up I should be *your* princess.

SOLNESS: *(Laughing a little.)* Dear, dear—did I say *that* too?

HILDA: Yes, you did. And when I asked how long I should have to wait, you said that you would come again in ten years—like a troll—and carry me off—to Spain or some such place. And you promised you would buy me a kingdom there.

SOLNESS: *(As before.)* Yes, after a good dinner one doesn't haggle about the halfpence. But did I really *say* all that?

HILDA: *(Laughs to herself.)* Yes. And you told me, too, what the kingdom was to be called.

SOLNESS: Well, what was it?

HILDA: It was to be called the kingdom of Orangia,[1] you said.

SOLNESS: Well, that was an appetizing name.

HILDA: No, I didn't like it a bit; for it seemed as though you wanted to make game of me.

SOLNESS: I'm sure *that* can't have been my intention.

HILDA: No, I should hope not—considering what you did next——

SOLNESS: What in the world did I do next?

HILDA: Well, that's the finishing touch, if you've forgotten *that* too. I should have thought one couldn't help remembering such a thing as that.

SOLNESS: Yes, yes, just give me a hint, and then perhaps—. Well?

HILDA: *(Looks fixedly at him.)* You came and kissed me, Mr. Solness.

SOLNESS: *(Open-mouthed, rising from his chair.)* I did!

HILDA: Yes, indeed you did. You took me in both your arms, and bent my head back, and kissed me—many times.

SOLNESS: Now, really, my dear Miss Wangel——!

HILDA: *(Rises.)* You surely don't mean to deny it?

SOLNESS: Yes, I do. I deny it altogether!

HILDA: *(Looks scornfully at him.)* Oh, indeed!

(She turns and goes slowly close up to the stove, where she remains standing motionless, her face averted from him, her hands behind her back. Short pause.)

SOLNESS: *(Goes cautiously up behind her.)* Miss Wangel!——

HILDA: *(Is silent and does not move.)*

SOLNESS: Don't stand there like a statue. You must have dreamt all this. *(Lays his hand on her arm.)* Now just listen——

HILDA: *(Makes an impatient movement with her arm.)*

SOLNESS: *(As a thought flashes upon him.)* Or——! Wait a moment! There is something under all this, you may depend!

HILDA: *(Does not move.)*

---

1. In the original "Appelsinia," "appelsin" meaning "orange."

SOLNESS: *(In a low voice, but with emphasis.)* I must have *thought* all that. I must have *wished* it—have *willed* it—have *longed* to do it. And then——. May not that be the explanation?

HILDA: *(Is still silent.)*

SOLNESS: *(Impatiently.)* Oh very well, deuce take it all—then I *did* do it, I suppose!

HILDA: *(Turns her head a little, but without looking at him.)* Then you admit it now?

SOLNESS: Yes—whatever you like.

HILDA: You came and put your arms round me?

SOLNESS: Oh yes.

HILDA: And bent my head back?

SOLNESS: Very far back.

HILDA: And kissed me?

SOLNESS: Yes, I did.

HILDA: Many times?

SOLNESS: As many as ever you like.

HILDA: *(Turns quickly towards him and has once more the sparkling expression of gladness in her eyes.)* Well, you see, I got it out of you at last!

SOLNESS: *(With a slight smile.)* Yes—just think of my forgetting such a thing as that.

HILDA: *(Again a little sulky, retreats from him.)* Oh, you've kissed so many people in your time, I suppose.

SOLNESS: No, you mustn't think *that* of me.

(HILDA seats herself in the arm-chair. SOLNESS stands and leans against the rocking-chair.)

SOLNESS: *(Looks observantly at her.)* Miss Wangel?

HILDA: Yes?

SOLNESS: How *was* it now? What came of all this—between us two?

HILDA: Why, nothing more come of it. You know that quite well. For then the other guests came in, and then—bah!

SOLNESS: Quite so! The others came in. To think of my forgetting *that* too!

HILDA: Oh, you haven't really forgotten anything: you're only a little ashamed of it all. I'm sure one doesn't forget things of that kind.

SOLNESS: No, one would suppose not.

HILDA: *(Lively again looks at him.)* Perhaps you've even forgotten what day it was?

SOLNESS: What day?

HILDA: Yes, on what day did you hang the wreath on the tower? Well? Tell me at once!

SOLNESS: H'm—I confess I've forgotten the particular day. I only know it was ten years ago. Some time in the autumn.

HILDA: *(Nods her head slowly several times.)* It was ten years ago—on the 19th of September.

SOLNESS: Yes, it must have been about that time. Fancy your remembering that too! *(Stops.)* But wait a moment—! Yes—it's the 19th of September to-day.

HILDA: Yes, it is; and the ten years are gone. And you didn't come—as you had promised me.

SOLNESS: Promised you? Threatened, I suppose you mean?

HILDA: I don't think there was any sort of threat in *that*.

SOLNESS: Well then, a little bit of a hoax.

HILDA: Was that all you wanted to do? To hoax me?

SOLNESS: Well, or to have a little joke with you! Upon my soul I don't recollect. But it must have been something of that kind; for you were a mere child then.

HILDA: Oh, perhaps I wasn't quite such a child either. Not such a mere chit as you imagine.

SOLNESS: *(Looks searchingly at her.)* Did you really and seriously expect me to come again?

HILDA: *(Conceals a half-teasing smile.)* Yes, indeed! I did expect *that* of you.

SOLNESS: That I should come back to your home, and take you away with me?

HILDA: Just like a troll—yes.

SOLNESS: And make a princess of you?

HILDA: That's what you promised.

SOLNESS: And give you a kingdom as well?

HILDA: *(Looks up at the ceiling.)* Why not? Of course it needn't have been an actual, every-day sort of a kingdom.

SOLNESS: But something else just as good?

HILDA: Yes, at least as good. *(Looks at him a moment.)* I thought if you could build the highest church-towers in the world, you could surely manage to raise a kingdom of one sort or another as well.

SOLNESS: *(Shakes his head.)* I can't quite make you out, Miss Wangel.

HILDA: Can't you? To me it seems all so simple.

SOLNESS: No, I can't make up my mind whether you mean all you say, or are simply having a joke with me.

HILDA: *(Smiles.)* Hoaxing you, perhaps? I, too?

SOLNESS: Yes, exactly. Hoaxing—both of us. *(Looks at her.)* Is it long since you found out that I was married?

HILDA: I've known it all along. Why do you ask me *that*?

SOLNESS: *(Lightly.)* Oh, well, it just occurred to me. *(Looks earnestly at her, and says in a low voice:)* What have you come for?

HILDA: I want my kingdom. The time is up.

SOLNESS: *(Laughs involuntarily.)* What a girl you are!

HILDA: *(Gayly.)* Out with my kingdom, Mr. Solness! *(Raps with her fingers.)* The kingdom on the table!

SOLNESS: *(Pushing the rocking-chair nearer and sitting down.)* Now, seriously speaking—what have you come for? What do you really want to do here?

HILDA: Oh, first of all, I want to go round and look at all the things that you've built.

SOLNESS: That will give you plenty of exercise.

HILDA: Yes, I know you've built a tremendous lot.

SOLNESS: I have indeed—especially of late years.

HILDA: Many church-towers among the rest? Immensely high ones?

SOLNESS: No. I build no more church-towers now. Nor churches either.

HILDA: What *do* you build then?

SOLNESS: Homes for human beings.

HILDA: *(Reflectively.)* Couldn't you build a little—a little bit of a church-tower over these homes as well?

SOLNESS: *(Starting.)* What do you mean by *that?*

HILDA: I mean—something that points—points up into the free air. With the vane at a dizzy height.

SOLNESS: *(Pondering a little.)* Strange that you should say *that*—for that's just what I'm most anxious to do.

HILDA: *(Impatiently.)* Then why don't you do it?

SOLNESS: *(Shakes his head.)* No, the people won't have it.

HILDA: Fancy their not wanting it!

SOLNESS: *(More lightly.)* But now I'm building a new home for myself—just opposite here.

HILDA: For yourself?

SOLNESS: Yes. It's almost finished. And on that there's a tower.

HILDA: A high tower?

SOLNESS: Yes.

HILDA: Very high?

SOLNESS: No doubt people will say that it's too high—too high for a dwelling-house.

HILDA: I'll go out and look at that tower the first thing to-morrow morning.

SOLNESS: *(Sits with his hand under his cheek and gazes at her.)* Tell me, Miss Wangel—what is your name? Your Christian name, I mean?

HILDA: Why, Hilda, of course.

SOLNESS: *(As before.)* Hilda? Ah?

HILDA: Don't you remember *that?* You called me Hilda yourself—that day when you misbehaved.

SOLNESS: Did I really?

HILDA: But then you said "*little* Hilda"; and I didn't like that.

SOLNESS: Oh, you didn't like that, Miss Hilda?

HILDA: No, not at such a time as that. But—"Princess Hilda"—that will sound very well, I think.

SOLNESS: Very well indeed. Princess Hilda of—of—what was to be the name of the kingdom?

HILDA: Pooh! I won't have anything to do with *that* stupid kingdom. I've set my heart upon quite a different one!

SOLNESS: *(Has leaned back in the chair, still gazing at her.)* Isn't it strange——? The more I think of it now, the more it seems to me as though I had gone about all these years torturing myself with—h'm——

HILDA: With what?

SOLNESS: With the effort to recover something—some experience, which I seemed to have forgotten. But I never had the least inkling of what it would be.

HILDA: You should have tied a knot in your pocket-handkerchief, Mr. Solness.

SOLNESS: In that case, I should simply have had to go racking my brains to discover what the knot could mean.

HILDA: Oh, yes, I suppose there are trolls of *that* kind in the world, too.

SOLNESS: *(Rises slowly.)* What a good thing it is that *you* have come to me now.

HILDA: *(Looks deeply into his eyes.) Is* it a good thing?

SOLNESS: For I've been so lonely here. I've been gazing so helplessly at it all. *(In a lower voice.)* I must tell you—I've begun to be so afraid—so terribly afraid of the younger generation.

HILDA: *(With a little snort of contempt.)* Pooh—is the younger generation a thing to be afraid of?

SOLNESS: It is indeed. And that's why I've locked and barred myself in. *(Mysteriously.)* I tell you the younger generation will one day come and thunder at my door! They'll break in upon me!

HILDA: Then I should say you ought to go out and open the door to the younger generation.

SOLNESS: Open the door?

HILDA: Yes. Let them come in to you on friendly terms, as it were.

SOLNESS: No, no, no! The younger generation—it means retribution, you see. It comes, as if under a new banner, heralding the turn of fortune.

HILDA: *(Rises, looks at him, and says with a quivering twitch of her lips.)* Can *I* be of any use to you, Mr. Solness?

SOLNESS: Yes, you can indeed! For you, too, come—under a new banner, it seems to me. Youth marshalled against youth——!

(DR. HERDAL *comes in by the hall-door.)*

DR. HERDAL: What—you and Miss Wangel here still?

SOLNESS: Yes. We've had no end of things to talk about.

HILDA: Both old and new.

DR. HERDAL: Have you really?

HILDA: Oh, it has been the greatest fun. For Mr. Solness—he has such a miraculous memory. All the least little details he remembers instantly.

(MRS. SOLNESS *enters by the door on the right.)*

MRS. SOLNESS: Well, Miss Wangel, your room is quite ready for you now.

HILDA: Oh, how kind you are to me!

SOLNESS: *(To MRS. SOLNESS.)* The nursery?

MRS. SOLNESS: Yes, the middle one. But first let us go in to supper.

SOLNESS: *(Nods to HILDA.)* Hilda shall sleep in the nursery.

MRS. SOLNESS: *(Looks at him.)* Hilda?

SOLNESS: Yes, Miss Wangel's name is Hilda. I knew her when she was a child.

MRS. SOLNESS: Did you really, Halvard? Well, shall we go? Supper is on the table.

(She takes DR. HERDAL'S *arm and goes out with him to the right.* HILDA *has meanwhile been collecting her travelling things.)*

HILDA: *(Softly and rapidly to* SOLNESS.*)* Is it true, what you said? *Can* I be of use to you?

SOLNESS: *(Takes the things from her.)* You are the very one I have most needed.

HILDA: *(Looks at him with happy, wondering eyes and clasps her hands.)* Oh heavens, how lovely——!

SOLNESS: *(Eagerly.)* What——?

HILDA: Then I *have* my kingdom!

SOLNESS: *(Involuntarily.)* Hilda——!

HILDA: *(Again with the quivering twitch of her lips.)* Almost—I was going to say.

(She goes out to the right. SOLNESS *follows her.)*

SECOND ACT

A prettily furnished small drawing-room in the house of SOLNESS. *In the back, a glass-door leading out to the veranda and garden. The right-hand corner is cut off transversely by a large bay-window, in which are flower-stands. The left-hand corner is similarly cut off by a transverse wall, in which is a small door papered like the wall. On each side, an ordinary door. In front, on the right, a console table with a large mirror over it. Well-filled stands of plants and flowers. In front, on the left, a sofa with a table and chairs. Further back, a bookcase. Well forward in the room, before the bay-window, a small table and some chairs. It is early in the day.*

SOLNESS *sits by the little table with* RAGNAR BROVIK'S *portfolio open in front of him. He is turning the drawings over and closely examining some of them.* MRS. SOLNESS *walks about noiselessly with a small watering-pot, attending to her flowers. She is dressed in black as before. Her hat, cloak and parasol lie on a chair near the mirror. Unobserved by her,* SOLNESS *now and again follows her with his eyes. Neither of them speaks.*

KAIA FOSLI *enters quietly by the door on the left.*

SOLNESS: *(Turns his head and says in an off-hand tone of indifference.)* Well, is that you?

KAIA: I merely wished to let you know I've come.

SOLNESS: Yes, yes, that's all right. Hasn't Ragnar come too?

KAIA: No, not yet. He had to wait a little while to see the doctor. But he's coming presently to hear——

SOLNESS: How is the old man to-day?

KAIA: Not well. He begs you to excuse him, for he must keep his bed to-day.

SOLNESS: Quite so; by all means let him rest. But now, get to your work.

KAIA: Yes. *(Pauses at the door.)* Do you wish to speak to Ragnar when he comes?

SOLNESS: No—I don't know that I've anything special to say to him.

(KAIA goes out again to the left. SOLNESS *remains seated, turning over the drawings.)*

MRS. SOLNESS: *(Over beside the plants.)* I wonder if *he* isn't going to die now, as well?

SOLNESS: *(Looks up at her.)* As well as who?

MRS. SOLNESS: *(Without answering.)* Yes, yes—depend upon it, Halvard, old Brovik's going to die too. You'll see that he will.

SOLNESS: My dear Aline, oughtn't you to go out for a little walk?

MRS. SOLNESS: Yes, I suppose I ought to. *(She continues to attend to the flowers.)*

SOLNESS: *(Bending over the drawings.)* Is she still asleep?

MRS. SOLNESS: *(Looking at him.)* Is it Miss Wangel you're sitting there thinking about?

SOLNESS: *(Indifferently.)* I just happened to recollect her.

MRS. SOLNESS: Miss Wangel was up long ago.

SOLNESS: Oh, was she?

MRS. SOLNESS: When I went in to see her, she was busy putting her things in order.

(She goes in front of the mirror and slowly begins to put on her hat.)

SOLNESS: *(After a short pause.)* So we've found a use for one of our nurseries after all, Aline.

MRS. SOLNESS: Yes, we have.

SOLNESS: That seems to me better than to have them all standing empty.

MRS. SOLNESS: That emptiness is dreadful; you're right there.

SOLNESS: *(Closes the portfolio, rises and approaches her.)* You'll find that we shall get on far better after this, Aline. Things will be more comfortable. Life will be easier—especially for *you.*

MRS. SOLNESS: *(Looks at him.)* After this?

SOLNESS: Yes, believe me, Aline——

MRS. SOLNESS: Do you mean—because *she* has come here?

SOLNESS: *(Checking himself.)* I mean, of course—when once we've moved into the new house.

MRS. SOLNESS: *(Takes her cloak.)* Ah, do you think so, Halvard? Will it be better then?

SOLNESS: I can't think otherwise. And surely you think so too?

MRS. SOLNESS: I think nothing at all about the new house.

SOLNESS: *(Cast down.)* It's hard for me to hear you say that; for you know it's mainly for your sake that I've built it.

(He offers to help her on with her cloak.)

MRS. SOLNESS: *(Evades him.)* The fact is, you do far too much for my sake.

SOLNESS: *(With a certain vehemence.)* No, no, you really mustn't say that, Aline. I can't bear to hear you say such things.

MRS. SOLNESS: Very well, then I won't say it, Halvard.

SOLNESS: But I stick to what *I* said. You'll see that things'll be easier for you in the new place.

MRS. SOLNESS: Oh heavens—easier for me—!

SOLNESS: *(Eagerly.)* Yes, indeed they will! You may be quite sure of that! For you see—there'll be so very, very much there that'll remind you of your own home——

MRS. SOLNESS: The home that used to be father's and mother's—and that was burnt to the ground——

SOLNESS: *(In a low voice.)* Yes, yes, my poor Aline. That was a terrible blow for you.

MRS. SOLNESS: *(Breaking out in lamentation.)* You may build as much as ever you like, Halvard—you can never build up again a real home for *me*!

SOLNESS: *(Crosses the room.)* Well, in Heaven's name, let us talk no more about it then.

MRS. SOLNESS: We're not in the habit of talking about it. For you always put the thought away from you——

SOLNESS: *(Stops suddenly and looks at her.)* Do I? And why should I do *that*? Put the thought away from me?

MRS. SOLNESS: Oh yes, Halvard, I understand very well. You're so anxious to spare me—and to find excuses for me too—as much as ever you can.

SOLNESS: *(With astonishment in his eyes.)* You! Is it *you*—yourself, that you're talking about, Aline?

MRS. SOLNESS: Yes, who else should it be but myself?

SOLNESS: *(Involuntarily, to himself.)* *That* too!

MRS. SOLNESS: As for the old house, I wouldn't mind so much about that. When once misfortune was in the air—why——

SOLNESS: Ah, you're right there. Misfortune will have its way—as the saying goes.

MRS. SOLNESS: But it's what came of the fire—the dreadful thing that followed——! *That* is the thing! That, that, that!

SOLNESS: *(Vehemently.)* Don't think about *that*, Aline.

MRS. SOLNESS: Ah, that's exactly what I can't help thinking about. And now, at last, I must speak about it, too; for I don't seem able to bear it any longer. And then never to be able to forgive myself——

SOLNESS: *(Vehemently.)* Yourself?

MRS. SOLNESS: Yes, for I had duties on both sides—both towards you and towards the little ones. I ought to have hardened myself—not to have let the horror take such hold upon me, nor the grief for the burning of my home. *(Wrings her hands.)* Oh, Halvard, if I'd only had the strength!

SOLNESS: *(Softly, much moved, comes closer.)* Aline—you must promise me never to think these thoughts any more. Promise me that, dear!

MRS. SOLNESS: Oh, promise, promise! One can promise anything.

SOLNESS: *(Clenches his hands and crosses the room.)* Oh, but this is hopeless, hopeless! Never a ray of sunlight! Not so much as a gleam of brightness to light up our home!

MRS. SOLNESS: This *is* no home, Halvard.

SOLNESS: Oh no, you may well say that. *(Gloomily.)* And God knows whether you're not right in saying that it will be no better for us in the new house, either.

MRS. SOLNESS: It will never be any better. Just as empty—just as desolate—there as here.

SOLNESS: *(Vehemently.)* Why in all the world have we built it then? Can you tell me that?

MRS. SOLNESS: No; you must answer that question for yourself.

SOLNESS: *(Glances suspiciously at her.)* What do you mean by *that*, Aline?

MRS. SOLNESS: What do I mean?

SOLNESS: Yes, in the devil's name! You said it so strangely—as if you had some hidden meaning in it.

MRS. SOLNESS: No, indeed, I assure you——

SOLNESS: *(Comes closer.)* Oh, come now—I know what I know. I've both my eyes and my ears about me, Aline—you may depend upon that!

MRS. SOLNESS: Why, what are you talking about? What is it?

SOLNESS: *(Places himself in front of her.)* Do you mean to say you don't find a kind of lurking, hidden meaning in the most innocent word I happen to say?

MRS. SOLNESS: *I*, do you say? I do that?

SOLNESS: *(Laughs.)* Ho-ho-ho! It's natural enough, Aline! When you've a sick man on your hands——

MRS. SOLNESS: *(Anxiously.) Sick*? Are you ill, Halvard?

SOLNESS: *(Violently.)* A half-mad man, then! A crazy man! Call me what you will.

MRS. SOLNESS: *(Feels gropingly for a chair and sits down.)* Halvard—for God's sake——

SOLNESS: But you're wrong, both you and the doctor. That's not what's the matter with me.

(He walks up and down the room. MRS. SOLNESS *follows him anxiously with her eyes. Finally he goes up to her.)*

SOLNESS: *(Calmly.)* In reality there's nothing whatever wrong with me.

MRS. SOLNESS: No, there isn't, is there? But then what is it that troubles you so?

SOLNESS: Why this, that I often feel ready to sink under this terrible burden of debt——

MRS. SOLNESS: Debt, do you say? But you owe no one anything, Halvard!

SOLNESS: *(Softly, with emotion.)* I owe a boundless debt to you—to you—to you, Aline.

MRS. SOLNESS: *(Rises slowly.)* What is behind all this? You may just as well tell me at once.

SOLNESS: But there *is* nothing behind it. I've never done you any wrong—not wittingly and wilfully, at any rate. And yet—and yet it seems as though a crushing debt rested upon me and weighed me down.

MRS. SOLNESS: A debt to me?

SOLNESS: Chiefly to you.

MRS. SOLNESS: Then you are—ill after all, Halvard.

SOLNESS: *(Gloomily.)* I suppose I must be—or not far from it. *(Looks towards the door to the right, which is opened at this moment.)* Ah! now it grows lighter.

(HILDA WANGEL *comes in. She has made some alterations in her dress, and let down her skirt.)*

HILDA: Good-morning, Mr. Solness!

SOLNESS: *(Nods.)* Slept well?

HILDA: Quite deliciously! As if in a cradle. Oh—I lay and stretched myself like—like a princess!

SOLNESS: *(Smiles a little.)* You were thoroughly comfortable then?

HILDA: I should think so.

SOLNESS: And no doubt you dreamed, too.

HILDA: Yes, I did. But *that* was horrid.

SOLNESS: Indeed?

HILDA: Yes, for I dreamed I was falling over a frightfully high, sheer precipice. Do you never have that kind of dream?

SOLNESS: Oh yes—now and then——

HILDA: It's tremendously thrilling—when you fall and fall——

SOLNESS: It seems to make one's blood run cold.

HILDA: Do you draw your legs up under you while you're falling?

SOLNESS: Yes, as high as ever I can.

HILDA: So do I.

MRS. SOLNESS: *(Takes her parasol.)* I must go into town now, Halvard. *(To* HILDA.*)* And I'll try to get one or two things that may be of use to you.

HILDA: *(Making a motion to throw her arms round her neck.)* Oh, you dear, sweet Mrs. Solness! You're really much too kind to me! Frightfully kind——

MRS. SOLNESS: *(Deprecatingly, freeing herself.)* Oh, far from it. It's only my duty, so I'm very glad to do it.

HILDA: *(Offended, pouts.)* But really, I think I'm quite fit to be seen in the streets—now that I've put my dress to rights. Or do you think I'm not?

MRS. SOLNESS: To tell you the truth, I think people would stare at you a little.

HILDA: *(Contemptuously.)* Pooh! Is that all? That only amuses me.

SOLNESS: *(With suppressed ill-humor.)* Yes, but people might take it into their heads that *you* were mad too, you see.

HILDA: Mad? Are there so many mad people here in town, then?

SOLNESS: *(Points to his own forehead.)* Here you see *one* at all events.

HILDA: You—Mr. Solness!

MRS. SOLNESS: Oh, don't talk like that, my dear Halvard!

SOLNESS: Haven't you noticed *that* yet?

HILDA: No, I certainly haven't. *(Reflects and laughs a little.)* And yet—perhaps in one single thing.

SOLNESS: Ah, do you hear *that*, Aline?

MRS. SOLNESS: What is that one single thing, Miss Wangel?

HILDA: No, I won't say.

SOLNESS: Oh yes, do!

HILDA: No thanks—I'm not so mad as all that.

MRS. SOLNESS: When you and Miss Wangel are alone, I daresay she'll tell you, Halvard.

SOLNESS: Ah—you think she will?

MRS. SOLNESS: Oh yes, certainly. For you've known her so well in the past. Ever since she was a child—you tell me.

(She goes out by the door on the left.)

HILDA: *(After a little while.)* Does your wife dislike me very much?

SOLNESS: Did you think you noticed anything of the kind?

HILDA: Didn't you notice it yourself?

SOLNESS: *(Evasively.)* Aline has become exceedingly shy with strangers of late years.

HILDA: Has she really?

SOLNESS: But if only you could get to know her thoroughly—Ah, she's so nice—and so kind—and so good at heart.

HILDA: *(Impatiently.)* But if she's all that—what made her say that about her duty?

SOLNESS: Her duty?

HILDA: She said that she would go out and buy something for me, because it was her *duty*. Oh I can't bear that ugly, horrid word!

SOLNESS: Why not?

HILDA: It sounds so cold, and sharp, and stinging. Duty—duty—duty. Don't *you* think so, too? Doesn't it seem to sting you?

SOLNESS: H'm—haven't thought much about it.

HILDA: Yes, it does. And if she's so nice—as you say she is—why should she talk in that way?

SOLNESS: But, good Lord, what would you have had her say, then?

HILDA: She might have said she would do it because she had taken a tremendous fancy to me. She might have said something like that—something really warm and cordial, you understand.

SOLNESS: *(Looks at her.)* Is that how you'd like to have it?

HILDA: Yes, precisely.

(She wanders about the room, stops at the bookcase and looks at the books.)

HILDA: What a lot of books you have!

SOLNESS: Yes, I've got together a good many.

HILDA: Do you read them all, too?

SOLNESS: I used to try to. Do you read much?

HILDA: No, never! I've given it up. For it all seems so irrelevant.

SOLNESS: That's just my feeling.

(HILDA wanders about a little, stops at the small table, opens the portfolio and turns over the contents.)

HILDA: Are all these drawings yours?

SOLNESS: No, they're drawn by a young man whom I employ to help me.

HILDA: Some one you've taught?

SOLNESS: Oh yes, no doubt he's learnt something from me, too.

HILDA: *(Sits down.)* Then I suppose he's very clever. *(Looks at a drawing.)* Isn't he?

SOLNESS: Oh, he's not bad. For *my* purpose——

HILDA: Oh yes—I'm sure he's frightfully clever.

SOLNESS: Do you think you can see that in the drawings?

HILDA: Pooh—these scrawlings! But if he's been learning from *you*——

SOLNESS: Oh, as far as that goes——there are plenty of people here that have learnt from *me*, and have come to little enough for all that.

HILDA: *(Looks at him and shakes her head.)* No, I can't for the life of me understand how you can be so stupid.

SOLNESS: Stupid? Do you think I'm so very stupid?

HILDA: Yes, I do indeed. If you're content to go about here teaching all these people——

SOLNESS: *(With a slight start.)* Well, and why not?

HILDA: *(Rises, half-serious, half-laughing.)* No indeed, Mr. Solness! What can be the good of that? No one but yourself should be allowed to build. You should stand quite alone—do it all yourself. Now you know it.

SOLNESS: *(Involuntarily.)* Hilda——!

HILDA: Well!

SOLNESS: How in the world did that come into your head?

HILDA: Do you think I'm so very far wrong then?

SOLNESS: No, that's not what I mean. But now I'll tell you something.

HILDA: Well?

SOLNESS: I keep on—incessantly—in silence and alone—brooding on that very thought.

HILDA: Yes, that seems to me perfectly natural.

SOLNESS: *(Looks somewhat searchingly at her.)* Perhaps you've already noticed it?

HILDA: No, indeed I haven't.

SOLNESS: But just now—when you said you thought I was—off my balance? In one thing you said——

HILDA: Oh, I was thinking of something quite different.

SOLNESS: What was it?

HILDA: I'm not going to tell you.

SOLNESS: *(Crosses the room.)* Well, well—as you please. *(Stops at the bay-window.)* Come here and I'll show you something.

HILDA: *(Approaching.)* What is it?

SOLNESS: Do you see—over there in the garden——?

HILDA: Yes?

SOLNESS: *(Points.)* Right above the great quarry——?

HILDA: That new house, you mean?

SOLNESS: The one that's being built, yes. Almost finished.

HILDA: It seems to have a very high tower.

SOLNESS: The scaffolding is still up.

HILDA: Is that your new house?

SOLNESS: Yes.

HILDA: The house you're soon going to move into?

SOLNESS: Yes.

HILDA: *(Looks at him.)* Are there nurseries in *that* house, too?

SOLNESS: Three, as there are here.

HILDA: And no child.

SOLNESS: And there never will be one.

HILDA: *(With a half-smile.)* Well, isn't it just as I said——

SOLNESS: That——?

HILDA: That you *are* a little—a little mad after all.

SOLNESS: Was that what you were thinking of?

HILDA: Yes, of all the empty nurseries I slept in.

SOLNESS: *(Lowers his voice.)* We *have* had children—Aline and I.

HILDA: *(Looks eagerly at him.)* Have you——?

SOLNESS: Two little boys. They were of the same age.

HILDA: Twins, then.

SOLNESS: Yes, twins. It's eleven or twelve years ago now.

HILDA: *(Cautiously.)* And so both of them——? You have lost both the twins, then?

SOLNESS: *(With quiet emotion.)* We only kept them about three weeks. Or scarcely so much. *(Bursts forth.)* Oh, Hilda, I can't tell you what a good thing it is for me that you have come! For now at last I have some one I can talk to!

HILDA: Can't you talk to—to *her,* too?

SOLNESS: Not about this. Not as I want to talk and must talk. *(Gloomily.)* And not about so many other things, too.

HILDA: *(In a subdued voice.)* Was that all you meant when said you needed me?

SOLNESS: That was mainly what I meant—at all events, yesterday. For to-day I'm not so sure. *(Breaking off.)* Come here and let us sit down, Hilda. Sit there on the sofa—so that you can look into the garden. *(HILDA seats herself in the corner of the sofa. SOLNESS brings a chair closer.)* Would you like to hear about it?

HILDA: Yes, I shall love to sit and listen to you.

SOLNESS: *(Sits down.)* Then I'll tell you all about it.

HILDA: Now I can see both the garden and you, Mr. Solness. So now, tell away! Go on!

SOLNESS: *(Points towards the bay-window.)* Out there on the rising ground—where you see the new house——

HILDA: Yes?

SOLNESS: Aline and I lived there in the first years of our married life. There was an old house up there that had belonged to her mother; and we inherited it, and the whole of the great garden with it.

HILDA: Was there a tower on *that* house, too?

SOLNESS: No, nothing of the kind. From the outside it looked like a great, dark, ugly wooden box; but, all the same, it was snug and comfortable enough inside.

HILDA: Then did you pull down the ramshackle old place?

SOLNESS: No, it was burnt down.

HILDA: The whole of it?

SOLNESS: Yes.

HILDA: Was that a great misfortune for you?

SOLNESS: That depends on how you look at it. As a builder, the fire was the making of me——

HILDA: Well, but——?

SOLNESS: It was just after the birth of the two little boys.

HILDA: The poor little twins, yes.

SOLNESS: They came healthy and bonny into the world. And they were growing too—you could see the difference from day to day.

HILDA: Little children do grow quickly at first.

SOLNESS: It was the prettiest sight in the world to see Aline lying with the two of them in her arms. But then came the night of the fire——

HILDA: *(Excitedly.)* What happened? Do tell me! Was any one burnt?

SOLNESS: No, not that. Every one got safe and sound out of the house——

HILDA: Well, and what then?

SOLNESS: The fright had shaken Aline terribly. The alarm—the escape—the break-neck hurry—and then the ice-cold night air—for they had to be carried out just as they lay—both she and the little ones——

HILDA: Was it too much for them?

SOLNESS: Oh no, *they* stood it well enough. But Aline fell into a fever, and it affected her milk. She would insist on nursing them herself; because it was her duty, she said. And both our little boys, they—*(clenching his hands)*—they—oh!

HILDA: They didn't get over *that*?

SOLNESS: No, *that* they didn't get over. That was how we lost them.

HILDA: It must have been terribly hard for you.

SOLNESS: Hard enough for me; but ten times harder for Aline. *(Clenching his hands in suppressed fury.)* Oh, that such things should be allowed to happen here on earth! *(Shortly and firmly.)* From the day I lost them, I had no heart for building churches.

HILDA: Didn't you like building the church-tower in our town?

SOLNESS: I didn't like it. I know how free and happy I felt when that tower was finished.

HILDA: *I* know that, too.

SOLNESS: And now I shall never—never build anything of that sort again! Neither churches nor church-towers.

HILDA: *(Nods slowly.)* Nothing but houses for people to live in.

SOLNESS: Homes for human beings, Hilda.

HILDA: But homes with high towers and pinnacles upon them.

SOLNESS: If possible. *(Adopts a lighter tone.)* Well, you see, as I said, that fire was the making of me—as a builder, I mean.

HILDA: Why don't you call yourself an architect, like the others?

SOLNESS: I haven't been systematically enough taught for that. Most of what I know, I've found out for myself.

HILDA: But you succeeded all the same.

SOLNESS: Yes, thanks to the fire. I laid out almost the whole of the garden in villa-lots; and *there* I was able to build entirely after my own heart. So I came to the front with a rush.

HILDA: *(Looks keenly at him.)* You must surely be a very happy man— situated as you are.

SOLNESS: *(Gloomily.)* Happy? Do *you* say that, too—like all the rest of them?

HILDA: Yes, I should say you must be. If you could only get the two little children out of your head——

SOLNESS: *(Slowly.)* The two little children—they're not so easy to forget, Hilda.

HILDA: *(Somewhat uncertainly.)* Do you still feel their loss so much—after all these years?

SOLNESS: *(Looks fixedly at her, without replying.)* A happy man, you said——

HILDA: Well now, *are* you not happy—in other respects?

SOLNESS: *(Continues to look at her.)* When I told you all this about the fire— h'm——

HILDA: Well?

SOLNESS: Was there not one special thought that you—that you seized upon?

HILDA: *(Reflects in vain.)* No. What thought should that be?

SOLNESS: *(With subdued emphasis.)* It was simply and solely by that fire that I was enabled to build homes for human beings. Cosy, comfortable, bright homes, where father and mother and the whole troop of children can live in safety and gladness, feeling what a happy thing it is to be alive in the world— and most of all to belong to each other—in great things and in small.

HILDA: *(Ardently.)* Well, and isn't it a great happiness for you to be able to build such beautiful homes?

SOLNESS: The price, Hilda! The terrible price I had to pay for it!

HILDA: But can you *never* get over that?

SOLNESS: No. That I might build homes for others, I had to forego—to forego for all time—the home that might have been my own. I mean a home for a troop of children—and for father and mother, too.

HILDA: *(Cautiously.)* But need you have done that? For all time, you say?

SOLNESS: *(Nods slowly.)* That was the price of this happiness that people talk about. *(Breathes heavily.)* This happiness—h'm—this happiness was not to be bought any cheaper, Hilda.

HILDA: *(As before.)* But may it not come right even yet?

SOLNESS: Never in this world—never. That is another consequence of the fire—and of Aline's illness afterwards.

HILDA: *(Looks at him with an indefinable expression.)* And yet you build all these nurseries?

SOLNESS: *(Seriously.)* Have you never noticed, Hilda, how the impossible—how it seems to beckon and cry aloud to one?

HILDA: *(Reflecting.)* The impossible? *(With animation.)* Yes, indeed! Is that how *you* feel too?

SOLNESS: Yes, I do.

HILDA: Then there must be—a little of the troll in you too?

SOLNESS: Why of the troll?

HILDA: What would *you* call it, then?

SOLNESS: *(Rises.)* Well, well, perhaps you're right. *(Vehemently.)* But how can I help turning into a troll, when this is how it always goes with me in everything—in everything!

HILDA: How do you mean?

SOLNESS: *(Speaking low, with inward emotion.)* Mark what I say to you, Hilda. All that I have succeeded in doing, building, creating—all the beauty, security, cheerful comfort—ay, and magnificence too—*(clenches his hands)*—oh, isn't it terrible even to think of——!

HILDA: *What* is so terrible?

SOLNESS: That all this I have to make up for, to pay for—not in money, but in human happiness. And not with my own happiness only, but with other people's too. Yes, yes, do you see that, Hilda? That is the price which my position as an artist has cost me—and others. And every single day I have to look on while the price is paid for me anew. Over again, and over again—and over again forever.

HILDA: *(Rises and looks steadily at him.)* Now I can see you're thinking of—of *her*.

SOLNESS: Yes, mainly of Aline. For Aline—she, too, had her vocation in life, just as much as I had mine. *(His voice quivers.)* But her vocation has had to be stunted, and crushed, and shattered—in order that mine might force its way to—to a sort of great victory. For you must know that Aline—she, too, had a turn for building.

HILDA: She? For building?

SOLNESS: *(Shakes his head.)* Not houses, and towers, and spires—not such things as I work away at——

HILDA: Well, but *what*, then?

SOLNESS: *(Softly, with emotion.)* For building up the souls of little children, Hilda. For building up children's souls in perfect balance, and in noble and beautiful forms. For enabling them to soar up into erect and full-grown human souls. That was Aline's talent. And there it all lies now—unused and unusable forever—of no earthly service to any one—just like the ruins left by a fire.

HILDA: Yes, but even if this were so——

SOLNESS: It *is* so! It *is* so! I know it.

HILDA: Well, but in any case it's not *your* fault.

SOLNESS: *(Fixes his eyes on her, and nods slowly.)* Ah, *that* is the great, the terrible question. *That* is the doubt that's gnawing me—night and day.

HILDA: That?

SOLNESS: Yes. Suppose the fault *was* mine—in a certain sense.

HILDA: Your fault! The fire!

SOLNESS: All of it; the whole thing. And yet, perhaps—I mayn't have had anything to do with it.

HILDA: (*Looks at him with a troubled expression.*) Oh, Mr. Solness, if you can talk like that, I'm afraid you must be—ill, after all.

SOLNESS: H'm—I don't think I shall ever be of quite sound mind on that point.

(RAGNAR BROVIK *cautiously opens the little door in the left-hand corner.* HILDA *comes forward.*)

RAGNAR: (*When he sees* HILDA.) Oh—I beg pardon, Mr. Solness—— (*He makes a movement to withdraw.*)

SOLNESS: No, no, don't go. Let's get it over.

RAGNAR: Oh, yes—if only we could.

SOLNESS: I hear your father is no better?

RAGNAR: Father is fast growing weaker—and therefore I beg and implore you to write a few kind words for me on one of the plans! Something for father to read before he——

SOLNESS: (*Vehemently.*) I won't hear anything more about those drawings of yours!

RAGNAR: Have you looked at them?

SOLNESS: Yes, I have.

RAGNAR: And they're good for nothing? And *I* am good for nothing, too?

SOLNESS: (*Evasively.*) Stay here with me, Ragnar. You shall have everything your own way. And then you can marry Kaia, and live at your ease—and—and happily too, who knows? Only don't think of building on your own account.

RAGNAR: Well, well, then I must go home and tell father what you say—I promised I would. *Is* this what I am to tell father—before he dies?

SOLNESS: (*With a groan.*) Oh tell him—tell him what you will for me. Best to say nothing at all to him! (*With a sudden outburst.*) I *cannot* do anything else, Ragnar!

RAGNAR: May I have the drawings to take with me?

SOLNESS: Yes, take them—take them by all means! They're lying there on the table.

RAGNAR: (*Goes to the table.*) Thanks.

HILDA: (*Puts her hand on the portfolio.*) No, no; leave them here.

SOLNESS: Why?

HILDA: Because I want to look at them too.

SOLNESS: But you *have* been—— (*To* RAGNAR.) Well, leave them here, then.

RAGNAR: Very well.

SOLNESS: And go home at once to your father.

RAGNAR: Yes, I suppose I must.

SOLNESS: (*As if in desperation.*) Ragnar—you *must* not ask me to do what's beyond my power! Do you hear, Ragnar? You *must* not!

RAGNAR: No, no. I beg your pardon——

(He bows, and goes out by the corner door. HILDA *goes over and sits down on a chair near the mirror.)*

HILDA: *(Looks angrily at* SOLNESS.*)* That was a very ugly thing to do.

SOLNESS: Do *you* think so, too?

HILDA: Yes, it was horribly ugly—and hard and bad and cruel as well.

SOLNESS: Oh, you don't understand my position.

HILDA: All the same——. No, you oughtn't to be like that.

SOLNESS: You said yourself, only just now, that no one but *I* ought to be allowed to build.

HILDA: *I* may say such things—but *you* mayn't.

SOLNESS: I most of all, surely, who have paid so dear for my position.

HILDA: Oh, yes—with what you call domestic comfort—and that sort of thing.

SOLNESS: And with my peace of soul into the bargain.

HILDA: *(Rising.)* Peace of soul! *(With feeling.)* Yes, yes, you're right in that! Poor Mr. Solness—you fancy that——

SOLNESS: *(With a quiet, chuckling laugh.)* Just sit down again, Hilda, and I'll tell you something funny.

HILDA: *(Sits down; with intent interest.)* Well?

SOLNESS: It sounds such a ludicrous little thing; for, you see, the whole story turns upon nothing but a crack in a chimney.

HILDA: No more than that?

SOLNESS: No, not to begin with.

(He moves a chair nearer to HILDA *and sits down.)*

HILDA: *(Impatiently, taps on her knee.)* Well, now for the crack in the chimney!

SOLNESS: I had noticed the split in the flue long, long before the fire. Every time I went up into the attic, I looked to see if it was still there.

HILDA: And it was?

SOLNESS: Yes; for no one else knew about it.

HILDA: And you said nothing?

SOLNESS: Nothing.

HILDA: And didn't think of repairing the flue either.

SOLNESS: Oh yes, I thought about it—but never got any further. Every time I intended to set to work, it seemed just as if a hand held me back. Not to-day, I thought—to-morrow; and nothing ever came of it.

HILDA: But why did you keep putting it off like that?

SOLNESS: Because I was revolving something in my mind. *(Slowly, and in a low voice.)* Through that little black crack in the chimney I might, perhaps, force my way upwards—as a builder.

HILDA: *(Looking straight in front of her.)* That must have been thrilling.

SOLNESS: Almost irresistible—quite irresistible. For at that time it appeared to me a perfectly simple and straightforward matter. I would have had it happen in the winter time—a little before midday. I was to be out driving Aline in the sleigh. The servants at home would have made a huge fire in the stove.

HILDA: For, of course, it was to be bitterly cold that day?

SOLNESS: Rather biting, yes—and they would want Aline to find it thoroughly snug and warm when she came home.

HILDA: I suppose she's very chilly by nature?

SOLNESS: She *is*. And as we drove home, we were to see the smoke.

HILDA: Only the smoke?

SOLNESS: The smoke first. But when we came up to the garden gate, the whole of the old timber-box was to be a rolling mass of flames.—That's how I wanted it to be, you see.

HILDA: Oh, why, *why* couldn't it have happened so!

SOLNESS: You may well say that, Hilda.

HILDA: Well, but now listen, Mr. Solness. Are you perfectly certain that the fire was caused by that little crack in the chimney?

SOLNESS: No, on the contrary—I'm perfectly certain that the crack in the chimney had nothing whatever to do with the fire.

HILDA: What!

SOLNESS: It has been clearly ascertained that the fire broke out in a clothes-cupboard—in a totally different part of the house.

HILDA: Then what's all this nonsense you're talking about the crack in the chimney?

SOLNESS: May I go on talking to you a little, Hilda?

HILDA: Yes, if you'll only talk sensibly,——

SOLNESS: I'll try to. *(He moves his chair nearer.)*

HILDA: Out with it, then, Mr. Solness.

SOLNESS: *(Confidentially.)* Don't you agree with me, Hilda, that there exist special, chosen people who have been endowed with the power and faculty of *desiring* a thing, *craving* for a thing, willing a thing—so persistently and so—so inexorably—that at last it *has* to happen? Don't you believe that?

HILDA: *(With an indefinable expression in her eyes.)* If that is so, we shall see one of these days—whether *I* am one of the chosen.

SOLNESS: It's not one's self alone that can do such great things. Oh, no—the helpers and the servers—they must do their part too, if it's to be of any good. But they never come of themselves. One has to call upon them very persistently—inwardly, you understand.

HILDA: What are these helpers and servers?

SOLNESS: Oh, we can talk about that some other time. For the present, let us keep to this business of the fire.

HILDA: Don't you think the fire would have happened all the same—even if you hadn't wished for it?

SOLNESS: If my house had been old Knut Brovik's, it would never have burnt down so conveniently for *him*. I'm sure of that; for he doesn't know how to call for the helpers—no, nor for the servers, either. *(Rises in agitation.)* So you see, Hilda—it's my fault, after all, the lives of the two little boys had to be sacrificed. And do you think it isn't my fault, too, that Aline has never been the woman she should and might have been—and that she most longed to be?

HILDA: Yes, but if it's all the work of those helpers and servers——?

SOLNESS: *Who* called for the helpers and servers? It was *I!* And they came and obeyed my will. *(In increasing excitement.) That's* what good people call having the luck on your side; but I must tell you what this sort of luck feels like! It feels like a great raw place here on my breast. And the helpers and servers keep on flaying pieces of skin off other people in order to close my sore. But still the sore is not healed—never, never! Oh, if you knew how it can sometimes gnaw and burn.

HILDA: *(Looks attentively at him.)* You *are* ill, Mr. Solness. Very ill, I almost think.

SOLNESS: Say *mad;* for that's what you mean.

HILDA: No, I don't think there's much amiss with your intellect.

SOLNESS: With *what,* then? Out with it!

HILDA: I wonder whether you weren't sent into the world with a sickly conscience.

SOLNESS: A sickly conscience? What devilry is that?

HILDA: I mean that your conscience is feeble—too delicately built, as it were—hasn't strength to take a grip of things—to lift and bear what's heavy.

SOLNESS: *(Growls.)* H'm! May I ask, then, what sort of a conscience one ought to have?

HILDA: I should like *your* conscience to be thoroughly robust.

SOLNESS: Indeed? Robust, eh? Is your own conscience robust.

HILDA: Yes, I think it is. I've never noticed that it wasn't.

SOLNESS: It hasn't been put very severely to the test, I should think.

HILDA: *(With a quivering of the lips.)* Oh, it wasn't such a simple matter to leave father—I'm so awfully fond of him.

SOLNESS: Dear me! for a month or two——

HILDA: I don't think I shall ever go home again.

SOLNESS: Never? Then why did you leave him?

HILDA: *(Half-seriously, half-banteringly.)* Have you forgotten again that the ten years are up?

SOLNESS: Oh, nonsense. Was anything wrong at home? Eh?

HILDA: *(Quite seriously.)* It *was* this something within me that drove and spurred me here—and allured and attracted me, too.

SOLNESS: *(Eagerly.)* There we have it! There we have it, Hilda! There's a troll in you too, as in me. For it's the troll in one, you see—it's *that* that calls to the powers outside us. And then you *must* give in—whether you will or no.

HILDA: I almost think you're right, Mr. Solness.

SOLNESS: *(Walks about the room.)* Oh, there are devils innumerable abroad in the world, Hilda, that one never *sees!*

HILDA: Devils, too?

SOLNESS: *(Stops.)* Good devils and bad devils; light-haired devils and black-haired devils. If only you could always tell whether it's the light or the dark ones that have got hold of you! *(Paces about.)* Ho, ho! Then it would be simple enough!

HILDA: *(Follows him with her eyes.)* Or if one had a really vigorous, radiantly healthy conscience—so that one *dared* to do what one *would.*

SOLNESS: *(Stops beside the console table.)* I believe, now, that most people are just as puny creatures as I am in this respect.

HILDA: I shouldn't wonder.

SOLNESS: *(Leaning against the table.)* In the sagas——Have you read any of the old sagas?

HILDA: Oh yes! When I used to read books, I——

SOLNESS: In the sagas you read about vikings, who sailed to foreign lands, and plundered and burned and killed men——

HILDA: And carried off women——

SOLNESS: ——and kept them in captivity——

HILDA: ——took them home in their ships——

SOLNESS: ——and behaved to them like——like the very worst of trolls.

HILDA: *(Looks straight before her with a half-veiled look.)* I think *that* must have been thrilling.

SOLNESS: *(With a short, deep laugh.)* To carry off women, eh!

HILDA: To *be* carried off.

SOLNESS: *(Looks at her a moment.)* Oh, indeed.

HILDA: *(As if breaking the thread of conversation.)* But what made you speak of these vikings, Mr. Solness?

SOLNESS: Because *those* fellows must have had robust consciences, if you like! When they got home again they could eat and drink, and be as happy as children. And the women, too! They often wouldn't leave them on any account. Can you understand that, Hilda?

HILDA: Those women I can understand exceedingly well.

SOLNESS: Oho! Perhaps you could do the same yourself?

HILDA: Why not?

SOLNESS: Live—of your own free will—with a ruffian like that?

HILDA: If it was a ruffian I had come to love——

SOLNESS: *Could* you come to love a man like that?

HILDA: Good heavens, you know very well one can't choose whom one's going to love.

SOLNESS: *(Looks meditatively at her.)* Oh no, I suppose it's the troll within one that's responsible for that.

HILDA: *(Half laughing.)* And all those blessed devils, that *you* know so well—both the light-haired and the dark-haired ones.

SOLNESS: *(Quietly and warmly.)* Then I hope with all my heart that the devils will choose carefully for you, Hilda.

HILDA: For me they *have* chosen already—once and for all.

SOLNESS: *(Looks earnestly at her.)* Hilda, you are like a wild bird of the woods.

HILDA: Far from it. I don't hide myself away under the bushes.

SOLNESS: No, no. There's rather something of the bird of prey in you.

HILDA: That's nearer it—perhaps. *(Very vehemently.)* And why not a bird of prey? Why shouldn't *I* go a-hunting—I, as well as the rest? Carry off the prey I want—if I can only get my claws into it, and have my own way with it.

SOLNESS: Hilda,—do you know what you are?

HILDA: Yes, I suppose I'm a strange sort of bird.

SOLNESS: No. You are like a dawning day. When I look at you, I seem to be looking towards the sunrise.

HILDA: Tell me, Mr. Solness—are you certain that you've never called me to you?—Inwardly, you know?

SOLNESS: *(Softly and slowly.)* I almost think I must have.

HILDA: What did you want with me?

SOLNESS: You are the younger generation, Hilda.

HILDA: *(Smiles.)* That younger generation that you're so afraid of.

SOLNESS: *(Nods slowly.)* And which, in my heart, I yearn towards so deeply. (HILDA *rises, goes to the little table, and fetches* RAGNAR BROVIK'S *portfolio.)*

HILDA: *(Holds out the portfolio to him.)* We were talking of these drawings——

SOLNESS: *(Shortly, waving them away.)* Put those things away! I've seen enough of them.

HILDA: Yes, but you have to write your approval on them.

SOLNESS: Write my approval on them? Never!

HILDA: But the poor old man is lying at death's door! Can't you give him and his son this pleasure before they're parted? And perhaps he might get the commission to carry them out, too.

SOLNESS: Yes, that's just what he would get. He's made sure of that—has my fine gentleman!

HILDA: Then good heavens—if that's so—can't you tell the least little bit of a lie for once?

SOLNESS: A lie? *(Raging.)* Hilda—take those devil's drawings out of my sight!

HILDA: *(Draws the portfolio a little nearer to herself.)* Well, well, well— don't bite me.—You talk of trolls—but I think you go on like a troll yourself. *(Looks round.)* Where do you keep your pen and ink?

SOLNESS: There's nothing of the sort in here.

HILDA: *(Goes towards the door.)* But in the office where that young lady is——

SOLNESS: Stay where you are, Hilda!—I ought to tell a lie, you say. Oh yes, for the sake of his old father I might well do that—for in my time I've crushed him, trodden him under foot——

HILDA: Him, too?

SOLNESS: I needed room for myself. But this Ragnar—he must on no account be allowed to come to the front.

HILDA: Poor fellow, there's surely no fear of that. If he has nothing in him——

SOLNESS: *(Comes closer, looks at her, and whispers.)* If Ragnar Brovik comes to the front he will strike *me* to the earth. Crush me—as I crushed his father.

HILDA: Crush you? Has he the ability for that?

SOLNESS: Yes, you may depend upon it *he* has the ability! He is the younger generation that stands ready to knock at my door—to make an end of Halvard Solness.

HILDA: *(Looks at him with quiet reproach.)* And yet you would bar him out. Fie, Mr. Solness!

SOLNESS: The fight I have been fighting has cost heart's blood enough.— And I'm afraid, too, that the helpers and servers won't obey me any longer.

HILDA: Then you must go ahead without them. There's nothing else for it.

SOLNESS: It's hopeless, Hilda. The luck is bound to turn. A little sooner or a little later. Retribution is inexorable.

HILDA: *(In distress putting her hands over her ears.)* Don't talk like that! Do you want to kill me? To take from me what is more than my life?

SOLNESS: And what is that?

HILDA: The longing to see you great. To see you, with a wreath in your hand, high, high up upon a church-tower. *(Calm again.)* Come, out with your pencil now. You must have a pencil about you!

SOLNESS: *(Takes out his pocket-book.)* I have one here.

HILDA: *(Puts the portfolio on the sofa-table.)* Very well. Now let us two sit down here, Mr. Solness.

(SOLNESS seats himself at the table.)

HILDA: *(Behind him leaning over the back of the chair.)* And now we'll write on the drawings. We must write very, very nicely and cordially—for this horrid Ruar—or whatever his name is.

SOLNESS: *(Writes a few words, turns his head and looks at her.)* Tell me one thing, Hilda.

HILDA: Yes?

SOLNESS: If you've been waiting for me all these ten years——

HILDA: What then?

SOLNESS: Why have you never written to me? Then I could have answered you.

HILDA: *(Hastily.)* No, no, no! That was just what I didn't want.

SOLNESS: Why not?

HILDA: I was afraid the whole thing might fall to pieces.—But we were going to write on the drawings, Mr. Solness.

SOLNESS: So we were.

HILDA: *(Bends forward and looks over his shoulder while he writes.)* Mind now! kindly and cordially! Oh how I hate—how I hate this Ruald——

SOLNESS: *(Writing.)* Have you never really cared for anyone, Hilda?

HILDA: *(Harshly.)* What do you say?

SOLNESS: Have you never cared for any one?

HILDA: For any one else, I suppose you mean?

SOLNESS: *(Looks up at her.)* For any one else, yes. Have you never? In all these ten years? Never?

HILDA: Oh yes, now and then. When I was perfectly furious with you for not coming.

SOLNESS: Then you did take an interest in other people, too?

HILDA: A little bit—for a week or so. Good heavens, Mr. Solness, you surely know how such things come about.

SOLNESS: Hilda—what is it you've come for?

HILDA: Don't waste time in talking. The poor old man might go and die in the mean time.

SOLNESS: Answer me, Hilda. What do you want of me?

HILDA: I want my kingdom.

SOLNESS: H'm——

(He gives a rapid glance towards the door on the left, and then goes on writing on the drawings. At the same moment MRS. SOLNESS *enters; she has some packages in her hand.)*

MRS. SOLNESS: Here are a few things I've got for you, Miss Wangel. The large parcels will be sent later on.

HILDA: Oh, how very, very kind of you!

MRS. SOLNESS: Only my simple duty. Nothing more than that.

SOLNESS: *(Reading over what he has written.)* Aline!

MRS. SOLNESS: Yes?

SOLNESS: Did you notice whether the   the book-keeper was out there?

MRS. SOLNESS: Yes, of course, *she* was there.

SOLNESS: *(Puts the drawings in the portfolio.)* H'm——

MRS. SOLNESS: She was standing at the desk, as she always is—when *I* go through the room.

SOLNESS: *(Rises.)* Then I'll give this to her, and tell her that——

HILDA: *(Takes the portfolio from him.)* Oh, no, let me have the pleasure of doing that! *(Goes to the door, but turns.)* What's her name?

SOLNESS: Her name is Miss Fosli.

HILDA: Pooh, that sounds so cold. Her Christian name, I mean?

SOLNESS: Kaia—I believe.

HILDA: *(Opens the door and calls out.)* Kaia, come in here! Make haste! Mr. Solness wants to speak to you.

*(*KAIA FOSLI *appears at the door.)*

KAIA: *(Looking at him in alarm.)* Here I am.

HILDA: *(Handing her the portfolio.)* See here, Kaia? You can take these home; Mr. Solness has written on them now.

KAIA: Oh, at last!

SOLNESS: Give them to the old man as soon as you can.

KAIA: I will go straight home with them.

SOLNESS: Yes, do. Now Ragnar will have a chance of building for himself.

KAIA: Oh, may he come and thank you for all——

SOLNESS: *(Harshly.)* I won't have any thanks. Tell him *that* from me.

KAIA: Yes, I will——

SOLNESS: And tell him at the same time that henceforward I don't require his services—nor yours either.

KAIA: *(Softly and quiveringly.)* Not mine either?

SOLNESS: You will have other things to think of now, and to attend to; and that's a very good thing for you. Well, go home with the drawings now, Miss Fosli. Quickly! Do you hear?

KAIA: (*As before.*) Yes, Mr. Solness.
(*She goes out.*)

MRS. SOLNESS: Heavens! what deceitful eyes she has.

SOLNESS: She? That poor little creature?

MRS. SOLNESS: Oh——I can see what I can see, Halvard.——Are you really dismissing them?

SOLNESS: Yes.

MRS. SOLNESS: Her as well?

SOLNESS: Wasn't that what you wished?

MRS. SOLNESS: But how can you get on without *her*——? Oh well, no doubt you have some one else in reserve, Halvard.

HILDA: (*Playfully.*) Well, *I* for one am not the person to stand at that desk.

SOLNESS: Never mind, never mind—it'll be all right, Aline. Now all you have to do is to think about moving into our new home—as quickly as you can. This evening we'll hang up the wreath—(*Turns to* HILDA)—right on the very pinnacle of the tower. What do you say to that, Miss Hilda?

HILDA: (*Looks at him with sparkling eyes.*) It'll be splendid to see you so high up once more.

SOLNESS: Me!

MRS. SOLNESS: For Heaven's sake, Miss Wangel, don't imagine such a thing! My husband!—when he always gets so dizzy!

HILDA: *He* get dizzy! No, I know quite well he doesn't.

MRS. SOLNESS: Oh, yes, indeed he does.

HILDA: But I've seen him with my own eyes right up at the top of a high church-tower.

MRS. SOLNESS: Yes, I hear people talk of that; but its utterly impossible——

SOLNESS: (*Vehemently.*) Impossible—impossible, yes! But there I stood all the same!

MRS. SOLNESS: Oh, how can you say so, Halvard? Why, you can't even bear to go out on the second-story balcony here. You've always been like that.

SOLNESS: You may perhaps see something different this evening.

MRS. SOLNESS: (*In alarm.*) No, no, no! Please God, I shall never see that! I'll write at once to the doctor—and I'm sure he won't let you do it.

SOLNESS: Why, Aline——!

MRS. SOLNESS: Oh, you know you're ill, Halvard. This *proves* it! Oh God—Oh God!
(*She goes hastily out to the right.*)

HILDA: (*Looks intently at him.*) Is it so, or is it not?

SOLNESS: That I turn dizzy?

HILDA: That *my* master builder *dares* not—*cannot*—climb as high as he builds?

SOLNESS: Is that the way you look at it?

HILDA: Yes.

SOLNESS: I believe there's scarcely a corner in me safe from you.

HILDA: *(Looks towards the bay-window.)* Up there, then. Right up there———

SOLNESS: *(Approaches her.)* You might have the topmost chamber in the tower, Hilda—there you might live like a princess.

HILDA: *(Indefinably, between earnest and jest.)* Yes, that's what you promised me.

SOLNESS: *Did* I really?

HILDA: Fie, Mr. Solness! You said, I should be a princess, and that you would give me a kingdom. And then you went and———Well!

SOLNESS: *(Cautiously.)* Are you quite certain that this is not a dream—a fancy, that has fixed itself in your mind?

HILDA: *(Sharply.)* Do you mean that you didn't do it?

SOLNESS: I scarcely know myself. *(More softly.)* But now I know *so much* for certain, that I———

HILDA: That you———? Say it at once!

SOLNESS: ———that I *ought* to have done it.

HILDA: *(In a bold outburst.)* Don't tell me *you* can ever be dizzy!

SOLNESS: This evening, then, we'll hang up the wreath—Princess Hilda.

HILDA: *(With a bitter curve of the lips.)* Over your new home, yes.

SOLNESS: Over the new house, which will never be a *home* for *me. (He goes out through the garden door.)*

HILDA: *(Looks straight in front of her with a far-away expression, and whispers to herself. The only words audible are:)*———frightfully thrilling———

THIRD ACT

A large, broad veranda attached to SOLNESS'S *dwelling-house. Part of the house, with outer door leading to the veranda, is seen to the left. A railing along the veranda to the right. At the back, from the end of the veranda, a flight of steps leads down to the garden below. Tall old trees in the garden spread their branches over the veranda and towards the house. Far to the right, in among the trees, a glimpse is caught of the lower part of the new villa, with scaffolding round so much as is seen of the tower. In the background the garden is bounded by an old wooden fence. Outside the fence, a street with low, tumble-down cottages.*

Evening sky with sun-lit clouds.

On the veranda a garden bench stands along the wall of the house, and in front of the bench a long table. On the other side of the table, an arm-chair and some stools. All the furniture is of wicker-work.

MRS. SOLNESS, *wrapped in a large white crape shawl, sits resting in the arm-chair and gazes over to the right. Shortly after,* HILDA WANGEL *comes up the flight of steps from the garden. She is dressed as in the last act and wears her hat. She has in her bodice a little nosegay of small common flowers.*

MRS. SOLNESS: *(Turning her head a little.)* Have you been round the garden, Miss Wangel?

HILDA: Yes, I've been taking a look at it.

MRS. SOLNESS: And found some flowers too, I see.

HILDA: Yes, indeed. There are such heaps of them in among the bushes.

MRS. SOLNESS: Are there really? Still? You see I scarcely ever go there.

HILDA: *(Closer.)* What! Don't you take a run down into the garden every day, then?

MRS. SOLNESS: *(With a faint smile.)* I don't "run" anywhere, nowadays.

HILDA: Well, but don't you go down now and then, to look at all the lovely things there?

MRS. SOLNESS: It has all become so strange to me. I'm almost afraid to see it again.

HILDA: Your own garden!

MRS. SOLNESS: I don't feel that it is *mine* any longer.

HILDA: What do you mean——?

MRS. SOLNESS: No, no, it *is* not—not as it was in my mother's and father's time. They have taken away so much—so much of the garden, Miss Wangel. Fancy—they've parcelled it out—and built houses for strangers—people that I don't know. And *they* can sit and look in upon me from their windows.

HILDA: *(With a bright expression.)* Mrs. Solness?

MRS. SOLNESS: Yes?

HILDA: May I stay here with you a little?

MRS. SOLNESS: Yes, by all means, if you care to.

(HILDA moves a stool close to the arm-chair and sits down.)

HILDA: Ah—one can sit here and sun oneself like a cat.

MRS. SOLNESS: *(Lays her hand softly on* HILDA'S *neck.)* It's nice of you to be willing to sit with *me*. I thought you wanted to go in to my husband.

HILDA: What should I want with him?

MRS. SOLNESS: To help him, I thought.

HILDA: No, thanks. And besides, he's not in. He's over there with his workmen. But he looked so fierce that I didn't dare to talk to him.

MRS. SOLNESS: He's so kind and gentle in reality.

HILDA: *He!*

MRS. SOLNESS: You don't really know him yet, Miss Wangel.

HILDA: *(Looks affectionately at her.)* Are you pleased at the thought of moving over to the new house?

MRS. SOLNESS: I *ought* to be pleased; for it's what Halvard wants——

HILDA: Oh, not just on that account, surely.

MRS. SOLNESS: Yes, yes, Miss Wangel; for it's simply my duty to submit myself to *him*. But very often it's dreadfully difficult to force one's mind to obedience.

HILDA: Yes, *that* must be difficult indeed.

MRS. SOLNESS: I can tell you it is—when one has so many faults as I have——

HILDA: When one has gone through so much as *you* have——

MRS. SOLNESS: How do you know about that?

HILDA: Your husband told me.

MRS. SOLNESS: To me he very seldom mentions these things.—Yes, I can tell you I've gone through more than enough trouble in my life, Miss Wangel.

HILDA: *(Looks sympathetically at her and nods slowly.)* Poor Mrs. Solness. First of all there was the fire——

MRS. SOLNESS: *(With a sigh.)* Yes, everything that was *mine* was burnt.

HILDA: And then came what was worse.

MRS. SOLNESS: *(Looking inquiringly at her.)* Worse?

HILDA: The worst of all.

MRS. SOLNESS: What do you mean?

HILDA: *(Softly.)* You lost the two little boys.

MRS. SOLNESS: Oh yes, the boys. But you see, *that* was a thing apart. That was a dispensation of Providence; and in such things one can only bow in submission—yes, and be thankful, too.

HILDA: Then are you so?

MRS. SOLNESS: Not always, I'm sorry to say. I know well enough that it's my duty—but all the same I *cannot*.

HILDA: No, no, I think that's only natural.

MRS. SOLNESS: And often and often I have to remind myself that it was a righteous punishment for me—

HILDA: Why?

MRS. SOLNESS: Because I hadn't fortitude enough in misfortune.

HILDA: But I don't see that——

MRS. SOLNESS: Oh, no, no, Miss Wangel—don't talk to me any more about the two little boys. We ought to feel nothing but joy in thinking of *them;* for they are so happy—so happy now. No, it's the *small* losses in life that cut one to the heart—the loss of all that other people look upon as almost nothing.

HILDA: *(Lays her arms on MRS. SOLNESS' knees and looks at her affectionately.)* Dear Mrs. Solness—tell me what things you mean!

MRS. SOLNESS: As I say, only little things. All the old portraits were burnt on the walls. And all the old silk dresses were burnt, that had belonged to the family for generations and generations. And all mother's and grandmother's lace—that was burnt too. And only think—the jewels too! *(Sadly.)* And then all the dolls.

HILDA: The dolls?

MRS. SOLNESS: *(Choking with tears.)* I had nine lovely dolls.

HILDA: And *they* were burnt too?

MRS. SOLNESS: All of them. Oh, it was hard—so hard for me.

HILDA: Had you put by all these dolls, then? Ever since you were little?

MRS. SOLNESS: I hadn't put them by. The dolls and I had gone on living together.

HILDA: After you were grown up?

MRS. SOLNESS: Yes, long after that.

HILDA: After you were married too?

MRS. SOLNESS: Oh yes, indeed. So long as he didn't see it.—But they were all burnt up, poor things. No one thought of saving them. Oh, it's so miserable to think of. You mustn't laugh at me, Miss Wangel.

HILDA: I'm not laughing in the least.

MRS. SOLNESS: For you see, in a certain sense there was life in them, too. I carried them under my heart—like little unborn children.

(DR. HERDAL, *with his hat in his hand, comes out through the door and observes* MRS. SOLNESS *and* HILDA.)

DR. HERDAL: Well, Mrs. Solness, so you're sitting out here catching cold?

MRS. SOLNESS: I find it so pleasant and warm here to-day.

DR. HERDAL: Yes, yes. But is there anything going on here? I got a note from you.

MRS. SOLNESS: *(Rises.)* Yes, there's something I must talk to you about.

DR. HERDAL: Very well; then perhaps we'd better go in. *(To* HILDA.*)* Still in your mountaineering dress, Miss Wangel?

HILDA: *(Gayly, rising.)* Yes—in full uniform! But to-day I'm not going climbing and breaking my neck. We two will stop quietly below and look on, doctor.

DR. HERDAL: What are we to look on at?

MRS. SOLNESS: *(Softly, in alarm, to* HILDA.*)* Hush, hush—for God's sake! He's coming! Try to get that idea out of his head. And let us be friends, Miss Wangel. Don't you think we can?

HILDA: *(Throws her arms impetuously round* MRS. SOLNESS' *neck.)* O, if we only could!

MRS. SOLNESS: *(Gently disengages herself.)* There, there, there! There he comes, doctor. Let me have a word with you.

DR. HERDAL: Is it about *him?*

MRS. SOLNESS: Yes, to be sure it's about him. Do come in.

(She and the doctor enter the house. Next moment SOLNESS comes up from the garden by the flight of steps. A serious look comes over HILDA's face.)

SOLNESS: *(Glances at the house-door, which is closed cautiously from within.)* Have you noticed, Hilda, that as soon as I come, she goes?

HILDA: I've noticed that as soon as you come, you make her go.

SOLNESS: Perhaps so. But I cannot help it. *(Looks observantly at her.)* Are you cold, Hilda? I think you look so.

HILDA: I've just come up out of a tomb.

SOLNESS: What do you mean by *that?*

HILDA: That I've got chilled through and through, Mr. Solness.

SOLNESS: *(Slowly.)* I believe I understand——

HILDA: What brings you up here just now?

SOLNESS: I caught sight of you from over there.

HILDA: But then you must have seen her too?

SOLNESS: I knew she would go at once if I came.

HILDA: Is it very painful for you that she should avoid you in this way?

SOLNESS: In one sense, it's a relief as well.

HILDA: Not to have her before your eyes?

SOLNESS: Yes.

HILDA: Not to be always seeing how heavily the loss of the little boys weighs upon her?

SOLNESS: Yes. Chiefly that.

(HILDA *drifts across the veranda with her hands behind her back, stops at the railing and looks out over the garden.*)

SOLNESS: *(After a short pause.)* Did you have a long talk with her?

(HILDA *stands motionless and does not answer.*)

SOLNESS: Had you a long talk, I asked?

(HILDA *is silent as before.*)

SOLNESS: What was she talking about, Hilda?

(HILDA *continues silent.*)

SOLNESS: Poor Aline! I suppose it was about the little boys.

HILDA: *(A nervous shudder runs through her; then she nods hurriedly once or twice.)*

SOLNESS: She will never get over it—never in this world. *(Approaches her.)* Now you're standing there again like a statue; just as you stood last night.

HILDA: *(Turns and looks at him with great serious eyes.)* I am going away.

SOLNESS: *(Sharply.)* Going away!

HILDA. Yes.

SOLNESS: But I won't allow you to.

HILDA: What am I to do *here* now?

SOLNESS: Simply to *be* here, Hilda!

HILDA: *(Measures him with a look.)* Oh, thank you. You know it wouldn't end there.

SOLNESS: *(Without consideration.)* So much the better.

HILDA: *(Vehemently.)* I *can't* do any harm to one I *know!* I can't take away anything that belongs to her.

SOLNESS: Who wants you to do that?

HILDA: *(Continuing.)* A stranger, yes! for that's quite a different thing. A person I've never set eyes on. But one that I've come into close contact with— ! No! Oh no! Ugh!

SOLNESS: Yes, but I never proposed you should.

HILDA: Oh, Mr. Solness, you know quite well what the end of it would be. And that's why I'm going away.

SOLNESS: And what's to become of me when you're gone? What shall I have to live for *then?*—After that?

HILDA: *(With the indefinable look in her eyes.)* It's surely not so hard for *you.* You have your duties to her. Live for those duties.

SOLNESS: Too late. These powers—these—these——

HILDA: ——devils——

SOLNESS: Yes, these devils! And the troll within me as well—they have drawn all the life-blood out of her. *(Laughs in desperation.)* They did it for my happiness. Yes, yes! *(Sadly.)* And now she's dead—for my sake. And I am chained alive to a dead woman. *(In wild anguish.)* I——I who *cannot* live without joy in life!

(HILDA walks round the table and seats herself on the bench with her elbows on the table, and her head supported by her hands.)

HILDA: *(Sits and looks at him awhile.)* What will you build next?

SOLNESS: *(Shakes his head.)* I don't believe I shall build much more.

HILDA: Not those cosy, happy homes for mother and father, and for the troop of children?

SOLNESS: I wonder whether there will be any use for such homes in the times that are coming.

HILDA: Poor Mr. Solness! And you have gone all these ten years—and staked your whole life—on that alone.

SOLNESS: Yes, you may well say so, Hilda.

HILDA: *(With an outburst.)* Oh, it all seems to me so foolish—so foolish!

SOLNESS: All what?

HILDA: Not to be able to grasp at your own happiness—at your own life! Merely because some one you know happens to stand in the way!

SOLNESS: One whom you have no right to set aside.

HILDA: I wonder whether one really *hasn't* the right? And yet, and yet——. Oh! If one could only sleep the whole thing away!

(She lays her arms flat down on the table, rests the left side of her head on her hand and shuts her eyes.)

SOLNESS: *(Turns the arm-chair and sits down at the table.)* Had *you* a cosy, happy home—up with your father, Hilda?

HILDA: *(Without stirring, answers as if half asleep.)* I had only a cage.

SOLNESS: And you're determined not to return to it?

HILDA: *(As before.)* The wild bird never wants to go into the cage.

SOLNESS: Rather range through the free air——

HILDA: *(Still as before.)* The bird of prey loves to range—

SOLNESS: *(Lets his eyes rest on her.)* If only one had the viking-spirit in life—

HILDA: *(In her usual voice; opens her eyes but does not move.)* And the other thing? Say what *that* was!

SOLNESS: A robust conscience.

(HILDA sits upon the bench with animation. Her eyes have once more the sparkling expression of gladness.)

HILDA: *(Nods to him.)* I know what you're going to build next!

SOLNESS: Then you know more than I do, Hilda.

HILDA: Yes, builders are such stupid people.

SOLNESS: What is it to be then?

HILDA: *(Nods again.)* The castle.

SOLNESS: What castle?

HILDA: *My* castle, of course.

SOLNESS: Do you want a castle now?

HILDA: Don't you owe me a kingdom, I'd like to know?

SOLNESS: You say I do.

HILDA: Well—you admit you owe me this kingdom. And you can't have a kingdom without a royal castle, I should think!

SOLNESS: *(More and more animated.)* Yes, they usually go together.

HILDA: Good! Then build it for me this moment!

SOLNESS: *(Laughing.)* Must you have that on the instant, too?

HILDA: Yes, to be sure! For the ten years are up now, and I'm not going to wait any longer. So—out with the castle, Mr. Solness!

SOLNESS: It's no light matter to owe you anything, Hilda.

HILDA: You should have thought of that before. It's too late now. So— *(tapping the table)*—the castle on the table! It's *my* castle. I will have it *at once!*

SOLNESS: *(More seriously, leans over towards her, with his arms on the table.)* What sort of castle have you imagined, Hilda?

(Her expression becomes more and more veiled. She seems gazing inwards at herself.)

HILDA: *(Slowly.)* My castle shall stand on a height—on a very great height— with a clear outlook on all sides, so that I can see far—far around.

SOLNESS: And no doubt it's to have a high tower?

HILDA: A tremendously high tower. And at the very top of the tower there shall be a balcony. And I will stand out upon it—

SOLNESS: *(Involuntarily clutches at his forehead.)* How can you like to stand at such a dizzy height——?

HILDA: Yes, I will! Right up there will I stand and look down on the other people—on those that are building churches, and homes for mother and father and the troop of children. And *you* may come up and look on at it, too.

SOLNESS: *(In a low tone.)* Is the builder to be allowed to come up beside the princess?

HILDA: If the builder *will.*

SOLNESS: *(More softly.)* Then I think the builder will come.

HILDA: *(Nods.)* The builder—he'll come.

SOLNESS: But he'll never be able to build any more. Poor builder!

HILDA: *(Animated.)* Oh yes, he will! We two will set to work together. And then we'll build the loveliest—the very loveliest—thing in all the world.

SOLNESS: *(Intently.)* Hilda, tell me what that is!

HILDA: *(Looks smilingly at him, shakes her head a little, pouts, and speaks as if to a child.)* Builders—they are such very—very stupid people.

SOLNESS: Yes, no doubt they're stupid. But now tell me what it is—the loveliest thing in the world—that we two are to build together?

HILDA: *(Is silent a little while, then says with an indefinable expression in her eyes.)* Castles in the air.

SOLNESS: Castles in the air?

HILDA: *(Nods.)* Castles in the air, yes! Do you know what sort of thing a castle in the air is?

SOLNESS: It's the loveliest thing in the world, you say.

HILDA: *(Rises with vehemence, and makes a gesture of repulsion with her hand.)* Yes, to be sure it is! Castles in the air—they're so easy to take refuge in. And so easy to build, too—*(looks scornfully at him)*—especially for the builders who have a—a dizzy conscience.

SOLNESS: *(Rises.)* After this day we two will build together, Hilda.

HILDA: *(With a half-dubious smile.)* A *real* castle in the air?

SOLNESS: Yes. One with a firm foundation under it.

(RAGNAR BOVIK comes out from the house. He is carrying a large, green wreath with flowers and silken ribbons.)

HILDA: *(With an outburst of pleasure.)* The wreath! Oh, that'll be glorious!

SOLNESS: *(In surprise.)* Have *you* brought the wreath, Ragnar?

RAGNAR: I promised the foreman I would.

SOLNESS: *(Relieved.)* Ah, then I suppose your father's better?

RAGNAR: No.

SOLNESS: Wasn't he cheered by what I wrote?

RAGNAR: It came too late.

SOLNESS: Too late!

RAGNAR: When she came with it he was unconscious. He has had a stroke.

SOLNESS: Why, then, you must go home to him! You must attend to your father!

RAGNAR: He doesn't need me any more.

SOLNESS: But surely you ought to be with him.

RAGNAR: *She* is sitting by his bed.

SOLNESS: *(Rather uncertainly.)* Kaia?

RAGNAR: *(Looking darkly at him.)* Yes—Kaia.

SOLNESS: Go home, Ragnar—both to him and to her. Give *me* the wreath.

RAGNAR: *(Suppresses a mocking smile.)* You don't mean that you your-self—

SOLNESS: I will take it down to them myself. *(Takes the wreath from him.)* And now, you go home; we don't require you to-day.

RAGNAR: I know you don't require me any more; but to-day I shall stop.

SOLNESS: Well, stop then, since you're bent upon it.

HILDA: *(At the railing.)* Mr. Solness, I will stand here and look on at you.

SOLNESS: At me!

HILDA: It will be fearfully thrilling.

SOLNESS: *(In a low tone.)* We'll talk about that another time, Hilda.

(He goes down the flight of steps with the wreath, and away through the garden.)

HILDA: *(Looks after him, then turns to RAGNAR.)* You might at least have thanked him, I think.

RAGNAR: Thanked him? Ought I to have thanked *him*?

HILDA: Yes, of course you ought!

RAGNAR: I think it's rather *you* I ought to thank.

HILDA: How can you say such a thing?

RAGNAR: *(Without answering her.)* But I advise you to take care, Miss Wangel! For you don't know *him* rightly yet.

HILDA: *(Ardently.)* Oh, I know him better than any one!

RAGNAR: *(Laughs in exasperation.)* Thank him, when he's held me down year after year! When he made father disbelieve in me—made me disbelieve in myself. And all merely that he might——!

HILDA: *(As if divining something.)* That he might——? Tell me at once!

RAGNAR: That he might keep her with him.

HILDA: *(With a start towards him.)* The girl at the desk!

RAGNAR: Yes.

HILDA: *(Threateningly, clenching her hands.)* That is not true! You're telling falsehoods about him!

RAGNAR: I wouldn't believe it either until to-day—when she said so herself.

HILDA: *(As if beside herself.)* What did she say? I *will* know! At once! at once!

RAGNAR: She said that he had taken possession of her mind—her whole mind—centred all her thoughts upon himself alone. She says that she can never leave him—that she will remain here, where *he* is——

HILDA: *(With flashing eyes.)* She won't be allowed to!

RAGNAR: *(As if feeling his way.)* Who won't allow her?

HILDA: *(Rapidly.)* *He* won't either!

RAGNAR: Oh no—I understand the whole thing now. After this she would merely be—in the way.

HILDA: You understand nothing—since you can talk like that! No, *I* will tell you why he kept hold of her.

RAGNAR: Well then, why?

HILDA: In order to keep hold of *you.*

RAGNAR: Has he told you so?

HILDA: No, but it is so. It *must* be so! *(Wildly.)* I will— I *will* have it so!

RAGNAR: And at the very moment when you came—he let her go.

HILDA: It was *you—you* that he let go! What do you suppose he cares about strange women like her?

RAGNAR: *(Reflects.)* Is it possible that all this time he's been afraid of me?

HILDA: *He* afraid! I wouldn't be so conceited if I were you.

RAGNAR: Oh, he must have seen long ago that I had something in me, too. Besides—cowardly—that's just what he is, you see.

HILDA: He! Oh yes, I'm likely to believe *that.*

RAGNAR: In a certain sense he *is* cowardly—he, the great master builder. He's not afraid of robbing others of their life's happiness—as he has done both for my father and for me. But when it comes to climbing a paltry bit of scaffolding—he'll do anything rather than *that.*

HILDA: Oh, you should just have seen him high, high up—at the dizzy height where I once saw him.

RAGNAR: Did you see that?

HILDA: Yes, indeed I did. How free and great he looked as he stood and fastened the wreath to the church-vane!

RAGNAR: I know that he ventured that, *once* in his life—one solitary time. It's a tradition among us younger men. But no power on earth would induce him to do it again.

HILDA: To-day he will do it again!

RAGNAR: *(Scornfully.)* Yes, I daresay!

HILDA: We shall see it.

RAGNAR: That neither you nor I will see.

HILDA: *(With uncontrollable vehemence.)* I *will* see it! I *will* and *must* see it!

RAGNAR: But he won't do it. He simply daren't do it. For you see he can't get over this infirmity—master builder though he be.

(MRS. SOLNESS *comes from the house on to the veranda.*)

MRS. SOLNESS: *(Looks around.)* Isn't he here? Where has he gone to?

RAGNAR: Mr. Solness is down with the men.

HILDA: He took the wreath with him.

MRS. SOLNESS: *(Terrified.)* Took the wreath with him! Oh God! Oh God! Brovik—you must go down to him! Get him to come back here!

RAGNAR: Shall I say you want to speak to him, Mrs. Solness?

MRS. SOLNESS: Oh yes, do! No, no—don't say that *I* want anything! You can say that somebody is here, and that he must come at once.

RAGNAR: Good. I will do so, Mrs. Solness.

(He goes down the flight of steps and away through the garden.)

MRS. SOLNESS: Oh, Miss Wangel, you can't think how anxious I feel about him.

HILDA: Is there anything in this to be so terribly frightened about?

MRS. SOLNESS: Oh yes; surely you can understand. Just think, if he were really to do it! If he should take it into his head to climb up the scaffolding!

HILDA: *(Eagerly.)* Do you think he will?

MRS. SOLNESS: Oh, one can never tell what he might take into his head. I'm afraid there's nothing he mightn't think of doing.

HILDA: Aha! Perhaps you think that he's—well——?

MRS. SOLNESS: Oh, I don't know what to think about him now. The doctor has been telling me all sorts of things; and putting it all together with several things I've heard him say——

(DR. HERDAL *looks out through the door.*)

DR. HERDAL: Isn't he coming soon?

MRS. SOLNESS: Yes, I think so. I've sent for him at any rate.

DR. HERDAL: *(Coming closer.)* I'm afraid you'll have to go in, my dear lady——

MRS. SOLNESS: Oh no! Oh no! I shall stay out here and wait for Halvard.

DR. HERDAL: But some ladies have just come to call on you—

MRS. SOLNESS: Good heavens, that too! And just at this moment!

DR. HERDAL: They say they positively must see the ceremony.

MRS. SOLNESS: Well, well, I suppose I must go to them after all. It's my duty.

HILDA: Can't you ask the ladies to go away?

MRS. SOLNESS: No; that would never do. Now that they're here, it's my duty to see them. But do you stay out here in the mean time, and receive him when he comes.

DR. HERDAL: And try to occupy his attention as long as possible——

MRS. SOLNESS: Yes, do, dear Miss Wangel. Keep as firm hold of him as ever you can.

HILDA: Wouldn't it be best for you to do that?

MRS. SOLNESS: Yes; God knows that is *my* duty. But when one has duties in so many directions——

DR. HERDAL: *(Looks towards the garden.)* There he's coming!

MRS. SOLNESS: And I have to go in!

DR. HERDAL: *(To* HILDA.*)* Don't say anything about *my* being here.

HILDA: Oh no! I dare say I shall find something else to talk to Mr. Solness about.

MRS. SOLNESS: And be sure you keep firm hold of him. I believe *you* can do it best.

(MRS. SOLNESS *and* DR. HERDAL *go into the house.* HILDA *remains standing on the veranda.* SOLNESS *comes from the garden up the flight of steps.)*

SOLNESS: Somebody wants me, I hear.

HILDA: Yes; it's I, Mr. Solness.

SOLNESS: Oh, is it you, Hilda? I was afraid it might be Aline or the Doctor.

HILDA: You're very easily frightened, it seems!

SOLNESS: Do you think so?

HILDA: Yes; people say that you're afraid to climb about—on the scaffoldings, you know.

SOLNESS: Well, that's quite a special thing.

HILDA: Then it's true that you're afraid to do it.

SOLNESS: Yes, I am.

HILDA: Afraid of falling down and killing yourself?

SOLNESS: No, not of that.

HILDA: Of what then?

SOLNESS: I'm afraid of retribution, Hilda.

HILDA: Of retribution? *(Shakes her head.)* I don't understand that.

SOLNESS: Sit down, and I'll tell you something.

HILDA: Yes, do—at once!

(She sits on a stool by the railing, and looks expectantly at him.)

SOLNESS: *(Throws his hat on the table.)* You know that I began by building churches.

HILDA: *(Nods.)* I know that well.

SOLNESS: For, you see, I came as a boy from a pious home in the country; and so it seemed to me that this church building was the noblest task I could set myself.

HILDA: Yes, yes.

SOLNESS: And I venture to say that I built those poor little churches with such honest and warm and heart-felt devotion that—that——

HILDA: That——? Well?

SOLNESS: Well, that I think he ought to have been pleased with me.

HILDA: *He?* What *he?*

SOLNESS: He who was to have the churches, of course! He to whose honor and glory they were dedicated.

HILDA: Oh, indeed! But are you certain, then, that—that he wasn't—pleased with you?

SOLNESS: *(Scornfully.) He* pleased with *me!* How can you talk so, Hilda? He who gave the troll in me leave to lord it just as it pleased. He who bade them be at hand to serve me, both day and night—all these—all these——

HILDA: Devils——

SOLNESS: Yes, of both kinds. Oh no, he made me feel clearly enough that he wasn't pleased with me. *(Mysteriously.)* You see, that was really the reason why he made the old house burn down.

HILDA: Was that why?

SOLNESS: Yes, don't you understand? He wanted to give me the chance of becoming an accomplished master in my own sphere—so that I might build all the more glorious churches for him. At first I didn't understand what he was driving at; but all of a sudden it flashed upon me.

HILDA: When was that?

SOLNESS: It was when I was building the church-tower up at Lysanger.

HILDA: I thought so.

SOLNESS: For you see, Hilda—up there, amid those new surroundings, I used to go about musing and pondering within myself. Then I saw plainly why he had taken my little children from me. It was that I should have nothing else to attach myself to. No such thing as love and happiness, you understand. I was to be only a master builder—nothing else. And all my life long I was to go on building for him. *(Laughs.)* But I can tell you nothing came of that.

HILDA: What did you do, then?

SOLNESS: First of all, I searched and tried my own heart——

HILDA: And then?

SOLNESS: Then I did the *impossible*—I no less than *he.*

HILDA: The impossible?

SOLNESS: I had never before been able to climb up to a great, free height. But that day, I did it.

HILDA: *(Leaping up.)* Yes, yes, you did!

SOLNESS: And when I stood there, high over everything, and was hanging the wreath over the vane, I said to him: Here me now, thou Mighty One! From this day forward I will be a free builder—I too, in my sphere—just as thou in thine. I will never build any more churches for thee—only homes for human beings.

HILDA: *(With great sparkling eyes.) That* was the song that I heard through the air!

SOLNESS: But afterwards his turn came.

HILDA: What do you mean?

SOLNESS: *(Looks disconsolately at her.)* Building homes for human beings is not worth sixpence, Hilda.

HILDA: Do you say *that* now?

SOLNESS: Yes, for now I *see* it. Men have no use for these homes of theirs—to be happy in. And I shouldn't have had any use for such a home, if I'd had one. *(With a quiet, bitter laugh.)* See, that is the upshot of the whole affair, however far back I look. Nothing really built; nor anything sacrificed for the chance of building. Nothing, nothing! the whole is nothing!

HILDA: Then you will never build anything more?

SOLNESS: *(With animation.)* On the contrary, I'm just going to begin.

HILDA: What, then? What will you build? Tell me at once!

SOLNESS: I believe there's only one possible dwelling-place for human happiness—and that's what I'm going to build now.

HILDA: *(Looks firmly at him.)* Mr. Solness—you mean our castles in the air.

SOLNESS: The castles in the air—yes.

HILDA: I'm afraid you would turn dizzy before we got half-way up.

SOLNESS: Not if I can mount hand in hand with you, Hilda.

HILDA: *(With an expression of suppressed resentment.)* Only with me? Won't there be others of the party?

SOLNESS: Who else should there be?

HILDA: Oh—that girl—that Kaia at the desk. Poor thing—don't you want to take her with you too?

SOLNESS: Oho! Was it about her that Aline was talking to you?

HILDA: Is it so—yes or no?

SOLNESS: *(Vehemently.)* I won't answer such a question! You must believe in me, utterly and entirely!

HILDA: All these ten years I've believed in you so fully—so fully.

SOLNESS: You must go on believing in me!

HILDA: Then let me see you stand free and high up!

SOLNESS: *(Sadly.)* Oh, Hilda—it's not every day that I can do that.

HILDA: *(Passionately.)* I will have you do it! I will have it! *(Imploringly.)* Just once more, Mr. Solness! Do the *impossible* once again!

SOLNESS: *(Stands and looks deep into her eyes.)* If I try it, Hilda, I will stand up there and talk to him as I did that time before.

HILDA: *(In rising excitement.)* What will you say to him?

SOLNESS: I will say to him: Hear me, Mighty Lord—thou may'st judge me as seems best to thee. But hereafter I will build nothing but the loveliest thing in the world——

HILDA: *(Carried away.)* Yes—yes—yes!

SOLNESS: —build it together with a princess, whom I love——

HILDA: Yes, tell him that! Tell him that!

SOLNESS: Yes. And then I will say to him: Now I shall go down and throw my arms round her and kiss her——

HILDA: —many times! Say that!

SOLNESS: —many, many times, I will say.

HILDA: And then——?

SOLNESS: Then I will wave my hat—and come down to the earth—and do as I said to him.

HILDA: *(With outstretched arms.)* Now I see you again as I did when there was song in the air!

SOLNESS: *(Looks at her with his head bowed.)* How have you become what you are, Hilda?

HILDA: How have you made me what I am?

SOLNESS: *(Shortly and firmly.)* The princess shall have her castle.

HILDA: *(Jubilant, clapping her hands.)* Oh, Mr. Solness——! My lovely, lovely castle. Our castle in the air!

SOLNESS: On a firm foundation.

(In the street a crowd of people have assembled, vaguely seen through the trees. Music of wind-instruments is heard far away behind the new house.)

(MRS. SOLNESS, with a fur collar round her neck, DOCTOR HERDAL, with her white shawl on his arm, and some ladies, come out on the veranda. RAGNAR BROVIK comes at the same time up from the garden.)

MRS. SOLNESS: *(To RAGNAR.)* Are we to have music, too?

RAGNAR: Yes. It's the band of the Masons' Union. *(To SOLNESS.)* The foreman asked me to tell you that he's ready now to go up with the wreath.

SOLNESS: *(Takes his hat.)* All right. I'll go down to him myself.

MRS. SOLNESS: *(Anxiously.)* What have you to do down there, Halvard?

SOLNESS: *(Curtly.)* I must be down below with the men.

MRS. SOLNESS: Yes, down below—only down below.

SOLNESS: That's where I always stand—on everyday occasions.

(He goes down the flight of steps and away through the garden.)

MRS. SOLNESS: *(Calls after him over the railing.)* But do beg the man to be careful when he goes up! Promise me that, Halvard!

DR. HERDAL: *(To MRS. SOLNESS.)* Don't you see that I was right? He's given up all thought of that folly.

MRS. SOLNESS: Oh, what a relief! Twice workmen have fallen, and each time they were killed on the spot. *(Turns to HILDA.)* Thank you, Miss Wangel, for having kept such a firm hold upon him. I should never have had my own way with him.

DR. HERDAL: *(Playfully.)* Yes, yes, Miss Wangel, you know how to keep firm hold on a man, when you give your mind to it.

(MRS. SOLNESS and DR. HERDAL go up to the ladies, who are standing nearer to the steps and looking over the garden. HILDA remains standing beside the railing in the foreground. RAGNER goes up to her.)

RAGNAR: *(With suppressed laughter, half whispering.)* Miss Wangel, do you see all those young fellows down in the street?

HILDA: Yes.

RAGNAR: They're my fellow-students come to look at the master.

HILDA: What do they want to look at *him* for?

RAGNAR: They want to see how he daren't climb to the top of his own house.

HILDA: Oh, *that's* what those boys want, is it?

RAGNAR: (*Spitefully and scornfully.*) He's kept us down so long, that man. Now we're going to see him keep quietly down below himself.

HILDA: You won't see that—not this time.

RAGNAR: (*Smiles.*) Indeed! Then where shall we see him?

HILDA: High—high up by the vane! That's where you'll see him!

RAGNAR: (*Laughs.*) Him! Oh yes, I daresay!

HILDA: His *will* is to reach the top—so at the top you shall see him.

RAGNAR: His *will* yes; that I can easily believe. But he simply *can't* do it. His head would swim round, long, long before he got half-way. He'd have to crawl down again on his hands and knees.

DR. HERDAL: (*Points across.*) Look! there goes the foreman up the ladders.

MRS. SOLNESS: And of course he's got the wreath to carry too. Oh, I do hope he'll be careful!

RAGNAR: (*Stares incredulously and shouts.*) Why, but it's——

HILDA: (*Breaking out in jubilation.*) It's the master builder himself.

MRS. SOLNESS: (*Screams with terror.*) Yes, it's Halvard! O my great God——! Halvard! Halvard!

DR. HERDAL: Hush! Don't shout to him!

MRS. SOLNESS: (*Half beside herself.*) I must go to him! I must bring him down again.

DR. HERDAL: (*Holds her.*) Don't move, any of you! Not a sound!

HILDA: (*Immovable, follows* SOLNESS *with her eyes.*) He climbs and climbs. Higher and higher! Higher and higher! Look! Just look!

RAGNAR: (*Breathless.*) He *must* turn now. He can't possibly help it.

HILDA: He climbs and climbs. He'll soon be at the top now.

MRS. SOLNESS: Oh, I shall die of terror. I can't bear to see it!

DR. HERDAL: Then don't look up at him.

HILDA: There, he's standing on the topmost planks! Right at the top!

DR. HERDAL: Nobody must move! Do you hear?

HILDA: (*Exulting, with quiet intensity.*) At last! At last! Now I see him great and free again!

RAGNAR: (*Almost voiceless.*) But this is im——

HILDA: So I have seen him all through these ten years. How secure he stands! Frightfully thrilling all the same. Look at him! Now he's hanging the wreath round the vane!

RAGNAR: I feel as if I were looking at something utterly impossible.

HILDA: Yes, it *is* the *impossible* that he's doing now! (*With the indefinable expression in her eyes.*) Can you see any one else up there with him?

RAGNAR: There is no one else.

HILDA: Yes, there is one he is striving with.

RAGNAR: You are mistaken.

HILDA: Then do you hear no song in the air, either?

RAGNAR: It must be the wind in the tree-tops.

HILDA: *I* hear a song—a mighty song! *(Shouts in wild jubilation and glee.)* Look, look! Now he's waving his hat! He's waving it to us down here! Oh, wave, wave back to him! For now it's finished! *(Tears the white shawl from the doctor, waves it, and shouts up to* SOLNESS.*)* Hurrah for Master Builder Solness!

DR. HERDAL: Stop! Stop! For God's sake——!

(The ladies on the veranda wave their pocket-handkerchiefs, and the shouts of "Hurrah" are taken up in the street below. Then they are suddenly silenced, and the crowd bursts out into a shriek of horror. A human body, with planks and fragments of wood, is vaguely perceived crashing down behind the trees.)

MRS. SOLNESS AND THE LADIES: *(At the same time.)* He's falling! He's falling!

*(*MRS. SOLNESS *totters, falls backwards, swooning, and is caught, amid cries and confusion, by the ladies. The crowd in the street breaks down the fence and storms into the garden. At the same time* DR. HERDAL, *too, rushes down thither. A short pause.)*

HILDA: *(Stares fixedly upwards, and says as if petrified.)* My Master Builder.

RAGNAR: *(Supports himself, trembling, against the railing.)* He must be dashed to pieces—killed on the spot.

ONE OF THE LADIES: *(Whilst Mrs. Solness is carried into the house.)* Run down for the doctor——

RAGNAR: I can't stir a foot——

ANOTHER LADY: Then call to some one!

RAGNAR: *(Tries to call out.)* How is it? Is he alive?

A VOICE: *(Below, in the garden.)* Mr. Solness is dead!

OTHER VOICES: *(Nearer.)* The head is all crushed.—He fell right into the quarry.

HILDA: *(Turns to* RAGNAR, *and says quietly:)* I can't see him up there now.

RAGNAR: This is terrible. So, after all, he could not do it.

HILDA: *(As if in quiet spell-bound triumph.)* But he mounted right to the top. And I heard harps in the air. *(Waves her shawl in the air, and shrieks with wild intensity.)* My—my Master Builder!

THE END.

—*Translated by Edmund Gosse and William Archer*

ACTIVITIES FOR WRITING AND DISCUSSION

1. Reread any passages where **symbols** appear, such as the high towers, the empty nursery rooms, Mrs. Solness's burned belongings (enumerated in Act III), the cracked chimney in the Solness's first house. Then analyze and discuss the symbols and their multiple meanings.

2. Throughout the play Solness expresses fear of the younger generation and the threat it poses to his professional supremacy. How do you explain his immediate attraction to Hilda, herself a member of the younger generation, when she appears in Act I?

3. Would the play have ended as it did if Hilda had not appeared? What does she introduce into Solness's life? What does she represent or symbolize in his imagination?

4. When Hilda was twelve or thirteen years old Solness promised to make her his "princess" and to buy her "a kingdom." Ten years later to the day she shows up at his house to collect on the promise. It isn't clear that she has done anything during the intervening years except *wait*. Skim the play for any information about Hilda's life between ages thirteen and twenty-three. Then imagine she kept a diary during those years and invent a few entries.

5. In Act II Solness says, "That I might build homes for others, I had to forego—to forego for all time—the home that might have been my own," suggesting a potential conflict between professional ambition and personal relationships. Consider this conflict carefully.
   a. Share a story or two of your own experiences (if any) with this conflict; or
   b. *Invent* a story that has this conflict at its center.
   c. How has Solness balanced—or failed to balance—professional ambition with personal relationships in his own life? How are the two connected in his mind? To focus your answer, look at one or more of his specific relationships, e.g., with Kaia, with Mrs. Solness, or with Ragnar.

6. Drawing on biographical details provided in the play and inventing others as needed, write Solness's obituary (a) as he might have composed it in anticipation of his death or (b) as his wife or some other character in the play might have written it. Discuss and interpret the results in class.

WORK AND THE QUALITY OF LIFE: ADDITIONAL ACTIVITIES FOR WRITING AND DISCUSSION

1. Reread all or a portion of your notebook. Mark any passages, however long or short, that strike you, for whatever reason. Beside each such passage, write a note explaining its significance for you. Finally, pick a favorite passage and either:
   a. Expand it into a new piece of writing, or
   b. Make notes of how you could expand or use it at some future date, or
   c. Rewrite it in a different form, e.g., a poem, dialogue, letter, memoir.

For a list of strategies for expanding or revising, see Chapter 9.

2. What is the purpose and value of work? How does work relate to happiness? Are the two complementary, or are they antithetical in some ways? These are important questions that everyone must answer for him- or herself. Identify and list a few such "life questions" that are compelling to you. Then:

    a. Bring together various characters and speakers from this thematic section and write a dialogue in which they (and you, if you wish) discuss your questions and some possible answers; or

    b. Address these questions in an essay.

3. Imagine Melville's Bartleby into the real-life **setting** of a contemporary workplace. With Bartleby or a 21st century version of him as your **protagonist,** and using either a first- or third-person narrator, write a short story about his experiences. (See Appendix A for a sample.) *Alternative:* Write a poem or short play on the same subject.

4. Explore the various meanings of "art" in Thomas Moore's "The Sacred Arts of Life" and Linda Hogan's "Waking Up the Rake." How do the two writers challenge or extend your own sense of the nature of "art"?

5. Several pieces in this thematic section are in unconventional literary forms (e.g., Jack Ridl's "Last Ditch" is a **prose poem** and Janice Lynch's "Sixty-Four Caprices" is a sequence of poetic **aphorisms**) or unusual **points of view** (both Lorrie Moore's "How to Become a Writer" and Jan Beatty's "A Waitress's Instructions on Tipping" address the reader directly using a second-person point of view). Borrowing any of these forms or points of view (or devising another of your own choosing that is equally unconventional) write a text of your own on some work-related topic. If you write in the second-person, think carefully about the identity of your intended audience (your "you") and what that audience might wish to gain or learn from your text.

6. The **speaker** in James Wright's poem, "Lying in a Hammock at William Duffy's Farm in Pine Island, Minnesota" says "I have wasted my life." Chekhov's "Gooseberries" invites us to ask whether the **protagonist** and his brother, Nikolay, have wasted their lives. Jean Thompson's protagonist in "Applause, Applause" finally admits to disliking his work, thereby suggesting that his life, too, has been wasted. On the other hand, in their writings Henry David Thoreau, Thomas Moore, and Linda Hogan discuss the necessity of creating personally and spiritually meaningful work. (Thoreau says he did not want to reach the end of his life and "discover that I had not lived.") Write an essay examining the concept of a "wasted life" in any one of these works or comparing its treatment in two or more works. Wherein does the "waste" consist? How is it represented in the particular text(s), and what alternatives (if any) are suggested or implied?

7. Review your entire notebook; as you do, make a running list of memorable or striking topics, e.g., "escape," "happiness," "competition," "fear of failure," etc. Then make a Topic/Form Grid (see Chapter 9), choose a favorite topic, and use one of the forms on your grid to create a new notebook entry about the topic. Should your chosen form not work, do a Topic/Form Shift to a different form on your grid.

Interchapter on Notebooks and Journals (VI)

Your Passing Thoughts: Ralph Waldo Emerson

Emerson has special talents unequalled. . . . His personal influence upon young persons greater than any man's. In his world every man would be a poet. . . .

—HENRY DAVID THOREAU

[A] moment is a concentrated eternity.

—EMERSON

This interchapter is more personal than the others. The words of Ralph Waldo Emerson (1803–1882) have punctuated much of this book. They provide the epigraph to the book as a whole: "Books are the best of things, well used; abused, among the worst. . . . They are for nothing but to inspire."

Essayist and poet, Emerson was among the most influential American writers of the nineteenth-century and was also an avid notetaker and journal writer. He began his first journal at age sixteen and eventually filled over 250 volumes (each 300 to 400 pages long) with thoughts, quotations, observations, facts, aphorisms, and germinal essays. These notes supplied most of the material for his published writings, which include *Nature* (1836), *Essays* (*First* and

Second Series, 1841 and 1844), *Poems* (1846), *Representative Men* (1850), *English Traits* (1856), and *The Conduct of Life* (1860). Emerson's views on reading and writing helped inspire this textbook and thus form a fitting close to it.

For me, Emerson's story begins with someone an ocean away and two generations removed from him who was not an Emersonian in name but in heart: Jules Renard (1864–1910; see page 844). Renard was a busy man. A writer, husband, parent, and public official, he could easily have lost himself in a cyclone of activity but for a life-changing event that occurred in his twenty-third year: he started keeping a journal. Renard developed the habit of carrying notepaper wherever he went and of pausing in the middle of his busy hours to record his passing thoughts. At the zoo he took notes on birds:

Tiny parakeets, like tie-pins that sing. (Renard 67)

In the park he noted his emotional reactions to nature:

I cannot look at the leaf of a tree without being crushed by the universe. (127)

Elsewhere he had a thought about composing and wrote:

I have an idea the way I look at a bird: I am always afraid it will fly away, and I don't dare touch it. (209)

Renard commented, "These notes are my daily prayer" (204). Notetaking was his way of slowing the moments of life so they could be savored and valued, a way of being simultaneously in time and in the transcendent.

Renard's notes provide a natural segue into the life and thought of Emerson and one of Emerson's important messages for us today:

Listen to and record your passing thoughts.

This message is vital, because to pay attention to your thoughts is to be "awake" in the Emersonian sense of the word: alive, aware, conscious.

To understand this consider two scenarios. In scenario #1 you race down the road to an appointment and arrive in record time but exhausted and stressed out. Are you happy about the trip? Not especially; all you have thought about is the slow drivers in front of you and the clock. At best, you may experience a brief spasm of relief at not being punished for tardiness. In scenario #2, you are enjoying the scenery as you drive to the appointment; you have a thought and pull off the road to write it down:

Slate mountains, gaslight clouds.

For a moment time stops: your blood pressure dips, your mind deserts the hustling traffic and wings its way into the mountains and clouds. You know then what William Blake meant when he wrote, "One thought fills immensity," because your own experience confirms it. You reach your destination a few minutes later than in scenario #1, but no one notices or cares; and you arrive feeling a little less like a robot and a bit more like a human being. Moreover, in the note you jotted down you have *made* something. During your trip you have indulged two of the human soul's basic needs: to reflect and to create.

Emerson heeded and wrote down his thoughts in just this way and tirelessly advised others to do the same: "Make your own Bible," he wrote. "Select & Collect all those words & sentences that . . . have been to you like the blast of trumpet out of Shakspear [sic], Seneca, Moses, John, & Paul" (*Emerson in His Journals* 148). Inspired by Emerson's stirring words, several years ago I began carrying a small notepad wherever I go—I still do—so that when a thought grabs me I can write it down. At times people look askance at me as I stop on the sidewalk to scribble something, or prop my notepad on the steering wheel to take a note as I zoom along the highway. Maybe I am a little crazy, certainly eccentric, but I don't mind. I take notes because I can't stop myself. I have been lit by the Emersonian fire.

What explains Emerson's incendiary effect on people in his own time and ours? Why does he make ordinary people like me believe that what we think is important—important enough to write down? The answer, I think, is in the story of Emerson's life. That life, particularly the early part of it, is a validation of *listening to yourself think,* a validation of self-trust.

Emerson the "sage of Concord" began life unremarkably, cutting a rather mediocre figure in the eyes of the world. His siblings all looked more promising as children than he did (Richardson 19). As a student at Harvard he was chosen class poet, but only after six of his classmates had declined the honor (Richardson 6). He graduated in the bottom half of his college class (number 30 out of 59; Allen 58). After that he taught briefly in an all girls' school—a bad choice, since young Waldo, growing up in a houseful of brothers—was awkward around girls and knew it. In his twenties he became a Unitarian minister, largely because it seemed the thing to do (both his father and paternal grandfather had been ministers), but he had to resign in 1832, at age twenty-nine, over doctrinal and philosophic differences with the church. Another failure. Making matters worse, his first wife, whom he loved passionately, died of tuberculosis less than two years into their marriage. As he was stumbling from job to job, Emerson was reading and writing voraciously on the side, educating himself. He knew that he *really* wanted to be a writer but was afraid to commit himself to so uncertain a vocation.

In short, Emerson at twenty-nine felt like many of us do from time to time: a bit like a cipher, a nonentity. He had read the great literature and knew, perhaps too well, the famous names: Plato, Shakespeare, Goethe, and other figures in the pantheon. Like many of *us*, who are deterred from doing something creative or adventurous by thoughts of our own insignificance, he seems to have doubted his ability to do what he truly *wanted* to do. Who was *he* to write? The crisis of vocation was a crisis of thought: he didn't trust his own thought and instinct enough; he didn't trust himself.

By the end of 1832 Emerson's spirits were at low ebb. In the words of a concerned brother, he was "sick" and "disheartened," his life "flying to pieces" (Richardson 5). He gave up his house, sold his furniture, and on Christmas Day, boarded a boat for Europe in quest of a new beginning.

And a new beginning it was. Nine months abroad gave Emerson badly needed distance from his past. More importantly, it helped awaken his slumbering sense of individual power. In England and Scotland he met the literary giants of the day, including Samuel Taylor Coleridge, Thomas Carlyle, and William Wordsworth. Instead of feeling eclipsed by these luminaries, as he half-expected, he was struck by their ordinariness. They were good writers, but they were only human. They were all "deficient" in important areas—notably, "insight into religious truth" (*Emerson in His Journals* 115). While he liked Carlyle, he found Wordsworth somewhat pompous and Coleridge disappointingly narrow-minded. In his journal Emerson wrote:

> Many things I owe to the sight of these men. I shall judge more justly, less timidly, of wise men forevermore. . . . it is an *idealized* portrait which always we draw of them. (115)

"An *idealized* portrait". . . . Till then Emerson had put the great writers on pedestals and imagined they *owned* poetry and thought. Now, encountering them face-to-face, he acquired a new perspective on fame and celebrity. Writing in his journal he affirmed that "fame is a conventional thing" (115). At the same time he felt new confidence in his own powers. What was exemplary in Wordsworth and the others was not their public renown but their frankness and self-trust—qualities independent of fame that he also found in himself. Emerson began to discard conventional ideas of "genius" for a more democratic one that would become the cornerstone of all this thought: Genius isn't the property of an elite few; it is innate in every human being.

What is genius? Nothing other than self-trust. "To believe your own thought . . .—that is genius" ("Self-Reliance" 138). Our passing thoughts—the thousands that dart evanescently through our minds each day—are sparks from what Emerson called the "universal soul" or "oversoul." Who you are is inscribed in your passing thoughts: they are the stuff of poetic inspiration and can point you toward your individual destiny. Moreover, the individual soul and the universal soul are coterminous; to honor your individual, private thought is to arrive, simultaneously, at the universal. "Speak your latent conviction, and it shall be the universal sense; for the inmost in due time becomes the outmost, and our first thought is rendered back to us by the trumpets of the Last Judgment" ("Self-Reliance" 138). Our intuitive thoughts are visitations of the divine.

The problem is, caught up in our routinized and conventional lives we reject most of these thoughts as "silly," "strange," or "inappropriate" or don't even notice them. Genius is the faculty of heeding the thought and recording it. Thus "In every work of genius we recognize our own rejected thoughts. . . ." ("Self-Reliance" 139). The great literature of the world is full of things that you and I have thought and that we instantly recognize when reading. The authors of the great literature honored the thoughts and wrote them down, while we had those same ideas but dismissed or ignored them.

In his own work and practice Emerson's cardinal rule was *trust your first thought,* however plain, awkward, or strange it might seem. If it occurs to you, any thought is important—not fixed or final but worth writing down as it may, at the least, be the prelude to other better thoughts. Not to miss the divine visitations, Emerson carried paper with him everywhere and took notes on all that he read, thought, and experienced, always striving to capture the passing thought in its fresh and original form. "For the best part . . . of every mind," he wrote, "is not that which a [person] knows, but that which hovers in gleams, suggestions, tantalizing unpossessed before him" (qtd. in Richardson 201).

Emerson had gone to Europe feeling unsure of himself and his abilities; by the time he returned home, in October 1833, he had found himself and his mission: to write; and to spread, as a public lecturer and essayist, the message of self-trust. Of his listeners and readers he asked: Why bask in the reflected genius of others— the great men and women of past and present—when you have your own genius—the universal soul—within you and speaking to you at all times of the day?

Emerson's younger contemporaries devoured this message. With Emerson's encouragement the young Thoreau started keeping a journal and adopted the habit of taking pencil and notepaper on his long daily walks for recording on-the-spot reflections and observations. Thoreau admonished himself to "Obey the spur of the moment. These accumulated it is that make the impulse and impetus of the life of genius. . . . Let the spurs of countless moments goad us incessantly into life" (*H. D. Thoreau: A Writer's Journal* 82–83).

In Brooklyn, New York, a brawny son of a carpenter-father and a semiliterate mother was also touched by Emerson and began disciplining himself to become the quintessential American poet. Walt Whitman read and reread Emerson's *Essays* during the 1840s and early 1850s when he was gestating what would become his great book and life's work, *Leaves of Grass.* "I was simmering, simmering, simmering," he later recalled; "Emerson brought me to a boil" (qtd. in Townsend 367). Like Emerson, Whitman learned to pause and jot down everything he saw, heard, felt, touched, and thought. He gathered notes everywhere, filing them away to form nascent poems and copying his poems and fragments of poems into notebooks. Whitman later summarized Emerson's unique effect on him:

The best part of Emersonianism is, it breeds the giant that destroys itself. Who wants to be any man's mere follower? lurks behind every page. No teacher ever taught, that has so provided for his pupil's setting up independently. . . . (qtd. in Harding 118)

In other words, for Emerson the job of the poet/writer was not to overwhelm and eclipse readers with his own brilliance but to inspire readers—all readers— to think and be poets themselves.

Emerson helped empower people like Whitman to work in their own individual ways, in calm defiance of social and literary conventions. Whitman largely invented free verse and wrote exuberantly of sex and the human body when such subjects were considered off-limits to poets, and he stuck firmly to his task through decades of public criticism and censure.

In Amherst, Massachusetts, Emily Dickinson also drew inspiration from Emerson. Emily Dickinson was largely unknown during her lifetime. She never made money from writing or gained any public reputation by it. In that respect she was much like you or me as *we* might reflect and write in the quiet obscurity of our own homes. She was a private person with no paid occupation, but she could as well have been a teacher, a carpenter, or a nurse stealing moments on the side to write. In Emersonian fashion she heeded all her passing thoughts as visitations of the divine and recorded them in nearly eighteen hundred poems. Rather than pushing to place her work in periodicals or publish them in books, she wove many of her poems into hand-sewn booklets (which remained unpublished till after her death) and shared individual poems with family and friends in her personal letters.

But for a lucky sequence of events that led to posthumous publication of her poems, Emily Dickinson might be as unknown today as she was during her lifetime. Would she have cared? I doubt it. For Emily Dickinson the life of the mind was the great thing. She was as drunk on it as Whitman was. Near the end of her life she wrote the following lines, which she incorporated into three different letters (Sewall 589):

> Take all away from me, but leave me Ecstasy,
> And I am richer then than all my Fellow Men. (Dickinson Poem #1640)

So to repeat: *Listen to and record your passing thoughts.* The stories of Emerson, Whitman, and Dickinson show that the ability to do so depends on self-trust, on learning from great examples without being intimidated by them, and on heeding the still small voice of "Yes" that comes from within over and against the societal "No" that comes from without. This message is tonic in a time like our own that places such emphasis on celebrity. You need only watch five minutes of a TV talk show or open a magazine to see that celebrity worship is about the *negation* of self-trust. Today more than ever we need to open our ears to our own thoughts.

At this point a question is appropriate: Suppose you listen to and write down your passing thoughts. What do you *do* with them? What did Emerson do? Emerson collected his notes (into some 250 notebooks, no less!) and habitually reread them—for amusement and pleasure, and to stimulate additional thought and writing. He compared his journal to a "Savings Bank." He deposited ideas there and earned interest on them by saving and rereading them:

> I grow richer because I have somewhere to deposit my earnings; and fractions are worth more to me because corresponding fractions are waiting here that shall be made integers by their addition. (*Emerson in His Journals* 119)

Hard-working professional writer though he was, I don't believe Emerson would have done any of this if it hadn't been *fun*—if he hadn't thrilled to the spectacle of seeing ideas grow. An idea written down is like a seed planted in the subconscious: it stays there and germinates and can blossom at surprising times and in unusual places—while you're housecleaning, taking a walk, mowing the lawn, doing dishes, enjoying a bath, or waiting for an appointment. That's part of the fun: the process can go on anywhere.

A short personal example will illustrate. I have long been fascinated by the contrast between the sheer volume of thought that passes through our heads and the little of it that we ever write down. Sophisticated as our technology becomes, the speed of thought still massively outpaces our ability to articulate the tiniest fraction of what we think. Some time ago I was thinking about this during a walk and paused to write the following in my notepad:

> Note-taking is good practice for those who can't write as fast as they think.

A month later I reread this note and a metaphor came to mind:

> Writing plods. A rickshaw.

The new version seemed better than the first, more striking and compact. A few weeks later I was in the yard raking leaves and the thought came back yet again, this time in the form of a comparison:

> Writing is to thought as rickshaw to rocket.

This version stuck. It said what I meant, and I liked the sound of it.

The point? I had fun shaping and honing my sentence to say exactly what I meant. Nor did I torture the idea; I just thought about it for a few minutes now and then (over a span of two months!) in my rereading and daily reflection. Finally, as an added benefit, it made activities like walking and raking leaves even more pleasant than they already are.

I'll end on a personal note. Like many people, I feel as if I am always on the run—between family, work, meetings, appointments, social obligations of all kinds, distractions. Emerson's message is about *time*. After years of complaining about time (there never seems to be enough of it) I've concluded that no one really gives us time or takes it away from us; we have to create it ourselves. Is there *time* to scribble down thoughts as Jules Renard did, or Emerson? Yes. It takes effort, but I think the rewards are worth it.

I teach writing professionally; but if I were an accountant, a plumber, an attorney, an engineer, a homemaker, a grocery clerk, a mechanic, retired, or unemployed I would still be carrying my notepad around, writing at stoplights and in grocery lines, whenever a thought comes. To be Emersonian is to be eccentric.

I once read where a certain poet—whose name I've forgotten—said that he never let himself walk faster than two miles per hour. (Try doing that for even five minutes and you'll see how hard it is!) He explained that the slow pace helped clear his head for thinking. At the time his statement baffled me. Was he serious? Slow down—when what we need is to go *faster*?

Now I understand what he meant. I've learned that if you like to think you actually *want* to move more slowly; you find yourself instinctively slowing down. (Perhaps the most subversive consequence of Emersonian habits is that they make you slow down while everyone else is speeding up.) I don't mind *waiting* anymore. If I'm stuck in highway construction or in a line somewhere, I just take out my notepad. In fact, strangely enough, I *like* having to wait, because it gives me more time to reflect.

The demand for speed will remain a constant in American life; we will always need to do more things more quickly and *will* do them more quickly. Electronic technology is taking care of that need, a material need. But over and against this is another need—call it a spiritual one—the need to slow down so we can hear ourselves think.

The best teachers teach us to wait, and Emerson was among the best of teachers.

Give yourself time.

Works Cited

Allen, Gay Wilson. *Waldo Emerson*. New York: Penguin, 1981.

Dickinson, Emily. *The Complete Poems of Emily Dickinson*. Ed. Thomas H. Johnson. Boston: Little, Brown, 1960.

Emerson, Ralph Waldo. *Emerson in His Journals*. Selected and edited by Joel Porte. Cambridge: The Belknap Press of Harvard UP, 1982.

———. "Self-Reliance." *The Portable Emerson*. Ed. Carl Bode in collaboration with Malcolm Cowley. New York: Viking Penguin, 1981. 138–164.

Harding, Walter. *A Thoreau Handbook*. New York: New York UP, 1961.

Renard, Jules. *The Journal of Jules Renard*. Ed. and trans. Louise Bogan and Elizabeth Roget. New York: George Braziller, 1964.

Richardson, Robert D., Jr. *Emerson: The Mind on Fire*. Berkeley: U of California P, 1995.

Sewall, Richard B. *The Life of Emily Dickinson*. Cambridge: Harvard UP, 1994.

Thoreau, Henry David. *H. D. Thoreau: A Writer's Journal*. Selected and edited by Laurence Stapleton. New York: Dover, 1960.

Trowbridge, John Townsend. *My Own Story: With Recollections of Noted Persons*. Boston: Houghton Mifflin, 1903.

Excerpts from Emerson's *Journals*

1

UNDATED

It is excellent advice both in writing and in action to avoid a too great elevation at first. Let one's beginnings be temperate and unpretending, and the more elevated parts will rise from these with a just and full effect. We were not made to breathe oxygen, or to talk poetry, or to be always wise.

FEBRUARY 1827

Much of what we learn, and to the highest purposes, of life is caught in moments, and rather by a sublime instinct than by modes which can be explained in detail.

BOSTON, AUGUST 24, 1828 [TO MISS EMERSON]

When I attended church, and the man in the pulpit was all clay and not of tuneable metal, I thought that if men would avoid that general language and general manner in which they strive to hide all that is peculiar, and would say only what was uppermost in their own minds, after their own individual manner, every man would be interesting.

AUGUST 18, 1830

The sun shines and warms and lights us and we have no curiosity to know why this is so; but we ask the reason of all evil, of pain, and hunger, and musquitoes and silly people.

JULY 15, 1831

The things taught in colleges and schools are not an education, but the means of education.

MAY 21, 1833

I like the sayers of No better than the sayers of Yes.

JANUARY 1, 1834

This Book is my Savings Bank. I grow richer because I have somewhere to deposit my earnings; and fractions are worth more to me because corresponding fractions are waiting here that shall be made integers by their addition.

APRIL 11, 1834

Went yesterday to Cambridge and spent most of the day at Mount Auburn; got my luncheon at Fresh Pond, and went back again to the woods. After much wandering and seeing many things, four snakes gliding up and down a hollow for no purpose that I could see—not to eat, not for love, but only gliding; then a whole bed of *Hepatica triloba*, cousins of the Anemone, all blue and beautiful, but constrained by niggard nature to wear their last year's faded jacket of leaves; then a black-capped titmouse, who came upon a tree, and when I would know his name, sang *chick-a-dee-dee;* then a far-off tree full of clamorous birds, I know not what, but you might hear them half a mile. I forsook the tombs, and found a sunny hollow where the east wind would not blow, and lay down against the side of a tree to most happy beholdings. At least I opened my eyes and let what would pass through them into the soul. I saw no more my relation, how near and petty, to Cambridge or Boston; I heeded no more what minute or hour our Massachusetts clocks might indicate—I saw only the noble earth on which I was born, with the great Star which warms and enlightens it. I saw the clouds that hang their significant drapery over us. It was Day—that was all Heaven said. The pines glittered with their innumerable green needles in the light, and seemed to challenge me to read their riddle. The drab oak-leaves of the last year turned their little somersets and lay still again. And the wind bustled high overhead in the forest top. This gay and grand architecture, from the vault to the moss and lichen on which I lay,—who shall explain to me the laws of its proportions and adornments?

April 12, 1834 9

All the mistakes I make arise from forsaking my own station and trying to see the object from another person's point of view.

April 13, 1834 10

We are always getting ready to live, but never living. We have many years of technical education; then many years of earning a livelihood, and we get sick, and take journeys for our health, and compass land and sea for improvement by travelling, but the work of self-improvement,—always under our nose,—nearer than the nearest, is seldom seldom engaged in. A few, few hours in the longest life.

May 21, 1834 11

I will trust my instincts. For always a reason halts after an instinct, and when I have deviated from the instinct, comes somebody with a profound theory teaching that I ought to have followed it. . . . "Our first and third thought coincide."

July 18, 1834 12

What is there of the divine in a load of bricks? What is there of the divine in a barber's shop? . . . Much. All.

October 14, 1834 13

Every involuntary repulsion that arises in your mind, give heed unto. It is the surface of a central truth.

December 22, 1834 14

It is very easy in the world to live by the opinion of the world. It is very easy in solitude to be self-centred. But the finished man is he who in the midst of the crowd keeps with perfect sweetness the independence of solitude.

July 21, 1836 15

Make your own Bible. Select and collect all the words and sentences that in all your reading have been to you like the blast of triumph out of Shakspear, Seneca, Moses, John and Paul.

OCTOBER 29, 1836

16

There is one advantage which every man finds in setting himself a literary task,—as these my lectures,—that it gives him the high pleasure of reading, which does not in other circumstances attain all its zest. . . . When the mind is braced by the weighty expectation of a prepared work, the page of whatever book we read becomes luminous with manifold allusion. Every sentence is doubly significant, and the sense of our author is as broad as the world. There is creative reading as well as creative writing.

NOVEMBER 12, 1836

17

How many attractions for us have our passing fellows in the streets, both male and female, which our ethics forbid us to express, which yet infuse so much pleasure into life. A lovely child, a handsome youth, a beautiful girl, a heroic man, a maternal woman, a venerable old man, charm us, though strangers, and we cannot say so, or look at them but for a moment.

AUGUST 2, 1837

18

An enchanting night of south wind and clouds; mercury at 73°; all the trees are wind-harps; blessed be light and darkness; ebb and flow, cold and heat; these restless pulsations of nature which by and by will throb no more.

FEBRUARY 17, 1838

19

How much self-reliance it implies to write a true description of anything, for example, Wordsworth's picture of skating; that leaning back on your heels and stopping in mid-career. So simple a fact no common man would have trusted himself to detach as a thought.

APRIL 1, 1838

20

Preaching, especially false preaching, is for able men a sickly employment. Study of books is also sickly; and the garden and the family, wife, mother, son, and brother are a balsam. There is health in table-talk and nursery play. We must wear old shoes and have aunts and cousins.

APRIL 26, 1838

21

Yesterday afternoon I went to the Cliff with Henry Thoreau. Warm, pleasant, misty weather, which the great mountain amphitheatre seemed to drink in with gladness. A crow's voice filled all the miles of air with sound. A bird's voice, even a piping frog, enlivens a solitude and makes world enough for us. At night I went out into the dark and saw a glimmering star and heard a frog, and Nature seemed to say, Well do not these suffice? Here is a new scene, a new experience. Ponder it, Emerson, and not like the foolish world, hanker after thunders and multitudes and vast landscapes, the sea or Niagara.

JUNE 8, 1838   22

A man must have aunts and cousins, must buy carrots and turnips, must have barn and woodshed, must go to market and to the blacksmith's shop, must saunter and sleep and be inferior and silly.

SEPTEMBER 29, 1838   23

Censure and Praise.—I hate to be defended in a newspaper. As long as all that is said is said *against* me, I feel a certain sublime assurance of success, but as soon as honied words of praise are spoken for me, I feel as one that lies unprotected before his enemies.

OCTOBER 5, 1838   24

Books.—It seems meritorious to read: but from everything but history or the works of the old commanding writers I come back with a conviction that the slightest *wood-thought,* the least significant native emotion of my own, is more to me.

NOVEMBER 14, 1838   25

What is the hardest task in the world? To think. . . .

JUNE 12, 1839   26

I know no means of calming the fret and perturbation into which too much sitting, too much talking, brings me, so perfect as labor. I have no animal spirits; therefore, when surprised by company and kept in a chair for many hours, my heart sinks, my brow is clouded and I think I will run for Acton woods, and live with the squirrels henceforward. But my garden is nearer, and my good hoe, as it bites the ground, revenges my wrongs, and I have less lust to bite my enemies. I confess I work at first with a little venom, lay to a little unnecessary strength. But by smoothing the rough hillocks, I smooth my temper; by extracting the long roots of the piper-grass, I draw out my own splinters; and in a short time I can hear the bobolink's song and see the blessed deluge of light and colour that rolls around me.

JUNE 22, 1839   27

It is one of the signs of our time, the ill health of all people. All the young people are nearsighted in the towns.

SEPTEMBER 14, 1839   28

How sad a spectacle, so frequent nowadays, to see a young man after ten years of college education come out, ready for his voyage of life,—and to see that the entire ship is made of rotten timber, of rotten, honeycombed, traditional timber without so much as an inch of new plank in the hull.

NOVEMBER 14, 1839   29

Systems.—I need hardly say to anyone acquainted with my thoughts that I have no System. When I was quite young, I fancied that by keeping a manuscript Journal by me, over whose pages I wrote a list of the great topics of human study, as, *Religion, Poetry, Politics, Love,* etc., in the course of a few years I should be able to complete a sort of encyclopædia containing the net value of all the definitions at which the world had yet arrived. But at the end of a couple of years, my Cabinet Cyclopædia, though much enlarged, was no nearer to a completeness than on its first day. Nay, somehow the whole plan of it needed alteration, nor did the following months promise any speedier term to it than the foregoing. At last I discovered that my curve was a parabola whose arcs would never meet, and came to acquiesce in the perception that, although no diligence can rebuild the universe in a model by the best accumulation of disposition of details, yet does the world reproduce itself in miniature in every event that transpires, so that all the laws of nature may be read in the smallest fact. So that the truth-speaker may dismiss all solicitude as to the proportion and congruency of the aggregate of his thoughts, so long as he is a faithful reporter of particular impressions.

JUNE 4, 1840   30

Waldo says, "The flowers talk when the wind blows over them." My little boy grows thin in the hot summer, and runs all to eyes and eyelashes.

SEPTEMBER 16, 1840   31

A sleeping child gives me the impression of a traveller in a very far country.

JULY, UNDATED (1841)   32

Let us answer a book of ink with a book of flesh and blood.

AUGUST, UNDATED (1841)   33

The trumpet-like lowing of a cow—what does that speak to in me? Not to my understanding. No. Yet somewhat in me hears and loves it well.

OCTOBER 9, 1841   34

The sum of life ought to be valuable when the fractions and particles are so sweet.

NOVEMBER 11, 1842   35

Do not be too timid and squeamish about your actions. All life is an experiment. The more experiments you make the better. What if they are a little coarse, and you may get your coat soiled or torn? What if you do fail, and get fairly rolled in the dirt once or twice? Up again you shall never be so afraid of a tumble.

MAY 20, 1843   36
    It is greatest to believe and to hope well of the world, because he who does so, quits the world of experience, and makes the world he lives in.

JANUARY, (1844) UNDATED   37
    Finish each day before you begin the next, and interpose a solid wall of sleep between two. This you cannot do without temperance.

MARCH, (1845) UNDATED   38
    Good manners require a great deal of time, as does a wise treatment of children. Orientals have time, the desert, and stars; the Occidentals have not.

MARCH, (1846) UNDATED   39
    What a discovery I made one day, that the more I spent the more I grew, that it was as easy to occupy a large place and do much work as an obscure place to do little; and that in the winter in which I communicated all my results to classes, I was full of new thoughts.

AUGUST, (1847) UNDATED   40
    Life consists in what a man is thinking of all day.

MAY (?) 1856 UNDATED   41
    Education. Don't let them eat their seed-corn; don't let them anticipate, ante-date, and be young men, before they have finished their boyhood. Let them have the fields and woods, and learn their secret and the base- and football, and wrestling, and brickbats, and suck all the strength and courage that lies for them in these games; let them ride bare-back, and catch their horse in his pasture, let them hook and spear their fish, and shin a post and a tall tree, and shoot their partridge and trap the woodchuck, before they begin to dress like collegians and sing in serenades, and make polite calls.

APRIL (?) 1859   42
    I am a natural reader, and only a writer in the absence of natural writers. In a true time, I should never have written.

MAY 25, 1862   43
    Resources or feats. I like people who can do things. When Edward and I struggled in vain to drag our big calf into the barn, the Irish girl put her finger into the calf's mouth, and led her in directly.

OCTOBER 1872   44
    Look sharply after your thoughts. They come unlooked for, like a new bird seen on your trees, and, if you turn to your usual task, disappear; and you shall never find that perception again; never, I say,—but perhaps years, ages, and I know not what events and worlds may lie between you and its return!

For further reading:
Emerson, Ralph Waldo. *The Heart of Emerson's Journals.* Ed. Bliss Perry.
   New York: Dover, 1995.

ACTIVITIES FOR WRITING AND DISCUSSION

1. Here are a few additional comments on "genius" to place alongside Emerson's:

[Genius is] the faculty of seizing and turning to account anything that strikes us.

—JOHANN WOLFGANG VON GOETHE

What is "genius"? Awareness of one's secret instinct and trusting to it, more than to anything others say and have said.

—VILHELM EKELUND

And so I do know what a genius is, a genius is some one who does not have to remember the two hundred years that everybody else has to remember.

—GERTRUDE STEIN

Genius is the ability to put into effect what is in your mind. There's no other definition of it.

—F. SCOTT FITZGERALD

Agree of disagree with Emerson's concept of genius and/or any of those implied in the above quotations. What are your own thoughts on the subject? Are geniuses different in *kind* from "the rest of us," or only in *intensity*? Refer to examples of people whom you consider to be "geniuses"—in whatever field—as you respond to these questions.

2. In your notebook relate some of your own experiences of encountering literary greatness in your readings. Think of a favorite author whose work you greatly admire. How has that author's presence affected your writing, for better and/or for worse? Has it intimidated or overwhelmed you? inspired you? some combination of both? Explain with a story.

3. In your notebook react to the following Emerson comment (on page 1032):

I will trust my instincts. For always a reason halts after an instinct, and when I have deviated from the instinct, comes somebody with a profound theory teaching that I ought to have followed it. . . . "Our first and third thought coincide."

First, what do you think Emerson means? Second, how does or doesn't his observation jibe with your own experience of "thoughts"?

4. In his notebook, *The Burning Brand,* the Italian writer Cesar Pavese writes:

> [G]enius is not a matter of discovering some external theme and treating it skillfully, but of finally achieving complete possession of one's own experience, own body, own memories—one's own rhythm, and expressing this rhythm, above and beyond the limitations of plot or subject matter, with the perennial fruitfulness of inexhaustible thought. (141)

How do you interpret this comment? How might one achieve "complete possession of one's own experience, own body, own memories"? Can a journal or notebook help? How?

5. Respond to Emerson's journal selections using any of the "Generic Ideas for Writing" found on pages 275 to 277.

Appendix A:
Sample Creative Writings

The samples below are not offered as masterpieces. (Sometimes the presence of a masterpiece does more to intimidate us as writers than it does to motivate us.) You can use these samples in at least two ways:

1. Use them as prompts for your own writing. Review them periodically, particularly when your own imaginative well runs dry. Remember the words of Emerson, which appear as an epigraph at the beginning of *Reading and Writing from Literature*:

[Texts] are for nothing but to inspire.

2. Use them to help select and revise your own favorite writings for a course portfolio or other presentation. Alone or with your small group or class, you can analyze the samples to determine what makes "successful" or "unsuccessful" writing. What do you like in a particular piece? What first gets your interest, and what makes you keep reading? What specific passages, long or short, do you find yourself annotating or underlining? What ideas does the sample give you for your own writing? What does the writer try that *you* might like to try?

Samples are keyed to the "Ten Ideas for Writing" introduced in Chapter 3. Terms in **boldface** are defined and illustrated in Part IV, "An Introduction to the Four Genres," and Appendix C, "Glossary of Literary Terms."

1. Converse with Specific Points in the Text that Strike You.

See sample in Chapter 3.

2. Write About Any Personal Connections You Have with the Reading.

"Grandpa Jack" by Tyler (see Chapter 2) is a good example.

Both of my grandfathers died before I was born. My Dad's father was bucked off a horse which broke his neck and caused his death soon after. My Mom's father had cancer and also died before I was born. Although my grandmothers married again, I never got to know my stepgrandfathers well at all. As a young boy I yearned for the companionship of a grandpa.

I grew up in a small neighborhood set in the heart of a beautiful valley. There was so much to do as a child. Pineview dam was directly behind the house, giving us ample amount of fun swimming in it. The "Honda" trails, as we called them, were nearby, and we rode our dirt bikes up and down the steep hills. It was a choice place for a young child to grow up, and I loved every minute of it. But there was still a vacancy in my life, and that was to have a grandpa. An elderly couple lived next door, and from the time I was born our lives wound together tightly. I believe my desire for a grandpa came true because my neighbor, Jack Hislop, took upon himself the role of a grandfather. Jack has been special to me for as long as I can remember. He gave me my first motorcycle, my first and only bolo decorated with Indian turquoise, and many other gifts throughout my youth. But most importantly he gave me the friendship of a grandpa.

As a little boy I would go over to visit him almost every day after school. One day I ran over to his house and found him lounging on the patio in his back yard. "Take a seat, partner," said Jack as he pulled up a chair for me. He fed me some cold watermelon and a large glass of "sodi water," as he called it. While I was enjoying the fruit Jack told me a story about when he was a young sheepherder. "I was no older than you, partner, maybe eleven years old," said Jack. "Me and Pa and a few of my brothers were high on Durphie's Peak taking the sheep down to a nearby watering hole." His eyes were flashing as he was trying to point out where they were, since the mountain was in a broadside view. "A few sheep took off up a narrow canyon, and I got roped into chasin' after 'em. I rode up the canyon a little way and seen 'em up ahead so I galloped my horse to catch 'em. When I caught those little rascals I started herding 'em back down to the watering hole. On the way down the canyon my horse started to get jittery because some bushes started to shake up ahead, and out charged a huge brown bear." Jack was standing now giving the motions of the incident. Jack blurted "Holy shit!" then apologized to me because his wife didn't like him to cuss. "The damn horse started to buck and my two dogs went into a barking frenzy. The bear was huge, it was at least ten feet tall when it reared up on its hind legs. The dogs distracted the bear long enough allowin' me to ride up and around to safety." Jack was really into the story because he made a sigh of relief as he told about his escape from the bear. "Damn bear killed old Dodger, one of my best dogs," said Jack with a sad look on his face, as if it had just happened.

Jack was drafted into the war during World War II and had many stories to tell about those experiences. The stories he told me about the war are engraved in my mind, and I am more sensitive about what happened in the war because Jack told me so many of his firsthand experiences. "There were dead bodies piled twenty feet high; hell, it smelled bad," said Jack as he plugged his nose to emphasize his point. Jack had a very sorrowful look on his face when he told me about the concentration camps. "When those skinny Jews were released they just started eatin' the grass, 'cause they were so hungry. I carried extra rations so I could give 'em something good to eat." Jack could go on and on with his war stories, and all I had to do was ask him to tell me a story. . . .

Jack's health was never very good. He had diabetes and heart trouble which caused him to have a great deal of pain. "I've got a pig valve in my heart—oink–oink," he would joke. As time went on Jack's health got worse, but our attachment grew stronger. Three years before he died he said, "I want ya to speak at my funeral, partner." I chuckled and told him he could never die. When Jack died his wife again asked me if I would speak. I don't think I could have said no. I was fourteen years old and scared to death to speak, but my love for Jack implored me to do it. I don't even remember what I said, but I do know that I declared my love for my Grandpa Jack.

3. Write a Letter to the Author and/or a Return Letter from the Author to Yourself.

See sample in Chapter 3.

4. Write an Imaginary Interview with the Author or with a Character in a Story, Novel, or Play.

John read some poetry by Walt Whitman and then began writing a response to it in the form of "What I like about this poet." Soon, however, he tired of this mode of writing and yearned to meet the poet "in the flesh." The result was the following "Interview with Walt Whitman." Before writing John read and reread "Song of the Open Road" (p. 603) and other poems in Whitman's book *Leaves of Grass* in order to get a sense of the poet's voice and probable style of speech. Stylistic features he noticed were Whitman's outspokenness, his taste for informal and robust language, and his habit of illustrating and expanding on ideas with long lists (such as the example in the third paragraph below).

Interview with Walt Whitman

I interviewed Walter Whitman at his print-shop in Brooklyn on a hot, humid day in mid–July. Mr. Whitman was relaxed and cordial. He is a man of 36, large-framed, in amazingly robust health, with a thick, matted beard and penetrating eyes. As we spoke he sat on the edge of a desk, his sleeves rolled to the elbows and his shirt collar open, the tools of his trade scattered around him. Mr. Whitman, it might be noted in passing, is a methodical man, softspoken, thinking before he speaks—creating an impression quite unlike that of the "barbaric yawp" that he affects in his poems.

Interviewer (I): Mr. Whitman, your book *Leaves of Grass* has been on the market now for two weeks and is causing something of a stir among critics. Not all the reactions, I might add, are favorable. For instance, Mr. Samuels of the *Daily Press* calls you a "hog" and says that you have no business writing poetry. What do you make of this?

WW: I never published *Leaves* with an eye to receiving compliments, or the favor of critics. The real audience of *Leaves* is profounder than the critics, and vaster: it is the great American public itself, the ordinary men and women—bus drivers, farmers, ferriers, mechanics, blacksmiths, boatmen and -women, clam-diggers, horse-dealers, slaves and freemen and freewomen. . . . On the pulse of these will the future of *Leaves* be decided.

I: Surely this is unlike any book of poetry any of us has seen before. Can you tell us something about the composition of *Leaves*?

WW: Gladly. But I'll probably not give you the answer you're wanting— no "pat" answer that will "finish" the matter, click the box shut, if you will. *Leaves* cannot be put in a box—the making of it can't be either; it doesn't give itself to formulae. First thing I did was throw out the rule-books, the sonnet treatises, the grammars and so on. Then I wrote, and wrote, and wrote—every day. Every chance I got I wrote. On the wharves or in the street, in the smithies and the shops, in the open air of farms where I happened to be, loafing, jotting down, in my leisurely way, all unhurried, nothing forced, getting a record of it all, big and little, I didn't discriminate. Then I stuffed what I wrote—all these pictures of America, of our times—into envelopes. And I never worried over the result. I knew all along I'd get a Poem out of it.

I: Your self-assurance and optimism about your craft are admirable, Mr. Whitman. I'm sure many poets would be envious.

WW: Maybe so. These poets have to see that making a poem isn't a logic-game. You don't just take a fancy mold of a sonnet or ballad or rhyme and dump words into it, so that the ideas are all corseted and constrained and dead. That's the way our poets write, and that's the undoing of 'em. They're stuck in the eighteenth century, or the seventeenth—in Europe—trying to out-Shakespeare Shakespeare, I suppose. That's the poetry *disease* today. That's the point I make in my "Preface" to *Leaves*. The true poems don't come from here [Mr. Whitman points to his head] but from here [he inscribes an imaginary circle from his heart to his pelvis]. That's the birthing room of a thousand poems—a thousand thousand poems—already written and still to be written.

5. Compose a Prequel or a Sequel to a Story.

See sample in Chapter 3.

6. Rewrite a Text from a Point of View Different from that Presented in the Original Text.

Gary Soto's poem "Oranges" (p. 474) describes—from a boy's **point of view**—an awkward incident during a first date. Angela retold the story from the girl's point of view:

Chocolate

My first date came
when I was twelve.
He was coming for me
I had been ready for hours
My parents had the light on
and the dog ready
Their way of saying who's boss.
At the last minute
my mother drowned my face
with rouge.
My father told me to remember
Who I was and what I'm worth.
My brother told me
the way to impress him
was to think big.
He came for me
He looked so nervous
We went to the drugstore
to get some candy
the whole way there
I wondered what he had
in his pockets besides those two oranges.
He told me to choose
whatever I wanted.
I remembered my brother
and picked up a chocolate
hoping he had the money.
His eyes fell
but he didn't say a word.
My heart ached as
he placed a nickel
and then one of his
precious oranges
on the counter.
I cried that night
for being so stupid
I had hurt him

and he had brushed it aside
I stared at the chocolate
wrapper stained brown like my
aching soul,
yet glittering
much like my soul
filled with the hope
That he'd call again.

7. Rewrite a Work into a Different Genre.

See sample in Chapter 3.

8. Borrow an Incident or Theme from a Work to Write a Piece of Your Own Based on a Similar Incident or Theme.

Herman Melville's "Bartleby, the Scrivener," with its theme of worker exploitation, inspired Meg to write a story of her own on the same theme. For her protagonist Meg created a woman named Candy, an overworked and undervalued worker in a law office at the end of the twentieth century. Candy related her story through a series of diary entries.

Dear Diary

January 15, 1999—Huge storm today. I sit at the office window, looking at the brick wall beyond. Snowflakes fall between my window and this wall. Wall and snowflakes. The snow is lovely but dreary. The wall is a symbol of the walled-in life I have come to live.

No one in this place knows me. The other women (they call themselves "girls" but they are all over 30) try, now and then, to include me in their conversations, but they sense I am not one of them. The men—Grady, Polk, and O'Hallahan—you can read their names on the glass windowpane of the office door—treat me like a coke machine. Deposit coins. Jingle jingle jingle. Wait for result. Ice cold pop with the flip top, ready to drink. They suppose I am brainless and without feelings. "Candy, honey, type this memo for me." "Candy, grab the file on Hilton." "Candy, call up Mr. Slater and schedule him for the fifth." O'Hallahan is the worst. Scummy old fart with cracked lips and banana nose. Always coming on to me. His breath stinks (Lord knows I've had opportunity enough to smell it) and I've come this close to slapping him. One of these days I will.

January 16, 1999—None of them—these people I spend eight hours a day with, sometimes longer—none of them knows me. I know them, but I am not known. I prefer it that way. The women, the "girls," think I'm stuck up, the "boys," as I call Messrs. Grady, Polk, and O'Hallahan—though not to their faces—think I am a brainless, not-bad looking sort of man-nikin. Not one you'd see in a window at I Magnum, but maybe at Pen-ney's or Sears. A button for them to push. A tool for them to use. A means to an end.

Little do they know I read. Yes, read. I actually have an intellectual life outside these doors. While Judy, Becky, and Amy race off to pore over the *Enquirer* and the *Star,* and O'Hallahan drools over his *Penthouse* (he keeps back issues stashed in his desk drawer—everyone knows it), I read Shakespeare and Emerson, Dickens and Faulkner, George Eliot and Vir-ginia Woolf and Alice Walker. It's a habit I've had all my life—reading the classics. I love to think. Just be by myself and think. That's why I remain unmarried: no thinking woman could attach herself to any man (and sur-vive). He'd drop her—fast and hard. "A thinking woman? That's some sort of contradiction in terms, isn't it?" So spake Stewart, my high school beau (for a day), who was obviously proud to have a fine phrase like "contra-diction in terms" in his vocabulary, though it twisted his tongue to say it. "Isn't that a con-thra-dikshun in shrterms?" Can't recall the context or what I said back—something sharp and clever enough to put Stewart out of my life forever.

January 17—I could have been a college professor. That's what my mama said to me.

"You could have been a college professor, Candy!"

"But I would prefer not to."

"Prefer not to!"

"Yes."

"Then, pray tell me, why you would prefer not to." Mama went to Mt. Holyoke and was fond of fancy phrases like "pray tell me."

I shrugged. "Cuz reading is too much fun. Why spoil it by turning it into a job?"

Mama had big dreams for me. I have big dreams for me, too, but they're not her dreams.

Anyway, dear diary, dearest confidant and affectionate friend: last night I discovered a classic, the classic, that will alter my life forever. One can't say for sure, of course, but I think it just might. "Bartleby," by Her-man Melville. Funny thing is, I vaguely remember my English professor assigning this story in college, but I didn't read it then because I pre-ferred not to. Jane Austen was more exciting to me. That was the year I didn't want to read anything by a man, it was a phase I was going through. A hard phase—all the books in English classes were by men, and since I preferred not to read any I nearly flunked. My imagination alone saved me. I could write my way through any problem.

Anyway—Bartleby. If I'd o' known about him, what he was like, in col-lege, I would have read him. He's like a woman—a fine, intelligent, sensi-tive woman. He's got common sense oozing out of his pores. I picture him as tall, pale, and munching ginger nuts. Quiet. Reading and thinking. Like those campy gurus in the far east who meditate and survive, quite well and healthy, on an olive a day. He's like me, an office clerk, a cog in the machine, a divine dare-devil philosopher, surrounded by <u>prudent</u> men. God, how I hate that word—"<u>prudence</u>." You can see that, diary, by the way I underline "prudence" and enclose it in angry squiggly quotation marks.

<u>Prudence</u>: always weighing, calculating, dividing and subdividing, adding and subtracting, bowing and scraping to the powers that be, conforming. Prudence is a person bending and conforming till all the individuality and roughness and uniqueness is sanded out of her; she becomes a neat little piece in a jigsaw puzzle. And you know how it is with jigsaws. Once the puzzle is complete the individual pieces become anonymous. A part of the vast machine of capitalism that is destroying us all.

What's it like being a piece in the jigsaw puzzle, a cog in the machine, the secretary who mans (I love that word—"mans"—how ironic!) the front desk in the office? the scrivener who copies out documents, like a sort of human photocopy machine?

I'll tell you, diary, and whoever else wants to listen: it's tiring. It's exhausting. It's dehumanizing.

Well, one day, when his "prudent" boss tells him to proofread a document, Bartleby just says, "I would prefer not to." Funny! The very phrase I have used myself on so many occasions. And, so on, day after day, Bartleby just stops working.

Wow! So what happens when a cog—even a little, bitty tiny one, in the machine stops working? Why, the whole machine stops, of course. Or at least the gears get clogged.

January 20—Bartleby will change my life. He already is. Today Grady told me (yelled at me from the other room, as he always does) to get the file on Zoomtechies, and I yelled back (politely, of course) "I would prefer not to." Silence. I felt a little tingle of excitement, anticipating.

"What the hell?" cries Grady, after a minute, "I said get the file on Zoom!"

"I heard you, Mr. Grady, and I said I would <u>prefer</u> not to get it."

A minute later Grady is striding in, all 200-plus macho pounds of him. He plants his fingers, palms spread, on my desk, and leans forward till his mug is just a few inches from mine. For a minute I think he's O'Hallahan, being so intimate, but his breath isn't <u>quite</u> as bad.

"Look, bitch . . ." He says it softly. Almost affectionate. Is he going to kiss me now?

But his nostrils flare. He glares at me. I look back, calmly, like Bartleby.

For a second everything is tense. He'd like to hit me, but how can he, with three other secretaries looking on? So he jerks himself upright, straightens his collar and tie (just like he's seen the tough boys do in movies) and goes to another desk, Mary's, knowing Mary will do what he tells her to.

[Later] It's now 5:30 P.M. The snow never stops; it's thick as a sheep's fleece. The office is empty except for me.

Bartleby's boss was a strange sort of guy. "Prudent"—yech! how I hate that word—but he couldn't fire Bartleby. He could never kick him out. Much as Bartleby preferred not to prop up his employer's miserable little law office, he—the employer—never put him out, like an old dog, to starve in the street. Because he knew Bartleby was a "king." I doubt very much that Bartleby's boss would have looked Bartleby in the eye the way Grady did me.

This is 1999, dear diary, and Grady's a different breed than the old gent in "Bartleby."

January 21—I've cleared out my desk. I even polished the surface—for spite. I have struck my little blow for emancipation and freedom and human dignity, knowing full well it's a feeble one. My hands are small and when I look at these little fists, they're no match for Grady's. Women were never made to fight anyway. Fighting is the crudest form of human behavior. Some day the human species will evolve to the point where fighting will become obsolete.

Tomorrow I will be jobless, out on the street. Not such a bad place.

At least I always have myself for company.

And you too, diary, I'll not forget you.

Yours,

—Candy.

(Candy is such an awful name. I've never realized it till now. Reminds me of "baby" or something. A name like Elizabeth or Margaret would be much better. Elizabeth has a royal sound to it—something imperial—and Margaret sounds like someone to be reckoned with. With a name like Elizabeth or Margaret my life might have been a whole lot different.)

9. Borrow the Genre or Form of a Work to Create a Piece of Your Own Cast in the Same Genre or Form.

Susan read Walt Whitman's poetry and followed it by writing a poem. She explains, "Whitman's 'Song of Myself,' a very emotional poem that created images in Walt's time and place, inspired me to write a piece in Whitmanian style, using contemporary images, while still maintaining the romantic tone that Whitman stressed."

Song of Ourselves

We celebrate ourselves, Walt,
you, I, all of us, grasping for perception, meaning
in this entrapment, awe inspired miracle,
from the deepest abyss of the earth,
to the empirical heights of the cosmos;
We keep watch.

A lonely doe crouches, staring at me from my hillside.
Her dark eyes reflect an eerie glow from the porch light.
She looks at me, through me,
knowing.
Hours pass.
I'm anxious, perplexed about my hillside occupant.
No movement from her perch.
The upstairs window elevates my eyes to hers;
Our gazes lock once again.
Am I in her yard?
Finally,
a gentle rain softly taps at the window pane.
I hurriedly glance up toward the sudden emptiness of the hillside.
I sigh . . . relieved?

A family waits for the subway in New York;
a group of cheap hoods attacks them for pocket change.
The family's son is stabbed through the heart
after lunging at his mother's assaulters.
The Mother,
hysterical, screaming in fear for her dying son,
rushes to a subway clerk, begging for help.
She's ignored.

A lost foreign boy knocks on a door
to ask for directions to a costume party,
but instead
gets a bullet through his chest.

The setting sun casts a soft illumination;
the shadows of things appear greater than life.
An orb weaving spider, its intricate web ablaze with sunset,
creeps up, hungrily,
seizing the unfortunate grasshopper nymph entrapped there.
The infant jerks uncontrollably as the fangs of the
venomous vampire
stab into its helpless form.
Another futile attempt at escape,
a final jerk—then stillness.
The spider's legs busily grope the lifeless body.

Survival, once again.

The infant's eyes question, search the face of the young mother.

The purple mountain crests up through the brown city haze.

The toddler giggles, attempts to gather the puppy into his small arms.

A rainforest smolders.

The children wait to talk to Santa Claus.

Men, women, children, humanity,
dash along the beach with buckets of sea water;
rush to quench the parched skin of a young, beached whale.

The kindergartener builds a tower of blocks,
all the way to the sky.

The sea surf roars, washes with a pile of garbage.
Plastic syringes leave imprints in the soft, wet sand.

The children wait to talk to Santa Claus.

The small girl, unsteady, finally balances the bicycle.

The space travelers orbit the earth,
watch the mysterious majesty of blueness.

The teenage boy flashes a grin and a driver's license.

The large and small quail hurriedly scamper;
tiny feet blur the roadway.

Humanity watches life and death each day,
from living room sofas.

The children wait to talk to Santa Claus.

Men armed with rifles
rush into the wilderness to kill,
chase a deer onto a frozen lake.
The frightened buck slips, straddling the frigid surface,
helplessly trapped.
He stares hopelessly into the eyes of the approaching men.
Rifles now discarded, they tie a rope about his fragile body,
gently pulling him along the ice to the shoreline,
then coaxing him back into the sanctuary of the brush;
they've finished hunting.

A group of Somali soldiers drags a trophy,
the body of an American killed in battle,

naked,
through the streets, laughing and cheering.
The body,
smoking from being set ablaze, causes a
jet black sunrise.

The autumn moonlight seeps softly, gently
through the nudeness of tree branches.
The dry leaves swirl about our feet.
Winter smells near, spring will follow.

Walt, we know who you were, and what you meant.
You waited for us.
You were there yesterday, here today, and tomorrow.
We searched and found you, I, ourselves.

10. Draft a Fictional Biography or Autobiography of a Character in a Story, Poem, Play, or Other Text.

Edith wrote an autobiography, in diary form, of Minnie Wright, the abused wife in Susan Glaspell's play *Trifles* (p. 259). The diary entries trace Minnie's development over a period of thirty years.

Dear Diary

April 7, 1886—Today was my 17th birthday. What a happy day! My parents gave me a beautiful white dress with blue hair ribbons. Mama said I was to wear them in the church choir program next Sunday. I can hardly wait, for I do love pretty things, and I do love to sing in the choir—makes me feel all warm and toasty inside. Maybe John will be there. He's new in town. I caught him staring at me last Sunday—I think he wants to walk me home. I've never had a boyfriend before, so the thought of it kinda gives me the "tingles." I wonder if he'll think I look pretty in my new dress.

May 2, 1886—Well, John finally got up the courage to walk me home from church yesterday. He seems awful quiet—didn't say much the whole way home, but I guess I talked enough for the both of us. I never did have trouble thinkin' of things to talk about, 'cause I just get so worked up over everything—the sun goin' down on the prairie, the new department store in town, the minister's sermon, the birds comin' back after winter, or just any old thing. Pa says conversation is my strong point. I don't know if John likes my white dress or not—probably he's too shy to say so. But it did make me feel so important to have a beau see me home!

June 25, 1886—Well, dear diary, you are never going to believe this, but I am gettin' married one month from today! I know it seems sudden, but John says there ain't no use in waitin'. I'm sure he must be right. Sometimes I get right dizzy when I think about bein' married. Most people seem to like it all right, so I guess I will too. John still don't say much, but he must like me or he wouldn't a decided we should get hitched. It *will* be fun to have babies and dress 'em up cute. I always did love babies. And you never know—once the babies come, maybe John will find his tongue a bit more. Then again—maybe not. Some folks just seems more bent on some things than other folks do.

July 25, 1887—Well dear diary, I haven't written much for a long time. It ain't that I don't have anything to write, but I guess it's partly two things: partly it's that bein' a wife is much more work than I ever thought it would be, and partly I guess I been puttin' off writing, hopin' I'd have something cheerful to write—hopin' maybe I'd find myself in the family way, or somethin' like that. But now I'm thinkin' it's not likely to happen any time soon. Every time I bring up the subject, John turns his head the other way and pretends he doesn't hear me. I'm beginning to think he doesn't want any children! Could that be? I don't like to think on it, so sometimes I go for short walks. Don't dare go for long walks, 'cause John gets powerful upset if he comes home and finds me gone somewhere.

March 4, 1888—I can't write too much today—got too much to do. I been feelin' a bit sad lately. John says he don't want me singin' in the choir no more—says it's prideful and a sin to show off in such a way. It's hard to think that havin' a little happiness is a sin, but perhaps he's right. He 'most generally is.

August 12, 1890—Been bakin' my usual batch of bread today, and thinkin' a mite more than usual. It's been *so* hot this week. I think I'll 'most melt away. Got my cherries all bottled a couple weeks ago. Soon it'll be time to do up the peaches. The corn's growin' pretty good. John does work hard, and I try to be a good wife to him. The thing that's hardest is bein' down in this here hollow where I can't see the road or any other houses, or nothin' but just the work that's gotta be done, day in and day out. Just the sameness is enough to make a body tired. Maybe, if we get a good crop, John will say we can go to town. I won't ask for a new dress, but maybe a new apron would be nice.

December 22, 1890—We been havin' one of the *coldest* winters I've ever seen in these parts. I make up a fire in the stove, but the heat seems to creep out at all the cracks before it even warms the room. I can't seem to get warm no matter what I do. John says it's too cold to work outside, so he sits inside all day and seems to get ornrier and ornrier. I've decided it's no use to try to talk to him, so I try to cheer myself up by workin' on my quilt blocks. I'm sure that when I get it all pieced it will be the prettiest thing in the house, and maybe then I'll get warm. Haven't been warm in such a long time. Goodness knows I won't be allowed to hold no quiltin' bee when I get it put together, so I'll just have to settle for tyin' knots in it. Stichin' it would be prettier, but I guess the knots'll do. At least they'll get the job done.

Mar. 1, 1891—The fetchingest little bird landed in the cherry tree this morning. He sang and sang until I thought my heart would just bust.

May 9, 1894—Made bread, did the laundry, hoed three rows of potatoes. Cloudy all day—no wind.

Sept. 12, 1896—Canned two bushel of peaches, mopped the floor, ironed the clothes. Seems cold tonight.

Dec. 24, 1898—Christmas tomorrow. Don't know if there'll be any singin' at Church. Too cold to go.

Mar. 10, 1902—John's been gone for three days, buyin' seed in the next county. I just seem to rattle around in here. Got to wishin' we might-a had a child to keep me a speck o' company. But perhaps it's no kinda life for a child.

Jan. 19, 1909—Found my piece quilt yesterday while cleanin' out the closet. Can't seem to work up the spirit to work on it much. It's been put away so long that it hurts me to look at it.

Dec. 26, 1912—Christmas yesterday. No one came to visit.

Apr. 7, 1916—My birthday. Almost forgot it, perhaps I should have. Seems I'm gettin' on. Bought myself a little canary from a peddlar man. He does sing pretty. Don't know what John will say.

Apr. 9, 1916—It should be spring, but we been havin' a blizzard for the last two days. Don't know why it's turned so cold again. Sewed a couple o' blocks on that quilt I started so long ago. It is right pretty.

Apr. 10, 1916—John couldn't stand for the singin' of my canary. Said it made him nervous. I put the poor little thing in a pretty box I'd been saving for somethin' special. I'll bury him tomorrow.

Apr. 11, 1916—I don't know what to do. I've done a awful thing. Couldn't help myself. God knows I didn't want to. Couldn't help myself. Couldn't stand it no more. My poor little bird. Wrung his neck. Need to finish my quilt. Going to knot it. Couldn't help myself. Gotta be free. Whatever shall I do. No one to talk to. So cold in here. Couldn't stand it no more. Going to knot it. Wrung his neck. God knows I didn't want to. So cold in here. . . .

Appendix B: Sample Essays About Literature

Essays about literature may assume a number of forms. This appendix illustrates three major kinds: explication, which is emphatically text-centered and focuses (generally) on a single literary text; the "reader-response" essay, which combines textual analysis with personal thoughts, feelings, and experience; and the comparison/contrast essay, which explores similarities and/or differences between two or more literary texts.

Sample #1. Angie writes an explication of Gary Soto's poem "Oranges" (p. 474); that is, she does a line-by-line analysis of the poem itself and what it means. Since "Oranges" is quite short, Angie is able to explicate, or "explain," the entire poem. In an explication of a longer text, such as a short story or play, you might focus on a particular scene, incident, or other crucial passage rather than the whole work.

"Oranges": Moving from Childhood to Adolescence

The poem "Oranges," by Gary Soto, suggests a beginning as well as an end. The beginning is the start of a new chapter in the lives of the speaker and the "girl"; they are starting to feel the emotions of adolescence in which the opposite sex is no longer viewed as repellent or "gross" but as somewhat mystical. At the same time, their childhood is ending; their new experience of dating seems to change how they look at

life. <u>This is a turning point in their lives,</u> though the
poet makes it seem so simple.

The thesis pro-
vides a context
for the ensuing
paragraphs

The nervousness and excitement of the boy are
evident early in the poem:

> She came out pulling
> At her gloves, face bright
> With rouge. I smiled,
> Touched her shoulder, and led
> Her down the street. . . .

Quotations of
more than four
lines are block-
indented

The girl's face is painted "bright/With rouge" for him.
He smiles, and leads the girl to a drugstore that sells
candy. The excitement of being able to buy a piece of
candy for this girl shows that he feels he is becoming
a man: "I turned to the candies/Tiered like bleachers,/And asked what she wanted." The mention of
"bleachers" suggests a performance. The speaker is
performing, trying to show the girl that he likes her
enough to give her whatever she wants.

Slash marks indi-
cate line breaks
when poetry is
printed out as
prose

The poem continues:

> . . . I fingered
> A nickel in my pocket,
> And when she lifted a chocolate
> That cost a dime,
> I didn't say anything.
> I took the nickel from
> My pocket, then an orange,
> And set them quietly on
> The counter.

Angie quotes the
poem to illustrate
her points. In
addition, she
discusses each
quotation to
make clear why
she has included
it

When the girl picks out the chocolate, which costs
more than what he has, the boy seems downhearted.
He gets his first real taste of responsibility in this new
sphere of life. He feels that he needs to impress the
girl in order to save his social status in this new and
frightening world; so he places one of his beloved oranges on the counter next to his hard-earned nickel in
hopes that the woman at the counter will understand.
"The lady's eyes met mine,/And held them, know-
ing/Very well what it was all/About." The woman,
watching this whole scene, probably remembers a
similar situation in her own life and takes pity on the
young boy.

The boy's happiness at being able to give the girl what she wants is incredible. In the beginning of the poem, he is walking with "a girl." Now that he has bought her a chocolate, he feels that she is his: "I took my girl's hand/In mine for two blocks,/Then released it to let/Her unwrap the chocolate." She suddenly changes from *a* girl to "my" girl, and he now gets the courage to hold her hand for two whole blocks.

Soto's poem ends:

> I peeled my orange
> That was so bright against
> The gray of December
> That, from some distance,
> Someone might have thought
> I was making a fire in my hands.

These last six lines suggest a metaphor for the boy's happiness. The orange could be interpreted as him peeling off his childhood to reveal this new part of his life. This new time is sweet, like the juices of an orange; and, also like an orange, it is "bright" with hope. The speaker's mood at this moment is "bright" like "a fire."

The girl, too, is experiencing a new time in her life. She tries to look good for this boy by wearing "gloves" and "rouge," no doubt watching her mother or maybe a sister. In the candy store, she seems flattered to be offered anything she likes: "Light in her eyes, a smile/Starting at the corners/Of her mouth." This is most likely the first time a boy has offered to buy her anything. When she sees the boy place one of his oranges on the counter with his nickel, she probably wonders whether she has offended or embarrassed him in any way. Though it is not mentioned in the poem, she may suppose she has already failed in trying to be like a grown-up. Once the boy takes her hand, however, she probably feels much better, as if the date has been a success.

"Oranges" is a narrative about a young boy and girl's first exposure to the world of dating. Through this experience, they learn lessons for their subsequent lives. A door has been opened for them to continue to grow and mature; at the same time, however, they must leave their simple childhoods behind.

The closing paragraph reinforces Angie's thesis & casts the experience depicted in the poem as one of simultaneous gain & loss

Sample #2. Many of the professionally written essays in Part V of *Reading and Writing from Literature* use narrative, or storytelling, as a means of illustrating ideas. For instance, Michael Dorris's "Life Stories" (p. 949) is composed primarily of stories about his early jobs and their effects on his development. In "The Hand," Joe discusses Dorris's essay in relationship to an early job experience of his own. Unlike Angie's essay, which focuses quite exclusively on the literary text itself, Joe's essay integrates literary analysis with his own personal experience.

The Hand

At the end of "Life Stories," Michael Dorris writes that his various school vacation jobs were "not so much to be held as to be weighed, absorbed, and incorporated, and, collectively, they carried me forward into adult life like an escalator, unfolding a particular pattern at once haphazard and inevitable" (954). In this statement, Dorris implies that those jobs were important not for making money, but because they provided him with valuable personal insight and revealed to him a pattern or script that his later life might follow.

Dorris begins his essay by talking about a rite of passage of the Plains Indians in which a male teen was to venture out into the wilderness alone and subsist there until he happened upon some "thing" that might transform him or give him insight into his life. "Through this unique prism," Dorris writes, "abstractly preserved in a vivid memory or song, a boy caught foresight of both his adult persona and of his vocation, the two inextricably entwined" (950). For Dorris, "this unique prism" was his collection of summer jobs.

The first job that Dorris describes is his position as a postal carrier, a job important for the opportunity it afforded him to do "casually sophisticated . . . work that required a uniform" (951). Entrusted with possibly "important correspondence," Dorris learned—the hard way—about responsibility on the job (951).

Another one of Dorris's jobs was his stint as Coordinator of Tribal Youth Programs, where he was to "coordinate" a group of "bored, disgruntled kids . . . who had nothing better to do each day than to show up . . . and hate whatever Program I had planned for them" (951). As that particular summer job progressed, Dorris came to understand the role that he was to play for the youths, and he came to greet each day with the "lightheadedness of anticipated exhaustion, that

MLA-style parenthetical references show the source & page numbers of quotations

Quotations are skillfully interwoven with the text

thrill of giddy dissociation in which nothing seems real or of great significance" (952).

Dorris values both of these jobs for what they offer him: unexpected challenges and unique perspectives. From there, he presumably moves on to deal with the rest of the unexpected challenges and unique perspectives that life affords him.

My experiences with jobs afforded me "personal, enabling insight" (950) in much the same way as Dorris's did. I'm not sure if my experiences were rites of passage or terms of a contract; but through my time spent as the managing editor of the *Iowa State Daily*, I came to understand certain conditions with which we must all live.

I wrote columns at the newspaper. In fact, I was the designated "fluff columnist"—the person responsible for commenting on the string found in coat pockets and combs found beneath couch cushions and which clouds looked like which president on a given day. The life of the fluff columnist on a newspaper is like that of a World War II bomber pilot: he fights the war from an infinitely high place while others slog through the trenches and do the work and report the minutes of school board meetings and take the shrapnel of barbed letters to the editor.

I became a mild hit, accepted by my peers and somehow deemed trustworthy by my readers. People began coming to me to have their stories told. A football player wanted to come out of the closet in my column, a philosophy professor wanted me to print his suicide note, and a co-ed wanted me to write a transcript of one of her sexual encounters. "I really hate sex," she told me on the Commons one afternoon, "and I think you could make that come across. I've never been in the paper before."

My life was running pleasantly out of tilt, happily imbalanced. I felt plugged into things. I got drunk most weekends and some weeknights, because that was what a writer did. I drank angostura bitters in my gin and tonic, because Hemingway drank angostura bitters in his gin and tonic. When I made clumsy, drunken passes at women, it was because Henry Miller made clumsy, drunken passes at women. I felt like I was a vital connection in the creative process and that, as such a connection, I needed to cultivate certain habits.

One Sunday morning, I was in the office filing my column when the report of an accident came over the

A thesis usually appears near the beginning of an essay—but not always. Joe's thesis appears several paragraphs into his essay; it states the connection between his own job experience & Dorris's

In this paragraph & others, Joe illustrates & enlivens his main point with examples & quotations

Like the simple word "Once," this phrase helps propel the writer (& his readers) into a specific longer story about his job experience

police scanner. It was early enough that no one else except the editor was in the office, so I was sent out with a camera to cover it. A train had struck a car in the middle of town. A man was dead. I was the first reporter on the scene.

Before I knew it, I was snapping pictures of the twisted wreckage of the car, which sat—still smoking—on the tracks, a sick convolution of metal and rubber enfolded back upon itself. In its midst was a hand held tentatively out toward the pavement, dripping blood in a steady patter that looked too red to be real. I circled the wreck, snapping photos; but the only evidence of there having been anything human inside the layered metal was the hand, stretched out like the one on the ceiling of the Sistine Chapel, reaching out for another. I snapped countless photos of the hand, knowing that I would get on the front page, reveling in the exaltation a trench reporter might feel at wading around in the viscera of a story. I was at the heart of the connection.

And then, the man's wife was brought to the scene. By some fluke, her mother had been listening to the police scanner that early Sunday morning as well. She was shielded from the accident by the throng of people that surrounded it, and she pushed her way up, past the police cars, past the people, up to where I was snapping photos.

She was repeating, "What happened? What happened? What happened?" and as she got closer to the wreck, as she was able to see the cataclysm of metal, the blob of car, she knew what it meant. I think she must have seen the hand. Maybe she saw me snapping pictures and composing the lead in my head. She screamed, and I felt it in my chest. Then she dropped to one knee, spattering the pavement with her vomit, and screamed once again through the thin torrent. She didn't cry; I didn't once hear her cry. She just screamed, over and over, mortally wounded; then she was guided off to the ambulance, away from the wreck. I faded into the crowd, drove back to the office, and developed the pictures of the hand. The wreck was front page news, along with my photo and story.

When the letters began coming in later that week, I laughed. People were calling me a ghoul and a sensationalist, and I couldn't have cared less. I was a vital connection. The city editor told me that I shouldn't take such things personally. "The fact of the matter is, you *are* a ghoul. And so am I, and so is everyone else in the newsroom," he told me at the bar later that week. He indicated the other people in the bar with a jerk of his head and added, "They don't understand that."

I didn't write on the paper the next semester and dropped out of school the semester after that. I avoided seeing any of my friends from the paper, but wondered in a sulking child's way if I was missed by them or by any of the readers. None of my self-pity mattered then or now, because I was a ghoul and still am, and only now am I comfortable with that truth.

Beyond the angostura bitters and the clumsy, drunken, poetic passes at women, is what Hemingway and Miller avoided saying directly, though it is a truth as blunt as any: a writer is a ghoul, a person who passes his hands over dead skin and then tells others how it feels.

The essay does not end in the usual way, with a neat conclusion, but with a blunt & disturbing metaphor. What is the effect? Does it matter that Joe does not return to Dorris's "Life Stories" at the end of his essay? Why or why not?

Sample #3. One common type of essay about literature is the comparison/contrast essay. In the next example, Sara compares the protagonists in two short stories, "The Story of an Hour" (p. 181) and "The Yellow Wallpaper" (p. 184).

Free at Last

There are strong similarities between "The Story of an Hour" and "The Yellow Wallpaper." Both stories feature women who are products of their times, confined by the constraints of both husband and society. The women grow in awareness of their situation and make a deliberate decision to free themselves from it.

The time frame of the stories, loosely from the late 1800's through the early 1900's, implies a standard of behavior and a conformity to male/female role models that influences the female protagonists in "The Story of an Hour" and "The Yellow Wallpaper." In this era, females were raised to be the helpmates of man. The clothes, etiquette, education, curricular activities, and household chores functioned to transform a girl into a young lady and to communicate her primary responsibilities as future wife and mother. Similarly, a young boy was trained to assume his birthright as wage earner and husband. Men and women followed closely dictated societal roles: men were the supporters, defenders, and rulers; women were the sup-

Sara deftly limits her thesis: rather than trying to compare everything about the two stories, she focuses on the two women protagonists & their move toward freedom

ported, defended, and governed. Men led; women followed. To venture beyond the confines of the prescribed role was a breach of conduct. Often the punishment was abandonment, alienation, or banishment by family or community. Just as men were instilled with virtues, such as bravery and stoicism, that complemented their role, so women were imbued with submissiveness. <u>These narrowly defined roles form the foundation for the conflict in "The Yellow Wallpaper" and "The Story of an Hour."</u>

Sara places the two characters in a historical & social context but does not lose sight of her focus: this last sentence returns us to the two stories

Long before the "hour" depicted in Chopin's story, Louise Mallard has been indoctrinated into the values and morals of her time period. She has been carefully prepared to fulfill the role of a wife. Within their marriage, she and Brently function in their prescribed roles. Louise is neither happy nor unhappy; she is comfortable. Her days pass predictably, and she feels no desire to change the pattern of her existence.

<u>The doctor's wife in "The Yellow Wallpaper" is a product of the same expectations and conformity.</u> She defers to the judgment of her husband and acquiesces in his decisions. "It is so hard to talk with John about my case," she writes, "because he is so wise, and because he loves me so" (190). Her rebellions are small and confined to his absence. The role modeling and constraints imposed by society form the background of her story and heighten her conflict as she comes into awareness of the self she has imprisoned.

Paragraph transitions are particularly important in comparison/contrast essays. These and other opening sentences of paragraphs keep the focus on connections <u>between</u> the two women rather than on either woman in isolation

<u>Just as Louise has been molded into the role of wife, so, too, has the doctor's wife.</u> Although neither is intentionally limited by her husband from achieving her potential as a woman, both are victims of a confining relationship. The tragic result is a loss of identity. Each woman can perceive herself only in terms of her husband. Because society dictated a submissive role for women, a woman seldom challenged her destiny. If she found her lot unpalatable, she kept the pain to herself. It would not occur to a woman to think in terms of her own development, needs, and expression. Only a crisis or some other catalyst could make her confront the identity she had repressed.

The crisis for Louise is the announcement of her husband's death. After the initial shock, she begins to contemplate her lack of remorse. As she gazes out the window towards the blue sky, she embarks on a process of self-discovery. She does not feel loss but a sense

of release from her confinement in an imposed role. She   MLA-style paren-
is "Free, free, free!" (182). Her awareness is sparked by   thetical reference
her ability to confront the identity she has repressed.
Louise's excitement over her freedom is in stark contrast to the apathy that defined her marriage role.

The doctor's wife's journey towards self-realiza-
tion is more tortured and lengthy than Louise's. She
does not experience a dramatic crisis that challenges
her to confront her inner self or open her eyes in sudden self-awareness. Her conformity to the established
norm exacts a price—illness. Her postpartum depression is a symptom of the repressed self. The wallpaper
serves as the catalyst for the journey into the depths
of her being. It symbolizes her overpowering illness
and represents an elaborate description of her struggle. The design in the paper illustrates her feelings.
The bars are the strings of steel in her mind that deny
her the courage and strength to move on with life and
that imprison her within her *role:*

> The front pattern *does* move—and no wonder! The   Quotations of
> woman behind shakes it!   more than four
>   lines are block-
> Sometimes I think there are a great many women   indented
> behind, and sometimes only one, and she crawls
> around fast, and her crawling shakes it all over. . . .
> And she is all the time trying to climb through. But
> nobody could climb through that pattern—it strangles
> so; I think that is why it has so many heads. (193)

The woman that the doctor's wife envisions in the
wallpaper, who is alternately trapped and freed, finally lures the wife deeper into herself. As she struggles to free the woman by ripping down the
wallpaper, she is struggling to free herself.

Both Louise and the doctor's wife become aware of   The conclusion re-
their inner selves through a process of discovery   iterates the main
brought on by an incident in their life. Their previous   similarities &
existence serves to contrast their former selves with   differences be-
their new revelations. Unfortunately, their realizations   tween the 2 char-
are dramatically extinguished: Louise dies when she   acters & their
sees her husband walk through the door; the doctor's   search for free-
wife joins the trapped woman in the wallpaper. Yet   dom
both endings represent a triumph. Louise's death is an
alternative to returning to her submissive self. The
doctor's wife's decision marks the severance of her
submission to her husband. Both women are free.

Appendix C:
Glossary of Literary Terms

Most of the terms below are also discussed in Part IV, "An Introduction to the Four Genres." For additional references and examples, consult the appropriate chapter in Part IV.

Abstract language   *See* concrete language.

Act   A major structural division within a play.

Alliteration   A sound effect in which consonant sounds are repeated, particularly at the beginnings of words or of stressed syllables. Examples: "*l*ow"/"*l*ong"; "*cr*acks"/"*cr*azes."

Allusion   A reference to something (such as a character or event in literature, history, or mythology) outside the literary text itself.

Anapest   A metrical foot composed of two lightly stressed syllables followed by a stressed syllable, e.g., in the énd. *See also* meter.

Antagonist   The main opponent of the protagonist in a story, play, or other narrative or dramatic work.

Aphorism   A terse statement of principle, truth, or opinion.

Argumentative essay   *See* essay.

Assonance   A sound effect in which identical or similar vowel sounds are repeated in two or more words in close proximity to each other. Example: "st*or*ms"/"m*or*ning."

Author   The writer of a literary work. *Compare* persona.

Ballad   A relatively short narrative poem, generally with an anonymous or impersonal narrator, that is usually written in rhymed four-line stanzas and that may include a refrain.

Blank verse   Verse composed in unrhymed iambic pentameter lines.

Caesura   A strong pause within a line of poetry.

Characters   The imaginary persons who appear in fictional narratives or dramatic works. A flat character is one who remains essentially unchanged throughout the story and tends to be less an individual than a type. A round character evolves or undergoes change in the course of the story and is more individualized and complex.

Citation   A reference made, in an essay, to another text. The citation may be included for diverse purposes: to illustrate a point or idea, to add support or authority to the writer's argument or reasoning, to bolster reader trust in the persona, or to add depth to the essay by expanding its range of literary reference.

Climax   The moment in the plot of a story or play at which tensions are highest or suspense reaches its height.

Concrete language   Language that describes or portrays specific or observable persons, places, or things rather than general ideas or qualities. Concrete language appeals to the senses, as in this example from Robert Frost's "Birches": "They [Birches] click upon themselves/As the breeze rises, and turn many-colored/As the stir cracks and crazes their enamel" (ll. 7–9). In contrast, **abstract language** refers to general ideas or qualities, as in this later passage from the same poem: "Earth's the right place for love:/I don't know where it's likely to get better" (ll. 52–53).

Conflict   A struggle among opposing characters or forces in fiction, poetry, or drama.

Connotation   An associative or suggestive meaning of a word in addition to its literal dictionary meaning (or "denotation"). The word "politician" denotes "a person actively involved in politics," while it connotes (for some people) a corrupt and conniving individual motivated exclusively by self-interest.

Consonance   A sound effect in which identical or similar consonant sounds, occurring in nearby words, are repeated with different intervening vowels. Example: "*crush*"/"*crash*."

Couplet   A pair of lines of poetry, usually rhymed; a two-line stanza.

Dactyl   A metrical foot consisting of one stressed syllable followed by two lightly stressed syllables, e.g., "póndĕrĭng."

Denotation   The dictionary definition of a word, without associative or implied meanings. *Compare* connotation.

Denouement   The moment of final resolution of the conflict in a plot.

Dialogue   The spoken conversation that occurs in a text.

Diction   Word choice. Diction can be described as formal or informal, abstract or concrete, general or specific, and literal or figurative.

End-stopped line   A line of poetry whose end coincides with the end of a phrase, clause, or sentence.

Enjambed line   A line of poetry that completes its grammatical unity and meaning by going into the next line without a pause.

Epic poem   A long narrative poem on a heroic subject.

Essay   A unified and relatively short work of nonfiction prose. An argumentative essay advances an explicit argument and supports it with evidence. An expository essay informs an audience or explains a particular subject. A personal or literary essay emphasizes elements that are ordinarily associated with "literary" texts–an engaging persona, an intellectual or emotional focus or theme that is usually implied rather than directly stated, and artful use of figurative language and other "literary" elements such as dialogue and narrative.

Exposition   The part of a plot of a short story or play that provides background information on characters, setting, and plot.

Expository essay   *See* essay.

Expressionism   A writing style or movement in which reality is exaggerated or distorted in order to render the world as we feel it rather than as we literally see it.

Falling action   The part of the plot of a short story or play, after the climax, in which action and suspense decline toward a denouement or resolution.

Feminine rhyme   *See* rhyme.

Figurative language   The term used to encompass all nonliteral uses of language.

Figure (or **trope**)   A word or phrase used in a way that significantly changes its standard or literal meaning. Some common kinds of figures are metaphor, simile, metonymy, irony, and paradox.

First-person narrator   *See* point of view.

Flashback   An interruption in the chronological presentation of a narrative or drama that presents an earlier episode.

Flat character   *See* characters.

Foot   *See* meter.

Free verse   Poetry that discards meter and usually dispenses with rhyme while keeping other poetic elements such as pronouncedly rhythmic phrasing, various types of patterned sound, and intensive use of figurative language.

Hero/Heroine   The main character in a narrative or dramatic work. Also called the "protagonist."

Hyperbole   A bold exaggeration used for rhetorical effect.

Iamb   A metrical foot consisting of a lightly stressed syllable followed by a stressed syllable, e.g., "around."

Irony   A type of incongruity. Dramatic irony involves an incongruity between what a character in a story or play *believes* and what we (the better-informed members of the audience) *know*. Verbal irony involves an incongruity between what is literally said and what is actually meant.

Limited point of view   *See* point of view.

Lyric poem   A poem, usually rather short, in which a speaker expresses a state of mind or feeling.

Masculine rhyme   *See* rhyme.

Metaphor   A figure or trope that makes an implicit comparison between dissimilar items in a way that evokes new or vivid ways of perceiving, knowing, and/or feeling. Example: "she is a green tree/in a forest of kindling" makes an implicit comparison between a young girl, indestructible in her zest for life, and an almost fireproof tree.

Meter   Rhythm that follows a regular repeating pattern of stressed and lightly stressed syllables. Within a poetic line, meters are measured in feet, with each repetition of the pattern comprising a separate foot. The most common meters are iambic (˘ ´), trochaic (´ ˘), anapestic (˘ ˘ ´), and dactylic (´ ˘ ˘). A line of three feet is described as trimeter, a line of four feet is tetrameter, and one of five feet is pentameter.

Metonymy   A figure or trope in which the literal term for one thing is used to stand for another with which it is closely associated. Example: "The White House says" instead of "The President says."

Monologue   A long speech by a single character.

Narrative poem   A poem that relates a story.

Narrator   The imaginary speaker, as distinct from the author him- or herself, who tells a story. *See also* point of view.

Octave   *See* stanza.

Ode   A lyric poem, composed in a lofty style, that is serious in subject and elaborate in stanza structure.

Omniscient narrator   *See* point of view.

One-act play   A relatively short play. Usually, though not always, a one-act dramatizes a single incident and includes fewer characters than multiple-act plays.

Oxymoron   A joining of two terms that are ordinarily conceived as opposites. Examples: "knowledgeable unknowing," "deafening silence."

Paradox   An apparently contradictory statement that proves, on examination, to be true. Example: "You must lose your life to gain it."

Persona   The "mask" or version of a self that an author projects in a particular text. The plural form of persona is **personae.**

Personal essay   *See* essay.

Personification   A figure or trope in which human qualities are ascribed to an abstract concept or inanimate object. Example: "Fortune smiled upon him."

Plot   The pattern of actions and events that combine to produce a total effect in readers or viewers of a narrative or dramatic work. Some critics divide plots into a rising action, which introduces the characters and establishes the conflict; a climax, in which the conflict reaches its height in the form of some decisive action or decision; a falling action, in which the conflict moves toward resolution; and a denouement or resolution, in which the conflicts are resolved.

Poem   A kind of literary text that is typically arranged in lines and composed in meter or free verse.

Point of view   The perspective from which a story is told. The two basic types are first-person and third-person. In a first-person narrative the narrator is a character within the story, while in a third-person narrative he or she is not a character in the story. Third-person narrators can be further classified (broadly) as either limited or omniscient. The limited narrator reports events and characters primarily through the consciousness of one character, while the omniscient functions as an all-knowing presence with access to the thoughts, feelings, and actions of any or all of the characters. An unreliable (or naive) narrator is a first-person narrator whose youth, naiveté, limited intelligence, or extreme subjectivity leads us to question the accuracy of his or her version of characters and events.

Prose poem   A poem that is shaped like prose (in paragraphs rather than lines) but that displays other features (such as pronouncedly rhythmic phrasing, various types of patterned sound, and intensive use of figurative language) characteristic of poetry.

Protagonist   The main character around whom a narrative or dramatic work centers. Also called the "hero" or "heroine."

Quatrain   *See* stanza.

Rhyme   An identity or similarity in sound patterns, the most familiar kind being the *end* rhyme that occurs between words at the ends of lines of poetry. When the end rhyme consists of a single stressed syllable ("sing"/"wing"), it is termed masculine; when the rhyme consists of a final stressed syllable followed by a lightly stressed ("whether"/"feather"), it is termed feminine. A slant, partial, or half rhyme occurs when the rhyming sounds are only approximately ("dizzy"/"easy"), rather than exactly, alike.

Rhythm   A distinct but variable pattern of stressed and lightly stressed sounds in poetry or prose.

Rising action   *See* plot.

Round character   *See* characters.

Scansion   The process of analyzing the metrical pattern of a poem.

Scene description   Text that describes what the stage looks like for a particular play.

Sestet   *See* stanza.

Setting   The place, time, and social context in which a story, poem, or play takes place.

Short story   A brief work of prose fiction.

Simile   A figure that makes an explicit (rather than implicit) comparison between dissimilar items in a way that evokes new or vivid ways of perceiving, knowing, and/or feeling. Example: "skin/worn, like the pages of her prayer book" makes an explicit comparison between an old woman's skin and the pages of a well-used book. *Compare* metaphor.

Slant rhyme   Also called a "half" or "partial" rhyme. *See* rhyme.

Sonnet   A fourteen-line lyric poem written in iambic pentameter and rhymed according to a preset conventional pattern. The **Italian** or **Petrarchan sonnet** is divided into an octave rhymed *abbaabba* and a sestet with a *cdecde* rhyme scheme or some variant. The **English** or **Shakespearean sonnet** falls into three quatrains rhymed *abab, cdcd, efef,* and a closing couplet rhymed *gg.*

Speaker   The "I" in a lyric poem.

Stage directions   In a play, text that describes the movements or gestures of characters onstage.

Stanza   A grouping of poetic lines arranged in a definite pattern that is repeated throughout the poem. Three-line stanzas are called tercets or triplets; stanzas of four lines, six lines, and eight lines are called (respectively) quatrains, sestets, and octaves.

Stream of consciousness   A narrative technique that tries to reproduce the exact flow of thoughts, feelings, and associations that go through a character's mind as he or she moves in the "stream" of time.

Symbol   Something that stands for something else. In literary analysis, something is said to be "symbolic" if it evokes an idea, quality, or concept larger than itself.

Synecdoche   A figure or trope in which a part of something is used to signify the whole or the whole is used to signify a part. Example: "All hands on deck" instead of "All sailors on deck."

Syntax   The arrangement of words within phrases, clauses, and sentences.

Tercet   *See* stanza.

Theme   A basic idea advanced (or implied) in a text.

Thesis   In a formal or academic essay, a sentence that articulates the main point that the text intends to address or argue.

Third-person narrator   *See* point of view.

Tone   The expression of a writer's attitudes toward a subject; the mood the writer has chosen for a piece.

Traditional verse   Poetry that employs meter and (often) rhyme. *See also* free verse.

Triplet   *See* stanza.

Trochee   A metrical foot consisting of one stressed syllable followed by a lightly stressed syllable, e.g., "dreary."

Trope   *See* figure.

Unreliable (or **naive**) **narrator**   *See* point of view.

Verbal irony   An incongruity between what a speaker says literally and the meaning that is implied in the larger context of the story, poem, or other work.

Voice   The felt authorial presence in a literary text.

Appendix D:
Notes on the Authors

Notes are included for all authors of short stories, essays, and plays and for authors represented by two or more poems.

Woody Allen (b. 1935)

Born in Brooklyn, New York, Woody Allen (real name Allen Stewart Konigsberg) attended college in New York City and began his career as a joke writer and comic. Though best known as a filmmaker (*Bananas, Sleeper, Annie Hall, Interiors, Manhattan, Bullets over Broadway*), the multitalented Allen is also an actor, short story writer, playwright, and jazz clarinetist. *Death Knocks* is reprinted from *Getting Even* (1971), a collection of Allen's comic stories, sketches, and plays.

Maya Angelou (b. 1928)

Maya Angelou has had a long and distinguished career as a poet, autobiographer, playwright, director, actress, singer, and producer for stage and screen. An African-American, Angelou grew up amid racial segregation in Stamps, Arkansas, and attended public schools there and in California. Later she studied dance and drama and worked as a performing artist, director, and producer in the United States and abroad. Her first book, the autobiographical *I Know Why the Caged Bird Sings* (1970), was widely praised. Angelou has produced several additional books of autobiography, including *Gather Together in My Name, The Heart of a Woman,* and *All God's Children Need Traveling Shoes,* and numerous collections of poems, such as *Poems: Maya Angelou, I Shall Not Be Moved,* and *On the Pulse of Morning.* She read the title poem of this last work at the 1993 inauguration of President Bill Clinton.

Margaret Atwood (b. 1939)

Margaret Atwood has been influential as an author and editor who has asserted the cultural identity of Canadian literature. Born in Ottawa, Ontario, Atwood attended the University of Ontario and did graduate work in the United States at Radcliffe College and Harvard. She published her first book of poems, *Double Persephone* (1961), when she was in her twenties. Since then she has been prolific as a writer of novels, poems, short stories, and nonfiction. Among her best-known novels are *The Edible Woman, Surfacing, Life before Man, The Handmaid's Tale,* and *Alias Grace.* Her short stories are collected in *Dancing Girls and Other Stories, Bluebeard's Egg and Other Stories, Murder in the Dark,* and *Wilderness Tips.*

Toni Cade Bambara (1939–1995)

Writer and social activist, Toni Cade Bambara was born in New York City and grew up in the neighborhoods of Harlem, Bedford-Stuyvesant, and Queens. She was educated, also in New York, at Queens College (bachelor's degree in theater and English literature) and City College (master's degree in modern American literature), and subsequently studied filmmaking and other arts in Europe. During the 1960s, Bambara became prominently associated with African-American writers who formed the Black Arts Movement, and much of her fiction and other work reflects and celebrates the folk-based language of African-American music, poetry, and prose. Her short story collections include *Gorilla My Love* and *The Sea Birds Are Still Alive.* Bambara also published two novels, *The Salt Eaters* and *If Blessing Comes,* wrote television and film scripts, and edited several anthologies, including *The Black Woman* and *Tales and Stories for Black Folks.*

William Blake (1757–1827)

Poet and artist, William Blake was born in London, the son of a hosier. Lacking any formal education, he began studying drawing at age ten, served an apprenticeship to an engraver, and for the rest of his life earned a modest income as an engraver and illustrator. Blake was writing verse in his teens and published his first volume of poems (*Poetical Sketches*) in 1783. In 1789 he began engraving, illustrating, and printing his own works, including *Songs of Innocence* and *The Book of Thel* (1789), *The Marriage of Heaven & Hell* (ca. 1790), and *Songs of Experience* (1794). Visionary, iconoclastic in style and outlook, and largely indifferent to the commercial success or failure of his writings, Blake also wrote and illustrated numerous books in verse that developed his own political and cosmological mythology. He died in relative obscurity; his poems were little read during his lifetime, and what reputation he had was chiefly as an artist and engraver.

Carol Bly (b. 1930)

A Minnesota native, Carol Bly is best known for her essays and short stories about rural and small-town Minnesotans. Born in Duluth, Bly earned her B.A.

degree from Wellesley College and did graduate study at the University of Minnesota. She married the poet Robert Bly and, before they were divorced, helped him produce an influential literary magazine, raised a family, and performed numerous tasks, paid and volunteer, in her community. In her forties she began writing essays ("letters," she called them) for Minnesota Public Radio that were collected and published as *Letters from the Country* in 1981. Bly has also written two volumes of short stories, *Backbone* (1985) and *The Tomcat's Wife and Other Stories* (1992). Bly's work both celebrates and critiques small-town life. As one reviewer explains, she distills "the essences of small-town life—its . . . satisfactions and impoverishments, the contradictory pleasures of community and isolation, and . . . the difficulty of coming to a full exercise of individual capacity without seeming an alien, even a threat, to one's neighbors."

Elizabeth Bowen (1899–1973)

Born in Dublin, Elizabeth Bowen grew up in County Cork and was educated in England, where she continued to live until permanently returning to Ireland in 1952. Author of several novels—including *The House in Paris, The Death of the Heart,* and *The Heat of the Day*—she was also a prolific writer of short stories, which were gathered in *Collected Stories of Elizabeth Bowen* (1981). "The Demon Lover" reflects Bowen's fascination with the occult.

Ray Bradbury (b. 1920)

Ray Bradbury was born in Waukegan, Illinois, and received no formal education beyond high school. From youth on, however, he aspired to write. In 1941 he published his first short story in the genre (science fiction) with which he was to become most intimately connected. Since then Bradbury has written prolifically for magazines, television, radio, theatre, and film. His many works include *The Martian Chronicles, The Golden Apples of the Sun, Fahrenheit 451, Dandelion Wine, Something Wicked This Way Comes,* and *The Stories of Ray Bradbury.*

Gwendolyn Brooks (b. 1917)

Born in Topeka, Kansas, Gwendolyn Brooks grew up in inner-city Chicago and graduated from high school and junior college there. She began writing poetry as a child, received encouragement from mentors, and published her first book of poetry, *A Street in Bronzeville,* in 1945. Her second book, *Annie Allen* (1949) was the first volume of poetry by an African-American to win a Pulitzer Prize. Though always focused on the experience of African-Americans, Brooks's work underwent an important evolution in the late 1960s, when she attended a conference with many new and younger black poets and began to write more exclusively to black audiences. In the late sixties and early seventies, her poetry became more self-consciously political as she championed the cause of black militants and feminists. Some of her books from this period are *Riot, Family Pictures,* and *Beckonings.* Brooks's poetry is a distinctive, energy-charged blend of many influences, including traditional Anglo-American rhymed verse, street talk, African chant, the biblical cadences of black Protestant preaching, and the improvisatory rhythms of jazz.

Raymond Carver (1938–1988)

In a career cut short by lung cancer, Raymond Carver established himself as a contemporary master of the short story. Born in Clatskanie, Oregon, the son of a sawmill worker and a waitress, Carver produced fiction that relentlessly chronicled the lives of working-class Americans. Collections of his short stories include *Will You Please Be Quiet, Please?, What We Talk About When We Talk About Love,* and *Cathedral.* Carver also wrote essays and poems, which are collected in *Fires: Essays, Poems, Stories, In a Marine Light,* and in the posthumously published *A New Path to the Waterfall.* The lean, spare, and often bleak character of his stories earned him the label "minimalist."

Anton Chekhov (1860–1904)

Anton Chekhov, a major short story writer and playwright, was born in rural Russia and earned a medical degree at Moscow University School of Medicine. Though he was educated as a physician, literature was his passion. At nineteen he began submitting humorous sketches to newspapers and magazines, and his first published collection of stories appeared in 1884. By the end of his life he had written some six hundred stories. During the last decade of his life Chekhov also produced several dramatic works that revolutionized the modern theater: *The Sea Gull, Uncle Vanya, The Three Sisters,* and *The Cherry Orchard.* Long plagued by tuberculosis, Chekhov died at a resort in Germany in 1904. Chekhov's work is characterized by a strict economy and objectivity. As he wrote, "The artist should be, not the judge of his characters and their conversations, but only an unbiased witness." This stance is evident in "Gooseberries," in which the writer presents us with "the characters and their conversations" while leaving judgment and interpretation to his readers.

Kate Chopin (1850–1904)

Born Katherine ("Kate") O'Flaherty in St. Louis, Missouri, Kate Chopin was educated at Sacred Heart Academy, a St. Louis boarding school. Her father died in a railroad accident when Kate was a child, and she was subsequently raised by her mother, grandmother, and great-grandmother, all widowed and independent women. In 1870 she married Oscar Chopin, a well-to-do Louisiana man, and lived with him and their growing family in New Orleans until 1879, when they moved to the Chopin plantation in central Louisiana. After Oscar's sudden death in 1882 Kate returned with her six children to St. Louis. There, in 1889, she began writing for publication, producing her first novel, *At Fault,* in 1890, and two collections of short stories—*Bayou Folk* (1894) and *A Night in Acadie* (1897). In 1899 she published the novel for which she is best known today, *The Awakening,* about a heroine whose voyage of self-discovery causes her to defy conventional notions of wifehood, motherhood, and womanhood. This book drew largely negative reviews from across the country, especially from male critics, who were angered by its controversial subject matter. Chopin's stories are mainly set against the culturally diverse background of rural Louisiana. They explore themes of female sexuality, the often imprisoning effects of social institutions and conventions on individual development, and the roles and status of women in nineteenth-century American society, a time when most married women were considered the legal property of their husbands.

Judith Ortiz Cofer (b. 1952)

Born in Hormigueros, Puerto Rico, Judith Ortiz Cofer grew up on a "border" between cultures. Her father was a career navy man, and during Cofer's childhood the family shuttled between Puerto Rico and the mainland United States, between Spanish language and English, and between Puerto Rican culture and American. Cofer describes the impact of this experience in "Primary Lessons" and other autobiographical writings. Some of Cofer's collections of poetry and prose are *Latin Women Pray, Silent Dancing: A Partial Remembrance of a Puerto Rican Childhood, The Latin Deli: Prose and Poetry,* and *The Year of Our Revolution.* She has also written a novel, *The Line of the Sun* (1989).

Sidonie-Gabrielle Colette (1873–1954)

Born in Burgundy, France, Sidonie-Gabrielle Colette was a child prodigy who read classics by the age of eight and excelled at composition. Strongly influenced by her mother—an intellectual, passionate, and independent woman—Colette herself led an exciting life that included careers as a music hall dancer, novelist, and journalist. Colette wrote dozens of books (many of which have been translated into English), including novels, short stories, and other works that blend autobiography with fiction in a manner distinctly her own. Her biographer notes that, while "most of Colette's writing reveals her to be more interested in women than in men," she neither argues on behalf of women nor denigrates men. "[S]he remains feminine, never feminist. . . ."

Emily Dickinson (1830–1886)

Emily Dickinson was born in Amherst, Massachusetts, where her father, Edward, was a prominent lawyer and leading citizen. She attended Amherst Academy and, briefly, the nearby Mount Holyoke Female Seminary. After leaving the seminary without graduating in 1848, Dickinson seldom went beyond the grounds of the family home in Amherst until the day of her death. There, in an upstairs room of the house, she wrote over 1,700 poems. She was wary of publication, terming it "the Auction of the Mind," and fewer than twenty of her poems appeared in print during her lifetime. Others were published posthumously by family members and friends, and her complete poems did not appear in a scholarly edition until the 1950s. Dickinson's reclusive circumstances gave her the privacy and freedom she wanted for reading, thinking, and writing. Moreover, she was not completely isolated from the world. She lived among family and servants, maintained passionate friendships, and read voraciously—newspapers, contemporary poetry and fiction, and classics (especially Shakespeare). Many of Dickinson's poems are written in the simple iambic meters (see Appendix C) of hymns, but her verbal compression, suggestiveness, and astonishing metaphors make it impossible to label her poetry as "traditional." Tough-minded, irreverent, and stubbornly faithful to her own intuitions, Dickinson constantly pushed the limits of language—reinventing it, when necessary, to suit her ends. In her brother's words, "She saw things directly and just as they were. She abhorred sham."

Michael Dorris (1945–1997)

Part white and part Modoc Indian, writer/teacher Michael Dorris was a prominent contemporary advocate of Native American studies. Educated at Georgetown University (B.A., 1967) and Yale University (M.Phil., 1970), Dorris founded the Native American Studies department at Dartmouth College in the 1970s. In 1981 he married Louise Erdrich, one of his former students and a writer with whom he later collaborated. Dorris's books include the novels *A Yellow Raft on Blue Water* and *Cloud Chamber; The Broken Chord: A Family's Ongoing Struggle with Fetal Alcohol Syndrome* (winner of the 1989 National Book Critics Circle Award); *The Crown of Columbus*, a novel he coauthored with Erdrich; and several works for young adults. His essays are gathered in *Paper Trail: Collected Essays, 1967–1992*.

William Faulkner (1897–1962)

A "self-made" writer in the fullest sense, William Faulkner grew from humble beginnings to become a major American novelist and the 1950 winner of the Nobel Prize for literature. Faulkner was born in New Albany, Mississippi, and moved as a child to Oxford, Mississippi, where he spent most of his life. In 1918, without finishing high school, he enlisted in the Royal Canadian Air Force. Upon his return to the United States he attended school briefly and did odd jobs while dreaming of a life as a writer. His first published book, *The Marble Faun* (1924), was a collection of poems, but during a stay in New Orleans he met story writer Sherwood Anderson, who encouraged him to write fiction. A first novel, *Soldier's Pay*, came out in 1926, followed soon after by the novels that began to earn Faulkner a wider reputation: *Sartoris* (1929), *The Sound and the Fury* (1929), and *As I Lay Dying* (1930). In these and subsequent works Faulkner found his subject matter—his own South, the corrupt and violent South of myth and history, which he evoked obsessively in the people and landscapes of a fictional county named "Yoknapatawpha." Faulkner also developed a poetic, metaphoric, and syntactically complex prose style that is unique in American literature. "Barn Burning" is reprinted from *Collected Stories* (1950).

Robert Frost (1874–1963)

Though Robert Frost was born in San Francisco, California, his poetry is closely associated with rural New England, where he lived most of his life. While still a boy he moved there with his mother and sister following his father's death. He graduated from high school in Lawrence, Massachusetts (and eventually married a high school classmate), did some college work at Dartmouth and Harvard, and dedicated himself to becoming a poet. Success, however, came late; well into his thirties, Frost did odd jobs to keep his growing family out of poverty, and in 1912 he had to move to England to find a positive reception for his writing. Recognition came, first in England and then in America, with his first two books, *A Boy's Will* (1913) and *North of Boston* (1914). After moving back to New England in 1915 Frost saw critical acclaim for his work grow, and he soon became one of the most famous and widely honored poets in the United States, winning four Pulitzer prizes and reading a poem at the inauguration of President John F. Kennedy. In Frost's work the ordinary rhythms of New England speech play with and against the poetic strictures of blank verse (see Appendix C) and rhyme. Much of the pleasure experienced in reading a Frost poem comes from the contrast between the spontaneous-sounding speech, on the one hand, and the attention to form, on the other. Frost's life was plagued by personal suffering and tragedy, and the tragic occasionally surfaces in his poetry, as in "Out, Out—." Poems like "Stopping by Woods on a Snowy Evening" evoke the scenes and images of rustic tranquility that are another familiar strain in Frost's work.

Athol Fugard (b. 1932)

A white native of South Africa, Athol Fugard is best known for his plays about apartheid and the deep political and racial divisions that have torn his country. Originally planning to enter a technical trade, Fugard excelled in academics and won a scholarship to the University of Cape Town; restless, however, he left school in 1953 and signed on as a crew member aboard a tramp steamer on which he was the only white seaman. Upon returning to South Africa he became a news writer, got married in 1956, and began both acting in and writing plays. He also helped organize an interracial theater in Cape Town at a time when such racial mixing was illegal in South Africa. Fugard's first major success, *Blood Knot* (1961), the first play performed in South Africa with a mixed cast, was followed by *Boesman and Lena, A Lesson from Aloes, "Master Harold" . . . and the Boys,* and *The Road to Mecca,* among many others. Though Fugard's work focuses on issues of racial tension and injustice, his more general themes are intolerance and prejudice of all kinds, as evidenced in *The Road to Mecca,* in which an eccentrically creative heroine incurs the wrath of her conformist neighbors.

Gabriel García Márquez (b. 1928)

Widely regarded as one of the greatest living storytellers, Colombian-born Gabriel García Márquez has worked as a professional journalist and has been a prolific writer of fiction, plays, screenplays, and nonfiction. His most famous novel, *One Hundred Years of Solitude* (1967)—which Chilean poet Pablo Neruda called "the greatest revelation in the Spanish language since the *Don Quixote* of Cervantes"—has been translated into over thirty languages. Among his other novels are *The Autumn of the Patriarch, Chronicle of a Death Foretold, Love in the Time of Cholera,* and *The General in His Labyrinth.* García Márquez was awarded the Nobel Prize for literature in 1982, and his *Collected Stories* were published in English translation in 1984. An author of "magical realism," a type of work that blends the fictional devices of realism and fantasy, García Márquez has remarked "that there's not a single line in all my work that does not have a basis in reality" and has described his work as "a *metaphor* for Latin America."

Charlotte Perkins Gilman (1860–1935)

Charlotte Perkins Gilman was born in Hartford, Connecticut, to a distinguished family of independent thinkers but suffered an unstable and impoverished childhood. Her father abandoned the family when Charlotte was a small child, and she and her brother were raised by their mother and moved nineteen times in eighteen years. In 1884 Charlotte married Charles W. Stetson, a painter. After the birth of their child, a daughter, Charlotte fell into a deep depression and received treatments from Philadelphia physician S. Weir Mitchell, a specialist in nerve disorders. Mitchell's prescription of complete rest nearly drove Charlotte mad, and in 1888 she left her husband, fled to California, and obtained a divorce. Subsequently she devoted herself to lecturing and writing and emerged as a leading feminist theorist. Her major works include *Women and Economics* (1898) *The Man-Made World: Our Androcentric Culture* (1911), and the utopian novel *Herland* (1915). Gilman committed suicide in 1935 while dying of breast cancer. Her autobiography, *The Living of Charlotte Perkins Gilman,* was published posthumously.

Susan Glaspell (1882–1948)

Susan Glaspell was a native Midwesterner who spent much of her creative life in New England. In 1915 she and her husband, George Cram Cook, were instrumental in creating the Provincetown Players in Massachusetts, a group of amateur writers and actors who inaugurated "modern" American theater and drama. Also a short story writer and novelist, Glaspell is best remembered today for her plays, in which she explored such issues as women's experience and relations between the sexes. Major works include *Suppressed Desires* (1915), *The Verge* (1921), and *Alison's House,* which won a Pulitzer Prize in 1930.

Ellen Goodman (b. 1941)

A Pulitzer Prize–winning journalist, Ellen Goodman was born in Newton, Massachusetts, and earned her B.A. degree from Radcliffe College. After a job doing research for *Newsweek* magazine, she shifted to newspaper work in the mid-1960s and became a columnist for *The Boston Globe.* As a syndicated columnist, Goodman has been largely concerned with issues of family relationships and values, divorce, feminism, and changing lifestyles—what she once called the "life-and-death issues" of contemporary American society. In 1980, she won the Pulitzer Prize for distinguished commentary. Among her books and collections of columns are *Close to Home, Turning Points, At Large, Keeping in Touch, Making Sense,* and *Value Judgments.*

Nadine Gordimer (b. 1923)

Novelist and short story writer, Nadine Gordimer was born in Springs, South Africa, and educated at private schools and the University of Witwatersrand.

Her first book, a collection of short stories (*Face to Face*), was published in 1949. Since then, Gordimer has published some fifteen additional story collections, among them *Selected Stories, Town and Country Lovers, Crimes of Conscience, Jump and Other Stories,* and *Reflections from South Africa.* She has also published numerous novels, including *The Lying Days, Occasion for Loving, The Late Bourgeois World, The Conservationist, My Son's Story,* and *The House Gun.* Called "the literary voice and conscience of her society," Gordimer produced most of her work as a white South African living under the system of apartheid (government enforced racial segregation) that dominated South Africa for nearly half a century, and her writings depict the enduring legacies, political and personal, of a racially divided society. In 1991, Gordimer was awarded the Nobel Prize for literature.

Francine du Plessix Gray (b. 1930)

The daughter of a French father and a Russian mother, Francine du Plessix Gray was born in Europe, immigrated to the United States in 1941, and became a naturalized United States citizen in 1952. After earning her B.A. degree from Barnard College in 1952, she worked as a reporter, editorial assistant, freelance writer, and book editor, before becoming a staff writer for the *New Yorker* magazine in 1968. Her books include *Divine Disobedience: Profiles in Catholic Radicalism, Hawaii: The Sugar Coated Fortress, Adam and Eve and the City: Selected Nonfiction, At Home with the Marquis de Sade: A Life,* and several novels, among them the autobiographical *Lovers and Tyrants* (1976), which depicts Gray's own struggle, as a woman, to become a writer. In the latter novel her protagonist observes: "Every woman's life is a series of exorcisms from the spells of different oppressors: nurses, lovers, husbands, gurus, parents, children, myths of the good life. The most tyrannical despots can be the ones who love us the most."

Thomas Hardy (1840–1928)

Thomas Hardy was born near Dorchester in rural Dorset, England. Though he trained as an architect, the young Hardy's passions for philosophy and poetry soon drove him to forsake architecture and become a writer. Beginning in the 1870s, he achieved widespread fame as a novelist, centering his fictional world in the countryside of his native Dorset (called "Wessex" in his novels). Among his best-known novels, published between 1874 and 1895, are *Far from the Madding Crowd, The Return of the Native, The Mayor of Casterbridge, Tess of the D'Urbervilles,* and *Jude the Obscure.* After 1896 he focused on writing poems, which were collected in *Wessex Poems* (1898) and two volumes, *Winter Words* and *Collected Poems,* published after his death. Like his novels, Hardy's poems reflect the traditions and rusticisms of the Dorset he knew in his youth.

Joy Harjo (b. 1951)

The work of Joy Harjo—poet, essayist, editor, children's book writer, and musician—has been closely tied to her identity as a Creek Indian. Harjo was born in Tulsa, Oklahoma, in the heart of the Creek Nation. She attended school at the Institute of American Indian Arts in Santa Fe, New Mexico, and graduated with a B.A. degree from the University of New Mexico, Albuquerque, in 1976. In 1978 she earned an M.F.A. in creative writing from the University of Iowa Writers Workshop, and since then she has continued both to write and to teach. Among her books are *She Had Some Horses* (1983), *Secrets from the Center of the World* (1989), *In Mad Love and War* (1990), and *The Woman Who Fell from the Sky: Poems* (1996). She has also co-edited an anthology of stories, *Reinventing the Enemy's Language: North American Native Women's Writing,* and recorded several albums with her band, Joy Harjo and Poetic Justice.

Nathaniel Hawthorne (1804–1864)

Nathaniel Hawthorne was born in Salem, Massachusetts, and was descended from New England Puritan stock, an influence which was to profoundly affect his novels and stories. After graduating from Bowdoin College in 1825, he spent twelve years in seclusion developing his craft as a writer. His first commercial success came with the short story collection *Twice-Told Tales* (1837), followed by *Mosses from an Old Manse* (1846) and several novels: *The Scarlet Letter* (1850, his masterpiece), *The House of the Seven Gables* (1851), and *The Blithedale Romance* (1852). Hawthorne called himself a writer of romances—stories which oppose strict realism and create their own reality. In a comment relevant to "The Minister's Black Veil," he once wrote that he intended to "keep the inmost Me behind its veil."

Edward Hoagland (b. 1932)

Novelist and essayist, Edward Hoagland was born in New York City and earned a bachelor's degree from Harvard University in 1954. He served in the U.S. Army from 1955 to 1957, began writing novels and nonfiction, and published the first of several novels, *Cat Man*, in 1956; but his main career has been as an essayist, particularly of nature and travel, beginning with *Notes from the Century Before: A Journal from British Columbia* (1969). Other nonfiction collections include *The Courage of Turtles: Fifteen Essays by Edward Hoagland* (1971), *The Moose on the Wall: Field Notes from the Vermont Wilderness, African Calliope: A Journey to the Sudan, The Edward Hoagland Reader* (1979), and *Balancing Acts.* Hoagland has also edited *The Penguin Nature Library* and published a collection of short stories, *The Final Fate of Alligators.*

Linda Hogan (b. 1947)

Born in Denver, Colorado, Linda Hogan is a member of the Chickasaw tribe, and her Native American heritage figures prominently in her poetry, essays, fiction, and plays. Hogan earned an M.A. degree from the University of Colorado at Boulder in 1978, and since then has taught at numerous schools and universities, such as the TRIBES program in Colorado Springs, the University of Minnesota, and the University of Colorado, Boulder. She has also held such jobs as dental assistant, homemaker, secretary, waitress, and volunteer worker at the Minnesota Wildlife Rehabilitation Clinic. Hogan says she has a focal interest in "studying the relationship between humans and other species, and trying to create world survival skills out of what I learn from this." Her writings include *Call-*

ing Myself Home (poems), *The Book of Medicines: Poems, Dwellings: Reflections on the Natural World, Solar Storms,* and *Power* (novels). She is also co-editor of the anthology, *Between Species: Women and Animals* (1997).

bell hooks (b. 1952)

Writer and social critic bell hooks (real name Gloria Watkins) is a prominent figure in contemporary African-American feminism. Hooks grew up in Kentucky, reading voraciously and gaining confidence in the importance of her own voice through writing and public speaking. With her first book, *Ain't I a Woman: Black Women and Feminism* (1981), hooks began articulating a vision for radical social change that she has since developed in *Talking Back: Thinking Feminist, Thinking Black, Teaching to Transgress: Education as the Practice of Freedom, Art on My Mind: Visual Politics, Reel to Real: Race, Sex, and Class at the Movies,* and other works. Though an "academic" (she has a Ph.D. and has taught at Yale and other prestigious institutions), hooks is known for her trenchant and accessible writing style. With her pen name, bell hooks honors her great-grandmother (Bell Hooks), "that figure in my childhood who . . . paved the way for me to speak."

Langston Hughes (1902–1967)

Regarded by some as the single most influential African American poet of the twentieth century, Langston Hughes was born in Joplin, Missouri, and started writing poetry as a boy. He graduated from high school in Cleveland and attended college for a year at Columbia University. Tiring of formal education, Hughes traveled to Africa and Europe in the early 1920s before returning to the United States and eventually settling in Harlem, New York. Harlem was then the scene of the "Harlem Renaissance" in black literature, theater, music, and other arts. Hughes became a literary leader of the Renaissance and a tireless champion of African-American culture and writers. He went on to write over a dozen volumes of poetry, including *The Weary Blues* (1926) and *Montage of a Dream Deferred* (1951), as well as novels, stories, screenplays, plays, and histories. Strongly influenced by jazz, the blues, and spirituals, Hughes wrote, as he put it, "to explain and illuminate the Negro condition in America."

Henrik Ibsen (1828–1906)

A major figure in nineteenth-century drama, Henrik Ibsen was born in Skien, Norway. His father went bankrupt when Henrik was a child, and Ibsen left home at age fifteen to work as a druggist's apprentice in the town of Grimstad, where he made intellectual friends and wrote his first play (*Catiline,* published 1850). Holding managerial positions with the Bergen and new Norwegian Theatres, Ibsen published over half a dozen plays between 1851 and 1862. Most of these early efforts, composed in verse and romantic-historical in nature, were artistic and financial failures. Feeling stifled by Norwegian society, Ibsen moved in 1864 to Italy, and he continued to live there and in Germany for the next twenty-seven years. In the 1870s, his craft evolved to a new level as he began writing plays in the prose of everyday speech and portrayed characters who were ordinary members of the Norwegian middle class. Major dramas in this vein include *A Doll's House* (1879), *Ghosts* (1881), *An Enemy of the People* (1882), and *The Wild Duck* (1884). In these so-called "problem" plays, Ibsen dramatized defects in social institutions and explored hypocritical social attitudes towards divorce, venereal disease, and other taboo subjects. Enormously controversial at the time, these plays solidified Ibsen's reputation as a great playwright and helped launch European theater into the modern era. Ibsen consistently denied any intent to "preach" overt messages in his plays, insisting that he merely sought to portray life conflicts and leave it to readers and viewers to draw their own conclusions.

Fenton Johnson (b. 1953)

Born in New Haven, Kentucky, Fenton Johnson earned a B.A. degree from Stanford University and an M.F.A. degree from the University of Iowa Writer's Workshop in 1983. He has worked as a journalist and writing consultant and has taught widely in universities and at workshops. Johnson's books, praised for their sensitive portrayal of culture and family life in his native Kentucky, include two novels (*Crossing the River* and *Scissors, Paper, Rock*) and *Geography of the Heart*, a memoir about his lover, Larry Rose, who died of AIDS in 1990.

James Joyce (1882–1941)

James Joyce is a central figure in modern literature. Born and classically educated in Dublin, Joyce spent most of his working life on the European Continent—in Paris, Zurich, and other cities. Dublin, however, furnished the themes, characters, and cultural backdrop for all of his writing. Joyce's first published book, *Chamber Music* (poems, 1907), was followed in 1914 by *Dubliners*, a collection of short stories. In 1914 the autobiographical novel *A Portrait of the Artist as a Young Man* also began to appear serially in the London journal *The Egoist*. Other works include the landmark and controversial *Ulysses* (1922), a densely woven modern epic of alienated urban humanity, and *Finnegans Wake* (1939).

Claire Kemp (b. 1936)

Born in Worcester, Massachusetts, Claire Kemp is a short story writer who lives in Florida.

Theodore (Ted) Kooser (b. 1939)

Born in Ames, Iowa, Ted Kooser earned a B.S. degree from Iowa State University in 1962, an M.A. degree from the University of Nebraska in 1968, and has worked for many years as an insurance underwriter and executive in Lincoln, Nebraska. His collections of poetry include *Official Entry Blank* (his first book, published in 1969), *A Local Habitation and a Name, Sure Signs: New and Selected Poems, The Windflower Home Almanac of Poetry* (editor), *One World at a Time*, and *Weather Central*. Though he does not consider himself a regionalist writer, Kooser says that most of his poetry reflects "my interest in my surroundings here on the Great Plains."

Elizabeth Larsen (b. 1964)

A graduate of Barnard College, Elizabeth Larsen is a Minneapolis-based journalist. She has been an editor of *Utne Reader,* in which "Buying Time" originally appeared, and has published extensively in print and online. She is currently writing a memoir about growing up with feminism.

D. H. Lawrence (1885–1930)

David Herbert Lawrence was born in Nottinghamshire, England, the son of a coal miner and a genteel and refined mother. He graduated from Nottingham University in 1908 and began writing poetry and fiction, including the major autobiographical novel, *Sons and Lovers* (1913). In 1912 he eloped with Frieda von Richthofen, the wife of a Nottingham professor, whom he later married and with whom he shared his intense and emotionally tempestuous life. In the 1910s Lawrence grew increasingly disaffected with the mechanized, routinized life of industrial society and began to wander widely in search of alternative modes of life. His journeys took him and Frieda to southern Europe, Ceylon, Australia, the southwestern United States, Mexico, and eventually back to Europe. Throughout this period he continued to write novels (*The Rainbow* and *Women in Love* are among the best) as well as the travel essays and poems that established him as one of the finest descriptive writers in English. He died, of tuberculosis, in France. Lawrence's writings exhibit deep and lifelong obsessions: an emphasis on the elemental force of human sexuality, a faith in the life-forming power of the unconscious as opposed to the sterility and deadness of life lived from the merely conscious mind, and a passion to restore connections among human beings and between human beings and the earth—connections that modern society, in Lawrence's view, has largely lost or destroyed.

Doris Lessing (b. 1919)

Doris Lessing was born in Persia, the daughter of English parents. When she was five the family moved to a farm in southern Rhodesia (now Zimbabwe). Lessing remained in Africa until 1949, when she and her second husband and their child moved to England. Her first novel, *The Grass Is Singing* (1950), portrays the horrors of black-white relations in Africa, and injustices—racial, political, gender-based—have remained focal concerns of her work. Major writings include *The Golden Notebook* (1962), which narrates the growth of one woman's feminist consciousness; the five-novel *Children of Violence* series (1952–1969); *Canopus in Argos: Archives* (1979–1983), a multivolume sequence of nonrealistic novels; *The Good Terrorist* (1986); and *African Lands* (1992). Among Lessing's short story collections are *The Habit of Loving* (1957), *African Stories* (1964), and *Stories* (1978).

Denise Levertov (1923–1997)

Often described as a "visionary" poet, the English-born Denise Levertov was descended from religious mystics on both her mother's side (Welsh) and her father's (Russian Jewish). Privately educated in England, she worked as a nurse in London during World War II and afterward briefly taught English in Holland. In the late 1940s, Levertov moved to the United States, where her poetry, which she described until then as "British Romantic," was heavily influenced by the style and American idiom of such writers as Ezra Pound and William Carlos Williams. Author of nearly twenty books of poetry (among them *Collected Earlier Poems 1940–1960, Poems 1960–1967, The Jacob's Ladder, O Taste and See, Life in the Forest, The Poet in the World,* and *Breathing the Water*), Levertov also published several volumes of essays and translations. Her poems celebrate the beauty and mystery of daily life and reflect her deep appreciation of the natural world.

Antonio Machado (1875–1939)

Regarded by many as the greatest poet of Spain since the seventeenth century, Antonio Machado was born in Seville and educated at a liberal school in Madrid. He published his first volume of verse in 1903 and obtained certification to teach in the Spanish secondary school system in 1907. For the next thirty years Machado was a writer and, as he put it, a "modest teacher" in various provincial public schools and in Madrid. Machado achieved national fame with his second book, *The Castilian Country* (1912), followed by other collections and *Complete Poems* (enlarged edition, 1928). During the 1930s, Machado became an impassioned spokesman for Spanish liberalism, publishing his views on a variety of public issues in the Madrid papers under the byline of "Juan de Mairena." A loyalist during the Spanish Civil War (1936–1939) he fled to France when the republican government of Spain fell to fascism, and there he died. Machado's poetry is known for its austerity, religious and philosophic concerns, and its vivid portrayal of the Spanish countryside. "The poet is a fisherman," he wrote, ". . . of fish capable of staying alive after being hauled out."

Naguib Mahfouz (b. 1911?)

Winner of the 1988 Nobel Prize for Literature, Naguib Mahfouz is generally regarded as Egypt's finest writer. He was born in Cairo (some sources say in 1911; others suggest 1912 or 1914), graduated from the University of Cairo, and did postgraduate study in philosophy. Many of Mahfouz's novels and stories depict the turbulence of Egypt's social and political past and the harsh lives of the Arab poor. Since the 1980s, Mahfouz's books (*Midaq Alley, The Thief and the Dogs, Miramar, Echoes of an Autobiography,* and many others) have been widely translated and become bestsellers in English-speaking countries.

Katherine Mansfield (1888–1923)

Born in New Zealand, Katherine Mansfield (born Kathleen Beauchamp) was educated in England and spent most of her working life there. Following a disastrous marriage in her twenties to a young musician, she obtained a divorce and in 1918 married the critic John Middleton Murry. Amid her family and personal problems and chronic ill health (she eventually died of tuberculosis), Mansfield devoted herself to writing. With such collections as *Bliss and Other Stories* (1920) and *The Garden Party and Other Stories* (1922), she established herself as a fiction writer of rare subtlety and as a daring experimenter with narrative technique. Today she is considered one of the major creators of the modern short story.

Guy de Maupassant (1850–1893)

A major influence on modern short story writers, Guy de Maupassant was born in Normandy, France, into a noble family. Following a restless youth, he fought in the Franco-Prussian War (1870–1871) and worked for nearly ten years as a government clerk in Paris. By then, writing had become his passion, and for seven years he apprenticed himself to the great French novelist, Gustave Flaubert, who was a family friend and who strongly influenced Maupassant's evolving style. With publication of his short story, "Boule de Suif" ("Ball of Fat"), in 1880, Maupassant gained instant fame; over the next decade he wrote and published hundreds of stories and articles and several novels. Maupassant's stories are populated by characters drawn from the French working and middle classes and are characterized by precise observation, unsentimental realism, and irony. His stories are often harsh in content and outlook, but typically objective in method, calculated to compel readers (as he put it) "to think, and to understand the deep, hidden meanings of events for themselves."

Terrence McNally (b. 1939)

Best known for his comedies and farces, playwright Terrence McNally was born in St. Petersburg, Florida, and graduated with a bachelor's degree from Columbia University. Subsequently he worked as a critic, editor, and stage manager as he was writing his first plays. His plays include *And Things That Go Bump in the Night, Bad Habits, The Ritz, Frankie and Johnny in the Claire de Lune* (which he rewrote for the Garry Marshall film *Frankie and Johnny*), *The Lisbon Traviata, Love! Valour! Compassion!*, and *Master Class*.

James Alan McPherson (b. 1943)

Born in Savannah, Georgia, James Alan McPherson earned his B.A. degree from Morris Brown College, a bachelor of laws degree from Harvard University, and an M.F.A. in creative writing from the University of Iowa (1969). In his early twenties he won first prize in a short story contest sponsored by the *Atlantic* magazine, and later he became a contributing editor to the *Atlantic*. Since 1981 McPherson has taught in the English Department at the University of Iowa. An African-American, McPherson has published two widely praised books of short stories, *Hue and Cry* (1969) and the Pulitzer Prize–winning *Elbow Room* (1977). While many of McPherson's characters are African-American, he has tried to transcend racial barriers in his work, regarding his characters less as "blacks" or "whites" than as individual people. McPherson's most recent books are *Crabcakes: A Memoir* and the anthology, *Fathering Daughters: Reflections by Men*, which he co-edited.

Herman Melville (1819–1891)

Born in New York City, Herman Melville attended school in New York City and Albany, where the family moved after his father failed in business. In 1839 he shipped as a cabin boy to Liverpool, an adventure he later described in his novel *Redburn* (1849). Starting in 1841, he spent eighteen months on a whaler in the South Seas, jumped ship, was captured by cannibals, escaped, and eventually returned to the United States on an American frigate in 1844. Melville's South Seas experiences furnished material for such enormously popular novels of adventure as *Typee* (1846) and *Omoo* (1847). After marrying in 1847, Melville settled in New York where he continued writing novels; and in 1851, while living on a farm near Pittsfield, Massachusetts, he published his masterpiece, *Moby-Dick*. After 1852 he wrote primarily short fiction and poetry. Melville's later works include *The Piazza Tales* (1856), which contains "Bartleby, the Scrivener"; *The Confidence Man*, a satire; *Battle Pieces*, a book of Civil War poems; *Clarel*, a long philosophical poem; and *Billy Budd*, a novella published posthumously in 1924.

N. Scott Momaday (b. 1934)

A member of the Kiowa Indian tribe, Navarre Scott Momaday was born in Lawton, Oklahoma, and grew up in Oklahoma and New Mexico. He earned his bachelor's degree from the University of New Mexico in 1958 and a Ph.D. from Stanford University in 1963. A poet, novelist, playwright, and artist, he won the 1969 Pulitzer Prize for fiction for *House Made of Dawn*. His other books include *The Way to Rainy Mountain*, *The Names*, *The Ancient Child*, *In the Presence of the Sun: Stories and Poems, 1961–1991*, *The Man Made of Words*, and *In the Bear's House*. Momaday's works are known for their celebration of Kiowa heritage and traditions and for their imaginative blending of legend, myth, history, and autobiography.

Lorrie Moore (b. 1957)

Born in Glen Falls, New York, Lorrie Moore graduated from St. Lawrence University and earned an M.F.A. degree from Cornell University in 1982. She has published widely in magazines (*The New Yorker, Ms., Cosmopolitan, Epoch*) and produced her first story collection, *Self-Help*, in 1985. In *Self-Help*, Moore experimented with writing several stories (including "How to Become a Writer") that mimic the "second person, mock imperative" voices of popular self-help manuals. Moore's other books include *Anagrams, Like Life*, and *Who Will Run the Frog Hospital?*

Thomas Moore (b. 1940)

Born in Detroit, Thomas Moore has been a professor of psychology and religious studies and a practicing psychotherapist. His books include *The Planets Within, Care of the Soul, Soulmates, The Re-Enchantment of Everyday Life*, and *The Soul of Sex*. Moore has also written numerous articles on Jungian and archetypal psychology for books and periodicals and has edited *A Blue Fire: Selected Writings* by archetypal psychologist James Hillman.

Gloria Naylor (b. 1950)

Born in New York City, Gloria Naylor earned her B.A. degree from Brooklyn College of the City University of New York in 1981 and an M.A. in African-

American Studies from Yale University in 1983. Her first novel, *The Women of Brewster Place* (1982), which won the American Book Award for best first novel, is about seven African-American women living in an urban ghetto in the northern United States. Her other books include *Linden Hills*, about residents of an upper-middle-class black neighborhood, *Mama Day, Bailey's Cafe*, and *The Men of Brewster Place* (1998). "Kiswana Browne" is reprinted from *The Women of Brewster Place*.

Joyce Carol Oates (b. 1938)

Born in Lockport, New York, Joyce Carol Oates was educated at Syracuse University and the University of Wisconsin. She taught at the Universities of Detroit and Windsor (Ontario) and since 1978 has been on the faculty at Princeton University. An extraordinarily prolific writer, Oates has published dozens of books, including novels (e.g., *Black Water, Bellefleur, A Garden of Earthly Delights, My Heart Laid Bare*), short stories, literary and social criticism, and plays. *Tone Clusters*, reprinted from her 1991 collection *Twelve Plays*, admits us to familiar Oates terrain: a place of instability and fear, the brutal side of American experience, a world in which people are repeatedly threatened—often violently—by dark forces from without and within. The play also exhibits the interest in formal experimentation that is characteristic of Oates's fiction and dramas.

Flannery O'Connor (1925–1964)

Flannery O'Connor was born in Savannah, Georgia, and attended school at Georgia State College for Women and the University of Iowa, from which she received an M.F.A. degree. As an undergraduate O'Connor was already writing and publishing stories. In 1952 she published her first novel, *Wise Blood*. Diagnosed in 1950 with lupus, an autoimmune disease that eventually claimed her life, O'Connor moved home to live with her mother on the family farm in Milledgeville. There she devoted mornings to writing and afternoons to reading, letter writing, and the raising of peacocks. Though she published a second novel, *The Violent Bear It Away*, in 1960, O'Connor's greatest success was as a writer of short stories, which are collected in *A Good Man Is Hard to Find* (1955) and two volumes published after her death, *Everything That Rises Must Converge* (1965) and *The Complete Stories* (1971). O'Connor was devoutly Catholic and emphasized the pervasive influence of her Catholicism on her work. She was never, however, sentimentally religious, but more (in the words of a fellow novelist) like "an Old Testament prophet, crying out in our modern wilderness," exposing faithlessness, secularization, and human hypocrisy. "Her instruments," wrote a reviewer for *Time* magazine, "are a brutal irony, a slam-bang humor and a style of writing as balefully direct as a death sentence."

Sharon Olds (b. 1942)

Born in San Francisco, Sharon Olds graduated with a B.A. degree from Stanford University and a Ph.D. from Columbia University in 1972. Her collections of poems include *Satan Says, The Dead and the Living, The Gold Cell, The Matter of This World, The Sign of Saturn, The Father,* and *The Wellspring.*

Mary Oliver (b. 1935)

Born in Cleveland, Ohio, Mary Oliver attended Ohio State University and Vassar College. *No Voyage and Other Poems* (1963) was her first book. It was followed by *The Night Traveler, Twelve Moons, Sleeping in the Forest,* and *American Primitive,* which won the Pulitzer Prize in 1984. *New and Selected Poems* won the National Book Award in 1992. Fellow poet Maxine Kumin has called Oliver an "indefatigable guide to the natural world" who is comfortable with being "on the margins of things, on the line between earth and sky, the thin membrane that separates human from what we loosely call animal." Oliver's most recent book is *West Wind* (1997), a collection of poems and prose poems.

Tillie Olsen (b. 1912/1913)

Tillie Olsen was born in Omaha, Nebraska. She married in her early twenties, had four children, and struggled for many years to write amid the competing demands of homemaking and earning a humble living at secretarial and other jobs. Not until the 1950s, with the help of a fellowship and a grant, was she able to concentrate on writing and finish her first short story collection, *Tell Me a Riddle* (1961). The title story of that volume won the O. Henry award for best American short story, and the book established Olsen's fame as a writer about the poor, the socially disenfranchised, and women. In a later nonfiction work, *Silences* (1978), Olsen examined how class, gender, race, and other circumstances compel people into unnatural "silences." Olsen has also published *Yonnondio: From the Thirties* (1974), a novel set during the Great Depression, and has edited two books about mothers and daughters.

Eugene O'Neill (1888–1953)

The son of a famous actor, Eugene O'Neill grew up around theater but only began writing plays in his mid-twenties. His formal schooling was minimal (he spent a year at Princeton in 1906–1907 and took a playwriting class at Harvard in 1914). Most of his early education came through voracious and idiosyncratic reading of poets, romantic philosophers, and other iconoclasts and a series of experiences as gold prospector, seaman, and beachcomber that took him to Central and South America, Africa, and other parts of the globe. Abroad and in his native New York, O'Neill befriended down-and-outers, prostitutes, vagabonds, alcoholics, and other socially marginal persons who were to pose the themes and provide many of the characters for his dramas. O'Neill's first plays (mostly one-acts) were written in the 1910s and performed by experimental theater groups, notably the Provincetown Players in Provincetown, Cape Cod, Massachusetts, and in New York. *Beyond the Horizon* (1920) earned him his first of four Pulitzer Prizes, and with *The Emperor Jones* (1920), *The Hairy Ape* (1922), and *Desire Under the Elms* (1924), O'Neill emerged as the first American playwright of international stature. In 1936 he won the Nobel Prize for Literature. His powerful autobiographical play *Long Day's Journey into*

Night was published posthumously in 1956. A fearless experimenter, O'Neill wrote plays of all lengths and in many forms and styles, including the expressionism (see Appendix C) of *The Hairy Ape.*

Cynthia Ozick (b. 1928)

Born in the Bronx, New York, Cynthia Ozick was educated at New York University and Ohio State University and worked briefly as an English teacher before devoting herself full-time to writing. Some of her best work reflects her strong cultural roots in Judaism. Most esteemed for her short stories—collected in *The Pagan Rabbi, Bloodshed,* and *Levitation*—Ozick has also published novels, a play, and several essay collections, including *Art & Ardor, Metaphor & Memory,* and *Fame & Folly.* "Existing Things" is reprinted from *Fame & Folly.*

Edgar Allan Poe (1809-1849)

The son of actor parents, Edgar Allan Poe was orphaned as a child and suffered a turbulent and lonely personal life. After a brief formal education and an abortive stint at West Point, Poe turned to writing and became one of the foremost literary editors and critics of his day. He also wrote poetry and tales of horror and the macabre, which were published in magazines and collected in *Tales of the Grotesque and Arabesque* (1840) and other volumes. Poe's influence cuts across literary genres and types. He did more than any other individual writer to establish the genre of the horror story; he wrote highly rhythmic, musical, and symbolic poetry that was internationally influential, especially in France; and his intricate stories of mystery and intrigue, such as "The Murders in the Rue Morgue" and "The Purloined Letter," make him the creator of the modern detective story.

Adrienne Rich (b. 1929)

An influential feminist poet and thinker, Adrienne Rich was born in Baltimore and grew up in an intellectual household. She graduated from Radcliffe College in 1951; in the same year her first book of poems, *A Change of World,* was published in the prestigious Yale Series of Younger Poets. In the decades since, Rich has published numerous volumes of poetry, as well as collections of essays and speeches. Her poems are collected in *The Fact of a Doorframe: Poems Selected and New 1950–1984, Time's Power: Poems 1985–1988, An Atlas of the Difficult World: Poems 1988–1991, Dark Fields of the Republic: Poems 1991–1995,* and *Midnight Salvage: Poems 1995–1998.* For Rich, poetry never stands apart from life; it is always "political" in the broadest sense—about one's position in the world and how one is situated in relationship to history and to institutions (for instance, the institutions of patriarchy). Her major autobiographical essay, "When We Dead Awaken: Writing as Re-Vision" (reprinted in her 1979 prose collection, *On Lies, Secrets, and Silence*), tells the story of her evolution into feminist consciousness. Additional prose is collected in *Of Woman Born: Motherhood as Experience and Institution; Blood, Bread, and Poetry;* and *What Is Found There: Notebooks on Poetry and Politics.*

Mary Robison (b. 1949)

Mary Robison was born in Washington, D. C., and graduated with an M.A. degree from Johns Hopkins University in 1977. She has been a writer in residence and a teacher at several colleges and universities. Her novels and short story collections include *Days, Oh!, An Amateur's Guide to the Night, Believe Them,* and *Subtraction.*

Milcha Sanchez-Scott (b. 1953)

Milcha Sanchez-Scott was born on the island of Bali, the daughter of a Colombian father and an Indonesian mother. She went to school in England and later at the University of California, San Diego, from which she graduated. Her published plays include *Latina, Dog Lady* and *The Cuban Swimmer* (both written in 1982 and produced for the first time in 1984), *Roosters,* and *Evening Star.*

Scott Russell Sanders (b. 1945)

Born in Memphis, Tennessee, Scott Russell Sanders earned his undergraduate degree at Brown University and his Ph.D. at Cambridge University. He has published work on subjects ranging from science fiction and literary criticism to biography and folklore. "In all of my work," he remarks, "regardless of period or style, I am concerned with the ways in which human beings come to terms with the practical problems of living on a small planet, in nature and in communities." Among his books, written in the 1980s and the 1990s, are *Fetching the Dead: Stories, Hear the Wind Blow: American Folksongs Retold, Secrets of the Universe, Staying Put: Making a Home in a Restless World,* and *The Country of Language.*

Arthur Schopenhauer (1788–1860)

A major nineteenth-century German philosopher, Arthur Schopenhauer was born into a wealthy family and earned his doctorate in 1813. The following year he moved to Dresden, where he wrote the book for which he is best known, *The World as Will and Idea* (1818). In this work and others, Schopenhauer articulated a pessimistic philosophy that placed him at odds with the then dominant and more optimistic philosophy of G. W. F. Hegel. Largely ignored for many years, he became embittered and resigned a lectureship at a prestigious university to pursue, after 1831, a reclusive life as a writer. Only in the last decade of his life did he begin to receive widespread recognition. Schopenhauer's work, blending philosophies of West and East and stressing the centrality of the irrational in human behavior, influenced Freud, among others.

Leslie Marmon Silko (b. 1948)

Leslie Marmon Silko was born in Albuquerque, New Mexico, and grew up in the nearby village of Old Laguna. She is of mixed blood, including white, Laguna, and Plains Indian, and her cultural origins and traditions are at the heart of her writing. After attending Catholic schools in Albuquerque, Silko graduated with a B.A. from the University of New Mexico and briefly attended law school before deciding to be a writer and teacher. She published her first story in 1969 and since then has produced a volume of poems and several books of fiction, including *Ceremony* (1977, a novel), *Storyteller* (1981, a collection of stories and short prose interwoven with poetry and photographs), and *Almanac of the Dead* (1991, a novel). She has also published two more books of nonfiction, *Sacred Water: Narratives and Pictures* (1993) and *Yellow Woman and a Beauty of the Spirit: Essays on Native American Life Today* (1996). Not just about characters, Silko's fiction is about the healing and protective powers inherent in storytelling itself. This emphasis on the functionality of storytelling is the focus of "Language and Literature from a Pueblo Indian Perspective," the Silko piece reprinted in *Reading and Writing from Literature.*

Gary Soto (b. 1952)

A noted Chicano poet, essayist, and fiction writer, Gary Soto grew up in a working-class family in Fresno, California. He was employed as a laborer during his childhood, and a strong identification with the working poor stamps much of his work. Soto graduated from California State University, Fresno, in 1974 and earned an M.F.A. in creative writing from the University of California, Irvine, in 1976. In 1977 he published his first book, *The Elements of San Joaquín,* a collection of poems depicting the Fresno of his childhood. Since then he has written several books of prose memoirs, including *Living Up the Street: Narrative Recollections* and *Lesser Evils: Ten Quartets,* and numerous volumes of poetry, including *Black Hair, Home Course in Religion,* and *New and Selected Poems* (1995).

Wole Soyinka (b. 1934)

Educated in England, Wole Soyinka is a Nigerian political activist who has had to flee his native land several times for criticizing the government. He is the author of *Swamp Dwellers, Death and the King's Horseman,* and over a dozen other plays that have made him Nigeria's leading playwright. In 1986 he was awarded the Nobel Prize for Literature. Though best known for his plays, Soyinka has also written novels, an autobiography, and several collections of poetry.

Brent Staples (b. 1951)

Born in Chester, Pennsylvania, Brent Staples earned a bachelor's degree from Widener University in 1973 and a Ph.D. in psychology from the University of Chicago in 1982. He worked as a reporter for the *Chicago Sun Times* before joining the editorial staff of the *New York Times* in 1985. His 1994 memoir, *Parallel Time: Growing Up in Black and White,* tells the story of his childhood growing up in Chester, a racially mixed and economically declining town. Staples is currently a member of the *Times* editorial board and writes on politics and culture.

Anna Swir (1909–1984)

Anna Swir (Swirszcynska) was born in Warsaw, Poland, the daughter of an impoverished painter, in whose studio she spent much of her childhood. She put herself through university in Warsaw, studying medieval and Baroque Polish

1090 APPENDIX D ~ *Notes on the Authors*

literature and publishing her first poems during the 1930s. During the World War II Nazi occupation of Poland, Swir was a member of the Resistance and narrowly escaped execution. The experience changed her profoundly; her poetry, previously rather impersonal, assumed heightened urgency and emotion. Swir is known as a crafter of miniature poems that are at once descriptive and personal. As her compatriot, Czeslaw Milosz, remarks, "Anna Swir achieves in her sensual and fierce poetry a nearly calligraphic neatness." Milosz and Leonard Nathan have translated a selection of Swir's poems into English under the title *Talking to My Body* (1996).

Wislawa Szymborska (b. 1923)

Wislawa Szymborska was born in Poland, educated at Jagellonian University (also in Poland), and currently lives in Cracow. For many years she was a poetry editor and columnist for a Polish literary weekly magazine. She published her first collection of poems in 1952. Her poems have been translated into English in *Sounds, Feelings, Thoughts: Seventy Poems* (1981), *View with a Grain of Sand* (1995), and *Poems, New and Collected, 1957–1997* (1998). Her poems have also been translated into Arabic, Hebrew, Japanese, Chinese, and other languages. In 1996 she was awarded the Nobel Prize for literature. Characteristically ironic and witty, Szymborska's poetry captures the experience of everyday life in deceptively simple language.

Jean Thompson (b. 1950)

Jean Thompson was born in Chicago and educated at the University of Illinois and Bowling Green State University in Ohio. She is the author of the novel, *My Wisdom,* and of the short story collections *Little Face* and *The Gasoline Wars.* She has taught for many years in the English department at the University of Illinois in Champaign-Urbana.

Henry David Thoreau (1817–1862)

Essayist, poet, and naturalist, Henry David Thoreau was born in Concord, Massachusetts. Though he graduated from Harvard in 1837, he was mainly self-taught, studying surveying and other practical arts and steeping himself in the literary classics of East and West. Above all Thoreau studied nature, both from a naturalist's perspective and from that of a poet who detected symbols of human experience in even the minutest natural phenomena. Thoreau matured into one of the era's great iconoclasts, a supreme example of a countercultural thinker. Disgruntled by the materialism of midcentury America, he built a small cabin at Walden Pond (near Concord) in 1845 and lived there, in simple relationship with nature, for two years. As he put it, he "chose to be rich by making his wants few." This experience furnished the material for *Walden* (1854), his most famous book. Other major writings include *A Week on the Concord and Merrimack Rivers* (1849) and the essay "Resistance to Civil Government" (1849), an argument for the sanctity of individual conscience in relation to political majorities that was to influence Mahatma Gandhi and Martin

Luther King, Jr., among others. Thoreau's *Journal,* which he kept for some twenty-three years, supplied the material for his published writings.

James Thurber (1894–1961)

American humorist James Thurber was born and grew up in Columbus, Ohio, and attended (but never graduated from) Ohio State University. In the 1920s he became a newspaper writer, worked briefly in France, and eventually settled in New York City, where he joined the staff of the recently founded *New Yorker* magazine, with which he was to maintain a lifelong association. Beginning in the late 1920s, Thurber's humorous sketches, stories, and line cartoons—distinguished by their simple style and often wildly imaginative subject matter—became a *New Yorker* fixture. His work is collected in such volumes as *My Life and Hard Times, Fables for Our Time, The Thurber Carnival,* and *My World—and Welcome to It,* which includes "The Secret Life of Walter Mitty."

Kurt Vonnegut, Jr. (b. 1922)

Born in Indianapolis, Indiana, Kurt Vonnegut attended Cornell University and the Carnegie Institute of Technology (now Carnegie-Mellon University) and earned an M. A. degree from the University of Chicago. During World War II he served in the U.S. Army in Europe, became a POW of the Germans, and survived one of the worst military atrocities of the war—the Allied firebombing of Dresden (a story later addressed in his novel, *Slaughterhouse Five*). Among Vonnegut's many books are novels (*Cat's Cradle, Slaughterhouse Five, Breakfast of Champions, Jailbird, Bluebeard, Timequake*); two collections of short stories (*Canary in a Cathouse* and *Welcome to the Monkey House*); and numerous plays, screenplays, essays, and speeches. Largely ignored by critics at the start of his career, Vonnegut became a countercultural icon in the late 1960s and 1970s, before gaining widespread critical recognition as a major American novelist. His radical experiments with style and form—blending elements of fantasy, science fiction, dark humor, and fierce social satire—coalesce around such basic human themes as happiness, the future, and the need to be humane in an inhumane world.

Alice Walker (b. 1944)

Alice Walker was born in Eatonton, Georgia, the youngest of eight children of black sharecropper parents. She attended Spelman College, a black women's school in Atlanta, and graduated in 1965 from Sarah Lawrence College in New York, where she began writing what would become some of her first published works. She participated in the civil rights movement in Mississippi in 1966 and taught college before obtaining a fellowship at the Radcliffe Institute in Cambridge, Massachusetts, in 1971. Walker's books include novels (*The Third Life of Grange Copeland, Meridian,* and *Possessing the Secret of Joy,* among others), collections of short stories (*In Love & Trouble* and *You Can't Keep a Good Woman Down*), poems (such as *Revolutionary Petunias*), and essay collections (*In Search of Our Mothers' Gardens: Womanist Prose, Living by the Word: Selected*

Writings, 1973–1987, and *Anything We Love Can Be Saved: A Writer's Activism.*).
The Color Purple, an epistolary novel (a novel in the form of a series of letters)
that won a Pulitzer Prize in 1983, shows Walker's characteristic interest in formal experimentation. Much of Walker's work is about strong and independent-
minded African-American women, such as Gracie Mae Still in the short story
"Nineteen Fifty-five."

Thomas S. Whitecloud (1914–1972)

Thomas St. Germain Whitecloud was born in New York City, the son of a white
mother and a Chippewa father. His parents divorced when Thomas was a child;
his father returned to the Lac Du Flambeau Reservation in Wisconsin, and
young Thomas grew up on both the reservation and in maintstream America.
Following a troubled youth, Whitecloud graduated from the University of Red-
lands in 1938, afterwards earning a medical degree from Tulane School of Medicine in New Orleans. Thereafter he worked as a physician, primarily in Texas
and Mississippi, and also wrote and lectured. Though he left behind numerous
unpublished stories, poems, and essays at his death, Whitecloud published only
one significant literary work, "Blue Winds Dancing," which appeared in *Scrib-
ner's Monthly* during his senior year of college.

Walt Whitman (1819–1892)

Born near Huntington, Long Island, Walt Whitman received virtually no formal education and worked at a variety of jobs during his youth and early manhood—as a printer, schoolteacher, journalist, and carpenter. As a poet he developed relatively late, not publishing his first book until 1855, when he was
thirty-six years old. Over time, however, this book, *Leaves of Grass,* revolutionized the writing of poetry in English and exerted significant impact on poets
worldwide. In an impassioned "Preface" to the book Whitman rejected the constraints of traditional verse, with its meter and rhyme, and advocated a poetry
that shapes itself freely out of the poet's own "beautiful blood and . . . brain."
An obsessive and fastidious rewriter, Whitman revised and expanded *Leaves of
Grass* for the rest of his life, taking the book through six different editions. During the Civil War he volunteered as a nurse, assisting and comforting the dying
and wounded in army hospitals in and around Washington, D.C. Out of this
experience he published *Drum-Taps,* a collection of vividly realistic war poems
that was later absorbed into *Leaves of Grass.* In addition to being a radical inno-
vator of poetic style, Whitman is famous for celebrating sex and the human
body as focal subjects for great poetry.

August Wilson (b. 1945)

August Wilson was born in Pittsburgh, Pennsylvania, the son of a black mother
and a white father. Abandoned by their father, August and his siblings were
raised by their mother in the Pittsburgh slums and, later, in a largely white
community where August suffered racial harassment at school. Wilson
dropped out of school at age fifteen and went on to work various jobs such as

short-order cook and stock clerk. He also frequented the public library, where he steeped himself in the works of Ralph Ellison, Langston Hughes, Richard Wright, and other African-American writers. While books helped give Wilson confidence to write himself, he was also inspired by many other influences in his African-American culture and heritage: street talk, the rhythms of ordinary speech and conversation, political movements, and especially the music and language of the blues. Wilson was already writing fiction and poetry in the 1960s when he got caught up in the Black Power movement and helped found a black activist theater in Pittsburgh. He also began writing plays. Later, moving to Minnesota, he worked with the Playwrights Center of Minneapolis and founded the Black Horizons Theatre Company. Wilson's first commercial success, *Ma Rainey's Black Bottom* (1984)—about the legendary black blues singer—was voted Best Play of the Year 1984–85 by the New York Drama Critics Circle. Wilson's aim is to write a cycle of ten plays about the experience of African-Americans, one for each decade of the twentieth century. Thus far he has completed several plays in the cycle, in addition to *Ma Rainey: Fences* and *The Piano Lesson* (both Pulitzer Prize winners), *Joe Turner's Come and Gone*, *Two Trains Running*, and *Seven Guitars*.

Tobias Wolff (b. 1945)

Born in Birmingham, Alabama, Tobias Wolff served in U.S. Army Special Forces during the Vietnam War and achieved the rank of first lieutenant. Following military service, he graduated with first-class honors from Oxford University in 1972 and earned a M.A. degree from Stanford University in 1978. Wolff published his first collection of short stories, *In the Garden of the North American Martyrs*, in 1981. Other short story collections include *Back in the World*, *The Stories of Tobias Wolff*, and *The Night in Question*. Wolff has also published two memoirs: *This Boy's Life*, about his teen years, and *In Pharaoh's Army: Memories of the Lost War*, which recounts his experiences fighting in the Vietnam War. *This Boy's Life* was made into a film in 1993.

William Butler Yeats (1865–1939)

Irish poet, playwright, and critic, William Butler Yeats was born near Dublin, the son of the lawyer and distinguished painter John Butler Yeats. William himself studied painting as a young man but soon abandoned art for writing, producing his first books of poems in the late 1880s. Yeats's poetry interweaves personal vision with history, mythology, psychology, mysticism, and other cultural influences. While many of his contemporaries wrote in free verse, Yeats breathed new life into old poetic forms, articulating his personal and symbolic vision in rhymed lines and tightly constructed stanzas. He was a leading advocate of Irish national art and served as president of the Irish National Theatre Society and codirector of Dublin's Abbey Theatre. In 1923 Yeats was awarded the Nobel Prize for Literature. Among his major collections of poetry are *In the Seven Woods* (1903), *The Wild Swans at Coole* (1917), *The Tower* (1928), and *Collected Poems* (definitive edition, 1956).

Author/Title Index

Subject Index

Text Credits